WYATT AND DASHWOOD'S
EUROPEAN UNION LAW

AUSTRALIA
Law Book Co.
Sydney

CANADA and USA
Carswell
Toronto

HONG KONG
Sweet & Maxwell Asia

NEW ZEALAND
Brookers
Wellington

SINGAPORE and MALAYSIA
Sweet & Maxwell Asia
Singapore and Kuala Lumpur

WYATT AND DASHWOOD'S

EUROPEAN UNION LAW

FIFTH EDITION

By

ANTHONY ARNULL
B.A. (Sussex), Ph.D. (Leicester)
Solicitor of the Supreme Court of England and Wales
Professor of European Law
Head of the School of Law
University of Birmingham

ALAN DASHWOOD
B.A. (Rhodes), M.A. (Oxon)
Of the Inner Temple, Barrister
Fellow of Sidney Sussex College, Cambridge
Professor of European Law, University of Cambridge

MICHAEL DOUGAN
M.A. (Cantab), Ph.D. (Cantab)
Professor of European Law and Jean Monnet Chair in EU Law
University of Liverpool

MALCOLM ROSS
LL.B. (Warwick), M.Phil (Leicester)
Professor of European Law
University of Sussex

ELEANOR SPAVENTA
Laurea (Rome), LL.M. (Cantab), D.Phil (Oxon)
Reader in Law and Director of the Durham European Law Institute (DELI)
University of Durham

and

DERRICK WYATT, Q.C.
M.A., LL.B. (Cantab.), J.D. (Chicago)
Of Lincoln's Inn, Barrister
Fellow of St. Edmund Hall, Oxford
Professor of Law, University of Oxford

London
Sweet & Maxwell
2006

First Edition	1980	Third Edition	1993
Second Impression	1981	Second Impression	1993
Third Impression	1986	Third Impression	1994
Second Edition	1987	Fourth Edition	2000
Second Impression	1990	Reprinted	2004
Third Impression	1991	Fifth Edition	2006

Published by
Sweet & Maxwell Limited of
100 Avenue Road, London NW3 3PF
(http://www.sweetandmaxwell.co.uk)
Typeset by J.P. Price, Chilcompton, Somerset
Printed and bound by MPG Books, Ltd, Bodmin, Cornwall

*A CIP catalogue record
for this book is available
from the British Library*

ISBN–10 0–421–92560–4
ISBN–13 978–0–421–92560–1

PREFACE

This book is the work of a team of authors, which for the first time includes Michael Dougan and Eleanor Spaventa. The core chapters retain the general shape and range of content that they were given in earlier editions, but they have been substantially revised, while new chapters have been added, and a few chapters have been dropped. Those we had in mind as readers when writing this edition were students taking degree level and equivalent courses in EU law, those who teach those courses, and those who practise the law. We do not claim to provide a comprehensive manual on the subject matter which we cover, but we have sought to be accurate, critical, pragmatic and occasionally original. We have enjoyed the process to a greater extent than most of our readers would imagine possible, and we hope that we have not buried all traces of that in the tenor and detail of our treatment. The coverage of the book remains broad, embracing constitutional, institutional and jurisdictional issues, the Community legal order, the internal market and competition law and policy. We do not believe that it can be validly claimed for any single volume that it comprise a "one stop shop" for those studying, teaching or practising EU law, but we do entertain the hope that our modest emporium is sufficiently well stocked to persuade the visitor to tarry a while before turning to primary sources and more specialised works.

Michael Dougan wrote the new Chapter 11 on the Constitutional Treaty; he also revised and updated Chapters 1–3 (history, institutions, legislative process), 4 (Union competences), adding a new section to this chapter on the categories of Union competence, 5 (sources, supremacy and direct effect), 6 (rights and remedies), and 10 (European Community and European Union). Tony Arnull revised and updated Chapters 12 (judicial architecture and judicial method) and 14 (preliminary rulings) and the majority of Chapter 13 (direct actions), to which editorial contributions were made by Michael Dougan, who also revised and updated the sections in Chapter 13 on failure to act, the plea of illegality and damages actions against the Community. Eleanor Spaventa revised and updated Chapter 7 (general principles of law), wrote the new Chapters 8 and 9 on fundamental rights and the Charter of Fundamental Rights (to the latter of which Tony Arnull made editorial contributions), revised and updated Chapters 15 and 16 (free movement of goods), and 18 (free movement of workers), and wrote the new Chapter 17 on Union Citizenship and the rights to move and reside in the Union. Malcolm Ross revised and updated the section on competition policy (Chapters 22–27), and received valuable research assistance from Francesco de Cecco with Chapter 26 (public and entrusted undertakings) and Chapter 27 (state aid), for which we are all extremely grateful. Derrick Wyatt revised and updated Chapter 19 (establishment and services), wrote (new) Chapter 20 (corporate establishment/cross-border acquisitions/ company law/tax), wrote the critical assessment of subsidiarity in Chapter 4, revised and updated the sections on international agreements in Chapter 5, and on intellectual property rights in Chapter 16, co-wrote with Eleanor Spaventa the section on non-discriminatory restrictions in Chapter 18, and wrote the conclusions of that section, and wrote the new section on common labelling rules and mutual recognition in Chapter 21. Alan Dashwood revised and updated Chapter 21 (completion of the internal market), adding new sections on freedom of movement under the Schengen Protocol and on the proposed Services Directive, and made editorial contributions to Chapters 1-4, 10 and 11. Finally, we would all like to express our thanks to Kate Brookson-Morris, for her valuable assistance in checking the proofs.

Anthony Arnull
Alan Dashwood
Michael Dougan
Malcolm Ross
Eleanor Spaventa
Derrick Wyatt

CONTENTS

PART 1

HISTORICAL INTRODUCTION

PART II

THE CONSTITUTIONAL ORDER

PART III

CONSTITUTIONAL FOUNDATIONS

PART IV

JURISDICTION OF THE COMMUNITY COURTS

PART V

THE FUNDAMENTAL RIGHTS OF UNION CITIZENS, THE INTERNAL MARKET AND BEYOND

PART VI

COMPETITION POLICY

Contents

TABLE OF EUROPEAN COURT OF JUSTICE AND COURT OF FIRST INSTANCE CASES (ALPHABETICAL)

TABLE OF CASES (EUROPEAN COURT OF JUSTICE)

TABLE OF CASES (EUROPEAN COURT OF FIRST INSTANCE)

E.C. COMMISSION DECISIONS

NATIONAL CASES

INTERNATIONAL TRIBUNAL CASES

TABLE OF E.C. TREATIES AND CONVENTIONS

Note. For convenience, all references to sections of the 1957 EEC and 1992 E.C. Treaties are tabled under the 1957 EEC Treaty only.

1957 Treaty Establishing the EEC—*cont.*
Art.226 ... 1–008, 5–003, 5–008,
5–014, 5–016, 5–024,
13–002, 13–003, 13–004,
13–006, 13–007, 13–009,
13–010, 13–012, 13–013,
13–014, 13–015, 13–019,
13–021, 13–053, 13–055,
13–060, 15–017, 15–020,
15–023, 16–041, 19–012,
21–011, 21–030, 21–031,
26–020
Art.226(2) 13–008
Arts 226–228 13–001
Art.227 .. 5–003, 5–016, 13–003,
13–019, 21–011
Art.228   5–043, 13–012, 13–019,
13–021, 13–022
Art.228(1) 13–011
Art.228(2) 13–011, 13–019,
13–020, 13–021
Art.229 25–020
Art.229a 12–013
Art.230 ... 1–008, 5–045, 6–012,
7–003, 9–020, 10–010,
11–029, 13–001, 13–009,
13–023, 13–024, 13–025,
13–027, 13–028, 13–029,
13–030, 13–031, 13–032,
13–033, 13–034, 13–034,
13–035, 13–036, 13–037,
13–043, 13–044, 13–047,
13–048, 13–049, 13–050,
13–051, 13–052, 13–052,
13–054, 13–055, 13–056,
13–057, 14–001, 14–013,
14–014, 14–017, 22–007,
27–037
Art.230(4) 11–029, 13–033,
27–035
Art.230(5) 13–029
Art.231   7–013, 13–030, 13–031
Art.232   1–008, 13–001, 13–009,
13–025, 13–026, 13–049,
13–050, 13–051, 13–052,
13–053, 13–057, 18–002,
21–009, 21–018
Art.233 .... 13–030, 13–031,
13–053, 21–009
Art.233(2) 13–031
Art.234 ... 5–002, 5–005, 5–010,
5–016, 5–031, 6–003,
6–011, 6–019, 7–013,
10–008, 10–009, 11–029,
12–010, 12–016, 13–001,
13–023, 13–054, 13–062,
14–001, 14–002, 14–003,
14–004, 14–005, 14–006,
14–007, 14–011, 14–012,
14–013, 14–014, 14–015,
14–016, 14–018, 22–007,
23–022, 25–007, 25–024,
27–037

1957 Treaty Establishing the EEC—*cont.*
Art.234(1) 14–013
Art.234(2) 14–008,
14–009
Art.234(3) 5–002
Art.235 .... 13–001, 13–031,
13–057, 13–063, 13–065
Art.236 .... 10–018, 12–013
Art.237 10–018
Art.238 5–043
Art.241 ...... 13–001, 13–054,
13–055
Art.242 .... 6–012, 14–014
Art.243   6–012, 13–013, 13–050
Art.244 5–016
Art.245 12–003
Arts 246–248 2–002
Art.249 ... 5–009, 5–016, 5–022,
5–023, 5–026, 5–027,
5–028, 5–031, 5–033,
5–034, 5–036, 10–007,
13–024, 13–036, 13–051,
13–061, 19–010, 25–019
Art.249(2) 5–003, 11–025,
11–026
Art.249(3) 11–025
Art.249(4) 11–026
Art.250(1) 3–012, 3–013
Art.250(2) 3–011
Art.251 ... 3–006, 3–007, 3–008,
4–027, 20–008
Art.251(2) 3–006
Art.251(3) 3–006
Art.251(4)   3–006, 3–007, 3–012
Art.251(5) 3–007, 3–012
Art.251(6) 3–007
Art.251(7) 3–007
Art.252 .... 3–008, 11–012
Art.252(c) 3–008
Art.252(d) 3–008
Art.252(e) 3–008
Art.253 .... 13–027, 21–019,
27–007
Art.254 .. 5–016, 5–036, 13–029
Art.254(1) 3–006
Art.255   3–007, 12–015, 17–032
Art.256 .... 5–016, 22–016
Arts 257–262 2–003
Arts 263–265 2–003
Art.266(1) 10–021
Arts 266–267 13–057
Art.269 ... 1–013, 2–004, 3–010
Art.269(2) 3–008
Art.272 .... 2–007, 2–015
Art.272(4) 2–015, 13–050
Art.272(5) 2–015
Art.272(6) 2–015
Art.272(7) 2–015
Art.272(8) 2–015
Art.272(9) 2–015
Art.276 2–002
Art.280(4) 3–007
Art.281 .... 10–019, 10–020

TABLE OF REGULATIONS

TABLE OF DIRECTIVES

TABLE OF COUNCIL DECISIONS

TABLE OF RULES OF PROCEDURE (OF THE EUROPEAN COURT OF JUSTICE AND COURT OF FIRST INSTANCE)

TABLE OF UK LEGISLATION

TABLE OF INTERNATIONAL TREATIES AND CONVENTIONS

PART I

HISTORICAL INTRODUCTION

PART 1

HISTORICAL INTRODUCTION

CHAPTER 1

FROM THE FOUNDING TREATIES TO THE TREATY ESTABLISHING A CONSTITUTION FOR EUROPE

Guide to this Chapter: It is difficult to understand the modern **1–001** European Union without knowing something of its origins and evolution. This chapter provides a brief overview of the historical development of European integration since the end of the Second World War. We begin with the establishment, by the six founding Member States, of the three original Communities: the European Coal and Steel Community (which has now expired); the European Atomic Energy Community; and (most importantly) the European Economic Community. These Communities created supranational institutions with real decision-making powers, capable of binding the Member States in those policy fields where they had agreed to act in common. From there, two major sets of developments have occurred, though they are closely inter-related. The first concerns the accession of new Member States, bringing the number of participating countries to 25. Further enlargements are envisaged in the short and longer terms, with the prospect of over 30 Member States well in sight. The second set of developments concerns reform of, and adaptations to, the substance of the Treaties. The first major instrument was the Single European Act (1986), which was concerned principally with kick-starting the process of economic integration after a period of stagnation. The next was the Maastricht Treaty (1992), which absorbed the existing Communities into a new European Union. While the Communities were granted competences over a broader range of economic and social policies (the "First Pillar"), the Union also acquired a mandate to act in the fields of foreign and security policy (the "Second Pillar") and justice and home affairs (the "Third Pillar"). The two subsequent Treaties—Amsterdam (1997) and Nice (2000)—contained further changes to the Union's institutions and activities, e.g. by reforming the decision-making procedures for exercising the competences conferred under the First Pillar. The most recent development is the Treaty establishing a Constitution for Europe (2004), which envisages a fundamental reorganisation of the Union's legal foundations and structure, together with a multitude of more detailed reforms to its institutions and activities. At the time of writing, the Constitutional Treaty has not yet been ratified by all the Member States. Indeed, having been rejected in popular referenda in two countries, it is not clear whether it will ever enter into force.

The Schuman Plan and the establishment of the ECSC

1–002   Although there was a certain ideological groundswell in favour of a "United Europe" shortly after the Second World War[1]—as evidenced by the call of the 1948 Hague Congress for Western European economic and political union—the first concrete steps towards integration were prompted by the spectre of Soviet expansion. Within days of the signature by France and the United Kingdom of the Dunkirk Treaty, providing for mutual assistance in the event of a renewal of hostilities with Germany, the breakdown of the Moscow Conference over the future of occupied Germany was to set the pattern for future strained relations between the USSR on the one side, and the United States, Great Britain and France on the other. Despite the indispensable United States defence commitment affirmed in the North Atlantic Treaty, Western Europe stood divided and vulnerable in the face of a Soviet Union whose wartime military potential had been scarcely diminished by demobilisation, and whose political influence had been enhanced by successful Communist Party coups in Bulgaria, Romania, Poland and Czechoslovakia.[2] It was in this context that Mr Robert Schuman, the French Foreign Minister, made an historic proposal to a ministerial meeting in London on May 9, 1950.[3] His proposal was for nothing less than the fusion of the coal and steel industries of France and Germany,

---

[1] On the historical context, see Milward, *The Reconstruction of Western Europe 1945–51* (1984). On the early history of the European Communities, see Palmer *et al.*, *European Unity* (1968) Introduction; Gladwyn, *The European Idea* (1967), Ch.4; Robertson, *European Institutions* (3rd ed., 1973), pp.5–17; Urwin, *The Community of Europe: A History of European Integration* (2nd ed., 1995).

[2] *NATO: Facts and Figures* (1971, Brussels), Ch.1.

[3] For the French text, see *Documents on International Affairs* (1949–50), pp.315–317. An English translation (from which the quotations in the text are extracted) appears in 22 Department of State Bulletin at pp.936, 937.

and any other countries wishing to participate, under a supranational High Authority. Not only would such a pooling of production make future conflict between France and Germany impossible, it would provide a sound basis for economic expansion. The implications of the scheme were clearly far-reaching, constituting, as Mr Schuman explained, "the first concrete foundation for a European Federation which is indispensable for the preservation of peace".

The Schuman Plan was enthusiastically endorsed by the Benelux countries, France, Germany and Italy, but the United Kingdom declined to participate, refusing to accept the supranational role of the projected High Authority. The Treaty Establishing the European Coal and Steel Community (or ECSC) was signed in Paris on April 18, 1951, and came into force on July 20 of the following year. It was concluded for a period of 50 years from that date and thus expired in July 2002.[4]

The strategy of the Treaty, inspired by the Schuman Declaration, **1–003** was to set limited and specific economic objectives as steps towards the long-term political objective of European unity. The preamble to the Treaty announced that Europe was to be built "through practical achievements which will first of all create real solidarity, and through the establishment of common bases for economic development". The economic community created pursuant to the Treaty was to constitute "the basis for a broader and deeper community among peoples long divided by bloody conflicts" and the foundations were to be laid "for institutions which will give direction to a destiny henceforward shared".

The central economic mechanism of the ECSC was a common market for coal and steel.[5] A definition of this mechanism, from a negative point of view, was given by Article 4 of the Treaty, which provided that the following were to be recognised as incompatible with the common market for coal and steel and should accordingly be abolished and prohibited within the Community:

    (a) import and export duties, or charges having equivalent effect, and quantitative restrictions on the movement of products;

    (b) measures or practices which discriminated between producers, between purchasers or between consumers, especially in prices and delivery terms or transport rates and conditions; and measures or practices which interfered with the purchaser's free choice of supplier;

    (c) subsidies or aids granted by States, or special charges imposed by States, in any form whatsoever;

---

[4] Art.97 ECSC. Since no steps were taken to renew the ECSC Treaty, the coal and steel sectors now come within the purview of the EC Treaty.

[5] Art.1 ECSC proclaims that the Community is "founded upon a common market, common objectives and common institutions".

(d) restrictive practices which tended towards the sharing or exploiting of markets.

Article 4 thus envisaged a Community-wide market for coal and steel free from interference by the Member States or by economic operators tending to impede the flow of trade or to distort the play of competition. The Community was empowered to carry out its task under the Treaty "with a limited measure of intervention", *inter alia*, by placing financial resources at the disposal of undertakings for investment and by bearing part of the cost of readaptation.[6] Only when circumstances so required was it authorised to exert direct influence upon production or upon the market, for instance, by imposing production quotas.[7]

The EDC and EPC—a false dawn

1-004   Significant as the founding of the ECSC may have been, it contributed little of itself to the increasingly pressing problem of incorporating West Germany into the defence network established by the Brussels and North Atlantic Treaties.

While the United States was enthusiastic for German participation, France was naturally chary of seeing her recently vanquished enemy so soon rearmed. At the instigation of Sir Winston Churchill and Mr Paul Reynaud,[8] the Consultative Assembly of the Council of Europe[9] called for the "immediate creation of a unified European Army, under the authority of a European Minister of Defence, subject to proper European democratic control and acting in full co-operation with the United States and Canada".[10]

After a French initiative known as the "Pleven Plan", the Treaty Establishing the European Defence Community (EDC) was signed—subject to ratification— by the Benelux countries, France, Germany and Italy.[11] Once again the United Kingdom held aloof. If the ECSC had been calculated to bind Germany to France industrially, the EDC was to provide the framework for German rearmament.

---

[6] Art.5 ECSC.

[7] *ibid.* second sub-para., third indent.

[8] Robertson, *European Institutions* (3rd ed., 1973), p.18.

[9] The Council of Europe is an inter-governmental organisation established in 1949. Its aim is to achieve greater unity among its members, and to this end it seeks agreement on common action "in economic, social, cultural, scientific, legal and administrative matters and in the maintenance and further realisation of human rights and fundamental freedoms". See Bowett, *The Law of International Institutions* (4th ed., 1982), p.168; Robertson, *European Institutions* (3rd ed., 1973), p.36.

[10] Resolution of the Consultative Assembly of the Council of Europe, August 11, 1950; *Documents on International Affairs* (1949–50), p.331. As is clear from the quotation cited in the text, the Council at times interprets the terms of its statute with some liberality. Robertson, *European Institutions* (3rd ed., 1973), p.19.

[11] May 27, 1952. See *Documents on International Affairs* (1952) pp.116–162. See also Furdson, *The European Defence Community: A History* (1979).

The projected Defence Community had two significant characteristics. First, it was to be endowed with a supranational institutional structure not unlike that of the Coal and Steel Community. Secondly, its statute assumed that it would be of a transitional nature, and would give way to some more comprehensive form of federal or confederal European Union.

The EDC Treaty provided for a European Army, composed of **1–005** units placed at the disposal of the Council of Ministers by the Member States. A Common Budget would be drawn up, and an executive body, the "Commissariat", would lay down common programmes in the field of armaments, provisioning and military infrastructure. The objects of the Community were to be purely defensive, within the context of the North Atlantic Treaty.

The transitional nature of the proposed Community was evidenced by the terms of Article 8(2), which provided that the institutional structure laid down in the Treaty would remain in force until displaced by the establishment of the federal or confederal organisation envisaged by Article 38.

This latter Article required the Assembly of the EDC to make proposals to the Governments of the Member States on the establishment of a directly elected Assembly, and the powers it should exercise. Particular regard was to be had to the principle that such a modified Parliamentary body should be able to constitute one of the elements in a subsequent federal or confederal structure.

These proposals were to be presented to the Governments of the **1–006** Six after the Assembly of the EDC assumed its functions, but within days of the signature of the Treaty the Consultative Assembly of the Council of Europe resolved that it would be "of great advantage if the basic principles of a European supranational political authority and the nature and limits of its powers were defined within the next few months, without waiting for the entry into force of the Treaty instituting the European Defence Community".[12] Despite the fact that the Assembly provided for in Article 38 of the EDC Treaty was not yet in existence, and that the Article only referred to the constitution of a future Parliamentary body, the Foreign Ministers of the Member States of the Coal and Steel Community requested the Members of the Coal and Steel Community Assembly to co-opt additional Members, reorganise the distribution of seats laid down in the Paris Treaty in accordance with that prescribed for the Assembly of the proposed EDC, and draw up a draft Treaty for a European

---

[12] Resolution of May 30, 1952. Texts Adopted (1952), and see *Report on the Constitutional Committee instituted to work out a Draft Treaty setting up a European Political Community* (Paris, December 20, 1952), p.6.

Political Community (EPC). On March 10, 1953, the "Ad Hoc Assembly" presented the requested draft.[13]

The "European Community" proposed by the Ad Hoc Assembly provided for the extensive political and economic integration of its Members. Its aims were as follows:

— to contribute towards the protection of human rights and fundamental freedoms in Member States;
— to co-operate with the other free nations in ensuring the security of Member States against all aggression;
— to ensure the co-ordination of the foreign policy of Member States in questions likely to involve the existence, the security or the prosperity of the Community;
— to promote the development of employment and the improvement of the standard of living in Member States, by means, in particular, of the progressive establishment of a common market.

To ensure the protection of human rights in the proposed Community, provision was made for the application—as part of the Community Statute—of the provisions of section I of the European Convention on Human Rights, along with the first Protocol to that Convention, signed in Paris on March 20, 1952.

The Institutions of the EPC were to comprise a bicameral legislature, a European Executive Council, a Council of National Ministers, a Court of Justice, and an Economic and Social Council. Financial resources would be derived from a combination of Community taxation and contributions from the Member States.

The hopes of those who saw the future of Western Europe in immediate federation were dashed when the French Parliament voted against ratification of the EDC Treaty. A change of Government in France, and an easing of tension between East and West,[14] contributed to the rejection of the Treaty by the combined votes of Gaullists, Communists, Socialists and Radicals.[15]

In the event, Germany's participation in the defence of Western Europe was achieved by other means. The Paris Agreements of October 23, 1954 provided for the recognition of the Federal Republic of Germany as a sovereign state, and for its subsequent accession to the North Atlantic Treaty.[16]

---

[13] See *Information and Official Documents of the Constitutional Committee of the Ad Hoc Assembly* (Paris, 1953), pp.53 *et seq.* For a brief but informative account of the events surrounding the preparation of the draft Treaty and its ultimate demise, see Griffiths, "Europe's First Constitution: The European Political Community, 1952–1954" in Martin (ed.) *The Construction of Europe* (1994).

[14] Robertson, *European Institutions* (3rd ed., 1973), p.21.

[15] Palmer *et al., European Unity* (1968) Introduction.

[16] *NATO: Facts and Figures* (Brussels, 1971), p.35. For the Protocol to the North Atlantic Treaty on the Accession of the Federal Republic of Germany, and the texts known collectively as the "Paris Agreements", see Apps 9 and 10.

The Spaak Report and the two Treaties of Rome

Despite the setback represented by the rejection of the EDC **1–007** Treaty, the Six were still convinced of the need for closer integration. At a Conference held in the Sicilian city of Messina in 1955, the Foreign Ministers of the ECSC countries expressed the belief that the time had come to make "a fresh advance towards the building of Europe", but that this must be achieved "first of all, in the economic field".[17] The two objectives were agreed of developing atomic energy for peaceful purposes, and establishing a European common market. An intergovernmental committee under the Chairmanship of the Belgian Foreign Minister, Mr Paul-Henri Spaak, was entrusted with the task of making proposals to this end. The United Kingdom was invited to participate in the work of the committee, but although a Board of Trade official was initially dispatched, he was recalled after a few weeks.

The Spaak Report was published in April 1956.[18] In the light of its conclusions two new Treaties were negotiated, one providing for the establishment of a European Economic Community (EEC) and the other for the establishment of a European Atomic Energy Community (Euratom). The EEC and Euratom Treaties were signed in Rome on March 25, 1957 and came into force on January 1, 1958.

The preamble to the EEC Treaty expresses the determination of the High Contracting Parties "to lay the foundation of an ever closer union among the peoples of Europe", and, from 1958, it has been that Treaty which has provided the main framework of the continuing process of European integration. As we shall see, successive amendments to the Treaty have greatly extended the range and variety of the governmental activities falling within its scope. This reached a point where it was thought appropriate to drop the adjective "Economic" from the name of the Community: it is now known simply as "the European Community" (or EC).[19] To avoid confusion, from here on we refer to the Community by that name, and to the Treaty as "the EC Treaty". When making an historical point, as in the present Chapter, we refer to "the original EEC Treaty".

The central mechanism of the EC was (and remains) a common market covering all economic sectors other than those falling within the purview of the ECSC Treaty (while it remained in force) or the Euratom Treaty.[20] The aim is to create, on a Community scale, economic conditions similar to those on the market of a single

---

[17] *Documents on International Affairs* (19550), p.163; Cmnd.9525.
[18] *Rapport des chefs de délégation aux ministres des affaires étrangères* (Brussels) April 21, 1956. A summarised translation of Part I of the Spaak Report, "The Common Market", was published by Political and Economic Planning as Broadsheet No.405 of December 17, 1956.
[19] The change of name was effected by the TEU (see below).
[20] See Art.305 EC.

state.[21] This involved the establishment of a customs union, through the elimination of all customs duties and quantitative restrictions (or quotas) in trade between the Member States and the erection of a common customs tariff (CCT), as well as the removal of barriers to the free movement of "the factors of production"—labour, business and capital. In addition, the Treaty contains rules designed to prevent competition from being restricted by arrangements between private operators, or by government subsidies or the activities of State monopolies. Legal machinery was provided for the harmonisation of national legislation that may have a bearing on the well-functioning of the common market. Other primordial features of the system are the common agricultural policy and the common transport policy, relating to sectors where a completely free market was thought impracticable; and provisions relating to the Community's external trade and the possibility of creating an "association" with a third country or an international organisation.[22]

A single set of institutions

1–008   The ECSC Treaty created four main institutions: a High Authority, a Special Council of Ministers, a Common Assembly and a Court of Justice. In accordance with the Schuman Plan, the leading role in the implementation of the Treaty was given to a supranational High Authority, whose members were under a duty to act with complete independence, in the Community interest.[23] The High Authority was empowered to take legally binding decisions[24]; and was authorised, *inter alia*, to procure funds,[25] to fix maximum and minimum prices for certain products,[26] and to fine undertakings in breach of the ECSC's rules on competition.[27] The Special Council of Ministers, a body composed of representatives of the Member States, was given the function of harmonising "the action of the High Authority and that of Governments, which are responsible for the general economic policies of their countries".[28] With limited exceptions, the role of the Council in the institutional system of the ECSC was confined to consultation with the High Authority and the giving (or withholding) of its assent (*avis conforme*) to actions which the latter proposed to take.

According to the EC and Euratom Treaties, the two later Communities were each to have, in their turn, four main institutions: an

---

[21] See the description of the common market in Case 15/81 *Schul v Inspecteur de Invoerrechten en Accijnzen* [1982] E.C.R. 1409, 1431–1432; [1981] 3 C.M.L.R. 229.
[22] As to the extension of the scope of the EC Treaty by the SEA, the TEU and the TA, see below.
[23] Art.9 ECSC, replaced by Merger Treaty, Art.10.
[24] Art.14 ECSC.
[25] Art.49 ECSC.
[26] Art.61 ECSC.
[27] Arts 65 and 66 ECSC.
[28] Art.26 ECSC.

Assembly, a Council, a Commission and a Court of Justice; but, to avoid unnecessary proliferation, a Convention was signed contemporaneously with the Treaties of Rome providing for there to be a single Assembly (now the European Parliament) and a single Court to carry out the functions assigned to those institutions under the three Community Treaties.[29] For some years after 1957, however, in addition to the High Authority and the Special Council of Ministers of the ECSC, there was a separate EC Council and Commission and a separate Euratom Council and Commission. That situation was brought to an end by the Treaty establishing a Single Council and a Single Commission of the European Communities (known as the "Merger Treaty") which was signed in April 1965 and came into force in July 1967.[30] From that time, the ECSC (while it remained in force), the EC and Euratom have been served by the same set of institutions whose powers vary depending on the Treaty under which they act for a given purpose.

As will be seen in Chapters 2 and 3, in the institutional structure of the Rome Treaties, and particularly of the EC Treaty, decision-making power is concentrated in the hands of the Council, and the role of the Commission is principally that of the initiator, and subsequently the executant, of Council decisions.[31] This difference, as compared with the institutional structure of the old ECSC, may be explained by the fact that, whereas the rules applicable to the coal and steel sectors were spelt out in considerable detail in the ECSC Treaty itself, in many areas of EC competence the Treaty merely establishes a framework for common action, leaving fundamental political choices to be made by the Community institutions. It was inevitable that the final say in respect of such choices be left to the Council, the institution in which Member States are directly represented.

Enlargement—from 6 to 15

Largely in response to the creation of the EC, Austria, Denmark, **1–009** Norway, Sweden, Switzerland, Portugal and the United Kingdom signed the Stockholm Convention on January 4, 1960, and the European Free Trade Association (or EFTA) came into being in May of that year. The primary object of the "Outer Seven" was to offset any detrimental effects to their trade resulting from the

---

[29] Convention on certain Institutions Common to the European Communities, March 25, 1957; see Sweet & Maxwell's *Encyclopedia of European Community Law, European Community Treaties*, Vol.I, Pt B8, B8–029.

[30] Treaty Establishing a Single Council and a Single Commission of the European Communities; see Sweet & Maxwell's *Encyclopedia*, B8–034.

[31] The Commission is also "guardian of the Treaties", with powers to ensure that the Member States and other Community institutions comply with their obligations: see, in particular, Art.211 EC, first indent and Arts 226, 230 and 232 EC. See further, Ch.13.

progressive elimination of tariffs inside the Community by a similar reduction within EFTA.

To a certain extent, EFTA was regarded as a stepping stone to possible future Community membership. As the White Paper that was published in July 1971 setting out the terms agreed, and the case for United Kingdom membership of the Communities explained: "From the outset . . . it was recognised that some members of the EFTA might eventually wish to join, and others to seek closer trading arrangements with, the European Communities".[32] Indeed, barely 14 months after the Stockholm Convention entered into force, the Macmillan Government applied for EC membership. This was to be the first of two applications thwarted by the opposition of President de Gaulle of France. After lengthy negotiations had taken place with the Six, the French President made it clear, in January 1963, that he would not consent to British accession.

Applications in 1967 by the United Kingdom, Denmark, Ireland and Norway met with a similar rebuff. Nevertheless, these four countries left their applications "lying on the table", and at the Hague Summit Conference of the Six in December 1969, summoned on the initiative of the new President of France, Mr Pompidou, it was agreed that "The entry of other countries of the continent to the Communities . . . could undoubtedly help the Communities to grow to dimensions more in conformity with the present state of world economy and technology . . . In so far as the applicant States accept the Treaties and their political objective . . . the Heads of State or Government have indicated their agreement to the opening of negotiations between the Community on the one hand and the applicant States on the other".[33]

Negotiations between the applicant States and the Six formally opened on June 30, 1970, and a Treaty of Accession was eventually signed on January 22, 1972. The provisions of the Treaty, and the detailed adaptations contained in the Act of Accession annexed to it, have served as a model, *mutatis mutandis*, for later enlargements. The only institutional changes required were those resulting from the need to accommodate the additional Member States. The elimination of customs duties and quotas between the prospective Member and the Six, and the adoption of the Common External Tariff, were to be phased in between April 1973 and July 1977. A transitional period was also to be allowed for the adoption of the Common Agricultural Policy, and for the build up of contributions

---

[32] See *The United Kingdom and the European Communities*, Cmnd.4715. After the accession of Denmark, Ireland and the United Kingdom of the European Communities, Austria, Finland, Norway, Portugal, Sweden and Switzerland entered into free trade agreements within the Nine. See *Seventh General Report on the Activities of the European Communities* (19730), p.400.

[33] *Third General Report on the Activities of the Communities* (1969) Annex: Documents on the Summit Conference, pp.497, 489.

to the Community budget. Although the United Kingdom would be compelled to forego Commonwealth preference as such, special arrangements were agreed for the access of New Zealand diary products and lamb, and the importation of sugar from Commonwealth suppliers. It was understood that association arrangements comparable with those already accorded to developing countries enjoying traditional relations with the original Six would be made with developing countries in the Commonwealth.[34]

On January 1, 1973, the Treaty of Accession entered into force, and Denmark, Ireland and the United Kingdom became Members of the three Communities. Norway, which had signed the Treaty on January 22, 1972, did not proceed to ratification, following an adverse result in a national referendum held on the issue of membership.

British membership of the Communities was briefly put in doubt **1–010** by the election in February 1974 of a Labour Government. Although the membership negotiations which were brought to a successful conclusion by the Conservative administration had been set in train by their predecessors, Labour in opposition declared themselves unable to accept the terms of entry finally agreed. When Labour returned to power, the Government of Mr Harold Wilson set out to "renegotiate" the agreed terms in respect of agriculture, contributions to the Community Budget, economic and monetary union, State aids to industry, movement of capital, the Commonwealth and developing countries, and value added tax, and on January 23, 1975 it was announced that a national referendum would be held on the results of the renegotiation. The Government declared itself satisfied with those results and felt able to recommend to the British people that they cast their votes in favour of continued membership of the European Communities.[35] This view was endorsed by an overwhelming majority of the votes in the referendum which followed on June 5, 1975.[36]

The transitional period for the accession of the three new Member States was barely half spent when a further application for membership was received from Greece. Negotiations commenced on July 27, 1976. The instruments relating to Greece's accession were signed in Athens on May 28, 1979 and Greece became the tenth Member State on January 1, 1981.[37]

Meanwhile, Spain and Portugal had also applied for membership. After long and sometimes difficult negotiations, the instruments of accession were signed in Madrid and Libson on June 12, 1985 and Spain and Portugal joined the Communities on January 1, 1986.[38]

---

[34] See [1973] O.J. L2/1.
[35] See *Membership of the European Community,* Cmnd.5999; *Report on Renegotiation,* Cmnd.6003.
[36] See Irving, "The United Kingdom Referendum" (1975–76) 1 E.L.Rev. 1.
[37] [1979] O.J. L291.
[38] [1985] O.J. L302.

The next enlargement, which took place on January 1, 1995, brought into the European Union (or "EU"), as it had by then become (see below), three States which had formerly belonged to EFTA: Austria, Finland and Sweden.[39] Norway had also applied for membership, and had taken part in the negotiations and signed the accession instruments; however, once again as in 1972, the referendum in that country on the ratification of the Treaty of Accession produced a negative result. So, by this stage, the original Six had become the Fifteen, comprising all the European States that escaped the imposition of Communist regimes protected by Soviet military power in the aftermath of the Second World War, with the exception of Iceland, Norway, Lichtenstein and Switzerland.

Amendments and development of the founding Treaties

1–011   Apart from the amendments contained in the Merger Treaty and in the Accession Treaties referred to above, the texts of the three founding Treaties have been amended or developed over the years by a series of Treaties, Decisions or Acts, the most significant of which are identified below.

The Budgetary Treaties of 1970 and 1975

1–012   These two Treaties, which were signed, respectively, on April 22, 1970 and on July 22, 1975, replaced the original budgetary procedure of the Communities with a new one giving important powers to the European Parliament.[40] The different roles in that procedure of the Council, which has the last word in respect of so-called "compulsory expenditure", and the Parliament, which has the last word in respect of "non-compulsory expenditure", are analysed in Chapter 2. The 1975 Treaty also created a new body, the Court of Auditors, to act as a financial watchdog for the Communities.

Own resources decisions

1–013   In the early years of the EEC and Euratom, the Communities' revenue came from direct financial contributions by the Member States, according to scales that were laid down by the Treaties. However, Article 269 EEC and Article 173 Euratom looked forward to the replacement of financial contributions by a system giving the Communities their "own resources".[41] A legislative procedure was

---

[39] [1994] O.J. C241/10. See also Council Decision 95/1 [1995] O.J. L1/1, adjusting the instruments of accession in the light of Norway's failure to ratify.

[40] The text of the 1970 Treaty is published at [1971] O.J. L2/1 and that of the 1975 Treaty at [1977] O.J. L359/1.

[41] The relevant provision of the EC Treaty, Art.200, was deleted as being obsolete by the TA. Different financial arrangements applied under the ECSC Treaty: see Arts 49 ECSC *et seq.*

provided for the establishment of such a system by a unanimous decision of the Council, acting on the basis of proposals by the Commission and after consulting the European Parliament, with the additional step that the Council decision be recommended to the Member States for adoption in accordance with their respective national requirements. That especially solemn procedure gives the decisions to which it applies a legal status only slightly inferior to the Treaties themselves.

A first own resources Decision was adopted in 1970.[42] This has been replaced by a series of Decisions, forming part of the package of measures governing the Union's finances, which it has become customary to re-negotiate every seven years. The multi-annual financial packages are discussed further in Chapter 2. The currently applicable own resources Decision was adopted in September 2000.[43] It is due to be replaced under the financial arrangements that will apply in respect of the period 2007 to 2013; political agreement on the new financial package was reached between the Governments of the Member States at the European Council of December 2005, though at the time of writing negotiations with the European Parliament and the Commission were still continuing.

Under the new arrangements, when they come into force, the principal categories of revenue constituting own resources are likely to remain unchanged, namely:

— levies and other charges imposed in respect of trade in agricultural products under the rules of the common agricultural policy;
— customs duties levied under the Common Customs Tariff on imports from third countries;
— the application of a uniform rate[44] to a uniform VAT assessment base determined in a uniform manner for Member States in accordance with Community rules;
— the application of a rate (variable from year to year, depending on the amount of additional revenue needed to balance the budget) to the sum of all the Member States' GNP.[45]

Of those four categories of own resources, only agricultural levies and customs duties (often referred to as "traditional own resources") have the true character of Community taxes. They are collected on behalf of the Communities by the Member States, which have the

---

[42] Council Decision 70/243 [1970] O.J. L94/19.
[43] Council Decision 2000/597/EC, Euratom of 29 September 2000 on the system of the European Communities' own resources, [2000] O.J. L253/46.
[44] *ibid.*, Art.2(1)(c) and (4).
[45] *ibid.*, Art.2(1)(d).

right to retain, by way of collection costs, 25 per cent of the amounts paid.[46] The VAT own resource does not give the Communities a fixed share of Member States' *actual* VAT receipts, since the prescribed rate is applied to an artificially constructed assessment basis. As for the GNP own resource, its purpose is, in part, to redress the economically regressive effect of the VAT resource, which, because it is related to consumption, falls more heavily on the less prosperous Member States, by shifting the burden towards those that are more prosperous. The GNP rate is fixed each year under the budgetary procedure, to cover the amount needed to balance the budget, after account has been taken of revenue from the other three resources.

It may be added that, from 1985 onwards, own resources Decisions have included a mechanism for the correction, in favour of the United Kingdom, of so-called "budgetary imbalances", *i.e.* the difference between payments to, and receipts from, the Community budget.[47] At the European Council in December 2005, the United Kingdom agreed to forego the budgetary correction to which it would otherwise have been entitled, in respect of expenditure resulting from the enlargement of the Union.[48]

A directly elected European Parliament

1–014   Article 190(4) EEC and the corresponding provisions of the other Treaties[49] lay down a solemn procedure for the enactment of rules for direct elections to the European Parliament. Under that procedure, an Act concerning the election of the representatives of the European Parliament by direct universal suffrage was approved by the Council in September 1976 and recommended to the Member States for adoption in accordance with their respective constitutional requirements.[50] The first elections were held in June 1979 and these have been followed by elections in 1984, 1989, 1994, 1999 and 2004. Further discussion of these developments is found in the section relating to the European Parliament in Chapter 2.

The Single European Act (SEA)

1–015   The Single European Act was signed on February 17, 1986 and entered into force on July 1, 1987.[51] Its odd-seeming title is explained by the fact that, within a single legal instrument, there were juxtaposed provisions amending the three EC Treaties and

---

[46] *ibid.*, Art.2(3).
[47] *ibid.*, Art.4.
[48] See further, Ch.2.
[49] Art.21(3) ECSC; Art.108(3) Euratom.
[50] Council Decision 76/787 [1976] O.J. L278/1.
[51] The SEA is published at [1987] O.J. L169/1.

provisions organising co-operation in the inter-governmental sphere of foreign policy.

The amendments to the Treaties contained in Title II of the SEA were the most extensive adopted up to that time. They included the introduction of a new "co-operation procedure" giving the European Parliament a significantly enhanced role in the legislative process, which is discussed in Chapter 3. One of the principal objectives of the SEA was to ensure the completion of the EC's internal market by the end of 1992.[52] The SEA also inserted into the EC Treaty a number of specific new legal bases for Community action, for example on: economic and social cohesion;[53] research and technological development;[54] and the protection of the environment.[55]

Title III of the SEA contained the Treaty provisions on European Cooperation in the sphere of foreign policy, known more shortly as "European Political Co-operation" (or EPC). Those provisions have been superseded by Title V of the Treaty on European Union, which constitutes the legal basis for the common foreign and security policy (see below).

The Treaty on European Union (TEU)

The TEU[56] (often referred to by the name of the Dutch city, **1–016** Maastricht, where it was signed in February 1992) entered into force on November 1, 1993.

The Treaty brought into being a new legal and political entity, the European Union. Article 1 TEU says that "[t]he Union shall be founded on the European Communities, supplemented by the policies and forms of co-operation established by this Treaty". That wording brings out the complex character of the Union and the preponderant influence of the three Communities (EC, Euratom and ECSC while it remained in force) within it. The clumsy phrase, "policies and forms of co-operation", refers to the legal arrangements provided by Title V and Title VI of the TEU, which organise the activity of the common institutions in two fields of activity the Member States could not agree to bring within the purview of the EC Treaty. Title V concerns the common foreign and security policy (or CFSP). Broadly speaking, that covers the *political* aspect of external relations (diplomatic contacts, election monitoring and other forms of political assistance to third countries, security activities such as peace-keeping and peace-making, prospectively

---

[52] See, in particular, Art.14 and Art.95 EC.
[53] Arts 158 to 162 EC.
[54] Arts 163 to 173 EC.
[55] Arts 174 to 176 EC.
[56] [1992] O.J. C191/1. Note that the numbering of the TEU, like that of the EC Treaty, was altered by the Treaty of Amsterdam.

even defence), to be distinguished from external *economic* relations (such as trade, development co-operation and emergency aid) which are within the competence of the EC. Those two branches of the EU's external relations competence require delicate consideration. In the TEU as originally concluded, Title VI grouped together, under the heading "Co-operation in the fields of justice and home affairs" (or JHA), a variety of matters concerning the treatment of third country nationals and aspects of law enforcement and the maintenance of public order. These included: aspects of the free movement of persons, such as asylum policy, the control of the Union's external frontiers, and immigration policy; combating drug addiction and international fraud; and co-operation between the Member States' judicial, customs and police authorities. As we shall see, certain of those matters have now been transferred to the EC Treaty, pursuant to the Treaty of Amsterdam (TA).

The image of a Greek temple façade, with three pillars joined by a pediment, is commonly used to illustrate the constitutional structure that was created by the TEU. The difference between the "First Pillar" (comprising the pre-existing Communities) and the "Second and Third Pillars" (respectively, Titles V and VI of the TEU) lies in the much lesser degree to which, in respect of the latter, the sovereign powers of the Member States have been curtailed. The "pediment" consists of the elements common to the three components of the Union, notably that they are served by a single institutional framework,[57] and that there is common machinery for the amendment of the Treaties,[58] as well as for enlargement.[59] The relationship between the EC and the EU is further explored in Chapter 10.[60]

1–017   Besides establishing the Union structure, the TEU effected a number of significant reforms within the EC system (the First Pillar), two of which may briefly be noticed here. First, an effort was made to tackle the problem of the "democratic deficit" in the system, by changing the rules on the appointment of the Commission and by introducing a new legislative procedure, commonly referred to as "co-decision", both measures being designed to enhance the role of the European Parliament: these are matters considered in Chapters 2 and 3. Secondly, the Treaty contained detailed provisions on the organisation of economic and monetary union (EMU), and a timetable for its realisation in three stages. It was specifically provided that the third stage, involving the introduction of a single

---

[57] Art.3 TEU.
[58] Art.48 TEU.
[59] Art.49 TEU.
[60] The structure created by the TEU has been much criticised. See, in particular, Everling, "Reflections on the Structure of the Union" (1992) 29 C.M.L.Rev. 1053; Curtin, "The Constitutional Structure of the Union: a Europe of Bits and Pieces" (1993) 30 C.M.L.Rev. 17.

currency, must start, at the latest, on January 1, 1999; and so, in the event, it did, with the introduction on that date of the "euro" as the currency of 11 out of the then 15 Member States.

The ratification process of the TEU was thrown off course by the negative outcome of the referendum that was held in Denmark in June 1992. Subsequent referenda in Ireland in June, and in France in September 1992, brought votes in favour of ratification, although in the latter case by a narrow margin. Political and economic uncertainty increased as a result of turbulence in the international money markets during the period immediately preceding and following the French referendum, and this led to the suspension by Italy and the United Kingdom of their membership of the exchange rate mechanism of the European Monetary System and to the reintroduction of exchange rate controls by Spain and Ireland. However, at an extraordinary meeting of the European Council at Birmingham on October 16, 1992, the Heads of State or Government reaffirmed their commitment to the TEU. It was agreed that the Community must develop together, on the basis of the TEU, while respecting, as the Treaty did, the identity and diversity of the Member States.[61]

That positive development was confirmed by the European Council held in Edinburgh on December 11 and 12, 1992. Agreement was reached in Edinburgh on texts establishing interpretations of various provisions of the TEU which the Danish authorities announced would make it possible to hold a second referendum, with a good prospect that Denmark would be in a position to ratify the Treaty. The European Council also approved texts on the application by the Council of the principle of subsidiarity (see Chapter 4) and on greater "openness" in the legislative process. Finally, there was agreement on the financial arrangements that were applied for the seven-year period to 1999 ("the Delors II package"[62]), and this, in turn, opened the way for the launching, early in 1993, of negotiations with the EFTA applicants for Community membership.[63]

There were more alarms and delays during 1993. Ratification of the TEU by the Parliament of the United Kingdom was achieved by the narrowest of margins; and in Germany the Treaty was the subject of a legal challenge before the Constitutional Court.[64] Thus, it was only on January 1, 1993, towards the end of the Belgian Presidency, that the TEU finally entered into force, and the EU appeared as a new player on the international stage.

---

[61] See Presidency Conclusions, Birmingham, October 1992, to which the text of the "Birmingham Declaration" is annexed.

[62] See the discussion, in Ch.2, of the financial arrangements under which relative peace has been preserved between the Council and the European Parliament in budgetary matters since 1988.

[63] See Presidency Conclusions, Edinburgh, December 1992.

[64] See Bundesvervassungsgericht, judgment of October 12, 1993, 2 BvR 2134 and 2 BvR 2153/92 [1994] 1 C.M.L.R. 57.

The Treaty of Amsterdam (TA)

1–018   To some of those who had been involved in the Intergovernmental Conference (IGC) on the TEU, the institutional reforms that were agreed seemed disappointing; and provision was made in Article N(2) of the Treaty (since deleted by the TA) for a new IGC to be convened as early as 1996, in order to consider further changes. However, the ambition to press ahead with further "deepening" of European integration was overtaken by other aims which became the primary focus of the 1996 IGC: to counteract the alienation of public opinion from the whole EU enterprise, which had become painfully apparent during the process of ratifying the TEU; and to effect the changes in the composition and functioning of the institutions of the Union, necessary in order to pave the way for an enlargement, by then perceived as politically ineluctable, that would bring in many (and eventually perhaps all) the countries of central and eastern Europe, as well as other applicants from the Mediterranean area (see below).[65]

The IGC on the Treaty of Amsterdam completed its work in June 1997, and the Treaty was signed in October of that year.[66] The ratification process went more smoothly than that of the TEU, and the TA entered into force on May 1, 1999.[67]

A major achievement of the TA was the reform of the Community legislative process, in ways that are considered in detail in Chapter 3. The TA also brought about a significant shift of matters relating to the treatment of third country nationals from the Third Pillar to the First Pillar: there is a new Title IV of Part Three of the EC Treaty on "Visas, asylum, immigration and other policies related to free movement of persons", which also includes provisions relating to judicial co-operation in civil matters. The reorganised Third Pillar is now focused on "Police and judicial co-operation in criminal matters", where the scope of Union powers has been notably extended. Another reform, which will be examined in Chapter 4, was the adoption of the principle of "closer co-operation". The idea behind the principle is that it should be possible for a limited number of Member States to establish, within the institutional framework of the Union, rules in relation to a certain matter, which will apply only to themselves, and not to the non-participating Member States.

The Treaty of Nice (TN)

1–019   There were, however, two important issues, regarded as relevant to the impending enlargement of the Union, on which the IGC on the Treaty of Amsterdam was unable to reach agreement: the size

---

[65] On the task of the IGC, see Dashwood (ed.), *Reviewing Maastricht Issues for the 1996 IGC* (Sweet & Maxwell, 1996).

[66] See the text of the TA as published in [1997] O.J. C340.

[67] On the TA, see e.g. Duff, *The Treaty of Amsterdam* (Sweet & Maxwell, 1997); Langrish, "The Treaty of Amsterdam: Selected Highlights" (1998) 23 E.L.Rev. 3.

and composition of the Commission; and the distribution of votes between the Member States when the Council acts by a qualified majority (the so-called "weighting" of votes in the Council).[68] Those matters, together with a possible extension of the policy areas in which the Council is empowered to act by a qualified majority (rather than by unanimity), were placed on the agenda of a new IGC which completed its work in December 2000. The TN was signed on February 26, 2001.[69] As with the Maastricht Treaty, the ratification process was thrown off course by a negative referendum result, this time in Ireland; but following a second popular vote in the Irish Republic, the TN finally entered into force on February 1, 2003.[70]

The TN carried through important reforms intended to adapt the institutional functioning of the Union to the challenges of further enlargement, for example in relation to: the scope of both qualified majority voting and the co-decision procedure (Chapter 3); the provisions on closer (renamed "enhanced") cooperation between groups of Member States (Chapter 4); and the structure and jurisdiction of the Union courts (Chapter 12). The other major issues of institutional concern were also addressed: the size and composition of the Commission; the weighting of votes in Council; and also the composition of the European Parliament. However, since the TN was finalised before it was decided when and in what order the various candidate countries would eventually accede to the Union, many of the relevant provisions on these issues sought merely to establish templates for future reform—the full details of which have since been finalised in the Treaties of Accession 2003 and 2005 (see below).

For example, a Protocol to the TN established a new weighting of votes within Council as between the then 15 Member States, envisaged to take effect during 2005; but Declarations annexed to the TN also set out the Member States' common position on this issue for the purposes of negotiating with the candidate countries. In the end, that common position was partly embodied in the Treaty of Accession 2003; the TN Protocol was therefore replaced by a new set of weightings applicable to the enlarged Union of 25 Member States, taking effect as from November 1, 2004. The common position was carried through to completion in the Treaty of Accession 2005; the weighting of votes in Council will thus be revised again upon the accession of Bulgaria and Romania. The TN provided the model for the current system—but the law is that contained in the EU and EC Treaties as amended by the TN *and* the later Treaties of Accession.

---

[68] The political and legal link established between those two matters is discussed in Ch.2.
[69] See the text of the TN as published at [2001] O.J. C80.
[70] On the TN, see e.g. St Bradley, "Institutional Design in the Treaty of Nice" (2001) 38 C.M.L.Rev. 1095; Dashwood, "The Constitution of the European Union After Nice: Law-Making Procedures" (2001) 26 E.L.Rev. 215.

Enlargement—from 15 to 25 (plus . . .)

1–020   We have mentioned several times the pressure for internal reform
of the Union's structure and functioning occasioned by its enlargement into central and eastern Europe. It was, in fact, the collapse of
the Communist regimes across that region, symbolised by the
dismantling of the Berlin Wall in 1989 and given concrete reality by
the withdrawal of the Red Army behind the borders of what was
once more to become Russia, which opened up the perspective of a
much more challenging enlargement than the EU had ever previously experienced.

In the light of those historic events, so-called "Europe Agreements" were concluded with a large number of central and eastern
European countries (CEECs): Bulgaria, the Czech Republic, Hungary, Poland, Romania, Slovakia and Slovenia, together with the three
Baltic Republics that were formerly part of the Soviet Union,
Estonia, Latvia and Lithuania. The Agreements established a close
"association" between the EU and each of those countries, and
explicitly held out the prospect of eventual accession. They were
bolstered by the adoption of pre-accession strategies to help each of
the countries concerned prepare for membership, *inter alia*, by
providing technical assistance on the harmonisation of their legislation and administrative structures and practices with those of the
Union. Other candidates for membership of the Union included
Cyprus, Malta and Turkey, with which the EC has longstanding
association agreements.[71]

The European Council held in Luxembourg in December 1997
decided that accession negotiations should formally be opened with
five of the CEECs, namely the Czech Republic, Estonia, Hungary,
Poland and Slovenia, as well as with Cyprus. However, the Helsinki
European Council in December 1999 reaffirmed "the inclusive
nature of the accession process, which now comprises 13 candidate
States within a single framework". Those States, it was said, "are
participating in the accession process on an equal footing". Clearly,
though, not all of the candidates were destined to fulfil the political
and economic criteria for membership of the Union at the same
time. The Helsinki Conclusions stated that "the Union should be in
a position to welcome new Member States from the end of 2002 as
soon as they have demonstrated their ability to assume the obligations of membership and once the negotiating process has been
successfully completed".[72]

1–021   As events turned out, the Treaty of Accession 2003 provided for
the accession to the Union of 10 new Member States (Cyprus, the
Czech Republic, Estonia, Hungary, Latvia, Lithuania, Malta, Poland,

---

[71] "Association" is a form of relationship involving "special, privileged links with a
non-member country": Case 12/86 *Demirel* [1987] E.C.R. 3719, para.9.
[72] See Presidency Conclusions, paras 3–13.

Slovakia and Slovenia) as from May 1, 2004.[73] This "Big Bang" enlargement took effect subject to two main sets of legal provisions.[74] In the first place, the Treaty of Accession 2003 contained numerous transitional provisions intended to ensure the smooth assimilation of the new Member States into the Union (e.g., in the field of the free movement of workers and freedom to provide services); as well as to provide a realistic timetable for the full application of Union law within those countries (as with certain aspects of agricultural, environmental, transport and energy policies). In the second place, the Treaty of Accession 2003 provided for more permanent adjustments to the EU and EC Treaties so as to accommodate the new Member States: for example, as regards the allocation of seats within the European Parliament, and (as we have seen) the weighting of votes within the Council of Ministers. A further Treaty of Accession, signed on April 25, 2005, envisages the accession of Bulgaria and Romania on January 1, 2007 (though the Council may decide to postpone accession by one or both countries for another year).[75] It likewise contains the necessary transitional and permanent adjustments to the existing body of EU law.

The 2007 accessions are not intended to represent the end of the Union's enlargement programme. In October 2005, accession negotiations were formally opened with Croatia and Turkey (though in the latter case, the negotiations are expected to last a considerable period of time). The former Yugoslav Republic of Macedonia was officially recognised as a candidate country by the European Council in December 2005. Other countries in the Western Balkans are acknowledged to be potential candidates (e.g.: Albania, Bosnia Herzegovina, and Serbia and Montenegro); while States such as the Ukraine have expressed their political ambition of becoming members of the EU in the future.

The Treaty establishing a Constitution for Europe 2004

This survey of the historical development of the EU would not be **1–022** complete without providing a brief introduction to the most ambitious of the projects for Treaty reform agreed by the Member States to date.

Even as they concluded the TN in December 2000, the Member States decided to adopt a "Declaration on the Future of the Union" highlighting the need for a more thorough reflection upon the EU's constitutional framework. The Laeken European Council held in December 2001 then agreed a "Declaration on the Future of the

---

[73] See the text of the Treaty of Accession 2003 as published at [2003] O.J. L236.
[74] For analysis, see Hillion, "The European Union is Dead. Long Live the European Union . . . A Commentary on the Accession Treaty 2003" (2004) 29 E.L.Rev. 583.
[75] See the text of the Treaty of Accession 2005 as published at [2005] O.J. L157.

European Union" laying down more precisely the parameters for this process of constitutional reflection, and establishing a "Convention on the Future of Europe" charged with preparing proposals for consideration at a future IGC. The Convention's work culminated in the presentation of a draft "Treaty establishing a Constitution for Europe" to the European Council in July 2003.[76] That text provided the basis for further (and sometimes very difficult) negotiations between the Member States, leading eventually to the signature of the Treaty establishing a Constitution for Europe (the Constitutional Treaty or CT) on October 29, 2004.[77]

Rather than integrating the changes envisaged by the CT into each and every relevant section of this book, we have decided to provide a comprehensive, detailed discussion of the entire reform package in Chapter 11. This is for two reasons. First, the process of ratifying the CT was thrown into disarray by negative referenda in France and the Netherlands, and the European Council meeting in June 2005 decided that it was necessary to have a "period of reflection and discussion" before deciding how best to proceed. It is therefore unclear at the time of writing when, or indeed whether, this Treaty will enter into force. Secondly, the CT seeks to reconstitute the Union upon an entirely new (and much simplified) set of legal foundations; and in the process, would carry out a multitude of more detailed reforms to many aspects of the Union's functioning and activities: for example, as regards the structure of and relations between the institutions, the range of competences exercised by the Union, the types of legal instrument available to it, the protection of human rights and fundamental freedoms, and the arrangements for enhanced cooperation between groups of Member States. Many of these changes can only properly be understood when considered within the overall context of the CT.

1–023 We have therefore decided that—in most cases—the best method of incorporating the CT into a textbook intended primarily to reflect the law of the EU as it stands at the time of writing, is for individual chapters to contain a list of the relevant reforms contained within the CT, from which the reader may then cross-refer to the appropriate sections of Chapter 11.

---

[76] For analysis, see e.g. Dougan, "The Convention's Draft Constitutional Treaty: Bringing Europe Closer to its Lawyers?" (2003) 28 E.L.Rev. 763; Kokott and Ruth, "The European Convention and its Draft Treaty Establishing a Constitution for Europe: Appropriate Answers to the Laeken Questions?" (2003) 40 C.M.L.Rev. 1315.

[77] See the text of the CT as published at [2004] O.J. C310. For analysis, see e.g. Dashwood, "The EU Constitution: What Will Really Change?" (2004/2005) C.Y.E.L.S. 33.

PART II

THE CONSTITUTIONAL ORDER

CHAPTER 2

THE INSTITUTIONS OF THE EUROPEAN UNION

Guide to this Chapter: This chapter begins by considering the 2–001
role of the European Council—the Union's supreme political
organ, responsible for providing impetus for the Union's development and defining its general political guidelines. The chapter
then addresses the Community's three main political institutions
as defined in Article 7 EC. First, the Council, composed of
Ministers from the Member States, through which the interests of
the Member States find expression, and are able to be reconciled,
at the level of the Union. Its primary functions are to exercise
(either alone or in conjunction with the European Parliament)
decision-making powers under the Treaty; to ensure the coordination of the Member State's general economic policies; to authorise the opening of negotiations for, and to conclude, agreements
under international law; and to adopt (in conjunction with the
European Parliament) the Community budget. Secondly, the
Commission, which is intended to represent the general interest
of the Community, in complete independence from any government or body. Its primary functions are to initiate the Community's
various legislative procedures by making proposals for legislative
acts; and to implement both the Treaty and Community legislative
acts through the exercise of delegated executive powers. The
Commission's role as "guardian of the Treaties", with responsibility for ensuring that the other institutions and the Member
States observe their Community law obligations, will be considered in Chapter 13. Thirdly, the European Parliament, the Union's
only directly elected institution. Its main functions (which have
expanded considerably since its inception) are to exercise

27

(in conjunction with the Council of Ministers) decision-making powers under the Treaty; to adopt (again together with the Council) the Community budget; and to exercise supervisory powers over the activities of the Commission (especially at the stage of appointing the Commission and through the possibility of adopting a motion of censure).

Article 7 of the EC Treaty

2–002   According to Article 7 EC, the tasks entrusted to the Community are to be carried out by five institutions—a European Parliament, a Council, a Commission, a Court of Justice and a Court of Auditors.[1] It is expressly provided that each of the institutions "shall act within the limits of the powers conferred on it by this Treaty". Thus the institutional system is founded on the idea of the "attribution of powers".[2] The Community institutions have only the powers given to them expressly or impliedly by the Treaties.

The founding Treaties endowed each of the European Communities with a separate set of institutions. However, as we have seen, a Convention on certain Institutions common to the European Communities, which came into force at the same time as the EC and Euratom Treaties, provided for there to be a single Assembly and a single Court of Justice exercising the various powers attributed to those institutions by the three Treaties. This was followed by the establishment, from July 1967, of a single Council of the European Communities, replacing the Special Council of Ministers of the ECSC, and the EC and Euratom Councils, and a Commission of the European Communities, replacing the High Authority of the ECSC, and the EC and Euratom Commissions.[3] The unity of the institutions is now maintained for the Union as a whole by the provision in Article 3, first paragraph of the TEU that the Union shall be served by a single institutional framework.[4]

Most of this chapter will be devoted to a closer examination of the Communities' three main *political* institutions—the Council, the Commission and the European Parliament. The Court of Justice will be dealt with further in Chapters 12 to 14, though it will quickly become evident that the Court's role in the development and functioning of the Community legal order is all-pervasive. A few words should be said about the Court of Auditors, which was created by the Financial Treaty of 1975, replacing the former Audit Board.

---

[1] The two surviving Community Treaties contain identical sets of provisions on the main institutions. References in this Chapter are to the EC Treaty.

[2] For further discussion of the legal implications of this principle, see Ch.4.

[3] The Treaty Establishing a Single Council and a Single Commission of the European Communities was signed on April 8, 1965 and entered into force on July 13, 1967. See Ch.1.

[4] See the discussion of the structure of the European Union in Ch.10.

The TEU "promoted" the Court of Auditors to paragraph (1) of Article 7 EC, thus giving it the full status of a Community institution: previously it was mentioned in a separate paragraph (3). Under powers which have been spelt out in progressively greater detail in the TEU and the TA, the Court of Auditors is required to examine the accounts of all Community revenue and expenditure and ensure their reliability, and the legality and regularity of the underlying transactions. Its annual report, and the replies of the institutions under audit to its observations, are essential elements in the exercise of giving a discharge to the Commission in respect of the implementation of the budget, and it may also, at any time, submit observations on specific questions and deliver opinions at the request of one of the Community institutions.[5]

Besides the five Community institutions listed in its first para- **2–003** graph, Article 7 mentions, in its second paragraph, the Economic and Social Committee and the Committee of the Regions. The role of these two bodies is to assist the Council and the Commission by giving advisory opinions. The Economic and Social Committee, which has been in existence since the establishment of the EC and Euratom, consists of representatives of the different categories of economic and social life and of the general interest, while the Committee of the Regions, which was created by the Treaty on European Union, consists of representatives of regional and local bodies.[6] Power to appoint the members of these Committees is given to the Council acting by qualified majority on the basis of lists of names put forward by each of the Member States. The decision to establish a Committee of the Regions represented a response to political demands in certain Member States, particularly those with a federal structure, that regional and local interests be given a direct line of communication to the Community institutions. However, more than 10 years after it was established, it cannot be said that the Committee has become a significant political force.

In addition to the five Community institutions and two advisory committees, other important bodies are created directly by the Treaties, notably the European Central Bank (ECB) established in accordance with Article 8 EC. The ECB's main tasks are to define and implement the Community's monetary policy, conduct foreign exchange operations, hold and manage the official foreign reserves of the Member States, and promote the smooth operation of payment systems.[7] The Treaty seeks to ensure that the ECB should be in a position to carry out its tasks independently, though the

---

[5] As to the composition and powers of the Court of Auditors, see Arts 246 to 248 EC. As to its role in the discharge of the Budget, see Art.276 EC.
[6] On the Economic and Social Committee, see Arts 257 to 262 EC. On the Committee of the Regions, see Arts 263 to 265 EC.
[7] Art.105(2) EC.

Court of Justice has confirmed that such independence does not have the consequence of separating the ECB entirely from the European Community, including the obligation to act within the limits of the powers conferred upon the ECB by the Treaty and its Statute.[8] Moreover, numerous additional bodies have been created pursuant to the Treaties, through acts of Community secondary legislation. These include the Community's decentralised agencies, which are public law bodies possessing their own legal personality, charged with executing technical, scientific or management tasks in particular fields of Community policy. Examples include the European Environment Agency (which collects and disseminates information on the state of the European environment);[9] the European Food Safety Authority (which is responsible for providing independent scientific advice on all matters relevant to food safety);[10] and the European Monitoring Centre on Racism and Xenophobia (which devises strategies to combat racism and xenophobia and shares good practice in integrating ethnic or religious minorities).[11]

Before turning to our detailed consideration of the Council, Commission and European Parliament, it is necessary to consider another body which, although not an institution in the sense of Article 7(1) TEU, may nevertheless be regarded as the supreme political authority of the Union: the European Council.

The European Council[12]

2–004   It was at the summit meeting of European Community leaders in Paris in December 1974 that the decision was taken to hold regular meetings at the highest political level, within a "European Council" (not to be confused with "the Council" composed of Ministers). The first European Council was held in Dublin in March 1975, and the series of meetings continued on an informal basis for some years. A legal basis for the activity of the European Council is now to be found in Article 4 TEU.

According to that Article, the European Council brings together the Heads of State or Government of the Member States and the President of the Commission, who are assisted by Ministers of Foreign Affairs and by a member of the Commission. The formula "Heads of State or Government" is designed to accommodate the constitutional position of the French President. Meetings are chaired by the Head of State or Government of the Member State holding the Presidency of the Council for the time being. There is a legal

[8] Case C–11/00 *Commission v European Central Bank* [2003] E.C.R. I–7147.
[9] See Reg.1210/90 [1990] O.J. L120/1.
[10] See Reg.178/2002 [2002] O.J. L31/1.
[11] See Reg.1035/97 [1997] O.J. L151/1.
[12] See further, Werts, *The European Council* (1992, North-Holland). Also Dashwood, "Decision-Making at the Summit" (2000) 3 C.Y.E.L.S. 79.

requirement that at least two meetings of the European Council be held per year, i.e. one in each six-monthly Presidency. However, it has become the established practice to hold four meetings of the European Council per year; additional meetings may also be called on an *ad hoc* basis.

The role of the European Council, which over the years has become increasingly significant, is essentially a political one. This is emphasised by Article 4 TEU which states in its first paragraph: "The European Council shall provide the Union with the necessary impetus for its development and shall define the general political guidelines thereof". To demonstrate the contribution European Councils have made to the strategic development of the Communities, it is enough to recall: the meeting in Fontainebleau in June 1984 when work was set in train which eventually bore fruit in the institutional reforms of the SEA; the meeting in Hanover in June 1988 when the project of establishing an economic and monetary union was relaunched; and the series of meetings at which the criteria for, and the modalities of, the accession to the Union of the countries of central and eastern Europe were laid down, from Copenhagen in June 1993 to Helsinki in December 1999. The Fontainebleau meeting illustrates another function of the European Council—that of unravelling knotty political problems which have defeated the efforts of the institutions. It was at that meeting that a solution was found to the long-running dispute about the level of the United Kingdom's net contribution to the Community budget.[13] European Councils also provide an opportunity for reviewing foreign policy questions, both those falling within the Communities' external competence and those which are the subject of the common foreign and security policy. The European Security and Defence Policy has, in particular, been developed through a series of Presidency Reports approved by the European Council.

Does the existence of the European Council, unforeseen by the original Treaties, distort the institutional structure of the Communities? The question is a legitimate one, since the task of leading the Member States along the road towards the ever closer union referred to in the preamble to the EC Treaty and in Article 1 TEU might have been thought to belong more particularly to the Commission. Experience, however, has shown that a strongly led Commission has nothing to fear and everything to gain from working in close

---

[13] The solution consisted of providing for an "abatement" of the amount payable by the United Kingdom under the rules for the calculation of the "own resources" which constitute the Communities' revenue. Provision has been made for this abatement in successive Council Decisions on own resources. The advantage from the United Kingdom's point of view of the solution devised at Fontainbleau is that unanimity is required for the adoption of own resources decisions: see Art.269 EC. At the European Council held under the British Presidency in December 2005, the United Kingdom agreed to an adaptation of the rules governing the abatement, by excluding from the calculation expenditure for the purposes of the enlargement of the Union to incorporate the countries of Central and Eastern Europe.

partnership with the European Council to achieve its medium-term objectives. Thus, political support from successive European Councils was an important factor in the implementation of the White Paper of 1985 on completing the internal market and in the realisation of plans for economic and monetary union with the introduction of the euro in January 1999.

The Council[14]

2–005   The first paragraph of Article 203 EC provides: "The Council shall consist of a representative of each Member State *at ministerial level*, authorised to commit the government of that Member State" (emphasis added). That wording allows Member States with a devolved structure to be represented, when the Council is dealing with matters falling within the competence of regional authorities, by a member of one of those authorities rather than by a minister in the central government.[15] In such a case, the regional minister concerned would have to be authorised to act on behalf of the Member State as a whole, so that his agreement to a matter on the Council agenda would bind that Member State both legally and politically. At all events, it is clear that a representative within the meaning of Article 203 EC must be a person holding political office, *i.e.* not a civil servant.

In law, the Council is a unitary institution: in other words, it is the same institution with the same powers under the Treaties, whatever the particular national responsibilities of the ministers attending a given meeting. However, the Council customarily meets in certain formations, determined in accordance with the matters on the agenda. The General Affairs and External Relations Council, which brings together Foreign Ministers, deals with issues affecting more than one of the Union's policies (such as negotiations on enlargement or broad institutional matters), the whole of the Union's external action (including common foreign and security policy, foreign trade and development cooperation) and generally provides a measure of co-ordination of the Council's multifarious activities. It also has the task of preparing for and following-up European Councils. Another Council with a wide remit is the Economic and Financial Affairs (or Ecofin) Council which, like the General Affairs Council, meets, in principle, monthly. The Ecofin Council is responsible for issues related to economic policy coordination, the monitoring of Member States' budgetary policy and public finances, the

---

[14] See further, Dashwood, "The Role of the Council of the European Union" in Curtin and Heukels (eds), *Institutional Dynamics of European Integration*, Vol. II (1994); Dashwood, "The Council of the European Union in the Era of the Amsterdam Treaty", in Heukels, Blokker and Brus (eds), *The European Union after Amsterdam* (1998).

[15] The United Kingdom could, for instance, be represented by a member of the Scottish Executive.

euro, financial markets and capital movements and economic relations with third countries. More specialised Council formations in which important legislative business is regularly transacted include the Councils on Agriculture and Fisheries; Competitiveness (including issues related to the internal market, industrial policy and research); the Environment; and Employment, Social Policy, Health and Consumer Affairs. In fact, during the 1990s, there were 22 separate Council configurations. However, this was reduced to 16 in June 2000, and then to just nine in June 2002, in an effort to promote coherence and consistency in the Council's activities.

Procedural changes, which began with the TEU, have put the principle of the unicity of the Council under some strain. Article 121 EC provided for certain decisions connected with the transition to the third stage of EMU and the establishment of a single currency to be taken by the Council "meeting in the composition of the Heads of State or Government" on the basis of recommendations put to it by the Council meeting in one of its ordinary formations (in practice, the Ecofin Council). It was a constitutional innovation that powers should be expressly reserved for the Council in a particular formation and that the basis for the exercise of those powers should consist of recommendations from the same institution meeting in a different formation. An important point to note in this context is that there is a clear distinction in law between the 25 Heads of State or Government taking decisions as a formation of the Council in the sense of Article 203 EC—which will be the case here—and the same leaders meeting as the European Council, with the President of the Commission as a twenty-sixth member. Another example of a power reserved for the Council in the composition of Heads of State or Government is that of nominating the Commission President.[16] There are also now situations in which the Treaties allow decisions to be taken by the Council without the participation of all 25 of its members, notably in the field of monetary policy or where a group of Member States is authorised to pursue "enhanced cooperation" between themselves within a given field of Community activity. These different instances of "flexibility" are further considered in Chapter 4.

Article 4 of the Council's Rules of Procedure[17] allows a member of the Council (*i.e.* a minister) unable to be present at a meeting, or part of it, to arrange to be represented. His or her place will usually be taken by the Permanent Representative or the Deputy Permanent Representative of the Member State concerned. Article 11(3) of the Rules of Procedure reproduces Article 206 EC which provides that, where a vote is taken, a Council member may act on behalf of not

---

[16] Art.214(2), first sub-para. EC.
[17] The Rules were first published in 1979: see [1979] O.J. L268/1. They are regularly amended and replaced. The latest version is to be found at [2004] O.J. L106/22.

more than one other member. The quorum, established by Article 11(4) of the Rules of Procedure, comprises a majority of the members of the Council entitled to vote on a given matter. The reference in Article 11(4) to "members of the Council" indicates that only ministers count for this purpose.

2–006   The Presidency of the Council is held in turn by the Member States for periods of six months, following the order laid down by the Council pursuant to Article 203, second paragraph EC.[18] The duties of the Presidency include, besides taking the chair at Council meetings, the convening of meetings[19] and the establishment of the provisional agenda, which must be circulated to other members of the Council at least a fortnight in advance and must contain an indication of the items on which a vote may be taken.[20] The Presidency has come to play an active role in managing the progress of Commission proposals through the Council. Negotiations between national delegations within the Council take place in relation to a series of compromise texts devised by the Presidency with a view to securing the necessary majority or unanimity for the adoption of the measure in question. A Presidency is expected to show objectivity in furthering proposals, without undue regard to its specific national interests. A certain rivalry has developed between Presidencies in seeking to achieve an impressive "score" of measures adopted, and this has undoubtedly been a factor in the acceleration of the legislative process.

The work of the Council is prepared by a Committee of Permanent Representatives (COREPER) who are senior national officials based in Brussels. The legal basis of COREPER's activities is Article 207(1) EC. The Committee operates at two levels, that of COREPER II, composed of the Permanent Representatives, who are of ambassadorial rank, and that of COREPER I, composed of the Deputy Permanent Representatives. The distribution of files between the two parts of COREPER is intended to reflect the more political nature of those given to COREPER II (e.g., external relations), and the more technical nature of those given to COREPER I (e.g., internal market legislation), but in practice even technical-seeming matters, such as the organisation of veterinary checks, may have political implications for some Member States. It might be noted that the business of the Agriculture and Fisheries

---

[18] See Decision 2005/902 [2005] O.J. L328/60, fixing the following order, as from January 2006: Austria, Finland, Germany, Portugal, Slovenia, France, Czech Republic, Sweden, Spain, Belgium, Hungary, Poland, Denmark, Cyprus, Ireland, Lithuania, Greece, Italy, Latvia, Luxembourg, Netherlands, Slovakia, Malta, United Kingdom, Estonia.

[19] Rules of Procedure, Art.1(1).

[20] Rules of Procedure, Art.3(1) and (2). The items on which a vote may be taken are indicated on the draft agenda by an asterisk. If no such indication is given, a matter cannot be put to the vote under Art.9 of the Rules of Procedure, except by unanimous agreement of the Council.

Council is prepared not only by COREPER (which usually confines itself to dealing with fisheries and food safety issues, and agri-budgetary questions), but also by the Special Committee on Agriculture (established in the early 1960s to take account of the highly technical nature of the agricultural dossier). In addition, with the extension of EU activity into new fields, the need was felt for the creation of bodies capable of providing the Council with specialised back-up, and composed of senior national officials. Notable examples are the Economic and Financial Committee, the Political and Security Committee (concerned with the common foreign and security policy, including the political control and strategic direction of crisis management operations) and the Co-ordinating Committee (concerned with police and judicial co-operation in criminal matters). The relationship between COREPER and these influential bodies is inevitably somewhat delicate; the contribution of the latter to the preparation of Council business is, however, stated by the relevant Treaty provisions to be "without prejudice to Article 207", thereby preserving the position of COREPER as the filter through which such business must pass.[21] The principle is important because, with so many different formations of the Council, there is a danger political coherence may be lost: COREPER is the only Council body able to take a horizontal view of the development of Community policies.

The business that comes to COREPER will have been prepared, in turn, by one of a large number of specialised committees and working groups made up of national officials. In addition to these standing groups, COREPER from time to time establishes *ad hoc* groups to deal with matters requiring specific expertise.

The Council, COREPER and working groups are assisted by an **2–007** independent body of civil servants, the General Secretariat. This has Article 207(2) EC as the legal basis for its activities. The TA enhanced the status of the Secretary General of the Council by combining the office with that of "High Representative for the CFSP".[22] The day-to-day running of the General Secretariat has been entrusted to the Deputy Secretary General.

Council agendas are divided into Part A and Part B.[23] Items listed in Part A (known as A-points) are those which COREPER has agreed may be adopted by the Council without discussion, though this does not exclude the possibility for a delegation to have a statement or a negative vote recorded in the minutes. Any member of the Council, or the Commission, may ask for an item to be taken off the list of A-points, in which case the item will be held over for a later Council, unless a simple majority of Council members decides

---

[21] See, respectively, Art.114(2) EC, Art.25 TEU and Art.36 TEU.
[22] See Art.26 TEU.
[23] Rules of Procedure, Art.3(6).

that it should remain on the agenda.[24] In the latter event, the item cannot be voted on unless the A-point list on which it appears was circulated within the 14-day time-limit.[25] The A-point procedure is often used for the formal adoption of texts which have been agreed in principle at an earlier Council.

Turning from the composition and organisation of the Council to its powers, these are described in the first two indents of Article 202 EC in an oddly cursory way. The first indent says the Council is to "ensure co-ordination of the general economic policies of the Member States" and the second indent that it is to "have power to make decisions".[26]

The Council's function of economic policy co-ordination is now carried out under the arrangements of the EC Treaty relating to Economic and Monetary Union (EMU). The guiding principles, stated in Article 4 EC, and reiterated in Article 98 EC, are those of "an open market economy with free competition, favouring an efficient allocation of resources". Among other things, the Member States have put themselves under a legal duty to avoid excessive government deficits, and the Council (in practice, Ecofin) has been empowered to intervene actively, to ensure compliance.[27]

The reference in the second indent of Article 202 EC to the Council's "power to take decision" highlights its essential role in the system of the EC and Euratom Treaties: that of the institution that has to decide for or against measures developing or extending the body of primary rules contained in the Treaties.[28] We return to the subject of decision making by the Council, including the vexed question of majority voting, in the next chapter.[29]

Consistently with its central role in the creation of law in the internal Community sphere, the Council has to agree to the acceptance by the EC of new obligations in international law resulting from the conclusion of agreements with third countries.[30] It is the Commission which negotiates with third countries on behalf of the Community, but Council authorisation is required for opening negotiations, and it is the Council that takes the decision to conclude

---

[24] Rules of Procedure, Art.3(8).

[25] Rules of Procedure, Arts 3(1) and (2). In theory, the members of the Council might decide *unanimously* that the item be put to the vote.

[26] The third indent of Art.202 EC which concerns implementing powers, is discussed below in connection with the powers of the Commission.

[27] See Art.104 EC and Protocol (No.5) on the excessive deficit procedure.

[28] In the "co-decision" procedure, which is discussed in Ch.3, the Council acts jointly with the European Parliament.

[29] Note that the Commission is given an independent power of decision on certain matters where, unusually, basic rules limiting the discretion of the legislator are found in the EC Treaty itself: e.g. under the (now obsolete) provisions for the completion of the customs union during the EC's transitional period, for which a detailed timetable was provided by the Treaty. The European Central Bank, too, has law-making powers on aspects of monetary policy: see Art.110 EC.

[30] The procedure for the negotiation and conclusion of agreements is found in Art.300 EC.

agreements. In some important cases, the assent (*avis conforme*) of the European Parliament also has to be obtained.

Another area in which the Council has important powers is that of the adoption of the Community budget. The Council and the European Parliament together constitute the budgetary authority of the Communities which has the annual task of elaborating and adopting the general budget, as well as any supplementary and amending budgets that may prove necessary in the course of the financial year.[31] The division of powers between the Council and the European Parliament in the budgetary procedure is further examined below.

The Commission

Unlike the Council, whose members directly represent the inter- 2–008 ests of their Governments, the Commission has a vocation to further the interests of the Community as a whole. The members of the Commission are required to be persons "whose independence is beyond doubt",[32] and the Treaty provides that they "shall, in the general interest of the Community, be completely independent in the performance of their duties".[33] They may not seek or take instructions from any government or other body, and each Member State has undertaken to respect that principle and not to seek to influence Commissioners in the performance of their tasks.[34] The rule that the Commission acts by a majority of its members[35] provides a further guarantee that its decisions will not reflect, even inadvertently, particular national viewpoints.

At the time of accession of Austria, Finland and Sweden to the EU, the number of Members of the Commission was fixed at 20.[36] This followed the convention (dating from the creation of a single Commission by the Merger Treaty) that one Commissioner be appointed from each of the smaller Member States, and two from each of the larger Member States (Germany, France, Italy, Spain and the United Kingdom). However, it became generally accepted, during preparations for the enlargement into central and eastern Europe, that a reduction in the number of Commissioners was necessary to prevent the institution from becoming unwieldy.[37] The issue proved fraught for both the larger Member States (who were

---

[31] The budgetary procedure is laid down by Art.272 EC.
[32] Art.213(1) EC.
[33] Art.213(2) EC.
[34] *ibid.*
[35] Art.219 EC.
[36] Art.213(1) EC.
[37] On the pros and cons, see Justus Lipsius, "The 1996 Intergovernmental Conference" (1995) 20 E.L.Rev. 265; Dashwood, *Reviewing Maastricht: Issues for the 1996 IGC* (Sweet & Maxwell, 1996), pp.152 *et seq.*

under pressure to sacrifice their second Commissioner) and the smaller ones (who feared that any further reduction in the number of Commissioners would mean their not being "represented" in the College at all). No agreement having been reached in the negotiations that led to the Treaty of Amsterdam, the new arrangements were finally put in place through the Treaty of Nice.[38] Beginning with the Barroso Commission which took office in November 2004, the Commission is to comprise one national of each of the Member States. However, once there are 27 Member States (i.e. after the intended accession of Bulgaria and Romania on January 1, 2007),[39] the next Commission to take up its duties after that date must have fewer members than the number of Member States. It will be for the Council, acting unanimously, to fix the precise number of Commissioners, as well as to lay down implementing arrangements for a rotation system between nationals of the different Member States, based on the principle of equality. Each successive College of Commissioners must be so composed as to reflect satisfactorily the demographic and geographical range of all the Member States of the Union.[40]

The procedure for the appointment of the President and Members of the Commission is found in Article 214 EC.[41] Amendments introduced by the TEU and the TA both enhanced the role of the European Parliament in the selection process, and gave the President-designate a greater say in the composition of his "team"; further amendments through the TN relaxed the applicable voting requirements within the Council.

The first step in the procedure is the nomination, by the Council meeting in the composition of Heads of State or Government, of the person they intend to appoint as President. They now do so by qualified majority vote (whereas previously, they were required to act by "common accord", a stricter voting rule even than unanimity, since it did not allow for abstentions). The nomination requires approval by the Parliament. Those to be appointed as Members of the Commission are then nominated by the Council acting by qualified majority and by common accord with the President-designate, which means the latter effectively has a veto. The whole slate of Commissioners is then subject to a vote of approval by the Parliament; and the final step in the procedure is the formal appointment of the President and Members by the Council acting by qualified majority.

---

[38] Art.213(1) EC as amended (and to be further amended) by Art.4 of the Protocol on enlargement of the European Union; and also (specifically as regards the period of entry into force) by the Treaty of Accession 2003.
[39] This date may be postponed, in accordance with the Treaty of Accession 2005, for a further year.
[40] Art.4(3) of the Protocol on enlargement of the EU.
[41] See Gonsalbo Bono, "The Commission after Amsterdam" in Heukels, Blokker and Brus (eds), *The European Union after Amsterdam* (1998).

The amended procedure is designed to ensure both a more **2–009** coherent Commission, and one more politically accountable to the European Parliament. To the latter end, the term of the Commission (five years, renewable) has been aligned on that of the Parliament: thus, each new College of Commissioners will be vetted by MEPs newly elected in the previous June. That the Parliament intends to take its new responsibilities seriously was well illustrated by the difficulties encountered in securing approval for the Barroso Commission in autumn 2004. The affair was sparked by the highly controversial, indeed offensive, views of the Italian nominee to the Justice, Freedom and Security portfolio (which encompasses responsibility for the Community's anti-discrimination policy) on issues concerning homosexuality and the role of women in society. At one point, after the President-designate attempted a show of political strength by vowing support for his "team" as nominated by the Member States, the scandal threatened to end in an unprecedented parliamentary rejection of the entire Commission. The matter was only resolved when both the Italian and Latvian nominees (the latter having also been severely criticised by MEPs) were replaced by figures more acceptable to the European Parliament. What was seen in some quarters as a crisis which had both delayed the appointment and damaged the credibility of the new Commission was interpreted by other commentators as a victory for democracy and accountability within the EU.

According to Article 217(3) EC, as amended by the TN, the Commission's Vice-Presidents are to be appointed from its members by the President, after obtaining the approval of the College. Previously, the number of Vice-Presidents was limited to a maximum of two; the Nice amendments permitted the Barroso Commission to appoint five Vice-Presidents. More generally, the TN sought to bolster the role of the President within the Commission. Under Article 217 EC, the Commission shall work under the political guidance of its President, who shall decide on its internal organisation in order to ensure that it acts consistently, efficiently and on the basis of collegiality.[42] The responsibilities incumbent upon the Commission shall be structured and allocated among its members by the President, who may reshuffle the allocation of those responsibilities during the Commission's term of office.[43] Furthermore, a Commissioner must resign if the President so requests, after obtaining the approval of the College.[44]

The Commission is assisted by a staff of permanent officials under a Secretary General, who are organised into Directorates General and various other services. In addition, each Commissioner has a

---

[42] Art.217(1) EC.
[43] Art.217(2) EC.
[44] Art.217(4) EC.

small personal staff (or *cabinet*) composed partly of political associates and seconded national officials and partly of seconded Community officials. Meetings of the heads of these personal staffs (the *Chefs de Cabinet*) prepare the weekly meetings of the Commission.

2–010   The various elements that define the complex role of the Commission are described in Article 211 EC in the following terms:

"In order to ensure the proper functioning and development of the common market, the Commission shall:

— ensure that the provisions of this Treaty and the measures taken by the institutions pursuant thereto are applied;

— formulate recommendations or deliver opinions on matters dealt with in this Treaty, if it expressly so provides or if the Commission considers it necessary;

— have its own power of decision and participate in the shaping of measures taken by the Council and by the European Parliament in the manner provided for in this Treaty;

— exercise the powers conferred on it by the Council for the implementation of the rules laid down by the latter."

In the present section we consider two aspects of the Commission's role: as the initiator of decisions; and as the institution that sees to their implementation once they have been adopted. Another important role, that of "guardian of the Treaties", is associated with the Commission's right to invoke against the Council or against a Member State judicial remedies which are discussed in Chapter 13.

The Treaties contain no general rule reserving to the Commission the right to put forward proposals for Community acts. The Commission's right of initiative is, accordingly, nothing but an inference drawn from the numerous Treaty provisions that empower the Council to act "on a proposal from the Commission". That form of words, or a similar one, is used by the EC Treaty in almost every case where the Council is given power to make new Community law. Thus, the Council is usually able to exercise its legislative powers only in relation to a text which has been formulated by the institution with a duty to act independently of specific national interests. The way in which the Commission's right of initiative, and its right to amend its own proposals at any time before their adoption by the Council, interacts with the right of the Council to amend those proposals, is discussed in Chapter 3.

One of the defining features of decision making under Titles V and VI of the TEU (the so-called "Second and Third Pillars") is that, in contrast to the Community system, the Commission does not enjoy an exclusive right of initiative. Thus, Article 22 TEU provides: "Any Member State or the Commission may refer to the Council any question relating to the common foreign and security policy and may submit proposals to the Council". As regards police and judicial co-operation in criminal matters, the Council is empowered to take the various kinds of measure provided for by Article 34(2) TEU "on the initiative of any Member State or of the Commission".[45] The feature of a shared right of initiative was retained, on a temporary basis, for decision making on the matters which were transferred by the TA from Title VI TEU to the new Title IV of Part Three of the EC Treaty on visas, asylum and immigration. Article 67(1) EC provided that, during a transitional period of five years from the entry into force of the TA, the Council should act, under most of the legal bases found in the new Treaty Title, "on a proposal from the Commission or on the initiative of a Member State". This deviation from the Community norm has now expired, and the Commission has regained its monopoly of initiative for the purposes of that Title.

The Commission is sometimes described as the "executive" of the **2–011** Communities but this is misleading. It implies that the Commission is like a government, with inherent or residual power to implement legislation, whereas Article 7(1), second sub-paragraph of the EC Treaty makes clear that it has only those powers of implementation that have been conferred on it either directly by the Treaties or by acts of the Council. Under the EC Treaty, although directly empowered to act for certain purposes (e.g., the establishment of the customs union and the supervision of State aids to industry), the Commission derives the bulk of its implementing powers from legislation enacted by the Council. In this regard, an important change introduced by the SEA was the insertion into Article 202 EC of a third indent establishing, as a general rule, that power to implement acts of the Council be conferred on the Commission. The Council is allowed to reserve implementing power for itself in specific cases, but the Court of Justice has said, "it must state in detail the grounds for such a decision".[46] In particular, the Council must properly explain, by reference to the nature and content of the basic instrument to be implemented, why exception is being made to the rule that, when implementing measures need to be taken at Community level, it is the Commission which is to be normally responsible for exercising that power.[47] Where delegation to the Commission does take place, the Court has stipulated that the essential elements of matters to be dealt with by the Commission under derived powers must be determined by the Council act directly based on the Treaty.[48] It would be a breach of the Treaty for

---

[45] See Ch.10.
[46] Case 16/88 *Commission v Council* [1989] E.C.R. 3457, 3485.
[47] Case C–257/01 *Commission v Council* [2005] E.C.R. I–345, para.51.
[48] Case 25/70, *Köster* [1970] E.C.R. 1161, 1170; [1972] C.M.L.R. 255. The same principle applies where the Council reserves for itself power to adopt implementing acts by a simpler procedure than the one prescribed by the Treaty for the basic act.

the Commission to be given a discretion co-extensive with that which the Council is required under the Treaty to exercise in accordance with a prescribed procedure.

The grant of powers to the Commission may cover, besides the management of the policy in question, the development, by subordinate legislation, of the rules contained in the basic Council act. This is most notably the case with the common agricultural policy where the Commission is responsible both for establishing the regulatory framework within which the competent national authorities are required to act and for the day-to-day management of agricultural markets, in close collaboration with those authorities. Competition policy provides another instructive example: this is an area where, unusually, the Commission has been given, pursuant to Regulation 1/2003,[49] administrative and coercive powers which can be used against individual undertakings; in addition, it has been empowered to adopt regulations exempting certain categories of restrictive agreements and practices from the automatic prohibition to which they would otherwise be subject under the rules of Article 81 EC.[50] Other areas in which the Commission has acquired an enhanced administrative role are those of research, where it implements the specific programmes developed within the various activities envisaged by the multi-annual framework programme, and economic and social cohesion where, in partnership with beneficiary Member States, it manages the resources made available through the structural funds.

The exercise by the Commission of powers of implementation which it has been granted under acts of the Council is frequently subjected to procedural requirements. Article 202, third indent, EC expressly preserves the Council's right to impose such requirements, while providing that the latter "must be consonant with principles and rules to be laid down in advance". A closed catalogue of forms of procedure has accordingly been laid down by what is known as the Council's Second Comitology Decision—all of which involve the submission of the Commission's draft implementing measures to a committee composed of national officials.[51] The degree of constraint placed on the Commission varies from one procedure to another: for instance, under the "advisory" procedure the Commission is required to take the utmost account of the opinion delivered by the Committee, but is not bound by it; whereas, under the "management" procedure, in the event of a negative opinion by the committee, the matter is referred to the Council which may, within a

---

[49] [2003] O.J. L1/1.

[50] See Ch.23.

[51] Decision 1999/468 [1999] O.J. L184/23. This replaced the First Comitology Decision 87/373 [1987] O.J. L197/33. For general judicial observations on the relationship between the comitology system and the principle of good administration, see Joined Cases C–154/04 and 155/04 *Alliance for Natural Health* (Judgment of July 12, 2005).

prescribed time-limit, substitute its own decision for that of the Commission.[52] It is for the Council, when it adopts an act conferring implementing power on the Commission, to determine which (if any) procedure should be attached to the exercise of that power. Article 2 of the Second Comitology Decision provides certain criteria for the guidance of the Council on which type of procedure is appropriate for various categories of implementing power, but the Court of Justice has held that these criteria are not strictly binding, though the Council is obliged to state its reasons for deviating from the guidance laid down in Article 2.[53] Furthermore, the Court has rejected the argument that, where implementation does not involve adopting subordinate legislation but simply applying rules to individual cases, only the advisory committee procedure is legally acceptable.[54]

The comitology system has frequently provoked discord among **2–012** the main Community institutions. For example, following the introduction of the co-operation and especially the co-decision legislative procedures,[55] the European Parliament raised concerns that it was effectively excluded from supervising the exercise of implementing powers delegated to the Commission under parent legislation which the Parliament had been closely or even jointly involved in adopting—thus distorting the inter-institutional balance, as intended by the Treaty, in favour of the Council. This prompted a series of political and legal disputes between the Parliament and the Council.[56] The difficulties were resolved, first, by the adoption of a *modus vivendi* between the three main political institutions seeking to offer the Parliament greater involvement in the scrutiny of Commission delegated powers, primarily through supplying more information about comitology activities;[57] and secondly, by making provision in the Second Comitology Decision for intervention by the Parliament if it considers that a draft implementing measure based on an instrument adopted by co-decision would exceed the powers thereby conferred.[58] Nevertheless, the comitology system remains highly contested, as evidenced by the Commission's 2002 proposal for

---

[52] See, respectively, Arts 3 and 4 of the Decision. In addition, there is provision for a "regulatory procedure" (Art.5) and a "safeguard procedure" (Art.6). Provisions designed to improve the transparency of comitology procedures are laid down by Art.7; *inter alia*, the principles and conditions on public access to documents now apply to the various committees.

[53] Case C–378/00 *Commission v Parliament and Council* [2003] E.C.R. I–937. See also Case C–122/04 *Commission v Council and Parliament* (Judgment of February 23, 2006).

[54] Case 16/88 *Commission v Council* [1989] E.C.R. 3457.

[55] See Ch.3.

[56] On Parliament's judicial challenges to the comitology system, see e.g. Case 302/87 *Parliament v Council* [1988] E.C.R. 5615; Case C–417/93 *Parliament v Council* [1995] E.C.R. I–1185; Case C–259/95 *Parliament v Council* [1997] E.C.R. I–5303.

[57] [1996] O.J. C102/1.

[58] Art.8 Decision 1999/468 [1999] O.J. L184/23. *cf.* Agreement between Parliament and Commission on procedures for implementing Decision 1999/468 [2000] O.J. L256/19.

amending the Second Comitology Decision.[59] This proposal would, in effect, remove the committees' power to block Commission proposals *ex ante*, when the latter is exercising implementing powers under legislation adopted through the co-decision procedure; if the Council and/or the Parliament were determined to object to the Commission's implementing measures, they would be obliged to bring an action for annulment *ex post* before the Court of Justice.[60] Such a system would tally with the Commission's apparent self-perception as the Community's true "executive" organ—but it would require the Council (and therefore the Member States) to sacrifice a tangible influence over the exercise of implementing powers at the Community level.[61]

The European Parliament[62]

2–013   The European Parliament has undergone more fundamental changes in its history than any of the other Community institutions. First, as to its name: it was called the "Assembly" in the founding Treaties, and continued to be referred to as such in Council acts until its change of name was officially recognised by the SEA.[63] Secondly, as to its composition: originally a nominated body, its members drawn from the parliamentary institutions of the Member States, the European Parliament was transformed into a body of representatives directly elected by universal suffrage in June 1979 when the first elections were held under rules which had been laid down by an Act annexed to a Council decision of 1976.[64] Thirdly, as to its powers, described in the founding Treaties as exercising "advisory and supervisory powers", the European Parliament has received significant new powers, in the budgetary sphere, under the Treaties of 1970 and 1975 and, in the legislative sphere, through the introduction of the co-operation procedure by the SEA and of the co-decision procedure by the TEU, and through the further development of the latter by the TA and TN.

The Act of 1976 was approved by the Council under the procedure prescribed by Article 190(4) EC. That procedure requires a proposal to be drawn up by the European Parliament "for elections by direct universal suffrage in accordance with a uniform procedure in all Member States" and empowers the Council, acting unanimously, after obtaining the assent of the Parliament, to lay down the

---

[59] COM (2002) 719 Final. See now COM(2004) 324 Final.
[60] On judicial review of the acts of Community institutions before the Community courts, see Ch.13.
[61] See further, on the Commission's attitude, e.g. COM (2002) 728 Final/2.
[62] See Jacobs and Corbett, *The European Parliament* (1990, Longman).
[63] SEA, Art.3(1) speaks, rather coyly, of the institutions "henceforth designated as referred to hereafter", and goes onto refer to "the European Parliament" in subsequent provisions.
[64] Decision 76/787 [1976] O.J. L278/1.

appropriate provisions, which must then be recommended to the Member States for adoption in accordance with their respective constitutional requirements. It did not prove possible in 1976 to agree a uniform electoral procedure and Article 7(2) of the Act, accordingly, states that, pending the entry into force of such a procedure (and subject to specific provisions of the Act, such as those relating to the timing of elections and the counting of votes), "the electoral procedure shall be governed in each Member State by its national provisions". The elections so far held have therefore been organised under national electoral laws, all of them based on variants of proportional representation, including now in the United Kingdom. The requirement of Parliamentary "assent" (which was added to Article 190(4) EC by the TEU) means that the Council is no longer in a position simply to impose its own conception of an appropriate electoral system. Thus, the European Parliament will have to give its formal approval to any uniform electoral system that may be adopted in the future.

According to Article 189 EC, the number of members of the European Parliament (or MEPs) shall not exceed 732. Like the qualified majority as defined by Article 148(2) EC, the number of seats given to the various Member States reflects, in a rough-and-ready way, differences in their populations: for example, 99 from Germany; 78 each from France, Italy and the United Kingdom; 54 each from Spain and Poland; whereas there are 24 each from Belgium, Hungary, the Czech Republic, Greece and Portugal; 13 from Ireland; six from Luxembourg; and five from Malta.[65] If Bulgaria and Romania join the Union as planned on January 1, 2007,[66] the Treaty of Accession 2005 envisages that the number of MEPs will temporarily rise above the maximum number ordinarily permitted under the Treaty (with the two new Member States being allocated 18 and 35 MEPs respectively). The allocation of MEPs between all 27 Member States would then have to be recalculated before the 2009–2014 parliamentary term.[67]

The MEPs are organised in cross-national political groups, broadly following the ideological divisions that are familiar in national politics. Thus, the two largest groups are the Socialist Group and the Group of the European People's Party and European Democrats (composed in the main of Christian Democrats from continental Member States). Article 191 EC emphasises the importance of political parties at European level as a factor for integration

---

[65] Art.190(2) EC (as amended by the Treaty of Accession 2003, and taking effect from the 2004 European Parliamentary elections).

[66] Or, in accordance with the Treaty of Accession 2005, on January 1, 2008.

[67] Art.21 of the Protocol concerning the conditions and arrangements for admission of the Republic of Bulgaria and Romania to the EU (annexed to the Treaty of Accession [2005] O.J. L157) envisages that this reallocation would take place in accordance with the provisions of the Treaty establishing a Constitution for Europe [2004] O.J. C310.

within the Union, and was amended by the TN so as to empower Council and the Parliament (using the co-decision procedure) to adopt rules governing, *inter alia*, the recognition and funding of such parties.[68]

2–014   Article 3(1) of the Act of 1976 provides for a fixed parliamentary term of five years.[69] This can be varied by up to a month either way, if the Council, acting unanimously after consulting the European Parliament, decides that elections are to be held during a period not exactly corresponding to the period chosen for the first elections in 1979, *i.e.* June 7 to 10.[70]

The increase in the powers of the European Parliament under successive Treaties was remarked on at the beginning of this section. The formal powers of the Parliament are broadly of three kinds: it participates in various ways, depending on the legal basis of the act in question, in the law-making process of the Communities; together with the Council, it constitutes the budgetary authority of the Communities; and it exercises political supervision over the performance by the Commission of its tasks. Besides these formal powers, the European Parliament evidently considers that it is entitled, as the collective voice of the Community electorate, to express reactions to political events both within the Communities and in the wider world. It does not have an independent right of initiative but brings its influence to bear on the Commission and, so far as it is able, on the Council, to provoke any action by those institutions that it considers necessary. For that purpose, the position of the European Parliament has been strengthened by the second paragraph of Article 192 EC, an amendment introduced by the TEU, which provides that it may, "acting by a majority of its members, request the Commission to submit any appropriate proposal on matters on which it considers that a Community act is required for the purpose of implementing this Treaty".[71]

The participation of the European Parliament in the law-making process will be discussed in Chapter 3. In the present chapter we confine our attention to the budgetary powers of the Parliament and to its role as political watchdog of the Commission.

In the budgetary sphere, as a result of the Treaties of 1970 and 1975, the European Parliament has become an equal partner of the Council. Their respective powers are determined by the distinction

---

[68] On which, see Reg.2004/2003 on the regulations governing political parties at European level and the rules regarding their funding [2003] O.J. L297/1.

[69] See also Art.190(3) EC.

[70] See Act, Art.10(2).

[71] *cf.* the Council's rarely used right under Art.200 EC to request the Commission to undertake studies and to submit to it any appropriate proposals. Note the 2003 inter-institutional agreement on "better law-making" concluded between the Parliament, the Council and Commission [2003] O.J. C321/1, para.9.

between "compulsory expenditure" (usually referred to by its French acronym, DO) and "non-compulsory expenditure" (or DNO). DO has been defined as "such expenditure as the budgetary authority is obliged to enter in the budget by virtue of a legal undertaking entered into under the Treaties or acts adopted by virtue of the said Treaties".[72] The Council has the last word on DO, which consists almost entirely of expenditure on the common agricultural policy, while the Parliament has the last word on DNO, which includes expenditure on the structural funds, on research and on aid to non-Community countries. At one time DNO accounted for only a small proportion of Community expenditure, but that proportion has risen very significantly with the doubling of expenditure on the structural funds between 1988 and 1993 and the high level of financial support for central and eastern European countries and the former Soviet Union. The increase not only in the amount but also in the political importance of DNO has reinforced the bargaining power of the European Parliament in financial matters.

The different roles assigned to the Council and the European 2–015 Parliament in the budgetary procedure laid down by Article 272 EC reflect the division of competence between them. On the basis of a provisional draft budget proposed by the Commission, the Council establishes the draft budget, which it is required to submit to the European Parliament before October 5 in the year preceding the one in which the budget is to be implemented.[73] At its first reading of the draft budget, the Parliament has the right to propose modifications of items classified as DO and to amend items classified as DNO.[74] The draft budget then returns to the Council for a second reading. Proposed modifications to DO which are not explicitly accepted by the Council stand as rejected (except for those involving no increase in total expenditure whose rejection requires a positive decision by the Council) and the Council may also modify any of the amendments to DNO adopted by the Parliament.[75] All Council decisions connected with the budgetary procedure are taken by a qualified majority. At its second reading of the draft budget, the Parliament may, acting by a majority of its members and three-fifths of the votes cast, amend or reject any of the modifications made by the Council to its amendments to DNO, but it no longer has any right to touch DO.[76] The procedure concludes with the formal declaration by the President of the European Parliament that the budget has been finally adopted.[77] However, the Parliament may "for important reasons", decide, by a majority of its members and two-

---

[72] See Inter-institutional Agreement of May 6, 1999, para.30 [1999] O.J. C172/1.
[73] Art.272(4) EC.
[74] *ibid.*
[75] Art.272(5) EC.
[76] Art.272(6) EC.
[77] Art.272(7) EC.

thirds of the votes cast, to reject the budget as a whole and ask for a new draft to be submitted to it.[78] Drastic as that power may seem, it has been used by the Parliament on three occasions, in respect of the general budgets for 1980 and 1985 and a supplementary and amending budget in 1982.

A complex mechanism to prevent DNO from increasing excessively from one year to another is provided by Article 272(9) EC. A "maximum rate of increase" is fixed by the Commission, through the mechanical application of a set of economic criteria; and the rate can only be altered if there is consensus between the two branches of the budgetary authority. The functioning of that mechanism was the subject of frequent disputes between the Council and the European Parliament, one of them, in respect of the 1986 budget, leading to proceedings before the Court of Justice and the annulment by the Court of the act of the President of the Parliament declaring the budget to have been finally adopted.[79] In 1988, however, the package of financial measures (known as the "Delors I" package) was adopted, with the aim of ensuring adequate resources to achieve the objectives of the SEA, within a framework of budgetary discipline. The measures included an Inter-Institutional Agreement (or IIA) between the European Parliament, the Council and the Commission containing "financial perspectives" by which annual ceilings were fixed for various categories of expenditure over the period 1988 to 1992. It is now the established practice for each set of financial perspectives to cover a period of seven years, thus providing a degree of financial stability and making medium-term planning of expenditure possible. The Delors I package has been followed by IIAs, covering, respectively, the periods of the financial packages known as "Delors II" (1993 to 1999) and "Agenda 2000" (2000 to 2006); and, at the time of writing, agreement had been reached between the Heads of State or Government of the Member States on an "Enlargement" package covering the years 2007 to 2013.[80] The financial perspectives have provided a basis for the orderly development of expenditure in accordance with agreed priorities. Thanks to the series of IIAs, relative peace has reigned between the two branches of the budgetary authority since 1987, and this in spite of the fact that unforeseen events, notably in Central and Eastern Europe and the former Soviet Union, have made it necessary for some of the ceilings of the financial perspectives to be raised.

2–016   The recourse to IIAs is interesting not only as a technique of budgetary policy but also from a legal point of view. An IIA is not an agreement in international law, since the parties—Community

---

[78] Art.272(8) EC.

[79] Case 34/86 *Council v European Parliament* [1986] E.C.R. 2155; [1986] 3 C.M.L.R. 94.

[80] The latter brought a successful end to the British Presidency, at the European Council of December 2005.

institutions—do not have international legal personality. It should rather be regarded as a pact between equal partners in a constitutional order about the way in which they will exercise co-ordinate powers. In fact, this kind of arrangement between institutions seems to be characteristic of the Community order: other examples are the Joint Declaration of 1975 on the institution of a conciliation procedure,[81] and the IIA of 1999 between the Parliament, Council and Commission concerning internal investigations by the European Anti-Fraud Office.[82] It remains unclear just how far such arrangements create legal or merely political obligations, though the Court of Justice has suggested that an IIA may be enforceable as between its parties where it is evident that they intended to enter into a binding commitment towards each other.[83] This perhaps constitutes a concrete expression of the obligation of loyal co-operation between the institutions. At all events, the parties to IIAs have generally behaved as if they expected their terms to be observed in good faith.

Detailed supervision by the European Parliament over the activities of the Commission is made possible by the regular attendance of members of the Commission at part-sessions of the Parliament, and of Commissioners or their officials at meetings of Parliamentary committees. There is an express Treaty obligation on members of the Commission to reply to written and oral questions[84] and, following the first enlargement of the Communities in 1973, a question time, clearly influenced by the British model, was introduced. The Treaty also requires the Commission to submit an annual general report to the Parliament,[85] and the practice has developed of publishing, in conjunction with that report, other reports of a more specialised character relating, for instance, to the agricultural situation in the Community or to competition policy, which are an important source of information.

Although not obliged by the Treaty to do so, the Council replies to written questions from the European Parliament and, through the President or any other member of the Council, to oral questions. Council Presidents are invited to appear before Committees of the Parliament and they attend part-sessions to represent the views of the Council or to give an account of their management of Council business. Before Parliamentary Committees, the Council may be represented by the Secretary-General, the Deputy Secretary-General or other senior officials, acting on instructions from the Presidency.[86]

---

81 [1975] O.J. C89/1.
82 [1999] O.J. L136/15.
83 Case C–25/94 *Commission v Council* [1996] E.C.R. I–1469.
84 Art.197 EC, third para.
85 Art.200 EC.
86 As to all this, see Art.197 EC, fourth para. and Rules of Procedure of the Council.

The supervisory powers of the European Parliament were reinforced by the TEU in three ways. First, the Parliament was given the right, under Article 193 EC, to set up temporary Committees of Inquiry to investigate "alleged contraventions or maladministration in the implementation of Community law", except where the matter is *sub judice*. It is interesting to note that the text does not explicitly limit the scope of such investigations to contraventions or maladministration for which Community institutions or bodies are allegedly responsible. Secondly, Article 194 EC confirms an established practice by giving any citizen of the Union or any resident of a Member State the right to petition the European Parliament on a matter within Community competence which affects him or her directly. Thirdly, under Article 195 EC, the European Parliament appoints an Ombudsman who is empowered to receive complaints concerning instances of maladministration in the activities of Community institutions or bodies (other than the Court of Justice or the Court of First Instance acting judicially). If the Ombudsman establishes a case of maladministration, he or she must give the institution concerned three months in which to inform him or her of its views and then forward a report to the European Parliament and to the institution, while also informing the complainant of the outcome. The Ombudsman is appointed after each election for the duration of the newly elected Parliament's term of office.

The effectiveness of the European Parliament's supervision of the Commission does not depend only on the moral authority of its democratic mandate: Article 201 EC puts into the hands of the Parliament the supreme political weapon of a motion of censure by which it can force the resignation of the College of Commissioners. If a motion of censure is tabled, three days must elapse before a vote is taken; and, for the motion to be carried, there must be a two-thirds majority of the votes cast, representing a majority of the members of the Parliament. In the past it was sometimes claimed that the power to dismiss the Commission by a vote of censure was too powerful a weapon ever to be used. If that claim was ever plausible, the events of March 1999 showed that it is no longer so: the Commission presided over by Jacques Santer resigned *en masse*, following an adverse report by a Committee of Experts which had been appointed to investigate claims of fraud, mismanagement and nepotism within certain Directorates General. The resignation was evidently precipitated by pressure from the European Parliament, where it had become clear that a motion of censure would otherwise, in all likelihood, be adopted. That episode, it has been said, marked the coming of age politically of the Parliament.[87] Together with the more recent affair surrounding the appointment of the Barroso

---

[87] See Editorial Comment (1999) 36 C.M.L.Rev. 270.

Commission in November 2004, it suggests that the Parliament does indeed take its role of supervising the Commission seriously—even when the political stakes for the Union as a whole are very high.

However, the resignation of the Santer Commission also suggested a potential weakness in the Parliament's political supervision over the Commission: the power of censure can only be exercised against the entire Commission, not against any individual member(s) of the College. This potential weakness was alleviated, to some degree, through the Framework Agreement on relations between the Parliament and Commission concluded by the two institutions in July 2000.[88] Under that agreement, where the Parliament expresses lack of confidence in any given member of the College, the President of the Commission will seriously consider whether he should request that member to resign. The significance of that understanding has increased since the TN conferred upon the Commission President the power to force the resignation of individual Commissioners (with the approval of the College).[89] A new Framework Agreement approved by the Parliament in May 2005 provides that, if the Commission President refuses to request the member's resignation, he or she shall explain that decision to the Parliament.[90] However, the Council has expressed concerns that any such informal understanding between the Parliament and Commission in fact brings about a shift in the institutional balance established under Article 201 EC, and reserves the right to take appropriate action should the framework agreement actually impinge upon the institutional equilibrium created by the Treaties.[91]

Impact of the Constitutional Treaty (CT)

The CT contains significant reforms affecting many of the topics **2–017** covered in this chapter, including:

- — formal recognition of the European Council as an EU institution, clarification of its policy and decision-making powers, and the introduction of a semi-permanent Presidency (para.11–006);
- — reorganisation of the Council of Ministers' formations, changes to the rules on their rotating Presidency, and provisions guaranteeing greater openness in the Council's legislative deliberations (para.11–007);

---

[88] [2001] O.J. C121/122, para.10.
[89] Art.217(4) EC. See further above.
[90] See para.3 of the revised framework agreement as contained in A6–0147/2005.
[91] Council statement concerning the framework agreement on relations between the European Parliament and the Commission [2005] O.J. C161/1.

— further revisions to the future size and composition of the Commission, together with minor modifications to the system for its appointment (para.11–009);

— the introduction of a Minister for Foreign Affairs, associated in an institutionally novel manner with both the Council of Ministers and the Commission (para.11–010);

— a more flexible system for the future allocation among Member States of seats in the European Parliament (para.11–008);

— a formal presumption that the Commission enjoys a monopoly of initiative as regards legislative acts (though not as regards non-legislative measures), subject to a shared right of initiative with the Member States as regards police and judicial cooperation in criminal matters (currently governed by Title VI TEU) (para. 11–011);

— introduction of a "citizens' right of initiative", i.e. to request the Commission to submit proposals on matters of popular concern (para. 11–011);

— drawing a clearer distinction between exercise by the Commission of delegated legislative powers and of purely executive implementing powers, including a new system of supervision by the Council and Parliament (in the former case) and a new legal basis for the comitology system (in the latter case) (para. 11–026);

— reform of the Union's budgetary procedure, with an increased role for the European Parliament (para. 11–016).

Further reading

Andenas and Türk (eds), *Delegated Legislation and the Role of Committees in the EC* (Kluwer, 2000).

de Búrca, "The Institutional Development of the EU: A Constitutional Analysis" in Craig and de Búrca (eds), *The Evolution of EU Law* (OUP, 1999).

Dashwood, "Decision-making at the Summit" (2000) 3 C.Y.E.L.S. 79.

Dehousse, "European Institutional Architecture After Amsterdam: Parliamentary System or Regulatory Structure?" (1998) 35 C.M.L.Rev. 595.

Joerges and Vos (eds), *EU Committees: Social Regulation, Law and Politics* (Hart Publishing, 1999).

Lenaerts, "Constitutionalism and the Many Faces of Federalism" (1990) 38 A.J.C.L. 205.

Lenaerts, "Some Reflections on the Separation of Powers in the European Community" (1991) 28 C.M.L.Rev. 11.

Lenaerts, "Regulating the Regulatory Process: Delegation of Powers in the European Community" (1993) 18 E.L.Rev. 23.

Raworth, "A Timid Step Forwards: Maastricht and the Democrat-isation of the European Community" (1994) 19 E.L.Rev. 16.

St Clair Bradley, "The European Parliament and Comitology: On the Road to Nowhere?" (1997) 3 E.L.J. 230.

St Clair Bradley, "Institutional Design in the Treaty of Nice" (2001) 38 C.M.L.Rev. 1095.

CHAPTER 3

THE LEGISLATIVE PROCESS

Guide to this Chapter: The legislative process of the EC is **3–001** characterised by a complex and variable interaction between (principally) the Commission, the European Parliament and the Council. In almost all situations, the Commission enjoys a monopoly over the initiation of legislative proposals. This is meant to ensure that the general interest of the Community (rather than the concerns of individual Member States) predominates in the legislative procedure; to that end, the Commission also has procedural advantages with respect to the amendment of its proposals. Once a proposal has been submitted by the Commission, the conduct of the legislative process is determined by two main variables. The first is the relationship between the Council and the Parliament. In a handful of situations, the Council can proceed to adopt legislation without any formal involvement by the Parliament; in other cases, the Council need only consult the Parliament before taking its decisions. However, beginning with the Treaty on European Union and thanks also to the Treaties of Amsterdam and Nice, the procedure applicable across many fields of Community activity is so-called "co-decision", under which the Council and the Parliament enjoy equal authority as joint legislators. This ensures that Community legislation receives dual democratic legitimation: through the representation of the Member States in the Council, and through the representation of Union citizens in the Parliament. Other available procedures (such as "co-operation") have declined in importance; or (as with "assent") are normally reserved for special categories of decisions. The second main variable concerns the voting requirements within the Council itself. While certain politically and financially sensitive fields still require a unanimous vote in the Council (and thus preserve for each Member State a national "veto"), considerations of efficiency have gradually led the Member States to accept that most Council decisions should be taken by qualified majority vote. In the light of the enlargement into central and eastern Europe, the Treaty of Nice 2000 and Treaty of Accession 2003, with effect from November 1, 2004, replaced the old definition of a qualified majority with a more complex system based on a "triple threshold": decisions must be supported by a qualified majority of votes divided among the Member States in rough proportion to their populations; those votes must be cast by a simple majority of the Member States; and it is possible to request verification that the Member States voting in favour in fact represent a specified proportion of the total Union population. This chapter concludes with discussion of some of the ways in which the three main institutions might interact during the legislative process: for example, as regards the Commission's right to withdraw, and the Council's power to amend, a given legislative proposal.

Legislative procedures

3–002   The EC Treaty provides the constitutional framework for a very large volume of legislative activity by the political institutions of the EU. Legislation can also be enacted under the Euratom Treaty but this, for the most part, is only of concern to the specific economic sector of atomic energy. In addition, under Titles V and VI of the TEU, there are special procedures for adopting the legally binding instruments available for pursuing the objectives of the common foreign and security policy and of police and judicial co-operation in criminal matters: the salient points of difference between Second and Third Pillar decision making, and that under the First Pillar, are considered in Chapter 10. The present Chapter is solely concerned with the legislative process of the European Community.

There is no single institution that constitutes the Community's legislature. The different institutions—Council, Commission and European Parliament (together with the consultative bodies, the Economic and Social Committee and the Committee of the Regions)—are assigned their respective roles in more or less elaborate law-making procedures. The technique used in the EC Treaty is to specify in the particular provision authorising action by the Community for a given purpose, which is known as the "legal basis", the precise procedural steps to be followed in taking such action.

As was noted in the previous chapter, it is a hallmark of the Community system that the legislative process almost always requires a formal Commission proposal to set it in motion.[1] There is

---

[1] We draw attention there to the important, but temporary, exception to this principle under Title IV of Part 3 of the EC Treaty, relating to certain matters transferred to the First Pillar from the Third Pillar (which is now spent).

thus an inbuilt bias towards a text formulated (in principle) independently of particular national or sectoral interests, to further the wider interests of the Community as a whole. Another constant feature is the Council's power of final decision: no primary legislation can be enacted without receiving the positive approval (expressed according to the voting rule prescribed by the Treaty) of the institution that comprises representatives of the Member States. This gives concrete reality to the claim that the latter have "pooled" their sovereignty, rather than surrendering it. Also, the participation, in the definitive phase of decision making, of those who will ultimately be responsible for the implementation of Community law on the ground (the EC institutions themselves having no coercive machinery) is a guarantee of the effectiveness of the system.[2]

The principal difference between legislative procedures is marked by the role given to the European Parliament. In the simplest procedure of all, that prescribed by Article 133 EC for legislating on the common commercial policy, the Parliament is not legally required to play any part at all: the Council acts by a qualified majority on a proposal from the Commission.[3] Usually, however, in the Community order at its present stage of development, the power-conferring provisions of the Treaty provide for the adoption of law-making acts either by the procedure known as "consultation" or by that known as "co-decision". The two procedures, in the form in which they apply under the EC Treaty as amended most recently by the TA and TN will be examined in detail below. Briefer consideration will be given to other procedures which are either more limited in their application or are now mainly of historical interest.[4]

The consultation procedure

In the original EEC Treaty, this was the only procedure giving the European Parliament a guaranteed role in the enactment of legislation. Under the procedure, a piece of legislation is proposed by the Commission, the European Parliament is consulted on the proposal and the Council takes the final decision, acting by a qualified majority or unanimity, as laid down by the relevant provision of the Treaty (and depending on whether the Council exercises its power of amendment, as to which, see below). **3–003**

---

[2] See Dashwood, "The Role of the Council of the European Union" in Curtin and Heukels (eds), *Institutional Dynamics of European Integration*, Vol. II (1994).

[3] The European Parliament may, however, be consulted on an optional basis (see below). The common commercial policy is concerned with the regulation of trade between the EC and third countries.

[4] For an historical perspective, see Dashwood "Community Legislative Procedures in the Era of the TEU" (1994) 19 E.L.Rev. 343; brought up to date in "European Community Legislative Procedures after Amsterdam" (1998) 1 C.Y.E.L.S. 25; and in "The Constitution of the European Union after Nice: law-making procedures" (2001) E.L.Rev. 215. See also Boyron, "Maastricht and the Co-decision Procedure: a success story" (1996) 45 I.C.L.Q. 293.

Although it has been, to a significant degree, superseded by co-decision, the consultation procedure continues to be used under the EC Treaty for legislation in several important policy areas, including the common agricultural policy,[5] harmonisation of indirect taxation,[6] certain aspects of the protection of the environment,[7] and matters connected with the establishment and functioning of EMU.[8]

As we shall see, co-decision was the procedure prescribed by the TA under most of the new legal bases in the EC Treaty which it created. An important exception was Article 67 EC, laying down the procedure for enacting legislation under the Treaty Title on "Visas, asylum, immigration and other policies related to free movement of persons", which has brought into the Community sphere a range of matters formerly covered by Title VI of the TEU (the Third Pillar). For an initial period of five years, following the entry into force of the TA, a variant of the consultation procedure applied—the variation being that the Member States shared the right of initiative with the Commission.[9] After the end of the five-year period, not only did the Commission recover its monopoly of the initiative, but the Council now also has the power to substitute co-decision for consultation in respect of "all or parts of the areas covered by this Title".[10] The Council in fact exercised this power so as to extend the co-decision procedure, with effect from January 1, 2005, to areas such as the abolition of internal border checks, the freedom of third country nationals to travel within the EU for up to three months, and illegal immigration and illegal residence.[11]

Where the Treaty provides for the consultation of the European Parliament, that requirement must be strictly complied with. In practice, work on a Commission proposal begins immediately within Council bodies, without waiting for the Parliament's Opinion: the Court of Justice has found that practice to be lawful, so long as the Council does not determine its position definitively before the Opinion of the Parliament is received.[12] The reason why the Council must normally await the Opinion before taking its final decision was explained by the Court in the *Isoglucose* case:

> "The consultation provided for in the third sub-paragraph of Article 43(2), as in other similar provisions of the Treaty, is the

---

[5] Art.37 EC.

[6] Art.93 EC.

[7] Art.175 EC. The matters in question comprise: provisions primarily of a fiscal nature; town and country planning; quantitative management of water resources or affecting, directly or indirectly, the availability of those resources; land use, with the exception of waste management; measures significantly affecting a Member State's choice between different energy sources and the general structure of its energy supply.

[8] e.g. Art.104(14) EC (excessive deficit procedure).

[9] The point was noticed in Ch.2.

[10] See Art.67(2) EC, second indent.

[11] Decision 2004/927 [2004] O.J. L396/45. See further Peers, "Transforming Decision-Making on EC Immigration and Asylum Law" (2005) 30 E.L.Rev. 285.

[12] Case C–417/93 *European Parliament v Council* [1995] E.C.R. I–1185; [1995] 2 C.M.L.R. 829.

means which allows the Parliament to play an actual part in the legislative process of the Community. Such power represents an essential factor in the institutional balance intended by the Treaty. Although limited, it reflects at Community level the fundamental democratic principle that the peoples should take part in the exercise of power through the intermediary of a representative assembly. Due consultation of the Parliament in the cases provided for by the Treaty therefore constitutes an essential formality disregard of which means that the measure concerned is void."[13]

In that case, the Court annulled a Regulation which the Council had **3–004** adopted on the basis of the provision which is now Article 37(2) EC without having received the opinion of the Parliament which had been requested some months previously. The Court rejected the Council's argument that the Parliament, by its own conduct in failing to give an opinion on a measure it knew to be urgent, had made compliance with the consultation requirement impossible. The judgment laid emphasis on the fact that the Council had not formally invoked the emergency procedure for which the Parliament's own rules provide, nor had it taken advantage of its right, under Article 196 EC, to request an extraordinary session of the Parliament: the implication seemed to be that, if the Council had exhausted all the procedural possibilities open to it, the adoption of the regulation, without waiting any longer for the Opinion, might well have been justified.

That was confirmed, some 15 years later, in a case relating to the Council Regulation laying down the arrangements for granting generalised trade preferences to developing countries during the year 1993.[14] The regulation had to be adopted before the end of 1992, to avoid disrupting trade with the countries concerned. On that occasion, the Council had requested the application of the European Parliament's urgency procedure and, when an Opinion was still not forthcoming, suggested that an extraordinary session be held in late December; having received a negative reply from the Office of the President of the Parliament, the Council proceeded without more ado to adopt the regulation. The action brought by the Parliament for the annulment of the regulation was rejected by the Court of Justice, on the ground that the failure punctually to render an Opinion amounted, in the circumstances, to an infringement of the duty of loyal co-operation which binds the institutions, by analogy with the duty of the Member States under Article 10 EC.

The consultation of the European Parliament takes place in relation to the Commission's original proposal. If the Commission

---

[13] Case 138/79 *Roquette Frères v Council* [1980] E.C.R. 3333, 3360.
[14] Case C–65/93 *European Parliament v Council* [1995] E.C.R. I–643; [1996] 1 C.M.L.R. 4.

amends its proposal, or the Council intends to exercise its power of
amendment, and this means that, considered as a whole, the
substance of the text which was the subject of the first consultation
will be altered, there is a duty to consult the Parliament a second
time.[15] Re-consultation is not required if the change is one of
method rather than of substance (e.g., the substitution, in a draft
regulation relating to officials' pay, of updated exchange rates); nor
if the change goes in the direction of wishes expressed by the
Parliament itself in its Opinion.[16] A new case for re-consultation,
acknowledged in the practice of the Council since the introduction
of the co-operation procedure by the SEA, is where the Council is
minded to amend the legal basis proposed by the Commission, and
the effect of this will be to substitute simple consultation for one of
the procedures that give the Parliament a more significant legislative
role.

3–005   Re-consultation, which is a legal requirement in certain circumstances, must not be confused with the conciliation procedure
instituted by a Joint Declaration of the European Parliament, the
Council and the Commission in 1975.[17] This was designed to provide
an opportunity, through a face-to-face meeting within a Conciliation
Committee, for the European Parliament and the Council to find
common ground in certain cases where the Council intends to depart
from the Opinion adopted by the Parliament. The act in question
must be one of "general application" (this would cover all acts of a
normative character, including, by definition, all regulations) and it
must have "appreciable financial implications".[18] Acts whose adoption is required pursuant to existing legislation are excluded, because
such legislation could itself have been the subject of conciliation.
There are also procedural requirements: the Commission must
indicate, in submitting its proposal, whether the act in question is a
suitable subject for the procedure; and the European Parliament's
request for conciliation must be made when it gives its Opinion.
Conciliation should normally be completed within three months, or
within an appropriate time-limit, to be fixed by the Council, if the
matter is urgent.[19] It must be stressed that the aim is to *seek* an
agreement between the Parliament and the Council: if there is a

---

[15] Case 41/69 *ACF Chemiefarma v Commission* [1970] E.C.R. 661, 702; Case 1253/79 *Battaglia
v Commission* [1982] E.C.R. 297; Case C–65/90 *European Parliament v Council* [1992]
E.C.R. I–4593. See also Opinion of Advocate General Mancini in Case 20/85 *Roviello* [1988]
E.C.R. 2805; Opinion of Advocate General Darmon in Case C–65/90 *European Parliament v
Council* [1992] E.C.R. I–4593.
[16] Case 1253/79 *Battaglia v Commission* [1982] E.C.R. 297.
[17] [1975] O.J. C89. The procedure laid down by the Joint Declaration is in practice resorted to
only where the legislative role of the Parliament is restricted to that of being consulted. It
must be distinguished from the mandatory conciliation provided for as an element of the
co-decision procedure.
[18] Joint Declaration, point 2.
[19] Joint Declaration, point 6.

sufficient *rapprochement*, the Parliament may give a fresh Opinion and the Council then proceeds to take definitive action;[20] however, even in the absence of agreement, the Council retains its legal right to adopt, according to the applicable voting procedure, the measure it considers appropriate. For the European Parliament, the advantage of the procedure is that it allows influence to be exerted in the final phase of decision making, and this has been done with some effect, for example in respect of the amendments to the Financial Regulation that were adopted in 1988.[21]

It should finally be noted that there is nothing to prevent the Council from consulting the European Parliament, and it often does so, where this is not required by the Treaty. In such a case, if the Parliament fails, for some reason, to give an Opinion, the Council is free to withdraw the request, but, it is thought, reasonable notice should be given to the Parliament before such withdrawal.

The co-decision procedure
Under this procedure, first introduced into the EC Treaty by the **3–006** TEU, and refined and streamlined by the TA, the European Parliament is treated, from a formal point of view at least, as the equal legislative partner of the Council. The Commission submits its proposal to both institutions at the same time,[22] and the final "product" of the law-making process is a joint act of the Parliament and the Council, which the President of each institution is required to sign.[23] The unofficial designation "co-decision" is meant to underline that partnership: it is in common use, but is not found in the text of the Treaty which speaks, awkwardly, of "the procedure referred to in Article 251".

The procedure entails successive "readings" of a proposal for legislation, offering a series of opportunities for interaction between the three main political institutions, and designed to channel the European Parliament and the Council towards approval of a joint text. The various possible stages are outlined below, and are also illustrated by the diagram below. We say "possible" stages, because the procedure does not have to run its full course, if agreement between the co-legislators can be reached earlier. Some of the amendments effected by the TA were intended precisely to facilitate such an outcome.[24] In practice, it has become common for proposals to be adopted at first or second reading; only a minority need to be taken to the stage of compulsory conciliation.

---

[20] Joint Declaration, point 7.
[21] Reg.610/90 [1990] O.J. L70/1.
[22] Art.251(2) EC.
[23] Art.254(1) EC.
[24] See amendments to paras (2) and (3) of Art.251 EC, enabling a definitive decision to be taken at an early stage in the procedure (as described below).

CO-DECISION PROCEDURE
(Article 251 EC)

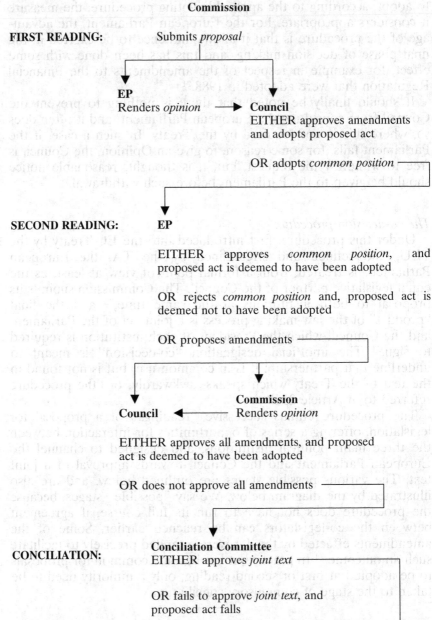

Commission

FIRST READING: Submits *proposal*

EP
Renders *opinion* ⟶ **Council**
                  EITHER approves amendments
                  and adopts proposed act

                  OR adopts *common position*

SECOND READING: **EP**

                  EITHER approves *common position*, and
                  proposed act is deemed to have been adopted

                  OR rejects *common position* and, proposed act is
                  deemed not to have been adopted

                  OR proposes amendments

                  Commission
Council ⟵ Renders *opinion*

EITHER approves all amendments, and proposed
act is deemed to have been adopted

OR does not approve all amendments

CONCILIATION: **Conciliation Committee**
                  EITHER approves *joint text*

                  OR fails to approve *joint text*, and
                  proposed act falls

                EITHER both adopt
     EP   **Council**

                OR act is deemed
                not to have been adopted

The first reading commences with the submission of the Commission's proposal to the European Parliament and the Council. The Parliament renders an opinion, which may or may not contain amendments. The Council then has a choice, to be exercised by qualified majority decision: it may definitively adopt the proposed act in conformity with the opinion (*i.e.* incorporating the Parliament's amendments, if any); or, if it does not approve all of the amendments contained in the opinion, or wishes to make others, it may adopt a "common position", which must be communicated to the Parliament with a full explanation of the underlying reasons. The Commission, too, must inform the Parliament fully of its position.[25]

At second reading, the common position of the Council replaces the Commission's proposal as the text which is the object of the interaction between the co-legislative institutions. The choice is now for the European Parliament between: (a) expressly approving the common position (or doing so tacitly by taking no decision within the prescribed period of three months); or (b) rejecting the common position (this requires an absolute majority of MEPs, not merely of those voting); or (c) proposing amendments to the common position (by the same majority).[26] Approval or rejection by the Parliament at this stage has the effect of concluding the procedure one way or the other: the act in question is deemed to have been adopted in accordance with the common position; or, as the case may be, not to have been adopted. In the (more likely) eventuality that amendments are proposed, these must be forwarded to the Council, as well as to the Commission which is required to deliver an opinion on them. The ball is then, once again, in the Council's court. It may, within three months, approve all of the proposed amendments (by a qualified majority, or by unanimity in respect of those on which the Commission has delivered a negative opinion), in which case the act will be deemed to have been adopted in the form of the common position as amended. Otherwise, the President of the Council, in agreement with the President of the Parliament, must, within six weeks, convene a meeting of the Conciliation Committee provided for by paragraph (4) of Article 251 EC.[27]

The procedure of the first and second readings involves interaction between the Council and the European Parliament at arm's **3–007**

---

[25] Art.251(2) EC, first sub-para. An early example of a measure adopted at first reading was Dir.1999/103 of the European Parliament and the Council amending Council Dir.80/181 on the approximation of the laws of the Member States relating to units of measurement [2000] O.J. L34/17. The Directive, proposed by the Commission on February 5, 1999, was definitively adopted in a little over 10 months, on January 24, 2000.

[26] Art.251(2) EC, second sub-para. For an example of a measure deemed to have been adopted pursuant to point (a) of the sub-para., following approval by the Parliament of the Council's common position, see Reg.141/2000 of the European Parliament and of the Council on orphan medicinal products [2000] O.J. L18/1.

[27] Art.251(3) EC. The TA substituted the six-week time-limit for the less precise obligation to convene a meeting of the Conciliation Committee "forthwith".

length. As described in the preceding paragraphs, they will have had three separate opportunities for reaching agreement, but if they fail to do so Article 251 EC provides the remedy of direct negotiation within the Conciliation Committee, to break the deadlock. The Committee is composed of the members of the Council or their representatives (normally, the appropriate COREPER, depending on the subject-matter of the act in question) and an equal number of representatives of the European Parliament. Its task is, within six weeks, to reach agreement on a joint text, by a qualified majority on the Council side and by a majority on the Parliament side. The Commission has a role in the proceedings as honest broker. The negotiations within the Committee take place in relation to the common position, which must be addressed on the basis of the amendments proposed by the Parliament. The parties are thus required to focus on the texts formally established by each of them during the earlier phases of the procedure.[28] However, the ECJ held in the *European Low Fares Airline Association* case that, so as to make the co-decision procedure effective, the Conciliation Committee must enjoy a wide discretion: it is charged, not with coming to an agreement on the Parliament's proposed amendments to the Council's common position, but rather with reaching an agreement on a joint text; for these purposes, Article 251 EC does not include any restriction as to the content of the measures chosen by the Conciliation Committee to enable such agreement to be reached. In this case, the Conciliation Committee had not exceeded its powers by agreeing modifications to the Council's common position on certain provisions of a draft regulation on air transport, as regards which the Parliament had not previously proposed any amendments.[29]

If conciliation is successful, the joint text agreed by the Committee is submitted to the co-legislators, who have a further six weeks in which formally to adopt the act in question, in accordance with that text. Should either of them fail to do so, the act will fall.[30] That will also be the result if the Conciliation Committee is unable to agree a joint text within the six-week deadline.[31]

---

[28] The last sentence of Art.251(4) EC was added by the TA. It is understood there had been occasions when there was disagreement between the two sides, as to the parameters of the discussion within the Committee.

[29] Case C–344/04 *European Low Fares Airline Association* (Judgment of January 10, 2006).

[30] Art.251(5) EC.

[31] Art.251(6) EC. Under the co-decision procedure as provided for by the TEU, if the Conciliation Committee failed to approve a joint text, it remained possible for the Council to confirm unilaterally the common position it had agreed prior to conciliation, with the option of including some or all of the European Parliament's amendments; the measure would then become law, unless it was rejected, within six weeks, by a majority of MEPs. By abolishing this so-called "third reading", the TA has formally placed the Parliament on an equal footing with the Council, both being required to give their positive approval to legislation. In a case where the Council sought to exercise its former power at third reading, relating to a proposed directive on open network provision (ONP) for voice telephony, the European Parliament imposed its veto by an overwhelming majority.

The various time-limits prescribed by Article 251 EC are very important, to prevent the legislative process from becoming too lengthy, and to avoid a loss of political momentum. There is, however, provision in paragraph (7) of the Article for the periods of three months to be extended by a maximum of one month, and those of six weeks by a maximum of a fortnight, at the initiative of either the European Parliament or the Council.

Co-decision was originally prescribed by the EC Treaty as amended by the TEU, for enacting legislation relating to the internal market,[32] where it replaced the co-operation procedure (discussed below). It was also provided for under several of the legal bases created by the TEU, in policy areas where specific authorisation for action by the Community was previously lacking.[33] The TA took matters still further: all of the provisions of the EC Treaty prescribing co-operation (with the exception of those found in the Treaty Title on Economic and Monetary Policy) were amended,[34] by substituting co-decision; and the procedure was substituted for consultation in certain cases.[35] Co-decision was, moreover, the legislative procedure chosen by the authors of the TA for almost all the new legal bases established pursuant to that Treaty, including in areas of considerable political sensitivity.[36] Further (more modest) extensions of the co-decision procedure were implemented under the TN:[37] for example, as regards incentive measures to combat

---

[32] Notably, under the general power of approximation conferred by Art.95 EC.

[33] See Art.152(4) EC on public health; Art.153(4) EC on consumer protection; Art.156 EC on trans-European networks. See also Art.151(5), first indent EC on culture; and Art.166(1) EC on the multiannual framework programmes for research. Under both of the latter, as provided for by the TEU, the Council was required to act by unanimity (see below). Another legal basis into which co-decision was introduced by the TEU was Art.175(3) EC on general action programmes setting out priority objectives for policy on the environment.

[34] Co-decision is substituted for co-operation in the following provisions: Art.12, second para., EC on discrimination on grounds of nationality; Art.71(1) EC on the common transport policy; Art.80 EC on sea and air transport; Art.137(2) EC on conditions of employment; Art.148 EC on implementation of the European Social Fund; Art.150(4) EC on vocational training; Art.162, first para., EC on implementing decisions for the purposes of the European Regional Development Fund; Art.172, second para., EC on the implementation of the research framework programme; Art.175(1) EC on the environment; Art.179 EC on development co-operation.

[35] Art.42 EC on social security for migrant workers; Art.46(2) EC on the co-ordination of national provisions derogating, on grounds of public policy, public sector or public health, from the right of establishment and the freedom to supply services; Art.47(2) EC on the co-ordination of provisions governing certain aspects of the taking up and pursuit of self-employed activities.

[36] Art.129 EC on incentive measures in the field of employment; Art.141(3) EC on equal opportunities and equal treatment for men and women in matters of employment and occupation; Art.152(4) on various public health measures; Art.255 EC on access to documents; Art.280(4) EC on countering fraud against the financial interests of the Community; Art.285(1) EC on the production of Community statistics; Art.286(2) EC on data protection. The glaring exception is legislation for the purposes of the new Treaty Title on "Visas, Asylum, Immigration and other Policies Related to Free Movement of Persons" (as to which, see above).

[37] See Dashwood, "The constitution of the European Union after Nice: law-making procedures" (2001) E.L.Rev. 215.

various forms of discrimination;[38] soft-law measures designed to combat social exclusion and modernise social protection;[39] and the regulation and funding of political parties at the European level.[40] The trend is thus towards the recognition of co-decision as the standard procedure for enacting Community measures which are genuinely legislative in character. If that could be achieved, it would be a great constitutional gain, in terms both of simplifying and helping to legitimate the process of Community law-making.

Unfortunately, in a few matters, the extension of co-decision has been purchased at the price of requiring the Council to act, throughout the procedure, by unanimity instead of by a qualified majority.[41] That is liable to distort the process of decision making, and to diminish the ability of the European Parliament to influence the final outcome, since at second reading the Council may be found less willing than usual to shift from its common position, which would have had to accommodate the particular viewpoints of all delegations.[42]

Other procedures

3–008   Brief mention must be made of the co-operation procedure (officially, "the procedure referred to in Article 252"),[43] because of its historical significance. The introduction of the procedure by the SEA was the first step towards enhancing the legislative role of the European Parliament beyond the simple consultation provided for by the original EEC Treaty. In the SEA, co-operation was closely associated with the project of completing the internal market by the end of 1992. As we have seen, internal market measures were brought within the scope of co-decision by the TEU, but co-operation survived under the regime of that Treaty for enacting EC legislation on, among other things, transport, aspects of environment

---

[38] Art.13(2) EC.

[39] Art.137(2) EC.

[40] Art.191 EC.

[41] See Art.42 EC and Art.47(2) EC. The legal basis for action by the Community in the field of culture, Art.151(5) EC, which was enacted by the TEU, retains the requirement of unanimity in the context of the co-decision procedure. Similar requirements in Art.166(1) EC on the adoption of the multinational framework programme for research, and in Art.18(2) EC on facilitating EU citizens' rights of free movement and residence, were dropped (respectively) by the TA and by the TN.

[42] For a positive assessment of the way in which the co-decision procedure (in the version provided for by the TEU) has functioned in practice, see Boyron, "Maastricht and the Co-decision Procedure: a success story" (1996) 45 I.C.L.Q. 293; and, by the same author, "The Co-decision Procedure: rethinking the constitutional fundamentals" in Craig and Harlow, *Lawmaking in the European Union* (Kluwer, 1998).

[43] For a fuller treatment of the co-operation procedure, see Dashwood "Community Legislative Procedures in the Era of the TEU" (1994) 19 E.L.Rev. 343. See also the discussion of the procedure in De Ruyt, *L'Acte unique europ'een* (Editions de l'Universite de Bruxelles, 1987), pp.124 *et seq.* On the application of the procedure to internal market legislation, see Schwarze (ed.), *Legislation for Europe 1992* (Nomos, 1989).

policy, and development co-operation. Now it has been superseded in those policy areas too: it was allowed by the TA to survive only in a few provisions relating to economic and monetary policy (regarded, seemingly for political reasons, as untouchable by the IGC which negotiated that Treaty).[44] Like co-decision, of which it was the forerunner, the co-operation procedure involves two readings: the main differences are that it contains no procedure for compulsory conciliation; and, at the end of the day, the Council cannot be prevented from adopting a text that ignores the Parliament's wishes, although it may be required, in so doing, to act by unanimity.[45]

Under the assent procedure, the Council acts on a proposal by the Commission, after obtaining the assent (*avis conforme*) of the European Parliament. This is a form of co-decision, since the act in question can only pass into law if the Council and the Parliament give their positive approval. The difference, as compared with the co-decision of Article 251 EC, is that there is no series of formal interactions between the two institutions: a common orientation is reached within the Council, and this is presented to the Parliament, effectively, on a take-it-or-leave-it basis.

The procedure is, therefore, unsuitable for enacting complex legislative measures. It was replaced, pursuant to the TA, by co-decision in the legal basis for adopting provisions with a view to facilitating the exercise of EU citizens' right to move and reside freely in the territory of the Member States,[46] but not, unfortunately, in the legal basis for the enactment of basic legislation on the structural funds, under which resources are transferred to the less prosperous regions of the Community.[47] On the other hand, the retention of assent as the method prescribed by Article 190(4) EC, for deciding on the electoral system of the European Parliament, does not appear objectionable, since here it is the Parliament itself which initiates the process by drawing up a proposal for the Council, so that a measure of interaction does take place. In addition, the procedure is, of course, perfectly suitable for deciding on matters that only require a "yes" or "no" answer from the Parliament, such as the accession of new Member States,[48] or the conclusion of especially important international agreements.[49]

---

[44] Provisions in which co-operation will, for the time being, survive are: Art.102(2) EC, Art.103(2) EC and Art.106(2) EC.

[45] Unanimity is required in two situations: where the Parliament has formally rejected the common position (Art.252(c), second para. EC); or where the Commission, having re-examined its proposal by taking into account the Parliament's amendments, forwards to the Council a text which the latter is unwilling to adopt without amendment (Art.252(d) and (e) EC).

[46] Art.18(2) EC.

[47] Art.161 EC.

[48] Art.49 TEU.

[49] Art.300(3), second sub-para., EC.

In giving its assent on the electoral procedure and on applications for membership the European Parliament is required, by the relevant legal bases, to act by an absolute majority of its component members; and on other matters by the majority of votes cast. For the Council, the voting rule prescribed in connection with the assent procedure is normally unanimity, but a qualified majority will be sufficient for deciding on some of the international agreements to which Article 300(3) EC applies.[50]

What may be termed the "organic law" procedure appears as a variant of either the consultation or the assent procedures. Its unique feature is that the Council, acting unanimously on a proposal from the Commission, and after consulting or, as the case may be, with the assent of, the European Parliament, takes a decision which it then recommends to the Member States for adoption in accordance with their respective constitutional requirements. Such a relatively "heavy" procedure (with what amounts to national ratification of a Community act) can only be justified for the purposes of decisions which are structural in character, just falling short of amendments to the Treaty. For the use of the organic law procedure with consultation, see Article 22 EC on provisions to strengthen or add to the rights of EU citizens as laid down by Part Two of the EC Treaty; and Article 269 EC, second paragraph, on own resources. For its use with assent, see Article 190(4) EC on provisions relating to the system of European Parliamentary elections.

Concluding on the legislative procedures, it may be noted that, besides the main ones mentioned here, there are multiple variants in the Treaty. This is an unsatisfactory situation, making the system unintelligible to the average EU citizen. However, a start was made by the TA (and continued by the TN) towards simplifying and rationalising the legislative process, notably through the virtual abolition of co-operation, and the extension of co-decision that was remarked on above.

Majority decisions by the Council

3–009	The general voting procedure, laid down by Article 205(1) EC, is that, save as otherwise provided by the Treaty, the Council shall act by a majority of its members (i.e. by a "simple majority"). However, there are few cases where the Treaty confers powers on the Council without specifically providing that acts shall be adopted either by a qualified majority or by unanimity. Effectively, the use of a simple majority is restricted to procedural decisions of the Council.

---

[50] e.g. "agreements establishing a specific institutional framework by organising cooperation procedures" or "agreements having important budgetary implications for the Community" in a field where unanimity is not required for the adoption of internal rules: para.(3) of Art.300 EC, read together with para.(1), second sub-para. and para.(2), second sentence.

The definition of a qualified majority within the Council has become one of the EU's most controversial institutional questions. In the Community of 15, a qualified majority consisted of 62 votes out of 87 (approximately 71.26 per cent). The allocation of votes to the various Member States was weighted so as to correspond to differences in the size of their populations.[51] However, the correspondence was only very rough, so that the system gave disproportionate voting power to the smaller Member States at the expense of the larger ones: for example, Germany with a population of around 80 million held 10 votes, while Ireland with a population of less than four million held three votes. It was evident that, were such an approach to have been maintained after the accession of the (mostly small and medium-sized) countries of central and eastern Europe, the influence of the larger Member States would have been even more severely diminished. Linked to this controversy over the qualified majority threshold within the Council was the problem of the size of the Commission: if the larger Member States were to sacrifice their traditional second Commissioner in the interests of a more efficient College, they expected some form of compensation when it came to the allocation of Council votes.[52] The negotiating conference which led to the TA tried but failed to find a solution to this conundrum; the blueprint for reform was laid down by the TN,[53] though the final arrangements were only agreed under the Treaty of Accession 2003.[54] Following a brief transitional period between May 1 and October 31, 2004 (in fact, a simple mathematical adjustment of the old approach), the new rules for calculating a qualified majority in Council within the Union of 25 came into force on November 1, 2004.

The Nice/Accession system of qualified majority voting is based on the so-called "triple threshold" now contained in the amended version of Article 205 EC. The *first* threshold is still based on a weighted allocation of votes. A qualified majority now consists of at least 232 votes out of 321 (a slight rise to approximately 72.27 per cent); the allocation of votes to the various Member States still corresponds to differences in the size of their populations.[55] But the correspondence is now a little less rough: for example, Germany's 29 votes can be compared with Ireland's seven votes. Perhaps the most

---

[51] Germany, France, Italy and the United Kingdom had 10 votes each; Spain had eight votes; Belgium, Greece, the Netherlands and Portugal had five votes; Austria and Sweden had four votes; Denmark, Ireland and Finland had three votes; Luxembourg had two votes.

[52] See Ch.2.

[53] Protocol on the enlargement of the EU, and Declaration on the enlargement of EU.

[54] [2003] O.J. L236.

[55] Germany, France, Italy and the United Kingdom have 29 votes each; Spain and Poland have 27 votes each; the Netherlands has 13 votes; Belgium, Hungary, the Czech Republic, Greece and Portugal have 12 votes each; Austria and Sweden have 10 votes each; Denmark, Ireland, Lithuania, Finland and the Slovak Republic have seven votes each; Estonia, Cyprus, Slovenia, Latvia and Luxembourg have four votes each; Malta has three votes.

glaring distortion is between the larger Member States themselves: Spain and Poland each secured 27 votes, even though their populations are each only around half that of Germany. The *second* threshold is that the votes in favour must, in any case, have been cast by a majority of Member States. This is intended to reassure the smaller countries that they cannot be outvoted by a minority coalition of larger Member States, since (in theory) just 12 Member States could have sufficient weighted votes to cross the first voting threshold.[56] It should be noted that, in the rather rare cases where the Council may act without a proposal from the Commission, the second threshold is raised to at least two-thirds of the Member States. The *third* threshold is that any member of the Council may request verification that the Member States who constitute the qualified majority on the basis of the previous two calculations furthermore represent at least 62 per cent of the total EU population.[57] If that is not the case, the decision in question cannot be adopted. This is intended to ensure that Council decisions are representative, not only of a weighted majority of Member States' votes, but also of a weighted majority of the Union's population; and in particular, to reassure the larger Member States that the Council cannot be driven towards a particular decision by a coalition of small and medium-sized countries. Another important point should be made about calculating a qualified majority vote: where the Treaty provides for the Council to act by unanimity, abstentions by the Member States do not prevent the act in question from being adopted;[58] whereas to obtain a qualified majority, positive votes are needed in all three thresholds, so that any purported abstention will contribute to a blocking minority.

3–010   If Bulgaria and Romania join the Union as planned on January 1, 2007,[59] the Treaty of Accession 2005 envisages that they should have 10 and 14 votes in the Council (respectively); and the qualified majority for the purposes of the first threshold would rise to at least 255 out of a new total of 345 votes (a more significant rise to approximately 73.91 per cent).[60]

The EC Treaty provides for special qualified majorities in certain cases, more particularly in connection with decisions that have to be

---

[56] e.g. Belgium, Spain, Hungary, the Netherlands, Poland, the United Kingdom, the Czech Republic, Germany, Greece, France, Italy, plus any other Member State.

[57] For these purposes, the Council's Rules of Procedure contain the relevant population figures for each Member State. Those figures are revised with effect from January 1 each year, in accordance with data provided by the Statistical Office of the European Communities: see, e.g. Decision 2006/34 [2006] O.J. L22/32.

[58] Art.205(3) EC.

[59] Or, in accordance with the Treaty of Accession 2005, on January 1, 2008.

[60] Art.22 of the Protocol concerning the conditions and arrangements for admission of the Republic of Bulgaria and Romania to the EU (annexed to the Treaty of Accession [2005] O.J. L157) envisages that this reallocation would take place in accordance with the provisions of the Treaty establishing a Constitution for Europe [2004] O.J. C310.

taken within the context of economic and monetary union. For example, when the Council takes steps under Article 104 EC against a Member State found to be running an excessive government deficit, the Member State concerned will not be entitled to vote, and the qualified majority will consist of two-thirds of the weighted votes of the other members of the Council. Similarly, only the Member States participating in the single currency have a right to vote on matters connected with its establishment and management, and two-thirds of the weighted votes of those Member States constitute a qualified majority.[61]

Since the end of the second stage of the EC's transitional period (December 31, 1965), the qualified majority has been the voting procedure prescribed in the core areas of Community competence: those of the common market and the common policies in agriculture and transport. The range of matters that could be decided by a qualified majority was extended by the SEA, most notably in the case of Article 95 EC, the legal basis for adopting measures for the approximation of national provisions where such measures have as their object the establishment and functioning of the internal market. With the further extension of qualified majority decisions by the TEU, the TA and the TN, the rule of unanimity has been confined to certain matters of special political sensitivity, such as the harmonisation of indirect taxation,[62] and to decisions of a fundamental character, such as the exercise of the "default mechanism" provided for by Article 308 EC.[63]

Despite the opportunities for majority voting offered by the EC Treaty, until the early 1980s the Council only regularly took decisions in this way on budgetary and staff matters, acting by consensus in other cases. The tedious process of negotiating a compromise acceptable to all delegations represented an impediment to progress in the development of the EC in the decade following the end of the transitional period. That has now changed and it has become the normal practice for the Council to act by a qualified or simple majority where the Treaty allows.[64] The change in practice reflected a new political climate, influenced by the perception that rapid progress towards completing the internal market was necessary to enable the Community to deal on equal terms with its main international competitors. The trend towards majority voting

---

[61] Art.122(5) EC.
[62] Art.93 EC.
[63] See Ch.4. Other typical examples are Art.175(2) EC (sensitive aspects of environmental policy); Art.137(2) EC (sensitive aspects of social policy); and Art.269 EC (own resources).
[64] See Dewost in Capotorti *et al.* (eds), *Du droit international au droit communautaire; Liber amicorum Pierre Pescatore* (Nomos, 1998), pp.167 *et seq;* Dashwood in Schwarze (ed.) *Legislation for Europe 1992* (Nomos, 1989), pp.79 *et seq.*

predated the entry into force of the SEA,[65] but it certainly received a fresh impetus from the introduction of new legal bases providing for majority decisions.

In connection with majority voting, something must be said about the so-called "Luxembourg Compromise". This was an "agreement to disagree", reached at a special meeting of the Council in January 1966, to resolve a political crisis precipitated in part because of the shift to decision making by qualified majority for many purposes, which was foreseen under the EEC Treaty from the beginning of the final stage of the transitional period. The text of the Luxembourg Compromise[66] included a provision to the effect that when, in case of a decision that can be taken by a majority vote, very important interests of a Member State are at stake, the Council will attempt, within a reasonable time, to reach a solution acceptable to all its members. It was noted that, in the view of the French delegation, the discussion in such cases must continue until unanimous agreement is reached, a view not shared by the other delegations. This arrangement left the Council's legal powers fully intact, while influencing its practice. In assessing that influence, it is useful to draw a distinction between the encouragement that was undoubtedly given to the search for consensus within the Council, and formal invocation of the Compromise by a Member State to prevent a vote from being taken on a particular occasion.[67] In fact, Member States have formally invoked the Compromise only about a dozen times, and the political price for doing so is considered to be high. The outcome may also be uncertain: thus in 1982, when the United Kingdom sought to block the adoption of the agricultural price package in order to put pressure on the other Member States to agree a reduction of the British contribution to the Community budget, its purported "veto" was swept aside and a vote was taken;[68] whereas in 1985, Germany successfully invoked the Compromise to forestall a decision on the reduction of cereal prices. Whether the Luxembourg Compromise can be said still to "exist" is not a question to which a legal answer can be given: it all depends on whether, in a concrete case, enough of the Member States to constitute a blocking minority can be persuaded, by the Member State claiming a vital interest, to refrain from voting. However, such cases, if they occur at all in future, will be very rare; more importantly, the Compromise has

---

[65] Evidence of the trend can be found in Council answers to Written Questions of the European Parliament: see, e.g. the answers to Written Questions No.1121/86 (Elles) [1986] O.J. C306/42; Written Questions No.2126/86 (Fontaine) [1987] O.J. C82/43.

[66] The full text of the Luxembourg compromise is published in Bulletin of the EEC, March 1966, pp.8–10.

[67] Dashwood in Schwarze (ed.) *Legislation for Europe 1992* (Nomos, 1989), pp.82–83.

[68] A lesson from that episode is that the very important interest which is claimed must be directly linked to the particular measure under consideration. The United Kingdom had indicated that it was invoking the Luxembourg Compromise, not to protect important interests threatened by the price package, but as a purely tactical move.

ceased to influence the Council towards acting by consensus, since, as we have seen, voting, if legally permissible, is now the normal practice.[69]

The interaction between the institutions

The Commission's right to alter or withdraw its proposal
The Commission is expressly empowered, as long as the Council **3-011** has not acted, to alter its proposal at any time during the procedures leading to the adoption of a Community act.[70] There are various reasons why it may choose to do so.

In the first place, the Commission may independently form the view that the proposal needs to be improved or completed; or perhaps to be updated, in order to keep abreast of scientific developments, especially if it has been lying on the Council's table for some time. Or account may have to be taken of changes in the legal situation: for instance, after the entry into force of the SEA, the Commission substituted what was then Article 100a (now Article 95) EC as the legal basis of a large number of proposals originally based on other provisions of the Treaty.

Secondly, the Commission may respond to an Opinion rendered by the European Parliament under the consultation procedure, or at first reading under the co-decision procedure, by incorporating into its proposal some or all of the amendments put forward by the Parliament. At second reading under the co-decision procedure, the Commission indicates its acceptance, or otherwise, of the Parliament's amendments, not by amending its own proposal, but by delivering an opinion, as required pursuant to Article 151(2)(c) EC.[71]

Thirdly, the Commission may alter its proposal in order to facilitate decision making within the Council. Decisions are reached by the Council through negotiations between national delegations in working groups, in COREPER and at ministerial level. These negotiations involve progressive adaptation of the Commission's proposal in order to take account of Member States' particular interests and difficulties. The process is managed by the Presidency,

---

[69] Concerns were expressed in the last edition of this book about the potential impact of the TA, which included a variant of the Luxembourg Compromise for the purposes of authorising closer cooperation by qualified majority vote under Art.11 EC and Art.40 TEU. However, such concerns appear to have been neutralised by the TN, which amended the procedure for authorising which is now known as "enhanced cooperation" under Art.11 EC and Art.40a TEU, so as to remove that variant of the Luxembourg Compromise. See further, Ch.4.

[70] Art.250(2) EC.

[71] Art.250(2) EC, as the more general provision, must be read consistently with the specific requirements of the co-decision procedure.

aided by the General Secretariat of the Council, with the aim of achieving a balanced compromise text, commanding the qualified majority or unanimity required for the adoption of the measure in question. The Commission is represented at meetings of Council bodies where its proposals are under discussion,[72] and it may play a vital part in the development of the Presidency compromise, both by providing technical assistance and by indicating amendments it is able to accept. In some cases, final amendments to the proposal are made orally by the Commissioner attending the Council meeting where a measure is adopted, who will have been mandated by the College of Commissioners to act within a certain margin of man-oeuvre. The Court of Justice has confirmed the legality of the practice of oral amendment, provided that the Commissioner concerned acts within the scope of this mandate.

There is no explicit provision of the Treaty enabling the Commission to withdraw a proposal which it has submitted to the Council. However, it is generally agreed that, within certain limits, the Commission has such a power.[73] One view is that withdrawal may be regarded as the extreme case of amendment, but the better view is, perhaps, that both amendment and withdrawal are corollaries of the right of initiative: the latter would be incomplete if the Commission, having put forward a proposal which it no longer considered appropriate, was unable to remedy the situation. At the same time, the power of withdrawal must not be used to prevent other institutions from performing the roles the Treaty has given them in the legislative procedure. Thus it would be an abuse of power for the Commission to withdraw a proposal which is on the point of being adopted by the Council, in order to prevent that institution from exercising its own power of amendment (as to which, see below). Similarly, it is submitted, under the co-decision procedure the Commission has no right to withdraw its proposal once the Council has adopted its common position. This seems to follow from the clear terms in which the Treaty specifies the options open to the European Parliament and the Council at second reading, and the legal consequences that ineluctably follow from the course of action chosen.

The Council's power of amendment

3–012   The Council has a general power to amend proposals of the Commission, when acting definitively under the consultation procedure or adopting a common position at first reading under the co-

---

[72] Art.5(2) of the Council's Rules of Procedure [2004] O.J. L106/22 provides: "The Commission shall be invited to take part in meetings of the Council . . . . The Council may, however, decide to deliberate without the presence of the Commission".

[73] See Mégret *et al.*, *Le droit de la CEE* (Editions de l'Université de Bruxelles, 1979), Vol.9, pp.135–136.

decision procedure but, in so doing, it must act unanimously.[74] The rule requiring unanimity for the amendment of Commission proposals was of limited practical significance during the period when the Council habitually acted by consensus; now, however, with the extension of the range of matters that can be decided by a qualified majority, and with majority decisions being taken as a matter of course where the Treaty permits, the rule has come into its own as a pivotal element of the Council/Commission relationship. This is because, if the Council is unwilling to adopt a proposal without making certain changes, the only way of avoiding the unanimity rule is for a compromise to be negotiated that the Commission can make its own; the compromise will then have the legal status of an amended Commission proposal and be capable of being enacted by a qualified majority. The Commission is thus able to maintain direct influence over the progress of its proposal, right up to the final outcome of the negotiations within the Council.

The right of the Council to amend the Commission's proposal by unanimity does not extend to the substitution of an entirely new proposal, since that would be to usurp the right of initiative.[75] It is submitted that Council amendments, however radical, will not be *ultra vires*, as long as the subject-matter of the measure in question remains the same. For instance, in a draft directive concerning animal welfare, the Council may decide to establish different criteria of welfare from those proposed by the Commission; but it would not be entitled to transform the directive into one fixing quality standards for fresh meat.

The requirement of unanimity for the amendment of Commission *proposals* does not extend to cases where the decision-making process is initiated by the submission to the Council of a *recommendation* by the Commission.[76] That is the case, for example, where the Commission seeks authorisation to negotiate an international agreement with a non-Member country. The Commission makes a recommendation to the Council, which decides whether to authorise the opening of negotiations and, if so, whether any negotiating directives should be issued to the Commission; in so doing, the Council is free to act by a qualified majority, even if it departs from the Commission's recommendation as to what the parameters of the negotiations should be.[77]

That model was followed in the case of various key decisions, in relation to the establishment and functioning of EMU. These include, notably, decisions in connection with the excessive deficit

[74] Art.250(1) EC.
[75] Mégret *et al., Le droit de la CEE* (Editions de l'Université de Bruxelles, 1979), Vol.9, p.133.
[76] This follows from the wording of Art.250(1) EC, which says, "Where, in pursuance of this Treaty, the Council acts *on a proposal from the Commission . . .*" (emphasis added).
[77] See Art.133(3) EC on agreements in the field of the common commercial policy; and Art.300(1) EC on international agreements in general.

procedure (as to the existence of an excessive deficit in a Member State; recommendations for bringing such a deficit to an end; measures for deficit reduction; the imposition of sanctions),[78] and the transition to the third stage of EMU (fulfilment of the conversion criteria;[79] grant of derogations).[80] Such an increase in the number of cases where the Council acts on a simple recommendation by the Commission might seem to represent a significant rebalancing of powers, to the Commission's disadvantage. However, it should be noted that the Council decisions in question are essentially executive in character: where *legislative* acts have to be adopted for the purposes of EMU (e.g., for the further elaboration of the excessive deficit procedure[81] or for the irrevocable fixing of exchange rates),[82] the Council acts in the traditional way, on the basis of a Commission proposal.

The general rule requiring unanimity for the amendment of a Commission proposal is subject to an express exception in respect of Article 251(4) and (5) EC. The exception relates to decisions adopted by the Council in accordance with a joint text agreed with the European Parliament in the Conciliation Committee provided for under the co-decision. The Council under the co-decision procedure is thus able to adopt by a qualified majority a text representing the result of a successful conciliation, regardless of whether the Commission has altered its proposal accordingly: indeed, from the end of the first reading, the Commission's proposal ceases to be relevant to the final outcome of the procedure.

The European Parliament's participation

3–013   There is a great difference between the ability of the European Parliament to influence the final shape of a measure enacted under the consultation procedure, and its influence where the prescribed legislative procedure is co-decision. We have seen that, where consultation of the European Parliament is required by the legal basis of a proposal, the Council must be formally seised of the Opinion rendered by the Parliament before proceeding to the adoption of the act in question (apart from urgent cases, where all procedural possibilities for obtaining the Opinion have been tried unsuccessfully); and that, if either the Commission or the Council is minded to amend a proposal in a way that would alter the substance of the text on which the Parliament has been consulted, adoption may have to be postponed pending re-consultation. However, the

---

[78] Art.104 EC.
[79] Art.121(2) EC.
[80] Art.122(1) EC.
[81] Art.104(14) EC.
[82] Art.123(4) EC.

Council, having considered the Parliament's Opinion, is under no legal obligation to follow it. In practice, the most effective way for the European Parliament to influence the final shape of legislation on a matter for which the consultation procedure is prescribed is by putting political pressure on the Commission to incorporate elements of the Opinion into an amended proposal. If the Commission responds favorably, the Council will then be faced with a text which it will only be able to amend further by unanimity.[83]

At first reading under the co-decision procedure, the traditional interplay between the Commission and the Council, based on the former's monopoly of the initiative and the two institutions' respective powers of amendment, still predominates. The main task of the Council Presidency is to negotiate a compromise text that commands a qualified majority among the delegations, and to which the Commission will rally, amending its proposal so that recourse to the adoption of a common position by unanimity can be avoided. However, through informal contacts, and through the Opinion rendered at first reading, the Presidency and the Council will be aware of the major concerns of the European Parliament, which will have to be accommodated, if the act in question is ultimately to receive the approval of the co-legislators; and due account will already be taken of those concerns in the negotiations within Council bodies. All three institutions will, moreover, be alert to any possibility of securing a first reading adoption.[84]

From the beginning of the second reading, we have seen, the Commission's proposal is effectively spent, and the politically significant interaction is that between the European Parliament and the Council, in relation to the common position. As amended by the Treaty of Amsterdam, the co-decision procedure no longer gives the Council even the theoretical possibility of acting unilaterally: if it wishes to see a measure adopted, it simply has to take into the common position the amendments that represent the Parliament's "bottom line". On the other hand, it is a fact of life for the Parliament that, once a political deal has been negotiated within the Council at first reading, the scope for securing amendments will be limited. General experience provides reason for optimism that the necessary give-and-take will be forthcoming between the co-legislators, to enable the procedure to function effectively.[85] However, the co-decision procedure has also witnessed moments of inter-institutional tension: for example, July 2005 witnessed the first occasion on which the Parliament simply rejected a Council common position by absolute majority at second reading, in the case of the proposed directive on the patentability of computer software, after

---

[83] Under the rule in Art.250(1) EC (considered above).
[84] As in the case of Dir.1999/103 [2000] O.J. L34/17.
[85] See Shackleton, "The Politics of Co-Decision" (2000) 38 J.C.M.S. 325.

many MEPs reacted angrily to the perception that neither the Commission nor the Council had taken seriously the concerns expressed by the Parliament in its opinion at first reading.[86]

Legal basis disputes

3–014   One of the striking characteristics of the EC Treaty is its multiplicity of legal bases, each conferring the necessary competence upon the Community institutions to adopt binding decisions and undertake other action in the relevant field, and each setting out its own framework of principles and rules: for example, as regards the applicable legislative procedure to be followed by the institutions; but also as regards matters such as the degree of competence conferred upon the Community, and its impact upon the Member States' power to adopt independent regulatory action (as discussed in Chapter 4).

Given that it is not always easy to identify a given policy initiative with one single legal basis, disputes are liable to arise from time to time as to which legal basis is the appropriate Article to use for the adoption of a proposed measure. In the early 1990s, for example, there was a series of cases in which the Council found itself at odds with the Commission and/or the European Parliament over the correct legal basis for various Community measures regulating the disposal of industrial waste: should the basis be Article 95 EC, since disparities between national provisions could result in different levels of costs for industry in the different Member States, thus distorting competition on the internal market; or should it be Article 175 EC, which confers law-making powers for the protection of the environment?[87] The choice between those two possible legal bases had a crucial impact upon the relative powers of the various institutions in the decision making process: since the TEU, Article 95 EC used the co-decision procedure, whereas Article 175 EC at that time employed the co-operation procedure.

The Court of Justice has been called upon to help resolve such legal basis disputes. The relevant principles were established in the *Waste Directive* case (and have been affirmed in many rulings since).[88] Community legislation must be based on the correct Treaty Article or it will be struck down as invalid. For these purposes, the choice of legal basis must be based on objective factors amenable to judicial review and, in particular, on the aim and content of the measure in question. If the measure concerns two different policy

---

[86] See COM(2002) 92 Final.
[87] e.g. Case C–300/89 *Commission v Council* [1991] E.C.R. 2867. *cf.* Case C–155/91 *Commission v Council* [1993] E.C.R. I–939; Case C–187/93 *European Parliament v Council* [1994] E.C.R. I–2857; [1995] 2 C.M.L.R. 309.
[88] Case C–155/91 *Commission v Council* [1993] E.C.R. I–939.

areas, and one is identifiable as the main or predominate purpose, whereas the other is merely incidental, the act must be adopted under the legal basis required by that main or predominate purpose. Exceptionally, however, a measure may concern two policy areas which are indissolubly linked, without one being secondary in relation to the other: in that event, it should be based on both the relevant Treaty Articles;[89] though this may not be possible where there are irreconcilable differences in the applicable legislative procedures.[90]

It is worth noting that some commentators relied on the *Titanium Dioxide* case as authority for the proposition that, where the dispute involved a choice between two legal basis with different legislative procedures, the Court would favour the legal basis which offered the greatest opportunity for Parliament to participate in the legislative process, and which thus increased the democratic legitimacy of the Treaty system.[91] However, in the more recent *Bovine Registration Regulation* case, the Court expressly rejected Parliament's argument that the measure in question should have been adopted under Article 95 EC (using co-decision) rather than Article 37 EC (mere consultation) because directly elected MEPs should be more closely involved in the adoption of protective measures against the spread of the BSE disease.[92]

With the progressive extension of co-decision by the TA and TN, legal basis disputes concerning the participation of the European Parliament in the legislative process are becoming less problematic.[93] However, as the *Bovine Registration Regulation* case illustrates, the potential for such legal basis disputes remains. Moreover, legal basis disputes will still arise from time to time inspired by other important differences between Treaty Articles (such as the degree of Community regulatory competence within a given policy field).[94]

Impact of the Constitutional Treaty (CT)
The CT contains significant reforms affecting the various topics **3–015** covered in this chapter, including:

— further extensions to the scope of the co-decision procedure with the European Parliament (renamed the "ordinary legislative procedure"), together with a simplified Treaty

---

[89] e.g. Case C–94/03 *Commission v Council* (Judgment of January 10, 2006); Case C–178/03 *Commission v Parliament and Council* (Judgment of January 10, 2006).
[90] e.g. Case C–338/01 *Commission v Council* [2004] E.C.R. I–4829.
[91] Case C–300/89 *Commission v Council* [1991] E.C.R. I–2867.
[92] Case C–269/97 *Commission and Parliament v Council* [2000] E.C.R. I–2257.
[93] e.g. the legislative procedure for both internal market and environmental measures is now, for most purposes, co-decision.
[94] See Ch.4.

amendment procedure to facilitate its future application to additional legal bases;
— abolition of the co-operation procedure, being replaced in some cases with consultation and in others with the ordinary legislative procedure;
— a new definition of qualified majority voting within Council to replace the triple threshold agreed under the Treaty of Nice 2000 and Treaty of Accession 2003;
— further extensions to the scope of qualified majority voting, together with a simplified Treaty amendment procedure to facilitate its future application to additional legal bases;
— introduction of a new "emergency brake" procedure, within the system of qualified majority voting applicable to certain legal bases considered especially sensitive by the Member States.

Further reading

Andenas and Usher (eds), *The Treaty of Nice and Beyond* (Hart Publishing, 2003).
Arnull and Wincott (eds), *Accountability and Legitimacy in the European Union* (OUP, 2003).
Boyron, "Maastricht and the Co-Decision Procedure: a Success Story" (1996) 45 I.C.L.Q. 293.
Cullen and Charlesworth, "Diplomacy By Other Means: The Use of Legal Basis Litigation as a Political Strategy By the European Parliament and Member States" (1999) 36 C.M.L.Rev. 1243.
Dashwood, "Community Legislative Procedures in the Era of the Treaty on European Union" (1994) 19 E.L.Rev. 343.
Dashwood, "Community Decision-Making After Amsterdam" (1998) 1 C.Y.E.L.S. 25.
Dashwood, "The Constitution of the European Union After Nice: Law-Making Procedures" (2001) 26 E.L.Rev. 215.
Mancini, *Democracy and Constitutionalism in the European Union* (Hart Publishing, 2000).
Moberg, "The Nice Treaty and Voting Rules in the Council" (2002) 40 J.C.M.S. 259.
O'Keeffe and Twomey (eds), *Legal Issues of the Maastricht Treaty* (Wiley, 1994).
O'Keeffe and Twomey (eds), *Legal Issues of the Amsterdam Treaty* (Hart Publishing, 1999).
Shackleton, "The Politics of Co-Decision" (2000) 38 J.C.M.S. 325.
Wouters, "Institutional and Constitutional Challenges for the European Union: Some Reflections in the Light of the Treaty of Nice" (2001) 26 E.L.Rev. 342.

CHAPTER 4

UNION COMPETENCES

Guide to this Chapter: This chapter deals with the trio of **4–001** principles set out in Article 5 EC which govern the existence and exercise of Community competences. First, the principle of attribution of competences, which makes clear that the Community enjoys only those decision making powers conferred upon it by the Treaty; it lacks any inherent or self-authenticating competences. Problems arise with this principle because certain Treaty provisions have, historically, been interpreted by the institutions in a relatively generous manner—giving rise to the phenomenon commonly known as "competence creep". However, there is some evidence in recent case law that the Court of Justice takes seriously its role in enforcing the principle of attribution of powers. Closely related to this principle is the question of what type of competence the Treaty has conferred upon the Community in any given field. The accepted model divides Community powers into three types, depending on their impact upon the exercise of the Member States' own regulatory competences: exclusive, shared and supporting. Secondly, the principle of subsidiarity, which attempts to guide the Community institutions towards exercising their non-exclusive competences only where collective action would have some appreciable advantage as compared to leaving matters to the Member States acting individually. There has again been much debate about how far the Court of Justice is able or willing to enforce this principle through judicial means. Recent judgments suggest that the Court feels increasingly comfortable about verifying that the political institutions have taken due account of the requirements of subsidiarity, but the Court will surely remain reluctant to second-guess their choices about the appropriateness or otherwise of

exercising supranational rather than purely domestic competences. Thirdly, the principle of proportionality, which ensures
that—even if the Community has competence, and may legitimately exercise it—any action taken by the Community should
not go beyond what is necessary to achieve its own objectives.
Whereas in ordinary administrative law disputes, the Court of
Justice is often prepared to intervene where it is evident that the
Community could have reached the same result using means less
injurious of Member State or individual interests, in the context of
constitutional disputes, case law makes clear that the scope for
judicial review will be more limited where the legislature is called
upon to make complex choices of economic or social policy. The
chapter closes with an examination of the principle of flexibility—
the idea that not all Member States are obliged to participate (or
to do so fully) in all aspects of Community policy making. The
Treaty itself provides some ad hoc examples, such as the United
Kingdom's opt-out from the single currency. But our discussion
concentrates on the "enhanced co-operation" provisions introduced at Amsterdam and reformed at Nice, which envisage a
controlled system of regulatory differentiation within the EU legal
order, whereby groups of Member States may pursue closer
integration between themselves in certain fields (albeit subject to
strict substantive and procedural conditions).

A constitutional order of States

4–002   We shall see in Chapter 5 how the Court of Justice in its case law
since *Van Gend en Loos*,[1] established the constitutional character of
the order brought into being by the EU Treaties.[2] Those "constitutionalising" principles comprise, notably, the direct effect of many of
the provisions of Community law and their primacy over conflicting
national law. In adhering to the new legal order resulting from the
Treaties, the Member States have, in the words of the Court,
"limited their sovereign rights in ever wider fields".[3] They have
accepted that, in a whole range of policy areas central to a modern
political economy, they may or must act together through the
common institutions, according to the procedures and with the legal
consequences which the Treaties prescribe.

At the same time, it is a central feature of the EU system that the
constituent entities of the Union retain the quality of states, in both
the legal and the political senses. Thus, the continuing status of EU
Members as full subjects of public international law is unquestioned;

---

[1] Case 26/62 [1963] E.C.R. 1, 12.
[2] See Mancini, "The Making of a Constitution for Europe" (1989) 26 C.M.L.Rev. 595.
[3] Opinion 1/91 *EEA Agreement* [1991] E.C.R. I–6079, para.21.

and, for their own peoples, they remain the principal focus of collective loyalty and the principal forum of democratic political activity. Moreover, the TEU expressly provides in Article 6(3) that "[t]he Union shall respect the national identities of its Member States". Accordingly, it seems appropriate to describe the unique polity created by the Treaties as "a constitutional order of states".[4]

The paradoxical fact that belonging to the EU in no way casts doubt on Members' existence as States, is due to the delicate checks and balances built into the system. One important factor is the role of the Council at the heart of the legislative process. As we have seen in Chapter 3, whether under the simple consultation procedure or the more complex (and more democratically legitimate) co-decision procedure, new law that builds on the primary rules of the Treaties cannot normally be enacted without receiving the positive approval of the institution composed of representatives of the Member States.[5] Another factor is the Union's lack of coercive powers exercisable in relation to individuals and businesses. The great exception is competition policy where, as will be shown in Chapter 25, the Commission is able, among other things, to send its officials on "dawn raids" against undertakings suspected of breaking the rules, and to punish infringements with fines and other penalties. In the main, however, the law made in Brussels and Strasbourg is implemented on the ground in the Member States by officials wearing national hats (and thus accountable through the national political process). The monopoly of coercion, one of the hallmarks of statehood, has thus been left by the Treaties almost completely undisturbed.[6]

In addition, an *acquis* of the TEU has been the legal reinforcement of the position of the Member States through Treaty amendments enacting certain "conservatory principles" (as they are here called) which provide a counterweight to the constitutionalising principles developed by the Court. These principles, enshrined in Article 5 EC, are concerned to identify the Union as an organisation with only limited competences; and to establish some of the ground-rules governing the very existence and legitimate exercise of such regulatory powers as have been conferred by the Member States upon the Community.

---

[4] The description was first used in Dashwood (ed.), *Reviewing Maastricht: Issues for the 1996 IGC* (Sweet & Maxwell, 1996), p.7.

[5] We say "normally", to cover the few cases where the EC Treaty gives the Commission an independent power of decision: see Ch.2.

[6] For a fuller treatment, see Dashwood, "States in the European Union" (1998) 23 E.L.Rev. 201.

Article 5 EC

4–003   Article 5 EC provides:

"The Community shall act within the limits of the powers conferred on it by this Treaty and of the objectives assigned to it therein.

In areas which do not fall within its exclusive competence, the Community shall take action, in accordance with the principle of subsidiarity, only if and in so far as the objectives of the proposed action cannot be sufficiently achieved by the Member States and can therefore, by reason of the scale or effects of the proposed action, be better achieved by the Community.

Any action taken by the Community shall not go beyond what is necessary to achieve the objectives of this Treaty."

The principles enshrined in the three paragraphs of the Article are known as, respectively, those of the attribution (or conferral) of powers,[7] of subsidiarity and of proportionality. They have always been immanent in the constitutional order, but were erected into express organising principles through the insertion of Article 5 into the EC Treaty by the TEU.

An interpretation of the Article 5 EC principles was agreed by the European Council at its Edinburgh meeting in December 1992, as one of the measures designed to secure the final ratification of the TEU, after the period of uncertainty that had followed the negative outcome of the first referendum in Denmark.[8] The Edinburgh text was a purely political document, describing the "overall approach" to be taken by the Council.[9] It was supplemented in October 1993 by another such text, the Inter-institutional Agreement between the European Parliament, the Council and the Commission on the procedure for implementing the principle of subsidiarity.[10] Subsequently, a "Protocol on the application of the principles of subsidiarity and proportionality", giving legal force to the main elements of the earlier texts, was annexed to the EC Treaty by the TA.[11]

---

[7] This was how the Court of Justice referred to the principle in Opinion 2/94 [1996] E.C.R. I–1759, para.24.
[8] The crisis surrounding the ratification of the TEU is described in Ch.1.
[9] See Annex 1 to Part A of the Presidency Conclusions: Bull EC 12–1992, p.13. Hereinafter, "the Edinburgh text".
[10] Bull EC 10–1993, p.128.
[11] Protocol No.7 to the Final Act of the TA. Hereinafter, "the Amsterdam Protocol".

The principle of the attribution of powers[12]

The existence of Union competence

Article 7 EC, which identifies the main institutions of the Com- **4–004**
munity, has always included a sub-paragraph providing: "Each
institution shall act within the limits of the powers conferred upon it
by this Treaty".[13] The addition to the Treaty of Article 5, first
paragraph, EC made explicitly clear that the principle of the
attribution of powers applies not only to the institutions but to the
Community as such. The paragraph means, as the Court of Justice
put it bluntly in Opinion 2/94, that the Community "has only those
powers which have been conferred on it".[14] Or, in the crude but
telling language of the Edinburgh text, "national powers are the rule
and the Community's the exception".[15] To make the point another
way, the Community order is not a self-authenticating one: new
powers cannot be generated within the order itself, above and
beyond those conferred by the constitution-making authority, acting
in accordance with the procedure provided for by Article 48 TEU.[16]

The technique of attribution employed in the EC Treaty is (in
most cases) highly specific.[17] Article 2 of the EC Treaty identifies the
"tasks" of the Community, and Articles 3 and 4 its "activities"; but
they contain no power-conferring provision, and so cannot be used
as legal bases for enacting particular measures. The characteristic
approach is for provisions giving the institutions law-making powers
to be included with the group of substantive provisions that define,
in more or less detail, the action the Community is authorised to
take in a given area of policy: the powers thus conferred are
exercisable, under the conditions specified, in that particular area
and not elsewhere.[18] The relevant legal basis will lay down the
procedure to be followed for enacting measures (this will normally
be consultation or co-decision); and it may also prescribe a measure
of a certain kind (e.g. only harmonisation or, conversely, no harmonisation), and the form(s) of legal instrument that may be used (e.g.
only directives).

However, the principle of attribution of powers does sometimes
give rise to constitutional problems. The difficulties arise from the
existence, within the Treaty, of certain legal bases which are

---

[12] For an extensive treatment of the attribution principle in the EC Treaty, see Dashwood,
"The Limits of European Community Powers" (1996) 21 E.L.Rev. 113.
[13] See Art.7(1), second sub-para., EC.
[14] Opinion 2/94 [1996] E.C.R. I–1759, para.23.
[15] Para.1.15 of Annex 1 to Part A of the Presidency Conclusions: Bull EC 12–1992.
[16] Because it is not a State, the Community lacks what German scholars call *Kompetenz
Kompetenz*, the ability to pull itself up legally by its own bootstraps.
[17] Opinion 2/94 [1996] E.C.R. I–1759, para.25.
[18] The contrasting attribution technique adopted under Titles V and VI TEU is considered in
Ch.10.

relatively ambiguous and open-ended in their potential scope of application; together with a willingness on the part of the main political institutions to exploit that ambiguity so as to extend the scope of Community action. This is the so-called "competence creep". Two Treaty provisions have created particular controversy: Article 95 EC on the completion of the internal market, and the "default mechanism" contained in Article 308 EC.

Article 95 EC was introduced by the SEA to enable the Community to adopt the legislation necessary to complete the internal market using qualified majority voting in Council, rather than unanimity as required under the legal basis already provided by Article 94 EC. In its current version, Article 95 EC states that the Council shall, acting in accordance with the co-decision procedure and after consulting the Economic and Social Committee, adopt the measures for the approximation of the provisions laid down by law, regulation or administrative action in Member States which have as their object the establishment and functioning of the internal market.

4–005 To some extent, the adoption of harmonising measures to complete the internal market will always imply that the Community must simultaneously make choices about other policy objectives. After all, when adopting harmonisation measures intended to replace divergent national rules on product specifications and marketing practices, the Community must decide not merely to approximate but to do so at a particular pitch and taking account of competing societal concerns (e.g.) about protection of the environment, employees or consumers. By that process, Article 94 EC had already witnessed an inevitable form of "competence creep" as the Community legislature adopted extensive legislation dealing not only with the internal market per se, but also with a broader range of social policy issues which (quite naturally) "flanked" the process of economic integration. Since Article 94 EC required unanimity, such competence creep at least occurred with the consent of every Member State. Moreover, the Treaty at that time did not provide any other legal bases determining the scope of or limits to Community action in those flanking policy fields.

Now, however, Article 95 EC operates in a very different political and constitutional environment. Since decisions are taken by a qualified majority, there is no guarantee that a broad construction of the circumstances in which legislation can be considered to help complete the internal market will actually command support from all the Member States. Moreover, successive Treaty amendments have introduced many additional legal bases (e.g., on environmental, employment and consumer policies), which confer specific powers for Community action in such fields. Controversy over the correct interpretation of the scope of the powers conferred upon the Community pursuant to Article 95 EC was made even more acute by

the judgment of the German Federal Constitutional Court in
Brunner, where it warned against the Community claiming for itself
functions and powers which were not clearly specified in the
Treaties.[19]

This set the scene for the important dispute over the Tobacco
Advertising Directive 98/43 (adopted under Article 95 EC, together
with closely related legal bases on the freedom of establishment and
freedom to provide services).[20] Article 3(1) of the Directive provided
that all forms of advertising and sponsorship of tobacco be banned
within the Community; while Article 3(2) gave Member States the
option of excluding diversification products (such as jeans and shoes
bearing the same name as well known tobacco brands) from the
scope of this general prohibition; and Article 3(5) excluded from the
material scope of the Directive certain types of advertising (such as
communications intended exclusively for professionals in the tobacco
trade). Article 5 stated that the Directive shall not preclude Member
States from laying down, in accordance with the Treaty, such stricter
requirements concerning the advertising and sponsorship of tobacco
products as they deem necessary to guarantee the health protection
of individuals. Germany had voted against the measure in the
Council, and subsequently brought an action for its annulment
before the Court of Justice. The gist of the German Government's
complaint was that Directive 98/43 was not really designed to
promote the operation of the internal market, but rather to regulate
public health; as to the latter, Article 152 EC explicitly excludes
harmonisation of the laws and regulations of the Member States.

In its judgment in *Germany v Parliament and Council*, the Court **4–006**
held that Article 95 EC could not be construed as conferring upon
the Community legislator a general power to regulate the internal
market: measures that can be adopted under the Article must have
the specific object of improving the conditions for the establishment
and functioning of the internal market—and they must be designed
to remove genuine obstacles to free movement or distortions of
competition, not purely abstract risks. Directive 98/43 could not be
said to fulfil those criteria. By prohibiting tobacco advertising not
only in media such as newspapers and magazines, which are traded
between Member States, but also on articles such as hotel and
restaurant posters, parasols and ashtrays, it went beyond the scope of
Article 95 EC. Moreover, the Directive did not ensure free movement for compliant products: it permitted the Member States to
enact more stringent welfare provisions but failed to guarantee
access to the entire single market for products conforming to the
Community standards. Similarly, Directive 98/43 could not be said to
contribute to the removal of appreciable distortions of competition.

---

[19] [1994] 1 C.M.L.R. 57.
[20] Dir.98/43 [1998] O.J. L213/9.

The competitive advantages enjoyed by advertising agencies and producers of advertising media established in Member States with fewer restrictions were too remote and indirect; and the admittedly appreciable distortions which arose in the field of sports sponsorship could not justify the more extensive prohibition contained in the Directive. Furthermore, by imposing a wide-ranging ban on tobacco advertising, the Directive was not actually removing any distortion of competition between Member States, but simply restricting forms of competition across the Community by limiting the means available for economic operators to enter or remain in the market. The Court concluded that Directive 98/43 should be annulled on the grounds that it had been adopted on an incorrect legal basis and (implicitly) in breach of the principle of attribution of powers contained in Article 5 EC.[21] The Court's rejection of the proposition that Article 95 EC conferred a general power to regulate the internal market, its emphasis on the need for measures adopted under Article 95 EC to make a positive contribution to the internal market, and the fact that it emphasised that the Directive in issue did not guarantee free movement for compliant products, seemed to imply that Article 95 EC could not provide a legal base for a measure which claimed to remove obstacles to trade in a product or service by prohibiting the product or service itself. In *Swedish Match*, however, the Court held that Article 95 EC authorises the Community legislature to intervene by "appropriate measures" to deal with actual or potential obstacles to trade, and that such "appropriate measures" may consist in prohibiting the marketing of a product or products; other appropriate measures would include requiring all the Member States to authorise the marketing of the product or products concerned, or subjecting such an obligation of authorisation to certain conditions.[22]

The judgment in the *Tobacco Advertising* case provides a striking example of the judicial enforcement of the principle of attribution of powers. By annulling the directive, the Court of Justice seemed to be signalling its intention to act as a true constitutional court whose role is to police the fine boundaries between Community and Member State competence established in the Treaty, and thus preserve the delicate system of checks-and-balances which is essential to the proper functioning of the Union. But the dispute that gave rise to the proceedings also reminds us of the role played by the Member

---

[21] Case C–376/98 *Germany v Parliament and Council* [2000] E.C.R. I–8419. Also: Case C–74/99 *Imperial Tobacco* [2000] E.C.R. I–8599. A new Tobacco Advertising Directive was subsequently adopted, intended to comply with the ECJ's judgment: see Dir.2003/33 [2003] O.J. L152/16. Germany has brought a further action seeking partial annulment of this measure: see Case C–380/03 *Germany v Parliament and Council* (pending)

[22] Case C–210/03 *Swedish Match* [2004] E.C.R. I–11893, esp. at paras 33, 34. This judgment seems to represent some retreat from the position in the *Tobacco Advertising* case. Accepting that obstacles to trade may be eliminated by eliminating the relevant trade does come close to approval of a general power to regulate the internal market.

States themselves in contributing to the problem of "competence creep". It was the Member States at the Maastricht inter-governmental conference that drafted Article 152 EC in a way specifically designed to place strict limits on Community competence in the field of public health; but a majority of the Member States subsequently attempted to bypass exactly those same limits, through recourse to Article 95 EC, in order to achieve what they regarded as valuable welfare objectives.

The second legal basis which has given rise to competence **4–007** problems is Article 308 EC, which states that, if action by the Community should prove necessary to attain, in the course of the operation of the common market, one of the objectives of the Community and the Treaty has not provided the necessary powers, the Council shall, acting unanimously on a proposal from the Commission and after consulting the European Parliament, take the appropriate measures. This is another provision which has, through a combination of textual ambiguity and institutional connivance, been used historically to extend the scope of Community action beyond the limits apparently set by the express provisions of the Treaty. For example, the Community's regional, environmental and development co-operation policies were all developed through recourse to Article 308 EC; only subsequently was the Treaty equipped with specific power-conferring provisions in these fields.[23] Article 308 EC was also used, not entirely appropriately, for providing technical assistance to countries other than developing countries (until the insertion of Article 181a into the Treaty by the TN).[24]

Article 308 EC still requires unanimity among the Member States in the Council; but this may be cold comfort (e.g.) to domestic parliaments who might witness their own executives signing up to Community action in fields not clearly envisaged under the Treaty, but which will still have a direct impact upon the exercise of national competences. Again, however, the Court of Justice has recognised the need to avoid Article 308 EC from being used blatantly to undermine the principle of attribution of powers. The leading case is Opinion 2/94, where the Court was asked whether the Community was competent to accede to the European Convention for the Protection of Human Rights and Fundamental Freedoms (the European Convention). It was found by the Court that "[n]o Treaty provision confers on the Community institutions any general power to enact rules on human rights or to conclude international conven-tions in this field".[25] Was it, then, possible to fall back on Article 308

---

[23] See, respectively, Part Three, Title XVII (Economic and Social Cohesion) and Title XIX (Environment), which date from the amendment of the Treaty by the SEA; and Title XX (Development Cooperation), dating from the amendment by the TEU.

[24] The unsuitability of Art.308 EC as a legal basis for the latter category of measures is due to the difficulty of demonstrating a connection with "the course of operation of the Common Market".

[25] Opinion 2/94 [1996] E.C.R. I–1759, para.27.

EC? The Court stressed that Article 308 EC "cannot be used as a basis for the adoption of provisions whose effect could, in substance, be to amend the Treaty".[26] Recourse to Article 308 EC was not possible in the instant case because accession to the European Convention would entail entry into "a distinct international institutional system", with fundamental implications for both the Community and the Member States; such a modification of the EC system of human rights protection would be "of constitutional significance", and thus could be brought about only by means of a Treaty amendment.[27]

While the emphasis in the Court's reasoning was on institutional considerations, the Opinion contains guidance as to the substantive limits of the default mechanism in Article 308 EC. The Article, the Court said, "cannot serve as a basis for widening the scope of Community powers beyond the general framework created by the provisions of the Treaty as a whole and, in particular, by those that define the tasks and the activities of the Community".[28] We take that to mean that a proposed measure is unlikely to qualify for adoption under Article 308 EC unless it relates to matters which, while not being specifically authorised, fall broadly within the purview of the activities referred to in Articles 3 and 4 of the Treaty, interpreted in the light of the different elements constituting the task of the Community, as defined by Article 2 EC. Thus, for example, the CFI in *Yusuf* held that Article 308 EC could not, taken alone, provide the legal basis for the imposition of economic and financial sanctions in respect of individuals suspected of contributing to the funding of terrorism, since the fight against international terrorism cannot be made to refer to one of the objects expressly entrusted to the Community under Articles 2 and 3 EC.[29] By contrast, Article 308 EC is an appropriate legal basis for the enactment of Community secondary measures which do not seek to approximate (and thereby replace, at least partially) national laws affecting the functioning of the internal market, in the sense of Article 95 EC, but rather to introduce new legal phenomena at the Community level (such as intellectual property forms) which will take effect alongside existing

---

[26] Opinion 2/94 [1996] E.C.R. I–1759, para.30. The same view has been firmly taken by the German Budesvervassungsgericht (Federal Constitutional Court). The Court indicated in its *Brunner* judgment that a measure based on Art.308 EC which exceeded the scope of the democratic authorisation given in respect of the transfer of legislative competence to the Community would not be considered binding in Germany: see [1994] 1 C.M.L.R. 57.

[27] Opinion 2/94 [1996] E.C.R. I–1759, paras 34 and 35.

[28] Opinion 2/94 [1996] E.C.R. I–1759, para.30.

[29] Case T–306/01 *Yusuf* (Judgment of September 21, 2005). However, the CFI was willing to accept the combined use of Arts 60, 301 and 308 EC, in the light of a common position adopted pursuant to the CFSP.

national legislation, whilst still promoting the sound operation of the internal market.[30]

The categories of Union competence

Closely related to the question of whether Community compe- **4–008** tence actually exists for a given purpose in accordance with the principle of attribution of powers under Article 5 EC is that of the "nature" of the competence that has been conferred upon the Community. This relates, more particularly, to the different sorts of legal consequences which the existence or the exercise of a Community competence may have upon national regulatory competences in the policy area concerned. In the absence of any explicit indications within the Treaty itself, we adopt the model laid down by the Treaty establishing a Constitution for Europe, which represents a consensus among the Member States in favour of dividing Community competences into three principal categories.[31]

(a) Exclusive competence. The first category comprises areas of **4–009** *exclusive Community competence.* In such areas, Community law takes the view that regulatory authority belongs to the Community alone: the Member States have lost the right to act autonomously. Exclusive Community competence is very much the exception. Indeed, there are only three uncontroversial cases: the regulation of external trade under the common commercial policy, which is based upon Article 133 EC;[32] the conservation of marine biological resources;[33] and monetary policy for those Member States which have adopted the euro. These are all situations where the exclusivity of the Community's competence arises *a priori*: given the nature of the activities in question, it would make no practical sense for regulatory authority to be shared with the Member States. Attempts to extend the category of exclusivity beyond these areas have met with failure. For example, in several cases, Advocates General have tried to persuade the Court of Justice to find that the Community's competence to adopt harmonising legislation for the completion of the internal market under Article 95 EC was exclusive.[34] Yet the

---

[30] e.g. Opinion 1/94 [1994] E.C.R. I–5267; Case C–377/98 *Netherlands v Parliament and Council* [2001] E.C.R. I–7079. *cf.* Case C–66/04 *United Kingdom v Parliament and Council* (Judgment of December 6, 2005). Note also Case C–436/03 *Parliament v Council* (pending); Case C–217/04 *United Kingdom v Parliament and Council* (pending).

[31] [2004] O.J. C310. See further Ch.11.

[32] e.g. Opinion 1/75 *Local Cost Standard* [1975] E.C.R. 1255. Certain important qualifications to the exclusivity of Community competence under Art.133 EC were added by the TN: for details, see Cremona, "A Policy of Bits and Pieces? The Common Commercial Policy After Nice" (2001) 4 C.Y.E.L.S. 61.

[33] e.g. Joined Cases 3, 4 and 6/76 *Kramer* [1976] E.C.R. 1279; [1976] 2 C.M.L.R. 440; Case C–25/94 *Commission v Council (FAO)* [1996] E.C.R. I–1469.

[34] e.g. in Case C–233/94 *Germany v Parliament and Council (Deposit Guarantee Schemes Directive)* [1997] E.C.R. I–2405; Case C–376/98 *Germany v Parliament and Council (Tobacco Advertising Directive)* [2000] E.C.R. I–8419; Case C–377/98 *Netherlands v Parliament and Council (Biotech Directive)* [2001] E.C.R. I–7079.

Court in its *Tobacco Labelling Directive* judgment held that Article 95 EC merely confers upon the Union "a certain competence" for improving the functioning of the Internal Market—expressly rejecting the claim that Article 95 EC was characterised by exclusivity.[35]

The crucial point about areas of exclusive Community competence is that the Member States are precluded from exercising any independent legislative initiative; they may only act if, and in so far as, the Community authorises them to do so. Such authorisation is usually express: for example, within the context of the common commercial policy, Regulation 2603/69 provides that exports from the Community to third countries shall not be subject to any quantitative restrictions or measures having equivalent effect; but Article 11 of the Regulation grants the Member States the right to restrict external trade on grounds identical to those contained in Article 30 EC.[36] However, authorisation may also be implied, for instance, where the Community has failed to exercise its exclusive competence and a situation of urgency arises which demands some form of public action. The Court recognised in the *Fisheries Conservation* case that, in such situations, the Member States may be regarded as implicitly authorised by the Community to adopt necessary regulatory measures acting as "trustees of the common interest", provided that they act in close consultation and cooperation with the Commission.[37]

4–010 (b) Shared competence. The second category is that of *shared competence*. Here, EC law recognises that both the Community and the Member States are competent to regulate the relevant sectors; however, the actual exercise of Community regulatory power is liable to curtail the scope for exercising national regulatory power with respect to the same matters. Shared competence is the normal relationship between Community and Member State powers in matters governed by the EC Treaty. It applies to the legal bases dealing with (e.g.): the internal market;[38] visas, asylum and immigration policy;[39] social policy;[40] environmental policy;[41] consumer policy;[42] agriculture;[43] and transport.[44]

---

[35] Case C–491/01 *ex parte British American Tobacco* [2002] E.C.R. I–11453, para.179.
[36] Reg.2603/69 establishing common rules for exports, [1969] O.J. L324/25. See: Case C–83/94 *Peter Leifer* [1995] E.C.R. I–3231. Also: Case 41/76 *Donckerwolcke* [1976] E.C.R. 1921; Case C–394/97 *Sami Heinonen* [1999] E.C.R. I–3599. Further: Cremona, "The External Dimension of the Single Market: Building (on) the Foundations" in Barnard & Scott (eds), *The Law of the Single European Market: Unpacking the Premises* (Hart Publishing, 2002).
[37] Case 804/79 *Commission v UK* [1981] E.C.R. 1045.
[38] In particular, Arts 94 and 95 EC.
[39] Under Title IV, Part Three EC.
[40] See Art.137 EC.
[41] See Art.175 EC.
[42] See Art.153 EC.
[43] See Art.37 EC.
[44] See Title V EC.

Where the Community has not yet exercised its shared regulatory competence, the Member States remain free to exercise theirs—provided they comply with any obligations imposed upon them by directly effective provisions of the Treaty, such as in the field of free movement of goods, persons, services or capital. A good example is the famous decision in *Cassis de Dijon*, which concerned German rules on the alcohol content of fruit liqueurs. The Court held that, in the absence of Community secondary legislation addressing this issue, each Member State was free to adopt its own regulatory standards—provided that the applicable national measures did not create unjustified obstacles to the free movement of fruit liqueurs lawfully marketed in other Member States and imported into the national territory.[45]

Where the Community has already exercised its shared regulatory competence, the Member States in principle remain free to exercise theirs—but now they must respect not only the obligations resulting from primary Treaty provisions, but also any obligations imposed by the relevant Community legislation. This includes the possibility for Community measures to have so-called "pre-emptive effects", i.e. to occupy the relevant regulatory field, and prevent Member States from legitimately exercising their own competence therein.

Such pre-emptive effects are sometimes total: they effectively prevent the Member State from lawfully adopting divergent national regulatory standards, unless and until the relevant Community legislation is revised or repealed. A good example is the *Dim-Dip Headlights* case, which concerned a Community Directive seeking to promote the free movement of cars within the internal market by listing exhaustively the types of device which could lawfully be incorporated into car lighting systems.[46] The United Kingdom subsequently attempted to prohibit the use on British roads of any car which did not use dim-dip headlights—a lighting system which was considered to offer superior road safety standards, but was not actually referred to in the directive, since it had not been sufficiently commercially developed at the time that measure was adopted. The Court of Justice held that the directive had effected a total harmonisation of the relevant field. The United Kingdom was not permitted unilaterally to deviate from the common standards agreed by the Community legislator, either by requiring cars to use dim-dip headlights instead of the headlights referred to in the directive, or even by permitting cars to use dim-dip headlights instead of the headlights referred to in the directive. To that extent, fully pre-emptive Community secondary legislation appears similar, in terms of its impact upon national regulatory competence, to the type of *a priori* exclusivity which applies under the Treaty itself to fields such

---

[45] Case 120/78 [1979] E.C.R. 649.
[46] Case 60/86 *Commission v United Kingdom* [1988] E.C.R. 3921.

as the common commercial policy and the protection of marine biological resources. The difference is that, in the areas of *a priori* exclusivity, autonomous action by the Member States is prohibited irrespective of whether the Community has acted or not; whereas in areas of shared competence, the exercise of national regulatory power is prohibited only to the extent of any incompatibility with a particular legislative measure that has been adopted by the Community and remains in force.[47]

In other situations, the pre-emptive effects of Community legislation need only be partial: while imposing certain obligations on Member States as to how they must exercise their own regulatory competences, the Community measure nevertheless leaves the national authorities a margin of discretion to make their own independent policy choices, even within the occupied field. This is the case, for example, with Community legislation which provides for only minimum harmonisation: the Community act establishes a regulatory "floor of rights", above which the Member States remain competent to enact higher standards of protection (e.g.) in favour of consumers, workers, or the environment, provided that those more stringent national measures continue to respect the primary rules contained within the Treaty itself. A good illustration is the dispute in *Finalarte*.[48] The Working Time Directive provides that workers must enjoy a certain number of paid holidays per year; but expressly states that the measure lays down only minimum requirements, and preserves each Member State's right to apply more favourable rules for the protection of the health and safety of workers.[49] On that basis, German legislation guaranteed longer paid leave to employees, over and above the basic standards of the Working Time Directive. In such circumstances, it was clear that any dispute must focus not on Germany's basic freedom to enact more stringent standards of health and safety than the Community legislation; but rather on whether the application of those national rules to workers posted within Germany by foreign undertakings created unlawful obstacles to the freedom to provide services within the domestic territory.[50]

Finally, in certain areas of shared competence, owing to the particular nature of the authorised activity, the actual exercise of Community competence may have no pre-emptive effect at all. There is case law which establishes that action by the Community in the fields of humanitarian aid or development co-operation does not have the consequence of precluding autonomous action by the

---

[47] This distinction may have important legal implications, e.g. for the Community institutions' obligation to respect the principle of subsidiarity when amending a fully pre-emptive legislative regime (see further below).

[48] Cases C–49, 50, 52–54 and 68–71/98 *Finalarte* [2001] E.C.R. I–7831.

[49] Dir.93/104 [1993] O.J. L307/18.

[50] Under Art.49 EC. See further Ch.19.

Member States with respect to the same subject-matter, as would be the case in other policy areas.[51] The explanation lies in the fact that, in those fields, the competences of the Community and the Member States are perfectly parallel: the exercise of either competence leaves open the full range of possibilities for the future exercise of the other. Thus, it would not interfere with the implementation of a Community regulation establishing a programme of financial and technical aid to a given developing country, if the United Kingdom, say, were to commence a similar programme of assistance to that country; nor would a pre-existing programme of Member State aid inhibit the Community from coming onto the scene as an additional donor. In our view, these areas of "parallel competence" also include economic, financial and technical assistance to third countries other than developing countries,[52] as well as research and technological development.[53]

(c) Competence to support, coordinate or supplement actions of the Member States. The third main category of Community competence is confined to supporting, coordinating or supplementing action by the Member States, in fields where the determination of policy is the preserve of the latter. In such fields, the Community's role is typically to adopt broad guidelines or incentive measures, or to facilitate the exchange of information about best practice. Where it is given power to adopt legally binding acts, these are not capable of harmonising national laws or having pre-emptive effects *vis-à-vis* domestic competence. Regulatory power, therefore, remains in the Member States' hands, and Community action merely complements domestic policies. A good illustration is Article 149 EC, first introduced by the Maastricht Treaty, which states that the Community shall contribute to the development of quality education by encouraging co-operation between Member States and, if necessary, by supporting and supplementing their action, while fully respecting the responsibility of the Member States for the content of teaching and the organisation of education systems and their cultural and linguistic diversity; the Council and the European Parliament, acting under the co-decision procedure, are empowered to adopt incentive measures,[54] *excluding* any harmonisation of the laws and regulations of the Member States. Such supporting competence also applies

4–011

---

[51] Joined Cases C–181/91 and C–248/91 *European Parliament v Council and Commission* [1993] E.C.R. I–3685; Case C–316/91 *European Parliament v Council* [1994] E.C.R. I–625.
[52] See Art.181a EC. This is an activity for all relevant purposes indistinguishable from development co-operation.
[53] Such was the view taken by the authors of the Constitutional Treaty: see Art. I–14(3) of that instrument.
[54] e.g. Community programmes such as Socrates and Leonardo da Vinci, which seek to encourage and facilitate cross-border mobility for education and training purposes.

(e.g.) under the legal bases on vocational training;[55] cultural policy;[56] most aspects of public health;[57] employment policy;[58] and industrial policy.[59]

Nevertheless, the Court of Justice has held that, even in areas of supporting competence, Member States must still respect the "horizontal" principles imposed under primary Community law (i.e. principles that apply to all the policy areas within the scope of the EC Treaty), such as those relating to the free movement of goods, persons, services and capital, and to non-discrimination on grounds of nationality. Consider, by way of illustration, the famous judgment in *Gravier*, which concerned Belgian rules requiring foreign students whose parents lived abroad to pay an additional enrolment fee in order to attend vocational training courses at universities and technical colleges; the fee was not levied on foreign students whose parents lived within Belgium, or on Belgian students regardless of their parents' domicile.[60] The Court held that educational organisation and policy are not as such included in the spheres which the Treaty has entrusted to the Community institutions. Indeed, since the case was pre-Maastricht, the Community did not enjoy even the limited competence now contained in Article 149 EC; the only relevant Treaty provision was ex-Article 128 EEC empowering the Council to lay down general principles for implementing a common vocational training policy. That was treated by the Court as sufficient to establish that vocational training falls within the scope of application of the Treaty, thus bringing into play the principle of equal treatment on grounds of nationality contained in Article 12 EC. By discriminating against students from other Member States as regards the conditions for admission to vocational training courses within its territory, Belgium was found to be in breach of its obligations under Article 12 EC.

The *Gravier* case, and the latter authorities that have extended the principle that the conditions of access must be the same for all Member State nationals to the whole of the higher education sector, can be seen as a further instance of "competence creep".[61] In its practical impact on the financing of higher education, the principle represents a significant intrusion upon the organisation of education systems, in apparent contradiction to the express wording of Article

---

[55] See Art.150 EC.
[56] See Art.151 EC.
[57] See Art.152 EC.
[58] See Title VIII EC.
[59] See Art.157 EC.
[60] Case 293/83 *Gravier v City of Liège* [1985] E.C.R. 593.
[61] e.g. Case 24/86 *Blaizot* [1988] E.C.R. 379; Case 42/87 *Commission v Belgium* [1988] E.C.R. 5445; Case C–47/93 *Commission v Belgium* [1994] E.C.R. I–1593; Case C–65/03 *Commission v Belgium* [2004] E.C.R. I–6427; Case C–147/03 *Commission v Austria* (Judgment of July 7, 2005).

149 EC. There is a troubling inconsistency, of which the Court of Justice has shown little awareness, between the tendency of the horizontal principles to curtail the policy-making autonomy of the Member States in areas of supporting competence such as education and public health, and the strict limits the Treaty imposes on regulatory action by the Community in those areas.

The principle of subsidiarity[62]

Origins of subsidiarity—a response to expanding Community competence

The principle of subsidiarity, though not under that name, was **4–012** first introduced as a principle of the Community legal order by the SEA, which introduced an Environmental Title into the (then) EEC Treaty, and provided that the Community should take action to the extent to which environmental objectives "can be attained better at Community level than at the level of the individual Member States".[63]

Subsidiarity in its present form was introduced by the Maastricht amendments to the EEC Treaty.[64] Subsidiarity was a response to the wide and expanding scope of Community law-making competence and to the increasing exercise of that competence. We have already seen how various factors contributed to an expansion in the scope of Community law-making competences. The adoption of qualified majority voting subsequent to the amendments introduced by the SEA also contributed, since 1987, to an increase in the exercise of that competence in practice. On one measure, the annual number of binding acts adopted by the Community institutions more than doubled between 1986 and 1992, from 311 to 752.[65] In the run up to the agreement on the Maastricht amendments, some Member States, including Spain, France and Italy, had sought a reference to

---

[62] There is an extensive literature on the principle of subsidiarity, much of it now overtaken by events. For a selection of views, see Constantinesco, "Who's afraid of Subsidiarity?" (1991) 11 Y.E.L. 33; Emiliou, "Subsidiarity: An Effective Barrier against the Enterprises of Ambition?" (1992) 17 E.L.Rev. 383; Toth, "The Principle of Subsidiarity in the Maastricht Treaty" (1992) 29 C.M.L.Rev. 1079; Cass, "The Word that Saves Maastricht? The Principle of Subsidiarity and the Division of Powers within the European Community" (1992) 29 C.M.L.Rev. 1107; Mattina, "Subsidiarité, Démocratie et Transparence" (1992) 4 R.M.U.E. 203; Gonzalez, "The Principle of Subsidiarity" (1995) 20 E.L.Rev. 355; Wyatt, "Subsidiarity—Is it too Vague to be Effective as a Legal Principle?" in Nicolaidis and Weatherill (eds), *National Models and the Constitution of the European Union* (OUP/European Studies at Oxford/Whose Europe?), p.86 (*www.europeanstudies.ox.ac.uk*).

[63] Art.130R(4) EEC.

[64] Now Art.5(b) of the (renamed) EC Treaty.

[65] See Estella, *The EU Principle of Subsidiarity and its Critique* (OUP, 2002), p.20.

subsidiarity in the preamble of the EC Treaty.[66] The main advocates of subsidiarity as a legally binding principle inhibiting the exercise of Community competence had been Germany and the United Kingdom.[67]

Three uses of subsidiarity

4–013 The broad idea underlying the principle of subsidiarity is a simple one: that public powers should normally be located at the lowest tier of government where they can be exercised effectively.[68]

In constitutional texts like the TEU and the EC Treaty, the principle can be used in a variety of ways.[69] It may, for instance, serve as a general political value permeating the constitutional order: that is the significance of the reference in Article 1, second paragraph of the TEU, to the union in the course of being created among the peoples of Europe, as one "in which decisions are taken . . . as closely as possible to the citizen". The principle may also guide the hand of the constitution-maker in allocating powers within a complex order, between the central authorities and the component entities. Examples in the EC Treaty would be the field of social policy, where Article 137 EC makes explicitly clear that the leading role belongs to the Member States, that of the Community being merely to "support and complement" their activities; and also the legal bases on employment, education and other matters, where the limited and supplementary character of Community action has already been noted.[70] Finally, the principle may organise the exercise of concurrent powers: its effect here is to require that, in matters where the constitution allows action to be taken either by the central authorities or by component entities, the choice should, other things being equal, fall on the latter.

---

[66] Elorza, "Subsidiariedad" in *Breve diccionario del Tratado de la Unión Europea, Política*, Vol. VI, 29 Otoño, 1992, p.126. Also Estella, *The EU Principle of Subsidiarity and its Critique* (OUP, 2002), p.85.

[67] Estella, *The EU Principle of Subsidiarity and its Critique* (OUP, 2002), p.85; Cloos, Reinesch, Vinges and Weyland, *Le Traité de Maastricht: Genèse, Analyse, Commentaires*, (Bruylant, 1993), p.149. And see Schilling, "A New Dimension of Subsidiarity: Subsidiarity as a Rule and a Principle" (1994) 14 Y.E.L. 203, referring to Case, "The Word that Saved Maastricht? The Principle of Subsidiarity and the Division of Powers within the European Community" (1992) 29 C.M.L.Rev. 1107.

[68] See the famous formulation of the principle by Pope Pius XI in his Encyclical of 1931, *Quadragesimo Anno*, where he wrote, ". . . it is an injustice, a grave evil and a disturbance of the right order, for a larger and higher association to arrogate to itself functions which can be performed efficiently by smaller and lower societies" (Catholic Truth Society, London, 1936). On the historical background, see Emiliou, "Subsidiarity: An Effective Barrier against the Enterprises of Ambition?" (1992) 17 E.L.Rev. 383.

[69] See the analysis of van Gerven, "Les Principes de 'Subsidiarité, Proportionnalité et Coopération' en Droit Communautaire Européen", a paper delivered in the author's capacity as President of the Académie royale des sciences, lettres et beaux-arts de Belgique, at the general meeting of the Academy on December 21, 1991.

[70] See above.

That last-mentioned function of the subsidiarity principle is the one provided for by the second paragraph of Article 5 EC. Once it is established that the Community enjoys competence in accordance with the principle of attribution of powers, the principle of subsidiarity is then designed to assist in deciding whether or not the Community should exercise that competence in practice—based upon the criterion that, in cases where the Treaty leaves the matter open, one should prefer action by the Member States acting individually, unless one can demonstrate some need for collective action at the Community level instead.

Subsidiarity has no application to areas falling within the Community's exclusive competence

According to Article 5, second paragraph, EC, the principle of **4–014** subsidiarity shall not apply to areas falling within the Community's exclusive competence. On the one hand, to apply the subsidiarity principle in such situations would be pointless, since the option of leaving it to the Member States to pursue the objectives in question has been specifically disallowed by the Treaty system. On the other hand, in accordance with the definition of exclusivity given above, only a small number of fields of Community activity are thereby excluded from the potential application of the subsidiarity test, i.e. aspects of the common commercial policy; the preservation of marine biological resources; and monetary policy for Member States participating in the single currency. Thus, for example, the Court has expressly held that the test of subsidiarity applies to the exercise of Community competence to complete the internal market under Article 95 EC.[71] This is true even in situations where the Community has already exercised its shared competence to enact secondary legislation in the relevant field, with at least some pre-emptive effects, and now wishes to repeal and replace that legislation with a revised regulatory code.[72]

The Article 5 test of subsidiarity

For those other fields of Community law characterised by shared **4–015** or supporting competence, the test of subsidiarity prescribed by Article 5, second paragraph, EC is that "the objectives of the proposed action cannot be sufficiently achieved by the Member States and can therefore, by reason of the scale or effects of the proposed action, be better achieved by the Community". The test, therefore, has a dual aspect: the impossibility of attaining the

---

[71] e.g. Case C–377/98 *Netherlands v Parliament and Council* [2001] E.C.R. I–7079; Cases C–154–155/04 *Alliance for Natural Health* (Judgment of July 12, 2005).
[72] e.g. Case C–491/01 *ex parte British American Tobacco* [2002] E.C.R. I–11453.

objectives in question by action at Member State level; and the superior efficacy of action at Community level. Using "qualitative or, wherever possible, quantitative indicators", it must be shown that both aspects of the test are satisfied, in order to justify action by the Community.[73] The following guidelines have been provided by the Amsterdam Protocol:

— the issue under consideration has transnational aspects which cannot be satisfactorily regulated by action by Member States;

— action by Member States alone or lack of Community action would conflict with the requirements of the Treaty (such as the need to correct distortion of competition or avoid disguised restrictions on trade or strengthen economic and social cohesion) or would otherwise significantly damage Member States' interests;

— action at Community level would produce clear benefits by reason of its scale or effects compared with action at the level of the Member States.[74]

Another point emphasised in the Protocol is that subsidiarity is a dynamic concept, allowing action by the Community "to be expanded where circumstances so require, and conversely, to be restricted or discontinued where it is no longer justified".[75] Thus, the principle must not be applied crudely as a brake on the exercise of Community powers. Events such as the BSE crisis and the discovery of dioxins in certain foodstuffs may, for instance, point to the need for a new programme of food safety measures.[76] On the other hand, existing proposals should be withdrawn, and legislation repealed, where these are found no longer to meet the test in Article 5, second paragraph, EC.[77]

Implementation of the principle

4–016   Primary responsibility for ensuring the effective application of the subsidiarity principle falls on the Commission, the Council and the European Parliament, as the institutions with the leading roles in the Community's legislative process. When putting forward a proposal on a matter for which the Community is not exclusively competent, the Commission must provide a justification as regards subsidiarity,

---

[73] Amsterdam Protocol, Arts 4 and 5, read together.
[74] *ibid.*
[75] Amsterdam Protocol, Art.3.
[76] See the Commission's Report, "Better Lawmaking 1999" COM(1999) 562 Final, p.2.
[77] An extensive review of existing proposals and legislation was initiated by the Commission in 1994: see COM(94) 533 Final, pp.15 *et seq.*

in the accompanying Explanatory Memorandum.[78] The issue of the compliance with Article 5 EC generally (*i.e.* the attribution and proportionality principles, as well as subsidiarity) of Commission proposals, and of any amendments to them, must be specifically addressed by the Council and the European Parliament in the ordinary course of the relevant procedures;[79] and, in the case of co-decision, there is a formal requirement that the Parliament be informed of the Council's views as to the application of Article 5 EC, by way of the statement of reasons communicated, at the end of the first reading, along with its common position.[80] Last but not least, reasons demonstrating the compliance of a measure with the principles of subsidiarity and proportionality must be given in its preamble.[81] An express reference to the principles is not, however, required.

The Edinburgh text called for the Commission to submit, to the European Council and the European Parliament, an annual report on the application of Article 5 EC; and this was transformed into a binding obligation by the Amsterdam Protocol.[82] From 1995 onwards, the report has been expanded to cover all action aimed at improving Community law-making.[83] The series of reports provides evidence, including statistical evidence, of the seriousness of the efforts being made by the political institutions, in particular the Commission, to give concrete substance to the Article 5 EC principles.[84]

It was hotly debated, in the early days following the insertion of Article 5 into the EC Treaty by the TEU, whether the principle of subsidiarity was justiciable.[85] As an eminent commentator pointed out, there is nothing in the text of Article 5 EC to suggest the contrary, nor that the Court of Justice does not have power to interpret the provisions of the Article.[86] Any doubts should by now have been dissipated by the available case law.[87] **4–017**

---

[78] Amsterdam Protocol, Art.9, second indent.
[79] *ibid.*, Art.11.
[80] *ibid.*, Art.12.
[81] *ibid.*, Art.4.
[82] See Art.9, fourth indent.
[83] The reports are, accordingly, entitled "Better Lawmaking".
[84] See, e.g. "Better Lawmaking 1999" COM(1999) 562 Final; or more recently, "Better Lawmaking 2004" COM(2005) 98 Final. Note also the Commission's periodic "culls" of pending legislative proposals: COM(2005) 462 Final provides a relatively large-scale example (though this particular exercise was not specifically justified by reference to the principle of subsidiarity, but rather on grounds such as promoting greater economic competitiveness or having failed to undertake an appropriate impact assessment).
[85] See, e.g. Toth, "Is subsidiarity justiciable?" (1994) 19 E.L.Rev. 268.
[86] Lord Mackenzie-Stuart, "Subsidiarity—A Busted Flush?" in Curtin and O'Keefe, *Constitutional Adjudication in European and National Law: Essays for the Hon. Mr Justice T. F. O'Higgins*, p.19.
[87] See also Arnull, *The European Union and its Court of Justice* (Oxford, 1999), at pp.551–552, where the justiciability of the subsidiarity principle is treated as a *fait accompli*.

An issue of pure law would be whether a given measure falls within an area of exclusive Community competence: a wrong characterisation, leading to the non-application of the subsidiarity test, would clearly provide grounds for challenging the measure's validity. Another orthodox ground for challenge would be the failure of the law-making institutions to provide, in the preamble to an instrument adopted under non-exclusive powers, an adequate explanation of why it was considered necessary. Advocate General Léger has noted "how useful . . . it could be, for the purpose of ensuring proper application of the principle of subsidiarity for the obligation to state reasons laid down in Article 190 of the Treaty to be enforced with particular rigour whenever the Community legislature takes action to lay down new rules".[88] He went on to conclude: "All measures adopted by the Community should thus indicate, either implicitly or explicitly, but in any event clearly, on what basis the authority concerned is acting—even if only to state, where this is the case, that the principle of subsidiarity does not come into play".[89] Unfortunately, the Court appears to be rather more easily satisfied.[90] Previously, in a case on the validity of the Council Directive concerning certain aspects of the organisation of working time,[91] it accepted, as justification for Community-wide action, the fact that "the Council has found that it is necessary to improve the existing level of protection as regards the health and safety of workers and to harmonise the conditions in this area while maintaining the improvements made".[92] That seems hardly sufficient, given that the relevant Treaty provisions[93] clearly contemplate the possibility of pursuing those same objectives through action at Member State level.

Litigants have also raised directly the substantive issue of compliance with the dual test in Article 5, second paragraph, EC. In a series of recent judgments—concerning the validity of the Biotechnological Inventions Directive,[94] the Second Tobacco Labeling Directive,[95] and the Food Supplements Directive,[96] respectively—the Court has indeed engaged with this issue and assessed whether the

---

[88] Case C–233/94 *Germany v European Parliament and Council* [1997] E.C.R. at I–2427, para.87 Opinion; [1997] 3 C.M.L.R. 1379.

[89] *ibid.*, para.90 Opinion.

[90] The judgment in Case C–233/94 goes out of its way to stress that there is no need for the subsidiarity principle to be referred to expressly. The relevant passage reads like a rebuttal of the Advocate General: see para.28 of the Judgment.

[91] Dir.93/104 [1993] O.J. L307/18.

[92] Case C–84/94 *United Kingdom v Council* [1996] E.C.R. I–5755, para.47; [1996] 3 C.M.L.R. 671.

[93] See Arts 136 and 137 EC.

[94] Case C–377/98 *Kingdom of the Netherlands v European Parliament and Council* [2001] E.C.R. I–7079.

[95] Case C–491/01 *ex parte British American Tobacco* [2002] E.C.R. I–11453.

[96] Joined Cases C–154/04 and C–155/04 *Alliance for Natural Health* (Judgment of July 12, 2005).

exercise of Community competence under Article 95 EC was justified from the perspective of subsidiarity. In each case, the Court held that the purpose of the disputed measure was to eliminate obstacles to trade and distortions of competition within the internal market resulting from the multifarious development of national laws. It was evident that that objective could not satisfactorily be achieved by the Member States alone (after all, leaving the Member States to their own devices had created the obstacles and distortions in the first place), and in fact required action at the Community level. These cases are significant because, really for the first time, the Court had engaged in judicial review based upon substantive (rather than purely procedural) compliance with the principle of subsidiarity. But, in some respects, they were "easy cases" for the Court: the emergence of cross-border obstacles to trade and/or distortions of competition is a *sine qua non* for the very existence of Community competence under Article 95 EC, and equally, their emergence would seem to support the conclusion that only action coordinated under the auspices of the Community can provide an effective regulatory solution; thus, compliance with the principle of attribution of powers might plausibly be equated with satisfaction of the principle of subsidiarity. The Court has not yet revealed its attitude towards the subsidiarity test in other, more difficult, situations involving legislation adopted under the legal bases (e.g.) dealing with environmental or social policy measures, i.e. where the prior existence of Community competence is not dependent upon some cross-border trigger, and satisfaction of the principle of subsidiarity cannot automatically be inferred from compliance with the principle of attribution of powers. In such situations, the Court will surely allow the political institutions a wide discretion in weighing up the pros and cons as to whether action should be taken at Community or at national level. Judicial review is likely to be confined to examining whether the assessment reached by the responsible institution has been vitiated by manifest error or abuse of powers, or whether the institution has manifestly exceeded the limits of its discretion.[97]

A critical assessment

Views differ as to the effectiveness of subsidiarity as a brake on **4–018** Community action in the hands of the political institutions and the Court of Justice. As we shall see in Chapter 11, the Constitutional Treaty contains a Protocol on Subsidiarity and Proportionality which seeks to confirm and strengthen application of subsidiarity, and provides for closer monitoring of the application of the principle by national parliaments and by the Court of Justice. With those reforms

---

[97] As with the principle of proportionality: see below.

in mind, the European Union Committee of the House of Lords (the upper chamber of the United Kingdom Parliament) undertook in the Session 2004–2005 an assessment of subsidiarity monitoring in order "to focus Parliamentary and public attention on subsidiarity monitoring" and to advise the House of Lords on how, if the Constitutional Treaty comes into force, the House might fulfil its a new obligations.[98] A written question posed by the Committee to the British Government gives some indication of the balance of the evidence received by the Committee: "Looking at the written evidence we have received it seems that most people believe that thus far the principle of subsidiarity has not acted as an effective 'brake' on the exercise of law-making powers at the Community level. Do you agree and if so why is this?" The reply by the Minister for Europe gave a firm endorsement of subsidiarity in practice:

> "The Government believes that . . . the EU's general direction has been positively influenced by the institutions' increasing application of subsidiarity. In particular the Government believes that the principle of subsidiarity has worked as an effective tool in influencing the formulation of European legislation."[99]

The Committee contrasted with the Government's view that "the institutions are applying the principle in practice as part of the policy-making and legislative process", an alternative view, to the effect "that subsidiarity has so far received only token attention from the EU institutions and has certainly not served as a founding principle to encourage self-restraint on the part of the Community institutions in their law making activities".[1] The Committee noted this division of opinion, and expressed the hope that the new Protocol to the Constitution Treaty would "provide a vehicle for highlighting and invigorating subsidiarity compliance across the Union".[2] In its summary of recommendations, the Committee expressed the hope "that the Court will take a more critical approach to subsidiarity, particularly in ensuring that the justification for action at Union level is adequate".[3] There is certainly room for a more critical approach to subsidiarity on the part of the Court of Justice, and for a more rigorous approach to application of the

---

[98] House of Lords EU Committee "Strengthening national parliamentary scrutiny of the EU—the Constitution's subsidiarity early warning mechanism", Report with Evidence, 14th Report of Session 2004–05, *www.publications.parliament.uk/pa/ld200405/ldselect/ldeucom/101/10102.htm* (hereafter "Report").

[99] Report, Minutes of Evidence, p.66.

[1] Report, para.77, citing evidence submitted by Professors Weatherill and Wyatt of the University of Oxford.

[2] Report, para.84.

[3] *ibid.*, para.244.

principle to proposals for legislation on the part of the Commission, Council and Parliament.

As we have noted, subsidiarity is first and foremost a political principle, to be interpreted and applied by the Community institutions. Yet it is equally a fundamental principle of the Community legal order, to be interpreted in light of its text, its aim and the principle of effectiveness. It is textually possible to interpret the dual test for subsidiarity in a way which minimises or eliminates its potential to inhibit Community action. Thus, a proposal for Community-wide rules on any subject-matter at all within Community competence might be said to pass the dual test, on the grounds that Member States cannot sufficiently achieve the objectives of the proposal (the adoption of Community-wide rules), while the scale or effects of the proposed action (Community-wide rules) can be better (indeed only) achieved at Community level. Commission references to subsidiarity in explanatory memoranda to some measures seem to imply such an approach.[4] And support for this approach might be derived from the terms in which the Court rejected the argument that the adoption of Directive 93/104 concerning certain aspects of the organisation of working time contravened the principle of subsidiarity. The Court stated that once the Council had found that it was necessary to improve the existing level of protection as regards the health and safety of workers and to harmonise conditions in this area, achievement of that objective through the imposition of minimum requirements necessarily presupposed Community-wide action.[5]

Yet such an approach is to say the least open to serious criticism. **4–019** To interpret the principle of subsidiarity as laying down a requirement for the exercise of Community competence which all proposed Community legislation is bound to pass would deprive the principle of useful effect. The rationale of the tests is to determine *whether* the scale or effects of the proposed action would be such as to justify the adoption of Community-wide rules, rather than leaving policy

---

[4] See e.g. the Communication from the Commission to the Council, the European Parliament, the Economic and Social Committee and the Committee of the Regions on certain Community measures to combat discrimination (1999/C 369/03), paragraph on subsidiarity: "The draft directives would lay down a set of principles on equal treatment covering key issues, including protection against harassment, the possibility for positive action, appropriate remedies and enforcement measures. These principles would be applied in all Member States, thus providing certainty for individuals about the common level of protection from discrimination they can expect. Common standards at Community level can only be achieved through co-ordinated action." For criticism of the "circularity" of the subsidiarity reasoning in the explanatory memorandum to the Proposal for a Council Directive to improve access to justice in cross-border disputes by establishing minimum common rules to legal aid and other financial aspects of civil proceedings, COM(2002) 13 Final, and generally, see Spaventa, "The Principle of Subsidiarity and the New Proposed Protocol" (Portuguese translation) in AAVV, *Uma Constituição para a Europa* (Coimbra, Livraria Almedina, 2004).
[5] Case C–84/94 *United Kingdom v Council* [1996] E.C.R. I–5755, paras 47 and 55.

choices over the subject-matter in issue to national or sub-national authorities of Member States. Community legislation by its very nature produces a Community-wide legal outcome. The core task of subsidiarity is to distinguish proposed Community measures whose objectives are to produce a Community-wide outcome from proposed measures which *must* produce a Community-wide outcome if their objectives are to be achieved. The objectives of proposed Community action, referred to in the definition of subsidiarity, which cannot sufficiently be achieved by the Member States, but which can be better achieved at Community level, are thus objectives which can *only* be achieved by Community-wide action.

This interpretation of the two tests for subsidiarity is supported by the guidelines which were adopted for its implementation by the Community institutions, first in the "soft law" form adopted at the Edinburgh summit of 11–12 December 1992, and subsequently in the 1997 Amsterdam Protocol on Subsidiarity and Proportionality. Two of these guidelines are particularly worthy of remark. The first is that the issue under consideration has transnational aspects which cannot be satisfactorily regulated by action by Member States. The second is that actions by Member States alone or lack of Community action would conflict with the requirements of the Treaty (such as the need to correct distortions of competition, or avoid disguised restrictions on trade, or strengthen economic and social cohesion); or would otherwise significantly damage Member States' interests. The references to transnational aspects, to distortion of competition, and disguised restrictions on trade, support an interpretation of subsidiarity which requires that Community action in areas of non exclusive competence be confined to the achievement of objectives which can be achieved only by Community-wide action. Reference to the requirements of the Treaty as including economic and social cohesion, and the indication that Community action would comply with the principle of subsidiarity where its lack "would otherwise significantly damage Member States' interests" seem to support a broader approach to subsidiarity, and indeed to establish a subjective and open-ended opportunity for any proposed measure to be treated as compliant with that principle. Yet such a literal construction would seem to be inappropriate. The words referred to should be construed in light of the aim of the Protocol, and the aim of the guidelines in which the words are to be found, which is to secure implementation of the subsidiarity principle. The words referred to should thus be interpreted as meaning that any requirements of the Treaty as regards economic and social cohesion, and any significant damage to Member States' interests, be requirements and/or damage which could only be remedied by Community-wide action.

The substantive content of subsidiarity might thus be simply summarised: in areas of non-exclusive competence, the Community should act if, and only if, the objectives of the proposed action can only be achieved by Community-wide action; in such circumstances, the objectives in question cannot be sufficiently achieved by the Member States, and can be better achieved by the Community. Application of this principle, on the other hand, is not necessarily straightforward, in that it is possible for rational individuals to come to different conclusions as regards the same proposed action. One reason for this is that the *objectives* of proposed action may be mixed; some objectives may not require Community-wide action, other objectives may require such action.

Take, for example, a proposed internal market measure which **4–020** would harmonise certain national rules which have the aim of protection of public health. Suppose: (a) that the principal aim of the measure is public health; (b) that the measure makes a very modest contribution to the internal market, and that contribution is clearly a secondary aim, but the latter contribution is sufficient for competence to be established pursuant to Article 95 EC.[6] In such a case it would, in principle, be rational (in the sense of within the range of options open to a rational decision maker taking into account all relevant legal and factual considerations) for the Community institutions to reason: (i) that the *principal* objectives of the proposed action (public health objectives) could *not* be better achieved at the Community level; (ii) that these objectives *could* be sufficiently achieved at the national level;[7] (iii) that the (secondary) internal market objectives of the measure *could* be better achieved at Community level (this will invariably be the case);[8] (iv) that the benefits of Community-wide action would be very modest, since any positive effects on trade and market conditions resulting would be slight; and (v) that their *overall* assessment was thus that the measure did not comply with the principle of subsidiarity. A contrary conclusion in identical circumstances might (just) be equally rational. Different assessments might be possible of the respective weights to be attached to the various objectives of the proposed act. Even a modest contribution to the internal market might be seen as significant, and the internal market objectives of the measure might thus be seen as equal to, or more significant than, the public health objectives, despite the fact that that public health objectives were in themselves and in principle matters for national competence rather than Community competence, and only matters appropriate for

---

[6] It follows from Case C–376/98 *Germany v Parliament and Council* [2000] E.C.R. I–8419 that where a directive adopted under Article 95 EC pursues trade and health aims it is necessary only that the directive makes a genuine contribution to the internal market, and not that the primary objective of the measure is to make such a contribution (see esp. paras 76–84 and para.88); and see Case C–491/01 *ex parte British American Tobacco* [2002] E.C.R. I–11453, paras 61 and 62.

[7] It is to be noted that public health remains an area of primarily national competence, and that the Title on public health excludes Community harmonisation: see Art.152(4)(c) EC.

[8] Case C–376/98 *Germany v Parliament and Council* [2000] E.C.R. I–8419; Case C–377/98 *Netherlands v Parliament and Council* [2001] E.C.R. I–7079.

regulation under Article 95 EC by virtue of the overall contribution of any relevant measure to the internal market.

It was to facilitate analysis of such issues in a transparent and systematic way that procedural requirements were introduced—first in the Edinburgh Conclusions and in the 1993 Inter-institutional Agreement, and later in the Amsterdam Protocol—which would apply to subsidiarity appraisal during the legislative process. The procedural requirements laid down by the Amsterdam Protocol[9] were that: (i) each institution must ensure that subsidiarity is complied with; (ii) for any proposed legislation, the reasons on which it is based shall be stated with a view to justifying its compliance with the principle of subsidiarity; (iii) the reasons for concluding that a Community objective can be better achieved by the Community must be substantiated by qualitative or, wherever possible, quantitative indicators; (iv) compliance with subsidiarity should only be established where action at the Community level would produce *clear* benefits compared with action at the level of the Member States; (v) the Commission should justify the relevance of its proposals with regard to the principle of subsidiarity, and wherever necessary, the explanatory memorandum accompanying a proposal shall give details in this respect; (vi) the European Parliament shall consider the consistency of Commission proposals with the principle of subsidiarity; and (vii) in the course of the co-decision and co-operation procedures, the European Parliament shall be informed of the Council's position on the application of the principle of subsidiarity, by way of a statement of the reasons which led the Council to adopt its common position.

Two of the procedural requirements listed above are worthy of further remark. The first is the requirement that reasons for concluding that a Community objective can be better achieved by the Community must be substantiated by qualitative or, wherever possible, quantitative indicators. Quantitative indicators (such as trade statistics and results of market research) can be of particular assistance when assessing whether any possible transnational aspects of a proposed act can or cannot be satisfactorily regulated at the national or sub-national level, or when assessing possible distortions of competition or disguised restrictions on trade which will allegedly be remedied by the proposed action. Furthermore, subject matter such as transnational effects, distortions of competition, and disguised restrictions on trade are particularly susceptible to quantitative analysis, even though this seems rarely to have been undertaken in any detail during the legislative process.

4–021   The second procedural requirement worthy of remark is that action at the Community level would produce *clear benefits* compared with action at the level of the Member States. This requirement is described as procedural since the reference to *clear* benefits

---

[9] These requirements are similar to those set out in the Edinburgh Conclusions and the 1993 Inter-institutional Agreement.

stipulated a standard akin to a standard of proof. If the question of benefits at the Community level was in doubt, that doubt was to be resolved in favour of the exercise of national or sub-national policy choices. This "standard of proof" may be derived from the basis of the principle of subsidiarity, which is that decisions be taken "as closely as possible to the citizen".[10] Since the European level is (within the Community/Union legal order) as distant as it is possible to get from the citizen, this principle might well be said to create a mild presumption against action at the European level, and it is consistent with this presumption that it be demonstrated that Community action would produce *clear* benefits compared with action at the level of the Member States.

The Amsterdam Protocol stated that "compliance with the principle of subsidiarity shall be reviewed in accordance with the rules laid down by the Treaty".[11] If legislation is adopted by the institutions contrary to the principle of subsidiarity, this is a matter which in principle can be raised before the Court of Justice. It has always been difficult to imagine the Court annulling a Community act on the ground that the institutions had been wrong to conclude that the objectives of the proposed action could be better achieved by action at the Community level than at the level of the Member States, as a result of the wide discretion, or margin of appreciation, accorded to the institutions in the making of complex assessments.[12] Nevertheless, even in the case of acts involving a complex assessment, the Court is entitled to examine the accuracy of the findings of fact and law made by the authority concerned,[13] and as noted above, in the context of subsidiarity, the Court has been prepared to address the question whether "the objective of the proposed action could be better achieved at Community level".[14] Yet in a case where the objectives of the act in question related to both the internal market and public health, and the latter objective was almost certainly the dominant objective, the Court considered only whether the internal market objective of moving future emerging obstacles to trade could be better achieved at Community level.[15] This is in contrast to the assessment of proportionality of the act in question, which took account of public health objectives as well as internal market objectives.[16]

---

[10] Art.1 TEU.

[11] Art.13 of the Amsterdam Protocol.

[12] Wyatt, "Subsidiarity and Judicial Review" in O'Keeffe and Bavasso (eds) *Liber Amicorum in Honour of Lord Slynn of Hadley* (Kluwer, 2000).

[13] e.g. Case C–120/97 *Upjohn* [1999] E.C.R. I–223, para.34.

[14] Case C–491/01 *ex parte British American Tobacco* [2002] E.C.R. I–11453, para.180.

[15] *ibid.*, paras 181 and 61.

[16] *ibid.*, paras 122–141. This cannot be explained by the way the case was argued since the applicants contended that there was no evidence for the proposition that the Member States were precluded from taking such steps to protect public health as they might wish to take, thus denying that the public health objectives of the act could be better achieved at the Community level.

Annulment of a binding act for failure to comply with an essential procedural requirement relating to application of the principle of subsidiarity has always been a much more likely possibility than annulment for manifest error of assessment. It has been noted that the Court's approach to the requirement that the statement of reasons of an act indicate compliance with subsidiarity has been undemanding. The Court could and, in our opinion should, at the outset, have required more detail in the statement of reasons of an act relating to compliance with subsidiarity, in particular as regards relevant transnational aspects, as regards the existence or otherwise of qualitative and quantitative indicators, and as regards reasons why (if this was the case) it had not been possible to substantiate compliance by reference to quantitative indicators. The texts of explanatory memoranda accompanying proposals for legislation invariably contain brief and self-serving references to subsidiarity, as do references to subsidiarity in the preambles of legislation; these practices can only have been encouraged by the Court's undemanding approach to the requirement that the statement of reasons for binding measures cover subsidiarity. Furthermore, it is established that the failure to take account of matters which it is essential to take into account will amount to a ground for annulment.[17] Thus, the failure to address transnational aspects etc., during the legislative process, would amount to infringement of an essential procedural requirement. In the case on the Working Time Directive, the United Kingdom argued that the institutions had neither fully considered nor demonstrated that there were transnational aspects etc., but the Court did not appear to consider the contention as relevant.[18]

The principle of proportionality

4–022　　Long before its importation into the third paragraph of Article 5 EC, the principle of proportionality had become a familiar tool of judicial review in the field of the Community's administrative law. In that field, as we shall see in a later chapter,[19] the principle has been used mainly for two purposes: controlling the extent to which measures, adopted by the Community authorities in furtherance of objectives of the Treaty, are permitted to override the interests of particular individuals; and limiting the leeway Member States have been given to protect important public interests, through derogations from certain fundamental rules of the Community system. The case

---

[17] Case 191/82 *FEDIOL v Commission* [1983] E.C.R. 2913, para.30; scrutiny to determine whether an institution has omitted to take into consideration any essential matters part of normal powers of review of the Court of Justice.

[18] Case C–84/94 *United Kingdom v Council* [1996] E.C.R. I–5755, para.46. A similar argument was made in Case C–491/01 *ex parte British American Tobacco* [2002] E.C.R. I–11453, but the point was not referred to by the Court.

[19] See Ch.7.

law establishes that, in applying the principle of proportionality, it must be ascertained, first, whether the means employed by the competent authority are suitable for the purpose of achieving the desired objective and, secondly, whether they do not go beyond what is necessary to achieve that objective.[20]

In the context of Article 5 EC, the logic of the proportionality principle remains the same, though it is here operating on the constitutional plane as regards the exercise of the Community's legislative powers. Assuming that Community competence exists in accordance with the principle of attribution of powers, and that the Community should legitimately exercise that competence in accordance with the principle of subsidiarity, the proportionality test provides an answer to the next question: "What should be the intensity or nature of the Community's action?".[21] Proportionality, in effect, guides the legislator towards choosing the form of Community action which, while being well designed to achieve its objective, will intrude, to the smallest praticable extent, on the powers of the Member States.

The Edinburgh text went into some detail in describing the elements relevant to an evaluation of proportionality for the purposes of Article 5, third paragraph, EC,[22] and many of these figure in the Amsterdam Protocol, from which they derive legal force. Among other things, it is stated that "[t]he form of Community action must be as simple as possible, consistent with the satisfactory achievement of the objective of the measure and the need for effective enforcement . . . Other things being equal, directives should be preferred to regulations and framework directives to detailed measures". Care must be taken "to respect well established national arrangements and the organisation and working of Member States' legal systems".[23] Examples of the steps taken by the political institutions in adapting their legislative practice to these requirements can be found in the Commission's annual "Better Lawmaking" Reports.[24]

As one of the instruments deployed by Article 5 EC to help preserve the balance between the Community and its Member States, the principle of proportionality usually has a stronger political flavour than in its usual administrative law setting. Not surprisingly, therefore, when the principle was invoked by the United Kingdom in the *Working Time Directive* case, the Court of Justice

---

[20] See, e.g. Joined Cases 279, 280, 285 and 286/84 *Rau v Commission* [1987] E.C.R. 1069, para.34; [1988] 2 C.M.L.R. 704; cited with reference to Art.5 EC in Case 426/93 *Germany v Council* [1995] E.C.R. I–3723, para.42.

[21] See Edinburgh text, Bull EC 12–1992, point I.15.

[22] *ibid.*, point I.19.

[23] See Amsterdam Protocol, Arts 6 and 7.

[24] See, e.g. "Better Lawmaking 1999" COM(1999) 562 Final; or more recently, "Better Lawmaking 2004" COM(2005) 98 Final.

saw fit to adopt the technique of "marginal review"[25] (for manifest
error, misuse of powers or manifest excess of jurisdiction) which, we
have suggested, would be similarly appropriate in dealing with issues
of subsidiarity.[26] Applying the two traditional aspects of the proportionality principle, the Court found that, with one exception (the
specification of Sunday as a rest day), the measures on the organisation of working time contained in the Directive were apt for the
purpose of enhancing workers' health and safety; and that the
Council did not commit any manifest error in concluding that the
objectives of the Treaty could not have been achieved by less
restrictive forms of Community action.[27] A similar "hands off"
approach to judicial review based upon the principle of proportionality, in the sort of constitutional contexts envisaged by Article 5,
third paragraph, EC, can be seen in other judgments from the Court
of Justice.[28]

Flexibility: a new organising principle[29]

4–023 A development complementing the "conservatory principles" set out
in Article 5 EC has been the formal acceptance of the principle of
flexibility as part of the constitutional machinery of the EU. We use
the term "flexibility" in this chapter to designate legal arrangements
under which it is recognised that one or more of the Member States
may, in principle, remain permanently outside certain activities or
practices being pursued within the single institutional framework of
the Union, either because they choose to do so or because they do
not meet the criteria for participation.[30]

So defined, flexibility is to be distinguished from the long-
established practice of allowing a transitional period before new

---

[25] This term is used by Schermers and Waelbroek, *Judicial Protection in the European Communities* (5th ed., Kluwer, 1992), when discussing the use of the technique in the judicial control of decisions based on broad economic assessments.

[26] See above.

[27] Case C–84/94 *United Kingdom v Council* [1996] E.C.R. I–5755, paras 59–66.

[28] e.g. Case C–233/94 *Germany v Parliament and Council* [1997] E.C.R. I–2405; Case C–491/01 *ex parte British American Tobacco* [2002] E.C.R. I–11453; Case C–434/02 *Arnold André* [2004] E.C.R. I–11825; Case C–210/03 *Swedish Match* [2004] E.C.R. I–11893; Case C–344/04 *European Low Fares Airline Association* (Judgment of January 10, 2006).

[29] For an analysis of the flexibility principle, from a political science perspective, see Edwards and Philippart, *Flexibility and the Treaty of Amsterdam: Europe's New Byzantium?*, CELS Occasional Paper No.3 (1997). See also Dashwood (ed.), *Reviewing Maastricht: Issues for the 1996 IGC* (Sweet & Maxwell, 1996) pp.158–164, 195–201; Stubb, "A Categorisation of Differentiated Integration" (1996) 34 J.C.M.S. 238; Kortenberg, "Closer Co-operation in the Treaty of Amsterdam" (1998) 35 C.M.L.Rev. 833; Gaja, "How Flexible is Flexibility under the Amsterdam Treaty?" (1998) 35 C.M.L.Rev. 855; Usher, "Flexibility and Enhanced Co-operation" in Heukels, Blokker and Brus (eds), *The European Union After Amsterdam*, p.253; Hederman-Robinson, "The Area of Freedom, Security and Justice with Regard to the UK, Ireland and Denmark: the 'Opt-in Opt-outs' under the Treaty of Amsterdam" in O'Keefe and Twomey (eds), *Legal Issues of the Amsterdam Treaty* (Hart Publishing, 1999).

[30] The term "variable geometry" is also found, especially in the older literature, in the sense of "flexibility" used here.

Member States are required to apply the whole body of EU law; or that of prescribing differential periods for the implementation of new legislation, taking account of the fact that a particular Member State may face special difficulties of adjustment.[31] Such derogations from the rules generally applicable under the Treaties differ from the flexibility principle in that they apply only on a temporary basis, and are accorded in recognition of objective socio-economic factors, not merely the political preferences of the State concerned.[32]

Indeed, the principle of flexibility is meant to recognise the difficulty of maintaining a workable consensus between the Member States about how best to exercise the Community's regulatory competences, especially given the dramatic growth both in the fields of activity in which the EU has become involved (including many sensitive policy areas such as the environment, education and public health), and in the simple number of Member States (thus representing a more heterogeneous body of political opinion about how best to tackle emerging economic and social problems). Rather than accept either that Community activity must proceed at the pace of the "lowest common denominator", or that more integrationist Member States will pursue their ambitions through new institutional arrangements lying altogether outside the Union, flexibility embodies a compromise: those Member States that are determined to pursue deeper integration between themselves may do so, but they are encouraged to employ the institutional structure and tools of the Union's own legal order. The main challenge posed by this compromise is to ensure that no irreparable harm is done to the legal fabric of the Union, or to the well functioning of its institutions, through an excessive fragmentation or incoherence in the Community's activities.

The legitimation of flexibility as an organising principle of the constitutional order was achieved by the TEU; and the vital role the principle will be called upon to play in an increasingly complex and differentiated Union has since been underlined by the TA and TN. We distinguish between two main types of flexibility: primary and secondary.

Primary flexibility
In cases of what we call "primary flexibility", the relevant legal **4–024** arrangements are to be found in Treaty provisions. Thus, the policy areas in which flexibility may operate, the decision making procedures to be followed and the Member States that may benefit from "opt-outs", will all have been determined at the level of the Union's

[31] *cf.* Art.15 EC.
[32] See the distinctions drawn in Dashwood (ed.), *Reviewing Maastricht: Issues for the 1996 IGC* (Sweet & Maxwell, 1996), pp.41–43.

constitutional authority; in other words, the matter will have been specifically negotiated within an Intergovernmental Conference, and ratified in accordance with the Member States' constitutional requirements, as part of an accession or amendment exercise.[33]

The earliest examples of primary flexibility date from the TEU. One such consisted of the Protocol and Agreement on Social Policy, which the TEU annexed to the EC Treaty.[34] Their combined effect was to enable the Member States, with the exception of the United Kingdom, to have recourse to the institutions, procedures and mechanisms of the EC Treaty, for the purpose of exercising certain powers going beyond those provided for in the Social Provisions Chapter of the Treaty itself. That is now history, since the change of government in the United Kingdom in 1997 brought the abandonment of the "opt-out", so that the relevant provisions could be incorporated into the EC Treaty by the TA.[35] Of more lasting significance are the arrangements which excuse two classes of Member States from participation in the single currency, following the (otherwise obligatory) transition to the third stage of EMU at the beginning of 1999. One class comprises "Member States with a derogation", i.e. those which do not yet fulfil the conditions for the adoption of a single currency.[36] The other class comprises Denmark and the United Kingdom, whose respective positions are governed by separate Protocols:[37] Denmark was given the right, if it notified the Council that it would not be taking part in the third stage, to treatment corresponding, for most purposes, to that of Member States with a derogation; while it was expressly recognised "that the United Kingdom shall not be obliged or committed to move to the third stage of economic and monetary union without a separate decision to do so by its government and Parliament".[38]

Another very important case of primary flexibility has been established by the TA. We have noted that the TA introduced into Part Three of the EC Treaty a Title IV on "Visas, asylum, immigration and other policies related to free movement of persons", which covers, among other things, aspects of the treatment of third country nationals previously dealt with under Title VI TEU (the Third Pillar). There is also a Protocol, annexed to the TEU and the EC Treaty by the TA,[39] which provides for the incorporation into

---

[33] Thus, on the basis of either Art.48 or Art.49 TEU.
[34] See Protocol No.14 to the Final Act of the TEU.
[35] They are now found in the EC Treaty, Ch.1 of Title XI of Part Three.
[36] Art.122 EC. Greece was such a Member State, at the time of the transition to a single currency. Sweden, it seems, was allowed to deem itself to be similarly unqualified. The 10 Member States which joined in 2004 fall into the category of "Member States with a derogation".
[37] Respectively, Protocols Nos 11 and 12 to the Final Act of the TEU. Hereinafter, "UK Protocol" and "Danish Protocol".
[38] UK Protocol, opening recital.
[39] Protocol No.2 to the Final Act of the TA. Hereinafter "the Schengen Protocol".

the EU framework of the so-called "Schengen acquis". That consists of the body of law derived from an Agreement ("the Schengen Agreement") originally signed in 1985 by France, Germany and the Benelux countries, but to which, by the time of the TA, all of the Member States except Ireland and the United Kingdom had become signatories.[40] The Schengen Agreement represented an attempt to proceed, more rapidly than seemed possible by acting through the Community institutions, to the complete abolition of checks on persons crossing the borders between the countries concerned. Pursuant to the TA, the different elements of the Schengen acquis have been brought within the compass of either the EC Treaty (in particular, Title IV of Part Three) or Title VI TEU, depending on their subject-matter.[41] The significance of all this for present purposes lies in the flexibility arrangements made for the benefit of Ireland and the United Kingdom; and also for Denmark, even though it is a party to Schengen. As for Ireland and the United Kingdom, they are bound neither by the consequences of the Schengen incorporation nor by the new Title IV, unless they are willing and able to take advantage of the complex provisions on opting in (which, in the case of the Schengen *acquis*, though not of measures building upon it, requires the unanimous agreement of the Council composed of the participating Member States).[42] As for Denmark, its legal position, in respect of the elements of the Schengen *acquis* which have been given a legal basis in Title IV is to remain unchanged: the relevant provisions and decisions do not, in other words, acquire (for it) the quality of EC law.[43] Nor will Denmark take part in the adoption of measures under Title IV; and if it decides to implement any such measures in its national law, this will give rise, *vis-à-vis* the participating Member States, to an international obligation, not an EC one.[44] The theoretically unsatisfactory result is therefore that the same set of rules will apply within the four walls of the Community order to 22 Member States

---

[40] The Schengen *acquis* is defined in an Annex to the Schengen protocol as comprising: the Schengen Agreement itself, of 1985; the Implementing Convention, signed in 1990; the series of Accession Protocols and Agreements with eight other Member States of the EU; and decisions and declarations adopted by the Schengen Executive Committee, as well as acts of the organs on which the Committee has conferred decision-making powers. Iceland and Norway are also associated with the implementation of the Schengen *acquis*; see Schengen Protocol, Art.6.

[41] The Council was given the task of assigning appropriate legal bases to the provisions and decisions included in the *acquis*: Schengen Protocol, Art.2. See Decision 1999/435 concerning the definition of the Schengen *acquis* [1999] O.J. L176/1; Decision 1999/436 determining the legal basis for each of the provisions or decisions which constitute the Schengen *acquis* [1999] O.J. L176/17.

[42] Schengen Protocol, Arts 4 and 5. The provisions relating to the opt-out from Title IV of Part Three, EC Treaty, are found in Protocol No.4 to the Final Act of the TA.

[43] Schengen Protocol, Art.3.

[44] Protocol No.5 to the Final Act of the TA.

(plus Ireland and/or the United Kingdom, if they opt in),[45] but to Denmark with the entirely different character of rules of international law.[46]

Secondary flexibility (enhanced co-operation)

4–025   "Secondary flexibility" was an innovation of the TA, in the form of the mechanism there referred to as "closer co-operation". The novelty of the mechanism is that it allows flexibility arrangements to be established by internal legislative procedures, and therefore not in policy areas which have been pre-selected for such treatment at Treaty level. The original Amsterdam provisions were significantly amended by the TN, and the whole mechanism renamed "enhanced co-operation". It is worth analysing the original and the amended provisions in turn.

4–026   **(a) Closer co-operation under the Amsterdam Treaty.** The provisions on closer co-operation introduced by the Treaty of Amsterdam were divided between the TEU and the EC Treaty. Title VII TEU set out the basic principles of the closer co-operation regime in respect of both the First and Third Pillars; Article 11 EC then laid down additional rules on closer co-operation relating more particularly to the First Pillar.[47]

The general idea of closer co-operation was that a majority of the Member States could choose, in the future and in respect of a range of Community activities, to pursue deeper integration between themselves using the institutional and legislative framework provided under the Treaties.

To this end, the Treaties imposed a range of substantive conditions. The basic parameters of closer co-operation were established: on the one hand, such co-operation had to respect the principle of attribution of powers and could not expand the Community's competences beyond those identified by the Treaty; on the other hand, it could not concern areas which fell within the exclusive competence of the Community, nor citizenship of the Union. Within those confines, closer co-operation had to further the objectives and protect the interests of the Union, and to respect the principles and the single institutional framework of the Union. More specifically, closer co-operation could only be used as a last resort where the objectives of the Treaty could not be attained by ordinary procedures. In any case, closer co-operation could not affect the *acquis*

---

[45] On the transitional provisions applicable to the Member States which acceded to the Union in 2004, as contained in the Treaty of Accession 2003, see Adinolfi, "Free Movement and Access to Work of Citizens of the New Member States: The Transitional Measures" (2005) 42 C.M.L.Rev. 469.

[46] For a full analysis, see de Zwaan, "Opting Out and Opting In" (1998) 1 C.Y.E.L.S. 107.

[47] The TA made no provision for closer co-operation as regards the Second Pillar.

communautaire, nor Community policies, actions or programmes adopted under the Treaty. Finally, closer co-operation could neither discriminate between nationals of Member States, nor constitute a discrimination or restriction of intra-Community trade, nor distort conditions of competition between the Member States.

On the procedural front, any proposed closer co-operation had to concern at least a majority of the Member States. Those Member States had to submit a request to the Commission, which could decide whether to refer a proposal to the Council. If not, the Commission needed only to explain its reasons for this decision. If a proposal was made, the Council could authorise closer co-operation acting by qualified majority and after having consulted the European Parliament. However, the Treaty gave every Member State a right of veto over the initial authorisation of closer co-operation by the Council: it was possible for any country to oppose closer co-operation "for important and stated reasons of national policy". In that event, the Council could, acting by a qualified majority, refer the matter for a unanimous decision by the Council meeting in the composition of the Heads of State or Government. Once an action of closer co-operation had been established, measures were to be adopted according to the relevant procedures set out in the Treaties. However, whilst all members of the Council could take part in its deliberations relating to such matters, decisions would be taken according to a restricted formation, compromising only the representatives of the participating Member States.[48] For that purpose, the qualified majority threshold represented the proportion of the weighted votes of the participating Member States corresponding to the threshold fixed by Article 205(2) EC. Unanimity was constituted by the absence of negative votes only of those Member States.

Finally, the Amsterdam Treaty sought to regulate the relationship between participating and non-participating Member States. Where a closer co-operation was authorised, it could not affect the competences, rights, obligations and interests of non-participants. Conversely, non-participants could not impede the implementation of closer co-operation measures by participating Member States. In any case, closer co-operation had in principle to be open to all countries and allow them to become parties at any time (provided they complied with the basic authorising decision and any measures adopted under the closer co-operation action). Member States wishing to participate in a closer co-operation action had to notify their intention to the Council and Commission. The latter would give its opinion, on the basis of which the former would then reach a decision on admitting the newcomer, and on any specific arrangements for its participation. For these purposes, the Council was again to act in its restricted formation.

---

[48] Further: Dashwood, "Community Decision-Making After Amsterdam" (1998) 1 C.Y.E.L.S. 25.

4–027 (b) Enhanced co-operation under the Nice Treaty. The Treaty of Nice has now reformed the closer co-operation system, renaming it "enhanced co-operation": the complex and fragmented Amsterdam provisions have been simplified and reorganised; the possibility of entering into an enhanced co-operation action has been extended, albeit under limited circumstances, to the Second Pillar; and certain of the substantive and procedural hurdles applicable to enhanced co-operation under the First and Third Pillars have been relaxed. The general provisions are now contained in Title VII TEU; and the specifically First Pillar provisions in Articles 11 and 11a EC.[49]

Some of the Nice changes are largely hortatory: for example, enhanced co-operation must be aimed at reinforcing the process of European integration; the Council and Commission must ensure that activities undertaken on the basis of enhanced co-operation are consistent with each other and with the activities of the Union; the Commission and participating Member States must ensure that as many Member States as possible are encouraged to take part in the enhanced co-operation. More significantly, it is now provided that enhanced co-operation must respect the *acquis communautaire* (watering down the Amsterdam requirement that closer co-operation must not affect the *acquis communautaire*).[50] In similar vein, enhanced co-operation must not undermine the internal market or economic and social cohesion (replacing the Amsterdam provision whereby closer co-operation could not affect Community policies, actions or programmes in general). In particular, there is no longer any express prohibition against enhanced co-operation concerning Union citizenship; and the specific direction that enhanced co-operation should not discriminate between nationals of the Member States has likewise been suppressed.

Crucially for the Union's development post-enlargement into Central and Eastern Europe, enhanced co-operation need now involve a minimum of only eight Member States (and thus a potential minority in the expanded Union, whereas under Amsterdam closer co-operation had to concern at least a majority of Member States). Furthermore, enhanced co-operation will remain a last resort—but this is to be established within the Council, according to the criterion that the objectives of the proposed enhanced co-operation cannot be attained within a reasonable period by applying the relevant Treaty provisions. Another vital amendment applies to the procedure for authorising an enhanced co-operation under the First Pillar: the existing national veto held by every Member State

---

[49] For general comments, see e.g. St Bradley, "Institutional Design in the Treaty of Nice" (2001) 38 C.M.L.Rev. 1095; Stein, "The Treaty of Nice and Enlargement of the EU with Special Regard to Enhanced Co-operation" (2001) 25 *Polish Yearbook of International Law* 277.

[50] Similarly, enhanced co-operation must respect (rather than must not affect) the competences, rights and obligations of non-participating countries.

has been removed. Instead, any Member State objecting to a proposed enhanced co-operation might request that the matter be referred to the European Council—after which the Council can still reach its decision by qualified majority vote.[51] However, where a proposed enhanced co-operation under the First Pillar relates to an area subject to co-decision between Parliament and Council under Article 251 EC, the Council must obtain the assent of the Parliament before authorising the enhanced co-operation to proceed (whereas under the original Amsterdam provisions, the Parliament was merely consulted on all closer co-operation proposals). Finally, authorisation for a non-participating Member State to join an existing enhanced co-operation is to be granted by the Commission (whereas the original Amsterdam provisions reserved such decisions to Council).

The significance of secondary flexibility for the Community legal order
Despite the liberalisation of their substantive and procedural **4–028** conditions by the TN, at the time of writing, the provisions on enhanced co-operation had still not been used in practice.

One might point out that the Schengen Protocol presents itself as an instance of "applied" closer co-operation, as provided for pursuant to the TA,[52] but that seems misconceived. Such assimilation disguises the constitutional significance of the difference between primary and secondary flexibility. Nor can it be said that all the conditions for closer co-operation are fulfilled in the case of the Schengen Protocol. In particular, the requirement of a unanimous decision to admit Ireland or the United Kingdom to the whole, or any part, of the Schengen *acquis,* flouts the condition that a given co-operation must be open to all Member States and must allow all of them to become parties at any time. In contrast, unanimity is not required by Article 5 of the Schengen Protocol for participation by Ireland or the United Kingdom in measures that build upon the Schengen Protocol.

There is, though, a generally applicable lesson that can be learned from the experience of Schengen. It is that, if a sufficiently large group of Member States is determined to proceed with closer co-operation in a certain field, and cannot do so within the Union order, they will act outside it, storing up legal complexities for the future. Sensibly and sparingly used, the Amsterdam/Nice enhanced co-operation mechanism (where applicable) seems a better alternative.

---

[51] Note that the national veto remains, even after Nice, in respect of the new enhanced co-operation provisions applicable to the Second Pillar. Further, e.g. Dashwood, "The Constitution of the European Union After Nice: Law-Making Procedures" (2001) 26 E.L.Rev. 215.
[52] See Schengen Protocol, sixth recital and Arts 1 and 5(1), second sub-para.

This is not to say that enhanced co-operation is free of potential problems. After all, there is now the possibility that Member States will coalesce into shifting regulatory groupings, each legislating for wider and/or deeper integration on any given subject, but only for itself. Thus, the Community is faced with the prospect of social, consumer or environmental policies which no longer consist of a body of (more or less) common provisions applicable throughout all the Member States, subject of course to the requirement that the internal market must not be undermined. One can therefore envisage the emergence of ever more complex regulatory patterns: instruments applying throughout the whole Community lay down certain common standards, while additional layers of obligation are added by new measures, each embracing different combinations of Member States. Such a model may well respond to the political need to accommodate greater diversity within the enlarged Union, but would also have serious implications for many established assumptions within the Treaty order: for example, as regards the efficient functioning and democratic legitimacy of the Community's legislative process.[53]

However, it is also possible that the greatest significance of the enhanced co-operation provisions will not be formal, but indirect, i.e. concerning how the Community institutions and the Member States manage the Treaty's more traditional decision making processes. In particular, the existence of the enhanced co-operation mechanism may perhaps provide the impetus for compromise between conflicting national viewpoints, and therefore (paradoxically) the maintenance of a single Community-wide legislative programme: Member States unconvinced of the wisdom of a given initiative may be persuaded to join in nevertheless, rather than suffer the inconvenience of having to opt in at a later stage.[54]

Impact of the Constitutional Treaty (CT)
4-029   The CT contains significant reforms affecting the various topics covered in this chapter, including:

— formal identification of the generic categories of Union competence and a description of their impact upon Member State regulatory powers—based around the concepts of

[53] e.g. Edwards and Philippart, *Flexibility and the Treaty of Amsterdam: Europe's New Byzantium?*, C.E.L.S. Occasional Paper No.3 (CUP, 1997); J Shaw, "The Treaty of Amsterdam: Challenges of Flexibility and Legitimacy" (1998) 4 E.L.J. 63; Walker, "Sovereignty and Differentiated Integration in the European Union" (1998) 4 E.L.J. 355.
[54] e.g. Edwards and Philippart, *Flexibility and the Treaty of Amsterdam: Europe's New Byzantium?*, C.E.L.S. Occasional Paper No.3 (CUP, 1997); Wessels, "Flexibility, Differentiation and Closer Cooperation: The Amsterdam Provisions in the Light of the Tindemans Report" in Westlake (ed.), *The European Union Beyond Amsterdam: New Concepts of European Integration* (Routledge, 1998).

exclusive, shared and supporting/supplementary competences—which are then linked to individual legal bases for Union action (para.11–018);

— changes to the substantive and procedural requirements of the flexibility clause currently contained in Article 308 EC (para.11–018);

— a new monitoring system for the principle of subsidiarity, based on greater input by the national parliaments into the Union's legislative processes, including a "yellow card system" permitting formal objections on subsidiarity grounds (paras 11–019–020);

— standing for national parliaments to bring challenges to Union legislative acts before the Court of Justice, specifically on subsidiarity grounds (para. 11–029);

— minor modifications to the existing provisions on primary flexibility, but a major overhaul of the enhanced co-operation provisions (paras 11–021–022).

Further reading

de Búrca, "The Principle of Proportionality and its Application in EC law" (1993) 13 Y.E.L. 105.

de Búrca and Scott (eds), *Constitutional Change in the EU: From Uniformity to Flexibility?* (Hart Publishing, 2000).

Dashwood, "The Limits of European Community Powers" (1996) 21 E.L.Rev. 113.

Dashwood, "States in the European Union" (1998) 23 E.L.Rev. 201.

Davies, "Subsidiarity: the Wrong Idea, in the Wrong Place, at the Wrong Time" (2006) 43 C.M.L.Rev. 63.

Dougan, "Minimum Harmonisation and the Internal Market" (2000) 37 C.M.L.Rev. 853.

Edwards and Philippart, *Flexibility and the Treaty of Amsterdam: Europe's New Byzantium*, C.E.L.S. Occasional Paper No.3 (CUP, 1997).

Estella, *The EU Principle of Subsidiarity and its Critique* (OUP, 2002).

Gaja, "How Flexible is Flexibility Under the Amsterdam Treaty?" (1998) 35 C.M.L.Rev. 855.

Schutze, "Organised Change Towards an 'Ever Closer Union': Article 308 EC and the Limits to the Community's Legislative Competence" (2003) 22 Y.E.L. 79.

Shaw, "The Treaty of Amsterdam: Challenges of Flexibility and Legitimacy" (1998) 4 E.L.J. 63.

Slot, "Harmonisation" (1996) 21 E.L.Rev. 378.

Soares, "Pre-emption, Conflicts of Powers and Subsidiarity" (1998) 23 E.L.Rev. 132.

Toth, "Is Subsidiarity Justiciable?" (1994) 19 E.L.Rev. 268.

Von Bogandy and Bast, "The European Union's Vertical Order of Competences: The Current Law and Proposals For Its Reform" (2002) 39 C.M.L.Rev. 227.

Walker, "Sovereignty and Differentiated Integration in the European Union" (1998) 4 E.L.J. 355.

Weatherill, "Beyond Preemption? Shared Competence and Constitutional Change in the European Community" in O'Keeffe and Twomey (eds) *Legal Issues of the Maastricht Treaty* (Wiley, 1994).

Weatherill, "Better Competence Monitoring" (2005) 30 E.L.Rev. 23.

de Witte, Hank and Vos (eds), *The Many Faces of Differentiation in EU Law* (Intersentia, 2001).

PART III

CONSTITUTIONAL FOUNDATIONS

CHAPTER 5

SOURCES, SUPREMACY AND DIRECT EFFECT OF COMMUNITY LAW

Guide to this Chapter: Principal subject-matter of this chapter is **5–001** the relationship between Community law and the legal orders of the Member States. After noting certain definitional problems which arise in the case law and academic literature, and acknowledging the debt owed by Community law to public international law in this field, we embark upon a detailed analysis of two fundamental principles of Community constitutional law (both developed by the Court of Justice). The first is the principle of supremacy of Community over national law. According to the Court of Justice, supremacy demands that, in the event of a conflict between Community and domestic law, the former must prevail over and take effect in preference to the latter. However, the higher courts of several Member States (including the United Kingdom, Germany and France) have proved reluctant to recognise the unconditional supremacy of Community law within their own national constitutional systems—giving rise to certain conceptual tensions with the Court of Justice, though these have only rarely had any serious practical consequences for the enforcement of Community law within the Member States. The second fundamental principle is the direct effect of Community law provisions which are sufficiently clear, precise and unconditional to produce independent effects within the national legal orders; supplemented by the principle of consistent interpretation of national law with those Community provisions which are not of themselves capable of producing direct effect. The three primary types of Community measure—Treaty provisions, regulations and directives—are all apt to enjoy direct effect. However, the precise rules applicable to each type of measure differ. The most important and problematic issue is the potential for unimplemented directives to have "horizontal direct effect" in litigation between two private parties—a question rendered more complex by the apparently inconsistent and sometimes confusing case law of the Court of Justice. The chapter closes with a brief overview of the potential for international agreements entered into between the Community and third States or international organisations to have direct effect within the Community and national legal orders.

The sources of Community law

5–002   The title of this chapter refers to *Community law,* rather than *Union law,* and the reason for this is that the law capable of being invoked by individuals before the national courts of the Member States and the ECJ is predominantly that part of the law of the EU which comprises the law of the European Communities.[1] This follows in part from the subject-matter of EC law, which includes in particular the law of the single market, of social policy, and of competition policy. And it follows in part from the legal provisions which define the jurisdiction of the ECJ, the most significant of which are to be found in the Treaties establishing the European Communities.[2] The term European *Community* law is used here simply because it is more specific than the all-embracing term European *Union* law.

The sources of Community law are as follows:

— the Treaties establishing the three Communities, as supplemented and amended from time to time, and the secondary legislation made thereunder;
— related Treaties concluded between Member States;[3]
— international Agreements concluded between the Community and third countries;[4]
— measures emanating from bodies which have been established by an international agreement between the Community and third countries, and which have been entrusted with responsibility for its implementation;[5]

---

[1] Predominantly, but not entirely, as illustrated by the judgment in Case C–105/03 *Pupino* (Judgment of June 16, 2005) as regards judicial co-operation in criminal matters pursuant to the Third Pillar. See further Ch.10.

[2] Art.46 TEU indicates the limited extent to which the provisions of the EC Treaty concerning the jurisdiction of the Court of Justice apply to the TEU. See further Chs 10 and 14.

[3] International agreements which are not based on the Treaties establishing the Communities do not fall within the scope of Art.234 EC or Art.150 Euratom: see Case 44/84 *Hurd v Jones* [1986] E.C.R. 29, para.20.

[4] Appropriately worded provisions of such agreements may be invoked before the courts of Member States, e.g. Case 104/81 *Kupferberg* [1982] E.C.R. 3641. See further below.

[5] Case C–192/89 *Sevince* [1990] E.C.R. I–3461, para.10.

— international treaties binding upon all the Member States, where the responsibilities of the latter have been assumed by the Community;[6]

— decisions of the Member States having legal effect within the sphere of operation of the Treaties;[7]

— judgments of the Court of Justice and the Court of First Instance;[8]

— general principles of law, including respect for human rights and fundamental freedoms;[9]

— recommendations adopted on the basis of the EC Treaty inasmuch as they may cast light on the interpretation of national law or Community law,[10] and certain other non-binding acts (e.g. joint declarations of the Commission and Council recorded in the minutes of a session at which a Community act was adopted,[11] or recommendations of a Joint Committee entrusted with the administration and implementation of an international agreement between the Community and third countries[12]) which may similarly be held to cast light on the interpretation of national law or Community law.

For the purposes of simplicity, where consideration of the above mentioned sources requires reference to the Treaties and to the secondary legislation made thereunder, discussion will be limited to the legal effects of the Treaty establishing the European Community, and the secondary legislation—regulations, directives and decisions—made thereunder.

Legal effects of the Treaty and secondary legislation—in general

Member States are bound to carry out the obligations imposed by the EC Treaty and secondary legislation made thereunder. Breach of these obligations may give rise to an action before the Court of **5–003**

---

[6] Cases 21–24/72 *International Fruit* [1972] E.C.R. 1219.

[7] e.g. the "acceleration" decisions of May 12, [1960] O.J. 1960 1217; and May 15, [1962] O.J. 1284. See Case 22/70 *ERTA* [1971] E.C.R. 263.

[8] Decisions of the Court under Art.234 EC are binding on the referring court: see Case 29/68 *Milchkontor* [1969] E.C.R. 165; Case 52/76 *Benedetti* [1977] E.C.R. 163. *Stare decisis* applies in the United Kingdom as regards both the ECJ and the CFI by virtue of s.3(1) of the European Communities Act 1972. A ruling of the Court under Art.234 EC on the invalidity of a Community act is binding *erga omnes*: see Case 66/80 *International Chemical Corporation* [1981] E.C.R. 1191. Prior decisions of the Court of Justice may extinguish the duty to refer under Art.234(3): see Case 283/81 *CILFIT* [1982] E.C.R. 3415. See further Ch.14.

[9] See Chs 7 and 8.

[10] Case 113/75 *Frecassetti* [1976] E.C.R. 983; Case 90/76 *Van Ameyde* [1977] E.C.R. 1091; Case C–322/88 *Grimaldi* [1989] E.C.R. 4407.

[11] Case C–310/90 *Nationale Raad van de Orde van Architecten v Ulrich Egle* [1992] E.C.R. I–177. But see Case C–292/89 *Antonissen* [1991] E.C.R. I–773.

[12] Case C–188/91 *Deutsche Shell AG v Hauptzollamt Hamburg-Harburg* [1993] E.C.R. I–363.

Justice at the suit of either the Commission, or another Member State.[13]

The legal impact of Community law in the Member States, however, springs from its capacity, indeed its tendency, to give rise to rights in individuals which national courts are bound to safeguard. From the outset, though, it is appropriate to identify two definitional problems which complicate this field.

The first concerns the rather confusing terminology which describes provisions of Community law as being either "directly applicable" or "directly effective". The latter expression describes a provision which is clear and unconditional and bestows a legal right on a natural or legal person, exercisable against another natural legal person, or against the authorities of a Member State. Establishing direct effect is a matter of interpretation, and it is clear that specific provisions of the Treaty, as well as specific provisions of regulations, directives or decisions, may be endowed with this quality. It has been argued that direct effect, in the sense of practical operation for all concerned, is to be presumed unless established to the contrary.[14] Direct applicability, on the other hand, is that attribute of a regulation which ensures its access, in its entirety, to the national legal order, without the need for specific incorporation.[15] Reproduction of the text of a regulation in the text of national legislation is not only unnecessary, but in principle impermissible.

A degree of terminological confusion could be said to arise because the expressions "directly applicable" and "directly effective" are sometimes used interchangeably, even by the Court.[16] While specific provisions of the Treaty, and of directives and decisions, may be directly effective, these instruments as a whole are not "directly applicable" in the same sense as regulations are described as being "directly applicable" by the Treaty. That said, it would be pedantic to do more than note the point, and no misunderstanding is in practice likely to arise, since the context will invariably make clear what is meant.

5–004   The second definitional problem concerns the precise meaning of the concept of "direct effect" itself. Throughout much of the case law and scholarly discourse, the tendency of a provision of Community law to have direct effect has been equated with the creation of an individual right enforceable before the national courts by its intended beneficiary (or any member of the intended class of beneficiaries). Thus, for example, the direct effect of Article 28 EC

---

[13] Arts 226 and 227 EC. See further Ch.13.

[14] Pescatore, "The Doctrine of 'Direct Effect': An Infant Disease of Community Law" (1983) 8 E.L.Rev. 155.

[15] Art.249(2) EC: "A regulation . . . shall be directly applicable and binding in its entirety".

[16] See the ruling in Case 2/74 *Reyners* [1974] E.C.R. 631, to the effect that Art.43 EC is directly applicable. In similar vein, see Case 17/81 *Pabst* [1982] E.C.R. 1331; Case 104/81 *Kupferberg* [1982] E.C.R. 3641.

on the free movement of goods necessarily implies an individual right for traders not to burdened by unjustified hindrances to cross border trade, and the ability of such traders to challenge national measures infringing that right before the domestic courts.[17] Similarly, the direct effect of Article 39 EC on the free movement of workers necessarily implies an individual right for migrant Union citizens not to be discriminated against on grounds of nationality as regards their terms and conditions of employment, and the ability of such workers to challenge public or private measures infringing that right before the national courts.[18]

However, certain rulings suggest that the Court's understanding of direct effect—or at least, of the capacity of Community law to produce independent effects within the national legal systems— stretches beyond the creation of individual rights to embrace also the protection of some diffuse public interest. In such cases, it might appear that the claimant is vested not with any subjective personal right, but rather, with a right of standing to invoke the relevant provisions of Community law before the national courts. Consider, for example, the Member State's obligation to carry out environmental impact assessments under Directive 85/337.[19] The Court held in judgments such as *Kraaijeveld* that, where the Community has imposed on Member States the obligation to pursue such a course of conduct, the useful effect of that directive would be weakened if individuals were prevented from relying on it before their national courts, and if the latter were prevented from taking it into consideration as an element of Community law in order to rule whether the national legislature had kept within the limits of its discretion. That case concerned an action brought by a local business challenging the legality of the decision of a Dutch local authority to approve dyke reinforcement works.[20] Both the nature of the Member State's obligation, and the economic motivation of the claimant, make it difficult to describe this as an example of direct effect understood in its narrow sense as the creation and enforcement of a personalised individual right. It is surely more natural in such situations to speak of direct effect in a broader sense of conferring rights of standing upon individuals to invoke provisions of Community law which seek to protect the general interest.[21]

However, any such dividing line, within the concept of direct effect, between the narrow sense of creating individual rights, and a

---

[17] See Ch.16.
[18] See Ch.18.
[19] Dir.85/337 on the assessment of the effects of certain public and private projects on the environment [1985] O.J. L175/40.
[20] Case C–72/95 *Kraaijeveld* [1996] E.C.R. I–5403. Similarly, e.g. Case C–435/97 *World Wildlife Fund* [1999] E.C.R. I–5613; Case C–287/98 *Linster* [2000] E.C.R. I–6917.
[21] See further, e.g. Prechal and Hancher, "Individual Environmental Rights: Conceptual Pollution in EU Environmental Law?" (2001) 2 Y.E.E.L. 89.

broader understanding which embraces also the mere invocability of Community law, is not necessarily easy to maintain. After all, the Court of Justice, in the subsequent case of *Wells*, suggested that individuals whose interests are adversely affected by the Member State's failure to carry out an environmental impact assessment under Directive 85/337 must be entitled to seek damages before the national courts in respect of their losses—a remedy which is more usually associated with the vindication of personal rights than with protection of the public interest.[22] The difficulty is also well illustrated by the judgment in *Muñoz*. The claimant alleged that a rival undertaking was selling grapes in the United Kingdom in breach of certain Community regulations on quality standards for fruit and vegetables. Under English law, enforcement of those regulations was reserved exclusively to a public authority, which refused to exercise its monopoly powers in this particular dispute. The claimant therefore initiated its own proceedings before the domestic courts, arguing that the Community regulations were directly effective and could be enforced not only by the competent public authorities but also by interested individuals. The Court held that the purpose of the regulations was to keep unsatisfactory products off the market, for the protection of both consumers and rival undertakings. The full effectiveness of those quality standards implied that it must be possible to enforce obligations contained in the regulations by means of civil proceedings brought against a trader by one of its competitors—thus supplementing enforcement by the Member State itself.[23] Was *Muñoz* merely a case of recognising the claimant's right of standing to invoke the regulations before the national courts, to enhance their enforcement in the general interest? Or, by conferring direct effect upon those regulations, did the Court of Justice actually create an individual right to fair competitive conditions vested in the class of economic rivals (and, by implication, to some form of compensatory remedy in respect of any losses which may have been incurred)?

5–005   Similar definitional problems within the concept of "direct effect" arise when one considers those Community provisions which do not (in any meaningful sense) bestow rights, or impose obligations, on individuals, or public authorities; but instead authorise public authorities to take action which they would not otherwise be authorised to take. Again, it appears difficult to describe such provisions as "directly effective" in any narrow sense; but they may nevertheless be susceptible to direct application in national courts. It

---

[22] Case C–201/02 *Wells* [2004] E.C.R. I–723.

[23] Case C–253/00 *Muñoz* [2002] E.C.R. I–7289. See further Ward, "Judicial Review of Environmental Misconduct in the European Community: Problems, Prospects and Strategies" (2000) 1 Y.E.E.L. 137; Dougan, *National Remedies Before the Court of Justice* (Hart Publishing, 2004) Ch.1.

may be recalled that the Advocate General in *van Gend en Loos* referred to Treaty provisions being "clearly intended to be incorporated into national law and to modify or supplement it",[24] and this approach is echoed in the words of the Court of Justice in *Costa v ENEL* to the effect that the "EEC Treaty has created its own legal system which, on the entry into force of the Treaty, became an integral part of the legal systems of the Member States and which their courts are bound to apply".[25] Consider, for example, Article 234 EC directly bestowing upon national courts the competence to refer questions to the Court of Justice for a preliminary ruling. National rules may establish the relevant details of procedure,[26] but they neither create, nor may they condition, the capacity to make the reference. Article 234 EC is not directly effective in the sense of giving rise to rights in individuals which national courts are bound to safeguard;[27] but it is nevertheless directly effective in the sense that it has direct application within the national legal order.

The same point may be made concerning *principles* derived from the Treaty which have legal effects as regards the application of national law by national courts, without those principles comprising rights in themselves which can be invoked by individuals. The extent to which national courts are under a duty to interpret national rules as far as possible in accordance with Treaty provisions will be examined later in this chapter. There is no doubt that national courts are under a duty to interpret national rules in accordance with the provisions of the EC Treaty, and of directives if it is possible for them to do so, even if those provisions are not themselves directly effective (e.g.) because they are not sufficiently clear, precise or unconditional.[28] Certain non-binding acts may also be held to cast light on the interpretation of national law or Community law. The responsibility of national courts and tribunals to respect such principles in the exercise of their responsibilities under national law cannot on the face of it be attributed solely or even mainly to the direct effect of the applicable substantive provisions of the Treaty or secondary legislation. According to the Court of Justice, the duty of consistent interpretation is derived rather from the general obligation in Article 10 EC "to ensure fulfillment of the obligations" arising out of the Treaty.[29] More recent cases go even further, stating that the duty of consistent interpretation must be considered, more

---

[24] [1963] E.C.R. 1, 20.
[25] [1964] E.C.R. 585, 593; and see Case 17/67 *Neumann* [1967] E.C.R. 441, 453.
[26] Consider, e.g. Case C–472/99 *Clean Car Autoservice* [2001] E.C.R. I–9687.
[27] Apart, perhaps, in circumstances where the third paragraph of Art.234 EC imposes a duty on national courts to make a reference.
[28] e.g. Case C–54/96 *Dorsch Consult* [1997] E.C.R. I–4961.
[29] e.g. Case 14/83 *Von Colson* [1984] E.C.R. 1891; Case C–106/89 *Marleasing* [1990] E.C.R. I–4135.

fundamentally, to be "inherent in the system of the Treaty".[30] In either case, this is another illustration of a provision or principle of Community law which is directly effective—but not in the sense of creating rights for individuals (whether to a personal benefit, or of standing and invocability).[31]

Nature of the Community legal order

5-006   The European Community is a developed form of international organisation which displays characteristics of an embryonic federation. Analysis of the nature of the Community legal system is of intrinsic interest, and may facilitate the solution of practical problems. The debt owed by Community law to public international law is considerable, and usually understated.[32] Underpinning the Community legal system are the doctrines of (i) direct applicability/direct effect, and (ii) the supremacy of Community law. Both doctrines are derived from international law.[33] Equally, however, the relationship between Community law and national law clearly lends itself to comparison with the relationship between State and federal law in a federal system. In the *Simmenthal* case, the Court of Justice held that Community law was competent to "preclude the valid adoption"[34] of inconsistent national legislation. This is a controversial formulation, and seems to equate the relationship between Community law and national law to a constitutional relationship, thereby distancing Community law from international law, which does not determine the validity of provisions of national law. As an eminent international lawyer has put it: "International tribunals cannot declare the internal invalidity of rules of national law since the international legal order must respect the reserved domain of domestic jurisdiction".[35] In the *IN.CO.GE.'90 Srl* case,[36] however, the Court of Justice qualifies the *Simmenthal* formulation to the effect that Community law precludes the "valid adoption" of subsequent inconsistent national legislation. While a national court faced with a conflict between Community law and a provision of subsequently adopted national legislation is obliged to "disapply" the

---

[30] e.g. Case C–160/01 *Mau* [2003] E.C.R. I–4791, para.34; Cases C–397/01 to C–403/01 *Pfeiffer* [2004] E.C.R. I–8835, para.114.

[31] Especially where the duty of consistent interpretation works against the individual, within the context of litigation against the defaulting Member State: see further below.

[32] Wyatt, "New Legal Order or Old?" (1982) 7 E.L.Rev. 147; De Witte, "Retour a 'Costa': La primauté du droit communautaire a la lumière du droit international" (1984) 20 R.T.D.E. 425.

[33] For direct applicability, see *Jurisdiction of the Courts of Danzig* (1928) P.C.I.J. Ser. B, No.15. For the principle that treaty obligations take priority over national law, see Vienna Convention on the Law of Treaties, Art.27; *Treatment of Polish Nationals in Danzig* (1932) P.C.I.J. Rep. Ser. A/B, No.44, p.24.

[34] Case 106/77 [1978] E.C.R. 629, 643.

[35] Brownlie, *Principles of Public International Law* (5th ed., Clarendon Press, 1998), p.40, citing *Interpretation of the Statute of the Memel Territory* P.C.I.J. Ser. A/B, No.49, p.236.

[36] Joined Cases C–10/97–22/97 [1998] E.C.R. I–6307.

incompatible provision of national law, it cannot "be inferred from the judgment in *Simmenthal* that the incompatibility with Community law of a subsequently adopted rule of national law has the effect of rendering that rule of national law non-existent".[37]

The European Court has contrasted the EEC Treaty with "ordinary international treaties",[38] and even before the establishment of the EEC, Advocate General Lagrange, in the *Fedechar* case,[39] involving the Coal and Steel Community Treaty, had floated the argument that the Court of Justice was not "an international court but the court of a Community created by six States as a model which is more closely related to a federal than to an international organisation", though he then dismissed the international court versus federal court argument as an "academic discussion". The Court of Justice referred in the event to a "rule of interpretation generally accepted in both international and national law".[40] More significantly, in *Commission v Luxembourg and Belgium*,[41] the Court rejected an argument based on international law that a default by the Commission in its obligations to a Member State had the effect of suspending the reciprocal obligations of the latter.[42] The Court has subsequently rejected the proposition that a default by one Member State suspends the reciprocal obligations of other Member States.[43] Yet this conclusion is perfectly consistent with the public international law basis of the Community legal system; the International Court of Justice has similarly held that the regime established by the Vienna Convention on Diplomatic Relations, which provides "the necessary means of defence against, and sanction for, illicit activities by members of diplomatic missions" excludes measures of self-help in the event of alleged illicit activities by such persons.[44] The principle affirmed by the International Court of Justice is that the provision of procedures capable of providing a remedy for the breach of an international obligation may be held to oust the customary law right of self-help.

---

[37] *ibid.*, para.21.
[38] Case 6/64 *Costa v ENEL* [1964] E.C.R. 585.
[39] Case 8/55 [1954–56] E.C.R. 245.
[40] [1954–6] E.C.R. 292, 299. For consideration of internationalist, federalist, and functionalist theories of the Community legal order, see Dagtoglou, "The legal nature of the European Community" in *Thirty Years of Community Law* (EC Publication, 1983).
[41] Cases 90 and 91/63 [1964] E.C.R. 625.
[42] For the doctrine in international law, see *Tacna-Arica Arbitration* 2 RIAA 921 (1925); *US-France Air Services Arbitration* 54 I.L.R. 303; Vienna Convention on the Law of Treaties, Art.60.
[43] Case 232/78 *Commission v France* [1979] E.C.R. 2729, para.9; also Case C–5/94 *Hedley Lomas* [1996] E.C.R. I–2553, para.20; Case 14/96 *Paul Denuit* [1997] E.C.R. I–2785.
[44] *US v Iran (Hostages)* (1980) I.C.J. Rep, p.3, paras 83–90. The Court acknowledges that brief arrest or detention of a diplomat caught committing an offence would be permissible: see para.87.

5–007   The truth is that there are certain legal characteristics of the
Community legal order which may be encountered both in international organisations established by "ordinary" international
treaties, and in federal systems. Thus, the principles of direct
applicability/direct effect, the supremacy of Community law, and the
predominance of judicial remedies over self-help—all of which are
features of the Community system—support analysis of the Community both as a highly developed order of public international law,
and as an incipient federal constitutional system. Perhaps the
Community at its present stage should be seen in this light. But the
"federalism" of the Community system must at the present time be
qualified as incipient, or undeveloped. A federal State is normally
characterised, *inter alia*, by the central government's legal monopoly
over foreign relations. In the Community, there is no real equivalent
of the "central government", and the Commission and Council
certainly enjoy no such monopoly, though the Community enjoys
substantial competence in the field of external relations. The Community is based upon international treaties concluded between
States, and the efficacy of Community law is, in some Member
States, still dependent upon its status as international law. In a
federal system, State courts resolve conflicts exclusively upon the
basis of federal supremacy rules. In the Community, national courts
resolve conflicts between national law and Community law upon the
basis both of national law and of Community law. Community law is
thus applied to the extent that it has been incorporated into national
law in accordance with national constitutional requirements. Nevertheless, it has been said with some force that the European Court
"has sought to 'constitutionalise' the Treaty, that is to fashion a
constitutional framework for a federal type structure in Europe".[45]
Consistently with this approach, the Court itself has said that: "The
EEC Treaty, albeit concluded in the form of an international
agreement, none the less constitutes the constitutional charter of a
Community based on the rule of law".[46] It is unexciting but accurate
to conclude that the Community and Union comprise a hybrid, and
as such different elements in this unique institutional and legal order
can be expected to reflect different traditions and inspirations.
Citizenship of the Union, comprising a bundle of rights exercisable
by all those holding the nationality of a Member State, clearly draws
its inspiration from the federal ideal.[47] By way of contrast, the
provisions in the Treaty on European Union, and the EC Treaty, for
the suspension of the rights of a Member State, including its voting

---

[45] Mancini, "The Making of a Constitution for Europe" (1989) 26 C.M.L.Rev. 595, 596. See
also Lenaerts, "Fundamental Rights to be included in a Community Catalogue" (1991) 16
E.L.Rev. 367.
[46] Opinion 1/91 *Draft Agreement between EEC and EFTA* [1991] E.C.R. I–6079, para.21.
[47] Arts 17–22 EC. See further Ch.17.

rights in the Council, if it is found to be guilty of a serious and persistent breach of such fundamental principles as respect for human rights and the rule of law,[48] are reminiscent of provisions to be found in the charters of international organisations for the suspension or expulsion of recalcitrant members.[49] Even participation in European Monetary Union (which is almost certainly the most federalising aspect of EU to date) is subject to conditions, which must be satisfied by Member States prior to entry, while some Member States remain undecided as to the desirability of joining.

The supremacy of Community law

International law by its nature binds the State in its executive, **5–008** legislative and judicial activities, and no international tribunal would permit a respondent State to plead provisions of its law or constitution as a defence to an alleged infringement of an international obligation.[50] The same is true of EC law, "over which no appeal to provisions of internal law of any kind whatever can prevail",[51] and the Court of Justice has always declined to accept a plea of *force majeure* where a Member State has attempted to comply with Community obligations, but failed as a result of delays in the legislative process. The Court's judgment in *Commission v Belgium* is illustrative.[52] Belgian indirect taxation of home grown and imported timber discriminated against the latter, contrary to Article 90 EC. In its defence to an action by the Commission under Article 226 EC, the Belgian Government argued that it had introduced draft legislation to the Chamber of Representatives two years previously, to remedy the situation, but that it had yet to be passed. It pointed out that, under the principle of the separation of powers prevailing in Belgium, it could do no more. The Court was unmoved. "The obligations arising from Article [90] of the Treaty", it observed, "devolve upon States as such and the liability of a Member State under Article [226] arises whatever the agency of the State whose action or inaction is the cause of the failure to fulfil its obligations, even in the case of a constitutionally independent institution".[53] Similarly, the Court has consistently held that a Member State may not plead provisions, practices or circumstances existing in its internal legal order to justify a failure to comply with the obligations and time-limits laid down in a directive.[54]

---

[48] Art.7 TEU; Art.309 EC. See further Ch.10.
[49] See e.g. Arts 5 and 6 of the UN Charter.
[50] *Treatment of Polish Nationals in Danzig* (1932) P.C.I.J. Rep, Ser. A/B, No.44, p.24. Vienna Convention on the Law of Treaties 1969, Art.27.
[51] Case 48/71 *Commission v Italy* [1972] E.C.R. 527, 535.
[52] Case 77/69 [1970] E.C.R. 237. The Court has taken the same position in a consistent line of cases, see e.g. Case 254/83 *Commission v Italy* [1984] E.C.R. 3395.
[53] Case 77/69 [1970] E.C.R. 237, para.15.
[54] See e.g. Case C–303/92 *Commission v Netherlands* [1993] E.C.R. I–4739, para.9; Case C–298/97 *Commission v Spain* [1998] E.C.R. I–3301, para.14.

The duty of Member States to take all appropriate measures to ensure the fulfilment of obligations arising under the Treaty or secondary legislation is laid down explicitly in Article 10 EC, and this duty devolves directly upon national courts where directly effective provisions of Community law are involved.[55] This factor was emphasised in *Costa v ENEL*,[56] in which it was argued that the Court's ruling would be irrelevant to the outcome of the national proceedings, since the national tribunal which had made the reference would be bound to apply national law in any event. The Court responded with an analysis of the Community legal system, and an affirmation of its supremacy over national law:

> "By contrast with ordinary international treaties, the EEC Treaty has created its own legal system which, on the entry into force of the Treaty, became an integral part of the legal systems of the Member States and which their courts are bound to apply.
>   By creating a Community of unlimited duration, having . . . powers stemming from a limitation of sovereignty, or a transfer of powers from the States to the Community, the Member States have limited their sovereign rights, albeit within limited fields, and have thus created a body of law which binds both their nationals and themselves."[57]

As the Court acknowledged in *Costa*, the supremacy of Community regulations is implicit in the legal characteristics attributed to them in Article 249 EC.[58] Not only does direct applicability require their access to the national legal order without the favour of specific incorporation, but they have the capacity to create a legal regime whose rules and aims national legislation is bound to respect.[59] Their very nature precludes their modification by inconsistent measures of national law.

5–009   That the duty of national courts to give precedence to Community law over national law extends to national legislation adopted after the incorporation of the relevant Community rules into the national legal order was made clear in *Simmenthal*:

> "Furthermore, in accordance with the principle of the precedence of Community law, the relationship between provisions of the Treaty and directly applicable measures of the institution

---

[55] See e.g. Case 45/76 *Comet* [1976] E.C.R. 2043, para.12.
[56] Case 6/64 [1964] E.C.R. 585. And see Case 17/67 *Neumann* [1967] E.C.R. 441, 453.
[57] Case 6/64 [1964] E.C.R. 585, 593.
[58] "The precedence of Community law is confirmed by Article [249 EC], whereby a regulation 'shall be binding' and 'directly applicable in all Member States' ": Case 6/64 [1964] E.C.R. 585, 594.
[59] See further, below.

on the one hand and the national law of the Member States on the other is such that those provisions and measures not only by their entry into force render automatically inapplicable any conflicting provision of current national law but—in so far as they are integral part of, and take precedence in, the legal order applicable in the territory of each of the Member States—also preclude the valid adoption of new national measures to the extent to which they would be incompatible with Community provisions . . . It follows from the foregoing that every national court must, in a case within its jurisdiction, apply Community law in its entirety and protect rights which the latter confers on individuals and must accordingly set aside any provision of national law which may conflict with it, whether prior or subsequent to the Community rule."[60]

In *IN.CO.GE.Srl*,[61] the Commission relied upon the above passage to argue that a Member State had no power whatsoever to adopt a fiscal provision that is incompatible with Community law, with the result that such a provision and the corresponding fiscal obligation must be treated as non-existent. But the Court rejected this argument, saying:

"In *Simmenthal*, the issue facing the Court related in particular to the consequences of the direct applicability of a provision of Community law where that provision was incompatible with a subsequently adopted provision of national law . . . It cannot . . . be inferred from the judgment in *Simmenthal* that the incompatibility with Community law of a subsequently adopted rule of national law has the effect of rendering that rule of national law non-existent. Faced with such a situation, the national court is, however, obliged to disapply that rule, provided always that this obligation does not restrict the power of the competent national courts to apply, from among the various procedures available under national law, those which are appropriate for protecting the individual rights conferred by Community law . . ."[62]

This distinction between the disapplication of incompatible national rules, and their nullity within the domestic legal order, leads us to consider certain other limitations to the practical effect of the principle of supremacy. Such limitations derive from two very different sources: Community law itself; and the constitutional framework of individual Member States.

---

[60] Case 106/77 [1978] E.C.R. 629, 643–644.
[61] Cases C–10/97 to C–22/97 [1998] E.C.R. I–6907.
[62] *ibid.*, paras 20–21.

5–010   Dealing first with Community law itself, it is clear from the Court's case law that the principle of supremacy is not totally unconditional. In certain situations, the imperative of disapplying national rules which are incompatible with provisions of Community law must be balanced against other equally fundamental principles of the Treaty system, such as the need for legal certainty and the protection of legitimate expectations. For example, *Kühne and Heitz* raised the question under which circumstances the principle of supremacy might require national authorities to reopen decisions which have become final following an unsuccessful challenge before the domestic courts, where it becomes apparent from a subsequent judgment of the Court of Justice that those decisions were based on a misinterpretation of Community law. It was held that legal certainty is one of the general principles of Community law, and implies that administrative bodies should not be required, in principle, to reopen a decision which has become final upon the expiry of reasonable limitation periods or the exhaustion of available legal remedies—even if that decision is incompatible with certain provisions of Community law. However, in the special circumstances of the case (where the national court of last instance had refused to make a reference to the ECJ under Article 234 EC, the claimants had complained to the Dutch authorities as soon as they became aware of the subsequent ECJ judgment, and Dutch law gave administrative bodies the power to reopen final decisions), Community law could also require the national authorities to revisit their apparently final decision.[63]

The important point is that, in cases such as *Kühne and Heitz*, Community law itself determines the scope and limits of the principle of supremacy—by examining the role of that principle relative to other basic tenets of the Community legal order. By contrast, it is in principle impermissible for national courts or tribunals to condition the supremacy of Community provisions unilaterally upon the requirements of domestic law (however fundamental).[64] Yet this brings us precisely to our second type of limitation on the principle of supremacy: however well established in the jurisprudence of the Court of Justice, supremacy may well be denied its full practical effect by national courts, which sometimes feel constrained to temper the rigour of the Treaty's requirements. In such situations, discharge of the national courts' primary responsibility—to maintain the integrity of their own domestic legal order—may lead them to defy their Treaty obligation to ensure the supremacy of Community law.

---

[63] Case C–453/00 *Kühne & Heitz* [2004] E.C.R. I–837. *cf.* Case C–234/04 *Kapferer v Schlank & Schick* (Opinion of November 10, 2005; Judgment pending). Consider also, e.g. Case C–108/01 *Asda Stores* [2003] E.C.R. I–5121; and the case law on national limitation periods (such as Case C–188/95 *Fantask* [1997] E.C.R. I–6783) discussed in detail in Ch.6.

[64] e.g. Case 11/70 *Internationale Handelsgesellschaft* [1970] E.C.R. 1125.

This potential conflict may be illustrated by the position of the **5–011** courts in the United Kingdom. Section 2 of the European Communities Act 1972 provides for the recognition of all directly enforceable Community law, and its application in preference to any Act of Parliament "passed or to be passed". This was a clear attempt to give legislative force, within the United Kingdom, to the principle of supremacy. However, this attempt appeared to clash with certain fundamental principles of British constitutional law: the sovereignty of the institution of Parliament, which prevents any given Parliament from curtailing the fullest legislative prerogatives of any subsequent Parliament; and implies that any measure passed after 1972 which conflicts with the requirements of Community law should have the effect of repealing the European Communities Act.[65] Under traditional constitutional doctrine, the latest expression of Parliamentary will must prevail—yet that risked bringing the United Kingdom into semi-perpetual breach of the principle of supremacy under Community law. The House of Lords resolved this dilemma in the *Factortame* and *Equal Opportunities Commission* litigation through the fiction of the "implied supremacy clause": every Act of Parliament passed since 1972 is deemed to incorporate a section to the effect that its provisions are without prejudice to any directly effective requirements of Community law.[66] By this expedient, the House of Lords reached a compromise whereby, for most practical purposes, the principle of supremacy will be respected and enforced by the English courts; but its justification under British constitutional law remains the sovereignty of Parliament, as expressed in 1972 Act with sufficient force as to abrogate the normal doctrine of implied repeal in respect of that particular legislation.[67] However, this compromise logically requires that, if Parliament were *expressly* to derogate from section 2 of the European Communities Act 1972, the English courts would be obliged be give effect to that subsequent provision of national law, rather than enforce the unconditional supremacy of Community law.[68]

This conflict between supremacy as conceived by the Court of Justice (on the one hand) and its reception into the national constitutional environment (on the other hand) is even better

---

[65] cf. *Madzimbamuto v Lardner-Burke* [1969] 1 A.C. 645.

[66] *R v Secretary of State for Transport, ex parte Factortame (No.2)* [1990] 3 W.L.R. 818; and *R v Secretary of State for Employment, ex parte Equal Opportunities Commission* [1995] 1 A.C. 1.

[67] For a view on the constitutional implications of these cases, see Craig, "Supremacy of the United Kingdom Parliament after Factortame" (1991) 11 Y.E.L. 221.

[68] cf. Lord Denning in *Macarthys Ltd v Smith* [1979] 3 All E.R. 325. For more recent judicial discussion on the relationship between supremacy, Parliamentary sovereignty and the common law: *Thoburn v Sunderland City Council* [2002] 4 All E.R. 156; *Gouriet v Secretary of State for Foreign and Commonwealth Affairs* (Court of Appeal Judgment of March 5, 2003).

illustrated by the German experience.[69] Prompted by concerns about
the level of fundamental rights protection guaranteed within the
Community legal system against acts adopted pursuant to the
Treaties, the Federal Constitutional Court in its so-called *Solange I*
judgment of 1974 suggested that, in the event of a conflict between
Community law and the basic rights contained in the German
Constitution, the latter would prevail.[70] However, in the light of the
evolution of the Court of Justice's case law on fundamental freedoms as general principles of Community law and the affirmation by
the Community institutions of the importance of human rights
within the Treaty system, the Federal Constitutional Court moder-
ated its position in the so-called *Solange II* ruling: so long as the
Community generally ensures an effective protection of fundamental
rights, substantially similar to the level guaranteed under German
law, the national courts should refrain from exercising their jurisdiction to review the legality of Community acts according to the
German Constitution.[71] However, views appeared to harden again
when the Federal Constitutional Court was called upon to assess the
constitutional legality of German ratification of the Treaty on
European Union. The famous *Brunner* judgment affirmed that the
supremacy of Community law within the German legal system is not
unconditional. In particular, the Federal Constitutional Court
asserted its ultimate jurisdiction to police the compatibility of
Community measures with the German Constitution, not only as
regards the protection of fundamental rights, but also as concerns
the principle that the Union enjoys merely attributed and limited
competences.[72] This judgment was followed by one of the most
dramatic illustrations of how national attitudes can determine the
practical effectiveness of the principle of supremacy. The "Bananas
litigation" concerned a Community regulation establishing a common organisation of the market in bananas, the legality of which
under both Community law and the GATT was challenged and
upheld before the Court of Justice. Disgruntled German banana
importers, however, continued their battle before the national
tribunals—leading to a series of rulings in which the German
administrative and tax courts, relying on the *Brunner* judgment,
declared the Community regulations unlawful and thus inapplicable
within the domestic territory. The crisis culminated in the *Bananas*
judgment of the Federal Constitutional Court in 2000, in which that

---

[69] See further, e.g. Herdegen, "Maastricht and the German Constitutional Court: Constitutional Restraints for an 'Ever Closer Union' " (1994) 31 C.M.L.Rev. 235; Everling, "Will
Europe Slip on Bananas? The Bananas Judgment of the Court of Justice and National
Courts" (1996) 33 C.M.L.Rev. 401; Schmid, "All Bark and No Bite: Notes on the Federal
Constitutional Court's Bananas Decision" (2001) 7 E.L.J. 95.
[70] [1974] 2 C.M.L.R. 540.
[71] [1987] 3 C.M.L.R. 225.
[72] [1994] 1 C.M.L.R. 57.

institution ultimately refused to exercise its reserved jurisdiction to review the legality of the relevant measures of Community secondary law: given that the general level of fundamental rights protection under the Treaties remains substantially similar to that guaranteed under the German constitution, the conditions for recognising the principle of supremacy as established in *Solange II* and *Brunner* had been respected.[73]

The judicial authorities of many other Member States have 5–012 encountered similar difficulties incorporating the principle of supremacy into their own national legal systems—though the basic position is more or less the same as in the United Kingdom and Germany, i.e. that the principle of supremacy is recognised and enforced in everyday practice, even if not as securely embedded in constitutional theory as the Court of Justice might demand.[74] A good recent example comes from the French *Conseil constitutionnel*, in a series of decisions delivered in 2004 concerning the compatibility with the French Constitution of national legislation intended to implement certain Community directives.[75] It was held that the jurisdiction of the *Conseil constitutionnel* to carry out judicial review was limited to examining whether there is a contradiction between domestic legislation adopted so as to implement a Community directive (which in fact represents a constitutional obligation) and an express provision of the French Constitution; but in the absence of such a conflict, the jurisdiction to determine whether the relevant directive complies with both respect for fundamental rights and the principle of attributed powers lies with the Court of Justice alone. One assumes that the *Conseil constitutionnel* does not intend to judicially review the compatibility of Community legislation with the express provisions contained in the French Constitution (e.g., on fundamental rights) where these are substantially equivalent to the general principles of Community law safeguarded by the Court of Justice itself. If so, that would bring the French position on supremacy close to that of the German Federal Constitutional Court.[76]

Academic views differ on the seriousness of such difficulties surrounding the reception of the principle of supremacy into national law. On the one hand, many commentators view the supremacy debate as a process of constructive dialogue between the Community and national judges about the Union's evolving legal order—reminding the Court of Justice of the importance of protecting fundamental rights against potential infringements by the Union

---

[73] (2000) 21 H.R.L.J. 251.
[74] For extensive analysis and discussion: Alter, *Establishing the Supremacy of European Law* (OUP, 2001).
[75] See, e.g. Decision No.2004–496 (June 10, 2004); Decision No.2004–497 (July 1, 2004).
[76] Further: Dutheil de la Rochère (2005) 42 C.M.L.Rev. 859.

institutions, or of enforcing the limits to Union competences which are intended to safeguard national sovereignty.[77] On the other hand, some commentators warn against the dangers of recognising (let alone encouraging) the right of national courts to dictate the course of Community policy under the threat of rebellion against the principle of supremacy; and indeed, question the legitimacy of a "dialogue" in which the domestic judges unilaterally reject Treaty obligations freely entered into by their elected politicians.[78] In any event, there are signs that the Court of Justice may be adopting a more aggressive approach to national courts which chose to defy their obligation to disapply any provision of domestic law conflicting with directly effective Community law. As we shall see in the next chapter, the ruling in *Köbler* established that Member States may be obliged to make reparation to individuals for losses incurred by a sufficiently serious breach of the Treaty perpetrated by the national supreme court.[79] Given the unconditional nature of the principle of supremacy, it is arguable that any refusal to respect that obligation would cross the high threshold for establishing liability—thus increasing the political pressure on national courts to think long and hard before taking the drastic step of refusing to enforce provisions of Community law adjudged valid according to the Treaties themselves.

The legal effect of Treaty provisions

Implementing Treaty provisions by national legislation

5–013   It has already been noted that the Court of Justice considers that the EC Treaty has created its own legal system which, on its entry into force, became an integral part of the legal systems of the Member States and which their courts are bound to apply.[80] It follows that Member States are bound to introduce constitutional amendments and/or legislation which recognise the full force and effect of Community law, including in particular its supremacy and direct effect. Where provisions of the EC Treaty are not directly effective, Member States are clearly obliged to adopt legislative measures of implementation where this is necessary to achieve compliance with the Treaty. But where Treaty provisions are directly

---

[77] Consider the analyses, e.g. of MacCormick, "The Maastricht-Urteil: Sovereignty Now" (1995) 1 E.L.J. 259; Weiler and Haltern, "Constitutional or International? The Foundations of the Community Legal Order" in Slaughter, Stone Sweet and Weiler (eds), *The European Court and National Courts: Doctrine and Jurisprudence* (Hart Publishing, 1998).

[78] e.g. Reich, "Judge-made 'Europe à la carte'" (1996) 7 European Journal of International Law 103.

[79] Case C–224/01 *Köbler* [2003] E.C.R. I–10239.

[80] Case 6/64 *Costa v ENEL* [1964] E.C.R. 585.

effective, and are recognised and enforceable as such under national law, is there any further obligation to adopt national measures of implementation? The answer to this question appears to be that it will be necessary to adopt such measures where otherwise the full and complete implementation of the Treaty would not be achieved. For example, it appears from a case initiated by the Commission against the Republic of France that a Member State may be required to repeal provisions of national law which discriminate on grounds of nationality, notwithstanding the fact that Article 39 EC prohibiting discrimination on grounds of nationality as regards access to employment, and the provisions of Regulation 1612/68 having the same effect, are directly applicable. This is because the ambiguous state of affairs resulting from the maintenance in force of the national legislation in question itself comprises a "secondary" obstacle to equal access to employment which itself contravenes Article 39 EC.[81] In a subsequent case against the Republic of Italy alleging that Italian rules restricting access by foreign nationals to certain occupations in the field of tourism infringed Community law, the Court said:

> "It must be observed in that regard that directly applicable provisions of the Treaty are binding on all the authorities of the Member States and they must therefore comply with them without its being necessary to adopt national implementing provisions. However, as the Court held in its judgment . . . in Case 72/85 (*Commission v Netherlands* . . .), the right of individuals to rely on directly applicable provisions of the Treaty before national courts is only a minimum guarantee and is not sufficient in itself to ensure the full and complete implementation of the Treaty . . ."[82]

The reference in the above quotation to *Commission v Netherlands*[83] is curious since the latter case concerns an action brought against the Netherlands for failing to take the necessary measures to ensure the implementation of EC staff *regulations* providing for the co-ordination of national pension schemes with the Community pension scheme as regards Community officials. As has been noted above, and is explained further below, in principle, regulations are directly applicable and binding in their entirety, and national legislative implementation is both unnecessary and impermissible. That is the position in principle, but in the case in point, the staff regulations

---

[81] Case 167/73 *Commission v French Republic* [1974] E.C.R. 359. The Court relied upon Case 167/73, and adopted similar reasoning, in Case 159/78 *Commission v Italy* [1979] E.C.R. 3247.
[82] Case 168/85 *Commission v Republic of Italy* [1986] E.C.R. 2945, para.11.
[83] Case 72/85 [1986] E.C.R. 1219.

(despite their direct applicability) could not have full force and effect unless national implementing rules were adopted to provide for the actual transfer of pension rights accrued under national law to the Community scheme. It was in this context that the Court stated that the right of individuals to rely upon the staff regulations before their national courts represented only a minimum guarantee which was not sufficient in itself to ensure the full and complete implementation of the regulations. In a subsequent *Commission v Italy*[84] case, the Court of Justice considered an allegation by the Commission that an exemption from VAT for domestic goods under Italian legislation was not extended to imports, contrary to Article 90 EC. In the course of its judgment, the Court stated:

> "the Court has consistently held (see *inter alia* the judgment . . . in Case 143/83 *Commission v Kingdom of Denmark* [1985] E.C.R. 427) that the principles of legal certainty and the protection of individuals require, in areas covered by Community law, that the Member States' legal rules should be worded unequivocally so as to give the persons concerned a clear and precise understanding of their rights and obligations and enable national courts to ensure that those rights and obligations are observed."[85]

5–014 The case cited above by the Court, *Commission v Denmark*, in fact concerned the failure to adopt unambiguous legislation implementing a *directive*, and it seems that at least in certain circumstances a Member State will be under a duty to implement a Treaty provision by national measures in a way which seems analogous to implementing a directive. In later proceedings against Italy, once more alleging that certain features of the Italian VAT system were being applied in such a way as to infringe Article 90 EC, the Court referred both to the principle that reliance upon the direct applicability of Article 90 EC represented only a minimum guarantee and was not sufficient in itself to ensure the full and complete implementation of the Treaty, and to the principle that in areas covered by Community law, national legal rules should be worded unequivocally so as to give the persons concerned a clear and precise understanding of their rights and obligations.[86] It followed that compliance with the directly applicable provision in question required the Italian authorities to enact national rules specifying the rights of importers as regards VAT which flowed from the terms of Article 90 EC. In the latter case the duty to enact the national rules in question amounted to a duty to *disapply* national rules which were incompatible with the

---

[84] Case 257/86 [1988] E.C.R. 3249.
[85] *ibid.*, para.12.
[86] Case C–120/88 *Commission v Italy* [1991] E.C.R. I–621, paras 10–11.

Treaty. But the duty to implement the Treaty by adopting national measures is not confined in all cases to a duty to *disapply* inconsistent national rules; it may on occasion amount to a further duty to adopt positive rules and procedures to ensure that individuals can exercise the rights contemplated by the Treaty. The case of *Commission v Kingdom of Spain* is illustrative.[87] In this case, the Commission brought an action under Article 226 EC for, *inter alia*, a declaration that, by failing to establish a procedure for examining qualifications acquired by a Community national in another Member State as a tourist guide and comparing them with those required by Spain in order to enable the diploma issued by that other Member State to be recognised, the Kingdom of Spain had failed to comply with, in particular, Articles 39 and 43 EC. Advocate General Lenz referred to the case law of the Court of Justice to the effect that a Member State which receives a request to admit a person to a profession to which access, under national law, depends upon the possession of a diploma or a professional qualification, must take into consideration the diplomas and other evidence of qualifications which the person concerned has acquired in order to exercise the same profession in another Member State by making a comparison between the specialised knowledge and abilities certified by those diplomas and the knowledge and qualifications required by the national rules. He went on:

> "With regard to the adjustment of national law to those principles, the Commission implicitly assumes that the defendant Member State must incorporate those principles in the provisions concerning the profession of tourist guide by means of express rules.
>
> That view is correct. The principles of legal certainty and the protection of individuals require that, in areas covered by Community law, the Member States' legal rules should be worded unequivocally so as to give the persons concerned a clear and precise understanding of their rights and obligations and to enable national courts to ensure that those rights and obligations are observed."[88]

The Court held that, by failing to establish a procedure for examining qualifications acquired by a Community national who holds a diploma as tourist guide issued in another Member State and comparing them with those required by Spain, the Spanish State had failed to fulfil its obligations under Articles 39, 43 and 49 EC.

---

[87] Case C–375/92 [1994] E.C.R. I–923. See also to similar effect in the context of a regulation, Case 72/85 *Commission v Netherlands* [1986] E.C.R. 1219.

[88] Paras 26 and 27 of Advocate General Lenz's Opinion in Case C–375/92 [1994] E.C.R. I–923. He refers to Case C–120/88 *Commission v Italy* [1991] E.C.R. I–621.

It follows that Member States are obliged to adopt national rules to implement provisions of the Treaty which are not directly applicable, where necessary, and to adopt national rules to implement directly applicable provisions of the Treaty in those cases where direct applicability will not secure the full and complete implementation of the Treaty provision in question. Member States must, moreover, repeal national rules which contradict directly applicable Treaty provisions, since the maintenance in force of such contradictory provisions gives rise to a state of uncertainty which prejudices the exercise by individuals of the rights which they derive directly from the Treaty. It is possible, however, that where a ruling of a superior court has made it clear that the direct applicability of the Treaty has the effect of disapplying a particular provision of national law, this will in itself ensure the full and complete implementation of the Treaty provision in question, without the need for national legislative confirmation of the position.[89]

Interpreting national legal provisions so that they are consistent with Treaty provisions

5–015   As has been mentioned, certain non-binding acts may cast light on the interpretation of national law or Community law. And as will be explained below, national courts are under a duty to interpret national law in accordance with the relevant provisions of Community directives, as far as it is possible for them to do so. But to what extent are national courts obliged by Community law to interpret national law in accordance with provisions of the *Treaty*? It was explained above that the national authorities of Member States are under a duty to repeal national legislation which is incompatible with the Treaty, and are obliged to remove any ambiguities or uncertainties which leave individuals in doubt as to the scope of their rights under the Treaty. Furthermore, the meaning and scope of national legislation is a matter for national courts and tribunals, and this has been recognised by the Court of Justice.[90] And it is established that national courts are under a duty pursuant to Article 10 EC "to ensure fulfilment of the obligations arising out of" the Treaty.[91] It would seem to follow that, if it is possible under national law for a superior court to resolve an ambiguity in national law in such a way as to ensure that the national law in question is consistent with, rather than incompatible with, a provision of the Treaty, the national court is obliged to interpret the national law in this way.

---

[89] The Court has said that the scope of national laws must be assessed in the light of the interpretation given to them by national courts: see Case C–382/92 *Commission v United Kingdom* [1994] E.C.R. I–2495, para.4; Case C–300/95 *Commission v United Kingdom* [1997] E.C.R. I–2649, para.37.
[90] See above.
[91] See further, Ch.6.

The Court's case law indeed supports this view. In *Murphy v An Bord Telecom Eireann*, a case involving the interpretation of Article 141 EC, the Court regarded the duty to set aside national rules incompatible with the direct applicability of that Treaty article as arising only if it proved impossible to construe national rules in a way which accorded with the requirements of the provision in question.[92]

But it seems that the duty of consistent interpretation of the Treaty only arises in a case in which failure to interpret the national rules in accordance with Community law will actually lead to a breach of the Treaty. In *ICI v Colmer*,[93] a taxpayer alleged that a provision of national tax law would in certain circumstances hinder the right of establishment of nationals of Member States, contrary to Article 43 EC, unless interpreted in the way favoured by the taxpayer. However, it was accepted on all sides that, in the circumstances of the case in point, no hindrance to the right of establishment of nationals of Member States could arise. The Court, having noted that the situation in issue lay outside the scope of Community law, ruled:

> "Accordingly, when deciding an issue concerning a situation which lies outside the scope of Community law, the national court is not required, under Community law, either to interpret its legislation in a way conforming with Community law or to disapply that legislation. Where a particular provision must be disapplied in a situation covered by Community law, but that same provision could remain applicable to a situation not so covered, it is for the competent body of the State concerned to remove that legal uncertainty in so far as it might affect rights deriving from Community rules."[94]

Direct applicability of Treaty provisions

(a) Invoking Treaty provisions against Member States (vertical 5–016 direct effect). The judicial source of the principle that certain provisions of the Treaty may be invoked by individuals in national courts is the judgment in *van Gend en Loos*.[95] Dutch importers challenged the rate of import duty charged on a chemical product imported from the Federal Republic of Germany, alleging that reclassifying it under a different heading of the Dutch customs tariff

---

[92] Case 157/86 [1988] E.C.R. 673, para.11. Similarly, e.g. Case C–262/97 *Engelbrecht* [2000] E.C.R. I–7321, paras 39–40.
[93] C–264/96 [1998] E.C.R. I–4695.
[94] *ibid.*, para.34.
[95] Case 26/62 [1963] E.C.R. 1.

had resulted in an increase in duty prohibited under Article 25 EC, which (at that time) provided that "Member States shall refrain from introducing between themselves any new customs duties on imports . . . or any charges having equivalent effect, and from increasing those which they already apply in their trade with each other". The *Tariefcommisie*, an administrative tribunal having final jurisdiction in cases involving such customs duties, asked the Court of Justice whether the Article in question had "direct application within the territory of a Member State, in other words, whether nationals of such a State can, on the basis of the Article in question, lay claim to individual rights which the courts must protect". The Netherlands Government, in its submissions to the Court, argued that an infringement of the Treaty by a Member State could be submitted to the Court only under the procedure laid down by Articles 226 and 227 EC, i.e. at the suit of the Commission or another Member State.[96] This general argument, to the effect that the provisions of the Treaty simply give rise to rights and obligations between Member States in international law, was rejected by Advocate General Roemer, who argued that anyone "familiar with Community law" knew that "in fact it does not just consist of contractual relations between a number of States considered as subjects of the law of nations".[97] This follows from the fact that the Community was authorised to make rules of law capable of bestowing rights and obligations on private individuals as well as on Member States.[98] The Court, in a judgment which was to prove of considerable importance for the development of Community law, stated:

> "The objective of the EEC Treaty, which is to establish a Common Market, the functioning of which is of direct concern to interested parties in the Community, implies that this Treaty is more than an agreement which merely creates mutual obligations between the contracting states. The task assigned to the Court of Justice under Article [234], the object of which is to ensure uniform interpretation of the Treaty by national courts and tribunals, confirms that the States have acknowledged that Community law has an authority which can be invoked by their nationals before those courts and tribunals.
>
> The conclusion to be drawn from this is that the Community constitutes a new legal order of international law for the benefit of which the States have limited their sovereign rights, albeit within limited fields, and the subjects of which comprise not only Member States but also their nationals. Independently of the legislation of Member States, Community law therefore not

---

[96] Case 26/62 [1963] E.C.R. 1, 6. On these actions, see further Ch.13.
[97] Case 26/62 [1963] E.C.R. 1, 20.
[98] The Advocate General cited in support of this proposition Arts 244, 249, 254 and 256 EC.

only imposes obligations on individuals but is also intended to confer upon them rights which become part of their legal heritage. These rights arise not only where they are expressly granted by the Treaty, but also by reason of obligations which the Treaty imposes in a clearly defined way upon individuals as well as upon the Member States and the institutions of the Community."[99]

This reasoning has been criticised for deducing the direct applicability of Treaty provisions "essentially without any legal basis in the Treaty".[1] The above passage of the Court certainly appears to rely more upon rhetoric than tight legal reasoning to persuade the reader. But it would be wrong to consider that the approach of the Court in *van Gend en Loos* amounted to an improper exercise of its judicial powers. Perhaps the strongest argument in favour of the Court's approach is to be found in its reference to the task assigned to the Court of Justice under Article 234 EC. In relevant part, this latter Article provides for the Court of Justice to give preliminary rulings on, *inter alia*, the interpretation of the Treaty, in response to requests from national courts which find that such an interpretation is necessary to enable them to give judgment in the national proceedings. This Article at the very least leaves open the possibility that Treaty provisions might have some legal consequences when pleaded before national courts. The possibility that those legal consequences might have been held to be limited in certain respects, e.g. to providing guidance to national courts on the interpretation of national rules meant to implement the provisions of the Treaty, does not render illegitimate the Court's actual conclusion, that provisions of the Treaty could give rise to rights in individuals which they could invoke in national courts. Furthermore, the rhetorical style of the above passage should not be allowed to detract from the underlying soundness of its analysis. The Treaty did set up institutions endowed with legislative powers which could bind individuals, and the Treaty did contemplate issues of Community law being invoked before national courts, which are empowered and in certain cases required to refer questions of Community law to the ECJ for decision. Whatever else the Treaty of Rome was, it was not an ordinary international treaty, and the Court of Justice should not be accused of judicial alchemy for acknowledging the fact.

---

[99] Case 26/62 [1963] E.C.R. 1, 12.
[1] Rasmussen, *European Court of Justice* (Gadjura, Copenhagen, 1998), p.78. For "sceptical" assessments of the role of the Court of Justice in developing the direct effect doctrine, see Neill, *The European Court of Justice: A Case Study in Judicial Activism*, evidence submitted to the House of Lords Select Committee on the European Communities, Sub-committee on the 1996 Inter-Governmental Conference, *1996 Inter-Governmental Conference, Minutes of Evidence, House of Lords, Session 1994–95*, 18th Report, p.218; Hartley, "The European Court, Judicial Objectivity and the Constitution of the European Union" (1996) 112 L.Q.R. 95. For a well considered assessment from a somewhat different perspective, see Tridimas, "The Court of Justice and Judicial Activism" (1996) 21 E.L.Rev. 199.

Since *van Gend en Loos* was a point of departure for so much that followed in the development of the Community legal order, it merits a little further attention. Although the Advocate General had taken the view that certain Treaty provisions were "clearly intended to be incorporated into national law and to modify or supplement it",[2] he had not numbered among them Article 25 EC, since its application required the resolution of complex issues of interpretation. To hold such a provision directly applicable, he pointed out, would create uncertainties in the law: enterprises would be far more likely to rely upon national customs legislation than upon the text of the Treaty. The Court's approach was less cautious:

> "The wording of Article [25] contains a clear and unconditional prohibition which is not a positive but a negative obligation. This obligation, moreover, is not qualified by any reservation on the part of States which would make its implementation conditional upon a positive legislative measure enacted under national law. The very nature of this prohibition makes it ideally adapted to produce direct effects in the legal relationship between Member States and their subjects."[3]

The *van Gend en Loos* judgment affirms the existence of the "new legal order" in which individuals, as well as Member States, may have rights and obligations, and it lays down the criteria to be applied in deciding whether or not a particular provision may be invoked by individuals in national courts. These criteria were to be applied subsequently in numerous cases,[4] and were summed up as follows by Advocate General Mayras in *Reyners v Belgian State*:[5]

— the provision in question must be sufficiently clear and precise for judicial application;[6]
— it must establish an unconditional obligation;[7]
— the obligation must be complete and legally perfect, and its implementation must not depend on measures being subsequently taken by Community institutions or Member States with discretionary power in the matter.[8]

---

[2] He cited Arts 81, 82, 84, 234, and 256 EC.
[3] Case 26/62 [1963] E.C.R. 1, 13.
[4] Provisions of the EC Treaty were held directly effective, e.g. in the following cases: Case 6/64 *Costa* [1964] E.C.R. 585; Case 57/65 *Lutticke* [1966] E.C.R. 205; Case 28/67 *Molkerei-Zentrale* [1968] E.C.R. 143; Case 27/67 *Fink-Frucht* [1968] E.C.R. 223; Case 13/68 *Salgoil* [1968] E.C.R. 453; Case 33/70 *SACE* [1970] E.C.R. 1213; Case 18/71 *Eunomia* [1971] E.C.R. 811; Case 127/73 *SABAM* [1974] E.C.R. 51.
[5] Case 2/74 *Reyners* [1974] E.C.R. 631.
[6] See *e.g.* Case 26/62 *van Gend en Loos* [1963] E.C.R. 1; Case 6/64 *Costa v ENEL* [1964] E.C.R. 585; Case 33/70 *SACE* [1970] E.C.R. 1213; Case 18/71 *Eunomia* [1971] E.C.R. 811; Case 41/74 *Van Duyn* [1974] E.C.R. 1337.
[7] See e.g. Case 26/62 *van Gend en Loos* [1963] E.C.R. 1; Case 6/64 *Costa v ENEL* [1964] E.C.R. 585; Case 57/65 *Lutticke* [1966] E.C.R. 205.
[8] See e.g. Case 26/62 *van Gend en Loos* [1963] E.C.R. 1; Case 57/65 *Lutticke* [1966] E.C.R. 205; Case 33/70 *SACE* [1970] E.C.R. 1213; Case 18/71 *Eunomia* [1971] E.C.R. 811; Case 41/74 *Van Duyn* [1974] E.C.R. 1337.

The second requirement, that the obligation be unconditional, was **5–017** of considerable importance during the transitional period (1958–1970), during which time national restrictions on the free movement of goods, persons and services were to be progressively abolished.[9] These conditional prohibitions in the Treaty became unconditional on the expiry of the transitional period, and national measures in force when the Treaty came into effect could be challenged in the national courts.[10]

The first and third requirements, that a legal provision be clear and precise, and be independent of measures to be taken subsequently by the Community institutions or the Member States, may be illustrated by reference to *Salgoil*,[11] in which the Court denied direct effect to Article 32(1), last sentence (the Article is now repealed), and Article 33 (now repealed), of the Treaty. These provisions required Member States to phase out quantitative restrictions on imports, by converting bilateral quotas into global quotas, and by progressively increasing their total value. The rate of liberalisation was prescribed for products where "the global quotas amounted to less than 3 per cent of the national production of the State concerned". The Court conceded that these provisions laid down obligations which were not subject to the adoption of measures by the institutions of the Community, but pointed out that: "Some discretion does fall to be exercised by the Member States from the obligation to 'convert any bilateral quotas . . . into global quotas' and from the concepts of 'total value' and 'national production.' In fact, since the Treaty gives no indication as to the data . . . or as to the methods applicable, several solutions may be envisaged".[12] It followed, in the Court's view, that the provisions in question were insufficiently precise to be considered directly effective.

It must be emphasised that the fact that provisions of Community law may require the appreciation of complex issues does not preclude their being directly effective, providing the requisite conditions are satisfied. Thus, Article 90(1) EC prohibits the imposition "on the products of other Member States" of "any internal taxation of any kind in excess of that imposed directly or indirectly on similar domestic products". The second paragraph of that Article adds that: "no Member State shall impose on the products of other Member States any internal taxation of such a nature as to afford indirect

---

[9] See e.g. Art.7 EC (now repealed); Arts 13(1) and (2) EC (now repealed).
[10] Ranbow, "The End of the Transitional Period" (1969) 6 C.M.L.Rev. 434. For obligations directly effective as of the end of the transitional period, see e.g. Case 77/72 *Capolongo* [1973] E.C.R. 611; Case 74/76 *Ianelli and Volpi* [1977] E.C.R. 557; Case 59/75 *Manghera* [1976] E.C.R. 91; Case 41/74 *Van Duyn* [1974] E.C.R. 1337; Case 2/74 *Reyners* [1974] E.C.R. 631; Case 33/74 *Van Binsbergen* [1974] E.C.R. 1299.
[11] Case 33/68 [1968] E.C.R. 453.
[12] *ibid.*, 461.

protection to other products". In *Fink-Frucht*,[13] the Court considered whether or not this latter provision was directly effective. It decided that it was, in face of the arguments of the Federal Republic of Germany that the paragraph was "vague and incomplete" and that the "value-judgments" it required should not be forced on national courts.[14] In the Court's view, the provision contained a straightforward prohibition against protection; "it established an unconditional obligation, and no action was required on the part of the institutions of the Community or the Member States for its implementation". "Although this provision involves the evaluation of economic factors", observed the Court, "this does not exclude the right and the duty of national courts to ensure that the rules of the Treaty are observed whenever they can ascertain . . . that the conditions necessary for the application of the Article are fulfilled".[15]

5–018   **(b) Invoking Treaty Provisions against private individuals and companies (horizontal direct effect).**   In the cases discussed above, the Court of Justice was called upon to consider whether or not a provision of the Treaty had modified the legal position of an individual *vis-à-vis* the State. Beginning with the judgment in *SABAM*,[16] we see a new development: the acknowledgment that provisions of the Treaty are capable of modifying the rights of private parties (individuals or companies) *inter se*. Thus, in *SABAM*, the Court observed that the prohibitions of Articles 81(1) and 82 EC, concerning anti-competitive behaviour by economic undertakings, "tend by their very nature to produce direct effects in relations between individuals", and "create direct rights in respect of the individuals concerned which the national courts must safeguard".[17] It might have been arguable that Articles 81 and 82 EC, being explicitly concerned with private action, could be treated as special cases. However, the Court's later decisions suggest a more general principle.

One line of case law has concerned the Treaty provisions on the free movement of persons. In *Walrave and Koch v Association Union Cycliste Internationale*,[18] motorcyclists who earned their living "pacing" pedal cyclists in international events asked a Netherlands court for a declaration that certain rules of the defendant association infringed the Treaty's prohibition of discrimination on grounds of nationality. The national court sought a preliminary ruling. Doubts were expressed by the Commission[19] in argument as to whether the

---

[13] Case 27/67 [1968] E.C.R. 223.
[14] *ibid.*, 229.
[15] *ibid.*, 232.
[16] Case 127/73 [1974] E.C.R. 51.
[17] *ibid.*, 62.
[18] Case 36/74 [1974] E.C.R. 1405.
[19] *ibid.*, 1410.

prohibition in question applied to private action, as opposed to State action, and the Court addressed itself to the question as follows:

> "It has been alleged that the prohibition in these Articles refer only to restrictions which have their origin in acts of an authority and not to those resulting from legal acts of persons or associations who do not come under public law.
>
> Articles [12, 39 and 49 EC] have in common the prohibition, in their respective spheres of application, of any discrimination on grounds of nationality.
>
> Prohibition of such discrimination does not only apply to the acts of public authorities, but extends likewise to rules of any other nature aimed at regulating in a collective manner gainful employment and the provision of services."[20]

It followed, in the Court's view, that the provisions of the Articles in question could be taken into account by a national court in judging the validity and the effects of the rules of a sporting association. The horizontal direct effect of the free movement of persons provisions has been extended still further in the more recent case of *Angonese*, which involved an action brought by a migrant Community worker challenging the discriminatory recruitment practices of a private Italian bank. The Court of Justice affirmed that the principle of equal treatment as regards employment laid down in Article 39 EC is capable of governing the conduct of private persons, and not merely in situations concerning collective regulation of the relevant sphere of employment or services.[21]

Another line of case law concerns the Treaty provision on equal **5–019** pay between men and women. *Defrenne v Sabena* concerned proceedings before the Belgian courts initiated by a former air hostess against her former employer alleging infringement of Article 141 EC.[22] The text of the latter Article provided, at the time, that during the first stage "[e]ach Member State shall . . . ensure and subsequently maintain the application of the principle that men and women should receive equal pay for equal work". The original six Member States had not complied with this obligation by January 1, 1973; nor had the then new Member States (Denmark, Ireland and the United Kingdom) been in a position to do so when they acceded on that date. The Belgian court asked the Court of Justice whether the Article in question entitled workers to undertake proceedings before national courts in order to ensure its observance. The Court

---

[20] *ibid.*, 1418.
[21] Case C–281/98 *Angonese* [2000] E.C.R. I–4139.
[22] Case 43/75 [1976] E.C.R. 455. The judgment provoked a great deal of discussion at the time: see Wyatt (1975–76) 1 E.L.Rev. 399; Crisham (1977) 14 C.M.L.Rev. 102; Allott [1977] C.L.J. 7.

replied in the affirmative: even though the complete implementation
of the equal pay principles could not be achieved without legislative
elaboration at the Community or national level, the requirement was
nevertheless apt for national judicial application in cases of "direct
and overt discrimination which may be identified solely with the aid
of the criteria based on equal work and equal pay referred to by the
Article in question".[23] It might be thought that the greatest obstacle
in the way to finding that the equal pay principle in the Treaty could
impose a direct obligation on employers was that it was framed in
terms of an obligation imposed on Member States. But the Court
reasons to the effect that the reference to "Member States" is a
reference which is not confined to national legislative authorities,
and the term "cannot be interpreted as excluding the intervention of
the courts in the direct application of the Treaty".[24] Thus, the duty
of the Member States to ensure and subsequently maintain the
application of the principle of equal pay includes the duty of the
courts of Member States to enforce the principle of equal pay in
those cases which come before them. This approach paradoxically
draws upon traditional principles of state responsibility in international law (to the effect that all acts of the legislative, executive
and judicial organs of the State may in principle be attributed to the
State) to produce a result which is far from traditional, and which is
rather, in our view, intellectually attractive. "In fact", went on the
Court, "since Article [141] is mandatory in nature, the prohibition
on discrimination between men and women applies not only to the
action of public authorities, but also extends to all agreements which
are intended to regulate paid labour collectively, as well as to
contracts between individuals".[25]

Although judgments such as *Angonese* and *Defrenne v Sabena*
illustrate that Treaty provisions such as those on the free movement
of workers and equal pay between men and women may be
enforceable in national courts against natural and legal persons as
well as Member States, it does not follow that every Treaty provision
which is capable of having direct effect will be both horizontally and
vertically applicable. Everything depends on an interpretation of the
relevant provision—including its specific objective and broader
context—to determine whether horizontal direct effect would actually be appropriate. Thus, for example, the Court has held that
Article 28 EC on the free movement of goods catches obstacles to
cross-border trade erected by public authorities and other bodies
controlled or underpinned by the Member State;[26] but does not

---

[23] Case 43/75 [1976] E.C.R. 455, 473: *e.g.* discrimination in national legislation or in collective
labour agreements, which could be detected on the basis of a purely legal analysis of the
situation.
[24] Case 43/75 [1976] E.C.R. 455, 475.
[25] *ibid.*, 476.
[26] e.g. Case 249/81 *Commission v Ireland* [1982] E.C.R. 4005; Case 222/82 *Apple and Pear
Development Council* [1983] E.C.R. 4083; Cases 266–267/87 *Royal Pharmaceutical Society*
[1989] E.C.R. 1295; Case C–292/92 *Hünermund* [1993] E.C.R. I–6787.

prohibit obstacles erected through the conduct of purely private bodies.[27] The Court believes that the latter category of obstacles are more appropriately dealt with—if at all—under the Treaty provisions on fair competition (which have horizontal direct effect) than those on the free movement of goods (which are therefore limited to vertical direct effect).[28]

(c) The Exceptional case—the prospective effect of a ruling on the 5–020 interpretation of a directly effective Treaty provision. Although the Court in *Defrenne* held that Article 141 EC was directly applicable— at least in part—it also held that the Article could not be relied upon to support claims in respect of pay periods prior to the date of its judgment, except as regards workers who had already brought legal proceedings or made equivalent claims. This was a step of some considerable significance. In normal circumstances a judicial decision defines the meaning and scope of the rule in issue as it should have been understood and applied from the time the rule came into force, and the rule as so interpreted is applicable to legal relationships arising and established prior to the judgment in question. But in *Defrenne*, the Court seems to have been moved by the pleas of Ireland and the United Kingdom that if claims to back pay based on Article 141 EC could be made they would have disastrous economic effects in these countries. It responded as follows:

"Although the practical consequences of any judicial decision must be carefully taken into account, it would be impossible to go so far as to diminish the objectivity of the law and compromise its future application on the ground of the possible repercussions which might result, as regards the past, from such a judicial decision.

However, in the light of the conduct of several of the Member States and the views adopted by the Commission and repeatedly brought to the notice of the circles concerned, it is appropriate to take exceptionally into account the fact that, over a prolonged period, the parties concerned have been led to continue with practices which were contrary to Article [141 EC], although not yet prohibited under their national law.

The fact that, in spite of the warnings given, the Commission did not initiate proceedings under Article [226 EC] against the Member States concerned on grounds of failure to fulfil that obligation was likely to consolidate the incorrect impression as to the effects of Article [141 EC].

---

[27] e.g. Case C–159/00 *Sapod Audic* [2002] E.C.R. I–5031.
[28] e.g. Cases 177–178/82 *van de Haar* [1984] E.C.R. 1797; Case 311/85 *Vereniging van Vlaamse Reisbureaus* [1987] E.C.R. 3801; Case 65/86 *Bayer v Süllhöfer* [1988] E.C.R. 5249.

In these circumstances, it is appropriate to determine that, as the general level at which pay would have been fixed cannot be known, important considerations of legal certainty affecting all the interests involved, both public and private, make it impossible to re-open the question as regards the past."[29]

In other words, the *unexpectedness* of the Court's ruling militated against its retrospective application. The legal basis of the decision is the principle of "legal certainty", which holds that parties acting reasonably on the basis of the law as it stands ought to be able to do so in the confidence that their legal position will not be changed retrospectively.[30] Analogous principles have been applied by the Supreme Court of the United States, which has declared in certain cases that constitutional rulings will have only prospective effect.[31]

The subsequent case law of the Court of Justice confirms that derogation from the normal principle whereby a ruling on the interpretation of Community law is binding as regards the past as well as the future is permissible only in quite exceptional circumstances, where the Court considers that compliance with it breaches the principle of legal certainty.[32] In considering whether that principle necessitates the imposition of a temporal limit on the effects of ruling on a request for interpretation, the Court must ascertain: (a) whether there is a risk of economic repercussions owing in particular to the large number of legal relationships entered into in good faith on the basis of national rules considered to be validly in force; and (b) whether individuals and national authorities have been prompted to adopt practices which do not comply with Community law by reason of "objective significant uncertainty regarding the precise scope of the rule of Community law interpreted by the Court . . . if it finds that the attitude adopted by other Member States or the Commission contributed to that uncertainty, that will have a particular bearing on its assessment of the matter in that regard".[33]

5–021   The Court has limited the temporal effects of a judgment on the meaning of a Treaty provision in only a small number of cases. For example, in *Blaizot*,[34] the Court was called upon to rule for the first time whether or not university education could be regarded as

---

[29] Case 43/75 [1976] E.C.R. 455, paras 71–74.
[30] On legal certainty and legitimate expectations as general principles of Community law, see further Ch.7.
[31] In so doing, it has emphasised three criteria: (i) the purpose to be served by the new rule; (ii) the extent of reliance by law enforcement authorities on the old rule; and (iii) the effect on the administration of justice of a retrospective application of the new rule. See e.g. *Stovall v Denno* 388 U.S. 293, 297; L.Ed. 2d 1199; 87 S.Ct. 1967.
[32] For a helpful general statement of the law see A.G. Cosmas in Joined Cases C–197/94 and C–252/94 *Bautiaa* [1996] E.C.R. 505, paras 40–41 Opinion.
[33] *ibid.*, para.41 Opinion.
[34] Case 24/86 *Blaizot* [1988] E.C.R. 379.

constituting vocational training for the purposes of the application of the principle that there be no discrimination on grounds of nationality as regards enrolment fees for access to vocational training courses. The Court admitted that, in so holding, it was recognising developments in the Community's vocational training policy, and noted that the conduct of the Commission "might reasonably have led the authorities concerned in Belgium to consider that the relevant Belgian legislation was in conformity with Community law". The Court concluded that, in such circumstances, pressing considerations of legal certainty precluded any reopening of the question of past legal relationships where that would retroactively throw the financing of university education into confusion and might have unforeseeable consequences for the proper functioning of universities. It followed that the direct effect of Article 12 EC could not be relied on in support of claims regarding supplementary enrolment fees improperly charged prior to the date of this judgment, except in respect of students who brought legal proceedings or submitted an equivalent claim before that date. The circumstances are similar to those in *Defrenne*, in that the Court's judgment broke new ground, and the conduct of the Commission had contributed to a mistaken view of the law on the part of national authorities.

The Court had reason to limit the temporal effects of yet another judgment on the interpretation of Article 141 EC on equal pay in *Barber*.[35] In that case, the Court held that the Treaty's guarantee of equal pay applied with direct effect to pensions paid under "contracted out" pension schemes, i.e. schemes recognised in the United Kingdom in substitution for the earnings-related part of the State pension. Nevertheless, the Court limited the temporal effects of its judgment. It was not this time the conduct of the Commission which contributed to a mistaken view of the law on the part of national authorities and private parties, but provisions of Council directives which in certain respects authorised Member States to defer the compulsory implementation of the principle of equal treatment as regards occupational social security schemes and contracted-out schemes such as the one in issue. In the light of these provisions, the Court considered that the Member States and the parties concerned were reasonably entitled to consider that the Treaty's guarantee of equal pay did not apply to pensions paid under contracted-out schemes and that derogations from the principle of equality between men and women were still permitted in that sphere.

A final example is the judgment in *Bosman*, where the Court considered the compatibility of rules of national sporting associations for the transfer of players between clubs, and held that Article 39 EC precluded the application of rules laid down by sporting

---

[35] Case C–262/88 *Barber* [1990] E.C.R. I–1889.

associations, under which a professional footballer who is a national
of one Member State may not, on the expiry of his contract with a
club, be employed by a club of another Member State unless the
latter club has paid to the former club a transfer, training or
development fee. But the Court limited the temporal effects of its
judgment, because the specific features of the rules laid down by the
sporting associations for transfers of players between clubs of
different Member States, together with the fact that the same or
similar rules applied to transfers both between clubs belonging to the
same national association and between clubs belonging to different
national associations within the same Member State, may have
caused uncertainty as to whether those rules were compatible with
Community law.[36]

But in numerous cases the Court of Justice has refused to limit the
temporal effects of a judgment, whether on the interpretation of a
Treaty provision, or of secondary legislation, on the grounds that the
conditions referred to above as justifying such an exceptional course
of action were not satisfied.[37]

The legal effects of Community acts

5–022   One of the most striking characteristics of the legal order established by the Treaty is the competence vested in the Community
institutions to enact legislation for the purpose of carrying out the
objectives of the Treaty. Article 249 EC states:

> "In order to carry out their tasks and in accordance with the
> provisions of this Treaty, the European Parliament acting
> jointly with the Council, the Council and the Commission shall
> make regulations and issue directives, take decisions, make
> recommendations or deliver opinions."

Since regulations and directives are of particular significance as
general measures of legislation, they will be examined in detail in the
following sections of this chapter.

Regulations

5–023   **(a) The legal character of Regulations.**   Article 249 EC states: "A
regulation shall have general application. It shall be binding in its
entirety and directly applicable in all Member States."

---

[36] Case C–415/93 *Bosman* [1995] E.C.R. I–4921, paras 139–145.
[37] See e.g. Case 69/80 *Worringham and Humphreys* [1981] E.C.R. 767; Joined Cases 142 and
143/80 *Essevi and Salengo* [1981] E.C.R. 1413; Case C–200/90 *Dansk Denkavit* [1992]
E.C.R. I–2217; Joined Cases C–367/93 to C–377/93 *Roders* [1995] E.C.R. I–2229; Case
C–137/94 *ex parte Cyril Richardson* [1995] E.C.R. I–3407; Case C–126/95 *Hallouzi-Choho*
[1996] E.C.R. I–4807; Case C–35/97 *Commission v France* [1998] E.C.R. I–5325; Case
C–184/99 *Grzelczyk* [2001] E.C.R. I–6193; Case C–209/03 *Bidar* [2005] E.C.R. I–2119.

At first sight, this description of regulations appears to attribute to them the characteristics of those Treaty provisions capable of giving rise to rights in individuals which national courts are bound to safeguard.[38] Even a cursory scrutiny of the *Official Journal*, however, reveals that each and every provision of each and every regulation does not give rise to rights in individuals against other individuals or against Member States. This unsurprising phenomenon is perhaps best explained by understanding the reference to direct applicability in Article 249 EC as concerning the process of incorporation of regulations into the national legal order. This description emphasises that national courts must take cognisance of regulations as legal instruments whose validity and recognition by national courts must not be conditioned on national procedures of incorporation into the national legal order. But whether or not particular provisions of such an instrument in fact give rise to rights in individuals which national courts must safeguard is a matter of interpretation of the provisions concerned, in light of the criteria established by the Court of Justice with respect to the direct effect of provisions of the Treaty.

This approach is consistent with the decided cases. In earlier rulings, it is true, the Court did not go out of its way to clarify the matter. For example, in *Politi v Italian Ministry of Finance*,[39] an Italian court asked the Court of Justice whether certain provisions of an agricultural regulation were (i) directly applicable, and (ii) if so, whether they created rights for individuals which national courts were bound to safeguard. The question presented to the Court reflects neatly the distinction indicated above; the Court's response did not. "Under the terms of the second paragraph of Article [249]", it declared, "regulations 'shall have general application' and 'shall be . . . directly applicable in all Member States.' Therefore, by reason of their nature and their function in the system of the sources of Community law, regulations have direct effect and are as such capable of creating individual rights which national courts must protect."[40] Advocate General Roemer in *Leonesio v Italian Ministry of Agriculture and Forestry* was more willing to separate the issues of direct applicability and direct effect (at least in the sense of creating rights for individuals). He pointed out that simply to acknowledge the status of a Community legal instrument as a regulation did not solve the problem of whether certain of its provisions bestowed enforceable rights on individuals as against the Member State—the solution to which "depends on the questions whether an area of discretion was left to the national authorities in the matter of

---

[38] See above on the relationship between direct applicability, direct effect and the creation of individual rights/mere rights of invocability.

[39] Case 43/71 [1971] E.C.R. 1039.

[40] *ibid.*, para.9. Similarly, e.g. Case 93/71 *Leonesio* [1972] E.C.R. 287 (contrasting the Court's judgment with the Opinion of Advocate General Roemer).

implementation and in what manner the national provisions were to
supplement the measures adopted".[41] That approach has since been
vindicated by the Court of Justice. For example, it was held in *Monte
Arcosu* that although, by virtue of the very nature of regulations,
their provisions generally have immediate effect in the national legal
systems without its being necessary for the national authorities to
adopt measures of application, some of their provisions may none
the less necessitate, for their implementation, the adoption of such
measures by the Member States. In such situations, given the
discretion enjoyed by the Member States, it cannot be held that
individuals may derive rights from the relevant provisions of the
regulation in the absence of measures adopted by the national
authorities.[42]

The circumstances in which national provisions might properly
supplement a Community regulation are further addressed below.
The important point for now is that the mere status of an instrument
qua regulation cannot determine whether any of its provisions in fact
enjoy direct effect—which is a question dependent upon detailed
interpretation of those specific provisions.

5–024 **(b) The permissible scope for implementation of regulations by
National rules.** A corollary of the proposition that regulations must
be recognised as legal instruments without the need for their terms
to be transposed into national law by national implementing rules, is
that such transposition, unless authorised in a particular case,[43] is
impermissible, in as much as it tends to disguise from those subject
to the law the Community source of their rights and obligations.
That the legislative duplication of regulations might in itself be
inconsistent with Community law was made clear in *Commission v
Italy*,[44] in which the Italian Government had failed to implement
certain EEC regulations concerning slaughter premia and the withholding of milk supplied from the market, resulting in an action by
the Commission under Article 226 EC. Not only did the Commission
complain of the delay of the Italian Government in instituting the
scheme, but also of the technique of reproducing the texts of
regulations in Italian legislation. This, said the Court, itself constituted a default, since by adopting this procedure, the Italian
Government had brought into doubt both the legal nature of the
applicable provisions and the date of their coming into force. The
Court reiterated its position in *Fratelli Variola v Italian Finance
Ministry*. "No procedure is permissible", it emphasised, "whereby the

---

[41] Case 93/71 [1972] E.C.R. 287, 300.
[42] Case C–403/98 *Monte Arcosu* [2001] E.C.R. I–103. Consider also Case C–253/00 *Muñoz*
[2002] E.C.R. I–7289 (discussed above).
[43] Case 31/78 *Bussone* [1978] E.C.R. 2429; Case 230/78 *Zuccheri* [1979] E.C.R. 2749.
[44] Case 39/72 [1973] E.C.R. 101.

Community nature of a legal rule is concealed from those subject to it".[45]

It is to be noted that what the Court of Justice found legally objectionable in the foregoing cases was the legislative duplication in national implementing rules of the texts of Community regulations. It does not follow, and it is not the case, that regulations do not ever require supplementary national rules to be adopted to ensure the effective application of regulations in the various Member States. Reference has already been made to *Commission v Netherlands*,[46] in which the Court held that the Netherlands was in breach of its obligations for failing to take the necessary measures to ensure the implementation of EC staff *regulations* providing for the co-ordination of national pension schemes with the Community pension scheme for Community officials. In the circumstances, the staff regulations (despite their direct applicability) could not have full force and effect unless national implementing rules were adopted to provide for the actual transfer of pension rights accrued under national law to the Community scheme. In this context, the Court held that the right of individuals to rely upon the staff regulations before their national courts represented only a minimum guarantee which was not sufficient in itself to ensure the full and complete implementation of the regulations. Furthermore, the Court has acknowledged that, where Community regulations require imple-mentation by national measures, the incorporation of the texts of such regulations may be justified for the sake of coherence and in order to make them comprehensible to the persons to whom they apply.[47] It is not uncommon for Community regulations to be supplemented by quite extensive national rules designed to ensure that the Community rules and national rules can be applied in an effective and comprehensible way. For example, the adoption of Council Regulation 2137/85 on the European Economic Interest Grouping (EEIG)[48] was followed in the United Kingdom by a Statutory Instrument which, amongst other things, laid down the detailed rules which under the regulation were to be left to Member States to adopt, and specified how relevant provisions of domestic Company Law and Insolvency Law applied to the EEIG.[49] The Finance Act 1990 made necessary provision for the taxation of the members of an EEIG.[50] The authorities in the United Kingdom are certainly conscious of the peculiar characteristics of EC regulations. In Department of the Environment Circular 13/94 on the application of Council Regulation 259/93 on the supervision and control of

---

[45] Case 34/73 [1973] E.C.R. 981, para.11.
[46] Case 72/85 [1986] E.C.R. 1219.
[47] Case 272/83 *Commission v Italy* [1985] E.C.R. 1057, para.27.
[48] [1985] O.J. L199/1.
[49] The European Economic Interest Grouping Regulations 1989, SI 1989/638.
[50] s.69 and Sch.11.

shipments of waste within, into and out of the EC, the Department states "The Waste shipment Regulation is directly applicable—that is, *most of its provisions do not require transposition*[51] into national legislation. There are some matters, however, which require national legislation *to give full effect to the provisions of the Regulation.*[52] In the United Kingdom, the legislation in question comprises a Statutory Instrument, The Transfrontier Shipment of Waste Regulations 1995".[53]

Giving full effect to the provisions of a Community regulation may require the imposition of penalties to secure enforcement of breaches of the regulation. In this connection the Court of Justice has held:

> "where a Community regulation does not specifically provide any penalty for an infringement or refers for that purpose to national laws, regulations and administrative provisions, Article [10] of the EC Treaty requires the Member States to take all measures necessary to guarantee the application and effectiveness of Community law. For that purpose, while the choice of penalties remains within their discretion, they must ensure in particular that infringements of Community law are penalised under conditions, both procedural and substantive, which are analogous to those applicable to infringement of national law of a similar nature and importance and which, in any event, make the penalty effective, proportionate and dissuasive . . ."[54]

The above formulation has been interpreted by the Court as meaning that, when Member States are fulfilling such responsibilities as indicated above, they are required to comply with the general principles of Community law, in particular the principle of proportionality.[55]

5–025 **(c) Regulations may have vertical and horizontal effect.** Since regulations constitute direct legislation by the Community, which are binding in their entirety, not only may individuals rely on specific provisions against other individuals and Member States, but they may also invoke the general objective and purpose of the legal

---

[51] Emphasis added. The passage appears to contemplate, though, that some provisions at least will actually require transposition. In principle they should not require *transposition*, though supplementary national rules may be necessary to ensure that the aims of the regulation are fully achieved.

[52] Emphasis added.

[53] SI 1137/1994. See para.2 of Circular 13/94.

[54] Case C–177/95 *Ebony Maritime* [1997] E.C.R. I–1111, citing Case 68/88 *Commission v Greece* [1989] E.C.R. 2965; Case C–326/88 *Hansen* [1990] E.C.R. I–2911; and Case C–36/94 *Siesse* [1995] E.C.R. I–3573. See also Ch.6.

[55] Case C–2/97 *Borsana* [1998] E.C.R. I–8597, para.49, referring to identical wording in Case C–326/88 *Hansen* [1990] E.C.R. I–2911. See also Ch.7.

regime established by a regulation to challenge the application of conflicting national legal provisions. This pre-emptive quality of regulations has become most obviously apparent in the context of the common agricultural policy, where the Court has ruled on several occasions that national measures have been incompatible with the legal regime established by a Community regulation (as opposed to incompatible with specific provisions vesting rights in individuals).[56] Thus, national measures which hinder agricultural producers from selling on the market at a price equal to the target price may be challenged by individuals concerned in the national courts, although producers have no "right" to sell at that price. They may nevertheless invoke the encroachment by national legislation on a Community legal regime from which they are entitled to benefit.[57] As the Court explained in *Amsterdam Bulb*:

> "From the moment that the Community adopts regulations under Article [34] of the Treaty establishing a common organisation of the market in a specific sector the Member States are under a duty not to take any measure which might create exemptions from them or affect them adversely.
>
> The compatibility with the Community regulations of the provisions referred to by the national court must be considered in the light not only of the express provisions of the regulations *but also of their aims and objectives*."[58]

In certain cases, the terms of a regulation may preclude the enactment of national legislation entirely in the field in question. Thus, in *Hauptzollamt Bremen-Freihafen v Waren-Import-Gesellschaft Krohn and Co.*, the Court declared: "In so far as the Member States have conferred on the Community legislative powers in tariff matters, in order to ensure the proper functioning of the common market in agriculture, they no longer have the power to issue independent provisions in this field".[59]

Regulations, in short, are to be treated as "law" in every sense of the word. National courts must take judicial notice of them in their entirety; specific provisions contained therein may bestow on individuals rights against other individuals, or companies, or national authorities; and their effect in a particular area may be to pre-empt the valid exercise of national legislative competence.

---

[56] See, *e.g.* Case 60/75 *Russo* [1976] E.C.R. 45; Case 77/76 *Fratelli Cucchi* [1977] E.C.R. 987. Also Wyatt [1977] C.L.J. 216, 217.
[57] Case 77/76 *Fratelli Cucchi* [1977] E.C.R. 987.
[58] Case 50/76 *Amsterdam Bulb* [1977] E.C.R. 137, para.8 (emphasis added).
[59] Case 74/69 [1970] E.C.R. 451, 458. And see Case 40/69 *Bollmann* [1979] E.C.R. 69, 79.

Directives

5–026 (a) The duty to implement directives by binding national rules. Article 249 EC states:

> "A directive shall be binding, as to the result to be achieved, upon each Member State to which it is addressed, but shall leave to the national authorities the choice of form and methods."

The choice left to Member States of the "form and methods" for the implementation of directives allows a Member State to choose the legislative format which it considers appropriate.[60] Thus, the legislation adopted to implement a directive need not use the same words as the directive itself.[61] National implementing rules should, however, give persons concerned a clear and precise understanding of their rights and obligations and enable national courts to ensure that those rights and obligations are observed.[62] As the Court of Justice put it in *Commission v Greece*:

> "the Court has consistently held that it is particularly important, in order to satisfy the requirement of legal certainty, that individuals should have the benefit of a clear and precise legal situation enabling them to ascertain the full extent of their rights and, where appropriate, to rely on them before the national courts."[63]

Implementation of a directive requires the transposition of the requirements of the directive by binding measures of national law; neither the adoption of administrative practices, which by their nature may be altered at the whim of the authorities and lack the appropriate publicity, nor the publication of administrative circulars,

---

[60] Case 163/82 *Commission v Italy* [1983] E.C.R. 3723, 3286–3287.
[61] Case 247/85 *Commission v Belgium* [1987] E.C.R. 3029, para.9; Case 262/85 *Commission v Italy* [1987] E.C.R. 3073, para.9; Case 252/85 *Commission v France* [1988] E.C.R. 2243, para.5.
[62] Case 257/86 *Commission v Italy* [1988] E.C.R. 3249, 3267.
[63] Case C–236/95 [1996] E.C.R. I–4459 (citing prior case law). The Court held a Greek Presidential Decree inadequate to implement a directive, because its general wording does not specifically bestow the relevant rights on the relevant parties, despite case law of the Council of State interpreting the Presidential Decree in conformity with the Directive. But the Court has said that the scope of national laws must be assessed in the light of the interpretation given to them by national courts: see Case C–382/92 *Commission v United Kingdom* [1994] E.C.R. I–2495, para.4; Case C–300/95 *Commission v United Kingdom* [1997] E.C.R. I–2649, para.37. Case C–236/95 must be taken to turn on its special facts. Provisions of Community law are on occasion too vague to be capable of confident interpretation without the benefit of the Court's case law, and it is the intervention of the latter which ensures legal certainty, as witnessed, e.g. by the doctrine of prospective effect (discussed above).

which do not have binding effects, will be enough to satisfy the requirements of Article 249 EC.[64] Despite the consistent case law, Member States have persisted until recently with the argument that transposition by means of administrative circulars was enough.[65] Appropriate national measures must be adopted within the time-limit specified in the directive. Problems at the national level, such as an overcrowded legislative timetable, cannot justify failure to meet this deadline. The Court has held on numerous occasions that "a Member State may not plead provisions, practices or circumstances existing in its internal legal system in order to justify a failure to comply with the obligations and time-limits laid down in a directive".[66] However, the Court has held that directives do not require legislative implementation where there exist general principles of constitutional or administrative law which render specific legislation superfluous, provided that those principles guarantee the application of the directive, are clear and precise, are made known to those subject to the law, and are capable of being invoked by the courts.[67] It follows that legislation is also superfluous where national legislative provisions in force afford similar guarantees that a directive will be effectively implemented. In the United Kingdom, Directive 76/207 on equal treatment for men and women as regards access to employment, vocational training and promotion, and working conditions,[68] is implemented by a prior piece of legislation, the Sex Discrimination Act 1975. On occasions, a directive will require that legislative measures of transposition refer to the underlying directive, and in such a case, failure to include a reference to the directive in national implementing legislation will amount to a distinct breach of Community law.[69]

5-027 In addition to transposing the substantive obligations of a directive, Member States are bound to introduce enforcement mechanisms to secure compliance, such as provisions for private law remedies or penalties. Even if a directive makes no express provision for such enforcement mechanisms, Member States are nevertheless obliged under Articles 10 and 249 EC to take all measures necessary to guarantee the application and effectiveness of Community law.[70] Furthermore, both in general terms, and in the context of enforcement mechanisms adopted to secure the implementation of directives, the Court has held that Member States must, "in order to

---

[64] Case 102/79 *Commission v Belgium* [1980] E.C.R. 1473; Case 96/81 *Commission v Netherlands* [1982] E.C.R. 1791; Case 145/82 *Commission v Italy* [1983] E.C.R. 711.
[65] In Case C–262/95 *Commission v Germany* [1996] E.C.R. I–5729, Germany initially argued that certain notices circulars and administrative provisions amounted to transposition, but abandoned its argument in light of the Court's case law: see paras 7 and 15.
[66] Case C–298/95 *Commission v Germany* [1996] E.C.R. I–6747 (citing previous case law).
[67] Case 29/84 *Commission v Germany* [1986] E.C.R. 1661.
[68] [1976] O.J. L39/40.
[69] Case C–360/95 *Commission v Spain* [1997] E.C.R. I–7337.
[70] Case C–5/94 *ex parte Hedley Lomas* [1996] E.C.R. I–2553, para.19.

secure the full implementation of directives in law and not only in fact, establish a specific legal framework in the area in question".[71] The Court has further held that, in adopting national measures to implement a directive, Member States are required to comply with the general principles of Community law, in particular the principle of proportionality.[72]

Implementation of directives in the United Kingdom is achieved either by primary or secondary legislation, the latter normally pursuant to section 2(2) of the European Communities Act 1972. Initially, there was a tendency to transpose directives by translating their requirements, to a greater or lesser extent, into the legal language which it was believed would have been used had they been "home grown". An example is the transposition of the product liability directive,[73] which was implemented in Part I of the Consumer Protection Act 1987, which in part substituted for the language of the directive the language of the Parliamentary draftsman.[74] But transposing directives by adopting the language and techniques of English law to ensure the fulfilment of requirements formulated by the European institutions in a distinctly different style has its pitfalls. It might be said that those subject to the law are better able to understand their legal position by having their rights and obligations set out in the manner characteristic of domestic legislation. If such domestic legislation could be regarded as definitive as regards the rights and obligations of those subject to the law, this proposition would have considerable force. But that is not the legal position. As will be explained below, national rules implementing a directive are to be interpreted as far as possible so as to be consistent with the terms of the relevant directive, while if a Member State fails properly to implement a directive, an individual may invoke against the national authorities of that State those provisions of the directive which are unconditional and sufficiently precise for judicial implementation. The effect of the foregoing is that the rights and obligations of natural and legal persons, and of authorities of Member States, cannot be said with certainty to be definitively stated by national transposing rules which reformulate the requirements of Community law into the language of the national draftsman. No prudent legal adviser would in all cases feel confident that he or she could interpret such national implementing rules without taking

---

[71] Case C–340/96 *Commission v United Kingdom* [1999] E.C.R. I–2023, paras 27–30 (system of undertakings established to enforce drinking water quality standards inadequate to the extent that implementing legislation did not set out such a specific legal framework as contemplated by the Court's case law).

[72] Case C–2/97 *Borsana* [1998] E.C.R. I8597, para.49.

[73] Dir.85/374 on the approximation of the laws of the Member States concerning liability for defective products [1985] O.J. L210/29.

[74] The Commission unsuccessfully challenged certain aspects of this implementation—as regards the so-called "state of the art" defence—in Case C–300/95 *Commission v United Kingdom* [1997] E.C.R. I–2649.

account of relevant terms of the relevant directive. Litigation on the scope of the national implementing rules would be likely to involve consideration of not only the terms of those rules, but also the terms of the relevant directive, and of any case law of the ECJ on those terms. In short, translating the requirements of directives into national legal language does not in all cases guarantee improved legal certainty for individuals. It may simply present all concerned with two legal texts to interpret instead of one. It is these considerations, amongst others, which have led to increased use of a technique of transposition sometimes called "copy-out", but which we prefer, in the interests of precision, to describe as "selective word for word incorporation".

A further consideration which has led to increased use of word for **5–028** word incorporation is that the drafting techniques of the Community institutions do on occasion lead to texts the precise meaning of which cannot be determined with sufficient precision to enable confident reformulation into national legal language of a Member State. Transposition by the incorporation, word for word, of key provisions of the directive, presents those subject to the law, and national courts, with a single text comprising both Community law and national law. This presents a simpler interpretative task than that which results from the consideration of two differently worded texts—the relevant provision of the directive, and the relevant provision of the national transposing legislation. Word for word incorporation may also mean that a reference from an English court on the meaning of the directive will provide a ruling on the meaning of the national implementing provisions. A good example of selective word for word incorporation is to be found in the transposition of the amended waste framework directive, Directive 75/442,[75] as amended by Directive 91/156,[76] which was implemented by the Waste Management Licensing Regulations 1994.[77] While it is not suggested that transposition could or should be entirely achieved by word for word incorporation, the apparent readiness of Government to adopt this approach on a selective basis is to be welcomed.

The period available for Member States to adopt necessary measures of implementation is specified in the directive in question. Since the purpose of such a period is to give Member States the necessary time to adopt transposition measures, they cannot be faulted for not having transposed the directive into their internal

---

[75] [1975] O.J. L194/47.

[76] [1991] O.J. L78/32.

[77] SI 1994/1056. The 1994 Regulations introduce into domestic environmental law the concept of "Directive waste", which is defined by reference to the definition in the Directive and to the potentially waste substances listed in Annex I of the Directive, which is reproduced as Part II of Sch.4 to the Regulations. For other examples of transposition of environmental directives by selective word for word incorporation, see Wyatt "Litigating Community Environmental Law", 10 J.E.L. 9–14.

legal order before expiry of that period.[78] Nevertheless, it follows from Articles 10 and 249 EC, and from the directive itself, that during the period allowed for implementation, Member States are required to refrain from adopting measures liable seriously to compromise the result prescribed.[79]

5–029 **(b) The duty of national courts to construe national rules in accordance with relevant directives.** Even before the European Court indicated that there was any *obligation* upon national courts to seek to construe national legislation in accordance with directives, examples could be found of national courts seeking preliminary rulings on the meaning of directives in order to give an appropriate construction to national implementing rules.[80] It was in *von Colson*,[81] and *Harz*,[82] that the Court first referred to the principle that national courts were under an obligation so to interpret national law. It did so in the context of national implementation of Directive 76/207 on equal treatment for men and women in employment. The Court stated:

> "the Member States' obligation arising from a directive to achieve the result envisaged by the directive and their duty under Article [10] of the Treaty to take all appropriate measures, whether general or particular, to ensure the fulfilment of that obligation, is binding on all the authorities of Member States including, for matters within their jurisdiction, the courts. It follows that, in applying the national law and in particular the provisions of a national law specifically introduced in order to implement Directive No 76/207, national courts are required to interpret their national law in the light of the wording and the purpose of the directive in order to achieve the result referred to in the third paragraph of Article [249 EC]."[83]

The Court qualified this statement two paragraphs later in its judgment:

> "it is for the national court to interpret and apply the legislation adopted for the implementation of the directive in conformity

---

[78] Case C–129/96 *Inter-Environnement Wallonie* [1997] E.C.R. I–7411, para.43.
[79] *ibid.*, para.50. See also, e.g. Case C–14/02 *ATRAL* [2003] E.C.R. I–4431; Case C–157/02 *Rieser Internationale Transporte* [2004] E.C.R. I–1477; Case C–316/04 *Stichting Zuid-Hollandse Milieufederatie* (Judgment of November 10, 2005); Case C–144/04 *Mangold* (Judgment of November 22, 2005).
[80] Case 32/74 *Friedrich Haaga GmbH* [1974] E.C.R. 1201; Case 111/75 *Impresa Costruzioni* [1976] E.C.R. 657.
[81] Case 14/83 *von Colson* [1984] E.C.R. 1891.
[82] Case 79/83 *Dorit Harz* [1984] E.C.R. 1921.
[83] Case 14/83 *von Colson* [1984] E.C.R. 1891, para.26; Case 79/83 *Dorit Harz* [1984] E.C.R. 1921, para.26.

with the requirements of Community law, *in so far as it is given discretion to do so under national law.*"[84]

Although the judgment in *von Colson* introduced the idea of consistent interpretation into Community law, it also suggested certain restrictions on the scope of that principle: first, that consistent interpretation applied only to national legislation specifically introduced to implement a directive; secondly, that whether the domestic judge engaged in the process of consistent interpretation was a matter of discretion whose parameters were determined by national law itself; and thirdly, that consistent interpretation applied primarily in vertical disputes, when an individual sought to rely on an unimplemented directive against the defaulting Member State.

In the subsequent case of *Marleasing*, however, the Court rejected all three such restrictions.[85] It is clear from that case (and many others since) that consistent interpretation applies to all domestic legislation which is relevant to the subject-matter of the directive at issue, regardless of the date at or purpose for which that domestic legislation was introduced.[86] Moreover, consistent interpretation is a duty imposed upon the national courts by Community law, which must be discharged regardless of the limits of their discretion under domestic law alone. And this duty of consistent interpretation is activated even within the context of horizontal disputes between two private parties—a development which is crucially important given that (as we shall see) directly effective provisions of directives are in principle incapable of being enforced in such situations.[87] Indeed, the ruling in *Aslanidou* illustrates that the duty of consistent interpretation arises even in disputes where the Member State, having failed correctly to implement a directive within the applicable time limit, nevertheless requests the national court to interpret existing legislation in conformity with that directive, to the potential detriment of the other (private) party to the proceedings.[88]

However, *Marleasing* also highlighted an important limitation on **5–030** this case law: national courts are only obliged to interpret domestic legislation in conformity with Community directives *in so far as it is possible to do so.*[89] The duty of consistent interpretation, therefore, does not require national courts to distort any reasonable meaning of the words, or, as the Court expressly confirmed in *Pupino*, to

[84] Case 14/83 *von Colson* [1984] E.C.R. 1891, para.28; Case 79/83 *Dorit Harz* [1984] E.C.R. 1921, para.28. (emphasis added).
[85] Case 106/89 *Marleasing* [1990] E.C.R. 4135.
[86] Also, e.g. Case C–334/92 *Wagner Miret* [1993] E.C.R. I–6911.
[87] Also, e.g. Case C–2/97 *Borsana* [1998] E.C.R. I–8597; Case C–343/98 *Collino* [2000] E.C.R. I–6659; Cases C–397–403/01 *Pfeiffer* [2004] E.C.R. I–8835; Case C–350/03 *Schulte* (Judgment of October 25, 2005).
[88] Case C–142/04 *Aslanidou* (Judgment of July 14, 2005).
[89] Case 106/89 *Marleasing* [1990] E.C.R. 4135, para.8.

adopt a construction which is simply *contra legem*.[90] What is expected, as the Court explained in its ruling in *Pfeiffer*, is that the domestic courts will consider national law *as a whole* in order to assess to what extent it may be applied so as not to produce a result contrary to that sought by a Community directive.[91] Nevertheless, the Court is well aware of the possibility that, in some cases, it may not be possible to achieve the result intended by a Community directive through the medium of consistent interpretation.[92] In such situations, in the absence of straightforward direct effect of the relevant provisions of that directive, the only solution is to seek to hold the Member State liable in damages in accordance with the *Francovich* case law.[93]

The case law demonstrates that Community law imposes certain other restrictions on the scope of the duty of consistent interpretation. First, there has been some debate about whether national courts are obliged to discharge their duty of consistent interpretation even before the deadline for transposition of the relevant directive has expired. On the one hand, it could be argued that the Member State's obligations during this time are limited to the negative duty to refrain from acts liable seriously to compromise the result envisaged by the directive.[94] On the other hand, it could equally be submitted that the more positive duty of consistent interpretation should be activated even before the deadline for transposition has expired, at least where the Member State has already adopted specific implementing measures.[95] The Court's attitude is not yet entirely clear, but the ruling in *Centrosteel* contains a dictum to the effect that the duty of consistent interpretation arises where the national court is seised of a dispute falling within the scope of the directive *and* arising from facts postdating the expiry of the period for transposing that directive into domestic law.[96] The ECJ may deliver a more definitive ruling on this issue in the case of *Adeneler*; certainly, Advocate General Kokott argued strongly in favour of imposing the duty of consistent interpretation upon the national courts, as regards existing domestic legislation, even before the expiry of the relevant directive's deadline for transposition.[97]

---

[90] See Case C–105/03 *Pupino* (Judgment of June 16, 2005), para.47.
[91] Cases C–397–403/01 *Pfeiffer* [2004] E.C.R. I–8835.
[92] e.g. Case C–91/92 *Paola Faccini Dori v Recreb Srl* [1994] E.C.R. I–3325; Case C–192/94 *El Corte Inglés* [1996] E.C.R. I–1281; Case C–235/03 *QDQ Media* [2005] E.C.R. I–1937.
[93] Discussed in detail in Ch.6.
[94] See above.
[95] *cf.* Advocate General Kokott in Case C–313/02 *Wippel* [2004] E.C.R. I–9483; Advocate General Tizzano in Case C–144/04 *Mangold* (Opinion of June 30, 2005; Judgment of November 22, 2005).
[96] Case C–456/98 *Centrosteel v Adipol* [2000] E.C.R. I–6007, para.17. Also, e.g. Cases C–240–4/98 *Océano Grupo Editorial* [2000] E.C.R. I–4941; Cases C–397–403/01 *Pfeiffer* [2004] E.C.R. I–8835.
[97] To be precise, as from the date of the directive's entry into force: see Case C–212/04 *Adeneler* (Opinion of October 27, 2005; Judgment pending).

Secondly, the duty of consistent interpretation is in any case limited by the general principles of Community law, in particular, the principles of legal certainty and non-retroactivity. Thus, a directive cannot, of itself and independently of national legislation adopted by a Member State for its implementation, have the effect of determining or aggravating the liability in criminal law of persons who act in contravention of the provisions of that directive—whether through straightforward direct effect, or through the medium of consistent interpretation.[98] Thus, for example, *Arcaro* concerned an Italian citizen charged before the criminal courts with having discharged dangerous substances into the aquatic environment. The prosecution was based on Italian legislation adopted to implement a Community environmental protection directive but which had failed to do so correctly. The national court was unsure whether nevertheless to construe the Italian measure so as to conform with the directive and thereby criminalise the defendant's behaviour. The Court of Justice advised the national court that the duty of consistent interpretation reached its limit where this would lead to the imposition upon a private party of obligations laid down in an incorrectly implemented directive.[99]

(c) The vertical direct effect of directives. By "vertical" direct 5–031 effect is meant the capacity of a provision of a directive to be invoked by private individuals or companies against authorities of a Member State (but not against other individuals or companies). It was initially considered that directives gave rise exclusively to rights and obligations as between the Member States and the Community institutions.[1] Yet the Court gave an early indication that directives might be capable of direct effect when, in *Grad v Finanzamt Traunstein*,[2] it indicated that decisions addressed to Member States might have such effects. Since decisions, like directives, are binding on those to whom they are addressed, the Court's reasoning seemed applicable both to decisions and to directives. In *Grad*, the Court said that it did not follow from the fact that, by virtue of Article 249 EC, regulations were directly applicable and therefore by their nature capable of producing direct effects, that other categories of legal measures mentioned in that Article could never produce

---

[98] Case 80/86 *Criminal proceedings against Kolpinghuis Nijmegen* [1987] E.C.R. 3969.
[99] Case C–168/95 *Criminal proceedings against Luciano Arcaro* [1996] E.C.R. I–4705. Also, e.g. Cases C–387/02, C–391/02 and C–403/02 *Berlusconi* [2005] E.C.R. I–3565; Case C–384/02 *Allan Bang* (Judgment of November 22, 2005).
[1] See e.g. *Joseph Aim* [1972] C.M.L.R. 901 (Cour d'Appel de Paris); *Firma Baer Getreide BmbH* [1972] C.M.L.R. 539 (Hessischer Verwaltunggerichtschof); and even after the development of the ECJ's case law, *Cohn-Bendit* [1979] Dalloz Jur 155 (Conseil d'Etat); and *Kloppenburg*, Judgment of April 25, 1985 (Bundesfinanzhof). See (1985) 10 E.L.Rev. 303.
[2] Case 9/70 [1970] E.C.R. 825; also Case 20/70 *Transports Lesage* [1970] E.C.R. 861; Case 23/70 *Haselhorst* [1970] E.C.R. 881.

similar effects. "In particular", said the Court, "the provision according to which decisions are binding in their entirety on those to whom they are addressed enables the question to be put whether the obligation created by the decisions can only be invoked by the Community institutions against the addressee or whether such a right may possibly be exercised by all those who have an interest in the fulfilment of this obligation".[3] In the Court's view, to adopt the alternative solution would call into question the binding nature of decisions, and diminish their useful effect. While the effects of a decision might not be identical with those of a provision contained in a regulation, this difference did not preclude the possibility that the end result, namely the right of the individual to invoke the measure before the courts, might be the same as that of a directly applicable provision of a regulation. In the Court's view, this conclusion was reinforced by the wording of Article 234 EC, pursuant to which national courts were empowered to refer to the Court of Justice all questions regarding the validity and interpretation of all acts of the institutions without distinction; this implied that individuals could invoke such acts before national courts. In each particular case, it must be ascertained whether the nature, background and wording of the provision in question were capable of producing direct effects in the legal relationships between the addressee of the act and third parties.

These principles were to provide the basis for the Court's later case law on the direct effect of directives, starting with its judgment in *van Duyn v Home Office*.[4] This case concerned a provision of a directive allowing, *inter alia*, the deportation of a worker of another Member State on public policy grounds based exclusively on the personal conduct of the individual concerned. The Court noted that the provision laid down an obligation which is not subject to any exception or condition and which, by its very nature, did not require the intervention of any act on the part either of the institutions of the Community or of the Member States, and concluded that the provision conferred on individuals rights which were enforceable by them in the courts of a Member State and which the national courts were bound to protect.[5] Similar reasoning was adopted in later cases.[6] Individual discretionary decisions of the national authorities, as well as legislative provisions, could be challenged by individuals relying upon the direct effect of provisions of directives.[7] In the *Ratti* case, the Court added a further reason for appropriately worded

---

[3] Case 9/70 [1970] E.C.R. 825, para.5.
[4] Case 41/74 [1974] E.C.R. 1337.
[5] *ibid.*, paras 13–15.
[6] See e.g. Case 36/75 *Rutili* [1975] E.C.R. 1219; Case 51/76 *Verbond van Nederlandse Ondernemingen v Inspecteur der Invoerrechten en Accijnzen* [1977] E.C.R. 113; Case 38/77 *Enka* [1977] E.C.R. 2203.
[7] Case 41/74 *van Duyn* [1974] E.C.R. 1337; Case 36/75 *Rutili* [1975] E.C.R. 1219.

provisions of directives being held to be directly effective: a Member State which had not adopted the implementing measures required by the directive in the prescribed period could not rely upon its own failure to perform the obligations which the directive entailed.[8] This was a kind of estoppel argument and it paved the way for the Court's later rulings excluding reliance upon directives against private individuals.[9] The Court has confirmed its jurisprudence on the direct effect of directives in a consistent case law.[10] The current formulation of the test for direct effect applied by the ECJ appears as follows in *Cooperativa Agricola Zootecnica S. Antonio v Amministrazione delle finanze dello Stato*:

"The Court has consistently held ... that, whenever the provisions of a directive appear, as far as their subject-matter is concerned, to be unconditional and sufficiently precise, those provisions may be relied upon before the national courts by an individual against the State where that State has failed to implement the directive in national law by the end of the period prescribed or where it has failed to implement the directive correctly.

A Community provision is unconditional where it sets forth an obligation which is not qualified by any condition, or subject, in its implementation or effects, to the taking of any measure either by the Community institutions or by the Member States . . .

Moreover, a provision is sufficiently precise to be relied on by an individual and applied by a national court where it sets out an obligation in unequivocal terms."[11]

The second condition laid down above, which includes the require- **5–032** ment that a Community provision not be subject, in its implementation of effect, to the taking of any measure either by the Community institutions *or by the Member States*, may mean that a provision of a directive becomes directly effective because a Member State has partially implemented the directive in question, thereby removing what would otherwise have been a bar to the direct effect of that provision. Thus, a directive may not be directly effective as regards any particular remedy, such as reinstatement for dismissal contrary to its terms; but if a Member State chooses to make the remedy of

---

[8] Case 148/78 *Criminal proceedings against Tullio Ratti* [1979] E.C.R. 1629. This ground appears in subsequent case law as a feature in the Court's reasoning in support of the direct effect of directives.
[9] See further, below.
[10] Case 8/81 *Becker* [1982] E.C.R. 53; Case 255/81 *Grendel* [1982] E.C.R. 2301; Case 5/84 *Direct Cosmetics* [1985] E.C.R. 617; Case 152/84 *Marshall v Southampton and South-West Hampshire Area Health Authority* [1986] E.C.R. 723.
[11] Case C–246/94 [1996] E.C.R. I–4373.

damages available, the directive may be relied upon to set aside a provision of national law which prevents the remedy of damages under national law from being effective.[12] Even if the above conditions appear to be satisfied, it must be added that a provision of a directive will not be enforceable by a national *judicial* authority if intended by the legislator to be given effect by national administrative authorities.[13] Nevertheless, a provision of a directive which satisfies the conditions for direct effect, and has not been implemented by national law, is binding on all the organs of the administration, including decentralised authorities and municipalities,[14] and other bodies which, irrespective of their legal form, have been given responsibility by the public authorities and under their supervision for providing a public service.[15]

It is to be noted that a provision of a directive may only be relied upon by individuals before national courts where the Member State has failed properly to implement that provision within the period prescribed for that purpose.[16] Where a directive has been properly implemented by national measures, its effects extend to individuals through the medium of those implementing measures.[17] And where a directive has been properly implemented by national measures, it is not open to the litigant to side-step the appropriate provisions of national law and rely upon the direct effect of the provisions of the directive.[18] However, the Court in its *Marks & Spencer* ruling rejected any absolute proposition that, if a Member State has correctly implemented the provisions of a directive into domestic law, individuals are thereby deprived of any possibility of relying before the national courts on the rights which they may derive from those provisions. In fact, the adoption of national measures correctly implementing a directive does not necessarily exhaust the effects of the latter measure; Member States remain bound *actually* to ensure full application of the directive *even after* the adoption of implementing measures. Individuals are therefore entitled to rely before national courts on the precise and unconditional provisions of a directive whenever the full application of the directive is not in fact secured, i.e. not only where the directive has not been implemented or has been implemented incorrectly, but also where the national measures correctly implementing the directive are not being applied

---

[12] Case 14/83 *von Colson* [1984] E.C.R. 1891; Case 79/83 *Dorit Harz* [1984] E.C.R. 1921; Case C–271/91 *Marshall v Southampton and South-West Hampshire Area Health Authority* [1993] E.C.R. I–4367.
[13] Case 815/79 *Cremonini and Vrankovich* [1980] E.C.R. 3583.
[14] Case 103/88 *Fratelli Constanzo v Commune di Milano* [1989] E.C.R. 1839, paras 31 and 32.
[15] Case C–188/89 *Foster v British Gas* [1990] E.C.R. I–3313; Cases C–253/96 to C–258/97 *Helmut Kampelmann* [1997] E.C.R. I–6907.
[16] Case 148/78 *Criminal proceedings against Tullio Ratti* [1979] E.C.R. 1629; Case 8/81 *Becker* [1982] E.C.R. 53; Case 126/82 *Smit* [1983] E.C.R. 73.
[17] Case 102/79 *Commission v Belgium* [1980] E.C.R. 1473; Case 8/81 *Becker* [1982] E.C.R. 53.
[18] Case 270/81 *Felicitas* [1982] E.C.R. 2771.

in such a way as to achieve the result sought by it (e.g.) because the national administrative authorities are in fact applying the domestic implementing legislation in a manner which is inconsistent with the parent directive.[19]

Conversely, it should be noted that Member States remain obliged to implement directives into domestic law, notwithstanding the fact that, in the absence of such implementation, the provisions concerned would be directly effective. The direct effect of a directive is a consequence of the failure of a Member State properly to implement the directive, by ensuring that its provisions are given full force and effect through the medium of binding national rules, and national judicial recognition of direct effect does not remedy the Member State's failure to adopt appropriate legislative measures.[20]

(d) No horizontal direct effect for directives. The Court has held 5–033 that, while directives may be invoked against the State (vertical direct effect), they can never be invoked against private individuals (horizontal direct effect).[21] The legal effects of directives (and presumably decisions addressed to Member States) thus differ from those of both Treaty provisions and regulations, and the reasons for this merit consideration.

Before the judgment in the *Ratti* case,[22] there was nothing in the Court's case law to suggest that the legal effects of a directly effective provision in a directive would be any different from those of a directly effective Treaty provision. Since the Court had held that Treaty provisions were capable of binding individuals, as well as States,[23] it would have followed that directives could have similar effects. There were several arguments, however, which could be made against this conclusion.[24] First, since there was no legal requirement to publish directives, it might seem to be implied that directives could only bind those to whom they were addressed. Secondly, it was arguable that to allow directives to be pleaded against individuals would assimilate directives to regulations, which would run counter to Article 249 EC. Thirdly, there was the argument that to allow directives to be pleaded against individuals would be contrary to the principle of legal certainty, since those subject to obligations contained in directives might be unsure whether to rely upon national implementing legislation, or upon the underlying directives. While none of these arguments were conclusive, there was a further argument, of a political, rather than a legal,

---

[19] Case C–62/00 *Marks & Spencer* [2002] E.C.R. I–6325.
[20] e.g. Case 96/81 *Commission v Netherlands* [1982] E.C.R. 1791.
[21] Case 152/84 *Marshall v Southampton and South-West Hampshire Area Health Authority* [1986] E.C.R. 723.
[22] Case 148/78 *Criminal proceedings against Tullio Ratti* [1979] E.C.R. 1629.
[23] See further, above.
[24] See, in general, Easson (1979) 4 E.L.Rev. 67, 70–73; Craig (1997) 22 E.L.Rev. 519, 519–524.

nature: the courts in some Member States were having difficulty in accepting that directives could have direct effect at all;[25] for the ECJ to go even further and recognise horizontal direct effect for directives might further diminish the credibility of the Court of Justice in such Member States, and lead to the uneven enforceability of directives in the Community.

The Court laid the conceptual foundations for its later compromise solution in 1979, in the *Ratti* case, in which the Court declared that:

"a Member State which has not adopted the implementing measures required by the directive in the prescribed period *may not rely, as against individuals, on its own failure to perform the obligations which the directive entails.*"[26]

The italicised words indicate that the legal basis for the direct effect of directives was that a State could not rely upon its own wrong as a defence to an action based upon a directive before its own courts. This doctrine seemed to restrict the application of directives by national courts to actions against defaulting Member States, and to rule out actions against individuals. The Court's case law following *Ratti* incorporated the above mentioned formulation.[27]

The Court's judgment in *Marshall*[28] seemed to lay speculation to rest. The appellant in the national proceedings, Miss Marshall, was an employee of an Area Health Authority in the United Kingdom. She had been dismissed at the age of 62, since she had passed "the normal retirement age" (of 60) applied by the Authority to female employees. An exception had in fact been made for Miss Marshall to work until the age of 62. The normal retiring age for male employees was 65.

5–034   Miss Marshall instituted proceedings against the Authority alleging sex discrimination contrary to the principle of equality of treatment laid down in Directive 76/207.[29] The Area Health Authority argued before the Court of Justice: (1) that the directive could not be relied upon against individuals; and (2) that the Authority, although a public authority emanating from central Government, had acted, not in its capacity as a State authority, in dismissing Miss Marshall, but in its capacity as employer. The Court held that since a directive under Article 249 EC was binding only upon "each Member State to which it was addressed", it could not of itself

---

[25] See Pescatore (1983) 8 E.L.Rev. 155.

[26] Case 148/78 *Criminal proceedings against Tullio Ratti* [1979] E.C.R. 1629, para.22 (emphasis added).

[27] See e.g. Case 8/81 *Becker* [1982] E.C.R. 53.

[28] Case 152/84 *Marshall v Southampton and South-West Hampshire Area Health Authority* [1986] E.C.R. 723.

[29] [1976] O.J. L39/40.

impose obligations upon an individual. However, this did not preclude an individual relying upon a directive against the State, regardless of the capacity in which the latter was acting, whether as an employer or as a public authority. The United Kingdom had argued that the possibility of relying on provisions of the directive against the Authority would give rise to arbitrary and unfair distinctions between the rights of State employees and those of private employees. The Court of Justice did not find this argument convincing. On the contrary, such a distinction might easily be avoided if the Member State concerned implemented the directive in national law.

The *Marshall* decision allows the invocation of "private law" **5–035** directives against the State, but rules out such actions against private parties. While the compromise may be justifiable on policy grounds, the Court's reasoning seems plausible rather than compelling. The Court says that directives bind the State, and therefore cannot be invoked against individuals. Yet this very argument failed in *Defrenne*[30] to prevent Article 141 EC being held to bind private parties as well as the State. What is true of the Treaty should also, it is thought, be true of directives, for the obligation to comply with a directive is itself a Treaty obligation, and the Court has held that directives have an effect no less binding than that of any other rule of Community law.[31]

That is not to say that the Court's ruling in *Marshall* could not be justified on legal grounds. On the contrary, there has always been a case to be made against the horizontal effect of directives based on the principle of legal certainty. Private individuals should clearly not be placed in unreasonable doubt as to their obligations by requiring the scrutiny of overlapping texts at both the national and Community level as a prerequisite to a complete appreciation of the law. The fact that individuals may be bound by Treaty provisions and by regulations does not give rise to the same risk of uncertainty. The Treaty is a single document with a limited number of provisions which may directly bind individuals; the threat to legal certainty is insignificant. As for regulations, it has always been clear that they constitute direct Community legislation; they are as capable of binding individuals as any provisions of national law, and are only subject to national implementation where they so provide. In this latter respect, regulations may be distinguished from directives, and decisions addressed to Member States, which must always be implemented by national legislation, resulting in the duplication of the substance of Community texts, and possible legal uncertainty for individuals. By way of contrast, the principle of legal certainty cannot properly be invoked by a national authority as a ground for denying

---

[30] Case 43/75 *Defrenne v Sabena* [1976] E.C.R. 455. See further, above.
[31] Case 79/72 *Commission v Italy* [1972] E.C.R. 667; Case 52/75 *Commission v Italy* [1976] E.C.R. 277.

the legal effects of a directive, irrespective of the capacity in which the authority is alleged to be bound. National authorities exercise power derived from the Member States, and the Member States are in a position to take appropriate measures to ensure legal certainty from their point of view, either in the course of the legislative process in which they participate, or through an action for annulment if they consider that the vagueness of a directive prejudices its legality.

A disadvantage of the Court's approach in *Marshall*, however, is that it rules out horizontal effect even in cases where such effect could not prejudice the legal security of individuals, for example in cases where the direct effect of provisions of a "private law" directive have already been established in proceedings against the authorities of a Member State. An alternative approach would have been a case-by-case approach, allowing the possibility of horizontal direct effect, but also allowing the principle of legal certainty to be pleaded as a complete defence to private individuals in some cases, and as justifying prospective effect for the Court's rulings in others.

While the Court of Justice ruled out horizontal direct effect for directives, it nevertheless adopted a broad view of the concept of "Member State" for the purpose of the principle in *Marshall* that directives might be invoked against the Member States but not against individuals. In *Foster v British Gas* the Court held that:

> "a body, whatever its legal form, which has been made responsible, pursuant to a measure adopted by the state, for providing a public service under the control of the state and which has for that purpose special powers beyond those which result from the normal rules applicable in relations between individuals is included in any event among the bodies against which the provisions of a directive capable of having direct effect may be relied upon."[32]

5–036 The ruling in *Marshall* did not prevent continued debate on the question of horizontal direct effect for directives. Two Advocates General indicated in subsequent Opinions that they favoured horizontal direct effect for directives.[33] In *Paola Faccini Dori v Recreb Srl*,[34] the Court once again considered this controversial question.

---

[32] See Case C–188/89 [1990] E.C.R. I–3313, para.20. The court pointed out that its previous case law indicated that Directives could be relied upon against tax authorities (e.g. Case 8/81 *Becker* [1982] E.C.R. 53); local or regional authorities (e.g. Case 103/88 *Constanzo* [1989] E.C.R. 1839); and constitutionally independent authorities responsible for the maintenance of public order and safety (e.g. Case 222/84 *Johnston v RUC* [1986] E.C.R. 1651).

[33] Advocate General Van Gerven in Case C–271/91 *Marshall v Southampton and South-West Hampshire Area Health Authority* [1993] E.C.R. I–4367; Advocate General Jacobs in Case C–316/93 *Vaneetveld* [1994] E.C.R. I–763.

[34] Case C–91/92 [1994] E.C.R. I–3325.

The national proceedings arose from a contract for an English language correspondence course concluded off business premises at Milan Central Railway Station by Miss Faccini Dori. She later thought better of the transaction, and wrote purporting to cancel the contract, indicating that she relied on the right of cancellation provided under Directive 85/577.[35] This Directive had not been transposed into Italian law at the material time, and an Italian court asked for a preliminary ruling on the question whether the directive was nevertheless capable of taking effect as between individuals. In addition to the parties, seven Member States and the Commission made written and/or oral observations in the proceedings before the European Court. All the Member States except Greece argued against horizontal direct effect; as did the Commission. Advocate General Lenz's Opinion pronounced in favour of horizontal direct effect, but only for the future. He pointed out that under the EEC Treaty the publication of directives was not mandatory, and argued that the "basic condition for a burden imposed on the citizen by legislative measures is their *constitutive publication* in an official organ".[36] But in the case of directives adopted following the entry into force of the Maastricht Treaty on November 1, 1993, he thought that the situation was fundamentally different, since Article 254 EC required directives to be published in the *Official Journal.* No objection based on the absence of publication could thereafter be raised against horizontal direct effect.

The Court of Justice confirmed its judgment in *Marshall* that a directive cannot of itself impose obligations on an individual and could not therefore be relied upon as such against an individual. The basis for the Court's case law on the vertical direct effect of directives was that a directive was binding under Article 249 EC only in relation "to each Member State to which it is addressed". That case law sought to prevent "the State from taking advantage of its own failure to comply with Community law".[37] But, in the view of the Court of Justice:

> "The effect of extending that case law to the sphere of relations between individuals would be to recognise a power in the Community to enact obligations for individuals with immediate effect, whereas it has competence to do only where it is empowered to adopt regulations.
>
> It follows that, in the absence of measures transposing the directive within the prescribed time-limit, consumers cannot derive from the directive itself a right of cancellation as against traders with whom they have concluded a contract or enforce such a right in a national court."[38]

---

[35] [1985] O.J. L372/31.
[36] Para.64 of the Opinion.
[37] Case C–91/92 [1994] E.C.R. I–3325, para.22.
[38] *ibid.*, paras 24–25.

Thus, the Court accepted the legal analyses pressed upon it by half-a-dozen Member States, and by the Commission. These arguments were essentially to the effect that the Court's clear and recent judgment in *Marshall* was correct, and should be adhered to. While the Court endorsed *Marshall*, it also emphasised the duty of a national court to interpret national law, whether adopted before or after a relevant directive, and whether the dispute was vertical or horizontal in nature, as far as possible in accordance with the directive.[39] Where the result prescribed by the directive could not be achieved by way of interpretation, the Court recalled the duty of Member States to make good the damage caused to individuals through failure to transpose a directive, where the requisite conditions for such liability were fulfilled.[40]

5–037 **(e) The "incidental" direct effect of directives.** While the case law has repeatedly emphasised that a directive cannot of itself impose obligations on an individual, the Court appears to accept that the enforcement of an unimplemented directive vertically against the Member State will sometimes have certain "incidental effects" for private parties—but without amounting to some sort of prohibited horizontal direct effect for the relevant directive.

Consider, for example, an action for judicial review of a national authority's decision to grant planning permission for certain mining works to be carried out, on the grounds that that decision was adopted without the Member State having conducted an environmental impact assessment as required under Directive 85/337.[41] On its face, such an action is clearly based on the vertical direct effect of the Directive by the claimant against the public body; but it is readily apparent that, should the action succeed, it will adversely affect the interests of the third (private) party which was granted the flawed planning permission. The Court in *Wells* held that, in such circumstances, the fact that a third (private) party will suffer certain adverse repercussions for its rights cannot justify preventing an individual from invoking the provisions of the Directive against the delinquent Member State.[42] Consider, along similar lines, the *Medicines Control Agency* case.[43] This involved an action for judicial review of a decision of the Medicines Control Agency granting a marketing authorisation to a company in respect of a proprietary medicinal product, initiated by a competing undertaking which held an original marketing authorisation for a proprietary medicinal product bearing the same name, on the grounds that the authorisation had been

---

[39] See further, above.
[40] See Ch.6 for detailed analysis.
[41] [1985] O.J. L175/40.
[42] Case C–201/02 *Delena Wells* [2004] E.C.R. I–723.
[43] Case C–201/94 [1996] E.C.R. I–5819.

granted by the Agency contrary to the provisions of a Community directive.[44] The Court of Justice held that the holder of the original marketing authorisation could rely upon the relevant provisions of the directive in proceedings before a national court in order to challenge the validity of an authorisation issued by the competent national authority to one of its competitors. Or again, an undertaking which tenders for a public contract and has its tender rejected on grounds inconsistent with the directly effective provision of a Community directive may rely upon that directive to challenge the rejection of its tender, and it seems that this is the case even if the public contract has been awarded to a third party.[45]

However, it can sometimes be very difficult to draw any plausible distinction between (on the one hand) the vertical enforcement of an obligation imposed upon the Member State, which has some merely incidental effect upon a private party, and (on the other hand) recognising that the unimplemented directive has had some more straightforward form of horizontal direct effect between individuals. This difficulty is well illustrated by the Court's case law on the legal effects of Directive 83/189 concerning the notification of draft technical regulations.[46]

Directive 83/189 is designed to protect the free movement of **5–038** goods through a system of preventive control.[47] Article 8 requires Member States to notify all draft technical regulations (as defined in the Directive) to the Commission; Article 9 then provides that such regulations cannot enter into force during certain specified periods. This is intended to give the Commission an opportunity to prevent unlawful obstacles to free movement from arising in the first place, by persuading the Member State to amend its proposed regulations; the Commission also has the option of proposing centralised harmonisation measures which would reduce or eliminate even lawful obstacles to free movement. The Court held in *CIA Security* (as regards Article 8) and *Unilever Italia* (as regards Article 9) that the effectiveness of the Directive's system of preventive control would be greater if breach of the obligation either to notify or to suspend constituted a "substantial procedural defect" such as to render the

---

[44] Dir.65/65 O.J. Sp. Ed. 1965–66; as amended in particular by Dir.87/21 [1987] O.J. L15/36.
[45] Case 103/88 *Fratelli Costanzo* [1989] E.C.R. 1839. The question nevertheless arises of the extent to which Community law recognises that individuals who have ostensibly derived rights under national law from legislative or administrative measures which have been adopted in contravention of the terms of a directive may have legitimate expectations which may or must be respected by national courts and other authorities which are subsequently called upon to disapply the national measure in question.
[46] [1983] O.J. L109/8. Dir.83/189 itself has now been repealed and replaced by Dir.98/34 [1998] O.J. L204/37.
[47] Thus supplementing the more traditional system whereby the Commission and private parties can challenge trade barriers erected by Member States *ex post* by relying on Art.28 EC. See Ch.16.

relevant technical regulations inapplicable to individuals.[48] However, both cases clearly involved horizontal disputes. In *CIA Security*, A claimed that B had marketed alarm systems which did not comply with domestic law; B brought an action under national rules prohibiting unfair trading practices, claiming that the domestic regulations had themselves been adopted by Belgium in breach of Article 8 Directive 83/189. Thanks to their substantial procedural defect, the domestic regulations were to be treated as inapplicable to B—even within the context of its horizontal litigation against A. *Unilever Italia* concerned a contract for the supply of olive oil by C to D. When D refused to accept delivery because the oil did not comply with labelling requirements imposed by recent Italian legislation, C initiated legal proceedings, claiming that the domestic rules were themselves adopted in breach of Article 9 Directive 83/189. Thanks again to their substantial procedural defect, the Italian specifications were to be treated as inapplicable to C—even within this private law dispute between two economic undertakings.

These judgments—clearly involving horizontal litigation about the rights and obligations of private parties *inter se*—cannot be explained in the same way as cases such as *Wells* or the *Medicines Control Agency*. And indeed, the Court in *Unilever Italia* clearly recognised the tension between its approach to Directive 83/189 and its broader case law on the horizontal direct effect of unimplemented directives. Its attempt to resolve this tension was reasoned as follows. Whilst it is true that a directive cannot of itself impose obligations on an individual and cannot therefore be relied on as such against an individual, that case law does not apply where non-compliance with Directive 83/189, which constitutes a substantial procedural defect, renders a technical regulation inapplicable. In such circumstances, Directive 83/189 does not in any way define the substantive scope of the legal rule on the basis of which the national court must decide the case before it. In fact, the Directive creates neither rights nor obligations for individuals.[49]

On one level, it is of course true that Directive 83/189 does not provide for a traditional regulatory code, aimed at governing relations between private individuals, such as one usually finds in fields such as consumer or employment law. Directive 83/189 is concerned rather with a procedural relationship between the Member State and the Commission. Thus, it is also true that the black letter of the Directive does not define the substantive legal rules for determining disputes under national law about unfair trading or contractual performance. In that sense, the Court is correct to observe that the Directive does not seek to create rights or obligations for individuals.

---

[48] Case C–194/94 *CIA Security* [1996] E.C.R. I–2201; Case C–443/98 *Unilever Italia* [2000] E.C.R. I–7535.

[49] Case C–443/98 *Unilever Italia* [2000] E.C.R. I–7535, paras 50–51.

But such reasoning is not entirely convincing. After all, the consequence of rendering the Belgian or Italian technical regulations inapplicable was precisely to transform Directive 83/189 into a measure which determined the substantive legal rules applicable to each case. In particular, the effect of the Directive *as construed by the Court* was to create rights and obligations for private parties, to the extent that one undertaking could now enforce claims and another undertaking was now bound by duties not recognised as such under existing Belgian or Italian law.[50]

It would perhaps be tempting to dismiss the case law on Directive 5–039
83/189 as an unfortunate anomaly. Yet there are other judgments which also hint at some sort of "incidental effect" by unimplemented directives upon private parties. For example, in *Ruiz Bernáldez*, the Court suggested that an obligation to compensate third party victims of car accidents, derived from a Community directive, could be imposed upon insurers even in the face of inadequate national implementing measures.[51] Similarly, in *Pafitis*, the Court ruled that the duty to hold a general meeting of shareholders before raising company capital, again derived from a Community directive, could be enforced in litigation between two groups of private parties so as to set aside incompatible provisions of domestic law.[52] Certain commentators argue that such judgments can best be explained on the basis either that the Court of Justice believed the national judges would resolve any apparent conflict between Community and domestic rules through the duty of consistent interpretation, or that the Court of Justice did not explicitly rule out the possibility of horizontal direct effect because the referring tribunals did not explicitly ask for advice on the issue.[53]

Other commentators have instead taken these various "incidental effects" rulings at face value and tried to construct some broader conceptual framework, capable both of explaining this diverse body of case law as a coherent phenomenon, and of reconciling it with the basic prohibition on directives having horizontal direct effect. One theory which seems to have garnered widespread support involves drawing a distinction between cases of "substitution" (involving the direct and immediate application of Community law) and cases of "exclusion" (involving the mere setting aside of incompatible national rules). In the former situation, the principle of direct effect sets out certain threshold criteria for the justiciability of Community legal norms, including the prohibition on horizontal direct effect for

---

[50] See further Dougan (2001) 38 C.M.L.Rev. 1503.
[51] Case C–129/94 *Ruiz Bernáldez* [1996] E.C.R. I–1829. Similarly, e.g. Case C–537/03 *Candolin* (Judgment of June 30, 2005).
[52] Case C–441/93 *Pafitis* [1996] E.C.R. I–1347.
[53] See further Dougan, "The Disguised Vertical Direct Effect of Directives?" [2000] C.L.J. 586.

unimplemented directives. In the latter situation, it is argued that the principle of supremacy alone provides a sufficient legal mechanism for determining the status of domestic law *vis-à-vis* Community legal norms, without any need to examine the threshold requirements inherent in the concept of direct effect, and may thus result in the imposition of fresh legal obligations upon private parties.[54] If correct, such a theory should obviously have a much broader potential scope of application than the handful of "incidental effects" rulings thus far delivered by the Court of Justice. However, it is difficult to find firm support in the decided cases for such a far-reaching qualification to the rulings in *Marshall* and *Faccini Dori*. After all, in several judgments which could have been classified as mere "exclusion" (rather than a more complex "substitution"), the Court either ruled out any horizontal application of the relevant directive, or merely instructed the national judges to resolve the dispute through the duty of consistent interpretation.[55]

5–040   Consider, most recently, the *Pfeiffer* dispute. This involved German legislation which, by and large, correctly implemented the Working Time Directive rules concerning the maximum 48-hour working week.[56] However, the national legislation also contained a derogation permitting collective agreements to prescribe longer working hours in the case of contracts involving significant periods of "duty time" (*in casu*, emergency workers required to make themselves available to their employer at the place of employment and able to act as and when the need arose). Having established that this derogation was incompatible with the requirements imposed under the Working Time Directive, the next question concerned the potential legal effects of the misimplemented Directive for the purposes of a horizontal dispute involving two private parties. The Court of Justice (sitting as a Grand Chamber) reopened oral proceedings and sought further observations in response to a structured series of questions on precisely this issue. One view would have been to argue that the Working Time Directive could legitimately be invoked so as to set aside the conflicting rule of German law creating an exception in favour of certain collective agreements: that would not involve horizontal direct effect for the Directive, since the employees are not seeking to substitute any new rule

---

[54] For support from various Advocates General, e.g. the Opinions in Cases C–240–4/98 *Océano Grupo Editorial* [2000] E.C.R. I–4941; Case C–343/98 *Collino v Telecom Italia* [2000] E.C.R. I–6659; Case C–287/98 *Linster* [2000] E.C.R. I–6917. For academic support, e.g. Lenz, Sif Tynes and Young, "Horizontal What? Back to Basics" (2000) 25 E.L.Rev. 509; Tridimas, "Black, White and Shades of Grey: Horizontality of Directives Revisited" (2002) 21 Y.E.L. 327.

[55] Consider the rulings in, e.g. Cases C–240–4/98 *Océano Grupo Editorial* [2000] E.C.R. I–4941; Case C–456/98 *Centrolsteel v Adipol* [2000] E.C.R. I–6007; Case C–343/98 *Collino v Telecom Italia* [2000] E.C.R. I–6659; Case C–233/01 *Lo Bue* [2002] E.C.R. I–9411.

[56] Dir.93/104 [1993] O.J. L307/18.

derived from the Directive which does not already exist under German law; it would merely be an example of the exclusionary effects *vis-à-vis* incompatible domestic norms which flow inexorably from the overarching supremacy of Community law. But the Court, having affirmed that the relevant provisions of the Working Time Directive were sufficiently clear, precise and unconditional to enjoy direct effect in principle, affirmed that directives cannot of themselves impose obligations upon individuals and cannot therefore be relied upon as such against individuals. Instead, it was for the national court to interpret existing German law so far as possible to achieve an outcome consistent with the objectives pursued by the Working Time Directive.[57]

Pfeiffer might well undermine the descriptive force of theories such as substitution-exclusion, but it does not suggest anything more satisfactory in their place, which raises suspicions that the Court of Justice has simply created a confusing and inconsistent body of case law on the "incidental effects" of unimplemented directives that is hardly conducive to the cause of legal certainty.

(f) Directives embodying general principles of Community law. The law on when directives can produce legal effects in horizontal situations has been further confused by another recent development, based upon the idea that the obligations imposed by a given directive merely reflect a general principle of Community law, and the latter principle can be enforced as against private individuals, even if the relevant directive has not been properly implemented into national law. 5–041

The main judgment here is *Mangold*.[58] It concerned Directive 2000/78, which was adopted under Article 13 EC and lays down a general framework for combating discrimination, *inter alia*, on grounds of age in the field of employment and occupation.[59] Article 2 of the Directive contains the basic prohibition on age discrimination; but Article 6 permits Member States to objectively justify certain differences in treatment. Germany was given until December 2, 2006 to transpose these provisions into national law. *Mangold* involved the German legislation for protecting workers employed under fixed-term contracts of employment: as a general rule, such contracts may only be concluded if there are "objective grounds" for doing so; but thanks to a derogation taking effect on January 1, 2003

---

[57] Joined Cases C–397/01 to C–403/01 *Pfeiffer* [2004] E.C.R. I–8835. For comments, see Dougan, "Legal Developments" in *Journal of Common Market Studies Annual Review 2004–2005* (Blackwell Publishing, 2006); Prechal (2005) 42 C.M.L.Rev. 1445. Consider also Joined Cases C–387/02, C–391/02 and C–403/02 *Berlusconi* [2005] E.C.R. I–3565 (contrasting the Advocate General's Opinion with the ECJ's ruling).

[58] Case C–144/04 *Mangold* (Judgment of November 22, 2005).

[59] Dir.2000/78 [2000] O.J. L303/16.

and running until December 31, 2006, fixed-term contracts could be concluded without showing any "objective grounds" where the worker was aged 52 or above.

The ECJ found that these German rules amounted to *prima facie* discrimination under Article 2 Directive 2000/78 which could not be objectively justified under Article 6 of that measure. However, the case involved two issues relating to the potential effects of the unimplemented Directive within the national legal system. First, the deadline for transposition of the Directive into German law had not yet expired; as we know, directives cannot have direct effect until such deadlines have elapsed. Secondly, the actual dispute in *Mangold* was horizontal: a private employer had hired a worker aged 56 on a fixed-term contract, relying upon the German rules; the legality of that fixed-term contract was challenged by the worker, relying on Directive 2000/78. To overcome these twin obstacles, the Court observed that the principle of non-discrimination on grounds of age must in fact be regarded as a general principle of Community law; Directive 2000/78 does not in itself lay down the principle of equal treatment as regards employment and occupation. As such, observance of the general principle of equal treatment on grounds of age cannot be made conditional upon expiry of the implementation period in respect of Directive 2000/78; it is the responsibility of national courts to provide the legal protection which individuals derive from Community law, if necessary, by setting aside any incompatible provision of domestic law.

5–042   *Mangold* is another judgment which suggests that the Court is actively exploring new avenues for avoiding the heavily criticised strictures of its case law on the legal effects of unimplemented directives: the national courts are not enforcing a directive against an individual, only the general principle of Community law which the directive embodies.[60] To be fair, *Mangold* is not entirely without precedent: after all, the Court has long held that the Equal Pay Directive[61] merely elaborates on the provisions of Article 141 EC and, as such, can be relied upon even in horizontal disputes against national rules which do not fully comply with the requirements imposed by Community law.[62] But that concerned a Treaty provision, not a general principle of Community law; it was not obvious before *Mangold* that general principles of Community law were capable of creating rights and obligations between private parties.[63]

---

[60] For comments, see Dougan, "Legal Developments" in *Journal of Common Market Studies Annual Review 2005–2006* (Blackwell Publishing, 2006); Editorial, "Horizontal Direct Effect: a Law of Diminishing Coherence?" (2006) 43 C.M.L.Rev. 1.

[61] Dir.75/117 [1975] O.J. L45/19.

[62] e.g. Case C–381/99 *Brunnhofer* [2001] E.C.R. I–4961.

[63] On this issue, see Ch.7.

How far will the ECJ be prepared to carry this idea? Speculation will surely focus on which other directives should be considered merely to embody some general principle of Community law which is enforceable even in the absence of proper transposition into national law. In this regard, the Court in *Mangold* clearly anticipated that its ruling should apply not only to equal treatment as regards age, but also the other forms of discrimination referred to in Directive 2000/78 (such as religion, disability and sexual orientation). Moving beyond Directive 2000/78: surely (say) the principle of equal treatment on grounds of sex is recognised as a general principle of Community law which gives rise to enforceable rights, and should be capable of doing so *à la Mangold* even in horizontal disputes where the Equal Treatment Directive[64] has not been correctly implemented into national law; whereas (e.g.) even if a principle such as consumer protection were to be treated as one of the general principles of Community law, it is surely too nebulous to be capable of creating justiciable individual rights and obligations independently of the various directives adopted by the Community legislature to deal with specific categories of consumer disputes.

But we should not let our speculation run away with itself altogether, by seeing in *Mangold* a virtual replacement-in-waiting for the lop-sided direct effect of whole swathes of directives. After all, national law must respect the general principles of Community law *not* in the abstract *but only* where it falls within the scope of the Treaty, in particular, by either derogating from or implementing one of the Member State's obligations.[65] In *Mangold* itself, this requirement was satisfied because the German rules on fixed-term employment contracts were intended to implement the provisions of the Framework Agreement on Fixed Term Work as put into effect by Directive 1999/70.[66] In the absence of such Community secondary legislation, one assumes that the German rules on fixed-term contracts would not have fallen within the scope of Community law at all, and the general principle of equal treatment on grounds of age would have been inapplicable. Thus, the latter cannot act as a substitute for Directive 2000/78 in every case; it can only do so as regards those situations which, because they are already regulated at the supranational level, are capable of bringing the relevant national legislation within the scope of Community law so as to become subject to its general principles.

Thus, as an alternative to the horizontal direct effect of an unimplemented directive, the *Mangold* approach seems merely to bring another layer of arbitrariness to a field of Community law already characterised by an undesirable degree of inconsistency and confusion.

---

[64] Dir.76/207 [1976] O.J. L39/40.
[65] See further Ch.7.
[66] Dir.1999/70 [1999] O.J. L175/43.

The legal effects of international agreements binding on the Community and of customary international law

Direct effect of international agreements which introduce asymmetry of obligations or create special relations with the Community

5–043   The EC Treaty makes provision for the conclusion of agreements between the Community and non-Member countries.[67] The stage has long been reached when it could be said that:

> "As far as the Community is concerned, an agreement concluded by the Council with a non-member country in accordance with the provisions of the EC Treaty is an act of a Community institution, and the provisions of such an agreement form an integral part of Community law."[68]

Equally, decisions of a Council of Association adopted to give effect to the international agreement under which it was established, are regarded as an integral part of the Community legal system.[69] The Court has also held that if an international agreement to which the Community is party provides for an international court to settle disputes between the Community and non-member countries, the decisions of that court would bind the Court of Justice when it was called upon to rule, by way of preliminary ruling or in a direct action, on the interpretation of the international agreement as part of the Community legal order.[70]

Appropriately worded provisions of an international agreement between the Community and a non-member country may have direct effect:

> "The Court has consistently held that a provision of an agreement concluded by the Community with non-member countries must be regarded as directly effective when, having regard to its wording and the purpose and nature of the agreement itself, the provisions contains a clear and precise obligation which is not subject, in its implementation or effects, to the adoption of any subsequent measure."[71]

---

[67] See in particular Arts 133, 300 and 310 EC. The Community may also conclude agreements pursuant to powers implied from its internal competence, see e.g. Case 22/70 *AETR* [1971] E.C.R. 263; Opinion 1/76 [1977] E.C.R. 741; Opinion 2/91 [1993] E.C.R. 1061; Opinion 1/94 [1994] E.C.R. I–5267; Opinion 2/92 [1995] E.C.R. I–521; Case C–476/98 *Commission v Federal Republic of Germany* [2002] E.C.R. I–9855.

[68] Case C–162/96 *Racke GmbH & Co v Hauptzollamt Mainz* [1998] E.C.R. I–3655, para.41, citing Case 12/86 *Demirel v Stadt Schwäbisch Gmünd* [1987] E.C.R. 3719, para.14.

[69] Case 30/88 *Greece v Commission* [1989] E.C.R. 3711, para.12; Case C–192/89 *S. Z. Sevince v Staatssecretaris van Justitie* [1990] E.C.R. I–3461, para.9.

[70] Opinion 1/91 on EC-EFTA Agreement [1991] E.C.R. I–6079, paras 39 and 40.

[71] Case C–416/96 *Nour Eddline El-Yassini v Secretary of State for Home Department* [1999] E.C.R. I–1209, citing Case 12/86 *Demirel v Stadt Schwäbisch Gmünd* [1987] E.C.R. 3719, para. 14; Case C–18/90 *ONEM v Kziber* [1991] E.C.R. I–199, para.15; and Case C–162/96 , *Racke GmbH & Co. v Hauptzollamt Mainz* [1998] E.C.R. I–3655, para.31.

The Court has held provisions of various agreements between the Community and non-member countries to be directly effective.[72] This conclusion was not inevitable from a legal point of view and is open to criticism on policy grounds since it may place Community traders at a disadvantage compared with counterparts in non-member countries. While the latter may invoke provisions of international agreements in their favour before the courts of the Member States, Community traders might be unable to do likewise in the States which refuse to recognise that such international agreements have direct effect. The Court of Justice has recognised that such an imbalance in implementation might exist, but has not regarded the failure of national courts in non-Member countries to accord direct effect to the provisions of such agreements as amounting to a lack of reciprocity in implementing the agreements in question.[73] The Court has described those international agreements whose provisions are capable of having direct effect as "agreements concluded between the Community and non-member countries which introduce a certain asymmetry of obligations, or create special relations of integration with the Community".[74]

GATT 1947 and WTO Agreements do not have direct effect and do not provide a basis to review the validity of Community measures
Policy reasons such as those referred to above, namely, the **5-044** relative disadvantage of Community operators compared with counterparts in non-member countries, might have carried more weight as regards the legal effects of the General Agreement on Tariffs and Trade (GATT 1947) and of World Trade Organization Agreements. The Court regarded GATT 1947 as binding on the Community, taking the view that under the EEC Treaty the Community assumed the powers previously exercised by Member States with respect to GATT 1947.[75] But the Court rejected arguments that direct

---

[72] See e.g. Case 87/75 *Conceria Daniele Bresciani v Amministrazione Italiana delle Finanze* [1976] E.C.R. 129 (Art.2(1) of the Youndé Convention); Case 17/81 *Pabst & Richarz KG v Hauptzollamt Oldenburg* [1982] E.C.R. 1331 (Art.53(1) of the EEC-Greece Association Agreement); Case 104/81 *Hauptzollamt Mainz v C.A. Kupferberg & Cie KG a.A.* [1982] E.C.R. 3641 (Art.21 of the EEC-Portuguese Association Agreement); Case 12/86, *Demirel v Stadt Schwäbisch Gmünd* [1987] E.C.R. 3719 (Art.12 of the EEC-Turkey Association Agreement); Case C–192/89 *S. Z. Sevince v Staatssecretaris van Justitie* [1990] E.C.R. I–3461 (certain provisions of certain decisions of the Association Council); Case C–126/95 *A. Hallouzi-Choho v Bestuur van de Sociale Verzekeringsbank.* [1996] E.C.R. I–4807 (Art.41(1) of the EEC-Morocco Co-operation Agreement); Case C–416/96 *Nour Eddline El-Yassini v Secretary of State for Home Department* [1999] E.C.R. I–1209 (Art.40(1) of the EEC-Morocco Cooperation Agreement).

[73] See Case 104/81 *Hauptzollamt Mainz v C.A. Kupferberg & Cie KG a.A.* [1982] E.C.R. 3641, para. 18.

[74] Case C–149/96 *Portugal v Council* [1999] E.C.R. I–8395, citing as an example of such an agreement, the EEC-Portuguese Association Agreement in issue in *Kupferberg,* previous footnote.

[75] Cases 21–24/72 *International Fruit Company v Produktschap voor Groenten en Fruit* [1972] E.C.R. 1219; Case 9/73 *Schlüter v Hauptzollamt Lörrach* [1973] E.C.R. 1135; Cases 267–269 *Societa Petrolifera Italiana* [1983] E.C.R. 801; Cases 290–291/81 *Compagnia Singer* [1983] E.C.R. 847.

effect could be attributed to GATT 1947 as regards Article II, Article XI, the Protocols concluded within the framework of the GATT, and those provisions of the GATT which determined the effect of those Protocols.[76] The World Trade Organization Agreement of 1994 included the General Agreement on Trade in Services (GATS) and the Agreement on Trade Related Aspects of Intellectual Property Rights (TRIPs), in addition to GATT 1994 on goods. Council Decision 94/800/EC,[77] by which the Community approved the agreements reached in the Uruguay Round multilateral negotiations, states in the eleventh recital to its preamble that "the Agreement establishing the World Trade Organization, including the Annexes thereto, is not susceptible to being directly invoked in Community or Member State courts". While a reference in the preamble, unaccompanied by any indication to similar effect in the text of the Decision, cannot be of determinative legal significance, the preamble is certainly consistent with the view that neither the Community nor the Member States had any intention of establishing an international legal regime having direct effects.[78] As regards GATS it is to be noted that in their Schedule of Commitments the Community and its Member States have excluded direct effect.[79] It has been suggested that the language of the TRIPs agreement lends itself to direct effect,[80] and in *Hermès* Advocate General Tesauro considered that the WTO agreement could be given direct effect on the basis of reciprocity and that Article 50(6) of TRIPs (concerning judicial revocation or cessation by lapse of time of provisional measures of protection) had direct effect.[81] In *Portugal v Council*[82] the Court of Justice held that the WTO agreements are not in principle among the rules in the light of which the Court is to review the legality of measures adopted by the Community institutions. The

---

[76] Cases cited in previous footnote.

[77] [1994] O.J. L336/1.

[78] See the Opinion of Advocate General Cosmas in Case C–183/95 *Affish* [1997] E.C.R. I–4315, para.127 (reference in preamble not determinative but the learned Advocate General appears to think it has some weight), and the Opinion of Advocate General Elmer in Cases C–364/95 and C–365/95 95 *T. Port GmbH and Co. v Hauptzollamt Hamburg-Jonas* [1998] E.C.R. I–1023 (the learned Advocate General appears to think the recital has at least some weight). Advocate General Tesauro in Case C–53/96 *Hermès International (société en commandite par actions) v FHT Marketing Choice BV* [1998] E.C.R. I–3603 states at para.24 of his Opinion that "the statement in question appears only in the preamble to the Council Decision approving the WTO Agreements, not in the operative part of the Decision, and this significantly reduces its effect, in legal terms, of course".

[79] The Introductory Note to the Schedule states that "The rights and obligations arising from the GATS, including the schedule of commitments, shall have no self-executing effect and thus confer no rights directly to individual natural persons or juridical persons." See Eeckhout (1997) 34 C.M.L.Rev. 11, 34.

[80] Eeckhout, *loc. cit.* previous footnote, at p.33.

[81] Opinion of Advocate General Tesauro, cited above, esp. at paras 34 to 37. The learned Advocate General considered that in the absence of reciprocity Community traders would be placed at a disadvantage compared with their foreign competitors; see para.31 of his Opinion.

[82] Case C–149/96 *Portugal v Council* [1999] E.C.R. I–8395.

Court noted that while the WTO Agreements differ significantly from the provisions of GATT 1947, in particular by reason of the strengthening of the system of safeguards and the mechanism for resolving disputes, the system resulting form those agreements "nevertheless accords considerable importance to negotiation between the parties".[83] The Court noted that pursuant to the Understanding on Rules and Procedures Governing the Settlement of Disputes, *inter alia*, if a member of the WTO fails to fulfil its obligation to implement recommendations and rulings of the dispute settlement body, it is, if so requested, and on the expiry of a reasonable period at the latest, to enter into negotiations with any party having invoked the dispute settlement procedures, with a view to finding mutually acceptable compensation.[84] If the courts of members were required to refrain from applying rules of domestic law inconsistent with the WTO agreements, this would have the consequence of depriving the legislative or executive organs of the contracting parties of the possibility afforded by the Understanding of entering into negotiated arrangements, even on a temporary basis. The Court also noted that some of the contracting parties, which are among the most important commercial partners of the Community, have concluded from the subject-matter and purpose of the WTO agreements that they are not among the rules applicable by their courts when reviewing the legality of their rules of domestic law. Significantly, the Court added that "To accept that the role of ensuring that Community law complies with those rules devolves directly on the Community judicature would deprive the legislative or executive organs of the Community of the scope for manoeuvre enjoyed by their counterparts in the Community's trading partners."[85] It followed that the WTO agreements could not be relied upon to review the legality of measures adopted by the Community institutions. The Court noted that the latter interpretation corresponded with the statement in the preamble to Decision 94/800, referred to above, according to which WTO agreements and Annexes are not susceptible to being directly invoked in the Community or Member State courts.[86] In *Dior*[87] the issue discussed in the Opinion of Advocate General Tesauro in *Hermès* arose for decision—whether or not Article 50(6) of TRIPs was directly effective. The Court of Justice, referring to its reasoning in *Portugal v Council*, held that "the provisions of TRIPs, an annex to the WTO Agreement, are not such as to create rights upon which individuals may rely directly before the courts by virtue of Community law."[88]

---

[83] *ibid.*, para.36.
[84] Case C–149/96, paras 36–39.
[85] Case C–149/96, para.46. Also, e.g. Case C–377/02 *Van Parys* (Judgment of March 1, 2005).
[86] Case C–149/96, para.49.
[87] Joined Cases C–300/98 and C–392/98 *Parfums Christian Dior SA v TUK Consultancy BV* [2000] E.C.R. I–11307.
[88] Joined Cases C–300/98 and C–392/98, para.44.

*The Nakajima exception—provisions of an international agreement
lacking direct effect may provide the basis for judicial review of
Community measures where that is the intent of the Community
legislature*

5–045   Provisions of an international agreement which do not have direct
effect may nevertheless have legal effects where Community legislation expressly or impliedly so provides. Thus the Court held in *Fediol*
that the definition in a common commercial policy regulation[89] of
"illicit commercial practices" as "any international trade practices
attributable to non-member countries which are incompatible with
international law or with the generally accepted rules" had the
consequence that individuals could rely on provisions of the GATT
in order to obtain a ruling on whether conduct contained in a
complaint lodged under the relevant regulation constituted an illicit
commercial practice within the meaning of that regulation.[90] Again,
in *Nakajima*, the Court held that where the Community adopts
legislation in order to comply with the international obligations of
the Community, such as GATT 1947 and its Anti-Dumping Code,
the Court will regard provisions of that legislation which are
inconsistent with those international obligations as being covered by
the words "infringement of this Treaty or of any rule of law relating
to its application" which appear as a ground if annulment in Article
230 EC.[91] In the so-called "bananas" litigation, the Court of Justice
confirmed that since GATT 1947 lacked direct effect, it was only if
the Community intended to implement a particular obligation
entered into within the framework of GATT, or if the Community
act expressly referred to specific provisions of GATT, that the Court
could review the legality of the Community act in question from the
point of view of the GATT rules.[92] The so-called *Nakajima* exception
has been applied in a number of cases.[93] The Commission argued in
Egenberger[94] that the Court should replace the *Nakajima* exception
with the principle that Community measures should be interpreted

---

[89] Council Reg. No.2641/84 on the strengthening of the common commercial policy with
regard in particular to protection against illicit commercial practices [1984] O.J. L252/1.
[90] Case 70/87 *Fédération de l'industrie de l'huilerie de la CEE (Fediol) v Commission of the
European Communities* [1989] E.C.R. 1781, at paras 19 and 20.
[91] Case C–69/89 *Nakajima All Precision Co. Ltd v Council of the European Communities*
[1991] E.C.R. I–2069, at paras 29 to 31.
[92] Case C–280/93 *Federal Republic of Germany v Council of the European Union* [1994] E.C.R.
I–4973, at para.111; see also Case C–149/96 *Portugal v Council* [1999] E.C.R. I–8395,
para.49; Case C–307/99 *OGT Fruchthandelsgesellschaft mbH v HZA Hamburg-St.Annen*
[2001] E.C.R. I–3159, para.27.
[93] See e.g. Case C–76/00 *Petrotub* [2003] E.C.R. I–79 (validity of Community anti-dumping
legislation in light of anti-dumping code); Case C–352/96 *Italy v Council* [1998] E.C.R.
I–6937 (legality of Council Regulation on tariff quotas for imports of rice in light of
Art.XXIV(6) of the GATT and the Understanding on the Interpretation of Art.XXIV of
the GATT).
[94] Case C–313/04 *Franz Egenberger GmbH Molkerei und Trockenwerk v Bundesanstalt für
Landwirtschaft und Ernährung* Judgment of July 11, 2006.

consistently with international law. Advocate General Geelhoed rejected this argument. He did think that the scope of the exception was unclear. He thought it artificial to confine its application to cases where the preamble of EC legislation revealed an intent to implement a WTO obligation, and considered it should also apply where such an intent clearly appeared from a comparison between the content of the contested EC provision and that of the WTO obligation in issue. The Court of Justice did not address the point.

Interpretation of Community measures in light of international agreements and customary international law

It is to be noted that provisions of international agreements, such **5–046** as GATT 1947 and the WTO agreements, which are not directly effective, may be taken into account in interpreting relevant provisions of Community legislation.[95] In *Commission v Germany*, the Court of Justice considered an argument that provisions of an EC inward processing regulation precluded the application of the measures provided for by the International Dairy Agreement, an agreement concluded under the GATT. The Court stated that:

> "the primacy of international agreements concluded by the Community over provisions of secondary Community legislation means that such provisions must, so far as is possible, be interpreted in a manner that is consistent with those agreements."[96]

The Court has also had recourse to principles of customary international law for the purpose of interpreting Community measures. In *Poulsen* the Court considered the terms of an EEC regulation laying down technical measures on the conservation of fishery resources, noting that:

> "As a preliminary point, it must be observed, first, that the European Community must respect international law in the

---

[95] Case 92–71 *Interfood GmbH v Hauptzollamt Hamburg-Ericus.* [1972] E.C.R. 231, at para.6 (GATT agreements relevant to interpretation of common external tariff); Case C–79/89 *Brown Boveri & Cie AG v Hauptzollamt Mannheim.* [1991] E.C.R. I–1853, at paras 15 to 19 (decision of GATT Committee on Customs Valuation relevant to interpretation of EEC Regulation on customs value); Case C–70/94 *Fritz Werner Industrie-Ausrüstungen GmbH v Federal Republic of Germany* [1995] E.C.R. I–3819, para.23, and Case C–83/94 *Criminal proceedings against Peter Leifer, Reinhold Otto Krauskopf and Otto Holzer* [1995] E.C.R. I–3231, at para.24 (interpretation of EC Export Regulation under Common Commercial Policy in light of GATT).

[96] Case 61/94 [1996] E.C.R. I–3989, para.52. The reasoning in this case is a little curious. The Court deduces the conclusion cited above from the propositions that; (a) secondary Community legislation must be interpreted as far as possible in accordance with the Treaty; and (b) an implementing regulation should be interpreted as far as possible in accordance with a basic regulation. But in each of these cases the superior norm comprises such within the Community legal order.

exercise of its powers and that, consequently, Article 6 above-
mentioned must be interpreted, and its scope limited, in the
light of the relevant rules of the international law of the sea.

In this connexion, account must be taken of the Geneva
Conventions of April 29, 1958 on the Territorial Sea and
Contiguous Zone . . . and on Fishing and Conservation of the
Living Resources of the High Seas . . . in so far as they codify
general rules recognised by international custom, and also of
the United Nations Convention of December 10, 1982 on the
Law of the Sea . . . It has not entered into force, but many of its
provisions are considered to express the current state of
customary international maritime law . . ."[97]

Extension of Nakajima to principles of customary international law

5-047   In *Racke*,[98] the approach taken by the Court in *Nakajima*[99] was
extended to principles of customary international law codified in the
Vienna Convention on the Law of Treaties. The plaintiff in the
national proceedings challenged the validity of an EEC regulation
suspending trade concessions under the EEC-Yugoslavia Co-
operation Agreement on the ground that such suspension was
inconsistent with relevant provisions of the Vienna Convention on
the Law of Treaties. These provisions referred to the doctrine of
rebus sic stantibus, whereby a party may unilaterally terminate a
treaty in the event of fundamental change of circumstances. It
appeared from the preamble to the suspension regulation that it was
based on the conviction of the Council that a "radical change in the
conditions" under which the Co-operation Agreement had been
concluded had occurred. The Court of Justice, purporting to apply
Nakajima by analogy, denied that the case concerned the direct
effect of rules of international law, and emphasised that the case
concerned a regulation which had been taken pursuant to the
relevant rules of international law, and could thus be challenged if
the Council made manifest errors of assessment concerning the
conditions for applying those rules; the Court concluded that no
such manifest errors had been made. The present writer considers
that *Racke* stretches the principles applied by the Court in *Fediol*
and *Nakajima* too far, even if the standard of review adopted by the

---

[97] Case C-286/90 *Anklagemyndigheden v Peter Michael Poulsen and Diva Navigation Corp.*
[1992] E.C.R. I-6019, paras 9 and 10. The 1982 Convention has since entered into force,
but the text of the judgment cited indicates that the Court of Justice is taking account of
the Treaties cited as evidence of customary international law, and that it is the relevant
principles of customary international law in light of which it is interpreting Community law.
[98] Case C-162/96 *A. Racke GmbH & Co. v Hauptzollamt Mainz* [1998] E.C.R. I-3655.
[99] Case C-69/89 *Nakajima All Precision Co. Ltd v Council of the European Communities*
[1991] E.C.R. I-2069.

Court was not excessively intrusive. The latter cases can be justified on the basis of the proposition that non-directly effective provisions of international agreements may nevertheless govern the scope of Community legislation where that legislation expressly or impliedly so provides. The reference to "radical change of conditions" in the preamble to the regulation is not of itself a convincing indication of a legislative intention to condition the efficacy of the regulation on a judicial assessment of its compatibility with international law. Moreover, the considerations referred to in *Portugal v Council*, above, and based in that case on the Understanding on Rules and Procedures Governing the Settlement of Disputes, to the effect that allowing reliance upon WTO Agreements to challenge the legality of measures adopted by the Community institutions, would have the consequence of depriving legislative and executive organs of contracting parties of the possibility of entering into negotiated arrangements, are not without relevance to a context such as that in issue in *Racke*. Differences of opinion between States as regards their respective rights and obligations in international law are normally resolved by negotiation, unless the parties have consented in advance to international adjudication, or consent to such adjudication in the circumstances of the particular case. For the Court of Justice to act, in effect, as a form of compulsory international adjudication in such cases, could place the Community and its Member States at a disadvantage when dealing with third countries with no comparable internal judicial constraints on their action.

"Indirect Review" of Security Council Resolutions by the Community Courts when reviewing the legality of Community implementing measures

In *Ahmed Ali Yusuf*, the CFI considered a challenge to an EC **5–048** regulation implementing several resolutions of the United Nations Security Council.[1] The Applicants contended, *inter alia*, that the regulation infringed their fundamental rights. The CFI considered that if it annulled the contested regulation, on the ground that the latter infringed their fundamental rights, such annulment would indirectly mean that the relevant resolutions of the Security Council themselves infringed those fundamental rights. "In other words", said the CFI, "the applicants ask the Court to declare by implication that the provision of international law at issue infringes the fundamental rights of individuals, as protected by the Community legal

---

[1] Case T–306/01 *Yusuf et al. v Council and Commission*, (Judgment of September 21, 2005), nyr, appeal pending Case C–415/05 P; and on the same issue Case T–315/01 *Kadi v Council and Commission*, (Judgment of September 21, 2005), appeal pending Case C–402/05P. For more detailed consideration of the facts of this case and its fundamental rights aspect, see Ch.8, para.8–014.

order".[2] The CFI considered that the resolutions of the Security Council at issue fell, in principle, outside the ambit of the Court's judicial review and that the Court had no jurisdiction to call into question, even indirectly, their lawfulness in the light of Community law. On the contrary, the Court was bound, so far as possible, to interpret Community law in a manner compatible with the obligations of the Member States under the Charter of the United Nations. However, the CFI entered an important caveat:

> "None the less, the Court is empowered to check, indirectly, the lawfulness of the resolutions of the Security Council in question with regard to *jus cogens*, understood as a body of higher rules of public international law binding on all subjects of international law, including the bodies of the United Nations, and from which no derogation is possible."[3]

The CFI scrutinised the relevant resolutions and the procedure which led up to them in light of *jus cogens*, and concluded that the contentions of the applicants as regards infringements of their fundamental rights must be rejected.

The approach of the CFI is not altogether satisfactory. It proceeds on the basis that to judicially review the contested regulation on the basis of Community fundamental rights norms would indirectly amount to review of the relevant Security Council resolutions. This is not self-evident. Compliance of Community acts with general principles of Community law is a matter of competence. If a Community act implementing a Security Council resolution were annulled for lack of competence, this might amount to implicit reproach for or criticism of the relevant resolution, but it would not in any legal sense amount to review of that obligation, not least because it would not even be implicit in the Court's judgment that the norms applied to the relevant Community act were binding on the Security Council. In order to avoid what it regards as indirectly reviewing the Security Council by reference to Community norms, the CFI proceeds to indirectly review the Security Council by reference to fundamental principles of *international law*, which clearly do purport to be norms applicable to the Security Council. On the face of it, this is an exercise which lies outside the jurisdiction of the Community Courts. A possibly preferable alternative approach would be to acknowledge that the application of Community constraints on competence to Community measures implementing Security Council resolutions does not amount to judicial review of any description of those resolutions. At the same time, when considering the question of compliance by Community

---

[2] *ibid.*, para.267.
[3] *ibid.*, para.277.

measures implementing Security Council resolutions with Community fundamental rights norms, full account should be taken of the aims of those measures, and of all the circumstances attending the adoption of the relevant Security Council resolutions, including the need to maintain international peace and security and to uphold the integrity and effectiveness of the United Nations, which has been charged with special responsibility for the achievement of that task.

The duty of national courts to interpret national rules in light of non-directly effective provisions of international agreements binding on the Community

In *Hermès*[4] the Court applied by analogy the principle applied in **5–049** *Poulsen* and *Commission v Germany* to national rules implementing Community rules falling with the scope of the TRIPs Agreement. Article 50 of the latter Agreement provides that judicial authorities shall have the authority to order prompt and effective provisional measures. TRIPs is a "mixed" agreement, falling within the scope of both Community competence and national competence, and was adopted by the Community and the Member States jointly. Article 50 only falls within Community competence to the extent that it covers subject-matter over which the Community has exercised internal competence. Under Article 99 of Regulation 40/94 on the Community Trade Mark,[5] rights arising from a Community trade mark may be safeguarded by the adoption of "provisional, including protective measures". The Court reasoned that:

> "since the Community is a party to the TRIPs Agreement and since the agreement applies to the Community trade mark, the courts referred to in Article 99 of Regulation 40/94, when called upon to apply national rules with a view to ordering provisional measures for the protection of rights arising under a Community trade mark, are required to do so, as far as possible in the light of the wording and purpose of Article 50 of the TRIPs Agreement . . ."[6]

In the above passage, the Court holds that the duty of consistent interpretation is incumbent upon national courts when they are protecting rights under *Community trade mark law*. The rationale is that since relevant Community rules must be interpreted in accordance with treaties such as TRIPs, national rules implementing those

---

[4] Case C–53/96 *Hermès International (société en commandite par actions) v FHT Marketing Choice BV* [1998] E.C.R. I–3603.
[5] [1994] O.J. L11/1.
[6] Case C–53/96 *Hermès International (société en commandite par actions) v FHT Marketing Choice BV* [1998] E.C.R. I–3603, para.28.

Community rules must be similarly interpreted by national courts. In *Christian Dior*,[7] the Court cites the above paragraph for a rather broader proposition—that the duty of consistent interpretation applies, not just in the field of the *Community* trade mark, but in *the field of trade marks*.[8] In *Schieving-Nijstad*[9] Advocate General Jacobs confesses that it is not easy to understand why Community law governs the effects of Article 50 of the TRIPs Agreement not only where a Community trade mark is involved but also in situations concerning national trade marks.[10] The Court's extension of its reasoning in *Hermès* to cover trade marks has been rightly criticised.[11]

In *Dior* the Court contrasted the duty of national courts in a field to which TRIPs applies and in respect of which the Community has already legislated ("as is the case with the field of trade marks"), namely, the duty of consistent interpretation, with their obligations in a field in which TRIPs applies but in respect of which the Community has not yet legislated and which consequently falls within the competence of Member States. In the latter situation:

"... the protection of intellectual property rights, and measures adopted for that purpose by the judicial authorities, do not fall within the scope of Community law. Accordingly, Community law neither requires nor forbids that the legal order of a Member State should accord to individuals the right to rely directly on the rule laid down by Article 50(6) of TRIPs or that it should oblige the courts to apply that rule of their own motion."

The above wording is a little curious. The contrast made by the Court is between the duty of national courts when acting within the scope of Community law on the one hand, and outside the scope of Community law on the other. As regards the first situation, the Court refers to the application of national rules in light of Article 50(6) of TRIPs; as regards the second situation the Court refers to the right of individuals to rely directly on Article 50(6) and the obligation of courts to apply that rule. The contrast is asymmetrical. Nevertheless, it seems that the conclusion which is to be drawn is that the legal effects of Article 50 of the TRIPs Agreement in a field in respect of which the Community has not yet legislated are to be determined by national law rather than Community law.[12]

[7] Joined Cases C–300/98 and C–392/98 *Parfums Christian Dior SA v TUK Consultancy BV* [2000] E.C.R. I–11307.
[8] *ibid.*, para.47.
[9] Case C–89/99 [2001] E.C.R. I–5851.
[10] Opinion, para.40.
[11] Eeckhout *External Relations of the European Union* (OUP, 2004), p.242.
[12] Case C–89/99 *Schieving-Nijstad* [2001] E.C.R. I–5851, Opinion of Advocate General Jacobs, para.39; Eeckhout, *op. cit.,* p. 243, "In cases coming within the scope of national law, whether or not there is direct effect or consistent interpretation or any other type of effect, depends on national law."

Jurisdiction of the Court of Justice to interpret international agreements concluded jointly by Member States and by the Community

As noted in para.5–043, above, an agreement concluded by the **5–050** Council with a non-Member country or countries in accordance with the EC Treaty is an act of a Community institution, and the provisions of such an agreement form an integral part of Community law. It follows that the Court of Justice has jurisdiction to interpret such agreements. As is apparent from the cases considered above, a potential difficulty in regarding all provisions of all international agreements between the Community and non-member countries as part of the Community legal order is that while some such agreements fall within the competence of the Community and the Community alone, others fall partly within Community competence and partly within national competence, and are concluded by both the Community and the Member States. The latter are described as mixed agreements. In *Demirel*[13] the Court considered the scope of a mixed agreement—the EEC/Turkey Association Agreement. Germany and the United Kingdom objected to the jurisdiction of the Court to interpret the provisions on freedom of movement for workers, since granting freedom of movement to nationals of non-member countries fell within national competence rather than Community competence. The Court rejected this argument on the ground that freedom of movement for workers fell within Community competence,[14] and the fact that it also involved the exercise of national competence did not exclude its jurisdiction to interpret the provisions in question. There must be a real question as to the competence of the Court of Justice to interpret provisions of a mixed agreement falling solely within national competence, and in principle the Court of Justice lacks jurisdiction to interpret such provisions.[15] In *Hermès* the Court of Justice received a request for a preliminary ruling on the meaning of Article 50 of TRIPs. As indicated in the above discussion of this case, TRIPs is a mixed agreement.[16] The Court held that it had jurisdiction to interpret this provision on several grounds. The first was that national courts would be obliged to take account of it when ensuring the protection of rights arising under the Community trade mark.[17] The Court

---

[13] Case 12/86 *Demirel v Stadt Schwäbisch Gmünd* [1987] E.C.R. 3719.
[14] Para.9 of the Court's judgment. An unconvincing argument, since the provisions of the Treaty on the free movement of workers apply only to nationals of Member States.
[15] For an interesting discussion see Advocate General Tesauro in Case C–53/96 *Hermès International (société en commandite par actions) v FHT Marketing Choice BV* [1998] E.C.R. I–3603, at paras 10 to 21 of his Opinion; a discussion of the position as regards TRIPS, but one which raises more general issues of principle.
[16] Case C–53/96, para.23, referring to Opinion 1/94 on WTO Agreement [1994] E.C.R. I–5267, in particular para.104.
[17] Para.28.

added that it was immaterial that the dispute in the main proceedings concerned trade marks whose international registrations designated the Benelux, since (a) it was for the national court hearing the dispute to assess the need for a preliminary ruling, and (b) where a provision such as Article 50 of TRIPs could apply both to situations falling within the scope of national law and to situations falling within the scope of Community law, it was clearly in the Community interest that, in order to forestall future differences of interpretation, that provision should be interpreted uniformly, whatever the circumstances in which it was to apply.[18] In *Dior*,[19] the Court responded to a question "designed to ascertain whether the scope of the judgment in . . . *Hermès* . . . relating to the jurisdiction of the Court of Justice to interpret Article 50 of TRIPs, is restricted solely to situations covered by trade-mark law".[20] The Court, repeating its reasoning in *Hermès*,[21] went on to refer to the obligation of close co-operation incumbent upon the Member States and the Community institutions in fulfilling the commitments undertaken by them under joint competence when they concluded the WTO Agreement, including TRIPs,[22] as follows:

> "Since Article 50 of TRIPs constitutes a procedural provision which should be applied in the same way in every situation falling within its scope and is capable of applying both to situations covered by national law and to situations covered by Community law, that obligation requires the judicial bodies of the Member States and the Community, for practical and legal reasons, to give it a uniform interpretation.
>
> Only the Court of Justice, acting in co-operation with the courts and tribunals of the Member States pursuant to Article [234] of the Treaty is in a position to ensure such uniform interpretation."[23]

5–052 The Court concluded that the jurisdiction of the Court of Justice to interpret Article 50 of TRIPs was thus not restricted solely to situations covered by trade-mark law.[24] The reasoning leading to this

---

[18] Para.32.

[19] Joined Cases C–300/98 and C–392/98 *Parfums Christian Dior SA v TUK Consultancy BV* [2000] E.C.R. I–11307.

[20] *ibid.*, para.32.

[21] *ibid.*, paras 34, 35.

[22] *ibid.*, para.36, citing Opinion 1/94 [1994] E.C.R. I–5267, para.108, which states: "Next, where it is apparent that the subject-matter of an agreement or convention falls in part within the competence of the Community and in part within that of the Member States, it is essential to ensure close cooperation between the Member States and the Community institutions, both in the process of negotiation and conclusion and in the fulfilment of the commitments entered into. That obligation to cooperate flows from the requirement of unity in the international representation of the Community . . ."

[23] *ibid.*, para.38.

[24] *ibid.*, para.39.

conclusion is not entirely satisfactory. If the legal effects of Article 50 of the TRIPs Agreement in a field in respect of which the Community has not yet legislated (and therefore a field outside the scope of Community law) are to be determined by national law rather than Community law, then the need for an interpretation of Article 50 of TRIPs in a field outside the field of trade-mark law, and therefore outside the scope of Community law, could only arise if national law chose to treat such a situation *as if it fell within the scope of Community law.* If the Court of Justice wished to confirm that it would have jurisdiction to interpret TRIPs in such a case, reference to its settled case law would have been enough. In cases where national law applies Community law to national situations to which Community law would not otherwise apply, the Court of Justice will interpret Community law in order to forestall future differences of interpretation. The Court of Justice made this point in *Hermès,* citing the relevant case law of the Court.[25] Recourse to the duty of co-operation between the national courts and the European Court is thus superfluous. But more than that, the concept of two-way co-operation leads the Court to the observation that *national courts* as well as the European Court are obliged to give TRIPs a uniform interpretation, for practical and *legal* reasons. Thus in the part of its judgment falling under the title "Jurisdiction of the Court to interpret Article 50 of TRIPs", the Court reaches the conclusion that the Court of Justice is entitled to give an interpretation of Article 50 of TRIPs outside the scope of Community law on the basis of a proposition that both the national courts and the European Court are bound to give Article 50 a uniform interpretation both in situations within the scope of Community law and in situations outside the scope of Community law. Yet, as discussed above, in the part of its judgment entitled "Direct effect of Article 50(6) of TRIPs", the Court goes on to say that *recourse* or not by national courts to TRIPs in fields outside the scope of Community law is a matter for *national law.* The different strands in the Court's reasoning do not quite connect. One just about possible way of connecting up the strands is to concentrate solely on what the Court actually says, and to ignore the parts of its judgment in which it says it. What the Court says in *Dior* is: (a) TRIPs is not directly effective;[26] (b) in a field covered by TRIPs but outside the scope of Community law it is for national law to determine whether individuals can rely on Article 50(6) of TRIPs or whether national courts should apply that provision on their own motion;[27] (c) in a field

---

[25] Case C–53/96 *Hermès International (société en commandite par actions) v FHT Marketing Choice BV* [1998] E.C.R. I–3603, para.32; citing Case C–130/95 *Giloy v Hauptzollamt Frankfurt am Main-Ost* [1997] E.C.R. I–4291, para.28, and Case C–28/95 *Leur-Bloem v Inspecteur der Belastingdienst/Ondermingen* [1997] E.C.R. I–4161, para.34.

[26] Joined Cases C–300/98 and C–392/98 *Parfums Christian Dior SA v TUK Consultancy BV* [2000] E.C.R. I–11307, para.44.

[27] *ibid.,* para.48.

covered by TRIPs, and in respect of which the Community has legislated, national courts are obliged to apply national rules so far as possible in light of the wording and purpose of Article 50 of TRIPs;[28] (d) Article 50 of TRIPs should be applied in the same way in every situation falling within its scope whether a situation is covered by national law or Community law and national courts are bound to give it a uniform interpretation.[29] On this view the duty of consistent interpretation applies to all situations falling within the scope of Article 50 of TRIPs whether or not that situation also falls within the scope of Community law. It is not suggested that this reading of *Dior* is a preferable outcome, simply a possible overall reading of the Court's judgment.

Impact of the Constitutional Treaty (CT)

5–053   The CT contains several reforms affecting the topics covered in this chapter, in particular:

— a far-reaching reorganisation of the Union's available legal instruments, based upon drawing a formal distinction between legislative and non-legislative acts (paras 11–025–026);

— this would include the replacement of existing regulations and directives with a new system of (legislative) "European laws" and "European framework laws", and (non-legislative) "European regulations", as well as (also non-legislative) "European decisions";

— codification of the principle of supremacy ("primacy") within the Constitution, though without any express mention of direct effect (paras 11–031–032).

Further reading

Betlem, "The Doctrine of Consistent Interpretation: Managing Legal Uncertainty" (2002) 22 O.J.L.S. 397.

von Bogdandy, Arndt and Bast, "Legal Instruments in European Union Law and their Reform: A Systematic Approach on a Empirical Basis" (2004) 23 Y.E.L. 91.

Coppel, "Rights, Duties and the End of Marshall" (1994) 57 M.L.R. 859.

Craig, "Once Upon a Time in the West: Direct Effect and the Federalisation of EEC Law" (1992) 12 O.J.L.S. 453.

Drake, "Twenty Years After *von Colson*: the Impact of 'Indirect Effect' on the Protection of the Individual's Community Rights" (2005) 30 E.L.Rev. 329.

---

[28] *ibid.*, para.47.
[29] *ibid.*, para.37.

Dougan, "The Disguised Vertical Direct Effect of Directives?" [2000] C.L.J. 586.

Dougan, Annotation of *Unilever Italia* (2001) 38 C.M.L.Rev. 1503.

Editorial, "Horizontal Direct Effect: A Law of Diminishing Coherence?" (2006) 43 C.M.L.Rev. 1.

Eeckhout *External Relations of the European Union* (OUP, 2004), esp. Chs 8 and 9.

Hilson and Downes, "Making Sense of Rights: Community Rights in EC Law" (1999) 24 E.L.Rev. 121.

Kuijper and Bronckers, "WTO Law in the European Court of Justice" (2005) 42 C.M.L.Rev. 1313.

Lenz, Sif Tynes and Young, "Horizontal What? Back to Basics" (2000) 25 E.L.Rev. 509.

Maltby, "*Marleasing*: What is All the Fuss About?" (1993) 109 L.Q.R. 301.

Mancini, "The Making of a Constitution for Europe" (1989) 26 C.M.L.Rev. 595.

Prechal, "Does Direct Effect Still Matter?" (2000) 37 C.M.L.Rev. 1047.

Prechal, *Directives in EC Law* (2nd ed., OUP, 2005).

Prinssen and Schrauwen (eds), *Direct Effect: Rethinking a Classic of EC Legal Doctrine* (Europa Law Publishing, 2002).

Tridimas, "Horizontal Effect of Directives: A Missed Opportunity?" (1994) 19 E.L.Rev. 621.

Tridimas, "Black, White and Shades of Grey: Horizontality of Directives Revisited" (2002) 21 Y.E.L. 327.

Weatherill, "Breach of Directives and Breach of Contract" (2001) 26 E.L.Rev. 177.

de Witte, "Direct Effect, Supremacy, and the Nature of the Legal Order" in Craig and de Búrca (eds), *The Evolution of EU Law* (OUP, 1999).

CHAPTER 6

RIGHTS AND REMEDIES

Guide to this Chapter: In most situations, Community law is **6–001** enforced through the national courts and according to domestic rules governing judicial procedures and remedies. However, Community law imposes two main limits to national competence over such standards of judicial protection. First, the principle of equivalence requires that Community law actions cannot be treated less favourably than comparable actions derived from purely domestic law. Secondly, the principle of effectiveness demands that national remedies and procedural rules cannot in any case render the exercise of Community law rights virtually impossible or excessively difficult. This chapter focuses on the application of the principles of equivalence and effectiveness to certain important categories of judicial protection before the national courts: limitation periods for the bringing of proceedings; interim relief against allegedly invalid national and Community measures; the recovery of charges and taxes imposed contrary to Community law; and the *Francovich* action for damages against the Member State for a breach of its Treaty obligations which causes loss to individuals. This chapter also touches upon the Community's increasing tendency to enact secondary legislation specifically addressing the standards of judicial protection applicable to certain categories of substantive Community law right.

Introduction

6-002 While the significance of the EU Courts and Institutions should not be underestimated in facilitating the application of Community law in the Member States, it must be noted that the Community legal system is in large part administered by national authorities, with the result that national agencies, courts and tribunals are entrusted with the application of sometimes subtle combinations of Community law and national law, based on variations of the following:

— rules of Community law incapable of direct application incorporated into national law in discharge of Community obligations, and enforced by the application of appropriate national procedures, remedies or penalties;

— rules of Community law incapable of direct application which have not been incorporated into national law, but which are taken into account in interpreting national rules and enforcing national remedies or penalties, or which are enforced by an action for damages under Community law, in accordance with appropriate national rules relating to damage actions against the State;

— directly applicable rules of Community law, supplemented by directly applicable Community procedural rules (and perhaps further supplemented by national procedural rules and national remedies);

— directly applicable rules of Community law, supplemented by national procedural rules and national remedies.

Rules of Community law incapable of direct application

6-003 Where non-directly applicable rules of Community law are incorporated into national law, the Community source of the national rules in question may be relevant for the purposes of interpreting and giving effect to relevant national legal rules.[1] In appropriate circumstances, the failure of a Member State to incorporate non-directly applicable rules of Community law into national law will give rise to an action in damages by an individual in accordance with Community law and appropriate provisions of national procedural and remedial law.[2] It may be that a provision of Community law bestows legal competence directly upon a national agency, court or tribunal, without giving any individual a specific right to call upon the agency court or tribunal to take advantage of that competence. Article 234 EC falls into this category, empowering national courts and tribunals to make references for preliminary ruling to the ECJ.[3] Although this

---

[1] See further Ch.5.
[2] See the discussion of the *Francovich* case law below.
[3] Though individuals would seem to have the right to call upon national courts or tribunals to take appropriate account of Art.234 EC in the course of proceedings to which they are party, and the third paragraph of Art.234 EC would seem to give a right to parties to a proceeding to call upon a national court from which no judicial remedy lies to make a reference to the ECJ. On Art.234 EC, see further Ch.14.

provision may be implemented by national procedural rules, the Court of Justice has never suggested that the admissibility of a reference from a national court depended upon anything other than compliance with the terms of the Article in question. Article 234 EC can properly be described as a provision of Community law which has direct application, in the sense that the competence it bestows upon national courts is not dependent on the enactment of national implementing rules. However, Member States would seem in principle to be obliged to repeal any national procedural rules which might directly or indirectly impede recourse by national courts or tribunals to the preliminary ruling procedure,[4] but otherwise to be free to adopt appropriate national rules governing the procedure for making a reference.[5] It is clear that in the absence of such national procedural rules, domestic courts or tribunals are free to make references in reliance directly upon the Treaty, and that the Court of Justice may make "practice directions" on the form of such references.[6]

Directly applicable provisions of Community law supplemented by directly applicable Community procedural rules

Community regulations may not only vest rights in individuals as against national authorities; they may also provide detailed procedural rules for the enjoyment of those rights,[7] including rules specifying the standard and burden of proof necessary to sustain a claim to the payment of money.[8] Directly applicable Community rules prohibit agreements which restrict competition and affect inter-State trade, and the abuse of a dominant position,[9] and Community regulations provide for the imposition of penalties by the Commission on undertakings which carry on such activities, and lay down procedural rules concerning such matters as hearings and time-limits relating to the imposition of such penalties.[10] Procedures and a time-limitation period have been laid down in connection with the application of Article 88 EC.[11]

6–004

---

[4] On the general duty of Member States to implement Treaty obligations, see Ch.5.

[5] e.g. Case C–472/99 *Clean Car Autoservice* [2001] E.C.R. I–9687.

[6] See the Note for Guidance on References by National Courts for Preliminary Rulings in 1996 [1997] 1 C.M.L.R. 78; revised in 2005 [2005] O.J. C143/1.

[7] See, e.g. for the buying-in of cereals by intervention agencies, and procedural conditions for the exercise by individuals of the right to sell to intervention agencies, Reg.1766/92 on the common organisation of the market in cereals [1992] O.J. L181/21; and Reg.689/92 fixing the procedure and conditions for the taking-over of cereals by intervention agencies [1992] O.J. L74.

[8] See, e.g. Reg.3719/88 laying down common detailed rules for the application of the system of import and export licences and advance fixing certificates for agricultural products [1988] O.J. L331/1; Reg.1162/95 laying down special detailed rules for the application of the system of import and export licences for cereals and rice [1995] O.J. L117/2.

[9] Arts 81 and 82 EC See further Chs 23 and 24.

[10] In particular, Reg.1/2003 [2003] O.J. L1/1. See further Ch.25.

[11] In particular, Reg.659/1999 [1999] O.J. L83/1. See further Ch.27.

It is important to establish whether or not Community regulations lay down comprehensive procedural rules in a specific area, since if they do not, the national authorities may be free, within the limits imposed by the ECJ, to supplement Community law with the rules of the domestic forum.[12]

Directly applicable Community law supplemented by national procedural rules and remedies—the general principles

6–005   While Community secondary legislation may, and sometimes does, provide procedural rules for the enforcement of Community rights, Community law more often than not vests rights in individuals (either against the State, or against other private parties), without prescribing explicitly the procedural rules applicable in national courts or tribunals, or the remedies for infringement of these rights. In a consistent case law, the Court of Justice has laid down two principles to be applied where individuals derive rights from the direct effect of Community law, but Community law does not prescribe procedural or remedial rules for the enjoyment of such rights. The first principle is that of equivalence: the procedural rules applying to enforcement of Community right must be no less favourable than those which apply to similar domestic actions. The second principle is that of effectiveness: the application of national procedural rules must not render the enforcement of Community rights virtually impossible or excessively difficult.[13] The Court summarised its case law as follows in *Peterbroeck v Belgian State*:[14]

> "the Court has consistently held that, under the principle of co-operation laid down in Article [10] of the Treaty, it is for the Member States to ensure the legal protection which individuals derive from the direct effect of Community law. In the absence of Community rules governing a matter, it is for the domestic legal system of each Member State to designate the courts and tribunals having jurisdiction and to lay down the detailed procedural rules governing actions for safeguarding rights which individuals derive from the direct effect of Community law. However, such rules must not be less favourable than those

---

[12] Case 31/69 *Commission v Italian Republic* [1970] E.C.R. 25.
[13] For full discussion of these principles, see: Lonbay and Biondi (eds), *Remedies for Breach of EC Law* (Wiley, 1997); Ward, *Judicial Review and the Rights of Private Parties in EC Law* (OUP, 2000); Kilpatrick, Novitz and Skidmore (eds), *The Future of Remedies in Europe* (Hart Publishing, 2000); Dougan, *National Remedies Before the Court of Justice* (Hart Publishing, 2004).
[14] Case C–312/93 [1995] E.C.R. I–4599, para.12.

governing similar domestic actions nor render virtually impossible or excessively difficult the exercise of rights conferred by
Community law . . ."[15]

The Court went on to indicate, in very general terms, the factors to
be taken into account in determining the extent to which the
application of national procedural rules could be regarded as
compatible with Community law:

"For the purposes of applying those principles, each case which
raises the question whether a national procedural provision
renders application of Community law impossible or excessively
difficult must be analysed by reference to the role of that
provision in the procedure, its progress and its special features,
viewed as a whole, before the various national instances. In the
light of that analysis the basic principles of the domestic judicial
system, such as protection of the rights of the defence, the
principle of legal certainty and the proper conduct of procedure, must, where appropriate, be taken into
consideration."[16]

As regards the principle of equivalence, it is in principle for the **6–006**
domestic courts to ascertain whether the procedural rules intended
to safeguard Community rights are not less favourable than those
intended to safeguard comparable national rights.[17] However, the
Court of Justice can provide a national court with guidance as to the
interpretation of Community law in this regard, which may be of use
to it in undertaking the assessment in question, and in this connection the Court has stated that the principle of equivalence requires
that the national rule at issue be applied without distinction, whether
the infringement alleged is of Community law or national law, where
the purpose and cause of action are similar.[18] This does not mean,

---

[15] *ibid.*, para.12. The Court referred to the following cases: Case 33/76 *Rewe v Land-
wirtschaftskammer fuer das Saarland* [1976] E.C.R. 1989; Case 45/76 *Comet v Produktschap
voor Siergewassen* [1976] E.C.R. 2043; Case 68/79 *Hans Just v Danish Ministry for Fiscal
Affairs* [1980] E.C.R. 501; Case 199/82 *Amministrazione delle Finanze dello Stato v San
Giorgio* [1983] E.C.R. 3595; Joined Cases 331/85, 376/85 and 378/85 *Bianco and Girard v
Directeur Général des Douanes des Droits Indirects* [1988] E.C.R. 1099; Case 104/86
Commission v Italy [1988] E.C.R. 1799; Joined Cases 123/87 and 330/87 *Jeunehomme and
EGI v Belgian State* [1988] E.C.R. 4517; Case C–96/91 *Commission v Spain* [1992] E.C.R.
I–3789; and Joined Cases C–6/90 and C–9/90 *Francovich v Italian Republic* [1991] E.C.R.
I–5357. The same passage as that cited in the text appeared in a judgment delivered the
same day as *Peterbroeck*: Cases C–430/93 and C–431/93 *van Schijndel* [1995] E.C.R. I–4705,
para.17.
[16] Case C–312/93 *Peterbroeck* [1995] E.C.R. I–4599, para.14. Also: Cases C–430/93 and
C–431/93 *van Schijndel* [1995] E.C.R. I–4705, para.19.
[17] Case C–326/96 *Levez v Jennings (Harlow Pools)* [1998] E.C.R. I–7835, para.39.
[18] *ibid.*, para.41. Also, e.g. Case C–261/95 *Palmisani* [1997] E.C.R. I–4025; Case C–132/95
Jensen and Korn [1998] E.C.R. I–2975; Case C–78/98 *Preston* [2000] E.C.R. I–3201; Case
C–34/02 *Pasquini* [2003] E.C.R. I–6515.

however, that (e.g.) a Member State must extend its most favourable rules in the field of employment law to an action for equal pay; the national court must consider both the purpose and the essential characteristics of allegedly similar domestic actions in order to reach its conclusion.[19]

As regards the principle of effectiveness, an important element of the case law concerns the right to a fair and public hearing within a reasonable time by an independent and impartial tribunal established by law, as found in Article 6 of the European Convention on Human Rights and Article 47 of the Charter of Fundamental Rights of the European Union, and recognised by the ECJ as a general principle of Community law.[20] Thus, for example, Member States may not provide for a right of appeal, against administrative decisions alleged to infringe Community law rights, before a tribunal which is empowered only to make non-binding recommendations to the relevant public authority;[21] nor may national law seek to oust the jurisdiction of the competent national tribunal to judicially review decisions of a public authority which the Member State seeks to certify as matters of national security.[22]

There can be no doubt that it is for national law to specify the appropriate court, and the appropriate remedy, to enable an individual or undertaking to enforce rights under Community law, but this principle cannot preclude a national court from applying directly effective rules of Community law in all cases falling within its jurisdiction. The problem arose in stark form in the *Simmenthal* case.[23] Should an Italian court refuse to apply national legislation already held by the Court of Justice to be incompatible with Community law, or should the Italian court only do so after referring the question to the Italian Constitutional Court? The Court of Justice ruled that:

> "A national court which is called upon, within the limits of its jurisdiction, to apply provisions of Community law is under a duty to give full effect to those provisions, if necessary refusing of its own motion to apply any conflicting provisions of national legislation, even if adopted subsequently, and it is not necessary for the court to request or await the prior setting aside of such provisions by legislative or other constitutional means."[24]

---

[19] *ibid.*, para.43.
[20] In particular: Case 222/84 *Johnston v Chief Constable of the RUC* [1986] E.C.R. 1651. Also, e.g. Case 178/84 *Commission v Germany* [1987] E.C.R. 1227; Cases C–174 and 189/98P *van der Wal* [2000] E.C.R. I–1; Case C–228/98 *Dounias* [2000] E.C.R. I–577; Case C–54/99 *Église de Scientologie* [2000] E.C.R. I–1335; Case C–7/98 *Krombach* [2000] E.C.R. I–1935.
[21] e.g. Case C–424/99 *Commission v Austria* [2001] E.C.R. I–9285.
[22] e.g. Case 222/84 *Johnston v Chief Constable of the RUC* [1986] E.C.R. 1651.
[23] Case 106/77 *Amministrazione delle Finanze dello Stato v Simmenthal* [1978] E.C.R. 629.
[24] *ibid.*, para.24.

It follows that if a national tribunal is acting within its subject-matter jurisdiction (e.g., tax matters or sex discrimination), it must give effect to Community rights affecting that subject-matter, even if its jurisdiction under national law is limited to rights specified under certain national enactments.[25] However, the Court of Justice seems more reluctant to insist that a national court should assume jurisdiction in entirely novel situations which lie beyond its *prima facie* field of competence as determined under the domestic legal system.[26]

The scope of the duty of a national court in a particular case to **6–007** give effect to Community law will be deducible in principle from the proposition referred to in *Peterbroeck* above: the national court may apply national procedural rules providing they are no less favourable than those governing similar domestic actions and that they do not render virtually impossible or excessively difficult the exercise of rights conferred by Community law. The latter proviso imposes a duty on national courts and tribunals to ensure the effective protection of Community rights, even if this means applying procedural standards more favourable to those enforcing Community rights than those enforcing rights of purely domestic origin. Indeed, the Court has stated that the existence of effective judicial protection is a general principle of Community law.[27] Thus, the Court has held that it is a corollary of the direct effect of the Treaty that an authority of one Member State taking a decision on the right of a national of another Member State to access to employment in that State must give reasons for its decision, and that the latter decision be subject to judicial review to assess its compatibility with Community law.[28] For these purposes, however, the principle of effectiveness will not require a national court to substitute its own judgment for that of a national authority where the national authority applying Community law is called upon to make complex assessments, and has a wide measure of discretion. In such a case judicial review may be restricted to verifying that the action taken by the national authority is not vitiated by a manifest error or a misuse of powers

---

[25] By way of example, direct claims under Art.141 EC may be made before Industrial Tribunals in the United Kingdom: see, e.g. *Pickstone v Freemans* [1987] 3 All E.R. 756, 777; *Greater Glasgow Health Board v Wright and Hannah* [1991] I.R.L.R. 187; *McKechnie v UBM Building Supplies* [1991] I.R.L.R. 283; *Livingston v Hepworth Refractories* [1992] I.R.L.R. 63.

[26] e.g. Case C–54/96 *Dorsch Consult* [1997] E.C.R. I–4961; Case C–76/97 *Walter Tögel* [1998] E.C.R. I–5357; Case C–111/97 *EvoBus Austria* [1998] E.C.R. I–5411; Case C–258/97 *Hospital Ingenieure* [1999] E.C.R. I–1405. Cf. Case C–462/99 *Connect Austria* [2003] E.C.R. I–5197; Case C–15/04 *Koppensteiner* (Judgment of June 2, 2005).

[27] Case 222/86 *Unectef v Heylens* [1987] E.C.R. 4097, para.14; Case 222/84 *Johnston v RUC* [1986] E.C.R. 1651, 1663. More recently, e.g. Case C–34/02 *Pasquini* [2003] E.C.R. I–6515; Case C–125/01 *Pflücke* [2003] E.C.R. I–9375.

[28] Case 222/86 *Unectef v Heylens* [1987] E.C.R. 4097. However, the duty to give reasons does not apply to national measures of general scope (e.g. Case C–70/95 *Sodemare* [1997] E.C.R. I–3395); or to provisional decisions which represent only a preliminary stage in the overall administrative procedure (e.g. Case C–127/95 *Norbrook Laboratories* [1998] E.C.R. I–1531).

and that the authority has not clearly exceeded the bounds of its discretion.[29]

It is true that in one case the Court stated that it was incumbent upon national courts to make available national remedies to secure the implementation of Community law, but added that they were not obliged to create *new* remedies for this purpose.[30] One would expect this to be correct, since the creation of new legal remedies would require legislative, rather than judicial action, but the proposition is contradicted by the judicial development of the principle of Member State liability for breach of Community law.[31] Even to regard the foregoing proposition as the general rule understates the extent to which Community law is capable of modifying the application of national procedures and remedies. For example, a national rule which subjects the availability of a domestic remedy to a condition which is incompatible with Community law must be set aside,[32] and in such a case, the practical effect is to make available a remedy which, if not new, is at any rate something of a hybrid. This is all the more so when the conditions for making available such a remedy are governed in part by national law, and in part by principles of Community law, which are in turn derived in part by analogy with the rules and principles to be applied in direct actions before the Court of Justice.[33]

6-008   The consequences in individual cases of the principle of effectiveness may extend to all national procedural and remedial rules, including (e.g.) the standard and burden of proof. The principal Treaty basis for this principle is Article 10 EC,[34] which requires Member States to take all "appropriate" measures to ensure the fulfilment of the obligations arising out of the Treaty or resulting from action taken by the Community institutions. Although the Court has suggested on occasion that what is "appropriate" is for the Member State in question to decide,[35] this would render the obligation nugatory, and an objective interpretation is more in accordance with principle.[36] It follows that all national procedural and remedial rules are subject in principle to Community minimum

---

[29] Case C–120/97 *Upjohn v The Licensing Authority established by the Medicines Act 1968* [1999] E.C.R. I–223.

[30] Case 158/80 *Rewe-Handelsgesellschaft Nord v Hauptzollamt Kiel* [1981] E.C.R. 1805.

[31] See further, below.

[32] Case 199/82 *Amministrazione delle Finanze dello Stato v SpA San Giorgio* [1983] E.C.R. 3595; Case C–213/89 *R v Secretary of State for Transport, ex parte Factortame* [1990] E.C.R. I–2433.

[33] See below, in particular, as regards injunctive relief.

[34] e.g. Case C–312/93 *Peterbroeck* [1995] E.C.R. I–4599.

[35] Case 50/76 *Amsterdam Bulb* [1977] E.C.R. 137, para.32.

[36] The Court has held that although the "choice of form and methods" in implementing directives is left to the Member States, they are nevertheless obliged to choose the most appropriate form and method to ensure the effective functioning of directives, account being taken of their aims: Case 48/75 *Royer* [1976] E.C.R. 497, para.73.

standards, and support for this may be found in *Rhein-mühlen-Dusseldorf*,[37] in which the Court of Justice acknowledged the competence of national authorities to adopt the standard of proof they thought fit for the purpose of assessing claims for export refunds, but added that complete reliance on shipment without a Community transit document as proof of exportation might nevertheless constitute an abuse of their discretion.

Whether or not Community law provides implicit procedural rules may be difficult to establish without the benefit of a reference to the Court of Justice. In certain cases, the Court has interpreted Community law as implicitly placing the burden of proof on the one party or the other in national proceedings. Thus, the Court has held that it is for the national authorities of a Member State to prove that national trading rules inhibiting imports may be justified under Article 30 EC.[38] Again, in the context of equal pay, the Court has held that if an employer applies a system of pay which is totally lacking in transparency, it is for the employer to prove that this practice in the matter of wages is not discriminatory, if a female worker establishes, in relation to a relatively large number of employees, that the average pay for women is less than that for men.[39] It seems that Community law may mitigate the burden of proof normally incumbent upon one party to adversarial proceedings where the other party is better placed to collect and verify the data which will determine the outcome of the proceedings in question.[40]

Against the background of the foregoing, consideration will be given to the effect of the principles of equivalence and effectiveness in certain specific contexts: national rules governing time-limits; injunctive relief; and the recovery of money levied without lawful authority. In these cases, national procedures and remedies are made available under conditions derived from national law but subject to (sometimes significant) modification as a result of the application of the Community's standards of effective judicial protection. Member State liability for breach of Community law will also be examined. It is more difficult to explain the development of Member State liability for breach of Community law in terms of the principle that national remedies must be made available, but in a form which ensures the effective protection of Community rights; it would be more accurate to speak not of a national remedy modified by a principle of Community law, but rather of a remedy derived from Community law, to be made available under procedural conditions derived from national law. Finally, mention will made of

---

[37] Case 6/71 [1971] E.C.R. 823.
[38] See further, Ch.16.
[39] Case 109/88 *Handels-og Kontorfunktionaererernes Forbund* [1989] E.C.R. 3199; also, e.g. Case 170/84 *Bilka v Weber* [1986] E.C.R. 1607.
[40] Case 28/94 *Netherlands v Commission* [1999] E.C.R. I–1973, para.41.

cases in which Community legislation has sought to harmonise the
national procedural and remedial rules which govern the enforcement before national courts and tribunals of rights derived from
Community law.

Directly applicable Community law and national time-limits

6–009   The principles applicable to the application of national time-limits
in proceedings to enforce Community law are the general principles
referred to above, that is to say, the principles of equivalence and
effectiveness. It is in principle for the national court to decide
whether a national time-limit complies with the principle of equivalence, in accordance with interpretative guidance from the Court of
Justice.[41]

Reasonable national time-limits are consistent with the principle
of effective judicial protection. This was explained in *Denkavit* by
Advocate General Jacobs, as follows:

> "The imposition by a Member State of a reasonable time-limit
> for taking legal proceedings to challenge a decision cannot be
> considered to make reliance on Community law virtually impos-
> sible or excessively difficult. Such time-limits are an application
> of the principle of legal certainty protecting both individuals
> and administrations."[42]

It will be rare for a national time-limit complying with the principle
of equivalence to fall foul of Community law on the grounds that it
nevertheless breaches the principle of effectiveness. The procedural
rule in issue in the national proceedings in one of the seminal cases
establishing the principle of effectiveness—the *Comet* case[43]—was a
30-day time-limit, and there is no indication in the Court's judgment
that this period was considered inadequate.[44] Nevertheless, the
Court of Justice has ruled that national law will infringe the principle

---

[41] Consider, e.g. Case C–326/96 *Levez v Jennings (Harlow Pools)* [1998] E.C.R. I–7835, paras
39–53, where considerable guidance is given to the Employment Appeal Tribunal on the
application of the principle of equivalence in the context of the rule limiting a claimant's
entitlement to arrears of remuneration or damages for breach of the principle of equal pay.

[42] Case C–2/94 *Denkavit Internationaal BV v Kamer van Koophandel en Fabrieken voor
Midden-gelderland* [1996] E.C.R. I–2827, para.64 Opinion (citing Case 33/76 *Rewe v
Landwirtschaftskammer Saarland* [1976] E.C.R. 1989; Case 45/76 *Comet v Produktschap voor
Siergewassen* [1976] E.C.R. 2043; Case 199/82 *Amministrazione delle Finanze dello Stato v
San Giorgio* [1983] E.C.R. 3595).

[43] Case 45/76 *Comet v Produktschap voor Siergewassen* [1976] E.C.R. 2043.

[44] AG Jacobs notes in Case C–2/94 *Denkavit Internationaal BV v Kamer van Koophandel en
Fabrieken voor Midden-gelderland* [1996] E.C.R. I–2827, para.68 Opinion, that "In upholding the right of Member States to lay down reasonable time-limits the Court did not suggest
that the time-limit was too short. Such a short time-limit is in any event no more restrictive
than the one-month time-limit laid down by Art.33 of the E.C.S.C. Treaty for actions
against decisions or recommendations of the Commission".

of effectiveness, for example, where a limitation period of two months within which employees can bring a claim in respect of wages unpaid by their insolvent employer is not justified by overriding interests of legal certainty relating to the proper functioning of the relevant public authority charged with guaranteeing payment of such wages.[45]

The requirements imposed by the principle of effectiveness in this **6–010** field, it must be noted, were thrown into confusion by the ruling in *Emmott*.[46] The case concerned a claim based upon Ireland's failure correctly to implement Directive 79/7 on equal treatment for men and women in matters of social security, initiated outside the applicable national time-limit of three months, but where the claimant had been dissuaded by the competent minister from bringing her action in the first place.[47] The Court held that, owing to the particular nature of directives, "until such time as a directive has been properly transposed, a defaulting Member State may not rely on an individual's delay in initiating proceedings against it in order to protect rights conferred upon him by the provisions of the directive and that a period laid down by national law within which proceedings must be initiated cannot begin to run before that time".[48] It was always difficult to see the precise justification for this broad proposition, which could have led the courts to set aside otherwise reasonable national limitation periods in broad categories of dispute. It was therefore no surprise that the Court of Justice distinguished *Emmott* in subsequent cases.[49] In the *Johnson* case,[50] the Court stated that it was clear "that the solution adopted in *Emmott* was justified by the particular circumstances of that case, in which a time bar had the result of depriving the applicant of any opportunity whatever to rely on her right to equal treatment under the directive".[51] The point was explained by Advocate General Jacobs as follows in *Denkavit*:[52]

"It seems to me that the judgment in *Emmott*, notwithstanding its more general language, must be read as establishing the

---

[45] Case C–125/01 *Pflücke* [2003] E.C.R. I–9375. Consider also, e.g. Case C–78/98 *Preston* [2000] E.C.R. I–3201.

[46] Case C–208/90 *Emmott v Minister for Social Welfare and the Attorney General* [1991] E.C.R. I–4269.

[47] [1979] O.J. L6/4.

[48] Case C–208/90 *Emmott v Minister for Social Welfare and the Attorney General* [1991] E.C.R. I–4269, para.23.

[49] See, e.g. Case C–338/91 *Steenhorst-Neerings v Bestuur van de Bedrijfsvereniging voor Detailhandel, Ambachten en Huisvrouwen* [1993] E.C.R. I–5475; Case C–410/92 *Elsie Rita Johnson v Chief Adjudication Officer* [1994] E.C.R. I–5483; Case C–188/95 *Fantask A/S e.a. v Industriministeriet (Erhvervsministeriet)* [1997] E.C.R. I–6783; Case C–231/96 *Edilizia Industriale Siderurgica Srl (Edis) v Ministero delle Finanze.* [1998] E.C.R. I–4951.

[50] Case C–410/92 *Elsie Rita Johnson v Chief Adjudication Officer* [1994] E.C.R. I–5483.

[51] *ibid.*, para.26.

[52] Case C–2/94 *Denkavit Internationaal BV v Kamer van Koophandel en Fabrieken voor Midden-gelderland* [1996] E.C.R. I–2827.

principle that a Member State may not rely on a limitation period where a Member State is in default both in failing to implement a directive and in obstructing the exercise of a judicial remedy in reliance upon it, or perhaps where the delay in exercising the remedy—and hence the failure to meet the time-limit—is in some other way due to the conduct of the national authorities. Seen in those terms the *Emmott* judgment may be regarded as an application of the well established principle that the exercise of Community rights must not be rendered 'excessively difficult' . . ."

This is certainly a satisfactory explanation to be attributed to the *Emmott* ruling, not least because it brings the case within the well-established principle of effectiveness, which applies whether or not the right relied upon before a national court is derived from a directive or from another source of Community rights. In this regard, the decision in *Levez* is instructive.[53] There, the Court held that a national rule applicable in an equal pay claim, under which entitlement to arrears of remuneration was restricted to the two years preceding the date on which the proceedings were instituted, was not in itself open to criticism.[54] However, the order for reference indicated that the claimant in the national proceedings (who alleged that she had been paid less than her male predecessor) was late in bringing her claim because of inaccurate information provided by her employer regarding the level of remuneration received by her male predecessor. The Court of Justice considered that to allow an employer to rely on a national rule such as that in issue would, in the circumstances of the case before the national court, be "manifestly incompatible with the principle of effectiveness".[55]

Just as the Court was engineering the demise of its own broad and bothersome *Emmott* principle, the case law witnessed the growth of other important elements within the effectiveness principle insofar as it applies to national time-limits. For example, the Court has made clear that Member States cannot reduce the duration of their limitation periods so as specifically to disadvantage the exercise of Treaty rights which have been the subject of proceedings before the ECJ.[56] Moreover, Member States cannot in any case shorten the duration of the limitation period applicable to the exercise of a Community law right in a manner which has retroactive effects, without including adequate transitional provisions allowing claimants

---

[53] Case C–326/96 *Levez v Jennings (Harlow Pools)* [1998] E.C.R. I–7835.
[54] *ibid.*, para.20.
[55] *ibid.*, paras 27 to 34. Consider also, e.g. Case C–327/00 *Santex* [2003] E.C.R. I–1877; Case C–481/99 *Heininger* [2001] E.C.R. I–9945.
[56] e.g. Case 309/85 *Bruno Barra* [1988] E.C.R. 355; Case 240/87 *Deville* [1988] E.C.R. 3513; Case C–228/96 *Aprile* [1998] E.C.R. I–7141; Case C–343/96 *Dilexport* [1999] E.C.R. I–579.

to initiate their actions under the old limitation periods, in accordance with the principle of legitimate expectations.[57]

Directly applicable Community law and interim relief

There can be no doubt that the principle of effectiveness may have **6–011** the effect of requiring national courts and tribunals to adapt national remedies in order to secure the effective enforcement of Community rights. An important example of this is the judgment of the Court of Justice in the *Factortame* case.[58] The House of Lords asked whether Community law either obliged or authorised a national court to grant interim relief against a national measure pending a judgment of the Court of Justice under Article 234 EC on the compatibility of such a measure with Community law. The House of Lords specified circumstances in which, *inter alia*, the national court had no power to give interim protection to the rights claimed by suspending the application of a national measure.[59] The question thus asked directly whether Community law could authorise or require the provision of a remedy which could not be granted under national law. The Court of Justice subtly reformulated the issue as follows:

> "the House of Lords seek essentially to ascertain whether a national court which, in a case before it concerning Community law, considers that the sole obstacle which precludes it from granting interim relief is a rule of national law, must disapply that rule."[60]

Thus the Court of Justice presented the issue as not so much involving the capacity of Community law to create judicial remedies, as the limits on the capacity of national law to impede the application of Community law. The Court of Justice, referring to the principle of the supremacy of Community law, and to the duty of national courts to ensure the legal protection which individuals derive from the direct effect of provisions of Community law, continued:

---

[57] e.g. Case C–228/96 *Aprile* [1998] E.C.R. I–7141; Case C–343/96 *Dilexport* [1999] E.C.R. I–579; Case C–62/00 *Marks & Spencer* [2002] E.C.R. I–6325; Case C–255/00 *Grundig Italiana* [2002] E.C.R. I–8003. Similar principles also apply to the revision of national rules on, e.g. the payment of interest (Cases C–216 and 222/99 *Prisco* [2002] E.C.R. I–6761); and unjust enrichment (Case C–147/01 *Weber's Wine World* [2003] E.C.R. I–11365).

[58] Case C–213/89 *R v Secretary of State for Transport, ex parte Factortame* [1990] E.C.R. I–2433.

[59] The House of Lords proceeded on the basis that no injunctive relief could be made available under English law; but see *M v Home Office* [1994] 1 A.C. 377; [1993] 3 All E.R. 537.

[60] Case C–213/89 *R v Secretary of State for Transport, ex parte Factortame* [1990] E.C.R. I–2433, para.17.

"The Court has also held that any provision of a national legal system and any legislative, administrative or judicial practice, which might impair the effectiveness of Community law by withholding from the national courts having jurisdiction to apply such law the power to do everything necessary at the moment of its application to set aside national legislative provisions which might prevent, even temporarily, Community rules from having full force and effect are incompatible with those requirements, which are the very essence of Community law . . . Consequently, the reply to the question raised should be that Community law must be interpreted as meaning that a national court which, in a case before it concerning Community law, considers that the sole obstacle which precludes it from granting interim relief is a rule of national law must set aside that rule."[61]

This judgment confirms the principle that national remedies must be made available in order to secure the effective enforcement of Community rights, and that any qualifying rules of national law which render those remedies inadequate in the judgment of the national court seised of the case must be set aside. The result is a hybrid remedy, based on national law, but taking on Community characteristics in certain categories of case.

The Court of Justice in *Factortame* did not address the question of the *criteria* to be applied in granting or withholding interim injunctive relief, although the second question referred by the House of Lords asked what those criteria were. The Court perhaps proceeded on the basis that, since the sole ground for the House of Lords refusing relief appeared to be the provision of English law precluding such relief against the Crown, addressing the question of the criteria to be applied in granting or withholding relief would have been superfluous. However, later case law of the Court of Justice indicates that Community law does lay down criteria for the grant of interim relief in situations where individuals rely before national courts on Community law to challenge Community (and perhaps also national) measures.

6–012   The leading cases, *Zuckerfabrik*[62] and *Atlanta*,[63] arose in the context of challenges to national measures giving effect to Community acts, thereby amounting to challenges to the underlying

---

[61] *ibid.*, paras 20 and 23. Interestingly, the Court made no reference to cases such as Case 45/76 *Comet v Produktschap voor Siergewassen* [1976] E.C.R. 2043 on the principle of effectiveness; but instead relied upon its judgment in Case 106/77 *Simmenthal v Amministrazione dello Stato* [1978] E.C.R. 629 on the supremacy and direct effect of Community law (discussed above).

[62] Cases C–143/88 and C–92/89 89 *Zuckerfabrik Süderdithmarschen and Zuckerfabrik Soest* [1991] E.C.R. I–415.

[63] Case C–465/93 *Atlanta Fruchthandelsgesellschaft mbH v Bundesamt für Ernährung und Forstwirtschaft* [1995] E.C.R. I–3761.

Community acts. As we shall see in Chapter 14, the Court of Justice held in *Foto-Frost*[64] that, while a national court does not have jurisdiction to invalidate a Community act (such jurisdiction being reserved exclusively to the Court of Justice itself), different considerations might apply if an applicant sought to suspend a Community act pending a ruling on its invalidity by the ECJ. In that case, the Court had not specified with precision the circumstances in which a national court could suspend a Community act, and had not indicated whether those circumstances were defined by Community law or by national law. It might have been assumed that such questions could be left entirely to national law, subject to the principles of equivalence and effectiveness. But the consequence of this might have been the *over*protection of the rights of individuals, at the expense of the uniform application of Community law; in Member States in which interim relief could and would be readily granted against the administration, the practical consequence might be the paralysis of a Community legal regime as a result of the (albeit temporary) suspension of the relevant Community legislation.

Community law does of course make provision for interim relief in *direct* actions before the Court of Justice for the judicial review of Community acts, pursuant to Articles 230, 242 and 243 EC.[65] In such actions, the Court of Justice (or the Court of First Instance) will suspend the act in question where there is a *prima facie* case, and urgency resulting from the likelihood of irreparable damage to the applicant. Where these conditions are satisfied, the urgency is balanced against the possibility of irreparable damage to the Community should the act be suspended but the applicant's case fail. The requirement of a *prima facie* case is not in principle onerous. The question posed is whether it can reasonably be asserted that the plea is without foundation. If the answer is "no", there is a *prima facie* case, and the Court moves on to urgency and balancing.[66]

In *Zuckerfabrik* and *Atlanta*, the Court, in specifying the criteria to be applied by national courts when considering whether to suspend national measures implementing Community rules, draws an analogy with the test under Articles 242 and 243 EC for interim relief in direct actions before the Community Courts. But it substitutes a somewhat different preliminary hurdle. Instead of the *prima facie* case requirement, as that requirement is understood in the context of applications for interim relief in direct actions, the Court holds that a national court must be satisfied that *serious doubts* exist as to

---

[64] Case 314/85 *Foto-Frost v Hauptzollamt Lubeck-Ost* [1987] E.C.R. 4199.
[65] See further Ch.13.
[66] Case T–29/92 R *SPO v Commission* [1992] E.C.R. II–2161, para.34; Joined Cases C–239/96 R and C–240/96 R *United Kingdom v Commission* [1996] E.C.R. I–4475, paras 51–53 and 61. While the test for *prima facie* case is not onerous, it seems that some account may be taken of the strength of the applicant's case: see Joined Cases C–239/96 R and C–240/96 R *United Kingdom v Commission* [1996] E.C.R. I–4475, para.70.

the validity of the Community act in question. This approach appears to require the national court to go somewhat further by way of preliminary assessment of the merits than do the Community Courts, which in analogous circumstances consider whether factors have been established which are likely to cast doubt on the conclusions reached by the Community authority.[67] In *Atlanta*, as regards the balancing stage, the Court of Justice stressed the Community interest, and the need for the national court to take into account the cumulative effect which would arise if a large number of courts were also to adopt interim measures for similar reasons. While these principles are derived from those developed by the Court of Justice in direct actions, they also appear adapted to erect hurdles slightly more difficult for the litigant before the national court to clear than for the litigant before the Community Courts. This no doubt reflects concern by the Court of Justice that the over-hasty grant of interim measures by national courts might prejudice the uniform application of Community law.

6–013   It is quite possible—though not yet settled beyond doubt—that the criteria referred to above also amount to a minimum standard of protection for those defending the application of *national* measures challenged on the grounds that they infringe Community law. In *Zuckerfabrik* and *Atlanta*, the Court of Justice, referring to *Factortame*, stated that the interim legal protection which Community law ensures for individuals before national courts must remain the same, irrespective of whether they contest the compatibility of national legal provisions with Community law or the validity of secondary Community law, in view of the fact that the dispute in both cases is based on Community law itself.[68]

In any case, there can be no doubt that national courts granting injunctive relief in accordance with the rules laid down in *Factortame*, *Zuckerfabrik* and *Atlanta* are making available hybrid remedies, derived in part from national law, and in part from Community law. Indeed, the propensity of the Court to extrapolate principles applicable in direct actions to the context of national proceedings for the enforcement of Community law makes it possible to contemplate novel forms of interim relief being made

---

[67] Case T–29/92 R *SPO v Commission* [1992] E.C.R. II–2161, para.34: "Whilst the judge hearing the application for interim measures cannot make a close examination of all the pleas and arguments in the main action . . . he must nevertheless consider the arguments put forward by the applicants in their application for interim measures and at the hearing, in order to determine whether there is any evidence to cast doubt on the conclusions reached by the Commission".

[68] Cases C–143/88 and C–92/89 *89 Zuckerfabrik Süderdithmarschen and Zuckerfabrik Soest* [1991] E.C.R. I–415, para.20; Case C–465/93 *Atlanta Fruchthandelsgesellschaft mbH v Bundesamt für Ernährung und Forstwirtschaft* [1995] E.C.R. I–3761, para.24. The approach of the Court of Justice is not far distant from that of the House of Lords in *Factortame* when the reference came back after the ruling of the ECJ: see Lord Goff at [1991] 1 All E.R. 107, 120h.

available before national courts as a consequence of the development of similar principles by the Community courts in direct actions. For example, in *Antonissen*,[69] the President refused to rule out the possibility that a request for an advance payment of compensation might amount to a proper subject of an interim application.[70]

Recovery of charges and taxes levied contrary to Community law
When a charge is imposed contrary to Community law, the **6–014** question arises of the extent to which an action for recovery is governed by national law, or Community law. In this context, once again, the dominant principles are those of equivalence and effectiveness. Entitlement to the repayment of charges levied by a Member State contrary to Community law is a consequence of, and an adjunct to, the rights conferred on individuals by the Community provisions prohibiting such charges. The Member State is therefore in principle required to repay charges levied in breach of Community law.[71] In the leading case in this area of the law, *San Giorgio*,[72] the Court of Justice considered a national rule which precluded the payment of duties or taxes unduly paid where such duties or taxes had been passed on to third parties. Under the national rule in question, duties or taxes were presumed to have been passed on whenever the goods in respect of which a charge had been levied had been transferred to third parties, in the absence of documentary proof to the contrary. The Court of Justice confirmed that national courts might legitimately take into account the fact that unduly levied charges had been incorporated into the price of goods and thus passed on to purchasers. However, any requirement of proof which has the effect of making it "virtually impossible or excessively difficult" to secure the repayment of charges levied contrary to Community law would be incompatible with Community law. That was particularly so in the case of presumptions or rules of evidence placing upon the taxpayer the burden of establishing that the charges had not been passed on to other persons, or in the case of special limitations concerning the form of evidence to be adduced, such as the exclusion of any kind of evidence other than documentary evidence. Once it was established that the levying of the charge was incompatible with Community law, the national court must be

---

[69] Case C–393/96P *Antonissen v Council* [1997] E.C.R. I–441.
[70] *ibid.*, paras 35–41.
[71] Case 177/78 *Pigs and Bacon Commission v McCarren* [1979] E.C.R. 2161; Case 68/79 *Hans Just* [1980] E.C.R. 501; Case 199/82 *San Giorgio* [1983] E.C.R. 3595; Cases 331, 376 and 378/85 *Bianco* [1988] E.C.R. 1099; Cases C–192–218/95 *Comateb* [1997] E.C.R. I–165. Further, e.g. Dougan, "Cutting Your Losses in the Enforcement Deficit: A Community Right to the Recovery of Unlawfully Levied Charges?" (1998) 1 C.Y.E.L.S. 233.
[72] Case 199/82 *Amministrazione delle Finanze dello Stato v SpA San Giorgio* [1983] E.C.R. 3595.

free to decide whether or not the burden of the charge had been passed on, wholly or in part, to other persons.

Furthermore, the Court emphasised that national rules rendering recovery virtually impossible could not be justified on the basis that they were not discriminatory, in as much as recovery of taxes unduly paid under national law was also virtually impossible:

> "It must be pointed out in that regard that the requirement of non-discrimination laid down by the Court cannot be construed as justifying legislative measures intended to render any repayment of charges levied contrary to Community law virtually impossible, even if the same treatment is extended to taxpayers who have similar claims arising from an infringement of national tax law. The fact that rules of evidence which have been found to be incompatible with the rules of Community law are extended, by law, to a substantial number of national taxes, charges and duties or even to all of them is not therefore a reason for withholding the repayment of charges levied contrary to Community law."[73]

In *Comateb*,[74] the question arose once more of the extent to which national rules could be regarded as establishing a presumption that charges unduly paid had been passed on to third parties, thereby providing national authorities with a defence in an action for recovery. The Court stated that the exception to the right to recover charges unduly levied, referred to in *San Giorgio*, which applied in cases where the charge had been passed on to other persons, applied only in a case in which the national court determined, in the light of the facts of the case, that the burden of the charge had been transferred in whole or in part by the trader to other persons, and that reimbursement to the trader would amount to unjust enrichment.[75] There could be no presumption that the charges had been passed on and that it was for the taxpayer to prove the contrary.[76] Even the fact that there was a legal obligation to incorporate the charge in the cost price of the product concerned did not mean that national authorities could rely upon a presumption to the effect that the entire charge had been passed on, and that was true even if the obligation to incorporate the charge in the cost price carried some form of penalty.[77] Indeed, so strict is the case law concerning allocation of the burden of proof that the Court now seems to expect the national authorities to demonstrate on a case-by-case basis the

---

[73] *ibid.*, para.17.
[74] Joined Cases C–192/95 to C–218/95 *Comateb* [1997] E.C.R. I–165.
[75] *ibid.*, paras 21–29.
[76] *ibid.*, para.25.
[77] *ibid.*, para.26.

existence of both passing on and unjust enrichment, and has limited the claimant's possible obligations to co-operation as regards access to relevant documentation (such as the undertaking's balance sheets).[78] In any event, if it transpires that the burden of the unlawful charge was passed on only in part, the national authorities remain obliged to reimburse the trader the amount which has not been passed on.[79]

In general, national procedural conditions which may lawfully be taken into account in relation to the repayment of charges and taxes levied contrary to Community law include time-limits;[80] unjust enrichment resulting from taxes or charges being passed on to third parties;[81] damage to the trade of taxpayers resulting from the imposition of the unlawful charge;[82] and any benefits accruing to a person paying unlawful taxes or charges by virtue of the payment.[83] If national authorities exact money payments in contravention of Community law, the question whether interest is payable on repayment is one for national, not Community law.[84] A Member State may not, however, adopt provisions making repayment of a tax held to be contrary to Community law by a judgment of the Court, or whose incompatibility with Community law is apparent from such a judgment, subject to conditions relating specifically to that tax which are less favourable than those which would otherwise be applied to repayment of the tax in question.[85]

Damages as a remedy for breach of Community law

There were early suggestions in the Court's case law that breach of **6–015** Community law by a Member State might give rise to liability in damages.[86] In *Francovich*,[87] the Court delivered a judgment which

---

[78] e.g. Case C–343/96 *Dilexport* [1999] E.C.R. I–579; Cases C–441 and 442/98 *Mikhailidis* [2000] E.C.R. I–7145; Case C–147/01 *Weber's Wine World* [2003] E.C.R. I–11365; Case C–129/00 *Commission v Italy* [2003] E.C.R. I–14637.

[79] Joined Cases C–192/95 to C–218/95 *Comateb* [1997] E.C.R. I–165, para.28.

[80] See, e.g. Case C–343/96 *Dilexport Srl v Amministrazione delle finanze dello Stato* [1999] E.C.R. I–579.

[81] As discussed just above. Loss of the unjust enrichment is also a relevant factor when national authorities seek recovery of subsidies paid contrary to Community law: see, e.g. Case C–298/96 *Oelmühle Hamburg* [1998] E.C.R. I–4767.

[82] Case 68/79 *Just v Ministry for Fiscal Affairs* [1980] E.C.R. 501, para.26; Joined Cases C–192/95 to C–218/95 *Comateb* [1997] E.C.R. I–165, paras 29–34. Damage to traders resulting from the unlawful imposition of national taxes or charges might also give rise to an action for damages: Joined Cases C–192/95 to C–218/95 *Comateb* [1997] E.C.R. I–165, para.34.

[83] Case 177/78 *Pigs and Bacon Commission v McCarren* [1979] E.C.R. 2161.

[84] Case 26/74 *Roquette Frères v Commission* [1976] E.C.R. 677, paras 11 and 12; Joined Cases C–279/96, C–280/96 and C–281/96 *Ansaldo Energia* [1998] E.C.R. I–5025, para.28. But an action in damages might lie for loss arising from non-payment of interest; *cf.* Case C–66/95 *ex parte Sutton* [1997] E.C.R. I–2163, paras 34–35.

[85] Case 240/87 *Deville* [1988] E.C.R. 3513; Case C–231/96 *Edis v Ministero delle Financze* [1998] E.C.R. I–4951.

[86] Case 6/60 *Humblet* [1960] E.C.R. 559; Case 60/75 *Russo v AIMA* [1976] E.C.R. 45.

[87] Joined Cases C–6/90 and C–9/90 *Andrea Francovich and Danila Bonifaci v Italian Republic* [1991] E.C.R. I–5357.

"caused a minor legal earthquake, perhaps comparable to that caused by the ruling of the House of Lords in *Donogue v Stevenson*".[88]

The *Francovich* case concerned a directive on the protection of employees in the event of the insolvency of their employer,[89] which had not been implemented by Italy within the time-limit specified, a default which had been established by the Court in previous enforcement proceedings brought by the Commission against that Member State.[90] The Court held that the principle of Member State liability for harm caused to individuals by breaches of Community law for which the Member State can be held responsible is inherent in the scheme of the Treaty. The Court stated in succinct terms the conditions for liability in a case such as that in issue:

"Although State liability is thus required by Community law, the conditions under which that liability gives rise to a right to reparation depend on the nature of the breach of Community law giving rise to the loss and damage. Where, as in this case, a Member State fails to fulfil its obligation under the third paragraph of Article [249] of the Treaty to take all the measures necessary to achieve the result prescribed by a directive, the full effectiveness of that rule of Community law requires that there should be a right to reparation provided that three conditions are fulfilled. The first of those conditions is that the result prescribed by the directive should entail the grant of rights to individuals. The second condition is that it should be possible to identify the content of those rights on the basis of the provisions of the directive. Finally, the third condition is the existence of a causal link between the breach of the State's obligation and the loss and damage suffered by the injured parties. Those conditions are sufficient to give rise to a right on the part of individuals to obtain reparation, a right founded directly on Community law."[91]

The judgment in *Francovich* was undoubtedly a bold and significant development of the law. The principle of Member State liability which it propounded could not be explained as a corollary or "adjunct" of the direct effect of a provision of Community law (as for example, with the right in principle to recover sums of money levied contrary to Community law),[92] since the provision of the

---

[88] Wyatt, "Injunctions and Damages against the State for Breach of Community Law: A Legitimate Judicial Development" in Andenas and Jacobs (eds) *European Community Law in the English Courts* (Clarendon Press, Oxford, 1998), p.93.

[89] Dir.80/987 [1980] O.J. L283/23.

[90] Case 22/87 *Commission v Italy* [1989] E.C.R. 143.

[91] Joined Cases C–6/90 and C–9/90 *Andrea Francovich and Danila Bonifaci v Italian Republic* [1991] E.C.R. I–5357, paras 38–41.

[92] As discussed above.

directive relied upon by the plaintiff in *Francovich* was held by the Court not to be directly effective. The liability was thus based not on the breach of a directly applicable Community right, but the failure to bring into existence an enforceable right in national law by way of transposition of the directive—that failure nevertheless giving rise to enforceable rights in individuals. *Francovich* nevertheless raised many questions about the future scope of this right to damages: for example, whether *Francovich* liability was actually confined to breach of the duty to implement non-directly effective norms derived from directives; or, if the action for damages was indeed potentially more far-reaching, whether liability would follow automatically from breach (as appeared to be the case in *Francovich* itself), or might be conditional on the existence of fault/culpability of one kind or another.[93]

Important guidance on these issues came as a result of the **6–016** requests for preliminary rulings in *Factortame III and Brasserie du Pêcheur*.[94] Proceedings in the former case arose from the adoption of United Kingdom rules which had sought to reserve the British flag for vessels owned by British nationals. That these rules amounted to an infringement of the right of establishment of Spanish fishermen under Article 43 EC had been established by a judgment of the Court of Justice.[95] The fishermen had from the start claimed damages for the losses they had sustained. The *Brasserie du Pêcheur* proceedings resulted from the application of German rules which had had the effect of excluding from the German market beer produced other than in accordance with German "pure beer" requirements. The German rules were held by the Court to be contrary to Article 28 EC in enforcement proceedings brought by the Commission.[96] A French brewery sought compensation for alleged loss of profits which would have been made on exports to Germany, but for the exclusionary effects of the German rules. These proceedings were, if anything, more controversial than the judgment in *Francovich*. The German Government argued before the Court of Justice that "an extension of Community law by judge-made law going beyond the bounds of the legitimate closure of lacunae would be incompatible with the division of competence between the Community institutions and the Member States laid down by the Treaty, and with the principle of the maintenance of

---

[93] For discussion, e.g. Craig, "*Francovich*, Remedies and the Scope of Damages Liability" (1993) 109 L.Q.R. 595; Steiner, "From Direct Effects to *Francovich*: Shifting Means of Enforcement of Community Law" (1993) 18 E.L.Rev. 3.

[94] Joined Cases C–46 and 48/93 [1996] E.C.R. I–1029. For discussion, e.g. Craig, "Once More Unto the Breach: The Community, the State and Damages Liability" (1997) 113 L.Q.R. 67; Emiliou, "State Liability Under Community Law: Shedding More Light on the *Francovich* Principle?" (1996) 21 E.L.Rev. 399; Deards, "Curiouser and Curiouser? The Development of Member State Liability in the Court of Justice" (1997) 3 E.P.L. 117.

[95] Case C–221/89 *Factortame II* [1991] E.C.R. I–3905.

[96] Case 178/84 *Commission v Germany* [1987] E.C.R. 1227.

institutional balance".[97] This came close to arguing that the Court would exceed its competence if it developed Community law in the way in which, in the event, it actually did.

The national courts asked the Court of Justice to specify the conditions under which a right to reparation of loss or damage caused to individuals by breaches of Community law attributable to a Member State was guaranteed by Community law. In its response, the Court drew a parallel between liability of the Member State, and liability of the Community institutions themselves under Article 288(2) EC.[98] Where the Community acted in a legislative context characterised by the exercise of a wide discretion, the Community only incurred liability if the institution concerned had manifestly and gravely disregarded the limits on its powers. This strict approach was justified by the need to ensure that the legislative process was not unduly hindered by the prospect of damages actions. Where national authorities had a wide discretion, comparable to that of the Community institutions in implementing common policies, the conditions under which the Member State might incur liability must in principle be the same as for the Community itself. The Court considered, as regards the proceedings in issue, that both the United Kingdom and Germany had a wide discretion in adopting the national rules in question and, accordingly, they would be liable only if three conditions were satisfied:

- the rule of law relied upon must be intended to confer rights on individuals;
- the breach must be sufficiently serious;
- there must be a direct causal link between the breach and the damage suffered.

As regards the question whether the breach was sufficiently serious, the Court said that the test for liability was whether the Member State had "manifestly and gravely disregarded the limits on its discretion".[99] The Court went on to indicate the factors which should be taken into consideration by a national court in determining whether a breach of Community law was to be regarded as sufficiently serious to ground liability:

---

[97] Report for the Hearing in Joined Cases C–46 and 48/93, para.32.
[98] On damages under Art.288(2) E.C., including the converse influence of the *Francovich* case law upon the jurisprudence on Community liability, see Ch.13. One might note that such an analogy had been widely canvassed in academic literature and in arguments in the proceedings in question; as early as 1985, the Court of Appeal had drawn a parallel between Community liability under Art.288(2) E.C. and Member State liability for breach of directly applicable Treaty provisions (see *Bourgoin v MAFF* [1985] 3 All E.R. 585).
[99] Joined Cases C–46 and 48/93 [1996] E.C.R. I–1029, para.55.

"The factors which the competent court may take into consideration include the clarity and precision of the rule breached, the measure of discretion left by that rule to the national or Community authorities, whether the infringement and the damage caused was intentional or involuntary, whether any error of law was excusable or inexcusable, the fact that the position taken by a Community institution may have contributed towards the omission, and the adoption or retention of national measures or practices contrary to Community law. On any view, a breach of Community law will clearly be sufficiently serious if it has persisted despite a judgment finding the infringement in question to be established, or a preliminary ruling or settled case-law of the Court on the matter from which it is clear that the conduct in question constituted an infringement."[1]

The ruling in *Factortame III and Brasserie du Pêcheur* thus made **6–017** clear, first, that the potential scope of *Francovich* liability was not limited to a failure to implement the non-directly effective provisions of a directive, but could be incurred on the basis of *any* breach by the Member State of its Treaty obligations; and, secondly, that considerations of culpability would be relevant to determining whether such liability had been engaged—at least as regards disputes involving legislation adopted by the Member State in breach of directly effective Treaty provisions. The Court subsequently applied its *Factortame III/Brasserie du Pêcheur* conditions to other categories of dispute: for example, those concerning decisions of the national administration taken in breach of the Treaty itself;[2] and cases involving the incorrect (rather than total non-)implementation of directives by the Member State.[3] Yet that merely raised a new question: why did the Member State's simple failure to implement a directive (as in *Francovich*) seem to be governed by different substantive conditions than every other type of Treaty infringement? The situation became clearer in the light of *Dillenkofer*, which (like *Francovich*) involved a claim for damages against a Member State for having failed to take any measures to transpose a directive within the prescribed deadline. The Court held that, in substance, the two sets of substantive conditions set out in *Francovich* and *Factortame III/Brasserie du Pêcheur* were the same; the requirement of a sufficiently serious breach, although not expressly mentioned in *Francovich*, was nevertheless evident from the circumstances of that case.[4]

---

[1] *ibid.*, paras 56 and 57.
[2] Case C–5/94 *ex parte Hedley Lomas* [1996] E.C.R. I–2553.
[3] Case C–392/93 *ex parte British Telecommunications* [1996] E.C.R. I–1631.
[4] Cases C–178–179 and 188–190/94 *Dillenkofer* [1996] E.C.R. I–4845.

Dillenkofer therefore generalised the three substantive conditions required in *Factortame III/Brasserie du Pêcheur* for imposing liability upon the Member States. Subsequent case law has explored each of these conditions in greater detail: for example, as regards exactly when any given provision of Community law is intended to confer rights on individuals;[5] and as regards the factors which national courts might take into account when determining the existence of a causal link between breach and damage.[6] But most attention has focused on the definition of a "sufficiently serious breach". Here, rulings such as *Factortame III/Brasserie du Pêcheur* and *Dillenkofer* had suggested that there was a fundamental distinction between situations where the Member State had an appreciable degree of discretion in complying with its Treaty obligations (in which case, the claimant must demonstrate that the Member State has perpetrated a manifest and grave disregard on the limits of its powers, taking into account the various factors listed in *Factortame III/Brasserie du Pêcheur*); and situations where the Member State had no appreciable degree of discretion in complying with the Treaty (in which case, the mere breach of Community law should be considered sufficiently serious, without more ado). However, more recent rulings, such as *Haim* and *Larsy*, suggest that, even in the latter category of situation, it is still necessary for national courts to take into account the full range of factors listed in *Factortame III/Brasserie du Pêcheur*.[7] Thus, there might well be an insufficiently serious breach, even though the Member State had no real discretion in discharging its Treaty obligations, for example because the relevant Community provisions were ambiguous and the Member State acted reasonably and in good faith. Indeed, Advocate General Léger in *Köbler* argued that, in the light of such case law, the decisive factor for establishing *Francovich* liability seems simply to be whether the error of law at issue can be considered excusable or inexcusable.[8]

6–018 Two further issues concerning the *Francovich* action for damages need to be considered. The first concerns what actually happens to the action for damages, assuming liability has been established in accordance with the substantive conditions derived from *Factortame III/Brasserie du Pêcheur*. The starting point here is that "it is in accordance with the rules of national law on liability that the State must make reparation for the consequences of the harm caused";[9]

---

[5] e.g. Case C–222/02 *Peter Paul* [2004] E.C.R. I–9425. *cf.* Case C–511/03 *Ten Kate* (Judgment of October 20, 2005).
[6] e.g. Case C–319/96 *Brinkmann* [1998] E.C.R. I–5255; Case C–140/97 *Rechberger* [1999] E.C.R. I–3499.
[7] Case C–424/97 *Haim* [2000] E.C.R. I–5123; Case C–118/00 *Larsy* [2001] E.C.R. I–5063.
[8] Case C–224/01 *Köbler* [2003] E.C.R. I–10239, para.139 Opinion. *cf.* the approach of the EFTA Court in Case E–9/97 *Sveinbjörnsdóttir* (Judgment of December 10, 1998); and the approach of the House of Lords in *ex parte Factortame (No.5)* [2000] 1 A.C. 524.
[9] Joined Cases C–6/90 and C–9/90 *Andrea Francovich and Danila Bonifaci v Italian Republic* [1991] E.C.R. I–5357, para.42.

subject to the proviso that any conditions laid down by national law remain subject to the principles of equivalence and effectiveness.[10] Thus, for example, in a case concerning Italian legislation designed to facilitate damages actions pursuant to the *Francovich* ruling, the Court held that a one-year time-limit for such actions was consistent with Community law from the point of view of effectiveness, provided it also met the requirement of equivalence.[11] As regards the actual quantum of damages, the Court of Justice in *Factortame III/Brasserie du Pêcheur* set out the following principle:

> "Reparation for loss or damage caused to individuals as a result of breaches of Community law must be commensurate with the loss or damage sustained so as to ensure the effective protection for their rights."[12]

That said, in the absence of relevant Community provisions, it is again for the domestic legal system of each Member State to set the criteria for determining the extent of reparation, subject to the Community principles of equivalence and effectiveness. In this connection, the Court in *Factortame III/Brasserie du Pêcheur* noted that the national court may enquire whether the injured person showed reasonable diligence in order to avoid the loss or damage or limit its extent and whether, in particular, "he availed himself in time of all the legal remedies available to him".[13] On the other hand, the Court held that a national rule which totally excluded loss of profit as a head of recoverable damage cannot be accepted in cases concerning a breach of Community law; especially in the context of economic or commercial litigation, such a total exclusion of lost profits would be such as to make reparation of the damage suffered by the claimant practically impossible.[14]

The second issue concerns the range of bodies in respect of whose infringement of Community law the Member State may incur liability under *Francovich*. The basic principle was established by the Court in *Factortame III/Brasserie du Pêcheur*: the right to reparation applies to any case in which a Member State breaches Community law, whichever is the authority of the Member State whose act or omission was responsible for the breach. The Court justified this

---

[10] *ibid.*, paras 42–43.
[11] Case C–261/95 *Palmisani* [1997] E.C.R. I–4025.
[12] Joined Cases C–46 and 48/93 [1996] E.C.R. I–1029, para.82.
[13] *ibid.*, para.84. Provided those alternative legal remedies are adequate, e.g. Cases C–397 and 410/98 *Metallgesellschaft* [2001] E.C.R. I–1727.
[14] Joined Cases C–46 and 48/93 [1996] E.C.R. I–1029, para.87. *cf.* Case C–271/91 *Marshall v Southampton and South-West Hampshire Area Health Authority* [1993] E.C.R. I–4367, which precludes a limit on compensation for loss sustained as a result of a dismissal from employment tainted by sex discrimination. For the duty to make adequate reparation, see also Joined Cases C–94/95 and C–95/95 *Bonifaci* [1997] E.C.R. I–3969; Case C–373/95 *Maso* [1997] E.C.R. I–4051; Case C–261/95 *Palmisani* [1997] E.C.R. I–4025, para.35.

principle by the fact that, under international law, a State which incurs liability for breach of an international commitment is viewed as a single entity, irrespective of whether the breach is attributable to the legislature, the judiciary or the executive. According to the Court, that principle must apply *a fortiori* in the Community legal order since all national authorities are bound in performing their tasks to comply with the rules laid down by Community law which directly govern the situation of individuals. In addition, the Court observed that, having regard to the fundamental requirement that Community law be uniformly applied, the obligation to make good damage caused to individuals by breaches of the Treaty could not depend upon domestic rules as to the division of powers between constitutional authorities.[15]

6-019 *Francovich* liability may therefore be attributed to the Member State on the basis of acts of the national legislature;[16] acts of the national executive (such as administrative decisions taken by central government departments);[17] acts of local or regional authorities (e.g. within a federal system);[18] and acts adopted by autonomous bodies governed by public law (such as professional regulatory agencies).[19] Perhaps most controversially, the ruling in *Köbler* established that decisions of a national supreme court may, in certain circumstances, also give rise to a right to reparation against the Member State.[20] In particular, the Court of Justice found that the full effectiveness of the Treaty would be called into question, and the protection of rights derived from Community law would be weakened, if individuals were unable to obtain reparation in respect of infringements resulting from judicial decisions delivered at last instance as regards which there could be no further possibility of correction.[21] However, when applying the substantive conditions for reparation, liability in respect of an infringement of the Treaty resulting from a judicial decision delivered at last instance should be incurred only in exceptional cases where the national court has manifestly breached Community law—taking into account the usual *Brasserie* factors, but also whether

---

[15] Joined Cases C-46 and 48/93 [1996] E.C.R. I-1029, paras 31f.

[16] e.g. as in Cases C-46 and 48/93 *Factortame III/Brasserie du Pêcheur* [1996] E.C.R. I-1029 itself.

[17] e.g. Case C-5/94 *ex parte Hedley Lomas* [1996] E.C.R. I-2553.

[18] e.g. Case C-302/97 *Konle* [1999] E.C.R. I-3099. Further, e.g. Anagnostaras, "The Allocation of Responsibility in State Liability Actions for Breach of Community Law: A Modern Gordian Knot?" (2001) 26 E.L.Rev. 139.

[19] e.g. Case C-424/97 *Haim* [2000] E.C.R. I-5123.

[20] Case C-224/01 *Köbler* [2003] E.C.R. I-10239. *cf.* Case C-173/03 *Traghetti del Mediterraneo* (Opinion of October 11, 2005; Judgment pending).

[21] In reaching that conclusion, the Court dismissed arguments that *Francovich* liability might undermine the principle of *res judicata*, or the independence of the judiciary. The Court also noted that the principle of liability for judicial decisions was accepted by the legal orders of most Member States; and had been established under the case law of the European Court of Human Rights.

the domestic court had abrogated its obligation to make a preliminary reference under Article 234 EC.[22] It remains to be seen whether infringements of the Treaty perpetrated via decisions delivered by lower courts and tribunals will furnish the basis for Member State liability under *Francovich*.[23]

This discussion leads on to an important but still uncertain question: the availability of damages under Community law in respect of the conduct of purely private parties who have contravened an enforceable obligation imposed by or pursuant to the Treaty. Such individuals cannot be treated as public bodies whose actions are attributable to the Member State for the purposes of bringing a *Francovich* action. Nor does it seem possible to bring an action for reparation directly against a private party on the basis of the *Francovich* case law (which is, after all, tailored to the administrative law liabilities of public authorities exercising their powers in the general interest).[24] Nevertheless, Advocate General van Gerven in *Banks* suggested that the ECJ should adapt the *Francovich* case law to the context of private law relations, such as those created in the field of competition law, so as to permit those whose rights are infringed by another individual to bring an action for damages in accordance with substantive conditions laid down by Community (rather than domestic) law.[25]

This question was presented to the Court in *Courage v Crehan*,[26] which concerned a beer tie agreement between a brewery and a publican alleged to contravene Article 81 EC on anti-competitive agreements. The publican's action for damages against the brewery was dismissed by the English courts on the grounds that anti-competitive agreements are to be treated as unlawful, and under domestic law, the parties to an unlawful contract cannot seek compensation or restitution *inter se*. Asked to determine whether this restriction on the availability of damages was compatible with Community law, the ECJ observed that the full effectiveness of Article 81 EC would be jeopardised if it were not open to any individual to claim damages for loss caused to him or her by a contract liable to restrict competition. There should not therefore be any absolute bar to an action for damages being brought by a party

---

[22] Indeed, the judgment seems to suggest that *Francovich* liability for judicial decisions will be incurred only in extreme and really very unlikely circumstances, e.g. where the claimant can demonstrate that the judges of the national supreme court were motivated by improper purposes.

[23] Especially bearing in mind the duty to exhaust available remedies (such as rights of appeal). However, consider Case C–129/00 *Commission v Italy* [2003] E.C.R. I–14637; Serena Rossi and Di Federico (2005) 42 C.M.L.Rev. 829.

[24] See further Dougan, "What is the Point of *Francovich*?" in Tridimas and Nebbia (eds), *European Union Law for the Twenty-First Century: Rethinking the New Legal Order (Volume I)* (Hart Publishing, 2004).

[25] Case C–128/92 *Banks v British Coal Corporation* [1994] E.C.R. I–1209.

[26] Case C–453/99 *Courage v Crehan* [2001] E.C.R. I–6297.

to a contract which is held to violate the competition rules; but in the absence of relevant Community rules, national law must lay down the detailed rules governing such actions, subject to the principles of equivalence and effectiveness.

Courage v Crehan is therefore a very significant but also rather ambiguous judgment. On the one hand, it is clear that the ECJ did not intend to go so far as the Advocate General had suggested in *Banks*: there was no bold attempt to create a "private *Francovich*" with its own substantive conditions for incurring liability as a matter of Community law. On the other hand, the Court made clear that the proper enforcement of certain Treaty provisions would require national courts to ensure the availability in principle of damages actions; and Community law would supervise the detailed conditions for awarding such compensation in accordance with the standards of equivalence and effectiveness. That reasoning should not be restricted to infringements of Article 81 (or 82) EC. The ECJ should also be prepared to guarantee the effective judicial protection, for example, of an EU citizen who suffers discrimination on grounds of nationality by his or her private employer, in breach of Article 39 EC on the free movement of workers, where national law imposes unduly restrictive conditions for the award of compensation.[27]

Harmonisation of procedural rules and remedies

6–020   The foregoing sections of this chapter have been concerned with modifications to the scheme of procedures and remedies normally applicable as a consequence of general principles derived from the EC Treaty. But in certain cases, the Community legislator has intervened to bring about more systematic alignment of national procedures and remedies.

Sometimes such intervention is based upon concerns that differences in national remedies and procedural rules hamper the proper functioning of the internal market, for example, by distorting the conditions of competition between traders through significant discrepancies in the levels of judicial protection available in different Member States. Thus, in the field of public procurement, two directives[28] harmonise the remedies available at national level when proceedings are taken to review the decisions of contracting authorities/entities on the ground that such decisions have infringed Community law in the field procurement or national rules implementing that law. The harmonised rules cover, *inter alia*, the availability of interim relief and compensatory damages.

---

[27] Art.39 EC now being established as being capable of having horizontal direct effect against private employers: Case C–281/98 *Angonese* [2000] I–4139. See further Ch.18.

[28] Dir.89/665 (review procedures for award of public supply and public works contracts) [1989] O.J. L395/33; Dir.92/13 (procurement procedures of entities operating in the water, energy, transport and telecommunications sectors) [1992] O.J. L76/14.

Other instances can be found in the field of Community social policy, where legislative intervention was thought desirable so as to enhance the protection of individual rights, particularly as regards vulnerable categories of citizens. For example, it was noted above how the Court of Justice held that the Treaty's guarantee of equal pay for equal work may affect the burden of proof in national legal proceedings; Council Directive 97/80 now lays down harmonised rules on the burden of proof in cases of discrimination based on sex.[29]

Furthermore, in the recent case of *Commission v Council*,[30] the Court confirmed that, although criminal law and criminal procedure generally fall outside the Community's competence, this does not prevent the Community legislature from adopting measures relating to national criminal law, which it considers necessary to ensure that the rules it lays down (*in casu*) on environmental protection are fully effective; in particular, where the application of effective, dissuasive and proportionate criminal penalties by the competent domestic authorities is essential for combating serious environmental offences. There is no reason to restrict this ruling to the field of environmental protection; one assumes that the Community legislature enjoys the competence to prescribe criminal penalties for other serious infringements of Treaty obligations, for example as regards the internal market, anti-discrimination law or agricultural policy.[31]

Significant legislative intervention in the domestic standards of judicial protection may also be seen in the fields of judicial co-operation in civil and criminal matters, as provided for under Title IV of Part Three of the EC Treaty and Title VI TEU (respectively), where the adoption of common minimum standards for the conduct of proceedings is seen as an important step towards Member States recognising and enforcing each other's judicial rulings within the area of freedom, security and justice. On that basis, there are Union acts dealing with issues such as access to legal aid in cross-border disputes;[32] and the standing of victims in criminal proceedings.[33]

Impact of the Constitutional Treaty (CT)

The CT contains few reforms affecting the topics covered in this **6–021** chapter, but:

— Member States would be expressly obliged to provide remedies sufficient to ensure effective legal protection in the fields covered by EU law (see Art.I–29(1) CT);

---

[29] Dir.97/80 [1998] O.J. L14/6. Extended to the United Kingdom by Dir.98/52 [1998] O.J. L205/66.

[30] Case C–176/03 *Commission v Council* (Judgment of September 13, 2005).

[31] A view supported by the Commission: see COM(2005) 583 Final.

[32] Dir.2003/8 [2003] O.J. L26/41.

[33] Framework Decision 2001/220 [2001] O.J. L82/1.

— the legal bases for Community harmonisation of civil and criminal procedural rules would be revised (see Ss.3 and 4, Ch.IV, Title III, Pt III CT).

Further reading

Biondi, "The European Court of Justice and Certain National Procedural Limitations: Not Such a Tough Relationship" (1999) 36 C.M.L.Rev. 1271.

Craig, "Once More Unto the Breach: The Community, the State and Damages Liability" (1997) 113 L.Q.R. 67.

Dougan, *National Remedies Before the Court of Justice* (Hart Publishing, 2004).

van Gerven, "Bridging the Unbridgeable: Community and National Tort Laws after *Francovich* and *Brasserie*" (1996) 45 I.C.L.Q. 507.

van Gerven, "Of Rights, Remedies and Procedures" (2000) 37 C.M.L.Rev. 501.

Himsworth, "Things Fall Apart: The Harmonisation of Community Judicial Procedural Protection Revisited" (1997) 22 E.L.Rev. 291.

Hoskins, "Tilting the Balance: Supremacy and National Procedural Rules" (1996) 21 E.L.Rev. 365.

Kakouris, "Do the Member States Possess Judicial Procedural 'Autonomy'?" (1997) 34 C.M.L.Rev. 1389.

Kilpatrick, Novitz and Skidmore (eds), *The Future of Remedies in Europe* (Hart Publishing, 2000).

Komninos, "New Prospects for Private Enforcement of EC Competition Law: *Courage v Crehan* and the Community Right to Damages" (2002) 39 C.M.L.Rev. 447.

Lonbay and Biondi (eds), *Remedies for Breach of EC Law* (Wiley, 1997).

Odudu and Edelman, "Compensatory Damages for Breach of Article 81" (2002) 27 E.L.Rev. 327.

Prechal, "Community Law in National Courts: The Lessons From *Van Schijndel*" (1998) 35 C.M.L.Rev. 681.

Ross, "Beyond *Francovich*" (1993) 56 M.L.R. 55.

Szyszczak, "Making Europe More Relevant to its Citizens: Effective Judicial Process" (1996) 21 E.L.Rev. 351.

Tridimas, "Liability for Breach of Community Law: Growing Up and Mellowing Down?" (2001) 38 C.M.L.Rev. 301.

Ward, *Judicial Review and the Rights of Private Parties in EC Law* (OUP, 2000).

CHAPTER 7

GENERAL PRINCIPLES OF COMMUNITY LAW

Guide to this Chapter: This Chapter examines the general 7–001
principles of Community law, unwritten principles deriving from
the common constitutional traditions of the Member States and
developed by the European Court of Justice. The general
principles are binding upon the EU institutions whenever they act,
on the Member States when they implement Community law and
when they act within the scope of Community law. This chapter
focuses on the principle of loyal co-operation, proportionality,
legitimate expectations, non-discrimination and good administration. Subsidiarity is only dealt with briefly as it is fully analysed in
Chapters 4 and 11. Fundamental rights, also general principles of
Community law, are of such constitutional importance that they
deserve to be dealt with in detail and are therefore the subject of
the next two chapters.

Function of general principles in the Union legal order

General principles operate at two levels. They define and limit the 7–002
scope of the competences of the Union Institutions to adopt binding
acts.[1] They also place obligations on Member States when the latter
are acting within the scope of Union obligations, e.g. when Member
States invoke exceptions to fundamental Treaty freedoms, or adopt
national rules or administrative acts to implement Union legislation.

---

[1] But the application of human rights and fundamental freedoms is not necessarily *limited* to
defining the scope of EU competence to adopt binding acts. Under the TEU the Union
"shall respect fundamental rights . . ." (Art.6(2)), and such rights are applicable to e.g. the
operational conduct of the common foreign and security policy under Title V of the TEU,
though the Court of Justice is not given jurisdiction over alleged breaches.

Sources of general principles

7–003　　The EC Treaty has from the outset expressly laid down certain general legal principles, such as the duty of co-operation which binds both Member States and the institutions in ensuring fulfilment of the obligations arising from the Treaty;[2] and the principle of non-discrimination on grounds of nationality.[3] Some general principles, such as proportionality, equality and legitimate expectation, are wholly or mainly the product of judicial development, though the principle of proportionality is now expressly recognised in the Treaty as a constitutional principle of the Union legal order, and the Union has been given competence to legislate to fight discrimination other than that on grounds of sex and nationality. Fundamental rights travelled a similar road to proportionality; first recognised by the Court's case law, then endorsed by declarations of the institutions, and finally written into the fundamental law of the EU. General principles such as these have important legal effects. They place limits on the administrative and legislative competence of the Community institutions, they govern the interpretation of provisions of Community law,[4] and they bind the Member States when the latter act within the scope of operation of Union law.

The Court can hardly be said to have exceeded its jurisdiction by its recourse to the general principles of law. No Treaty regime, let alone the "new legal order" of the Community, could be interpreted and applied in a legal vacuum. International tribunals have long been regarded as competent to draw upon the general principles of municipal law as a source of international law,[5] and the competence of the Court of Justice in the interpretation and application of Community law could surely have been intended to be no less. The Treaty might be said to imply as much. Article 220 EC provides that "The Court of Justice shall ensure that in the interpretation and application of this Treaty the law is observed." While this formulation implies commitment to the rule of law, it has been argued that this implies a *corpus juris* outwith the express Treaty texts.[6] Other provisions are consistent with the proposition that the general principles of law constitute a source of Community law. Article 230 EC includes among the grounds of invalidity of Community acts infringement of "any rule of law" relating to the Treaty's application, an expression wide enough to encompass the principles under

---

[2] Art.10 EC see below.

[3] Art.12 EC see below.

[4] Case 316/86 *Hauptzollamt Hamburg-Jonas v Krucken* [1988] E.C.R. 2213, para.22; Joined Cases 201 and 202/85 *Klensch* [1986] E.C.R. 3466, para.10; Joined Cases C–90/90 and C–91/90 *Neu v Secrétaire d'Etat àl'Agriculture* [1991] E.C.R. I–3617, para.12.

[5] See Wyatt, "New legal Order, or Old?" (1982) 7 E.L.Rev. 147 at 157. *cf.* Art.38 of the Statute of the International Court of Justice, which lists as a source of international law, "the general principles of law recognized by civilized nations".

[6] See Pescatore, "Fundamental Rights and Freedom in the System of the European Communities" [1970] A.J.I.L. 343 at 348.

consideration. Furthermore, Article 288(2) EC provides that the non-contractual liability of the Community shall be determined "in accordance with the general principles common to the laws of the Member States", which amounts to express recognition of the role of the general principles of Community law. In the sections of this Chapter which follow, particular principles will be examined.

The general principle of sincere or loyal co-operation
Article 10 of the EC Treaty provides that Member States shall 7–004 take all appropriate measures, whether general or particular, to ensure fulfilment of the obligations arising out of the Treaty or resulting from action taken by the institutions of the Community. They are obliged to facilitate the achievement of the Community's tasks, and to abstain from any measure which could jeopardise the attainment of the objectives of the Treaty. This provision is worthy of remark in this context, since it has been developed as a general principle binding upon the Community institutions as well as the Member States. In *Hilmar Kellinghusen* the Court stated:

"As to Article 5 [now 10] of the Treaty, it should be borne in mind that, according to the case-law of the Court, the relations between the Member States and the Community institutions are governed, under that provision, by a principle of sincere co-operation. That principle not only requires the Member States to take all the measures necessary to guarantee the application and effectiveness of Community law, but also imposes on the Community institutions reciprocal duties of sincere co-operation with the Member States."[7]

The principle of sincere, or loyal[8] co-operation inherent in Article 10 of the Treaty requires the Union institutions, and above all the Commission, which is entrusted with the task of ensuring application of the provisions of the Treaty, to give active assistance to any national judicial authority dealing with an infringement of Community rules. That assistance, which takes various forms, may, where appropriate, consist in disclosing to the national courts documents acquired by the institutions in the discharge of their duties.[9] The

---

[7] Joined Cases C–36/97 and C–37/97 *Hilmar Kellinghusen v Amt für Land- und Wasserwirtschaft Kiel* and *Ernst-Detlef Ketelsen v Amt für Land- und Wasserwirtschaft Husum* [1998] E.C.R. I–6337, para.31; Case C–275/00 *EC v First NV and Franex NV* [2002] E.C.R. I–10943, para.49.

[8] The French text refers to the obligation of "loyauté" or to "loyale" co-operation. The English text has sometimes rendered this as "sincere" co-operation, and sometimes as "loyal" co-operation.

[9] Case C–2/88 Imm. *J.J. Zwartveld* [1990] E.C.R. I–3365, para.17; Case T–353/94 *Postbank NV v Commission* [1996] E.C.R. I–921, para.64.

Commission is obliged to respond as quickly as possible to requests from national courts.[10] As far as the Member States are concerned, the principle of loyal co-operation has been used by the ECJ as a funding block to build the entire Community/Union constitutional architecture. Thus, in *Von Colson*, the Court held:

> "However, the Member States' obligation arising from a directive to achieve the result envisaged by the directive and their duty under Article 5 [now 10] of the Treaty to take all appropriate measures, whether general or particular, to ensure the fulfilment of that obligation, is binding on all the authorities of Member States including, for matters within their jurisdiction, the courts."[11]

As we have seen in Chapters 5 and 6, Article 10 EC has been directly or indirectly instrumental to establishing the doctrine of supremacy, direct effect, the duty of consistent interpretation, as well as the general principles of equivalence and effectiveness in relation to national procedural autonomy and *Francovich* damages.[12] The principle of loyal co-operation has been held to be inherent also in the TEU, even though it is not expressly mentioned there.[13]

Subsidiarity as a general principle

7–005 Subsidiarity has been discussed in detail in Chapter 4, on Union Competences. Brief mention is made of subsidiarity here, as a "general principle", since however unwilling the Court of Justice has been to enforce application of the principle through the mechanism of judicial review of Community acts, the fact remains that subsidiarity lays down conditions for the exercise of Community competence, and non-compliance with subsidiarity may in principle lead to the annulment of a Community act. This is accepted by the Court of Justice, which has on a number of occasions considered claims that Community acts should be annulled on grounds of compliance with subsidiarity.[14] Subsidiarity is not, however, any more than the principle of sincere or loyal co-operation laid down in Article 10 EC, a general principle derived from the common constitutional traditions of the Member States; it is derived from Article 5 EC.[15] And

---

[10] Case C–39/94 *Syndicat Français de l'Express International (SFEI) v La Poste* [1996] E.C.R. I–3547, at para.50; Case C–275/00, *EC v First NV* [2002] E.C.R. 1–10943, para.49.

[11] Case 14/83 *Von Colson* [1984] E.C.R. 1891, para.26.

[12] Chs 5 and 6 above.

[13] C–105/03 *Pupino* [2005] E.C.R. I–5285.

[14] See Ch.4, pp.97 and 98.

[15] It is true that it has always been possible to argue that proportionality was also derived from the Treaty, even before it was given a specific Treaty basis, along with subsidiarity, in what is now Art.5 EC.

whereas general principles of law proper bind not only the Community institutions, but also the Member States when they implement Community law,[16] subsidiarity by its nature binds the Community to defer in certain circumstances to Member State action, which is an obligation which cannot fall to be performed by Member States when they implement Community obligations or otherwise act within the scope of Community law. Community obligations may fall to be performed by Member States where subsidiarity leads to no action being taken by the Community, but these obligations are existing obligations pursuant to Article 10 of the EC Treaty which would have been displaced by the Community action which would have been taken had it not been for the principle of subsidiarity.[17]

In principle, subsidiarity would seem relevant to the interpretation of Community acts, at least those adopted after the principle took effect within the Community legal order.[18] Since the Community institutions take account of the principle in framing Community legislation, it would seem logical to apply the principle in interpreting that legislation. Furthermore, if two interpretations are possible, one consistent with subsidiarity, and the other not, one would expect the Court to prefer the former—that is the normal approach of the Court where there is a risk of conflict between a provision of a Community act and a general principle of law. Differing views on this point have been expressed by Advocates General,[19] but it now seems clear from the judgment of the Court of Justice *AvestaPolarit Chrome Oy*,[20] that the principle of subsidiarity may be invoked as a guide to the interpretation of Community secondary legislation. It also seems that the Commission takes into account subsidiarity along with the other circumstances of the case when deciding whether to dismiss a complaint for want of sufficient Community interest; this is surely correct in principle.[21]

---

[16] See above at p.235, and discussion below at p.240.

[17] Amsterdam Protocol on Subsidiarity and Proportionality, point (8), "Where the application of the principle of subsidiarity leads to no action being taken, Member States are required in their action to comply with the general rules laid down in Art.10 of the Treaty . . .". For the principle of sincere or loyal co-operation laid down in Art.10, see above.

[18] Art.5 EC (ex 3b) cannot have retroactive effect, see Joined Cases C–36/97 and C–37/97 *Hilmar Kellinghusen v Amt für Land- und Wasserwirtschaft Kiel* and *Ernst-Detlef Ketelsen v Amt für Land- und Wasserwirtschaft Husum* [1998] E.C.R. I–6337, para.35.

[19] In Case C–188/95 *Fantask A/S e.a. v Industriministeriet (Erhvervministeriet)*. [1997] E.C.R. I–6783, Advocate General Jacobs rejects the argument that the text should be interpreted in light of the principle of subsidiarity, see para.28 of the Opinion. The Directive in any event predated the incorporation of subsidiarity into the Community legal order. Advocate General Alber in C–318/96 *SPAR Österreichische Warenhandels AG v Finanzlandesdirectktion für Salzburg* [1998] E.C.R. I–785, at para.59 of his Opinion, implies that subsidiarity is relevant to the interpretation of the directive under consideration. In Case C–103/01 *Commission v Federal Republic of Germany* [2003] E.C.R. I–5369, at para.40 of his Opinion, Advocate General Ruiz-Jarabo Colomer observes that the Commission's interpretation does not breach the principle of subsidiarity.

[20] C–114/01 [2003] E.C.R. I–8725, paras 55–57.

[21] Case T–5/93.*Roger Tremblay and François Lucazeau and Harry Kestenberg v Commission of the European Communities* [1995] E.C.R. II–185, para.61.

Proportionality

7–006   The principle of proportionality, shortly stated, holds that "the individual should not have his freedom of action limited beyond the degree necessary for the public interest".[22] It applies to the acts of the Union institutions; to the acts of the Member States when they implement Community law; and to the acts of the Member States when they act within the field of Community law, for instance when they seek to limit one of the rights conferred on individuals by the Treaty.[23]

The principle of proportionality as a limit to the actions of the institutions

7–007   The Union's institutions are bound to comply with the principle of proportionality, and indeed breach of such obligation constitutes one of the grounds for annulment of the contested act. The duty for the institutions to act in a proportionate way—when legislating but also when taking decisions which affect individuals—originally found recognition in the express words of the Treaty only in specific contexts. Thus e.g. the Treaty has always provided, in connection with the establishment of a common organisation of agricultural markets, that such common organisation may include all measures *required* to attain the objectives specified by the Treaty;[24] and the provision made for the harmonisation of indirect taxation is for "such harmonisation as is *necessary* to ensure the establishment and the functioning of the internal market . . .".[25] Notwithstanding the sectorial references to the principle in the Treaty, the Court from a very early stage, found that the principle of proportionality was one of the general principles of Community law which applied regardless of the field in which action was taken, even though the intensity with which it is applied might vary according to the amount of discretion enjoyed by the institutions. Where a Community institution has a wide discretionary power, e.g. in the context of the common agricultural policy, the Court of Justice will only interfere if a measure is manifestly inappropriate having regard to the objective which the competent institution is seeking to pursue.[26]

The Court has given a number of different formulations of the principle of proportionality; one more or less standard formulation is as follows:

---

[22] Case 11/70 *Internationale Handelsgeselklschaft* [1970] E.C.R. 1125, at 1127, *per* Advocate General Dutheillet de Lamothe.

[23] On the different standards of review according to when the principle is invoked, see De Burca "The Principle of Proportionality and its application in EC Law" (1993) 13 Y.E.L. 105.

[24] Art.34(2) EC.

[25] Art.93 EC.

[26] Case 265/87 *Schrader* [1989] E.C.R. 2237, paras 21, 22; Case 331/88, *Ex Parte Fedesa* [1990] E.C.R. I–4023, para.14; Case C–375/96 *Galileo Zaninotto v Ispettorato Centrale Repressione Frodi—Ufficio di Conegliano—Ministero delle risorse agricole, alimentari e forestali* [1998] E.C.R. I–6629, para.64.

"In order to establish whether a provision of Community law is consonant with the principle of proportionality it is necessary to establish, in the first place, whether the means it employs to achieve the aim correspond to the importance of the aim, and, in the second place, whether they are necessary for its achievement."[27]

A somewhat fuller formulation of the principle is to the effect that:

". . . the principle of proportionality, which is one of the general principles of Community law, requires that measures adopted by Community institutions do not exceed the limits of what is appropriate and necessary in order to attain the objectives legitimately pursued by the legislation in question; when there is a choice between several appropriate measures recourse must be had to the least onerous, and the disadvantages caused must not be disproportionate to the aims pursued . . ."[28]

The principle has operated, *inter alia*, to invalidate a provision of a **7–008** regulation providing for the forfeiture of a security for any failure to perform a contractual undertaking, irrespective of the gravity of the breach.[29] The Court held that the:

"Absolute nature . . . of the above-mentioned regulation is contrary to the principle of proportionality in that it does not permit the penalty for which it provides to be made commensurate with the degree of failure to implement the contractual obligations or with the seriousness of the breach of those obligations."[30]

Thus where Community legislation makes a distinction between a primary obligation (such as the export of a commodity from the Community), compliance with which is necessary in order to attain the objective sought, and a secondary obligation (such as the duty to apply for an export licence), essentially of an administrative nature, it cannot, without breaching the principle of proportionality, penalise failure to comply with the secondary obligation as severely as failure to comply with the primary obligation.[31]

---

[27] Case 66/82 *Fromancais* [1983] E.C.R. 395, para.8; Case C–369/95 *Somalfruit SpA, Camar SpA v Ministero delle Finanze, Ministerio del Commercio con l'Estero* [1997] E.C.R. I–6619.
[28] Case C–157/96 *R v Minister of Agriculture, Fisheries and Food ex parte National Farmers' Union* [1998] E.C.R. I–2211, para.60; Case C–375/96 *Galileo Zaninotto v Ispettorato Centrale Repressione Frodi—Ufficio di Conegliano—Ministero delle Risorse Agricole, Alimentari e Forestali* [1998] E.C.R. I–6629, para.63.
[29] Case 240/78 *Atalanta* [1979] E.C.R. 2137.
[30] [1979] E.C.R. 2137 at p. 2151.
[31] Case 181/84 *R v Intervention Board for Sugar ex parte Man (Sugar)* [1985] E.C.R. 2889, para.20; Case 21/85 *Maas v Bundesanstalt für Landwirtschaftliche Marktordnung* [1986] E.C.R. 3537, para.15; Case C–161/96 *Südzucker Mannheim/Ochsenfurt AG v Hauptzollamt Mannheim* [1998] E.C.R. I–281, para.31.

If the principle was, to start with, of jurisprudential derivation, however, it was incorporated in an express provision of the Treaty at Maastricht. Article 5 EC, which states that the Community shall take action in accordance with the principle of subsidiarity, adds that: "Any action by the Community shall not go beyond what is necessary to achieve the objectives of this Treaty." Furthermore, a Protocol on the application of the principle of proportionality and subsidiarity was added by the Amsterdam Treaty. Point 1 of such Protocol states that each institution shall ensure "compliance with the principle of proportionality, according to which action by the Community shall not go beyond what is necessary to achieve the objectives of the Treaty". Application of this principle to determine whether the scale of Community action contemplated is necessary to achieve the purpose of the draft legislation under consideration could in principle rule out the legislation in question, or have a significant limiting effect on its content, and provide the possibility of annulment if the Community legislator overstepped the mark. The point may be illustrated, hypothetically, by reference to the unfair contract terms directive.[32] The directive is an internal market measure based on Article 95 EC. The directive harmonises the laws of Member States as regards unfair terms in consumer contracts. The preamble indicates that one of the problems caused for the single market by the existence of different national rules on unfair consumer contracts is that consumers from one Member State may be deterred from purchasing goods and services in another Member State because they may be unaware of the rules of that State. If the foregoing—adverse effect on direct cross-border purchases—were regarded as the *only* mischief identified as flowing from the disparities between national rules referred to it, it might be said that the directive was disproportionate in regulating *all* consumer transactions, and that the aim of the directive could be achieved by laying down harmonised rules for cross-border transactions. While such questions involve large elements of policy, and a wide measure of discretion, it is not impossible to envisage the Court of Justice intervening in a case where there is a clear lack of proportion between the wide scope of Community legislation, and the relatively narrow ambit of the aim identified in the preamble of the measure in question.

The principle of proportionality as a limit to Member States actions

7–009   When Member States are implementing Community law, for instance, by enacting legislation pursuant to a directive, they must exercise whatever discretion they have in compliance with the principle of proportionality. Thus, e.g. the Court found that the

---

[32] O.J. 1993 L95/29.

power left to the Member States to derogate form harmonised labelling rules on grounds of protection of public health and the consumers, needs to be exercised consistently with the principle of proportionality. National rules which absolutely, and without exceptions, precluded any reference to "slimming" and "medical recommendations" in product labels were found to be not proportionate as there were least restrictive means to ensure that buyers would not be misled and that those statements would not be used in a fraudulent way.[33] The same reasoning applies in the case in which a regulation leaves some discretion to the Member State—since the Member State here acts as a "delegated power" it has to comply with the general principles of Community law, including the principle of proportionality.[34]

Furthermore, Member States are also bound by the general principles of Community law, including proportionality, when acting within the field of Community law. This is particularly the case when the national authorities seek to limit the free movement rights enshrined in Articles 28, 39, 43, 49 and 56 EC by relying on the mandatory requirements doctrine or on the Treaty derogations. In this context, the Court has consistently held that a rule which impacts on one of those rights not only has to pursue an interest consistent with Community law, but it has also to be proportionate to that end.[35] Furthermore, following the direct effect of the provisions on Union citizenship contained in Article 18 EC the principle of proportionality also applies to the limits imposed on the right to reside and move of non-economically active Union citizens. In this field, and as we shall see in Chapter 17 below, the principle of proportionality acts as an hermeneutic principle which might call into question national rules which, even though consistent with secondary legislation enacted at Community level, produce results which are out of proportion with the sought aim. Thus in *Baumbast*,[36] the Court found that to deprive a Union citizen who had resided for several years in another Member State of his right to reside only because he lacked cover for emergency treatment was out of proportion with the legitimate aim of ensuring that he would not become an "unreasonable burden" on the welfare system of that State. Following this case law, an increasing number of national rules will be subjected to the proportionality scrutiny, and the principle will become even more central in the assessment of the compatibility of national legislation with Community law.

---

[33] Case C–239/02 *Douwe Egberts NV v Westrom Pharma NV and Christophe Souranis* and *Douwe Egberts NV v FICS-World BVBA* [2004] E.C.R. I–7007.
[34] Joined Cases C–480/00 to 482/00, C–484/00, C–489/00 to C–491/00 and C–497/00 to C–499/00 *Azienda Agricola Ettore Ribaldi v Azienda di Stato per gli interventi nel mercato agricolo (AIMA), Ministero del Bilancio e della Programma Economica* [2004] E.C.R. I–2943.
[35] e.g. Case 60/00 *Carpenter* [2002] E.C.R. I–6279.
[36] Case C–413/99 *Baumbast and R* [2003] E.C.R. I–7091, and see below Ch.17.

Furthermore, and even though it is for the Member State to decide the penalties imposed for breaches of its rules, the principle of proportionality also applies to criminal and administrative sanctions imposed for breach of rules in any way connected with the exercise of a Community right. This is the case in relation, for instance, to penalties imposed to secure compliance with formalities relating to establishing a right of residence under Community law,[37] or providing evidence of entitlement to drive based on recognition of a valid driving licence issued in another Member State.[38]

Legal certainty and legitimate expectation

7–010   The principle of legal certainty requires that those subject to the law should be able to clearly ascertain their rights and obligations. The related concept of legitimate expectation constitutes what has been described as a corollary[39] to this principle: those who act in good faith on the basis of the law as it is or as it seems to be should not be frustrated in their expectations.

The principle of legal certainty requires that Community rules must enable those concerned to know precisely the extent of the obligations which are imposed upon them.[40] In one case the Court appears to say that the latter principle requires that the Commission must adhere to the interpretation of an EC regulation which is dictated by the normal meaning of the words used, but it is certainly not an invariable principle of interpretation that the normal meaning be attributed to the words in a text.[41] Nevertheless, the Court of Justice in a consistent case law has held that ambiguity or lack of clarity in measures alleged to impose charges should be resolved in favour of the taxpayer. In *Gondrand Frères* the Court declared:

> "The principle of legal certainty requires that rules imposing charges on the taxpayer must be clear and precise so that he may know without ambiguity what are his rights and obligations and may take steps accordingly."[42]

---

[37] Case C–265/88 *Messner* [1989] E.C.R. 4209.

[38] Case C–193/94 *Skanavi and Chryssanthakopoulos* [1996] E.C.R. I–929, paras 35–38; Case C–29/95 *Pastoors* [1997] E.C.R. I–285 (higher penalty for non-resident permissible in principle but must not be disproportionately higher).

[39] Case C–63/93 *Duff v Minister for Agriculture and Food, Ireland, and the Attorney General* [1996] E.C.R. I–569, para.20. Case T–73/95 *Estabelecimentos Isidoro M. Oliveira SA v Commission* [1997] E.C.R. II–381, para.29.

[40] Case C- 233/96 *Kingdom of Denmark v Commission* [1998] E.C.R. I–5759, para.38.

[41] *ibid*. In interpreting a provision of Community law it is necessary to consider not only its wording but also, where appropriate, the context in which it occurs and the objects of the rules of which it is part, see, in particular, Case C–340/94 *De Jaeck v Staatssecretaris van Financiën* [1997] E.C.R. I–461, para.17.

[42] Case 169/80 [1981] E.C.R. 1931 at 1942. See also Case C–143/93 *Gebroeders van Es Douane Agenten BV v Inspecteur der Invoerrechten en Accijnzen* [1996] E.C.R. I–431, para.27; Case C–177/96 *Belgian State v Banque Indosuez and European Community* [1997] E.C.R. I–5659, para.27. But where a regulation authorizes the total or partial suspension of imports, a power to impose charges, as a less drastic measure, may be implied, Case 77/86 *ex parte National Dried Fruit Association* [1988] E.C.R. 757.

It seems, however, that rules may present some difficulties of interpretation, without thereby infringing the principle of legal certainty, at any rate where the difficulties result from the complexity of the subject-matter, and where a careful reading of the rules in question by one professionally involved in the area allows the sense of the rules to be grasped.[43] The failure of the Commission to amend a regulation concerning tariff nomenclature where it was required to do so, and which resulted in uncertainty on the part of individuals as to their legal obligations, had the consequence that the regulation could not thereafter be applied.[44] The principle is capable of operating in favour of Member States, and a provision laying down a time-limit, particularly one which may have the effect of depriving a Member State of the payment of financial aid, application for which has been approved and on the basis of which it has already incurred considerable expenditure, should be clearly and precisely drafted so that the Member States may be made fully aware of the importance of complying with the time-limit.[45]

The principle of legal certainty also applies when Member States **7–011** adopt rules when required or authorised to do so pursuant to Community law. Thus Member States are bound to implement directives in a way which meets the requirements of clarity and certainty, by enacting appropriate national rules, and mere administrative practices will be inadequate for this purpose.[46] In *Raija-Liisa Jokela*, a case involving Finnish legislation adopted in accordance with an EC regulation, the Court described the principle of legal certainty as requiring that "legal rules be clear and precise, and aims to ensure that situations and legal relationships governed by Community law remain foreseeable".[47]

The principle of legal certainty militates against administrative and legislative measures taking effect without adequate notice to persons concerned. As the Court declared in *Racke*:

> "A fundamental principle in the Community legal order requires that a measure adopted by the public authorities shall not be applicable to those concerned before they have the opportunity to make themselves acquainted with it."[48]

---

[43] Case C–354/95 *R v Minister of Agriculture, Fisheries and Food, ex parte National Farmers' Union* [1997] E.C.R. I–4559, para.57.

[44] C–143/93 *Gebroeders van Es Douane Agenten BV v Inspecteur der Invoerrechten en Accijnzen* [1996] E.C.R. I–431.

[45] Case 44/81 *Commission v Germany* [1982] E.C.R. 1855.

[46] Case 102/79 *Commission v Belgium* [1980] E.C.R. 1473 at 1486. And see above at Ch.5.

[47] Joined Cases C–9/97 and C–118/97 [1998] E.C.R. I–6267, para.48.

[48] Case 98/78 [1979] E.C.R. 69 at 84. And see Case 84/81, *Staple Dairy Products* [1982] E.C.R. 1763 at 1777; Case 108/81 *Amylum* [1982] E.C.R. 3107 at 3130. Case 77/71 *Gervais-Danone* [1971] E.C.R. 1127; Case 158/78 *Biegi* [1979] E.C.R. 1103; Case 196/80 *Ango-Irish Meat* [1981] E.C.R. 1103. A regulation is deemed to be published throughout the Community on the date appearing on the issue of the *Official Journal* containing the text of the regulation, unless the date of actual issue was later, Case C–337/88 *SAFA* [1990] E.C.R. I–1.

This principle argues against the retroactive application of Community measures, and this is indeed the general principle, but it is not invariable. As the Court explained in *Decker*:

"Although in general the principle of legal certainty precludes a Community measure from taking effect from a point in time before its publication, it may exceptionally be otherwise where the purpose to be achieved so demands and where the legitimate expectations of those concerned are duly respected."[49]

7-012 Thus a public statement of intention to alter monetary compensatory amounts justifies a later regulation altering the rate retrospectively to the earlier date.[50]

The principle of legitimate expectations, which may be invoked as against Community rules only to the extent that the Community has previously created a situation which can give rise to a legitimate expectation,[51] operates in particular to protect individuals where they have acted in reliance upon measures taken by the Community institutions, as the *Mulder* case illustrates. In order to stabilise milk production, Community rules provided for dairy farmers to enter into non-marketing agreements for a period of five years, in return for which they received a money payment. In 1984 milk quotas were introduced, whereby milk producers would pay a super levy on milk produced in excess of a quota determined by reference to their production during the 1983 marketing year. No provision was made for the grant of quota to those who did not produce during 1983 because of the existence of a non-marketing agreement. Having been urged to suspend milk production under Community rules, farmers were then excluded from milk production when their non-marketing period came to an end. One such farmer challenged the regulations in this regard. The Court of Justice held that the relevant regulation was invalid to the extent that no provision for allocation of quota was made in such cases. The basis of the ruling was the principle of legitimate expectations. As the Court explained:

---

[49] Case 99/78 [1979] E.C.R. 101, at 111. See also Case 276/80 *Pedana* [1982] E.C.R. 517 at 541; Case 258/80 *Runi* [1982] E.C.R. 487 at 503. Procedural rules are generally held to apply to all proceedings pending at the time when they enter into force, while substantive rules are usually interpreted as applying to situations existing before their entry into force only insofar as it clearly follows from the terms, objectives or general scheme that such an effect must be given to them, Cases 212–217/80 *Salumi* [1981] E.C.R. 2735.

[50] Case 338/85 *Pardini* [1988] E.C.R. 2041, paras 24–26.

[51] Case C–375/96 *Galileo Zaninotto v Ispettorato Centrale Repressione Frodi—Ufficio di Conegliano—Ministero delle risorse agricole, alimentari e forestali* [1998] E.C.R. I–6629, para.50. The CFI held that three essential conditions have to be met in order to claim legitimate expectations: (i) precise, consistent and unconditional assurances given by the institution to the individual; (ii) those assurances must be as such as to create a legitimate expectation; (iii) the assurances must comply with the applicable rules, e.g. Case T–282/02 *Cementbouw Handel and Industrie BV v Commission*, (Judgment of February 23, 2006) nyr (para.77).

"where such a producer, as in the present case, has been encouraged by a Community measure to suspend marketing for a limited period in the general interest and against payment of a premium he may legitimately expect not to be subject, upon the expiry of his undertaking, to restrictions which specifically affect him because he availed himself of the possibilities offered by the Community provisions."[52]

On the basis of the same principle, if an undertaking purchases grain for denaturing with a view to qualifying for a Community subsidy, it is not permissible to discontinue or reduce the subsidy without giving the interested party a reasonable opportunity of denaturing the grain in question at the old rate.[53] Again, if the Community induces prudent traders to omit to cover their transactions against exchange risk, by establishing a system of compensatory amounts which in practice eliminate such risks, it must not withdraw such payments with immediate effect, without providing appropriate transitional measures.[54] Similar reasoning protected certain former Community officials in receipt of pensions which had increased in value over a number of years as a result of the Council's failure to adjust the exchange rates used to calculate the amounts due. The Council sought to rectify the situation and phase out the advantages which had accrued, over a 10-month period. The Court held that respect for the legitimate expectations of those concerned required a transitional period twice as long as that laid down by the Council.[55] And if the Commission brings about a situation of uncertainty for an individual, and the individual in consequence does not comply with certain requirements, the Commission may be precluded from relying upon those requirements without notifying the individual and clarifying the situation.[56]

Considerations of both legal certainty and legitimate expectation **7–013** may argue in favour of modifying the temporal effects of judicial and administrative decisions which would normally apply with retroactive effect. It has already been noted that in exceptional circumstances considerations of legal certainty may preclude the retroactive effect

---

[52] Case 120/86 [1988] E.C.R. 2321, para.24. For a survey of the case law of the Court see Sharpston, "Legitimate Expectation and Economic Reality" (1990) 15 E.L.Rev. 103.

[53] Case 48/74 *Deuka* [1975] E.C.R. 421; Case 5/75 *Deuka* [1975] E.C.R. 759.

[54] Case 74/74 *CNTA* [1975] E.C.R. 533; and prudent traders are deemed to know the contents of the *Official Journal*, see Case C–174/89 *Hoche* [1990] E.C.R. I–2681, at para.35. But an overriding public interest may preclude transitional measures from being adopted in respect of situations which arose before the new rules came into force but which are still subject to change, Case 74/74 *CNTA* [1975] E.C.R. 533, para.44; Case 152/88 *Sofrimport* [1990] E.C.R. I–2477, paras 16 and 19.

[55] Case 127/80 *Grogan* [1982] E.C.R. 869; Case 164/80 *De Pasquale* [1982] E.C.R. 909; Case 167/80 *Curtis* [1982] E.C.R. 931.

[56] Case T–81/95 *Interhotel—Sociedade Internacional de Hotéis SARL v Commission of the European Communities.* [1997] E.C.R. II–1265, paras 49–58

of a judgment of the Court of Justice concerning the direct effect of a provision of Community law.[57] Similar considerations explain Article 231 EC, which allows the Court of Justice to determine which of the legal effects of a regulation declared to be void by the Court shall nevertheless be considered as definitive. The Court applies Article 231 by analogy to acts other than regulations and in preliminary rulings on invalidity under Article 234 EC, denying retroactivity in appropriate cases to ensure legal certainty and respect for legitimate expectations. Thus in the *Simmenthal* case the Court annulled a Commission decision fixing the minimum selling prices for frozen beef put up for sale by intervention agencies. However, "for reasons of legal certainty and taking special account of the established rights of the participants in the invitation to tender whose tenders have been accepted" the Court ruled that the annulment must be restricted to the specific decision to reject the applicant's tender which stemmed from the decision in question.[58] It is established that any Community institution which finds that a measure which it has just adopted is tainted by illegality has the right to withdraw it within a reasonable period, with retroactive effect, but that right may be restricted by the need to fulfil the legitimate expectations of a beneficiary of the measure, who has been led to rely on its legality.[59]

Respect for vested rights is itself an aspect of the principles of certainty and legitimate expectations. In *Rossi* the Court stressed that:

> "The Community rules could not, in the absence of an express exception consistent with the aims of the Treaty, be applied in such as way as to deprive a migrant worker or his dependants of the benefit of a part of the legislation of a Member State."[60]

7–014 Yet traders may not rely upon legitimate expectations to insulate them from changes in legal regimes subject to constant adjustments. As the Court explained in *Eridania*, in the context of the common agricultural policy:

> ". . . an undertaking cannot claim a vested right to the maintenance of an advantage which is obtained from the establishment of a common organisation of the market and which it enjoyed at a given time."[61]

---

[57] Above at Ch.5.
[58] Case 92/78 [1979] E.C.R. 777, esp. at 811. See Ch.13.
[59] Case C–90/95P *Henri de Compte v European Parliament* [1997] E.C.R. I–1999, para.35, and cases there cited.
[60] Case 100/78 [1979] E.C.R. 831 at 844.
[61] Case 230/78 [1979] E.C.R. 2749 at 2768. See also Case C–375/96 *Galileo Zaninotto v Ispettorato Centrale Repressione Frodi—Ufficio di Conegliano—Ministero delle risorse agricole, alimentari e forestali.* [1998] E.C.R. I–6629, para.50 (common agricultural policy). The same principle has been stated in the context of the common commercial policy, Case C–284/94 *Kingdom of Spain v Council* [1998] E.C.R. I–7309, para.43.

The Court has said on numerous occasions that a wrongful act on the part of the Commission or its officials, and likewise a practice of a Member State which does not conform with Community rules, is not capable of giving rise to legitimate expectations on the part of an economic operator who benefits from the situation thereby created.[62] But it is possible that the broad scope of this proposition may be limited by the conclusion which is often drawn from it in the case law to the effect that it follows that the principle of the protection of legitimate expectations cannot be relied upon against a *precise*[63] provision of Community law, or an *unambiguous*[64] provision of Community law. Another limitation on recourse to the principle of legitimate expectations is to the effect that "the principle of the protection of legitimate expectations may not be relied upon by an undertaking which has committed a manifest infringement of the rules in force".[65]

Where Community or national subsidies are paid to undertakings in contravention of Community law, the principle of legitimate expectations may preclude recovery.[66] This will not be the case, however, where a beneficiary was in a position to appreciate that the State aid was paid contrary to mandatory provisions of Community law.[67] Circumstances in which legitimate expectations may preclude recovery of State aid include long delay on the part of the Commission in taking a decision, and aid comprising measures which do not self-evidently constitute State aid and which could not readily be identified as such by the beneficiary.[68]

Non-discrimination

A further principle binding upon the Community in its administra- **7–015** tive and legislative activities is that prohibiting discrimination, whereby comparable situations must not be treated differently, and

---

[62] Case 188/92 *Thyssen* [1983] E.C.R. 3721; Case 5/82 *Maizena* [1982] E.C.R. 4601 at 4615; Case 316/86 *Hauptzollamt Hamburg-Jonas v Firma P. Krücken* [1988] E.C.R. 2213 at 2239; Joined Case C–31/91 to C–44/91 *SpA Alois Lageder v Amministrazione delle Finanze dello Stato* [1993] E.C.R. I–1761, para.34 Case T–336/94 *Efisol SA v Commission*, [1996] E.C.R. II–1343, para.36.
[63] Case 316/ *Hauptzollamt Hamburg-Jonas v Krucken* [1988] E.C.R. 2213.
[64] Joined Case C–31/91 to C–44/91 *SpA Alois Lageder v Amministrazione delle Finanze dello Stato* [1993] E.C.R. I–1761, para.35.
[65] Case 67/84 *Sideradria v Commission* [1985] E.C.R. 3983, para.21; Joined Cases T–551/93, T–231/94, T–233/94 and T–234/94 *Industria Pesdquera Campos v Commission* [1996] E.C.R. II–247, para. 76; Case T–73/95 *Estabelecimentos Isidoro M. Oliveira SA v Commission* [1997] E.C.R. II–381, para.28.
[66] Joined Cases 205–215/82 *Deutsche Milchkontor GmbH v Federal Republic of Germany.* [1983] E.C.R. 2633, paras 30–33; Case 5/89 *Commission v Germany* [1990] E.C.R. I–3437, paras 13–16.
[67] Case 5/89 *Commission v Germany* [1990] E.C.R. I–3437.
[68] Case 223/85 *Rijn-Schelde-Verolme (RSV) Machinefabrieken en Scheepswerven NV v Commission* [1987] E.C.R. 4617; Case C–39/94 *Syndicat Français de l'Express International (SFEI) v La Poste* [1996] E.C.R. I–3547, para.70, and paras 73 to 77 of the Advocate General's Opinion; Case C–148/04 *Unicredito Italiano Spa* Judgment of 15/12/05, not yet reported. On State aids, see Ch.26.

different situations must not be treated in the same way, unless such treatment is objectively justified.[69]

The principle is applied in the relationships between the Community institutions and its officials. As the Court stated in the *Ferrario* case:

"According to the Court's consistent case law the general principle of equality is one of the fundamental principles of the law of the Community civil service."[70]

On this basis in *Sabbatini* and *Airola* the Court invalidated differentiation between Community officials on grounds of sex in the payment of expatriation allowances.[71] And in *Noonan* the Court said that it would only be lawful to treat candidates with a university qualification differently to those who had none where there were essential differences between the situations in law and in fact of the two categories.[72] However, the Community cannot be called to account for inequality in the treatment of its officials for which it is not itself responsible. In *Souasio* it was alleged that a Community dependent child tax allowance paid only once in respect of each child, even where both parents were employed by the Community, was contrary to the principle of equality, since it did not take into account tax allowances which might be claimed by a spouse who did not work for the Community, under national law. The Court rejected this argument:

"The principle of equality does not require account to be taken of possible inequalities which may become apparent because the Community and national systems overlap."[73]

7–016 The principle of non-discrimination provides a basis for the judicial review of measures adopted by the Community in all its various activities. Thus the Court has invalidated a regulation which provided substantially more severe criteria for the determination of the origin of cotton yarn than for the determination of the origin of cloth and fabrics.[74] The Court has also required consistency in the

---

[69] Case 106/83 *Sermide* [1984] E.C.R. 4209 para.28; and a consistent case law, see e.g. Case C–354/95 *R v Minister for Agriculture, Fisheries and Food, ex parte National Farmers' Union* [1997] E.C.R. I–4559 para.61.

[70] Cases 152 etc.,/81 [1983] E.C.R. 2357 at 2367.

[71] Case 20/71 *Sabbatini* [1972] E.C.R. 345; Case 21/74 *Airola* [1972] E.C.R. 221; see also *Razzouk and Beydoun* [1984] E.C.R. 1509; however the Court has so far refused to include in the principle of non-discrimination the right not to be discriminated against on grounds of sexual orientation and found that registered partnerships are not comparable to marriages, Case C–122/99 and C–125/99 *D and Sweden v Council* [2001] E.C.R. I–4319.

[72] Case T–60/92 *Noonan v Commission* [1996] E.C.R. II–215, para.32.

[73] [1980] E.C.R. 3557 at 3572.

[74] Case 162/82 *Cousin* [1983] E.C.R. 1101.

Commission's policy of imposing fines upon undertakings for the infringement of production quotas for steel.[75]

The principle of non-discrimination has been held to add a gloss to Article 34(2) EC, which provides that the common organisations of the agricultural markets "shall exclude any discrimination between producers or consumers within the Community". In *Codorniu* the Court held the foregoing principle includes the prohibition of discrimination on grounds of nationality laid down in the first paragraph of Article 12 EC,[76] which states that "[w]ithin the scope of application of this Treaty, and without prejudice to any special provisions contained therein, any discrimination on grounds of nationality shall be prohibited".[77] In *Ruckdeschel*[78] and *Moulins*[79] proceedings arose from challenges in national courts to the validity of the Council's action in abolishing production refunds on maize used to make quellmehl and gritz, while continuing to pay refunds on maize used to make starch, a product in competition with both quellmehl and gritz. Producers of the latter product argued that they had been placed at a competitive disadvantage by the Council's discriminatory, and hence unlawful, action. Their pleas were upheld. Referring to Article 34(3) EC, the Court observed:

> "While this wording undoubtedly prohibits any discrimination between producers of the same product it does not refer in such clear terms to the relationship between different industrial or trade sectors in the sphere of processed agricultural products. This does not alter the fact that the prohibition of discrimination laid down in the aforesaid provision is merely a specific enunciation of the general principle of equality which is one of the fundamental principles of Community law. This principle requires that similar situations shall not be treated differently unless differentiation is objectively justified."[80]

---

[75] Case 234/82 *Ferriere di roe Volciano* [1983] E.C.R. 3921.

[76] Case C–309/89 *Codorníu SA v Council of the European Union* [1994] E.C.R. I–1853, para.26.

[77] The reference to "without prejudice to any special povisions contained therein" refers particularly to other provisions of the Treaty in which the application of the general principle of non-discriminatiion on gorunds of nationality is given concrete form in respect of specific situations, such as free movement of workers, the right of establishment and the freedom to povide services, see Case C–186/87 *Cowan* [1989] E.C.R. 195, para.14. Art.12 EC "applies independently only to situations governed by Community law in regard to which the Treaty lays down no specific prohibition of discrimination," see Case 305/87 *Commission v Greece* [1989] E.C.R. 1461 para.13.

[78] Cases 117/76 and 16/77 [1977] E.C.R. 1753.

[79] Cases 124/76 and 20/77 [1977] E.C.R. 1795.

[80] Cases 117/76 and 16/77 *Ruckdeschel* [1977] E.C.R. 1753 at 1769; Joined Cased 124/76 and 20/77 *Moulins* [1977] E.C.R. 1795 at 1811. And see Case 300/86 *Landschoot v Mera* [1988] E.C.R. 3443; Case C–37/89 *Weiser* [1990] E.C.R. I–2395; Case C–2/92 *Bostock* [1994] E.C.R. I–955, para.23. The principle applies as between identical or comparable situations, Case T–48/89 *Beltrante* [1990] E.C.R. II–493 para.34.

The *Wagner* case[81] affords a helpful illustration of objective criteria justifying differentiation between apparently similar situations. Community rules provided for reimbursement of storage costs in respect of sugar in transit between two approved warehouses situated in the same Member State, but not in respect of sugar in transit between two approved warehouses in different Member States. The Court rejected the argument that this was discriminatory, since the difference in treatment was based on requirements of supervision which could be objectively justified. The Court's ruling is a reminder that the principle of non-discrimination is only infringed by differences in treatment where the Community legislator treats *comparable* situations in different ways.[82] It follows that an allegation of discrimination cannot be based on differences in treatment of products subject to different market organisations which are not in competition with each other.[83]

7–017   The principle whereby Community rules may treat differently apparently similar situations where objective justification exists for such differentiation allows a challenge to the validity of the rules in question once the circumstances constituting objective justification have ceased to obtain.[84] Pending such challenge the Community institutions are bound to continue to apply the measure in question.[85] But it would seem to follow that even in the absence of a challenge, the Community institutions are bound to take steps to amend the rules in question.

The principle of non-discrimination has also been invoked in the budgetary context,[86] and the "equality of States" has been resorted to as a general principle of the interpretation of the Treaties.[87]

As it is the case with the other general principles, the Court has found that the principle of non-discrimination applies also to the Member States when they act within the scope of Community law. As we have seen in Chapter 5, in *Mangold* the Court found the principle of non-discrimination on grounds of age to be a general principle of Community law.[88] The Court did not give much explanation as to why discrimination on grounds of age should be elevated to the rank of general principle, but it is likely that all the areas in which the Community can act to fight discrimination according to Article 13 EC now constitute general principles of Community law.

[81] Case 8/82 [1983] E.C.R. 271.
[82] See e.g. Case 6/71 *Rheinmühlen Düsseldorf* [1971] E.C.R. 719; Case 283/83 *Racke* [1984] E.C.R. 3791.
[83] Cases 292 and 293/81 *Jean Lion* [1982] E.C.R. 3887.
[84] Case T–177/94 and T–377/94 *Henk Altmann and Margaret Casson v Commission* [1996] E.C.R. II–2041, paras 121–123.
[85] *ibid.*
[86] Case 265/78 *Ferwerda* [1980] E.C.R. 617.
[87] Case 128/78 *Commission v United Kingdom* [1979] E.C.R. 419; Case 231/78 *Commission v United Kingdom* [1979] E.C.R. 1447 at 1462.
[88] Case C–144/04 *Mangold* [2005] E.C.R. I–9981.

Furthermore, according to the *Mangold* ruling, such general principles are also of horizontal application, i.e. they can be invoked against a private party regardless of whether there is national legislation in place.

Other general principles

As said in the introduction we are going to deal with fundamental **7–018** rights as general principles of Community law in the next chapter. Here we will just refer to some other principles elaborated by the Court; some of those have also been codified in the Charter and will be the subject of further analysis in Chapter 9.

The right to be heard

In *Transocean Marine Paint*[89] the Court invoked the general **7–019** principle that a person whose interests are affected by a decision taken by a public authority must be given an opportunity to make his or her point of view known. In *Eyckeler & Malt AG* the Court of First Instance referred to respect for the rights of the defence as a fundamental principle of Community law which must be guaranteed, even in the absence of any rules governing the procedure in question, and held that the principle required not only that the person concerned should be placed in a position in which they may effectively make known their views on the relevant circumstances, but also that they should at least be able to put their own case on the documents taken into account by the decision making authority.[90] Not all determinations are subject to these principles however. Thus the right to a fair hearing does not extend to the work of a Medical Committee engaged in the medical appraisal of an individual.[91]

The right to counsel

The right to be assisted by counsel has been recognised by the **7–020** Court as a general principle of law. In *Demont*,[92] a staff case, the Court held that the refusal of the Commission to allow the applicant's counsel, as well as the applicant, access to the disciplinary file in the course of proceedings which resulted in a disciplinary measure

---

[89] Case 17/74 [1974] E.C.R. 1063. See also case 264/82 *Timex* [1985] E.C.R. 849; Case 85/87 *Dow Benelux* [1989] E.C.R. 3137; Case C–49/88 *Al-Jubail Fertiliser* [1991] E.C.R. I–3187. The principle may be invoked by a Member State as well as by an individual, see Case 259/85 *France v Commission* [1987] E.C.R. 4393.
[90] Case T–42/96 [1998] E.C.R. II–401, paras 76–80. But there is no right to be heard in a legislative process, see Case T–521/93 *Atlanta AG* [1996] E.C.R. II–1707, para.70.
[91] Case T–154/89 *Vidranyi* [1990] E.C.R. II–455. We shall examine the right to be heard also in Ch.9.
[92] Case 115/80 [1981] E.C.R. 3147.

being taken, amounted to a breach of a fundamental legal principle which the Court would uphold. The Court emphasised that respect for the rights of the defence was all the more important when the disciplinary proceedings were likely to result in particularly severe disciplinary measures.[93]

The freedom to conduct a business

7–021   The Court has recognised that the right to exercise an economic activity is one of the general principles of Community law, subject to those limitations on the exercise of that right which may be justified in the general interest.[94]

The principle of good administration

7–022   The principle of "good administration" or "sound administration" is often invoked before and by the Court. On one occasion the Court referred to the duty to allow a person the right to be heard as "a general principle of good administration",[95] but the principle does more than describe other principles. For example, in the *Lucchini* case the Court stigmatised the failure to respond to a communication as a "neglect of the rules of good administration" and reduced a fine accordingly.[96] In the context of a procedure to investigate the compatibility of a proposed State aid with the common market, the CFI said that "the interests of legal certainty and sound administration require the Commission to be aware, as far as possible, of the particular circumstances of every trader who considers himself injured by the grant of aid proposed".[97]

In principle, it is contrary to the principle of good administration for a competent authority to reject a tender on the ground that it is ambiguously drafted without exercising its power to seek clarification.[98]

Further reading

Bernitz and Nergelius (eds), *The General Principles of European Community Law* (Aspen, 2000).

Boyron, "General Principles of Law and National Courts: Applying a *Jus Commune?*" (1998) 28 E.L.Rev. 171.

---

[93] Case 115/80 [1981] E.C.R. 3147 at 3158; as we shall see in Ch.9 this principle has been codified in the Charter.
[94] Case 234/85 *Keller* [1986] E.C.R. 2897; Case C–370/88 *Marshall* [1990] E.C.R. I–4071; Case T–521/93 *Atlanta AG* [1996] E.C.R. II–1707, para.62; this is also codified in the Charter, see below Ch.9.
[95] Cases 33 and 75/79 *Kuhner* [1980] E.C.R. 1677 at 1698.
[96] Case 179/82 [1983] E.C.R. 3083 at 3095.
[97] Case T–11/95 *BP Chemicals Limited v Commission* [1998] E.C.R. II–1707, para.75.
[98] Case T–54/99 *max.mobil Telekommunication Service GmbH v Commission* [2002] E.C.R. I–2365, para.48; see also below Ch.27.

de Burca, "The Principle of Proportionality and its Application in EC Law" (1993) 13 Y.E.L. 105.

Craig, "Sustantive Legitimate Expectations in Domestic and Community Law" (1996) 55 C.L.J. 289.

Jacobs, "Recent Developments in the Principle of Proportionality in European Community Law", in E. Ellis (ed.) *The Principle of Proportionality in the Laws of Europe* (Hart Publishing, 1999).

Rodriguez Iglesias, "Reflections on the General Principles of Community Law" (1998) C.Y.E.L.S. 1.

Sharpston, "Legitimate Expectations and Economic Reality" (1990) 15 E.L.Rev. 103.

Tridimas, "Proportionality in European Community Law: Searching for the Appropriate Standard", E. Ellis (ed.) *The Principle of Proportionality in the Laws of Europe* (Hart Publishing, 1999).

Tridimas, *The General Principles of EU Law* (OUP, 2006).

Usher *The General Principles of Community Law* (Longman, 1998).

Usher "The Reception of General Principles of Community Law in the United Kingdom" (2005) E.L.Rev. 489.

CHAPTER 8

FUNDAMENTAL RIGHTS

Guide to this Chapter: Fundamental rights form part of the **8–001** general principles of Community law and because of their import- ance deserve separate space. This chapter examines the evolu- tion of the case law of the European Court of Justice, whilst the Charter of Fundamental Rights will be the subject of the next chapter. We will start by examining the evolution of the case law of the European Court of Justice which held that fundamental rights formed part of the general principles of Community law which it would guarantee. We will then look at the scope of application of fundamental rights which apply not only to the Union institutions but also to the Member States when they act within the field of Community law. Next, this chapter analyses some problems concerning fundamental rights protection arising from the EU institutional framework. We will then examine the relationship between the European Court of Justice and the European Court of Human Rights. Whilst the European Conven- tion on Human Rights is not part of Community law, the ECJ has recognised its primary importance as a source in identifying the rights protected at Community level, and it has looked at the case law of the European Court of Human Rights to establish the appropriate level of protection of those rights. However, the protection afforded at Community level has not always been deemed appropriate: this has led to a lively doctrinal debate as well as to a ruling of the European Court of Human Rights which held that, at least in some cases, it can hold the Member States collectively responsible for a breach of the Convention provoked by an act of the EU institutions.

Evolution of the concept

8–002   Unlike the abortive Treaty for the establishment of a European Political Community, which provided explicitly for the application of Section I of the European Convention on Human Rights,[1] the EEC Treaty made no provision for the protection of human rights as such. Nevertheless, after an initial resistance,[2] the Court of Justice soon made it clear that fundamental rights were implicitly recognised by Community law, and that they were capable of limiting the competence of the Community. Thus in *Stauder*,[3] the claimant argued that a Commission Decision which conditioned the distribution of butter at reduced prices on the disclosure of the name of the recipient breached his right to dignity as protected by the German Constitution. The German court made a reference to the Court enquiring whether such rules conflicted "with the general principles of Community law in force". In other words the national court enquired not whether the Community decision was compatible with the German Constitution,[4] but rather whether there were general principles of *Community* law which could be applied in the case at stake to the advantage of the applicant. Put in this way, the question did not affect nor threaten the principle of supremacy. The Court replied that on its true construction the Decision in question did not require the disclosure of the names of beneficiaries to retailers, and added that: "Interpreted in this way the provision at issue contains nothing *capable of prejudicing the fundamental rights . . . protected by the Court*".[5] The Court thus recognised that even though fundamental rights were not mentioned in the original Treaties, they were nonetheless part of the general principles of Community law.

This was confirmed in the *Internationale Handelsgesellschaft* case, in which the Court stated:

> "In fact, respect for fundamental rights forms an integral part of the general principles of law protected by the Court of Justice. The protection of such rights, whilst inspired by the constitutional traditions common to the Member States, must be ensured within the framework of the structure and objectives of the Community."[6]

---

[1] One of the initiatives which predated the EEC Treaty but which failed to secure the support of all potential signatories. See Ch.1.
[2] Case 1/58 *Stork v High Authority* [1959] E.C.R. 17; Case 36–40/59 *Geitling v High Authority* [1960] E.C.R. 425; Case 40/64 *Sgarlata v Commission* [1965] E.C.R. 215.
[3] Case 29/69 *Stauder* [1969] E.C.R. 419.
[4] In *Stork, Geitling* and *Sgarlata* the ECJ had been asked to rule as to the compatibility of ECSC and Community decisions with national constitutional law; not surprisingly the ECJ held that national constitutional law and the fundamental rights guarantees contained therein were not relevant.
[5] Para.7, emphasis added.
[6] Case 11/70 [1970] E.C.R. 1125, para.4.

In *Internationale*, the Court not only restated its intention to review the acts of the Community institutions in relation to fundamental rights, but it also identified in the "common constitutional traditions" one of the sources to ascertain the content of those rights. In *Nold*, whilst restating the importance of national constitutions, it also held that "international treaties for the protection of human rights on which the Member States have collaborated or of which they are signatories", would supply useful guidelines.[7] It was always clear that of the treaties referred to, the European Convention on Human Rights was of special significance in this respect and the Court has said as much in a consistent case law.[8]

The readiness of the Court of Justice to interpret Community law **8-003** as containing implicit human rights guarantees which operated as limits on the permissible scope of Community action has generally been attributed to a desire to persuade national constitutional courts that it was not necessary to subject Community acts to scrutiny pursuant to national constitutional provisions guaranteeing human rights and fundamental freedoms. Notwithstanding the Court's prompt response to the national constitutional courts' concerns, it took some time before the latter, and especially the German *Bundesverfassungsgericht*, renounced to case-by-case jurisdiction over fundamental rights compliance of Community acts. Thus, as we have seen in Chapter 5, in the so-called *Solange I* case,[9] delivered a few weeks after *Nold*, the German Court held that in the "hypothetical case" of a conflict between a provision of Community law and the fundamental rights contained in the German Constitution, the latter would take precedence so long as (*solange*) the Community institutions would not remove the conflict. It was only in 1987, in the so-called *Solange II* case,[10] that the German Court declared itself satisfied with the general level of fundamental rights protection afforded by the ECJ and held that it would not exercise its jurisdiction to review acts of the Community institutions in relation to the German Constitution. This, as long as (*solange*) the

---

[7] Case 4/73 [1974] E.C.R. 491, para.13.
[8] Case 222/84 *Johnston v Royal Ulster Constabulary* [1986] E.C.R. 1651, para.18; Case C–260/89 *Elliniki Radiophonia Tiléorassi AE (ERT) v Dimotiki Etairia Pliroforissis* [1991] E.C.R. I–2925, para.41; Opinion 2/94 [1996] E.C.R. I–1759, para.33; Case C–299/95 *Kremzow v Austria* [1997] E.C.R. I –2629, para.14.
[9] *Internationale Handelsgesellschaft* [1974] 2 C.M.L.R. 540 (*Solange I*); see also *Steinike und Weinling* [1980] 2 C.M.L.R. 531; and *cf.* also the Italian Constitutional Court rulings Sentenza 7/3/64, n.14 (in F. Sorrentino, *Profili Costituzionali dell'Integrazione Comunitaria*, 2nd ed., Giappichelli Editore 1996, p.61) and *Società Acciaierie San Michele v High Authority* (27/12/65, n.98), [1967] C.M.L.R. 160.
[10] *Wünsche Handelsgesellschaft* [1987] 3 C.M.L.R. 225, (*Solange II*).

Community institutions, and especially the ECJ, were to guarantee the effective protection of fundamental rights.[11]

The response of the political institutions

8–004   The Court's case law was endorsed by the Parliament, the Council and the Commission in their Joint Declaration of April 5, 1977, where they declared themselves bound by fundamental rights as general principles of Community law.[12] Treaty endorsement came later, first in the preamble of the Single European Act and then more forcefully in the Maastricht Treaty. Thus, Article F(2) of the Treaty on European Union provided that the Union shall respect fundamental rights, as guaranteed by the European Convention and as they result from the constitutional traditions common to the Member States, as general principles of Community law. The latter provision appeared in Title I of the Union Treaty and, under Article L, it therefore did not fall within the jurisdiction of the Court of Justice. The Treaty of Amsterdam, whilst maintaining unaltered the text of Article F(2) (renumbered 6(2)), amended Article L (renumbered Article 46), by providing that the Court's jurisdiction extends to "Article 6(2) with regard to action of the institutions, insofar as the Court has jurisdiction under the Treaties establishing the European Communities and under this Treaty". The Treaty of Amsterdam also added Article 7 TEU which provides for a procedure in cases in which a Member State is found to be in serious and persistent breach of fundamental rights. In this case the rights of the Member State in question, including the voting rights, may be suspended by the Council acting with unanimity but without taking into account the vote of the Member State in question.[13] The Treaty of Nice has added a new paragraph to this article (so-called Haider clause)[14] according to which the Council acting with a majority of

---

[11] See discussion on supremacy in Ch.5; as said above the Maastricht decision (*Brunner v EU Treaty* [1994] 1 C.M.L.R. 57) subsequently cast some doubts as to whether the German Constitutional Court would continue to refuse jurisdiction in such cases; however this was confirmed in the decision following the banana litigation, see Federal Constitutional Court, Decision 7/6/00 [2000] *Human Rights Law Journal* 251. See also the French *Conseil Constitutionnel*, Decision No.2004–496 (June 10, 2004); Decision No.2004–497 (July 1, 2004); the Polish Constitutional Court ruling in *Trybunal Konstytucyjny, arrêt du 27.04.05, P 1/05, Dziennik Ustaw 2005.77.680*, as reported by *Réflets—Informations rapides sur les développements juridiques présentant un intérêt communautaire*, No. 2/2005, p.16, also available on http://curia.eu.int/en/coopju/apercu—reflets/lang/index.htm.

[12] O.J. 1977 C103/1. Note that the declaration was referred to by the German Constitutional Court in the ruling in *Wünsche Handelsgesellschaft* [1987] 3 C.M.L.R. 225, (*Solange II*) as one of the indications that the fundamental rights protection in the EC had reached a satisfactory level and that they would as a result cease to exercise their power of scrutiny over EC law.

[13] There is a corresponding provision in the EC Treaty (also added by the Treaty of Nice), Art.309 TEC.

[14] The clause was introduced as a result of the realisation in relation to the Haider affaire that the Art.6 TEU threshold of "actual and persistent" fundamental rights breach was very high and did not allow the EU to react to potential risks of fundamental rights breaches.

four-fifths can make a recommendation to one Member State when there is a *clear risk* of a serious breach of the principles contained in Article 6 TEU. The ECJ has jurisdiction over the procedural provisions of Article 7 TEU. Lastly, According to Article 49 TEU the respect for the principles enshrined in Article 6 TEU (respect for liberty, freedom, democracy, rule of law and fundamental rights) is a precondition for joining the Union. Finally, in 2000, the Commission, Council and European Parliament, proclaimed the Charter of Fundamental Rights (see next chapter), a non-legally binding catalogue of fundamental rights recognised by the EU.[15]

The scope of application of fundamental rights

As with the other general principles, fundamental rights apply in **8–005** three different situations. First of all, they apply to the acts of the EU institutions; secondly, they apply to acts of the Member States when they implement Community law; and thirdly, they apply to acts of the Member States in fields which fall within the scope of Community law.

Fundamental rights as a limit to the acts of the institutions

As stated above, despite the lack of any mention of fundamental **8–006** rights in the original Treaties, the Court has, since *Stauder*, held the institutions to be bound by fundamental rights as general principles of Community law. Thus breach of fundamental rights is one of the grounds of review that might lead to the annulment of any measure having legal effects adopted by the EU institutions.[16] It has already been stressed that in determining the existence and the content of fundamental rights, the Court takes particular account of the European Convention on Human Rights (ECHR or Convention), and of the jurisprudence of the European Court of Human Rights.[17] However, because of the principle of supremacy, and since the Union is not yet party to the ECHR,[18] in relation to Union/Community acts the standard set by the European Court of Justice is the only applicable one. It is not surprising then that this is the area which has provoked more criticism and a heated scholarly debate. In particular, the Court has been accused of having adopted too low of

---

[15] Charter of Fundamental Rights (2000) O.J. C364/1; other initiatives in the field of fundamental rights include the establishment of a Fundamental Rights Agency, see Commission Proposal for a Council Regulation establishing a European Union Agency for Fundamental Rights, COM(2005) 280 Final; see generally Alston and de Schutter (eds) *Monitoring Fundamental Rights in the EU* (Hart Publishing, 2005).
[16] See Ch.13.
[17] e.g. Case C–94/00 *Roquette Frères* [2002] E.C.R. I–9011, where the ECJ "updated" its interpretation of the scope of Art.8 of the Convention in order to take into account subsequent case law of the ECtHR.
[18] See below para.8–015.

a standard, and to have privileged the needs of economic integration over fundamental rights protection.[19] Thus, some authors have noted that whilst the Court has been ready to hold national measures falling within the scope of Community law to be incompatible with the latter because of a fundamental rights breach, in relation to the acts of the Community institutions the Court has used a lighter touch of review.

For instance, in the *Banana* cases the Court refused to annul a Regulation which established a new regime for bananas imports and which favoured African, Caribbean and Pacific (ACP) producers at the expense of Latin American producers.[20] The regime had been introduced, in breach of the GATT/WTO agreement,[21] to favour former European colonies. The new regime introduced discriminatory treatment of producers as well as a system of quotas for importers. Those quotas were calculated according to the amount of bananas that the trader had imported from the ACP countries before the introduction of the regime. Whilst this suited almost all European importers, who had always imported their bananas from the ACP countries, it damaged German importers who had traditionally imported their bananas from Latin American countries. Since they had never imported from ACP countries they were in fact not eligible for most of the ACP quotas. The economic livelihood of those importers was therefore threatened by the new Community regime. Both the German Government and German importers attacked the new regime on several grounds,[22] *inter alia*, breach of the principle of non-discrimination; breach of the right to property; breach of the right to pursue a trade and business. In relation to the latter claim, the Court found that whilst the German importers were indeed affected, the "substance" of their right remained intact and therefore there was no breach of their fundamental rights. As we have seen in Chapter 5, this decision gave rise to a renewed clash with the German courts which were wholly unimpressed by the level

---

[19] Coppel and O'Neill, "The European Court of Justice: Taking Rights Seriously?" (1992) 12 Legal Studies 227; and in response see Weiler and Lockhart " 'Taking Rights Seriously' Seriously: The European Court of Justice and its Fundamental Rights Jurisprudence" (1995) 32 C.M.L.Rev. 51 and 579. And for a mote sophisticated approach de Burca, "The Language of Rights and European Integration" in Shaw and More (eds) *New Legal Dynamics of European Integration* (Clarendon Press, 1995), p.29.

[20] Reg.404/93 on the common organisation of the market in bananas [1993] O.J. L47/1.

[21] The system was declared in breach of the GATT agreement, EC-Banans III case (WT/DS27/R), report of Dispute Settlement Body of 25/09/97; as a result, the system was amended by Reg.1637/98 ([1998] O.J. L210/28), which again was found not to be fully compliant with the WTO agreement, Dispute Settlement Body (WT/DS27/2W) report 6/5/99 which authorised retaliation by the United States and Ecuador; the Community eventually introduced WTO compatible measures to take effect from 1/1/06, Reg.2587/2001 [2001] O.J. L345/13.

[22] Case C–280/93 *Germany v Council* [1994] E.C.R. I–4973; there was a partial concession in Case C–68/95 *T Port I* [1996] E.C.R. I–6065. See also Peers "Taking Supremacy Seriously" (1998) E.L.Rev. 146.

of protection afforded by the Court. A small constitutional crisis ensued as it was not clear whether the German constitutional court would decide to apply its own (higher) standard of protection or whether it would refuse to scrutinise the Regulation consistently with the *Solange II* doctrine. The issue was eventually settled in the latter way.[23] Similarly, but less controversially, in the *Biotechnology* directive case,[24] the Court refused to accept the Netherlands claim that to allow for the patentability of biotechnological inventions involving human DNA or tissue, breached the right to human dignity.

It is not only in relation to legislative and regulatory acts that the scrutiny of fundamental rights is of relevance. Indeed, the most contentious cases in relation to fundamental rights protection arise in relation to the acts of the institutions in their capacity as employers as well as in relation to the powers of the Commission in competition law proceedings.

In relation to the institutions' behaviour as employers, the Court **8–007** has readily accepted that those institutions are obliged to respect fundamental rights. In this respect it has recognised, *inter alia*, the right to hold a religious belief,[25] the right to strike and the right of trade unions,[26] and the right not to be subject to medical examination without consent,[27] the right of freedom of expression.[28] It has, however, failed to recognise the right for same sex couples registered under national law to be treated on equal footing with married couples in relation to employment related benefits.[29] Thus in *D and Sweden*, D was in a same sex registered partnership recognised by Swedish law as being equivalent to a marriage; the Council, his employer, refused to award him benefits to which married officials were entitled, on the grounds that D was not "married" within the meaning of the Staff Regulations. One of D's complaints was that such interpretation of the Regulations breached the principle of non-discrimination on grounds of sex.[30] The Court considered that

---

[23] Federal Constitutional Court, Decision 7/6/00 [2000] Human Rights Law Journal 251; and see Schmid "All Bark and No Bite: Notes on the Federal Constitutional Court's 'Banana Decision' " (2001) E.L.J. 95.

[24] C–377/98 *Netherlands v Council* (biotechnology directive) [2001] E.C.R. I–7079.

[25] Case 130/75 *Prais v Council* [1976] E.C.R. 1589.

[26] *cf.* on the right to strike Joined Cases 44, 46 and 49/74 *M. L. Acton v Commission* [1975] E.C.R. 383; Joined Cases T–576 to 582/93 *M. Browet v Commission* [1994] E.C.R. II–677, IA–191. On the rights of trade unions, see Case T–349/00 *Lebedef v Commission* [2001] E.C.R. II–1031, IA–225, where the CFI annulled the new operational rules because one of the trade unions had been left out of the negotiations.

[27] Case C–404/92 *X v Commission* [1994] E.C.R. I–4737 (AIDS test case) overruling Case T–121/89 *X v Commission* [1992] E.C.R. II–2195.

[28] e.g. Case T–34/96 and 163/96 *Connolly v Commission* [1999] E.C.R. II–463, upheld by ECJ in Case C–273/99P *Connolly v Commission* [2001] E.C.R. I–1575; Case T–82/99 *Cwick v Commission* [2000] E.C.R. II–713, upheld by the ECJ in case C–340/00P *Commission v Cwick* [2001] E.C.R. I–10269.

[29] Joined Cases C–122/99 and C–125/99 *D and Sweden v Council* [2001] E.C.R. I–4319; the ECJ.

[30] The Court had previously ruled that discrimination on grounds of sexual orientation did not fall within the scope of sex discrimination (Art.141 TEC), Case C–249/96 *Grant v South West Trains Ltd* [1998] E.C.R. I–621.

the situation of people in a same sex registered partnership was not comparable to that of married (and necessarily heterosexual) people, since the situation as to recognition of partnerships varied greatly amongst the Member States. The narrow interpretation given by the ECJ seems at odds both with an earlier ruling of the European Court of Human Rights which held that discrimination on grounds of sexual orientation comes within the scope of Article 14 of the Convention;[31] and with the ECJ's own liberal case law in relation to transsexuals.[32]

In relation to competition law, fundamental rights have been instrumental to curtail the broad powers of investigation vested in the Commission by Regulation 17 (which has now been repealed and substituted with Regulation 1/2003). Thus for instance in the *AM & S* case,[33] the Court recognised that the principle of confidentiality between lawyer and client was a fundamental right and therefore it annulled part of a Commission decision requiring the applicants to disclose letters protected by legal privilege. In *Hoechst* and *Dow Benelux*,[34] the Court found that the right to private life enshrined in Article 8 of the European Convention on Human Rights did not extend to business dwellings; however, it also found that protection from interference from public authorities in the life of any person, natural or legal, was a general principle of Community law which it would protect. The exclusion of business dwellings from the scope of Article 8 of the ECHR attracted criticism following the European Court of Human Rights, ruling in *Niemietz*[35] to the effect that Article 8 ECHR was applicable also to business premises. However, such criticism seems to be misguided: it should be borne in mind that when the matter arose in front of the ECJ, there was as yet no case law of the Court of Human Rights on whether Article 8 should be construed as extending to business premises or not. It is thus very likely that the ECJ might have not wanted to interfere with the interpretation that the other European Court might decide to adopt in the future. This reading of the ruling is supported by the fact that the European Court of Justice recognised, in the very same cases, a right substantially equivalent to the right to private life as a general

---

[31] *Salgueiro da Silva Mouta v Portugal* (Appl. No.33290/96), (1999) E.H.R.R. 176. The provision of non-discrimination contained in Art.14 ECHR is not a free-standing provision, and it can only be relied upon in conjunction with another Convention article. It would have not been difficult, however, for the ECJ to rely on Art.1 Protocol 1 (right to property), at least in those cases in which registered partnerships are allowed and equated to marriage in the State of origin. It is rather striking that Mischo relied on the fact that the ECtHR ruling post-dated the facts of the case to exclude its application to the case, see Joined Cases C–122/99 and C–125/99 *D and Sweden v Council* [2001] E.C.R. I–4319, para.96 of the Opinion.

[32] Case C–13/94 *P v S Cornwall County Council* [1996] E.C.R. I–2143; Case C–117/01 *K.B.* [2004] E.C.R. I–541; see below para.8–012.

[33] 155/79 [1982] E.C.R. 1575.

[34] 46/87 and 227/88 [1989] E.C.R. 2859; Case 85/87 [1989] E.C.R. 3137.

[35] *Niemietz v Germany* (1993) Series A Vol.251, 16 E.H.R.R. 97.

principle of Community law, even though not deriving from the ECHR, and that, as soon as the chance arose, the Court brought its interpretation into line with that adopted by the European Court of Human Rights.[36]

A similar situation arose in the *Orkem* case, where the ECJ found **8–008** that the right to fair trial provided by Article 6 ECHR did not encompass the right not to give evidence against oneself.[37] However, the Court also found that the Commission could not compel the undertaking to "provide it with answers which might involve an admission on its part of the existence of an infringement which it is incumbent upon the Commission to prove",[38] since otherwise the right to defence, a general principle of Community law, would be compromised. In the case at stake, the Court found that such right had been breached by the Commission. Some years later the European Court of Human Rights faced with a similar question in the *Funke* case found that Article 6 did indeed encompass a right not to give evidence against oneself.[39] The ECJ subsequently held that it had to take into account the developments following from the *Funke* ruling, although it also found that that was not necessary in the case at stake, thus arguably interpreting the terms of the ruling rather restrictively.[40]

Article 6(1) of the ECHR provides that in the determination of his or her civil rights and obligations or of any criminal charge against him or her, everyone is entitled to a fair and public hearing within a reasonable time by an independent and impartial tribunal established by law. Whether this provision is as such applicable to administrative proceedings before the Commission relating to competition policy or not, it is a general principle of Community law that the Commission must act within a reasonable time in adopting decisions following administrative proceedings relating to competition policy and State aids.[41] A similar principle governs the proceedings of the CFI when it reviews decisions of the Commission on

---

[36] Case C–94/00 *Roquette Frères Sa v Directeur général de la concurrence, de la consomation et de la répression des fraudes* [2002] E.C.R. I–9011, esp. para.29.

[37] Case 374/87 *Orkem v Commission* [1989] E.C.R. 3283.

[38] Case 374/87 *Orkem v Commission* [1989] E.C.R. 3283, para.35.

[39] *Funke v France* (1993) Series A, No.256-A, 16 E.H.R.R. 297.

[40] Case C–238/99P *Limburgse Vinyl Maatschappij (LVM) v Commission* [2002] E.C.R. I–8375, annotated by Wesseling, (2004) 41 C.M.L.Rev. 1141; see also Case T–112/98 *Mannesmannröhren-Werke AG v Commission* [2001] E.C.R. II–729 where the CFI made clear that the Convention does not as such apply to Community law, albeit reiterating the *Orkem* ruling.

[41] e.g. Joined Cases T–213/95 and T–18/96 *SCK, FNK v Commission* [1997] E.C.R. II–1739, para.56; Case T–67/01 *JCB Service v Commission* [2004] E.C.R. II–49, para.36 and ff; Case C–238/99 P *Limburgse Vinyl Maatschappij (LVM) v Commission* [2002] E.C.R. I–8375. But the ECJ has also made clear that it is not prepared to annul a Commission's decision on the sole grounds that it exceeded a reasonable time-limit; rather it is only when the length of the procedure came at the expense of the right to defence that the Court will be prepared to annul the Commission's decision, e.g. Joined Cases C–204/00P, C–205/00P C–211–00P, C–213/00P, C–217/00P, C–219/00P *Aalborg Portland v Commission* [2004] E.C.R. I–123 where the procedure leading to the upheld contested decision lasted 8½ years.

competition matters, and the ECJ will secure enforcement of this principle through the appeals procedure. As the Court explained in *Baustahlgewebe GmbH v Commission*, having referred to Article 6(1) of the ECHR:

"The general principle of Community law that everyone is entitled to fair legal process, which is inspired by those fundamental rights . . . and in particular the right to legal process within a reasonable period, is applicable in the context of proceedings brought against a Commission decision imposing fines on an undertaking for infringement of competition law. It is thus for the Court of Justice, in an appeal, to consider pleas on such matters concerning the proceedings before the Court of First Instance."[42]

The duration of the proceedings being considered by the ECJ was approximately 5 years and 6 months.[43] The Court noted that such a duration was, at first sight, considerable, but added that the reasonableness of such a period must be appraised in the light of the circumstances specific to each case and, in particular, the importance of the case for the person concerned, its complexity and the conduct of the applicant and of the competent authorities; these criteria were derived from judgments of the European Court of Human Rights, to which the Court referred by way of analogy.[44] The Court noted in particular: that the appellant had not contributed in any significant way to the protraction of the proceedings;[45] that about 32 months had elapsed between the end of the written procedure and the decision to open the oral procedure; and that about 22 months had elapsed between the close of the oral procedure and the delivery of the judgment of the CFI.[46] The ECJ held that the proceedings before the CFI did not satisfy the requirements concerning completion within a reasonable time.[47] Having regard to all the circumstances of the case, the Court held that a sum of ECU 50,000 constituted reasonable satisfaction for the excessive duration of the proceedings, and the latter sum was deducted from the ECU 3,000,000 fine determined by the CFI.[48] This judgment amounts to a public reprimand of the CFI and sends a strong signal that the European Court has no intention of allowing the Community Courts in future to fall short of the standards which they are charged with upholding.

---

[42] Case C–185/95 P *Baustahlgewebe GmbH v Commission* [1998] E.C.R. I–8417, paras 20–22.
[43] Para.28.
[44] Para.29.
[45] Para.40.
[46] Para.45.
[47] Para.47.
[48] Para.141.

Fundamental rights and Member States' implementing powers

Fundamental rights as general principles of Community law apply **8–009** to the acts of the Member States when they are implementing Community law, i.e. when they are enacting administrative acts in order to enforce a regulation, or when they enact administrative and legislative acts to implement a directive. In those cases, the Member States are acting as "delegated powers" and are therefore bound by the general principles of Community law.

An instructive example of the applicability of general principles of Community law to national authorities when they implement Community rules is to be found in the *Wachauf* case.[49] Under Community regulations concerned with milk quotas, it was provided that the milk quota should be transferred when the holding to which the quota related was transferred. A producer acquired a quota in the first place by virtue of his having produced milk during the applicable reference year. The issue in *Wachauf* was whether a transfer of quota from lessee to lessor on the expiry of the lease in accordance with the applicable regulation would be consistent with the general principles of Community law where it had been the lessee's milk production which had secured entitlement to the milk quota. The Court of Justice referred to the *Hauer* case to support applicability of fundamental rights in the Community system, subject to such proportionate restrictions as might be imposed in the general interest. The Court stated:

> "Having regard to those criteria, it must be observed that Community rules which, upon the expiry of the lease, had the effect of depriving the lessee, without compensation, of the fruits of his labour and of his investments in the tenanted holding would be incompatible with the requirements of the protection of fundamental rights in the Community legal order. Since those requirements are also binding on the Member States when they implement Community rules, the Member States must, as far as possible, apply those rules in accordance with those requirements."[50]

The same principle has been affirmed in the case of directives: in exercising their discretion when implementing a directive, Member States must, so far as possible, respect fundamental rights as general principles of Community law.[51] This principle is now established case law and, as we shall see in the next chapter, has been codified by the

---

[49] Case 5/88 [1989] E.C.R. 2609.

[50] [1989] E.C.R. 2609, para.19. See also Case C–2/92 *Bostock* [1994] E.C.R. I–955, and Case C–351/92 *Manfred Graff v Hauptzollamt Köln Rheinau* [1994] E.C.R. I–3361.

[51] C–20/00 and C–64/00 *Bokker Aquaculture Ltd v Scottish Ministers* [2003] E.C.R. I–7411, para.88; see Joined Cases C–465/00, C–138/01 and C–139/01 *Österreichischer Rundfunk* [2003] E.C.R. I–4989.

Charter. However, until the Charter comes into force, it is not clear how far it stretches. The reference to "so far as possible" might be read as a mere interpretative obligation upon national courts similar to that imposed by the duty of consistent interpretation, whereby the national court when applying a non-directly effective piece of Community law, must interpret national law insofar as possible so as to comply with the aim of the Community legislation at stake.[52] If that were the case then, the national court would not be able to set aside a national rule which, in implementing Community law, breaches a fundamental right protected by Union law. Rather, the national judge's duty would be limited to interpreting national law "insofar as possible" consistently with the general principles.[53] This interpretation would be more limited than that adopted by the Court in relation to acts falling within the scope of Community law, and would therefore introduce some inconsistency in the system. Furthermore, the Court in *ERT* held that the *Wachauf* principle meant that the Community could not "accept measures which are incompatible with observance of the human rights thus recognised and guaranteed".[54] It seems then that the reference to "so far as possible" should be considered as an oversight in drafting rather than a limitation of the scope of application of fundamental rights to the acts of the Member States.[55] This is further confirmed by the fact that Article II–111(1) of the Charter seems to impose a directly enforceable obligation upon Member States to comply with the Charter when implementing Union law.

Member States acting within the scope of Community law

8–010   Fundamental rights as general principles of Community law bind the Member States also when the latter are acting "within the scope" of Community law, i.e. where the State's action limits or has an impact on one of the rights guaranteed by the Treaty and in particular when the Member States seek to limit the enjoyment of one of the free movement provisions either by relying on the mandatory requirements doctrine[56] or on one of the express Treaty derogations contained in Articles 30,[57] 39(3),[58] and 46 EC.[59] When

---

[52] See Ch.5 above.

[53] This is the view espoused by Hartley *The Foundations of European Community Law* (5th edn., OUP, 2003), 146, n.60.

[54] Para.41.

[55] Consider also that in some cases the Court does not limit the national court's obligation to "insofar as possible"; e.g. Case C–276/01 *J. Steffensen* [2003] E.C.R. I–3735. *cf.* also the ruling in Case 144/04 *Mangold* [2005] E.C.R. I–9981, see Ch.7 above.

[56] Case C–368/95 *Familiapress* [1997] E.C.R. I–3689, para.24.

[57] Case C–260/89 *Elliniki Radiophonia Tiléorassi AE (ERT) v Dimotiki Etairia Pliroforissis* [1991] E.C.R. I–2925, para.42.

[58] Case 36/75 *Rutili v French Minister of the Interior* [1975] E.C.R. 1219.

[59] Case C–260/89 *Elliniki Radiophonia Tiléorassi AE (ERT) v Dimotiki Etairia Pliroforissis.* [1991] E.C.R. I–2925, para.42.

an individual is exercising one of the rights conferred by the Treaty, he or she falls within the scope of Community law and therefore any interference with the Treaty right must not only to be justified, but it also has to be consistent with the general principles of Community law, and in particular with fundamental rights. Accordingly, a national rule which limits a free movement right, maybe for a legitimate policy reason, but which infringes fundamental rights as guaranteed by the general principles of Community law has to be set aside by the national court.

For instance, in *Rutili* the French authorities granted to Mr Rutili, an Italian national working in France, a resident permit which allowed him to reside only in one part of the French territory because of his political and trade union activities. The French Government pleaded that such restrictions were justified according to the public policy derogation contained in Article 39(3) EC. In adopting a restrictive interpretation of the public policy derogation the Court expressly referred to the ECHR.[60] Some years later, in *ERT*,[61] the Court was more explicit. In this case, a company complained against the Greek national monopoly on broadcasting (a service covered by Article 49 EC) arguing that the impossibility for private operators to provide broadcasting services was a limitation on the free movement of services which also affected freedom of expression as guaranteed by Article 10 ECHR. In examining the Greek Government's contention that such rules were justified under Article 46 EC, the Court held that national rules can be justified by one of the Treaty derogations "only if they are compatible with the fundamental rights the observance of which is ensured by the Court".[62] The Court later extended this doctrine to all limitations to the free movement provisions (i.e. also to mandatory and imperative requirements), and not only those justified by the Treaty derogations.

The extension of the scope of fundamental rights as general principles of Community law to cover Member States acts that merely limit (or regulate) a free movement right has been criticised since it expands significantly the scope of Community law by allowing for the direct effect of fundamental rights in all those situations which have an even remote link with Community law. A good example of such expansion can be found in the case of *Carpenter*.[63] Here Mrs Carpenter, a third country national, married a British national after having overstayed her leave to enter the

---

[60] Case 36/75 *Rutili v French Minister of the Interior* [1975] E.C.R. 1219, para.32.
[61] Case C–260/89 *Elliniki Radiophonia Tiléorassi AE (ERT)* [1991] E.C.R. I–2925.
[62] Case C–260/89 *Elliniki Radiophonia Tiléorassi AE (ERT)* [1991] E.C.R. I–2925, para.43.
[63] Case C–60/00 *Mary Carpenter v Secretary of State for the Home Department* [2002] E.C.R. I–6279. For interpretation of Reg.1612/68 on freedom of movement for workers in light of respect for family life, see Case C–413/99 *Baumbast, R v Secretary of State for the Home Department* [2002] E.C.R. I–7091, para.72.

United Kingdom. She then applied for and was refused leave to remain in the United Kingdom as the spouse of a British national. A deportation order had also been made. Her husband ran a business selling advertising space in medical and scientific journals and offering various services to the editors of those journals. A significant proportion of the business was conducted with advertisers established in other Member States. Mr Carpenter travelled occasionally to other Member States for the purposes of his business. The Court held that since Mr Carpenter was providing services within the meaning of Article 49 EC,[64] it was clear "that the separation of Mr and Mrs Carpenter would be detrimental to their family life and, therefore, to the conditions under which Mr Carpenter exercises a fundamental freedom".[65] The Court went on:

> "A Member State may invoke reasons of public interest to justify a national measure which is likely to obstruct the exercise of the freedom to provide services only if that measure is compatible with the fundamental rights whose observance the Court ensures . . .
> The decision to deport Mrs Carpenter constitutes an interference with the exercise by Mr Carpenter of his right to respect for his family life within the meaning of Article 8 of the [ECHR], which is among the fundamental rights which . . . are protected in Community law."[66]

8–011 The Court, referring to the case law of the European Court of Human Rights, concluded that a decision to deport Mrs Carpenter in circumstances such as those in the main proceedings, did not strike a fair balance between the competing interests, that is, on the one hand, the right of Mr Carpenter to respect for his family life, and, on the other hand, the maintenance of public order and public safety.

The *Carpenter* case is a good example of the expansion of Community law arising from the Court's case law on fundamental rights: the rule in itself would have been justified according to the mandatory requirements doctrine, since control of migration fluxes is clearly a public interest consistent with Community law. However, since the application of the rule did interfere with Mr Carpenter's right to family life in a way that the ECJ deemed disproportionate, it needed to be set aside. As a result, through the medium of Community law, fundamental rights become directly effective even in situations where they would not be so according to national law.

---

[64] See Ch.19.
[65] The reference to a fundamental freedom is a reference to a fundamental internal market freedom, i.e. a free movement right, see Chs 16–20.
[66] Paras 40, 41.

Take the case of the United Kingdom by way of example: here a statutory rule which is inconsistent with the Human Rights Act 1998 is valid and enforceable against an individual until Parliament, using the fast track procedure provided under the Act, amends the rule. However, if the situation falls within the scope of Community law, as it was the case in *Carpenter*, then the national court is under a duty not to apply that rule to the case at issue without having to wait for Parliament to change the law.

Furthermore, in the *Carpenter* case the basis for the application by the Court of the principle of respect for family life was the conclusion by the Court of Justice that Mr Carpenter was exercising a fundamental internal market freedom, to which the deportation would be detrimental. In the *Akrich* case,[67] the Court went a step further. Here, Mr Akrich married Mrs Akrich, a British national, whilst illegally present in the United Kingdom. The couple then went to Ireland in order to trigger the Treaty so that Mr Akrich, upon returning to the United Kingdom, would gain the right to residence as a spouse of a Community national who returned to the United Kingdom after having exercised her freedom to move.[68] The United Kingdom authorities nonetheless denied Mr Akrich leave to enter and reside in the United Kingdom on the grounds that Mr and Mrs Akrich had moved temporarily to Ireland with the sole purpose of triggering the Treaty so that Mr Akrich could derive a right to reside in the United Kingdom from Community law and thus evade the provisions of UK immigration law. The Court found that Mr Akrich did not fall within the scope of Community law, since he was not lawfully resident within the Community when he moved to Ireland. Nonetheless the Court instructed the national court to have regard to the right to respect for family life as guaranteed by Article 8 ECHR. The soundness of the Court's conclusion is questionable and its reasoning seems contradictory. If the situation of the spouses fell outside the scope of the free movement provisions of the Treaty, the essential basis for applying human rights guarantees *as an element of Community law* would seem to have been lacking. The only way to explain the ruling is to understand the Court to have separated two issues: first of all, the possibility for Mr Akrich to rely on (then) Article 10 Regulation 1612/68 which grants a right of entry and residence in the Member State where the worker is migrating to their spouses and children. This article could not apply since Mr Akrich was not lawfully present in the territory of any of the Member States before moving to follow his wife. Secondly, the Court must have considered Mrs Akrich's right to move (and come back) as a Community worker. Since she had moved she was clearly

---

[67] Case C–109/01 *Secretary of State for the Home Department v Hacene Akrich* [2003] E.C.R. I–9607.
[68] See Chs 17 and 18, below.

covered by Article 39 EC; and not to allow her husband to follow her would clearly affect her desire to migrate (albeit to migrate back to her country of origin) and thus impact on her free movement rights. For this reason the rule had to be both justified and respect Mrs Akrich's right to family life. In this way, the two conflicting statements—that the case did not fall within the scope of Community law and that the national court should have due regard to fundamental rights—can be reconciled.[69]

8–012   A further significant feature of the *Carpenter* and *Akrich* cases was that the Court of Justice defined the scope of right to family life as a general principle of Community law by reference to the case law of the European Court of Human Rights.[70] Any distinction in principle or difference in practice between Convention rights inspiring and influencing the content of general principles of Community law, on the one hand, and the Court of Justice applying the ECHR, and the case law of the European Court of Human Rights, on the other, would seem to have disappeared. This is even more visible in the case of *K.B.*[71] Here, *K.B.* attacked UK legislation which prevented those who had undergone gender reassignment from amending their birth certificates to reflect their change of sex. As a result, post-operative transsexuals were effectively prevented from marrying a person of the other sex, since only their sex of birth would be taken into account. The ECJ had already ruled that, unlike discrimination on grounds of sexual orientation,[72] discrimination against transsexuals fell within the scope of application of Article 141 EC (equal pay for men and women).[73] *K.B.* argued that the fact that she could not marry her partner who was a post-operative man constituted discrimination on grounds of sex prohibited by Article 141 EC. This was the case because in the event of K.B.'s death, her partner would be deprived of a widower's pension on the grounds that the couple was not married; however the reason why the were not married was because UK legislation prevented K.B.'s partner from amending his birth certificate to reflect his change of sex. The British legislation preventing those who had undergone gender reassignment from amending their birth certificate had just been declared inconsistent with the ECHR.[74] The European Court of Justice put great weight on the Strasburg Court's ruling and held that:

> "Article 141 EC, in principle, precludes legislation, such as that at issue before the national court, which, in breach of the

---

[69] See further Spaventa "Annotation on *Akrich*" (2005) C.M.L.Rev. 225.

[70] *Carpenter*, para.42; *Akrich*, para.60.

[71] Case C–117/01 *K.B.* [2004] E.C.R. I–541.

[72] Case C–249/96 *Grant v South West Trains Ltd* [1998] E.C.R. I–621.

[73] Case C–13/94 *P v S Cornwall County Council* [1996] E.C.R. I–2143.

[74] *Goodwin v UK* (Appl. No.28957/95) (2002) 35 E.H.R.R. 18; the ECtHR found that the British legislation at issue breached the right to respect for private life enshrined in Art.8 of the Convention, and the right to marry enshrined in Art.12.

European Convention for the Protection of Human Rights and Fundamental Freedoms, [. . .], prevents a couple such as K.B. and R. from fulfilling the marriage requirement which must be met for one of them to be able to benefit from part of the pay of the other."[75]

It is clear that a broad interpretation of the scope of the Treaty in the free movement cases, and of the meaning of what constitutes sex discrimination falling within the scope of Article 141 EC, come to the benefit of individuals, who see their fundamental rights recognised through the medium of Community law. However, such case law also has the effect of reducing Member States' regulatory autonomy and relocating the balancing exercise between fundamental rights and competing interests in the hands of the ECJ, a step not necessarily welcomed by the Member States.[76]

Another, related problem, occurs when the rights guaranteed by the Treaty directly clash with (non-economic) rights guaranteed by the common constitutional traditions and the ECHR. In those cases, the Court has been willing to admit that the need to protect fundamental rights constitutes a legitimate aim justifying a restriction to Treaty rights;[77] however, the limitation must be proportionate and the balance between conflicting interests is a matter for Community rather than national law. For instance, and as we shall see in more detail in Chapter 16, in *Schimidberger*,[78] a trader attacked the Austrian Government's decision not to block a demonstration on the motorway which had the effect of interrupting the flow of goods on wheels for several days. The trader's right to transport goods guaranteed by Article 28 EC therefore directly clashed with the demonstrators' right to freedom of expression, a right recognised and guaranteed by the Austrian Constitution as well as by the ECHR. The Court held that fundamental rights might take precedence even over the Treaty free movement provisions, and found that in the case at stake the interference with the traders' right to free movement was proportionate.[79]

---

[75] Case C–117/01 *K.B.* [2004] E.C.R. I–541, operative part of the ruling.

[76] See the discussion about the horizontal provisions of the Charter in the next Chapter.

[77] e.g. Case C–368/95 *Familiapress* [1997] E.C.R. I–3689; Case C–36/02 *Omega* [2004] E.C.R. I–9609.

[78] Case C–112/00 *Schmidberger* [2003] E.C.R. I–5659, see Ch.16, below.

[79] A more complex and delicate case is currently pending in front of the ECJ. In that case the Court will have to balance the right to take industrial action at Community level with the right to freedom of establishment, see Case C–438/05 *International Transport Workers' Federation and The Finnish Seamen's Union v Viking Line*, case pending; and the ruling of the UK Court of Appeal which referred the case to the ECJ, *Viking v ITWF* [2006] 1 C.M.L.R. 27 (on the interim relief issue).

The institutional structure of the Union and fundamental rights

8–013   Despite the Court's willingness to protect fundamental rights in the Community system, some concerns have been raised in relation to the compatibility of certain features of the Union system with fundamental rights and in particular with the right to a fair trial and effective judicial protection enshrined in Article 6 of the ECHR. In particular, some problems arise in relation to some characteristics of the competition law enforcement system; to the role of the Advocate General in direct proceedings; and to the exclusion and limitation of the jurisdiction of the ECJ in relation to Second and Third Pillar instruments.

In relation to competition law proceedings, as we shall see in the relevant chapter,[80] the Commission is responsible both for carrying out the investigation on competition law breaches, and imposing a fine should it find that a breach of competition law has occurred. According to Regulation 1/2003, such fine—which can be very high[81]—is not of a criminal nature.[82] However, the European Court of Human Rights, in deciding whether proceedings are of a criminal nature, adopts a substantial rather than a formal criterion. Thus, if the national legal system qualifies the offence as criminal in nature, Article 6 is automatically applicable. Otherwise the European Court of Human Rights will look at several factors in order to decide whether a "charge" is a "criminal charge" for the purposes of the Convention. Amongst those factors, are the nature of the offence and the severity of the penalty imposed. If a fine is substantial, punitive in nature, and aimed at deterring future breaches, it might be qualified as a criminal sanction.[83] In the case in which European competition fines were to be qualified as criminal sanctions, then the fine-imposing powers of the Commission might be problematic in relation to Article 6 ECHR. The CFI has so far refused to consider such fines as criminal in nature,[84] even though both the CFI and the ECJ have held that the guarantees provided for in Articles 6 and 7 ECHR apply, to a certain extent, also to the Commission's investigatory power.[85]

---

[80] Ch.25.

[81] The fine can be up to 10 per cent of global turnover for the preceding year.

[82] Art.23(5) Reg.1/2003 on the implementation of the rules on competition laid down in Arts 81 and 82 of the Treaty, [2003] O.J. L1/1; Reg.17 also provided that the fine was not a criminal sanction. The Court has held that penalties/fines imposed in relation to the CAP are not of a criminal nature, see e.g. Case 137/85 *Maizena* [1987] E.C.R. 4587; C–210/00 *Käserei Champignon Hofmeister* [2002] E.C.R. I–6453.

[83] A fine for breach of competition law was qualified as a criminal sanction by the European Commission of Human Rights in *Societé Stenuit v France* (Appl. No.11598/85) [1992] 14 E.H.R.R. 509; also see obiters in *Lilly France S. A. v France* (Appl. No.53892/00), judgment of 3/12/02, and *Neste St. Petersburg v Russia* (Appl. No.69042/01).

[84] e.g. Case T–64/02 *Dr Hans Heubach GmbH & Co KG v Commission* Judgment of 29/11/05, not yet reported.

[85] e.g. T–220/00 *Cheil Jedang v Commission* [2003] E.C.R. II–2473, para.44, on non-retroactivity of sanctions.

A further problem with the institutional organisation of the EU relates to the role of the Advocate General in court proceedings, at least in direct proceedings. Here, the rules of procedure of the Court do not allow the parties to reply to the Advocate General's opinion. In *Emesa*, another competition law case, Emesa sought leave to submit observations on the Advocate General's opinion. It relied on a European Court of Human Rights case, *Vermeulen*, in which the Strasbourg Court held that the fact that the parties could not reply to the submissions of the Belgian *Procureur Général* in proceedings before the *Cour de Cassation*, infringed the right to adversarial proceedings and thus Article 6 ECHR. The ECJ distinguished the role of the Advocate General from that of the Procureur General. It held:

> "the Opinion of the Advocate General brings the oral pro-
> cedure to an end. It does not form part of the proceedings
> between the parties, but rather opens the stage of deliberation
> by the Court. It is not therefore an opinion addressed to the
> judges or to the parties which stems from an authority outside
> the Court or which 'derives its authority from that of the
> Procureur Général's department [in the French version, "minis-
> tère public"]' [. . .]. Rather, it constitutes the individual reas-
> oned opinion, expressed in open court, of a Member of the
> Court of Justice itself."[86]

Whilst the ECJ reasoning seems persuasive in distinguishing the role of the *Procureur* from that of the Advocate General, a subsequent ruling of the European Court of Human Rights cast some doubts on the compatibility of the lack of possibility of rebuttal to the Advocate General's Opinion with Article 6 ECHR. In *Kress*,[87] a case concern-ing the French *Commissaire du Government*, whose role is very similar to that of the Advocate General,[88] the European Court of Human Rights held:

> "[. . .] the concept of a fair trial also means in principle the
> opportunity for the parties to a trial to have knowledge of and
> comment on all evidence adduced or observations filed, even by
> an independent member of the national legal service, with a
> view to influencing the court's decision."[89]

In the case at issue the European Court of Human Rights found that **8–014** there was no breach of Article 6 ECHR since the parties could ask the *Commisaire* to indicate the general tenor of his submissions; and

---

[86] Case C–17/98 *Emesa Sugar Free Zone NV and Aruba*, order of the Court, [2000] E.C.R. I–665, para.14.
[87] *Kress v France* (Appl. No.39594/98).
[88] In fact the French Government resisting the application held that were the ECtHR apply the *Vermeulen* ruling to the *Commisaire du Government* it would be "condemning" the European Community judicial system, *cf.* para.62.
[89] *Kress v France* (Appl. No.39594/98), para.74.

it was open to the parties to reply to the *Commissaire's* submissions.
This is not possible however in the Community legal system. As a
result of the *Kress* ruling, the institution of the Advocate General
came under attack again. In *Kaba II* the applicant claimed that the
fact that in the first ruling concerning his situation he was not able to
rectify some allegedly wrong factual assessment reached by the
Advocate General was a breach of Article 6(1) of the Convention as
interpreted by the European Court of Human Rights in *Kress*.
Advocate General Ruiz-Jarabo Colomer in *Kaba II*, defended the
role of the Advocate General and attacked the European Court of
Human Rights for its *Kress* ruling.[90] The European Court of Justice
avoided the issue by inverting the order of the questions and thus
limiting itself to examine the issue of substance. Admittedly, in the
case of preliminary rulings the problem is much reduced by the fact
that the case is decided by the national court which can therefore
ensure that the ECJ ruling is not based upon a misunderstanding of
the facts or of the national rules applicable, and, if that is the case,
can refer a new question to the ECJ. However, the issue is more
delicate in relation to direct proceedings. Here, the fact that the
parties are unable to reply to the Advocate General's submissions
seems to be in direct conflict with the European Court of Human
Rights assessment of the scope of Article 6(1) ECHR. This might
become a real problem when and if the Charter comes into force,
since according to Article 52 the Community standard of protection
of those rights which derive from the Convention cannot fall below
the Convention's standard;[91] and/or in the case in which the Union
should accede to the Convention.

However, the serious problem concerning the right to effective
judicial protection in the EU arises in relation to Second and Third
Pillar measures, and measures adopted under the Community pillar
to give effect to Second Pillar measures. In relation to the latter, it is
worth examining a recent case concerning a Community Regulation
giving effect to a Common Position adopted under second pillar
competence, which in turn gave effect to a UN Security Council
resolution. The Security Council Resolution in question established
that the assets of anyone associated with Usama Bin Laden, or with
Al Qaeda, should be frozen, and instructed the UN Sanctions'
Committee to maintain an updated list of people and organisations
whose assets should be frozen.[92] The European Council considered
that action at Union level was necessary to give effect to the Security
Council Resolutions; it therefore adopted a Common Position (a
Second Pillar measure which is not subject to judicial review)[93]
providing that any fund relating to Usama Bin Laden or to any

---

[90] Case C–466/00 *Kaba* (Kaba II) [2003] E.C.R. I–2219, Opinion, esp. paras 104–107.
[91] See Ch.9.
[92] Resolution 1333 (2000) and see also UN Security Council Resolution 1267 (1999).
[93] Common Position 2001/154/CFSP concerning additional restrictive measures against the
Taliban and amending Common Position 96/746/CFSP [2001] O.J. L57/1.

person associated with him as designated by the Sanctions Committee should be frozen. Since Common Positions are not capable of producing direct effects, the Community subsequently adopted a Regulation providing for the freezing of assets of those designated by the UN Sanctions Committee.[94] Mr Yusuf brought proceedings challenging the freezing of his assets under the Regulation on the grounds that he was not linked to the Taliban regime.[95] His claim rested on two main grounds: first of all, the Community did not have competence to enact the Regulation.[96] Secondly, the Regulation breached his fundamental rights as protected by Community and Union law, and in particular the right to a fair hearing. In Mr Yusuf's submission his right to fair hearing had been breached since he had not been told why the sanctions had been imposed on him; he was not communicated the evidence and facts relied against him; and he had had no opportunity to defend himself. The CFI found that, even though the European Community legal order protected the right to a fair hearing, in this case it had no power to scrutinise whether the inclusion of the applicants in the Annex to the Regulation was justified. It relied on the fact that to review the lawfulness of the Regulation and inclusion of the applicants in the list according to the general principles of Community law would have amounted to an indirect review of the Security Council Resolution. In the view of the CFI, principles of international and Community law prevented it from such indirect review of a Security Council Resolution (an act of international law), since that was not within its jurisdiction. However, the CFI held that it was entitled to assess the compatibility of the Security Council Resolution with *jus cogens* (i.e. mandatory principles of international law). Even though it found that the right to effective judicial protection had been limited (if not altogether excluded), such "lacuna in the judicial protection available to the applicants is not in itself contrary to *jus cogens*".[97] The *Yusuf* ruling is incredibly complex in that it examines

---

[94] Reg.467/2001 prohibiting the export of certain goods and services to Afghanistan, strengthening the flight ban and extending the freeze of funds and other financial resources in respect of the Taliban of Afghanistan, and repealing Reg.337/2000 [2001] O.J. L67/1; the Regulation contains an annex with the list of those whose assets should be frozen. This list can be amended by the Commission according to the findings of the UN Sanctions Committee.

[95] Case T–306/01 *Yusuf v Council and Commission*, judgment of 21/9/05, nyr, appeal pending Case C–415/05 P; and on the same issue Case T–315/01 *Kadi v Council and Commission*, judgment of 21/9/05, appeal pending Case C–402/05P.

[96] On this point see Ch.5, above.

[97] Case T–306/01 *Yusuf v Council and Commission*, judgment of 21/9/05, nyr, para.341. The CFI also held "Moreover, the question whether an individual or organisation poses a threat to international peace and security, like the question of what measures must be adopted *vis-à-vis* the persons concerned in order to frustrate that threat, entails a political assessment and value judgments which in principle fall within the exclusive competence of the authority to which the international community has entrusted primary responsibility for the maintenance of international peace and security." (para.339). It is debatable whether such blanket cheque to executive authorities (albeit acting in an international forum) in determining sanctions capable of affecting individual rights is satisfactory and sound.

the relationship between international and Community law when international law indirectly impinges on fundamental rights. Without entering the debate as to whether the Court's reasoning is satisfactory, it is clear that, in this case, the effect of using Community competence to give effect to UN resolutions is to deprive individuals of the fundamental right to judicial protection, the right to have the claims against them assessed by an independent body. In other words, rightly or wrongly, there is a domino effect whereby the implementation of international law through Community law ends up knocking down guarantees that might have been available had the UN Resolution been implemented through national law rather than through a Community Regulation.

A similar problem, arises in relation to measures adopted under the Second and Third Pillars, when those measures have an effect on individual rights, but are not amenable to judicial review because of the exclusion (or limitation as the case might be) of the Union Courts' jurisdiction.[98] Thus for instance, in the case of *SEGI*, an organisation defined as terrorist by a common position, was unable to challenge its inclusion in the contested list because the CFI (and ECJ) lack jurisdiction over such instruments.[99] The Constitutional Treaty would have remedied this significant gap in fundamental rights protection by providing for the ECJ jurisdiction in relation to CFSP measures providing for "restrictive measures against natural and legal persons",[1] and for almost universal jurisdiction in relation to measures adopted in the field of criminal law.[2] Lacking ratification of the Constitutional Treaty the responsibility to ensure the right to effective judicial protection in these fields will therefore lie with national courts and with the European Court of Human Rights. It is now time to turn to the relationship between the EU and the ECHR and to look at the European Court of Human Rights' view of its own jurisdiction over acts adopted by the EU institutions.

Relationship between the EU and the ECHR

8–015   As we have seen above, the ECHR does not directly apply to the EU since it has not been ratified by it. Thus, the Convention merely serves as a source (the main one) for the identification of those rights which are to be considered protected as general principles of Community law; and the case law of the Court of Human Rights is

---

[98] Joint positions are excluded from the Court's jurisdiction; in relation to the other instruments listed in Art.34(2), the Court's jurisdiction in voluntary, i.e. dependent upon a declaration from the Member State. See Chs 10 and 14.

[99] *cf.* Case T–338/02 *Segi v Council*, order of 7/06/04, appeal pending (Case C–355/04 P).

[1] Article III–376 CT.

[2] But maintaining the exclusion of jurisdiction in relation to the review of the validity and proportionality of operations carried out by the police or other law-enforcement services of a Member State or the exercise of the responsibilities incumbent upon Member States with regard to the maintenance of law and order and the safeguarding of internal security (Article III–377 CT).

looked at to determine the appropriate minimum level of protection. However, the fact that the Union is not party to the Convention has given rise to some controversy, in that some commentators, as well as some claimants, have argued that the protection of fundamental rights afforded by the ECJ through the general principles sometimes falls below that afforded by the European Court of Human Rights. If and when that is the case, the applicant is left with no remedy since he or she cannot bring a complaint in front of the European Court of Human Rights (as it would be possible were the situation a domestic rather than a Community one). Furthermore, and as we have seen, the institutional framework of the Union might fall short of fundamental rights guarantees. In those cases, membership of the Community might have the effect of weakening the protection of fundamental rights by removing that minimum floor of rights which should be a common denominator for all Member States. In order to solve these problems, it has been suggested that the Community should accede to the Convention, and be bound by the same instrument which binds all of its Member States and membership of which is a precondition for acceding the Union.

In exploring this possibility, the Council asked the ECJ to rule as to whether accession would be possible under the current Treaty provisions using as legal base Article 308 EC which provides for the residual competence of the Community.[3] In its Opinion 2/94, after having restated that compliance with fundamental rights is a condition for the lawfulness of Community acts, the Court held:

> "Access to the Convention would, however, entail a substantial change in the present Community system for the protection of Human Rights in that it would entail the entry of the Community into a distinct international institutional system as well as integration of all the provisions of the Convention into the Community legal order. Such a modification of the system for the protection of human rights in the Community, with equally fundamental institutional implications for the Community and for the Member States, would be of constitutional significance and would therefore be such as to go beyond the scope of Article 235 [now 308]. It could be brought only by way of Treaty amendment."[4]

Whilst Article I–9 of the Constitutional Treaty provides for such competence, neither the Amsterdam nor the Nice Treaty did. Thus,

---

[3] See Ch.4.

[4] Opinion 2/94 (Accession to the ECHR), [1996] E.C.R. I–1759, paras 34 and 35; and see C.E.L.S. Occasional Paper No.1 "The Human Rights Opinion of the ECJ and its Constitutional Competence", Cambridge 1996; O'Leary "Accession by the European Community to the European Convention on Human Rights—The Opinion of the ECJ" (1996) E.H.R.L.R. 362.

for the time being the Union cannot accede to the Convention. This is not to say, however, that the Convention cannot have some effects beyond those highlighted above. In particular, some claimants have argued that the fact that the Convention does not bind the Union does not deprive it of its effects since the Member States and the national authorities are always bound by the ECHR, even when they are enforcing/implementing a Community decision. According to this view, national authorities would be under an obligation to refuse to apply/implement a piece of Community law if it conflicted with one of the Convention rights. It is clear that this approach would place a significant limit on the doctrine of supremacy of Community law and that there is an inherent tension between such principle and the need to ensure that Member States do not escape their Convention obligations through the medium of Community/Union law. This balance is not an easy one to strike, and the European Court of Human Rights has progressively taken a more intervention-ist stance.

8–016   The first case in which the relationship between Community/national and Convention law was examined is *M & Co.*[5] There the claimant tried to rely on the reasoning outlined above in attacking the acts of the German authorities which were enforcing a European Commission's decision taken within the field of competition law. On that occasion, the European Commission of Human Rights (then in charge of deciding on the admissibility of the case in front of the European Court of Human Rights), partially rejected such reasoning. It first noted that, according to Article 1 of the Convention, Member States are responsible for *any* violation of the Convention, whether it is a consequence of domestic or international law. However, it also found that the Community system both secured and controlled compliance with fundamental rights. To require the Member State to check whether the Convention rights had been respected in each individual case would be contrary to the very idea of transferring powers to an international organisation. The *M & Co.* ruling lays down the so-called doctrine of equivalent protection (not dissimilar from that espoused by national constitutional courts): since the Community system affords fundamental rights protection as well as the possibility to enforce such rights in front of the CFI/ECJ, the national courts/authorities do not need to check case by case whether such protection is adequate, and the European Court of Human Rights will refuse jurisdiction.[6]

Some years later, however, in the *Matthews* ruling, the European Court of Human Rights allowed for the Convention to have some effect in a field occupied by Community law. In this case, Ms

---

[5] (1990) 64 Ecm.H.R.R. 138.
[6] The ECtHR had no problem asserting jurisdiction when the national rule under attack was reproducing Community law, Case *Cantoni v France* (1997–V) E.C.H.R.R. 1614.

Matthews was a Gibraltar national who complained about the fact that Gibraltar nationals did not have the right to vote for the European Parliament's elections. She argued that, even though the exclusion from the right to vote followed from a Council decision rather than a unilateral act of the United Kingdom, the United Kingdom was still responsible for the effect of the decision which deprived her of the right to vote guaranteed by Article 3 of Protocol No. 1.[7] The main question for the Court was whether, notwithstanding the fact that the European Parliament was an organ of the Community, the United Kingdom was under an obligation to "secure" elections to it. The Court of Human Rights found that even though the Council decision could not be challenged in front of it, since the Community itself is not party to the Convention, the Member States' responsibility to secure the rights in the Convention continued even after the transfer of sovereignty to an international organisation. Noting that in this case the European Court of Justice did not have jurisdiction to review the Council decision, as this was primary law having the same status as the Treaty, the European Court of Human Rights held that the United Kingdom, together with all the other Members of the Community, was responsible for possible violations of the Protocol. It then found that such Protocol had been violated and, as a result, the Community subsequently amended its rules to allow Gibraltar citizens to vote at the European Parliament elections. The ruling in *Matthews* signals the European Court of Human Rights' willingness to intervene at least in those cases in which the ECJ lacks jurisdiction since in those cases the protection afforded by the Community is not equivalent to that afforded by the Convention. In *Bosphorus*,[8] the European Court of Human Rights further curtailed the scope of the doctrine of equivalent protection. Here the case at issue related to a Community Regulation implementing a UN Security Council Resolution; consistent with the Regulation, the Irish authorities impounded the claimant's aircraft on the grounds that it was owned by a company established in Serbia, which was the target of the UN sanctions. The claimant argued that since it leased the aircraft from the Serbian company before the sanctions came into force, the impoundment constituted a disproportionate interference with its right to property. The ECJ found that the public interest of securing a resolution to the Serbian conflict outweighed the claimant's right to property, and that therefore the impoundment was consistent with fundamental rights. When the claimant seized the European Court of Human

---

[7] Art.3 recites "The High Contracting Parties undertake to hold free elections at reasonable intervals by secret ballot, under conditions which will ensure the free expression of the opinion of the people in the choice of the legislature".

[8] *Bosphorus v Ireland* (Appl. No.45036/98), judgment of 30/06/05, noted (2005) E.H.R.L.R. 649.

Rights, the preliminary question was whether the European Court of Human Rights had jurisdiction over the issue: after all the case related to a Community measure over which the ECJ had jurisdiction. The European Court of Human Rights restated the doctrine of equivalent protection; it however added that:

"any such presumption [of equivalence] can be rebutted if, in the circumstance of a *particular case*, it is considered that the protection of Convention rights was *manifestly deficient*. In such cases, the interest of international co-operation would be outweighed by the Convention's role as a 'constitutional instrument of European public order' in the field of fundamental rights." (emphasis added)

8–017 Following the rulings in *Matthews* and *Bosphorus*, it is clear that despite the fact that the Union is not part to the Convention, the European Court of Human Rights is willing to assert jurisdiction to ensure that Union law does not fall systematically below the standards required by the Convention. However, if it is true that the European Court of Human Rights now allows for the possibility that claimants rebut the presumption of equivalent protection, the threshold for successfully doing so is set at a high level since a mere infringement of Convention's rights is not enough to trigger the European Court of Human Rights' intervention: rather the protection must be "manifestly deficient". That is most likely to be the case when the ECJ has no jurisdiction, and in particular in the case of Common Positions adopted under the Second and Third Pillar.

Further reading
Alston (ed.), *The EU and Human Rights* (OUP, 1999).
Bamforth, "Sexual Orientation after *Grant v South West Trains*" (2000) M.L.R. 694–718.
de Burca "The Language of Rights and European Integration" in Shaw and More (eds) *New Legal Dynamics of European Integration* (Clarendon Press, 1995), p.29.
CELS Occasional Paper No.1, "The Human Rights Opinion of the ECJ and its Constitutional Competence", Cambridge, 1996.
Coppel and O'Neill, "The European Court of Justice: Taking Rights Seriously?" [1992] Legal Studies 227.
Harmsen, "National Responsibility for European Community Acts under the European Convention on Human Rights: Recasting the Accession Debate" (2001) E.P.L. 625.
Jacobs, "Human Rights in the European Union: The Role of the Court of Justice" (2001) 26 E.L.Rev. 331.
King, "Ensuring Human Rights of Inter-governmental Acts in Europe" (2000) E.L.Rev. 79.

Lawson, "Confusion and Conflict? Diverging Interpretation of the European Convention on Human Rights in Strasbourg and Luxembourg" in Lawson and de Bloijs (eds), *The Dynamics of the Protection of Human Rights in Europe* (essays in honour of Schermers, Kluwer, 1994).

Neuwhal and Rosas (eds), *The European Union and Human Rights* (1995).

O'Leary, "Accession by the European Community to the European Convention on Human Rights—The Opinion of the ECJ" (1996) E.H.R.L.R. 362.

Spaventa, "Remembrance of Principles Lost: on Fundamental Rights, the Third Pillar and the scope of Union law" (2006) Y.E.L. forthcoming.

Weiler and Lockhart " 'Taking Rights Seriously' Seriously: the European Court of Justice and its Fundamental Rights Jurisprudence" [1995] C.M.L.Rev. 51 and 579.

Williams, *EU Human Rights Policies. A Study in Irony* (OUP, 2004).

de Witte "The Past and Future Role of the European Court of Justice in the Protection of Human Rights" in Alston (ed.) *The EU and Human Rights* (OUP, 1999), 859.

CHAPTER 9

THE CHARTER OF FUNDAMENTAL RIGHTS

Guide to this Chapter: The Charter of Fundamental Rights of **9–001** the European Union was officially proclaimed by the Council, the Parliament and the Commission in December 2000. It was then included in the Constitutional Treaty with a few amendments. Even though for the time being it is not legally binding, it is a legally relevant, and constitutionally significant, document. This chapter provides an examination of its substantive provisions, its scope and its legal value. The Charter is narrower in scope than the general principles and it applies only to the acts of the Union institutions and to the Member States when they implement Community law. Thus, the Charter, unlike the general principles, does not apply to the Member States when they act within the scope of Community law. Should the Charter come into force, this would create a dichotomy in the application of fundamental rights. However, as we shall see when analysing the legal status of the Charter, this is most likely to be just a formal dichotomy.

Background to the drafting of the Charter

In the previous chapter we saw that in the absence of any written **9–002** catalogue of rights, the task of identifying the fundamental rights applicable at Community level fell primarily upon the European Court of Justice. As a result of the Court's case law, the issue of fundamental rights protection in the (then) European Economic Community became a matter of political discussion. The first resolution inviting the Commission to elaborate proposals on funda- mental rights in the light of the UN International Covenant of 1966, and of the political and civil rights contained in the UN Charter was issued in 1977 a few months after the institutional endorsement by the Parliament, Council and Commission of the Court's case law.[1] The issue of fundamental rights was further discussed in relation to the draft EU Treaty adopted by the European Parliament in 1984,[2] Article 4 of that draft providing for an express fundamental rights guarantee, as well as for a procedure for breach of fundamental rights not dissimilar from that currently contained in Article 7 TEU. As we saw in the previous chapter, each Treaty amendment after the Single European Act also included new provisions with a fundamental rights relevance. Eventually in 1999 it was decided that the Union should equip itself with its own fundamental rights document.[3] Thus, the Cologne European Council in its Conclusions held that ". . . at the present stage of development of the European Union, the fundamental rights applicable at Union level should be consolidated in a Charter and thereby made more evident".[4] This declaration was complemented by an Annex IV, which detailed the mandate as well as outlining the composition of the body which would be entrusted with the drafting of the Charter. According to the mandate the Charter was to contain: the fundamental rights contained in the European Convention on Human Rights (ECHR or Convention) and in the constitutional traditions common to the Member States (i.e. the general principles of Community law), together with the fundamental rights pertaining to Union citizens (e.g. political representation, consular protection, as well as free movement). In addition the mandate stated that account should be taken of the economic and social rights contained in the European Social Charter[5] and in the Community Charter of the Fundamental Social Rights of Workers.[6]

---

[1] Joint declaration of European Parliament, the Council and the Commission Concerning the protection of fundamental rights and the European Convention for the Protection of Human Rights and Fundamental Freedoms [1977] O.J. C103/1.

[2] Draft European Union Treaty adopted by the European Parliament on February 14, 1984 (the Spinelli draft); see Capotorti, Hilf, Jacobs, and Jacqué, *The European Union Treaty. Commentary on the draft adopted by the European Parliament on February 14, 1984* (Clarendon Press, 1986), esp. p.39.

[3] For an analysis of the reasons which might have led to this decision, see Paciotti "La Carta: i contenuti e gli autori", in Manzella, Melograni, Paciotti, Rodotà, *Riscrivere i diritti in Europa* (Il Mulino, 2001).

[4] Cologne European Council, 3 and June 4, 1999, Presidency Conclusions, 150/99 REV 1, para.44.

[5] The European Social Charter is an instrument adopted by the Council of Europe (the body which adopted the ECHR) in 1961 and revised in 1996. Whilst the ECHR focuses on civil and political rights, the Social Charter focuses on economic and social rights (e.g. housing, education, employment, etc.). The enforcement mechanisms for the latter are different from those provided for in relation to the ECHR and the European Court of Human Rights has no jurisdiction over the Social Charter.

[6] This is a non-binding instrument adopted at Community level by 11 out of the then 12 Member States (the United Kingdom was the exception). In 1999 the United Kingdom signed the Charter, and now all of the Member States are signatories.

As far as the composition of the body entrusted with the drafting of the Charter was concerned, Annex IV of the Cologne Conclusions stated that it should be comprised of representatives of the Heads of State and Government and of the President of the Commission, as well as representatives of the European Parliament and of the national parliaments. The Cologne Council, however, left it to the following European Council to be held in Tampere, to decide the precise composition of the body. The Tampere Council set up a "Convention" composed by 62 people:[7] 15 representatives of the Heads of States or Government of the Member States, one representative of the Commission, 16 representatives of the European Parliament, and 30 representatives of the national parliaments (two for each Member State). The number of EP representatives was set so as to counterbalance the number of representatives of the Community executive (15 + 1); whilst the number of representatives of national parliaments was set at two for each Member State so as to ensure that those Member States which have a bicameral system could have a representative from each chamber. The inclusion of representatives from national parliaments, which had previously been excluded from any direct participation to the legislative and political processes of the EU, was by far the most significant innovation. This move was aimed at providing the Convention with stronger democratic legitimacy than the traditional inter-governmental process adopted in drafting primary Community legislation. For the same reason, the Convention proceedings were to be as transparent as possible, with all documents published on the internet. Furthermore, the Convention accepted representations from a number of institutions, including non-governmental organisations, as well as from the then applicant countries, and the proceedings were attended by two observers each from the ECJ and from the European Court of Human Rights.[8]

The introduction of the Convention method was seen as a revolutionary step in European Governance and it was reproduced in the drafting of a Treaty establishing a Constitution for Europe.[9] Indeed, the Constitutional Treaty provides that the Convention method is to be used in future amendments.[10] The Convention met for the first time on December 17, 1999, and delivered the completed Charter on October 2, 2000. The Charter was then solemnly

---

[7] Tampere European Council, 15 and October 16, 1999, Annex to the Presidency Conclusions, *http://ue.eu.int/ueDocs/cms—Data/docs/pressData/en/ec/00200-r1.en9.htm*.

[8] The observers from the ECJ did not submit any documents, the observers from the ECtHR made a submission; see Comments of the Council of Europe observers on the Draft Charter, document CHARTE 4861/00 CONTRIB 356, 13/11/00.

[9] See below, Ch.11.

[10] Article VI-443 CT; in some cases the Convention method can be derogated from, see Articles IV-443 and ff. CT, and see Ch.11 below. On the significance of the Convention process, De Burca "The Drafting of the European Union Charter of Fundamental Rights" (2001) E.L.Rev. 126.

proclaimed by the European Parliament, the Commission and the Council at the Nice European Council on December 7, 2000.[11] As a result the Charter was not and is not, for the time being, legally binding. The Constitutional Treaty incorporated the entire Charter (including the Preamble) in its second part; it also amended the numbering and the provisions on its interpretation and application. We will consider the Charter as proclaimed in Nice, highlighting the amendments introduced in the Constitutional Treaty.[12]

The Charter—structure and substantive provisions

9–003   The structure of the Charter is innovative in that it departs from the traditional division between civil and political rights on the one hand, and economic and social rights on the other. Instead it adopts a "horizontal" approach to fundamental rights placing them (at least theoretically) all at the same level, highlighting the indivisible nature of fundamental rights.[13] For this reason the Charter is divided in chapters according to six fundamental values:[14] Dignity (Articles 1–5); Freedom (Articles 6–19); Equality (Articles 20–26); Solidarity (Articles 27–38); Citizenship (Articles 39–46); and Justice (Articles 47–50). Those are complemented by the Preamble and by the general provisions (so called horizontal provisions, Articles 51–55) which set out the scope of application of the Charter. As we shall see below, the Charter, unlike the European Convention on Human Rights, contains a general derogating provision which theoretically applies to all Charter rights. However, Article 52 provides also for the ECHR minimum floor guarantee, whereby the Charter can never fall below the level of protection afforded by the Convention. Accordingly, when Charter rights derive from Convention rights, their scope cannot be less extensive that the scope of Convention rights. In order to understand the scope of some of the Charter rights it is therefore necessary to look at the Convention.

As stated above, the mandate of the Convention was to codify existing rights, not to create new ones. Whilst the main sources of such rights had been identified by the Cologne Council, the list there provided was not considered exhaustive and the Convention drew extensively from the case law of the ECJ and of the European Court of Human Rights, and from secondary and primary Community legislation, as well as from other international Conventions and

---

[11] Charter of Fundamental Rights (2000) O.J. C364/1.

[12] Since for the time being the Constitutional Treaty has not been adopted we will use the original Charter numbering, with the Constitutional Treaty numbering in brackets.

[13] On indivisibility of fundamental rights, *cf.* Kenner "Economic and Social Rights in the EU Legal Order: The Mirage of Indivisibility" in Hervey and Kenner (eds) *Economic and Social Rights under the EU Charter of Fundamental Rights—A Legal Perspective* (Hart Publishing, 2003), p.1.

[14] The CT version of the Charter is divided in Titles rather than Chapters.

Treaties. As we shall see, this allowed the Convention to codify also the so-called new generation of rights. The fact that the Charter aims to be a comprehensive document of the rights recognised by the Union entailed a substantial degree of duplication with rights contained in other TEC provisions as well as internal duplication. The reason for these duplications was to ensure that *all rights* which are recognised by the Union would be clearly visible. It is not obvious, however, that such duplication has not come at the expense of clarity, especially since Article 52(2) provides that those rights which duplicate rights contained elsewhere in the Treaty have the same scope as the latter.

The Charter is accompanied by "explanations" which clarify both the scope of each of the Charter rights/provisions and where they are derived from.[15] The source of the rights is especially important for those rights deriving from the ECHR since, as we said above and as we shall see in more detail below, Article 52(3) makes clear that the meaning and scope of the rights corresponding to Convention rights must be at least the same as those laid down by the ECHR.

Preamble

The Preamble reaffirms the Union's values as well as its founding **9-004** principles and its aims. It then states that it is necessary to "strengthen the protection of fundamental rights in the light of the changes in society, social progress and scientific and technological developments by making those rights *more visible* in a Charter".[16] In this way, the Preamble stresses the non-innovative nature of the Charter. It then identifies, in a non-exhaustive manner, the sources of such fundamental rights. It mentions the common constitutional traditions, international obligations common to the Member States, the ECHR, the European Community and Council of Europe Social Charters, as well as the case law of the ECJ and the European Court of Human Rights. The Constitutional Treaty added a sentence explicitly referring to the explanations which accompany the Charter, indicating that they must be used as a guide to its interpretation. The Preamble also makes clear that enjoyment of the rights contained in the Charter entails responsibilities and duties towards other persons, the human community and future generations. It concludes by stating that the Union recognises the rights, freedoms and principles set out in the Charter.

---

[15] The original explanations can be found on the Council's documents website (*www.europa.eu.int*), or as an official publication of the European Communities ISBN 92-824-1955-X (2001); the amended explanations can be found in the Constitutional Treaty (in Declarations concerning provisions of the Constitution), Declaration 12 concerning the explanations relating to the Charter of Fundamental Rights, [2004] O.J. C310/424.

[16] Emphasis added.

Chapter I—Dignity

9–005   The first Title of the Charter deals with those rights which are essential to protect the very essence of any fundamental right.

Article 1 (II–61) provides that *human dignity* is inviolable and that it shall be respected and protected. Human dignity is generally seen as the basis for enjoyment of any fundamental right. Thus, according to the explanations to the Charter, no provision of the Charter may be used to harm the dignity of another person and dignity is part of the substance of the Charter rights which therefore has *always* to be respected even when Charter rights are limited. The ECJ recognised that the right to human dignity is a general principle of Community law in the biotechnology case (see below).[17]

Article 2 (II–62) provides for the *right to life* as well as for the *prohibition of the death penalty and execution*. It substantially reproduces right to life as enshrined in Article 2(2) of the Convention and in Protocol No. 6 on the death penalty,[18] and it has at least the same scope as the Convention rights.[19] Thus, even though this is not explicitly stated in the Charter, the right to life can be limited only in (exhaustively) listed circumstances, i.e. defence from unlawful violence, to make a lawful arrest or to prevent someone lawfully detained from escaping, or in order to quell a riot or insurrection. The prohibition on the death penalty can be derogated from in time of war or in time of imminent threat of war.

Article 3 (II–63), entitled right to the *integrity of the person*, contains the so-called new generation rights.[20] As well as providing for a general right to physical and mental integrity, Article 3 prescribes limits to be respected in the fields of medicine and biology, such as the principle of informed consent,[21] the prohibition of eugenic practices, the prohibition on making the human body, or its parts as such, a source of financial gain, as well as the prohibition

---

[17] Case C–377/98 *Netherlands v Council* (biotechnology directive) [2001] E.C.R. I–7079. Even though it is not expressly mentioned in the Convention, the right to dignity informs the interpretation of all Convention rights; e.g. *Tyrer v UK* (Appl. No.5856/72) (1979–80) 2 E.H.R.R. 1.

[18] See also Declaration No.1 on the abolition of the death penalty annexed to the Treaty of Amsterdam.

[19] Art.2(1) ECHR provides for the possibility of death penalty; however the ECtHR has recently revisited its previous case law and held that following the adoption of Protocol No.6, and changes in attitudes towards the death penalty, the exception in Art.2 is no longer applicable and capital punishment is no longer admissible, *cf. Öcalan v Turkey* (Appl. No.46221/99) (2003) 37 E.H.R.R. 10. See also Protocol No.13 ECHR on the abolition of death penalty in all circumstances, signed by all Member States but not yet ratified by France, Italy Spain and Poland.

[20] They are called new generation rights because they result from scientific developments; however, it should be remembered that they are inherent in other rights: thus for instance the principle of informed consent is inherent in Art.8 ECHR (respect for private life), e.g. *Glass v UK* (Appl. No.61827/00) (2004) 39 E.H.R.R. 15.

[21] The principle of informed consent to medical practices has been recognised by the ECJ in Case C–404/92 *X v Commission* [1994] E.C.R. I–4737 (AIDS test case) reversing Case T–121/89 *X v Commission* [1992] E.C.R. II–2195.

on reproductive cloning.[22] It is open to the legislature to afford more extensive protection: thus, and as highlighted by the explanations, it would be open to the legislature to prohibit other forms of cloning. The prohibition on the marketability of the human body and its parts has already given rise to litigation in the case of *Netherlands v Council*.[23] Here, the Netherlands sought the annulment of the biotechnology directive,[24] *inter alia*, on the grounds that by allowing for the patentability of elements isolated from the human body or otherwise produced by means of a technical process, including the sequence or partial sequence of a gene, it breached the principle of human dignity and of non-marketability of the human body and its parts. The Court drew a distinction between inventions which combine a natural element with a technical process, which can be patented, and mere discoveries of DNA sequences which are not as such patentable. The Court held that given the safeguards provided for in the Directive, the patentability of DNA-based inventions did not conflict with the principle of human dignity and non-commercialisation of the human body.

Article 4 (II–64) prohibits *torture* and *inhuman or degrading* **9–006** *treatment* and *punishment*. It reproduces exactly the wording of Article 3 of the Convention and it is an *absolute* right that can never be derogated from, not even in time of war.[25] Thus, even though the horizontal provisions theoretically apply to all Charter rights, because of the Convention floor guarantee, the Charter derogations cannot be validly invoked in relation to Article 4.[26]

Article 5 (II–65) prohibits *slavery and forced labour*. Article 5(1) provides that no one shall be held in slavery (which is a legal condition) and servitude (which is a *de facto* status);[27] since it reproduces Article 4 of the ECHR it has to be construed accordingly and cannot therefore be derogated for any reason, not even in time of war. Article 5(2) prohibits forced and compulsory labour, and again shall be construed in relation to Article 4(2) of the Convention

---

[22] Those principles are contained in the Convention for the Protection of Human Rights and Dignity of the Human Being with regard to the application of Biology and Medicine (Oviedo Convention, ETS 164); and in its additional protocol on the Prohibition of Cloning Human Beings.
[23] Case C–377/98 *Netherlands v Council* (biotechnology directive) [2001] E.C.R. I–7079.
[24] Directive 98/44/EC on the legal protection of biotechnological inventions [1998] O.J. L213/13.
[25] Of course is then a matter of interpretation to decide what is to be defined as "torture", "inhuman" and "degrading". See e.g. *Ireland v UK* (Appl. No.5310/71) (1979–80) 2 E.H.R.R. 25; and *Aksoy v Turkey* (Appl. No.21987/93) (1997) 23 E.H.R.R. 553. See also European Convention for the Prevention of Torture (ETS 126). The House of Lords, reversing a ruling of the Court of Appeal, has stated that evidence obtained through torture or inhuman and degrading treatment is not admissible in British courts, *A v Secretary of State for the Home Department* [2006] 1 All E.R. 575.
[26] See below, paras 9–022 *et seq.*
[27] cf. *Siliadin v France* (Appl. No.73316/01), judgment of 26/7/05.

that excludes from the definition of "forced and compulsory labour" work done in the course of lawful detention; military service or service done instead of military service; work required in the case of public emergencies or calamities; and work which forms part of normal civic obligations. Article 5(3) adds an explicit prohibition on trafficking in human beings that reflects both the Europol Convention and the framework decision on human trafficking.[28]

Title II—Freedoms

9–007   Title II of the Charter is devoted to *freedoms*, ranging from traditional Convention rights to social rights. It includes principles which would not be judicially enforceable.

Article 6 (II–66) provides for the right to *liberty and security* and it reproduces the first sentence of Article 5 of the ECHR. In order to understand the scope of the article it is necessary to look at the Convention. Thus, Article 5(1) ECHR contains an exhaustive list of exceptions to the right to liberty which, in order to be consistent with the Convention, have to be prescribed by law.[29] Accordingly, the right to liberty might be limited because of detention following conviction by a court and lawful arrest (and there are further conditions for the detention/arrest to be consistent with the Convention); detention of a minor for educational supervision or lawful detention to bring her or him in front of the competent authority; lawful detention for medical purposes (to avoid the spreading of infectious diseases; or detention of mentally ill people, alcoholics and drug addicts and vagrants). Article 5 of the Convention also contains minimum procedural guarantees as well as the principle of compensation for unlawful detention. The explanations provide that Article 6 should be respected "in particular" in the exercise of Union competences in criminal matters (and by Member States when they implement Union measures adopted in that field).

Article 7 (II–67) provides for the right to respect for *private and family life, home and communications*. It reproduces the first sentence of Article 8 ECHR apart from using the word "communications" rather than "correspondence", so as to reflect technological

---

[28] Art.2(1) EC [1995 P] C 313/2 as amended by the Protocol amending the Europol Convention [2003] O.J. C2/01; *cf.* also Framework Decision 2002/629/JHA on combating trafficking in human beings [2002] O.J. L203/1 and Council Directive 2004/81 on the residence permit issued to third-country nationals who are victims of trafficking in human beings or who have been the subject of an action to facilitate illegal immigration, who co-operate with the competent authorities [2004] O.J. L261/19. The Directive does not apply to the UK, Ireland and Denmark.

[29] And in order to decide whether a derogation has been prescribed by law, the ECtHR has recourse to a substantial assessment aimed at guaranteeing the rule of law and dispose of any arbitrariness, e.g. *Amuur v France* (Appl. No.19776/92) (1996) 22 E.H.R.R. 533.

developments. Again, it is impossible to understand the scope of this provision without looking at the list of legitimate limitations contained in the Convention article. Thus public authorities can interfere with the right to privacy only in accordance with the law and for listed reasons (national security, public safety; economic well-being of the country; prevention of disorder and crime; protection of health, morals or the rights and freedoms of others); and the interference must in any event be limited to what is necessary in a democratic society. Article 8 ECHR has been broadly construed by the European Court of Human Rights to include rights as diverse as the right to have one's birth certificate modified following gender reassignment;[30] the right not to be separated from one's family;[31] the right not to be subject to surveillance, including audio and video surveillance;[32] and so on. In other words, Article 8 ECHR provides protection from any interference with one's private sphere, and therefore any such interference needs to be justified according to one of the listed grounds of derogation.[33]

Article 8 (II–68) provides for the right to the protection of **9–008** *personal data*, and is a new generation right (albeit implicit in the right to privacy)[34] deriving from the TEC and the data protection directives.[35] It provides that personal data have to be processed fairly, either for legitimate reasons provided by law or with the consent of the person concerned who shall also have access to such data and the right to have it rectified. It also provides for an independent authority that shall ensure compliance with these rules;

---

[30] e.g. *Goodwin v UK* (2005) 35 E.H.R.R. 18; the same right was recognised by the European Court of Justice in Case C–117/01 *K.B.* [2004] E.C.R. I–541, see above Ch.8, para.8–012. Sexuality is considered part of one's private sphere, e.g. *Smith and Grady v UK* (Appl. No.33895/96 and 33896/96) (2001) 31 E.H.R.R. 24.

[31] e.g. *Elsholz v Germany* (Appl. No. 25735/94) (2002) 34 E.H.R.R. 58; and *cf.* e.g. Case C–60/00 *Mary Carpenter* [2002] E.C.R. I–6279; Case C–413/99 *Baumbast and R* [2002] E.C.R. I–7091.

[32] e.g. *Vetter v France* (Appl. No.59842/00), judgment 31/5/05.

[33] The Community's commitment to the right to privacy might well be called into question by the Proposal for a Directive on the retention of data processed in connection with the provision of public electronic communication services and amending Directive 2002/58, COM(2005) 438 final. For a critical appraisal of the Commission's proposal COM(2005) (438 final) see Opinion of the European Economic and Social Committee on the proposal for a Directive on the retention of data processed in connection with the provision of public electronic communication services and amending Dir.2002/58, TEN/230; and Opinion of the Data Protection Supervisor on the proposal for a Directive on the retention of data processed in connection with the provision of public electronic communication services and amending Directive 2002/58, [2005] O.J. C298/1.

[34] e.g. *Rotaru v Romania* (Appl. No. 28341/95), judgment of 4/5/00; and see Joined Cases C–465/00 and C–138 and 139/01 *Rechnungshof v Osterreichischer Rundfunk* [2003] E.C.R. I–4989.

[35] Directive 95/46 on the protection of individuals with regard to the processing of personal data and on the free movement of such data [1995] O.J. L281; and Directive 2002/58 concerning the processing of personal data and the protection of privacy in the electronic communications sector [2002] O.J. L 201/37.

the Union has its own authority, the European Data Protection Supervisor.[36]

Article 9 (II–69) provides for the right to *marry and the right to found a family*, in accordance with national laws. It is a modernised version of Article 12 ECHR, which states that "men and women have a right to marry and to found a family". By severing the right to found a family from the right to marry, and omitting any reference of the sex of the partners, Article 9 seeks to leave open the door for recognition of other types of partnerships (such as civil partnerships) and for same-sex marriages.[37] Of course, for the time being, the definition and regulation of marriage is entirely for the Member States. However, Article 9 might still be relevant when the Member States implement Union/Community law. Thus, for example, it is not clear how the right in Article 9 will relate to the Residency Directive,[38] which does not impose on Member States any obligation to recognise civil partnerships contracted in another Member State unless there is a domestic equivalent. The Directive does, however, impose a duty to "facilitate" the entry of Union citizens' partners: refusing entry to a registered partner (without there being a public policy/security/health reason) could then be construed as an interference with Article 9 of the Charter that applies when Member States are implementing Union law.

Article 10 (II–70) provides for freedom of *thought, conscience and religion*, and the right to change belief or religion as well as the freedom to manifest, alone or with others, religion or belief "in worship, teaching, practice and observance". This provision corresponds to Article 9 ECHR, and therefore the limitations provided for therein apply also in relation to Article 10 of the Charter. Thus, those rights can be derogated from only when prescribed by law and to the extent to which a limitation is necessary in a democratic society in order to protect public safety, public order, health or morals and for the protection of the freedom of others. Article 10(2)

---

[36] The Community has entered into agreements with the United States to transfer passengers name records of all carriers operating to or through the US territory, see Council Decision 2004/496 and Commission Decision 2004/535; Parliament brought an action for annulment of these agreements on the grounds of, inter alia, breach of Art.8 ECHR. AG Léger found that the Commission's and the Council's decision should be annulled because of infringement of Directive 95/46 and wrong legal basis respectively; he found however that the agreement did not constitute a disproportionate interference with the right to privacy. The Court annulled the decisions because of lack of competence and wrong legal basis but it did not examine the fundamental rights issue. Case C–317/04 *Parliament v Council* and Case C–318/04 *Parliament v Commission* judgment of 30/05/06.

[37] The ECJ refused to equate the situation of a same-sex partnership to that of a marriage in Joined Cases C–122/99 and C–125/99 *D and Sweden v Council* [2001] E.C.R. I–4319.

[38] Directive 2004/38 on the right of citizens of the Union and their family members to move and reside freely within the territory of the Member States [2004] O.J. L229/35, Art.3 and see below Ch.17, para.17–08; even more problematic is Directive 2003/86 on the right to family reunification [2003] O.J. L251/12 which merely authorises Member States to allow long-term unmarried partners in the country for family reunification purposes (Art.4(3)).

provides for the "recognition" of the right of conscientious objection in accordance with national law. It is derived from national legislation and constitutional practices, and the use of the word "recognises" suggests that the right to conscientious objection is entirely dependent upon the right provided for in domestic contexts. Article 10 has been criticised because it fails to expressly recognise the right "not to hold a religious belief",[39] despite the fact that the European Court of Human Rights has recognised such right to be inherent in Article 9 ECHR.[40]

Article 11 (II–71) provides for the right to *freedom of expression* **9–009** *and information* which includes the right to hold opinions as well as to impart information and ideas without interference from public authorities. It corresponds to Article 10 ECHR and so any limitation to the right of expression must be prescribed by law and be limited to what is necessary in a democratic society for the protection of national security, territorial integrity, public safety, prevention of disorder and crime, protection of health and morals, reputation or rights of others (i.e. libel), for preventing breaches of confidence and for maintaining the authority and impartiality of the judiciary.[41] Freedom of expression entails any form (written, oral, artistic, pictorial, broadcasting, etc.) and type of expression: thus, it encompasses not only freedom of the press and the freedom to hold opinions, including political opinions, but also commercial expression (and advertising in particular).[42] The Court of First Instance (CFI) and the ECJ in the past have adjudicated on the matter in relation to publications of EU officials that the institutions considered prejudicial to the reputation of the EU.[43]

Article 11(2) provides that freedom and pluralism of the media shall be respected, a principle which, even though not expressly provided for in the ECHR, has been recognised as inherent in freedom of expression by both the European Court of Human Rights[44] and the ECJ.[45] Article 10 ECHR also recognises the possibility of licensing of broadcasting, televisions, and cinemas; the

---

[39] *cf.* Amnesty International Comments on the Draft Charter, CHARTE 4446/00, CONTRIB 300.

[40] *Buscarini v San Marino* (Appl. No.24645/95) (2000) 30 E.H.R.R. 208.

[41] On Art. 10 ECHR, *cf. Handyside v UK* (Appl. No.5493/72) (1970–80) 1 E.H.R.R. 737.

[42] In the Community context, see e.g. Case C–368/95 *Familiapress* [1997] E.C.R. I–3689.

[43] e.g. Case T–34/96 and T–163/96 *Connolly v Commission* [1999] E.C.R. II–463, [1999] ECR-SC I-A-87, upheld in Case C–274/99 P *Connolly v Commission* [2001] E.C.R. I–1611; T–82/99 *Cwick v Commission* [2000] E.C.R. II–713, upheld in Case C–340/00P *Commission v Cwick* [2001] E.C.R. I–10269; Art.17 of the Commission's Staff Regulations was amended in 2004 to guarantee a more effective right to freedom of expression (see new Art.17 and 17a which have substituted the system of prior authorisation for publication with a system of notification and silence/assent).

[44] e.g. *Informationsverein Lentia v Austria* (Appl. Nos 13914/88, 15041/89, 15717/89, 15779/89 and 17207/90) (1994) 17 E.H.R.R. 93.

[45] *cf. e.g.* Case C–288/89 *Gouda* [1991] E.C.R. I–4007, para.23; Case C–368/95 *Familiapress* [1997] E.C.R. I–3689, para.24.

explanations make clear that such possibility remains but shall be exercised consistently with EU competition law.[46]

Article 12 (II–72) provides for the right to freedom of *peaceful assembly* and to *freedom of association* at all levels,[47] and in particular in *political, trade union and civic matters*, which also implies the right for everyone to join trade unions.[48] This provision corresponds to Article 11 ECHR and therefore those rights can be limited only according to the Convention's derogations. As usual those must be prescribed by law, and be necessary in a democratic society in the interest of national security, public safety, the prevention of disorder or crime, the protection of health or morals; or for the protection of the rights and freedoms of others. Lawful restrictions can be imposed by members of the armed forces, the police or the administration of the State. Article 12(2) provides that "Political parties at Union level contribute to expressing the political will of the citizens of the Union".[49] This provision corresponds to Article 191 EC (and I–46(4) of the Constitutional Treaty), although the latter is phrased slightly differently, mentioning also the political parties' role in forming European political awareness.

9–010   Article 13 provides that the *arts and scientific research* shall be free of constraint and that *academic freedom* shall be respected. This right is not explicitly spelled out in the Convention, but it has always been interpreted as part of freedom of expression.[50] The explanations indicate that it must be exercised having regard to the principle of human dignity and it shall be subject to the same limitations as contained in Article 10 ECHR.

Article 14 provides for the *right to education*, and the right to have *access to vocational and continuing training*. This corresponds to the common constitutional traditions as well as to Article 2 of the first Protocol to the ECHR. The reference to vocational and continuing training is new to the Charter. Article 14(2) provides that the right to education includes the "possibility to receive free compulsory education". According to the explanations this provision means that compulsory education shall be provided free of charge by the State, and that children (and their parents) shall have the right to choose whether to take advantage of such education. Article 14(3) provides that the right to found educational establishments with due respect for democratic principles shall be recognised; the same goes for the right of the parents to choose their children's education in conformity with their religious, philosophical and pedagogical beliefs. This

---

[46] *cf. e.g.* Case C–260/89 *Elliniki Radiophonia Tiléorassi AE (ERT)* [1991] E.C.R. I–2925.
[47] *cf. e.g.* Case C–112/00 *Schmidberger* [2003] E.C.R. I–5659; Case C–415/93 *Bosman* [1995] E.C.R. I–4921, para.79.
[48] See also Art.28 below.
[49] *cf. e.g.* Case T–222/99 *Martinez v Parliament* [2001] E.C.R. II–2823.
[50] e.g. *Hertel v Switzerland* (Appl. No.25181/94) (1999) 28 E.H.R.R. 534; *Müller v Switzerland* (Appl. No.10737/84) (1991) 13 E.H.R.R. 485.

article is of limited importance given that the Union has only complementary/supplementary competences in the field of education.[51] Thus, it is mostly aimed at guaranteeing that the Union in its policies respects the principles enshrined in this article.

Article 15(1) (II–75) provides for the right to *engage in work* and to *pursue a freely chosen* or *accepted occupation*.[52] This right has been recognised by the European Court of Justice from the very first cases concerning fundamental rights protection: thus, in both *Nold* and *Hauer* the Court recognised that the Community protected the right to choose an occupation, even though that right was not unfettered and could be limited in the public interest provided the substance of the right was left untouched.[53]

Article 15(2) provides for the Union citizens' right to engage in an economic activity (either in an employed or self-employed capacity) and to seek work in any of the Member States; it reproduces existing economic free movement rights contained in Articles 39, 43 and 49 EC, and therefore, according to Article 52(2) Charter, must be exercised under the conditions and within the limits provided for in the TEC (or in the Constitutional Treaty as the case might be).[54]

The third paragraph of Article 15 provides that third country nationals who lawfully work in the Union are entitled to conditions of employment "equivalent" to those of Union citizens. In 2001, the Commission put forward a proposal relating to the conditions of employment for third country nationals which provided also for the right to equal treatment of lawfully resident third country nationals;[55] however, the Council failed to reach an agreement and the proposal was dropped. For the time being then Article 15(3) is of little relevance, but it constitutes nonetheless a very important statement of principle since it binds the Union to equal treatment should it legislate on the matter.[56]

Article 16 (II–76) provides for the recognition of the *freedom to* **9–011** *conduct a business* in accordance with Union law, and national law and practices. Articles 15 and 16 substantially deal with the freedom to exercise an economic activity, recognised in the case law of both European Courts as well as in national constitutional traditions. In

---

[51] Arts 149 and 150 EC.

[52] This right is not expressly included in the ECHR but the ECtHR has included the right to pursue economic activities in the right to property provided by Art.1 of the Protocol to the ECHR, *cf. Dogan v Turkey* (Appls. Nos 8803–11/02, 8813/02, 8815–19/02) (2005) 41 E.H.R.R. 15.

[53] Case 4/73 *Nold v Commission* [1974] E.C.R. I–491; Case 44/79 *Hauer* [1979] E.C.R. 3727; also e.g. Case 234/85 *Keller* [1986] E.C.R. I–2897.

[54] *cf.* relevant chapters on free movement.

[55] Proposal for a Council Directive on the conditions of entry and residence of third-country nationals for the purposes of paid employment and self-employed economic activities, COM (2001) 386 final, Art.11(1)(f).

[56] Of course, only when and if the Charter should become legally binding, although Commission and Parliament consider themselves already bound by it; see below, para.9–028.

assessing whether a limitation to those rights is justified (for instance a piece of secondary legislation that prohibits trade in a certain substance), the principle of proportionality is of particular importance.

Finally, Article 17 (II–77) provides for the right to *property* (long recognised by the ECJ),[57] and it substantially reproduces the provisions of Article 1(1) of the first Protocol to the ECHR,[58] including the possibility of expropriation on public interest grounds subject to due compensation.[59] Furthermore, the Charter adds an express recognition of intellectual property, which must be protected.[60] Article 17 also provides that the use of property can be *regulated* by law insofar as this is necessary for the general interest, thus codifying the case law of the ECJ[61] as well as common constitutional traditions and the case law of the European Court of Human Rights.[62]

As pointed out above, the Charter disposes of the traditional partition between civil and political rights on the one hand, and socio-economic rights on the other. Thus having dealt with economic freedoms, it leaps to the right to *asylum*.[63] Article 18 (II–78) provides that such a right shall be guaranteed with due respect of the rules of the Geneva Convention on refugees and in accordance with the (Constitutional) Treaty. Respect for the Geneva Convention is already a pre-condition for the exercise of Community competence under Title IV of Pt 3 TEC.[64] According to the Protocol on Asylum,[65] Member States' nationals cannot, as a matter of principle, obtain asylum in any of the Member States, since the Member States are satisfied that the level of fundamental rights protection within

---

[57] *cf.* Case 44/79 *Hauer* [1979] E.C.R. 3727.

[58] It is interesting to note that the Charter departs from the ECHR Protocol in not limiting the enjoyment of the right of property to "peaceful enjoyment" and not mentioning the general principles of international law. Art.1(2) of the Protocol explicitly provides for the right of the State to regulate property and to impose taxes, other contributions and penalties.

[59] For a recent discussion on the right to property, see Case C–84/95 *Bosphorus* [1996] E.C.R. I–3953, and Ch.8 above.

[60] *cf.* also Art.30 TEC.

[61] e.g. Case 44/79 *Hauer* [1979] E.C.R. 3727.

[62] e.g. *Mellacher v Austria* (Appl. Nos 10522/83, 10011/84, and 11070/84) (1990) 12 E.H.R.R. 391.

[63] *cf.* also Joint Position 96/196/JHA on the harmonised application of the definition of the term "refugee" in Art.1 of the Geneva Convention of July 28, 1951 relating to the status of refugees, [1996] O.J. L63/2; Council Directive 2003/9 laying down minimum standards for the reception of asylum seekers [2003] O.J. L31/18 (the UK has opted in this directive); Council Reg.343/2003 establishing the criteria and mechanisms for determining the Member State responsible for examining an asylum application lodged in one of the Member States by a third-country national [2003] O.J. L50/1 (the UK and Ireland have both opted in); and Council Directive 2005/85 on minimum standards on procedures for granting and withdrawing refugee status [2005] O.J. L326/13.

[64] It should be remembered that Ireland and the United Kingdom are not bound by measures adopted under Title IV TEC unless they decide on a case-by-case basis to opt in, and Denmark has opted out altogether from Title IV TEC. See Ch.4, para.4–024.

[65] Protocol on asylum for nationals of Member States of the EU, added by the Treaty of Amsterdam.

the Union is adequate and therefore each Member State constitutes a "safe country of origin" for asylum purposes. The only cases in which an asylum request from the national of a Member State can be taken into account is when (i) the Member State of origin is derogating from the ECHR pursuant to Article 15 ECHR; (ii) the procedure provided for in Article 6 TEU (procedure for serious and persistent breach of fundamental rights) has been initiated; (iii) the Council has determined the existence of a serious and persistent breach pursuant to Article 6 TEU; (iv) the Member State so decides unilaterally, in which case the Council shall be informed immediately and the application shall be dealt with on the basis of the presumption of being "manifestly unfounded" (although the receiving Member State retains the final decision on the matter).

Finally, Article 19 (II–79) provides for protection in the event of *removal, expulsion* and *extradition*. It prohibits collective expulsions, as well as deportation in cases in which there is a serious risk that the person removed would be subjected to the death penalty, or to torture or inhuman and degrading treatment or punishment. This is consistent with the prohibition of the death penalty contained in Article 2 and the prohibition on torture and inhuman treatment contained in Article 4, as well as with the case law of the European Court of Human Rights.[66] As a result the Union would not be able to enter into extradition agreements with countries which practise the death penalty, without inserting appropriate safeguards.[67]

Chapter III—Equality

Chapter III is concerned with equality, and accordingly Article 20 (II–80) provides that *everyone is equal before the law*. The principle of equality requires that comparable situations should be treated equally, and that non-comparable situations should be treated in different ways; it corresponds to established constitutional traditions in all of the Member States, and has been recognised by the case law of the ECJ.[68]   **9–012**

Article 21 (II–81) provides for the more general prohibition of *discrimination*. The provision contains a non-exhaustive list of prohibited grounds of discrimination, i.e. sex, race, colour, ethnic or

---

[66] e.g. *Soering v UK* (Appl. No.14038/88) (1989) 11 E.H.R.R. 439; in *D v UK* (Appl. No.30240/96) (1997) 24 E.H.R.R. 423, the ECtHR accepted the applicant's contention that his removal from the United Kingdom would constitute inhuman treatment prohibited by Art.3 ECHR since he was terminally ill with AIDS and he would not receive adequate treatment and care in his country of origin.

[67] *cf.* e.g. Art.13 of the Agreement on Extradition between the EU and the US (2003) O.J. L181/27. On the Union external competence under Title VI TEU (police and judicial co-operation in criminal matters) see Ch.10 below.

[68] e.g. Case 283/83 *Racke* [1984] E.C.R. 3791; Case C–15/91 *EARL* [1997] E.C.R. I–1961; Case C–292/97 *Karlsson* [2000] E.C.R. 2737; Case C–144/04 *Mangold* [2005] E.C.R. I–9981.

social origin, genetic features, language,[69] religion or belief,[70] political or any other opinion, membership of a national minority, property, birth, disability, age and sexual orientation.[71] It is thus slightly broader in scope than Art.13 EC (and III–124) which provides for competence to adopt measures intended to fight discrimination on grounds of sex, racial or ethnic origin, religion or belief, disability, age or sexual orientation.[72] Surprisingly, Article 21 does not explicitly mention gender discrimination, which is a broader concept than sex discrimination and encompasses in a clearer way also discrimination against transsexuals. Discrimination against transsexuals has been to a certain extent equated by the ECJ to sex discrimination and therefore Article 21, which in any case is not exhaustive,[73] prohibits also that type of discrimination. It could be argued however that, given that the Charter should make rights more visible to the citizen, it would have been appropriate for Article 21 to say so expressly.

Article 21(2) prohibits discrimination on grounds of nationality: however, like Art.12 EC, this applies only within the scope of the TEC/Constitution, and subject to the conditions contained therein; it is thus mainly a right pertaining to Union citizens.

Article 22 (II–82) requires the Union to respect *cultural, religious* and *linguistic* diversity. It is a very likely example of a "principle" which, according to the new version of Article 52 (II–112), is judicially cognisable only in interpreting acts of the Union institutions and acts of the Member States implementing Union law, and in assessing the validity of such acts. In other words Article 22, contrary to Article 21, does not constitute a free standing right.

9–013   Article 23 (II–83) provides for additional protection against *sex discrimination*: thus despite the fact that discrimination on grounds of sex is already prohibited by Article 21, Article 23 provides that "equality between women and men must be ensured in all areas, including employment, work and pay". This article is based on

---

[69] But in the field of employment conditions relating to linguistic knowledge required by the nature of the post are allowed, see Art.3 Reg.1612/68 on freedom of movement for workers within the Community (as amended) [1968] O.J. Sp. Ed. L257/2, and the Treaty does not prohibit a policy for the protection and the promotion of a language of a Member State, see Case 379/87 *Groener* [1989] E.C.R. 3967.

[70] See Case 130/75 *Prais v Council* [1976] E.C.R. 1589.

[71] Discrimination on grounds of sexual orientation was excluded from the scope of the prohibition on grounds of sex (and therefore from the scope of the Treaty) in Case C–249/96 *Grant v South West Trains Ltd* [1998] E.C.R. I–621. Following the adoption of Art.13 TEC and the ruling in Case C–144/04 *Mangold* [2005] E.C.R. I–9981, it is likely that discrimination on grounds of sexual orientation is now prohibited as a general principle of Community law. See Ch.7, para.7–017, above.

[72] Two directives have so far been adopted using the competence conferred in Art.13 TEC: Directive 2000/43 implementing the principle of equal treatment between persons irrespective of racial or ethnic origin [2000] O.J. L180/22; and Directive 2000/78 establishing a general framework for equal treatment in employment and occupation [2000] O.J. L303/16.

[73] Case C–13/94 *P v S Cornwall County Council* [1996] E.C.R. I–2143; Case C–117/01 *K.B.* [2004] E.C.R. I–541.

existing EC Treaty provisions, and in particular on Articles 2 and 3(2) EC, and on Article 141 EC.[74] Article 23 is broader in scope than Article 141 EC, since it applies also beyond the field of employment.

Article 23(2) provides that "the principle of equality shall not prevent the maintenance or the adoption of measures providing for *specific* advantages for the under-represented sex".[75] Therefore, consistently with Article 141(4) EC,[76] the Union and the Member States when implementing Union law are allowed to enact "positive discrimination" measures aimed at achieving substantive rather than just formal equality between the sexes. In the context of employment, the Court has imposed two conditions which must be satisfied if positive discrimination measures are to be compatible with the general principle of equality: such measures cannot give priority automatically and unconditionally to the under-represented sex; and they must also allow for an objective assessment of the specific personal situations of all candidates.[77] This is the case since such measures derogate from the (formal) principle of equality, and therefore have to comply with the principle of proportionality, i.e. remain within the limits of what is necessary to achieve the purported aim (substantive equality). Thus, for instance, a measure that provides that if men and women are equally qualified for a job precedence should be given to the woman if women are under-represented in that job, is inconsistent with Community law since it is "absolute" and "unconditional" in its application.[78] However, rules that provide that when women are under-represented and a woman and a man candidate are equally qualified, the woman shall be granted preferential treatment unless there are other considerations that might tilt the balance in favour of the male candidate, are compatible with the principle of equal treatment.[79] In other words, in order to be compatible with Community law, a positive discrimination policy must always allow for an objective assessment of the specific personal circumstances of all candidates. Since, as said

---

[74] Art.141 TEC has been implemented through Directive 76/207 on the implementation of the principle of equal treatment for men and women as regards access to employment, vocational training and promotion, and working conditions [1976] O.J. L39/40, as amended by Directive 2002/73 [2002] O.J. L269/15 (see in particular Art.2(8) previously 2(4)); and Arts I–3, III–116, III–214 of the Constitutional Treaty. See e.g. Case 43/75 *Defrenne v Sabena* (Defrenne II) [1976] E.C.R. 455, and Case C–50/96 *Deutsche Telekom AG v Lilli Schröder* [2000] E.C.R. I–743, where the Court clarified that the economic aim of sex equality is secondary to its social aim, which constitutes the expression of a "fundamental human right" (para.57). Discrimination on grounds of gender reassignment has been held to constitute discrimination on grounds of sex, see Case C–13/94 *P v S Cornwall County Council* [1996] E.C.R. I–2143 and Case C–117/01 *K.B.* [2004] E.C.R. I–541.
[75] Emphasis added.
[76] This provision was introduced with the Treaty of Amsterdam.
[77] *cf.* recently Case C–319/03 *Briheche* [2004] E.C.R. I–8807, esp paras 22–24.
[78] Case C–450/93 *Kalanke* [1995] E.C.R. I–3051.
[79] See Case C–158/97 *Badek* [2000] E.C.R. I–1875; and Case C–409/95 *Marschall* [1997] E.C.R. I–6363.

above, Article 23 partially reproduces existing TEC provisions, it must be exercised under the conditions and according to the limits provided therein. It could well be questioned whether Article 23 was really necessary: on the one hand, by singling out sex discrimination, it weakens the general prohibition on discrimination contained in Article 21. On the other hand, the relationship between Article 21 and Article 23 is made more difficult because, unlike Article 23, Article 21 does not contain a provision authorising "positive action". Such positive action, however, is authorised by the race and ethnic origin anti-discrimination directive,[80] and by the framework anti-discrimination directive.[81] The result is thus confusing, also given that the anti-discrimination directives pre-date both the completion and the proclamation of the Charter. Thus, it could be argued that the fact that the Charter refers to the possibility to enact positive measures to achieve substantive equality in relation only to sex discrimination precludes the possibility of enacting such measures in relation to other forms of discrimination (and eventually would even invalidate the positive action clauses in the directives). Or, which is preferable and consistent with existing case law,[82] it could be argued that Article 23(2) is redundant since the principle of equal treatment must always be interpreted as aimed at achieving substantive and not only formal equality.[83]

9–014   Article 24 provides for the *rights of the child*. Article 24(1) provides that children "shall have the right to such protection and care as it is necessary for their well-being. They may express their views freely. Such views shall be taken into consideration on matters which concern them in accordance to their age and maturity". Article 24(2) lays down the general principle that public authorities and private institutions must take the child's best interests as the primary consideration. Article 24(3) provides that children shall have a right to maintain a personal relationship and contact with both parents, unless that is contrary to the child's interests. Whilst family law falls primarily within the competence of the Member States, this article is relevant in relation to cases of cross-border divorce, i.e. when the parents end up living in different countries.[84] In relation to Union citizenship, the Court has already found that a third country

---

[80] Directive 2000/43 implementing the principle of equal treatment between persons irrespective of racial or ethnic origin [2000] O.J. L180/22.

[81] Directive 2000/78 establishing a general framework for equal treatment in employment and occupation [2000] O.J. L303/16.

[82] The ECJ has accepted the compatibility of positive action with equal treatment even before the Amsterdam Treaty entered into force, see Case C–409/95 *Marschall* [1997] E.C.R. I–6363.

[83] See generally Ellis *EU Anti-Discrimination Law* (OUP, 2005); Fredman *Discrimination law* (OUP, 2001).

[84] See also Council Reg.2201/2003 concerning jurisdiction and the recognition and enforcement of judgments in matrimonial matters and the matters of parental responsibility, repealing Regulation (EC) No.1347/2000, [2003] O.J. L338/1.

national who is the primary carer of a Union citizen who has not reached the age of majority and who has the right to reside in the host-Member State, derives a right to reside in the same State from his or her child.[85] The Charter provision is broader since it refers to the right of the child to maintain contact with both parents, and not only with the carer. As a result, Article 13 of Directive 2004/34 which provides for the right to reside of the divorced spouse/separated partner, needs to be interpreted having regard to the child's right to have a relationship and direct contact also with the parent who is not the primary carer.

Article 25 deals with the *rights of the elderly*, and provides that the Union recognises and respects the rights of the elderly to lead a life of "dignity and independence and to participate in social and cultural life". According to the explanations, this is a mere principle rather than a free standing right; however, as we saw in Chapter 7, the right not to be discriminated against on grounds of age has been elevated to the status of general principle of Community law by the ECJ.[86]

Article 26 provides for the *integration of persons with disabilities*, according to which the "Union recognises and respects the right of people with disabilities to benefit from measures designed to ensure their independence, social and occupational integration and participation in the life of the community". The explanations to the Charter (as modified by the Constitutional Treaty) clarify that Article 26 constitutes a principle rather than a right.

Chapter IV—Solidarity

Chapter IV is concerned with solidarity, and most of the rights **9–015** listed therein are in fact "principles" that must inspire the Union's legislative action rather than free-standing rights. The new version of Article 52 (II–112) clarifies that in the case of "principles", judicial proceedings can be brought only to challenge Union action, or its implementation by the Member States, on the grounds that the Union/implementing Member State failed to comply with one of the stated principles. Solidarity rights are in most cases merely aspirational, i.e. they are not free-standing rights. Most of the rights/principles listed in this part derive from the European Social Charter, like the ECHR an instrument of the Council of Europe,[87] and from the Community charter on the rights of workers, a soft law instrument adopted through a declaration by all of the Member States.[88]

---

[85] e.g. Case C–413/99 *Baumbast and R* [2002] E.C.R. I–7091; Case C–200/02 *Chen* [2004] E.C.R. I–9925, see Ch.17 below.

[86] Case C–144/04 *Mangold* [2005] E.C.R. I–9981.

[87] The ECtHR does not have jurisdiction over the Social Charter, and the mechanisms for enforcement are different from those relating to the ECHR.

[88] Originally the United Kingdom did not sign up to the Charter; however it did so in 1998.

Article 27 (II–87) provides for the *workers' right to information and consultation* within the undertaking. The Charter does not detail the extent of the workers' right to be informed, rather referring to Union law and national laws and practices. There is an extensive body of Community secondary legislation which provides for the workers' right to consultation, and the basic principle is that workers (or their representatives) should be informed and/or consulted in relation to all events relating to the undertaking that might have an impact on the workers' employment situation. Those events include: the economic situation and the development of the undertaking; structural developments and changes especially when there is a threat to employment or when it is likely that there are going to be substantial changes in the organisation of the work or in contractual relations;[89] when there is a transfer of undertaking;[90] or when the employer is contemplating collective redundancies.[91] Generally speaking, the promotion of dialogue between employers and labour, of which the Union secondary legislation is clearly an expression, is one of the aims of the European Community social policy (Article 136 EC), and Article 137 EC expressly confers on the Community complementary competence in relation to information and consultation of workers.[92]

Article 28 (II–88) provides for the right of *collective bargaining and action*: thus workers and employers have the right to negotiate and enter into collective agreements as well as the right to collective action, including the right to strike. Those rights must be exercised in accordance with Union and national law, and it is the latter which regulates the conditions for the right to strike; thus, for the time being this provision is directly relevant only in relation to the Union

---

[89] Council Directive 2002/14 establishing a general framework for informing and consulting employees in the European Community [2002] O.J. L80/29. In relation to Community scale undertakings and Community scale groups of undertakings, see Directive 94/45 on the establishment of European Works Council or a procedure in Community-scale undertakings or Community-scale groups of undertakings for the purposes of informing and consulting employees [1994] O.J. L254/64, and Case C–440/00 *Kühne and Nagel* [2004] E.C.R. I–887. The ECtHR has held that Art.11 ECHR (freedom of association) encompasses a right for trade unions to be heard, but not the right for trade unions to be treated in a particular way and leaves it to the Member States to decide the means by which to secure the right to be heard; see *National Union of Belgian Police v Belgium* (Appl. No.4464/70), (1979–80) 1 E.H.R.R. 578.

[90] *cf.* Art.7 Directive 2001/23 on the approximation of the laws of the Member States relating to the safeguarding of employees' rights in the event of transfer of undertakings, business, or parts of undertakings or business [2001] O.J. L82/16.

[91] Directive 98/59 on the approximation of the laws of the Member States relating to collective redundancies [1998] O.J. L225/16; on the extent to which the trade unions must be involved in those circumstances see e.g. Case C–383/92 *Commission v UK* [1994] E.C.R. I–2435.

[92] See Ch.4 above.

institutions' duties as employers.[93] Whilst the right to strike is not recognised explicitly by the ECHR (since this is concerned with civil and political rights), Article 11 on freedom of association recognises the right to form and join trade unions,[94] and the European Court Human Rights has recognised that, at least to a certain extent, the right to strike is inherent in Article 11.[95] Furthermore the right to collective bargaining and action are also recognised by the European Social Charter, the Community Social Charter,[96] several International Labour Organisation instruments,[97] as well as several of the national constitutions.[98] The right to take collective action might interfere with other Community fundamental rights and, in particular, with the free movement provisions.[99]

Article 29 (II–89) provides for *free access to placement services.* **9–016** The right to placement services, based on existing provisions of the European and Community Social Charters,[1] is seen as a condition for the effective exercise of the right to work and in order to increase workers' mobility (and their chances of finding employment) the Commission has established the European Employment Services (EURES),[2] a network for the exchange of information in relation to employment services aimed at increasing workers' mobility.[3] There has been considerable debate as to whether such right should have been included in a fundamental rights Charter, and indeed it is not clear that this can be really defined as a free-standing right rather than a principle.

[93] *cf.* on the right to strike against Community institutions, Joined Cases 44, 46 and 49/74 *M.L. Acton v Commission* [1975] E.C.R. 383; Joined Cases T–576 to 582/93 *M. Browet v Commission* [1994] E.C.R. II–677, IA–191. On the rights of trade unions see Case T–349/00 *Lebedef v Commission* [2001] E.C.R. II–1031, IA–225, where the CFI annulled the new operational rules because one of the trade unions had been left out of the negotiations. See also Case T–191/02 *Lebedef v Commission* judgment of 12/4/05, not yet reported. (Appealed Case C–265/05P, not yet decided).

[94] And the Member States' positive obligation to protect those rights include an obligation to prohibit employers from providing financial incentives to employees who forfeit their right to be represented by trade unions; see *Wilson and National Union of Journalists v UK* (Appl. No.30668/96, 30671/96, 30678/96) [2002] 35 E.H.R.R. 20.

[95] *Schmidt and Dahlström v Sweden* (Appl. No.5589/72) [1978–9] 1 E.H.R.R. 632.

[96] Art.6 and paras 12–14 respectively.

[97] e.g. ILO Declaration on Fundamental Principles and Rights at Work, June 1998.

[98] e.g. Art.39 of the Italian Constitution; Art.27 of the Czech Constitution; Art.28 of the Spanish Constitution; para.8 and 9 of the Preamble to the French Constitution; Art.54 of the Portuguese Constitution.

[99] Case C–438/05 *International Transport Workers' Federation and The Finnish Seamen's Union v Viking Line et al*, case pending; and see the ruling of the Court of Appeal which referred the case to the ECJ, *Viking v ITWF* [2006] 1 C.M.L.R. 27 (on the interim relief issue).

[1] Art.1(3) European Social Charter; point 13 of the Community Charter of the Fundamental Social Rights of Workers.

[2] Commission Decision 93/569 on the implementing of Council Regulation (EEC) No.1612/68 on freedom of movement for workers within the Community as regards, in particular, the clearance of vacancies and applications for employment, establishing a network entitled Eures (European Employment Services) [1993] O.J. L274/32.

[3] See EURES Charter, (2003) O.J. C106/03.

Article 30 (II–90) provides for the right to *protection in the event of unjustified dismissal*; this right must be exercised in accordance with Union and national laws. Article 30 thus provides that the worker has a right to a judicial remedy, i.e. the right to review, as well as the right to compensation or reinstatement, in relation to unjustified dismissal. This right is enshrined in several of the workers' protection directives.[4]

Article 31 (II–91) provides for the right to *fair and just working conditions*. This encompasses the right to working conditions that respect health, safety and dignity of the worker, as provided in Directive 89/391 on safety and health at work;[5] and the right to maximum working hours, the right to daily and weekly rest periods, and the right to an annual period of paid leave, as guaranteed by the working time Directive.[6] The right to dignity at work encompasses the right not to be harassed, especially, but not only, sexually and racially (also provided by the relevant Community secondary legislation),[7] as well as the right not to be discriminated against.

Article 32 (II–92) deals with the rights of children and young people in the context of employment. Thus, it lays down a general prohibition of *child labour*, and establishes that the minimum age for admission to employment should not be lower than the minimum school leaving age, except for limited derogations. Directive 94/33 on the protection of young people at work[8] provides that in any event the minimum age for work shall be no less than 15 (or higher if the leaving school age is higher), although Member States may provide for limited exception for children of at least 14 and 13 years of age (Art. 4). The derogations concern employment for the purposes of cultural, sporting or advertising activities. Article 32(2) provides for the protection of *young people at work*; thus minors admitted to work need to be afforded working conditions appropriate to their age and need to be protected against economic exploitation as well as from any work which would harm their safety, their health or their

---

[4] e.g. Directive 2001/23 relating to the safeguarding of employees' rights in the event of transfers of undertakings, business or parts of undertakings or businesses [2001] O.J. L82/16.

[5] Directive 89/391 on the introduction of measures to encourage improvements in the safety and health of workers at work [1989] O.J. L183/1; see also Communication from the Commission "Adapting to Change in Work and Society: A New Community Strategy on Health and Safety at Work 2002–2006" COM(2002) 118 final.

[6] Directive 2003/88 concerning certain aspects of the organisation of working time (which repealed Directive 93/104) [2003] O.J. L299/9.

[7] See Directive 2000/43 implementing the principle of equal treatment between persons irrespective of racial or ethnic origin [2000] O.J. L180/22, Art.2(3); and Dir.2000/78 establishing a general framework for equal treatment in employment and occupation [2000] O.J. L303/16, Art.2(3); Directive 76/207 on the implementation of the principle of equal treatment for men and women as regards access to employment, vocational training and promotion, and working conditions [1976] O.J. L39/40, as amended by Directive 2002/73 [2002] O.J. L269/15, Art.2(2) third indent.

[8] Directive 94/33 on the protection of children at work [1994] O.J. L216/12.

physical, mental, moral or social development or interfere with their education. Article 32 might be relevant in informing the Union's external policy: thus for instance the Union provides for a system of bonus tariffs for developing countries which respect given ILO Conventions, including Convention 138 on minimum age for work.[9]

Article 33 (II–93) provides for the right to *family and professional life*, and it states that the family shall enjoy legal, economic and social protection. Paragraph 2 details this by providing that, in order to reconcile family and professional life, everyone has the right to protection from dismissal for reasons connected with maternity, as well as the right to paid maternity leave and to parental leave following the birth or adoption of a child. This maternity and parental protection is based on existing Community legislation;[10] it should be remembered that dismissal on grounds of pregnancy constitutes direct discrimination on grounds of sex and therefore is also prohibited by Articles 21 and 23.[11] Parental leave is available to men as well as women, although it does not need to be paid. It is interesting to note that the Ombudsman relied also on this provision of the Charter to initiate an investigation on the Commission's failure to provide for parental leave.[12] **9–017**

Article 34 (II–94) provides for the right to *social security and social assistance*. Article 34(1) provides for the recognition of entitlement to several social security benefits, whilst Article 34(2) provides that everyone (i.e. not only Union citizens) residing and moving legally within the Union is entitled to social benefits and social advantages. Union migrant workers are entitled to social advantages and benefits at the same level as host-citizens and are also entitled to export some social security benefits to the Member State where they move to so as not to lose entitlement because of migration.[13] As for third country nationals, as we saw above the Council was unable to agree

---

[9] Reg.1154/98 applying the special incentive arrangements concerning labour rights and environmental protection provided for in Arts 7 and 8 of Regulation No.3281/94 and 1256/96 applying multiannual schemes of generalised tariff preferences in respect of certain industrial and agricultural products originating in developing countries [1998] O.J. L160/1; on the possible problems arising from imposing Charter values in the EU external policies see Wouters "The EU Charter of Fundamental Rights—Some Reflections on its External Dimension" (2001) MJ 3; and more generally Bartels *Human Rights Conditionality in the EU's International Agreements* (OUP, 2005); and Alston (ed.) *The EU and Human Rights* (OUP, 1999), esp. sections F and G.

[10] See Directive 92/85 on the introduction of measures to encourage improvements in the safety and health of work of pregnant workers and workers who have recently given birth or are breast-feeding [1992] O.J. L348/91; Directive 96/34 on the framework agreement on parental leave concluded by UNICE, CEEP and ETUC [1996] O.J. L145/4.

[11] See e.g. Case 177/88 *Dekker* [1990] E.C.R. I–394; Case C–32/93 *Webb* [1994] E.C.R. I–3567; and also Art.2(7) Directive 76/207, as amended by Directive 2002/73.

[12] See European Ombudsman press release 19/2001, and decision OI/4/2001/ME.

[13] See Reg.1408/71on the application of social security schemes to employed persons, to self-employed persons and to members of their families, as amended Consolidated text in Annex A Regulation 118/97 [1997] O.J. L28/1; the Regulation will soon be replaced by Reg.883/2004 on the co-ordination of social security systems [2004] O.J. L166/1.

on the Commission's proposal that would have, *inter alia*, extended to legally resident and working non-Union citizens the right not to be discriminated against in relation to social security provision.[14] However, following the adoption of Regulation 859/2003 third country nationals who move from one Member State where they are lawfully resident to another Member State (or in situations where there is a cross-border element) are also covered by Regulation 1408/71.[15]

Article 34(3) recognises the right to social assistance and housing, so as to ensure a "decent existence for those who lack sufficient resources"; this right is to be exercised in accordance with Union and national law. As we shall see in Chapter 17, Union citizens who are not economically active are entitled to draw on the social assistance system of a Member State other than that of their nationality only to a limited extent.

9–018   Article 35 (II–95) provides for the right to *health care* and states that everyone has the right to access preventive health care and medical treatment under the conditions established by national law and practices. It should be recalled that Article 152(4)(c) EC excludes the possibility of harmonising measures intended to protect and improve health,[16] limiting the Community's competence to incentive measures. Thus, the first part of Article 35 is of very limited application, and might be primarily relevant in the interpretation of Article 22 Regulation 1408/71 that provides for a qualified right to seek health treatment in a Member State other than that where the person concerned is insured. The second part of the same article reproduces Article 152(1) EC by providing that a high level of health protection shall be ensured in the definition and implementation of all health policies.[17]

Article 36 (II–96) recognises *access to services of general economic interest* as provided by national law and practices and in accordance with the Treaty, in order to promote the social and territorial cohesion of the Union. This provision draws on Article 16 EC which also provides that Member States and the Community shall take care

---

[14] See Commission's proposal for a Council Directive on the conditions for entry and residence of third country nationals for the purposes of paid employment and self-employment economic activities, COM(2001) 386 final, Art.11. This said, most of the Member States already provide for equal benefits for lawful workers/self-employed.

[15] Reg.859/2003, [2003] O.J. L124/1 which however does not apply to Denmark; the Danish, and UK / Ireland opt out create some problems of co-ordination with the Charter. Reg.859/2003 was an indirect result of the case *Gaygusuz v Austria* (Appl. No.17371/90) (1997) 23 E.H.R.R. 364.

[16] This does not mean that Community law does not impact on health care provision; apart from Art.22 Reg.1408/71, the Court has interpreted Art.49 EC as granting a (limited) right to seek treatment abroad at the expenses of the State of origin, e.g. Case C–157/99 *Geraets-Smits* and *Peerbooms v Stichting* [2001] E.C.R. I–5473; Case C–385/99 *Müller Fauré* and *van Riet* [2003] E.C.R. I–4509; and Case C–372/04 *Watts*, judgment of 16/5/06, not yet reported. See Ch.19 below.

[17] See Commission Communication on the Precautionary Principle, COM (2000) 1 final.

that "such services operate on the basis of principles and conditions which enable them to fulfil their mission". Services of general economic interest include postal and telecommunication services, water and electricity, transportation services etc. It should be noted that Article 36 does not provide a right to such services: rather, like Article 16 EC, it is aimed at informing Community/Union policy and at ensuring that liberalisation of such services does not come at the expenses of citizens' access to them.

Article 37 (II–97) provides that a *high level of environmental protection* and the improvement of the environment must be integrated into the policies of the Union and ensured in accordance with the principle of sustainable development. This provision is based on existing EC provisions, in particular Article 174, and, like the preceding two articles, is a good example of a "principle", i.e. it is not a free-standing right but is "judicially cognisable" only in assessing the validity of Community secondary legislation and Member States' implementing measures.

Finally, Article 38 (II–98) provides that Union policies shall ensure a *high level of consumer protection*. This "principle" draws on Article 153 EC. The inclusion of the provisions relating to services of general economic interest, environmental protection and consumer protection in a fundamental rights document has been criticised as not relevant to such document. Thus, it could be argued that the main interests that those articles seek to achieve are already protected elsewhere in the TEC; and that a repetition is confusing and, in many respects, misleading since those principles are of very limited application as far as citizens are concerned.[18] As we have seen, this is a criticism that applies throughout the Charter. It is all the more disappointing, however, that mere policy aims should be stated alongside fundamental social rights.

Chapter V—Citizens' rights

Chapter V deals with Union citizens' rights. It reproduces existing **9–019** rights contained in the TEC, in secondary legislation or emerging from the Court's case law. Those rights are dealt with extensively in Chapter 17; for this reason it is sufficient to provide a brief list of the rights contained in Charter. The latter lists as citizens' rights: electoral rights (right to vote and stand as a candidate at elections of the European Parliament and at municipal elections);[19] rights to good administration (good administration, access to documents,

---

[18] Not least because of the restrictive rules on standing; the requirement to prove individual concern makes it impossible to bring actions at Community level for the protection of diffuse interests, such as environmental protection; *cf.* Case T–585/93 *Greenpeace* [1995] E.C.R. II–2205 upheld in appeal Case C–321/95 P *Greenpeace* [1998] E.C.R. I–1651.

[19] Arts 39 and 40.

European ombudsman, right to petition);[20] rights to free movement and residence;[21] and the right to diplomatic and consular protection.[22] Those rights have the same scope as the TEC rights.

Chapter VI—Justice

9–020   Chapter VI deals with rights concerning the administration of justice. It draws primarily on the ECHR, the common constitutional traditions and the case law of the European Court of Justice.

Article 47 (II–107) provides for the right to *an effective remedy and to a fair trial*, and is based on Articles 6 and 13 of the ECHR.[23] Consistently with the Charter's scope, its application is limited to violation of rights and freedoms guaranteed by Union law, and it provides that in relation to the latter, everyone has the right to an effective remedy before a tribunal (which is here used in the continental sense of any court of law, not in the more limited English sense). The explanations to the Charter make clear that this article does not "intend" to change the system of judicial review laid down in the Treaty (Article 230 EC) and in particular the rules on standing. As we shall see in Chapter 13, those are rather strict. The Constitutional Treaty provides for a relaxation of the rules on standing in relation to acts which do not require national implementation, where it might be therefore almost impossible for individuals to challenge the validity of a Community measure in front of a national court.[24] However, since the Constitutional Treaty has failed so far to come into force, there is a (recognised) gap in fundamental rights protection when Community legislation cannot be challenged in any court of law. It could therefore be argued that, if the Charter came into force and maybe even regardless of that, the ECJ should change its case law so as to ensure the right to an effective remedy, at least in those situations where access to a national court is not possible or is excessively difficult.

Article 47(2) provides for the right to a fair and public hearing within a reasonable time, by an independent tribunal previously established by law, and for the right to be advised, defended and represented. This is a codification of existing case law, since the ECJ has been called several times, especially in competition law proceedings,[25] to adjudicate as to the compatibility of the Community system

---

[20] Arts 41 to 44.

[21] Art.45.

[22] Art.46.

[23] The right to an effective remedy has been long recognised by the Court, especially in relation to national rules implementing Community legislation or national rules relating to rights conferred by Community law; e.g. Case 222/84 *Johnston v Chief Constable of Royal Ulster* [1986] E.C.R. 1651; Case 222/86 *Heylens* [1987] E.C.R. 4097.

[24] See e.g. Case T–177/01 *Jégo-Quéré* [2002] E.C.R. II–2365, reversed in Appeal Case C–263/02 P, [2004] E.C.R. I–3425; and Case C–50/00 P *UPA* [2002] E.C.R. I–6677. In relation to the second and third pillar the problem is even more pronounced, see above Ch.8, para.8–013.

[25] See para.8–013, Ch.8 above; e.g. Case C–185/95 P *Baustahlgewebe v Commission* [1998] E.C.R. I–8417.

of judicial protection with the principles of a fair trial. However, and as we saw in the previous chapter, there are open questions regarding the extent to which some of the features of the Union institutional framework satisfy the standard required to guarantee the right to effective judicial protection. This might be the case for the role of the Commission in administering heavy fines for breaches of competition law; for the lack of a right to respond to the Advocate General's opinion in direct proceedings; and more importantly in relation to measures adopted in the field of Common Foreign and Security Policy, or as a result of it, and in the field of police and judicial co-operation in criminal matters, where the jurisdiction of the Court is more limited if not altogether excluded.[26]

Article 47(3) provides that "legal aid shall be made available for **9–021** those who lack sufficient resources insofar as such aid is necessary to ensure effective access to justice". Article 94 of the rules of procedure of the CFI provides that legal aid shall be granted to those who, because of their economic circumstances, are unable to meet wholly or in part the costs of the procedure, unless the action is manifestly unfounded or manifestly inadmissible.[27] The application for legal aid suspends the effluxion of time for bringing an action, and the decision as to the availability of legal aid is taken by the President of the Court by means of an order, which cannot be appealed. For proceedings before the ECJ the decision concerning legal aid is taken by a formation of the Court after having heard the Advocate General and the Judge Rapporteur's proposal. The Court decides by means of an order and takes into consideration whether there is "manifestly no cause of action".[28] Since the Charter applies to Member States when they implement Union/Community law, legal aid shall be available as a matter of Union law in relation to litigation concerning Member States' implementation of Directives and Regulations, as well as in relation to cross-border litigation following the adoption of Directive 2003/8.[29]

Article 48 (II–108) provides for the *presumption of innocence and right of defence*, according to which a person charged shall be presumed innocent until proved guilty according to law, and for the rights of the defence of anyone who has been charged.[30] It draws on Article 6(2) and (3) of the ECHR, and accordingly must be construed as encompassing the guarantees contained therein. Thus,

---

[26] See para.8–013, Ch.8 above.

[27] Arts 94 *et seq.* of the CFI Rules of Procedure.

[28] Art.76 of the ECJ rules of procedure.

[29] Council Directive 2003/8 to improve access to justice in cross-border disputes by establishing minimum common rules relating to legal aid for such disputes [2003] O.J. L26/41. The Directive appeared as Directive 2002/8 but a corrigendum ([2003] O.J. L32/15) rectified the mistake.

[30] The presumption of innocence applies also to competition law proceedings; *cf. e.g.* Joined Cases T–67/00, T–68/00, T–71/00, T–78/00 *JFE Engineering v Commission* [2004] E.C.R. II–2501, esp. para.178.

according to Article 6(3) everyone charged shall have, as minimum rights, the right to be informed promptly and in a language she or he understands of the nature and cause of the accusation against her/ him; to have adequate time and facilities for the preparation of her/ his defence; to defend him/herself in person or through legal assistance (and to have legal aid as detailed above); to have witnesses against her/him cross-examined as well as to have the right to have witnesses on his/her behalf give evidence under the same conditions as witnesses against him/her; and to have an interpreter free of charge when she/he cannot understand or speak the language used in court. These are minimum procedural rights,[31] and national legislation would often provide for a more generous regime. Given that, at least for the time being, the Union does not have direct criminal competence (i.e. it does not have the power to prosecute and adjudicate on individuals' criminal liability) Article 49 is relevant for assessing the validity of legislative acts of the Union[32] and of the Member States when they prosecute individuals as a result of breaches of measures implementing Union law.[33]

Article 49 (II–109) provides for the *principles of legality and proportionality of criminal offences and penalties*. Article 49(1) states that no one can be held guilty of a criminal offence which was not a crime at the time it was committed (*nullum crimen sine lege*);[34] that the penalty cannot be heavier than that which was applicable at the time when the offence was committed;[35] and that if after the commission of a criminal offence the law provides for a lighter penalty then that penalty shall be applicable (this principle is not contained in the ECHR).[36] Article 49(2) provides that that article

---

[31] See also Commission Proposal for a Council Framework Decision on certain procedural rights in criminal proceedings throughout the EU, COM(2004) 328 final, and the European Parliament's amendments (A6–0064/2005 Final).

[32] e.g. Case C–303/05 *Advocaten voor de Wereld*, case pending, in which the Belgian Court of Arbitration is enquiring, *inter alia*, as to the compatibility of Framework Decision 2002/584/JHA on the European Arrest Warrant [2002] O.J. L190/1 with Art.6(2) ECHR insofar as the Framework decision disposes of the requirement of double criminality (i.e. the principle according to which in cases of extradition the offence must be a criminal offence in both the requesting and requested State).

[33] Even though there is no competence under the first pillar to adopt measures in the field of criminal law, a Community measure might require Member States to impose a criminal sanction for breaches of the obligations imposed in Community law, at least in the field of environmental law. See Case C–176/03 *Commission v Council* (Criminal liability for offences against the environment) [2005] E.C.R. I–7879, and Ch.4.

[34] And, accordingly, a Directive cannot be interpreted in a way that would create or aggravate criminal liability; see e.g. Case 80/86, *Kolpinghuis* [1987] E.C.R. 3969; Joined Cases C–387/02, C–391/02 and C–403/02 *Berlusconi* [2005] E.C.R. I–3565, and above, Ch.5.

[35] The Commission is bound by the principle of non-retroactivity of criminal sanctions when acting in its administrative capacity in competition law proceedings; however, that principle does not prevent it from raising the level of fines after the behaviour has taken place, *cf.* Case T–64/02 *Dr Hans Heubach GmbH & Co. KG v Commission* judgment of 29/11/05, not yet reported. Were the fines to be qualified as criminal penalties this would not be possible.

[36] Advocate General Kokott found that this was a general principle of Community law in Joined Cases C–387/02, C–391/02 and C–403/02 *Berlusconi* [2005] E.C.R. I–3565, Opinion paras 154 *et seq.*; the Court did not examine the issue.

does not prejudice trial and punishment for crimes that when committed were criminal according to the general principles recognised by the community of nations. Thus, like Article 7(2) ECHR, this exception allows for the prosecution of crimes against humanity. Article 49(3) provides that "the severity of penalties must not be disproportionate to the criminal offence", and it is an expression of the general principle of proportionality that applies in all areas of Community law as well as to Member States when implementing or acting within the scope of Community law.[37] The Court has held that the principle of proportionality also applies in relation to Member States' penalties for breaches of rules in any way connected with the exercise of Treaty rights.[38]

Article 50 (II–110) provides for the right not to be *tried or punished twice* in criminal proceedings for an offence for which one has already been finally acquitted or convicted within the Union in accordance with the law.[39] It is the so-called *"ne bis in idem"* rule codified in Article 4 of Protocol No.7 of the ECHR which allows for the reopening of the case if there is new evidence or newly discovered facts or if there has been a fundamental defect in the previous proceedings which could affect the outcome of the case.

The horizontal provisions: interpretation and scope of application of the Charter

Chapter VII contains the general provisions on the interpretation and application of the Charter (commonly referred to as horizontal provisions). Chapter VII is, legally speaking, the most complex part of the Charter, and the horizontal provisions have been criticised because of their lack of clarity. The aim of the drafters was to ensure that the Charter would not be used to encroach on Member States' competence and that the balancing exercise inherent in such matters would not be relocated in the hands of the ECJ when the Member States were merely acting within the scope of Union law. The result   9–022

---

[37] Thus penalties provided by Community law must be proportionate, e.g. Case C–356/97 *Molkereigenossenschaft Wiedergeltingen* [2000] E.C.R. I–5461.

[38] e.g. Case C–265/88 *Messner* [1989] E.C.R. 4209; Case C–193/94 *Skanavi and Chrysanthakopoulos* [1996] E.C.R. I–929, paras 35–38; Case C–29/95 *Pastoors* [1997] E.C.R. I–285.

[39] In Union law the principle is provided in several pieces of legislation; e.g. Arts 3 and 4 of Council Framework Decision 2002/584/JHA on the European arrest warrant and the surrender procedure between Member States, [2002] O.J. L190/1; Arts 54 to 58 of the Schengen Convention; and see Case C–187/01 *Gözütok* [2005] E.C.R. I–1345 and Case C–469/03 *Miraglia* [2005] E.C.R. I–2009. The *ne bis in idem* principle applies beyond the confines of criminal law; thus for instance it applies also to competition law proceedings; cf Joined Cases T–305/94, T–306/94, T–307/94, T–313/94, T–314/94, T–315/94, T–316/94, T–318/94, T–325/94, T–328/94, T–329/94 and T–335/94 *Limburgse Vinyl Maatschappij NV v Commission* [1999] E.C.R. II–931; and to Commission's proceedings for infringement of Community law against Member States, Case C–416/02 *Commission v Spain* [2005] E.C.R. I–7487.

is far from satisfactory, highlighting a degree of political schizo-phrenia in relation to fundamental rights policy which results in a dichotomy in the sources of fundamental rights: when the Member States implement Union law, the applicable standard would be the Charter. However, when the Member States act within the field of Community law, the applicable standard would be that of the general principles. The Constitutional Treaty introduced some amendments to the horizontal provisions: it is a matter of debate whether those changes were necessary, or whether they were politi-cally motivated. We will look at the original provisions as well as at the amendments introduced by the Constitutional Treaty.

Article 51—field of application

9–023   According to Article 51 (II–111) the Charter is addressed to the EU's institutions, bodies (offices and agencies),[40] with due regard to the principle of subsidiarity and to the Member States only when they *implement* Union law. Union and Member States shall respect the rights, observe the principles and promote the application of the Charter in accordance with their respective powers (and respecting the limits of the Union's powers as conferred by the TEU/Constitutional Treaty). The second paragraph, as reinforced by the Constitution, provides that the Charter does not extend the field of application of Union law beyond the powers of the Union or establish any new power or task for the Union, or modify powers and tasks defined in the Treaties/Constitutional Treaty. It is clear that the main worry of the drafters was to ensure that the Charter would not be used to expand the competences of the Union, and that it would not become a vehicle through which the ECJ would acquire general human rights jurisdiction. For this reason, the Charter is narrower in its application than the general principles: it applies to Member States only when they *implement* Union law, rather than when they "act within the scope" of Union law.[41] Thus, the Charter applies only when the Member States are implementing a directive or taking measures to implement a regulation, and not when an individual falls within the scope of Union law by virtue of having moved. Whilst the drafters' intention is clear, the wording of the article gives rise to some concerns, in particular in relation to the reference to subsidiarity and to the distinction between rights and principles. As to the former, the Charter does not confer new competences on the Union and therefore cannot be used as a legal

---

[40] The reference to offices and agencies has been added by the Constitutional Treaty.

[41] It is rather unfortunate that the explanation of Art.51 does not really reflect this choice as it refers to the fact that fundamental rights apply only when the Member States "act in the scope of Union law", and it then refers to *ERT* (C–260/89 [1991] E.C.R. I–2925), which is a free movement case in which the Member State was merely acting within the scope of Community law.

basis for any Union action. Since the principle of subsidiarity is aimed at regulating the exercise of Union competences, it is not clear what its significance is in relation to the Charter. The most likely explanation is that it is a political statement, with no real legal significance, aimed at reinforcing the fact that the Charter cannot be used to extend the competences of the Union. As for the latter, the distinction between rights (to be respected) and principles (to be observed), a distinction which is also present in Article 52, has being criticised since it does little to make the Charter easy to read. The idea behind such a distinction is to clarify that some of the provisions are purely aspirational and are relevant as yardsticks against which to measure the Union's legislative activity. This is normal in constitutional documents, and therefore not particularly surprising. However, it could be argued that either the principles should have not been included in a fundamental rights documents (since they are not fundamental rights, at least not in a traditional sense); or that the language of the Charter should have been consistent with that distinction (rights are sometimes referred to as principles, and vice versa); or that the drafters could have left it to the courts to clarify that some of the Charter's statements are not free-standing rights.

Article 52—Scope of the Charter's provisions

Article 52 (II–112) deals with the *scope* of the Charter and it was **9–024** substantially amended in the Constitution, in that the latter added four new paragraphs, whilst the first three paragraphs remained the same as in the original version.

Article 52(1) contains the general derogation clause, according to which any limitation on the rights and freedoms recognised in the Charter shall respect the *essence* of those rights; shall be proportionate; and must be necessary to "genuinely meet objectives of general interest recognised by the Union or the need to protect the rights and freedoms of others". Article 52(2) clarifies that rights recognised in the Treaties/other parts of the Constitutional Treaty shall be exercised under the conditions and within the limits defined in the Treaties/Constitutional Treaty. Article 52(3) provides the minimum floor guarantee, according to which insofar as the Charter rights correspond to rights guaranteed by the ECHR, their meaning and scope shall be the same as that laid down by the Convention (which shall be interpreted as also including its Protocols).[42] The Union is, however, entitled to provide more extensive protection. The general derogation clause constitutes a significant departure from the structure followed in the ECHR. The Convention provides for possible

---

[42] See explanation to the Charter; the Protocols to the Convention are an integral part of the Convention over which the ECtHR has jurisdiction.

grounds of limitation on an article-by-article basis: this means that
some rights (e.g. torture, slavery) can never be derogated from; some
rights can be limited only in exhaustively listed situations (e.g. right
to life; right to fair trial); and some articles can be limited in order to
pursue legitimate public interests, which are also listed (e.g. right to
private life, freedom of expression etc.). The scheme of the Convention achieves therefore two aims: first, the scope of the rights and
their possible limitations is made clearer to the individual; secondly,
it defines when and how those rights can be limited, therefore
delimiting legislative discretion. The Charter unfortunately does not
achieve either aim: having a general clause means that the citizen is
not able to assess the possible limitations without referring to the
Convention. Furthermore, it means that the absolute nature of some
of the rights is disguised; and that new generation rights that should
be absolute are not so clearly defined since they are not contained in
the Convention. Take for instance the prohibition on trafficking:
short of slavery and forced labour, trafficking is not explicitly
prohibited by the Convention.[43] Of course, it is not a right which can
be derogated from since any limitation of it would undermine the
very *essence* of the prohibition.[44] However, it would have been
preferable to have this expressly set out. As to the second aim, that
of clearly curtailing legislative discretion by listing interests and
occasions in which rights can be derogated from, Article 52 not only
does not achieve this, but fails to mention that any limitation must
be necessary in a "democratic society" in order to be legitimate. So,
overall, the choice of a general derogation clause is unsatisfactory;
however, it is possible that the inclusion of such a provisions is due
in part to the fact that the Charter is much broader in scope than the
Convention. In other words, whilst in relation to some of the more
clearly defined rights (civil and political as well as social) it would
have been easy to provide for article-by-article limitations, that
might have been more difficult for statement of principles (e.g.
environmental and consumer protection).

9–025   As noted above, the Constitutional Treaty added four other
paragraphs to Article 52 which, unfortunately, do nothing to increase
visibility and clarity. The new Article 52(4) provides that insofar as
the Charter rights result from the constitutional traditions common
to the Member States, they have to be interpreted in "harmony"
with those traditions. The explanations state that this is a codification of the Court's case law which, as we have seen, refers to the
common constitutional traditions as a *source* of rights. However,

---

[43] It is prohibited by the Council of Europe Convention against Trafficking in Human Beings
(ETS 196), which has not entered into force yet and also, since it is not a Protocol to the
ECHR, is not relevant in assessing the scope of the Charter's rights.
[44] Same problem—if not even more pronounced—arises in relation to the prohibition of
eugenic practices in Art.3 Charter.

Article 52(4) seems not to codify the Court's case law: rather it seems more aimed at curtailing the Court's hermeneutic autonomy in interpreting the Charter.

Article 52(5) reaffirms the distinction between principles and rights and spells out the consequence of such distinction by stating that principles may be implemented through legislative/executive acts of the Union, and by acts of the Member States when they are implementing Union law; and that they are judicially cognisable only in the interpretation of such acts and in the ruling of their validity. Thus, for instance, whilst the principle of environmental protection contained in Article 37 does not give rise to a free-standing right, if the Union were to adopt an act in blatant defiance of such principle, such act could be held invalid by the Court. And, if the Union act were to be drafted in uncertain terms, then the interpretation which enhances environmental protection would have to be favoured.

Article 52(6) provides that "full account shall be taken of national law and practice as specified in this Charter", and seems a rather redundant provision probably dictated by political needs rather than by legal necessities.

Finally, Article 52(7) provides that the explanations to the Charter shall be given due regard by Union and national courts. In this way, the explanations acquire a hybrid status: they are not "legally binding" and yet they seem to aim to curtail the judiciary's hermeneutic freedom.[45]

Article 53—Level of protection

Article 53 (II–113) reinforces the minimum floor guarantee; thus **9–026** it states that nothing in the Charter shall be interpreted as "restricting or adversely affecting human rights and fundamental freedoms as recognised, in their respective fields of application, by Union law and international law and by international agreements to which the Union, the Community or all of the Member States are party, including the European Convention on Human Rights, and by the Member States' Constitutions". The reference to the Member States' Constitutions rather than to the common constitutional traditions has raised fears as to the consistency of this provision with the principle of supremacy according to which Union law (or at least Community law) shall always take precedence even over conflicting national constitutional law.[46] Take the *Biodirective* case where the

---

[45] The explanations to the Charter state that "Although they do not as such have the status of law, they are a valuable tool of interpretation intended to clarify the provisions of the Charter".

[46] This problem has been extensively analysed by Liisberg "Does the EU Charter of Fundamental Rights Threaten the Supremacy of Community law?" (2001) 38 C.M.L.Rev. 1171, who gives a negative answer to the question. The explanations merely refer to national law, a concept much broader than national Constitutions.

Dutch Government brought proceedings against the Directive on the grounds, *inter alia*, that it infringed human dignity as guaranteed by the Dutch Constitution. Would Article 53 require the ECJ to apply the higher Dutch standard? And how is Article 53 going to apply when different national constitutions privilege different conflicting interests (e.g. right to life/right to dignity, right to health/right of the unborn)?

Article 54 (II–114)—Abuse of Rights

9–027 The final provision states "Nothing in the Charter shall be interpreted as implying any right to engage in any activity or to perform any act aimed at the destruction of any of the rights and freedoms recognised in the Charter or at their limitation to a greater extent than is provided for therein." It is almost identical to Article 17 ECHR and therefore should be construed in a similar way: thus, it is aimed at ensuring that individuals/groups and States do not use the Convention to destroy rights contained therein; it is not aimed at depriving individuals of the rights conferred by the Convention.[47]

The legal value of the charter

9–028 The Charter has no formal legal status since it was merely proclaimed by the Union Institutions. The Laeken declaration which convened the Convention on the Future of Europe, instructed that Convention to consider "whether the Charter of Fundamental Rights should be included in the basic treaty and to whether the European Community should accede to the European Convention on Human Rights".[48] The Charter, amended in its Preamble and horizontal provisions, was then included in Part II of the Treaty establishing a Constitution for Europe, and would become legally binding if the Constitutional Treaty entered into force. If, for the time being, the Charter is not (formally) legally binding, it does not mean, however, that it is devoid of legal significance. The EU political institutions have all referred to the Charter, and so have Advocates General and the CFI. The European Commission, before the proclamation of the Charter, issued a Communication stating that:

">. . . it is reasonable to assume that the Charter will produce *all* its effects, legal and others, *whatever its nature* . . . [I]t is clear that it would be difficult for the Council and the Commission,

---

[47] See e.g. *Lawless v Ireland* (No.3) (1979/80) 1 E.H.R.R. 15.
[48] Leaken Declaration on the Future of Europe, Annex 1 to the Presidency Conclusions of the Laeken European Council, 15 and December 15, 2001, SN 300/1/01 REV; *http://ue.eu.int/ueDocs/cms—Data/docs/pressData/en/ec/68827.pdf*, see below, Ch.11.

who are to proclaim it solemnly, to ignore in the future, in their legislative function, an instrument prepared at the request of the European Council by the full range of sources of national and European legitimacy acting in concert."[49]

Subsequently the Commission made clear that it would scrutinise any proposal and any draft instrument for compatibility with the Charter.[50]

The European Parliament has included a reference to the Charter in its Rules of Procedure. Thus, Rule 34 provides that during the examination of a legislative procedure "the Parliament shall pay particular attention to respect for fundamental rights and in particular that the legislative act is in *conformity* with the European Union *Charter of Fundamental Rights*". Rule 96 provides that Parliament shall conduct its business according to the principle of transparency in line with, *inter alia*, Article 42 of the Charter.[51]

Given the Commission and the European Parliament's commit- **9–029** ment to the Charter, it is hardly surprising that it has become common for the preamble to Community legislation to state that that legislation complies with the Charter. Thus, for example, recital 31 of the preamble to Directive 2004/38 on the right of Citizens of the Union and their family members to move and reside freely within the territory of the Member States, declares that "This Directive respects the fundamental rights and freedoms and observes the principles recognised in particular by the Charter on Fundamental Rights of the European Union." Numerous Community acts declare such compatibility. Such a declaration might have legal effects, since it reflects a legislative intent that the act in question comply with the Charter any incompatible provision of the act in question might be held to be invalid.[52]

Moreover, the Charter, although not formally legally binding, has had an impact on the Community judicial process. For instance, Advocate General Alber referred to the Charter less than two months from when it was adopted,[53] and it has now become usual for

---

[49] Communication from the Commission on the legal nature of the Charter of Fundamental Rights of the European Union, COM(2000) 644 final, point 10, emphasis added.

[50] SEC(2001) 380/3, *Communication de M. le Presient et de M. Vittorino*, Application de la Charte des droits fondamentaux de l'Union Europeenne. See also *Communication from the Commission*, Compliance with the Charter of Fundamental Rights in Commission Legislative proposals, Methodology for systematic and rigorous monitoring, COM(2005)172 final.

[51] Rules of Procedure, July 2004, *www2.europarl.eu.int/omk/sipade2?PUBREF=-//EP/ /NONSGML+RULES-EP+20040720+0+DOC+PDF+V0//EN*. See also European Parliament Resolution on the impact of the Charter of Fundamental Rights of the European Union and its future status (2002/2139(INI)) (2003) O.J. 300E 11/12/03P 432.

[52] A broad analogy might be drawn with the so-called *Nakajima* exception. Although non-directly effective international agreements may not be relied upon to call into question the legality of Community measures, the position is different where Community legislation expressly or impliedly otherwise provides, e.g. by a reference in the preamble to measure in question. See Ch.5, p.192.

[53] Opinion, Case C–340/99 *TNT Traco Spa* [2001] E.C.R. I–4109, para.94.

Advocates General to refer to the Charter to strengthen their submissions as to the fact that a right is recognised at Union level.[54] Slightly more unusual, and maybe questionable, is the use of the Charter to *exclude* the existence of a given fundamental right. Thus, in *D and Council* Advocate General Mischo relied on Article 9 of the Charter, together with the explanatory memorandum, to exclude the existence of a right to equal treatment of same-sex couples.[55] The CFI has also referred to the Charter in several of its judgments.[56] For instance, in the *Jégo-Quéré* case, the CFI relied on Article 47 of the Charter (right to effective judicial remedy) in order to relax the test for standing to challenge acts of the Community institutions.[57] The Court of Justice has also recently referred for the first time to the Charter, relying both on the fact that the preamble of the directive under challenge referred to it,[58] and on the fact that the Charter's principle aim is to "reaffirm *existing* rights".[59] Thus, it is clear that the Charter produces legal effects even if it is not legally binding. This result might be doctrinally justified by the fact that the Charter does not introduce new rights but rather renders existing rights more visible.[60]

This said, the situation is far from satisfactory. First of all, it is not clear how the Union institutions' "proclamation" relates to Opinion

---

[54] e.g. *cf.* Advocate General Jacobs' opinion in case C–377/98 *Netherlands v Council* (Biotechnology) [2001] E.C.R. I–7079, esp. para.197, in relation to the right to dignity; Advocate General Poiares Maduro's Opinion in Case C–160/03 *Spain v Eurojust*, [2005] E.C.R. I–2077 in relation to linguistic diversity; Advocate General Kokott's Opinion in Case C–105/03 *Pupino* [2005] E.C.R. I–5285, in relation to the right to fair trial and the rights of children; Advocate General Geelohed in Case C–209/03 *Bidar* [2005] E.C.R. I–2119, in relation to limitations to fundamental rights; Advocate General Léger's Opinion in Case C–277/02 *EU-Wood Training GmbH v Sonderabfall-Management-Gesellschaft Rheinland-Pfalz mbH*, [2004] E.C.R. I–11957 in relation to environmental protection; Advocate General Tizzano's Opinion in Case C–173/99 *BECTU* [2001] E.C.R. I–4881.

[55] Opinion, in Case C–122/99 and 125/99 *D and Sweden v Council* [2001] E.C.R. I–4319, para.125; see also his opinion in Case C–20/00 and C–64/00 *Booker Aquaculture et al.* [2003] E.C.R. I–7411, para.125–127. And indeed the fact that codification could lead to "fossilisation" of fundamental rights protection, impeding their development lead some to criticise the Charter as being too detailed. Finally the Charter has been referred to also by the ECtHR to develop its own case law in a more liberal fashion, e.g. in order to extend the principle of non-discrimination to transsexuals, see *Goodwin v UK* (2005) 35 E.H.R.R. 18; and *I. v UK* (2003) 36 E.H.R.R. 53; see also Spanish Constitutional Court ruling of 30/11/00.

[56] e.g. Case T–211/02 *Tideland Signal Ltd* [2002] E.C.R. II–3781, para.37; Case T–116/01 *P & O European Ferries* [2003] E.C.R. II–2957, para.209; Case T–223/00 *Kyowa Hakko* [2003] E.C.R. II–2553, para.104.

[57] Case T–77/01 *Jégo-Quéré* [2002] E.C.R. II–2365; the new test proposed by the CFI was reversed by the ECJ which restates its previous case law C–50/00 *UPA* [2002] E.C.R. I–6677.

[58] Directive 2003/86 on the right to family reunification (2003) O.J. L151/12.

[59] Case C–540/03 *European Parliament v Council* (family reunification), judgment of 27/06/06, not yet reported, para.30, emphasis added; see also para.58.

[60] Consider also that the Court has had no problems referring to the Community Social Charter as an aid to interpretation despite the fact that the latter is not legally binding; e.g. Case C–14/04 *Dellas* judgment of 1/12/05, not yet reported; Joined Cases C–397/01 to 403/01 *Pfeiffer* [2004] E.C.R. I–8835.

2/94 where the Court held that "no Treaty provision confers on the Community institutions any general power to *enact rules on human rights* or to conclude international conventions in this field".[61] As shown above, whilst it is true that the Charter is not formally legally binding, it is far from being a legally irrelevant document and the "proclamation" has the effect of bypassing national parliaments, since it does not need to be ratified.

Another issue which deserves brief consideration concerns the **9–030** relationship between the Charter and the case law of the ECJ relating to the scope of fundamental rights as general principles of Community law. We have seen that the scope of the Charter appears to be narrower than the scope of the fundamental rights case law, since the latter apply also to Member States when acting within the scope of Community and Union law, whilst the former applies only to Member States when they implement Community law. However, nothing in the Charter prevents the ECJ from continuing to apply its previously developed case law, in the form of general principles, to the Member States acting within the scope of Community law. Indeed, as we shall see Chapter 11, the Constitutional Treaty expressly mentions fundamental rights as general principles of Community law. Despite the drafters' intentions then, it is very unlikely that the Court will refuse to recognise as a general principle of Community law a right which is expressly recognised by the Charter.

Further reading
AA. VV., (2001) M.J. 1, special issue on the Charter.
Arnull, "Form Charter to Constitution and Beyond: Fundamental Rights in the New European Union" (2003) P.L. 774.
Ashiagbor, "Economic and Social Rights in the European Charter of Fundamental Rights" (2004) E.H.R.L.R. 62.
Basselink, "The Member States, the National Constitutions and the Scope of the Charter" (2001) M.J. 69.
Curtin and van Ooik, "The Sting is Always in the Tail. The Personal Scope of Application of the EU Charter of Fundamental Rights" (2001) M.J. 103.
de Burca and de Witte (eds), *Social Rights in Europe* (OUP, 2005).
de Burca, "The Drafting of the European Union Charter of Fundamental Rights" (2001) E.L.Rev. 126.
de Burca, "Human Rights: The Charter and Beyond" Jean Monnet Working Paper No. 10/01.
de Witte, "The Legal Status of the Charter: Vital Question or Non-Issue?" (2001) M.J. 81.

---

[61] Opinion 2/94 Accession to the ECHR [1996] E.C.R. I–1759, emphasis added.

Eechout, "The EU Charter of Fundamental Rights and the Federal Question" (2002) C.M.L.Rev. 945–994.

Heringa, and Verhey, "The EU Charter: Text and Structure" (2001) M.J. 11.

Hervey and Kenner (eds), *Economic and Social Rights under the EU Charter of Fundamental Rights—a legal perspective* (Hart Publishing, 2003).

Knook, "The Court, the Charter and the Vertical Division of Powers in the EU" (2005) C.M.L.Rev. 367.

Lanaerts and de Smijter, "The Charter and the Role of the European Courts" (2001) M.J. 90.

Lemmens, "The Relationship between the Charter of Fundamental Rights of the European Union and the European Convention on Human Rights—Substantive Aspects" (2001) M.J. 49.

Liisberg, "Does the EU Charter of Fundamental Rights Threaten the Supremacy of Community Law?" (2001) 38 C.M.L.Rev. 1171.

Peers and Ward (eds), *The Charter of Fundamental Rights* (Hart Publishing, 2004).

Wounters, "The EU Charter of Fundamental Rights—Some Reflections on its External Dimension" (2001) M.J. 3

CHAPTER 10

EUROPEAN COMMUNITY AND EUROPEAN UNION

Guide to this Chapter: So far, our attention has focused on the **10–001** legal order of the European Community—its institutional relations, decision-making procedures and powers, the principles govern- ing its relationship with the national legal systems, and the general principles of Community law identified by the ECJ. But the European Community constitutes only the first (albeit the most important and developed) of the three "pillars" of the wider European Union. This Chapter examines the key characteristics of the other two pillars: the common foreign and security policy; and police and judicial cooperation in criminal matters. Despite some degree of convergence thanks to the TA and TN, those two pillars differ from the Community legal order in several important respects: as regards, for example, the relative dominance of the Council *vis-à-vis* the Commission and European Parliament within the inter-institutional balance; the reliance on unanimity rather than qualified majority voting for decision-making by the Council under primary powers; the types of legal instrument available to the Union in order to achieve its objectives; the limited jurisdiction of the Court of Justice to review Union acts and deliver prelimin- ary rulings; the express preclusion of direct effect for certain Union measures, and uncertainty as to the constitutional status of other of the Court's "constitutionalising principles"; and the detailed rules for engaging in enhanced cooperation. All three pillars, however, remain linked by a unified "pediment"—a collec- tion of common principles and procedures which transcend the individual sub-orders of the Union. These comprise: a single institutional framework for the Union; a common body of funda- mental values and principles (such as liberty, democracy and respect for human rights); a series of common objectives for the Union which are intended to provide a coherent reference point for its multifarious activities; and common procedures for amend- ment of, and accession to, the three Treaties upon which the

Union is founded. The Chapter closes with some brief observations on the legal personality of the Community and the Union within the domestic legal orders and under public international law.

The Union architecture

10–002   The European Union came into being with the entry into force of the TEU on November 1, 1993.[1]

It has been pointed out that the term "European Union" has long been in use as a generic description of a (possible) ulterior stage of the integration process, transcending the Community model.[2] However, the historic entity that is the EU owes its existence, more mundanely, to the course of the negotiations that culminated in agreement on the text of the TEU, at the Maastricht meeting of Heads of State or Government in December 1991.[3] During the negotiations, it became an issue whether certain policy areas to be covered by the Treaty should be brought within the compass of the EC; and, to the extent that they were not, what the relationship should be between those policy areas and the Community order. The four areas principally in question were citizenship, economic and monetary union, foreign and security policy, and justice and home affairs. The solution eventually adopted was that the powers relating to citizenship and to economic and monetary union should be integrated into the EC Treaty, while those on the common foreign and security policy (CFSP) and on co-operation in the fields of justice and home affairs (JHA) should be placed in separate Titles (respectively, Titles V and VI) of the TEU; at the same time, the three Communities would be linked to each other, as well as to the CFSP and JHA, in a new overarching structure, the EU. Within that structure, the same group of institutions would operate with differing

---

[1] For early, critical reactions, see Everling, "Reflections on the Structure of the Union" (1992) 29 C.M.L.Rev. 1053; Noël, "Reflections on the Maastricht Treaty" (1992) 27 *Government and Opposition* 148; Curtin, "The Constitutional Structure of the Union: A Europe of Bits and Pieces" (1993) 30 C.M.L.Rev. 17. A more measured response is that of Weiler, "Neither Unity Nor Three Pillars: The Trinity Structure of the Treaty on European Union" in Monar, Ungerer and Wessels (eds), *The Maastricht Treaty on European Union* (1993). See also Curtin and Dekker, "The EU as a 'Layered' International Organisation: Institutional Unity in Disguise" in Craig and de Búrca (eds), *The Evolution of EU Law* (1999).

[2] By de Witte, "The Pillar Structure and the Nature of the European Union: Greek Temple or French Gothic Cathedral?" in Heukels, Blokker and Brus (eds), *The European Union after Amsterdam* (1998), p.57. He cites Toth, *The Oxford Encyclopedia of European Community Law, Vol.I: Institutional Law* (1990), p.248.

[3] The TEU, in its final form, brought together two texts that were negotiated separately by parallel conferences. One text, relating to what was known as "political union" was negotiated by personal representatives of the Foreign Ministers of the Member States under the auspices of the General Affairs Council, while the other text, relating exclusively to economic and monetary union, was negotiated by personal representatives of Finance Ministers under the auspices of the Economic and Financial Affairs Council.

powers under differing procedures, and with differing legal consequences, depending on the substantive policies being pursued.[4]

The structure was preserved, indeed strengthened, by the TA,
though it was modified in an important respect.[5] As we have noted
in previous chapters, the TA caused a large part of the subject-
matter of the former JHA (in effect, everything to do with the
control of Member States' external frontiers and the treatment of
third country nationals, as well as judicial co-operation in civil
matters) to be transferred from Title VI TEU to the new Title IV of
Part Three of the EC Treaty. Title VI TEU, as amended, is now
devoted entirely to police and judicial co-operation in criminal
matters (PJC). The material scope of the Title has thus been
curtailed, but in that narrower field the common institutions have
been given powers that are more concrete and far-reaching than
originally under the TEU.

The general character of the relationship between the EU and the
European Communities, and that of the various component elements of the Union *inter se*, can be gathered from Article 1, third
paragraph of the TEU, which provides: 10–003

> "The Union shall be founded on the European Communities,
> supplemented by the policies and forms of co-operation estab-
> lished by this Treaty. Its task shall be to organise, in a manner
> demonstrating consistency and solidarity, relations between the
> Member States and between their peoples."

The three Communities pre-date the EU by many years: the ECSC
(though now expired) came into being in July 1952; the EC and
Euratom in January 1958. Until November 1993, they were formally
distinct, each resting on its own free-standing Treaty. The description of the Union as being "founded" on the Communities indicates
that the latter must now be regarded as having been subsumed into
the former; but also that they constitute overwhelmingly its most
important component, the CFSP and PJC providing complementary
elements.

---

[4] On the political union negotiations and their outcome, see de Schoutheete de Tervarent in
Louis (ed.), *L'Union européenne après Maastricht* (journée d'études Bruxelles, February 21,
1922), p.17; Timmermans, *ibid.*, p.49. For a commentary on the "political union" aspect of
the Treaty in the draft put forward by the Luxembourg Presidency to the European Council
in June 1991, see Vignes (1991) R.M.C. p.504. The Addendum on the TEU in de Cockborne
et al., *Commentaire Mégret* (2nd ed.) Vol.1 (1992, Editions de l'Université de Bruxelles)
contains at pp.369 *et seq.*, a commentary on the Preamble and Common Provisions of the
TEU.

[5] On the Union structure post-Amsterdam, see de Witte, "The Pillar Structure and the Nature
of the European Union: Greek Temple or French Gothic Cathedral?" in Heukels, Blokker
and Brus (eds), *The European Union after Amsterdam* (1998); and, for a more negative
reaction, Gormley, "Reflections on the Architecture of the European Union after the Treaty
of Amsterdam" in O'Keefe and Twomey (eds), *Legal Issues of the Amsterdam Treaty* (1999).
See also Curtin and Dekker, "The EU as a 'Layered' International Organisation: Institutional Unity in Disguise" in Craig and de Búrca (eds), *The Evolution of EU Law* (1999).

The foundational quality of the Communities, and more particularly the EC, *vis-à-vis* the Union can be seen as both substantive and ideological. Thus, the great bulk of EU activity (covering the fields of economic and social policy, in their internal and external aspects, and much besides) falls within the scope of application of the EC Treaty. At the same time, the Community model of European integration has been taken over as standard for the Union as a whole, though not (or not yet) applicable in all its parts. An explicit objective of the Union is "to maintain in full the *acquis communautaire* and build on it with a view to considering to what extent the policies and forms of co-operation introduced by this Treaty may need to be revised with the aim of ensuring the effectiveness of the mechanisms and the institutions of the Community".[6] There is thus an obligation to protect the Community model, and to contemplate the possibility of extending it to the areas that are subject to the special institutional and procedural arrangements established by the TEU. The first results of this were found in the TA, most conspicuously in the transfer of matters from Title VI TEU to the EC Treaty; and the TN continued the trend as regards the remaining Third Pillar competences, though its impact was more limited. On the other hand, the dynamic of the Second Pillar is towards stronger divergence from the Community model.

10–004 It is stated, by Article 47 TEU, that, subject to the provisions amending the Community Treaties (found in Titles II to IV TEU), and to the Final Provisions (in Title VIII), "nothing in this Treaty shall affect the Treaties establishing the European Communities or the subsequent Treaties and Acts modifying or supplementing them". Article 47 is one of the provisions of the TEU which the Court of Justice has jurisdiction to apply. The Court has thus been given the role of policing the frontier between the EC, on the one hand, and the CFSP and PJC, on the other. For example, in Case C–170/96 *Commission v Council*,[7] the issue was whether a measure on the granting of airport transit visas to third country nationals ought to have been given a legal basis in the EC Treaty, rather than in Title VI TEU. In rejecting an objection to the admissibility of the action, the Court said it had to ensure that acts which, in the Council's view, fell within the scope of Title VI, did not encroach upon the powers conferred by the EC Treaty on the Community. More recently, the Court annulled a Council act adopted under the Third Pillar, which had identified a number of environmental offences in respect of which the Member States were obliged to prescribe criminal penalties, on the grounds that, considered in the light of both its aims and its primary content, the disputed measure could have properly been adopted on the basis of Article 175 EC.

---

[6] Art.2, first para., fifth indent, TEU.
[7] Case C–170/96 *Commission v Council* [1998] E.C.R. I–2763; [1998] 2 C.M.L.R. 1092.

Again, therefore, the Council had infringed Article 47 TEU by encroaching upon the Community's powers under the First Pillar.[8] It remains to be seen whether that analysis can be applied to the interaction between the Second Pillar and the First, given that Article 3 TEU appears to contemplate that the external relations powers of the Union should be used in a complementary way.[9]

The second sentence of Article 1, third paragraph of the TEU speaks of the Union's task as being "to organise, in a manner demonstrating consistency and solidarity, relations between the Member States and between their peoples". Two organisational values are there highlighted: "consistency", presumably as between activities carried on under the different institutional arrangements that may be applicable;[10] and "solidarity", implying a commitment in principle to systematic co-operation and common action, wherever possible and appropriate.

There are commentators on the TEU who have argued that the **10–005** Treaty did not give rise to any kind of new legal order: the so-called "Union" was simply a framework for enhanced intergovernmental co-operation in the fields of activity covered by Titles V and VI, as Title III of the SEA had been in respect of the former EPC.[11] We do not share that conception of the Union. It seems clear to us that the intention of the Treaty is to create a complex order, in which powers have been allocated among the common institutions, and as between those institutions and the Member States, under arrangements— found respectively in the Community Treaties and in Titles V and VI TEU—which are sufficiently differentiated to be regarded as three distinct sub-orders.[12] That follows from the operative language of Article 1, first paragraph TEU, which is identical to that of Article 1 EC,[13] from the definition of the Union just considered, and from the provisions organising the "complementary" sub-orders internally, and the principles that govern their relationship with the Community sub-order, which are analysed below.

The image of a Greek temple façade, conventionally used to illustrate the structure of the Union, was mentioned in the discussion

---

[8] Case C–176/03 *Commission v Council* (Judgment of September 13, 2005).
[9] At the time of writing, the issue was before the Court of Justice in Case C–91/05 *Commission v Council* [2005] O.J. C115/10.
[10] See also Art.3 TEU on the single institutional framework, which is considered below.
[11] The thesis is vigorously propounded by Koenig and Pechstein, *Die Europäische Union* (1995). For an opposite view, see Von Bogdandy and Netterheim, "Ex pluribus unum: Fusion of the European Communities into the European Union" (1996) 2 E.L.J. 267; "Die Europäische Union: Ein einheitlicher Verband mit eigener Rechtsordnung" (1996) 31 *Europarecht* 3; and Von Bogdandy, "The Legal Case for Unity: The European Union as a Single Organisation with a Single Legal System" (1999) 36 C.M.L.Rev. 887.
[12] Our conception is close to that of de Witte, "The Pillar Structure and the Nature of the European Union: Greek Temple or French Gothic Cathedral?" in Heukels, Blokker and Brus (eds), *The European Union after Amsterdam* (1998).
[13] "By this Treaty, the HIGH CONTRACTING PARTIES *establish* among themselves a EUROPEAN UNION" (emphasis added).

of the TEU in Chapter 1. In that image, the "First Pillar" represents the Communities, the "Second Pillar", the CFSP as provided for by Title V TEU, and the "Third Pillar", PJC as now provided for by Title VI TEU; while the pediment represents the various legal elements that link those three together as components of the Union. There has been criticism of the image,[14] and it is evidently defective: likening the Union's component orders to pillars, exaggerates the separation between them,[15] and makes it hard to convey the idea that the structure is "founded" on the European Communities. Nevertheless, "pillar talk" is pervasive and inescapable; and the image, if not pressed too far, provides a rough but helpful guide to understanding. Our version of it presents the First Pillar as being situated in the middle, and also as much more solid than the other two.

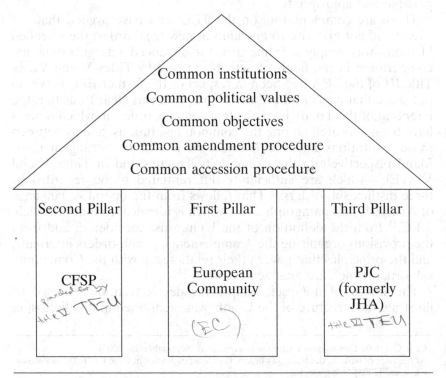

14 By de Witte, "The Pillar Structure and the Nature of the European Union: Greek Temple or French Gothic Cathedral?" in Heukels, Blokker and Brus (eds), *The European Union after Amsterdam* (1998), pp.52–53; Gormley, "Reflections on the Architecture of the European Union after the Treaty of Amsterdam" in O'Keefe and Twomey (eds), *Legal Issues of the Amsterdam Treaty* (1999), pp.57–58. Suggested alternatives have been a gothic cathedral (see de Witte, *op.cit.*, pp.64–65; Kapteyn and Verloren van Themaat (ed. Gormley), *Introduction to the Law of the European Communities* (3rd ed., 1998), p.47); and a "Trinity . . . in which 'oneness' and 'separateness' co-exist simultaneously" (see Weiler, "Neither Unity nor Three Pillars: The Trinity Structure of the Treaty on European Union" in Monar, Ungerer and Wessels (eds), *The Maastricht Treaty on European Union* (1993), p.62).

15 We return to this point when discussing the single institutional framework, below.

In the remainder of this chapter, we examine, first, the "pillars" (i.e. what it is that differentiates the European Communities legally from the CFSP and PJC) and, secondly, the unifying elements that constitute the "pediment" of the Greek façade. We conclude with some remarks on the legal personality and capacity of the Communities and the Union.

The three pillars

It has rightly been said by de Witte: **10–006**

> "The *essence* of the pillar structure is the variation in the allocation of powers among the institutions. The Member States consider that primary responsibility for certain matters should remain in the hands of the national executives meeting in the Council."[16]

Nevertheless, we believe that the epithet "intergovernmental", still commonly applied to the institutional and procedural arrangements of the CFSP and PJC, is misleading. As we shall see, under those arrangements, especially as reformed by the TA, the first tentative steps have been taken towards the Member States' acceptance of the discipline of acting in common—though their sovereign rights are, and are likely to remain, much less severely curtailed than under the First Pillar.[17] It is possible to identify several main differences between the Second and Third Pillars (on the one hand) and the First Pillar (on the other hand).

The first such difference lies in the rules governing the interaction between the political institutions. The Council has a more than usually dominant role under the Second and Third Pillars; this leaves the other institutions correspondingly reduced opportunities for influencing the development of policy and making their mark on the measures finally adopted, although there was an adjustment of the balance in their favour by the TA. The Commission must be "fully associated" with the work carried out in the fields of the CFSP and PJC;[18] and it has a right of initiative, but not the exclusive right it enjoys for most purposes under the EC Treaty.[19] Member States also have a right of initiative, which in practice is normally exercised by

---

[16] de Witte, "The Pillar Structure and the Nature of the European Union: Greek Temple or French Gothic Cathedral?" in Heukels, Blokker and Brus (eds), *The European Union after Amsterdam* (1998), p.66.

[17] In Opinion 1/91, the Court said that, for the benefit of the new legal order established by the Community Treaties, "the States have limited their sovereign rights, *in ever wider fields*" (emphasis added): [1991] E.C.R. I–6079, para.21.

[18] Art.27 and Art.36(2) TEU.

[19] Art.22(1) and Art.34(2) TEU. Under the former Art K.3(2) TEU there were certain matters where the Member States had an exclusive right of initiative.

the Council's Presidency. It is also the Presidency that has been entrusted with implementing decisions taken under Title V TEU, assisted by the Secretary General of the Council in the capacity of "High Representative for the CFSP", and again in association with the Commission.[20] In Title VI matters, it seems that implementation remains entirely in the hands of the Member States. As for the European Parliament, it must be consulted by the Presidency "on the main aspects and the basic choices" of the CFSP, and have its views "duly taken into consideration", as well as being kept regularly informed of developments;[21] however, it is not directly involved in decision making on specific matters. That is in contrast to the position under Title VI TEU, as amended by the TA, where the Council is required to consult the Parliament before adopting most kinds of measure; though here, too, there is a difference as compared with the consultation procedure of the EC Treaty, since the Council has power to impose a time-limit of not less than three months for the delivery of the Parliament's opinion, after which it may act.[22] The Parliament also has the right to be regularly informed of discussions in the areas covered by Title VI, and to ask questions of the Council or make recommendations to it; and there must be an annual Parliamentary debate on progress made in those areas.[23]

10–007   Secondly, both Title V and Title VI TEU equip the institutions with a different set of legal instruments from those available under Article 249 EC. The binding instruments provided by Article 12 TEU for pursuing the objectives of the CFSP are common strategies (decided on by the European Council), and joint actions and common positions (adopted by the Council). Their function is either to give formal expression to policy positions or, in the case of joint actions, to organise operational activity, such as peacekeeping. In contrast to EC regulations and directives, they are not designed to lay down rules. For the purposes of PJC, the Council has the following at its disposal:

(a) "common positions defining the approach of the Union to a particular matter";

(b) "framework decisions for the purpose of approximation of the laws and regulations of the Member States", of which it is said, as in the case of Community directives, that they "shall be binding upon the Member States as to the result to be achieved but shall leave to the national authorities the choice of form and methods";

---

[20] Art.18 TEU.
[21] Art.21 TEU.
[22] Art.39 TEU.
[23] *ibid.*

(c) "decisions", which can be used for any purpose consistent with the objectives of Title VI, other than approximation; and

(d) "conventions which [the Council] shall recommend to the Member States for adoption in accordance with their respective constitutional requirements".[24]

There is thus no PJC instrument equivalent to a Community regulation that could be used to enact legislation directly applicable in all of the Member States, in the sense of neither requiring nor permitting implementation by the national authorities.[25] It is also stated expressly, as regards both framework decisions and the residual category of decisions, that they "shall not entail direct effect".

The third main difference is found in the Council's voting rules. Whereas, under the EC Treaty, the trend is towards extending qualified majority voting to an ever wider range of matters,[26] in principle decisions under Titles V and VI TEU are taken by the Council acting unanimously.[27] Here too, however, the TA brought changes. In CFSP matters, the Council may act by a qualified majority when implementing a common strategy, a joint action or a common position (the basic instrument in each case requiring unanimity). After the TN, the Council may also act by qualified majority when appointing a special representative (mandated to act in relation to specific policy issues).[28] As to PJC, there is provision in Article 34(2)(c) TEU for measures implementing, "at the level of the Union", decisions other than framework decisions, to be taken by the Council acting by a qualified majority; while Article 34(2)(d) TEU says that "[m]easures implementing conventions shall be adopted within the Council by a majority of two-thirds of the Contracting Parties". The reference in the latter case to adoption "within", rather than by, the Council, indicates that the measures in question are acts, not of the institution itself, but of the representatives of the governments of the Contracting States; accordingly they have the legal quality of international agreements in simplified form.

Fourthly, and of great significance because case law has been so **10–008** influential in shaping and developing the Community order, the Court of Justice has no jurisdiction under the Second Pillar, and only

---

[24] Art.34(2) TEU. *cf.* the more meagre armoury provided by the original Art.K.3(2) TEU.
[25] See the discussion in Ch.5.
[26] See the discussion in Ch.3.
[27] Art.23(1) and Art.34(2) TEU.
[28] The derogations from the unanimity rule in Art.23(2) TEU are subject to the variant of the Luxembourg compromise discussed in Ch.3. Nor do they apply to decisions which have military or defence implications. Note that, under Art.207 EC as amended by the TN, QMV now also applies for the appointment of the Secretary-General of the Council (High Representative for the CFSP).

a limited one under the Third Pillar.[29] The latter jurisdiction was conferred on the Court by the (TA.[30] That step, though (as we shall see) it falls short of establishing the rule of law in Title VI matters at the level of the Union, provides a clear example of the communitarising dynamic referred to above.

Pursuant to Article 35(1) TEU, the Court of Justice has jurisdiction to give preliminary rulings on the validity and interpretation of framework decisions and of decisions, on the interpretation of Title VI conventions, and on the validity and interpretation of the measures implementing them; but only where questions are referred to it by the courts or tribunals of Member States which have made a declaration signifying their acceptance of this jurisdiction.[31] In making such a declaration, a Member State must specify whether the possibility of requesting preliminary rulings is to be restricted to courts or tribunals of final resort, or to be available throughout the judicial hierarchy;[32] in either case, the Treaty does not itself place courts or tribunals of final resort under a duty corresponding to that imposed by the third paragraph of Article 234 EC, but there was a Declaration by the Amsterdam Conference noting that Member States could reserve the right to provide for such a duty in their national law.[33]

It must be possible for the Court of Justice, in giving preliminary rulings on the validity, or as the case may be the interpretation, of the secondary Title VI measures referred to in Article 35(1) TEU, to interpret any relevant provisions contained in the Title itself. However, from the wording of the paragraph, the Court does not seem to have been empowered to respond to requests from national courts for preliminary rulings relating directly to those primary provisions.

10–009   Paragraph (5) of Article 35 TEU provides:

> "The Court of Justice shall not have jurisdiction to review the validity or proportionality of operations carried out by the police or other law enforcement services of a Member State or the exercise of the responsibilities incumbent upon Member States with regard to the maintenance of law and order and the safeguarding of internal security."

---

[29] See Art.46 TEU. See also the discussion of the Court's jurisdiction contained in Ch.14.

[30] For a full discussion of this jurisdiction, see Arnull, "Taming the Beast? The Treaty of Amsterdam and the Court of Justice" in O'Keeffe and Twomey (eds), *Legal Issues of the Amsterdam Treaty* (1999) pp.117–120.

[31] Art.35(2) TEU. For recent examples of preliminary rulings delivered under Art.35 TEU, see Cases C–187 and 385/01 *Gözütok and Brügge* [2003] E.C.R. I–1345; Case C–469/03 *Miraglia* [2005] E.C.R. I–2009.

[32] Art.35(3) TEU.

[33] Declaration No.10. For recent decisions of the German and Polish courts (concerning the European Arrest Warrant) which help illustrate the problems which may arise from the ECJ's limited jurisdiction to deliver preliminary rulings under the Third Pillar, see Editorial, "Arrested Development" (2005) 30 E.L.Rev. 605.

That appears to be stating the obvious: no jurisdiction "to review the validity or proportionality" of Member State measures of any kind is given by Article 35(1) TEU. If it were asked to conduct such a review the Court would doubtless follow its long-standing practice in cases under Article 234 EC,[34] and confine itself to an abstract ruling on the applicable Title VI measures, leaving any appropriate conclusions, in respect of actions taken by the national authorities, to be drawn in the main proceedings. Paragraph (5) does not say, and there are no good reasons for interpreting it as meaning, that jurisdiction under Article 35(1) must be refused, wherever it appears from the order for reference that the proceedings for the purposes of which a ruling by the Court is being sought, are concerned with the legality of police or other internal security operations.[35]

Courts in Member States which have chosen not to make a declaration under Article 35(2) TEU accepting the Court's jurisdiction are not themselves able to request preliminary rulings on the interpretation or validity of Title VI measures; but there is no legal impediment to their recognising the persuasive authority of such rulings in cases that have come to the Court from other Member States, and they are likely in practice to do so.[36] That likelihood is tacitly recognised by Article 35(4) TEU, which allows statements of case or written observations to be submitted in proceedings arising under the Article by any Member State, whether or not it has made a declaration pursuant to paragraph (2).

Besides the optional preliminary rulings procedure, there are two **10–010** other heads of jurisdiction for the Court of Justice provided by Article 35 TEU. Paragraph (6) enables the Court to review the legality of framework decisions and decisions, in actions brought by a Member State or the Commission, on similar grounds to those that apply under Article 230 EC, and subject to the same two-month time-limit. That natural and legal persons have not been given *locus standi* is unsurprising, since both kinds of instrument in question are expressly stated not to entail direct effect.[37] Under paragraph (7), the Court may rule on a dispute between Member States regarding

---

[34] See Ch.14.

[35] *cf.* Art.68(2) EC, which excludes the Court's Art.234 EC jurisdiction in respect of Council measures taken with a view to ensuring the absence of controls on persons crossing internal borders, where these relate to "the maintenance of law and order and the safeguarding of internal security".

[36] *cf.* the Protocol on the opt-out for the United Kingdom and Ireland from Title IV of Part Three of the EC Treaty (Protocol No.4 to the Final Act of the Amsterdam Conference). Art.2 of the Protocol provides that, *inter alia*, no decision of the Court of Justice interpreting any provision of Title IV or any measure adopted under it "shall be binding upon or applicable in the United Kingdom or Ireland"; or "shall in any way affect the competitiveness, rights and obligations of those States"; or "shall in any way affect the *acquis communautaire* nor form part of Community law as they apply to the United Kingdom or Ireland".

[37] It is hard to see how, in the absence of direct effect, the criterion of direct and individual concern, applicable under Art.230 EC, could be satisfied.

the interpretation or the application of Title VI instruments, which the Council has been unable to settle within six months of having the matter referred to it; and it also has jurisdiction in disputes between Member States and the Commission regarding the interpretation or application of conventions established under Article 35(2)(d) TEU. The paragraph (7) jurisdiction thus gives pride of place to the political resolution of inter-Member State disputes, with recourse to the Court only if this fails. Taking the two paragraphs together, the Commission can be seen as the junior partner of the Member States in preserving legality under Title VI (in contrast with its role as guardian of the EC Treaty).[38]

The (fifth) main difference between the First Pillar (on the one hand) and the Second and Third Pillars (on the other hand) concerns the legal effects of their respective provisions and instruments within the national legal systems, and follows from their respective Treaty bases. The location of the CFSP and PJC in Titles of the TEU, and not in the EC Treaty, sets them apart from the new legal order, the principles of which the Court of Justice has been working out in the remarkable series of judgments that began with *Van Gend en Loos*.[39] The "essential characteristics" of that legal order, as we have seen, are its primacy over the law of the Member States and the potential direct effect of Community law provisions in relations between individuals and with the Member States.[40] But there is uncertainty about how far those (and other) constitutionalising principles of the Community legal order are applicable also in respect of the CFSP or PJC.

For example, it is clear from the express provisions of Article 34(2) TEU that framework decisions and decisions as used in the Third Pillar are incapable of having direct effect; while it seems evident that common positions and conventions are simply not apt to enjoy direct effect in any case. But what of the duty of consistent interpretation as developed by the Court of Justice under Community law since *von Colson* and *Marleasing*:[41] could a national court be obliged, as a matter of Union law, to construe its existing domestic legislation, so far as possible, to achieve the results laid out in a Third Pillar framework decision or decision (even though the latter is not in principle capable of having any direct effect)? This issue was addressed in *Pupino*,[42] which concerned the possible interpretation of Italian legislation dealing with the protection during criminal trials of young children who had been the victims of maltreatment, so as to comply with the requirements set out in

---

[38] Art.211, first indent, EC.
[39] Case 26/62 [1963] E.C.R. 1.
[40] See Ch.5.
[41] Case 14/83 *von Colson* [1984] E.C.R. 1891; Case 106/89 *Marleasing* [1990] E.C.R. 4135. For detailed discussion, see Ch.5.
[42] Case C–105/03 *Pupino* (Judgment of June 16, 2005).

Framework Decision 2001/220 on the standing of victims in criminal proceedings.[43] The Court of Justice held that, even though the Treaty on European Union contains no provision equivalent to Article 10 EC, the duty of loyal co-operation between the Union and its Member States nevertheless applies to the Third Pillar—since otherwise, it would be difficult for the Union to carry out its tasks effectively. That the duty of consistent interpretation thus applies within the scope of PJC also follows from the binding character of framework decisions under Article 34(2) TEU; and from the need to ensure that the Court's jurisdiction to give preliminary rulings at the request of competent national courts has any useful effect. Of equal significance is the fact that the Court limited this duty of interpretation (as in the First Pillar) by reference to the general principles of (not only *Community*, but now also *Union*) law—such as legal certainty, the non-retroactivity of criminal liability, and respect for human rights and fundamental freedoms. The ruling in *Pupino* thus demonstrates that, even if certain of the Court's constitutionalising principles as developed in the sphere of Community law have been excluded from the scope of CFSP and PJC, other such principles may yet apply in those fields. One might therefore speculate (e.g.) about whether the *Francovich* principle of Member State liability can apply within the Third Pillar, where failure to implement a framework decision intended to create individual rights causes loss to one of its intended beneficiaries;[44] or whether the general principles of Union law, since (unlike framework decisions and decisions) they are not specifically excluded from having direct effect, may be relied upon as an independent source of rights before the domestic courts (say) to challenge the legality of national measures implementing or derogating from a PJC instrument.[45]

Finally, it is possible for Member States to engage in enhanced co-operation, in particular as reformed by the TN, within the fields covered by the Second and Third Pillars—but under different conditions from those applicable to the First Pillar.[46] The rules governing enhanced co-operation within the CFSP are set out in Articles 27a to 27e TEU. Thus, for example: the enhanced co-operation may only relate to implementation of a joint action or common position, and may not relate in any case to matters having military or defence implications; the request for an enhanced co-operation is made directly to the Council, not through the Commission, which has the power merely to express its opinion on the proposal; authorisation to embark upon the enhanced co-operation

---

[43] [2001] O.J. L82/1.
[44] See further, Ch.6.
[45] See further, Ch.7.
[46] See the analysis of enhanced co-operation under the First Pillar contained in Ch.4. The general principles contained in Title VII TEU apply to enhanced co-operation across all three pillars.

is granted by the Council acting by qualified majority, but each Member State retains its Luxembourg Compromise-style veto. The rules governing enhanced co-operation as regards PJC are set out in Articles 40 to 40b TEU. Thus, for example: Member States wishing to launch an enhanced co-operation have an effective right of appeal to the Council, in situations where the Commission refuses their request to make a proposal to the Council; and the European Parliament is merely consulted on any proposed enhanced co-operation under the Third Pillar.

The pediment

10–011   The main unifying elements, represented by the pediment of the Greek temple image, are: the single institutional framework within which all Union activities are carried on; a set of fundamental political and constitutional values, and machinery (first provided by the TA) to help ensure that these are upheld by all the Member States; common objectives, stated in a way that implies an "inter-pillar" approach; and common procedures for the amendment of the founding Treaties (the three Community Treaties and the TEU), and for accessions to the Union.

The single institutional framework

10–012   Prior to the TEU, co-operation in the matters that would be brought within the Second and Third Pillars was carried on outside the Community institutions (as they then were). European Political Cooperation (or EPC), the forerunner of the CFSP, was organised on the basis of Title III of the SEA.[47] The partners to EPC were described as "High Contracting Parties", not Member States; and their Foreign Ministers, when discussing EPC matters, did not constitute "the Council" (though such discussions might take place "on the occasion of meetings of the Council").[48] A Secretariat was established in Brussels to assist in preparing and implementing EPC activities and in administrative matters,[49] but was kept strictly apart from the Council's General Secretariat, and staffed by national officials on secondment from the various Foreign Ministries. As for the matters which came to be grouped under the JHA rubric of the Third Pillar, structured co-operation had for some time been taking place in a range of intergovernmental working parties, but without a Treaty basis.

Article 3 TEU states, in its first paragraph, that "[t]he Union shall be served by a single institutional framework which shall ensure the

---

[47] Title III SEA was repealed by Art.P(2) TEU.
[48] See the former Art.30(3)(a) SEA.
[49] See the former Art.30(10)(g) SEA.

consistency and the continuity of the activities carried out in order to attain its objectives while respecting and building upon the *acquis communautaire*". The second paragraph of Article 3 lays particular emphasis on "the consistency of the Union's external activities as a whole in the context of its external relations, security, economic and development policies". There must, in other words, be a coherent overall approach to the aspects of a complex international situation (as in Bosnia and subsequently in Kosovo) that belong to the domain of the CFSP, and those aspects falling within the external relations competence of the EC. Responsibility for ensuring the necessary consistency is placed on the Council and the Commission, which "shall co-operate to this end",[50] to ensuring the implementation of the policies mentioned in the paragraph, "each in accordance with its respective powers".

From the two following Articles of the TEU, the "single institutional framework" can be seen to comprehend the European Council and the five main institutions identified by Article 7 EC.

A Treaty basis for the European Council was first provided by Article 2 of the SEA. That provision was replaced by Article 4 TEU, which defines the role and composition of the European Council, fixes the rhythm of its meetings and imposes upon it reporting obligations to the European Parliament.[51] The reference in the first paragraph of the Article to the "Union", must be interpreted in the sense of Article 1, third paragraph: it follows that the European Council has been entrusted with providing "the necessary impetus", and "defining the general political guidelines" for the development of the EC no less than of the CFSP and PJC; and Presidency Conclusions from successive European Councils show that is exactly how the latter have understood their task.[52]

According to Article 5 TEU: "[t]he European Parliament, the **10–013** Council, the Commission, the Court of Justice and the Court of Auditors shall exercise their powers under the conditions and for the purposes provided for, on the one hand, by the provisions of the Treaties establishing the European Communities and of the subsequent Treaties and Acts modifying and supplementing them and, on the other hand, by the other provisions of this Treaty". The grammatical construction of the provision ("on the one hand, . . . and, on the other hand") places the powers derived by the five

---

[50] The duty of co-operation was an addition to Art.3 by the TA, after friction between the two institutions experienced in the early years of the CFSP.
[51] See further the discussion contained in Ch.2.
[52] See, e.g. Part III of the December 1999 Helsinki Conclusions. A similar point is made by de Witte, "The Pillar Structure and the Nature of the European Union: Greek Temple or French Gothic Cathedral?" in Heukels, Blokker and Brus (eds), *The European Union after Amsterdam* (1998), p.60. See also Glaesner, "The European Council" in Curtin and Heukels (eds), *The Institutional Dynamics of European Integration—Essays in Honour of Henry G. Schermers* (1994), pp.112–115.

institutions from the TEU on an equal footing with those derived
from the Community Treaties. For that reason, the view (which has
been widely held,[53] and which the authors of this work once
shared),[54] that the institutions retain their Community character and
are merely "borrowed" by the Union, seems mistaken. A metaphor
that reflects, more accurately than that of "borrowing", the text of
Article 5 TEU and the institutional reality, would be that institutions
born under the Community Treaties, as amended, have been "legally
adopted" by the Union.[55]

We have seen that the respective powers, and the mutual interaction, of the institutions differ significantly between the three pillars.
The implications of the creation of a single institutional framework
serving the Union as a whole are, nevertheless, profound, in both
formal and substantial terms. This is especially clear in relation to
the Council, because of its central role in decision making on the
CFSP and PJC, as well as in the Community sphere.

Broadly speaking, the Council's mode of operation, as defined by
the Treaties and its own Rules of Procedure, and elaborated in its
working practices, is the same across the whole spectrum of Union
activities. Thus, draft measures, whether based on First, Second or
Third Pillar powers, undergo technical examination in the appropriate Council working party, and then proceed by way of the Committee of Permanent Representatives (COREPER) to the
ministerial level, for political consideration, where necessary, and
formal adoption. The same Council agenda may contain items for
discussion (so-called "B-points") belonging to different pillars: for
instance, CFSP matters, and trade or development co-operation
matters falling within the EC's external relations competence,
appear alongside each other on agendas of the General Affairs and
External Relations Council. Similarly, A-point lists may contain

---

[53] See, among others, Timmermans in Louis (ed.) *L'Union européenne après Maastricht*
(Journée d'études Bruxelles, February 21, 1992), p.51; Constantinesco, "La structure du
Traité instituant l'Union européenne" (1993) 29 C.D.E. 251, 267–268; Everling, "Reflec-
tions on the Structure of the Union" (1992) 29 C.M.L.Rev. 1053, 1061; Heukels and De
Zwaan, "The Configuration of the European Union: Community Dimensions of Institu-
tional Interaction" Curtin and Heukels (eds), *The Institutional Dynamics of European
Integration—Essays in Honour of Henry G. Schermers* (1994), p.227.
[54] See the 3rd ed. of this book, at p.657.
[55] de Witte, "The Pillar Structure and the Nature of the European Union: Greek Temple or
French Gothic Cathedral?" in Heukels, Blokker and Brus (eds), *The European Union after
Amsterdam* (1998), pp.58f, though he does not use the suggested metaphor, expresses a
similar view. The Council has acknowledged its adoption by the Union through rechristen-
ing itself "Council of the European Union": see Decision 93/591 [1993] O.J. L281/18. This,
despite the fact that Art.1 of the Merger Treaty continues to refer to "[a] Council of the
European Communities"; as does Art.9 of the same Treaty, to "[a] Commission of the
European Communities". The justification for the Council's change of name lies in reading
Art.1 of the Merger Treaty together with Arts 3 and 5 TEU.

items for adoption without discussion from all three pillars, regardless of the particular formation in which the Council may be meeting.[56]

There are specialised committees composed of senior national **10–014** officials—the Political and Security Committee and the Coordinating Committee—which, among their other tasks, contribute to the preparation of Council decisions under the Second and Third Pillars, respectively;[57] that, however, is without prejudice to the role of COREPER as the body with general responsibility for the final preparation and presentation of all agenda items to the Council.[58] Article 19(1) of the Council's Rules of Procedure says that COREPER "shall in any case ensure consistency of the Union's policies and actions and see to it that the following principles and rules are observed:

  (a) the principles of legality, subsidiarity, proportionality and providing reasons for acts;
  (b) rules establishing the powers of Union institutions and bodies;
  (c) budgetary provisions;
  (d) rules on procedure, transparency and the quality of drafting.[59]

A footnote to the italicised phrase makes clear that COREPER's duty to ensure consistency and the observance of those principles applies "in particular for matters where substantive preparation is undertaken in other fora".

Moreover, the standing invitation for the Commission to take part in meetings of the Council applies irrespective of the legal basis of the matter being discussed.[60] Commission representatives will, therefore, regularly be present at all levels of Council decision making on CFSP or PJC measures, and may contribute actively to the debate.

A last point on the single institutional framework is that it has brought matters covered by Titles V and VI TEU within the field of responsibility of the Council's General Secretariat. The national officials and Ministers dealing with such matters in Council bodies, accordingly, have the benefit of independent advice and assistance from the same corps of permanent civil servants with which they are accustomed to working in the European Community context.

---

[56] See de Witte, "The Pillar Structure and the Nature of the European Union: Greek Temple or French Gothic Cathedral?" in Heukels, Blokker and Brus (eds), *The European Union after Amsterdam* (1998), p.61. On the organisation of the Council's agenda, see further, Ch.2.
[57] See, respectively, Art.25 and Art.36(1) TEU.
[58] Art.207(1) EC.
[59] Council Rules of Procedure [2004] O.J. L106/22.
[60] *ibid.*, Art.5(2).

Fundamental values and principles

10–015   Article 6 TEU provides:

(1) The Union is founded on the principles of liberty, democracy, respect for human rights and fundamental freedoms, and the rule of law, principles which are common to the Member States.

(2) The Union shall respect fundamental rights, as guaranteed by the European Convention for the Protection of Human Rights and Fundamental Freedoms signed in Rome on November 4, 1950 and as they result from the constitutional traditions common to the Member States, as general principles of Community law.

(3) The Union shall respect the national identities of its Member States.

(4) The Union shall provide itself with the means necessary to attain its objectives and carry through its policies.

The principles that encapsulate the fundamental political values of the EU are stated in paragraph (1) of the Article. The paragraph was added by the TA; in the version of the Article found in the original TEU, there was only an oblique reference to the fact that Member States' "systems of government are founded on the principle of democracy". That change has an echo in Article 49 TEU, where respect for the principles set out in Article 6(1) TEU has been made a condition which States applying for membership of the Union must fulfil. With the prospect of enlargements which were and are likely to bring into the Union some countries where democracy and the rule of law are recent and fragile growths, it may have seemed wise to spell out in black and white that commitment to those principles is, for an applicant, a qualification as indispensable as being "European".

Article 7 TEU (as introduced by the TA and revised by the TN) provides for a degree of human rights enforcement against Member States at the Union level. According to Article 7(1) TEU, on a reasoned proposal by one third of the Member States, or by the Parliament or the Commission, the Council (acting by a majority of four-fifths of its members after obtaining the assent of Parliament) may determine that there is a "clear risk of a serious breach by a Member State of principles mentioned in Article 6(1)" and address appropriate recommendations to that State. Before making such a determination, the Council shall hear the Member State in question, and may call on independent persons to report on the situation in that Member State. Article 7(2) TEU then provides for the Council, meeting in the composition of the Heads of State or Government, and acting unanimously on a proposal by one-third of the Member States or by the Commission, after obtaining the assent of the

European Parliament, to determine that a Member State is guilty of a "serious and persistent breach" of the Article 6(1) principles. Again, the government of the Member State concerned must have been invited to submit its observations. Following such a determination, the Council may, by qualified majority decision, suspend certain of the rights enjoyed by that Member State under the TEU and the EC Treaty, including its voting rights (though its obligations must be left intact). Due consideration must be given to the consequences such suspensions may have for the legal situation of individuals.[61] The Council may decide subsequently, again by a qualified majority, to vary or revoke any suspension measures it has taken, in response to changes in the situation.[62] For the purposes of the relevant Council decisions, the vote of the representative of the targeted Member State will not be taken into account.[63]

A certain degree of scepticism may be felt as to the practical value of that machinery. The unanimity necessary at the level of the Heads of State or Government (excepting only the Member State in the dock) for a determination as to the existence of a serious and persistent breach, under Article 7(2) TEU, seems most unlikely to be achieved—the less so, the larger the Union becomes. The introduction of the suspension machinery might be seen as unfortunate in principle, too: it detracts from the *sui generis* nature of the Union, making it appear like just another international organisation; it also places the enforcement of the Article 6(1) TEU principles at the mercy of high political manouvres, threatening to discredit the Union should it in fact fail to respond to a Member State's "serious and persistent breach".[64]

We have seen that the fundamental human rights, guaranteed by **10–016** the ECHR and by the constitutional traditions common to the Member States, have been recognised by the Court of Justice as applying within the European Community order, with the force of general principles of law.[65] The effect of Article 6(2) TEU is to render the obligation to respect fundamental rights applicable to all Union activities, and therefore also to those that take place under the Second and Third Pillars. However, pursuant to Article 46(d) TEU, the jurisdiction of the Court only extends to Article 6(2) "with regard to action of the institutions, in so far as the Court has jurisdiction under the Treaties establishing the European Communities and under this Treaty". The limitation on the justiciability of human rights infringements calls for two comments.

First, the reference in Article 46(d) TEU to "action of the institutions" must not be interpreted as purporting to override the

---

[61] Art.7(3) TEU.
[62] Art.7(4) TEU.
[63] Art.7(5) TEU.
[64] In any case, note the Commission's proposal for a Regulation establishing a "European Union Agency for Fundamental Rights" COM(2005) 280 Final.
[65] See Ch.8.

case law that requires respect for fundamental rights on the part of the authorities of the Member States, when they are acting as executants of Community policies or taking advantage of deroga-tions allowed by the EC Treaty.[66] Such an interpretation would be incompatible with Article 47 TEU, since Article 6(2) TEU is found among the Common Provisions in Title I of the TEU, against the effects of which the Community Treaties are protected.[67]

Secondly, the Court's lack of jurisdiction under the Second Pillar, though it manifestly weakens the effect of Article 6(2) TEU in respect of actions taken for the purposes of the CFSP, does not render the provision nugatory. The legal obligation of the Union to respect human rights is a factor likely to be invoked in Council debates, and which may influence their outcome; as may have been the case, for example, when it was decided that the powers granted to the EU Administrator of the city of Mostar in Bosnia-Herzegovina, should be made subject to a form of judicial review, by a specially appointed Ombudsman.[68]

The two remaining paragraphs of Article 6 TEU require only brief notice. The obligation in paragraph (3) for the Union to "respect the national identities of its Member States" was mentioned in Chapter 4: it applies equally under all three pillars. Paragraph (4) puts the Union under an obligation to provide itself with the means necessary to attain its objectives and carry through its policies. This will come into play as a political makeweight in discussions about the level of "own resources" to be made available to the Union under the financial packages which are agreed periodically.[69]

Common objectives

10–017   According to Article 2 TEU, the Union is to set itself the following objectives:

— to promote economic and social progress and a high level of employment and to achieve balanced and sustainable development, in particular through the creation of an area without internal frontiers, through the strengthening of economic and social cohesion and through the establish-ment of economic and monetary union, ultimately including a single currency in accordance with the provisions of this Treaty;

---

[66] e.g. Case 5/88 *Wachauf* [1989] E.C.R. 2609; [1991] 1 C.M.L.R. 328; Case C–260/89 *ERT* [1991] E.C.R. I–2925.
[67] As distinct from Titles II, III and IV which contain the provisions amending the three Community Treaties, and Title VII the TEU's Final Provisions: these are excluded from the saving effect of Art.47 TEU.
[68] See Decision 94/976 [1994] O.J. L312/34.
[69] On the current "Agenda 2000" package, see Chs 1 and 2.

— to assert its identity on the international scene, in particular through the implementation of a common foreign and security policy including the progressive framing of a common defence policy, which might lead to a common defence, in accordance with the provisions of Article 17;

— to strengthen the protection of the rights and interests of the nationals of its Member States through the introduction of a citizenship of the Union;

— to maintain and develop the Union as an area of freedom, security and justice, in which the free movement of persons is assured in conjunction with appropriate measures with respect to external border controls, asylum, immigration and the prevention and combating of crime;

— to maintain in full the *acquis communautaire* and build on it with a view to considering to what extent the policies and forms of co-operation introduced by this Treaty may need to be revised with the aim of ensuring the effectiveness of the mechanisms and the institutions of the Community.

The second paragraph of the Article imposes a requirement on the Union, in the course of attaining its objectives in conformity with the conditions and the timetable provided for, to respect the principle of subsidiarity as defined in Article 5 EC.

A first point to note about the statement of objectives in Article 2 TEU is its completeness. The first four indents contain succinct summaries of the concrete activities that can be carried on under all three pillars. This is the clearest possible refutation of the conception of the Union as a mere organising framework for co-operation on Title V and VI matters. It confirms the conception of a comprehensive Union order.

Secondly, the objectives mentioned in the second and fourth indents are ones that presuppose inter-pillar activity. Although the second indent places particular emphasis on the CFSP, for the Union "to assert its identity on the international scene" calls for the co-ordinated exercise of the full range of external relations powers conferred by the Treaties, as Article 3 TEU goes on to make clear. Similarly, the measures referred to in the fourth indent, "to maintain and develop the Union as an area of freedom, security and justice", are ones that will entail action under both Title IV of Part Three of the EC Treaty and Title VI TEU.[70]

The obligation stated in the fifth indent, to maintain in full, and to build on, the *acquis communautaire*, which confirms the centrality of the Community Pillar in the Union architecture, was considered earlier in this chapter.

---

[70] See, for confirmation, the explicit references to Third Pillar measures in Art.61 EC.

Common amendment and accession procedures

10–018   Prior to the TEU, there were separate procedures under each of
the three European Community Treaties, for the amendment of
each of those Treaties,[71] and for the accession of new Member States
to the Community in question.[72] The relevant provisions were
repealed by the TEU, and replaced by standard procedures "for the
amendment of the Treaties on which the Union is founded", and for
the admission of States to membership of the Union.

The common amendment procedure is found in Article 48 TEU.
Proposals for amendment may come from any Member State or
from the Commission, and must be submitted to the Council. After
consulting the European Parliament, the Commission (if not itself
the initiator of the proposal) and the European Central Bank (in
case of institutional changes in the monetary area), the Council may
decide (by a simple majority, presumably, since no voting rule is
specified)[73] to deliver an opinion in favour of calling an intergovernmental conference (IGC). If it does so, the IGC is convened by the
President. The amendments to be made to the Treaties are determined by common accord, and enter into force after being ratified
by all Member States in accordance with their respective constitutional requirements.

Article 49 TEU lays down the common accession procedure.
Applications for membership of the Union must be addressed to the
Council, which acts by unanimity, after consulting the Commission
and receiving the assent of the European Parliament. The conditions
of admission, and any necessary adjustment to the Treaties, have to
be agreed between the Member States and the applicant; and the
agreement is then submitted for ratification by all the contracting
States. In practice, the Council exercises its powers in respect of
membership applications in two phases: there is, first, a decision on
the principle of admission, which allows negotiations to be set in
train; and, once these have been completed successfully, and the
accession instruments are ready for signature, a formal decision is
taken,[74] accepting the application.

Legal personality and capacity

10–019   Under the present heading, we consider the status of the Communities and the Union in the domestic legal orders of the Member
States, on the one hand, and in public international law, on the
other. These are interesting issues, but it is important to be clear

---

[71] Respectively, the former Art.98 ECSC, Art.236 EC and Art.204 Euratom.
[72] Respectively, the former Art.98 ECSC, Art.237 EC and Art.205 Euratom.
[73] *cf.* Art.205(1) EC. It is suggested that rule would apply by analogy, since the qualified
majority voting rule applicable under the TEU is that of Art.205(2) EC.
[74] In the case of the accession of Austria, Finland and Sweden it was necessary to adjust the
accession instruments to take account of Norway's failure to ratify the Accession Treaty.

that they have no particular relevance to the public powers of legislation, administration and adjudication exercisable by the common institutions within the Union's own order.

Each of the two remaining European Communities is expressly declared, by its respective founding Treaty, to have legal personality.[75] There is also an explicit statement as to the legal capacity of the Community in the national orders:

> "In each of the Member States, the Community shall enjoy the most extensive legal capacity accorded to legal persons under their laws; it may, in particular, acquire or dispose of movable and immovable property and may be a party to legal proceedings."[76]

In addition, the Euratom Treaty acknowledges the capacity of that Community to act in the international order.[77] Article 101, first paragraph Euratom provides:

> "The Community may, within the limits of its powers and jurisdiction, enter into obligations by concluding agreements or contracts with a third State, an international organisation or a national of a third State."

Curiously, the EC Treaty contains no equivalent provision expressly **10–020** recognising the external capacity of the Community. However, the Court of Justice has chosen, with some audacity, to interpret the bare reference in Article 281 EC to the legal personality of the EC as meaning "that in its external relations the Community enjoys the capacity to establish contractual links with third countries over the whole field of objectives defined in Part One of the Treaty".[78] The Court's reasoning was that the generality of the grant of legal personality, evidenced by the position of Article 281 EC at the head of Part Six of the Treaty devoted to General and Final Provisions, must entail acknowledgement of the external capacity of the EC in all policy areas falling within its competence. Effectively, therefore, the position of the EC as a subject of international law, has been assimilated by the Court to that of Euratom.

Of course, neither Article 281 EC, nor the more explicit provisions of the Euratom Treaty, could actually have given the Communities

---

[75] Art.281 EC; Art.184 Euratom. *cf.* Art.6, first para, ECSC (now expired).
[76] Art.282 EC; Art.185 Euratom is in identical terms. *cf.* Art.6, third para., ECSC (now expired).
[77] As had the ECSC Treaty before it: see Art.6, second para., ECSC.
[78] Case 22/70 *Commission v Council (AETR)* [1971] E.C.R. 263, para.14; [1971] C.M.L.R. 335. For a full discussion of this and other aspects of the famous *AETR* case, see Dashwood, "Implied External Competence of the EC" in Koskennienni (ed.), *International Law Aspects of the European Union* (1998).

international legal personality and capacity: the existence of the former, and the extent of the latter, are matters for international law itself to determine. However, the intentions of the States which have formed the entity in question, as manifested in the foundational instrument, weigh heavily in such a determination; and these can be gathered not only from texts like Article 101, first paragraph Euratom but also, and more particularly, from the goals the entity has been set, and from the nature and scope of the powers conferred on its institutions.[79] The Communities manifestly fulfil the criteria for possession of legal personality that were laid down by the International Court of Justice in the *Reparations for Injuries* case; and recognition of their capacity to pursue their objectives on the international plane has been confirmed by decades of practice.

The TEU contains no provision stating that the Union established pursuant to that Treaty shall have legal personality. Two proposals for the insertion of such a provision into the Treaty were considered at different moments by the IGC negotiating the future TA: one idea was that the Union be given legal personality which would be juxtaposed with the existing personalities of the Communities;[80] while the more radical suggestion (of the Dutch Presidency) was for a single legal personality of the Union as a whole, into which those of the Communities would be assimilated. In the event, however, neither proposal won acceptance.

10–021   On the other hand, the TA did introduce a Council procedure which may (though it need not) be used when an international agreement, on a matter falling within Title V or Title VI of the TEU, is called for. That procedure was amended by the TN, and Article 24 TEU currently provides:

"(1) When it is necessary to conclude an agreement with one or more States or international organisations in implementation of this title, the Council may authorise the Presidency, assisted by the Commission as appropriate, to open negotiations to that effect. Such agreements shall be concluded by the Council on a recommendation from the Presidency [. . .]

---

[79] The leading case is the Advisory Opinion of the International Court of Justice on *Reparation for Injuries Suffered in the Service of the United Nations* I.C.J. Reports, 1949, p.174 (hereinafter "the *Reparation for Injuries*" case). The Opinion draws a distinction between attribution of legal personality in principle, and the scope of the capacity enjoyed by a given international organisation: see, in particular, pp.178–184. The criteria of legal personality for international organisations have been summarised by Brownlie as follows: (1) a permanent association of States, with lawful objects, equipped with organs; (2) a distinction between the organisation and its Member States; (3) the existence of legal powers exercisable on the international plane and not solely within the national systems of one or more States (see *Principles of Public International Law* (4th ed., 1990), pp.680–683).
[80] This was part of a rather elaborate draft provision, under the heading "Endowing the Union with legal personality", included in the text which was submitted by the Irish Presidency to the European Council in Dublin in December 1996; see CONF 2500/96, pp.87–89.

(4) The provisions of this Article shall also apply to matters falling under Title VI [. . .]

(5) No agreement shall be binding on a Member State whose representative in the Council states that it has to comply with the requirements of its own constitutional procedure; the other members of the Council may agree that the agreement shall nevertheless apply provisionally.

(6) Agreements concluded under the conditions set out by this Article shall be binding on the institutions of the Union."

Article 38 TEU cross-refers to Article 24 TEU, so far as concerns agreements on PJC matters.

There are two ways in which the provisions of Article 24 TEU could be interpreted.[81] One possible interpretation would be that the Article merely establishes a simplified procedure, enabling the institutional machinery of the Treaty to be used for the purpose of negotiating and concluding, on behalf of the Member States, international agreements to which they, and not the Union, become parties. The reference, in the second sentence, to national ratification procedures, and to the possibility of provisional application in respect of "the other members of the Council", would tend to support that construction. The other possibility would be that Article 24 TEU acknowledges the capacity of the Union as such to enter into international agreements relating to Title V or Title VI matters. In favour of that interpretation was the fact that the power to authorise the opening of negotiations and to conclude any agreement, is expressed to belong to the Council, and not to the representatives of the governments of the Member States meeting within the Council.

The practice that has developed confirms the second interpretation. A significant, and increasing, number of agreements have been negotiated and concluded under the procedure laid down by Article 24 TEU, all of them in the name of the Union.[82] This is an indication that the Member States and their international partners have accepted that the Union is endowed with external capacity, and necessarily therefore legal personality, at least for the purposes of Titles V and VI TEU. Indeed, applying the criteria of the *Reparation for Injuries* judgment, a good case could be made, quite independently of Article 24 TEU, for the Union's possession of international

---

[81] See Dashwood, "External Relations Provisions of the Amsterdam Treaty" (1998) 35 C.M.L.Rev. 1019, 1038–1041. Reprinted in O'Keeffe and Twomey (eds), *Legal Issues of the Amsterdam Treaty* (1999), pp.218–221.

[82] For a recent example of a CFSP agreement, see [2005] O.J. L256/57 (Agreement between the EU and the Democratic Republic of the Congo on the status and activities of the EU Police Mission in the Democratic Republic of the Congo); and for recent examples of highly important PJC agreements, see [2003] O.J. L181/25 (Agreements between the EU and the USA on extradition and on mutual legal assistance in criminal matters).

legal personality, in view of its objectives, which manifestly have an external dimension, as well as its single institutional framework. Further support for this analysis can be found in the fact that ambassadors from third countries are now regularly accredited to the Union, rather than to the Communities.[83]

In the result, despite the silence, or at best the equivocation, of the TEU, we take it as established that the Union possesses functional international personality and capacity. It is no impediment to such recognition that the Communities, which constitute the major component of the Union, each have their own distinctive personalities. After all, within the legal order created by the EC Treaty, there are, besides the Community, two entities endowed with legal personality, namely the European Central Bank[84] and the European Investment Bank.[85] Complex though the Community's relationship with each of the Banks may be, their co-existence as legal persons is not seen as problematic in itself.[86]

The Union has not been given legal capacity within the domestic orders of the Member States, but that is unlikely to be felt as more than a minor inconvenience. In the private law relationships that call for such capacity (e.g. procurement contracts or the acquisition or disposal of real property) the interests of the Union and of the Community will normally be indistinguishable.

Impact of the Constitutional Treaty (CT)

10–022   The CT would significantly reform the various topics covered in this chapter, including:

— repeal of the existing Treaties and abolition of their three pillar structure, so the Union would be reconstituted upon a single Treaty based upon a unitary legal order (para.11–005);
— the preservation of special arrangements in the field of CFSP within that unitary legal order: for example, as regards the inter-institutional balance, the range of available legal instruments, the jurisdiction of the Union courts, and the potential for enhanced co-operation (para.11–005);

[83] There is, moreover, a tendency for CFSP instruments to refer to the Union as if it were an international actor with rights and obligations: see, e.g. the Joint Action on the participation of the Union in the implementing structures of the peace plan for Bosnia-Herzegovina [1995] O.J. L309/2.
[84] Art.266, first para., EC.
[85] Art.107(2) EC.
[86] As to the EIB, see Case 85/86 *Commission v Governors of the EIB* [1988] E.C.R. 1281. On the relationship between the ECB and the European Community, see Zilioli and Solmayr, "The European Central Bank: an Independent Specialised Organisation of Community Law" (2000) 37 C.M.L.Rev. 591. Also Case C–11/00 *Commission v ECB* [2003] E.C.R. I–7147.

— the almost total assimilation of PJC into the "Community method": for example, as regards the inter-institutional balance, the available legal instruments, the jurisdiction of the Union courts, and the potential for enhanced co-operation (para.11–005);
— a restatement of the Union's basic aims, objectives, values and principles (para.11–017);
— express provision for voluntary withdrawal by any Member State from the Union (para.11–033);
— the introduction of simplified procedures for amending certain parts of the Constitution (para.11–034);
— express conferral of legal personality upon the Union (para.11–005).

Further reading

Arnull, "Taming the Beast? The Treaty of Amsterdam and the Court of Justice" in O'Keeffe and Twomey (eds), *Legal Issues of the Amsterdam Treaty* (Hart Publishing, 1999).

Dashwood, "Issues of Decision-making in the European Union after Nice" in Arnull and Wincott (eds), *Accountability and Legitimacy in the European Union* (OUP, 2003).

Denza, *The Intergovernmental Pillars of the European Union* (OUP, 2002).

Everling, "Reflections on the Structure of the European Union" (1992) 29 C.M.L.Rev. 1053.

de Witte, "The Pillar Structure and the Nature of the European Union: Greek Temple or French Gothic Cathedral?" in Heukels, Blokker and Brus (eds) *The European Union after Amsterdam* (Aspen, 1998).

Wessel, "The International Status of the European Union" (1997) E.F.A.Rev. 109.

Wessel, "Revisiting the International Status of the European Union" (2000) E.F.A.Rev. 507

CHAPTER 11

THE TREATY ESTABLISHING A CONSTITUTION FOR EUROPE

Guide to this Chapter This Chapter provides a summary of the **11–001** relevant reforms to the primary law of the European Union contained in the Treaty establishing a Constitution for Europe 2004. Even though that Treaty is unlikely to enter into force (at least not in the near future and in its current form), it is nevertheless worthy of serious consideration by students of the existing Treaties—not least because it represents a consensus between the Member States about the major constitutional problems facing the Union, together with an acceptable compromise package of reforms for addressing them. After some background to the process of constitutional reform, the approach we adopt is not to give a systematic Title-by-Title description of the entire Constitutional Treaty, but instead to highlight the provisions which are of greatest importance for the topics covered in the various chapters of this book: the Union's basic constitutional architecture; the Union's institutions; its legislative procedures; its competences; the protection of human rights and fundamental freedoms; the Union's legal instruments; reforms to the Union's judicial system; and a final section covering other issues of general significance (such as codification of the principle of supremacy, withdrawal from the Union, and the procedures for amending the Constitutional Treaty).

Background

The Intergovernmental Conference (IGC) which was concluded in **11–002** December 2000, as well as agreeing the Treaty of Nice, adopted a "Declaration on the Future of the Union" (annexed to the Final

Act), which highlighted the need for a more thorough reflection upon the Union's constitutional framework.[1]

The Laeken European Council held a year later, in December 2001, adopted a "Declaration on the Future of the European Union" (the Laeken Declaration) which laid down the parameters for this process of constitutional reflection.[2] The Laeken Declaration identified two main challenges for the EU: responding to the perceived lack of democracy and legitimacy among the Union's own citizens; and defining the identity and role of the Union in a post-Cold War, globalised and multi-polar, world. It went on to raise a large number of questions relating to the reforms needed in order to address these challenges, which were gathered under four principal headings: a better division and definition of competence in the EU; simplification of the Union's instruments; more democracy, transparency and efficiency in the Union; and the drive towards a Constitution for European citizens. Building on the perceived success of the Convention which had drafted the Charter of Fundamental Rights, the Laeken Declaration also established a "Convention on the Future of Europe" to deliberate on these myriad questions, and prepare a set of proposals for presentation to the Member States at a future IGC. This Convention—under the Presidency of the former French President Valérie Giscard d'Estaing—was composed of representatives of the Member States, the European Parliament, the national parliaments and the Commission. Its work commenced in February 2002, and culminated in the presentation of a draft "Treaty establishing a Constitution for Europe" to the European Council in July 2003.[3]

The Italian Presidency, which launched the IGC in autumn 2003 to approve the new Treaty, as required by Article 48 TEU, failed to achieve agreement on a final text at the meeting of Heads of State or Government held in December of that year; this was due primarily to controversies over revising the definition of QMV within the Council of Ministers. All outstanding problems were resolved and political agreement on a final text was reached under the Irish Presidency in June 2004, paving the way for signature of the Treaty establishing a Constitution for Europe at a ceremony in Rome on October 29, 2004.[4]

11–003   Thus began the arduous process of ratification. Although the document purports to establish a "constitution" for the EU, its form remains that of a treaty agreed between the Member States as High Contacting Parties under international law, a political and legal

---

[1] See Presidency Conclusions of December 8, 2000.
[2] See Presidency Conclusions of December 14, 2001.
[3] The full text is published at [2003] O.J. C169.
[4] The full text is published at [2004] O.J. C310. For an overview of the entire constitutional reform process, see Craig, "Constitutional Process and Reform in the EU: Nice, Laeken, the Convention and the IGC" (2004) 10 E.P.L. 653.

ambiguity well captured by referring to the document as the "Constitutional Treaty" (CT). According to Article IV–447 CT, the Treaty must be ratified by the High Contracting Parties in accordance with their respective constitutional requirements, and shall enter into force on November 1, 2006, provided that all the instruments of ratification have been deposited; or, failing that, on the first day of the second month following the deposit of the instrument of ratification by the last signatory State to take this step. Declaration No.30 adopted at the IGC and annexed to the Final Act states that if, two years after the signature of the Constitutional Treaty, four-fifths of the Member States have ratified it and one or more Member States have encountered difficulties in proceeding with ratification, the matter will be referred to the European Council.

At first, ratification by national parliaments (and, in the case of Spain, through a popular referendum) proved unproblematic.[5] However, the ratification process descended into crisis following negative results in popular referenda held first in France (May 29, 2005), then in the Netherlands (June 1, 2005). In the light of those events, the European Council meeting in June 2005 decided that the date initially planned for a report on ratification of the Treaty (November 1, 2006) was now untenable. The European Council called for a period of reflection and discussion across all Member States, and resolved to return to the issue of ratification in the first half of 2006, to make an overall assessment of the national debates and agree on how to proceed.[6]

In the meantime, opinion has been deeply divided about the best **11–004** way forward.[7] For example, some actors and commentators believe that the Constitutional Treaty is effectively dead: the only real option is to make the existing post-Nice arrangements work as best they can in the enlarged Union; possibly also "cherry picking" some of the more uncontroversial reforms proposed under the Constitution and adopting them (so far as possible) through secondary legislation, changes to institutional rules of procedure and new interinstitutional agreements.[8] Other actors and commentators have not given up hope that the Constitutional Treaty may yet enter into force: Member States such as Luxembourg have pressed ahead with their ratification procedures and secured positive votes;[9] it is possible

---

[5] Note also that the compatibility of the new Treaty with the constitutions of several Member States (including Spain and France) had to be clarified by their respective national constitutional courts: see the comments on France by Azoulai and Agerbeek (2005) 42 C.M.L.Rev. 871; and on Spain by Castillo de la Torre (2005) 42 C.M.L.Rev. 1169.

[6] See the Declaration by the Heads of State or Government of the Member States of the European Union on the Ratification of the Treaty establishing a Constitution for Europe (June 18, 2005).

[7] See further, Editorial, "What Now?" (2005) 42 C.M.L.Rev. 905.

[8] Consider, e.g. the Council's moves towards greater transparency in its legislative deliberations through amendments to its Rules of Procedure (discussed further below).

[9] Also, at the time of writing, Belgium, Cyprus and Malta.

that (as with the Danes over Maastricht and the Irish over Nice) a second referendum will eventually be held in both France and the Netherlands, with changed political circumstances (and, if necessary, appropriate declarations about the implications of the Constitution) increasing the chances of popular approval.

Much of the political uncertainty comes from the fact that it is very difficult to understand precisely *why* the French and Dutch electorates proved hostile to the Constitutional Treaty.[10] Domestic issues (such as the unpopularity of the prevailing government) certainly played some role; so too did concerns over recent and future enlargements of the Union, and a perceived threat to national identity and/or political influence. But it cannot be denied that the French and Dutch referenda also highlighted problems not only with the new Constitution (e.g., the sheer size and complexity of the document); but also with aspects of the existing EU which the Constitution would not have changed (such as a perceived neo-liberal bias in the relationship between economic and social policy).

It is therefore unclear at the time of writing when or indeed whether the Constitutional Treaty will enter into force. Nevertheless, the instrument deserves serious consideration by students of the existing Treaties—not least because it represents a consensus between the Member States about the major constitutional problems facing the Union, together with an acceptable compromise package of reforms for addressing them. The present chapter will therefore highlight the principal features of the Constitutional Treaty which impact upon topics covered elsewhere in this book.[11]

The Union's constitutional architecture

11–005   The CT would repeal and replace the existing Treaties upon which the EU is founded (including the Treaties of Rome and Maastricht).[12] In the process, it would bring to an end the current structure of the EU based upon the "three pillars plus pediment"; and abolish the European Community as a distinct legal entity.[13]

---

[10] See the post-referenda opinion polls conducted at the request of the Commission in both France and the Netherlands (Flash Eurobarometer Poll Nos 171 and 172, respectively).

[11] Many important aspects of the EU are not substantially affected by the CT, and thus are not addressed in this chapter, e.g. Union citizenship as dealt with under Arts I–10 and III–125–129 CT; e.g. the accession procedure as contained in Art.I–58 CT. Reasons of space preclude discussion of many other more significant reforms contained in the CT, e.g. the extension of Union competence under the area of freedom, security and justice as contained in Chapter IV, Title III, Part III CT; e.g. the reorganisation of the Union's competences in the field of external relations as contained in Title V, Part III CT; e.g. the introduction of new legal bases for Union action in fields such as energy and intellectual property under Arts III–256 and III–176 CT (respectively).

[12] Art.IV–437 CT. Art.IV–438 CT contains provisions on succession and legal continuity. Art.IV–439 CT refers to certain transitional provisions in respect of the Union institutions (see further below). Note also Protocol No.33 on the acts and treaties which have supplemented or amended the EC Treaty and TEU, which deals, *inter alia*, with the Single European Act and the Treaties of Amsterdam and Nice.

[13] *cf.* Ch.10 on the existing pillar structure, and the relationship between the EC and the EU.

Instead, there would be a unitary EU based upon a single Treaty-Constitution.[14] Besides its preamble, the CT is divided into four parts: Part I sets out the Constitution's core principles; Part II contains the Charter of Fundamental Rights; Part III contains provisions on the substantive policies of the Union, together with more detailed institutional, procedural and financial provisions; and Part IV consists of General and Final Provisions. In addition, the CT is supplemented by a long list of protocols, annexes and declarations. According to Article I–7 CT, this newly constituted EU would possess its own legal personality.[15]

However, it is important to stress that abolition of the existing pillar structure and the creation of an integral Union does not imply that the EU's multifarious activities would thenceforth be governed by a uniform system of inter-institutional relations, including a single procedure for decision making. The CT preserves strongly differentiated institutional and procedural arrangements, in particular, for the Union's activities in the areas of the CFSP (the present Second Pillar); and also, although less so, for activities in the area of PJC (the present Third Pillar).[16]

The Union's institutions

European Council

Article I–19 CT formally recognises the European Council, for the **11–006** first time, as a Union institution.[17] According to Article I–21(1) CT, the European Council shall provide the Union with the necessary impetus for its development and shall define the general political directions and priorities thereof. That provision also states that the European Council shall not exercise legislative functions; however, various provisions of the CT, relating to matters of a "constitutional" or "high politics" character, give the European Council a power to take legally binding decisions: for example, on the future composition of the European Parliament as regards the allocation of MEPs between Member States;[18] on the future rotation of Commissioner posts between Member States (including the power to increase the number of Commissioners);[19] on the final appointment of the Commission after its nominees have received the consent of the European Parliament;[20] and on the strategic interests and objectives of the Union in the external relations field.[21]

---

[14] Art.I–1 CT.
[15] *cf.* Ch.10 on the existing legal personalities of the EC and the EU.
[16] See further, below.
[17] *cf.* discussion of the existing legal framework of the European Council in Ch.2.
[18] Art.I–20(2) CT.
[19] Art.I–26(6) CT.
[20] Art.I–27(2) CT.
[21] Art.III–293 CT.

One politically sensitive issue addressed by the Convention and the IGC concerned the Presidency of the European Council. Many felt that the current system of rotation between Member States created problems of consistency and continuity in defining the Union's political agenda, which was liable to experience a shift in direction every six months, as a different Member State took over the helm. In practical terms, moreover, the task of the European Council President has simply become too big for a person who is acting at the same time as his or her Head of Government to give the attention that it requires. It was therefore decided that the European Council should acquire a more stable presidency. According to Article I–22 CT, the President of the European Council is to be elected by the European Council,[22] for a term of two-and-a-half years (renewable once). The President will be responsible for chairing European Council meetings, ensuring the preparation of and continuity in the work of the European Council, facilitating cohesion and consensus within the European Council, presenting reports to the European Parliament after European Council meetings, and representing the EU externally at his or her level as regards the CFSP.[23] The President of the European Council may not hold a national office—but there is no explicit bar to holding another office within the Union itself. While in theory that would leave open the possibility for the same person to be President of the European Council and of the Commission, such an accumulation of offices might be thought to be inconsistent with the institutional balance intended by the CT.

Council of Ministers

11–007   Article I–24 CT expressly refers to two Council configurations— General Affairs and Foreign Affairs—and empowers the European Council[24] to establish a list of other Council configurations.[25] Two further reforms are of greater importance.

First, Article I–24(6) CT provides that the Council shall meet in public when it deliberates and votes on a draft legislative act.[26] There has, historically, been widespread criticism of the Council's perceived secrecy and, in particular, suspicion that Member States horse-trade over controversial measures in the Council, then blame "Brussels" in the face of an unpopular response at home. In fact, some of the Council's deliberations are already open to the public, in particular,

---

[22] Acting by QMV.
[23] Though without prejudice to the powers of the new Minister for Foreign Affairs (discussed below).
[24] Acting by QMV.
[25] Pending which, see Art.3 Protocol No.34 on the transitional provisions relating to the institutions and bodies of the Union. On the current position within the Council, see Ch.2.
[26] See also Art.I–50(2) CT.

when the Council is acting under the co-decision procedure with the European Parliament.[27] Even despite the faltering of the Constitution's ratification process, a strong feeling emerged that the more far-reaching principle of transparency contained in Article I–24(6) CT was sufficiently important as to warrant immediate action. The Council therefore decided in December 2005 to increase the number of public debates it holds on important new legislative proposals other than those governed by the co-decision procedure, as well as on important non-legislative initiatives affecting the interests of the Union and its citizens.[28]

Secondly, Article I–24(7) CT states that the Presidency of Council configurations[29] shall be held by the Member States on the basis of equal rotation, in accordance with conditions established by the European Council.[30] The draft text of those conditions was agreed at the IGC and is to be found in Declaration 4 annexed to the Final Act. The Presidency should be held by pre-established groups of three Member States for a period of 18 months. Groups are to be made up on the basis of equal rotation, taking into account the diversity of Member States and their geographical balance. Unless they decide otherwise, each member of the group shall in turn chair for six months the relevant Council configurations, with the other members assisting the Chair on the basis of a common programme. It is anticipated that this arrangement should facilitate greater coherence and continuity in the Council's activities.

European Parliament

In accordance with Article IV–439 CT and Protocol No.34, the **11–008** composition of the European Parliament during its 2004–2009 term shall not be affected by the entry into force of the Constitution.[31]

However, sufficiently in advance of the 2009 elections, the European Council[32] must adopt a decision under Article I–20(2) CT establishing the Parliament's composition. For these purposes, the number of MEPs shall not exceed 750, divided between Member States on a degressively proportional basis, with a minimum of six

---

[27] See Art.8 of the Council's Rules of Procedure [2004] O.J. L106/22.
[28] See Council conclusions of December 21, 2005, "Improving Openness and Transparency in the Council" (15834/05).
[29] Other than Foreign Affairs, which is presided over by the new Minister for Foreign Affairs (discussed below).
[30] Acting by QMV.
[31] On the current composition of the European Parliament, see Ch.2. Note Art.21 of the Protocol concerning the conditions and arrangements for admission of the Republic of Bulgaria and Romania to the EU annexed to Treaty of Accession 2005 [2005] O.J. L157, which would amend Art.1 of Protocol No.34 annexed to the CT so as to allow for the election of MEPs from the two new Member States, in derogation from the normal maximum permitted number of MEPs, with effect until the end of the 2004–2009 parliamentary term.
[32] Acting unanimously, on the Parliament's initiative and with its consent.

and maximum of 96 MEPs per Member State. This new system of allocating MEPs to Member States through secondary legislation is intended to offer greater flexibility, particularly in the light of future enlargements, as compared to the existing approach (whereby changes to the allocation of MEPs to Member States requires formal amendment of the Treaty itself).

European Commission

11-009   The composition of the Commission is dealt with by Article I–26 CT.[33] The first new Commission appointed under the CT would consist of one national per Member State.[34] However, subsequent Commissions appointed under the Constitution would consist of a number of members equal to two-thirds of the number of Member States.[35] Those members are to be selected on the basis of equal rotation between the Member States, and reflect the demographic and geographical range of all Member States. The detailed system is to be established by the European Council, acting unanimously.[36]

The procedure for appointing the Commission is contained in Article I–27 CT: the Commission President is to be proposed by the European Council (acting by QMV) and "elected" by the European Parliament (by a majority of its members); the Commissioners are to be proposed by the Council of Ministers by common accord with the Commission President-elect, and the entire Commission[37] requires the consent of the European Parliament, before finally being appointed by the European Council (again acting by QMV). When proposing its candidate for Commission President, the European Council is expressly instructed to take into account the elections to the European Parliament—a reform which is intended to increase the political influence of the MEPs, and hence the incentive for citizens to vote at the European parliamentary elections.[38]

Minister for Foreign Affairs

11-010   One of the Convention's principal objectives was to furnish the Union with an institutional framework capable of executing its external policies more effectively and coherently. The end result is

---

[33] On the current composition of the Commission, see Ch.2. Note that the impact of the entry into force of the CT upon the existing Commission (in particular, the appointment of the first MFA) is dealt with under Art.4 of Protocol No.34 on the transitional provisions relating to the institutions and bodies of the Union.
[34] Including the President and the new Minister for Foreign Affairs.
[35] Including the President and the Minister for Foreign Affairs. The European Council, acting unanimously, may decide to alter this number.
[36] Note also Declaration No.6 annexed to the Final Act, intended to assuage Member State nerves about the balanced functioning of a Commission in which not all nationalities are represented.
[37] Including the President and the Minister for Foreign Affairs.
[38] *cf.* the current arrangements for appointment of the Commission as discussed in Ch.2.

the post of Minister for Foreign Affairs (MFA)—an amalgamation of the existing functions of the High Representative for the CFSP and the Commissioner for External Relations.

According to Article I–28(2) CT, the MFA shall conduct the Union's CFSP.[39] In particular, he or she will enjoy a power of initiative as regards CFSP proposals; and will be responsible for implementing the CFSP under mandate from the Council.[40] The MFA will, moreover, preside over the Foreign Affairs Council, whether it is considering CFSP or other external relations matters such as the common commercial policy.[41] But the chief constitutional novelty of the MFA is that he or she will simultaneously be associated with the Council of Ministers *and* a member of the Commission (in fact, one of its Vice-Presidents). In the latter capacity, according to Article I–28(4) CT, the MFA shall ensure the consistency of the Union's external action, with responsibility within the Commission for external relations and coordinating other aspects of the Union's external action. When the Convention's proposals were first published, doubts were expressed about whether the same person could really owe their institutional loyalty to both the Council and the Commission. However, the final text of the CT makes clear that the MFA should be bound by the Commission's procedures *only* when discharging his or her responsibilities under Article I–28(4) CT, and *only* to the extent that this is consistent with his or her position within the Council. In other words, the MFA may well be "double-hatted"—but his or her Council hat will sit on top of the Commission one at the final stage of decision making by the Foreign Affairs Council. According to Article I–21(2) CT, the MFA shall take part in the work of the European Council, although without formally becoming a member of it.

According to Article I–28(1) CT, the MFA is to be appointed by the European Council by QMV, with the agreement of the Commission President.[42] However, as one of the Vice-Presidents of the Commission, he or she must also be approved, collectively with the remainder of the College, by the European Parliament.[43] Moreover, in the event of a motion of censure being passed by the Parliament against the Commission, the MFA must resign from his or her duties within the Commission (but will remain in post for those responsibilities associated with the Council).[44]

---

[39] *cf.* Art.I–22(2) CT on external representation of the Union by the President of the European Council, without prejudice to powers of the MFA (dealt with above).
[40] See further the detailed provisions on external action in general and the CFSP in particular contained in Title V, Part III CT.
[41] Art.I–28(3) CT.
[42] The European Council may end his or her term of office by the same procedure. This applies also in situations where the Commission President requests the MFA to resign: see Art.I–27(3) CT.
[43] See above.
[44] Arts I–26(8) and III–340 CT.

The Union's legislative procedures

Initiation of the legislative process

11–011   According to Article I–26(2) CT, *legislative* acts of the Union[45] may be adopted only on the basis of a Commission proposal, except where the Constitution provides otherwise. The main exception to the general principle that the Commission enjoys a monopoly over the initiation of Union legislation is contained in Articles I–42(3) and III–264 CT: in the field of PJC, acts may also be adopted on the initiative of one-quarter of the Member States.[46]

However, the CT contains no such presumption as regards *non-legislative* acts.[47] Here, each legal basis determines whether the Commission and/or some other body enjoys the right of initiative. For example, Articles I–40(6) and III–299 CT provide that, in the field of the CFSP, proposals for Union measures (all of which are non-legislative in nature) may be made either by a Member State or by the new MFA (acting alone or with Commission support).[48]

Another point to note is that, in addition to the existing power of the Council and the Parliament to request the Commission to consider submitting a given legislative proposal,[49] Article I–47(4) CT introduces a further innovation: at least one million citizens from a significant number of Member States may invite the Commission to submit appropriate proposals for the purposes of implementing the Constitution. The detailed conditions for exercising this "citizens' initiative" (including the minimum number of Member States whose citizens must be involved) are to be laid down by future secondary legislation.

Role of the European Parliament

11–012   Article I–46(2) CT contains a concise statement of the Union's dual basis of democratic legitimacy: *citizens* are directly represented at the Union level in the European Parliament; *Member States* are represented in the European Council and the Council of Ministers, those representatives being themselves democratically accountable either to their national parliaments or their citizens.

In accordance with this dual basis for democratic legitimacy, the CT is to be applauded for further extending the co-decision procedure[50]—now renamed the "ordinary legislative procedure" and

---

[45] On the definition of legislative acts, see further below.
[46] *cf.* the current position under the Third Pillar as discussed in Ch.10.
[47] On the definition of non-legislative acts, see further below.
[48] *cf.* the current position under the Second Pillar as discussed in Ch.10.
[49] Now contained in Arts III–345 and III–332 CT (respectively).
[50] On the current scope of the co-decision procedure, see Ch.3.

described in full under Article III–396 CT—so as to cover fields such as agricultural policy (currently subject to mere consultation of the Parliament by the Council),[51] and the common commercial policy (as regards which the Parliament is currently denied any formal right of participation).[52]

Nevertheless, certain legal bases would remain governed by procedures giving the European Parliament a more limited role (now referred to as "special legislative procedures").[53] For example, the consultation procedure would be retained in fields such as the harmonisation of indirect taxation;[54] and the Parliament's consent would be required in areas such as the adoption of general anti-discrimination measures.[55]

However, Article IV–444 CT introduces a "passerelle clause" or simplified revision procedure whereby, as regards legal bases contained in Part III CT which provide for legislative acts to be adopted by the Council in accordance with a special legislative procedure, the European Council (acting unanimously and with the consent of the European Parliament) may decide to provide instead for the future application of the ordinary legislative procedure. Any such proposal must be notified to the national parliaments, each of which has an effective right to veto the proposal within a six-month period.[56]

One might note that, as a result of these reforms, the co-operation procedure introduced by the SEA and currently contained in Article 252 EC would cease to exist (being replaced under some legal bases by the ordinary legislative procedure, and in others by mere consultation).[57] This was accepted by the Convention and the IGC as a useful step towards reducing the sheer number of legislative procedures employed by the Union.

Voting rules within the Council of Ministers

According to Article I–23(3) CT, the Council of Ministers shall act **11–013** by QMV, except where the Constitution provides otherwise.

The definition of QMV was perhaps the most difficult issue to be addressed by the Convention and the subsequent IGC. In accordance with Article IV–439 CT and Protocol No.34, the existing rules on QMV as established by the TN will continue to have effect until

---

[51] Art.III–231 CT.
[52] Art.III–315 CT.
[53] On the current situation, see again Ch.3.
[54] Art.III–171 CT.
[55] Art.III–124 CT.
[56] Arts IV–444(2) and (3) CT. Cp. Art.6 of the Protocol on the role of national parliaments in the EU.
[57] On the co-operation procedure under the existing Treaties, see Ch.3.

October 31, 2009.[58] Then, as from November 1, 2009, the new rules set out in Article I–25(1) CT would come into operation. Those rules consist of a new form of triple threshold: where the Council acts on a proposal from the Commission, a qualified majority shall be defined as at least 55 per cent of the members of the Council, comprising at least 15 of them and representing Member States comprising at least 65 per cent of the population of the Union.[59]

So far as concerns the first and second thresholds—at least 55 per cent of Council members, comprising at least 15 Member States—both are based upon the numerical number of Member States, but their inter-relationship will vary depending on the size of the Union at any given time. For example, in the EU25, "55 per cent" is around 14 Member States, so that the crucial threshold would in fact be "at least 15". However, in the EU27, which it is assumed will exist by the time the new voting rules would come into effect, 55 per cent is indeed around 15 Member States, so that the two thresholds closely correspond. Yet future enlargements would refocus attention again: for example, in an EU of 31 countries, "55 per cent" would require at least 17—not 15—Member States.

So far as concerns the third threshold—the Member States voting in favour must represent at least 65 per cent of the EU population—Article I–25(1) CT further states that a blocking minority must in any case include at least four Council members, failing which the qualified majority shall be deemed attained. This is intended to reassure the smaller Member States that (e.g.) Germany, France and the United Kingdom—which together make up over 44 per cent of the total Union population—cannot form an automatic blocking minority without the support of at least one additional Member State (even if it is a small country such as Luxembourg or Malta).

11–014   Furthermore, Declaration No.5 annexed to the Final Act adopted at the IGC contains the draft text of a decision which is to be adopted by the Council of Ministers on the day the Constitutional Treaty enters into force. This decision sets out certain rules intended by the Member States to facilitate a smooth transition from the existing Nice definition of QMV to the new definition contained in

---

[58] On the existing definition of QMV, see Ch.3. Note Art.22 of the Protocol concerning the conditions and arrangements for admission of the Republic of Bulgaria and Romania to the EU annexed to Treaty of Accession 2005 [2005] O.J. L157, which would amend Art.2 of Protocol No.34 annexed to the CT so as to accommodate the votes of the two new Member States within the Council of Ministers during this transitional period. Moreover, Art.2(4) Protocol No.34 contains transitional arrangements to deal with those provisions of the CT where the European Council/Council of Ministers would vote in a restricted formation (e.g. within an enhanced co-operation initiative under Art.I–44(3)); the listed provisions of the CT would also enter into force only as from November 1, 2009.

[59] Under Art.I–25(2) CT, higher thresholds would be applicable where the Council does not act on the basis of a proposal from the Commission or MFA (e.g. where it acts on the initiative of a group of Member States as regards PJC matters in accordance with Art.III–264 CT).

Article I–25 CT. As such, it will take effect on November 1, 2009 and remain in force until at least 2014, when the Council may decide to repeal it. The decision basically deals with "narrow majorities": if Council members representing at least three-quarters of the Union population, or at least three-quarters of the Member States, necessary to constitute a blocking minority in accordance with Article I–25 CT indicate their opposition to the adoption of the relevant act by QMV, the Council shall do all in its power to reach (within a reasonable period and without prejudice to any mandatory time-limits laid down by Union law) a satisfactory solution which addresses the concerns raised by the relevant Council members. It is anticipated that this decision will seldom be formally invoked in practice, since the Council normally strives to achieve as broad as possible a consensus among the Member States.

The CT would affect not only the definition but also the scope of QMV,[60] extending its application to issues such as the taking up and pursuit of self-employed activities;[61] incentive measures in the field of culture;[62] and across the field of border controls, asylum and immigration.[63] However, unanimity would still be retained as regards certain especially sensitive legal bases: for example, the harmonisation of indirect taxation;[64] the enactment of general anti-discrimination measures;[65] and the exercise of primary powers in the field of the CFSP.[66] But, as with the ordinary legislative procedure, Part IV CT includes a "passerelle clause" (simplified revision procedure) whereby the European Council (acting unanimously and with the consent of the European Parliament) may decide that legal bases contained in Part III which are governed by unanimity in the Council of Ministers may thenceforth be converted to QMV. Again, any such proposal must be notified to the national parliaments, each of which has an effective right to veto the proposal within a six-month period.[67]

Note that, according to Article I–21(4) CT, except where otherwise provided, the European Council shall reach decisions by consensus; where applicable, the definition of a qualified majority is based on that for the Council of Ministers—but for these purposes, the European Council President and the Commission President do not vote.[68]

---

[60] On the existing scope of QMV, see Ch.3.

[61] Art.III–141 CT.

[62] Art.III–280 CT.

[63] Arts III–265–267 CT. *cf.* the use of the passerelle clause under Art.67 EC, by the Council in 2004, as regards the abolition of internal border checks, the freedom of third country nationals to travel within the Union for up to three months, and illegal immigration and illegal residence (discussed further in Ch.3).

[64] Art.III–171 CT.

[65] Art.III–124 CT.

[66] Arts I–40(6), I–41(4) and III–300 CT.

[67] Arts IV–444(1) and (3) CT. *cf.* Art.6 of the Protocol on the role of national parliaments in the EU.

[68] Arts I–25(3)-(4) CT.

Emergency brake procedures

11–015   Under a few legal bases, the CT introduces a new "emergency brake" procedure—in effect, a variant of the ordinary legislative procedure which deviates, in particular, from the general rules applicable to QMV in Council.

Articles III–270(3)-(4) CT provide a good illustration. Where a Council member considers that draft legislation establishing minimum rules of criminal procedure, within the context of PJC and as provided for under Article III–270(2) CT, would affect fundamental aspects of its criminal justice system, it may request that the draft be referred to the European Council, thus suspending the ordinary legislative procedure. Within four months, the European Council may either refer the draft back to the Council, permitting the ordinary legislative procedure to resume its course; or else request the Commission (or the group of Member States from which the draft legislation originated) to submit a new draft—in which case, the original proposal shall be deemed not to have been adopted.

If, within that four-month period the European Council has taken no action, or (where applicable) within 12 months of the new draft having been submitted the legislation has not been adopted, *and* at least one-third of the Member States wish to establish an enhanced co-operation on the basis of the draft act, authorisation to proceed with that enhanced co-operation shall be deemed to have been granted (without having to comply with the usual procedural requirements applicable to the initiation of enhanced co-operation).[69]

Similar "emergency brakes" are to be found in the provisions concerning the cross-border coordination of social security systems;[70] and the definition of certain criminal offences and sanctions.[71]

Budgetary procedure

11–016   The CT would alter the Union's financial principles and budgetary procedure in several important respects.[72] Space precludes any detailed examination of the provisions to be found in Articles I–53 to I–56 CT and Articles III–402 to III–415 CT, but some of the principal reforms are as follows. First, the system of "financial perspectives", which in the existing practice form part of a "soft law" text (the current Inter-Institutional Agreement on budgetary discipline and improvement of the budgetary procedure) would be formalised under the Constitution as the Union's "multi-annual

---

[69] *cf.* Arts I–44(2) and III–419(1) CT. The new rules on enhanced co-operation are set out below.

[70] Art.III–136(2) CT—though without any provisions on the simplified initiation of enhanced co-operation.

[71] Arts III–271(3)-(4) CT.

[72] On the existing financial principles and budgetary procedure, see Chs 1 and 2.

financial framework". Secondly, the budgetary procedure itself would be simplified into a variant of the ordinary legislative procedure, with the Commission presenting a draft budget (rather than an initial draft) and the Council and Parliament engaging (where necessary) in a process of conciliation in accordance with strict deadlines. Thirdly, the existing distinction between compulsory expenditure and non-compulsory expenditure would be abolished. The European Parliament would thus obtain greater influence over the budget as a whole (though it would, incidentally, lose its existing power to have the final say over non-compulsory expenditure).

The Union's competences

Right from the outset of the Constitutional Treaty, the text makes **11–017** clear that the Union is an organisation of derived and limited powers, "on which the Member States confer competences to attain objectives they have in common"; the Union "shall coordinate the policies by which the Member States aim to achieve these objectives, and shall exercise on a Community basis the competences they confer on it".[73] Articles I–2 and I–3 CT state, in a concise fashion, the Union's basic values and objectives. However, as with the existing Treaties, the Union can only take action to uphold its values and pursue its objectives where a specific legal basis contained in the Constitution empowers it to do so, and only under the specific conditions—institutional and otherwise—laid down in that legal basis. Thus, the underlying legal framework governing the existence and exercise of Union competences has not changed; the CT's reforms affect only the detailed application of that framework.[74]

Principle of conferral (attribution of powers)

Article I–11 CT contains a restatement and linguistic strengthen- **11–018** ing of the basic principle of conferral (attribution of powers), currently set out in Article 5(1) EC.

There was much discussion before and during the Convention about how to overcome the problem of legal bases such as Articles 95 and 308 EC, whose open-ended nature (combined with a good dose of institutional connivance) have given rise to the problem of "competence creep".[75] In the end, Article 95 EC has become Article III–172 CT but without any significant amendments.[76] Perhaps it was felt that the new judicial wind blowing since the *Tobacco Advertising Directive* judgment was a sufficient safeguard for Member State

---

[73] Art.I–1(1) CT.
[74] For discussion of the existing framework of Union competences, see Ch.4.
[75] See the detailed analysis in Ch.4.
[76] Though its relationship to existing Art.94 EC/new Art.III–173 CT is to be reformed.

competences.[77] By contrast, Article 308 EC would be replaced by Article I–18 CT, which provides that if action by the Union should prove necessary, within the framework of the policies defined in Part III, to attain one of the objectives set out in the Constitution, and the Constitution has not provided the necessary powers, the Council (still acting unanimously on a Commission proposal, though now with the Parliament's consent) shall adopt the appropriate measures. On the one hand, the reference to action in furtherance of the Union's objectives *in toto* makes the potential scope of application of Article I–18 CT much broader than that of Article 308 EC, which refers only to action in furtherance of the common market. On the other hand, the comparatively restrictive wording of Article 308 EC rarely acted in itself as a practical barrier to its liberal employment by the Community across a wide range of policy fields; it seems more likely that extensive recourse to Article I–18 CT—and with it any further "competence creep"—will be rendered unnecessary by the sheer range of sector-specific legal bases under which the Union is now empowered to act. In that regard, it is significant that measures based on Article I–18 CT shall not entail harmonisation of national laws in cases where the Constitution excludes such harmonisation— thus preventing Article I–18 CT being used to undermine the distinction between shared and supporting (complementary) competences. In any case, it is expressly provided under Article I–18 CT that the Commission must draw national parliaments' attention to proposals made thereunder, using the new procedure for monitoring the subsidiarity principle.[78]

In what is arguably one of the Constitution's most successful exercises in clarifying and explaining the nature of Union power, for the benefit of specialist practitioners and the interested public alike, Article I–12 CT offers—for the first time—generic definitions of the meaning of exclusive, shared and supporting (complementary) Union competences. Each of those definitions is then linked to the individual legal bases contained in Part III of the Constitutional Treaty, i.e. setting out in greater detail the principles governing Union activity within the relevant field, and more precise rules on the impact of Community competence upon national regulatory powers (e.g., whether harmonising measures adopted in fields of shared competence may be fully pre-emptive or should consist only in the setting of minimum standards).[79] The generic definitions contained in Article I–12 CT, and their respective scopes of application, are very similar to the model we adopted in Chapter 4—

---

[77] Case C–376/98 *Germany v Parliament and Council (Tobacco Advertising Directive)* [2000] E.C.R. I–8419.
[78] See further below.
[79] See, e.g. Arts III–210 CT (social policy), III–234 CT (environment) and III–235 CT (consumer policy).

though some of the Constitution's choices, in particular, about what constitutes an exclusive Union competence might seem to go beyond the pre-existing academic consensus, which was in turn based on the available case law.[80] One might note that the Union's coordinating powers in relation to the Member States' economic and employment policies, and in the field of CFSP, are accorded a special status falling outside the scope of those generic categories.[81]

Principle of subsidiarity

According to Article I–5(1) CT, the Union must respect the **11–019** national identities of the Member States, inherent in their fundamental political and constitutional structures, including regional and local self-government.

Beyond this hortatory principle, the CT contains important changes to the manner in which subsidiarity is to be monitored and enforced within the Union.[82] Article I–11(3) CT states that the Union institutions shall apply the principle of subsidiarity as laid down in the Protocol on the application of the principles of subsidiarity and proportionality, and that the national parliaments shall ensure compliance with that principle in accordance with the procedure set out in that Protocol.

Article 4 of the Protocol seeks to increase the flow of information about the Union's legislative activities to the national parliaments. Thus, the Commission must notify all its legislative proposals to the national parliaments at the same time as to the Union institutions themselves. Similar obligations apply to the other institutions and bodies: for example, the Council is obliged to notify national parliaments of draft legislative acts originating from a group of Member States in the field of PJC. Legislative resolutions of the European Parliament and positions of the Council must also be forwarded to the national parliaments.[83]

In addition, Articles 6 and 7 of the Protocol introduce a so-called "yellow card" system to help ensure respect for the principle of subsidiarity. Each national parliament has the power to object to any given legislative proposal by means of a "reasoned opinion", specifically on the grounds that it infringes the principle of subsidiarity, within a deadline of six weeks from the date of transmission of the

---

[80] In particular, the reference in Art.I–13(1) CT to establishing the competition rules necessary for the functioning of the internal market; and the rather shoddy definition of exclusive external competence contained in Art.I–13(2) CT.

[81] See Arts I–12(3)-(4) and I–15–16 CT.

[82] The principle itself, as set out in Art.I–11(3) CT remains substantially unchanged, save for express reference to objectives being sufficiently achieved by the Member States "either at central level or at regional and local level". For detailed discussion of the existing subsidiarity principle, see Ch.4.

[83] Note also the provisions of the Protocol on the role of national parliaments in the EU.

draft. The Union institutions (and other relevant bodies) would be obliged to consider all such reasoned opinions; but if one-third or more of the national parliaments object, then the draft legislation must be formally reviewed. That threshold is lowered to one-quarter, in the case of drafts proposed by the Commission or a group of Member States in the field of PJC. For these purposes, each national parliament has two votes: both votes may be used by a unicameral legislature; the votes are to be divided out between the chambers in a bicameral legislature. After the necessary review, the Commission (or other institution/body from which the draft legislation originated) must give reasons for its decision either to maintain, amend or withdraw the proposal. Reasoned opinions from national parliaments cannot have a veto effect on the progress of the Union's own legislative processes.

11–020   This "yellow card" system reflects the view held by the Convention and the IGC that compliance with the principle of subsidiarity would be most effectively achieved through a system of *ex ante* input into the legislative procedure as it unfolds, rather than *ex post* review of legislation after it has already been adopted.[84] Doubts have in fact been expressed about just how well the "yellow card" system as established by the Protocol could work. For example, is six weeks really enough time for national parliaments to consider and formulate a response to draft Union legislation? And will it be possible to divide objections specifically on grounds of subsidiarity from other complaints based rather on, say, the principle of proportionality, or the simple desirability of the proposed regulatory standards? Nevertheless, we believe that the requirement for reasoned opinions on the part of the national parliaments, and for reasons to be given if the competent institution at the Union level decides to maintain, amend or withdraw the draft legislative act in question, would seem likely, at least to some extent, to formalise and perhaps systematise subsidiarity scrutiny at both the Union level, and the level of national parliaments. Even if the competent institution (e.g., the Commission) decided to maintain a draft to which objection had been made by the requisite number of national parliaments, it would be open to other institutions (e.g., the Council and the European Parliament) to take into account and, if they considered it appropriate, act upon, the reasoned opinions of the national parliaments. The EU Committee of the UK House of Lords has expressed the view that "the raising of a yellow card would have a significant effect on the EU institutions . . . [I]f national parliaments operate the mechanism effectively it would be hard for the Commission and the

---

[84] Though see below on Art.8 of the Protocol.

Council to resist such sustained political pressure".[85] More fundamentally, giving teeth to the principle of subsidiarity by entrusting
national parliaments with responsibility for monitoring its application could increase the accountability and legitimacy of the EU's
lawmaking bodies, and enhance in an unprecedented way the sense
of "ownership" of the European project at national level.

One might point out that the Commission undertook a pilot study
of the "yellow card" system proposed under the new Constitutional
Treaty by inviting national parliaments to express their opinion on
the compatibility with the principle of subsidiarity of the Commission's 2004 package of proposals on the European railway system.[86]
It seems that around half the domestic parliamentary chambers
which responded expressed the view that the proposals breached the
principle of subsidiarity—crossing the threshold which would, under
the CT, require the Commission formally to review its position—
though (perhaps a little unpromisingly) this did not prevent the
European Parliament from subsequently voting in favour of the
original package.[87]

Although it appears unlikely that the Constitutional Treaty will
come into force, that fact need not necessarily prevent the introduction of subsidiarity monitoring by national parliaments. Voluntary
co-operation between the national parliaments and the Community
institutions, perhaps formalised by joint declarations establishing the
agreed framework, would be sufficient to put in place machinery
close in content and effects to that contemplated by the CT's
Protocol on the application of the principles of subsidiarity and
proportionality. The House of Lords EU Committee expressed the
view that "even if the Constitutional Treaty does not enter into
force, the provisions relating to national parliaments and to subsidiarity can and should provide a stimulus to greater and more
effective scrutiny by all national parliaments in the EU".[88] In fact,
national parliaments, acting under the auspices of COSAC,[89] have
already agreed to reinforce their scrutiny of Community legislative

---

[85] House of Lords EU Committee, "Strengthening National Parliamentary Scrutiny of the EU:
The Constitution's Subsidiarity Early Warning Mechanism", Report with Evidence, 14th
Report of Session 2004–05, *www.publications.parliament.uk/pa/ld200405/ldselect/ldeucom/
101/10102.htm* (at para.126).

[86] See generally "Further Integration of the European Rail System: Third Railway Package":
COM(2004) 140 Final.

[87] As reported on *www.euobserver.com* on September 28, 2005.

[88] House of Lords EU Committee, "Strengthening National Parliamentary Scrutiny of the EU:
The Constitution's Subsidiarity Early Warning Mechanism", Report with Evidence, 14th
Report of Session 2004–05, *www.publications.parliament.uk/pa/ld200405/ldselect/ldeucom/
101/10102.htm* (at para.281).

[89] The Conference of Community and European Affairs Committees of Parliaments of the
EU.

proposals and raise objections with the Commission on grounds of breach of the principle of subsidiarity, in an effort to increase political pressure for taking Article 5(2) EC seriously, even if this lacks the legal force of the "yellow card" provisions contained in the CT.[90]

Finally, one might note that the CT makes special provision for future participation by the national parliaments in evaluating the activities of Eurojust, and scrutinising the activities of Europol, within the context of PJC.[91]

Flexibility and enhanced co-operation

11–021   The examples of "primary flexibility" found under the existing Treaties would be retained under the new Constitutional Treaty.[92] Thus, for example, Denmark and Malta would keep their Protocols on the ownership of second homes;[93] while Ireland and Malta would keep their Protocols on the prohibition of abortion.[94] However, several such provisions would be revised. For example, the Constitution continues to contain permanent opt-outs from the third stage of EMU for unwilling Member States together with temporary derogations for as-yet-unable Member States;[95] but also envisages new provisions to increase economic integration among those Member States which already use the euro.[96] Similarly, the opt-out/opt-in provisions applicable to the UK and Ireland as regards the common policies on visas, asylum, immigration and judicial co-operation in civil matters would be slightly extended;[97] while Denmark's opt-out would be extended more substantially so as to cover not only the current Title IV issues but also PJC measures.[98] The CT also envisages special forms of flexibility within the context of the Common Security and Defence Policy.[99]

---

[90] See Contribution and Conclusions adopted by the XXXIV COSAC (October 9–11, 2005) available at *www.cosac.org*.

[91] Arts I–42(2), III–273 and III–276 CT. Note also: Art.III–259 CT, making further (though strictly unnecessary) reference to the subsidiarity "yellow card" system specifically as regards PJC measures; Arts III–260–261 CT on the participation of national parliaments in evaluation and co-operation activities within the area of freedom, security and justice.

[92] On primary flexibility under the existing Treaties, see Ch.4.

[93] See Protocol No.26 and Art.61 Protocol No.9 (respectively).

[94] See Protocol No.31 and Art.62 Protocol No.9 (respectively).

[95] See, in particular, Protocol Nos 13 and 14 dealing with the UK and Denmark (respectively).

[96] Arts I–15(1) and III–194–6 CT.

[97] So as to cover also measures concerning the collection, storage, processing, analysis and exchange of data within the framework of cross-border police co-operation under Art.III–275(2)(a) CT. See Protocols 18 and 19.

[98] Together with an option to convert its own peculiar approach to flexibility into an opt-out/opt-in regime similar to that of the UK and Ireland. See Protocol No.20.

[99] Arts III–310–312 CT.

"Secondary flexibility" would be substantially revised by the CT: the new enhanced co-operation regime is contained in Articles I–44 and III–416–423 CT.[1]

As regards enhanced co-operation *outside* the scope of the CFSP,[2] the CT would see certain changes to the substantive conditions for launching an enhanced co-operation. For example, under Article I–44(2) CT, the number of Member States required to engage in a new enhanced co-operation would change from a fixed number of eight to a floating number of one-third—which in the enlarged Union could actually make enhanced co-operation more difficult to initiate by raising the threshold to at least nine countries in a Union of 25 or 27. There would also be certain changes to the procedural requirements for initiating an enhanced co-operation. For example, the CT would abolish the lingering possibility that a Member State which objects to the initiation of enhanced co-operation by QMV within the Council may have the matter referred to the European Council for further discussion.[3] Moreover, under Article III–418(1) CT, when an enhanced co-operation is being established, the Council's authorising decision may impose certain objective conditions for participation; thus, Member States must be not only willing, but also (where appropriate) able to take part in the enhanced co-operation. In any case, the role of the European Parliament will be further bolstered: under Article III–419(1) CT, authorisation to proceed with an enhanced co-operation is to be granted by the Council only with the consent of the European Parliament (whereas under the existing First Pillar rules, Parliament's assent is required only when the relevant proposal relates to a legal basis governed by co-decision; and under existing Article 40a(2) TEU, there is mere consultation with the Parliament across the entire scope of PJC).

One of the most important changes introduced by the new **11–022** Constitution is an enhanced co-operation "passarelle clause". According to Article III–422 CT, if unanimity in Council applies under the legal basis to which the enhanced co-operation relates, then Council (acting unanimously and in its restricted enhanced co-operation formation) may move instead to QMV; while if the relevant legal basis uses a special legislative procedure for the adoption of laws and framework laws,[4] then Council (again acting unanimously and in its restricted enhanced co-operation formation, after consulting the European Parliament) may move instead to the ordinary legislative procedure.[5]

---

[1] On secondary flexibility under the existing Treaties, see Ch.4.
[2] Depillarisation means that there would thenceforth be no specific provisions on enhanced co-operation in the field of PJC.
[3] *cf.* the existing provisions contained in Art.11(2) EC.
[4] On which, see further below.
[5] *cf.* Declaration No.27: the Conference declares that Member States may indicate, when they make a request to establish enhanced co-operation under Art.III–419 CT, if they intend already at that stage to make use of the passerelle clause under Art.III–422 CT.

The rules for subsequent participation in an existing enhanced co-operation, now contained in Article III–420(1) CT, would also be reformed. In particular, if the Commission twice considers that the applicant Member State does not fulfil the conditions for participation, the Member State (in effect) has a right of appeal to the Council, which may authorise its participation (acting by QMV and in its restricted enhanced co-operation formation).[6]

The IGC agreed to a major extension of enhanced co-operation *within* the scope of the CFSP. Article 27b TEU currently provides that enhanced co-operation under Title V TEU must relate to the mere implementation of a joint action or common position as already agreed within the general framework of the CFSP; and also states that enhanced co-operation under Title V TEU must not relate to matters having military or defence implications.[7] The new Constitution would suppress both those limitations entirely, and permit the ordinary enhanced co-operation provisions to apply within the scope of the CFSP—subject to certain special adjustments to reflect the special character of this field of Union activity. For example, authorisation to initiate an enhanced co-operation would be granted by the Council acting unanimously.[8] There are also special rules on Member States subsequently joining an existing enhanced co-operation under the CFSP.[9]

Human rights and fundamental freedoms

Incorporation of the Charter of Fundamental Rights

11–023   According to Article I–9(1) CT, the Union shall recognise the rights, freedoms and principles set out in the Charter of Fundamental Rights which constitutes Part II.

In principle, incorporation of the Charter as a legally binding document represents a major achievement for the Convention and the IGC—but they also agreed to certain amendments of the text of the Charter (especially to its preamble and the horizontal provisions), in the face of reservations expressed by Member States such as the United Kingdom and Ireland.[10]

Several of these amendments are largely cosmetic. For example, the amended text of Article II–111(2) CT provides that the Charter does not extend the field of application of Union law beyond the

---

[6] With the higher QMV thresholds referred to in Art.I–25(2) CT applicable, because the Council is not acting on a proposal from the Commission.
[7] See Ch.10.
[8] Art.III–419(2) CT.
[9] Art.III–420(2) CT.
[10] On the Charter's existing horizontal provisions, and its legal status under Community law, see the detailed analysis in Ch.9.

powers of the Union or establish any new power or task for the Union, or modify powers and tasks defined in the other Parts of the Constitution. A new provision contained in Article II–112(4) CT states that, insofar as the Charter recognises fundamental rights as they result from the constitutional traditions common to the Member States, those rights shall be interpreted in harmony with those traditions. Similarly, according to new Article II–112(6) CT, full account shall be taken of national laws and practices as specified in the Charter.

More controversially, new Article II–112(5) CT states that the provisions of the Charter which contain principles may be implemented by legislative acts and executive acts taken by institutions of the Union, and by acts of the Member States when they are implementing Union law, in the exercise of their respective powers. However, they shall be judicially cognisable only in the interpretation of such acts and in any ruling on their legality. This is a clumsy attempt to ensure that exhortatory principles—usually embodying certain social and cultural aspirations, rather than conferring more traditional civil and political liberties, or concrete economic and social rights—cannot in themselves form the basis of directly effective individual rights, enforceable even in the absence of the necessary implementing measures at Union or national level; but should instead act merely as useful yardsticks against which to measure the relative success (or otherwise) of Union/national legislative activity. The problem is that there is no definitive guidance as to what constitutes a "principle" for the purposes of Article II–112(5) CT, either in the Charter itself or in the accompanying explanations (as revised by the Convention), which are contained in Declaration 12 annexed to the Final Act of the IGC. According to new Article II–112(7) CT, due regard must be paid to those explanations by the courts of the Union and of the Member States when interpreting the relevant provisions of the Charter.[11]

Notwithstanding the formal incorporation of the Charter as Part II of the Constitution, Article I–9(3) CT states that fundamental rights as guaranteed by the European Convention for the Protection of Human Rights and Fundamental Freedoms (ECHR) and as they result from the constitutional traditions common to the Member States shall constitute general principles of the Union's law—thus preserving the Court's existing case law, and also the legal basis for continuing to develop that case law in the future, lest the incorporated Charter should act as a constraint upon the flexible evolution of the Union's human rights jurisprudence in response to new social and moral problems.[12]

---

[11] The Charter's own preamble was revised to similar effect: see fifth recital.
[12] On fundamental rights as general principles of Community law, see the detailed analysis in Ch.8.

Legal basis for accession by the EU to the ECHR

11–024   Article I–9(2) CT imposes upon the Union an obligation to accede to the ECHR. However, it is expressly stated that such accession shall not affect the Union's competences as defined in the Constitution. This would overcome the legal objections to accession under Union law as identified by the Court of Justice in *Opinion 2/94.*[13] The remaining obstacles to the Union's accession would concern rather the institutional framework of the ECHR itself.[14]

The Union's legal instruments

11–025   Another of the main areas addressed by the Convention and the IGC, in pursuit of simplifying and clarifying the Union's operation, concerns legal instruments. These reforms have two goals. The first is to reduce the number of different legal instruments employed by the Union institutions, especially by abolishing the special types of measure currently used in the Second and Third Pillars (such as joint actions, framework decisions and conventions).[15] The second goal is to create a clearer distinction between *legislative* acts and *non-legislative* acts. This distinction—drawn in Article I–33(1) CT—has implications across a number of fields. For example, as regards the Union's decision making procedures, the fact that the Constitution provides for the adoption of legislative acts activates the presumptions contained in Article I–34(1) CT that the Commission enjoys the right to initiate the legislative process and that the relevant measure will be adopted by the ordinary legislative procedure involving equal participation from the Council and the European Parliament.[16] Moreover, the national parliaments' right to object to Union measures on the grounds of an alleged incompatibility with the principle of subsidiarity applies only as regards legislative acts;[17] and the distinction between legislative and non-legislative measures is crucial to the new rules on the standing of natural and legal persons to bring an action for annulment directly before the Union courts.[18]

Article I–33 CT describes two types of legislative act. "European laws" correspond to existing regulations as defined under Article 249(2) EC. "European framework laws" correspond to existing directives as defined under Article 249(3) EC.

---

[13] Opinion 2/94 [1996] E.C.R. I–1759. *cf.* Ch.4.
[14] Note also Protocol No.32 relating to Art.I–9(2) of the Constitution on the accession of the Union to the ECHR; and Declaration No.2 on Art.I–9(2) CT.
[15] On the Community's existing legal instruments, see Ch.5. On the legal instruments employed under the Second and Third Pillars, see Ch.10.
[16] Though, in accordance with Arts I–34(2)-(3) CT, the Constitution may rebut those presumptions by providing either for another body to enjoy the right to initiate the legislative procedure, or for legislative acts to be adopted according to a special legislative procedure (such as mere consultation of the European Parliament).
[17] See further, above.
[18] See further, below.

Besides non-binding recommendations and opinions, Article I–33 **11–026**
CT also describes two types of non-legislative act. "European
regulations" may take the form of *either* current regulations under
Article 249(2) EC *or* current directives under Article 249(3) EC—
but in either case are deemed non-legislative in nature. "European
decisions" correspond to current decisions under Article 249(4)
EC—but are also deemed non-legislative in nature. It is specifically
envisaged that such European decisions may be adopted without
reference to any specific addressee(s); this formalises existing practice whereby the Union institutions sometimes adopt so-called *"sui
generis"* decisions binding *omnes partes*.

These non-legislative acts can be adopted in three main categories
of situation. First, they may be adopted directly under the Constitution where provided for by a specific legal basis. This is true, in
particular, of the European Council and the Council acting in the
field of the CFSP.[19] Secondly, Article I–36 CT provides that the
Council and/or the Parliament, when adopting legislative measures,
may delegate to the Commission the power to adopt European
regulations intended to supplement or amend certain "non-essential
elements" of the parent act. The latter must explicitly define the
objectives, content, scope and duration of the Commission's delegated powers; and lay down the conditions to which the delegation is
subject (such as the possibility of the delegated powers being
revoked by Council and/or Parliament). Thirdly, Article I–37 CT
provides that, where uniform conditions for implementing legally
binding Union acts are needed, those acts shall confer implementing
powers (i.e. the ability to adopt European regulations or European
decisions) upon the Commission or, in duly justified specific cases,
upon the Council.[20] That Article also provides a new legal basis for
the comitology system, including a greater role for the Parliament in
setting out the relevant rules: European laws—adopted by the
ordinary legislative procedure—shall law down in advance the rules
and general principles concerning mechanisms for control by Member States of the Commission's exercise of implementing powers.[21]

The Union's judicial system

General reforms
The Union's present judicial architecture, and the jurisdiction of **11–027**
the Union courts, are the subject of detailed discussion in Chapters
12–14 of this book.

---

[19] See, e.g. Arts I–40–41 and III–294–313 CT.
[20] And in any case upon the Council within the field of the CFSP (in accordance with
Art.I–40 CT).
[21] On the existing comitology arrangements, see Ch.2.

One of the most obvious changes made by the Constitutional Treaty to the Union's judicial system is contained in Article I–29(1) CT: the "Court of Justice of the European Union" shall include the Court of Justice (currently the Court of Justice of the European Communities), the General Court (currently the Court of First Instance of the European Communities (CFI)) and any specialised courts (currently designated "judicial panels", as introduced by the TN). Moreover, Article III–355 CT would require the Member States to consult a panel before appointing members of the Court. In particular, Article III–357 CT provides for that panel to give an opinion on candidates' suitability for appointment. The panel is to comprise seven persons chosen from among former members of the Court of Justice and the CFI, members of national supreme courts and lawyers of recognised competence, one of whom is to be proposed by the European Parliament. The Council of Ministers is to lay down the panel's operating rules and appoint its members.

Otherwise, however, the Union's basic judicial architecture is not significantly modified by the CT.

11–028   That said, the CT would introduce several changes to the detailed jurisdiction of the Union courts. For example, the procedure for imposing sanctions upon defaulting Member States within the context of enforcement proceedings would be simplified in two ways.[22] First, where the Member State has already been found by the Court to be in breach of its obligations, the Commission would no longer be required to issue a reasoned opinion, only to give the Member State an opportunity to submit its observations. Secondly, where the proceedings relate to an alleged failure to notify domestic measures transposing a European framework law, the Commission would be able *in its initial application to the Court* to request the imposition of a financial penalty. In the latter situation, the Treaty would prevent the Court from imposing a sanction exceeding the amount specified by the Commission (though if the sanction proved inadequate, there would appear to be nothing to prevent the Commission from going back to the Court to ask for a harsher sanction).

As regards the jurisdiction to deliver preliminary rulings, the CT would expressly provide that, as regards cases involving a person in custody, the competent Union court must act "with the minimum of delay"—presumably in accordance with the accelerated procedure provided for under the Rules of Procedure.[23] Moreover, there would

---

[22] See Art.III–362 CT. On the existing rules for enforcement proceedings, see Ch.13.

[23] Art.III–369 CT. When agreeing the Hague Programme in December 2004, the European Council invited the Commission to bring forward a proposal, after consulting the Court, for an amendment to the Statute enabling all references concerning the area of freedom, security and justice to be dealt with speedily when the CT enters into force: see Presidency Conclusions, Annex I, point 3.1. *cf.* Art.104a of the Court's Rules of Procedure. On the existing rules for preliminary rulings, see Ch.14.

be a significant extension of the Court's jurisdiction within the area of freedom, security and justice, by suppressing most of the existing limitations on the Court's jurisdiction as regards PJC contained in the TEU: for example, those which give Member States the option of whether to accept the Court's jurisdiction to deliver preliminary rulings, or to limit that jurisdiction to references from courts of last instance; and those which limit the standing of various Union institutions, and natural and legal persons, to seek the judicial annulment of Third Pillar acts.[24] However, Article III–376 CT would continue to exclude the Court's jurisdiction over the CFSP—save as regards proceedings designed to ensure that the CFSP is not used as an improper legal basis for Union acts which could properly have been pursued elsewhere under the Constitution;[25] and annulment actions challenging European decisions imposing restrictive measures against natural and legal persons pursuant to the CFSP.[26] One might also note that the Court's limited jurisdiction to conduct judicial review in situations where a Member State has been the subject of a fundamental rights determination under existing Articles 7 and 46 TEU would be retained in the CT.[27]

Standing of NPAs under the action for annulment

For lawyers, one of the most interesting issues addressed by the **11–029** Convention and the IGC concerns the action for annulment now contained in Article III–365 CT.[28] This action is reformed in several ways: for example, by expressly extending the Court's jurisdiction to cover acts of the European Council which are intended to produce legal effects *vis-à-vis* third parties;[29] by permitting annulment actions also against the wider category of Union bodies, offices or agencies established by or pursuant to the Constitution, again where their acts are intended to produce legal effects *vis-à-vis* third parties;[30] by conferring upon the Committee of the Regions "semi-privileged applicant" status, i.e. able to bring annulment actions for the purposes of protecting its own prerogatives;[31] and by recognising

---

[24] However, the "internal security" provision currently contained in Art.35(5) TEU would survive intact as Art.III–377 CT. On the existing PJC rules, see Chs 10 and 14.

[25] *cf.* Art.III–308 CT.

[26] On the existing CFSP rules, see Ch.10.

[27] With certain revisions: see Arts I–59 and III–371 CT. On the existing position, see Ch.10.

[28] On the existing action for annulment under Art.230 EC, see Ch.13.

[29] Art.III–365(1) CT. *cf.* the extension of actions for failure to act to cover the European Council: Art.III–367 CT.

[30] *cf.* Art.III–365(5) CT, which provides that legislation creating Union bodies and agencies "may lay down specific conditions and arrangements concerning actions brought by natural or legal persons against acts of these bodies, offices or agencies intended to produce legal effects in relation to them". Note also the extension of actions for failure to act to cover Union bodies, offices and agencies: Art.III–367 CT.

[31] Art.III–365(3) CT. Art.8 of the Protocol on the application of the principles of subsidiarity and proportionality specifically refers to the standing of the Committee of the Regions to bring actions for annulment in respect of legislative acts for the adoption of which the Constitution provides that the Committee be consulted.

standing for national parliaments (albeit through the medium of their Member States) to seek the annulment of Union legislative acts on the grounds that they breach the principle of subsidiarity.[32]

However, perhaps the most significant reform relates to the standing of natural and legal persons to bring actions for annulment. As discussed in Chapter 13, in cases such as *UPA* and *Jégo-Quéré*, the Court of Justice was asked, but refused, to reconsider its very strict approach to the *locus standi* of non-privileged applicants under Article 230(4) EC, in particular, as regards the definition of "individual concern".[33] The problem of access to justice was deemed particularly acute as regards self-executing Community acts, whose full legal effects do not depend upon the adoption of national implementing measures; the absence of such a measure, capable of having its validity tested in a domestic court, might deprive applicants of the opportunity of challenging the validity of the underlying Community act, by way of a reference to the ECJ for a preliminary ruling under Article 234 EC. The Constitutional Treaty addresses this problem in minimalist fashion, in Article III–365(4) CT: any natural or legal person may institute proceedings against an act addressed to that person or which is of direct and individual concern to him or her, *and against a regulatory act which is of direct concern to him or her and does not entail implementing measures*. It seems that the term "regulatory acts" is intended to refer to non-legislative acts, i.e. European regulations and European decisions; it is only in respect of such measures, and only where they are self-executing, that the hurdle of having to demonstrate "individual concern" has been suppressed. In all other situations, that restrictive requirement remains in place, and the CT seems to place the onus for securing adequate access to justice firmly upon the Member States: the latter are obliged (under Article I–29(1) CT) to "provide remedies sufficient to ensure effective legal protection in the fields covered by Union law".

11–030 Although minimalist, Article III–365(4) CT could nevertheless have significant consequences in practice. The effect on the workload of the Courts could be potentially severe, as "[t]he vast majority of EC law-making takes the form of executive [i.e. regulatory] as opposed to (normative) legislative measures".[34] The Commission would be particularly affected, since its acts would always be regulatory under the CT. Moreover, Article III–365(4) CT would also focus attention on the difficult problem of how to draw a clear distinction between legislative and regulatory acts. This may be

---

[32] Art.8 of the Protocol on the application of the principles of subsidiarity and proportionality.

[33] Case C–50/00 *Unión de Pequeños Agricultores* [2002] E.C.R. I–6677; Case C–263/02P *Jégo-Quéré* [2004] E.C.R. I–3425.

[34] Ward, "*Locus standi* under Article 230(4) of the EC Treaty: Crafting a Coherent Test for a 'Wobbly Polity' " (2003) 22 Y.E.L. 45, 56.

illustrated by comparing *UPA* with *Jégo-Quéré*. The regulation concerned in the latter case, which was adopted by the Commission to conserve fish stocks, would have been a regulatory act had the CT been in force. However, the Council regulation in issue in *UPA*, which reformed the common organisation of the olive oil market, would probably have been legislative, with the result that the less stringent test applicable to regulatory acts would not have applied to it. It is doubtful whether such a fine distinction should produce such a radical effect on the availability of judicial remedies.[35]

Entry into force of the CT would therefore seem unlikely, of itself, to put an end to arguments over standing before the Union courts for the purposes of bringing actions for annulment. The ability of the Union courts to contribute through effective judicial review to the Union's accountability and legitimacy[36] would be immeasurably enhanced if they were to find in the CT a license to break free from the interpretative straightjacket imposed by the existing case law.

Finally, one might note that the plea of illegality (to be found in Article III–378 CT) would be extended so as to cover not only regulations adopted by the institutions expressly listed in Article 241 EC, but any "act of general application adopted by an institution, body, office or agency of the Union".[37] It is clear from the expanded list of potential authors of the relevant acts that the latter need not be legislative in nature (i.e. European laws or framework laws); non-legislative acts which nevertheless have general application would also be capable of falling within the scope of Article III–378 CT.

Some other major issues

Codification of supremacy

According to Article I–6 CT, the Constitution and law adopted by **11–031** the institutions of the Union in exercising competences conferred on it shall have primacy over the law of the Member States.

This provision has given rise to much critical comment. For example, it has been argued that, by making reference to the principle of supremacy without also alluding to the principle of direct effect, the Constitution offers only an incomplete and indeed potentially misleading description of the relationship between Union law and the national legal systems.[38] Indeed, it has been suggested

---

[35] See Usher, "Direct and Individual Concern—An Effective Remedy or a Conventional Solution?" (2003) 28 E.L.Rev. 575, 599.

[36] See Lenaerts and Corthaut, "Judicial Review as a Contribution to the Development of European Constitutionalism" (2003) 22 Y.E.L. 1.

[37] On the existing rules for the plea of illegality, see Ch.13.

[38] For detailed discussion of both supremacy and direct effect within the existing Community legal order, see Ch.5.

that, by setting out the principle of supremacy in such an unconditional fashion, Article I–6 CT might provide a legal basis for the
Court of Justice to overrule its unsatisfactory case law on the direct
effect of directives, in particular, by holding that unimplemented
directives have primacy over national law even in disputes between
two private parties.[39] From another perspective, fears have been
expressed that, by referring to the supremacy of legal acts adopted
by the institutions "in exercising competences conferred on [the
Union]", Article I–6 CT might encourage national courts to engage
in their own unilateral assessment of whether any given act falls
within the competence rules established by the Constitution.[40]

All such speculation must be read subject to Declaration No.1,
annexed to the Final Act adopted by the IGC: the Member States
noted that Article I–6 CT "reflects existing case law of the Court of
Justice of the European Communities and of the Court of First
Instance". The provision, it seems, was intended to be a cosmetic
exercise which should not affect substantive debates about the
proper scope and potency of the principle of supremacy as
developed in the case law relating to the legal order of the
Community.

11–032   However, because it refers to *existing* case law, Declaration No.1
does nothing to resolve the issue as to whether, in an integral Union
where the formal separation of the Community Pillar from the
Second and Third Pillars has been abolished, the principle of the
primacy of Union law, as codified in Article I–6 CT, should extend
to the fields of the CFSP and PJC.[41] That such is the intended effect
of Article I–6 CT might be thought to follow from its position in
Title I of Part I of the CT as well as from its unqualified language.
So far as concerns PJC, the application of the primacy principle
might not be seen as unduly controversial, since the progressive
assimilation of the Third Pillar to the Community model of the First
Pillar has been under way since the TA. However, the CFSP is a
different case. There are two good reasons for thinking that Article
I–6 CT could not be meant to extend to this area. The first reason
concerns the exclusion of the jurisdiction of the Court of Justice
from nearly all aspects of the CFSP: it would be contrary to the
jurisdictional system of the CT for Member State courts to be
required to apply CFSP provisions directly, and to disapply any
incompatible national provisions, without any possibility of obtaining
guidance from the Court of Justice. Secondly, Article I–6 CT must
be read together with Article I–16 CT. CFSP competence is singled
out by the latter provision as being distinct from the other areas of

---

[39] On this case law, see Ch.5.
[40] On the difficulties which have already surfaced in certain Member States, see Ch.5.
[41] On the extent to which the Court's "constitutionalising principles" currently extend from
the First to the Second and Third Pillars, see Ch.10.

Union competence. The non-application of the primacy principle, it could be argued, must have been one of the particular features of CFSP competence which that provision was designed to preserve.[42]

Voluntary withdrawal from the EU

Even though the current Treaties have been concluded for an **11–033** indefinite period and contain no express provisions permitting a Member State to exit the Union, it is beyond doubt that—politically and legally—nothing can prevent a country from seceding should it wish to do so. Nevertheless, the Convention and the IGC believed it would enhance legal certainty by defining the right to withdraw in a more explicit fashion. According to Article I–60(1) CT, any Member State may decide to withdraw from the Union in accordance with its own constitutional requirements. The procedure for withdrawal is then set out in Article I–60(2)–(4) CT. It involves, in particular, the negotiation of an agreement between the Union and the Member State concerned, setting out the arrangements for the latter's withdrawal and the framework of its future relationship with the Union, as well as a timetable for the Constitution's ceasing to apply within its territory. Pursuant to Article I–60(5) CT, should the withdrawing State subsequently change its mind, its application for readmission will be treated like any other accession to the Union.[43]

Amendment procedures

The ordinary procedure for revising the Constitutional Treaty is **11–034** contained in Article IV–443 CT.[44] Proposals for amendment are submitted to the European Council, which may decide to examine the proposals, either by convening a Convention charged with drawing up recommendations for consideration by an IGC, or by defining for itself the terms of reference for that IGC. The IGC shall determine the amendments by common accord, and those will enter into force after being ratified by all the Member States in accordance with their respective constitutional requirements. If, after two years, four-fifths of the Member States have ratified the amendments and one or more Member States have encountered difficulties in ratification, the matter shall be referred to European Council.

We have already mentioned the simplified revision procedures contained in Article IV–444 CT, i.e. the "passerelle clauses" for converting unanimity in Council into qualified majority voting, and/ or a special legislative procedure into the ordinary one, as regards

---

[42] See further, Editorial, "The CFSP under the EU Constitutional Treaty: Issues of Depillarisation" (2005) 42 C.M.L.Rev. 325.

[43] The accession procedure is now contained in Art.I–58 CT.

[44] *cf.* the existing procedure for amending the Treaties, discussed in Ch.10.

legal bases falling within the scope of Part III.[45] In addition, Article IV–445 CT provides another simplified revision procedure as regards detailed provisions governing internal Union policies under Title III, Part III—in other words, the internal market; economic and monetary union; the area of freedom, security and justice; and other fields of internal shared and complementary competences. Such provisions may be amended (on a proposal from any Member State, the Commission or the European Parliament) by unanimous decision of the European Council (after consulting the Commission and the Parliament).[46] That decision must then be approved by all Member States in accordance with their respective constitutional requirements; and must not, in any case, increase the Union's existing competences as defined under the CT.

Thus, it remains true that in no case can the Union's fundamental constitutional arrangements be amended without the unanimous agreement of its Member States.

Further reading
This list of selected further reading covers *both* the Convention's draft Constitutional Treaty of July 2003 *and* the final Constitutional Treaty signed by the Member States in October 2004.

Albi and van Elsuwege, "The EU Constitution, National Constitutions and Sovereignty: An Assessment of a European Constitutional Order" (2004) 29 E.L.Rev. 741.

Barents, "The Court of Justice in the Draft Constitution" (2004) 11 M.J. 121.

Birkinshaw, "Constitutions, Constitutionalism and the State" (2005) 11 E.P.L. 31.

Craig, "Competence, Clarity, Conferral, Containment and Consideration" (2004) 29 E.L.Rev. 323.

Dashwood, "The Draft EU Constitution: First Impressions" (2002–2003) 5 C.Y.E.L.S. 419.

Dashwood and Johnston, "The Institutions of the Enlarged EU under the Regime of the Constitutional Treaty" (2004) 41 C.M.L.Rev. 1481.

Dashwood, "The EU Constitution: What Will Really Change?" (2004/2005) 7 C.Y.E.L.S. 33.

Dougan, "The Convention's Draft Constitutional Treaty: Bringing Europe Closer to its Lawyers?" (2003) 28 E.L.Rev. 763.

Dougan, "The Convention's Draft Constitutional Treaty: a 'Tidying-Up Exercise' That Needs Some Tidying-Up of Its Own . . ." *Federal Trust Constitutional Online Essay 27/03* available at *www.fedtrust.co.uk/eu—constitution.htm*.

---

[45] See above.
[46] And the European Central Bank, in the case of institutional changes in the monetary area.

Dyèvre, "The Constitutionalisation of the European Union: Discourse, Present, Future and Facts" (2005) 30 E.L.Rev. 165.

Editorial, "A Constitution for Europe" (2004) 41 C.M.L.Rev. 899.

Kokott and Ruth, "The European Convention and its Draft Treaty establishing a Constitution for Europe: Appropriate Answers to the Laeken Questions?" (2003) 40 C.M.L.Rev. 1315.

Lenaerts and Gerard, "The Structure of the Union According to the Constitution for Europe: The Emperor is Getting Dressed" (2004) 29 E.L.Rev. 289.

Tridimas, "The European Court of Justice and the Draft Constitution: a Supreme Court for the Union?" in Tridimas and Nebbia (eds), *EU Law for the Twenty-First Century: Re-Thinking the New Legal Order, Volume I* (Hart Publishing, 2004).

Usher, "Direct and Individual Concern: an Effective Remedy or a Conventional Solution?" (2003) 28 E.L.Rev. 575.

Von Bogdandy, "The Prospect of a European Republic: What European Citizens are Voting On" (2005) 42 C.M.L.Rev. 913.

Weatherill, "Competence Creep and Competence Control" (2004) 23 Y.E.L. 1.

Williams, "EU Human Rights Policy and the Convention on the Future of Europe: A Failure of Design" (2003) 28 E.L.Rev. 794.

PART IV

JURISDICTION OF THE COMMUNITY COURTS

CHAPTER 12

JUDICIAL ARCHITECTURE AND JUDICIAL METHOD

Guide to this Chapter: This chapter provides an introduction to **12–001** the structure and particular characteristics of the Union's judicial system. The main task of the Courts is to ensure that, in the interpretation and application of the Treaties, the law is observed. This task is discharged in accordance with the detailed provisions conferring jurisdiction upon the Courts to hear direct actions against the Community institutions (and other bodies established pursuant to the Treaties), as well as the Member States, and to deliver preliminary rulings to assist national courts in the interpretation and application of Community law within the domestic legal orders. The Union has two main Courts of its own: the Court of Justice and the Court of First Instance (to which may be attached various "judicial panels" exercising jurisdiction in specialised categories of dispute). We will discuss the membership of the Courts, and some of the important features which affect their functioning: for example, the multi-lingual nature of judicial proceedings; the role of the Advocate General; and the practice of delivering a single judgment with no dissenting opinions. We will also consider some important aspects of the Courts' judicial method: for example, the tools of interpretation called upon by the judges, especially the importance of teleological interpretation; the degree to which the Court of Justice considers itself bound by a doctrine of precedent as regards its own caselaw; and the degree to which the Court of First Instance considers itself bound by rulings from the Court of Justice.

Background

The Court of Justice of the European Communities, which sits in **12–002** Luxembourg, plays a central role in the system created by the Treaties and has made a vital contribution to the Community's development.[1] Some of the concepts which are fundamental to the way in which the Community functions are to be found, not in the Treaties themselves, but in the case law of the Court. The approach taken by the Court to the discharge of its responsibilities has not escaped criticism. In a paper published in January 1995 entitled "The European Court of Justice: A Case Study in Judicial Activism", Sir Patrick Neill QC suggested that many of the Court's decisions were "logically flawed or skewed by doctrinal or idiosyncratic policy considerations". Sir Patrick Neill's views were considered by the House of Lords Select Committee on the European Communities in the course of its enquiry into the 1996 intergovernmental conference (IGC). Many of those who gave evidence to the Select Committee took a more positive view of the Court's role and the Neill thesis was comprehensively rejected by the Select Committee itself,[2] which observed:

> "A strong and independent Court of Justice is an essential part of the structure of the European Union. We agree with those witnesses who stressed the important role of the Court in the consolidation of democratic structures and upholding the rule of law in the European Community. We note the criticisms of 'judicial activism' which have been levelled against the Court but these appear to be based mainly on cases where the Court has made Community law effective against defaulting Member States at the instance of individuals seeking to enforce their rights. We accept that enforceable remedies are essential to the application of Community legal obligations, with a high degree of uniformity throughout the Member States."

The geographical enlargement of the Union and the expansion of the substantive scope of the Treaties have resulted in a significant growth in the number of cases brought before the Court. Increases in the productivity of the Court have not been sufficient to keep up.

---

[1] See further Arnull, *The European Union and its Court of Justice* (2nd ed., 2006); Dehousse, *The European Court of Justice* (1998); de Búrca and Weiler (eds), *The European Court of Justice* (2001). Although sometimes referred to as the European Court of Justice or the European Court, the Court of Justice should not be confused with the International Court of Justice, which is the principal judicial organ of the United Nations and sits in the Hague, the Netherlands, or the European Court of Human Rights, which was established under the European Convention on Human Rights and sits in Strasbourg, France. The International Court of Justice and the European Court of Human Rights are not institutions of the EU.

[2] See *1996 Inter-Governmental Conference* (Session 1994–95, 21st Report, HL Paper 105), para.256. Sir Patrick Neill's paper is published in the Minutes of Evidence taken before the Select Committee (Session 1994–95, 18th Report, HL Paper 88), p.218. It was also published as a pamphlet by the European Policy Forum in August 1995. Sir Patrick Neill was not without supporters. See e.g. Hartley, "The European Court, Judicial Objectivity and the Constitution of the European Union" (1996) 112 L.Q.R. 95. For an earlier analysis of the Court from a similar perspective, see Rasmussen, *On Law and Policy in the European Court of Justice* (1986).

The result has been growing delays in disposing of cases and the accumulation of a substantial backlog.[3] The first serious attempt to address this problem came with the Single European Act (SEA), where provision was made for the establishment of a court of first instance to relieve the pressure on the Court of Justice by dealing at first instance with certain categories of case. The Court of First Instance of the European Communities (CFI) and the Court of Justice are sometimes referred to collectively as the Community judicature/Courts or the Union judicature/Courts. The CFI is discussed in more detail below.

A further major reform of the Union's legal system (or judicial **12–003** architecture, as it is often called) was effected by the Treaty of Nice, which allowed a series of changes to be made without the need for further amendments of the Treaties.[4] As a result, a system which remained relatively stable for many years now seems to have entered an era of almost permanent review and reform. It has been remarked that this is, "perhaps paradoxically, appropriate to a mature system".[5]

The Community Courts are required by Article 220 EC to "ensure that in the interpretation and application of this Treaty the law is observed".[6] The Treaty proceeds to equip them with a series of specific powers in order to enable them to comply with that duty. The proceedings which may be brought before the Courts fall broadly speaking into two categories. *Direct actions* are proceedings which start and finish in Luxembourg. Some are considered only by the Court of Justice; some, depending on the status of the applicant, commence in the CFI and may proceed on appeal to the Court of Justice.[7] By contrast, *references for preliminary rulings* represent an episode in proceedings which will have begun—and will finish—in one of the national courts of the Member States. Where the national judge encounters a question of European law which needs to be resolved before judgment can be given, provision is made for the question to be referred to the Court of Justice for an answer known as a preliminary ruling. When the ruling has been given, it is for the national court to apply it to the facts of the case. Some national

---

[3] Statistics relating to the activities of the Court are available on its website, *http://europa.eu.int/cj/index.htm*.

[4] See generally Eeckhout, "The European Courts after Nice" in Andenas and Usher (eds), *The Treaty of Nice and Beyond* (2003), 313; Gormley, "The Judicial Architecture of the European Union after Nice" in Arnull and Wincott (eds), *Accountability and Legitimacy in the European Union* (2002), 133; Johnston, "Judicial Reform and the Treaty of Nice" (2001) 38 C.M.L.Rev. 499; Dashwood and Johnston (eds), *The Future of the Judicial System of the European Union* (2001); Arnull, "Modernising the Community Courts" (2000) 3 C.Y.E.L.S. 37.

[5] Jacobs, "Recent and Ongoing Measures to Improve the Efficiency of the European Court of Justice" (2004) 29 E.L.Rev. 823, 830.

[6] Art.220 was amended at Nice to refer specifically to the CFI and to the creation of judicial panels attached to the CFI.

[7] See Art.225(1) EC.

courts are obliged to seek preliminary rulings on questions of European law they are called upon to decide. The CFI has no jurisdiction at present to give such rulings, though this may change in the future.

The main rules relating to the Community Courts are to be found in the Treaties themselves and the Statute of the Court of Justice, which was annexed as a protocol to the TEU, the EC Treaty and the Euratom Treaty by the Treaty of Nice. Apart from Title I, which concerns the members of the Courts,[8] the Council can amend the Statute by unanimous vote.[9] Detailed effect is given to the Statute by the Rules of Procedure of the two Courts. The Court's Rules are adopted by the Court itself. The CFI has its own Rules of Procedure, which it establishes in agreement with the Court of Justice. Both the Court's Rules and those of the CFI require the approval of the Council, which it grants by qualified majority vote.[10] At Nice, the Member States rejected a request by the Court that changes to the Rules should no longer require the approval of the Council.

The creation by the Member States at Maastricht of a European Union with stronger intergovernmental features than the original Communities led to the insertion in the TEU of a provision limiting the scope of the powers of the Court of Justice. Article L TEU made it clear that the powers conferred on the Court by the three Community Treaties did not extend to Title V TEU on the common foreign and security policy, the so-called second pillar of the Union, or (except in limited circumstances)[11] to Title VI TEU, the so-called third pillar of the Union, which was concerned at the outset with co-operation in the fields of justice and home affairs. The conduct of foreign policy is an area in which many national courts are reluctant to interfere, but the Court's exclusion from Title VI was more controversial because of the potential of measures taken under that Title to affect the rights of individuals. At Amsterdam, Title VI TEU was renamed "Provisions on police and judicial co-operation in criminal matters" and its scope extended. The Court of Justice was given important new powers to rule on disputes concerning its application and Article L (now 46) TEU was amended accordingly. A further change was made at Nice to give the Court jurisdiction over "the purely procedural stipulations in Article 7" of the TEU (suspension of Member States' rights) acting at the request of the Member State concerned. The Court's jurisdiction under the Second

---

[8] Title I applies to members of the CFI by virtue of Art.47 of the Statute.

[9] See Art.245 EC.

[10] See Arts 223, last para., and 224, 5th para., EC respectively.

[11] Art.K.3 TEU made provision for conventions drawn up by the Member States in the areas referred to in Art.K.1 to "stipulate that the Court of Justice shall have jurisdiction to interpret their provisions and to rule on any disputes regarding their application, in accordance with such arrangements as they may lay down".

and Third Pillars is the subject of further discussion in Chapters 10 and 14.

The Court of Justice

The members

The Court of Justice currently consists of 25 Judges[12] and is **12–004** assisted by eight Advocates General.[13] The Judges and Advocates General are sometimes referred to collectively as the members of the Court. The general function of a Judge needs no further explanation here. The distinctive role played by the Advocate General in proceedings before the Court is considered below. The Court sits in four different formations:[14]

— the full Court, for which the quorum is 15. The Court is required to sit in plenary session in cases concerning removal of members of the Commission and Court of Auditors and the Ombudsman. The full Court may also hear cases which it considers to be of exceptional import-ance. Recourse to the full Court is now wholly exceptional.
— the Grand Chamber consisting of 13 Judges (quorum nine). The Court is required to sit in that formation when a Member State or a Community institution that is party to the proceedings so requests.
— chambers of five or three Judges, according to the import-ance or difficulty of the case.

Before the Treaty of Nice, there was nothing in the Treaties about the national composition of the Court. In practice, however, one Judge has always been appointed from each Member State. The first paragraph of Article 221 EC now provides: "The Court of Justice shall consist of one judge per Member State". A party is not entitled to ask for a formation of the Court to be changed because it objects to its national composition.[15] There is always one Advocate General from each of the five largest Member States.[16] The remaining three posts rotate among the other Member States.

The rule that there must be one Judge per Member State is not without practical problems, particularly since the enlargement of the

---

[12] Art.221 EC.
[13] Art.222 EC. The Council may, acting unanimously, increase the number of Advocates General, but the Treaty does not envisage an automatic increase on the accession of new Member States.
[14] Statute, Arts 16 and 17.
[15] Statute, Art.18.
[16] France, Germany, Italy, Spain and the United Kingdom.

Union to 25 Member States. In a report on the application of the Treaty on European Union published as part of the preparations for the 1996 IGC,[17] the Court observed that "any significant increase in the number of judges might mean that the plenary session of the Court would cross the invisible boundary between a collegiate court and a deliberative assembly. Moreover, as the great majority of cases would be heard by chambers, this increase could pose a threat to the consistency of the case law". The Court acknowledged, however, that "the presence of members from all the national legal systems on the Court is undoubtedly conducive to harmonious development of Community case law, taking into account concepts regarded as fundamental in the various Member States and thus enhancing the acceptability of the solutions arrived at. It may also be considered that the presence of a Judge from each Member State enhances the legitimacy of the Court".[18] The introduction of the Grand Chamber at Nice was intended to alleviate some of the managerial problems which might otherwise have resulted from the 2004 enlargement by reducing the need to have recourse to the full Court.

12–005   Judges and Advocates General "rank equally in precedence according to their seniority in office".[19] The rules relating to their appointment are the same. Thus, according to Article 223 EC, they must be "persons whose independence is beyond doubt and who possess the qualifications required for appointment to the highest judicial offices in their respective countries or who are jurisconsults of recognised competence". In practice, the members of the Court have come from a variety of backgrounds, including the national judiciary, the civil service, the Bar and universities. It has been suggested[20] that a member's professional background can have at least as significant an influence on his or her approach to a case as his/her national origin. British critics sometimes object to the appointment of members without judicial experience. It may be noted, however, that under the ECSC Treaty no legal qualifications whatsoever were required for appointment and two of the original members of the Coal and Steel Court did not possess any. It has also been pointed out that "in all the original six Member States the holder of a University chair of law may be translated to the bench,

---

[17] See "The Proceedings of the Court of Justice and Court of First Instance of the European Communities", May 22 to 26, 1995, No.15/95.

[18] Para.16.

[19] Rules, Art.6. Where there is equal seniority in office, precedence is determined by age. Advocates General have sometimes become Judges (e.g. Mancini, Slynn, Gulmann) and Judges have sometimes become Advocates General (e.g. Trabucchi, Capotorti). La Pergola began his career at the Court as a Judge, then became an Advocate General and subsequently reverted to being a Judge. Only Judges take part in the election of the Court's President, who directs the judicial business and administration of the Court and presides at hearings of the full Court. The President must be a Judge.

[20] By a former President of the Court, Judge Due of Denmark, in an interview broadcast on BBC Radio in 1990.

sometimes at the highest levels".[21] In its report on the 1996 IGC,[22] the House of Lords Select Committee on the European Communities said that "a Treaty amendment which would exclude professors or administrators would narrow the range of professional experience available to the Court and would be seen as trying to impose on other Member States a particularly British view of the best background for senior judicial office".

According to Article 223 EC, the members of the Court are appointed "by common accord of the governments of the Member States for a term of six years", which is in principle renewable. It is worth emphasising that the Members are not appointed by the Council of Ministers or by any single Member State. This means that a Member's appointment can in theory be blocked by any of the Member States. It is sometimes suggested that members should instead be chosen from a list of national nominees by a Judicial Appointments Board composed of very senior members of the judiciaries of the Member States.[23] The advantage of such a system is said to be that it would distance the selection of members from the domestic political process. As referred to in Chapter 11, the Constitutional Treaty makes a rather half-hearted gesture in that direction.[24]

In a resolution on the functioning of the TEU adopted on May 17, 1995 as part of the preparations for the 1996 IGC,[25] the European Parliament argued that its assent should be required to nominations to the Court. In its own report on the functioning of the TEU, the Court expressed opposition to the introduction of any such procedure on the ground that prospective appointees would be unable to respond to questions without prejudging questions they might have to decide in the exercise of their judicial functions. The Court's view that such a procedure would be unacceptable was shared by the House of Lords Select Committee.[26] The Parliament's suggestion has not been taken up by the Member States.

The role of the Advocate General

Each case which comes before the Court is assigned to an **12–006** Advocate General.[27] His or her role is normally to present an independent and impartial opinion on the case to the Court. This is

---

[21] Brown and Kennedy, *Brown and Jacobs' The Court of Justice of the European Communities* (5th ed., 2000), p.49.
[22] Para.260.
[23] See Koopmans, "The Future of the Court of Justice of the European Communities" (1991) 11 Y.E.L. 15, 26; Dashwood, evidence to the House of Lords Sub-Committee on the 1996 IGC (Session 1994–95, 18th Report, HL Paper 88), p.259. See also Convention on the future of Europe document on the functioning of the institutions, CONV 477/03, January 10, 2003.
[24] See Arts III–355–357 CT [2004] O.J. C310.
[25] See [1995] O.J. C151/56, point 23(ii).
[26] See para.261 of its report on the 1996 IGC.
[27] Art.10(2) RP.

done after the parties have concluded their submissions and before
the Judges begin their deliberations. The Opinion will be fully
reasoned in the manner of a reserved judgment in the higher English
courts. It will set out any relevant facts and legislation, discuss the
issues that have been raised, situating them in the evolving pattern of
the Court's case law, and recommend a decision to the Judges.

The office of Advocate General is thought to have been modelled
on that of the *commissaire du gouvernement* in the French Conseil
d'Etat, although it has now developed in such a way that it is better
to regard it as *sui generis*. Because the Advocate General has no
counterpart in the English legal system, those whose background is
in the common law sometimes search for analogies to elucidate his
or her role. A popular analogy is with a judge of first instance, but
that comparison is useful only because of its inappropriateness. First,
the Advocate General does not sit alone but hears the case with the
Judges. Secondly, the Opinion only contains a recommendation: it is
the Judges who actually decide the case. Thirdly, since the Opinion
constitutes the last stage in the oral part of the procedure,[28] the
parties are not entitled to comment on the views expressed by the
Advocate General. The inability of the parties to respond to issues
addressed in the Opinion, even those which have not been raised in
argument, is consistent with the continental principle that a court is
deemed to know the law.[29] According to that view, the task of a
court is to apply the relevant legal rules to the facts presented by the
parties and if necessary it will engage in its own legal research.[30] The
Court is sometimes willing to reopen the oral procedure pursuant to
Article 61 of the Rules where a party wishes to respond to the
Advocate General's Opinion,[31] but has rejected the view that closing
the oral procedure after the Advocate General has delivered his or
her Opinion involves an infringement of the right to a fair trial
enshrined in Article 6(1) of the European Convention on Human
Rights.[32] This difficult question is discussed further in Chapter 8.

There is good reason to believe that a persuasive Opinion will
strongly influence the subsequent deliberation. Lord Slynn, who
served as an Advocate General and later as a Judge at the Court, has

[28] Rules, Art.59.
[29] "*Jura novit curia*" or "*curia novit legem*".
[30] See Advocate General Jacobs in Joined Cases C–430/93 and C–431/93 *van Schijndel and van Veen v SPF* [1995] E.C.R. I–4705, 4717–4718.
[31] See e.g. Case C–35/98 *Staatssecretaris van Financiën v Verkooijen*, Order of September 17, 1999. The Advocate General delivered a second Opinion on December 14, 1999. *cf.* Case C–163/90 *Administration des Douanes et Droits Indirects v Legros* [1992] E.C.R. I–4625; Case C–140/02 *R v MAFF* [2003] E.C.R. I–10635, para.37.
[32] See Case C–17/98 *Emesa Sugar (Free Zone) NV v Aruba*, Order of February 4, 2000. See also the lengthy discussion of the compatibility of the office of Advocate General with the ECHR in the Opinion of Advocate General Ruiz-Jarabo Colomer in Case C–466/00 *Kaba II* [2003] E.C.R. I–2219.

written:[33] "As an Advocate General, one always hoped that the function had some utility; as a judge I now know that it is very valuable in this kind of court to have a detailed first-round assessment on which the judges can work. The research, the analysis of fact and law, the direction indicated by the Advocate General—even if not followed—are of considerable help". In the majority of cases, the judgment and its rationale follow the Advocate General's Opinion fairly closely. Indeed, in a change from its previous practice, the Court now often refers expressly to the Opinion of the Advocate General where it agrees with it, sometimes without even adding any reasons of its own.[34] However, it has become widely acknowledged that an Advocate General's Opinion is not necessary in every case the Court is called upon to decide. The fifth paragraph of Article 20 of the Statute accordingly now provides: "Where it considers that the case raises no new point of law, the Court may decide, after hearing the Advocate General, that the case shall be determined without a submission from the Advocate General."

Language

Cases may in principle be conducted in 21 languages: Czech, **12–007** Danish, Dutch, English, Estonian, Finnish, French, German, Greek, Hungarian, Irish, Italian, Latvian, Lithuanian, Maltese, Polish, Portuguese, Slovak, Slovene, Spanish or Swedish.[35] Judgments and Opinions are published in all these languages except Irish. In direct actions,[36] the general rule is that the choice of language lies with the applicant. However, where the defendant is a Member State or a natural or legal person having the nationality of a Member State, the language of the case is the official language of that State. In references for preliminary rulings,[37] which constitute an interlude in

---

[33] *Introducing a European Legal Order* (1992), pp.157–158. See also the remarks of Judge Robert Lecourt, a former President of the Court, in a speech delivered on October 9, 1973 on the occasion of the retirement of Advocate General Roemer: "Pour avoir une idée vraie du rôle des conclusions, c'est au délibéré qu'il faut avoir accès. On y decouvrirait l'intérêt de cet ultime répit entre le débat de l'audience et la médiation du juge et l'utile décantation du conflit judiciare qui en résulte. On y apprécierait qu'une voix autorisée et libre, s'élevant au-dessus des parties, ait pu analyser avec le recul nécessaire l'argumentation de chacune et pris le risque de porter sur le litige un premier jugement. On relèverait, enfin, l'importance de cette tension de l'ésprit que provoque, en chaque juge, des orientations qui alimenteront les éventuelles confrontations du délibéré, en l'absence de votre personne, mais non dans le silence de votre voix."

[34] See e.g. Case C–59/92 *Hauptzollamt Hamburg-St Annen v Ebbe Sönnichsen* [1993] E.C.R. I–2193, para.4; Case C–36/92P *SEP v Commission* [1994] E.C.R. I–1911, para.21; Case C–119/97P *Union Française de l'Express v Commission* [1999] E.C.R. I–1341, para.81. In Case T–14/98 *Hautala v Council* [1999] E.C.R. II–2489, para.20, the CFI quoted from the Opinion of the Advocate General in another case.

[35] Rules, Art.29(1). See Jacobs, "Recent and Ongoing Measures to Improve the Efficiency of the European Court of Justice" (2004) 29 E.L.Rev. 823, 827–829.

[36] i.e. actions which start and finish before the Court. See Ch.13.

[37] See Ch.14.

proceedings starting and finishing in a national court, the language of the case is that of the referring court. The submissions of the parties, both written and oral, must be made in the language of the case. The Member States may use their own official languages when intervening in a case or taking part in a reference for a preliminary ruling. The Registar of the Court arranges for translation into the language of the case.

Inside the Court, French is the working language. At hearings, members of the Court are entitled to put questions to the parties in any of the Court's procedural languages. The Advocates General draft their Opinions in their own languages. The difficulty of providing translation of documents directly from each official language into all the others following the 2004 enlargement led the Court to adopt five so-called pivot languages (English, French, German, Italian and Spanish) via which some translations are now produced. Opinions are now produced in one of these pivot languages as well as in the language of their author (where different) in order to aid the process of translation into the other official languages.

Deliberation and judgment

12–008   The process of reaching a decision is usually conducted in French. The authentic version of the judgment in the language of the case, if it is one other than French, will therefore be a translation. An attempt is usually made to reach a consensus on the outcome. Every Judge taking part in the deliberations is obliged to give his or her view and the reasons for it and to cast a vote. The final decision on a case is, if necessary, taken by majority vote, but all the Judges who took part in the deliberations are required to sign the judgment. There are no dissenting judgments. Moreover, under Article 35 of the Statute, the deliberations of the Court take place in secret. Only the Judges taking part attend. The collegiate character of the Court's judgments helps to protect the Judges from the various forms of political pressure to which they might otherwise be subject. However, the resulting judgment may perhaps have the look of a "committee document", lacking in elegance and sometimes even in coherence.

The Court of First Instance

The establishment of the Court of First Instance

12–009   The CFI was set up in 1988 by a decision of the Council adopted under powers conferred on it by the SEA. The Council's decision was repealed by the Treaty of Nice[38] and its provisions incorporated into the EC and Euratom Treaties and the Statute.

---

[38] With the exception of the provision giving the CFI jurisdiction to exercise the powers conferred on the Court by the ECSC Treaty, which expired in 2002.

The new Court commenced operations on October 31, 1989[39] with two basic objectives. One was to reduce the case load of the Court of Justice and thereby to reduce the amount of time taken by that Court to dispose of cases. The burgeoning case load of the Court of Justice had been giving rise to concern for a number of years. Increases in the Court's productivity had not kept pace with the growing number of new cases being brought and this was having a serious effect on the average duration of proceedings. By the end of 2000, it was taking the Court on average 21.6 months to deal with a reference for a preliminary ruling and 23.9 months to deal with a direct action. The CFI was also intended to improve the administration of justice by engaging in more detailed investigation of factual matters.[40] The fact-finding procedures of the Court of Justice had been widely criticised[41] and it was hoped that the CFI would develop into a specialised fact-finding tribunal with particular expertise in cases concerning the economic effects of complex factual issues. To that end, the CFI was given extensive investigatory powers in its Rules of Procedure, which it soon began to exercise with gusto.[42]

The jurisdiction of the Court of First Instance
The establishment of the CFI did not result in the creation of new **12–010** heads of jurisdiction, but simply in a redistribution of responsibility for dealing at first instance with certain cases brought under the existing heads. Under Article 225(1) EC and Article 51 of the Statute, the CFI now has jurisdiction in all direct actions brought by natural and legal persons. Thus, actions brought by private applicants against the Community or its institutions for annulment, failure to act and damages commence in the CFI. The CFI is also responsible for dealing with challenges to decisions of the Boards of Appeal established under the Community trade mark regulation,[43] which creates a Community trade mark existing alongside national trade marks but having equal effect throughout the Community. Responsibility for implementing the regulation belongs to OHIM, the Office for Harmonisation in the Internal Market (Trade Marks and Designs), which is based in Alicante, Spain. Appeal against decisions of the examiners and the various divisions of OHIM lies to independent Boards of Appeal within OHIM. Decisions of the Boards of Appeal are in turn amenable to judicial review before the

---

[39] Since then, the numbers of cases decided by the Court of Justice have borne the prefix "C", those decided by the CFI the prefix "T" (for the French word *tribunal*).
[40] See the fourth recital to the Council's decision.
[41] See e.g. House of Lords Select Committee on the European Communities, *A European Court of First Instance* (Session 1987–88, 5th Report, HL Paper 20), paras 35–36 and 63–65.
[42] See Vesterdorf, "The Court of First Instance of the European Communities After Two Full Years in Operation" (1992) 29 C.M.L.Rev. 897.
[43] Reg.40/94 [1994] O.J. L11/1.

CFI. Such cases have been growing steadily in number and may in time place heavy pressure on the CFI.[44]

Article 225 EC originally excluded actions brought by Member States or by Community institutions from the jurisdiction of the CFI. That exclusion was removed from the Treaty at Maastricht, but it was not until June 1, 2004 that the CFI acquired jurisdiction over a limited category of direct actions brought by Member States. The effect of Article 51 of the Statute is that the CFI now has jurisdiction in direct actions brought by Member States against:

(a) acts and omissions of the Commission, except those involving authorisation to participate in enhanced co-operation;[45] and

(b) acts and omissions of the Council concerning State aid,[46] anti-dumping and the protection of trade,[47] and the exercise of implementing powers, either where the Council has reserved such powers to itself or under "comitology" arrangements;[48] and

(c) acts and omissions of the European Central Bank.

This extension in the jurisdiction of the CFI reduces the risk that the same issue will be raised simultaneously before both Courts in separate proceedings brought by applicants of different status. Where this occurs, the third paragraph of Article 54 of the Statute entitles either Court to stay the proceedings in such circumstances,[49] but the consequences of recourse to that provision may not be entirely satisfactory. One drawback is that, if the CFI stays a challenge to a Community act brought by a private applicant, that applicant will not be entitled to take part in parallel proceedings before the Court of Justice brought by an institution or a Member State.[50] Where a Member State is challenging an act before the CFI and an institution is challenging the same act before the Court, the fourth paragraph of Article 54 of the Statute requires the CFI to decline jurisdiction so that the Court can resolve the issue. In these circumstances, the Member State would be entitled to take part in the proceedings before the Court.[51]

References for preliminary rulings under Article 234 EC continue to go directly to the Court of Justice. Until Nice, references were

---

[44] The first such action was Case T–163/98 *Proctor & Gamble v OHIM* [1999] 2 C.M.L.R. 1442.
[45] See Art.11a EC. On enhanced co-operation, see Ch.4.
[46] See Art.88(2) EC, third subparagraph.
[47] See Art.133 EC.
[48] See Art.202 EC, third indent.
[49] Where the Court of Justice decides to stay the proceedings, the proceedings before the CFI must continue.
[50] See Statute, Art.40, second paragraph.
[51] Statute, Art.40, first paragraph.

excluded by the Treaty from the jurisdiction of the CFI. There were essentially three reasons for this: (i) the importance of the preliminary rulings procedure for the uniform application of Community law; (ii) the fact that references only involve questions of law, questions of fact being a matter for the national court; and (iii) the difficulty of allowing for an appeal to the Court of Justice in cases which represent an interlude in national proceedings. The high standards the CFI had succeeded in maintaining and the continuing pressure imposed on the Court of Justice by references from national courts led the Member States to review the position at Nice. Article 225(3) EC now makes it possible for the CFI to be given a preliminary rulings jurisdiction in specific areas by means of an amendment to the Statute, but it incorporates various safeguards. First, the CFI will be able to refer the case on to the Court where it requires "a decision of principle likely to affect the unity or consistency of Community law". Secondly, preliminary rulings given by the CFI will exceptionally be subject to review by the Court "where there is a serious risk of the unity or consistency of Community law being affected". It is envisaged that the Court would deal with such cases under an emergency procedure to avoid too much further delay to the national proceedings.[52] At the time of writing, no action had been taken to amend the Statute pursuant to Article 225(3) EC.

The members of the Court of First Instance

Article 224 EC says that the CFI "shall comprise at least one **12–011** judge per Member State". That requirement was introduced at Nice and recognises the possibility that it may become necessary to have more CFI Judges than Member States. For the time being, the CFI consists of 25 members.[53] The number of Judges could be changed by amending the Statute. As for the qualifications for appointment, Art 224 EC says that the members of the CFI must be "chosen from persons whose independence is beyond doubt and who possess the ability required for appointment to high judicial office". Like the members of the Court of Justice, they are appointed by common accord of the Governments of the Member States for renewable terms of six years.

The CFI has the right to sit in plenary session but in practice it hardly ever does so, normally sitting in Chambers of five or three Judges.[54] The Statute[55] also permits the formation of a Grand Chamber. Like the Court of Justice, the CFI delivers a single

---

[52] The Court would have two months to decide whether or not the decision of the CFI should be reviewed: Statute, Art.62.
[53] Council Decision, Art.2; Nice Statute, Art.48.
[54] See Art.50, Nice Statute.
[55] Art.50.

collegiate judgment signed by all the Judges who took part in the case. There are no dissenting judgments. Certain straightforward cases assigned to a three-Judge chamber may now be dealt with by the Judge Rapporteur sitting as a single Judge[56] "where, having regard to the lack of difficulty of the questions of law or fact raised, to the limited importance of the case and to the absence of other special circumstances, they are suitable for being so heard".[57] The decision to delegate a case to a single Judge is taken by the Chamber before which the case is pending acting unanimously after hearing the parties.[58] Formal delegation to a single Judge is not often done because in practice simple cases are in any event handled by the Judge Rapporteur with minimal involvement from the two other members of the chamber. It is expressly excluded in certain areas of substantive law and "in cases which raise issues as to the legality of an act of general application".[59] In *Liberos v Commission*,[60] an appeal to the Court of Justice was upheld where a case was found to have been wrongly delegated to a single Judge because the legality of an act of general application was in issue.

As a rule, each member of the CFI performs the function of Judge.[61] As mentioned above, there are no full-time Advocates General in the CFI, but any of the Members (with the exception of the President) may be called upon to perform the function of Advocate General.[62] When the CFI sits in plenary session, it must be assisted by an Advocate General, who is designated by the President. A chamber of the CFI "may be assisted by an Advocate-General if it is considered that the legal difficulty or the factual complexity of the case so requires".[63] A Member who is called upon to act as Advocate General in a case may not then take part in deciding that case,[64] although he or she can of course perform the function of Judge in

---

[56] See Statute, Art.50; CFI Rules, Art.14(2)-(3). See the House of Lords Select Committee on the European Communities, *The Court of First Instance: Single Judge* (Session 1997–98, 25th Report, HL Paper 114). The first decision given by a single Judge was Case T–180/98 *Cotrim v CEDEFOP* [1999] E.C.R. II–1077. That case was decided about six months earlier than might otherwise have been expected. The Judge Rapporteur's role is normally to take the lead in progressing a case to judgment.

[57] CFI Rules, Art.14(2)(1). Actions for annulment, failure to act and damages must, in order to be eligible for delegation, "raise only questions already clarified by established case law or that form part of a series of cases in which the same relief is sought and of which one has already been finally decided".

[58] A case must be maintained before the chamber concerned where a Member State or a Community institution which is a party to the proceedings objects to its delegation to a single Judge: CFI Rules, Art.51(2).

[59] Such as competition, merger control, State aid, trade protection (e.g. anti-dumping), the common organisation of agricultural markets (with the exception of cases that form part of a series in which the same relief is sought and one of which has already been decided) and the Community trade mark regulation: CFI Rules, Art.14(2)(2)(a).

[60] Case C–171/00P [2004] 1 C.M.L.R. 21.

[61] See Art.2, CFI Rules.

[62] For an example, see Case T–51/89 *Tetra Pak Rausing v Commission* [1990] E.C.R. II–309.

[63] Art.18, CFI Rules.

[64] Council Decision, Art.2(3).

other cases where the same issues arise. In practice, Advocates General have to date been appointed relatively rarely by the CFI. However, the increase in the CFI's jurisdiction which is likely to result from the Treaty of Nice may make the appointment of Advocates General more frequent. It may even become desirable to endow the CFI with a permanent corps of Advocates General. If so, this could be achieved by the Council under Article 224 EC by means of an amendment to the Statute.

Appeals to the Court of Justice

By virtue of Article 225(1) EC, decisions of the CFI are "subject **12–012** to a right of appeal to the Court of Justice on points of law only, under the conditions and within the limits laid down by the Statute". That provision is expanded by the first paragraph of Article 58 of the Statute, which provides: "An appeal to the Court of Justice shall be limited to points of law. It shall lie on the grounds of lack of competence of the Court of First Instance, a breach of procedure before it which adversely affects the interests of the appellant as well as the infringement of Community law by the Court of First instance". An appeal can only be justified by an interest in having the operative part (as opposed to the reasoning) of the CFI's decision altered.[65] No appeal lies against certain procedural matters, such as decisions on the amount of costs or the party ordered to pay them[66] or on whether to grant legal aid.[67] A party may not put forward for the first time in an appeal a plea which it has not raised before the CFI, since that would mean "allowing that party to bring before the Court, whose jurisdiction in appeals is limited, a case of wider ambit than that which came before the Court of First Instance".[68]

In *Aalborg Portland v Commission*,[69] the Court offered an extended account of its role in appeals against decisions of the CFI, focusing in particular on the sometimes elusive distinction between questions of law and questions of fact:[70]

> "In an appeal, the Court's task is limited to examining whether, in exercising its power of review, the Court of First Instance made an error of law . . .

---

[65] Case C–49/92P *Commission v Anic* [1999] E.C.R. I–4125, para.168. The operative part is the passage in bold type at the end of a judgment formally giving the outcome of the case.

[66] Statute, Art.58.

[67] CFI Rules, Art.94(2).

[68] Case C–51/92 P *Hercules Chemicals v Commission* [1999] E.C.R. I–4235, para.58. (The suffix "P" after the number of the case stands for the French word *pourvoi* and denotes a decision given by the Court of Justice on appeal from the Court of First Instance.)

[69] Joined Cases C–204/00 P, C–205/00 P, C–211/00 P, C–213/00 P, C–217/00P and C–219/00P [2004] E.C.R. I–123, paras 47–51. See also Joined Cases C–2/01P and C–3/01P *BAI and Commission v Bayer* [2004] E.C.R. I–23, para.47.

[70] See Sonelli, "Appeal on points of law in the Community system" (1998) 35 C.M.L.Rev. 871.

An appeal may therefore be based only on grounds relating to the infringement of rules of law, to the exclusion of any appraisal of the facts. The Court of First Instance has exclusive jurisdiction, first, to establish the facts except where the substantive inaccuracy of its findings is apparent from the documents submitted to it and, second, to assess those facts . . .

It follows that the appraisal of the facts by the Court of First Instance does not constitute, save where the clear sense of the evidence produced before it is distorted, a question of law which is subject, as such, to review by the Court of Justice . . .

Article 225 EC, Article 5[8], first paragraph, of the EC Statute of the Court of Justice and Article 112(1)(c) of the Rules of Procedure of the Court of Justice provide, in particular, that where the appellant alleges distortion of the evidence by the Court of First Instance, he must indicate precisely the evidence alleged to have been distorted by that Court and show the errors of appraisal which, in his view, led to that distortion.

The requirements resulting from those provisions are not satisfied by an appeal which, without even including an argument specifically identifying the error of law allegedly vitiating the judgment of the Court of First Instance, simply repeats or reproduces verbatim the pleas in law and arguments already put forward before that Court, including those which were based on facts expressly rejected by that Court. Such an appeal amounts in reality to no more than a request for re-examination of the application submitted to the Court of First Instance, which the Court of Justice does not have jurisdiction to undertake . . ."

The Court will review the CFI's determination of the legal consequences which ensue from the facts it has established.[71] In one case,[72] Advocate General Mischo said that the question whether an applicant in annulment proceedings was directly and individually concerned was "undoubtedly a point of law". However, in competition cases, the Court will not interfere on grounds of fairness with the amount of any fine fixed by the CFI.[73]

Appeals must be brought within two months of the notification of the contested decision. There is at present no requirement that leave be obtained beforehand, but Article 225(1) EC ("under the conditions and within the limits laid down by the Statute") permits the Council to introduce such a requirement—known as a filtering system in Community parlance—by way of amendment to the

---

[71] Case C–136/92P *Commission v Brazzelli Lualdi* [1994] E.C.R. I–1981, para.49; Case C–7/95 P *Deere v Commission* [1998] E.C.R. I–3111, para.21.
[72] Case C–73/97P *Comafrica and Dole Fresh Fruit v Commission* [1999] 2 C.M.L.R. 87, 91.
[73] Case C–51/92P *Hercules Chemicals v Commission* [1999] E.C.R. I–4235, para.109.

Statute. Appeals may be lodged by any party which has been unsuccessful, in whole or in part, in its submissions. Interveners, other than the Member States and the Community institutions, may bring an appeal only where the decision of the CFI directly affects them. An appeal may also be brought by Member States and institutions which did not take part in the proceedings at first instance.[74] Where an appeal to the Court of Justice is successful, the decision of the CFI has to be quashed. The Court of Justice may then proceed to give final judgment in the matter, where the state of the proceedings so permits, or it may refer the case back to the CFI for judgment, in which case the CFI is bound by the decision of the Court of Justice on points of law.[75]

Judicial panels

Article 225a EC gives the Council a power to create a new type of **12–013** tribunal beneath the CFI in the Community judicial hierarchy. These new tribunals are known as judicial panels and have jurisdiction "to hear and determine at first instance certain classes of action or proceeding brought in specific areas". Their members must be "chosen from persons whose independence is beyond doubt and who possess the ability required for appointment to judicial office". They are appointed by the Council acting unanimously. The establishment of judicial panels means that the CFI no longer, in fact, sits in all cases as a court "of first instance".

In November 2004, the Council reached agreement on the establishment of the first judicial panel: the European Union Civil Service Tribunal.[76] The Tribunal was declared by the President of the Court of Justice to be duly constituted on December 2, 2005;[77] publication of that declaration in the *Official Journal* signalled the entry into force of Article 1 of Annex I to the Statute of the Court of Justice, according to which the Tribunal shall exercise at first instance jurisdiction in disputes between the Communities and their servants,[78] including disputes between any bodies or agencies and their servants in respect of which jurisdiction is conferred on the Court of Justice. This jurisdiction at first instance in staff cases is exercised in place of the CFI. There is a right of appeal on points of law only to

---

[74] Except in staff cases: Statute, Art.56. That right was exercised by a Member State (France) for the first time in Case C–73/97P *Comafrica and Dole Fresh Fruit v Commission* [1999] 2 C.M.L.R. 87. See also Case C–49/92P *Commission v Anic* [1999] E.C.R. I–4125, paras 171–172.

[75] See Statute, Art.61. Where a successful appeal is brought by a Member State or Community institution which did not take part in the proceedings at first instance, the Court of Justice may state which, if any, of the effects of the decision of the Court of First Instance which has been quashed are to be considered definitive as between the parties.

[76] See Decision 2004/752 [2004] O.J. L333/7.

[77] See [2005] O.J. L325/1.

[78] As referred to in Art.236 EC and Art.152 Euratom.

the CFI, whose own decisions are in turn "exceptionally . . . subject to review by the Court of Justice . . . where there is a serious risk of the unity or consistency of Community law being affected".[79] The Civil Service Tribunal held its first hearing on March 28, 2006.[80] In the context of the proposed regulation on the Community patent, the Commission has also proposed[81] the establishment, by 2010 at the latest, of a judicial panel to be called the Community Patent Court. Appeal from the Community Patent Court would lie, on questions of law and of fact, to the CFI.[82] Judicial panels offer a way of making significant reductions in the case load of the CFI. In 2005, staff cases represented over 32 per cent of the new cases brought before it, the second largest category, so the establishment of the Civil Service Tribunal will make a significant dent in the CFI's case load.

Judicial method

Methods of interpretation

12–014 The Court of Justice has become well known for interpreting provisions of Community law by reference, not just—or even principally—by reference to their wording, but also by reference to their spirit and the general scheme of the instrument of which they form part. In *CILFIT v Ministry of Health*,[83] the Court sought to explain its approach to the interpretation of Community provisions by reference to "the characteristic features of Community law and the particular difficulties to which its interpretation gives rise". The features underlined by the Court in that case included: (a) the fact that the different language versions of a Community provision are all equally authentic and may have to be compared; and (b) the need to place every provision of Community law in its context and to interpret it in the light of Community law as a whole, having regard to the objectives of Community law and its present state of development.

This does not mean that the Court takes no account of the wording of the provision it is called upon to interpret. Sometimes the Court will conclude that the ordinary meaning of the words used can be applied,[84] but there are two reasons why the wording cannot

---

[79] Art.225(2) EC.

[80] Case F–16/05 *Falcione v Commission* (Judgment of April 26, 2006).

[81] See COM(2003) 828 final. The latter proposal was accompanied by a proposal for a decision based on Art.229a EC conferring on the Union Courts and the judicial panels jurisdiction in disputes relating to the Community patent: see COM(2003) 827.

[82] See further Lavranos, "The new specialised courts within the European judicial system" (2005) 30 E.L.Rev. 261.

[83] Case 283/81 [1982] E.C.R. 3415, paras 17–20.

[84] See e.g. Case 152/84 *Marshall v Southampton and South-West Hampshire Area Health Authority* [1986] E.C.R. 723; Case 59/85 *Netherlands v Reed* [1986] E.C.R. 1283.

always be treated as decisive. One, mentioned by the Court in *CILFIT*, is the multi-lingual nature of Community law.[85] In *Regina v Bouchereau*, that factor was overlooked by the United Kingdom Government when it sought to rely on the use of the same term in the English text of separate provisions of a Community directive. The Court observed:[86] "A comparison of the different language versions of the provisions in question shows that with the exception of the Italian text all the other versions use different terms in each of the two articles, with the result that no legal consequences can be based on the terminology used". The Court treats all the language versions as having the same weight, regardless of the size of the Member States where they are spoken.[87] Another reason why a literal approach is often inappropriate concerns the way in which many Community provisions are drafted. Bingham J. (as he then was) explained in *Customs and Excise v ApS Samex* that,[88] "[t]he interpretation of Community instruments involves very often not the process familiar to common lawyers of laboriously extracting the meaning from words used but the more creative process of applying flesh to a spare and loosely constructed skeleton".

Thus, depending on the circumstances, the Court may give priority to factors other than language, such as the objectives of the provision concerned (so-called "teleological interpretation") and its legal context. These factors were treated as decisive in *Bouchereau*,[89] where the Court declared: "The different language versions of a Community text must be given a uniform interpretation and hence in the case of divergence between the versions the provision in question must be interpreted by reference to the purpose and general scheme of the rules of which it forms a part". The Court has made extensive use of the teleological and contextual approaches, not only to resolve divergences between different language versions but also to confirm

---

[85] See Van Calster, "The EU's tower of babel—the interpretation by the European Court of Justice of equally authentic texts drafted in more than one official language" (1997) 17 Y.E.L. 363.

[86] Case 30/77 [1977] E.C.R. 1999, para.13. *cf.* Case 29/69 *Stauder v Ulm* [1969] E.C.R. 419; Case 9/79 *Koschniske v Raad van Arbeid* [1979] E.C.R. 2717; Case C-298/94 *Henke v Gemeinde Schierke and Verwaltungsgemeinschaft 'Brocken'* [1996] E.C.R. I-4989; Joined Cases C-283/94, C-291/94 and C-292/94 *Denkavit Internationaal v Bundesamt für Finanzen* [1996] E.C.R. I-5063; Case C-64/95 *Lubella v Hauptzollamt Cottbus* [1996] E.C.R. I-5105; Case C-72/95 *Kraaijeveld v Gedeputeerde Staten van Zuid-Holland* [1996] E.C.R. I-5403; Joined Cases C-267/95 and C-268/95 *Merck v Primecrown* and *Beecham v Europharm* [1996] E.C.R. I-6285.

[87] See Case C-296/95 *The Queen v Commissioners of Customs & Excise, ex parte EMU Tabac* [1998] E.C.R. I-1605, para.36.

[88] [1983] 1 All E.R. 1042, 1056. See also Lord Denning in *Bulmer Ltd v Bollinger SA* [1974] Ch. 401, 425.

[89] Case 30/77 [1977] E.C.R. 1999, para.14. See also Joined Cases C-267/95 and C-268/95 *Merck v Primecrown* and *Beecham v Europharm* [1996] E.C.R. I-6285, para.22; Case C-375/97, *General Motors v Yplon* [1999] E.C.R. I-5421, paras 20–23; Case C-231/97 *van Rooij v Dagelijks bestuur van het waterschap de Dommel* [1999] E.C.R. I-6355, paras 24–29.

interpretations suggested by the wording,[90] to clarify ambiguity and to fill in gaps in the legal framework.[91]

12–015   The Court has traditionally made little use of *travaux préparatoires* (preparatory documents) as an aid to discovering the intentions of the authors of the Treaty, although this is a popular method of interpretation in international law.[92] The main reason for the Court's reticence is that the *travaux préparatoires* of the original Treaties were for many years not made public.[93] However, it is likely that this approach will in future be modified. The Court is willing to look at *travaux préparatoires* in cases concerning the interpretation of Community acts.[94] Increasing pressure for transparency[95] and the development of the internet have now brought many *travaux préparatoires* concerning subsequent amendments to the Treaties themselves into the public domain. This was particularly noticeable during the IGCs which resulted in the Treaties of Amsterdam and Nice. The proceedings of the Convention on the Future of Europe and the subsequent IGC generated a vast amount of documentation, much of it readily available on the internet, concerning the drafting of the Constitutional Treaty. This material is now routinely referred to in academic literature and will inevitably be drawn to the Court's attention by counsel. It seems inconceivable that the Court will be able to resist using it as an aid to the interpretation of Treaty provisions.

In principle the Court's approach to the interpretation of Community acts is similar to the one it takes in interpreting the Treaty. However, the Court may give less emphasis to the objective of a provision and to its legal context where there is a detailed legislative scheme, such as those that have been laid down in the fields of social security and agriculture.[96] Indeed, where the legislature has made its

---

[90] See e.g. Case C–260/90 *Leplat* [1992] E.C.R. I–643; Case C–84/95 *Bosphorus Hava Yollari AS v Minister for Transport, Energy and Communications, Ireland* [1996] E.C.R. I–3953.

[91] See e.g. Case 26/62 *Van Gend en Loos v Nederlandse Administratie der Belastingen* [1963] E.C.R. 1. *cf.* Case 314/85 *Foto-Frost v Hauptzollamt Lübeck-Ost* [1987] E.C.R. 4199, paras 16 and 17.

[92] See Art.32 of the Vienna Convention on the Law of Treaties.

[93] Some *travaux préparatoires* are now available at the Historical Archives of the European Union administered by the European University Institute in Florence (*www.iue.it/ECArchives/*). See Fonds CM3/NEGO (*The Rome Treaties Negotiations*) *wwwarc.iue.it/dcs/Fonds.html*.

[94] See Joined Cases C–68/94 and C–30/95 *France v Commission* [1998] E.C.R. I–1375, para.167; Case 15/60 *Simon v Court* [1961] E.C.R. 115, 125. *cf.* Case C–321/96 *Mecklenburg v Kreis Pinneberg—Der Landrat* [1998] E.C.R. I–3809, para.28; Schønberg and Frick, "Finishing, Refining, Polishing: on the use of *travaux préparatoires* as an Aid to the Interpretation of Community legislation" (2003) 28 E.L.Rev. 149.

[95] See e.g. Arts 207(3) and 255 EC; Case C–58/94 *Netherlands v Council* [1996] E.C.R. I–2169. The pressure has grown since the accession of Sweden, where the law on access to documents is highly developed. See Österdahl, "Openness v Secrecy: Public Access to Documents in Sweden and the European Union" (1998) 23 E.L.Rev. 336.

[96] By contrast, the Court has relied extensively on the teleological and contextual methods in interpreting the Community's detailed VAT legislation: see Farmer and Lyal, *EC Tax Law* (1994), pp.89–90.

intentions clear through the use of detailed provisions, the Court may feel bound to acknowledge the results, even if they render the act concerned unlawful.[97] Where legislation is less precise, its objectives and context will naturally assume greater prominence.[98] The Court sometimes also has recourse to the comparative analysis of the laws of the Member States on a given problem in order to find the solution which is best adapted to the needs of the Community. An example is *A M & S Europe Ltd v Commission*.[99] There, having examined the position in the Member States, the Court accepted that a limited doctrine of legal professional privilege applied in EC competition cases, notwithstanding the silence of the relevant provisions on the matter. On occasion Member States or Community institutions[1] make statements, which may be recorded in the Council minutes, when a measure is adopted about what they consider its scope to be. Whether or not they are made public, the Court has made it clear that such statements cannot affect the objective meaning of the measure.[2]

In addition to these maxims, there are certain more precise principles which should be mentioned for the sake of completeness. The first is that derogations from general provisions are normally interpreted strictly. This principle has been applied not only to provisions of the Treaty, such as Articles 30[3] and 39(3) EC,[4] but also to those contained in Community acts.[5] Secondly, the Court has said:[6] "When the wording of secondary Community legislation is open to more than one interpretation, preference should be given as far as possible to the interpretation which renders the provision consistent with the Treaty. Likewise, an implementing regulation must, if possible, be given an interpretation consistent with the basic regulation ... Similarly, the primacy of international agreements concluded by the Community over provisions of secondary Community legislation means that such provisions must, so far as is

---

[97] See Advocate General Jacobs in Case C–85/90 *Dowling* [1992] E.C.R. I–5305, 5320–5322.

[98] See e.g. Case C–13/94 *P v S and Cornwall County Council* [1996] E.C.R. I–2143. *cf.* Case 184/83 *Hofmann v Barmer Ersatzkasse* [1984] E.C.R. 3047.

[99] Case 155/79 [1982] E.C.R. 1575. See also Case 374/87 *Orkem v Commission* [1989] E.C.R. 3283.

[1] See e.g. the accompanying statements entered in the minutes of the Council when Reg.4064/89 on merger control was adopted: [1990] 4 C.M.L.R. 314.

[2] Case C–292/89 *Antonissen* [1991] E.C.R. I–745. See also Case C–25/94 *Commission v Council* [1996] E.C.R. I–1469, para.38; Joined Cases C–283/94, C–291/94 and C–292/94 *Denkavit v Bundesamt für Finanzen* [1996] E.C.R. I–5063, para.29; Hartley, "Five Forms of Uncertainty in European Community Law" [1996] C.L.J. 265, 274–278.

[3] See e.g. Case 95/81 *Commission v Italy* [1982] E.C.R. 2187, para.27; Joined Cases C–267/95 and C–268/95 *Merck v Primecrown* and *Beecham v Europharm* [1996] E.C.R. I–6285, para.23.

[4] See e.g. Case 30/77 *Regina v Bouchereau* [1977] E.C.R. 1999, paras 31–35.

[5] See e.g. Case 222/84 *Johnston v Chief Constable of the RUC* [1986] E.C.R. 1651, para.36; Case C–450/93 *Kalanke* [1995] E.C.R. I–3051, para.21.

[6] Case C–61/94 *Commission v Germany* [1996] E.C.R. I–3989, para.52. See also Case C–135/93 *Spain v Commission* [1995] E.C.R. I–1651, para.37.

possible, be interpreted in a manner that is consistent with those agreements". Finally, it may be noted that "procedural rules are generally held to apply to all proceedings pending at the time when they enter into force, whereas substantive rules are usually interpreted as not applying to situations existing before their entry into force".[7] However, amending legislation applies, unless otherwise stated, to the future consequences of situations which arose under the legislation previously in force.[8]

Precedent

12–016   The Court of Justice is not bound by its previous decisions but in practice it does not often depart from them. The Court's approach is epitomised by the extent of the freedom enjoyed by the national courts of the Member States to request preliminary rulings from the Court of Justice under Article 234 EC. Since the Court of Justice is not bound by its own previous decisions, the national courts are not precluded from taking that step merely because the point of Community law at issue has already been dealt with by the Court of Justice.[9] A corollary of the absence of a doctrine of binding precedent in Community law is that the distinction between the *ratio decidendi* of a judgment of the Court and its *obiter dicta* loses much of its significance.[10] The distinction is important in the common law because it is only the *ratio* of a case which is capable of binding other courts in the future. However, in principle everything that is said in a judgment of the Court of Justice expresses the Court's opinion and is therefore capable of having the same persuasive force.[11] Occasionally, however, the Court seeks to distinguish a case on which a party has sought to rely. In order to perform this exercise, the Court has to establish what the previous case, properly construed, in fact decided. This process is analogous to that of identifying the *ratio* of a judgment given by a common law court.[12]

---

[7] Case C–61/98 *De Haan Beheer v Inspecteur der Invoerrechten en Accijnzen* [1999] 3 C.M.L.R. 211, para.13.

[8] See Case C–60/98 *Butterfly Music Srl v CEMED* [1999] E.C.R. I–3939, para.24.

[9] See Joined Cases 28, 29 and 30/62 *Da Costa v Nederlandse Belastingadministratie* [1963] E.C.R. 31; Case 66/80 *International Chemical Corporation v Amministrazione delle Finanze dello Stato* [1981] E.C.R. 1191, para.14; Case 283/81 *CILFIT v Ministry of Health* [1982] E.C.R. 3415, paras 14 and 15; Case C–91/92 *Faccini Dori v Recreb* [1994] E.C.R. I–3325.

[10] See further Toth, "The Authority of Judgments of the European Court of Justice: Binding Force and Legal Effects" (1984) 4 Y.E.L. 1, 36–42; *cf.* Koopmans, "*Stare decisis* in European Law" in O'Keeffe and Schermers (eds), *Essays in European Law and Integration* (1982) 11, 22–24.

[11] Thus, the Court's ruling in Case 152/84 *Marshall v Southampton and South-West Hampshire Area Health Authority* [1986] E.C.R. 723 that directives could not have horizontal direct effect was reached in proceedings in which the respondent was a public authority. See Advocate General Roemer in Case 9/61 *Netherlands v High Authority* [1962] E.C.R. 213, 242. *cf.* Advocate General Warner in Case 112/76 *Manzoni v FNROM* [1977] E.C.R. 1647, 1661–1663.

[12] A good example is Case C–313/90 *CIRFS v Commission* [1993] E.C.R. I–1125.

Of course, like all courts the Court of Justice tries to be consistent in the decisions it reaches. Thus, in proceedings under Article 234 EC in which the Court is asked to rule on a point it has already dealt with, it will, in the absence of any suggestion that the previous case was wrongly decided, simply repeat its earlier ruling.[13] Indeed, where a question referred to the Court for a preliminary ruling is "identical to a question on which the Court has already ruled, or where the answer to such a question may be clearly deduced from existing case law", the Court is empowered by Article 104(3) of the Rules to give its decision by reasoned order in which, if appropriate, reference is made to its previous judgment or to the relevant case law. The same provision also empowers the Court to give its decision by reasoned order, this time after informing the court or tribunal which made the reference and hearing any observations submitted by the parties, "where the answer to the question referred to the Court for a preliminary ruling admits of no reasonable doubt".

The practice of the Court has been strongly influenced by its civil **12–017** law origins. In the civilian tradition, judicial decisions are not considered a formal source of law and judges do not feel compelled to analyse or reconcile earlier judgments in the manner of the common law judge.[14] As a result, the Court for many years rarely referred in its judgments to its previous decisions, even when repeating a passage verbatim. In due course references to its previous decisions became commonplace, but the analysis of them remained superficial and selective by the standards of English courts. The reader of the Court's judgments will be struck by the fact that previous decisions are often only cited by the Court where they support its argument. Authorities which point the other way are sometimes not mentioned at all, and sometimes even presented as if they support the line the Court has chosen to take.[15]

Perhaps as a consequence of the growing influence of the common law, there are signs in some more recent decisions of greater willingness on the part of the Court to confront the implications of earlier case law. The first unequivocal sign of a change in approach came in *HAG II*,[16] where the Court for the first time expressly overruled one of its own previous decisions. Following the advice of Advocate General Jacobs, the Court in that case abandoned the much-criticised doctrine of common origin laid down in *HAG I*,[17]

---

[13] See e.g. Case C–350/89 *Sheptonhurst Ltd v Newham Borough Council* [1991] E.C.R. I–2387, where the Court repeated its ruling in Case C–23/89 *Quietlynn Ltd v Southend Borough Council* [1990] E.C.R. I–3059. *cf.* Joined Cases C–418/93 etc. *Semeraro Casa Uno* [1996] E.C.R. I–2975.

[14] See Brown and Kennedy, *Brown and Jacobs' The Court of Justice of the European Communities* (5th ed., 2000), pp.343–344.

[15] See e.g. Case C–368/95 *Familiapress v Bauer Verlag* [1997] E.C.R. I–3689; Case C–358/89 *Extramet Industrie v Council* [1991] E.C.R. I–2501; Case C–70/88 *Parliament v Council* [1990] E.C.R. I–2041.

[16] Case C–10/89 *CNL-Sucal v HAG GF* [1990] E.C.R. I–3711.

[17] Case 192/73 *Van Zuylen v HAG* [1974] E.C.R. 731.

which limited the circumstances in which the owner of a trade mark in one Member State could restrain imports of products legally bearing the mark in another Member State. The Court said that it was "necessary to reconsider the interpretation given in [*HAG I*]"[18] and went on to make it clear that the doctrine of common origin no longer formed any part of the case law on intellectual property. In a subsequent case concerning the scope of Article 28 EC, *Keck and Mithouard*,[19] the Court also departed from previous case law, but it did so less candidly. The Court stated that it considered it "necessary to re-examine and clarify its case law on this matter" and concluded, "contrary to what has previously been decided", that certain types of national legislation which might appear to hinder imports were none the less compatible with the Treaty. Unlike *HAG II*, however, the Court did not make clear precisely what it was overruling. The effect of its judgment was therefore to leave the status of its previous decisions on the matter unclear. This aspect in particular of the *Keck* ruling attracted criticism,[20] which seemed to produce an effect. In *Cabanis-Issarte*,[21] a social security case, the Court made it clear that an earlier ruling[22] was to be regarded as confined to its facts and that a series of specified later cases based on it were no longer good law.[23] By contrast, in *Merck v Primecrown* and *Beecham v Europharm*,[24] the Court refused to depart from the rule laid down in a previous case, *Merck v Stephar and Exler*,[25] on the circumstances in which patent rights were to be considered exhausted. The Court undertook a detailed examination of the arguments for reconsidering the rule in *Merck v Stephar*, but concluded that it had struck the right balance in that case between the principle of the free movement of goods and the interests of patentees.

However, practice remains variable. In *Bergaderm and Goupil v Commission*,[26] a full Court of 11 Judges appeared to modify a fundamental principle of the law relating to the Community's liability in damages. The case was an appeal from a decision of a three-Judge chamber of the CFI.[27] The parties, the CFI and the Court's Advocate General had approached it on the basis that the principle in question remained valid. In its judgment, the Court

---

[18] At para.10.
[19] Joined Cases C–267 and C–268/91 [1993] E.C.R. I–6097.
[20] See e.g. Gormley, "Reasoning Renounced? The Remarkable Judgment in *Keck and Mithouard*" (1994) EBLR 63, 66; Reich, "The 'November Revolution' of the European Court of Justice: *Keck*, *Meng* and *Audi* revisited" (1994) 31 C.M.L.Rev. 459, 471.
[21] Case C–308/93 [1996] 2 C.M.L.R. 729.
[22] Case 40/76 *Kermaschek v Bundesanstalt für Arbeit* [1976] E.C.R. 1669.
[23] See also Case C–394/96 *Brown v Rentokil* [1998] E.C.R. I–4185, where the Court expressly overruled its decision in Case C–400/95 *Larsson v Fotex Supermarked* [1997] E.C.R. I–2757.
[24] Joined Cases C–267/95 and C–268/95 [1996] E.C.R. I–6285.
[25] Case 187/80 [1981] E.C.R. 2063.
[26] Case C–352/98 [2000] E.C.R. I–5291. See further Ch.13.
[27] Case T–199/96 [1998] E.C.R. II–2805.

failed to acknowledge the departure its decision represented from the law as it was previously understood, omitting to refer to its voluminous previous case law[28] on the subject. In the event, however, the Court's preferred line did not affect the outcome of the case as the appeal was dismissed.

Precedent and the Court of First Instance

The establishment of the CFI raised two new questions about the **12–018** status of judicial precedents in Community law: (a) is the CFI bound by its own previous decisions; and (b) is it bound by the decisions of the Court of Justice? The answer to the first question is that, like the Court of Justice itself, the CFI is not strictly bound by its own decisions but that it endeavours to be consistent. As for the second question, the CFI makes extensive reference to the Court's case law in its judgments and normally follows it. However, where the CFI believes it is liable to produce adverse results, it has not hesitated to look for ways of avoiding it.

One of the clearest statements of the attitude of the CFI to the case law of the Court of Justice is to be found in *NMB France v Commission* (*NMB II*),[29] where the CFI declared:[30] "the Court of First Instance is only bound by the judgments of the Court of Justice, first, in the circumstances laid down in the second paragraph of Article [61] of the Statute of the Court of Justice of the European Community, and, secondly, pursuant to the principle of *res judicata*". As we have seen, Article 61 of the Statute is concerned with the consequences where an appeal to the Court against a decision of the CFI is upheld. In the interests of completeness, the CFI might also have mentioned the second paragraph of Article 54 of the Statute. According to that provision, where the Court finds that an action which has been brought before it falls within the jurisdiction of the CFI, it must refer the action to the CFI, which "may not decline jurisdiction". In other words, the CFI is bound by the finding of the Court of Justice that the CFI has jurisdiction to hear the action. Neither Article 61 nor Article 54 of the Statute was relevant in the circumstances of *NMB II*, so the CFI went on to consider whether the status as *res judicata*[31] of a judgment of the Court of Justice, *NMB I*,[32] rendered the present action inadmissible. The CFI observed: "It is settled case law that this can be the case only if the proceedings disposed of by the judgment in [*NMB I*] were between

---

[28] Beginning with Case 5/71 *Zuckerfabrik Schöppenstedt v Council* [1971] E.C.R. 975.

[29] Case T–162/94 [1996] E.C.R. II–427 (Second Chamber, Extended Composition).

[30] Para.36. See also Joined Cases T–177/94 and T–377/94 *Altmann v Commission* [1996] E.C.R. II–2041, para.80.

[31] See further Toth, *The Oxford Encyclopaedia of European Community Law*, Vol.I (1990), pp.464–467.

[32] Case C–188/88 *NMB v Commission* [1992] E.C.R. I–1689.

the same parties, had the same purpose and were based on the same submissions as the present case . . . those conditions necessarily being cumulative".[33] Since those conditions were not satisfied, the CFI concluded that the judgment in *NMB I* could not affect the admissibility of *NMB II*. The judgment in the latter case confirms indications given by earlier cases that, while the CFI treats decisions of the Court of Justice as persuasive, it does not consider itself bound by them except in certain exceptional and clearly defined circumstances.[34]

Impact of the Constitutional Treaty (CT)

12–019   The CT contains reforms to several of the topics covered in this chapter, including:

— a renaming of the Court of First Instance and judicial panels as the General Court and specialised courts (respectively) (para.11–027);
— provision for consultation of an independent panel before appointment of Union judges by the Member States (para.11–027);
— modest reform of the Court's jurisdiction in the field of CFSP, but a more substantial extension of judicial supervision as regards PJC (para.11–028).

Further reading

General
Arnull, *The European Union and its Court of Justice* (2nd ed., 2006).
Arnull, "A Constitutional Court for Europe?" (2004) 6 C.Y.E.L.S. 1.
Brown and Kennedy, *The Court of Justice of the European Communities* (5th ed., 2000).
Dashwood, "The Advocate General in the Court of Justice of the European Communities" (1982) 2 Legal Studies 202.
de Búrca and Weiler (eds), *The European Court of Justice* (2001).
Dehousse, *The European Court of Justice* (1998).
Edward, "How the Court of Justice works" (1995) 20 E.L.Rev. 539.
Granger, "When Governments go to Luxembourg . . .: The Influence of Governments on the Court of Justice" (2004) 29 E.L.Rev. 3.

---

[33] Para 37 of the judgment in *NMB II*.
[34] For a dramatic example of an unsuccessful attempt by the CFI to change the direction of the case law on an important topic, see Case T–177/01 *Jégo-Quéré v Commission* [2002] E.C.R. II–2365, discussed in Ch.13.

Hartley, *The Foundations of European Community Law* (5th ed., 2003).

Lasok, *The European Court of Justice: Practice and Procedure* (2nd ed., 1994).

Lenaerts, Arts and Bray, *Procedural Law of the European Union* (1999).

Rasmussen, *On Law and Policy in the European Court of Justice* (1986).

Rasmussen, *The European Court of Justice* (1998).

Schønberg and Frick, "Finishing, Refining, Polishing: On the use of *travaux préparatoires* as an Aid to the Interpretation of Community Legislation" (2003) 28 E.L.Rev. 149.

Shapiro, "The European Court of Justice" in Craig and de Búrca (eds), *The Evolution of EU Law* (1999).

Slynn, *Introducing a European Legal Order* (1992).

Timmermans, "The European Union's Judicial System" (2004) 41 C.M.L.Rev. 393.

Toth, "The Authority of Judgments of the European Court of Justice: Binding Force and Legal Effects" (1984) 4 Y.E.L. 1.

Tridimas, "The Court of Justice and Judicial Activism" (1996) 21 E.L.Rev. 199.

Tridimas, "The role of the Advocate General in the Development of Community Law: Some Reflections" (1997) 34 C.M.L.Rev. 1349.

Judicial architecture

Arnull, "Modernising the Community Courts" (2000) 3 C.Y.E.L.S. 37.

Dashwood and Johnston (eds), *The Future of the Judicial System of the European Union* (2001).

Eeckhout, "The European Courts after Nice" in Andenas and Usher (eds), *The Treaty of Nice and Beyond* (2003).

Gormley, "The Judicial Architecture of the European Union after Nice" in Arnull and Wincott (eds), *Accountability and Legitimacy in the European Union* (2002).

House of Lords Select Committee on the European Communities, "A European Court of First Instance" (Session 1987–88, 5th Report).

Heffernan, "The Community Courts Post-Nice: A European *certiorari* Revisited" (2003) 52 I.C.L.Q. 907.

Jacqué and Weiler, "On the Road to European Union—A New Judicial Architecture: An Agenda for the Intergovernmental Conference" (1990) 27 C.M.L.Rev. 185.

Johnston, "Judicial Reform and the Treaty of Nice" (2001) 38 C.M.L.Rev. 499.

Kapteyn, "Reflections on the Future of the Judicial System of the European Union After Nice" (2001) 20 Y.E.L. 173.

Kennedy, "The Essential Minimum: The Establishment of the Court of First Instance" (1989) 14 E.L.Rev. 7 and (1990) 15 E.L.Rev. 54.

Lenaerts, "The Development of the Judicial Process in the European Community After the Establishment of the Court of First Instance" in Clapham (ed.), *Collected Courses of the Academy of European Law* (1990).

Rasmussen, "Remedying the Crumbling EC Judicial System" (2000) 37 C.M.L.Rev. 1071.

Sonelli, "Appeal on Points of Law in the Community System" (1998) 35 C.M.L.Rev. 871.

Turner and Muñoz, "Revising the Judicial Architecture of the European Union" (1999–2000) 19 Y.E.L. 1.

Vesterdorf, "The Community Court System Ten Years from Now and Beyond: Challenges and Possibilities" (2003) 28 E.L.Rev. 303.

CHAPTER 13

DIRECT ACTIONS

Guide to this Chapter: This chapter considers the Community **13–001** Courts' jurisdiction over a range of direct actions, i.e. those initiated and finally disposed of in Luxembourg. First, enforcement proceedings against Member States under Articles 226–228 EC. This allows (in particular) the Commission to establish before the Community Courts that a Member State has failed to comply with its obligations under the Treaty and, in appropriate cases, to seek the imposition of financial sanctions against that Member State (through a lump sum fine, recurrent penalty payments, or a combination of both). Secondly, the action for annulment of the unlawful acts of Community institutions under Article 230 EC. The most difficult issue arising under Article 230 EC concerns the standing of natural and legal persons to seek judicial review before the Community Courts. Unless the disputed act is addressed to the applicant, he or she must demonstrate that the act is nevertheless of "direct and individual concern" to him or her. These concepts have been interpreted in a highly restrictive fashion by the CFI and ECJ, so that the numbers of applicants able to secure access to judicial review directly before the Community Courts is relatively limited. The only alternative route to judicial review is by bringing an action before the national courts and (as we shall see in Chapter 14) asking the latter to make a reference to the ECJ under Article 234 EC querying the validity of the relevant Community act. However, that indirect route to judicial review poses problems of its own: for example, where the national court also refuses to recognise the applicant's standing under domestic law. The ECJ came under pressure from both its own Advocate General and the CFI to liberalise the definition of "individual concern" under Article 230 EC, but in its famous *UPA* ruling, the ECJ refused to make any substantive changes to the case law. We will then consider, thirdly, the action in respect of an unlawful failure to act by a Community institution under Article 232 EC; and fourthly, the plea of illegality under Article 241 EC, by which applicants may plead the illegality of an act indirectly during proceedings pending before the Community Courts concerning some other provision of Community law. Finally, we will deal with the action for non-contractual damages against the Community under Articles 235 and 288 EC. Such damages are usually sought as regards *unlawful* Community conduct. The legal principles here have changed since 2000: in its judgment in *Bergaderm*, the ECJ aligned the system governing the liability of the Community institutions more closely with that determining the liability of the Member States under the *Francovich* case law. But the Community institutions may also incur liability to compensate undertakings forced to bear a disproportionate burden of the consequences which result even from *lawful* Community conduct. That principle has been affirmed by the CFI, but the conditions required for such damages are very restrictive.

Infringement proceedings against Member States

13–002 One of the novel features of the Community legal order is the power given to the Commission to supervise compliance by the Member States with their obligations under the Treaties.[1] As far as the EC Treaty is concerned, that power derives principally from Article 226 EC,[2] which provides as follows:

> "If the Commission considers that a Member State has failed to fulfil an obligation under this Treaty, it shall deliver a reasoned opinion on the matter after giving the State concerned the opportunity to submit its observations.
> If the State concerned does not comply with the opinion within the period laid down by the Commission, the latter may bring the matter before the Court of Justice."

Article 226 EC may be contrasted with the now defunct Article 88 ECSC, which used to give the Commission the power to record in a binding decision the failure of the State concerned to fulfil its obligations. That State could then challenge the Commission's decision before the Court.

13–003 Article 226 EC is complemented by Article 227 EC, the first paragraph of which provides that "[a] Member State which considers that another Member State has failed to fulfil an obligation under

---

[1] See Audretsch, *Supervision in European Community Law* (2nd ed., 1986); Dashwood and White, "Enforcement Actions under Articles 169 and 170 EEC" (1989) 14 E.L.Rev. 388.
[2] An expedited procedure is applicable in the context of State aid under the second paragraph of Art.88(2) EC.

this Treaty may bring the matter before the Court of Justice". A Member State wishing to institute proceedings under Article 227 EC must first bring the matter before the Commission, which is required to give each of the States concerned the opportunity to submit its own case and its observations on the other party's case, both in writing and orally. The Commission must then deliver a reasoned opinion on the matter. Whether or not the respondent State complies with the reasoned opinion, the applicant State then has the right to refer the matter to the Court. The latter State may also bring the matter before the Court if the Commission does not deliver an opinion within three months of the date on which the matter was brought before it. In practice, the Member States have shown a marked reluctance to commence proceedings under Article 227 EC.[3] The Member States evidently prefer to rely on the Commission to act under Article 226 EC, sometimes taking part in its support when the matter is brought before the Court.[4]

The Commission publishes an annual Report on Monitoring the Application of Community Law.[5] The 20th Report, published in 2003 and covering the year 2002,[6] shows that the volume of complaints addressed to the Commission each year has been growing steadily and that they represent the chief source for detecting infringements of Community law by Member States.[7] In 2002, 1,431 complaints were received, accounting for 60.74 per cent of all infringements detected. The highest number of complaints concerned (in descending order) Germany, Spain and Italy; Denmark and Luxembourg were (again in descending order) the subject of the lowest number of complaints. Significant numbers of cases fall by the wayside as the procedure advances, so that, of the total number of cases in which infringement proceedings are formally launched, only a small fraction are ultimately referred to the Court of Justice. Be that as it may, the judicial statistics show that, in 2003, they represented by far the largest category of direct actions brought before the Court. In that year, an infringement was declared in the vast majority (77 out of 86) of the judgments given under Article 226 EC. Of the six founding Member States, Italy has most often been the subject of infringement proceedings before the Court. Greece,

---

[3] For rare examples, see: Case 141/78 *France v United Kingdom* [1979] E.C.R. 2923; Case C–388/95 *Belgium v Spain* [2000] E.C.R. I–3123. See also, e.g. Case C–145/04 *Spain v United Kingdom* (pending).

[4] Intervention involves taking part voluntarily in proceedings before one of the Community Courts in support of the relief sought by one of the parties. See Statute, Art.40; Rules, Art.93; CFI Rules, Arts 115–116.

[5] The reports are available online at *http://europa.eu.int/comm/secretariat—general/sgb/droit—com/index—en.htm#infractions*.

[6] COM(2003) 669 final, the latest available at the time of writing.

[7] "Routine checks regarding failure to notify the Commission of national measures transposing directives within the time allowed are another major source of information on infringements": 20th Report, p.6.

Austria and Spain also have poor records. The implications of these figures seem to be threefold. First, there seem to be considerable variations in the extent to which Member States comply with their Treaty obligations. Secondly, the infringement procedure is a fairly effective way of inducing Member States to tow the line. Thirdly, infringement actions impose a significant burden on the Court of Justice, even though some are relatively straightforward and are now dealt with by three-Judge chambers.

The procedure laid down in Article 226 EC falls into two distinct phases, the administrative phase (or pre-litigation procedure, as it is sometimes called in the Court's decisions) and the judicial phase.

The administrative phase

13–004   The administrative phase corresponds to the first paragraph of Article 226 EC, which requires the Commission to take two steps: it must give the State concerned "the opportunity to submit its observations" and then, if it is still not satisfied, it must consider whether to "deliver a reasoned opinion on the matter". The Court has said that the first paragraph of the article "pursues the following three objectives: to allow the Member State to put an end to any infringement, to enable it to exercise its rights of defence and to define the subject-matter of the dispute with a view to bringing an action before the Court".[8]

13–005   **(a) Detecting infringements.**   The Commission may become aware of a possible breach by a Member State of its obligations under the Treaty either through its own monitoring of the application of Community law or more often, as mentioned above, following a complaint by a private party. When a complaint is received it is registered by the Commission, which acknowledges receipt and informs the complainant of the procedure to be followed. The Commission also provides the complainant with information about the role of the national courts in ensuring the proper application of Community law. The complainant will subsequently be told what action has been taken in response to the complaint and notified of representations made to the national authorities concerned. The complainant will also be told whether or not infringement proceedings are to be instituted and if other proceedings on the same issue

---

[8] Case C–135/01 *Commission v Germany* [2003] E.C.R. I–2837, para.21. See also Joined Cases 142 and 143/80 *Amministrazione delle Finanze dello Stato v Essevi and Salengo* [1981] E.C.R. 1413, para.15; Case C–207/96 *Commission v Italy* [1997] E.C.R. I–6869, paras 17–18. The Court may be prepared to excuse a minor procedural breach where it did not prevent any of those objectives from being achieved: see Case C–362/01 *Commission v Ireland* [2002] E.C.R. I–11433, paras 18–22. The Commission is entitled to refuse the public access to documents connected with proceedings under Art.226 EC where disclosure might jeopardise the chances of a settlement: see Case T–105/95 *WWF UK v Commission* [1997] E.C.R. II–313; Case T–309/97 *Bavarian Lager Co v Commission* [1999] 3 C.M.L.R. 544.

are already under way. A decision to close the file without taking any further action or to institute proceedings is taken within one year of the date on which the complaint was registered, except in special cases the reasons for which are stated. Delays in processing complaints are often caused by the need to discuss the matter with the national authorities concerned.

The way in which the Commission deals with complaints by private parties about infringements by Member States of their obligations under the Treaty was the subject of several complaints to the European Ombudsman who, in April 1997, began an enquiry into the matter under Article 195 EC.[9] The Ombudsman found no maladministration, but the Commission agreed to extend to all cases a practice, previously applied in some cases only, of informing the complainant when it was minded to close a file and indicating its reasons for finding that Community law had not been infringed (except where a complaint was manifestly unfounded or the complainant appeared to have lost interest in the matter). This offers the complainant the opportunity to submit observations before the Commission comes to a definitive conclusion. The Ombudsman also suggested that, when acknowledging receipt of a complaint, the Commission should where appropriate provide information about extra-judicial mechanisms, such as national ombudsmen, for providing redress to aggrieved citizens.

In its White Paper on European Governance issued in July 2001,[10] the Commission offered guidance on the types of suspected infringement to which it would attach priority. It announced that it would:

"focus on:
- The effectiveness and quality of transposition of directives as the most effective way of avoiding individual problems arising at a later stage.
- Situations involving the compatibility of national law with fundamental Community principles.
- Cases that seriously affect the Community interest (e.g. cases with cross-border implications) or the interests that the legislation intended to protect.
- Cases where a particular piece of European legislation creates repeated implementation problems in a Member State.
- Cases that involve Community financing."

Cases falling within those categories would, the Commission said, be handled as a priority. In other cases, different forms of intervention

---

[9] See the European Ombudsman's Annual Report for 1997 at pp.270–274.
[10] COM(2001) 428, pp.25–26.

would be explored before formal infringement proceedings were launched.

13–006   The Commission also announced in its White Paper that it intended to codify its administrative rules on the handling of complaints. The need for further attention to be given to the matter was underlined by the report of the European Ombudsman for that year,[11] which recorded his decision on a complaint lodged in 1998. The complainant had made an allegation to the Commission that Greece had infringed its obligations, but the Commission eventually decided to close the case. The Ombudsman found that the Commission's letter to the complainant informing him of its decision implied that it had been reached because the Commission considered that there had been no infringement of Community law. The Ombudsman found, however, that the Commission had reached its decision in the exercise of its discretion notwithstanding evidence of a possible infringement. The Commission's failure to provide the complainant with adequate reasons for its decision to close the file constituted an instance of maladministration. The Ombudsman also criticised the Commission for failing to give the complainant enough time to submit observations on its intention to close the file.

The criticisms made by the Ombudsman in his 2001 report led the following year to the publication by the Commission in the *Official Journal* of a communication on relations with complainants in cases of alleged infringements of Community law by Member States.[12] In an Annex to the Communication, the Commission gave a detailed description of "the administrative measures for the benefit of the complainant with which it undertakes to comply when handling his/her complaint and assessing the infringement in question". The Annex deals with such matters as how to make a complaint, recording complaints, acknowledging receipt of correspondence, keeping complainants informed of the steps taken in response to their complaint and time-limits. It states that, in the absence of exceptional circumstances, "where a Commission department intends to propose that no further action be taken on a complaint, it will give the complainant prior notice thereof in a letter setting out the grounds on which it is proposing that the case be closed and inviting the complainant to submit any comments within a period of four weeks".[13] Commission decisions would be published on the internet and some would be the subject of a press release. The right of complainants to approach the Ombudsman if they consider that the Commission has been guilty of maladministration in handling a complaint is specifically mentioned.

The Commission emphasised in its communication that, as the Court had recognised, it enjoyed a discretion in deciding whether and

---

[11] European Ombudsman, *Annual Report 2001*, pp.116–119.
[12] [2002] O.J. C244/5.
[13] Annex, para.10.

when to commence infringement proceedings and whether to refer a case to the Court. The standard complaint form, referred to in the Annex to the communication, invites potential complainants to consider seeking redress from the national courts and administrative authorities, who may be able to act more quickly than the Commission and to offer a more immediate remedy, such as damages or a ruling on the validity of the contested national measure. The form notes that "any finding of an infringement by the Court of Justice [under Article 226 EC] has no impact on the rights of the complainant, since it does not serve to resolve individual cases".

(b) Pursuing infringements. When the Commission decides to **13–007** pursue a possible breach of Community law by a Member State, it will first raise the matter on an informal basis through the Permanent Representative of the State concerned in Brussels. If the Commission is not satisfied that Community law is being respected, the first formal step in the procedure is for a letter of formal notice to be sent to the Member State concerned. That letter gives the Member State the opportunity to submit its observations on the matter. It defines the subject-matter of the dispute and indicates to the Member State the essence of the Commission's case. It constitutes "an essential formal requirement of the procedure under Article [226 EC]".[14] The Commission is required to allow the Member State a reasonable period in which to reply to the letter of formal notice. What is reasonable depends on the circumstances of the case, but very short periods may sometimes be justified, particularly where there is an urgent need to remedy a breach or where the Member State concerned was aware of the Commission's view before the procedure started.[15] The Member State is not obliged to avail itself of the opportunity given to it by the letter of formal notice.[16] The Court has said that "No provision of Community law penalises failure to respond to the letter of formal notice within the period fixed by the Commission by rendering the Member State's observations inadmissible".[17]

The Court has rejected attempts by the Commission to treat as a letter of formal notice an opinion issued by it under Directive 83/189. That was the directive at issue in the *Unilever* case.[18] It required Member States to communicate draft technical regulations to the Commission and to take account of the Commission's comments. When certain Member States introduced such regulations without taking account of the Commission's observations, the

---

[14] *ibid.*, paras 8 and 9.
[15] Case 293/85 *Commission v Belgium* [1988] E.C.R. 305, para.14.
[16] See Case 211/81 *Commission v Denmark* [1982] E.C.R. 4547, para.9.
[17] Case C–362/01 *Commission v Ireland* [2002] E.C.R. I–11433, para.19.
[18] Case C–443/98 [2000] E.C.R. I–7535. See Ch.5.

Commission sought to have its comments treated as a letter of formal notice under Article 226 EC. Subsequent applications to the Court were dismissed as inadmissible.[19] The Court declared that, in order for a letter of formal notice to be issued, a prior infringement of its obligations by the Member State concerned must be alleged. However, when a detailed opinion under Directive 83/189 was delivered by the Commission, the Member State to which it was addressed could not have infringed Community law, since the national measure to which the opinion related only existed in draft form.

The letter of formal notice may lead to a further round of discussions between the Commission and the Member State concerned in an attempt to reach a settlement. If this does not prove possible, the Commission may decide to deliver a reasoned opinion on the matter. Although the Treaty uses the word "shall" in this context, it seems that the Commission is not obliged to take this step. In the first place, the Commission may only deliver a reasoned opinion where it "considers" that a Member State is in breach of Community law, which involves an essentially discretionary assessment. Secondly, the second paragraph of Article 226 EC makes it clear that, even if the Member State concerned fails to comply with the reasoned opinion, the Commission is not obliged, but merely empowered, to bring the matter before the Court.[20] There would therefore have been little point in imposing on the Commission an obligation to deliver a reasoned opinion whenever it took the view that a Member State was in breach of its obligations under the Treaty.[21]

13-008   In *Commission v Spain*,[22] the Court gave the following explanation of the relationship between the reasoned opinion and the letter of formal notice:

> "The letter of formal notice from the Commission to the Member State concerned and the reasoned opinion issued by the Commission delimit the subject-matter of the proceedings, so that it cannot thereafter be extended. Consequently, the reasoned opinion and the proceedings brought by the Commission must be based on the same complaints as those set out in the letter of formal notice initiating the pre-litigation procedure
>
> . . .
>
> However, that requirement cannot be carried so far as to mean that in every case the statement of complaints in the

---

[19] See Case C–341/97 *Commission v Netherlands* [2000] E.C.R. I–6611; Case C–230/99 *Commission v France* [2001] E.C.R. I–1169.
[20] See Case 247/87 *Star Fruit v Commission* [1989] E.C.R. 291, paras 11 and 12.
[21] See further Evans, "The Enforcement Procedure of Art.169 EEC: Commission Discretion" (1979) 4 E.L.Rev. 442; Dashwood and White, "Enforcement Actions under Articles 169 and 170 EEC" (1989) 14 E.L.Rev. 388, 398–399.
[22] Case C–358/01 [2003] E.C.R. I–13145, paras 27–29.

letter of formal notice, the operative part of the reasoned opinion and the form of order sought in the application must be exactly the same, provided that the subject-matter of the proceedings has not been extended or altered but simply limited . . .

The Court has also held that, although the reasoned opinion must contain a coherent and detailed statement of the reasons which led the Commission to conclude that the State in question has failed to fulfil one of its obligations under the Treaty, the letter of formal notice cannot be subject to such strict requirements of precision, since it cannot, of necessity, contain anything more than an initial brief summary of the complaints. There is therefore nothing to prevent the Commission from setting out in detail in the reasoned opinion the complaints which it has already made more generally in the letter of formal notice . . .”

In *Commission v Netherlands*,[23] the Court declared inadmissible a complaint mentioned in the letter of formal notice but which the Commission appeared to abandon in its reasoned opinion. An attempt by the Commission to reintroduce it in its subsequent application to the Court was regarded as “an extension of the subject-matter of the dispute as opposed to its extent as specified in the reasoned opinion”.[24] Its effect, in the view of the Court, was to deprive the defendant of the opportunity of terminating the alleged infringement or explaining itself prior to the Commission’s application to the Court.

The Commission is not required to indicate in the reasoned opinion the steps which need to be taken to eliminate the alleged infringement. However, the Commission must specifically indicate to the Member State concerned that it needs to adopt a certain measure if it intends to make failure to adopt that measure the subject of the action.[25] It must also lay down a deadline for compliance by the Member State.[26] That deadline determines the relevant date for the purposes of any subsequent proceedings before the Court,[27] for compliance with its obligations by the Member State concerned after the deadline has passed does not prevent the Commission from bringing the matter before the Court. Thus, in *Commission v Austria*,[28] the Court held that the quashing of the contested national measure with retrospective effect after the expiry of the deadline did not prevent the Commission from continuing

---

[23] Case C–350/02 [2004] E.C.R. I–6213.
[24] Para.28 of the judgment.
[25] Case C–328/96 *Commission v Austria* [1999] E.C.R. I–7479, para.39.
[26] See the second paragraph of Art.226 EC.
[27] See e.g. Case C–362/90 *Commission v Italy* [1992] E.C.R. I–2353.
[28] Case C–209/02 [2004] E.C.R. I–1211.

with the case. The Court has said that the Commission retains an interest in continuing with a case in these circumstances, since a judgment of the Court "may be of substantive interest as establishing the basis of a responsibility that a Member State can incur as a result of its default, as regards other Member States, the Community or private parties".[29]

13–009 As in the case of the letter of formal notice, the Commission must allow the Member State concerned a reasonable period within which to comply with the reasoned opinion. The Court does not have the power to substitute a different period for that laid down by the Commission,[30] but if it considers the period allowed too short, it may dismiss any subsequent application to the Court as inadmissible. In *Commission v Belgium*,[31] for example, Belgium was given eight days to reply to the letter of formal notice and 15 days to comply with the reasoned opinion. The Court ruled the Commission's application inadmissible. By contrast, in *Commission v Ireland*,[32] Ireland was given five days to amend legislation which had been on the statute book for over 40 years. The Court made it clear that it disapproved of so short a deadline, but declined to rule the application inadmissible. Member States are usually allowed a month or two to take the necessary steps. In *Commission v Belgium*,[33] the Court said that "very short periods may be justified in particular circumstances, especially where there is an urgent need to remedy a breach or where the Member State concerned is fully aware of the Commission's views long before the procedure starts".

None of the measures taken by the Commission during the administrative phase of the procedure under Article 226 EC has binding force. Such measures may not therefore be the subject of annulment proceedings under Article 230 EC.[34] The legality of those measures may be reviewed only in the context of a subsequent application by the Commission to the Court under Article 226 EC.[35] Moreover, as the Court of First Instance (CFI) explained in *SDDDA v Commission*,[36] "[t]he Commission is not bound to initiate an infringement procedure against a Member State; on the contrary, it has a discretionary power of assessment, which rules out any right

[29] See Case 39/72 *Commission v Italy* [1973] E.C.R. 101, para.11; Case C–29/90 *Commission v Greece* [1992] E.C.R. I–1971, para.12. On the liability of Member States to private parties for breaches of Community law, see Ch.6.
[30] Case 28/81 *Commission v Italy* [1981] E.C.R. 2577, para.6; Case 29/81 *Commission v Italy* [1981] E.C.R. 2585, para.6.
[31] Case 293/85 [1988] E.C.R. 305.
[32] Case 74/82 [1984] E.C.R. 317.
[33] Case 293/85 *Commission v Belgium* [1988] E.C.R. 305, para.14. See also Case C–328/96 *Commission v Austria* [1999] E.C.R. I–7479, paras 51–56.
[34] Case 48/65 *Lütticke v Commission* [1966] E.C.R. 19. The action for annulment is discussed below.
[35] *cf.* Joined Cases 76 and 11/69 *Commission v France* [1969] E.C.R. 523, para.36.
[36] Case T–47/96 [1996] E.C.R. II–1559, para.42.

for individuals to require it to adopt a particular position". No action for failure to act under Article 232 EC therefore lies against it should it decline to do so.[37] It is not for the Court to decide whether the Commission's discretion was wisely exercised.[38]

The Court has been willing to allow the Commission a degree of flexibility in the internal procedure it follows in deciding whether proceedings should be brought. In *Commission v Germany*,[39] it was argued that the proceedings were inadmissible because the issue of the reasoned opinion and the decision to commence proceedings before the Court had been delegated to a single Commissioner instead of having been the subject of a decision by the Commission acting as a college. The Commission explained that, because of the number of infringement proceedings, Commissioners did not have before them draft reasoned opinions when they decided to issue such measures. However, they did have available to them the facts of each case and details of the provisions of Community law which the Commission's services considered to have been breached. The decision to issue the reasoned opinion and to commence proceedings before the Court was therefore taken in full knowledge of the essential facts. Drafting of the reasoned opinion then took place at administrative level under the responsibility of the competent Commissioner. The Court ruled that this procedure was acceptable. It was true that the functioning of the Commission was governed by the principle of collegiate responsibility. It followed[40] "that both the Commission's decision to issue a reasoned opinion and its decision to bring an action for a declaration of failure to fulfil obligations must be the subject of collective deliberation by the college of Commissioners. The information on which those decisions are based must therefore be available to the members of the college. It is not, however, necessary for the college itself formally to decide on the wording of the acts which give effect to those decisions and put them in final form".

The judicial phase

If the Member State fails to comply with the reasoned opinion **13–010** within the deadline laid down in it, the Commission has the power to bring the matter before the Court of Justice. In principle, the Commission is not obliged to do so within any specific period, although the Court has recognised that the rights of the defence might be infringed if the duration of the pre-litigation procedure is

---

[37] Case 247/87 *Star Fruit v Commission* [1989] E.C.R. 291. The action for failure to act is discussed below.
[38] Case C–200/88 *Commission v Greece* [1990] E.C.R. I–4299, para.9.
[39] Case C–191/95 [1998] E.C.R. I–5449. See also Case C–272/97 *Commission v Germany* [1999] E.C.R. I–2175; Case C–198/97 *Commission v Germany* [1999] E.C.R. I–3257.
[40] Para.48.

excessive.[41] In *Commission v Germany*,[42] the Commission brought proceedings against Germany for failure to comply with various Council directives on waste. All had been substantially amended or repealed during the administrative or judicial phases of the proceedings. The Court said that it was "somewhat surprising[,] that the Commission brought its action more than six years after the entry into force of the basic German legislation on the shipment of waste, and did so at a time when the Community had in fact changed its policy in that field along the same lines as those followed by that legislation".[43] However, the Court ruled that the Commission was entitled to decide when it was appropriate to bring an action. It was not for the Court to review the exercise of that discretion. The Court therefore concluded that the action was admissible.

In *Commission v Italy*, Advocate General Mischo suggested that, in a case of an isolated failure by a Member State to apply a directive correctly, the Commission should only bring proceedings under Article 226 EC where the situation is particularly flagrant and a sustained effort to induce the State concerned to act has proved unsuccessful.[44] That suggestion was not taken up by the Court. It should be noted that the Commission's attitude to whether or not to bring proceedings does not affect the substance of the Member State's obligations under the Treaty or the rights which individuals may derive from them.[45]

If the Commission decides to make an application to the Court, it is not required to show any specific interest in doing so,[46] but it will be required to prove its allegation that the obligation in question has not been fulfilled.[47] The burden on the Commission is not easy to discharge. The Court requires the Commission to indicate not merely the legal basis of its complaint but also to give details of the facts and circumstances which are said to give rise to the alleged failure by the State concerned to comply with its obligations.[48] Where a Member State is required by a directive to inform the Commission of the steps taken to comply with it, failure to satisfy

[41] See Case C–96/89 *Commission v Netherlands* [1991] E.C.R. I–2461; Case C–187/98 *Commission v Greece* [1999] E.C.R. I–7713.
[42] Case C–422/92 [1995] E.C.R. I–1097. See also Case C–152/98 *Commission v Netherlands* [2001] E.C.R. I–3463, para.21. In Case C–52/00 *Commission v France* [2002] E.C.R. I–3827, para.34, the Court held that it was irrelevant that the Commission had consulted interested parties about possible amendments to the act alleged to have been infringed.
[43] Para.18.
[44] Case C–365/97 [1999] E.C.R. I–7773. See para.64 of the Opinion.
[45] See Joined Cases 142 and 143/80 *Amministrazione delle Finanze dello Stato v Essevi and Salengo* [1981] E.C.R. 1413, paras 16–18.
[46] Joined Cases C–418/00 and C–419/00 *Commission v France* [2002] E.C.R. I–3969, para.29.
[47] See e.g. Case C–434/01 *Commission v United Kingdom* [2003] E.C.R. I–13239.
[48] See e.g. Case C–347/88 *Commission v Greece* [1990] E.C.R. I–4747; Case C–52/90 *Commission v Denmark* [1992] E.C.R. I–2187; Case C–55/99 *Commission v France* [2000] E.C.R. I–11499; Case C–127/99 *Commission v Italy* [2001] E.C.R. I–8305; Case C–458/00 *Commission v Luxembourg* [2003] E.C.R. I–1553, paras 44–45.

that requirement may itself amount to a breach of Community law, but it will not entitle the Commission to assume that no implementing measures have in fact been adopted.[49] Moreover, the mere existence in a Member State of a situation which is inconsistent with a directive does not in itself entitle the Commission to conclude that the directive concerned has not been properly implemented. However, the persistence of such a situation may indicate a failure by the State concerned to comply with its obligations.[50]

If the Commission's application to the Court is successful, the **13–011** Court will declare that the Member State in question has failed to fulfil its obligations under the Treaty. The Court will specify the act or omission giving rise to the failure, but it has no power to tell the Member State what it must do to remedy the breach or to quash any national measure which it may have found unlawful. The Member State is required by Article 228(1) EC "to take the necessary measures to comply with the judgment of the Court of Justice". If it fails to do so, it exposes itself to further proceedings under Article 228(2) EC, which may result in the imposition of a financial penalty. This is discussed below.

The effect of the Court's ruling
Action to comply with the Court's judgment must be commenced **13–012** as soon as it is delivered and completed as soon as possible.[51] The effect produced by a ruling of the Court of Justice under Article 226 EC in the legal order of the Member State concerned was considered in *Procureur de la République v Waterkeyn*,[52] where it was held that: "if the Court finds in proceedings under Articles [226] to [228 EC] that a Member State's legislation is incompatible with the obligations which it has under the Treaty the courts of that State are bound by virtue of Article [228 EC] to draw the necessary inferences from the judgment of the Court. However, it should be understood that the rights accruing to individuals derive, not from that judgment, but from the actual provisions of Community law having direct effect in the internal legal order".

This means that a judgment of the Court under Article 226 EC does not in itself confer rights on individuals. Such a judgment merely establishes whether or not a given course of conduct by a Member State is compatible with Community law. However, where the Court decides that the Member State is in breach of its obligations under a provision of Community law which produces direct effect, the national courts must draw the appropriate consequences and protect rights claimed by individuals under that

---

[49] See Case 96/81 *Commission v Netherlands* [1982] E.C.R. 1791, paras 4–6.
[50] See Case C–365/97 *Commission v Italy* [1999] E.C.R. I–7773, para.68.
[51] See e.g. Joined Cases 227 to 230/85 *Commission v Belgium* [1988] E.C.R. 1, para.11.
[52] Joined Cases 314 to 316/81 and 83/82 [1982] E.C.R. 4337.

provision. The ruling of the Court of Justice under Article 226 EC establishes conclusively that the provision in question has been breached. Moreover, the Court's ruling in *Francovich*[53] makes it clear that a ruling of the Court under Article 226 EC establishing that a Member State has failed to comply with a provision of Community law, even one that does not have direct effect, may render the State concerned liable to pay compensation to anyone who has thereby suffered loss.

Interim measures

13–013   Although the Court has no power under Article 226 EC to order the State concerned to pursue or refrain from pursuing a particular course of conduct, somewhat anomalously such an order may be made in the context of an application for interim measures under Article 243 EC.[54] Interim measures are not, however, available in proceedings against a Member State for failure to take the steps necessary to comply with a previous ruling of the Court under Article 226 EC where the measures sought would merely repeat the substance of the Court's earlier ruling.[55]

According to the second subparagraph of Article 83(1) of the Court's Rules of Procedure, an application for interim measures under Article 243 EC "shall be admissible only if it is made by a party to a case before the Court and relates to that case". The result is that, in proceedings under Article 226 EC, no such application may be made before the Commission has brought the matter before the Court (although both steps may be taken simultaneously).[56] In particular, no application for interim measures can be made when the letter of formal notice is dispatched. Article 226 EC does not therefore permit rapid intervention by the Commission in urgent cases. It has been remarked that "a strengthening of the Commission's guardian role in the Community interest by a rapid intervention mechanism is not merely desirable but also essential".[57]

In *Commission v France*,[58] the Commission brought proceedings against France for failing to comply with two decisions requiring it to allow some beef and beef products to be imported from the UK. The Commission had required France to reply to the letter of formal notice and the reasoned opinion within short time-limits but had not

---

[53] Joined Cases C–6/90 and C–9/90 [1991] E.C.R. I–5357.
[54] See Case 61/77R *Commission v Ireland* [1977] E.C.R. 937 and 1411 (note in particular the remarks of Advocate General Reischl at pp.953–954); Case 246/89 R *Commission v United Kingdom* [1989] E.C.R. 3125.
[55] Joined Cases 24 and 97/80 R *Commission v France* [1980] E.C.R. 1319.
[56] See e.g. Case 246/89 R *Commission v United Kingdom* [1989] E.C.R. 3125.
[57] See Gormley (ed.), *Kapteyn and VerLoren van Themaat's Introduction to the Law of the European Communities* (3rd ed., 1998), p.454.
[58] Case C–1/00 [2001] E.C.R. I–9989.

applied to the Court for interim relief. It was argued that this amounted to an abuse of process because it put pressure on the French Government without observing the procedural and substantive conditions governing proceedings for interim relief. The Court found that, having regard to the circumstances of the case, the time-limits set by the Commission for replying to the letter of formal notice and the reasoned opinion were not unreasonable. The Commission had chosen the proceedings specifically envisaged by the Treaty for cases where it considered that a Member State had infringed the Treaty. The Treaty did not require the Commission to apply for interim relief in a case such as this.

Defences

(a) **General.**   One of the most promising types of defence open to a **13–014** Member State in proceedings against it under Article 226 EC is that the Commission has failed to respect the procedural requirements imposed on it by the Treaty. Thus, it may be said that the period within which the Member State was asked to respond to the letter of formal notice or to comply with the reasoned opinion was unreasonably short, or that the Commission's application to the Court introduces complaints that were not formulated in the reasoned opinion or the letter of formal notice.[59] If such an argument succeeds, the Commission's application will be found inadmissible, either wholly or in part.

In the absence of a defence of this nature, the essential question is whether, objectively speaking, the situation in the defendant State is consistent with the requirements of Community law. This may lead the State concerned to challenge the Commission's understanding of either Community law or the State's own national law. However, except in cases of force majeure (a concept which is construed narrowly),[60] the Court will not be interested in how any inconsistency may have arisen. The Commission is not required to show "inertia or opposition on the part of the Member State concerned"[61] or "to draw distinctions based on the nature or gravity of the infringement".[62]

Thus, it is no defence that national legislation, although technically incompatible with Community law, is in practice applied in accordance with the requirements of the Treaty. The Court has said

---

[59] See e.g. Case C–145/01 *Commission v Italy* [2003] E.C.R. I–5581 (application inadmissible because reasoned opinion and application to Court referred to provisions of Community law not cited in letter of formal notice).

[60] See Case 101/84 *Commission v Italy* [1985] E.C.R. 2629.

[61] Case C–215/98 *Commission v Greece* [1999] E.C.R. I–4913, para.15.

[62] Case C–140/00 *Commission v United Kingdom* [2003] E.C.R. I–10379, para.34; Case C–454/99 *Commission v United Kingdom* [2002] E.C.R. I–10323, para.27.

that the mere maintenance in force of such legislation "gives rise to
an ambiguous state of affairs by maintaining, as regards those
subject to the law who are concerned, a state of uncertainty as to the
possibilities available to them of relying on Community law".[63] The
need to avoid this type of uncertainty has also led the Court to
refuse to allow Member States to rely on the fact that the provisions
of Community law which have been breached are directly effective
and may therefore be relied on in the national courts, which must
accord them precedence over inconsistent provisions of national law.
The Court has stated that "the primacy and direct effect of the
provisions of Community law do not release Member States from
their obligation to remove from their domestic legal order any
provisions incompatible with Community law".[64] Nor can Member
States rely on a failure by the Community institutions to comply with
their own obligations under the Treaty. In *Commission v Luxembourg and Belgium*,[65] the Court said that "the Treaty is not limited
to creating reciprocal obligations between the different natural and
legal persons to whom it is applicable . . . [E]xcept where otherwise
expressly provided, the basic concept of the Treaty requires that the
Member States shall not take the law into their own hands.
Therefore the fact that the Council failed to carry out its obligations
cannot relieve the defendants from carrying out theirs". The appropriate remedy for a Member State in such circumstances would be a
direct action against the institution in question.

Similarly, a Member State may not justify a breach of Community
law on the ground that its object was to correct the effects of such a
breach by another Member State. The Court made it clear in
Commission v France[66] that "[a] Member State cannot under any
circumstances unilaterally adopt, on its own authority, corrective
measures or measures to protect trade designed to prevent [i.e.
obviate][67] any failure on the part of another Member State to comply
with the rules laid down by the Treaty". The Court pointed out that
a Member State which considers the action of another Member
State incompatible with Community law can take action at the
political level, invite the Commission to bring proceedings against
that State under Article 226 EC or take action itself under Article
227 EC. Moreover, reservations or statements made by the Member
State concerned in the course of the procedure leading to the

---

[63] Case 167/73 *Commission v French Republic* [1974] E.C.R. 359, para.41. See also Case
C–58/90 *Commission v Italy* [1991] E.C.R. I–4193, para.12.
[64] Case 104/86 *Commission v Italy* [1988] E.C.R. 1799, para.12.
[65] Joined Cases 90 and 91/63 [1964] E.C.R. 625, 631.
[66] Case 232/78 [1979] E.C.R. 2729, para.9. See also Case C–5/94 *The Queen v MAFF, ex parte
Hedley Lomas* [1996] E.C.R. I–2553, para.20; Case C–265/95 *Commission v France* [1997]
E.C.R. I–6959, para.63.
[67] Sic. The French text reads "...destinées à obvier à une méconnaissance éventuelle, par un
Etat membre, des règles du traité".

adoption of an act which is alleged to have been breached will not be taken into account by the Court, since "the objective scope of rules laid down by the common institutions cannot be modified by reservations or objections which Member States have made at the time the rules were being formulated".[68]

As the Court pointed out in *Commission v Ireland*,[69] "[i]t is well- **13–015** established in the case law of the Court . . . that a Member State may not plead internal circumstances in order to justify a failure to comply with obligations and time-limits resulting from Community law. Moreover, it has been held on several occasions . . . that practical difficulties which appear at the stage when a Community measure is put into effect cannot permit a Member State unilaterally to opt out of fulfilling its obligations". In particular, the Court has made it clear that the obligations arising from the Treaty "devolve upon States as such and the liability of a Member State under Article [226 EC] arises whatever the agency of the State whose action or inaction is the cause of the failure to fulfil its obligations, even in the case of a constitutionally independent institution".[70] Thus, it is no defence that draft legislation intended to give effect to the requirements of Community law lapsed due to the dissolution of the national parliament.[71]

It follows that proceedings under Article 226 EC could in principle be brought against a Member State if its courts failed to comply with their obligations under the Treaty, at least if the failure were deliberate or systematic. However, it might be less provocative to challenge the competent national authority's failure to introduce legislation which is sufficient to give effect to the requirements of Community law. In *Commission v Italy*,[72] the Commission sought a declaration that Italy had failed to fulfil its Treaty obligations by maintaining in force a legislative provision which, as construed and applied by the domestic administrative authorities and courts, was producing a result which was contrary to Community law. The Court said that, although the contested legislative provision was not self-evidently incompatible with Community law, its effect had to be determined in the light of the way it was interpreted by the national courts. The Court acknowledged that "isolated or numerically insignificant judicial decisions in the context of case law taking a different direction, or still more a construction disowned by the

---

[68] Case 39/72 *Commission v Italy* [1973] E.C.R. 101, para.22. See also Case 38/69 *Commission v Italy* [1970] E.C.R. 47, para.12.

[69] Case C–39/88 [1990] E.C.R. I–4271, para.11.

[70] Case 77/69 *Commission v Belgium* [1970] E.C.R. 237, para.15.

[71] *ibid*. See also e.g. Case 91/79 *Commission v Italy* [1980] E.C.R. 1099.

[72] Case C–129/00 [2003] E.C.R. I–14637. *cf.* Case C–224/01 *Köbler v Austria* [2003] E.C.R. I–10239, where the Court held that a Member State was obliged to make good damage caused to an individual by an infringement of Community law stemming from a decision of a national supreme court. The *Köbler* case is discussed in Ch.6.

national supreme court, cannot be taken into account". However, a "widely-held judicial construction" which, as here, had been confirmed by the supreme court, was relevant to the question whether the State concerned had failed to fulfil its obligations.[73] Where the case law on the meaning of national legislation was inconsistent, the Court held that, "at the very least, such legislation is not sufficiently clear to ensure its application in compliance with Community law".[74] The Court concluded that Italy had breached its obligations by failing to amend a provision "which is construed and applied by the administrative authorities and a substantial proportion of the courts, including the Corte suprema di cassazione" in a way which resulted in a situation which was contrary to Community law.

A Member State may even incur liability under Article 226 EC as a result of the actions of individuals if the Court takes the view that it has not taken appropriate steps to prevent such actions from interfering with the rights of others under Community law. This was established in *Commission v France*,[75] where the Commission argued that France had breached its Treaty obligations by failing to take effective action to prevent imports of fruit and vegetables from other Member States from being disrupted by acts of violence committed by farmers. The Court held that the Treaty required the Member States to take all necessary and appropriate measures to ensure that the fundamental principle of the free movement of goods was respected on their territory. Although the Member States had a margin of discretion in determining what measures were most appropriate to eliminate barriers to imports in a given situation, it was the responsibility of the Court to ensure that that margin had not been exceeded. The Court concluded that "in the present case the French Government has manifestly and persistently abstained from adopting appropriate and adequate measures to put an end to the acts of vandalism which jeopardise the free movement on its territory of certain agricultural products originating in other Member States and to prevent the recurrence of such acts".[76]

13–016 **(b) Failure to implement directives.** The growth in the use of directives since the advent of the single market programme highlighted the importance of ensuring compliance by Member States with the obligations they lay down.[77] In a declaration issued at

---

[73] Para.32.
[74] Para.33.
[75] Case C–265/95 [1997] E.C.R. I–6959.
[76] Para.65. The Court's decision led to the adoption of Reg.2679/98 on the functioning of the internal market in relation to the free movement of goods among the Member States [1998] O.J. L337/8. See further on this issue Ch.16.
[77] The Commission maintains an "Internal Market Scoreboard" showing the progress of Member States in implementing internal market directives. See *http://europa.eu.int/comm/internal—market/en/update/score/index.htm*.

Maastricht, the Member States stressed "that it is central to the coherence and unity of the process of European construction that each Member State should fully and accurately transpose into national law the Community directives addressed to it within the deadlines laid down therein". They called on the Commission to ensure, in exercising its powers, that Member States fulfilled their obligations in that regard.[78]

Many infringement actions concern alleged failures by Member States to give effect to directives. Such actions are often straightforward, the State concerned scarcely troubling to defend itself before the Court. Member States are not permitted in infringement proceedings to contest the validity of a directive they are accused by the Commission of having failed to implement properly.[79] This is because the Treaty provides a special remedy, the action for annulment, for challenging the validity of Community acts. Member States do not have to satisfy any standing requirements in order to bring an annulment action.[80]

Some infringement actions for failure to implement directives properly have, however, given rise to difficult questions about the meaning of the directive concerned and the precise steps which need to be taken to give effect to it. Some of the potential areas of dispute are apparent from the following summary of the obligations imposed by directives on Member States offered by the Court in *Commission v France*:[81]

> "While it is . . . essential that the legal situation resulting from national implementing measures is sufficiently precise and clear to enable the individuals concerned to know the extent of their rights and obligations, it is none the less the case that, according to the very words of the third paragraph of Article [249] of the Treaty, Member States may choose the form and methods for implementing directives which best ensure the result to be achieved by the directives, and that provision shows that the transposition of a directive into national law does not

---

[78] See Snyder, "The Effectiveness of European Community Law: Institutions, Processes, Tools and Techniques" (1993) 56 M.L.R. 19.

[79] A decision addressed to the State concerned is treated in the same way as a directive for this purpose: see Case C–52/00 *Commission v France* [2002] E.C.R. I–3827, para.28; Case C–194/01 *Commission v Austria* [2004] E.C.R. I–4579, para.41. The position may be different in the case of regulations, because the impact of such an act on a Member State may not initially be apparent: see further para.191 of the Opinion of Advocate General Jacobs in Case C–11/00 *Commission v European Central Bank* [2003] E.C.R. I–7147.

[80] The action for annulment is discussed below.

[81] Case C–233/00 [2003] E.C.R. I–6625, para.76. See also Case 29/84 *Commission v Germany* [1985] E.C.R. 1661, paras 22 and 23; Case C–217/97 *Commission v Germany* [1999] E.C.R. I–5087, paras 31 and 32; Case C–296/01 *Commission v France* [2003] E.C.R. I–13909, paras 54 and 55. A provision contained in a directive which concerns only relations between the Member States and the Commission does not, in principle, need to be transposed: Case C–296/01 *Commission v France* [2003] E.C.R. I–13909, para.92.

necessarily require legislative action in each Member State. The Court has thus repeatedly held that it is not always necessary formally to enact the requirements of a directive in a specific express legal provision, since the general legal context may be sufficient for implementation of a directive, depending on its content. In particular, the existence of general principles of constitutional or administrative law may render superfluous transposition by specific legislative or regulatory measures provided, however, that those principles actually ensure the full application of the directive by the national authorities and that, where the relevant provision of the directive seeks to create rights for individuals, the legal situation arising from those principles is sufficiently precise and clear and that the persons concerned are put in a position to know the full extent of their rights and, where appropriate, to be able to rely on them before the national courts . . ."

13–017 In *Commission v Austria*,[82] the Court emphasised that Member States were not released from their obligation to implement a directive "where they consider that their national provisions are better than the Community provision concerned and that the national provisions are therefore better able to ensure that the objective pursued by the directive is achieved".

The problems which may arise where national implementing legislation is regarded by the Commission as ambiguous were highlighted in *Commission v United Kingdom*.[83] In that case, the Commission argued that the United Kingdom Consumer Protection Act 1987 failed to give effect properly to a directive on liability for defective products. The United Kingdom pointed out that section 1(1) of the Act made it clear that its purpose was to give effect to the directive and required it to be construed accordingly. It maintained that the relevant provision of the Act, section 4(1)(e), was capable of being interpreted consistently with the directive. The Court held that the Commission had not succeeded in refuting that argument:[84] "the Court has consistently held that the scope of national laws, regulations or administrative provisions must be assessed in the light of the interpretation given to them by national courts . . . Yet in this case the Commission has not referred in support of its application to any national judicial decision which, in its view, interprets the domestic provision at issue inconsistently with the Directive".[85] The

---

[82] Case C–194/01 [2004] E.C.R. I–4579, para.39.
[83] Case C–300/95 [1997] E.C.R. I–2649. See also Case C–80/92 *Commission v Belgium* [1994] E.C.R. I–1019, para.7. *cf.* Case C–392/96 *Commission v Ireland* [1999] E.C.R. I–5901; Case C–252/01 *Commission v Belgium* [2003] E.C.R. I–11859.
[84] Para.37.
[85] *cf.* Case C–233/00 *Commission v France* [2003] E.C.R. I–6625, paras 84–87.

United Kingdom courts on the whole have a good record in interpreting national provisions consistently with directives they are designed to implement,[86] and this provided a further ground for rejecting the Commission's application:[87]

> "there is nothing in the material produced to the Court to suggest that the courts in the United Kingdom, if called upon to interpret section 4(1)(e), would not do so in the light of the wording and the purpose of the Directive so as to achieve the result which it has in view and thereby comply with the third paragraph of Article [249] of the Treaty . . . Moreover, section 1(1) of the Act expressly imposes such an obligation on the national courts."

The Court concluded that the Commission had failed to make out its allegation that the Act was inadequate to give effect to the directive.

The Commission was also unsuccessful in *Commission v Sweden*,[88] **13–018** where Sweden successfully defended itself against an allegation that it had failed to give effect properly to Directive 93/13 on unfair terms in consumer contracts.[89] The directive contained an annex giving "an indicative and non-exhaustive list of the terms which may be regarded as unfair". The Swedish legislation implementing the directive did not reproduce the annex. It appeared, along with a commentary, in the statement of reasons accompanying the legislation, but the Commission said this was not enough. The Court disagreed. In so far as the list did not limit the discretion of the national authorities to determine the unfairness of a term, it did not have to be reproduced in the domestic implementing legislation as long as its content was drawn to the attention of the public. Sweden claimed that, according to a well-established legal tradition in the Nordic countries, preparatory work constituted an important aid to the interpretation of legislation and could easily be consulted. Moreover, the public had been given information about contractual terms which might be regarded as unfair. The Commission had not disputed those claims. Its application was accordingly dismissed.

However, a Member State will not be able to avoid the need for legislative measures by relying on the principle of consistent interpretation.[90] In *Commission v Netherlands*,[91] the Commission alleged

---

[86] See generally Arnull, "Interpretation and precedent in English and Community law: evidence of cross-fertilisation?" in Andenas (ed.), *English Public Law and the Common Law of Europe* (1998).
[87] Para.38 of the judgment.
[88] Case C–478/99 [2002] E.C.R. I–4147. See also Case C–70/03 *Commission v Spain* [2004] E.C.R. I–7999.
[89] [1993] O.J. L95/29.
[90] See Ch.5.
[91] Case C–144/99 [2001] E.C.R. I–3541.

that the Netherlands had failed to take the steps necessary to transpose certain provisions of Directive 93/13. Although the Netherlands had not adopted any specific implementing provisions, it claimed that such provisions were not necessary as its national law already achieved the aims of the directive. Advocate General Tizzano explained[92] that the principle of consistent interpretation "does not solve the problem at issue here. It is designed to be of use pending the transposition of a directive into national law—or even after transposition if this is incorrect or incomplete—but it certainly cannot serve as an excuse for failure to transpose or for inadequate transposition". The Court pointed out that, while legislative action on the part of each Member State was not necessarily required, it was essential that the legal position under national law should be sufficiently precise and clear and that individuals should made fully aware of their rights. The Court declared that, even where the national courts were willing to interpret national law in a manner which satisfied the requirements of a directive, that was not adequate to meet the requirements of legal certainty. The Commission's application was therefore upheld. The circumstances were not the same as those of *Commission v United Kingdom*, discussed above, because there specific implementing legislation had been adopted which said it was to be interpreted in the light of the directive in question.

The effectiveness of infringement proceedings

13–019 Of the cases which result in a ruling of the Court adverse to the Member State concerned, most are in due course complied with, although sometimes only after considerable delay. However, the 1980s saw a marked increase in the number of rulings given by the Court against Member States for breach of Article 228 EC.[93] In order to give Member States an added incentive to comply with rulings against them under Article 226 EC, a new second paragraph was added to Article 228 EC at Maastricht giving the Court the power to impose financial sanctions on Member States which failed to do so.

Article 228(2) EC provides that the Commission, if it considers that the State concerned has not taken the measures necessary to comply with the Court's judgment:

---

[92] See [2001] E.C.R. I–3541, 3555.

[93] The explanation for this development may lie partly in the increased vigour with which the Commission, between the late 1970s and the early 1990s, pursued Member States which failed to comply with their Treaty obligations. See Dashwood and White, "Enforcement Actions under Articles 169 and 170 EEC" (1989) 14 E.L.Rev. 388, 399–400; Gormley (ed.), *Kapteyn and VerLoren van Themaat's Introduction to the Law of the European Communities* (3rd ed., 1998), p.454.

"shall, after giving that State the opportunity to submit its observations, issue a reasoned opinion specifying the points on which the Member State concerned has not complied with the judgment of the Court of Justice.

If the Member State concerned fails to take the necessary measures to comply with the Court's judgment within the time-limit laid down by the Commission, the latter may bring the case before the Court of Justice. In so doing it shall specify the amount of the lump sum or penalty payment to be paid by the Member State concerned which it considers appropriate in the circumstances.

If the Court of Justice finds that the Member State concerned has not complied with its judgment it may impose a lump sum or penalty payment on it.

This procedure shall be without prejudice to Article 227."

One drawback of this procedure is that the Commission may not ask for the imposition of a financial penalty in its initial application to the Court under Article 226 EC. Moreover, no additional penalties (other than further infringement proceedings under Article 226 EC) are envisaged if a Member State refuses to pay a sanction imposed on it.[94] On the other hand, although the Commission is required to follow an administrative procedure which corresponds to that laid down in Article 226 EC, involving an opportunity for the State concerned to submit its observations and the issue of a reasoned opinion, it is not required to specify the amount of any sanction it considers appropriate until it brings the case before the Court. It will also be noted that the Treaty does not set any limit to the amount of the penalty which the Court may impose.[95]

By the time the Maastricht Treaty was signed on February 7, 1992, **13–020** the Court of Justice had held in the famous *Francovich* case,[96] decided the previous November, that there was a principle "inherent in the system of the Treaty" that Member States were liable to compensate individuals for damage caused by breaches of Community law for which they were responsible. That principle deprived Article 228(2) EC of much of its significance, but there remain some

---

[94] *cf.*Art.88 ECSC, which provided that, where a Member State's failure to comply with its Treaty obligations had been established, the High Authority could, with the assent of the Council acting by a two-thirds majority, (a) suspend the payment of any sums which it might be liable to pay to the State in question under the Treaty, and (b) take measures, or authorise the other Member States to take measures, which would otherwise be prohibited as incompatible with the common market for coal and steel in order to correct the effects of the infringement. These apparently draconian sanctions were never imposed.

[95] Note, furthermore, that the Commission is entitled to limit the extent of the Member State's alleged failure to fulfil its obligations, so as to take account of partial measures to comply with the ECJ's original judgment, adopted during the course of the Art.228 EC proceedings: see Case C–177/04 *Commission v France* (Judgment of March 14, 2006).

[96] Joined Cases C–6/90 and C–9/90 [1991] E.C.R. I–5357. See Ch.6.

situations where the principle of State liability is unlikely to have much practical effect. The conditions laid down in *Francovich* and the Court's later case law on the principle of State liability may not be satisfied. The loss suffered by a potential plaintiff may be too small to justify the cost of bringing proceedings; causation may be hard to prove. In some cases, it may be undesirable to leave matters until a willing litigant emerges. In circumstances such as these, the imposition of a financial sanction under Article 228(2) EC may be particularly appropriate.

In 1996, the Commission issued its first "Memorandum on applying Article [228] of the EC Treaty",[97] in which it set out its views on how the second paragraph of that article might be applied. The Commission observed that the penalty payment, rather than the lump sum, was the "most appropriate instrument" for achieving the objective of the infringement procedure, which was "to secure compliance as rapidly as possible". The Commission stated that the amount of the penalty would be calculated on the basis of three criteria: (a) the seriousness of the infringement; (b) its duration; and (c) the need to deter further infringements. The Commission acknowledged that failure to comply with a judgment of the Court is always a serious matter, but said that it would also take account of the effects of the underlying infringement and the importance of the rules which had been infringed. In January 1997, the Commission issued further guidance on how it proposed to calculate the appropriate penalty in particular cases. It announced[98] that the amount of any penalty payments proposed to the Court would be calculated by multiplying coefficients reflecting the gravity and duration of the infringement by an "invariable factor" based on the gross domestic product of the Member State concerned and the weighting of votes in the Council.

The Commission's annual Reports on Monitoring the Application of Community Law give details of action taken by the Commission under Article 228(2) EC. The Reports suggest that the sanctions available under that provision play a useful role in encouraging Member States to comply with their obligations, most cases being resolved satisfactorily without a further judgment of the Court. The first case to proceed to judgment was *Commission v Greece*,[99] a judgment dated July 4, 2000 in which the Court decided to impose on Greece a penalty of €20,000 for each day of delay in taking the measures necessary to comply with a ruling given on April 7, 1992 finding Greece to be in breach of its obligations under two directives

---

[97] [1996] O.J. C242/6.
[98] See [1997] O.J. C63/2.
[99] Case C–387/97 [2000] E.C.R. I–5047.

on the disposal of waste.[1] While emphasising that they could not bind it, the Court in that case endorsed the guidelines on the calculation of sanctions laid down by the Commission, observing:[2] "Those guidelines . . . help to ensure that it acts in a manner which is transparent, foreseeable and consistent with legal certainty" and that they were "designed to achieve proportionality in the amounts of the penalty payments to be proposed by it". The Court stated that the Commission's suggestion that account should be taken of the defendant State's gross domestic product and the number of votes it had in the Council "appears appropriate in that it enables that Member State's ability to pay to be reflected while keeping the variation between Member States within a reasonable range".[3] The Court declared:[4]

> "the basic criteria which must be taken into account in order to ensure that penalty payments have coercive force and Community law is applied uniformly and effectively are, in principle, the duration of the infringement, its degree of seriousness and the ability of the Member State to pay. In applying those criteria, regard should be had in particular to the effects of failure to comply on private and public interests and to the urgency of getting the Member State concerned to fulfil its obligations."

In accordance with the Commission's application, the penalty **13–021** imposed by the Court was to run from the date of the second judgment rather than that of the first or the (subsequent) entry into force of the TEU. The judgment implies[5] that the date of the original judgment under Article 226 EC will normally be regarded as marking the starting date of the infringement for the purposes of fixing the amount of the penalty, not the date on which the underlying breach of the Treaty took place (in a case such as this, the expiry of the deadline for implementing the relevant directive).[6] Measures to give effect to the original ruling were finally adopted by the Greek authorities on February 26, 2001, so they paid a total penalty of €5,400,000 for the period between July 2000 and March 2001.

The Court imposed a penalty for a second time in *Commission v Spain*.[7] That case also involved a failure on the part of the State

---

[1] Case C–45/91 *Commission v Greece* [1992] E.C.R. I–2509.
[2] Para.87 of the judgment.
[3] Para.88.
[4] Para.92.
[5] See para.98. This view is also supported by the ruling in Case C–304/02 *Commission v France* (Judgment of July 12, 2005).
[6] In the *Greece* case, the defendant should have implemented both directives by January 1, 1981: see para.10 of the judgment.
[7] Case C–278/01 [2003] E.C.R. I–14141.

concerned to give effect to a directive on the protection of the environment, on this occasion by reducing the pollution of bathing water. Spain was found to have failed to comply with a judgment delivered on February 12, 1998[8] declaring it in breach of its obligation to implement the directive concerned. The Commission asked for the imposition of a daily penalty payment. However, as the state of bathing water was assessed on an annual basis, the Court held that the penalty payment should also be imposed on an annual basis. Otherwise a penalty might fall due for a period in respect of which the requirements of the directive were subsequently found to have been met. The Court thought that the amount of the penalty should take account of progress made by Spain in complying with the first judgment against it and of the difficulty of complying fully with that judgment in a short time. It therefore imposed a lower penalty than that proposed by the Commission and made it payable annually from the first assessment of the quality of bathing water following delivery of its (second) judgment until the year in which its first judgment was complied with.

In accordance with its 1996 memorandum, the Commission's settled practice under Article 228 EC was to suggest to the Court the imposition of penalty payments (rather than a lump sum) upon the defaulting Member State. However, the first indication of a change in attitude came with the institution of proceedings under Article 228(2) EC against France, which induced the latter Member State to lift its ban on the importation of British beef imposed during the BSE crisis and declared unlawful by the Court in December 2001.[9] The Commission announced in November 2002 that it would not be pursuing its application to the Court for the imposition of a penalty,[10] but according to the 20th Report on Monitoring the Application of Community Law,[11] "the British beef controversy prompted the Commission to consider the possibility of proposing that the Court of Justice should order not only a periodic penalty payment but also a fine, to give Member States an incentive to comply with judgments holding them to be in default".[12]

13–022 The issue arose more recently in another case involving France,[13] where the Commission asked the Court to impose a daily penalty payment running from the date of its second judgment until its first judgment[14] had been implemented. Advocate General Geelhoed

---

[8] Case C–92/96 *Commission v Spain* [1998] E.C.R. I–505.
[9] See Case C–1/00 *Commission v France* [2001] E.C.R. I–9989.
[10] See Commission press releases IP/02/1086 and IP/02/1671.
[11] COM(2003) 669 final, p.9.
[12] It should in any event be borne in mind that the Treaty gave those affected by the French ban a remedy in the French courts: see Case C–241/01 *National Farmers' Union v Secrétariat Général du Gouvernement* [2002] E.C.R. I–9079.
[13] Case C–304/02 *Commission v France* (Judgment of July 12, 2005).
[14] Case C–64/88 *Commission v France* [1991] E.C.R. I–2727.

took the view that the infringement[15] was so serious that the Court should impose both a lump sum and a penalty payment. As he pointed out:[16] "Where a Member State succeeds in complying with the obligations it neglected before such a penalty is payable, the final result may be that no sanction is imposed. Though effective in finally ensuring compliance, the imposition of a periodic penalty payment may not therefore always be an appropriate response to the infringement in question". The Court itself held that both a lump sum and penalty payments are intended to achieve the objective, pursued by Article 228 EC, of inducing a defaulting Member State to comply with a judgment establishing a breach of its obligations. Each measure is to be applied depending on its respective ability to meet that objective, according to the circumstances of each case: penalty payments seems particularly suited to inducing a Member State to put an end as soon as possible to a breach of obligations which would otherwise tend to persist; a lump sum is based more on an assessment of the effects on public and private interests of the failure of the Member State to comply with its obligations, in particular, where the breach has persisted for a long period since the judgment which initially established it. Recourse to both types of penalty in the same case is possible, especially where the breach of obligations both has continued for a long period and is inclined to persist. Moreover, the Court confirmed that it enjoys discretion, where appropriate, to depart from the Commission's suggestions: for example, to impose a lump sum on a Member State, even though the Commission did not propose doing so.[17]

The Commission has now replaced its 1996 and 1997 memoranda with a new 2005 communication on the application of Article 228 of the EC Treaty, in which it seeks to take into account the various principles sets out by the ECJ in its rulings against Greece, Spain and France (as well as updating the method of calculating sanctions to the enlarged Union).[18] The communication indicates an important change for the future in the Commission's approach to requesting sanctions under Article 228 EC: in principle, the Commission will now include in its applications to the Court under Article 228 EC a specification of *both* (a) a penalty by day of delay after delivery of the judgment under Article 228 EC, *and* (b) a lump sum penalising continuation of the infringement between the first judgment on non-compliance and the judgment under Article 228 EC.[19] This means

---

[15] Which involved failure to ensure compliance with Community measures on the conservation of fishery resources.

[16] Para.88 of his Opinion of April 29, 2004. A second Opinion was delivered on November 18, 2004, confirming his view that the Court was entitled to impose both a lump sum and a penalty payment, even where the Commission had only suggested a penalty payment.

[17] *cf.* Case C–119/04 *Commission v Italy* (Opinion of January 26, 2006; Judgment pending).

[18] SEC(2005)1658.

[19] Para.10.3 of the communication.

that, where a Member State rectifies its infringement before the judgment under Article 228 EC, so that penalty payments have lost their purpose, the Commission may still proceed with the case on the basis of the lump sum payment, which retains its objective of penalising the infringement up to the time of its rectification.[20]

The action for annulment

13–023   It would have been incompatible with the legal traditions of the founding Member States and with the rule of law for the exercise by the Community institutions of their law-making powers to have escaped judicial review. Article 230 EC therefore permits direct actions for the annulment of Community acts to be brought before the Community Courts.[21] It may also be possible to challenge the validity of Community acts in proceedings before the courts of the Member States, which must, where there is a serious doubt about the validity of the act in question, ask the Court of Justice for a preliminary ruling on the matter under Article 234 EC.[22] The preliminary rulings procedure is discussed in Chapter 14.

Article 230 EC, as amended at Maastricht, Amsterdam and Nice, provides as follows:

> "The Court of Justice shall review the legality of acts adopted jointly by the European Parliament and the Council, of acts of the Council, of the Commission and of the ECB, other than recommendations and opinions, and of acts of the European Parliament intended to produce legal effects *viv-à-vis* third parties.
>
> It shall for this purpose have jurisdiction in actions brought by a Member State, the European Parliament, the Council or the Commission on grounds of lack of competence, infringement of an essential procedural requirement, infringement of this Treaty or of any rule of law relating to its application, or misuse of powers.
>
> The Court shall have jurisdiction under the same conditions in actions brought by the Court of Auditors and by the ECB for the purpose of protecting their prerogatives.
>
> Any natural or legal person may, under the same conditions, institute proceedings against a decision addressed to that person or against a decision which, although in the form of a regulation or a decision addressed to another person, is of direct and individual concern to the former.

---

[20] Para.11 of the communication.
[21] The Court also has a limited annulment jurisdiction in relation to Title VI of the Treaty on European Union: see Art.35(6) TEU. See also Ch.10.
[22] See Case 314/85 *Foto-Frost v Hauptzollamt Lübeck-Ost* [1987] E.C.R. 4199.

The proceedings provided for in this article shall be instituted within two months of the publication of the measure, or of its notification to the plaintiff, or, in the absence thereof, of the day on which it came to the knowledge of the latter, as the case may be."

As explained in Chapter 12, jurisdiction in annulment actions brought by natural and legal persons and in a limited category of such actions brought by the Member States is now exercised by the CFI, from which appeal lies to the Court of Justice on points of law. Annulment actions brought by one institution against another for the time being commence in the Court of Justice, although it is possible that certain categories of such actions will also be transferred to the CFI in due course.[23]

Reviewable acts

Under the first paragraph of Article 230 EC, proceedings may be **13–024** brought against acts adopted jointly by the European Parliament and the Council and acts of the Council, of the Commission, and of the ECB, other than recommendations or opinions. According to Article 249 EC, the last two categories of act "have no binding force".[24] The other categories of act mentioned in Article 249 EC (regulations, directives and decisions) do have binding force and are susceptible to review under Article 230 EC provided they bring about a distinct change in the applicant's legal position.

In *Philip Morris International v Commission*,[25] the applicants, who were cigarette manufacturers, sought the annulment of two decisions of the Commission to commence legal proceedings against them in the USA as part of its efforts to combat the smuggling of cigarettes into the EU. The CFI dismissed the action as inadmissible on the basis that a decision to commence legal proceedings did not in itself determine definitively the obligations of the parties or alter the legal position. That only happened when the court in question gave judgment. The CFI's ruling was surprising. It seems inconsistent with the rule of law and the right to an effective remedy, which the Court has said the EC legal order guarantees,[26] for one of the arguments of the applicants was that the Commission had exceeded its powers in launching the US proceedings. The ruling of the CFI removed the

---

[23] See Art.225(1) EC; Statute, Art.51.

[24] Recommendations are not, however, entirely devoid of legal significance: see Case C–322/88 *Grimaldi v Fonds des Maladies Professionnelles* [1989] E.C.R. 4407.

[25] Joined Cases T–377/00, T–379/00, T–380/00, T–260/01 and T–272/01 [2003] E.C.R. II–1. See also Case T–353/00 *Le Pen v European Parliament* [2003] E.C.R. II–125.

[26] See e.g. Case C–50/00 P *Unión de Pequeños Agricultores v Council* [2002] E.C.R. I–6677; Case C–263/02 *Jégo-Quéré v Commission* [2004] E.C.R. I–3425; Art.47 of the Charter of Fundamental Rights.

most effective way of testing that argument before the Community Courts. The action for damages against the Community, which the CFI mentioned as a possible remedy for the applicants, would necessarily only come into play if the applicants lost in the US courts.[27] That might not become clear for several years after the expenditure of large amounts of time and money.

The question whether Article 230 EC can be used to challenge measures adopted by the Community institutions which produce legal effects, but which do not take the form of any of the binding acts referred to in Article 249 EC, was considered in the "ERTA" case.[28] The Commission sought the annulment of Council proceedings concerning the negotiation and conclusion by the Member States of a European road transport agreement. The Court stated that "Article [230 EC] treats as acts open to review by the Court all measures adopted by the institutions which are intended to have legal force". The Court said that it would be inconsistent with the purpose of Article 230 EC, which was to ensure that the law was observed in accordance with Article 220 EC, "to limit the availability of this procedure merely to the categories of measures referred to by Article [249 EC]". It concluded that "[a]n action for annulment must therefore be available in the case of all measures adopted by the institutions, whatever their nature or form, which are intended to have legal effects". Similarly, in *Les Verts v Parliament*[29] a French political grouping sought the annulment of two measures adopted by the European Parliament. At the material time, the Parliament was not mentioned in the first paragraph of Article 230 EC, but the Court held that it would be inconsistent with the spirit of the Treaty for measures adopted by the Parliament which produced legal effects *vis-à-vis* third parties to be excluded from the scope of the action for annulment.[30]

The ERTA principle was applied by the Court in *Commission v Council*,[31] which concerned a dispute over the procedure for dealing with Member States which have adopted the euro as their currency but which have run up excessive government deficits. The obligation of such Member States to avoid excessive government deficits is laid down in Article 104 EC, which gives the Commission the task of

---

[27] The action for damages is discussed further below.

[28] Case 22/70 *Commission v Council* [1971] E.C.R. 263, paras 39–42. See also Case C–366/88 *France v Commission* [1990] E.C.R. I–3571.

[29] Case 294/83 [1986] E.C.R. 1339. See also Case 34/86 *Council v Parliament* [1986] E.C.R. 2155; Case C–57/95 *France v Commission* [1997] E.C.R. I–1627.

[30] For examples of acts which were not intended to produce legal effects, and therefore could not be challenged under Art.230 EC, see e.g. Case 114/86 *United Kingdom v Commission* [1988] E.C.R. 5289; Case C–180/96 *United Kingdom v Commission* [1998] E.C.R. I–2265; Case C–443/97 *Spain v Commission* [2000] E.C.R. I–2415; Case C–208/03 P *Le Pen v European Parliament* (Judgment of July 7, 2005); Case C–301/03 *Italy v Commission* (Judgment of December 1, 2005).

[31] Case C–27/04 [2004] E.C.R. I–6649.

monitoring their budgetary situation and addressing opinions to the Council where it considers that an excessive deficit in a Member State exists. Under Article 104(6) EC, it is for the Council, acting on a recommendation from the Commission, to decide whether the Commission is right. Article 104(7) to (9) EC provides as follows:

> "7. Where the existence of an excessive deficit is decided according to paragraph 6, the Council shall make recommendations to the Member State concerned with a view to bringing that situation to an end within a given period. Subject to the provisions of paragraph 8, these recommendations shall not be made public.
>
> 8. Where it establishes that there has been no effective action in response to its recommendations within the period laid down, the Council may make its recommendations public.
>
> 9. If a Member State persists in failing to put into practice the recommendations of the Council, the Council may decide to give notice to the Member State to take, within a specified time-limit, measures for the deficit reduction which is judged necessary by the Council in order to remedy the situation.
>
> In such a case, the Council may request the Member State concerned to submit reports in accordance with a specific timetable in order to examine the adjustment efforts of that Member State."

In 2003, the Commission recommended that the Council take **13–025** decisions under Article 104(8) EC establishing that neither France nor Germany had taken adequate steps to bring excessive government deficits to an end following earlier Council recommendations under Article 104(7) EC. The Commission recommended that the Council give both States notice under Article 104(9) EC to take measures to reduce their deficits. At a meeting on November 25, 2003, the Council took votes on the Commission recommendations. Since the requisite majorities were not achieved, the decisions were not adopted. However, the Council adopted "conclusions" in respect of each Member State welcoming public commitments they had given to reduce their deficits and recommending that they put an end to their excessive deficits as rapidly as possible. They agreed to hold the excessive deficit procedure in abeyance for the time being, but to act under Article 104(9) EC if either of the States concerned failed to honour the commitments it had given. The Commission sought the annulment of the Council's conclusions and its decisions not to adopt formal instruments under Article 104(8) and (9) EC in accordance with the Commission's recommendations.

The Court rejected the Council's argument that the conclusions were texts of a political nature which did not entail any legal effects. They did more than merely confirm the situation resulting from the

Council's failure to adopt the acts recommended by the Commission: they made the suspension of the ongoing excessive deficit procedure conditional on compliance by the Member States concerned with the commitments they had given. Those commitments were unilateral in character and had been made outside the framework of the recommendations previously addressed by the Council to the States in question under Article 104(7) EC, which had in reality been modified. It followed that the Council's conclusions were intended to have legal effects and the Commission's application for their annulment was admissible.[32]

However, the Court dismissed as inadmissible the Commission's application for the annulment of the Council's decisions not to adopt the formal instruments sought by the Commission. The Commission had relied on *Eurocoton v Council*,[33] a dumping case,[34] where the Court held that the Council's failure to adopt a proposal for a regulation imposing a definitive anti-dumping duty submitted by the Commission "has all the characteristics of a reviewable act within the meaning of Article [230] of the Treaty, in that it produced binding legal effects capable of affecting the appellants' interests".[35] However, as the Court pointed out in that case, the Council's failure to adopt the proposal, together with the expiry shortly afterwards of the period laid down in the basic regulation within which this could be done,[36] "determined definitively the Council's position in the final phase of the anti-dumping proceedings".[37] As the Court explained in *Commission v Council*, the excessive deficit procedure was different, for it did not lay down any deadlines the expiry of which would prevent the Council from adopting at a later date the acts recommended by the Commission. It followed that "failure by the Council to adopt acts provided for in Article 104(8) and (9) EC that are recommended by the Commission cannot be regarded as giving rise to acts open to challenge for the purposes of Article 230 EC". The proper remedy for the Commission in circumstances such as these was an action for failure to act under Article 232 EC[38] (although, as the Council pointed out,[39] the conditions laid down in that article were not met in this case).

---

[32] The conclusions were subsequently quashed by the Court.

[33] Case C–76/01 [2003] E.C.R. I–10091.

[34] Dumping occurs when a product is imported into the Community from a non-member country at a price which is lower than its normal value in that country and the result is to cause injury to a Community industry. Dumped products may be the subject of regulations imposing anti-dumping duties.

[35] Para.67.

[36] Reg.384/96 on protection against dumped imports from countries not members of the European Community [1996] O.J. L56/1, under Art.6(9) of which anti-dumping investigations had to be concluded within 15 months of initiation.

[37] Para.65.

[38] See below.

[39] See para.25 of the judgment.

Finally, it should be noted that annulment proceedings cannot be brought against certain types of act which might be considered binding. For example, a provisional measure intended to pave the way for the final decision in a procedure involving several stages cannot be challenged; only the final act definitively laying down the adopting body's position is susceptible to review under Article 230 EC.[40] Nor can proceedings be brought against a measure which merely confirms a previous measure which has not been challenged within the two-month time-limit laid down in the last paragraph of Article 230 EC.[41]

Grounds of review

In order to succeed in an action for the annulment of a Community act, the applicant must establish that the contested act was unlawful. The second paragraph of Article 230 EC mentions four grounds, derived from French administrative law,[42] on which this may be done. In practice, those grounds overlap to a considerable extent and the Court does not distinguish rigidly between them. **13–026**

A measure may be annulled by the Court for *lack of competence* if the adopting institution lacked the authority to adopt it. This typically arises where the legal basis under which the adopting institution purported to act is found by the Court not to be wide enough to cover the contested measure.[43]

An example of a *breach of an essential procedural requirement* is failure to consult the Parliament prior to the adoption of an act where consultation is required by the Treaty.[44] Another example is failure to hear the views of interested parties before a decision which directly affects them is adopted.[45] In *Lisrestal v Commission*,[46] an application for the annulment of a decision reducing financial assistance initially granted under the European Social Fund, the CFI stated:

> "it is settled law that respect for the rights of the defence in all proceedings which are initiated against a person and are liable to culminate in a measure adversely affecting that person is a

---

[40] Case 60/81 *IBM v Commission* [1981] E.C.R. 2639.
[41] See e.g. Joined Cases 166 and 220/86 *Irish Cement Ltd v Commission* [1988] E.C.R. 6473, para.16; Case T–275/94 *CB v Commission* [1995] E.C.R. II–2169, para.27.
[42] See Advocate General Lagrange in Case 3/54 *ASSIDER v High Authority* [1954 to 1956] E.C.R. 63, a case decided under the ECSC Treaty.
[43] See e.g. Joined Cases 281, 283 to 285 and 287/85 *Germany, France, Netherlands, Denmark and United Kingdom v Commission* [1987] E.C.R. 3203; Case 264/86 *France v Commission* [1988] E.C.R. 973. *cf.* Case 45/86 *Commission v Council* [1987] E.C.R. 1493.
[44] Case 138/79 *Roquette Frères v Council* [1980] E.C.R. 3333.
[45] See e.g. Case 17/74 *Transocean Marine Paint Association v Commission* [1974] E.C.R. 1063; Case C–49/88 *Al-Jubail Fertilizer Company v Council* [1991] E.C.R. I–3187.
[46] Case T–450/93 [1994] E.C.R. II–1177, para.42.

fundamental principle of Community law which must be guaranteed, even in the absence of any specific rules concerning the proceedings in question . . . That principle requires that any person who may be adversely affected by the adoption of a decision should be placed in a position in which he may effectively make known his views on the evidence against him which the Commission has taken as the basis for the decision at issue."

Thus, a person must be heard if administrative proceedings have been brought against him. However, that requirement does not apply to the adoption of legislation of general application. In that context, the only obligations of consultation which the Community legislature must respect are those laid down in the legal basis of the contested act.[47]

13–027   Another important example of an essential procedural requirement is contained in Article 253 EC, which requires Community acts to contain an adequate statement of the reasons on which they are based. The Court explained in *Commission v European Parliament and Council*[48] that "absence of reasons or inadequacy of the reasons stated goes to an issue of infringement of essential procedural requirements within the meaning of Article 230 EC, and constitutes a plea distinct from a plea relating to the substantive legality of the contested measure, which goes to infringement of a rule of law relating to the application of the Treaty within the meaning of that Article". The contested act in that case contained a brief statement of reasons on the point at issue, but that statement had been developed in a declaration made by the Council when the act was adopted and which was published in the *Official Journal*. The Court held: "First, the statement of reasons for a Community measure must appear in that measure . . . and, second, it must be adopted by the author of the measure . . . so that, in the present case, a declaration adopted by the Council alone cannot in any event serve as a statement of reasons for a regulation adopted jointly by the Parliament and the Council".[49]

The amount of detail required by Article 253 EC depends on the nature of the act and the context in which it is intended to operate. In *R v Secretary of State, ex parte Omega Air*,[50] the Court summarised the effect of its case law on Article 253 EC as follows:

---

[47] See Case T–521/93 *Atlanta v European Community* [1996] E.C.R. II–1707, paras 70–74. The right to be heard does not apply to the Member States under Art.95(4) EC: Case C–3/00 *Denmark v Commission* [2003] E.C.R. I–2643, paras 47–50.
[48] Case C–378/00 [2003] E.C.R. I–937, para.34.
[49] Para.66.
[50] Joined Cases C–27/00 and C–122/00 [2002] E.C.R. I–2569, paras 46–47. See also Joined Cases C–71/95, C–155/95 and C–271/95 *Belgium v Commission* [1997] E.C.R. I–687, para.53; Case C–304/01 *Spain v Commission* [2004] E.C.R. I–7655.

"it should be borne in mind that it is settled case law that the statement of reasons required by Article 253 EC must be adapted to the nature of the act in question. It must disclose in a clear and unequivocal fashion the reasoning followed by the Community institution which adopted the measure in such a way as to make the persons concerned aware of the reasons for the measure and to enable the Court to exercise its power of review. It follows from the case law that it is not necessary for details of all relevant factual and legal aspects to be given. The question whether the statement of the grounds for an act meets the requirements of Article 253 EC must be assessed with regard not only to its wording but also to its context and to all the legal rules governing the matter in question . . .

The Court has also held that if the contested measure clearly discloses the essential objective pursued by the institution, it would be excessive to require a specific statement of reasons for the various technical choices made . . ."

The Court added that "the statement of reasons in a regulation of general application cannot be required to specify the various facts, frequently very numerous and complex, on the basis of which the regulation was adopted, nor *a fortiori* to provide a more or less complete evaluation of those facts . . . That is particularly the case where the relevant factual and technical elements are well known to the circles concerned".[51] The Court concluded that the reasoning of the contested act was adequate to satisfy Art 253. The reasoning contained in decisions is expected to be more detailed.

The third ground, *infringement of the Treaty or of any rule of law* **13–028** *relating to its application*, is the widest one and is capable of subsuming the other three. As we have seen, it covers the substantive legality of the contested measure.[52] It may therefore be invoked if a measure contravenes a provision of the Treaty or is inconsistent with a parent measure. It also covers infringements of general principles of law recognised by the Court.[53] The general principles constitute a body of unwritten rules to which the Community Courts have recourse in order to supplement the Treaties and acts made under them. They are discussed in more detail in Chapter 7.

---

[51] Para.51.
[52] See Case C–378/00 *Commission v European Parliament and Council* [2003] E.C.R. I–937, para.34.
[53] A Community act may also be declared void on this ground if it infringes an international agreement to which the Community is a party (even if the provisions of the agreement do not produce direct effect in the Community): Case C–377/98 *Netherlands v European Parliament and Council* [2001] 3 C.M.L.R. 49.

The last ground of invalidity mentioned in Article 230 EC is *misuse of powers*. This is a particularly difficult ground to establish: it is concerned with the purpose of a measure, not just its content,[54] and therefore requires the applicant to establish that the intentions of the defendant institution were different from those stated in the contested measure. In *R v Secretary of State, ex parte British American Tobacco*,[55] the Court said that "a measure is vitiated by misuse of powers only if it appears on the basis of objective, relevant and consistent evidence to have been taken with the exclusive or main purpose of achieving an end other than that stated or evading a procedure specifically prescribed by the Treaty for dealing with the circumstances of the case". In that case, the applicants challenged a directive on the manufacture, presentation and sale of tobacco products. The directive purported to be intended to improve the functioning of the internal market by ironing out differences between the laws of the Member States, but the applicants said it was in fact designed to protect public health, a field where the Community's competence was more limited. The Court rejected that argument, taking the view that "it has not in any way been established that it was adopted with the exclusive, or at least decisive, purpose of achieving an end other than that of improving the conditions for the functioning of the internal market in the tobacco products sector".[56]

Time-limits

13–029   Under the fifth paragraph of Article 230 EC, proceedings must be instituted "within two months of the publication of the measure, or of its notification to the plaintiff, or, in the absence thereof, of the day on which it came to the notice of the latter". Article 254 EC requires certain regulations, directives and decisions to be published in the *Official Journal*. Other directives and decisions are only required to be notified to those to whom they are addressed, but may in practice also be published in the *Official Journal*.

Where a measure is published in the *Official Journal*, the date of publication is that on which the issue concerned actually becomes available, which may not be the same as the date on the cover. This is so whether or not publication was compulsory and whether or not the measure came to the knowledge of the applicant before it was published. In *Germany v Council*,[57] the Court said that the wording

---

[54] See Case T–18/99 *Cordis v Commission* [2001] E.C.R. II–913, para.56 (Community not guilty of misuse of powers in adopting regulation allegedly containing infringements of WTO rules).

[55] Case C–491/01 [2002] E.C.R. I–11453. See also Joined Cases C–133/93, C–300/93 and C–362/93 *Crispoltoni* [1994] E.C.R. I–4863, para.27.

[56] Para.191.

[57] Case C–122/95 [1998] E.C.R. I–973, para.35. See also Case T–14/96 *BAI v Commission* [1999] E.C.R. II–139, paras 32–37.

of the fifth paragraph of Article 230 EC made it clear "that the criterion of the day on which a measure came to the knowledge of an applicant, as the starting point of the period prescribed for instituting proceedings, is subsidiary to the criteria of publication or notification of the measure".

Where a measure has not been published in the *Official Journal* and the time-limit runs from notification, it will be important to know precisely what the term "notification" entails. In *Commission v Socurte*,[58] the Court said that notification for these purposes "necessarily involves the communication of a detailed account of the contents of the measure notified and of the reasons on which it is based. In the absence of such an account, the third party concerned would be denied precise knowledge of the contents of the act in question and of the reasons for which it was adopted, which would enable him to bring proceedings effectively against that decision". That requirement could only be satisfied by sending the applicant the text of the measure in issue, not a brief summary of its contents. However, once a party is aware of the existence of a measure concerning it, it will be expected to request the text of the measure within a reasonable period. Once that period has expired, time will start running against the party concerned.[59]

The fifth paragraph of Article 230 EC must be read in the light of the Rules of Procedure of the Community Courts. Under Article 80(1)(a) of the Court's Rules and Article 101(1)(a) of the CFI's Rules, the day on which an event occurs is not counted as falling within the prescribed period of time. Furthermore, by virtue of Article 81(1) of the Court's Rules and Article 102(1) of the CFI's Rules, where the period of time allowed for commencing proceedings runs from publication of the contested measure, the period is calculated "from the end of the 14th day after publication thereof in the *Official Journal of the European Union*". Moreover, Article 81(2) of the Court's Rules and Article 102(2) of the CFI's Rules grant a 10-day extension of the prescribed time-limits "on account of distance".

In *Mutual Aid Administration Services NV v Commission*,[60] the CFI said: "It is settled case law that the time-limit prescribed for bringing actions under Article [230] of the Treaty is a matter of public policy and is not subject to the discretion of the parties or the Court, since it was established in order to ensure that legal positions are clear and certain and to avoid any discrimination or arbitrary treatment in the administration of justice". Failure to observe the time-limit therefore constituted "an absolute bar"[61] to the admissibility of an application.

---

[58] Case C–143/95 P [1997] E.C.R. I–1, para.31.
[59] See Case T–155/95 *LPN and GEOTA v Commission* [1998] E.C.R. II–2751.
[60] Joined Cases T–121/96 and T–151/96 [1997] E.C.R. II–1355, para.38.
[61] Para.39.

The effects of annulment

13–030   According to the first paragraph of Article 231 EC, where the
Court of Justice finds an action under Article 230 EC well founded,
it "shall declare the act concerned to be void".[62] The Courts have no
power to order the institution concerned to take any particular
steps,[63] but the institution is required by the first paragraph of
Article 233 EC to take the measures necessary to comply with the
Court's judgment.[64]

The scope of the defendant institution's obligations under the first
paragraph of Article 233 EC was considered in *Commission v
AssiDomän Kraft Products*.[65] That case was a sequel to the ruling of
the Court of Justice in the so-called "Wood Pulp" case,[66] a competition proceeding in which the Court partially annulled a decision of
the Commission. In the contested decision, the Commission found
that 43 undertakings, including the seven applicants in *AssiDomän*
("the Swedish addressees"), had infringed one of the competition
provisions of the Treaty.[67] The Commission imposed fines on almost
all the addressees of the decision.[68] In annulment proceedings
brought against the decision by 26 of its addressees, the Court
quashed provisions finding that there had been an infringement of
the Treaty and annulled or reduced the fines imposed on the
applicants. The Swedish addressees had not sought the annulment of
the decision and had paid the fines imposed on them. After the
Court had given judgment, they asked the Commission to refund the
fines they had paid in respect of findings which had now been
quashed by the Court. The Commission refused on the basis that the
Court had only annulled or reduced the fines imposed on the
applicants in "Wood Pulp" and that the decision was unaffected in
so far as it concerned the Swedish addressees.

After a ruling by the CFI in favour of the applicants,[69] an appeal
by the Commission was upheld by the Court of Justice.[70] Although

---

[62] Note that, where it is possible to sever and annul only the legally flawed elements of the
relevant act, the remainder may be allowed to stand, e.g. Case 17/74 *Transocean Marine
Paint* [1974] E.C.R. 1063; *cf.* Case C–376/98 *Germany v Parliament and Council* [2000]
E.C.R. I–8419. Conversely, a request for partial annulment, in the case of non-severable
provisions, may be grounds for declaring the entire action inadmissible, e.g. Case C–244/03
France v Parliament and Council [2005] E.C.R. I–4021; Case C–36/04 *Spain v Council*
(Judgment of March 30, 2006).
[63] See e.g. Case 15/85 *Consorzio Cooperative d'Abruzzo v Commission* [1987] E.C.R. 1005,
para.18; Case C–5/93 P *DSM v Commission* [1999] E.C.R. I–4695, para.36.
[64] See Toth, "The Authority of Judgments of the European Court of Justice: Binding Force
and Legal Effects" (1984) 4 Y.E.L. 1.
[65] See also Case T–89/00 *Europe Chemi-Con v Council* [2002] E.C.R. II–3651, para.32.
[66] Joined Cases C–89/85, C–104/85, C–114/85, C–116/85, C–117/85 and C–125/85 to C–129/85
Ahlström Osakeyhtiö v Commission [1993] E.C.R. I–1307. See Chs 21 and 22.
[67] Art.81(1) EC: see Ch.22.
[68] The Commission's power to impose fines on undertakings which infringe the Treaty
competition rules is discussed in Ch.24.
[69] Case T–227/95 [1997] E.C.R. II–1185. See also Case T–220/97 *H & R Ecroyd Holdings Ltd v
Commission* [1999] E.C.R. II–1677.
[70] Case C–310/97 P [1999] 5 C.M.L.R. 1253. See also Case C–239/99 *Nachi Europe v
Hauptzollamt Krefeld* [2001] E.C.R. I–1197.

drafted and published in the form of a single act, the CFI had treated the contested decision as a bundle of individual decisions affecting each of its addressees. The Court did not dissent from that approach. It made it clear that, although Article 233 EC required the defendant institution to ensure that any act intended to replace the act annulled was not vitiated by the same defects, it did not mean that the institution was required to "re-examine identical or similar decisions allegedly affected by the same irregularity, addressed to addressees other than the applicant".[71] A decision which had not been challenged by its addressee within the time-limit laid down in Article 230 EC became definitive as against that addressee. The purpose of that time-limit was "to ensure legal certainty by preventing Community measures which produce legal effects from being called in question indefinitely".[72] The Court explained that:

> "[w]here a number of similar individual decisions imposing fines have [sic] been adopted pursuant to a common procedure and only some addressees have taken legal action against the decisions concerning them and obtained their annulment, the principle of legal certainty . . . precludes any necessity for the institution which adopted the decisions to re-examine, at the request of other addressees, in the light of the grounds of the annulling judgment, the legality of the unchallenged decisions and to determine, on the basis of that examination, whether the fines paid must be refunded".[73]

Where Article 233 EC requires the adoption of a new measure to **13–031** replace the one declared void by the Court, the principle of legal certainty will generally mean that the new measure cannot be made retrospective. However, in exceptional cases this is permitted "where the purpose to be achieved so demands and where the legitimate expectations of those concerned are duly respected".[74] The Court's ruling may also lead to a claim for compensation against the Community in accordance with Article 235 EC and the second paragraph of Article 288 EC.[75]

In principle, a declaration by the Court under Article 230 EC that an act is void takes effect *erga omnes* and *ex tunc*, that is, with regard to the whole world and with retrospective effect. The second paragraph of Article 231 EC states: "In the case of a regulation, however, the Court of Justice shall, if it considers this necessary, state which of the effects of the regulation which it has declared void

---

[71] Para.56.
[72] Para.61.
[73] Para.63.
[74] See e.g. Case 108/81 *Amylum v Council* [1982] E.C.R. 3107.
[75] See the second paragraph of Art.233 EC. The second paragraph of Art.288 EC is discussed below.

shall be considered as definitive". This enables the Court to mini-
mise any disruption which might be caused by the gap left by the
disappearance of the measure which has been quashed. For example,
in a case in which the Court declared void certain provisions of a
regulation relating to the remuneration of Community officials, it
declared that those provisions should continue to have effect until
they were replaced "to avoid discontinuity in the system of
remuneration".[76] In *Timex v Council*, the Court declared void a
provision in a regulation imposing an anti-dumping duty. The aim of
the action had been to have the rate of the duty increased and to
secure the imposition of a duty on a wider range of products. The
Court therefore ruled that the provision in question should remain
in force until it had been replaced.[77] The Court applied the power
conferred on it by the second paragraph of Article 231 EC by
analogy in a case in which a directive was quashed. This, the Court
said, was justified by "important reasons of legal certainty, comparable to those which operate in cases where certain regulations are
annulled".[78]

Capacity to bring proceedings

13-032　In order to bring proceedings under Article 230 EC, an applicant
must show that he satisfies the conditions regarding standing, or
locus standi, laid down in the Treaty. Article 230 EC draws a
distinction in this respect between three categories of applicant: (a)
the Member States, the European Parliament, the Council and the
Commission ("privileged applicants"); (b) the Court of Auditors and
the ECB ("semi-privileged applicants"); and (c) natural and legal
persons ("non-privileged applicants").

13-033 **(a) Privileged applicants.**　Applicants falling within the first category automatically have standing to bring proceedings and do not
have to establish any particular interest.[79] To put the point another
way, such applicants are presumed to have an interest in the legality
of all Community acts. The right of the Commission to bring
proceedings is not affected by its position during the legislative
procedure.[80] Similarly, where a Member State seeks the annulment
of a measure adopted by the Council, its right to bring proceedings
is not affected by whether or not it voted for the measure when it
was adopted.[81] The term "Member State" in this context means the

---

[76] Case 81/72 *Commission v Council* [1973] E.C.R. 575, para.15.
[77] Case 264/82 [1985] E.C.R. 849, para.32.
[78] Case C–295/90 *Parliament v Council* [1992] E.C.R. I–4193, para.26.
[79] See Case 45/86 *Commission v Council* [1987] E.C.R. 1493, para.3.
[80] Case C–378/00 *Commission v European Parliament and Council* [2003] E.C.R. I–937,
para.28.
[81] Case 166/78 *Italy v Council* [1979] E.C.R. 2575, para.6.

governments of the Member States and does not include the governments of regions or autonomous communities, whatever their powers might be under national law. The Court has said that "[i]t is not possible for the European Communities to comprise a greater number of Member States than the number of States between which they were established".[82] Regional governments constitute legal persons for the purposes of Article 230 EC and may only bring proceedings where the conditions set out in the fourth paragraph of that article are satisfied.[83]

(b) Semi-privileged applicants. This category is now confined to **13–034** the Court of Auditors and the ECB.[84] Until the Treaty was amended at Nice, it also included the European Parliament. Indeed, prior to the Treaty of Maastricht, Article 230 EC conferred no right of action on the European Parliament at all, but the Court held in the "Chernobyl" case[85] that the Parliament had the right to seek the annulment of acts adopted by the Council or by the Commission where the purpose of the proceedings was to protect the Parliament's prerogatives, for example, its right to participate to the extent envisaged by the Treaty in the legislative process leading to the adoption of a Community act.[86] Thus, even in the absence in Article 230 EC of any reference to the European Parliament, that institution could both institute annulment proceedings and be the defendant in such proceedings.[87] The Court's case law on the status of the Parliament in annulment proceedings is now enshrined in the text of Article 230 EC.

(c) Non-privileged applicants. The standing of natural and legal **13–035** persons to institute annulment proceedings is limited and for this reason they are sometimes referred to as "non-privileged applicants". A natural person is an individual. According to the CFI, "an applicant is a legal person if, at the latest by the expiry of the period prescribed for proceedings to be instituted, it has acquired legal personality in accordance with the law governing its constitution . . .

---

[82] See Case C–95/97 *Région Wallonne v Commission* [1997] E.C.R. I–1787, para.6; Case C–180/97 *Regione Toscana v Commission* [1997] E.C.R. I–5245, para.6.

[83] See e.g. Case T–288/97 *Regione Autonoma Friuli-Venezia Giulia v Commission* [1999] E.C.R. II–1169. The conditions laid down in the fourth paragraph of Art.230 EC are considered below.

[84] The Constitutional Treaty would add the Committee of the Regions: see Art.III–365(3) and, further, Ch.11.

[85] Case C–70/88 *Parliament v Council* [1990] E.C.R. I–2041.

[86] The Court made it clear that such proceedings were not brought under Art.230 EC, but under a right of action created by the Court to ensure respect for the institutional balance established by the Treaties. Indeed, the Court had held less than two years previously that the Parliament had no right of action under Art.230 EC: see Case 302/87 *Parliament v Council* [1988] E.C.R. 5615. The Court followed that ruling on this point in the 'Chernobyl' case.

[87] See Case 294/83 *Les Verts* [1986] E.C.R. 1339.

or if it has been treated as an independent legal entity by the Community institutions".[88]

The fourth paragraph of Article 230 EC suggests that a non-privileged applicant[89] may only bring proceedings against three types of act, namely:

— a decision addressed to him or her;
— a decision in the form of a regulation which is of direct and individual concern to him or her;
— a decision addressed to another person[90] which is of direct and individual concern to the applicant.

The Treaty seems to imply that regulations cannot be challenged by private applicants. However, by talking about a "decision in the form of a regulation", the Treaty makes it clear that it is not the label attached to a measure but its substance which counts.[91] So if an applicant can show that a measure called a regulation is really a decision in disguise, he or she can clearly challenge its validity. This principle cuts both ways, so that a measure entitled a decision may be treated *as if it were a regulation* if it is does not have the characteristics of a real decision.[92] The apparent wish of the authors of the Treaty to exclude measures having the characteristics of true regulations from review at the suit of private applicants has produced some rather unsatisfactory results. The Court has therefore allowed private applicants to challenge such measures in certain circumstances. The question whether those circumstances should be widened is a matter of continuing controversy.

It is now necessary to look in more detail at three questions in particular: the distinction between regulations and decisions, the meaning of direct concern, and the meaning of individual concern. The discussion is to some extent historical, because recent developments can only properly be understood by reference to the position which prevailed previously.

13–036 *(i) The distinction between regulations and decisions.* According to Article 249 EC, "[a] regulation shall have general application. It shall be binding in its entirety and directly applicable in all Member States". The same article provides that "[a] decision shall be binding in its entirety upon those to whom it is addressed". In *Producteurs de*

---

[88] Case T–161/94 *Sinochem Heilongjiang v Council* [1996] E.C.R. II–695, para.31.
[89] A category which includes all natural and legal persons, regardless of their nationality or place of residence or establishment.
[90] For the purposes of the fourth paragraph of Art.230 EC, this expression includes the Member States: Case 25/62 *Plaumann v Commission* [1963] E.C.R. 95.
[91] See Joined Cases 16 and 17/62 *Producteurs de Fruits v Council* [1962] E.C.R. 471, 478.
[92] See Joined Cases T–480/93 and T–483/93 *Antillean Rice Mills v Commission* [1995] E.C.R. II–2305, para.65 (appeal dismissed: Case C–390/95 P [1999] E.C.R. I–769).

Fruits v Council,[93] the Court deduced from the terms of that article that "[t]he criterion for the distinction [between regulations and decisions] must be sought in the general 'application' or otherwise of the measure in question". Thus, regulations were said to be essentially legislative in nature and to apply to "categories of persons viewed abstractly and in their entirety".[94] By contrast, the Court said in *Plaumann v Commission*[95] that "decisions are characterised by the limited number of persons to whom they are addressed. In order to determine whether or not a measure constitutes a decision one must enquire whether that measure concerns specific persons".

The difficulty of satisfying the requirement of a decision may be illustrated by *Calpak v Commission*.[96] In that case, the Court dismissed as inadmissible a challenge by two Italian companies to a regulation restricting the amount of aid payable to processors of Williams pears preserved in syrup. There were only 38 processors of Williams pears in the Community, 15 in France and 23 in Italy. None the less, the Court said that the contested regulation was "by nature a measure of general application within the meaning of Article [249] of the Treaty. In fact the measure applies to objectively determined situations and produces legal effects with regard to categories of persons described in a generalised and abstract manner. The nature of the measure as a regulation is not called in question by the mere fact that it is possible to determine the number or even the identity of the producers to be granted the aid which is limited thereby".[97]

The strictness of this approach was somewhat mitigated by the Court's acceptance that, where the annulment of only some of the provisions of an act was sought, it was the proper classification of those provisions, and not that of the act as a whole, that was important. The Court was prepared to accept that a true regulation might contain provisions which amounted in substance to decisions and which could therefore be challenged by private applicants under Article 230 EC.[98] This was not, however, a conclusion that the Court would be willing to reach where the provisions in question were an "integral part" of a "legislative whole".[99]

The inability of private applicants to challenge true regulations **13–037** increasingly came to be regarded as unsatisfactory and, in some cases where regulations were challenged, the Court dealt with the

---

[93] *ibid.*

[94] *ibid.*

[95] Case 25/62 *Plaumann v Commission* [1963] E.C.R. 95.

[96] Cases 789–90/79 *Calpak* [1980] E.C.R. 1949.

[97] Para.9.

[98] See Joined Cases 16 and 17/62 *Producteurs de Fruits v Council* [1962] E.C.R. 471, 479. *cf.* Case C–29/99 *Commission v Council* [2002] E.C.R. I–11221, para.45: "partial annulment of a decision is possible if the elements whose annulment is sought may be severed from the remainder of the decision".

[99] Joined Cases 103–109/78 *Société des Usines de Beauport v Council* [1979] E.C.R. 17, para.16.

question of admissibility on the basis of direct and/or individual concern without considering the requirement of a decision. This led Advocate General Jacobs to argue in *Extramet Industrie v Council*[1] that "the Court should in my view make clear what is already implicit in the prevailing trend of its case law, namely that the requirement of a decision does not exist independently of the requirement of individual concern". The judgment of the Court in *Extramet* was less explicit, but in the landmark case of *Codorniu v Council*,[2] which concerned the validity of a regulation on the description and presentation of sparkling wines, the Court accepted that true regulations could in principle be challenged by non-privileged applicants if they could establish direct and individual concern.[3]

It is not only in relation to the requirement of a decision that the Court has taken a liberal approach to the interpretation of Article 230 EC. A similar approach was adopted in the "ERTA" case, as we have seen, and in the case law recognising the capacity of the Parliament to sue and to be sued at a time when Article 230 EC did not refer to that institution.[4] These developments may all be justified by the need to adapt the action for annulment to the way in which the Community has developed[5] and to address difficulties which the authors of Article 230 EC quite understandably failed to foresee. The thread which links them together is the need to ensure that the political institutions of the Community respect the limits of their powers and to give individuals a remedy when they fail to do so.

What about directives? Article 230 EC does not expressly grant private applicants the right to challenge such acts. However, in *Asocarne v Council* the Court reiterated that a directive was normally "an indirect mode of legislating or regulating".[6] It had of course been held in *Codorniu* that a regulation might, without losing its legislative character, be challenged by a private applicant who could establish direct and individual concern. This was a possibility for which the Treaty made no express provision either, so should the same not be true of directives? That logic was expressly accepted in *UEAPME v Council*[7] and *Salamander AG v Parliament*

---

[1] Case C–358/89 [1991] E.C.R. I–2501. *cf.* Case C–152/88, *Sofrimport v Commission* [1990] E.C.R. I–2477.

[2] Case C–309/89 [1994] E.C.R. I–1853. See Waelbroeck and Fosselard (1995) 32 C.M.L.Rev. 257; Usher (1994) 19 E.L.Rev. 636.

[3] Direct concern was not at issue in the case.

[4] See Case 294/83 *Les Verts* [1986] E.C.R. 1339; Case C–70/88 *Parliament v Council* [1990] E.C.R. I–2041.

[5] See Advocate General Jacobs in Case C–358/89 *Extramet* [1991] E.C.R. I–2501, 2519.

[6] Case C–10/95 P [1995] E.C.R. I–4149, para.29.

[7] Case T–135/96 [1998] E.C.R. II–2335, paras 67–68. See Adinolfi, "Admissibility of action for annulment by social partners and 'sufficient representativity' of European agreements" (2000) 25 E.L.Rev. 165. The directive at issue in *UEAPME* was adopted under the Agreement on Social Policy annexed to the Protocol on Social Policy agreed at Maastricht and itself annexed to the EC Treaty. The Protocol and Agreement were repealed by the Treaty of Amsterdam.

and Council,[8] where the CFI acknowledged that, notwithstanding the legislative nature of the directives at issue in those cases, it was necessary to consider whether the applicants were directly and individually concerned by them. *Extramet* and *Codorniu* were among the cases cited by the CFI on both occasions.

The apparent elimination of the requirement of a decision[9] means that the admissibility of annulment proceedings brought by private applicants usually now effectively turns on the impact on them of the contested act and, in particular, on whether they can establish direct and individual concern.

(ii) Direct concern. The Court stated in *Les Verts v Parliament*[10] that **13–038** a measure was of direct concern to an applicant where it constituted "a complete set of rules which are sufficient in themselves and which require no implementing provisions", since in such circumstances the application of the measure "is automatic and leaves no room for any discretion". Thus, in order to establish direct concern, an applicant must be able to show that, at the time the contested act was adopted, the effect it would produce on him or her was substantially certain. Where the applicant is only affected by a measure because of the way a third party has exercised a discretion conferred on him or her and it was not possible to say in advance how he or she would do so, the applicant will not therefore be able to establish direct concern. In *Alcan v Commission*,[11] for example, a decision addressed to two Member States refusing to grant them import quotas was held not to be of direct concern to an applicant where the allocation of any quota would have been a matter for the discretion of the Member States concerned.

A measure requiring implementation by a third party may be of direct concern to an applicant if the third party has no discretion in the matter.[12] Similarly, an applicant may be able to establish direct concern if, at the time the contested measure was adopted, there was no real doubt how any discretion left to a third party would be exercised. In *Piraiki-Patraiki v Commission*,[13] for example, the applicants sought the annulment of a Commission decision authorising France to impose a quota system restricting imports of cotton yarn from Greece during a specific period shortly after Greek accession.

---

[8] Cases T–172 and 175–177/98 *Salamander* [2000] E.C.R. II–2487, paras 27–31. *cf.* Joined Cases T–125/96 and T–152/96 *BI Vetmedica v Council and Commission* [1999] E.C.R. II–3427, para.143, where the CFI dismissed as unfounded a challenge by a private applicant to a directive without ruling on an objection of inadmissibility raised by the Council.

[9] But see Case C–50/00 P *Unión de Pequeños Agricultores v Council* [2002] E.C.R. I–6677, discussed below.

[10] Case 294/83 *Les Verts* [1986] E.C.R. 1339, para.31.

[11] Case 69/69 [1970] E.C.R. 385.

[12] See e.g. Case 113/77 *NTN Tokyo Bearing Company v Council* [1979] E.C.R. 1185.

[13] Case 11/82 [1985] E.C.R. 207. *cf.* Case C–404/96 P *Glencore Grain* [1988] E.C.R. I–2435; Case T–80/97 *Starway v Council* [2000] E.C.R. II–3099, para.68.

The Commission argued that the applicants were not directly concerned by the contested decision, since it required implementation by the French authorities, which were free not to make use of the authorisation. That argument was rejected by the Court, since the contested decision had been adopted in response to a request from the French authorities for permission to impose an even stricter quota system. In those circumstances, the Court concluded that "the possibility that the French Republic might decide not to make use of the authorisation granted to it by the Commission decision was entirely theoretical, since there could be no doubt as to the intention of the French authorities to apply the decision".[14]

Where the Commission pronounces *ex post facto* on the compatibility with Community law of a national measure which has already been adopted, the Commission's act will not be of direct concern to someone who objects to the national measure. This emerges from *DSTV v Commission*.[15] DSTV was a Danish TV company which transmitted a satellite TV service called "Eurotica Rendez-Vous" to viewers in various Member States, including the United Kingdom. The United Kingdom authorities took the view that the service infringed a directive on TV broadcasting and made an order imposing restrictions on it. Under the directive, the UK was required to notify the order to the Commission and it duly did so. If the Commission had found the order incompatible with Community law, the United Kingdom would have been required to repeal it. However, the Commission found the order compatible with Community law. DSTV challenged the Commission's decision, but the CFI found that it was not directly concerned. The order existed independently of the Commission's decision. That decision did not take the place of the United Kingdom order, nor did it retrospectively render it valid. It did not therefore directly affect the applicant's legal position.

13–039 *(iii) Individual concern.* The requirement of individual concern has always been a major obstacle to the admissibility of actions brought by private applicants. The starting point remains the well-known *Plaumann* formula,[16] according to a more recent version of which "[i]n order for a measure to be of individual concern to the persons to whom it applies, it must affect their legal position because of a factual situation which differentiates them from all other persons and distinguishes them individually in the same way as a person to whom it is addressed".[17]

---

[14] Para.9 of the judgment.
[15] Case T–69/99 [2000] E.C.R. II–4039.
[16] See Case 25/62 *Plaumann* [1963] E.C.R. 95, 107; Craig, "Legality, Standing and Substantive Review in Community Law" (1994) 14 O.J.L.S. 507, 508–511.
[17] Case 26/86 *Deutz und Geldermann v Council* [1987] E.C.R. 941, para.9.

The restrictive nature of that formula may be illustrated by *Greenpeace v Commission*, where several individuals and three associations concerned with the protection of the environment sought the annulment of a Commission decision granting Spain financial assistance for the construction of two electric power stations in the Canary Islands. The applicants invited the CFI to accept that standing could derive from a concern for the protection of the environment. The applicants claimed that in each Member State associations set up for the protection of the environment which were sufficiently representative of the interests of their members, or which satisfied certain formalities, were entitled to challenge administrative decisions alleged to breach rules on environmental protection.[18] The CFI refused to accept that the standing of the applicants should be assessed by reference to criteria other than those laid down in the case law.[19] It concluded that the individual applicants were affected by the contested measure in the same way as anyone living, working or visiting the area concerned and that they could not therefore be considered individually concerned. The same was true of the applicant associations, since they had been unable to establish any interest of their own distinct from that of their members, whose position was no different from that of the individual applicants. On appeal,[20] the Court declared that the approach taken by the CFI was "consonant with the settled case law of the Court of Justice".[21]

It is worth considering three types of case in particular in which the question whether the applicant is individually concerned may prove difficult to answer. The first is cases concerning so-called closed classes. The second is cases concerning the applicant's so-called specific rights. The third is cases where the applicant participated in one way or another in the procedure leading to the adoption of the contested act.

CLOSED CLASSES. In the *Plaumann* case, the Court made it clear **13–040** that an applicant would not be considered individually concerned merely because it carried on a particular commercial activity which could be practised by anyone. However, there was some support in the early case law for the view that an applicant could establish individual concern by showing that the contested act was only capable of affecting a finite group, or closed class, to which it

---

[18] In England, see e.g. *R v Inspectorate of Pollution, ex parte Greenpeace* (No.2) [1994] 4 All E.R. 329. For a comparison between the position in England and the United States, see Cane, "Standing, Representation, and the Environment" in Loveland (ed.), *A Special Relationship? American Influences on Public Law in the UK* (1995).

[19] See Case T–585/93 [1995] E.C.R. II–2205. See also Case T–219/95 *Danielsson v Commission* [1995] E.C.R. II–3051.

[20] Case C–321/95 P [1998] E.C.R. I–1651.

[21] Para.27. See also e.g. Case T–472/93 *Campo Ebro v Council* [1995] E.C.R. II–421; Case T–107/94 *Kik v Council and Commission* [1995] E.C.R. II–1717 (upheld on appeal: Case C–270/95 P [1996] E.C.R. I–1987).

belonged.[22] However, it is now clear that this is not in itself enough.[23] Membership of a closed class will not be treated as distinguishing an applicant individually unless the defendant institution was obliged to take into account the effect of the disputed act on members of the class concerned.[24]

The point is illustrated by *Piraiki-Patraiki v Commission*,[25] where the applicants challenged a Commission decision authorising France to restrict imports of cotton yarn from Greece during a specific period. The Court held that the contested decision was of individual concern to those of the applicants who, before it was adopted, had entered into contracts to be performed while it was in force and whose execution would not now be possible. The Court found that the Commission had been in a position to discover the existence of contracts of that kind. Moreover, it noted that Article 130 of the Greek Act of Accession required the Commission to take account of the effect on the parties to such contracts of the measures it was proposing to authorise.

The importance of that factor was emphasised in *Buralux v Council*,[26] where the Court rejected an appeal against a decision of the CFI dismissing as inadmissible a challenge to a Council regulation on the movement of waste. The applicants were three undertakings engaged together in the disposal of waste which originated in Germany and which had been exported to France. One of them had in 1989 concluded renewable five-year contracts for the disposal of waste with various German public bodies. In 1992 the French Minister for the Environment adopted a decree prohibiting the importation of household waste into France and the following year the Council adopted a regulation which authorised the Member States "to prohibit generally or partially or to object systematically to shipments of waste". The applicants took the view that the purpose of the regulation was to legitimise the French decree of the previous year and they brought proceedings for the regulation's annulment.

13-041   The Court upheld the CFI's conclusion that the applicants were not individually concerned, being affected in the same way as anyone operating in the business of waste transfer between Member States. Although the applicants were practically the only operators who transported waste from Germany to France, the regulation applied to waste shipments between all the Member States. *Piraiki-Patraiki*

[22] See e.g. Case 100/74 *CAM v Commission* [1975] E.C.R. 1393. The closed class test was sometimes used to distinguish regulations from decisions: see e.g. Joined Cases 41 to 44/70 *International Fruit Company v Commission* [1971] E.C.R. 411.
[23] Case T-298/94 *Roquette Frères v Council* [1996] E.C.R. II-1531. See also Case T-482/93 *Weber v Commission* [1996] E.C.R. II-609, paras 63-66.
[24] See Case C-300/00 *Federación de Cofradías de Pescadores de Guipúzcoa v Council and Commission*, above [2000] E.C.R. I-8797, para.46.
[25] Case 11/82 [1985] E.C.R. 207.
[26] Case C-209/94 P [1996] E.C.R. I-615.

was distinguishable because (among other things) the Commission had been obliged to take into account the negative effects on the undertakings concerned of the decision at issue in that case and to consider the contracts they had entered into and would not now be able to carry out.

So *Piraiki-Patraiki* does not apply where the institution concerned is not required by the legal basis of the contested act to take account of the consequences it is liable to have for the individuals affected by it. Moreover, in *Commission v Nederlandse Antillen*,[27] the Court emphasised that only some of the applications in *Piraiki* had been declared admissible: applicants who were unable to show that, prior to the adoption of the contested decision, they had entered into contracts with customers in France for the delivery of cotton yarn from Greece while the decision was in force were held not to be individually concerned by it. According to the judgment in *Nederlandse Antillen*, this meant that it was not enough for an applicant to show that the defendant institution was required, at the time the contested act was adopted, to take account of the negative effects it would have on the members of a particular class. In order to establish individual concern, applicants needed to show *in addition* that they were affected by the act "by reason of a factual situation which differentiates them from all other persons".[28] This will not be possible where the impact on all those affected by the act is the same.

SPECIFIC RIGHTS. The Community Courts are prepared to recog- **13–042** nise individual concern where the contested act affects an applicant's so-called specific rights. *Codorniu* itself is an example. There the Court ruled that the applicant was individually concerned by the contested regulation because it prevented it from using a term which it had registered as a trade mark in 1924 and had traditionally used both before and after that date. That factor, according to the Court, was enough to distinguish the applicant from all other traders affected by the regulation.

The expression "specific rights" first seems to have been used by the CFI in *Asocarne v Council*,[29] where a Spanish trade association sought the annulment of a directive on the financing of health inspections and controls of meat and poultry. The CFI maintained that, "[u]nlike the regulation in question in Case C–309/89 [*Codorniu*] ... the directive now under consideration has not affected *specific rights* of the applicant or its members. On the contrary, the applicant and its members are—like all traders in the Community operating in the sector in question—subject to the national measures

---

[27] Case C–142/00 P [2004] 2 C.M.L.R. 41.
[28] Para.76 of the judgment.
[29] Case T–99/94 [1994] E.C.R. II–871.

adopted for the purposes of transposing the directive".[30] On appeal, that finding was specifically endorsed by the Court of Justice, which repeated the expression "specific rights".[31] The precise meaning of the term remains unclear, but it clearly covers property rights in the traditional sense and intellectual property rights (patents, trade marks, copyright and the like). However, in order to confer individual concern, it seems that such a right must differentiate its owner from other individuals affected by the contested act.[32]

13–043 PROCEDURAL PARTICIPATION. There are certain particular contexts in which the Court has traditionally been willing to accord standing to natural and legal persons on the basis of their participation in the procedure leading to the adoption of an act adversely affecting them. The contexts in question all involve what have been termed[33] quasi-judicial determinations taken at the end of a procedure in the course of which interested parties are given the opportunity to express their views. Such procedures, which may begin with the lodging of a complaint, are particularly prominent in three fields: competition,[34] State aid[35] and dumping.[36]

The case law on standing in these contexts is generally regarded as distinct, but it has had some effect on the broader thrust of the case law. There now seems to be a general rule that a person's procedural participation will confer individual concern on him or her if—but only if—he or she enjoys specific procedural guarantees under the legal basis of the act.[37] Thus, sending a Community institution letters criticising a previous measure and seeking to influence its future conduct,[38] or commenting on proposed acts, will not in itself be enough to distinguish the correspondent individually, even if the institution concerned replies to them.[39] This seems right, since

[30] Paras 20–21 (emphasis added).
[31] Case C–10/95 P [1995] E.C.R. I–4149, para.43. See also Case C–87/95 P *CNPAAP v Council* [1996] E.C.R. I–2003, para.36; Case T–482/93 *Weber v Commission* [1996] E.C.R. II–609, para.69; Case T–194/95 *Area Cova v Council* [1999] E.C.R. II–2271, para.69; Case T–12/96 *Area Cova v Council and Commission* [1999] E.C.R. II–230, para.68.
[32] Case C–258/02 P *Bactria v Commission* [2004] 2 C.M.L.R. 42, paras 48–52. cf. Case C–142/00 P *Nederlandse Antillen* [2004] 2 C.M.L.R. 41. See also Case T–33/01 *Infront v Commission* (Judgment of December 15, 2005).
[33] See Hartley, *The Foundations of European Community Law* (5th ed., 2003), pp.372–377.
[34] See Bailey, "Scope of Judicial Review Under Article 81 EC" (2004) 41 C.M.L.Rev. 1327; Völcker, "Developments in EC Competition Law in 2003: An Overview" (2004) 41 C.M.L.Rev. 1027, 1061–1063 (judicial review in merger cases). Further: Ch.24.
[35] See Ch.26.
[36] See Reg.384/96 on protection against dumped imports from countries not members of the European Community [1996] O.J. L56/1.
[37] See e.g. Joined Cases T–125/96 and T–152/96 *BI Vetmedica v Council and Commission* [1999] E.C.R. II–3427.
[38] See Joined Cases T–481/93 and T–484/93 *Exporteurs in Levende Varkens v Commission* [1995] E.C.R. II–2941, para.59; Cases T–38/99 to T–50/99 *SAA v Commission* [2001] E.C.R. II–585, para.46.
[39] Case T–109/97 *Molkerei v Commission* [1998] E.C.R. II–3533, para.67.

otherwise anyone would be able to ensure that they would be individually concerned by sending the competent institution observations on draft measures. In the case of legislative measures, the interests of those liable to be affected are "deemed to be represented by the political bodies called upon to adopt those measures".[40] In *CSR Pampryl v Commission*,[41] the CFI stated: "in the absence of expressly guaranteed procedural rights, it would be contrary to the wording and spirit of Article 230 EC to allow any individual, where he has participated in the preparation of a legislative measure, subsequently to bring an action against that measure".

(d) The standing of representative bodies. One of the issues raised **13–044** in the *Greenpeace* case was the circumstances in which representative bodies have standing to seek the annulment of Community acts. The CFI provided a helpful summary of the position in *Federolio v Commission*,[42] in which a trade organisation representing undertakings active on the market for edible vegetable oils challenged a Commission regulation. The CFI explained:

"As regards, more specifically, actions brought by associations, these have been held to be admissible in at least three types of situation, namely:

(a) where a legal provision expressly grants trade associations a series of procedural rights . . .;

(b) where the association represents the interests of undertakings which would be entitled to bring proceedings in their own right . . .;

(c) where the association is differentiated because its own interests as an association are affected, in particular because its position as negotiator is affected by the measure which it seeks to have annulled . . .

In those three situations, the Court of Justice and the Court of First Instance have also taken into account the participation of the associations in question in the procedure."

The fact that a representative body has standing to challenge a Community act does not mean that all its members also have

---

[40] *ibid.*, para.60.

[41] Case T–114/99 [1999] E.C.R. II–3331, para.50.

[42] Case T–122/96 [1997] E.C.R. II–1559, paras 60–61. *cf.* Joined Cases T–447/93, T–448/93 and T–449/93 *Associazione Italiana Tecnico Economica del Cemento (AITEC) v Commission* [1995] E.C.R. II–1971, paras 58–62. See also Case T–114/92 *BEMIM v Commission* [1995] E.C.R. II–147, paras 28–30. Where a number of applicants (e.g. an association and some of its members) make a single application, it will be treated as admissible if one of the applicants fulfils the conditions laid down in Art.230 EC: see Case C–313/90 *CIRFS v Commission* [1993] E.C.R. I–1125, para.31.

standing. Whether an individual member has standing will depend on its own particular circumstances.[43] Indeed, the *Federolio* case shows that representative bodies may sometimes be accorded standing even where none of their members is directly and individually concerned by the contested act. However, this occurs only exceptionally: in that case, the CFI found that the requirements laid down by the case law were not met and dismissed the action as inadmissible. In his Opinion in the *Greenpeace* case, Advocate General Cosmas counselled against treating environmental associations as a special case. Otherwise, he observed, "[n]atural persons without *locus standi* under the fourth paragraph of Article [230] of the Treaty could circumvent that procedural impediment by setting up an environmental association". Moreover, he said, "the number of environmental associations capable of being created is, at least in theory, infinite".[44]

13–045 **(e) Interest in bringing proceedings.** Leaving aside any question of direct and individual concern, the defendant institution may argue that the applicant has no interest in challenging an act because annulment will not affect his or her rights or interests. For example, the contested act may already have been repealed or implemented. It does not, however, follow that an applicant has no interest in seeking the annulment of such an act and arguments of this nature have rarely succeeded. The position was helpfully summarised by the CFI in *Antillean Rice Mills v Commission*:[45]

> "It is settled law that a claim for annulment is not admissible unless the applicant has an interest in seeing the contested measure annulled . . . Such an interest can be present only if the annulment of the measure is of itself capable of having legal consequences . . .
>
> In that regard, it must be borne in mind that, under Article [233] of the Treaty, an institution whose act has been declared void is required to take the necessary measures to comply with the judgment. Those measures do not concern the elimination of the act as such from the Community legal order, since that is the very essence of its annulment by the Court. They involve, rather, the removal of the effects of the illegalities found in the judgment annulling the act. The annulment of an act which has already been implemented or which has in the mean time been

---

[43] Case C–70/97 P *Kruidvat v Commission* [1998] E.C.R. I–7183.

[44] [1998] E.C.R. I–1651, 1699.

[45] Joined Cases T–480/93 and T–483/93 [1995] E.C.R. II–2305, paras 59 and 60. See also Case T–102/96 *Gencor Ltd v Commission* [1999] 4 C.M.L.R. 971, paras 40–41; Case T–82/96 *ARAP v Commission* [1999] E.C.R. II–1889, paras 35–37; Joined Cases T–125/96 and T–152/96 *BI Vetmedica v Council and Commission* [1999] E.C.R. II–3427, paras 158–160; Case T–89/00 *Europe Chemi-Con v Council* [2002] E.C.R. II–3651, paras 34–35.

repeated from a certain date is thus still capable of having legal
consequences. Such annulment places a duty on the institution
concerned to take the necessary measures to comply with the
judgment. The institution may thus be required to take adequate steps to restore the applicant to its original situation or to
avoid the adoption of an identical measure . . ."

That case may be compared with *Proderec v Commission*,[46] where the
CFI held that the applicant had no interest in seeking the annulment
of the contested act since it had by then been withdrawn with
retroactive effect.

(f) The availability of a remedy in the national courts. Applicants **13–046**
have often argued that to dismiss their claim as inadmissible would
be incompatible with considerations such as the principle of the rule
of law, or the right of access to a court, or the right to a fair trial and
an effective remedy enshrined in Articles 6 and 13 of the European
Convention on Human Rights.[47] The Community Courts have
sometimes sought to rebut arguments of that type by pointing out
that the applicant could seek relief in national proceedings, when a
reference could be made to the Court of Justice for a preliminary
ruling.[48]

That consideration may appear persuasive where proceedings
have already been brought before a national court, either by the
applicant before the CFI or by someone else, by the time the CFI
gives judgment.[49] However, it may seem less so where there is no
national measure implementing the contested Community act which
can be challenged in the national courts. The Court was confronted
with a situation of this sort in *Unión de Pequeños Agricultores v
Council*,[50] where the applicant sought the annulment of a regulation
withdrawing aid granted to producers of olive oil. The applicant
argued that, because the contested regulation deprived it of a benefit
it had previously enjoyed, it did not call for any national measures of
implementation. Consequently the validity of the regulation could
not be called into question in proceedings before a national court.

---

[46] Case T–145/95 [1997] E.C.R. II–823. See also Case T–26/97 *Antillean Rice Mills v Commission* [1997] E.C.R. II–1347; Case T–326/99 *Olivieri* [2003] E.C.R. II–1985; Case T–141/03 *Sniace* (Judgment of April 14, 2005).
[47] See Harlow, "Access to Justice as a Human Right: The European Convention and the European Union" in Alston, Bustelo and Heenan (eds), *The EU and Human Rights* (1999).
[48] Similar issues arise in competition cases where the Commission refuses to pursue a complaint on the basis that the complainant's rights can be adequately protected in the national courts: see e.g. Case T–24/90 *Automec v Commission* (No.2) [1992] E.C.R. II–2223; Case T–114/92 *BEMIM v Commission* [1995] E.C.R. II–147; Joined Cases T–189/95, T–39/96 and T–123/96 *SGA v Commission* [1999] E.C.R. II–3587. In that context, however, the question goes not to the admissibility of the action but to its substance.
[49] See e.g. Cases T–172 and 175–177/98 *Salamander* [2000] E.C.R. II–2487, para.76.
[50] Case C–50/00 P [2002] E.C.R. I–6677 (hereafter *UPA*).

Unless the applicant were granted standing to bring annulment proceedings in the Community Courts, it would be deprived of its right to effective legal protection of its rights under Community law.

There was no doubt that the applicant was directly concerned by the contested regulation, so the case turned on the test of individual concern. Could an applicant be regarded as individually concerned on the ground that, in the absence of an alternative remedy before the national courts, it would otherwise be deprived of judicial protection? If not, could the applicant in this particular case be considered individually concerned? The case reached the Court of Justice by way of an appeal from the CFI, which had concluded, on the basis of the existing case law, that the applicant was not individually concerned: it was affected by the regulation in the same way as anyone else operating in the same market, now or in the future. Before the Court, Advocate General Jacobs argued in an important Opinion that the existing case law should be reconsidered. He rejected the idea that the absence of a remedy in the national courts could be treated as decisive, as this would require the Community Courts to conduct a detailed examination of the position in the competent Member State and would mean that an applicant's standing in Luxembourg might depend on which national courts had jurisdiction. Instead, he urged the Court to adopt a new, more liberal, test under which a person would be regarded as individually concerned by a Community measure "where, by reason of his particular circumstances, the measure has, or is liable to have, a substantial adverse effect on his interests".[51]

13–047   Before the Court gave judgment in *UPA*, the CFI intervened in support of Advocate General Jacobs in *Jégo-Quéré v Commission*,[52] another case in which a private applicant sought the annulment of a regulation. The regulation at issue in the latter case laid down a prohibition (on the use by fishing boats of nets with mesh below a certain size) which Member States would be required to enforce, but which did not itself need to be transposed into national law. A five-Judge formation of the CFI headed by its President abandoned its long-standing reluctance to relax the standing rules under Article 230 EC. Referring to the Opinion of Advocate General Jacobs in *UPA*,[53] the CFI observed: "The fact that an individual affected by a Community measure may be able to bring its validity before the national courts by violating the rules it lays down and then asserting their illegality in subsequent judicial proceedings brought against him does not constitute an adequate means of judicial protection. Individuals cannot be required to breach the law in order to gain

---

[51] Para.60 of the Opinion.
[52] Case T–177/01.
[53] See para.43.

access to justice".[54] The CFI stated that the strict existing test of individual concern should be reconsidered and declared:[55]

> "in order to ensure effective judicial protection for individuals, a natural or legal person is to be regarded as individually concerned by a Community measure of general application that concerns him directly if the measure in question affects his legal position, in a manner which is both definite and immediate, by restricting his rights or by imposing obligations on him. The number and position of other persons who are likewise affected by the measure, or who may be so, are of no relevance in that regard."[56]

This was bold move, because the new test laid down by the CFI was clearly inconsistent with the existing case law and the Court itself had not yet endorsed a departure from it.[57]

Indeed, when the Court gave judgment in *UPA*, it reaffirmed the existing case law. It noted that the appellant accepted that the contested regulation was of general application, that its specific interests were not affected by it and that it possessed no peculiar attributes which were such as to distinguish it from all other persons. For the Court, the question was therefore whether the appellant should be accorded standing "on the sole ground that, in the alleged absence of any legal remedy before the national courts, the right to effective judicial protection requires it".[58] The Court observed that "a measure of general application such as a regulation can, in certain circumstances, be of individual concern to certain natural or legal persons and is thus in the nature of a decision in their regard".[59] This represented a retreat from the position it had adopted in *Codorniu*, where it appeared to accept that a measure of general application might be of individual concern to an applicant without losing its legislative character.[60] The *UPA* approach may seem easier to reconcile with the wording of Article 230 EC, but in reality it serves only to complicate the analysis, for the Court was effectively saying that a regulation would automatically constitute a decision

---

[54] Para.45 of the judgment. See *Posti and Rahko v Finland*, App. No. 27824/95, judgment of September 24, 2002, para.64 (ECtHR).

[55] Para.51 of the judgment.

[56] The final sentence of that passage reiterated a point made by Advocate General Jacobs in *UPA*: see para.59 of his Opinion.

[57] It may not have been supported by all the members of the CFI. It is noteworthy that, notwithstanding its importance, the case was not referred to the plenary of the CFI and that, in Joined Cases T–377/00, T–379/00, T–380/00, T–260/01 and T–272/01 *Philip Morris International v Commission* [2003] 1 C.M.L.R. 21, decided in January 2003, a differently constituted formation of the CFI took a more restrictive approach. The *Philip Morris* case is discussed above.

[58] Para.33.

[59] Para.36.

[60] See Case C–309/89 *Codorniu v Council* [1994] E.C.R. I–1853, para.19.

with regard to the applicant if he or she could show that he or she was individually concerned by it. The logical difficulty of treating the same provisions as simultaneously both general and individual in scope was acknowledged by the Court as long ago as 1982.[61]

13–048   The Court endorsed the view of Advocate General Jacobs that standing could not be given to an applicant on the sole basis that he had no remedy before the national courts. That would mean that, in every case, the Community Courts would have to examine and interpret national procedural law, which was outside their jurisdiction when reviewing the legality of Community measures.[62] The Court acknowledged that individuals were "entitled to effective judicial protection of the rights they derive from the Community legal order".[63] However, it sought to show that the Treaty provided various means of challenging the validity of Community acts, devoting particular attention to the preliminary rulings procedure. The Court declared that it was the responsibility of the Member States "to establish a system of legal remedies and procedures which ensure respect for the right to effective judicial protection".[64] National courts were required, "so far as possible, to interpret and apply national procedural rules governing the exercise of rights of action"[65] in a way that enabled claimants to challenge national measures applying Community acts of general application by contesting the validity of such acts. The Court ended by observing that, if reform of the system currently in force were considered desirable, that was a matter for the Member States.[66]

The Court's injunction to the national courts in *UPA* was a classic *obiter dictum*, for the point of the case was that there was no national measure applying the contested regulation. It seems unreasonable for the Court to expect national judges to interpret their own rules in the light of the need to ensure effective judicial protection when it refused to do likewise in interpreting Article 230 EC. In practical terms, the ruling means that the Court is liable to find itself enmeshed in the details of national procedural law. Those are the very issues the Court claimed it had no jurisdiction to examine when reviewing the legality of Community acts directly.[67] That outcome might perhaps have been acceptable had the language of the Treaty made it unavoidable. However, as Advocate General Jacobs emphasised, "the notion of individual concern is capable of carrying a number of different interpretations".[68]

---

[61] See Case 45/81 *Moksel v Commission* [1982] E.C.R. 1129, para.18. See also Advocate General Jacobs in Case C–358/89 *Extramet* [1991] E.C.R. I–2501, 2517. The approach of the CFI on this point seems inconsistent: see Arnull, "Private Applicants and the Action for Annulment since *Codorniu*" (2001) 38 C.M.L.Rev. 7, 20–22.

[62] Para.43. See also paras 50–53 of the Opinion of Advocate General Jacobs.

[63] Para.39.

[64] Para.41.

[65] Para.42. *cf.* Case C–106/89 *Marleasing* [1990] E.C.R. I–4135.

[66] Para.45. The case was decided while the Convention on the Future of Europe was sitting.

[67] *cf.* the Opinion of Advocate General Jacobs, paras 57–58.

[68] *ibid.*, para.75.

The Court subsequently upheld an appeal brought by the Commission against the judgment of the CFI in *Jégo-Quéré*.[69] The Court's judgment contained strong criticism of the CFI for "removing all meaning from the requirement of individual concern set out in the fourth paragraph of Article 230 EC". The Court was silent on alternative tests, such as that put forward by Advocate General Jacobs in *UPA*, which offered a way of reconciling the open-textured language of Article 230 EC with the Union's values. Indeed, the Court did not dissent from Advocate General Jacobs' view that the case law showed "that the traditional interpretation of individual concern, because it is understood to flow from the Treaty itself, must be applied regardless of its consequences for the right to an effective judicial remedy".[70] Thus, the Court's traditional approach to the requirement of individual concern, pursuant to the *Plaumann* formula and notwithstanding all pressure for judicial reform, has been reaffirmed on several occasions.[71]

The action for failure to act

The action for annulment is complemented by the action for failure to act, for which provision is made in Article 232 EC. That article is in the following terms: **13–049**

> "Should the European Parliament, the Council or the Commission, in infringement of this Treaty, fail to act, the Member States and the other institutions of the Community may bring an action before the Court of Justice to have the infringement established.
>
> The action shall be admissible only if the institution concerned has first been called upon to act. If, within two months of being so called upon, the institution concerned has not defined its position, the action may be brought within a further period of two months.
>
> Any natural or legal person may, under the conditions laid down in the preceding paragraphs, complain to the Court of Justice that an institution of the Community has failed to

---

[69] See Case C–263/02 [2004] E.C.R. I–3425.

[70] Para.46 of the Opinion. The ECJ declared that, "even if it could be shown" (para.33) that the applicable national procedural rules did not offer the individual applicant an alternative remedy, he should not be permitted to challenge a measure of general application if he did not satisfy the standard test of individual concern. The Court's conclusion was unyielding: "an action for annulment before the Community Court should not on any view be available, even where it is apparent that the national procedural rules do not allow the individual to contest the validity of the Community measure unless he has first contravened it" (para.34).

[71] e.g. Case C–312/00 *Commission v Camar* [2002] E.C.R. I–11355; Case C–142/00 *Commission v Netherlandse Antillen* [2003] E.C.R. I–3483; Case C–167/02P *Rothley* [2004] E.C.R. I–3149.

address to that person any act other than a recommendation or an opinion.

The Court of Justice shall have jurisdiction, under the same conditions, in actions or proceedings brought by the ECB in the areas falling within the latter's field of competence and in actions or proceedings brought against the latter."

The Court has occasionally emphasised the parallel between the action for failure to act and the action for annulment. In *Chevalley v Commission*,[72] for example, it said that Articles 230 and 232 EC "merely prescribe one and the same method of recourse". Similarly, in the "Transport" case[73] the Court emphasised that "in the system of legal remedies provided for by the Treaty there is a close relationship between the right of action given in Article [230 EC] . . . and that based on Article [232 EC]". The analogy between the two articles should not, however, be pushed too far. In particular, the Court has accepted that the right to bring proceedings under Article 232 EC should not always be confined to failure to adopt an act having legal effects which could be challenged in annulment proceedings.

13-050 This emerges from the Court's treatment of failure to adopt preparatory acts which, although not open to review under Article 230 EC themselves,[74] constitute an essential step in the process leading to another act which itself produces legal effects. In the "Comitology" case,[75] for example, the Court observed that "[t]here is no necessary link between the action for annulment and the action for failure to act". It pointed out that the Parliament could bring proceedings against the Council under Article 232 EC if it failed to present a draft budget within the deadline laid down in Article 272(4) EC. The Court noted that, as a preparatory measure, the draft budget could not, once established, be challenged under Article 230 EC. If the Court had held that the Parliament had no right of action under Article 232 EC in these circumstances, it would be unable to challenge an unlawful failure by the Council to establish a draft budget, without which the Parliament could not exercise the power conferred on it by the Treaty to adopt the budget.

In *Asia Motor France v Commission*,[76] the Court held that, where the Commission declined to pursue a complaint by a natural or legal

---

[72] Case 15/70 [1970] E.C.R. 975, para.6. See also Case C-68/95 *T Port v Bundesanstalt für Landwirtschaft und Ernährung* [1996] E.C.R. I-6065, para.59. Actions for failure to act are distributed between the CFI and the Court of Justice in the same way as actions for annulment: Art.225(1) EC; Statute, Art.51.
[73] Case 13/83 *Parliament v Council* [1985] E.C.R. 1513, para.36.
[74] See Case 60/81 *IBM v Commission* [1981] E.C.R. 2639.
[75] Case 302/87 *Parliament v Council* [1988] E.C.R. 5615, para.16.
[76] Case T-28/90 [1992] E.C.R. II-2285, paras 29–30. *cf.* Case T-127/98 *UPS Europe v Commission* [1999] E.C.R. II-2633.

person that the Treaty competition rules had been infringed, the complainant could bring an action for failure to act if it had not been informed beforehand of the Commission's reasons and given the opportunity to submit further comments. The Commission was required to take that step by Article 6 of Regulation 99/63,[77] but where it did so the notification concerned could not be challenged under Article 230 EC because it was only a provisional measure intended to pave the way for the final decision.[78] However, that final decision could not be adopted in the absence of a notification under Regulation 99/63. If a complainant could not challenge an unlawful failure to issue such a notification, it might not be able to challenge a failure by the Commission to adopt the final decision because the Commission could say that, in the absence of the notification, it had no power to adopt such a decision.[79]

It may also be noted that, although a national court can use the preliminary rulings procedure to obtain a ruling from the Court of Justice that a Community act is invalid,[80] it cannot be used to obtain a ruling that a Community institution has failed to act. As the Court explained in *T Port*,[81] national courts therefore "have no jurisdiction to order interim measures pending action on the part of the institution. Judicial review of alleged failure to act can be exercised only by the Community judicature". The Court pointed out[82] that the Community Courts have the power under Article 243 EC to adopt interim measures in the framework of proceedings for failure to act.

In the "Transport" case,[83] the Court stated that an action under Article 232 EC would only lie in respect of "failure to take measures the scope of which can be sufficiently defined for them to be identified individually and adopted in compliance with the Court's judgment". In that case, the Parliament brought proceedings for a declaration that the Council had infringed the Treaty by failing to introduce, before the end of the transitional period, a common policy for transport dealing (among other things) with "the conditions under which non-resident carriers may operate transport services within a Member State".[84] The application was successful in

---

[77] [1963–1964] O.J. English Special Edition, p.47. See now Art.7(1), Reg.773/2004 [2004] O.J. L123/18, discussed in Ch.25.
[78] See Case C–282/95 P *Guérin Automobiles v Commission* [1997] E.C.R. I–1503, paras 33–38. A definitive decision rejecting a complaint may be the subject of an action for annulment. Moreover, if the Commission fails to adopt such a decision within a reasonable time, the complainant may bring proceedings against it for failure to act. That is so even if he has already brought such proceedings in order to obtain the notification provided for by Art.7(1) Reg.773/2004.
[79] Hartley, *The Foundations of European Community Law* (5th ed., 2003), p.388.
[80] See Ch.14.
[81] Case C–68/95 *T Port v Bundesanstalt für Landwirtschaft und Ernährung* [1996] E.C.R. I–6065, para.53.
[82] Para.60.
[83] Case 13/83 *Parliament v Council* [1985] E.C.R. 1513, para.37.
[84] See Art.71(1)(b) EC.

part only. The Court made it clear that it was irrelevant how difficult it might be for the institution concerned to comply with its obligations, but found that under the Treaty the Council enjoyed a discretion with regard to the implementation of the common transport policy. Although that discretion was subject to certain limits, the Court said that it was for the Council to determine "the aims of and means for implementing a common transport policy".[85] The Court concluded that the absence of such a policy "does not in itself necessarily constitute a failure to act sufficiently specific in nature to form the subject of an action under Article [232 EC]".[86] The Commission, which intervened in support of the Parliament, argued, however, that the common transport policy envisaged by the Treaty contained one element which was sufficiently well-defined to be regarded as imposing on the Council a specific obligation, namely a requirement to ensure freedom to provide services. The scope of that requirement could be determined by reference to the Treaty rules on services and the relevant directives and case law.[87] That argument found favour with the Court, which ruled that, in so far as the obligations laid down in the Treaty related to freedom to provide services, they were sufficiently well defined to be the subject of a finding of failure to act.

Standing

13–051 The distinction between privileged and non-privileged applicants which we encountered in the context of Article 230 EC is reproduced in Article 232 EC, the Member States and the Community institutions enjoying broader rights than natural and legal persons to institute proceedings for failure to act. Even before the reforms to Article 230 EC under the TN, Article 232 EC had placed the European Parliament on the same footing as the Member States, the Council and the Commission. This was confirmed in the "Transport" case,[88] where the Court emphasised that, in referring to "the other institutions of the Community", the first paragraph of Article 232 EC gave the same right of action to all the Community institutions, including the Parliament. The Court declared that "[i]t is not possible to restrict the exercise of that right by one of them without adversely affecting its status as an institution under the Treaty, in particular Article [7(1)]". It would seem to follow that the Court of Auditors, which was elevated to the status of an institution under Article 7(1) EC at Maastricht, is also entitled to bring proceedings under Article 232.

---

[85] Para.49 of the judgment.
[86] Para.53.
[87] See Ch.19.
[88] Case 13/83 *Parliament v Council* [1985] E.C.R. 1513, para.17.

Under the third paragraph of Article 232 EC, any natural or legal person may complain to the Court "that an institution of the Community has failed to address to that person any act other than a recommendation or an opinion". Thus, in *Chevalley v Commission*[89] the Court held that a definition of the Commission's position on a question, which would have amounted in substance to an opinion within the meaning of Article 249 EC, was not capable of forming the subject-matter of an action under the third paragraph of Article 232 EC. However, the decision in *Guérin Automobiles v Commission*[90] shows that a non-privileged applicant may bring proceedings under Article 232 EC where an institution fails to take a step which, although it could not itself have been challenged in annulment proceedings, constitutes a prerequisite for the adoption of an act which could.

Article 232 EC appears to require a non-privileged applicant to show that the act he or she alleges should have been adopted would have been addressed to him or her. If that requirement were applied strictly, however, there would be a gap in the system of remedies established by the Treaty: a natural or legal person would be unable to challenge a failure to adopt a measure which would have been of direct and individual concern to him or her had it been adopted and which he or she would therefore have been able to challenge under Article 230 EC. The Court has avoided that result by a flexible interpretation of the word "address". In *T Port v Bundesanstalt für Landwirtschaft und Ernährung*,[91] the Court explained: "just as the fourth paragraph of Article [230 EC] allows individuals to bring an action for annulment against a measure of an institution not addressed to them provided that the measure is of direct and individual concern to them, the third paragraph of Article [232 EC] must be interpreted as also entitling them to bring an action for failure to act against an institution which they claim has failed to adopt a measure which would have concerned them in the same way. The possibility for individuals to assert their rights should not depend upon whether the institution concerned has acted or failed to act". Notwithstanding earlier case law to the contrary,[92] it would

---

[89] Case 15/70 [1970] E.C.R. 975.
[90] Case C–282/95 P *Guérin Automobiles v Commission* [1997] E.C.R. I–1503.
[91] Case C–68/95 *T Port v Bundesanstalt für Landwirtschaft und Ernährung* [1996] E.C.R. I–6065, para.59. See also Case C–107/91 *ENU v Commission* [1993] E.C.R. I–599; Case T–95/96 *Gestevisión Telecinco v Commission* [1998] E.C.R. II–3407; Joined Cases T–79/96, T–260/97 and T–117/98 *Camar and Tico v Commission* [2000] E.C.R. II–2193. *cf.* Advocate General Darmon in Case C–41/92 *Liberal Democrats v Parliament* [1993] E.C.R. I–3153, 3172; Advocate General Dutheillet de Lamothe in Case 15/71 *Mackprang v Commission* [1971] E.C.R. 797, 807–808.
[92] See e.g. Case 134/73 *Holtz v Council* [1974] E.C.R. 1, para.5; Case 90/78 *Granaria v Council and Commission* [1979] E.C.R. 1081, para.14 (from the final sentence of which the word "not" has inadvertently been omitted in the English version); Case 60/79 *Producteurs de Vins de Table et Vins de Pays v Commission* [1979] E.C.R. 2429.

seem to follow that a natural or legal person may challenge a failure to adopt a regulation, or indeed a directive, if he or she can establish that he would have been directly and individually concerned by it, even though regulations are not addressed to anyone and directives can only be addressed to Member States. This would be consistent with the position under Article 230 EC.

The Court clarified in the *Ten Kate* case that Article 232 EC does not impose any obligation on a Member State to bring an action for failure to act for the benefit of one of its citizens.[93] On the other hand, Community law does not, in principle, preclude national law itself from containing such an obligation, or providing for liability to be imposed on the Member State for not having brought an action for failure to act under Article 232 EC. However, Article 10 EC would require the Member State in such circumstances to retain a degree of discretion under national law about the appropriateness of initiating an action under Article 232 EC, so as to avoid the risk that the Community Courts might be inundated with actions, some patently unfounded, such as would jeopardise the proper functioning of the Court of Justice.

Procedural aspects

13–052   Article 232 EC does not specify how soon proceedings must be instituted after the alleged failure to act has come to light. In a case decided under Article 35 ECSC, the counterpart of Article 232 EC, the Court held that proceedings for failure to act must be instituted within a reasonable period once it has become clear that the institution concerned has decided to take no action.[94] In the "Transport" case, however, the Court partially upheld an application made under Article 232 EC in January 1983 in respect of a failure to discharge an obligation which should have been fulfilled by the end of 1969, by which time the applicant was fully aware of the failure concerned. These cases may perhaps be distinguished on the ground that in the former the defendant had made it clear that it had decided not to take any action, whereas in the latter the defendant accepted the need for it to take further steps. It seems that it is only in the former type of case that proceedings must be brought within a reasonable period of the alleged failure to act having come to light.

According to the second paragraph of Article 232 EC, the institution concerned must first be "called upon to act". In the "Transport" case, the Council argued that that requirement had not been met. The Court disagreed, since the President of the Parliament had sent a letter to the Council which referred to Article 232

---

[93] The same is true of Art.230 EC: see case C–511/03 *Ten Kate* (Judgment of October 20, 2005).

[94] Case 59/70 *Netherlands v Commission* [1971] E.C.R. 639.

EC and which stated that the Parliament was calling on the Council to act pursuant to that provision. Moreover, annexed to the letter was a list of the steps which the Parliament considered necessary to remedy the failure. If the institution concerned has not "defined its position" within two months of having been called upon to act, an application may be made to the Court within a further period of two months. Thus, where the institution does define its position in time, it is not possible to bring the matter before the Court under Article 232 EC. In the "Transport" case the Court declined to treat as a definition of its position the Council's reply to the letter from the Parliament calling upon it to act. The Court observed[95] that the Council's reply "was confined to setting out what action it had already taken in relation to transport without commenting 'on the legal aspects' of the correspondence initiated by the Parliament. The reply neither denied nor confirmed the alleged failure to act nor gave any indication of the Council's views as to the measures which, according to the Parliament, remained to be taken".

The applicant will not normally be able to seek the annulment of the act by which the institution defines its position unless he or she would have had standing to challenge the measure requested under Article 230 EC had it been adopted. In *Nordgetreide v Commission*[96] the applicant, a private undertaking, sought the annulment of a refusal by the Commission to adopt an act which would have taken the form of a regulation. Since the measure requested "would have affected the applicant only in so far as it belongs to a category viewed in the abstract and in its entirety", it could not have been challenged by the applicant under Article 230 EC. The application was therefore declared inadmissible. However, the CFI takes a more liberal approach where an institution is requested to act but refuses to do so under a procedure laid down by regulation which requires it to rule on such requests. In those circumstances, the nature of the act requested seems to be irrelevant.[97]

Some of the Court's case law[98] suggests that the defendant **13–053** institution may define its position for the purposes of Article 232 EC simply by refusing to adopt the act requested by the applicant. However, the Court took a more relaxed stance in the "Comitology" case,[99] where it considered the question whether the Parliament had the right to institute annulment proceedings under Article 230 EC,

---

[95] Para.25 of the Judgment.

[96] Case 42/71 [1972] E.C.R. 105. See also Case T–166/98 *Cantina sociale di Dolianova v Commission* (pending); Joined Cases C–15/91 and C–108/91 *Buckl v Commission* [1992] E.C.R. I–6061; Case 48/65 *Lütticke v Commission* [1966] E.C.R. 19.

[97] See Case T–120/96 *Lilly Industries v Commission* [1998] E.C.R. II–2571, paras 61–63; *cf.* Joined Cases T–125/96 and T–152/96 *BI Vetmedica v Council and Commission* [1999] E.C.R. II–3427, paras 166–169.

[98] See e.g. Case 42/71 *Nordgetreide v Commission* [1972] E.C.R. 105.

[99] Case 302/87 [1988] E.C.R. 5615.

which did not at the material time expressly give it any such right. One of the arguments put forward by the Parliament was that, in the absence of any power to institute annulment proceedings, it would be unable to challenge an express refusal to act issued by the Council or the Commission after the Parliament had called upon them to act under Article 232 EC. The Court replied: "that argument is based on a false premise. A refusal to act, however explicit it may be, can be brought before the Court under Article [232 EC] since it does not put an end to the failure to act".[1] It is possible that the Court's statement in "Comitology" is limited to cases where the applicant would otherwise be deprived of a remedy because he or she is unable to challenge an express refusal to act under Article 230 EC.[2] However, Article 232 EC cannot be used to challenge a refusal by an institution to revoke a Community act which has not been challenged within the deadline laid down in Article 230 EC, since this would provide applicants "with a method of recourse parallel to that of Article [230 EC], which would not be subject to the conditions laid down by the Treaty".[3]

Where the failure is remedied within two months of the institution concerned having been called upon to act, no action may be brought before the Court. The steps taken need not be the same as those requested by the applicant, for "Article [232 EC] refers to failure to act in the sense of failure to take a decision or to define a position, and not the adoption of a measure different from that desired or considered necessary by the persons concerned".[4] Thus, an institution which proposes a particular legal basis for a measure cannot use Article 232 EC to challenge the choice of a different legal basis by the adopting institution.[5]

Where the defendant institution takes the steps requested over two months after being called upon to do so but before judgment is given, the Court will decline to give a ruling on the basis that "the subject-matter of the action has ceased to exist".[6] This is so even though, according to the second paragraph of Article 233 EC, a ruling by the Court under Article 232 EC is without prejudice to the liability of the institution concerned in damages under the second paragraph of Article 288 EC.[7] As the Court explained in *Buckl v Commission*,[8] "where the act whose absence constitutes the subject-

---

[1] Para.17 of the Judgment. *cf.* the Opinion of Advocate General Darmon at pp.5630–5631.

[2] See Due, "Legal Remedies for the Failure of European Community Institutions to Act in Conformity with EEC Treaty Provisions" (1990–91) 14 Fordham International Law Journal 341, 356; Hartley, *The Foundations of European Community Law* (5th ed., 2003), p.383.

[3] Joined Cases 10 and 18/68 *Eridania v Commission* [1969] E.C.R. 459, para.17.

[4] Joined Cases 166 and 220/86 *Irish Cement Ltd v Commission* [1988] E.C.R. 6473, para.17. Also, e.g. Case T–26/01 *Fiocchi Munizioni v Commission* [2003] E.C.R. II–3951.

[5] See Case C–70/88 *Parliament v Council* ("Chernobyl") [1990] E.C.R. I–2041.

[6] See Case 377/87 *Parliament v Council* [1988] E.C.R. 4017. Also, e.g. Joined Cases T–297/01 and T–298/01 *SIC v Commission* [2004] E.C.R. II–743.

[7] See below.

[8] Joined Cases C–15/91 and C–108/91 *Buckl v Commission* [1992] E.C.R. I–6061, para.15.

matter of the proceedings was adopted after the action was brought but before judgment, a declaration by the Court to the effect that the initial failure to act is unlawful can no longer bring about the consequences prescribed by Article [233 EC]. It follows that in such a case, as in cases where the defendant institution has responded within the period of two months after being called upon to act, the subject-matter of the action has ceased to exist". The Court's approach may be contrasted with its attitude in proceedings brought by the Commission under Article 226 EC where the Member State complies with its obligations after the expiry of the deadline laid down in the reasoned opinion.[9] Such cases are allowed to continue unless withdrawn by the Commission.

Where an application under Article 232 EC is upheld, the Court declares that the failure of the institution concerned to act is contrary to the Treaty. The Court cannot remedy the failure itself or order the institution concerned to take any particular steps, but the institution is required by the first paragraph of Article 233 EC "to take the necessary measures to comply with the judgment of the Court of Justice". The Court has said that those measures must be taken within a reasonable period of the judgment.[10]

The plea of illegality and non-existent acts

The strict time-limits and rules on standing laid down in Article **13–054** 230 EC are to some extent mitigated by the so-called plea of illegality, for which provision is made in Article 241 EC. That article provides as follows:

> "Notwithstanding the expiry of the period laid down in the fifth paragraph of Article 230, any party may, in proceedings in which a regulation adopted jointly by the European Parliament and the Council, or a regulation of the Council, of the Commission, or of the ECB is at issue, plead the grounds specified in the second paragraph of Article 230, in order to invoke before the Court of Justice the inapplicability of that regulation."

Article 241 EC allows the illegality of an act to be pleaded indirectly in proceedings which are pending before the Community Courts under some other provision.[11] Where, for example, a natural or legal person seeks the annulment of a decision addressed to him or her which is based on a regulation, he may contest the validity of that regulation even if he or she could not have challenged it directly

---

[9] See e.g. Case 39/72 *Commission v Italy* [1973] E.C.R. 101.
[10] See Case 13/83 *Parliament v Council* [1985] E.C.R. 1513, para.69.
[11] See Joined Cases 31 and 33/62 *Wöhrmann v Commission* [1962] E.C.R. 501.

under Article 230 EC. The CFI has explained that, "[s]ince the legality of the individual measure contested must be assessed on the basis of the elements of fact and of law existing at the time when the measure was adopted . . . the legality of the legislative measure which forms its legal basis must also be assessed at that time rather than at the time of its own adoption".[12]

The plea of illegality therefore represents a compromise between the principle of legal certainty, which would rule out a challenge to a Community act once the deadline laid down in Article 230 EC had expired, and the principle of legality, which would preclude reliance on unlawful acts. It is important to emphasise, however, that Article 241 EC does not give rise to a separate remedy. As the CFI explained in *CSF and CSME v Commission*,[13] "[t]he possibility afforded by Article [241] of the Treaty of pleading the inapplicability of a measure of general application forming the legal basis of the contested decision does not constitute an independent right of action and recourse may be had to it only as an incidental plea. More specifically, Article [241 EC] may not be invoked in the absence of an independent right of action". Since Article 241 EC applies only in proceedings before the Community Courts,[14] it does not affect the circumstances in which the validity of Community acts may be contested in the national courts. It seems, however, that a declaration of inapplicability made by the Court of Justice under Article 241 EC in a previous case would enable a national court to treat the act in question as invalid without referring the matter to the Court of Justice under Article 234 EC.[15]

Although Article 241 EC only refers to regulations, the Court said in *Simmenthal v Commission*[16] that:

> "Article [241] of the EEC Treaty gives expression to a general principle conferring upon any party to proceedings the right to challenge, for the purpose of obtaining the annulment of a decision of direct and individual concern to that party, the validity of previous acts of the institutions which form the legal basis of the decision which is being attacked, if that party was not entitled under Article [230] of the Treaty to bring a direct action challenging those acts [and] by which it was thus affected without having been in a position to ask that they be declared void."

13-055 The Court concluded that Article 241 EC extended to "acts of the institutions which, although they are not in the form of a regulation, nevertheless produce similar effects and on those grounds may not

---

[12] Joined Cases T–177/94 and T–377/94 *Altmann v Commission* [1996] E.C.R. II–2041, para.119.
[13] Case T–154/94 [1996] E.C.R. II–1377, para.16.
[14] See Joined Cases 31 and 33/62 *Wöhrmann v Commission* [1962] E.C.R. 501, 507.
[15] See Case 314/85 *Foto-Frost v Hauptzollamt Lübeck-Ost* [1987] E.C.R. 4199, para.16, where the Court refers to Art.241 EC. The *Foto-Frost* case is discussed in Ch.14.
[16] Case 92/78 [1979] E.C.R. 777, para.39.

be challenged under Article 230 EC by natural or legal persons other than Community institutions and Member States".[17] It seems to follow from *Simmenthal* that the plea of illegality may be invoked in relation to any act producing legal effects which natural and legal persons are unable to challenge directly under Article 230 EC, for example a decision addressed to a third party which is not of direct and individual concern to the person wishing to contest its validity. Conversely, in *TWD Textilwerke Deggendorf*,[18] it was held that the validity of a Community act may not be challenged in a national court by an applicant who would undoubtedly have had standing to contest its validity in a direct action under Article 230 EC but who failed to do so in time. In *TWD v Commission*,[19] the CFI said that, as a result, "[t]he objection of illegality provided for by Article [241] of the Treaty cannot be raised by a legal or natural person who could have brought proceedings under the second paragraph of Article [230 EC] but who did not do so within the period prescribed therein".

According to its express terms, the plea of illegality may be invoked by "any party", an expression which is clearly broad enough to cover Member States, notwithstanding their privileged status for the purpose of annulment proceedings. The case law suggests that a Member State may challenge the validity of a regulation indirectly in proceedings under both Articles 230[20] and 226 EC.[21] The rationale seems to be that "defects appertaining to a general regulation often do not clearly emerge until the regulation is applied to a particular case".[22] That rationale does not apply to acts addressed to a Member State and it is well-established that a Member State may not challenge the validity of a decision addressed to it once the deadline laid down in Article 230 EC has expired.[23] It is submitted that other privileged applicants (including the Council, Commission and Parliament) are in the same position, *mututis mutandis*, as the Member States. This is supported by the ruling in *Commission v European Central Bank*.[24] There, the ECB sought to rely on Article 241 EC so

---

[17] Para.40 of the Judgment. Thus, the Court held that Art.241 EC could be invoked in relation to notices of invitation to tender.

[18] Case C–188/92 [1994] E.C.R. I–833. Also, e.g. Case C–178/95 *Wiljo* [1997] E.C.R. I–585; Case C–239/99 *Nachi Europe* [2001] E.C.R. I–1197. See further Ch.14.

[19] Joined Cases T–244/93 and T–486/93 [1995] E.C.R. II–2265, para.103 (appeal dismissed: see Case C–355/95 P [1997] E.C.R. I–2549).

[20] See Case 32/65 *Italy v Council and Commission* [1966] E.C.R. 389.

[21] See Case 116/82 *Commission v Germany* [1986] E.C.R. 2519.

[22] See Advocate General Roemer in Case 32/65 *Italy v Council and Commission* [1966] E.C.R. 389, 414.

[23] See e.g. Case 156/77 *Commission v Belgium* [1978] E.C.R. 1881; Case C–183/91 *Commission v Greece* [1993] E.C.R. I–3131. *cf.* Case C–241/01 *National Farmers' Union* [2002] E.C.R. I–9079: a Member State is precluded from pleading before the national courts the illegality of a Community measure of which it is an addressee, once the time limit for bringing an action for annulment has expired.

[24] Case C–11/00 *Commission v European Central Bank* [2003] E.C.R. I–7147.

as to invoke the illegality of an anti-fraud regulation adopted by the Parliament and Council, within the context of an action for annulment brought by the Commission against an ECB act which was alleged to contravene that regulation. The Commission argued that the ECB should be prevented from relying on Article 241 EC, since it had failed to challenge the regulation under Article 230 EC within the two-month time-limit. The ECJ agreed that a regulation may become definitive as against any party as regards whom it must be considered an individual decision, where that party could have sought annulment of the regulation under Article 230 EC. But here, the disputed regulation was clearly of a legislative nature and could not be treated as a decision, or in any event, not as a decision of which the ECB was an addressee, so the plea of illegality under Article 241 EC was admissible.

Where a plea of illegality is successful, the Court does not formally annul the measure in question, but simply declares it inapplicable. This has the effect of depriving any act adopted under it of its legal basis. Nevertheless, although the Court's ruling in relation to the first measure is technically limited to the case in which it is made, it is tantamount in practical terms to a declaration of invalidity, for the institutions will immediately cease to apply the measure and the Community Courts will henceforth treat it as invalid.

13–056   Where the plea of illegality cannot be invoked and the deadline for bringing annulment proceedings has expired, any party may nevertheless argue that an act, regardless of its nature, is vitiated by such fundamental defects that it should be considered non-existent[25] and incapable of producing any legal effects.[26] This test is extremely difficult to satisfy, as the Court's judgment in *Commission v BASF*[27] makes clear. That case was an appeal by the Commission against a ruling of the CFI[28] that a Commission decision on the application of the Treaty competition rules was "vitiated by particularly serious and manifest defects" and was to be considered non-existent. The CFI had taken the view that the defects in question made it impossible to be certain of the exact date on which the contested measure took effect, the precise terms of the statement of reasons it was required by the Treaty to contain, the extent of the obligations it imposed on its addressees, the identity of those addressees or that of the authority which issued the definitive version of the act. The Court took a more lenient approach, observing:[29]

---

[25] Case 226/87 *Commission v Greece* [1988] E.C.R. 3611, para.16.
[26] See Case 15/85 *Consorzio Cooperative d'Abruzzo v Commission* [1987] E.C.R. 1005, para.10.
[27] Case C–137/92 P [1994] E.C.R. I–2555. See also Case C–199/92 P *Hüls v Commission* [1999] E.C.R. I–4287; Case C–227/92 P *Hoechst v Commission* [1999] E.C.R. I–4443; Case C–234/92 P *Shell International Chemical Company v Commission* [1999] E.C.R. I–4501; Case C–235/92 P *Montecatini v Commission* [1999] E.C.R. I–4539; Case C–245/92 P *Chemie Linz v Commission* [1999] E.C.R. I–4643.
[28] Joined Cases T–79/89 etc, *BASF v Commission* [1992] E.C.R. II–315.
[29] See paras 48–50 of the Judgment.

"It should be remembered that acts of the Community institutions are in principle presumed to be lawful and accordingly produce legal effects, even if they are tainted by irregularities, until such time as they are annulled or withdrawn.

However, by way of exception to that principle, acts tainted by an irregularity whose gravity is so obvious that it cannot be tolerated by the Community legal order must be treated as having no legal effect, even provisional, that is to say that they must be regarded as legally non-existent. The purpose of this exception is to maintain a balance between two fundamental, but sometimes conflicting, requirements with which a legal order must comply, namely stability of legal relations and respect for legality.

From the gravity of the consequences attaching to a finding that an act of a Community institution is non-existent it is self-evident that, for reasons of legal certainty, such a finding is reserved for quite extreme situations."

The Court concluded that the irregularities identified by the CFI were not serious enough to render the contested decision non-existent, although it went on to annul it. Unlike the ruling of the CFI, the judgment of the Court therefore had no implications for the validity of earlier decisions suffering from similar defects, in respect of which any challenge under Article 230 EC would by then have been out of time.

The action for damages
   Article 235 EC gives the Court of Justice jurisdiction in actions for **13–057** damages brought under the second paragraph of Article 288 EC,[30] which provides: "In the case of non-contractual liability, the Community shall, in accordance with the general principles common to the laws of the Member States, make good any damage caused by its institutions or by its servants in the performance of their duties". At Maastricht, a new third paragraph was inserted in Article 288 EC stating that the second paragraph also applies "to damage caused by the ECB or by its servants in the performance of their duties". That addition may not have been strictly necessary, for the Court held in *SGEEM and Etroy v EIB*[31] that the term "institutions" in the second paragraph of the article was not confined to the institutions listed in Article 7(1) EC, but extended to any Community body "established by the Treaty and authorised to act in its name and on its behalf".[32]

---

[30] See generally Heukels and McDonnell (eds), *The Action for Damages in Community Law* (1997).
[31] Case C–370/89 [1992] E.C.R. I–6211.
[32] Para.15. It therefore covered the European Investment Bank (on which see Arts 266–267 EC).

484   *Direct actions*

Thus, for example, it has been held that the acts of the Ombudsman may, in principle, provide the basis for an action in damages under Articles 235 and 288 EC.[33]

According to the Treaty, it is the Community as a whole whose liability is in issue in proceedings under the second paragraph of Article 288 EC. However, in *Werhahn v Council* the Court said that, "where Community liability is involved by reason of the act of one of its institutions, it should be represented before the Court by the institution or institutions against which the matter giving rise to liability is alleged".[34] Where the action relates to a legislative measure adopted by the Council on a proposal from the Commission, proceedings may be brought against both institutions jointly.[35]

The reference to the general principles common to the laws of the Member States in the second paragraph of Article 288 EC does not mean that the Community Courts must search in cases on non-contractual liability for a solution favoured by a majority of the Member States, still less that they have to apply the lowest common denominator. It means simply that the Community Courts must look to the national systems for inspiration in devising a regime of non-contractual liability adapted to the specific circumstances of the Community.[36] The principles traditionally applied by the Community Courts have in fact been relatively strict, with the result that the number of successful claims brought against the Community is fairly small. However, the case law has recently undergone some significant changes, the stimulus for which was the ECJ's acknowledgment, in *Brasserie du Pêcheur and Factortame*,[37] that "the conditions under which the State may incur liability for damage caused to individuals by a breach of Community law cannot, in the absence of particular justification, differ from those governing the liability of the Community in like circumstances. The protection of the rights which individuals derive from Community law cannot vary depending on whether a national authority or a Community authority is responsible for the damage". As we shall see, the crossover between the principles governing Member State liability, on the one hand, and Community liability, on the other hand, has become increasingly fertile.

It is well-established that the action for damages constitutes an independent or autonomous form of action. Its purpose is different from that of proceedings for annulment or failure to act and it is not necessary to have recourse to such proceedings before commencing

---

[33] Case C–234/02P *European Ombudsman v Lamberts* [2004] E.C.R. I–2803.
[34] Joined Cases 63 to 69/72 [1973] E.C.R. 1229, para.7.
[35] *ibid.*, para.8.
[36] See Advocate General Gand in Case 9/69 *Sayag v Leduc* [1969] E.C.R. 329, 339–340; Advocate General Roemer in Case 5/71 *Zuckerfabrik Schöppenstedt v Council* [1971] E.C.R. 975, 989.
[37] Joined Cases C–46/93 and C–48/93 [1996] E.C.R. I–1029, para.42. See Ch.6.

an action under the second paragraph of Article 288 EC.[38] That paragraph may normally be used as a means of challenging indirectly the legality of an act or a failure to act which has not been contested directly under Articles 230 or 232 EC or where proceedings under those articles have been dismissed as inadmissible. However, a claim for damages will not be entertained where its purpose is to secure exactly the same result as an action for annulment which has been found inadmissible.[39] In *Cobrecaf v Commission*,[40] for example, the CFI dismissed as inadmissible both an application for annulment and a claim for damages. It found that "the actual purpose of the applicants' alternative claim for damages is to secure payment of a sum corresponding exactly to the amount denied to it by reason of the disputed decision and that it is therefore designed to secure indirectly annulment of the individual decision rejecting the applicants' request for financial aid".[41]

Damage caused by servants of the Community in the performance of their duties

Where the applicant relies on an act performed by a Community **13-058** official in the performance of his or her duties, the Court applies a strict, perhaps unduly strict, test. In *Sayag v Leduc*,[42] a case concerning the corresponding provision of the Euratom Treaty,[43] the Court held that the Community was not liable for an accident caused by a servant while using his private car during the performance of his duties. The Court said that "[o]nly in the case of *force majeure* or in exceptional circumstances of such overriding importance that without the servant's using private means of transport the Community would have been unable to carry out the tasks entrusted to it, could such use be considered to form part of the servant's performance of his duties".

Damage caused by an institution of the Community

Of greater practical importance is the Community's potential **13-059** liability for loss caused by acts adopted by its institutions. For these purposes, we may deal with the case law in two main phases: the traditional case law, focused around the restrictive *Schöppenstedt* formula; and the more recent case law, aligning the rules on Community liability more closely to those on Member State liability.

---

[38] See e.g. Case 4/69 *Lütticke v Commission* [1971] E.C.R. 325; Case 5/71 *Zuckerfabrik Schöppenstedt v Council* [1971] E.C.R. 975.
[39] See Case 25/62 *Plaumann v Commission* [1963] E.C.R. 95; Case 175/84 *Krohn v Commission* [1986] E.C.R. 753.
[40] Case T-514/93 [1995] E.C.R. II-621.
[41] Para.60.
[42] Case 9/69 [1969] E.C.R. 329.
[43] The second paragraph of Art.188 Euratom.

13–060 **(a) The traditional case law under the *Schöppenstedt* formula.** The older case law on liability of the Community institutions drew a basic distinction between two main categories of act: administrative acts and legislative acts.

In the case of administrative acts, the general conditions to be satisfied for a claim to succeed were summarised in *New Europe Consulting v Commission*,[44] where the CFI explained that "the conduct of the Community institutions in question must be unlawful; there must be real and certain damage; and a direct causal link must exist between the conduct of the institution concerned and the alleged damage". One might note that the Community may also incur liability as a result of an omission, but only where the institution concerned had a legal obligation to act under a provision of Community law.[45] Thus, a failure by the Commission to bring proceedings against a Member State under Article 226 EC is not capable of fixing the Community with liability in damages because the Commission is not under any obligation to initiate such proceedings.[46]

The Stanley Adams saga provides a striking example of a successful claim against the Community arising out of both an act and an omission on the part of the Commission.[47] Stanley Adams was an employee of the Swiss pharmaceutical company, Hoffmann-La Roche. He believed that some of the company's practices were incompatible with the competition rules laid down in the EC Treaty. He therefore alerted the Commission and supplied it with copies of a number of internal company documents. The Commission subsequently commenced an investigation into the company's activities, in the course of which it handed over to the company edited copies of some of the documents supplied by Adams. The Commission ultimately adopted a decision imposing a substantial fine on the company for breach of Article 82 EC.[48]

In the meantime, the company, realising the Commission must have had an informant, attempted to discover his identity. The company's lawyer told the Commission that it was considering taking criminal proceedings against the informant for economic espionage under the Swiss Penal Code. The company eventually succeeded in identifying Adams from the copies of its own documents which had been handed to it by the Commission. Adams had by then left the

---

[44] Case T–231/97 [1999] 2 C.M.L.R. 1452, para.29. See also Case C–358/90 *Compagnia Italiana Alcool v Commission* [1992] E.C.R. I–2457, para.46; Case C–55/90 *Cato v Commission* [1992] E.C.R. I–2533, para.18.

[45] See e.g. Case C–146/91 *KYDEP v Council and Commission* [1994] E.C.R. I–4199, para.58.

[46] Case C–72/90 *Asia Motor France v Commission* [1990] E.C.R. I–2181, para.13.

[47] The story is recounted by Stanley Adams in *Roche versus Adams* (1984). See also Hunnings, "The Stanley Adams affair or the biter bit" (1987) 24 C.M.L.Rev. 65.

[48] The essence of the Commission's decision was upheld by the Court in Case 85/76 *Hoffmann-La Roche v Commission* [1979] E.C.R. 461.

company and moved to Italy, but he was arrested by the Swiss authorities as he attempted to enter Switzerland on a visit. While he was being held in custody, his wife committed suicide. He was subsequently released on bail, but was in due course found guilty of economic espionage and sentenced in his absence to a suspended term of one year's imprisonment. His conviction damaged his creditworthiness and led to the failure of a business he had established after leaving the company.

In proceedings against the Commission under the second para- **13–061** graph of Article 288 EC,[49] the Court found that two aspects of the Commission's conduct gave rise to liability: first, the disclosure to the company of the documents which enabled Adams to be identified; secondly, the failure to warn Adams of the risk that he would be prosecuted if he returned to Switzerland, a risk of which the Commission should have been aware following its discussions with the company's lawyer. However, the Court took the view that Adams was partly to blame for his misfortunes: he had not, for example, warned the Commission that he could be identified from the documents he had supplied and he had returned to Switzerland without enquiring as to the risks involved in doing so. The Court therefore decided that responsibility for the damage he had suffered should be apportioned equally between himself and the Commission.

The act and the omission which gave rise to liability in the *Adams* case were administrative, in the sense that they did not have general application. In such cases, it was enough for the applicant to establish illegality, damage and causation. But legislative measures, in the sense of acts having general application, may also give rise to non-contractual liability on the part of the Community. Where such measures involved choices of economic policy, however, the Courts traditionally applied a particularly stringent test of unlawfulness.[50] That test was laid down in *Zuckerfabrik Schöppenstedt v Council*,[51] where the Court stated: "Where legislative action involving measures of economic policy is concerned, the Community does not incur non-contractual liability for damage suffered by individuals as a consequence of that action . . . unless a sufficiently flagrant violation of a superior rule of law for the protection of the individual has occurred". Since nearly all Community legislation of a type liable to give rise to a claim in damages is concerned in some way with economic policy, the test laid down in the *Schöppenstedt* case was

---

[49] Case 145/83 *Adams v Commission* [1985] E.C.R. 3539.
[50] See Case 50/86 *Grands Moulins de Paris v Council and Commission* [1987] E.C.R. 4833, paras 7–8; Advocate General van Gerven in Joined Cases C–104/89 and C–37/90 *Mulder v Council and Commission* [1992] E.C.R. I–3061, 3103. It is not enough to establish liability that the measure in question has previously been declared void by the Court: see e.g. Joined Cases 83 and 94/76, 4, 15 and 40/77 *HNL v Council and Commission* [1978] E.C.R. 1209, para.4.
[51] Case 5/71 [1971] E.C.R. 975, para.11.

broad in scope. It also applied in the case of an unlawful failure to adopt a legislative act.[52]

Applying the *Schöppenstedt* formula involved defining what exactly constituted "legislative action". The case law set out certain guidelines. First, the term did not cover instruments of primary Community law, such as treaties concerning the accession of new Member States[53] or the Single European Act.[54] These are agreements concluded by the Member States, not acts of the institutions. Secondly, the CFI made it clear in *Schröder v Commission*[55] that "the concept of legislative measure within the meaning of the case law may apply to all the measures referred to by Article [249 EC] and not only to regulations". As in actions for annulment, the decisive question was not what the disputed act was called but whether it was of general application. In *Schröder*, the CFI concluded that the contested measures, even though they took the form of decisions, produced "with regard to the applicants effects which are those of a measure of general application, in the same way as a regulation".[56] The *Schöppenstedt* test was therefore applicable. The Court also applied that test in a claim for loss allegedly caused by a directive.[57] Conversely, the *Schöppenstedt* test did not apply where the contested act, although labelled a regulation, was not in fact a legislative measure of general application.[58] Because the action for damages and the action for annulment are independent remedies, the nature of a measure for the purposes of the former action was not affected by whether or not the applicant had standing to challenge it for the purposes of the latter action. Thus, in *Antillean Rice Mills v Commission*,[59] a decision which had been found to be of direct and individual concern to the applicants for the purposes of Article 230 EC was treated as a legislative measure in the context of a parallel claim for damages.

13–062   The *Schöppenstedt* formula also called for a definition of what constituted a "superior rule of law for the protection of individuals". Again, the case law established that this could include a provision of the Treaty, such as Article 34(2) EC prohibiting discrimination between producers and consumers in the Community in the context

---

[52] See Case T–113/96 *Dubois et Fils v Council and Commission* [1998] E.C.R. II–125, para.60.
[53] See Joined Cases 31 and 35/86 *Laisa v Council* [1988] E.C.R. 2285.
[54] See Case T–113/96 *Dubois et Fils v Council and Commission* [1998] E.C.R. II–125, para.41.
[55] Case T–390/94 [1997] E.C.R. II–501, para.54.
[56] Para.56. See also Case C–390/95 P *Antillean Rice Mills v Commission* [1999] E.C.R. I–769, para.60; Joined Cases T–481/93 and T–484/93 *Exporteurs in Levende Varkens v Commission* [1995] E.C.R. II–2941.
[57] See Case C–63/89 *Assurances du Crédit v Council and Commission* [1991] E.C.R. I–1799.
[58] See Case C–119/88 *Aerpo v Commission* [1990] E.C.R. I–2189; Case T–472/93 *Campo Ebro v Council* [1995] E.C.R. II–421 (appeal dismissed: see Case C–138/95 P [1997] E.C.R. I–2027).
[59] Case C–390/95 P *Antillean Rice Mills v Commission* [1999] E.C.R. I–769, para.62. See also Case C–152/88, *Sofrimport v Commission* [1990] E.C.R. I–2477.

of the common organisation of agricultural markets,[60] or a provision contained in a regulation.[61] An applicant was required only to show that the rule in question was for the protection of individuals generally, not that it was for the protection of a particular class of which he or she was a member.[62] Thus, the category was held to include general principles of law, such as proportionality, equal treatment, the protection of legitimate expectations and the right to be heard. Misuse of powers by an institution was also covered.[63] However, failure to respect the institutional balance laid down in the Treaties was not sufficient to render the Community liable, since the division of powers among the institutions is not intended to protect individuals.[64]

In order to succeed, the applicant was furthermore obliged to show that the superior rule of law in question had been breached in a manner that was sufficiently serious to fix the Community with liability. In *HNL v Council and Commission*,[65] the Court said that, in a legislative field which involved the exercise of a wide discretion, such as that of the Common Agricultural Policy, the Community would not incur non-contractual liability "unless the institution concerned has manifestly and gravely disregarded the limits on the exercise of its powers". Where the applicant was unable to show that such conduct had occurred, it was not possible to establish a sufficiently serious breach of a superior rule of law.[66] The Court went even further in *Amylum v Council and Commission*,[67] where it stated that a legal situation resulting from legislative measures involving choices of economic policy would only be sufficient to fix the Community with liability if the conduct of the institutions concerned "was verging on the arbitrary".

A consequence of that extremely strict test was that actions in respect of legislative measures conferring discretionary powers on the institutions have rarely been successful. The Court regarded the strictness of its approach as justified by two factors. The first was that, if liability were too easy to establish, the institutions would be

---

[60] See e.g. Joined Cases 83 and 94/76, 4, 15 and 40/77 *HNL v Council and Commission* [1978] E.C.R. 1209, para.5; Case 238/78 *Ireks-Arkady v Council and Commission* [1979] E.C.R. 2955, para.11.

[61] See Case 74/74 *CNTA v Commission* [1975] E.C.R. 533; Case C–152/88 *Sofrimport v Commission* [1990] E.C.R. I–2477.

[62] See Joined Cases 5, 7 and 13 to 24/66 *Kampffmeyer v Commission* [1967] E.C.R. 245, 262–263.

[63] See Joined Cases T–481/93 and T–484/93 *Exporteurs in Levende Varkens v Commission* [1995] E.C.R. II–2941, para.102, with references to earlier case law. See also Case T–489/93 *Unifruit Hellas v Commission* [1994] E.C.R. II–1201, para.42 (appeal dismissed: see Case C–51/95 P [1997] E.C.R. I–727).

[64] Case C–282/90 *Vreugdenhil v Commission* [1992] E.C.R. I–1937, paras 20–21.

[65] Joined Cases 83 and 94/76, 4, 15 and 40/77 *HNL v Council and Commission* [1978] E.C.R. 1209, para.6.

[66] See Case C–390/95 P *Antillean Rice Mills v Commission* [1999] E.C.R. I–769, paras 64–70.

[67] Joined Cases 116 and 124/77 [1979] E.C.R. 3497, para.19.

unduly hampered in the performance of the tasks conferred on them by the Treaty.[68] The second was that an individual who considered him- or herself injured by a Community act which had been implemented by the national authorities could challenge the act's validity before the national courts, who could make a reference to the Court of Justice under Article 234 EC. According to the Court, "[t]he existence of such an action is by itself of such a nature as to ensure the efficient protection of the individuals concerned".[69]

13–063 **(b) The more recent case law under *Bergaderm*.** The Court's traditional case law on Community liability was criticised not only for the restrictive nature of the *Schöppenstedt* formula, but also on several other grounds. For example, it seemed peculiar that administrative acts could attract liability on the basis of illegality alone, without any further requirements as to fault or culpability, even where those acts might equally involve the exercise of wide discretionary powers. After all, a Community institution might rightly consider its ability to discharge its responsibilities in the general interest hampered by the prospect of widespread liability, regardless of whether the act in question is considered to be administrative or legislative in nature. Furthermore, despite the Court's statement in *Brasserie du Pêcheur and Factortame* that the protection of the rights which individuals derive from Community law cannot vary depending on whether a national authority or a Community authority is responsible for the damage, it was evident that precisely such variations existed in the case law. As regards Member State liability, the key factor in determining liability was discretion, not the strict classification of the act as administrative or legislative in nature; the requirement of a "manifest and grave disregard" of the limits of a Member State's powers applied to any situation in which the national authorities exercised appreciable discretion in the general interest.[70]

Perhaps in the light of such criticisms, the ECJ in *Bergaderm* revised its approach to Community liability.[71] The case concerned a directive adopted by the Commission amending the list of substances which, if contained in cosmetic products, would require Member States to prohibit the marketing of those products in accordance with Directive 76/768.[72] The claimant company argued that, since it was the only undertaking affected by the Commission's directive, the latter should be considered an administrative act and its illegality per se could found the basis of a damages action. However, the CFI

---

[68] See e.g. Joined Cases 83 and 94/76, 4, 15 and 40/77 *HNL v Council and Commission* [1978] E.C.R. 1209, para.5.
[69] See Case 108/81 *Amylum v Council* [1982] E.C.R. 3107, para.14.
[70] For full discussion, see Ch.6.
[71] Case C–352/98P *Bergaderm* [2000] E.C.R. I–5291.
[72] [1976] O.J. L262/169.

found the act to be legislative in nature, and applied the *Schöppenstedt* formula. The undertaking appealed based, *inter alia*, upon an alleged error of law by the CFI in categorising the directive for the purposes of establishing damages liability. The ECJ observed that, as regards Member State liability, the right to reparation depends upon fulfilling three conditions: the rule of law infringed must be intended to confer rights on individuals; the breach must be sufficiently serious; and there must be a direct causal link between the breach and the damage sustained. As regards the requirement of a sufficiently serious breach, liability depends on the Member State, or the Community institution, manifestly and gravely disregarding the limits of its discretion; where the Member State or Community institution has considerably reduced, or even no, discretion, the mere infringement of Community law may be sufficient to establish the existence of a sufficiently serious breach. However, the general or individual nature of a measure adopted by the Community institution is not a decisive criterion for identifying the limits of that institution's discretion—so that the undertaking's appeal based on the strict categorisation of the disputed directive was misconceived.

It was, at first, unclear how far the ECJ in *Bergaderm* had intended to revise its case law on Community liability; after all, the Court of Justice did not expressly overrule the *Schöppenstedt* formula, and indeed there was no hint that a new approach to Community liability might be in the offing in either the judgment of the CFI,[73] or the opinion of the Advocate General.[74] Nevertheless, subsequent rulings have made it clear that the *Bergaderm* approach indeed represents the current law: the system of liability worked out in respect of the Member States under the *Francovich* case law, which was supposed, after all, to have been inspired by the jurisprudence under Articles 235 and 288 EC, now applies to the liability of the Community institutions themselves.[75] In some respects, this change might be seen as largely cosmetic: for example, the idea of a "superior rule of law for the protection of the individual" will in most cases prove identical to the concept of a "rule intended to confer rights on the individual". But in other respects, the change is quite fundamental: in particular, the mere illegality of an administrative act will no

---

[73] Case T–199/96 [1998] E.C.R. II–2805.

[74] Opinion of January 27, 2000. Consider also post-*Bergaderm* rulings such as Case T–178/98 *Fresh Marine v Commission* [2000] E.C.R. II–3331.

[75] e.g. Joined Cases T–198/95, T–171/96, T–230/97, T–174/98 and T–225/99 *Comafrica v Commission* [2001] E.C.R. II–1975; Case T–159/99 *Dieckmann and Hansen v Commission* [2001] E.C.R. II–3143; Case C–472/00 P *Commission v Fresh Marine* [2003] E.C.R. I–7541; Case T–166/98 *Dolianova* (Judgment of November 24, 2004); Case T–139/01 *Comafrica v Commission* (Judgment of February 3, 2005); Case C–198/03 P *Commission v CEVA Santé Animale* (Judgment of July 12, 2005); Case T–415/03 *Cofradía de pescadores de "San Pedro" de Bermeo v Council* (Judgment of October 19, 2005). For a good example of case law on Member State liability being cited to illuminate the system of Community liability, see Case T–364/03 *Medici Grimm v Council* (Judgment of January 26, 2006).

longer suffice to establish liability, without taking into account the degree of discretion enjoyed by the Community institution when discharging its functions.[76]

13–064   Of course, *Bergaderm* means that it has in fact become *more* difficult for claimants to establish Community liability than under the older case law, at least as regards those acts which would previously have been categorised as administrative in nature. However, it is also worth pointing out that there were already signs in the pre-*Bergaderm* case law of a modest relaxation in the Court's approach towards the restrictiveness of its "manifest and grave" test as regards unlawful legislative (discretionary) acts. For example, in *Commission v Stahl-werke Peine-Salzgitter*,[77] the Court acknowledged that it was not necessary to establish "conduct verging on the arbitrary" where the Community's liability for unlawful legislative acts was in issue. Similarly, in *Mulder v Council and Commission (Mulder II)*,[78] the Court upheld claims arising out of unlawful legislative acts even though the consequence was to expose the Community to liability to large numbers of other claimants in a position similar to that of the applicants.[79] That case is particularly striking because it arose within the framework of the Common Agricultural Policy, where the institutions enjoy wide discretionary powers.

Liability without fault

13–065   Under the laws of some Member States, the administration may incur liability in damages for loss caused by acts which are lawful. The idea, enshrined in the French doctrine of "égalité devant les charges publiques" and the German doctrine of "Sonderopfer", is that it is unfair to make a limited group of individuals bear the financial burden of measures taken in the general interest.[80] Although the Community Courts generally describe unlawfulness as a condition of the Community's liability under the second paragraph of Article 288 EC, the case law now recognises the possibility that the Community might in exceptional cases incur liability in damages for a lawful act. In *Dorsch Consult v Council and Commission*,[81] the CFI observed, having reviewed the case law of the Court of Justice, that:

---

[76] e.g. Case C–312/00 P *Commission v Camar* [2002] E.C.R. I–11355.

[77] Case C–220/91 P [1993] E.C.R. I–2393, para.51.

[78] Joined Cases C–104/89 and C–37/90 [1992] E.C.R. I–3061. See also Case C–152/88 *Sofrimport v Commission* [1990] E.C.R. I–2477.

[79] Because of the number of those affected by the Court's judgment, the Council adopted a regulation to facilitate the settlement of claims: see Reg.2187/93 providing for an offer of compensation to certain producers of milk and milk products temporarily prevented from carrying on their trade [1993] O.J. L196/6.

[80] See Bronkhorst, "The Valid Legislative Act as a Cause of Liability of the Communities" in Heukels and McDonnell (eds), *The Action for Damages in Community Law* (1997), p.156.

[81] Case T–184/95 [1998] E.C.R. II–667, para.80. See also Case T–195/00 *Travelex Global and Financial Services v Commission* [2003] E.C.R. II–1677.

"in the event of the principle of Community liability for a lawful act being recognised in Community law, such liability can be incurred only if the damage alleged, if deemed to constitute a 'still subsisting injury', affects a particular circle of economic operators in a disproportionate manner by comparison with others (special damage) and exceeds the limits of the economic risks inherent in operating in the sector concerned (unusual damage), without the legislative measure that gave rise to the alleged damage being justified by a general economic interest . . ."

The CFI found that, in the circumstances, those conditions were not satisfied. It did not therefore need to address the question whether the Community could in principle be liable in damages for the consequences of a lawful act. However, the CFI was more forthright in the case of *FIAMM*.[82] In 1999, the Dispute Settlement Board of the WTO granted authorisation for the USA to take retaliatory measures in the form of higher customs duties against certain Community imports, on the basis that the Community's 1998 reforms to the common organisation of the market in bananas remained incompatible with certain provisions of the GATT. Several Community undertakings whose exports to the USA were affected by the retaliatory measures brought an action under Articles 235 and 288 EC against the Council and Commission seeking compensation for their losses. Insofar as the applicants sought compensation on the basis that the Community institutions had acted *unlawfully*, their action failed on the grounds that, since the WTO agreements are not among the rules in the light of which the Community Courts are entitled to review the legality of Community measures, there was no basis upon which the applicants could establish that the Council or Commission had committed any unlawful act. However, the CFI held that the Community institutions may also, in principle, incur liability to compensate undertakings forced to bear a disproportionate burden of the consequences which result even from *lawful* Community action. For these purposes, the applicants were required to fulfil three conditions. First, actual damage must be sustained; this was satisfied insofar as there had in fact been an appreciable reduction in the applicants' exports to the USA. Secondly, there must be a direct causal link between the damage sustained and the conduct of the Community institutions; again, this was satisfied insofar as the adoption of the bananas regulations had led the USA

---

[82] Joined Cases T–69/00, T–151/00, T–301/00, T–320/00, T–383/00 and T–135/01 *FIAMM* (Judgment of December 14, 2005). See also Case T–383/00 *Beamglow v European Parliament* (Judgment of December 14, 2005) paras 169–217.

to impose its retaliatory measures against the applicants. Finally, the damage sustained must be unusual and special in nature; it was at this hurdle that the applicants' action for compensation failed, since the commercial losses they had incurred did not exceed the limits of the economic risks inherent in their export operations.

Thus, although *FIAMM* seems to have confirmed the principle of Community liability in respect of lawful acts, it has also indicated that the threshold for obtaining compensation in such circumstances is high indeed.

Concurrent liability of the Community and the Member States

13–066   Under the system established by the Treaties, it is common for Community legislation to require implementation by the national authorities of the Member States. If a person suffers damage as a result of such implementation, the question may arise whether he or she should commence proceedings against the competent national authorities in the national courts (which might have to ask the Court of Justice for a preliminary ruling), or against the Community under the second paragraph of Article 288 EC. It has been persuasively argued[83] that a claimant should in these circumstances have the right to choose whether to bring proceedings in the national courts or the Community Courts, but that solution would involve a departure from the case law.

The Court has held that, in some cases, proceedings under the second paragraph of Article 288 EC will only be admissible if the applicant has exhausted any cause of action he or she might have against the national authorities in the domestic forum.[84] It seems that such a cause of action must be pursued first where the actions of the national authorities, although based on Community legislation, are a more direct cause of the damage suffered by the applicant.[85] However, where the conduct in question is in fact the responsibility of a Community institution (e.g., where the national body was acting under its instructions), it is the Community Courts which have jurisdiction.[86] In any event, it is not necessary to exhaust any national rights of action that may be available where they are not capable of providing an effective means of protection for the applicant and compensating him for the damage he claims to have suffered.[87]

---

[83] See Wils, "Concurrent Liability of the Community and a Member State" (1992) 17 E.L.Rev. 191, 204–206.

[84] See e.g. Case 175/84 *Krohn v Commission* [1986] E.C.R. 753, para.27.

[85] See e.g. Case 133/79 *Sucrimex v Commission* [1980] E.C.R. 1299; Case C–282/90 *Vreugdenhil v Commission* [1992] E.C.R. I–1937.

[86] See e.g. Case 175/84 *Krohn v Commission* [1986] E.C.R. 753.

[87] *ibid.*, para.27; Case 20/88 *Roquette Frères v Commission* [1989] E.C.R. 1553, para.15.

Damage

In proceedings under the second paragraph of Article 288 EC, an **13–067** applicant may in principle recover actual financial loss[88] as well as loss of profits.[89] In order to succeed, the applicant must either quantify the loss which it claims to have suffered or point to evidence on the basis of which its nature and extent can be assessed.[90] It is also possible to recover damages for non-material injury, such as the effect on the applicant's integrity and reputation of defamatory remarks made by the defendant.[91] In staff cases, small amounts have been awarded for shock, disturbance and uneasiness.[92] Moreover, the Court has acknowledged that it may be asked "to declare the Community liable for imminent damage foreseeable with sufficient certainty even if the damage cannot yet be precisely assessed".[93] However, the applicant must take steps to mitigate any damage[94] and will not be able to recover compensation where it could have passed the loss on to its customers.[95] The applicant must also show that the damage it has suffered "exceeds the limits of the economic risks inherent in operating in the sector concerned".[96]

Where a claim under the second paragraph of Article 288 EC is successful, the Court does not normally make a specific award of damages. Instead, the judgment will usually establish the acts or omissions giving rise to liability and, if appropriate, make an award of interest. It will then order the parties to attempt to reach an agreement, within a specified period, on the amount of compensation payable. The judgment will require the parties to transmit to the Court a statement of their views, with supporting figures, if they are unable to reach agreement.[97]

---

[88] See Joined Cases 5, 7 and 13 to 24/66 *Kampffmeyer v Commission* [1967] E.C.R. 245; Case 74/74 *CNTA v Commission* [1975] E.C.R. 533.

[89] See e.g. Joined Cases 5, 7 and 13 to 24/66 *Kampffmeyer v Commission* [1967] E.C.R. 245. *cf.* Joined Cases 54 to 60/76 *Compagnie Industrielle du Comité de Loheac v Council and Commission* [1977] E.C.R. 645.

[90] See Case T–277/97 *Ismeri Europa Srl v Court of Auditors* [1999] E.C.R. II–1825, para.67.

[91] See e.g. Case T–277/97 *Ismeri Europa Srl v Court of Auditors* [1999] E.C.R. II–1825, paras 80–94.

[92] See e.g. Joined Cases 7/56 and 3 to 7/57 *Algera v Common Assembly* [1957 and 1958] E.C.R. 39, 66–67.

[93] Joined Cases 56 to 60/74 *Kampffmeyer v Commission and Council* [1976] E.C.R. 711, para.6. *cf.* Case T–230/95 *BAI v Commission* [1999] E.C.R. II–123.

[94] See Case 120/83 R *Raznoimport v Commission* [1983] E.C.R. 2573, para.14.

[95] See Joined Cases 64 and 113/76, 167 and 239/78, 27, 28 and 45/79 *Dumortier Frères v Council* [1979] E.C.R. 3091, para.15; Case 238/78 *Ireks-Arkady v Council and Commission* [1979] E.C.R. 2955, para.14; Joined Cases 241, 242 and 245 to 250/78 *DGV v Council and Commission* [1979] E.C.R. 3017, para.15; Joined Cases 261 and 262/78 *Interquell Stärke v Council and Commission* [1979] E.C.R. 3045, para.17 (the so-called "Gritz and Quellmehl" cases, after the products with which they were concerned). See Rudden and Bishop, "Gritz and quellmehl: pass it on" (1981) 6 E.L.Rev. 243.

[96] Case 59/83 *Biovilac v EEC* [1984] E.C.R. 4057, para.28.

[97] See e.g. the "Gritz and Quellmehl" cases (referred to above); Case 145/83 *Adams v Commission* [1985] E.C.R. 3539. *cf.* Case C–308/87 *Grifoni v EAEC* [1994] E.C.R. I–341, where the parties were unable to reach agreement and the Court had to quantify the precise amount of compensation to which the applicant was entitled.

Causation

13–068   The Court has said that the second paragraph of Article 288 EC
does not require the Community "to make good every harmful
consequence, even a remote one, of unlawful legislation".[98] The
applicant must therefore establish that the damage is a "sufficiently
direct consequence of the unlawful conduct".[99] In *Compagnia Italiana Alcool v Commission*,[100] the Court said that there was no causal
link between the damage allegedly suffered by the applicant and a
deficiency in the statement of reasons contained in a Commission
decision. As the Court explained, "[i]f that deficiency had not
existed, the damage allegedly suffered by [the applicant] would have
been the same". The chain of causation may be broken by, for
example, the actions of national authorities or by the behaviour of
the applicant itself. In this respect, traders are expected to behave in
a prudent manner and to apprise themselves of the conditions on the
markets in which they operate. If they fall short of this standard, the
Community will not be held responsible for any loss that ensues.[101]

Limitation

13–069   Article 46 of the Statute of the Court provides that "[p]roceedings
against the Communities in matters arising from non-contractual
liability shall be barred after a period of five years from the
occurrence of the event giving rise thereto". That period is suspended if the aggrieved party brings proceedings for annulment or
failure to act against the institution concerned.[102] The limitation
period does not start to run "before all the requirements governing
an obligation to provide compensation for damage are satisfied and
in particular before the damage to be made good has mater-
ialised".[103] Thus, where the liability of the Community derives from a
legislative measure, the limitation period does not begin "before the
injurious effects of that measure have been produced".[104] Where the
cause of the damage suffered by the applicant is an administrative
act or omission, the limitation period does not start to run until he
or she becomes aware of it.[105]

---

[98] Joined Cases 64 and 113/76, 167 and 239/78, 27, 28 and 45/79 *Dumortier Frères v Council*
[1979] E.C.R. 3091, para.21.
[99] *ibid.*
[100] Case C–358/90 [1992] E.C.R. I–2457, para.47.
[101] See Case 169/73 *Compagnie Continentale v Council* [1975] E.C.R. 117, paras 22–32; Case
26/81 *Oleifici Mediterranei v EEC* [1982] E.C.R. 3057, paras 22–24.
[102] See Joined Cases 5, 7 and 13 to 24/66 *Kampffmeyer v Commission* [1967] E.C.R. 245, 260.
[103] Joined Cases 256, 257 and 267/80 and 5/81 *Birra Wührer v Council and Commission* [1982]
E.C.R. 85, para.10; Case 51/81 *De Franceschi v Council and Commission* [1982] E.C.R. 117,
para.10.
[104] *ibid.*
[105] See Case 145/83 *Adams v Commission* [1985] E.C.R. 3539, paras 50–51.

Impact of the Constitutional Treaty (CT)

13–070 The CT contains significant reforms to several of the topics covered in this chapter, including:

— a more expeditious procedure for the imposition of sanctions upon defaulting Member States within the context of enforcement proceedings (para.11–028);
— broadening the range of bodies whose acts/failures to act are to be considered reviewable for the purposes of the action for annulment/action for failure to act (para.11–029);
— limited rights of standing for the national parliaments and the Committee of the Regions to bring actions for annulment for themselves (para.11–029);
— a modest liberalisation of the standing requirements for natural and legal persons to bring actions for annulment, in particular, through the partial suppression of the individual concern criterion (para.11–029);
— revisions to the drafting of the plea of illegality, in particular, as regards the authors of the act whose legality is under dispute (para.11–030).

Further reading

Infringement proceedings against Member States
Bonnie, "Commission Discretion under Article 171(2) EC" (1998) 23 E.L.Rev. 537.
Dashwood and White, "Enforcement Actions under Articles 169 and 170 EEC" (1989) 14 E.L.Rev. 388.
Evans, "The Enforcement Procedure of Article 169 EEC: Commission Discretion" (1979) 4 E.L.Rev. 442.
Everling, "The Member States of the European Community before their Court of Justice" (1984) 9 E.L.Rev. 215.
Rawlings, "Engaged Elites: Citizen Action and Institutional Attitudes in Commission Enforcement" (2000) 6 E.L.J. 4.
Snyder, "The Effectiveness of European Community Law: Institutions, Processes, Tools and Techniques" (1993) 56 M.L.R. 19.
Wennerås, "A New Dawn for Commission Enforcement Under Articles 226 and 228 EC: General and Persistent (GAP) Infringements, Lump Sums and Penalty Payments" (2006) 43 C.M.L.Rev. 31.

The action for annulment
Albors Llorens, *Private Parties in European Community Law: Challenging Community Measures* (Clarendon Press, 1996).

Albors Llorens, "The Standing of Private Parties to Challenge Community Measures: Has the European Court Missed the Boat?" [2003] C.L.J. 72.

Arnull, "Private Applicants and the Action for Annulment Under Article 173 of the EC Treaty" (1995) 32 C.M.L.Rev. 7.

Arnull, "Private Applicants and the Action for Annulment since *Codorniu*" (2001) 38 C.M.L.Rev. 7.

Gormley, "Judicial Review in EC and EU Law—Some Architectural Malfunctions and Design Improvements?" (2001) 4 C.Y.E.L.S. 167.

Greaves, "*Locus standi* under Article 173 EEC when Seeking Annulment of a Regulation" (1986) 11 E.L.Rev. 119.

Harding, "The Private Interest in Challenging Community Action" (1980) 5 E.L.Rev. 354.

Joliet, "The Reimbursement of Election Expenses: A Forgotten Dispute" (1994) 19 E.L.Rev. 243.

Lenaerts and Corthaut, "Judicial Review as a Contribution to the Development of European Constitutionalism" (2003) 22 Y.E.L. 1.

Lenaerts and Vanhamme, "Procedural Rights of Private Parties in the Community Administrative Process" (1997) 34 C.M.L.Rev. 531.

Maselis and Gilliams, "Rights of Complainants in Community Law" (1997) 22 E.L.Rev. 103.

Neuwahl, "Article 173, paragraph 4 EC: Past, Present and Possible Future" (1996) 21 E.L.Rev. 17.

Stein and Vining, "Citizen Access to Judicial Review of Administrative Action in a Transnational and Federal Context" (1976) 70 A.J.I.L. 219.

Usher, "Judicial Review of Community Acts and the Private Litigant" in Campbell and Voyatzi (eds), *Legal Reasoning and Judicial Interpretation of Community Law* (Trenton, 1996).

Usher, "Direct and Individual Concern—An Effective Remedy or a Conventional Solution?" (2003) 28 E.L.Rev. 575.

Van Nuffel, "What's in a Member State? Central and Decentralized Authorities before the Community Courts" (2001) 38 C.M.L.Rev. 871.

Ward, *Judicial Review and the Rights of Private Parties in EC Law* (2000).

Ward, "Judicial Architecture at the Cross-roads—Private Parties and Challenge to EC Measures Post-Jégo-Quéré" (2001) 4 C.Y.E.L.S. 413.

Ward, "*Locus standi* under Article 230(4) of the EC Treaty: Crafting a Coherent Test for a 'Wobbly Polity'"(2003) 22 Y.E.L. 45.

Other direct actions: failure to act; plea of illegality; damages actions

Barav, "The Exception of Illegality in Community Law: A Critical Analysis" (1974) 11 C.M.L.Rev. 366.

Due, "Legal Remedies for the Failure of European Community Institutions to Act in Conformity with EEC Treaty Provisions" (1990–91) 14 Fordham International Law Journal 341.

Heukels and McDonnell (eds), *The Action for Damages in Community Law* (1997).

Hilson, "The Role of Discretion in EC Law on Non-Contractual Liability" (2005) 42 C.M.L.Rev. 677.

Hunnings, "The Stanley Adams Affair or the Bitter Bit" (1987) 24 C.M.L.Rev. 65.

Odudu, Annotation of *Commission v European Central Bank* (2004) 41 C.M.L.Rev. 1073.

Tridimas, "Liability for Breach of Community Law: Growing Up and Mellowing Down?" (2001) 38 C.M.L.Rev. 301.

Vogt, "Indirect Judicial Protection in EC Law: The Case of the Plea of Illegality" (2006) 31 E.L.Rev. 364.

Wils, "Concurrent Liability of the Community and a Member State" (1992) 17 E.L.Rev. 191.

CHAPTER 14

PRELIMINARY RULINGS

Guide to this Chapter: This chapter considers the ECJ's **14–001** jurisdiction to deliver preliminary rulings under Article 234 EC. This is a crucial means by which national judges seek guidance from the Court about the proper interpretation of Community law as it is to be applied and enforced within the domestic legal orders. Preliminary references not only account for a substantial proportion of the Court's workload; they have also provided the Court with the opportunity to develop many of the fundamental principles of Community law (including direct effect and supremacy). We will consider the main issues which arise within the Article 234 EC procedure: for example, the nature of the questions which may be referred to the ECJ; and the range of courts and tribunals which are actually capable of making references. Particular attention will be paid to the situations in which national courts have a discretion about whether to make a reference, and those in which the national courts are under a positive obligation to do so. The latter includes the use of Article 234 EC not as a means to interpret Community secondary legislation, but to challenge its very validity. In this way, the Article 234 EC procedure provides a valuable complement to the action for annulment under Article 230 EC (which was analysed in Chapter 13). Finally, we will discuss the special arrangements governing preliminary references as regards Title IV of Part Three EC on visas, asylum and immigration policy; and as regards Title VI TEU on police and judicial co-operation in criminal matters.

Much of the responsibility for applying the rules laid down in the EC **14–002** Treaty and acts of the Community legislature belongs to the national courts of the Member States, but this gives rise to a potential problem. If the internal market is to work properly, the relevant rules must have the same effect in all the Member States. However, the nature of the judicial process and varying legal traditions mean that, left to their own devices, it would be highly unlikely that courts in, say, Edinburgh would always apply Community law in the same way as courts in, say, Athens. To help safeguard the uniform application of Community law, Article 234 EC therefore lays down a procedure which enables national courts to refer to the Court of Justice questions of Community law that they must decide before giving judgment.

It is hard to exaggerate the importance of this procedure. Courts can obviously only decide issues raised by cases brought before them. The reference procedure has brought before the Court of Justice a host of issues which it might not otherwise have had a chance to consider and has enabled it to influence directly the application of Community law in the Member States. The Court has described the procedure as "the veritable cornerstone of the operation of the internal market, since it plays a fundamental role in ensuring that the law established by the Treaties retains its Community character with a view to guaranteeing that the law has the same effect in all circumstances in all the Member States of the European Union".[1]

As the table below shows, 221 of the 474 new cases brought before the Court of Justice in 2005 were references from national courts. This reflects the growing practical importance of Community law in the Member States. However, there is quite a wide variation in the number of references from each Member State. In 2005, the highest number of references came from Germany (51), followed by the Netherlands (36). United Kingdom courts made 12 references. Historically, Germany is well ahead of all the other Member States, with a total of 1465 references, followed by Italy with 862 and France with 693 by the end of 2005. Once allowance has been made for length of membership, the variation seems to be due, mainly if not exclusively, to differences between Member States in the volume of economic activity in areas subject to Community law.[2] The large number of references made by German courts is widely thought to have increased the impact of German law and legal thinking on the development of Community law.

---

[1] See the Court's report on the application of the TEU in "The Proceedings of the Court of Justice and Court of First Instance of the European Communities", May 22–26, 1995 (No.15/95) para.11.

[2] See Tridimas and Tridimas, "National courts and the European Court of Justice: a public choice analysis of the preliminary reference procedure" (2004) 24 *International Review of Law and Economics* 125, 132–133.

New cases brought before the Court of Justice in 2005 14–003
(cumulative totals in brackets)

Direct actions	References for preliminary rulings				Appeals[a]	Total[b]
179	221				67	474
	From Germany	*From Italy*	*From the UK*	*From France*		
	51 (1465)	18 (862)	12 (408)	17 (693)		

[a] Includes appeals concerning interim measures and interventions.
[b] Includes other forms of procedure.
Source: Statistics Concerning the Judicial Activity of the Court of Justice, *http://europa.eu.int/cj/en/instit/presentationfr/index—cje.htm.*

Article 234 EC provides as follows:

"The Court of Justice shall have jurisdiction to give preliminary rulings concerning:

   (a) the interpretation of this Treaty;
   (b) the validity and interpretation of acts of the institutions of the Community and of the ECB;
   (c) the interpretation of the statutes of bodies established by an act of the Council, where those statutes so provide.

Where such a question is raised before any court or tribunal of a Member State, that court or tribunal may, if it considers that a decision on the question is necessary to enable it to give judgment, request the Court of Justice to give a ruling thereon.
Where any such question is raised in a case pending before a court or tribunal of a Member State, against whose decisions there is no judicial remedy under national law, that court or tribunal shall bring the matter before the Court of Justice."

As we shall see, a reference to the Court of Justice under Article 234 EC may in principle be made at any stage in the proceedings pending before the national court. The ruling of the Court of Justice is interlocutory in that it constitutes a step in the proceedings before the national court, which must apply the ruling to the facts of the case. It is in this sense that the ruling of the Court of Justice is preliminary. Thus, the national court must be in a position to take account of the ruling of the Court of Justice when giving judgment.

The Court of Justice has no jurisdiction to give a preliminary ruling if the proceedings before the referring court have already been terminated.[3]

The Court of Justice enjoys similar jurisdiction under the Euratom Treaty.[4] Provision for the Court of Justice to give preliminary rulings was also made in relation to a number of conventions drawn up between the Member States. An example is the 1968 Brussels Convention on jurisdiction and the enforcement of judgments in civil and commercial matters,[5] now replaced by a Council regulation adopted under Title IV of Part Three of the EC Treaty.[6] The preliminary rulings mechanisms applicable under the Brussels Convention did not operate in exactly the same way as Article 234 EC. In particular, while under Article 234 EC a reference may be made by any national court or tribunal, under the Brussels Convention that facility was available only to superior national courts and other courts when sitting in an appellate capacity. The model offered by the Brussels Convention was followed by the Member States when Title IV was introduced at Amsterdam, for Article 234 EC applies in that particular context in a modified form by virtue of Article 68 EC. Article 68 EC is considered in more detail below.[7]

Questions which may be referred

14–004   Article 234 EC enables any question of EC law to be referred to the Court of Justice for a preliminary ruling by any national court or tribunal which considers a decision on the question "necessary to enable it to give judgment". The question may be raised either by one of the parties or by the judge of his/her own motion.[8] A decision is "necessary" for these purposes if the national court sees it as a step, which need not be the final one, in its strategy for disposing of the case. The Community point need not be conclusive.[9] Questions which may be the subject of a reference include, as well as questions on the interpretation of the EC Treaty itself, questions on one of the amending Treaties or on one of the Treaties of Accession, and questions on the validity and interpretation of acts of the Community institutions, such as regulations, directives and decisions of

---

[3] Case 338/85 *Pardini v Ministero del Commercio con l'Estero* [1988] E.C.R. 2041, para.11. *cf.* Case C–3/90 *Bernini* [1992] E.C.R. I–1071; *Magnavision v General Optical Council* [1987] 2 C.M.L.R. 262 (DC).

[4] See Art.150 Euratom.

[5] See [1998] O.J. C27/1.

[6] Reg.44/2001, [2001] O.J. L12/1. Legal basis: Arts 61(c) and 67(1) EC.

[7] See also Ch.10.

[8] Case 166/73 *Rheinmühlen v Einfuhr- und Vorratsstelle Getreide* [1974] E.C.R. 33. See also Joined Cases C–87/90, C–88/90 and C–89/90 *Verholen* [1991] E.C.R. I–3757.

[9] See e.g. Case C–453/99 *Courage v Crehan* [2001] 5 C.M.L.R. 28; Case C–315/92, *Verband Sozialer Wettbewerb v Clinique Laboratories and Estée Lauder* [1994] E.C.R. I–317; Joined Cases 36 and 71/80 *Irish Creamery Milk Suppliers Association v Ireland* [1981] E.C.R. 735; *Polydor Ltd v Harlequin Record Shops Ltd* [1980] 2 C.M.L.R. 413 (CA).

the Council or Commission and non-binding measures such as recommendations.[10] Acts of the European Parliament may also be the subject of references to the Court of Justice.[11] Cases may be referred on the interpretation of an agreement concluded by the Community with a third State, since such an agreement constitutes, as far as the Community is concerned, an act of one of the institutions.[12] References may also be made on whether a provision of Community law produces direct effect, that is, whether it confers rights on individuals which national courts are bound to protect. However, the Court has no jurisdiction under Article 234 EC to give preliminary rulings on provisions of the TEU other than those which are specifically mentioned in Article 46 TEU.[13]

National courts remain free to bring matters of Community law before the Court of Justice under Article 234 EC whenever they feel it necessary to do so: they are not precluded from doing so by the fact that the point in question seems already to have been settled by the Court.[14] Indeed, a national court may if it wishes make more than one reference in the same proceedings. This was acknowledged in *Pretore di Salò v Persons Unknown*,[15] where the Court said that a second reference "may be justified when the national court encounters difficulties in understanding or applying the judgment, when it refers a fresh question of law to the Court, or again when it submits new considerations which might lead the Court to give a different answer to a question submitted earlier". In practice, more than one reference in the same case happens only exceptionally.[16]

---

[10] See e.g. Case C–322/88 *Grimaldi v Fonds des Maladies Professionnelles* [1989] E.C.R. 4407.

[11] See e.g. Case 208/80 *Lord Bruce of Donington* [1981] E.C.R. 2205.

[12] See Case 181/73 *Haegeman v Belgium* [1974] E.C.R. 449; Opinion 1/76 [1977] E.C.R. 741; Case C–321/97 *Andersson v Swedish State* [1999] E.C.R. I–3551. The Court has no jurisdiction under Art.234 to rule on the interpretation of the EEA Agreement as regards its application in the EFTA States, only to situations which come within the Community legal order. See also Case C–53/96 *Hermès v FHT* [1998] E.C.R. I–3603; Joined Cases C–300/98 and C–392/98 *Parfums Christian Dior v Tuk Consultancy* [2000] E.C.R. I–11307; Case C–245/02 *Anheuser-Busch v Budvar* [2004] E.C.R. I–10989 (Court has jurisdiction to interpret TRIPs Agreement, to which both the Community and its Member States are parties); Case C–439/01 *Cipra and Kvasnicka v Bezirkshauptmannschaft Mistelbach* [2003] E.C.R. I–745 (AETR Agreement forms part of Community law and Court has jurisdiction to interpret it).

[13] See Case C–167/94 *Grau Gomis* [1995] E.C.R. I–1023. Note that the Court has no jurisdiction to interpret provisions of Community law as regards its purported application with effect before the relevant Member State's accession to the EU: see Case C–321/97 *Andersson v Swedish State* [1999] E.C.R. I–3551; Case C–302/04 *Ynos kft* (Judgment of January 10, 2006).

[14] See Case 283/81 *CILFIT v Ministry of Health* [1982] E.C.R. 3415, para.15.

[15] Case 14/86 [1987] E.C.R. 2545.

[16] For examples, see *Pierik*, Case 117/77 [1978] E.C.R. 825 and Case 182/78 [1979] E.C.R. 1977; *Foglia v Novello*, Case 104/79 [1980] E.C.R. 745 and Case 244/80 [1981] E.C.R. 3045; *CILFIT*, Case 283/81 [1982] E.C.R. 3415 and Case 77/83 [1984] E.C.R. 1257; *Francovich*, Joined Cases C–6/90 and C–9/90 [1991] E.C.R. I–5357 and Case C–479/93 [1995] E.C.R. I–3843; *Factortame*, Case C–213/89 [1990] E.C.R. I–2433, Case C–221/89 [1991] E.C.R. I–3905 and Joined Cases C–46/93 and C–48/93 [1996] E.C.R. I–1029; *Kaba*, Case C–356/98 [2000] E.C.R. I–2623 and Case C–466/00 [2003] E.C.R. I–2219.

In *Dzodzi v Belgium*,[17] the Court of Justice held that it has jurisdiction under Article 234 EC to give preliminary rulings on the effect of provisions of Community law which are applicable in the action pending before the national court only because their scope has been extended by national law. The Court took the view that the proper functioning of the Community legal order made it imperative that provisions of Community law be given a uniform interpretation regardless of the circumstances in which they fell to be applied. It proceeded to deal with the substance of the questions which had been put to it.[18] The Court seems to have been concerned that, had it declined jurisdiction to give preliminary rulings in these circumstances, parallel lines of national case law might have developed, one concerning the interpretation of provisions of Community law applicable in their own right, the other concerning the interpretation of the same provisions when applicable solely by virtue of national law. The possibility that cases in the second category might have influenced cases in the first could in principle have jeopardised the uniform application of Community law.

14–005   This point is perhaps best explained by looking at a case where doubt was cast on the continued applicability of the *Dzodzi* approach, namely *Kleinwort Benson v City of Glasgow District Council*.[19] In that case, the English Court of Appeal made a reference on the interpretation of the Brussels Convention.[20] In the United Kingdom, rules based on the Brussels Convention had been laid down by Act of Parliament (the Civil Jurisdiction and Judgments Act 1982) to provide for the allocation of civil jurisdiction between England and Wales, Scotland and Northern Ireland. In *Kleinwort Benson*, the Court of Appeal asked the Court of Justice for guidance on the meaning of the Convention so that it could decide whether, under the 1982 Act, the dispute between the parties fell within the jurisdiction of the English or Scottish courts. The Court of Justice said it had no jurisdiction to answer. The national court had made the reference to enable it to apply, not the Convention, but its national law. Moreover, the relevant Act, although modelled on the Convention, did not wholly reproduce its terms. The Court concluded that the Act did not render the Convention applicable as such to cases which fell outside its scope. Moreover, the Act did not require United Kingdom courts to follow the interpretation of the Convention supplied by the Court of Justice, but merely to have regard to it when applying its national law. The reference procedure

---

[17] Joined Cases C–297/88 and C–197/89 [1990] E.C.R. I–3763, followed in Case C–231/89 *Gmurzynska-Bscher v Oberfinanzdirektion Köln* [1990] E.C.R. I–4003.
[18] Which concerned the rules on the free movement of persons.
[19] Case C–346/93 [1995] E.C.R. I–615.
[20] The reference was not made under Art.234 EC but under a special Protocol on the interpretation of the Convention by the Court of Justice. However, this has no bearing on the following discussion.

did not in the Court's view envisage that it should give purely advisory rulings which lacked binding effect.

In two subsequent cases, the Court appeared to retreat from the line taken in *Kleinwort Benson*. The *Dzodzi* approach continued to apply where a Member State had chosen to align its domestic legislation with Community law so as to apply the same treatment to purely internal situations as that accorded to situations governed by Community law. The cases in question[21] involved domestic rules on the imposition of tax. The Court explained that "where in regulating internal situations, domestic legislation adopts the same solutions as those adopted in Community law so as to provide for one single procedure in comparable situations, it is clearly in the Community interest that, in order to forestall future differences of interpretation, provisions or concepts taken from Community law should be interpreted uniformly, irrespective of the circumstances in which they are to apply".[22]

The Court's decision in *BIAO*[23] suggests that the decisive question is not whether the relevant Community provisions have been reproduced verbatim, but whether any interpretation given by the Court would be treated by the referring court as binding on it as a matter of national law. That decision (like *Leur-Bloem* and *Giloy*) was reached against the advice of Advocate General Jacobs, who pointed out[24] that it might mean that the Court has to take a view on questions of national law which are both complex and controversial. The Advocate General went on to explain[25] that "The referring court will not as a matter of Community law be bound by the Court's judgment, which will thus inevitably be (again as a matter of Community law) purely advisory. Such a consequence clearly alters the function of the Court as envisaged in the Treaty".

In any case, however, the Court has no jurisdiction under Article 234 EC to deliver interpretative rulings concerning provisions of Community law, where the subject-matter of the dispute is not connected in any way with any of the situations contemplated by the Treaties.[26] Thus, for example, in the *Vajnai* case, the Court dismissed a request for a preliminary ruling on the compatibility with Article 6

---

[21] Case C–28/95 *Leur-Bloem v Inspecteur der Belastingdienst/Ondernemingen Amsterdam 2* [1997] E.C.R. I–4161; Case C–130/95 *Giloy v Hauptzollamt Frankfurt am Main-Ost* [1997] E.C.R. I–4291. See also Case C–53/96 *Hermès v FHT* [1998] E.C.R. I–3603, paras 32 and 33 (TRIPS); Case C–1/99 *Kofisa Italia v Ministero delle Finanze* [2001] E.C.R. I–207; Case C–222/01 *BAT v Hauptzollamt Krefeld* [2004] E.C.R. I–4683, paras 39–41; Case C–3/04 *Poseidon Chartering* (Judgment of March 16, 2006), paras 16–18.

[22] Case C–28/95 *Leur-Bloem v Inspecteur der Belastingdienst/Ondernemingen Amsterdam 2* [1997] E.C.R. I–4161, para.32; Case C–130/95 *Giloy v Hauptzollamt Frankfurt am Main-Ost* [1997] E.C.R. I–4291, para.28. The Court's conclusion was reached against the advice of Advocate General Jacobs: see in particular pp I–4180 and I–4187.

[23] Case C–306/99 [2003] E.C.R. I–1, para.92.

[24] Para.57 of the Opinion.

[25] Para.61.

[26] e.g. Case C–299/95 *Kremzow* [1997] E.C.R. I–2629.

TEU, the Race Directive 2000/43,[27] and the Charter of Fundamental Rights,[28] of a rule of Hungarian criminal law penalising the public display of certain "totalitarian symbols", where the proceedings in question (against a Hungarian national) were wholly unconnected with Community law.[29]

Courts and tribunals of the Member States

14–006   The power to make a reference under Article 234 EC belongs to "any court or tribunal of a Member State". That notion has traditionally been interpreted broadly by the Court of Justice. In *Dorsch Consult Ingenieurgesellschaft v Bundesbaugesellschaft Berlin*, the Court said: "In order to determine whether a body making a reference is a court or tribunal for the purposes of Article [234] of the Treaty, which is a question governed by Community law alone, the Court takes account of a number of factors, such as whether the body is established by law, whether it is permanent, whether its jurisdiction is compulsory, whether its procedure is *inter partes*, whether it applies rules of law and whether it is independent".[30] Thus, in *Vaassen v Beamtenfonds Mijnbedrijf*,[31] a Dutch social security tribunal which gave "non-binding opinions" and which did not consider itself a court or tribunal under Dutch law was held to be a court or tribunal of a Member State for the purposes of Article 234 EC. The Court reached that conclusion because the members of the tribunal were appointed, its chairman designated and its rules of procedure laid down by the responsible minister. Moreover, the tribunal was a permanent body which heard disputes according to an adversarial procedure and it was bound to apply rules of law. By contrast, in *Corbiau v Administration des Contributions*,[32] the Court held that the notion of a court or tribunal for the purposes of Article 234 EC was confined to authorities which had no connection with the body which had adopted the measure being challenged in the main action. In that case, the reference had been made by a Luxembourg tax tribunal, who was linked organically with the national tax authorities, one of the parties to the action. He was therefore held not to be a court or tribunal within the meaning of Article 234 EC and the reference was dismissed as inadmissible.[33]

A body will not be considered a "court or tribunal of a Member State" within the meaning of Article 234 EC unless it is closely

---

[27] [2000] O.J. L180/22.
[28] [2000] O.J. C364/1.
[29] Case C–328/04 *Vajnai* (Judgment of October 6, 2005).
[30] Case C–54/96 [1997] E.C.R. I–4961, para.23. The requirement that the procedure should be *inter partes* is not absolute: see Case C–17/00 *De Coster* [2001] E.C.R. I–9445, para.14.
[31] Case 61/65 [1966] E.C.R. 261. See also Case C–195/98 *OG v Austria* [2000] E.C.R. I–10497.
[32] Case C–24/92 [1993] E.C.R. I–1277. Cf Case C–516/99 *Schmid* [2002] E.C.R. I–4573.
[33] See also, e.g. Case C–53/03 *Syfait* [2005] E.C.R. I–4609.

linked to "the organisation of legal remedies through the courts in the Member State in question". That requirement was laid down in *Nordsee v Reederei Mond*,[34] where an arbitrator appointed under a private contract was held not to be entitled to make a reference. The public authorities of the Member State concerned had not been involved in the decision by the parties to the contract to opt for arbitration, nor were those authorities automatically called upon to intervene in the proceedings before the arbitrator. However, the Court made it clear that a court or tribunal hearing an appeal against an arbitrator's award was entitled to make a reference under Article 234 EC.[35]

A body may only make use of the facility for which Article 234 EC provides if its functions are judicial rather than administrative in nature, in other words, if it is responsible for settling disputes through the application of rules of law.[36] Where a body exercises both judicial and administrative functions, it may not request a preliminary ruling when performing its administrative tasks.[37] In several recent cases, the Court has dismissed references as inadmissible on the basis that they have been made by bodies exercising non-judicial functions, such as registering contracts for the sale of land in the land register[38] or the transfer of a company's registered office in the commercial register.[39]

It is not clear whether this represents an attempt by the Court to reduce the burden of responding to references or whether it reflects increased recourse to the preliminary rulings procedure by national bodies which are not courts in the strict sense. In the *de Coster* case,[40] Advocate General Ruiz-Jarabo Colomer argued that the case law on what constituted a court or tribunal offered insufficient guidance to national bodies and was in need of rationalisation. He expressed concern about the number of bodies who might seek to refer in an enlarged EU and proposed a new, stricter test. He concluded that the body which had made the reference in that case was not a judicial one and was not therefore entitled to do so. The Court rejected the Advocate General's advice and applied the criteria set out in *Dorsch Consult*, concluding that the reference was admissible. It therefore seems to regard those criteria as striking the right balance between clarity and flexibility.

---

[34] Case 102/81 [1982] E.C.R. 1095. See para.13. See also Case C–125/04 *Dennit and Cordenier v Transorient-Mosaïque Voyages et Culture* (Judgment of January 27, 2005).

[35] See also Case C–393/92 *Almelo* [1994] E.C.R. I–1477. *cf.* Case C–126/97 *Eco Swiss China Time v Benetton International* [1999] E.C.R. I–3055.

[36] See e.g. Case C–111/94 *Job Centre* [1995] E.C.R. I–3361, paras 9–11; Case 138/80 *Borker* [1980] E.C.R. 1975, para.4.

[37] See Case C–192/98 *Ministero dei Lavori Pubblici* [1999] E.C.R. I–8583; Case C–440/98 *RAI* [1999] E.C.R. I–8597. *cf.* Case 14/86 *Pretore di Salò v Persons Unknown* [1987] E.C.R. 2545.

[38] Case C–178/99 *Salzmann* [2001] E.C.R. I–4421.

[39] Case C–86/00 *HSB-Wohnbau* [2001] E.C.R. I–5353. See also Case C–192/98 *ANAS* [1999] E.C.R. I–8583.

[40] Case C–17/00 [2001] E.C.R. I–9445.

The relationship between the Court of Justice and the national court

14–007   The relationship between the Court of Justice and the national court in proceedings under Article 234 EC is co-operative rather than hierarchical in nature. Both courts have distinct but complementary roles to play in finding a solution to the case which is in conformity with the requirements of Community law. A reference to the Court of Justice is not in any sense an appeal against the decision of the national court. There are technically no parties to the proceedings before the Court of Justice,[41] which may be regarded as a form of dialogue between that court and the referring court. The parties to the action before the referring court have the right, along with the Member States and the Commission, to submit written and oral observations to the Court of Justice in accordance with Article 23 of the Statute of the Court. That right is also extended to the Council or European Central Bank, where the validity of interpretation of an act of one of those bodies is in issue, and to the European Parliament and the Council where the validity or interpretation of an act adopted jointly by those institutions is in issue. In order to enable them to exercise that right, Article 23 requires the Court to notify the reference to those entitled to submit observations.[42] However, they only receive the reference itself, not any accompanying documents. The national court's order for reference should therefore be self-contained and self-explanatory.

The Court of Justice will not, in the context of a reference for a preliminary ruling, entertain a challenge to the jurisdiction of the referring court based on national law or to the facts set out by that court in its order for reference.[43] Nor will the Court of Justice rule on the application of the law to the facts or the compatibility of national law with the requirements of Community law.[44] These are matters within the exclusive jurisdiction of the national court in proceedings under Article 234 EC. The questions referred should be couched in terms which pose a general question of Community law rather than the concrete issue as it falls to be decided in the instant case. If they are not, the Court of Justice may reformulate them. Questions may also be reformulated if the Court of Justice considers this necessary to furnish the national court with all the elements of Community law which it requires to give judgment[45] or to avoid an

---

[41] See Case 69/85 *Wünsche v Germany* [1986] E.C.R. 947, para.14.

[42] As well as to the EFTA States which are parties to the EEA Agreement and the EFTA Surveillance Authority and sometimes non-member States, who also have the right in certain cases to submit observations: see Art.23 of the Statute, third and fourth paragraphs.

[43] See Case C–435/97 *WWF v Autonome Provinz Bozen* [1999] E.C.R. I–5613, paras 28–29; Case C–198/01 *Consorzio Industrie Fiammiferi v Autorità Garante* [2003] 5 C.M.L.R. 16, para.62.

[44] See e.g. Joined Cases C–332/92, C–333/92 and C–335/92 *Eurico Italia* [1994] E.C.R. I–711; Case C–295/97 *Piaggio v IFITALIA* [1999] E.C.R. I–3735.

[45] See e.g. Case 28/85 *Deghillage v Caisse Primaire d'Assurance Maladie* [1986] E.C.R. 991, para.13; Case C–221/89 *The Queen v Secretary of State for Transport, ex parte Factortame* [1991] E.C.R. I–3905.

issue which the Court would prefer not to address.[46] The Court will not, at the request of one of the parties to the main proceedings, examine questions which have not been submitted to it by the national court,[47] but it may consider provisions which the national court has not cited in the text of its question.[48]

In *Arsenal Football Club v Matthew Reed*, the referring court refused to follow the ruling given by the Court of Justice because it thought that Court had exceeded its jurisdiction under Article 234 EC. The case concerned an attempt by Arsenal to prevent Reed from selling souvenirs bearing official Arsenal logos outside its ground. It turned on the effect of a Community directive on trade marks and that issue was referred to the Court of Justice by the High Court.[49] The Court of Justice made it clear that there was an infringement in circumstances such as those of the main action.[50] However, the High Court gave judgment for Reed[51] on the basis that the Court had exceeded its jurisdiction under Article 234 EC by making findings of fact which were inconsistent with those made by the High Court before the reference was made.

The High Court's judgment was later overturned by the Court of Appeal,[52] but the case emphasises the delicate nature of the relationship between the Court of Justice and the national courts and the care the Court of Justice needs to take when drafting preliminary rulings.[53] The Court clearly thought that the national judge had underestimated the risk that the essential function of a mark might be compromised in a case such as this. However, it failed to express that view in sufficiently objective terms, crucial passages of its judgment referring directly to the parties to the main action. That does not mean, however, that the referring court was justified in giving a judgment which effectively ignored the guidance it had been given. The remedy for a national court which is confronted with a preliminary ruling it thinks is based on a misunderstanding or misrepresentation of the facts is to make a further reference.[54] Why did the High Court reject that course, given that, as the judge, Laddie J, acknowledged, "national courts do not make references to the ECJ with the intention of ignoring the result"?[55]

---

[46] e.g. the horizontal effect of directives before the *Marshall* case. See Ch.5.
[47] See Case C–189/95 *Franzén* [1997] E.C.R. I–5909, para.79; Case C–435/97 *WWF v Autonome Provinz Bozen* [1999] E.C.R. I–5613, paras 28–29.
[48] See Case C–439/01 *Cipra and Kvasnicka v Bezirkshauptmannschaft Mistelbach* [2003] E.C.R. I–745, para.22.
[49] See [2001] 2 C.M.L.R. 23.
[50] See [2003] 1 C.M.L.R. 12.
[51] See [2003] 1 C.M.L.R. 13.
[52] See [2003] 2 C.M.L.R. 25.
[53] See Arnull (2003) 40 C.M.L.Rev. 753.
[54] For a recent discussion, see Tridimas, "Knocking on heaven's door: fragmentation, efficiency and defiance in the preliminary rulings procedure" (2003) 40 C.M.L.Rev. 1, 31–33.
[55] (2003) 1 C.M.L.R. 11, para.28.

The authors of a leading text on the reference procedure[56] divide cases in which national courts have resisted rulings supplied by the Court of Justice into three categories:

— Those where there is a conflict between Community law and values enshrined in national constitutions;
— Those where the national court takes the view that the Court of Justice has exceeded its jurisdiction; and
— Those where the national court has disliked the ruling given by the Court of Justice and sought to avoid applying it to the case in hand.

The *Arsenal* case seems to fall into both the second and the third categories. Laddie J's sympathies were clearly with Reed, who would probably have won under the English law as it stood before the trade marks directive was implemented. Laddie J appears to have seized on an apparent excess of jurisdiction by the ECJ in order to avoid applying the guidance it gave.

The discretion conferred by the second paragraph of Article 234 EC

14-008 Under the second paragraph of Article 234 EC, inferior national courts enjoy a discretion in deciding whether or not to ask for a preliminary ruling. The mere existence of the right to do so does not deprive them of the right to reach their own conclusions on questions of Community law it may be necessary for them to decide.[57] Indeed, where the point raised is reasonably clear or it is possible to deduce from the case law of the Court of Justice a clear general approach to a particular question, it may be preferable for an inferior national court to decide the point itself.[58] However, where it seems likely that a reference will be made at some stage in the proceedings, it is sensible for that step to be taken sooner rather than later, for an early reference saves time and costs.[59] Moreover, as Bingham J. acknowledged in *Commissioners of Customs and Excise v Samex ApS*,[60] the Court of Justice is far better equipped than national courts to resolve issues of Community law:

"Sitting as a judge in a national court, asked to decide questions of Community law, I am very conscious of the

[56] Anderson and Demetriou, *References to the European Court* (Sweet & Maxwell, 2nd ed., 2002), pp.327–330.
[57] See Slade L.J. in *J Rothschild Holdings plc v Commissioners of Inland Revenue* [1989] 2 C.M.L.R. 621, 645 (CA).
[58] See *Pickstone v Freemans plc* [1987] 2 C.M.L.R. 572, 591 (CA) *per* Purchas L.J.
[59] This was acknowledged by Kerr L.J. in *R v Pharmaceutical Society of Great Britain, ex parte The Association of Pharmaceutical Importers* [1987] 3 C.M.L.R. 951, 972.
[60] [1983] 3 C.M.L.R. 194, 210–211 (HC).

advantages enjoyed by the Court of Justice. It has a panoramic view of the Community and its institutions, a detailed knowledge of the Treaties and of much subordinate legislation made under them, and an intimate familiarity with the functioning of the Community market which no national judge denied the collective experience of the Court of Justice could hope to achieve. Where questions of administrative intention and practice arise the Court of Justice can receive submissions from the Community institutions, as also where relations between the Community and non-Member States are in issue. Where the interests of Member States are affected they can intervene to make their views known . . . Where comparison falls to be made between Community texts in different languages, all texts being equally authentic, the multi-national Court of Justice is equipped to carry out the task in a way which no national judge, whatever his linguistic skills, could rival. The interpretation of Community instruments involves very often not the process familiar to common lawyers of laboriously extracting the meaning from words used but the more creative process of applying flesh to a spare and loosely constructed skeleton. The choice between alternative submissions may turn not on purely legal considerations, but on a broader view of what the orderly development of the Community requires. These are matters which the Court of Justice is very much better placed to assess and determine than a national court."

The proper functioning of the preliminary rulings procedure therefore depends to a large extent on the way in which inferior national courts exercise the discretion conferred on them by Article 234 EC. Since the scope of that discretion depends on the correct interpretation of Article 234 EC, only the Court of Justice is competent to make authoritative pronouncements on the matter. None the less, some national courts have purported to lay down guidelines of their own. An early attempt to do so was made by Lord Denning in *HP Bulmer Ltd v J Bollinger SA*.[61] Lord Denning's guidelines had a considerable influence on the practice of the English courts, but they attracted a certain amount of academic criticism because of their tendency to discourage references.[62] A more positive emphasis was given by Sir Thomas Bingham M.R. in the later case of *R v Stock*

---

[61] [1974] Ch. 401.
[62] See e.g. Dashwood and Arnull, "English courts and Article 177 of the EEC Treaty" (1984) 4 Y.E.L. 255, 263.

Exchange, ex parte Else (1982) Ltd.[63] In that case, the Master of the Rolls declared:

> "I understand the correct approach in principle of a national court (other than a final court of appeal) to be quite clear: if the facts have been found and the Community law issue is critical to the court's final decision, the appropriate course is ordinarily to refer the issue to the Court of Justice unless the national court can with complete confidence resolve the issue itself. In considering whether it can with complete confidence resolve the issue itself the national court must be fully mindful of the differences between national and Community legislation, of the pitfalls which face a national court venturing into what may be an unfamiliar field, of the need for uniform interpretation throughout the Community and of the great advantages enjoyed by the Court of Justice in construing Community instruments. If the national court has any real doubt, it should ordinarily refer."

It is well-established in the case law of the Court of Justice that the national court is in principle the sole judge of whether a preliminary ruling is necessary and of the relevance of the questions referred.[64] "Consequently, where the questions submitted concern the interpretation of Community law, the Court of Justice is, in principle, bound to give a ruling".[65] The fact that the issue referred is the subject of a pending infringement action against the State concerned is irrelevant.[66] Moreover, the Court of Justice made it clear in *Rheinmühlen*[67] that a national court cannot be deprived of its power to make a reference by the rulings of superior national courts. A decision to refer remains subject to the remedies normally available under national law (such as appeal), but the Court will act on the decision until it has been formally revoked.[68]

None the less, the Court explained in *Cipra* and *Kvasnicka v Bezirkshauptmannschaft Mistelbach* that[69]:

---

[63] [1993] 2 W.L.R. 70, 76; [1993] 1 All E.R. 420, 426 (CA). cf. *Trinity Mirror PLC v Commissioners of Customs and Excise* [2001] 2 C.M.L.R. 33, paras 48–56, where the Court of Appeal, influenced by the Opinion of Advocate General Jacobs in Case C–338/95 *Wiener v Hauptzollamt Emmerich* [1997] E.C.R. I–6495, declined to make a reference on the basis that there was "no real doubt" about the answer to the question of Community law that had arisen.

[64] See e.g. Case 297/88 *Dzodzi v Belgium* [1990] E.C.R. I–3763.

[65] Case C–256/97 *DMT* [1999] E.C.R. I–3913, para.10.

[66] Case C–457/02 *Niselli* [2004] E.C.R. I–10853, para.27.

[67] Case 166/73 [1974] E.C.R. 33, paras 3 and 4.

[68] See Case 146/73 *Rheinmühlen-Düsseldorf v Einfuhr- und Vorratsstelle Getreide* [1974] E.C.R. 139, para.3.

[69] Case C–439/01 [2003] E.C.R. I–745, para.19. See also Case C–60/98 *Butterfly Music Srl v CEMED* [1999] E.C.R. I–3939, para.13; Case C–421/97 *Tarantik v Directeur des Services Fiscaux de Seine-et-Marne* [1999] E.C.R. I–3633, para.33; Case C–415/93 *URBSFA v Bosman* [1995] E.C.R. I–4921, para.61.

"In exceptional circumstances, it can examine the conditions in which the case was referred to it by the national court, in order to assess whether it has jurisdiction . . . The Court may refuse to rule on a question referred for a preliminary ruling by a national court only where it is quite obvious that the interpretation of Community law that is sought bears no relation to the actual facts of the main action or its purpose, where the problem is hypothetical, or where the Court does not have before it the factual or legal material necessary to give a useful answer to the questions submitted to it."

The decision in *Foglia v Novello*,[70] cited by the Court in *Cipra*, began **14–009** a retreat from the more liberal attitude originally taken by the Court. In *Foglia*, the Court refused to entertain a reference made in the context of a collusive action brought in one Member State by parties who were not really in dispute with each other with the intention of challenging the law of another Member State as contrary to Community law. The Court's ruling in that case was heavily criticised[71] and was for many years applied with considerable restraint. However, it was given a new lease of life by the ruling in *Telemarsicabruzzo v Circostel*.[72] In that case, an Italian judge, the Vice Pretore di Frascati, referred two questions on the compatibility with the EC Treaty, and in particular the competition rules laid down in it, of provisions of Italian law restricting the right of private sector television channels to use certain frequencies. The orders for reference contained very little information about the factual background to the cases or the relevant provisions of Italian law. The Court emphasised that the need to give a useful ruling in proceedings under Article 234 EC made it essential for the national judge to define the factual and legislative background to the case, or at least the factual hypotheses on which the questions referred were based. These requirements were particularly important in the field of competition, characterized as it was by complex legal and factual situations. The Court pointed out that the orders for reference in the present cases contained no information on these matters. The information the Court had been able to glean during the course of the proceedings was not adequate to enable it to interpret the Treaty competition rules in the light of the circumstances of the case pursuant to the referring court's invitation. In those circumstances, the Court concluded that there were no grounds for ruling on the questions submitted by the Vice Pretore.

---

[70] Case 104/79 [1980] E.C.R. 745.
[71] See e.g. Barav, "Preliminary censorship? The judgment of the European Court in *Foglia v Novello*" (1980) 5 E.L.Rev. 443; Bebr, "The existence of a genuine dispute: an indispensable precondition for the jurisdiction of the Court under Art.177 EEC?" (1980) 17 C.M.L.Rev. 525 and "The possible implications of *Foglia v Novello II*" (1982) 19 C.M.L.Rev. 421.
[72] Joined Cases C–320/90, C–321/90 and C–322/90 [1993] E.C.R. I–393. See also Case C–83/91 *Meilicke v ADV/ORGA* [1992] E.C.R. I–4871.

The judgment in *Telemarsicabruzzo* was delivered by the full Court and was clearly intended to emphasise that, if the background to the case was not clearly set out by the referring court, the Court would decline to give a ruling. That message was subsequently reinforced in a series of cases in which inadequately explained references were dismissed by reasoned order as manifestly inadmissible under the abbreviated procedure for which provision is made in Article 92(1) of its Rules of Procedure.[73] In one case,[74] the Court rejected a reference as inadmissible where the relevance of Community law depended on an interpretation by the referring court of the national law of another Member State which the Government of that State regarded as implausible. The Court said it was unable to establish from the information supplied to it whether answering the referring court's questions would serve a useful purpose. In another case, the Court even refused to give a ruling when it thought the reference should have been withdrawn by the national court in the light of developments since it was made.[75]

However, there are some modern cases where the Court has been willing to deal with questions it might have been expected to reject. In *Vaneetveld*,[76] for example, the order for reference contained no information about the facts of the case. Nonetheless, following the advice of Advocate General Jacobs, the Court observed:[77] "It is true that the Court has held that the need to arrive at an interpretation of Community law which is useful for the national court requires that court to define the factual and legislative context of the questions, or at least to explain the factual hypotheses on which they are based . . . None the less, that requirement is less pressing where the questions relate to specific technical points and enable the Court to give a useful reply even where the national court has not given an exhaustive description of the legal and factual situation". The Court concluded that it had enough information to enable it to give a useful answer.

The Court may also treat possible deficiencies in the information supplied by the national court as having been cured during later stages of the proceedings. An example is *Arduino*,[78] where the Court

---

[73] See e.g. Case C–157/92 *Banchero I* [1993] E.C.R. I–1085; Case C–386/92 *Monin Automobiles I* [1993] E.C.R. I–2049. For the sequel to these cases, see Case C–428/93 *Monin Automobiles II* [1994] E.C.R. I–1707; Case C–387/93 *Banchero II* [1995] E.C.R. I–4663.

[74] Case C–153/00 *der Weduwe* [2002] E.C.R. I–11319.

[75] See Joined Cases C–422/93, C–423/93 and C–424/93 *Zabala Erasun* [1995] E.C.R. I–1567.

[76] Case C–316/93 [1994] E.C.R. I–763. See also Case C–412/93 *Leclerc-Siplec v TF1 Publicité and M6 Publicité* [1995] E.C.R. I–179; Case C–415/93 *URBSFA v Bosman* [1995] E.C.R. I–4921; Case C–295/97 *Piaggio v IFITALIA* [1999] E.C.R. I–3735; Case C–355/97 *Landesgrundverkehrsreferent der Tiroler Landesregierung v Beck* [1999] E.C.R. I–4977; Case C–67/96 *Albany International v Stichting Bedrijfspensioenfonds Textielindustrie* [1999] E.C.R. I–5751; Joined Cases C–115/97, C–116/97 and C–117/97 *Brentjens v Stichting Bedrijfspensioenfonds voor de Handel in Bouwmaterialen* [1999] E.C.R. I–6025; Case C–413/99 *Baumbast v Secretary of State* [2002] 3 C.M.L.R. 23, paras 31–34.

[77] Para.13.

[78] Case C–35/99 [2002] 4 C.M.L.R. 25, para.28.

observed: "The observations submitted by the governments of the Member States and the Commission . . . show that the information supplied in the order for reference enabled them effectively to state their views on the questions referred to the Court". The Court continued:[79]

> "Furthermore, the information in the order for reference was supplemented by the written observations lodged before the Court. All that information, which was included in the Report for the Hearing, was brought to the notice of the governments of the Member States and the other interested parties for the purposes of the hearing, at which they had an opportunity, if necessary, to amplify their observations."

The Court concluded[80] that "the information provided by the national court, supplemented where necessary by the abovementioned material, gives the Court sufficient knowledge of the factual and legislative background to the dispute in the main proceedings to enable it to interpret the relevant rules of the Treaty.

The modern case law therefore suggests that, where the referring **14–010** court sets out clearly what the case is about and gives a plausible explanation of why it needs an answer to the questions it has referred, the Court will normally proceed to answer them. However, it will not answer questions which are manifestly irrelevant,[81] nor will it respond where it takes the view that there is no real dispute between the parties to the main action.[82] Moreover, it will not normally spend time trying to identify what a case is about when this has not been properly explained by the national court. An exception is sometimes made where gaps in the information supplied are cured during subsequent stages of the proceedings, provided the dispute is genuine, the questions are relevant and those submitting observations have not been prevented from stating their views effectively.

In a Note for Guidance on References by National Courts for Preliminary Rulings issued in late 1996,[83] the Court summarised its case law and offered advice on what references should contain. The Note also contained guidance on the point in the proceedings at which references should be made—a matter which falls within the exclusive jurisdiction of the national court.[84] A revised Note on

---

[79] Para.29. See also Case C–476/01 *Felix Kapper* [2004] E.C.R. I–5205, paras 26–29.
[80] Para.30.
[81] See generally Barnard and Sharpston, "The changing face of Art.177 references" (1997) 34 C.M.L.Rev. 1113; O'Keeffe, "Is the spirit of Art.177 under attack? Preliminary references and admissibility" (1998) 23 E.L.Rev. 509.
[82] Though consider the Court's liberal approach to the allegedly fictitious / contrived dispute in Case C–144/04 *Mangold* (Judgment of November 22, 2005).
[83] [1997] 1 C.M.L.R. 78, (1997) 22 E.L.Rev. 55, (1997) 34 C.M.L.Rev. 1319, [1997] All E.R. (EC) 1.
[84] Case C–60/02 *X* [2004] E.C.R. I–651, para.28.

references from national courts for a preliminary ruling, issued by the Court of Justice in 2005, states that: "A national court or tribunal may refer a question to the Court of Justice for a preliminary ruling as soon as it finds that a ruling on the point or points of interpretation or validity is necessary to enable it to give judgment; it is the national court which is in the best position to decide at what sage of the proceedings such a question should be referred".[85] The Court stresses, however, that, because it cannot decide issues of fact or of national law, "a decision to seek a preliminary ruling should be taken when the proceedings have reached a stage at which the national court is able to define the factual and legal context of the question, so that the Court has available to it all the information necessary to check, where appropriate, that Community law applies to the main proceedings. It may also be in the interests of justice to refer a question for a preliminary ruling only after both sides have been heard".[86] Where national courts do not follow the advice contained in the Note, the Court now has the power to ask for clarification.[87] This reduces the delay involved in dismissing a reference as inadmissible, only for the case to be referred a second time.

Mandatory References

14–011   Where a question of Community law, within the meaning of the first paragraph of Article 234 EC, is raised in a case pending before a court or tribunal of a Member State against whose decisions there is no judicial remedy under national law, that court or tribunal is obliged, under the third paragraph of the Article, to refer the question to the Court of Justice. That paragraph is not confined to courts whose decisions are always final, such as the House of Lords. It covers any court, even if not the highest court, against whose decision there is no judicial remedy in the instant case.[88] In *Köbler v Austria*,[89] the Court held that non-compliance by a top national court with its obligations under the third paragraph of Article 234 EC might render the State in which it was situated liable in damages to an individual thereby deprived of his/her rights under Community law.[90]

---

[85] [2005] O.J. C143/1, at para.18.

[86] *ibid.*, at para.19.

[87] See Art.104(5), Rules of Procedure, in force since July 1, 2000. Conversely, the Court may give its decision by reasoned order where the answer to a question which has been referred to it "may be clearly deduced from existing case law" or "where the answer to the question . . . admits of no reasonable doubt": see Art.104(3) of the Rules.

[88] Case 6/64 *Costa v ENEL* [1964] E.C.R. 585. See also Case 107/76 *Hoffmann-La Roche v Centrafarm* [1977] E.C.R. 957 and Joined Cases 35 and 36/82 *Morson and Jhanjan v Netherlands* [1982] E.C.R. 3723. *cf.* Case C–337/95 *Parfums Christian Dior v Evora* [1997] E.C.R. I–6013.

[89] Case C–224/01 [2003] E.C.R. I–10239, para.55.

[90] On this issue, see Ch.6.

In the English legal system, a potential difficulty arises at the level of an appeal from the Court of Appeal to the House of Lords. Such an appeal can only be brought with the leave of the Court of Appeal or the House of Lords. If either of them grants leave, there is no problem, but what is the position if the Court of Appeal refuses to grant leave? In *Chiron Corporation v Murex Diagnostics*,[91] the Court of Appeal held that, where it refuses leave to appeal and the House of Lords is presented with an application for leave to appeal, then before refusing leave it should consider whether it needed to resolve an issue of Community law. If it decided that it did and that the answer to the question was unclear, it could either make a reference at that stage or grant leave and consider at a later stage whether to make a reference. The Court of Appeal thought that the possibility of making an application to the House of Lords for leave to appeal constituted a "judicial remedy" within the meaning of the third paragraph of Article 234 EC. The Court of Appeal could not therefore be considered a court of last resort itself for the purposes of that provision. Nor did it have jurisdiction to make a reference if the House of Lords refused leave, since by that stage it was *functus officio*.

The approach of the Court of Appeal was subsequently endorsed by the Court of Justice in *Lyckeskog*,[92] a reference from the Court of Appeal for Western Sweden, which wanted to know if it was a court of last resort for the purposes of the third paragraph of Article 234 EC. The referring court's decision in the main action would be subject to appeal to the Swedish Supreme Court, but only if the Supreme Court declared it admissible on grounds set out in the Swedish Code of Procedure. The Court ruled that the possibility of an appeal to the Supreme Court meant that the Court of Appeal could not be considered a court of last resort for these purposes, even where the merits of the appeal were only examined by the Supreme Court where it had declared the appeal admissible. The Court pointed out:[93]

> "If a question arises as to the interpretation or validity of a rule of Community law, the supreme court will be under an obligation, pursuant to the third paragraph of Article 234 EC, to refer a question to the Court of Justice for a preliminary

---

[91] [1995] All E.R. (EC) 88, [1995] F.S.R. 309. See Demetriou "When is the House of Lords not a judicial remedy?" (1995) 20 E.L.Rev. 628. *cf. R v Secretary of State, ex parte Duddridge* [1996] 2 C.M.L.R. 361.

[92] Case C–99/00 [2002] E.C.R. I–4839.

[93] Para.18.

ruling either at the stage of the examination of admissibility or at a later stage."

The obligation to refer is not affected by the fact that the Commission may have discontinued infringement proceedings raising the same issue as that which the national court is called upon to decide.[94] However, although the third paragraph of Article 234 EC states that a reference is obligatory "where any such question is raised", this does not mean that the obligation arises wherever a party contends that a question of Community law needs to be decided. In *CILFIT v Ministry of Health*,[95] the Court of Justice held that final courts are in the same position as other national courts in deciding whether they need to resolve a question of Community law before giving judgment. A final court is not therefore obliged to ask for a preliminary ruling where the answer to the question raised cannot affect the outcome of the case. Even where a question of Community law is relevant, the Court of Justice went on to hold in that case that a final court is under no obligation to refer if: (a) "previous decisions of the Court have already dealt with the point of law in question"[96] (although in that event the national court remains free to refer if it wishes the Court of Justice to reconsider its earlier ruling)[97]; or (b) the correct application of Community law is so obvious as to leave no scope for any reasonable doubt as to the manner in which the question raised is to be resolved. This is known as *acte clair*. However, before the national court reaches this conclusion, it must be convinced that the matter would be equally obvious to the courts of the other Member States and to the Court of Justice. In that regard, it must take account of the characteristic features of Community law and the particular difficulties to which its interpretation gives rise.[98] These criteria may also be relevant where an inferior national court is called upon to interpret Community law. This is because, where they are satisfied, such a court may properly decline, in the exercise of its discretion, to make a reference.[99]

14–012 What is the relationship between the *CILFIT* criteria and the *Köbler* case? If a top national court relies on *CILFIT* to avoid a reference and then in its judgment deprives one of the parties of its rights under Community law, does that party have a claim for damages against the State concerned? The issue was addressed in

---

[94] Case C–393/98 *Gomes Valente* [2001] E.C.R. I–1327.

[95] Case 283/81 [1982] E.C.R. 3415. More recently, e.g. Case C–495/03 *Intermodal Transports* (Judgment of September 15, 2005).

[96] Para.14.

[97] This applies *a fortiori* "when the question raised is substantially the same as a question which has already been the subject of a preliminary ruling in the same national proceedings": Case C–337/95 *Parfums Christian Dior v Evora* [1997] E.C.R. I–6013, para.29.

[98] On methods of interpretation, see Ch.12.

[99] *cf.* Case C–340/99 *TNT Traco v Poste Italiana* [2001] E.C.R. I–4109, para.35.

Köbler itself.[1] The Court's judgment suggests that the Member State is not liable where a national court mistakenly but in good faith concludes that the *CILFIT* criteria are satisfied and declines to make a reference. The Member State clearly would be liable, however, if it could be shown that the court in question had deliberately mis-construed the *CILFIT* criteria to avoid making a reference. However, that reasoning would appear inapplicable to lower courts: the remedy for a party who believes that such a court has deprived him/her of his/her rights under Community law is to appeal to a higher court.

Some commentators take the view that the *CILFIT* criteria are too strict. The authors of a report entitled *The Role and Future of the European Court of Justice*, published by the British Institute of International and Comparative Law in 1996, observed[2]: "Compliance with these requirements for *acte clair* is virtually impossible. In practice this test is completely unworkable". In one English case, the criteria were even described as "intimidating".[3] That view perhaps gives insufficient weight to the Court's acceptance that the Treaty imposed no obligation to refer where the Court had already dealt in previous decisions with the point at issue. In a development of previous case law,[4] the Court made it clear that this was so "irrespective of the nature of the proceedings which led to those decisions, even though the questions at issue are not strictly identical".[5] In circumstances such as these, there is no need to invoke the *acte clair* doctrine. The obligation laid down by the third paragraph of Article 234 EC helps to maintain uniformity by providing a safeguard against the incorrect application of Community law by national courts.

That view seems to have been accepted at Nice, where the Member States declined to pursue a suggestion that the obligation of the highest national courts to refer should be relaxed. It is submitted that any such relaxation beyond that enshrined in the *CILFIT* test could only be contemplated if there were some protection against abuse by national courts or misunderstanding on their part of the circumstances in which a reference ought to be made. Such protection might be afforded by extending the scope of Article 68(3) EC, which was introduced at Amsterdam and is currently confined to Title IV of Part Three of the EC Treaty. Article 68(3) EC allows the Council, the Commission or a Member State to ask the Court of

---

[1] See paras 118 and 123 of the Judgment.
[2] At p.76.
[3] Hodgson J in *R v Secretary of State for Transport, ex parte Factortame* [1989] 2 C.M.L.R. 353, 379.
[4] See Joined Cases 28 to 30/62 *Da Costa v Nederlandse Belastingadministratie* [1963] E.C.R. 31.
[5] Para.14.

Justice to give a ruling on the interpretation of Title IV or of acts of the institutions based on it. The ruling given by the Court in response to such a request does not apply to previous judgments of national courts and tribunals.[6] Article 68 EC is considered in more detail below.

It was held in *Hoffmann-La Roche v Centrafarm* that a national court is not required to refer to the Court a question of interpretation which is raised in interlocutory proceedings for an interim order, provided that each of the parties is entitled to institute proceedings (or to require proceedings to be instituted) on the substance of the case, and that during such proceedings the question provisionally decided at the interlocutory stage may be re-examined and referred to the Court of Justice.[7] This is so even where the criteria laid down in the *CILFIT* case are not satisfied and no judicial remedy is available against the interlocutory decision itself.

References on validity

14–013   Under the first paragraph of Article 234 EC, the Court of Justice may be asked for a preliminary ruling not only on the interpretation of acts of the Community institutions but also on their validity. The jurisdiction of the Court of Justice to rule on the validity of Community provisions under Article 234 EC complements its jurisdiction to review the legality of Community acts under Article 230 EC.[8] This means that a person affected by a Community act may sometimes challenge its validity independently of the direct action which may be available before the Court of Justice under Article 230 EC. However, the Court has imposed limits on the circumstances in which the validity of Community acts may be challenged in the national courts. The effect of the Court's decision in *TWD Textilwerke Deggendorf*[9] is that a natural or legal person who fails to challenge a Community act under Article 230 EC, even though he or she clearly has standing to do so, may not subsequently contest the validity of that act in proceedings before a national court. The *TWD* case concerned the Treaty rules on State aid and there was initially some doubt about whether it was confined to that context. The

---

[6] In other words, such rulings do not affect cases which have already been decided but apply only for the future. *cf.* the protocol on the interpretation of the Brussels Convention, mentioned above.

[7] Case 107/76 *Hoffmann-La Roche v Centrafarm* [1977] E.C.R. 957. The *Hoffmann-La Roche* judgment also refers to questions of validity, but must be considered superseded on that point by *Foto-Frost*: see Advocate General Lenz in *Zuckerfabrik Süderditmarschen* [1991] E.C.R. I–415, 483–489.

[8] See Ch.13.

[9] Case C–188/92 [1994] E.C.R. I–833.

Court made it clear that this was not so in *Wiljo v Belgian State*,[10] where it applied the *TWD* approach in a different context.[11]

The jurisdiction of the Court of Justice to rule on validity typically arises where a national measure, purportedly based on a Community act, is challenged in a national court on the ground that the Community act is itself invalid. Indeed, the Court said in the *UPA* case[12] that national courts were under a duty to apply their national law in a way that enabled claimants to challenge a national measure applying a Community act of general application on the basis that the act was invalid.

In *R v Secretary of State, ex parte British American Tobacco*,[13] the Court made it clear that a claimant's right to plead the invalidity of a Community act of general application before a national court did not depend on the existence of national implementing measures. In that case, the applicants sought judicial review in the High Court of "the intention and/or obligation" of the UK government to transpose a directive on tobacco products into national law. The Court held that a reference by the High Court on the validity of the directive was admissible, even though at the time of the application for judicial review the deadline for implementing the directive had not expired and the government had not yet adopted any implementing measures. The judgment may be seen in part as a reflection of the duty imposed on national courts in *UPA*. In *BAT*, however, the applicants had been granted permission to seek judicial review. The Court's judgment does not address the problems which may confront claimants where no national remedy is available to them and they lack standing to bring a direct action under Article 230 EC.

The Treaty appears to confer on inferior national courts the same discretion whether the question of Community law raised is one of interpretation or one of validity. However, in the controversial case of *Foto-Frost v Hauptzollamt Lübeck-Ost*[14] the Court of Justice held

---

[10] Case C–178/95 [1997] E.C.R. I–585. See also Case C–408/95 *Eurotunnel v SeaFrance* [1997] E.C.R. I–6315. *cf.* Case C–241/95 *The Queen v Intervention Board for Agricultural Produce, ex parte Accrington Beef* [1996] E.C.R. I–6699; Case C–239/99 *Nachi Europe* [2001] E.C.R. I–1197.

[11] For criticism of the *TWD* ruling, see e.g. Wyatt, "The relationship between actions for annulment and references on validity after *TWD Deggendorf*" in Lonbay and Biondi (eds), *Remedies for Breach of EC Law* (Wiley, 1997), Ch.6; Advocate General Tesauro in Case C–408/95 *Eurotunnel v SeaFrance* [1997] E.C.R. I–6315, 6328. *cf.* Tesauro, "The effectiveness of judicial protection and co-operation between the Court of Justice and the national courts" (1993) 13 Y.E.L. 1, 15–16. However, the preliminary rulings procedure is in several respects a less satisfactory mechanism for reviewing the legality of Community acts than the action for annulment. See Advocate General Jacobs in *TWD* at pp.840–844, Case C–358/89 *Extramet Industrie v Council* [1991] E.C.R. I–2501, 2523–2525 and *UPA*, below, paras 40–44.

[12] Case C–50/00 P *Unión de Pequeños Agricultores v Council* [2002] 3 C.M.L.R. 1, para.42. The case is discussed in Ch.13.

[13] Case C–491/01 [2002] E.C.R. I–11453.

[14] Case 314/85 [1987] E.C.R. 4199. See Bebr, "The reinforcement of the constitutional review of Community acts under Art.177 EEC Treaty" (1988) 25 C.M.L.Rev. 667.

that, while national courts were entitled to find that acts adopted by the institutions of the Community were valid, they had no power to declare such acts invalid. This was because "[d]ivergences between courts in the Member States as to the validity of Community acts would be liable to place in jeopardy the very unity of the Community legal order and detract from the fundamental requirement of legal certainty". The Court also pointed out that, if the matter were referred to it, the institution which adopted the contested act would be able to participate in the proceedings. This will rarely, if ever, be possible in proceedings before a national court.

The result is that, where a real and substantial doubt is raised in a national court on the validity of a Community measure, and where it is clear that a decision on the validity of the measure is necessary for the resolution of the case, then the issue must be referred. This is so even where similar provisions have been declared void by the Court of Justice in other cases[15] and even where the national court is not one of last resort. Where the national court is one of last resort, the *acte clair* doctrine laid down in *CILFIT* cannot operate to relieve it of its obligation to refer: that doctrine applies only to questions of interpretation. Thus, where in proceedings before a national court, whether or not it is one of last resort, there is a real possibility that a Community measure might be invalid, the matter must be referred to the Court of Justice.[16]

Some commentators[17] have objected to the ruling in *Foto-Frost* on the basis that it is incompatible with the terms of Article 234 EC, but the reasoning underlying the conclusion reached by the Court seems compelling.

14–014   The Court's judgment in *Foto-Frost* suggested[18] that national courts might have jurisdiction to declare Community acts invalid in interlocutory proceedings, where the urgency of the case might render it impractical to wait for a ruling from the Court of Justice. The powers of national courts in such proceedings were considered in more detail in *Zuckerfabrik Süderditmarschen v Hauptzollamt Itzehoe*.[19] The essential point at issue in that case was whether, and if so in what circumstances, a national court could suspend the operation of a national measure based on a Community regulation which was alleged to be invalid. The Court of Justice observed that the rights of individuals to challenge regulations in the national

[15] cf. *R v Intervention Board for Agricultural Produce, ex parte ED and F Man (Sugar) Ltd* [1986] 2 All E.R. 126 (QBD); *R v Minister of Agriculture, ex parte Fédération Européenne de la Santé Animale* [1988] 3 C.M.L.R. 207 and 661 (DC).
[16] See Case C–461/03 *Gaston Schul Douane-expediteur BV* (Judgment of December 6, 2005); Case C–344/04 *European Low Fares Airline Association* (Judgment of January 10, 2006).
[17] See e.g. Hartley, *Constitutional Problems of the European Union* (Hart, Oxford, 1999), pp.34–35.
[18] See para.19 of the Judgment.
[19] Joined Cases C–143/88 and C–92/89 [1991] E.C.R. I–415. See also the discussion in Ch.6.

courts would be compromised if they could not be suspended pending a ruling on their validity from the Court of Justice, which had exclusive jurisdiction to adjudicate on that question.[20] A request for a preliminary ruling was one of the means provided by the Treaty for reviewing the validity of Community acts. Another means was the action for annulment brought directly before the Court of Justice under Article 230 EC.[21] In such an action, the Court had the power under Article 242 EC to order the suspension of the contested act. As a result, "[t]he coherence of the system of interim legal protection therefore requires that national courts should also be able to order suspension of enforcement of a national administrative measure based on a Community regulation, the legality of which is contested".[22]

The Court observed that the suspension of administrative measures based on a Community regulation, whilst governed by national rules of procedure, had to be subject to conditions which were uniform throughout the Community so far as the granting of relief was concerned.[23] Since the power of the national courts to suspend administrative measures in these circumstances corresponded to the jurisdiction of the Court of Justice to grant interim measures in actions for annulment, the national courts could only be permitted to grant such relief "on the conditions which must be satisfied for the Court of Justice to allow an application to it for interim measures".[24] The Court concluded that[25]:

> "suspension of enforcement of a national measure adopted in implementation of a Community regulation may be granted by a national court only:
>
> (i) if that court entertains serious doubts as to the validity of the Community measure and, should the question of the validity of the contested measure not already have been brought before the Court, itself refers that question to the Court;
>
> (ii) if there is urgency and a threat of serious and irreparable damage to the applicant;
>
> (iii) and if the national court takes due account of the Community's interests."

In *Krüger v Hauptzollamt Hamburg-Jonas*,[26] the Commission argued that, when considering the Community interest, a national court

---

[20] See Case 314/85 *Foto-Frost* [1987] E.C.R. 4199.
[21] See Ch.13.
[22] Para.18.
[23] Para.26.
[24] Para.27.
[25] Para.33.
[26] Case C–334/95 [1997] E.C.R. I–4517.

which was minded to grant interim relief must give the Community institution which adopted the contested act an opportunity to express its views. The Court was not prepared to impose such a requirement on the national courts, simply observing that it was for the national court to decide on the most appropriate way of obtaining all the information it needed to assess the Community interest.

In *Atlanta Fruchthandelsgesellschaft v Federal Republic of Germany*,[27] the Court offered further clarification of the conditions laid down in *Zuckerfabrik*. Where a national court had serious doubts about the validity of a Community act and made a reference to the Court of Justice on that issue, it had to explain why it thought the act in question might be invalid. If the Court had already dismissed as unfounded an action for the annulment of the contested act, or previously held in proceedings under Article 234 EC that no doubt had been cast on the act's validity, the national court was not entitled to grant interim measures, and any such measures which had already been granted would have to be revoked, unless the new grounds of illegality put forward differed from those which had been rejected by the Court. The same applied, *mutatis mutandis*, where a challenge to the validity of an act had been dismissed by the Court of First Instance in a ruling which had become final and binding.

It was established in the *Nevedi* case that interim relief against the application of allegedly invalid Community measures may not be granted by national administrative authorities. The Court observed that such authorities are not in a position to comply with the conditions for granting such measures as defined by the Court in rulings such as *Zuckerfabrik* and *Atlanta*. In particular, the status of national administrative authorities is not generally such as to guarantee that they have the same degree of independence and impartiality as national courts; it is also uncertain that such authorities benefit from the exercise of the adversarial principle inherent to judicial proceedings, which allows account to be taken of the arguments put forward by the different parties before the necessary weighing of interests at stake in the dispute.[28]

The effects of the ruling of the Court of Justice

14–015   A ruling on interpretation given by the Court of Justice under Article 234 EC "is binding on the national court as to the interpretation of the Community provisions and acts in question".[29] The

---

[27] Case C–465/93 [1995] E.C.R. I–3761. *cf.* Case C–68/95 *T Port v Bundesanstalt für Landwirtschaft und Ernährung* [1996] E.C.R. I–6065.

[28] Case C–194/04 *Nevedi* (Judgment of December 6, 2005).

[29] Case 52/76 *Benedetti v Munari* [1977] E.C.R. 163, para.26. This obligation is reinforced for courts in the United Kingdom by s.3(1) of the European Communities Act 1972. For a detailed discussion of the effects of rulings given by the Court of Justice under Art.234, see Toth, "The authority of judgments of the European Court of Justice: binding force and legal effects" (1984) 4 Y.E.L. 1.

referring court is under a duty to give full effect to the provisions of Community law as interpreted by the Court of Justice. This may require it to refuse to apply conflicting provisions of national law, even if adopted subsequently.[30] Moreover, other courts are entitled to treat the ruling of the Court of Justice as authoritative and as thereby obviating the need for the same points to be referred to the Court of Justice again.[31]

A ruling by the Court under Article 234 EC declaring an act of one of the institutions void is also binding on the referring court.[32] Moreover, such a ruling entitles "any other national court to regard that act as void".[33] The consequences for the institutions of a preliminary ruling declaring a Community act void were considered by the Court of First Instance in *H & R Ecroyd Holdings Ltd v Commission.*[34] The Court of First Instance observed[35]:

> "when the Court of Justice rules in proceedings under Article 234 EC . . . that an act adopted by the Community legislature is invalid, its decision has the legal effect of requiring the competent Community institutions to adopt the measures necessary to remedy that illegality . . . In those circumstances, they are to take the measures that are required in order to comply with the judgment containing the ruling in the same way as they are, under Article 233 EC, in the case of a judgment annulling a measure or declaring that the failure of a Community institution to act is unlawful . . . [W]hen a Community measure is held to be invalid by a preliminary ruling, the obligation laid down by Article 233 EC applies by analogy."

This may mean that the institution concerned must not only adopt the legislative or administrative measures necessary to give effect to the Court's judgment but also consider whether the unlawful measure caused those affected by it damage which has to be made good. On the other hand, where the Court in proceedings under Article 234 EC rejects a challenge to the validity of a measure, it will rule that consideration of the questions raised has disclosed no factor of such a kind as to affect the validity of the contested act.[36] The

---

[30] See e.g. Case 106/77 *Amministrazione delle Finanze dello Stato v Simmenthal* [1978] E.C.R. 629; Case 170/88 *Ford España v Estado Español* [1989] E.C.R. 2305. However, on the relationship between preliminary rulings and the principle of *res judicata*, see Case C–453/00 *Kühne & Heitz* [2004] E.C.R. I–837; Case C–234/04 *Kapferer* (Judgment of March 16, 2006).

[31] See Joined Cases 28–30/62 *da Costa en Schaake* [1963] E.C.R. 31; Case 283/81 *CILFIT v Ministry of Health* [1982] E.C.R. 3415.

[32] Case 66/80 *International Chemical Corporation v Amministrazione delle Finanze dello Stato* [1981] E.C.R. 1191.

[33] *ibid.*, para.13.

[34] Case T–220/97 [1999] E.C.R. I–1677.

[35] Para.49.

[36] See e.g. Case C–323/88 *Sermes* [1990] E.C.R. I–3027.

national court is not of course entitled to declare the act invalid on the grounds rejected by the Court, but the effect of the ruling is to leave open the possibility of a subsequent challenge on other grounds.

A preliminary ruling on the interpretation of a rule of Community law "clarifies and defines where necessary the meaning and scope of that rule as it must be or ought to have been understood and applied from the time of its coming into force. It follows that the rule as thus interpreted may, and must, be applied by the [national] courts even to legal relationships arising and established before the judgment ruling on the request for interpretation".[37] Very exceptionally the Court of Justice may, in the interests of legal certainty, be led to limit the effects on past transactions of preliminary rulings on questions of both interpretation and validity.[38] Any such limitation will always be laid down in the ruling itself.[39]

The area of freedom, security and justice

14–016   Two of the central characteristics of Article 234 EC are that Member States are obliged to accept the mechanism it lays down and that all national courts can take advantage of it. Those characteristics were modified in special arrangements for preliminary rulings made by the Treaty of Amsterdam in the so-called area of freedom, security and justice (AFSJ). There are two sets of provisions on that subject: (a) Title IV of Part Three of the EC Treaty entitled "Visas, asylum, immigration and other policies related to free movement of persons"[40]; and (b) Title VI of the TEU entitled "Provisions on police and judicial co-operation in criminal matters."[41] The preliminary rulings mechanisms applicable under each of those Titles differ, both from each other and from the classic mechanism of Article 234 EC.[42]

Visas, asylum, immigration and other policies related to free movement of persons

14–017   The Court's preliminary rulings jurisdiction over Title IV of Part Three of the EC Treaty is limited by Article 68 EC.[43] That provision

---

[37] Case 61/79 *Amministrazione delle Finanze dello Stato v Denkavit Italiana* [1980] E.C.R. 1205, para.16.

[38] See e.g. Case 43/75 *Defrenne v SABENA* [1976] E.C.R. 455; Case 41/84 *Pinna v Caisse d'Allocations Familiales de la Savoie* [1986] E.C.R. 1; Case 24/86 *Blaizot v University of Liège* [1988] E.C.R. 379; Case 262/88 *Barber* [1990] E.C.R. I–1889. See further Ch.5.

[39] See Case 61/79 *Amministrazione delle Finanze dello Stato v Denkavit Italiana* [1980] E.C.R. 1205.

[40] Arts 61–69 EC.

[41] Arts 29–42 TEU. These provisions are also discussed in Ch.10, within the broader context of the Third Pillar as a whole.

[42] See Arnull, "Taming the beast? The Treaty of Amsterdam and the Court of Justice" in O'Keeffe and Twomey (eds), *Legal Issues of the Amsterdam Treaty* (Hart, Oxford, 1999), pp.115–120.

[43] Art.67(2) EC required the Council to consider "adapting the provisions relating to the powers of the Court of Justice" five years after the entry into force of the Treaty of Amsterdam, but nothing has so far been done.

requires national courts of last resort to seek preliminary rulings on Title IV questions and the validity and interpretation of acts of the institutions based on Title IV. Moreover, as already explained, the Council, the Commission and the Member States are entitled to ask the Court for a ruling on how the provisions of the Title and acts adopted under it should be interpreted.[44] However, lower national courts have no power to ask the Court for preliminary rulings in cases covered by Title IV. Thus, in the case of *Warbecq*, the Court declared that it lacked jurisdiction to respond to a request for a preliminary ruling from the Tribunal du travail de Charleroi (Belgium), since decisions of that tribunal were amenable to appeal under national law.[45]

The Member States were justifiably concerned at Amsterdam about the possibility that the Court would be inundated by references in the large number of immigration and asylum cases which come before national courts and Article 68 EC, where applicable, was always likely to reduce the number of references. However, there was a concomitant risk that the procedure would prove less effective in ensuring uniform application and protecting individual rights. Many of those involved in immigration and asylum cases do not have the resources to pursue them as far as courts of last resort.[46] By contrast, some cases might be taken to such courts purely in order to secure a reference to the Court of Justice.[47]

Under Article 68(2) EC, the Court does not have jurisdiction to rule on Council measures connected with the removal of controls on the movement of persons across internal borders "relating to the maintenance of law and order and the safeguarding of internal security".[48] This provision seems to be applicable only to cases covered by Article 68(1) EC. The Court's other powers, notably those it possesses under Article 230 EC, are accordingly unaffected by it. As a result, Council measures taken under Title IV remain fully susceptible to review in annulment proceedings.

It is submitted that the *Foto-Frost* principle does not apply to cases covered by Title IV. It would be intolerable if parties to national proceedings could not challenge the validity of acts adopted under Title IV without taking their case to a court of last resort. Even then, the Court of Justice could not be asked to rule on the validity of a

---

[44] See Art.68(3), last sentence.

[45] Case C–555/03 *Warbecq* [2004] E.C.R. I–6041. For recent examples of rulings delivered pursuant to Art.68 EC, see Case C–443/03 *Leffler* (Judgment of November 8, 2005); Case C–473/04 *Plumex* (Judgment of February 9, 2006).

[46] See JUSTICE, "The jurisdiction of the European Court of Justice in respect of asylum and immigration matters" (May 1997), p.7.

[47] A point made by the Community Courts in their discussion paper entitled "The Future of the Judicial System of the European Union" at p.24.

[48] *cf.* Art.35(5) TEU, discussed below. See also Art.2(1), third indent, of the Protocol integrating the Schengen Acquis into the framework of the EU, which is annexed to the TEU and the EC Treaty.

measure falling within the scope of Article 68(2) EC. The conclusion must therefore be that national courts are free to declare invalid acts adopted under Title IV (including those covered by Article 68(2) EC).

It should be noted that, by virtue of special protocols annexed to the TEU and the EC Treaty, Title IV does not apply to the United Kingdom, Ireland or Denmark unless they decide to "opt in". In the absence of such a decision, cases decided by the courts of those States are not affected by Title IV and they will therefore have no need to avail themselves of Article 68 EC. However, the UK and Ireland have "opted in" to Regulation 44/2001,[49] the regulation replacing the Brussels Convention, which is based on Title IV. The preliminary rulings mechanism applicable under the Brussels Convention gave a right to refer questions to the Court of Justice not only to national courts of last resort but also to other national courts when sitting in an appellate capacity.[50] The replacement of the Convention by Regulation 44/2001 therefore deprived some national courts of the right they previously enjoyed to refer to the Court questions on jurisdiction and the enforcement of judgments.

Police and judicial co-operation in criminal matters

14–018   The revised provisions of Title VI of the TEU on police and judicial co-operation in criminal matters are also designed to contribute to the establishment of the AFSJ.[51] Article 35(1) TEU gives the Court of Justice a preliminary rulings jurisdiction in relation to a range of measures adopted under Title VI,[52] although only at the request of national courts situated in Member States which have declared that they accept the involvement of the Court.[53] There is no provision for such declarations to be revoked once they have been made and they may not be limited to specific instruments.[54]

Under Article 35(3) TEU, Member States which have decided to accept the involvement of the Court of Justice may either confine

---

[49] [2001] O.J. L12/1. See recital 20 of the preamble.

[50] Protocol on the interpretation by the Court of Justice of the Convention of September 27, 1968 on jurisdiction and the enforcement of judgments in civil and commercial matters, Art.2(1) and (2). Art.4 of the Protocol contained a precursor to Art.68(3) EC.

[51] See Art.29 TEU.

[52] The first references under Art.35 TEU were made by German and Belgian courts respectively in Joined Cases C–187/01 and C–385/01 *Gözütok and Brügge* [2003] E.C.R. I–1345.

[53] See Art.35(2). *cf.* the Protocol on the interpretation by the Court of Justice of the Convention on the establishment of a European Police Office ("Europol") [1996] O.J. C299/1.

[54] Under Art.35(4), any Member State, whether or not it has made a declaration accepting the Court's jurisdiction, has the right to submit observations in cases referred under Art.35(1). There is no equivalent provision in Art.68 EC, but the same is presumably true under that provision also because it does no more than modify Art.234 EC to the extent specified: see Art.68(1) EC.

the right to refer to their courts and tribunals of last resort or extend it to any court or tribunal.[55] In neither case does the Treaty impose an obligation to refer on courts of last resort, but a declaration (No.10) adopted at Amsterdam notes that Member States may impose such an obligation as a matter of national law. It is therefore for national law to determine the scope of any such obligation. It follows that the decision of the Court in the *CILFIT* case applies only to the extent (if any) laid down by national law.[56]

Even where a reference is made from a Member State which has accepted the jurisdiction of the Court, Article 35(5) TEU prevents the Court from reviewing the validity or proportionality of national police operations or national measures concerned with "the maintenance of law and order and the safeguarding of internal security." Like its counterpart in Title IV of Part Three of the EC Treaty, Article 68(2) EC, Article 35(5) TEU poses a potential threat to the uniform application of the law. However, it is for the Court to define the precise scope of these provisions.

As with Article 68 EC, the question arises whether the *Foto-Frost* principle applies in the context of Article 35 TEU. The answer once again seems to be that it does not. It is obvious that it could not apply in a Member State which had not accepted the jurisdiction of the Court. For the reasons given above, the *Foto-Frost* principle could not apply either in cases falling within the scope of Article 35(5) TEU or in Member States which have restricted to national courts of last resort the right to refer questions to the Court of Justice. Even in a case brought in a Member State which had extended to all its courts the right to refer, the *Foto-Frost* principle would not be capable of ensuring the uniform application of the law because of the possibility that other Member States might not have extended the right to refer so widely.

Impact of the Constitutional Treaty (CT)

The CT contains reforms to several of the topics covered in this **14–019** chapter, including:

- an express obligation upon Member States to provide remedies sufficient to ensure effective legal protection in fields covered by Union law, which would include issues relating to individuals' standing to challenge Union acts via the national courts (para.11–029);
- the complete suppression of the restrictions on the Court's jurisdiction to deliver preliminary rulings in the fields

---

[55] For the position on the entry into force of the Treaty of Amsterdam, see [1999] O.J. C120/24.

[56] By contrast, it is submitted that the *CILFIT* decision does apply to Art.68(1) EC, since that provision is a specific application of Art.234 EC.

currently governed by Title IV of Part Three of the EC
Treaty (para.11–028);
— the (almost) complete suppression of the restrictions on the
Court's jurisdiction to deliver preliminary rulings on PJC as
currently provided for under Title VI TEU (para.11–028);
— an obligation for the Court to act promptly when requested
to deliver preliminary rulings in cases concerning persons in
custody (para.11–028).

Further reading

Allott, "Preliminary rulings—another infant disease" (2000) 25
E.L.Rev. 538.

Anderson and Demetriou, *References to the European Court* (Sweet
& Maxwell, 2nd ed., 2002).

Arnull, "The use and abuse of Article 177 EEC" (1989) 52 M.L.R.
622.

Arnull, "References to the European Court" (1990) 15 E.L.Rev. 375.

Barav, "Preliminary censorship? The judgment of the European
Court in *Foglia v Novello*" (1980) 5 E.L.Rev. 443.

Barnard and Sharpston, "The changing face of Article 177 references" (1997) 34 C.M.L.Rev. 1113.

Bebr, "The existence of a genuine dispute: an indispensable precondition for the jurisdiction of the Court under Article 177 EEC
Treaty?" (1980) 17 C.M.L.Rev. 525.

Bebr, "The reinforcement of the constitutional review of Community
acts under Article 177 EEC Treaty" (1988) 25 C.M.L.Rev. 667.

Dougan, *National Remedies Before the Court of Justice* (Hart, Oxford,
2004), Ch.6.

Kennedy, "First steps towards a European certiorari?" (1993) 18
E.L.Rev. 121.

Lefevre, "The interpretation of Community law by the Court of
Justice in areas of national competence" (2004) 29 E.L.Rev. 501.

de la Mare, "Article 234 in Social and Political Context" in Craig
and de Búrca (ed.), *The Evolution of EU Law* (OUP, Oxford,
1999).

O'Keeffe, "Is the spirit of Article 177 under attack? Preliminary
references and admissibility" (1998) 23 E.L.Rev. 509.

Snell, "European courts and intellectual property: a tale of Hercules,
Zeus and Cyclops" (2004) 29 E.L.Rev. 178.

Tridimas, "Knocking on heaven's door: fragmentation, efficiency and
defiance in the preliminary rulings procedure" (2003) 40
C.M.L.Rev. 9.

Walsh, "The appeal of an Article 177 EEC referral" (1993) 56
M.L.R. 881.

Wyatt, "The relationship between actions for annulment and references on validity after *TWD Deggendorf*" in Lonbay and Biondi
(eds), *Remedies for Breach of EC Law* (Wiley, 1997), Ch.6.

PART V

**THE FUNDAMENTAL RIGHTS OF UNION CITIZENS,
THE INTERNAL MARKET AND BEYOND**

CHAPTER 15

CUSTOMS DUTIES AND DISCRIMINATORY INTERNAL TAXATION

Guide to this Chapter: One of the main aims of the Treaty is to **15–001** ensure the free movement of goods, persons, services and capital within the Community. In this part, we analyse the free movement rights together with Union citizenship. We start with the free movement of goods and in this chapter we analyse fiscal barriers to intra-Community trade and discriminatory taxation. Fiscal barriers, prohibited by Article 25 EC, are customs duties and charges having equivalent effect to customs duties. Those are charges imposed for the sole reason that the goods have crossed a frontier. Customs duties and charges having equivalent effect can never be justified; this said, the Court has held that some charges, which might at first sight seem charges having equivalent effect, do not fall within the scope of Article 25 EC if they represent consideration for a service provided to the importer or if they represent the cost of mandatory inspections required by Community law. Discriminatory or protectionist taxation is prohibited by Article 90 EC. Discrimination arises when similar goods are taxed in a different way so as to benefit domestic products at the expenses of imported ones. Protectionist taxation arises when products which are in competition with each other are taxed in such a way so as to afford an advantage to domestic products. As we shall see, the assessment of whether internal taxation is compatible with Article 90 EC sometimes requires complex economic assessments and in some cases taxes which appear at first sight to have a more burdensome effect on imported products might be objectively justified by legitimate public policy aims. This chapter analyses the scope of Articles 25 and 90 EC, the relationship between the two as well as the relationship between those provisions and other Treaty provisions.

CUSTOMS DUTIES AND CHARGES HAVING EQUIVALENT EFFECT

Establishment of a customs union

15–002   Whereas a free trade area comprises a group of customs territories in which duties are eliminated on trade in goods originating in such territories, a customs union represents a further step in economic integration, since a common tariff is adopted in trade relations with the outside world.

Article 23(1) EC (ex 9(1)) provides that:

> "The Community shall be based upon a customs union which shall cover all trade in goods and which shall involve the prohibition between Member States of customs duties on imports and exports and of all charges having equivalent effect, and the adoption of a common customs tariff in their relations with third countries."[1]

The "goods" referred to include all products which have a monetary value and may be the object of commercial transactions. In *Commission v Italy* the Court rejected an argument adduced by the Italian Government that the free movement provisions of the Treaty could have no application to a charge levied on the export of goods of historic or artistic interest. The products covered by the Italian law in issue, said the Court, regardless of any other qualities which might distinguish them from other commercial goods, resembled such goods in that they had a monetary value and could constitute the object of commercial transactions—indeed, the Italian law recognised as much by fixing the charge in relation to the value of the object in question.[2] Coins may constitute "goods" if they do not constitute a means of payment in the Member States,[3] and substances or objects which comprise waste, whether recyclable or not, and whether they have a commercial value or not, also comprise "goods" for these purposes.[4]

---

[1] Former Art.9 was held to be directly applicable in conjunction with other Treaty Articles; see e.g., Cases 2 and 3/69 *Sociaal Fonds, etc. v Brachfeld and Chougol Diamond Co.* [1969] E.C.R. 211 (former Arts 9 and 12); Case 33/70 *SACE v Italian Ministry of Finance* [1970] E.C.R. 1213 (former Arts 9 and 13(2)); Case 18/71 *Eunomia v Italian Ministry of Education* [1971] E.C.R. 811 (former Arts 9 and 16).
[2] Case 7/68 [1968] E.C.R. 423.
[3] Case 7/78 *R v Johnson* [1978] E.C.R. 2247.
[4] Case C–2/90 *Commission v Belgium* [1992] E.C.R. I–4431.

The abolition as between the Member States of customs duties and charge having equivalent effect constitutes a fundamental principle of the common market applicable to all products and goods with the result that any exception, which in any event must be strictly interpreted, must be clearly laid down.[5]

The abolition of customs duties between the constituent territories **15–003** of a free trade area is normally restricted to goods originating in such territories, because otherwise member countries of the area maintaining high tariffs against non-Member countries would find their markets open to imports from such countries via the territories of lower tariff member countries of the area (a phenomenon known as trade deflection). The problem is avoided if all members adopt the same tariffs in their trade with third countries. And this is indeed the solution adopted in a customs union, such as the European Community. Thus the EC Treaty makes provision in Article 26 EC (ex 28) for a Common Customs Tariff, and provides in Article 23(2) that its free movement provisions—Articles 25 EC and Articles 28–31 EC (ex 30, 34, 36 and 37)—apply not only to goods originating in Member States, but also to products coming from third countries which are in free circulation in the Member States.

Article 24 EC (ex 10) thus provides that:

> "Products coming from a third country shall be considered to be in free circulation in a Member State if the import formalities have been complied with and any customs duties or charges having equivalent effect which are payable have been levied in that Member State, and if they have not benefited from a total or partial drawback of such duties or charges."

The "drawback" referred to in Article 24 is possible in the case of inward processing, when goods are imported for the purposes of processing followed by re-export.[6] In *Houben* the Court said of the latter Article:

> "That article draws no distinction between goods imported from a non-member country in circulation in the Member State where the import formalities were completed and the various duties paid and those which, after due completion of the import formalities and payment of the various duties in one Member State, are subsequently imported into another Member State."[7]

---

[5] Joined Cases 90/63 and 91/63 *Commission v Luxembourg and Belgium* [1964] E.C.R. 625; Joined Cases 80/77 and 81/77 *Commissionaires Réunis v Receveur des Douanes* [1978] E.C.R. 927, para.24; Case C–272/95 *Bundesantalt für Landwirtschaft und Ernährung v Deutsches Milch-Kontor GmbH* [1997] E.C.R. I–1905, para.36.

[6] See Reg.2913/92, O.J. [1992] L302/1, Arts 114 *et seq.*

[7] Case C–83/89 *Openbaar Ministerie and the Minister for Finance v Vincent Houben.* [1990] E.C.R. I–1161, para.10.

The Court has also made it clear, as regards the free movement of goods within the Community, that products which are in free circulation are "definitively and wholly assimilated to products originating in Member States".[8]

Customs duties on imports and exports are prohibited

15–004   Relevant provisions of the EC Treaty prior to the amendments which came into force on May 1, 1999 were as follows. Article 12 EC prohibited new customs duties on imports and exports and new charges having equivalent effect, and prohibited any increases in such duties or charges. Article 13 EC stated that customs duties on imports were to be abolished by the end of the transitional period (December 31 1969), as were charges having equivalent effect. Article 16 EC provided that Member States should abolish between themselves customs duties on exports and charges having equivalent effect by the end of the first stage (December 31, 1961). It is to be noted that in certain respects the drafting of the foregoing provisions represented the situation at the time the original Treaty came into force, and to this extent no longer served a useful purpose. The provisions referred to were replaced by the current Article 25 EC, which states:

> "Customs duties on imports and exports and charges having equivalent effect shall be prohibited between Member States. This prohibition shall also apply to customs duties of a fiscal nature."

Customs duties on imports and exports are thus prohibited, and it is proposed to deal first with these. This prohibition is directly applicable.[9–10] The Court of Justice emphasised the "essential nature" and the "importance" of the prohibition of customs duties and similar charges, contained in former Articles 9 and 12 EC (now Articles 23 and 25 EC), in *Commission v Luxembourg and Belgium*, basing its view on the respective provisions of these Articles in the scheme of the Treaty, Article 9 EC being placed at the beginning of

---

[8] Case C–130/92 *OTO SpA v Minstero delle Finanze* [1994] E.C.R. I–3281, para.16.

[9–10] Case 26/62 *Van Gend en Loos v Nederlandse Administratie der Belastingen* [1963] E.C.R. 1; Joined Cases 2 and 3/69 *Sociaal Fonds etc v Brachfeld and Chougol Diamond Co* [1969] E.C.R. 211; Case C–17/91 *Georges Lornoy en Zonen NV v Belgian State* [1992] E.C.R. I–6523; Case 18/71 *Eunomia di Porro & Co. v Italian Ministry of Education* [1971] E.C.R. 811 (former Art.16 directly applicable in conjunction with former Art.9); Case C–114/91 *Criminal proceedings against Gérard Jerôme Claeys* [1992] E.C.R. I–6559 (former Arts 12 and 13). Applicable equally to agricultural goods, see Cases 90 and 91/63 *Commission v Luxembourg and Belgium* [1964] E.C.R. 65. As of the end of the transitional period, trade in agricultural products in sectors lacking a common organisation of the market became subject to the free movement of goods provisions of the Treaty, see e.g. Case 48/74 *Charmasson v Minister for Economic Affairs and Finance* [1974] E.C.R. 1383.

the title relating to "Free Movement of Goods", and Article 12 EC at the beginning of the section dealing with the "Elimination of Customs Duties".[11] This reasoning loses none of its force as regards the current text and context of Articles 23 and 25 EC. The Court in *Luxembourg and Belgium* went on to say that any exception to such an essential rule would require to be clearly stated, and would receive a narrow construction.[12] Thus, to the extent that a Council Regulation concerning the common organisation of the market in wine authorised Member States to impose charges on intra-Community trade, it was held to be invalid by the Court of Justice in *Commissionaires Réunis v Receveur des Douanes*.[13] The Court's rigorous approach is reflected in a consistent case law. In *Sociaal Fonds voor de Diamantarbeiders* the Court was faced with a reference from an Antwerp magistrate, concerning a levy imposed under Belgian law on imported diamonds. The Belgian Government argued that the levy could not be regarded as infringing (former) Articles 9 and 12 EC, since it was devoid of protectionist purpose; in the first place, Belgium did not even produce diamonds, and in the second place, the purpose of the levy was to provide social security benefits for workers in the diamond industry. The following statement of the Court emphasised that the achievement of a single market between Member States requires more than the elimination of protection:

> "In prohibiting the imposition of customs duties, the Treaty does not distinguish between goods according to whether or not they enter into competition with the products of the importing country. Thus, the purpose of the abolition of customs barriers is not merely to eliminate their protective nature, as the Treaty sought on the contrary to give general scope and effect to the rule on elimination of customs duties and charges having equivalent effect in order to ensure the free movement of goods. It follows from the system as a whole and from the general and absolute nature of the prohibition of any customs duty applicable to goods moving between Member States that customs duties are prohibited independently of any considera-tion of the purpose for which they were introduced and the destination of the revenue obtained therefrom. The justification for this prohibition is based on the fact that any pecuniary charge—however small—imposed on goods by reason of the

---

[11] Cases 2 and 3/62 [1962] E.C.R. 425, at 431.
[12] Former Art.115 EC (now Art.134) permitted unilateral derogation from the free movement provisions of the Treaty, in cases of urgency, during the transitional period, but subse-quently, it has been necessary to secure a Commission authorisation.
[13] Joined Cases 80/77 and 81/77 [1978] E.C.R. 927.

fact that they cross a frontier constitutes an obstacle to the movement of such goods."[14]

The fact that the achievement of a single market between Member States is dependent on more than the suppression of measures calculated to protect domestic industry is well illustrated by the prohibition of customs duties on exports as well as imports. As Advocate General Gand pointed out in *Commission v Italy*:

> "What distinguishes customs duties on exports is not that they protect the national industry but that they increase the price of goods and thus tend to hinder their exportation and, without prohibiting trade in goods, to make it more difficult."[15]

Charges having equivalent effect on imports and exports are prohibited

15–005   As noted above, Article 25 EC prohibits charges having an effect equivalent to customs duties on imports and exports, and is directly applicable. The abolition of charges having an effect equivalent to customs duties on imports has been described by the Court of Justice as the "logical and necessary complement" to the elimination of customs duties proper.[16] Similar logic applies to charges having an equivalent effect on exports. The prohibition of charges having equivalent effect, like the prohibition of customs duties, constitutes a basic Treaty norm, and any exception must be clearly and unambiguously provided for.[17]

The concept of charges having equivalent effect must be interpreted in the light of the objects and purposes of the Treaty, in particular the provisions dealing with the free movement of goods,[18] and the Court described such charges on imports or exports in the following terms in *Commission v Italy*:

> "Consequently, any pecuniary charge, however small and whatever its designation and mode of application, which is imposed unilaterally on domestic or foreign goods by reason of the fact that they cross a frontier, and which is not a customs duty in the strict sense, constitutes a charge having equivalent effect within

---

[14] Joined Cases 2 and 3/69 *Sociaal Fonds voor de Diamantarbeiders v S.A. Ch. Brachfeld & Sons and Chougol Diamond Co* [1969] E.C.R. 211.

[15] Case 7/68 [1968] E.C.R. 423 at 434.

[16] Joined Cases 52 and 55/65 *Germany v Commission* [1966] E.C.R. 159 (former Art.13(2)); and see e.g., Joined Cases 2 and 3/69 *Chougol Diamond* [1969] E.C.R. 211; Case 24/68 *Commission v Italy* [1969] E.C.R. 193.

[17] Joined Cases 52 and 55/65 *Germany v Commission* [1966] E.C.R. 159.

[18] See e.g., Joined Cases 2 and 3/69 *Chougol Diamond* [1969] E.C.R. 211.

the meaning of Articles 9, 12, 13 and 16 of the Treaty, even if it is not imposed for the benefit of the State, is not discriminatory or protective in effect and if the product on which the charge is imposed is not in competition with any domestic product."[19]

The prohibition of such charges also applies if a Member State engages a private contractor to carry out customs procedures in connection with the transit of goods between Member States. Thus a transit charge paid under a private contract between such a contractor and a road haulier in respect of the above services will amount to a charge having equivalent effect prohibited by Community law.[20] Furthermore, in order to be qualified as a charge having equivalent effect the charge does not need to be levied for the benefit of the State nor does it matter that it is used to finance worthy causes.[21]

Whilst the definition of charge having equivalent effect refers to charges imposed "by reason of the fact that goods cross a frontier", the Court has found that Article 25 EC applies also to charges imposed in internal frontiers/administrative borders. In *Legros* the Court held that the description of charges having equivalent effect covered dock dues (comprising *ad valorem* duties on goods) imposed on the import of goods into the Rèunion region of France from another Member State, even though the dock dues in question also applied to goods entering Rèunion from Metropolitan France. The Court stated:

> "A charge levied at a regional frontier by reason of the introduction of products into a region of a Member State constitutes an obstacle to the free movement of goods which is at least as serious as a charge levied at the national frontier by reason of the introduction of the products into the whole territory of a Member State."[22]

The same system of dock dues as was in issue in *Legros* was the **15–006** subject of a preliminary ruling in *Lancry*, but this time the question posed was whether the imposition of the dues on goods from the

---

[19] Case 24/68 [1969] E.C.R. 193 at 201; Case 158/82 *Commission v Denmark* [1983] E.C.R. 3573, para.18; Case 340/87 *Commission v Italy* [1989] E.C.R. 1483; Case C–45/94 *Cára de Comercio, Industria y Navegaciön, Ceuta v Municipality of Ceuta* [1995] E.C.R. I–4385, para.28.
[20] Case C–16/94 *Edouard Dubois et Fils SA and Général Cargo Services SA v Garoner Exploitation SA* [1995] E.C.R. I–2421.
[21] e.g. Joined Cases 2 and 3/69 *Sociaal Fonds voor de Diamantarbeiders v S.A. Ch. Brachfeld & Sons and Chougol Diamond Co* [1969] E.C.R. 211; more recently see e.g. Joined Cases C–441/98 and C–442/98 *Michailidis* [2000] E.C.R. I–7145; Case C–389/00 *Commission v Germany* (shipment of waste) [2003] E.C.R. I–2001; Case C–293/02 *Jersey Produce Marketing Organisation Ltd* [2005] E.C.R. I–9543, para.55.
[22] Case 163/90 *Administration des Douanes et Droits Indirects v Léopold Legros.* [1992] E.C.R. I– 4625, para.16; see also Joined Cases C–485/93 and C–86/93 *Maria Simitzi v Dimos Kos.* [1995] E.C.R. I–2655, para.17.

same Member State, France, also amounted to charges having equivalent effect prohibited by the EC Treaty. The Court, perhaps surprisingly, rejected the argument of the Council of the European Union to the effect that the Treaty's prohibition on charges having equivalent effect to customs duties did not apply to charges internal to a Member State, as follows:

> "The unity of the Community customs territory is undermined by the establishment of a regional customs frontier just the same, whether the products on which a charge is levied by reason of the fact that they cross a frontier are domestic products or come from other Member States.
>
> Furthermore, the obstacle to the free movement of goods created by the imposition on domestic products of a charge levied by reason of their crossing that frontier is no less serious than that created by the collection of a charge of the same kind on products from another Member State.
>
> Since the very principle of a customs union covers all trade in goods, as provided for by Article 9 [now 23] of the Treaty, it requires the free movement of goods generally, as opposed to inter-State trade alone, to be ensured within the union. Although Article 9 *et seq.* makes express reference only to trade between Member States, that is because it was assumed that there were no charges exhibiting the features of a customs duty in existence within the Member States. Since the absence of such charges is an essential precondition for the attainment of a customs union covering all trade in goods, it follows that they are likewise prohibited by Article 9 *et seq.*"[23]

Similarly, in *Simitzi* the Court held that charges imposed on goods despatched from one region of a Member State to another region of that same Member State amounted to charges having equivalent effect to customs duties on exports.[24] In *Carbonati Apuani*,[25] the Court found that a charge imposed on marble leaving the district territory of Carrara (the town where it was escavated) was a charge having equivalent effect even though it applied also to marble destined for Italy, and in *Jersey* the Court adopted similar reasoning to charges imposed on Jersey potatoes exported to the UK.[26]

[23] Joined Cases C–363/93, etc., *René Lancry SA v Direction Générale des Souanes etc.* [1994] E.C.R. I–3957, esp. paras 27–29. See also Joined Cases C–485/93 and C–86/93 *Maria Simitzi v Dimos Kos.* [1995] E.C.R. I–2655, para.27.
[24] Joined Cases C–485/93 and C–86/93 *Maria Simitzi v Dimos Kos* [1995] E.C.R. I–2655, paras 26 and 27.
[25] Case C–72/03 *Carbonati Apuani Srl v Comune di Carrrara* [2004] E.C.R. I–8027.
[26] Case C–293/02 *Jersey Produce Marketing Organisation Ltd* [2005] E.C.R. I–9543.

Charges falling outside the scope of Article 25 EC: services provided to the importer and Community law obligations

A charge falling within the scope of Article 25 EC can never be **15–007** justified; however in some cases (narrowly interpreted) a charge might fall altogether outside the scope of Article 25 EC. This is the case in relation to charges imposed on traders to cover the costs of services actually rendered to the importer/exporter,[27] and in relation to charges imposed to discharge and obligation imposed by Community law.

In relation to the former, the Court has usually rejected the "consideration for services" argument in the case of unilateral measures, either because the services in question were rendered in the general interest (e.g. health inspections), rather than in the interests of traders themselves or, if the services did benefit traders, because they benefited them as a class in a way which was impossible to quantify in a particular case (e.g. compilation of statistical data).[28] Furthermore, in order to fall outside the scope of Article 25 EC the charge imposed as consideration for a service must reflect the cost of the service provided. Therefore a charge calculated according to the value of the good necessarily falls within the scope of Article 25 EC, since it bears no relation to the actual cost of the service provided.[29]

On the other hand, the position is rather different if charges are imposed to cover the cost of procedures (such as inspections) provided for by Community measures. Such charges will not amount to charges having equivalent effect prohibited by Community law,[30] at any rate where the Community measures reduce obstacles to intra-Community trade which would otherwise result from divergent national measures, where the fee charged does not exceed the actual cost of the operations involved,[31] and where there is a direct link between the amount of the fee and the cost of the actual inspection in respect of which the fee was charged.[32] Measures taken by a Member State under an international treaty to which all Member States are parties, and which encourage the free movement of goods, may be assimilated to Community measures, and fees covering costs may be charged accordingly.[33]

---

[27] e.g. Case 132/82 *Commission v Belgium* [1983] E.C.R. 1649.
[28] Joined Cases 52 and 55/65 *Germany v Commission* [1966] E.C.R. 159 (charge by national intervention agency for import licences); Case 24/68 *Commission v Italy* [1969] E.C.R. 193, 201 (fee to defray the costs of compiling statistical data); Case 39/73 *Rewe-Zentralfinanz v Landwirtschaftskammer* [1973] E.C.R. 1039, Case 87/75 *Bresciani v Italian Finance Administration* [1976] E.C.R. 129; Case 35/76 *Simmenthal v Italian Minister of Finance* [1976] E.C.R. 1871; Case 251/78 *Firma Denkavit Futtermittel Gmbh v Minister for Food* [1979] E.C.R. 3369 (fees to offset the costs of compulsory and sanitary inspections).
[29] Case 170/88 *Ford Espana* [1989] E.C.R. 2305.
[30] Case 46/76 *Bauhuis v Netherlands* [1977] E.C.R. 5; Case 18/87 *Commission v Germany* [1988] E.C.R. 5427; Case C-130/93 *Lamaire v NDALTP* [1994] E.C.R. I –3215, para.19.
[31] Case C–209/89 *Commission of the European Communities v Italian Republic*. [1991] E.C.R. I–1575, para.10.
[32] *ibid.*
[33] Case 89/76 *Commission v Netherlands* [1977] E.C.R. 1355.

A case neatly illustrating the difficulties of establishing whether or not national charges may be regarded as charges having equivalent effect was *Commission v Belgium*.[34] The development of Community transit procedures enabled importers to convey their goods from the frontier to public warehouses situated in the interior of the country without paying duties and taxes. In these warehouses, importers could have customs clearance operations carried out, and they also had the opportunity of placing their goods in temporary storage, pending their consignment to a particular customs procedure. The Belgian Government levied storage charges on goods deposited in such public warehouses in the interior of the Community. The Court held that these charges were charges having equivalent effect when they were imposed solely in connection with the completion of customs formalities, but that they were justified in cases where the trader elected to place his or her goods in storage. In the latter case, the Court accepted that the storage represented a service rendered to traders. A decision to deposit the goods could only be taken at the request of the trader concerned, and ensured storage of the goods without payment of duties. The Belgian Government argued that also in the former case—where the goods were cleared through customs without storage—a service was rendered to the importer. It was always open to the latter to avoid payment by choosing to have his or her goods cleared through customs at the frontier, where such a procedure was free of charge. By using a public warehouse, the importer could have the goods declared through customs near the places for which his products were bound. The Court acknowledged that the use of a public warehouse in the interior of the country offered certain advantages, but noted that such advantages were linked solely with the completion of customs formalities which, whatever the place, was always compulsory. Furthermore, the advantages in question resulted from the scheme of Community transit, not in the interest of individual traders, but in order to encourage the free movement of goods and facilitate transport in the Community. "There can therefore," concluded the Court, "be no question of levying charges for customs clearance facilities accorded in the interests of the Common Market."

15–008   It was noted above that Member States could charge for procedures for which provision is made by Community law,[35] while in the foregoing case it is said that no charges could be made for customs clearance facilities provided for by Community law. What is the dividing line between the Community procedures for which a charge might be made, and those customs clearance facilities which can be charged for? The case law is less than completely clear in this respect. In *Commission v Italy* in 1991 the Court, citing one of its

---

[34] Case 132/82 [1983] E.C.R. 1649.
[35] See above page 543.

previous rulings authorising charges for procedures provided for by Community law,[36] referred to "the compatibility with the Treaty rules of fees charged in connection with the completion of customs formalities, on condition that their amount does not exceed the actual cost of the operations in respect of which they are charged".[37] In *Dubois* in 1995 the Court, referring to *Commission v Belgium*, stated that:

> "Articles 9 and 12 of the Treaty require Member States to bear the cost of the controls and formalities carried out in connection with the movement of goods across frontiers."[38]

The explanation for this apparent contradiction is that a distinction is to be drawn between, on the one hand, the customs formalities applicable to all goods in transit pursuant to Community law, for which no charge may be made, and, on the other hand, any additional requirements applicable in the case of certain goods, such as, inspections of goods, or any additional facilities provided for by the authorities of a Member State. It is to be noted that the case referred to by the Court in *Commission v Italy* (1991), as authority for the above proposition concerning charges for "the completion of customs formalities" was a case concerning phytosanitary inspections,[39] while the action by the Commission against Italy in the case itself involved a system of charges payable by undertakings where customs formalities were completed outside the customs area or outside normal office hours. The Commission did not allege that the charges amounted in themselves to charges having equivalent effect to customs duties; only that they amounted to such charges because they were disproportionate to the service rendered in certain cases.[40]

As regards charges having equivalent effect on exports, the Court has held that an internal duty which falls more heavily on exports than on domestic sales amounts to a charge having equivalent effect to a customs duty.[41] Fees for inspections of plants charged only in respect of exported product, and not in respect of those intended for the home market, constitute charges having equivalent effect on exports, even if those inspections are carried out to meet the requirements of international conventions affecting only exported products. The contrary would be true only if it were established that the products intended for the home market derived no benefit from the inspections.[42]

---

[36] Case 89/76 *Commission v Netherlands* [1977] E.C.R. 1355, at para.16.
[37] Case C–209/89 [1991] E.C.R. 1991 page I–1575, para.10.
[38] Case C–16/94 *Edouard Dubois et Fils SA and Général Cargo Services SA v Garoner Exploitation SA* [1995] E.C.R. I–2421.
[39] Case 89/76 *Commission v Netherlands* [1977] E.C.R. 1355.
[40] The action was successful in this respect.
[41] Joined Cases 36 & 71/80 *Irish Creamery Milk Suppliers Assn. v Govt. of Ireland* [1981] E.C.R. 735.
[42] Case C–111/89 *Hillegom* [1990] E.C.R. I–1735.

Transit charges prohibited

15–009   The EC Treaty has been interpreted as prohibiting in the widest possible terms charges on goods originating in the EC or in free circulation, even when such charges are imposed on goods of one Member State introduced in another region of that same Member State.[43] But the Treaty does not expressly prohibit transit charges on third country goods which are not in free circulation in the Community. In *SIOT*[44] an Italian undertaking challenged before an Italian court charges imposed upon oil landed at Trieste for consignment via the transalpine oil pipe-line to Germany. The Italian court asked the Court of Justice whether such transit charges were compatible with Community law. The Court held that it was a necessary consequence of the Customs Union and the mutual interest of the Member States that there be recognised a general principle of freedom of transit of goods within the Community. The imposition of transit charges was incompatible with this principle, unless the charges in question represented the costs of transportation or of other services connected with transit, including general benefit derived form the use of harbour works or installations, for the navigability and maintenance of which public authorities were responsible. The Court's conclusion is unremarkable as regards as goods originating in Member States or as regards third country goods in free circulation. But it is to be noted that the oil in question did not originate in a Member State, and it is not clear that it was in free circulation in a Member State.[45] While the Treaty states that the elimination of customs duties and quantitative restrictions applies to products originating in Member States and to products coming from third countries which are in free circulation in Member States, the *SIOT* case implies that the above mentioned provisions apply by analogy to third country goods which are not in free circulation where such goods are in lawful transit in one Member State and destined for another. In the *Richardt* case[46] goods of third country origin in free circulation in France were mistakenly consigned via the community transit procedure applicable to third country goods not in free circulation (the external transit procedure) to Luxembourg for export to the Soviet Union. The Court of Justice confirmed the principle of freedom of transit without stating in so many words that the principle applied to goods in external community transit as well as to goods in free circulation. But the implication is that goods in external community transit or which would be so conveyed unless exempted from that procedure are subject to the application of

---

[43] See above at p.542.
[44] Case 266/81 [1983] E.C.R. 731.
[45] The reference by the Trieste Port Authority to external Community transit suggests that the goods were not in free circulation, [1988] E.C.R. 731 at 752.
[46] Case C–367/89 [1991] E.C.R. I–4621.

analogy of the provisions of the Treaty prohibiting customs duties and charges having equivalent effect, and indeed quantitative restrictions and measures having equivalent effect.

DISCRIMINATORY TAXATION

Discriminatory internal taxation prohibited

Article 90 EC

The first paragraph of Article 90 EC (ex 95) provides that no **15–010** Member State shall impose, directly or indirectly, on the product of any other Member State any internal taxation of any kind in excess of that imposed directly or indirectly on similar domestic products. Paragraph 2 adds that Member States shall furthermore impose no taxation of such a kind as to afford indirect protection to other products. The first paragraph is concerned with imports having such a close competitive relationship with similar domestic products as to merit the same tax treatment as that applicable to those products. The second paragraph contemplates imports which are not in such a close competitive relationship with relevant domestic products as to merit the same tax treatment, but which are nevertheless sufficiently interchangeable from the point of view of consumers to merit tax treatment which is even handed and free of any protective effect in favour of such domestic products. Although Article 90 EC refers to products "of other Member States", this has been held to include products from third countries which are in free circulation in Member States.[47] Furthermore, once a product has been imported from another Member State and placed on the market, it becomes a domestic product for the purposes of comparison of its tax position with an import from another Member State under Article 90 EC.[48]

(a) The Purpose of Article 90 EC. The Court has stated that the **15–011** Article is calculated to close any loopholes which internal taxation might open in the prohibition on customs duties and charges having equivalent effect.[49] The purpose of the Article has been explained as follows in a consistent line of cases:

> ". . . Article 95 [now 90] supplements the provisions on the abolition of customs duties and charges having equivalent effect. Its aim is to ensure free movement of goods between the Member States in normal conditions of competition by the

---

[47] Case 193/85 *Co-Frutta* [1987] E.C.R. 2085 at para.25.
[48] Case C–47/88 *Commission v Denmark* [1990] E.C.R. I–4509, para.17.
[49] Joined Cases 2 and 3/62 *Commission v Belgium and Luxembourg* [1962] E.C.R. 425 at 431.

elimination of all forms of protection which may result from the application of internal taxation that discriminates against products from other Member States. Thus Article 95 must guarantee the complete neutrality of internal taxation as regards competition between domestic products and imported products."[50]

The rule prohibiting discriminatory internal taxation on imported goods constitutes an essential basic principle of the common market,[51] and is directly applicable.[52]

15–012 (b) Member States free under Article 90(1) to choose system of internal taxation, providing its advantages are extended to imported products. Article 90 EC, first paragraph, prohibits discrimination against similar imported products, with respect to the rate of taxation, basis of assessment,[53] or detailed rules.[54] By way of example, in *Commission v Greece*,[55] the detailed rules for calculating the taxable value of imported used cars for the purposes of application of a consumer tax were held to be discriminatory and contrary to Article 90 EC, while in *Commission v France* disproportionately higher penalties for VAT offences regarding import transactions than for such offences regarding domestic transactions were held to contravene Article 90 EC.[56]

Article 90 EC leaves each Member State free to establish the system of taxation which it considers the most suitable in relation to each product, provided that the system is treated as a point of reference for determining whether the tax applied to a similar product of another Member State complies with the requirements of the first paragraph of that Article.[57] It matters not that tax concessions for domestic products rest, not directly upon national law, but on administrative instructions to the authorities.[58]

A system of taxation can be considered compatible with Article 90 EC only if it is proved to be so structured as to exclude any

---

[50] Case 252/86 *Bergandi* [1988] E.C.R. 1343, at para.24; Case C–45/94 *Cára de Comercio, Industria y Navegacion, Ceuta v Municipality of Ceuta* [1995] E.C.R. I–4385, para.29.
[51] Case 57/65 *Lütticke* [1966] E.C.R. 205 at 214.
[52] Case 57/65 *Lütticke* [1966] E.C.R. 205; Case 28/67 *Molkerei-Zentrale v Hauptzollamt Paderborn* [1968] E.C.R. 143; Case 45/75 *Rewe-Zentrale etc v Hauptzollamt Landau/Pfalz* [1976] E.C.R. 181; Case 74/76 *Iannelli & Volpi v Paolo Meroni* [1977] E.C.R. 557; Case C–119/89 *Commission v Kingdom of Spain* [1991] E.C.R. I–641, para.5.
[53] Case 54/72 *FOR v VKS* [1973] E.C.R. 193; Case 20/76 *Schottle & Sohne v Finanzampt Feudenstadt* [1977] E.C.R. 247; Case 74/76 *Iannelli & Volpi v Paolo Meroni* [1977] E.C.R. 557; Case C–68/96 *Grundig Italiana SpA v Ministero delle Finanze* [1998] E.C.R. I–3775.
[54] Case 169/78 *Commission v Italy* [1980] E.C.R. 385; Case 55/79 *Commission v Ireland* [1980] E.C.R. 385.
[55] Case C–375/95 [1997] E.C.R. I–5981.
[56] Case C–276/91 [1993] E.C.R. I–4413.
[57] Case 127/75 *Bobie-Getrankervertrieb v Hauptzollamt aachen-Nord* [1976] E.C.R. 1079.
[58] Case 17/81 *Pabst & Richarz* [1982] E.C.R. 1331.

possibility of imported products being taxed more heavily than domestic products, so that it cannot in any circumstances have discriminatory effect.[59] It follows that all manner of tax concessions or advantages available in respect of domestic products must be extended to similar imported products.

In the *Hansen* case[60] the question arose whether an importer of spirits into Germany was entitled to take advantage of tax relief available, *inter alia*, in respect of spirits made from fruit by small businesses and collective farms. The Court acknowledged that advantages of this kind could serve legitimate economic or social purposes, such as the use of certain raw materials, the continued production of particular spirits of high quality, or the continuance of certain classes of undertakings such as agricultural distilleries. However, Article 90 EC required that such preferential systems must be extended without discrimination to spirits coming from other Member States.[61]

The above principle was applied to the Republic of Italy when that country charged lower taxes on regenerated oil than on ordinary oil, on ecological grounds, while refusing to extend this advantage to imported regenerated oil. Italy argued that it was impossible to distinguish whether oil was of primary distillation, or regenerated. The Court of Justice refused to accept this argument as a justification. It was for importers to establish that their oil qualified for the relief in question, while the Italian authorities were to set standards of proof no higher than was necessary to prevent tax evasion. The Court of Justice observed that certificates from the authorities of exporting Member States could provide one means of identifying oil which had been regenerated.[62] Similarly, in *Commission v Greece*, the Greek government claimed that extending to imported cars the reduced rate of special consumer tax payable in respect of domestic cars using "anti-pollution technology" would require a technical test to be carried out on each import, which was not practical. The Court held that such considerations could not justify tax discrimination against imports, and held the tax contrary to Article 90 EC.[63] In *Outokumpu Oy* the Court considered a Finnish tax regime whereby domestic electricity was subject to a rates varying with the method of production and energy sources used while imported electricity was subject to a flat-rate tariff which in certain cases exceeded the lowest

[59] Case C–90/94 *Haahr Petroleum Ltd v Obenra Havn* [1997] E.C.R. I–4085, para.34; Case C–375/95 *Commission v Greece* [1997] E.C.R. I–5981, para.29; Case C–387/01 *Weigel* [2004] E.C.R. I–4981, para.86.
[60] Case 148/77 *H. Hansen v Hauptzollampt Flensburg* [1978] E.C.R. 1787. See also Case 26/80 *Schneider-Import* [1980] E.C.R. 3469; Case 277/83 *Commission v Italy* [1985] E.C.R. 2049, para.17; Case 196/85 *Commission v France* [1987] E.C.R. 1597.
[61] *ibid.*
[62] Case 21/79 *Commission v Italy* [1980] E.C.R. 1. See also Case 140/79 *Chemial Farmaceutici v DAF* [1981] E.C.R. 1; Case 46/80 *Vinal v Orbat* [1981] E.C.R. 77.
[63] Case C–375/95 [1997] E.C.R. I–5981, esp. para.47.

rate applicable to domestic electricity. The Court noted that while the characteristics of electricity may indeed make it extremely difficult to determine precisely the method of production of imported electricity and hence the energy sources used for that purpose, "the Finnish legislation at issue does not even give the importer the opportunity of demonstrating that the electricity imported by him has been produced by a particular method in order to qualify for the rate applicable to electricity of domestic origin produced by the same method."[64] The Court concluded that the tax was contrary to Article 90 EC.

15–013 **(c) Criteria for differentiating between products for tax purposes must not discriminate against similar imported products or products in partial or potential competition with imported products.** Even if a Member State applies to similar imported products the same tax regime which applies to domestic products, the effect in practice may be that imported products fall into higher taxed categories, while domestic goods fall into lower taxed categories. In *Commission v Greece* the Court considered Greek rules imposing the general VAT rate of 16 per cent on certain spirits (including ouzo, brandy, liqueurs), while imposing a higher rate of 36 per cent on others (including whisky, gin, vodka and rum). Spirits in the former category were produced in Greece, while those in the latter category were not, or to no significant extent. The Court proceeded on the basis that all the spirits in the former category were either similar products within the meaning of the first paragraph of Article 90 EC, or were partly or potentially in competition with products in the second category, and considered that the tax regime in question contravened Article 90 EC. The Court made the following observation:

> "The tax system established by the Greek legislation displays undeniably discriminatory or protective features. Although it does not establish any formal distinction according to the origin of the products, it is arranged in such a way that all the national production of spirits falls within the most favoured tax category. Those features of the system cannot be cancelled out by the fact that a fraction of imported spirits benefits from the most favourable rate ... It therefore appears that the tax system benefits national production and puts imported spirits at a disadvantage."[65]

It does not however follow automatically from the fact that all products falling within the most highly taxed category are imported

---

[64] Case C–213/96 [1998] E.C.R. I–1777, at para.39.
[65] Case C–230/89 [1991] E.C.R. I–1909, at para.10.

products that the tax regime is contrary to Article 90 EC, and the Court has emphasised on a number of occasions that "a system of taxation cannot be regarded as discriminatory solely because only imported products, in particular those from other Member States, come within the most highly taxed category."[66] The explanation for the apparent contradiction between the latter proposition and the quotation set out above from *Commission v Greece* is that differentiating between products on objective grounds consistent with Community law may lead to imports rather than domestic products falling into the highest taxed categories simply because of the characteristics of the imports. As the Court stated in *Haahr Petroleum*:

> ". . . at its present stage of development Community law does not restrict the freedom of each Member State to lay down tax arrangements which differentiate between certain products, even products which are similar within the meaning of the first paragraph of Article 95 [now 90] of the Treaty, on the basis of objective criteria, such as the nature of the raw materials used or the production processes employed. Such differentiation is compatible with Community law, however, only if it pursues objectives of economic policy which are themselves compatible with the requirements of the Treaty and its secondary legislation, and if the detailed rules are such as to avoid any form of discrimination, direct or indirect, in regard to imports from other Member States or any form of protection of competing domestic products."[67]

The Court has on a number of occasions considered progressive national taxes which at their higher level apply in practice exclusively to imports.

Humblot[68] arose from a challenge to a French special car tax payable by reference to "fiscal horsepower" or CV. Cars were subject in the first place to a tax which rose uniformly in proportion to increases in CV, and in the second place to a special tax levied at a single and considerably higher rate on cars rated at more than 16CV. No cars of more than 16CV were manufactured in France, all were imported. The Court emphasised that Member States were free to subject products such as cars to a system of tax which increases progressively in amount depending on an objective criterion, such as the power rating for tax purposes, which might be determined in

---

[66] Case 140/79 *Chemial Farmaceutici v DAF* [1981] E.C.R. 1, para.18; Case C–132/88 *Commission v Greece* [1990] E.C.R. I–1567, para.18;
[67] Case C–90/94 *Haahr Petroleum Ltd v Obenra Havn* [1997] E.C.R. I–4085, para.29, referring to a consistent case law.
[68] Case 112/84 [1985] E.C.R. 1367.

various ways. Such a system of domestic taxation would only be compatible with Article 90 EC, however, if it were free of any discriminatory or protective effect. France denied any protective effect, arguing that there was no evidence that a consumer who might have been dissuaded from buying a vehicle of more than 16CV would purchase a car of French manufacture of 16CV or less. The Court of Justice rejected this argument, noting that cars on each side of the 16CV line were in competition with each other. The substantial additional increase in tax on cars of more than 16CV was liable to cancel out advantages which certain cars imported from other Member States might have in consumers' eyes over comparable cars of domestic manufacture. "In that respect," said the Court, "the special tax reduces the amount of competition to which cars of domestic manufacture are subject and hence is contrary to the principle of neutrality with which domestic taxation must comply."

15–014   It fell to the Court to consider the successor tax to the above in the *Feldain* case.[69] The successor tax was progressive, but not uniformly progressive in two respects. Firstly, it progressed less sharply at the level which applied to top of the range French cars. According to the Court, "It thus exhibits a discriminatory or protective effect . . . in favour of cars manufactured in France."[70] Secondly, it incorporated a factor in calculating the power rating which had the effect of placing in the higher tax bands only imported vehicles. The Court noted that the factor in question was not justified by considerations relating to fuel consumption which France has argued as the basis for the system. "It must therefore be held that that method of determining the power rating for tax purposes is not objective in character and favours cars manufactured in France."[71]

In *Commission v Greece*[72] the Court considered another system of progressive taxation of cars, relating the tax payable to the cylinder capacity of the car. Greece argued that progression was justified by the fact that larger capacity cars were luxury products, and generated pollution. The progression was not uniform, increasing sharply at 1201 c.c., and then at 1801 c.c. Most cars produced in Greece were of 1300 c.c.; none were produced of more than 1600 c.c. capacity, and the tax rates which applied above that level applied exclusively to imports. The Court of Justice held that the system was compatible with Article 90 EC since a consumer deterred from buying a car of over 1800 c.c. would either buy one of 1600 to 1800 c.c. (all of which were of foreign manufacture), or one of below 1600 c.c. (which range included imports and cars of Greek manufacture). "Consequently,"

[69] Case 433/85 [1987] E.C.R. 3521.
[70] *ibid.* at para.14.
[71] *ibid.* at para.16.
[72] Case C–132/88 [1990] E.C.R. I–1567.

held the Court, "the Commission has not shown how the system of taxation at issue might have the effect of favouring the sale of cars of Greek manufacturer."[73] This reasoning would be sustainable if the Court had found that cars of over 1800 c.c. were not in competition with cars below 1600 c.c., though this is not self-evident, and the case referred to below, *Tarantik*, indicates that the reasoning is not so limited. In which case, in the words of the Court in *Humblot*, the tax in question "reduces the amount of competition to which cars of domestic manufacture are subject and hence is contrary to the principle of neutrality with which domestic taxation must comply".[74] To put the matter in a different way, the approach in *Commission v Greece* appears to condone a higher tax rate being imposed on an imported car of over 1800 c.c. than on a domestically produced car below 1600 c.c., because the competitive disadvantage of the 1800+ c.c. import may operate to the advantage of another import rather than a domestically produced car. Yet if the domestically produced car, and the 1800+ c.c. import, are "similar" within the meaning of Article 90(1) EC, they should be subject to the same tax, and if they are not subject to the same tax, the tax discrimination in question cannot be justified on the ground that *other* imports are not subject to the same discrimination. In the *Greek Spirits* case referred to above,[75] it certainly does not appear that tax discrimination as between Greek brandy and Scotch and Irish whisky could be justified by an absence of discrimination against French and German brandy. As noted above, compliance with Article 90(1) EC requires a national tax regime to exclude any possibility of imported products being taxed more heavily than domestic products, so that it cannot in any circumstances have discriminatory effects.[76] The result in the case might be justified on the ground that, although the effect of the progressive tax was to indirectly discriminate against certain imports, this was objectively justified by the nature of the tax regime; but this was not the approach taken by the Court.

The French rules on fiscal horsepower, which were amended after the *Feldain* judgment, were considered by the Court in several further cases, including *Tarantik*.[77] The fiscal horsepower arrangements referred to above in the context of the *Humblot* case by then included a 15–16 CV tax band, a 17–18 CV tax band, and a number of bands over 18 CV. The Court noted that, unlike the 15–16 CV

---

[73] *ibid.* at para.20.
[74] Case 433/85 [1987] E.C.R. 3521, para.14.
[75] See above, p.550.
[76] See above, para.15–011.
[77] Case C–421/97 *Yves Tarantik v Direction des Services Fiscauz de Seine-et-Marne* [1999] E.C.R. I–3633 ; and rules on taxation of used vehicles must take into account depreciation of imported vehicles and legislation cannot be drafted in general and abstract terms unless it ensures that any discriminatory effect be excluded, e.g. Case C–393/98 *Gomes Valente* [2001] E.C.R. I–1327; Case C–101/00 *Tulliasiamies and Siilin* [2002] E.C.R. I–7487.

band (which covered both imported and domestic cars), the tax bands above 18 CV covered exclusively imported vehicles. The Court also considered that certain vehicles in the 15–16 CV tax band could be considered similar to vehicles in the bands over 18 CV. The Court concluded *inter alia* that national rules such as those in issue would nevertheless be compatible with Article 90 EC if consumers have a choice such that the increase in the progression co-efficient between the 15–16 CV band and the bands above 18 CV is not of a nature such as to favour the sale of vehicles of domestic manufacture. This reasoning is the same as that in *Commission v Greece*,[78] and is open to criticism on the same ground.

While it is open to Member States to differentiate between like products on objective grounds consistent with the Treaty, they are not permitted to discriminate by conditioning tax concessions on requirements which can only be, or in fact only are, satisfied by national products.[79] Examples of such discrimination would be charging lower tax rates on those products which could be inspected on national territory at the manufacturing stage,[80] and charging lower rates on products without a designation of origin or provenance where no such protection was available for domestic products and the higher rate applied in practice only to imports.[81]

15–015 **(d) Article 90(1) EC—taxation in excess of that imposed "indirectly" on domestic products.** It will be recalled that Article 90 first paragraph, prohibits internal taxation of any kind in excess of that imposed directly or indirectly on similar domestic products. In *Molkerei-Zentrale v Hauptzollamt Paderborn*[82] the Court was asked for a definition of the "indirect" taxation in question. Advocate General Gand suggested that the charges in question must include all those imposed on raw materials and component goods and services. The Court agreed that the words "directly or indirectly" were to be construed broadly, and defined them as embracing all taxation which was actually and specifically imposed on the domestic product at earlier stages of the manufacturing and marketing process. This formulation might suggest that taxes on components, not being actually and specifically imposed on the product, might be excluded. This is not the case. As the Court's interpretation of the words "directly or indirectly" in Article 91 EC (ex 96) indicates,[83] "indirect" taxation indeed includes charges levied on raw materials

---

[78] Above at p.552.
[79] Case C–90/94 *Haahr Petroleum Ltd v Obenra Havn* [1997] E.C.R. I–4085, at para.30.
[80] Joined Cases 142 and 143/80 *Italian Finance Administration v Essevi SpA* [1981] E.C.R. 1413; see also Case 277/83 *Commission v Italy* [1983] E.C.R. 601.
[81] Case 319/81 *Commission v Italy* [1983] E.C.R. 601; see also Case 106/84 *Commission v Denmark* [1986] E.C.R. 833.
[82] Case 28/67 [1968] E.C.R. 143.
[83] Case 45/64 *Commission v Italy* [1965] E.C.R. 857.

and semi-finished products incorporated in the goods in question. Nevertheless, the Court entered a caveat in *Molkerei-Zentrale*: the effect of these charges diminished with the incidence of stages of production and distribution and tended rapidly to become negligible, and that fact ought to be taken into account by Member States when calculating the indirect charges applied to domestic products.

Although the taxation of undertakings manufacturing products will not in general be regarded as constituting taxation of the products themselves, the taxation of specific activities of an undertaking which has an "immediate effect" on the cost of the national imported product must by virtue of Article 90 EC be applied in a manner which is not discriminatory to imported products. Thus taxation imposed indirectly upon products within the meaning of Article 90 EC must be interpreted as including charges imposed on the international transport of goods by road according to the distance covered on the national territory and the weight of the goods in question.[84] Again, Article 90 EC applies to internal taxation which is imposed on the use of imported products were these products are intended for such use and have been imported solely for that purpose.[85]

(e) Article 90 EC does not place imports in a privileged tax position. The object of Article 90 EC is to abolish direct or indirect discrimination against imported products, but not to place them in a privileged tax position.[86] Internal taxation may therefore be imposed on imported products, even in the absence of a domestically produced counterpart. In *Stier*,[87] the Court of Justice held that although Article 90 EC does not prohibit Member States from imposing taxation on imported products which lack a domestic counterpart, it would not be permissible to impose on such imports charges of such an amount that the free movement of goods would be impeded. In *Commission v Denmark*[88] the Court held that such impediment to the free movement of goods would fall to be governed by Articles 28–30 EC, rather than within the framework of Article 90 EC. Yet, after *Commission v Denmark* the relationship between Article 90 and 28 EC was unclear. In particular, whilst it is consistent case law that Article 28 EC does not apply in relation to obstacles of a fiscal nature falling within the scope of Article 25 or Article 90 EC, it was not clear in what circumstances Article 28 EC would be triggered. This issue was clarified in *De Danske Billimportører*,[89] where the Court clarified that in order for Article 28 EC

15–016

---

[84] Case 20/76 *Schottle & Sohne v Finanzamt Freudenstadt* [1977] E.C.R. 247.
[85] Case 252/86 *Bergandi* [1988] E.C.R. 1343.
[86] Case 153/80 *Rumhaus Hansen* [1981] E.C.R. 1165; Case 253/83 *Kupferberg* [1985] E.C.R. 157.
[87] Case 31/67 [1968] E.C.R. 235.
[88] Case C–47/88 [1990] E.C.R. I–4509.
[89] Case C–383/01 *De Danske Billimportører* [2003] E.C.R. I–6065.

to be triggered the charge must be so high as to impede free movement.[90]

15–017 **(f) Domestic products may not claim equality with imports.** However, Article 90 EC does not prohibit the imposition on national products of internal taxation in excess of that on imported products.[91] It has been noted that Member States may differentiate for tax purposes between products, provided that discrimination against imports does not result. What if national law imposes a higher rate of tax on product X than on competing product Y, where product X is largely, but not entirely, imported, and where the higher rate of tax contravenes Article 90 of the EC Treaty? The position is that while importers of product X may claim the protection of Article 90 EC, domestic producers may legitimately be taxed at the higher rate. In one example Danish revenue laws imposed a lower rate of tax on aquavit than on other spirits, which other spirits were mainly, but not entirely, imported. In proceedings instituted by the Commission under Article 226 EC the Court held that these rules were contrary to Article 90 EC[92] and in later proceedings the Court emphasised that only importers could rely on Article 90 EC, and not domestic producers of those spirits subject to the "discriminatory" tax.[93]

15–018 **(g) Respective Scope of Article 90(1) and 90(2).** Whereas Article 90 EC, first paragraph, prohibits internal taxation in excess of that imposed on similar domestic products, paragraph 2 adds that Member States shall furthermore impose no taxation of such a kind as to afford indirect protection to other products. The respective scope of these two paragraphs is as follows. Under Article 90(1) EC it is necessary to consider as similar products those which have similar characteristics and which might meet the same needs from the point of view of consumers. The appropriate criterion is not the strictly identical nature of the products but their similar and comparable use.[94] The Court at one stage held that "similarity" within Article 90(1) EC existed when the products were normally, for tax, tariff or statistical purposes, placed in the same classification.[95] In a later case the Court confirmed that classification under

---

[90] See Ch.16, and para.15–024, below. The Court has also clarified that the non-applicability of Arts 25 and 90 EC by no means triggers the automatic applicability of Art.28 EC; see Joined Cases C–34/01 to C–38/01 *Enirisorse Spa* [2003] E.C.R. I–14243.
[91] Case 86/78 Case 86/78 *Grandes Distilleries Peureux v Directeur des Services Fiscaux* [1979] E.C.R. 89.
[92] Case 171/78 *Commission v Denmark* [1980] E.C.R. 447. And see Case 168/78 *Commission v France* [1980] E.C.R. 347.
[93] Case 68/79 [1980] E.C.R. 501.
[94] Case 169/78 *Commission v Italy* [1980] E.C.R. 385.
[95] Case 27/67 *Fink-Frucht v Hauptzollamt Munchen-Landsbergstrasse* [1968] E.C.R. 223. Case 28/69 *Commission v Italy* [1979] E.C.R. 187.

the same heading in the Common Customs Tariff (CCT) was an important consideration in assessing similarity under Article 90 EC.[96] But the Court has stressed that the fact that rum and whisky are given separate subdivisions under the (CCT) is not conclusive on the question of "similarity" under Article 90(1) EC,[97] and when asked by an Italian court whether it should apply the "tariff classification" test, or the broader economic approach referred to above, the Court reiterated the latter criterion, without adverting to the former.[98] Nevertheless, it would seem that CCT classification constitutes at least an indication one way or the other of "similarity" within the meaning of Article 90(1) EC.

In *John Walker*,[99] the Court held that in order to determine whether the products in question (fruit liqueur wines and whisky) were "similar" within the meaning of Article 90(1) EC, it was first necessary to consider objective characteristics of the respective products, such as their origin, method of manufacture, and their organoleptic qualities, in particular taste and alcohol content, and secondly it was necessary to consider whether both categories of beverages were capable of meeting the same needs from the point of view of consumers. Applying the first test, it was not sufficient that the same raw material, alcohol, was to be found in both products. For the products to be regarded as similar that raw material would have to be present in more or less equal proportions in both products. Since whisky contained twice the alcoholic content of fruit liqueur wines, the products could not be regarded as "similar" within the meaning of Article 90(1) EC.

Once similarity is established and Article 90(1) applies, the tax rates on the domestic product and the similar imported product must be the same. Article 90(2), by way of contrast, covers all forms of indirect tax protection in the case of products which, without being similar within the meaning of Article 90(1), are nevertheless in competition, even partial, indirect or potential, with products of the importing country. It is sufficient for the imported product to be in competition with the protected domestic product by reason of one or several economic uses to which it may be put, even though the condition of similarity for the purposes of Article 90(1) EC are not fulfilled.[1]

While Article 90(1) EC prohibits a higher tax on imported products than similar domestic products, Article 90(2) EC, because of the difficulty of making a sufficiently precise comparison between the products in question, employs a more general criterion, i.e. the

---

[96] Case 45/75 *Rewe-Zentrale etc. v Hauptzollamt Landau/Pfalz* [1976] E.C.R. 181.

[97] Case 169/78 *Commission v Italy* [1980] E.C.R. 385; Case 168/78 *Commission v France* [1980] E.C.R. 347; Case 106/84 *Commission v Denmark* [1986] E.C.R. 833

[98] Case 216/81 *Cogis SpA v Italian Finance Ministry* [1982] E.C.R. 2701.

[99] Case 243/84 [1986] E.C.R. 875.

[1] Case 169/78 *Commission v Italy* [1980] E.C.R. 385.

indirect protection afforded by a domestic tax system. It follows that a tax on an imported product need not be identical with the tax imposed on a domestic product with which it is in partial or indirect competition, as it would have to be if the products were in a sufficiently close competitive relationship to be regarded as similar within the meaning of Article 90(1) EC. In *Commission v Belgium*[2] it was alleged that VAT on wine (imported) at 25 per cent afforded indirect protection to beer (a domestic product) which was subject to VAT at 19 per cent. The Court rejected this argument, in view of the insignificant impact of the difference in tax on the difference in price between the two products. The Commission had not shown that the difference in question gave rise to any protective effect favouring beer intended for domestic consumption. It seems that what the Court was looking for was not complex market analysis, but a price difference which on a common sense basis would suggest an advantage for beer over wine. Protective effect need not, however, be shown statistically. It is sufficient for the purposes of Article 90(2) EC for it to be shown that a given system of taxation is likely, in view of its inherent characteristics, to bring about the protective effect referred to by the Treaty.[3] Furthermore, statistics showing import penetration by products allegedly discriminated against cannot rebut the inference of protective effect to be drawn from the inherent characteristics of a national tax system.[4] However, statistics are admissible to show that a tax system which is apparently neutral in fact burdens imports to a greater extent than domestic products.[5]

15–019 To illustrate the inter-relation between Article 90(1) and (2) EC, reference may be made to the great range of spirit drinks aquavit, geneva, grappa, whisky, etc. While these drinks have common generic factors (distillation, high alcohol level), there are different types of spirits, characterised by the raw material used, their flavour, and processes of manufacture.[6] Furthermore, spirits may be consumed in different forms: neat, diluted, or in mixtures.[7] They may also be consumed on different occasions, as aperitifs or digestifs, at meal times, or on other occasions.[8] The Court of Justice has held that among spirit drinks there exists an indeterminate number which can be regarded as similar products within the meaning of Article 90(1) EC, and that where it is impossible to identify a sufficient degree of similarity between the products concerned for the purposes of Article 90(1) EC, there exist nevertheless characteristics

---

[2] Case 356/85 [1987] E.C.R. 3299. And for the *"de minimis"* effect see Case 27/67 *Fink-Frucht* [1968] E.C.R. 223, 233.
[3] Case 170/78 *Commission v United Kingdom* [1980] E.C.R. 417.
[4] Case 168/78 *Commission v France* [1980] E.C.R. 347; Case 319/81 *Commission v Italy* [1983] E.C.R. 601.
[5] Case 319/81 *Commission v Italy* [1983] E.C.R. 601.
[6] Case 168/78 *Commission v France* [1980] E.C.R. 347; Case 169/78 *Commission v Italy* [1980] E.C.R. 385; Case 171/78 *Commission v Denmark* [1980] E.C.R. 447.
[7] Case 169/78 *Commission v Italy* [1980] E.C.R. 385.
[8] Case 168/78 *Commission v France* [1980] E.C.R. 347.

common to all spirits which are sufficiently marked for it to be said that they are all at least partly, indirectly or potentially in competition for the purposes of Article 90(2) EC.[9] The result is that in a case involving alleged discrimination between domestic spirits and imported spirits, it may not be necessary to distinguish between the application of Article 90(1) and that of Article 90(2) EC, since it cannot reasonably be denied that the products are in at least partial, indirect or potential competition.[10] It will however be necessary to distinguish between the application of Article 90(1) and (2) EC if the tax on the import in question is greater than that on the domestic product without being sufficient to be shown to afford indirect protection to domestic products. In such a case, Article 90(1) EC would be infringed if the products were similar, but Article 90(2) EC would not be infringed if they were not.

The fact that Article 90(2) EC embraces potential as well as actual competition significantly widens its ambit. In *Commission v United Kingdom*,[11] the United Kingdom argued that wine and beer could not be considered to be competing beverages, since beer was a popular drink consumed generally in public houses, while wine was generally consumed on special occasions. The Court of Justice stressed that it was necessary to examine not only the present state of the market in the United Kingdom but also possible developments in the free movement of goods within the Community and the further potential for the substitution of products for one another which might result from an intensification of trade. Consumer habits varied in time and space, and the tax policy of a Member State must not crystallise given consumer habits so as to consolidate an advantage acquired by the national industries concerned to respond to them. The Court held that to a certain extent at least wine and beer were capable of meeting identical needs and that there was a degree of substitution one for another.

And it must be admitted that in the case of some products found to have a competitive relationship it may be extremely difficult to establish the appropriate basis for comparison of the tax applied to the respective products, and the appropriate rate to be applied to ensure fiscal neutrality. A striking illustration is afforded by the above mentioned Court's decision in *Commission v United Kingdom*,[12] in which the Court attempted to establish the degree of indirect protection afforded to beer by the excessive taxation of wine. On the basis of tax per unit of volume, wine bore an overall tax burden of 400 per cent more than on beer. On the basis of alcoholic

---

[9] Case 319/81 *Commission v Italy* [1983] E.C.R. 601, referring to Case 168/78 *Commission v France* [1980] E.C.R. 347; Case 169/78 *Commission v Italy* [1980] E.C.R. 385; Case 171/78 *Commission v Denmark* [1980] E.C.R. 447.
[10] Case 168/78 *Commission v France* [1980] E.C.R. 347;
[11] Case 170/78 [1980] E.C.R. 417; [1983] E.C.R. 2265.
[12] *ibid.*

strength per unit of volume, wine was subject to a tax burden 100 per cent. in excess of that on beer. On the basis of tax as a proportion of the net price of the beverage free of tax, the court admitted that the evidence was difficult to assess, suggesting additional tax burdens of between 58 per cent and 286 per cent! The Court concluded that whichever criterion for comparison was used, the tax system offered indirect protection to national production, and that there was no need to express a preference for one or other of the criteria discussed! Though Article 90(2) EC was long ago held to be directly effective,[13] in such a case one might well sympathise with an importer challenging a national tax claim who seeks to quantify the amount by which his or her national tax demand offends Article 90(2) EC!

15–020 **(h) Only true fiscal charges subject to Article 90 EC.** It must be emphasised that while Article 90 EC permits the imposition of internal taxation on imports to the extent that domestic goods bear similar charges, it cannot justify any charges imposed with a view to assimilating the prices of imports to those of domestic goods. The point arose in *Commission v Luxembourg and Belgium*,[14] a proceeding under Article 226 EC in which the Commission alleged infringement of Articles 23 and 25 EC in respect of charges levied on the issue of import licences for gingerbread. The defendants argued that the charges compensated for the effect of measures of price support for domestically produced rye, and were accordingly justified under Article 90 EC. The purpose of the disputed charge, said the Court, was not to equalise charges which would otherwise unevenly burden domestic and imported products, but to equalise the very prices of such products.[15] A similar point arose in *Hauptzollamt Flensburg v Hermann C. Andresen & Co. KG*.[16] A charge was imposed on spirits imported into Germany, being a charge also applicable to domestic spirits, and calculated to defray (in the case of domestic spirits) the administrative and operating costs of the Federal Spirits Monopoly. The Court held that a charge such as this was not a true fiscal charge, and that Article 90 EC only permitted the imposition on imports of such elements of the price of domestic spirits which the monopoly was required by law to remit to the State Treasury.

Prohibition of customs duties and charges having equivalent effect, and prohibition of discriminatory internal taxation, mutually exclusive

15–021 The prohibitions of Articles 25 EC on the one hand, and Article 90 EC on the other, have often been contrasted by the Court. Article 25 applies to all charges exacted at the time of or by reason of

---

[13] Case 27/67 *Fink-Frucht* [1968] E.C.R. 223.
[14] Joined Cases 2 and 3/62 [1965] E.C.R. 425.
[15] See also Case 45/75 *Rewe-Zentrale* [1976] E.C.R. 181.
[16] Case 4/81 [1981] E.C.R. 2935.

importation which are imposed specifically on an imported product to the exclusion of the similar domestic product,[17] and it has also been held that pecuniary charges intended to finance the activities of an agency governed by public law can constitute charges having equivalent effect.[18] Article 90 EC applies to financial charges levied within a general system of internal taxation applying systematically to domestic and imported goods.[19] The application of these respective prohibitions has been held to be mutually exclusive, not only because one and the same charge could not have been both removed during the transitional period (as had originally been provided under Articles 13 and 14 of the EEC Treaty for customs duties and charges having equivalent effect), and by no later than the beginning of the second stage (as had originally provided for discriminatory internal taxation under Article 95 of the EEC Treaty),[20] but also because the requirement for customs duties and charges having equivalent effect is that they are abolished, while the requirement for discriminatory internal taxation is the elimination of any form of discrimination between domestic products and products originating in other Member States.[21] The Court has explicitly rejected the argument that an equalisation tax on an imported product which exceeds the charges applied to similar domestic products takes on the character of a "charge having equivalent effect" as to the difference.[22] It is thus established that "provisions relating to charges having equivalent effect and those relating to discriminatory internal taxation cannot be applied together, so that under the system of the Treaty the same imposition cannot belong to both categories at the same time."[23]

---

[17] Case 77/82 *Capolongo v Azienda Agricola Maya* [1973] E.C.R. 611; Joined Cases C–149/91 and C–150/91 *Sanders Adour SNC and Guyomarc'h Orthez Nutrition Animale SA v Directeur des Services Fiscaux des Pyrenées-Atlantiques* [1992] E.C.R. I–3889, para.15.

[18] Joined Cases C–149/91 and C–150/91 *Sanders Adour SNC and Guyomarc'h Orthez Nutrition Animale SA v Directeur des Services Fiscaux des Pyrenées-Atlantiques* [1992] E.C.R. I–3889, para.15; Case C–114/91 *Criminal proceedings against Gérard Jerôme Claeys* [1992] E.C.R. I–6559, para.13; Case C–144/91 *Gilbert Demoor en Zonen NV v Belgian State* [1992] E.C.R. I–6613, para.15; Case C–266/91 *Celulose Beira Industrial SA v Fazenda Pública* [1993] E.C.R. I–4337, para.10.

[19] Case 77/82 *Capolongo v Azienda Agricola Maya* [1973] E.C.R. 611; Case C–347/95 *Fazenda Pública v União das Cooperativas Abastecedoras de Leite de Lisboa, UCRL (UCAL)* [1997] E.C.R. I–4911.

[20] Case 10/65 *Deutschmann v Federal Republic of Germany* [1965] E.C.R. 469. And see Case 57/65 *Lutticke v Hauptzollamt Saarlouis* [1966] E.C.R. 205; Case 27/74 *Demag v Finanzamt Duisburg-Sud* [1974] E.C.R. 1037.

[21] Case 94/74 *IGAV v ENCC* [1975] E.C.R. 699.

[22] Case 25/67 *Milch- Fett- und Eierkontor v Hauptzollamt Saarbrucken* [1968] E.C.R. 207; Case 32/80 *Officier van Justitie v Kortmann* [1981] E.C.R. 251.

[23] Joined Cases C–78/90 etc., *Compagnie Commerciale de l'Ouest v Receveur Principal des Douanes de La Pallice Port* [1992] E.C.R. I–1847, para.22; Joined Cases C–149/91 and C–150/91 *Sanders Adour SNC and Guyomarc'h Orthez Nutrition Animale SA v Directeur des Services Fiscaux des Pyrenées-Atlantiques* [1992] E.C.R. I–3889, para.14; Case C–114/91 *Criminal proceedings against Gérard Jerôme Claeys* [1992] E.C.R. I–6559, para.12; Case C–144/91 *Gilbert Demoor en Zonen NV v Belgian State* [1992] E.C.R. I–6613, para.14; Case C–266/91 *Celulose Beira Industrial SA v Fazenda Pública* [1993] E.C.R. I–4337, para.9; Case C–347/95 *Fazenda Pública v União das Cooperativas Abastecedoras de Leite de Lisboa, UCRL (UCAL)* [1997] E.C.R. I–4911, para.17.

Since the respective fields of application of the Treaty's prohibition on obstacles to the free movement of goods are to be distinguished, obstacles which are of a fiscal nature or have equivalent effect and are covered by Articles 25 or 90 EC cannot fall within the prohibition of Article 28 EC, on quantitative restrictions and measures having equivalent effect.[24] However, an excessive tax impeding the free movement of goods which falls outside the scope of Article 25 EC because it lacks a domestically produced counterpart might fall within the scope of Articles 28–30 EC.

A charge which is imposed both on imported products and on domestic products but in practice applies almost exclusively to imported products because domestic production is extremely small does not amount to a charge having equivalent effect if it is part of a general system of internal dues applied systematically to categories of products in accordance with objective criteria irrespective of the origin of the products. It therefore constitutes internal taxation within the meaning of Article 90 EC.[25] Indeed, a charge comprises internal taxation even where there are no comparable domestic products at all, where the charge in question applies to whole classes of domestic or foreign products which are all in the same position irrespective of origin.[26] However, the Court has held that such a limited number of products as "groundnuts, groundnut products and Brazil nuts" cannot fall within the concept of such whole classes of products, a concept which implies a much larger number of products determined by general and objective criteria.[27]

But to fall within the scope of Article 90 EC a charge must be levied at the same marketing stage on both domestic goods and imports, and the chargeable event giving rise to the duty must be identical in each case,[28] and if there is an insufficiently close connection between the charges levied on domestic goods, and those levied on imports, in that they are determined on the basis of different criteria, they will fall to be classified under Article 25 EC, rather than Article 90 EC.[29]

The Court added a qualification in *Wohrmann v Hauptzollamt Bad Reichenhall*,[30] that *in the absence of any protective purpose,* an internal

---

[24] Case 74/76 *Iannelli & Volpi v Paolo Meroni* [1977] E.C.R. 557 at para.9.

[25] Case 193/85 *Co-Frutta v Amministrazione delle Finanze dello Stato* [1987] E.C.R. 2085, para.14; Case C–343/90 *Manuel José Lourenço Dias v Director da Alfândega do Porto* [1992] E.C.R. I–4673, para.53.

[26] Joined Cases 2 and 3/69 *Chougol Diamond Co.* [1969] E.C.R. 211.

[27] Case 27/67 *Fink-Frucht* [1968] E.C.R. 223; Case 158/82 *Commission v Denmark* [1983] E.C.R. 3573.

[28] Case 132/78 *Denkavit Loire Sarl v France* [1979] E.C.R. 1923; Joined Cases C–149/91 and C–150/91 *Sanders Adour SNC and Guyomarc'h Orthez Nutrition Animale SA v Directeur des Services Fiscaux des Pyrénées-Atlantiques* [1992] E.C.R. I–3889, para.17. But VAT levied on imports does not amount to a charge having equivalent effect, Case 249/84 *Profant* [1986] E.C.R. 3237.

[29] Case 132/80 *United Foods* [1981] E.C.R. 995.

[30] Case 7/67 [1967] E.C.R. 177.

tax could not be regarded as a charge having equivalent effect to a customs duty. This seems at first sight surprising, since the Court has often emphasised that a charge may have an effect equivalent to a customs duty under Article 25 EC independently of either its purpose or the destination of its revenue.[31] The significance of protective purpose in this context is that a charge applicable equally to domestic and imported products—and therefore ostensibly "internal taxation" under Article 90 EC—may nevertheless fall to be classified as a charge having equivalent effect, if the revenue from the charge is devoted exclusively to benefit domestic producers. In *Interzuccheri v Ditta Rezzano e Cavassa*,[32] the Court considered a charge imposed on sales of sugar, whether home produced or imported, the proceeds of which were used for the exclusive benefit of national sugar refineries and sugar beet producers. The Court held that such a charge, on the face of it internal taxation, could only be considered a charge having equivalent effect if:

— it had the sole purpose of financing activities for the specific advantage of the taxed domestic product;
— the taxed product and the domestic product benefiting from it were the same;
— the charges imposed on the domestic product were made good in full.

Since the charge in issue in the national proceedings financed sugar **15–022** beet producers, as well as sugar refiners, it would not seem to constitute a charge having equivalent effect, according to the Court's stringent criteria.

In the later case of *Commission v Italy*,[33] the Commission challenged the same Italian charge in contentious proceedings, arguing that if the charge were entirely offset by reimbursements in the form of aid, it amounted to a charge having an equivalent effect to a customs duty, while if it were only partly offset, it infringed Article 90 EC. Somewhat puzzlingly, the Court held that Italy had violated Article 90 EC, and that internal taxation would be regarded as indirectly discriminatory within the meaning of that Article if its proceeds were used *exclusively* or principally to finance aids for the sole benefit of domestic products. Yet in the later case of *Officier van Justitie v Kortmann*,[34] the Court confirmed the *Interzuccheri* proposition that an internal tax amounted to a charge having

---

[31] e.g. Case 63/74 *Cadskey* [1975] E.C.R. 281; Joined Cases 2 and 3/69 *Chougol Diamond Co.* [1969] E.C.R. 211.
[32] Case 105/76 [1977] E.C.R. 1029; Case 77/72 *Capolongo* [1973] E.C.R. 611; Case 94/74 *IGAV* [1975] E.C.R. 699; Case 77/76 *Fratelli Cucchi v Avez* [1977] E.C.R. 987; Case 222/78 *ICAP v Walter Beneventi* [1979] E.C.R. 1163.
[33] Case 73/79 [1980] E.C.R. 1533.
[34] Case 32/80 [1981] E.C.R. 251.

equivalent effect to a customs duty when in fact it was imposed solely on imported products to the exclusion of domestic products. The explanation for the apparent inconsistency seems to be that *Commission v Italy*[35] concerned a charge on one product (imported sugar) which was used to benefit sugar beet as well as sugar. Indeed, this was why it is clear from the Court's ruling in *Interzuccheri*[36] that the charge in question could not be regarded as a charge having equivalent effect. Thus the ruling in *Commission v Italy* that an equal charge imposed on both imported and domestic products may amount to discriminatory internal taxation if used *exclusively* or principally to finance aids for the sole benefit of domestic products (which appears to be categorising as discriminatory internal taxation that which is a charge having equivalent effect to a customs duty) would seem to be confined to cases where the domestic products benefited are not identical to the imported products subject to the charge. The proposition is of course unexceptionable insofar as it refers to the proceeds of a charge used principally (or indeed at all) to benefit domestic products alone. Where the products are identical, and the *Interzuccheri*[37] criteria are satisfied, the ostensible internal tax is to be categorised as a charge having equivalent effect to a customs duty. It will be noted that these problems only arise if a Member State has resort to ear-marked taxes, as Italy pointed out to the Court during the proceedings in *Commission v Italy*.[38]

The *Interzuccheri* formulation has been endorsed in a consistent subsequent case law.[39] The Court explained the rationale underlying its case law, and the manner in which an assessment is to be made of any advantages for domestic products which offset the burden of charges imposed upon such products, in *Celulose Beira Industrial SA (Celbi)*:

> "The *ratio decidendi* of the above case law on the intended use of the revenue from a charge applied without distinction as well as the offsetting of any burden from that charge rests on the finding that, in economic terms, the advantages financed by the revenue from such a charge constitute, for domestic products, the consideration for the amounts paid, the burden of which is thereby offset in full or in part. For imported products, on the other hand, which are excluded from those advantages, the charge represents a net additional financial burden.

---

[35] Case 73/79 [1980] E.C.R. 1533.
[36] Case 105/76 [1977] E.C.R. 1029.
[37] Case 105/76 [1977] E.C.R. 1029.
[38] Case 73/79 [1980] E.C.R. 1533.
[39] See e.g., Joined Cases C–78/90 etc., *Compagnie Commerciale de l'Ouest v Receveur Principal des Douanes de La Pallice Port* [1992] E.C.R. I–1847, paras, 24 and 26; Case C–266/91 *Celulose Beira Industrial SA v Fazenda Pública* [1993] E.C.R. I–4337, paras 12–14; ; Case C–347/95 *Fazenda Pública v Uniáo das Cooperativas Abastecedoras de Leite de Lisboa, UCRL (UCAL)* [1997] E.C.R. I–4911, paras 20–24; Case C–234/99 *Niels Nygård and Svineafgiftsfonden* [2002] E.C.R. I–3657, para.23.

In those circumstances, the criterion of whether the burden is offset, in order to be usefully and correctly applied, presupposes a check, during a reference period, on the financial equivalence of the total amounts levied on domestic products in connection with the charge and the advantages afforded exclusively to those products."[40]

As is so often the case when national courts, or the Court of Justice, for that matter, are called upon to apply Community law, this may involve complex issues of economic fact.

Discriminatory tax treatment of exports

The system adopted for taxing products in intra-Community trade **15–023** is based on the "destination principle," i.e. goods exported from a Member State receive a rebate of internal taxation paid, and are in turn subjected to internal taxation in the country of destination.[41] The purpose of Article 90 EC is to prevent this process being used to place a heavier burden on imports than on domestic goods, but the system is vulnerable to another, equally damaging abuse: the repayment to exporters of an amount exceeding the internal taxation in fact paid, which would amount to an export subsidy for domestic production. It is to counteract this possibility that Article 91 EC provides that where products are exported to the territory of any Member State, any repayment of internal taxation shall not exceed the internal taxation imposed on them, whether directly or indirectly.

The Court laid down guidelines as to the extent of repayments permissible under this Article in *Commission v Italy*,[42] a case arising from proceedings under Article 226 alleging excessive repayment of taxes levied on certain engineering products. The Commission claimed that the repayment of duties paid on licenses, concessions, motor vehicles and advertising, in connection with the production and marketing of the products in question, were ineligible for repayment under Article 91 EC. The Court ruled that the words "directly or indirectly" referred to the distinction between taxes which had been levied on the products themselves (directly), and taxes levied on the raw materials and semi-finished goods used in their manufacture (indirectly).[43] It followed that the charges referred

---

[40] Case C–266/91 *Celulose Beira Industrial SA v Fazenda Pública* [1993] E.C.R. I–4337, paras 17 and 18.
[41] Case C–213/96 *Outokumpu Oy* [1998] E.C.R. I–1777, Opinion of Advocate General Jacobs, para.46.
[42] Case 45/64 [1965] E.C.R. 857. For infringements of Art.96 (now Art.91) see Case C–152/89 *Commission v Luxembourg* [1991] E.C.R. I–3171; Case C–153/89 *Commission v Belgium* [1991] E.C.R. I–3171.
[43] On the similar wording in Art.90(1), see above at p.554, and Case 28/67 *Molkerei-Zentrale* [1968] E.C.R. 143 at 155.

to by the Commission could not be repaid consistently with Article 91 EC, for the simple reason that they were not taxes imposed on the products at all, but "upon the producer undertaking in the very varied aspects of its general commercial and financial activity."[44] The Court has also held that when a Member State employs a flat-rate system for determining the amount of internal taxation which can be repaid on exportation to another Member State, it is for that former State to establish that such a system remains *in all cases* within the mandatory limits of Article 91 EC.[45]

But whereas Article 25 EC applies to customs duties and charges having equivalent effect on both imports and exports, Article 90 EC, on its face, applies only to tax discrimination against imports. Nevertheless, in *Staten Kontrol v Larsen*,[46] the Court held that the rule against discrimination underlying Article 90 EC also applied when the export, rather than import, of a product constituted, within the context of a system of internal taxation, the chargeable event giving rise to a fiscal charge. It would be incompatible with the system of tax provisions laid down in the Treaty to acknowledge that a Member State, in the absence of an express prohibition laid down in the Treaty, were free to apply in a discriminatory manner a system of internal taxation to products intended for export to another Member State. Article 90 EC, it seems, prohibits internal taxation which either discriminates against imports or exports, as compared to domestic products.[47]

Furthermore, in *Hulst v Produktschap voor Siergewassen*,[48] the Court held that an internal levy applying to domestic sales and exports could have an effect equivalent to a customs duty when either its application fell more heavily on export sales than on sales within the country, or when the levy was intended to finance activities likely to give preferential treatment to the product intended for marketing within the country, to the detriment of that intended for export.

The relationship between Articles 25 and 90 EC, and other provisions of the Treaty

15–024   Where national measures are financed by a discriminatory internal tax, Article 90 EC is applicable to the latter, despite the fact that it forms part of a national aid, subject to scrutiny under Articles 87 and

---

[44] Case 45/64 [1965] E.C.R. 857, 866.
[45] Case 152/89 *Commission v Luxembourg* [1991] E.C.R. I–3171, para.36.
[46] Case 142/77 [1978] E.C.R. 1787.
[47] *cf.* Case 27/74 *Demag* [1974] E.C.R. 1037.
[48] Case 51/74 [1975] E.C.R. 79.

88 EC (ex 92 and 93).[49] Equally, Article 25 EC on the one hand, and Articles 87 and 88, on the other, are cumulatively applicable in such circumstances.[50] Articles 25 and 90 EC do not however overlap with Article 28 EC (ex 30). The Court held in *Ianelli & Volpi v Paolo Meroni* that:

> "However, wide the field of application of Article 30 [now 28 EC] may be, it nevertheless does not include obstacles to trade covered by other provisions of the Treaty. Thus obstacles which are of a fiscal nature or have equivalent effect and are covered by Articles 9 to 16 and 95 of the Treaty do not fall within the prohibition of Article 30."[51]

The relationship between Article 31 EC on state monopolies (ex 37), and Article 90 EC, was considered by the Court in *Grandes Distilleries Peureux*.[52] Whereas Article 31 EC was acknowledged to have provided an exception to certain rules of the Treaty—*in casu* Article 90 EC—during the transitional period, this was declared to be no longer the case. Where internal taxation is concerned, Article 90 EC apparently constitutes a *lex specialis*, even it seems in the case of activities which would otherwise qualify for scrutiny under Article 31 EC.

In *Staten Kontrol v Larsen*,[53] the Court held that, while a Member State was precluded under Article 90 EC from taxing exports more heavily than domestically traded goods, it was open to a Member State to tax exports in the same way as domestic goods, even if this led to taxes overlapping with those imposed in the country of destination: this latter problem would fall to be solved by harmonisation of national legislation under Articles 93 or 94 of the Treaty (ex 99 and 100). However, in *Gaston Schul*,[54] the Court held that a

---

[49] Case 47/69 *France v Commission* [1970] E.C.R. 487; Case 73/79 *Commission v Italy* [1980] E.C.R. 1547; Case 17/81 *Pabst and Richarz v Hauptzollamt Oldenburg* [1982] E.C.R. 1331; Case 277/83 *Commission v Italy* [1985] E.C.R. 2049; Case C–266/91 *Celulose Beira Industrial SA v Fazenda Pública* [1993] E.C.R. I–4337, para.21. Arts 25 and 90 EC are relevant even when the state aid has been authorized by the Commission, e.g. Case C–234/99 *Niels Nygård and Svineafgiftsfonden* [2002] E.C.R. I–3657, operative part of the ruling.

[50] Joined Cases C–78/90 etc., *Compagnie Commerciale de l'Ouest v Receveur Principal des Douanes de La Pallice Port* [1992] E.C.R. I–1847, para.32; Case C–144/91 *Gilbert Demoor en Zonen NV v Belgian State* [1992] E.C.R. I–6613, para.24; Case C–266/91 *Celulose Beira Industrial SA v Fazenda Pública* [1993] E.C.R. I–4337, para.21.

[51] Case 74/76 [1977] E.C.R. 557; Joined Cases C–78/90 etc., *Compagnie Commerciale de l'Ouest v Receveur Principal des Douanes de La Pallice Port* [1992] E.C.R. I–1847, para.20; Case C–17/91 *Georges Lornoy en Zonen NV v Belgian State* [1992] E.C.R. I–6523, para.14. But if Art.90 EC is inapplicable because an import lacks a domestic counterpart, Art.28 EC may apply to the tax in question, see Case C–47/88 *Commission v Denmark* [1900] E.C.R. I–4509.

[52] Case 86/78 [1979] E.C.R. 897.

[53] Case 142/77 [1978] E.C.R. 1787.

[54] Case 15/81 *Gaston Schul* [1982] E.C.R. 1409, and see Case 39/85 *Bergeres-Becque* [1986] E.C.R. 259; Case C–120/88 *Commission v Italy* [1991] E.C.R. I–621; Case C–119/89 *Commission v Spain* [1991] E.C.R. I–641; *Commission v Greece* [1991] E.C.R. I–691.

Member State was required by Article 90 EC when imposing value added tax on imports, to take into account value added tax paid but not refunded (and not refundable under the applicable VAT Directive) in the country of export. So far from the harmonisation of national tax provisions ousting Article 90 EC, the Court held that the applicable VAT Directive must be construed in accordance with the terms of Article 90 EC, which were mandatory and binding upon the Community institutions in the enactment of such legislation.

The common customs tariff and external relations

15–025   The preceding exposition has been concerned with the elimination of customs duties and other financial charges on trade between the Member States, but brief mention must be made of imports and exports between the Community and third countries.

Neither the relevant Articles of the Treaty, nor Regulation 950/68 of the CCT,[55] explicitly provided for the regulation of charges having an equivalent effect in trade relations between the Member States and third countries. Nevertheless, the Court held in *Sociaal Fonds voor de Dimantarbeiders v Indiamex*[56] that the unilateral imposition of such charges after the adoption of the CCT was inconsistent with the aim of the Treaty that Member States adopt a common policy in their trade relations with the outside world. The Court has confirmed this position in a consistent case law,[57] but has indicated that the Treaty does not preclude the levying of a charge having equivalent effect to a customs duty on imports which, having regard to all its essential characteristics, must be regarded as a charge already in existence on July 1, 1968, provided that the level at which it is levied has not been raised, and where the level has been raised, only the amount by which it has been raised must be regarded as incompatible with the Treaty.[58]

The Treaty itself has no provision analogous to Article 90 EC applying to imports from non-member countries.[59] International agreements between the EC and third countries, and the provisions of agricultural regulations, may prohibit customs duties, charges having equivalent effect, and discriminatory internal taxation, on

---

[55] [1969] O.J. Spec. Ed. 275. Repealed with effect from December 31, 1987 by Reg. 2658/87, O.J. 1987 L256/1.

[56] Joined Cases 37 and 38/73 [1973] E.C.R. 1609.

[57] Case C–125/94 *Aprile Srl, in liquidation, v Amministrazione delle Finanze dello Stato* [1995] E.C.R. I–2919, paras 35–37; Case C–109/98 *CRT France International SA v Directeur Régional des Impâts de Bourgogne* [1999] E.C.R. I–2237, para.22.

[58] Case C–126/94 *Société Cadi Surgeléles etc. v Ministre des Finances* [1996] E.C.R. I–5647.

[59] Case 148/77 *Hansen* [1978] E.C.R. 1787; Joined cases C–228/90 to C–234/90, C–339/90 and C–353/90 *Simba SpA v Ministero delle finanze* [1992] E.C.R. I–3713, para.14; Case C–130/92 *OTO SpA v Ministero delle Finanze* [1994] E.C.R. I–3281, paras 18 and 19; Case C–284/96 *Didier Tabouillet v Directeur des Services Fiscaux de Meurthe-et-Moselle* [1997] E.C.R. I–7471, para.23.

trade between the EC and third countries. It cannot be assumed without more that such provisions as these are to be construed as strictly as analogous provisions governing intra-Community trade, though a provision in an international agreement prohibiting charges having equivalent effect will be construed in the same way as the same term appearing in the EC Treaty if to give it more limited scope would deprive the agreement in question of much of its effectiveness.[60] But even where a provision of a regulation prohibits charges having equivalent effect on trade with third countries, and the Court takes the view that the concept is the same as that embodied in Article 25 EC, the requirement may be subject to derogation authorised by the Community institutions in a way that would not be possible were intra-Community trade involved.[61] And where health inspections are permitted by Community regulations on imports from third countries, the inspections may be more strict, and the fees charged higher, than in intra-Community trade, since Community law does not require Member States to show the same degree of confidence towards non member countries as they are required to show other Member States.[62]

Where an international agreement prohibits discriminatory internal taxation on imports from third countries, it will be a matter of interpretation whether or not the provision in question is intended to fulfil the same purpose in relations between the EC and third countries as Article 90 EC fulfils in respect of intra-Community trade. Thus, the Court held in *Pabst & Richarz v Hauptzollamt Oldenburg* that Article 53 of the Association Agreement between the EEC and Greece (this was before Greece had joined the Community), which prohibited discriminatory internal taxation, fulfilled, within the framework of the Association between the Community and Greece, the same function as that of Article 90 EC, and should be interpreted in the same way.[63] But in *Hauptzollamt Mainz v Kupferberg*,[64] which involved Article 21 of the EEC-Portugal free trade Agreement, also prohibiting discriminatory internal taxation, the Court observed that although Article 21 of the Agreement and Article 90 EC had the same object, they were nevertheless worded differently, and must be considered and interpreted in their own context. The Court concluded that the interpretation given to Article 90 EC of the Treaty could not be applied by way of simple analogy to the agreement on free trade. In *Metalsa Srl* the Court considered the interpretation to be given to Article 18 of the EEC-Austria Agreement, the wording of which was the same as that of Article 21

---

[60] Case C-163/90 *Administration des Douanes et Droits Indirects v Léopold Legros* 1992] E.C.R. I-4625, para.26.
[61] Case 70/77 *Simmenthal* [1978] E.C.R. 1543.
[62] Case 30/79 *Land Berlin v Wigei* [1980] E.C.R. 1331.
[63] Case 17/81 *Pabst & Richarz KG v Hauptzollamt Oldenburg* [1982] E.C.R. 1331.
[64] Case 104/81 *Hauptzollamt Mainz v Kupferberg* [1982] E.C.R. 3641.

of the EEC-Portugal Agreement. It distinguished *Pabst and Richarz*
and followed *Kupferberg*, and declined to extend to Article 18 the
same interpretation as that applied to Article 90 EC.[65] And in
Texaco A/S v Middelfart Havn and others the Court applied the same
reasoning to the identical terms of Article 18 of the EEC-Sweden
Agreement.[66]

Customs duties on trade with third countries are established by
the CCT,[67] which the Court has held must be interpreted in such a
way as to give effect to a single trading system with third countries,
and not in such a way that products are treated differently according
to the country by which they enter the Community.[68] But customs
duties are only chargeable under the CCT upon goods capable of
being lawfully traded within the Community, and not, for example,
upon smuggled narcotic drugs,[69] or counterfeit currency.[70]

Further reading
Framer and Lyal, *EC Tax Law* (2nd ed., OUP, Oxford, due 2007).
Lyons, *EC Customs Law* (OUP, Oxford, 2002).
Terra and Wattel, *European Tax Law* (4th ed., Kluwer Law Inter-
    national, the Hague, 2005).

---

[65] Case C–312/91 [1993] E.C.R. I–3751,
[66] Joined Cases C–114/95 and C–115/95 [1997] E.C.R. I–4263.
[67] See para.15–003, above.
[68] Case 153/79 *Gedelfi* [1980] E.C.R. 1713.
[69] Case 50/80 *Horvath* [1981] E.C.R. 385; Case 221/81 *Wolf* [1982] E.C.R. 3681; Case 240/81
    Einberger [1982] E.C.R. 3699.
[70] Case C–343/89 *Witzemann* [1990] E.C.R. I–4477.

CHAPTER 16

QUANTITATIVE RESTRICTIONS AND MEASURES HAVING EQUIVALENT EFFECT

Guide to this Chapter: In the previous Chapter we considered **16–001** fiscal barriers to trade. This chapter is concerned with non-fiscal barriers to trade. Articles 28 and 29 EC prohibit quantitative restrictions and measures having equivalent effect to quantitative restrictions to imports, exports and goods in transit. Article 30 EC allows the Member States to retain such measures in order to protect listed interests. The definition of quantitative restrictions did not give rise to problems: the concept was already known in international trade law before the establishment of the EEC, and aims at prohibiting quotas on imports/exports. The definition of measures having equivalent effect to a quantitative restriction on imports proved to be more complex. In the seminal case of *Dassonville*, the Court gave a broad interpretation of the concept that encompasses any direct or indirect, actual or potential obstacle to intra-Community trade. However, such broad interpretation lead to significant problems. First, the narrow grounds for justification contained in Article 30 EC proved inadequate to strike the correct balance between the legitimate regulatory needs of the Member States and the demands of the Treaty. In order to solve this problem, the Court held in the *Cassis the Dijon* ruling that Member States could rely on broader ground of public interest, the mandatory requirements, to justify non-directly discriminatory restrictions to intra-Community trade. Secondly, the broad *Dassonville* formula, even if coupled with the *Cassis de Dijon* mandatory requirements doctrine, led to further problems when almost any trading rule was found to constitute an obstacle to intra-Community trade in need of justification. As a result, the Court revisited its own case law in the *Keck* ruling, and introduced a distinction based on the "type" of rules: rules regulating the physical qualities of a product (product requirements) automatically fall within the scope of Article 28 EC. However, rules that merely discipline the *way* a product is sold (selling arrangements) in principle fall outside the scope of Article 28 EC, unless directly or indirectly discriminatory. The *Keck* ruling brought much needed clarification: however, it reignited the debate as to the appropriate scope of Article 28 EC. This chapter deals with these issues, as well as with the scope of Articles 29 and 30 EC; the scope of the mandatory requirements doctrine; the relationship between the free movement of goods provisions and other Treaty provisions; and the relationship between Article 28 EC and intellectual property (IP) rights. The co-existence of different national systems of IP law is capable of conflicting with the objective of creating a single market. For example, a company holding patent or trade mark rights protected under the law of two Member States might use its rights in each to prevent products which it itself had placed on the market in one of the Member States being imported into the other. Articles 28–30 EC have been interpreted as preventing holders of IP rights from using them to prevent the import of goods into one Member State from the territory of another where the holder of the rights in question has consented to their being placed on the market. This principle is known as "exhaustion" of IP rights, and is examined in some detail in this Chapter. Harmonisation of IP rights is considered in outline by way of introduction and reference is made to specific harmonising legislation where appropriate.

INTRODUCTION

16–002 A quantitative restriction, or a quota, is a measure restricting the import of a given product by amount or by value. In order to obviate the risk of importers ordering goods, only to have them excluded at the frontier because the quota has been filled, a licensing system may be adopted, whereby a government agency formally authorises particular importers to import stated quantities, or money's worth, of goods.[1] Since quotas are capable of disturbing the flow of international trade to a greater extent than tariffs,[2] and indeed found favour during the 1930s as a means of restricting imports without infringing international agreements prohibiting the introduction of customs duties,[3] it is hardly surprising that the authors of the Spaak Report considered their elimination as a "fundamental element" in the creation of a common market.[4] Accordingly, the EEC Treaty in its original text provided for the abolition of quantitative restrictions and measures having equivalent effect on imports and exports,[5] in the former case by the end of the transitional period,[6] and in the case of exports by the end of the first stage.[7] "Standstill" provisions prevented Member States from introducing new quantitative restrictions or measures having equivalent effect,[8] or making more restrictive those measures already in existence when the Treaty entered into force.[9] The current provisions on quantitative restrictions and measures having equivalent effect are set out in Articles 28 and 29 EC. Article 28 EC provides:

"Quantitative restrictions on imports and all measures having equivalent effect shall be prohibited between Member States."

Article 29 EC provides:

"Quantitative restrictions on exports, and all measures having equivalent effect, shall be prohibited between Member States."

The Court has said that the principle of the free movement of goods is one of the fundamental principles of the Treaty, and that the principle is implemented by Article 28 *et seq.* EC.[10] Article 28 EC

---

[1] Jackson, *World Trade and the Law of GATT* (Bobbs-Merrill, Indianapolis, 1969), p.305.

[2] The volume of imports cannot expand to meet increased demand, nor can the improvement of efficiency of manufacturers in exporting countries secure their access to the protected markets, Wilcox, *A Charter for World Trade* (Macmillan Co, 1949), pp.81 *et seq.*; K. Dam, *The GATT* (University of Chicago Press, Chicago, 1970), p.147; Jackson, *op. cit.*, pp.309–310.

[3] Jackson, *op. cit.*, p.306.

[4] *Rapport des Chefs de Délégation aux Ministres des Affaires Etrangères* (1956), p.35.

[5] The Spaak Report points out that one result of the removal of restrictions on imports would be increased interdependence of the Member States. This would require, as a necessary corollary, that importing countries be able to rely on continuity of supplies from exporting countries, *Rapport*, p.38.

[6] Former Arts 30, 32 and 33.

[7] Art.29 EC. For detailed treatment of Arts 28–30 EC see Oliver (assisted by Jarvis), *Free Movement of Goods in the European Community, under Arts 28 to 30 of the EC Treaty*, (4th ed., Sweet & Maxwell, 2003).

[8] Ex Art.31.

[9] Ex Art.32. There was no explicit standstill for quantitative restrictions and measures having equivalent effect on exports, but Art.29(1) EC prohibited such measures outright.

[10] Case C–265/95 *Commission v France* [1997] E.C.R. I–6959, paras 24 and 27.

has direct effect and creates individual rights which national courts must protect.[11] The prohibition on quantitative restrictions and measures having equivalent effect is applicable without distinction to products originating in Member States and to those coming from non-member countries which are in free circulation.[12] Articles 28–30 EC apply to all trade in goods, subject only to the exceptions provided in the Treaty itself.[13] In *Campus Oil* the Irish Government argued unsuccessfully that oil, being of vital national importance, should be regarded as impliedly exempt from Article 28 EC. The Court held that goods could not be considered to be exempt merely because they were of particular importance for the life or economy of the Member State.[14] Coins which constitute legal tender do not fall within Articles 28–30 EC; coins which no longer constitute legal tender do.[15] Electricity is a good for the purposes of Articles 28–30 EC.[16] Waste, whether recyclable or not, falls within Articles 28–30 EC.[17] But where the supply of goods is incidental to the provision of services Articles 28–30 EC do not apply.[18] The re-import of goods falls within Articles 28–30 EC,[19] but not where the goods are exported for the sole purpose of re-importation in order to circumvent national legislation.[20] The provisions of Articles 28–30 EC also take effect within the framework of EC regulations on the common organisation of the markets for the various agricultural products.[21] Where national procedures are contrary to Articles 28–30 EC, any charge made by the national authorities for completion of such procedures is likewise unlawful.[22]

While Articles 28 and 29 EC prohibit quantitative restrictions and measures having equivalent effect, Article 30 EC provides that these latter Articles shall nevertheless not preclude prohibitions or restrictions on imports exports or goods in transit which are justified on such grounds as public policy, public security or public health.

---

[11] Case 74/76 *Ianelli & Volpi v Meroni* [1977] E.C.R. 557, para.13.
[12] Case Case 41/76 *Donckerwolcke* [1976] E.C.R. 1921; Case 288/83 *Commission v Ireland* [1985] E.C.R. 1761; Case 212/88 *Levy* [1989] E.C.R. 3511.
[13] For exceptions under Art.30 EC and the so-called "mandatory requirements" see paras 16–036 and 16–044, below. See also Art.296 EC, dealing with trade in arms, munitions and war materials.
[14] Case 72/83 [1984] E.C.R. 2727, para.17.
[15] Case 7/78 *Thompson* [1978] E.C.R. 2247.
[16] in Case C–393/92 *Almelo v Energiebedrijf IJsselmij* [1994] E.C.R. I–1477, para, 28; Case C–158/94 *Commission of the European Communities v Italian Republic.* [1997] E.C.R. I–5789, para.17.
[17] Case C–2/90 *Commission v Belgium* [1992] E.C.R. I–4431.
[18] Case C–257/92 *Schindler* [1994] E.C.R. I–1039; Case C–55/93 *Johannes Gerrit Cornelis van Schaik* [1994] E.C.R. I–4837, para.14.
[19] Case C–240/95 *Rémy Scmit* [1996] E.C.R. I–3179.
[20] Case 229/83 *Leclerc* [1985] E.C.R. 1.
[21] Joined Cases 3/76, 4/76 and 6/76 *Kramer* [1976] E.C.R. 1279, paras 53 and 54; Case C–228/91 *Commission v Italy* [1993] E.C.R. I–2701, para.11; Case C–265/95 *Commission v France* [1997] E.C.R. I–6959, para.36.
[22] Case 50/85 *Schloh* [1986] E.C.R. 1855.

Furthermore, national measures which are on the face of it covered by Articles 28 and 29 EC may be held to fall outside the scope of those provisions where they are justified on such grounds as consumer protection, fiscal supervision or environmental protection. In this chapter consideration will first be given to national measures which in principle comprise quantitative restrictions and measures having equivalent effect, without reference to the question of possible justification, while justification under Article 30 EC, or otherwise, will be considered in later sections of this chapter.[23-24]

QUANTITATIVE RESTRICTIONS ON IMPORTS

The notion of a quantitative restriction is well understood, and **16–003** definition poses little difficulty. As the Court explained in *Geddo*, "The prohibition on quantitative restrictions covers measures which amount to a total or partial restraint of, according to the circumstances, imports, exports, or goods in transit."[25] Thus, when the Italian authorities suspended imports of pork into Italy from other Member States in June 1960, the Court ruled that such a measure amounted to an infringement of the "standstill" provision of Article 31, first paragraph, of the Treaty, as the text of the Treaty stood at the time.[26] A total prohibition on imports is considered a zero quota, and therefore is qualified as a quantitative restriction. For instance, in *Henn and Darby* a statutory prohibition in the United Kingdom on the import of pornographic material was held to amount to a quantitative restriction contrary to Article 28 EC, subject to possible justification under Article 30 EC,[27] and a restriction in the United Kingdom on imports of main crop potatoes was held to amount to a quantitative restriction.[28]

Measures having equivalent effect to quantitative restrictions on imports

Directive 70/50/EEC

The concept of a measure having equivalent effect to a quantita- **16–004** tive restriction is rather more complex than that of a quantitative

---

[23-24] Paras 16–036 and 16–044.

[25] Case 2/73 *Geddo v Ente Nazionale Risi* [1973] E.C.R. 865 at 879.

[26] Case 7/61 *Commission v Italy* [1961] E.C.R. 317.

[27] Case 34/79 [1979] E.C.R. 3795.

[28] Case 118/78 *Meijer* [1979] E.C.R. 1387, Case 231/78 *Commission v United Kingdom* [1979] E.C.R. 1447.

restriction. Article 2(1) of Directive 70/50[29] prohibits measures, other than those applicable equally to domestic or imported products, which hinder imports that could otherwise take place, including those "which make importation more difficult or costly than the disposal of domestic production." This provision was relied upon by the Court in terms in *Ianelli*.[30] In other cases the Court has relied upon the principle involved without reference to the Directive. Thus in *Commission v Italy*[31] the Court held that an import deposit scheme was contrary to Article 28 EC because its effect was to render imports "more difficult or burdensome" than internal trans-actions, and thereby produced restrictive effects on the free move-ment of goods. With respect to imports, Article 2(2) of Directive 70/50 provides that measures having equivalent effect include those which "make imports or the disposal, at any marketing stage, of imported products subject to a condition—other than a formality—which is required in respect of imported products only, or a condition differing from that required from domestic products and more difficult to satisfy." This provision was cited with approval in *Rewe-Zentralfinanz v Landwirtschaftskammer*,[32] in which the Court declared that health inspections of plant products at national frontiers constituted a measure having equivalent effect, where similar domestic products were not subject to a similar examination. Although the Article refers to measures other than formalities, the Court has held that national measures requiring import or export licences in intra-Community trade—even though such licences are granted automatically—infringe the prohibition of Articles 28 and 29 EC.[33]

Article 2(3) lists examples of the national measures covered by the definitions contained in Articles 2(1) and 2(2). Thus Article 2(3)(g) refers to measures which make the access of imported products to the domestic market conditional upon having an agent or repre-sentative in the territory of the importing Member State. This provision was relied upon by the Commission in an action against the Federal Republic of Germany.[34] German legislation provided that pharmaceutical products could be placed on the market only by

---

[29] [1970] O.J. Spec. Ed. 17. While strictly speaking this measure applies to measures in force at the end of transitional period, it provides valuable guidance on the meaning of measures having equivalent effect.

[30] Case 74/76 *Ianelli & Volpi SpA v Meroni* [1977] E.C.R. 557.

[31] Case 95/81 *Commission v Italy* [1982] E.C.R. 2187.

[32] Case 4/75 *Rewe-Zentralfinanz v Landwirtschaftskammer* [1975] E.C.R. 843.

[33] Cases 51–54/71 *International Fruit* [1971] E.C.R. 1107; Case 53/76 *Bouhelier* [1977] E.C.R. 197; Case 68/76 *Commission v French Republic* [1977] E.C.R. 515; Case 124/81 *Commission v United Kingdom* [1983] E.C.R. 203.

[34] Case 247/81 *Commission v Germany* [1984] E.C.R. 1111. See also Case 87/85 *Laboratoires de Pharmacie Legia* [1986] E.C.R. 1707. Art.2(3) contains a list of examples and cannot be pleaded to defeat the purpose of Art.28 EC; Case 103/84 *Commission v Italy* [1986] E.C.R. 1759.

a pharmaceutical undertaking having its headquarters in the area in which that legislation was applicable. The Court held—without reference to the Directive—that the legislation in question was likely to involve additional costs for undertakings which found no good reason for having a representative of their own established in Germany, and which sold directly to customers. The legislation was therefore likely to hinder trade within the Community and amounted to a measure having equivalent effect. Again, Article 2(3)(s) refers to national measures which "confine names which are not indicative of origin or source to domestic products only."[35] However, even names which are indicative of origin or source may only be confined to domestic products if the geographical area of origin of a product confers upon it a specific quality and characteristic of such a nature as to distinguish it from all other products.[36] It follows that making the application of a designation of quality which is neither an indication of origin or source conditional upon one or more stages of the production process taking place on national territory, amounts to a measure having equivalent effect.[37]

Article 3 of Directive 70/50 covers measures governing the marketing of products which deal in particular with the presentation or identification of products and which apply equally to domestic and imported products, where the restrictive effect of such measures on the free movement of goods exceed the effects intrinsic to trade rules. This is stated to be the case, in particular, where the restrictive effects on the free movement of goods are out of proportion to their purpose, or where the same objective can be attained by other means which are less of a hindrance to trade. This provision has been cited by the Court of Justice.[38] It is to be noted that the tenth recital to the preamble of Directive 70/50 might suggest that Article 3, despite referring to measures which "are equally applicable" to domestic and imported products, only covers national measures which are indirectly discriminatory, since the recital refers to imports which are "either precluded or made more difficult or costly than the disposal of domestic production." The Court's so-called *Cassis* case law[39] (developed without specific reference to Article 3) would suggest that Article 3 applies to obstacles to the free movement of goods where they are the consequence of national rules which lay down requirements to be met by goods (such as requirements as to composition, labelling, packaging, etc.) even if those rules apply without distinction to all products, unless their application can be

---

[35] Case 12/74 *Commission v Germany* [1975] E.C.R. 181; Case 13/78 *Eggers* [1978] E.C.R. 1935; Joined Cases C–321/94 –324/94 *Jacques Pistre* [1997] E.C.R. I–2343.
[36] Case 12/74 *Commission v Germany* [1975] E.C.R. 181; Case 13/78 *Eggers* [1978] E.C.R. 1935.
[37] Case 13/78 *Eggers* [1978] E.C.R. 1935.
[38] Case 75/81 *Blesgen* [1982] E.C.R. 1211.
[39] See below at para.16–006 *et seq.*

justified by a public-interest objective taking precedence over the free movement of goods.[40] And the Court appears to consider that such obstacles do not amount to discrimination, either direct or indirect, though the extension to imports of such national measures could indeed be said to indirectly discriminatory.[41]

Evolution of the Court's case law

16–005 **(a) The *Dassonville* case.** It was clear from the Court's early case law that a national rule requiring import licences for the import of goods from other Member States would amount to a measure having equivalent effect to a quantitative restriction, even if the requirement was a formality.[42] This was consistent with the view that it was a characteristic of such measures that they applied specifically to imports and burdened them in some way. But it was in the judgment of the Court in *Procureur du Roi v Dassonville* that one finds the first attempt to lay down a general definition of measures having equivalent effect to quantitative restrictions on imports. The defendants in the national proceedings imported into Belgium Scotch whisky which they had purchased from French distributors. Belgian legislation required such goods to be accompanied by a certificate of origin made out in the name of the Belgian importer, and the goods in question were without such certificates, which could have been obtained only with the greatest difficulty once the goods had been previously imported into France. On a reference for a preliminary ruling the Court of Justice stated:

> 5. All trading rules enacted by Member States which are capable of hindering, *directly or indirectly, actually or potentially*, intra-Community trade are to be considered as measures having an effect equivalent to quantitative restrictions.
>
> 6. In the absence of a Community system guaranteeing for consumers the authenticity of a product's designation of origin, if a Member State takes measures to prevent unfair practices in this connection, it is however subject to the condition that these measures should be reasonable and that the means of proof required should not act as a hindrance to trade between member states and should, in consequence, be accessible to all community nationals.

---

[40] See in particular Joined Cases C–267 and C–268/91 *Bernard Keck and Daniel Mithouard* [1993] E.C.R. I–6097.

[41] In Joined Cases C–267/91 and C–268/91 *Keck*, the Court's reference in para.16 to "certain selling arrangements" not hindering trade in the absence of discrimination, in law or in fact, implies that the requirements as regards composition and labelling etc., referred to in para.15 are not regarded as being directly or indirectly discriminatory. For the view that such latter measures might properly be regarded as indirectly discriminatory, see below at p.592.

[42] Joined Cases 51–54/71 *International Fruit* [1971] E.C.R. 1107.

7. Even without having to examine whether or not such measures are covered by Article 36 [now 30], they must not, in any case, by virtue of the principle expressed in the second sentence of that Article, constitute a means of arbitrary discrimination or a disguised restriction on trade between Member States.

8. That may be the case with formalities, required by a Member State for the purpose of proving the origin of a product, which only direct importers are really in a position to satisfy without facing serious difficulties."[43]

While the definition of measures having equivalent effect in paragraph 5 of the above judgment is stated in rather broad terms, it does not necessarily follow that it was intended to cover measures which reduce in one way or another the overall volume of trade, but without placing any particular burden on imports. Much depends on the notion of "hindering . . . intra-Community trade", and it is not self-evident that such trade can be regarded as being hindered by a national measure which is neutral as regards inter-State and intra-State trade and as between channels of inter-State trade. The national measure in issue in *Dassonville* was of course far from being trade-neutral. As the Court indicates in paragraphs 7 and 8 of its judgment set out above, the national measure in issue in that case imposed a considerably greater burden on one category of imports (imports from a Member State into which the goods had already been imported), than on another category of imports (imports directly from the country of origin). And since there is no indication that the latter category of imports were burdened less than domestic transactions as regards proof of origin, the national measure also placed a greater burden on the former category of imports than on comparable domestic transactions. In such circumstances it is not surprising that the measures were regarded as comprising "a means of arbitrary discrimination or a disguised restriction on trade" within the meaning of Article 30 EC of the Treaty.

(b) The *Cassis* ruling. Prior to the judgment of the Court of Justice **16–006** in the *Cassis* case[44] it was generally assumed—and the Court's case law was consistent with this assumption—that Article 28 EC had no application to a national measure unless the measure in question discriminated in some way, formally or materially, between either imports and domestic products, or between channels of intra-Community trade.

The *Cassis* case involved the intended importation into Germany of a consignment of the alcoholic beverage "Cassis de Dijon". Under

---

[43] Case 8/74 *Procureur du Roi v Dassonville* [1974] E.C.R. 837, paras 5–8, emphasis added.
[44] Case 120/78 *Rewe-Zentral AG v Bundesmonopolverwaltung für Branntwein* ("Cassis de Dijon") [1979] E.C.R. 649.

German legislation fruit liqueurs such as "Cassis" could only be marketed if they contained a minimum alcohol content of 25 per cent, whereas the alcohol content of the product in question was between 15 per cent and 20 per cent. A German court asked the Court of Justice whether legislation such as that in issue was consistent with Article 28 EC of the Treaty. Before the Court of Justice the Federal Republic of Germany argued that the legislation in question was discriminatory in neither a formal nor a material sense; any obstacles to trade resulted simply from the fact that France and Germany had different rules for the minimum alcohol contents of certain drinks. The Court's judgment makes no reference at all to the issue of discrimination. Rather, it regards incompatibility with Article 28 EC as flowing from the very fact that the "Cassis" could not be placed lawfully on the German market, and addresses itself at once to the question whether there existed any justification for the restriction.

> "In the absence of common rules relating to the production and marketing of alcohol . . . it is for the Member States to regulate all matters relating to the production and marketing of alcohol and alcoholic beverages on their own territory.
>
> Obstacles to movement within the Community *resulting from disparities between the national laws* relating to the marketing of the products in question must be accepted *in so far as those provisions may be recognised as being necessary in order to satisfy mandatory requirements* relating in particular to the effectiveness of fiscal supervision, the protection of public health, the fairness of commercial transactions and the defence of the consumer."[45]

The Court rejected the arguments of the Federal Republic of Germany relating to the protection of public health and to the protection of the consumer against unfair commercial practices, and continued:

> "It is clear from the foregoing that the requirements relating to the minimum alcohol content of alcoholic beverages do not serve a purpose which is in the general interest and such as to take precedence over the requirements of the free movement of goods, which constitutes one of the fundamental rules of the Community."[46]

In the paragraphs which follow the Court describes the restrictive effect of national rules such as those in issue in terms which seem to

---

[45] Case 120/78 *Rewe-Zentral AG v Bundesmonopolverwaltung für Branntwein* ("Cassis de Dijon") [1979] E.C.R. 649, paras 8, 9, emphasis added.
[46] *ibid.*, para.14.

make the existence of an element of discrimination irrelevant in establishing violation of Article 28 EC, or to presume it to exist from the very fact of exclusion of products lawfully produced and marketed in one of the Member States.

> "In practice, the principal effect of requirements of this nature is to promote alcoholic beverages having a high alcohol content by excluding from the national market products of other Member States which do not answer that description.
>
> It therefore appears that the unilateral requirement imposed by the rules of a Member State of a minimum alcohol content for the purposes of the sale of alcoholic beverages constitutes an obstacle to trade which is incompatible with the provisions of Article 30 [now 28] of the Treaty. There is therefore no valid reason why, *provided that they have been lawfully produced and marketed in one of the Member States, alcoholic beverages should not be introduced into any other Member State;* the sale of such products may not be subject to a legal prohibition on the marketing of beverages with an alcohol content lower than the limit set by the national rules."[47]

The judgment in this case was one of the great formative events in the establishment of the internal market. The ruling in *Cassis* is notable for two main reasons: first of all, it lays down the principle of mutual recognition;[48] and secondly, it lays down the mandatory requirements doctrine. Thus once the goods have been lawfully produced in one of the Member States they should be able to circulate freely in the Community, and be marketed everywhere in the Community, *unless* there is a valid reason to stop them. The importing Member State can impose its own rules on imported products only to the extent to which that is necessary to protect a mandatory requirement of public interest, such as consumer protection, fiscal supervision, etc.[49]

The mutual recognition principle has been one of the founding **16–007** stones of the internal market: it allowed for free movement of goods, whilst at the same time leaving in place the regulatory differentiation, an aspect also of cultural diversity, that characterises the European Community. Thus, the Commission's communication on Cassis de Dijon clarified that following the *Cassis* ruling, "the Commission's work of harmonisation will henceforth have to be directed mainly at national laws having an impact on the functioning

---

[47] *ibid.*, para.14, emphasis added.
[48] The Court has held that the lack of a mutual recognition clause in rules on product requirements (composition, etc) is per se a breach of Community law, Case C–184/96 *Commission v France* (paté de foie gras) [1998] E.C.R. I–6197.
[49] See below para.16–044.

of the common market where barriers to trade to be removed arise from national provisions which are admissible under the criteria set by the Court".[50]

As a result of the *Cassis* ruling, then, the need for positive integration (the setting of one standard for all the European countries)[51] is reduced to the minimum thanks to the fact that market integration in significant areas can be achieved via mutual recognition (negative integration). An example might serve to illustrate this point: take by way of example blue cheese; this is traditionally produced in many Member States according to different rules: e.g. gorgonzola in Italy, stilton in the UK, roquefort in France. If each of the Member States were allowed to prevent import of blue cheese produced according to rules different from its own, there would be 25 different markets. The only way to achieve a single market would then be to have only *one* Community standard for blue cheese (positive integration), with the consequent loss of both regulatory and product diversity. On the other hand, thanks to Article 28 EC as interpreted by the Court, there is no need to impose *one* standard: different regulatory traditions, and different products, can co-exist since each product can gain access to the other Member States' markets without having to be modified (negative integration). Thus, it is only when the Member States successfully invoke a justification for imposing their own rules on imported product (i.e. when they successfully rely on the mandatory requirements doctrine) that there will be the need to remove such barriers through harmonisation.

If the principle of mutual recognition is one of the founding blocks of the internal market, the mandatory requirements doctrine is hardly less important. The broad interpretation given to Article 28 EC would have given rise to significant problems if the Court had not accepted that the Member States could still impose their own rules on imported products when there was a mandatory requirement of public interest which justified such rules. Take for instance the case of rules on labeling (which are measures having equivalent effect falling within the scope of Article 28 EC): it is in the interest of consumer protection that product labels should be understood by consumers and Member States should be allowed to require that labels are in the language spoken in their territory. However, consumer protection is not mentioned in Article 30 EC. The mandatory requirements doctrine addresses this problem: as we shall see in more detail later, it allows the Member State to invoke broader public interest grounds to justify the imposition of its rules to imported products. However, such grounds of public interest can be invoked only if the rules are not directly discriminatory, i.e. apply in law to domestic and imported products alike.

---

[50] [1980] O.J. C256/2.
[51] For harmonisation see Ch.21 on completing the internal market.

(c) From *Cassis* to *Keck*. The ruling in *Cassis* was confirmed in later 16–008
case law; for instance, in *Gilli & Andres*,[52] a case concerning national
legislation prohibiting the marketing of vinegar containing acetic
acid derived otherwise than from the acetic fermentation of wine.
The defendants in the national proceedings were prosecuted for
being in possession of apple vinegar for sale for gain. In this case the
Court slightly modified one of its observations in *Cassis*:

> "In practice, the principal effect of provisions of this nature is
> to protect domestic production by prohibiting the putting on to
> the market of products from other Member States which do not
> answer the descriptions laid down by the national rules."[53]

If discrimination was the distinguishing feature of national measures
prima facie contrary to Article 28 EC before the *Cassis* judgment,
emphasis after that case was placed upon the protective effect of
national rules which excluded from the market of one Member State
goods lawfully produced and marketed in the territory of another.
As the Commission stated in its above mentioned Communication
on *Cassis*:

> "Any product imported from another Member State must in
> principle be admitted to the territory of the importing Member
> State if it has been lawfully produced, that is, conforms to rules
> and processes of manufacture that are customarily and tradi-
> tionally accepted in the exporting country, and is marketed in
> the territory of another."[54]

Examples of measures held by the Court to fall within the scope of
the *Cassis* formulation (subject to justification in accordance with the
Treaty)[55] are national rules imposing a labelling requirement[56]:
national rules prohibiting use of the additive nisin in cheese[57];
national rules regulating the dry matter content, moisture content,
and salt content, of bread[58]; national rules requiring silver products
to be hall-marked[59]; national rules requiring margarine to be sold in
cube-shaped packets[60]; national rules restricting or prohibiting certain forms of advertising[61]; national rules prohibiting the retail sale

---

[52] Case 788/79 *Gilli and Andres* [1980] E.C.R. 2071.
[53] *ibid.*, para.10.
[54] [1980] O.J. C256/2.
[55] As to which, see below at para.16–016 *et seq.*
[56] Case 27/80 *Fietje* [1980] E.C.R. 3839; Case 94/82 *De Kikvorsch* [1983] E.C.R. 947.
[57] Case 53/80 *Eyssen* [1981] E.C.R. 409.
[58] Case 30/80 *Kelderman* [1981] E.C.R. 517; Case C–358/95 *Tommaso Morellato v USL No.11, Prodenone* [1997] E.C.R. I–1431; Case C–17/93 *Van der Veldt* [1994] E.C.R. I–3537
[59] Case 220/81 *Robertson* [1982] E.C.R. 2349; Case C–293/93 *Houtwipper* [1994] E.C.R. I–4249; Case C–166/03 *Commission v France* [2004] E.C.R. I–6535.
[60] Case 261/81 *Rau* [1982] E.C.R. 3961.
[61] Case 286/81 *Oosthoek's etc.* [1982] E.C.R. 4575.

of certain products unless marked with their country of origin[62]; national rules prohibiting the marketing under the designation "beer" of beers manufactured in other Member States in accordance with rules different to those applicable in the Member State of import, and prohibiting the import of beers containing additives whose use is authorised in the Member State of origin but forbidden in the Member State of import[63]; national rules prohibiting the use of common wheat flour in the production of pasta products[64]; national rules restricting the term "yoghurt" to fresh yoghurt and prohibiting its application to deep frozen yoghurt[65]; national rules restricting the name "Edam" to cheese having a minimum fat content of 40 per cent[66]; national rules providing that sales offers involving a temporary price reduction may not state the duration of the offer or refer to previous prices[67]; and advertisements relating to prices in which the new price is displayed so as to catch the eye and reference is made to a higher price shown in a previous catalogue or brochure.[68]

There can be no doubt that the *Cassis* formulation may cover national measures which the Court regards as discriminatory and at times the notions of protective effect and indirect discrimination appear to coalesce—indeed, the concepts should be treated as the same. Thus in *Prantl* the Court declared:

> ". . . even national legislation on the marketing of a product which applies to national and imported products alike falls under the prohibition laid down in Article 30 [now 28] . . . if in practice it produces protective effects by favouring typical national products and, by the same token, operating to the detriment of certain types of products from other Member States."[69]

16–009 Nevertheless, the Court made it clear in the *Cinéthèque* case[70] that the *Cassis* formulation was not limited in its application to national measures which are proved to have or are assumed to have some discriminatory purpose or effect. The case concerned French rules which provided that video-cassettes of films could not be distributed within one year of the release of the films in question at the cinema. The Court made the following observations:

---

[62] Case 207/83 *Commission v United Kingdom* [1985] E.C.R. 1201.
[63] Case 178/84 *Commission v Germany* [1987] E.C.R. 1227.
[64] Case 407/85 *Drei Glocken GmbH* [1988] E.C.R. 4233.
[65] Case 298/87 *SMANOR SA* [1988] E.C.R. 4489.
[66] Case 286/86 *Deserbais* [1988] E.C.R. 4907.
[67] Case C–362/88 *GB-INNO-BM* [1990] E.C.R. I–667.
[68] Case 126/91 Case C–126/91 *Schutzverband gegen Unwesen in der Wirtschaft e.V. v Yves Rocher GmbH* [1993] E.C.R. I–2361.
[69] Case 16/83 *Prantl* [1984] E.C.R. 1299, para.21.
[70] Joined Cases 60 and 61/84 *Cinéthèque* [1985] E.C.R. 2605.

". . . such a system, if it applies without distinction to both video-cassettes manufactured in the national territory and to imported video-cassettes, does not have the purpose of regulating trade patterns; its effect is not to favour national production as against the production of other Member States, but to encourage cinematograph production as such.

Nevertheless, the application of such a system may create barriers to intra-Community trade in video-cassettes because of the disparities between the systems operated in the different Member States and between the conditions for the release of cinematographic works in the cinemas of those States. In those circumstances a prohibition of exploitation laid down by such a system is not compatible with the principle of the free movement of goods provided for in the Treaty unless any obstacle to intra-Community trade thereby created does not exceed what is necessary in order to ensure that attainment of the objective in view and unless that objective is justified with regard to Community law."[71]

The stage was reached where a wide range of commercial and marketing rules applied by national authorities in the Member States were potentially covered by the prohibition on measures having equivalent effect to quantitative restrictions, even if the national rules in question did not differentiate between domestic goods and imports, and were not intrinsically more difficult for imports to comply with than for domestic goods. Thus, e.g. national rules on advertising and promotion were regarded as being capable of amounting to measures having equivalent effect if there was a possibility that they might affect the prospects of importing products from other Member States. As the Court explained in *Oosthoek's Uitqeversmaatschappij BV*[72]:

"Legislation which restricts or prohibits certain forms of advertising and certain means of sales promotions may, although it does not directly affect imports, be such as to restrict their volume because it affects marketing opportunities for the imported products. The possibility cannot be ruled out that to compel a producer either to adopt advertising or sales promotion schemes which differ from one Member State to another or to discontinue a scheme which he considers to be particularly effective may constitute an obstacle to imports even if the legislation in question applies to domestic products and imported products without distinction."[73]

---

[71] *ibid.*, paras 21, 22.
[72] Case 286/81 *Oosthoek's Uitqeversmaatschappij BV* [1981] E.C.R. 4575.
[73] *ibid.*, para.15, advertising falls now within the *Keck* selling arrangements exemption, see below para.16–011.

Yet it must be said that the Court's case law on the application of the abovementioned principles was not entirely consistent. In *Blesgen*[74] the Court considered that a legislative provision that concerned only the sale of strong spirits for consumption on the premises in all places open to the public and did not concern other forms of marketing the same drinks had in fact no connection with the import of the products and for that reason was not of such a nature as to impede trade between Member States. In *Quietlynn*[75] the Court referred to *Blesgen* in holding that national provisions prohibiting the sale of lawful sex articles from unlicensed sex establishments did not constitute a measure having equivalent effect. Yet it is difficult to reconcile the approach in these cases with the reasoning of the Court in the Sunday trading cases.

In *Torfaen BC v B & Q Plc*[76] the Court of Justice relied upon the *Cinéthèque* case in support of the proposition that a prohibition on Sunday trading was not compatible with the principle of the free movement of goods provided for in the Treaty unless any obstacle to Community trade thereby created did not exceed what was necessary in order to ensure the attainment of the objective in view and unless that objective was justified with regard to Community law.[77] Furthermore, the Court stated in *Marchandise*[78] that a prohibition on the employment of workers in retail shops on Sundays after 12 noon might have negative repercussions on the volume of sales and hence on the volume of imports (though the Court regarded any such restrictions as being justified). It is difficult to see the difference in principle, as regards potential effect on imports, between restrictions such as those in issue in *Blesgen* and *Quietlynn* on the one hand, and those in *Torfaen* and *Marchandise*, on the other, though differences in degree there may be.

16–010   Thus the concept of the non-discriminatory trade restriction developed by the Court covered (subject to justification) national measures defining not only the composition of products, and their labelling and packaging, but also methods of advertising and sales promotion, and indeed all manner of terms and conditions under which goods were marketed in Member States. As will be seen in the following section, the Court was to re-define the scope of the *Cassis* doctrine in the *Keck* case, in which the Court distinguished between national rules dealing with the composition, packaging and labelling of goods, etc., as regards which the *Cassis* case law held good, and national rules prohibiting "certain selling arrangements", which the

---

[74] Case 75/81 *Blesgen* [1982] E.C.R. 4575, para.15.
[75] Case C–23/89 *Quietlynn* [1990] E.C.R. I–3059.
[76] Case 145/88 *Torfaen BC v B & Q Plc* [1989] E.C.R. 3851.
[77] See also Case C–16/91 *Council of the City of Stoke-on-Trent and Norwich City Council v B & Q plc* [1992] E.C.R. I–6635.
[78] Case C–332/89 [1991] E.C.R. 1027; see also Case C–312/89 *Union Départementale des Syndicats CGT de l'Aisne v Conforama* [1991] E.C.R. I–997.

Court held would fall within the scope of Article 28 EC only if they discriminated in law or in fact between domestic goods and imports.[79]

This is perhaps an appropriate point at which to analyse the problems arising from an over broad interpretation of Article 28 EC (or of the other free movement provisions). An interpretation of Article 28 EC that goes beyond a prohibition of directly and indirectly discriminatory rules, as well as rules which have a specific effect on intra-Community trade, is problematic because it leads to national courts and the Court of Justice deciding whether national legislative bodies have excessively burdened trade by enacting and maintaining in force national rules, which, while neutral from an intra-Community trade perspective, nevertheless tend to reduce the overall level of sales of domestic goods and imports alike (such as the Sunday trading rules), or to inconvenience producers or traders who might for example have chosen to adopt a sales promotion scheme under the law of one Member State and to seek to extend it to the territory of another Member State where such schemes are subject to restrictions not applicable in the first Member State (such as the rules referred to by the Court in the *Oosthoek's* case). Judicial resolution of the question whether any impact on imports caused by such measures is justified by the purpose of the measure in question (whether it be protection of shop-workers or consumer protection) involves making value judgments on broad policy questions, and places judges at the outer limits of their legitimate judicial role, where the judiciary risks substituting its assessment for that of the legislature.[80] Whilst in the case where there is a clear impact on intra-Community trade (either because the measure is directly or indirectly discriminatory or because it specifically affects imports or exports), the judiciary is entitled and indeed required to balance different interests, that is not the case in relation to measures that do not have a specific impact on intra-Community trade and that merely express societal and cultural preferences.

Given the above, it is not surprising that following the ruling in *Torfaen* there was a lively scholarly debate as to the appropriate scope of Article 28 EC. Some authors suggested that Article 28 EC should be construed as encompassing only a prohibition on discriminatory (in law or in fact) restrictions. Most of the case law, it was argued, could be reconciled with such an approach since the concept of indirect discrimination is broadly construed to encompass all measures that might place imports at a disadvantage, such as composition requirements, labeling requirements, etc. Other authors suggested a more careful assessment of the "effect on intra-

---

[79] See below at para.16–011 *et seq.*

[80] See also Bernard *Multilevel Governance in the European Union* (Kluwer Law International, 2002), esp. Ch.2, and see also below at p.592.

Community trade" which is in any case required by the *Dassonville*
formula. Thus, the problem did not lie with the original definition of
a measure having equivalent effect, but with the Court's misunderstanding that measures which merely reduce the volume of sales
could have such an effect.[81] Finally, another part of the scholarship
proposed a distinction according to the type of rules[82]; in particular,
White[83] proposed to distinguish between rules concerning the physical characteristics of the products, which should always be caught by
Article 28 EC and rules concerning the *way* a product is sold. The
former are an obstacle to intra-Community trade since they require
producers to modify their product in order to comply with the rules
imposed by the country of destination. However, rules concerning
how and when a product can be sold do not have any specific effect
on intra-Community trade, unless they are directly or indirectly
discriminatory.[84] It is this distinction that was embraced by the Court
in the ruling in *Keck*, which we shall now consider.

16–011 **(d) The *Keck and Mithouard* judgment.**   The facts giving rise to the
national proceedings in *Bernard Keck and Daniel Mithouard*[85] were
that Mr Keck and Mr Mithouard were prosecuted for reselling
products in an unaltered state at prices lower than their actual
purchase price contrary to French legislation. In their defence, they
contended that a general prohibition on resale at a loss was
incompatible with, *inter alia*, Article 28 EC of the Treaty, and a
reference *inter alia* on that question was made to the Court of
Justice. In its judgment, the Court re-defined its *Cassis* case law to
date as follows:

> 12. National legislation imposing a general prohibition on
>   resale at a loss is not designed to regulate trade in goods
>   between Member States.
> 13. Such legislation may, admittedly, restrict the volume of
>   sales, and hence the volume of sales of products from other

---

[81] L. Gormley " 'Actually or Potentially, Directly or Indirectly?' Obstacles to the Free
Movement of Goods" (1989) 9 Y.E.L. 197; "Some Reflections on the Internal Market and
Free Movement of Goods" (1989) 12 LIEI 9; "Recent Case Law on the Free Movement of
Goods: Some Hot Potatoes" (1990) 27 C.M.L.Rev. 825, and to a certain extent J. Steiner
"Drawing the line: Uses and Abuses of Article 30 EEC" (1992) 29 C.M.L.Rev. 749,and
W.P.J. Wils "The Search for the rule in Article 30 EEC: Much Ado About Nothing?"
(1993) 18 E.L.Rev. 475.
[82] K. Mortelmans "Article 30 of the EEC Treaty and Legislation Relating to Market
Circumstances: Time to Consider a New Definition?" (1991) 28 C.M.L.Rev. 115, 129–131;
E.L. White "In Search of the Limits to Article 30 of the EEC Treaty"(1989) 26 C.M.L.Rev.
235.
[83] E.L. White "In Search of the Limits to Art.30 of the EEC Treaty"(1989) 26 C.M.L.Rev.
235.
[84] And see Advocate General Tesauro's opinion in Case C–292/92 *R Hünnermund v
Landesapothekerkammer Baden-Wurttemberg* [1993] E.C.R. I–6787, which was the opinion
on which the Court based its *Keck* ruling.
[85] Joined Cases C–267 and C–268/91 *Keck and Mithouard* [1993] E.C.R. I–6097.

Member States, in so far as it deprives traders of a method of sales promotion. But the question remains whether such a possibility is sufficient to characterize the legislation in question as a measure having equivalent effect to a quantitative restriction on imports.

14. In view of the increasing tendency of traders to invoke Article 30 [now 28] of the Treaty as a means of challenging any rules whose effect is to limit their commercial freedom even where such rules are not aimed at products from other Member States, the Court considers it necessary to re-examine and clarify its case law on this matter.

15. It is established by the case law beginning with "Cassis de Dijon" (. . .) that, in the absence of harmonisation of legislation, obstacles to free movement of goods which are the consequence of applying, to goods coming from other Member States where they are lawfully manufactured and marketed, rules that lay down requirements to be met by such goods (such as those relating to designation, form, size, weight, composition, presentation, labelling, packaging) constitute measures of equivalent effect prohibited by Article 30 [now 28]. This is so even if those rules apply without distinction to all products unless their application can be justified by a public-interest objective taking precedence over the free movement of goods.

16. By contrast, contrary to what has previously been decided, the application to products from other Member States of national provisions restricting or prohibiting certain selling arrangements is not such as to hinder directly or indirectly, actually or potentially, trade between Member States within the meaning of the *Dassonville* judgment (. . .), so long as those provisions apply to all relevant traders operating within the national territory and so long as they affect in the same manner, in law and in fact, the marketing of domestic products and of those from other Member States.

17. Provided that those conditions are fulfilled, the application of such rules to the sale of products from another Member State meeting the requirements laid down by that State is not by nature such as to prevent their access to the market or to impede access any more than it impedes the access of domestic products. Such rules therefore fall outside the scope of Article 30 [now 28] of the Treaty."

The above passages from the judgment of the Court contrast on the one hand, national rules laying down requirements to be met by goods themselves (product requirements), and on the other hand, rules which lay down "certain selling arrangements". The former continue to be governed by the *Cassis* case law and have therefore to be always justified by the mandatory requirements/Treaty deroga-tions.[86] The latter, notwithstanding the previous case law of the Court, are no longer held to hinder trade and to require justification provided that they apply to all relevant traders operating within the national territory, and so long as they affect in the same manner, in law and in fact, the marketing of domestic products and of those from other Member States.

In paragraph 17 of its *Keck* ruling the Court gives some indication as to why selling arrangements should be caught by the Treaty only when directly or indirectly discriminatory: in the Court's view, provided they are not discriminatory, selling arrangements neither prevent the access of imports to the market nor impede the access of imports more than that of domestic products. Non-discriminatory selling arrangements only restrict imports to the extent that they restrict the overall volume of sales of both domestic goods and imports,[87-88] and it may be questioned whether such measures could ever be said to impede the *access* of products to the market at all. Rather, such measures deprive traders of a sales opportunity which affects equally all products which have secured access to the market and are the subject of transactions on that market. The Court also indicates, in the first of the paragraphs cited from its judgment above, that its reference to "certain selling arrangements" does not cover measures which are designed to regulate trade in goods between Member States.[89] The Court in *Keck* concluded that Article 28 EC did not apply to legislation of a Member State imposing a general prohibition on resale at a loss, which the Court clearly regarded as comprising "selling arrangements" of the type referred to above.[90]

Given that product requirements always fall within the scope of Article 28 EC and must therefore always be justified, whilst selling arrangements are in need of justification only if they are directly or indirectly discriminatory, it is important to distinguish the two. In *Familiapress*, the Court held that a rule which prohibited the marketing of magazines containing prize competitions fell within the scope of Article 28 EC without there be any need to assess whether it was discriminatory. Even though the rule concerned a method of sale promotion, i.e. a selling arrangement, it also bore on the content of the product, and was therefore to be considered as a product requirement. The trader could not in fact import its magazines in Austria, the country of destination, without altering the content of

---

[86] Consistent case law, e.g. Case C–358/01 *Commission v Spain* [2003] E.C.R. I–13145; Case C–143/03 *Commission v Italy*, judgment of 14/10/04, unreported.

[87-88] Para.13 of Judgment.

[89] Case C–158/94 *Commission of the European Communities v Italian Republic* [1997] E.C.R. I–5789, para.31.

[90] For an analogous case concerning sales at low profit margins, see Case C–63/94 *Groupement National des Négociants en Pommes de Terre de Belgique* [1995] E.C.R. I–2467.

the periodicals.[91] Thus, if a rule can be qualified at the same time as a product requirement and as a selling arrangement, it will fall automatically within the scope of Article 28 EC by virtue of being a product requirement.

(i) The academic debate on the *Keck* ruling: market access *vis-à-vis* 16–012 discrimination. We saw above that the scholarship was highly critical of the turn taken by the Court in the Sunday Trading cases; however, not everyone welcomed the Court's chosen solution to the problem. In particular, it was feared that the Court might have gone a step too far in the opposite direction and might have chosen too narrow an approach to Article 28 EC.

The case in favour of rethinking the *Keck* ruling was forcefully made by Advocate General Jacobs in *Leclerc Siplec*,[92] where he proposed an alternative to the *Keck* test. Advocate General Jacobs argued that the ruling in *Keck* produced two main shortcomings. First of all, it was not appropriate to introduce a rigid distinction between different categories of rules and to impose different tests. In his opinion, the difference in the effect that selling arrangements might have on intra-Community trade is one of degree, not one of quality. Thus, if some selling arrangements might well have little impact (such as the prohibition on advertising outside pharmacies in *Hünermund*), other rules (such as rules severely limiting the outlets in which a product can be sold) might have a very restrictive impact on intra-Community trade. Secondly, it is inappropriate to introduce a discriminatory test, since an obstacle to intra-Community trade does not cease to exist merely because the rules affect domestic producers to the same extent. A discriminatory test would lead to fragmentation of the single market across national borders, since traders would have to adapt their arrangements to meet the demands of different Member States. Restrictions to trade should not be tested against local conditions, but against the aim "of access to the entire Community market".[93] In his opinion, the guiding principle which provides the appropriate test for the scope of Article 28 EC should be that "all undertakings which engage in a legitimate economic activity in a Member State should have unfettered access to the whole of the Community market, unless there is a valid reason for denying them full access to a part of that market".[94] In order to limit the breadth of this principle, and to avoid a new Sunday Trading trap, Advocate General Jacobs suggested the introduction of a form of *de minimis* test. Thus, in his opinion, only rules which

---

[91] Case C–368/95 *Familiapress* [1997] E.C.R. I–3689.
[92] Case C–412/93 *Société d'importation Éduard Leclerc-Siplec v TF1 Publicité SA* [1995] E.C.R. I–179.
[93] *ibid.*, para.40 of the Opinion.
[94] *ibid.*, para.41 of the Opinion.

impose a *substantial* restriction on access should be scrutinised in relation to the mandatory requirements doctrine. Of course, the *de minimis* would not apply to directly discriminatory rules, since in that case the Treaty provides for an outright prohibition. Similarly, product requirements always have a substantial effect on intra-Community trade and thus would always be scrutinised since they always affect market access.

As we shall see below, Advocate General Jacobs' suggestion was not taken on board by the Court; however, it gained favour with part of the scholarship that, with a few modifications, argued that a market access test would be better apt at ensuring that Article 28 EC catches all barriers to intra-Community trade, regardless of discrimination.[95] Moreover, a market access test would bring the case law on goods in line with the case law on the other free movement provisions, where the Court has accepted that barriers to market access fall within the scope of the Treaty and therefore need to be justified.[96]

Other authors, however, have favourably received the *Keck* ruling, and in particular the return to a discriminatory approach.[97] Thus, some argue that the scope of Article 28 EC, and indeed of the other free movement provisions, should be confined to a prohibition on discriminatory rules since the Treaty does not contain any indication as to the preferred level/type of regulation. In other words, all that the Treaty requires is that Member States do not create obstacles to the free flow of goods (and to the other free movement provisions) by having rules which are directly or indirectly discriminatory. Provided this condition is satisfied, it is for the Member States, not for the judiciary, to decide on the appropriate level of regulation. For those reasons, those who support a discriminatory approach welcomed the *Keck* ruling as a step in the right direction. Thus, they argue, following *Keck* the scope of Article 28 EC has been narrowed down to a prohibition on discrimination. Product requirements are always caught by Article 28 EC since they are inherently indirectly discriminatory: the imposition of rules concerning the physical qualities of a product on imported goods have a heavier effect on

---

[95] S. Weatherill "After *Keck*: some thoughts on how to clarify the clarification" (1996) 33 C.M.L.Rev. 885, 897, also criticising the *Keck* distinction based on the type rather than on the effect of the rules, suggested that non-discriminatory measures should escape scrutiny if they impose "no direct or substantial hindrance to the access of imported goods or services". On almost the same lines C. Barnard "Fitting the remaining pieces into the goods and persons jigsaw? (2001) 26 E.L.Rev. 34, with the only difference that the test would apply also to discriminatory rules since those always either prevent or substantially impede market access.

[96] See Chs 18 and 19, below.

[97] N. Bernard "Discrimination and Free Movement in EC Law" (1996) 45 I.C.L.Q. 83; N. Bernard "La libre circulation des marchandises, des personnes et des services dans le Traité CE sous l'angle de la compétence" (1998) 33 C.D.E. 11, 34–35; N. Bernard *Multi Level Governance in the European Union* (Kluwer Law International, London, 2002), 168; and J. Snell *Goods and Services in EC Law* (OUP, Oxford, 2002).

the latter than on domestic products. This is the case because the imported product has already been regulated in the country of production and in order to comply with further product rules the importer would have to modify its product. Goods produced and sold in the domestic market however, have to comply with only the domestic regulatory standard. Selling arrangements on the other hand are caught only when directly or indirectly discriminatory. So, according to this view, and even though the Court has not expressly said so, Article 28 EC is now limited to a prohibition of discriminatory restrictions.

As we shall see below, neither the market access view nor the discriminatory view is entirely supported by the case law. The latter, disregards the fact that some rules (residual rules) are caught regardless of discrimination; and that product requirements are always caught by Article 28 EC even when there is no domestic production of similar or competing goods, therefore excluding discrimination.[98] The market access theory is also not entirely convincing: whilst it is certainly true that product requirements also constitute a barrier to market access and might be seen to fall within the scope of Article 28 EC for that reason, other rules (such as restrictions on internet sales) that clearly affect market access have been found to fall outside its scope unless discriminatory.[99]

(e) The case law after the *Keck* judgment. The scale of the case law 16–013 caught by the words "contrary to what has previously been decided" became apparent as the Court applied the *Keck* reasoning in its subsequent cases. In *Punto Casa SpA* the Court considered Italian rules restricting the Sunday opening hours of shops; the Court held that Article 28 EC did not apply to national legislation on the closure of shops which applies to all traders operating within the national territory and which affects in the same manner, in law and in fact, the marketing of domestic products and of those from other Member States.[1]

In *Lucien Ortscheit GmbH*, the Court considered a national rule prohibiting advertisements containing an offer to obtain specified medicinal products by individual importation. This the Court held to fall within the scope of Article 28 EC because it applied solely

---

[98] In relation to discriminatory taxation, the Court has clearly held that in the absence of similar or comparable domestic production there cannot be any discrimination; e.g. Case C–47/88 *Commission v Denmark* [1990] E.C.R. I–4509. See Ch.15, para.15–016. And in Case C–391/92 *Commission v Greece* (processed milk for infants) [1995] E.C.R. I–1621, para.17, the Court, against the advice of Advocate General Lenz, has excluded that the absence of domestic production, a "purely fortuitous factual circumstance", is enough for there to be a finding of discrimination.

[99] Case C–322/01 *Deutscher Apothekerverband eV v 0800 DocMorris NV, Jacques Waterval* [2003] E.C.R. I–4887, and see below p.599.

[1] Joined Cases C–69/93 and C–258/93 *Punto Casa Srl* [1994] E.C.R. I–2355. See also Joined Cases C–410/91 and C–402/92 *Tankstaton 't Heukske vof* [1994] E.C.R. I–2199.

to *foreign* medicinal products, and was therefore directly discriminatory.[2] In *Hünermund* the Court considered a restriction imposed on advertising by pharmacists outside their pharmacy of quasi-pharmaceutical products which they were authorised to sell, and held that it did not fall within Article 28 EC because it did not affect the marketing of goods from other Member States differently from that of domestic products.[3] In *Leclerc-Siplec* the Court held that legislation which prohibits television advertising in a particular sector concerns selling arrangements for products belonging to that sector in that it prohibits a particular form of promotion of a particular method of marketing products, and that a prohibition such as that in issue did not fall within the scope of Article 28 EC, since it affected the marketing of imports and domestic goods in the same manner.[4] In *De Agostini*[5] the Court considered an outright ban on advertising aimed at children less than 12 years of age and on misleading advertising. The Court noted that the national measures in issue applied to all relevant traders operating within national territory, but added that it could not be excluded that an outright ban, applying in one Member State, of a type of promotion for a product which is lawfully sold there might have a greater impact on products from other Member States. It followed that such a ban was not covered by Article 28 EC, unless it were shown that the ban did not affect in the same way, in fact and in law, the marketing of national products and of products from other Member States. In that case it would be necessary to consider the question of justification.[6]

The Court has applied the "selling arrangements" analysis to national rules which restrict the distribution of certain products to certain types of outlet. Thus in *Commission v Greece* the Court considered Greek rules which required processed milk for infants to be sold exclusively by pharmacies. The Court took the view that the legislation,

> ". . . the effect of which is to limit the commercial freedom of traders irrespective of the actual characteristics of the product referred to, concerns the selling arrangements of certain goods, inasmuch as it prohibits the sale, other than exclusively by pharmacies, of processed milk for infants and thus generally determines the points of sale where they may be distributed."[7]

---

[2] Case C–320/93 *Lucien Ortscheit GmbH* [1994] E.C.R. I–5243, para.9.
[3] Case C–292/92 *Ruth Hünermund v Landesapothekerkammer Baden-Württemberg* [1993] E.C.R. I–6787, para.23.
[4] Case C–412/93 *Société d'Importation Edouard Leclerc-Siplec* [1995] E.C.R. I–179, para.23. For a thought provoking critique of the reasoning in *Keck* see the Opinion of Advocate General Jacobs at paras 38 *et. seq.*, and p.592, above.
[5] Joined Cases C–34/95, C–35/95 and C–36/95 *Konsumentombudsmannen (KO) v De Agostini (Svenska) Förlag AB* [1997] E.C.R. I –3843.
[6] *ibid.*, paras 39–45.
[7] Case C–391/92 *Commission v Greece* [1995] E.C.R. I–1621, Ch.15.

Since the legislation applied without distinction according to the origin of the products in question to all of the traders operating within the national territory, and did not affect the sale of products originating in other Member States any differently from that of domestic products, the Court concluded that it did not fall within Article 28 EC. The Court noted that this conclusion was not affected by the fact, pointed out by the Commission, that Greece did not itself produce processed milk for infants, and the Court added that the situation would be different "only if it was apparent that the legislation in issue protected domestic products which were similar to processed milk for infants from other Member States or which were in competition with milk of that type." But the Commission had not shown this to be the case.[8] Similar reasoning has been applied in the case of national rules confining tobacco sales to authorised retailers,[9] and national rules which require authorisation for the distribution of bovine semen.[10]

However useful the *Keck* distinction between selling arrangements and product requirements is, the case law needed some fine tuning. The main problem, identified already in 1995 by Advocate General Jacobs, and widely commented upon by the scholarship, concerns advertising restrictions and selling techniques that are particularly useful, and effective, for long distance transactions.

As mentioned above, in *Hünnermund* the Court qualified rules **16–014** regulating advertising as selling arrangements.[11] This might well have been a (non intentional) mistake that had more to do with the fact that the rules at issue in that case (a prohibition of advertising just outside pharmacies) clearly did not have any effect on intra-Community trade. However, other advertising rules might well have important effects on intra-Community trade. First of all, advertising is crucial to penetrate new markets, since without it the consumer might not be aware of a new product/brand. Take the example of alcopops or MP3 players: if the producers of such products were not allowed to advertise them, it would be almost impossible, and probably not economically viable, to penetrate a new market (or indeed create a new demand for a product that was previously not there). Secondly, in relation to heavily branded products, advertising might be as, if not more important, than the physical qualities of the products. Take, by way of example, the case of perfumes: there, branding is crucial, much more so than the scent itself might be. The effect of forcing a producer to elaborate different advertising campaigns for each of the Member States might be as market

---

[8] *ibid.*, paras 15–19.
[9] Case C–387/93 *Banchero* [1995] E.C.R. I–4663, paras 37 and 44.
[10] Case C–162/97 *Gunnar Nilsson* [1998] E.C.R. I–7477; see also Case C–416/00 *Morellato* [2003] E.C.R. I–8343.
[11] Case C–292//92 *Ruth Hünermund v Landesapothekerkammer Baden-Württemberg* [1993] E.C.R. I–6787, para.23.

partitioning as the imposition of domestic product requirements on imported goods. In other words, in the case of heavily branded products, advertising, the image of the product, the perception that the consumer has of a particular brand, might be more important than the intrinsic qualities of the product itself. For this reason, to exclude advertising from the scope of Article 28 EC unless it is discriminatory in fact or in law might have the effect of leaving in place significant barriers to intra-Community trade.

A similar problem arises in relation to rules that discipline the way a product is sold (a selling arrangement) when such way is especially useful in penetrating new markets. That would be the case, for instance, in relation to internet sales where producers have a way to penetrate a new market without having to bear the commercial risks inherent in doing so. Thus, even a small producer can attempt to penetrate a foreign market through the internet because it does not have to bear the costs and the risk of setting up a distribution system, or a retail network.

It is especially in relation to those cases that the *Keck* distinction based on the type of rules, rather than on their effects, has proven to be inadequate. For this reason, as we saw above, Advocate General Jacobs, as well as several authors, have suggested that the determinant factor in order to decide whether a rule falls within or outside the scope of Article 28 EC should be whether the rule restricts market access in a significant way. Whilst the Court has so far refused to depart from the *Keck* product requirement/selling arrangement distinction, it has, as said above, tuned its approach to deal with these problems.

The first indication of a less rigid approach to selling arrangements came in the case of *TK-Heimdienst*.[12] Here, Austrian rules restricted the possibility to do sales on rounds of given groceries to those traders who had an establishment in the administrative district where the sale on rounds took place or in a district bordering with it. The Court was asked by the national court whether those rules were to be considered restrictions falling within the scope of Article 28 EC. For the purposes of the case, it was accepted that traders established in bordering districts in other Member States would be allowed to do sales on rounds under the same conditions as the Austrian traders. The rules were clearly selling arrangements and the issue was whether they were indirectly discriminatory or not. Advocate General La Pergola found that there was no discrimination since traders established in bordering States could do sales on rounds under the same conditions as Austrian traders; furthermore, the rules had no effect on intra-Community trade since it was not realistic to think that a baker established in Paris would want to go

[12] Case C–254/98 *Schutzverband gegen unlauteren Wettbewerb v TK-Heimdienst Sass GmbH* [2000] E.C.R. I–151.

and sell her/his bread in Austria. Having taken a substantive and realistic approach to the question of discrimination, the Advocate General found that there was no way the rules at issue could have an affect on intra-Community trade. The Court, however, favoured a purely abstract assessment of the rules at issue: since a residence/ establishment requirement is always indirectly discriminatory (national traders being more likely than foreign traders to have an establishment within the national territory),[13] the Austrian rules were to be so qualified. Furthermore, the Court found that the rules were not justified and were therefore incompatible with Article 28 EC.[14]

In *Gourmet*,[15] Swedish legislation imposed an almost complete ban **16–015** on the advertising of alcoholic products. The question for the Court was whether, as contended by the Swedish government, the advertising ban fell within the *Keck* exception since it was a selling arrangement that applied to domestic and imported products alike, or whether, as contended by *Gourmet*, it instead fell within the scope of Article 28 EC. The Court held:

> 18. It should be pointed out that, according to paragraph 17 of its judgment in *Keck and Mithouard*, if national provisions restricting or prohibiting certain selling arrangements are to avoid being caught by Article 30 [now 28] of the Treaty, they must not be of such a kind as to prevent access to the market by products from another Member State or to impede access any more than they impede the access of domestic products.
> [. . .]
> 21. [. . .] in the case of products like alcoholic beverages, the consumption of which is linked to traditional social practices and to local habits and customs, a prohibition of all advertising directed at consumers in the form of advertisements in the press, on the radio and on television, the direct mailing of unsolicited material or the placing of posters on the public highway is liable to impede access to the market by products from other Member States more than it impedes access by domestic products, with which consumers are instantly more familiar."

---

[13] An establishment requirement is always considered to be indirectly discriminatory, see Ch.19 on services.

[14] A more reasonable approach was taken in Case C–441/04 *A-Punkt Schmuckhandels GmbH v C Schmidt*, (Judgment of February 23, 2006), where the Court left it to the national court to determine whether a prohibition on doorstep sales of silver jewelry affected market access for imported products more than market access for domestic products. See also Case C–20/03 *M Burmnajer* [2005] E.C.R. I–4133.

[15] Case C–405/98 *Gourmet International Products* [2001] E.C.R. I–1795; see A. Biondi, "Advertising alcohol and the free movement principle: the *Gourmet* decision" (2001) 26 E.L.Rev. 616. See also Ch.19 below.

The Court then found that the advertising ban was caught by Article 28 EC, and left it to the national court to determine whether it constituted a proportionate measure to safeguard the legitimate aim of protecting the population from the harmful effects of alcohol abuse.

It should be noted that the Court's reasoning is ambiguous in that it is based both on a market access rationale and on the potential discriminatory effects of an outright ban of advertising, that might render access to the market of foreign alcoholic products more difficult than access to the market of domestic products with which consumers are more familiar. Thus, the ruling can be interpreted in two ways: first, restrictions that *prevent* market access are caught by Article 28 EC without there be any need to prove a discriminatory effect. A total ban on advertising always has the effect of preventing access to a market. Or, a total ban on advertising by its nature puts imported products at a disadvantage and therefore is caught by Article 28 EC. No matter which reading of the case is chosen, it is clear that in the case of a total ban on advertising there is no need to prove a discriminatory effect. The case might be usefully compared with the *De Agostini* ruling where the Court held that in the case of a partial ban on advertising, a ban on television advertising directed at children, where other means of advertising are allowed (e.g. billboard, advertising on publications, etc.), discrimination needs to be established before the rule can be held to fall within the scope of Article 28 EC and therefore be in need of justification. This said, subsequent case law seems to indicate that the Court has not accepted a market access test in relation to Article 28 EC (whilst it has clearly accepted such test in relation to the other free movement provisions).

In *DocMorris*,[16] the main defendant was a company established in the Netherlands which sold medicinal products over the internet. The company sold both prescription and non-prescription drugs. In relation to the former it would sell the drugs only on production of a prescription. In order to determine whether a drug was a prescription only drug it would have regard to both the Dutch legislation and the rules of the place where the consumer was established, always applying the strictest rule, meaning that it would not sell a drug without prescription if such prescription was required in the Netherlands, and it would not sell a drug without prescription if prescription was required in the place where the consumer was located, even if Dutch law did not require such prescription. The drugs would either be posted by courier or could be collected in a pharmacy located in the Netherlands. The company also provided advice

---

[16] Case C–322/01 *Deutscher Apothekerverband eV v 0800 DocMorris NV, Jacques Waterval* [2003] E.C.R. I–4887; see also Case C–497/03 *Commission v Austria* (sale by mail), judgment of 28/10/04, unreported.

through the internet, by phone and by post. The company sold its drugs also to German consumers; as a result *Deutscher Apothekerverband*, a German association protecting the interests of pharmacists, brought proceedings on the grounds that the internet sale of drugs breached German legislation. The national court requested a preliminary ruling from the Court as to the compatibility with Article 28 EC of the German legislation which, *inter alia*, prohibited the sale of medicinal products outside pharmacies, therefore prohibiting postal and internet sales of drugs. The Court found that the rules were selling arrangements; it then turned to the question of discrimination. After having acknowledged that the ban applied in law in the same way to German and foreign pharmacies, it held:

> "72. A prohibition such as that at issue in the main proceedings is more of an obstacle to pharmacies outside Germany than to those within it. Although there is little doubt that as a result of the prohibition, pharmacies in Germany cannot use the extra or alternative method of gaining access to the German market consisting of end consumers of medicinal products, they are still able to sell the products in their dispensaries. However, for pharmacies not established in Germany, the internet provides a more significant way to gain direct access to the German market. A prohibition which has a greater impact on pharmacies established outside German territory could impede access to the market for products from other Member States more than it impedes access for domestic products."

The Court then examined whether the rules at issue were justifiedand found that a ban on sale outside pharmacies of prescription drugs was justified by public health concerns, whilst in the case of non-prescription drugs such a ban was disproportionate.

The ruling in *DocMorris* clarified the ruling in *Gourmet*: it is clear that were the Court to have moved to a market access test it should have not assessed the discriminatory effect of the rules, since a prohibition on the marketing of a product over the internet clearly restricts market access. Instead, the Court decided to restate the *Keck* approach: selling arrangements are caught by Article 28 EC only insofar as they affect in law or in fact imported products more than domestic products. We have seen above that a total ban on advertising is to be qualified as inherently indirectly discriminatory. Rules banning internet sales should also be so qualified: by nature foreign producers which do not have a network of retail outlets in the market of destination are more affected than domestic producers by a ban on sale over the internet.

In *Douwe Egberts* the Court examined the compatibility with **16–016** Article 28 EC of rules which prohibited any reference in advertising of foodstuff to "slimming" and "medical recommendations, attestations, declarations or statements of approval". After having mentioned the *Keck* ruling, the Court referred to pre-*Keck* case law[17] and held that it could not be "ruled out that to compel a producer to discontinue an advertising scheme which he considers to be particularly effective may constitute an obstacle to imports". This seems a regression to pre-*Keck* case law; the Court however then continued: "Moreover, an absolute prohibition of advertising the characteristics of a product is liable to impede access to the market by products from other Member States more than it impedes access by domestic products, with which consumers are more familiar".[18] If one focuses on the latter statement, then the ruling can be easily reconciled with what was said above: the rules at issue constituted an absolute ban on the advertising of the characteristics of the product. For this reason, and as with any absolute ban, they can be considered indirectly discriminatory and thus in need of justification.

This said, given the importance of advertising and its effect on market penetration it would have been preferable if rules concerning advertising had not been included in the category of "certain selling arrangements" that are caught only if discriminatory. In any event, however, *Gourmet*, *DocMorris* and *Douwe Egberts* demonstrate that the *Keck* distinction between product requirements and selling arrangements is not as rigid as some authors feared[19]: the Court is willing to look at whether the rules might put foreign traders at a disadvantage and therefore have a specific effect on intra-Community trade. If that is the case, then such rules fall within the scope of Article 28 EC and have to be justified. Furthermore, the fine-tuning of the *Keck* distinction between product requirements and selling arrangements is complemented by Article 49 EC which guarantees the free movement of services within the European Community. As we shall see in Chapter 19, the scope of Article 49 EC is broader than that of Article 28 EC, in that the former catches any hindrance/discouragement to the provision of cross-border services. As it happens, advertising and internet provision, are also services since both imply the sell/purchase of services from a third person (the advertising agency, the internet provider, etc.). Thus, the rules in *Gourmet* were scrutinised also having regard to Article 49 EC: even had they been found not to be indirectly discriminatory under Article 28 EC, they would have still required justification as a restriction to the provision of cross-border services. In this way, even if an advertising/internet restriction were to fall outside Article 28 EC, it might be caught by Article 49 EC, and therefore need to be justified.[20]

---

[17] Case C–241/89 *SARPP* [1990] E.C.R. I–4695.

[18] Case C–239/02 *Douwe Egberts NV* [2004] E.C.R. I–7007, paras 52 and 53.

[19] See also P. Koutrakos "On Groceries, Alcohol and Olive Oil: More on the Free Movement of Goods after *Keck*" (2001) 26 E.L.Rev. 391.

[20] This provided the service provision is not entirely ancillary to the sale of goods; *cf.* Case C–71/02 *Karner* [2004] E.C.R. I–3025, para.46.

Residual rules: other rules that might be caught by Article 28 EC

Not all national measures which affect intra-Community trade can **16–017** be classified as either rules relating to the goods themselves on the one hand, or selling arrangements, on the other: bans on sale or use[21]; inspections[22]; registration[23] and authorisation requirements[24]; licence requirements[25]; restrictions on transport[26]; and obligations to provide data for statistics,[27] cannot be comfortably categorised under either heading. Whilst, however, product requirements are always deemed to have an (at least potential) effect on intra-Community trade, and directly and indirectly discriminatory restrictions always fall within the scope of application of Article 28 EC (whether selling arrangements or not), in the case of "residual" rules, an investigation might be necessary as to the (at least potential) effect of the measure on intra-Community trade. Thus, when the measure does not distinguish according to the origin of the goods, and its purpose is not to regulate trade in goods with other Member States, the restrictive effects which it might have on the free movement of goods might be too uncertain and indirect for the obligation which it imposes to be regarded as being capable of hindering trade between Member States.[28] This is not, however, to say that there is a *de*

---

[21] Case C–293/94 *Criminal proceedings against Brandsma* [1996] E.C.R. I–3159; Case C–400/96 *J. Harpegnies* [1998] E.C.R. I–5121; Case C–473/98 *Kemikalienspektionen v Toolex Alpha AB* [2000] E.C.R. I–5681.

[22] Case C–105/94 *Ditta A Celestini* [1997] E.C.R. I–2971.

[23] Case C–55/99 *Commission v France* [2000] (Registration for reagents) E.C.R. I–1149; Case C–390/99 *Canal Satélite Digital SL v Administración General del Estado* [2002] E.C.R. I–607. In this case the Court excluded that the *Keck* ruling could apply because of "the need in certain cases to adapt the products in question to the rules in force in the Member State in which they are marketed" (para.30); to the same effect also Case C–14/02 *ATRAL SA V Belgium* [2003] E.C.R. I–4431.

[24] Case C–120/95 *N Decker v Caisse de Maladie des Employés Privés* [1998] E.C.R. I–1831.

[25] Case C–189/95 *Criminal proceedings against H. Franzén* [1997] E.C.R. I–5909; it is not clear whether an obligation to store semen in authorised centres is a selling arrangements or not, *cf. Case* C–323/93 *Société Civile Agricole du Centre d'Insémination de la Crespelle v Coopérative d'Elevage et d'Insémination Artificielle du Département de la Mayenne* [1994] E.C.R. I–5077, where the Court unusually refers to Case C–169/91 *Council of the City of Stoke-on-Trent and Norwich City Council v B & Q plc* [1992] E.C.R. I–6635 (one of the Sunday Trading cases) rather than to *Keck*.

[26] Case C–350/97 *W Monsees v Unabhängiger Verwaltungssenat für Kärnten* [1999] E.C.R. I–2921.

[27] Case C–114/96 *René Kieffer and Roman Thill* [1997] E.C.R. I–3629.

[28] The "effect to uncertain and indirect" doctrine has been referred to e.g. in Case C–69/88 *H. Krantz GmbH & Co v Ontvanger der Directe Belastingen and Netherlands State* [1990] E.C.R. I–583, in relation to the tax collector's seizure powers (para.11); Case C–93/92 *CMC Motorradcenter GmbH v Pelin Baskiciogullari* [1993] E.C.R. I–5009, in relation to rules establishing a duty to communicate relevant information to the counter-party to a contract (para.12); Case C–379/92 *Peralta* [1994] E.C.R. I–3453, in relation to an obligation for vessels to carry costly equipment (para.24); Case C–96/94 *Centro Servizi Spediporto Srl v Spedizioni Marittima del Golfo Srl* [1995] E.C.R. I–2883 on road haulage tariffs; Case C–266/96 *Corsica Ferries France SA v Gruppo Antichi Ormeggiatori del Porto di Genova Coop. A.r.l. et al.* [1998] E.C.R. I–3949 on mooring tariffs; Case C–44/98 *BASF v Präsident des Deutschen Patentamts* [1999] E.C.R. I–6269, in relation to an obligation to translate patents in order to benefit of the exclusive right. The doctrine applies also to Art.29 EC, Case C–412/97 *ED Srl v I Fenocchio* [1999] E.C.R. I–3845 in relation to a rule prohibiting the issue of a summary payment to be served outside the national territory.

minimis test, but rather—as explained by Advocate General La Pergola[29]—that in these cases, the causal link between the rule and an effect on intra-Community trade might be lacking.

The investigation of the Court will thus be directed at assessing whether the link between rule and intra-Community effect, necessary in any case in order to trigger the application of Article 28 EC, exists at all, i.e. whether the effect of the rule is not "too uncertain and indirect" to exclude the application of the free movement of goods provisions. On the other hand, a *de minimis* test, often rejected by the Court, would imply the exclusion of the applicability of Article 28 EC when the measure would have "non-appreciable" effects on intra-Community trade.[30] In the latter case, there is *an* effect—however small or potential—on intra-Community trade. In the former case, there is *no* effect at all. This could be because, for instance, the effect does not depend on the rules at issue, but rather on the unforeseeable decisions of economic operators[31]; because the impact of the rule on the price of the goods is so minimal as not to be able to affect intra-Community trade[32]; or because there is not even a risk that the rules might affect intra-Community trade.[33]

The "effect too uncertain and indirect doctrine" creates some confusion as to the relationship between this doctrine and selling arrangements which escape scrutiny under Article 28 EC. Thus, it is not clear whether non-discriminatory selling arrangements fall outside the scope of the Treaty because there is no effect on intra-Community trade; or because they fall outside the definition of a measure having equivalent effect in that they are recognised as falling within the inherent regulatory competence of the Member States. The latter is a more convincing explanation for two reasons. First of all, the "effect too uncertain and indirect" doctrine predates the ruling in *Keck*. Thus, if non-discriminatory selling arrangements had no effect on intra-Community trade, the Court would have had no need to impose a different test for this type of rules. The focus in the case of selling arrangements is on the *type* of rule, not on its *effect*. Secondly, and more importantly, it would be difficult to maintain that a restriction on advertisement has only a remote effect

---

[29] Opinion in Case C–44/98 *BASF v Präsident des Deutschen Patentamts* [1999] E.C.R. I–6269. See also Advocate General Fenelly's Opinion in Case C–67/97 *Bluhme* [1998] E.C.R. I–8033, para.19. Advocate General Fenelly in his opinion in Case C–266/96 *Corsica Ferries France SA v Gruppo Antichi Ormeggiatori del Porto di Genova Coop. A.r.l. et al.* [1998] E.C.R. I–3949, has identified in the fact that the measure must have some "protective effect" the necessary element in order to trigger Art.28 EC. This is lacking when the effects on the cost of importing goods is entirely incidental. However, the definition of what is to be considered as protective effect is not necessarily easy. Moreover it is debatable whether any protectionist effect or intent is needed in order to trigger Art.28 EC.

[30] Case 16/83 *Prantl* [1984] E.C.R. 1299, para.20.

[31] Case C–44/98 *BASF v Präsident des Deutschen Patentamts* [1999] E.C.R. I–6269.

[32] Case C–266/96 *Corsica Ferries France SA v Gruppo Antichi Ormeggiatori del Porto di Genova Coop. A.r.l. et al.* [1998] E.C.R. I–3949.

[33] Case C–93/92 *CMC Motorradcenter GmbH v Pelin Baskiciogullari* [1993] E.C.R. I–5009.

on intra-Community trade, since it might considerably affect the volume of sales. In that case, there might not be a *specific* effect on intra-Community trade, but there is *an* effect. On the other hand, rules which benefit from the effect too uncertain and indirect doctrine do not even lead to a contraction on the volume of sales.[34] This is not to say, however, that the Court could not have chosen a test capable of accommodating both types of rules. But it has not and for the reasons outlined above it seems more consistent to consider the two tests as distinct.

Failure to Act: The Member States' duty to protect the rights conferred by Article 28 EC

Member States might be infringing Article 28 EC not only when **16–018** imposing rules which are liable to affect intra-Community trade, but also when failing to take appropriate steps to ensure that obstacles to free movement created by actions of individuals are removed. In *Commission v France*, the Commission brought proceedings against France alleging that the latter's failure to take any action against the unlawful behaviour of French farmers, who repeatedly engaged in violent actions to prevent imports of Spanish strawberries, constituted a breach of the Treaty.[35] The Court accepted the Commission's plea, although it recognised that, in these cases, Member States retain a wide margin of discretion as to the action needed to deal with obstacles to free movement created by private actions. Article 28 EC,[36] together with Article 10 EC, imposes not only a duty of non-interference upon Member States, but also a positive duty to ensure that the Treaty freedom may—in practice—be enjoyed by its right-holders. This approach is entirely consistent with fundamental rights theory, according to which States have not only a negative duty of non-interference with individuals' fundamental rights, but might also have a positive duty to guarantee the effective enjoyment of those rights.

---

[34] Contrast Advocate General Cosmas' Opinion in C–63/94 *Groupement National des Négociants en Pommes de Terre de Belgique v ITM Belgium Sa and Vocarex SA* [1995] E.C.R. I–2467, esp. para.26.

[35] Case C–265/95 *Commission v France* (Riots) [1997] E.C.R. I–6959. The ECJ has in principle accepted that, if the Member State is unable to use the means at its disposal to deal with possible public order or public security problems caused by its citizens, then it can rely on the Treaty derogations, Case 231/83 *H. Cullet et Chambres Syndicale des réparateurs automobiles et détaillants de produits pétroliers v Centre Leclerc à Toulouse et Centre Leclerc à Saint-Orens-de-Gameville* [1985] E.C.R. 35. For an application of this case law by the English courts, see *R v chief Constable of Sussex, ex parte International Trader's Ferry Ltd (ITF)* [1997] 2 All E.R. 65, also in [1997] 2 C.M.L.R. 164, upheld in the HL, [1999] 1 All E.R. 129, and [1999] 1 C.M.L.R. 1320. For a critical assessment of *Commission v France* and *ITF*, C. Barnard and I. Hare "The Right to Protest and the Right to Export: Police discretion and the Free Movement of Goods" (1997) 60 M.L.R. 394; G. Orlandini "The Free Movement of Goods as a Possible 'Community' Limitation on Industrial Conflict" (2000) E.L.J. 341.

[36] It is likely that the reasoning in Case C–265/95 *Commission v France* (Riots) [1997] E.C.R. I–6959 could be applied also to the other free movement provisions.

The outcome of the ruling was later codified in Council Regulation 2679/98/EC, which clarifies that the Member States may be in breach of Article 28 EC for their inaction.[37] The term comprises cases in which a Member State, in the presence of an obstacle created by private individuals, fails to take "necessary and proportionate action" with a view to removing the obstacle. More importantly, the Regulation clarifies that it does not affect fundamental rights as recognised in the Member States. This provision is consistent with the Court's view that, when acting in the field of Community law, Member States must respect fundamental rights, although the reference to national fundamental rights (as opposed to fundamental rights as general principles of Community law) seems to suggest that, should a clash arise, Member States would have to rely on the public policy derogation. However, a more recent ruling shows the Court's unwillingness to follow the approach enshrined in the Regulation.

In *Schmidberger*,[38] an Austrian court made a preliminary reference in order to ascertain the compatibility with Article 28 EC of a decision authorising a demonstration on the Brenner motorway, a major transit route between Italy and the rest of continental Europe. The claimants argued that the demonstration was an obstacle to the free movement of goods since it impeded road transport of goods coming from Italy. The Court found that the demonstration, which resulted in the closure of the motorway, was capable of restricting intra-Community trade and was thus a measure having equivalent effect. It then turned to assess whether such a restriction could be justified, and whether the free movement provisions should be construed as taking precedence over fundamental rights as enshrined in the European Convention of Human Rights (ECHR) and recognised by national constitutions (in this case, freedom of expression and assembly). The Court held that, since fundamental rights are general principles of Community law which bind both the Community and the Member States, the protection of those rights justifies a restriction of "the obligations of Community law, even under a fundamental freedom guaranteed by the Treaty".[39] Thus, at least in cases in which the fundamental right clashing with the free movement right is recognised by the ECHR, the Member States are not required to rely on the public policy derogation.[40] The scope of

---

[37] Council Regulation 2679/98/EC of December 7, 1998 on the functioning of the internal market in relation to the free movement of goods among the Member States, [1998] O.J. L337/8.

[38] Case C–112/00 *Schmidberger* [2003] E.C.R. I–5659; and see A. Biondi "Free trade, a mountain road and the right to protest: European economic freedoms and fundamental individual rights" (2004) E.H.R.L.R. 51.

[39] *ibid.*, para.74. *cf.* Case C–50/96 *Deutsche Telekom Advocate General v Lilli Schroder* [2000] E.C.R. I–743, para.57, where the Court held that the economic aim pursued by Art.141 EC, is secondary to the social aim pursued by that provision which is the expression of a fundamental right (of equality between men and women).

[40] They might be under a duty to do so if there is no "common" view in the Community as to the scope of the fundamental right (such as it is the case for abortion and the right to life).

the free movement provisions is thus, not surprisingly, *inherently limited* by the proportionate enjoyment by other of their (not necessarily economic) rights.

Other characteristics of the prohibition on measures having equivalent effect to quantitative restrictions on imports

(a) Intra-state or regional restrictions. When a national measure **16–019** has limited territorial scope because it applies only to a part of national territory, it cannot escape being characterised as discriminatory or protective for the purpose of the rules on the free movement of goods on the ground that it affects both the sale of products from other parts of the national territory and the sale of products imported from other Member States. For such a measure to be characterized as discriminatory or protective, it is not necessary for it to have the effect of favouring national products as a whole or of placing only imported products at a disadvantage.[41] Thus a Danish prohibition on keeping and importation into Laesø of any bee but the Laesø brown bee, for reasons of conservation, and having the effect of excluding bees both from other parts of Denmark and from other Member States, was held to amount to a measure having equivalent effect, though a measure justified on environmental grounds.[42] In relation to Article 29 EC, the Court has held that rules which impose obstacles to the flaw of goods from one part of the national territory (in this case Jersey) to another part of the national territory (the United kingdom) fell within the scope of the Treaty since there is nothing to rule out the possibility that the goods could be re-exported after having been moved within the national territory. Thus, the mere potentiality of an intra-Community element is enough to trigger Article 29 EC.[43]

(b) Only conduct attributable to the state comprise measures having 16–020 equivalent effect. The measures defined by the Court amounting to measures having equivalent effect are invariably described as "national" measures, or trading rules "of the Member States" or measures "enacted by Member States." This would seem to exclude the conduct of private individuals and undertakings unsupported by State action of a legislative, executive or judicial character. The Court has condemned as a measure having equivalent effect a campaign funded by a Member State to promote the sale of

---

[41] Joined Cases C–1/90 and C–176/90 *Aragonesa de Publicidad Exterior SA* [1991] E.C.R. I–4151, para.24. See also Joined Cases C–277/81, C–318/91 and C–319/81 *Ligur Carni Srl and Genova Carni Srl v Unità Sanitaria Locale n. XV di Genova and Ponente SpA v Unità Sanitaria Locale n. XIX di La Spezia and CO.GE.SE.MA Coop a r l.* [1993] E.C.R. I–6621.

[42] Case C–67/97 *Ditlev Bluhme* [1998] E.C.R. I–8033.

[43] Case C–293/02 *Jersey Produce Marketing Organisation Ltd* [2005] E.C.R.I–9543.

domestic goods with a view to limiting imports, despite the fact that the campaign was conducted by a private company limited by guarantee. The management committee of the company was appointed by the national authorities, and the aims and outlines of the campaign were decided upon by those authorities. The Court held that the Member State in question could neither rely upon the fact that the campaign was conducted by a private company, nor upon the fact that the campaign was based upon decisions which were not binding upon undertakings, to avoid liability under Article 28 EC.[44] The Court observed in another case that a body established and funded by the Government with a view, *inter alia*, to promoting the sale of domestic products could not under Community law enjoy the same freedom as regards methods of advertising as that enjoyed by producers themselves or producer's associations of a voluntary character.[45]

16–021 **(c) The State has a positive duty to safeguard the rights conferred by Article 28 EC, including a duty to leave time to traders to adjust to regulatory changes.** We saw above that a Member State which abstains from taking action or fails to adopt adequate measures to prevent obstacles to the free movement of goods which are created, in particular, by actions of private individuals on its territory aimed at products originating in other Member State, will infringe Article 28 EC, read in conjunction with Article 10 EC.[46] Furthermore, the Court has also held that Article 28 EC imposes on Member States constraints on *how* to regulate, even when the rules to be introduced, whilst restrictive of intra-Community trade, are justified by a mandatory requirement/Treaty derogation. Thus the principle of proportionality, always to be complied with when acting within the scope of Union law, requires that when Member States introduce important changes in their regulatory system they allow enough time to traders to adapt to the changes. This might well require the existence of a transitional period before the changes can start having effects. Thus, for instance, a Member State must provide for such transitional period when introducing a mandatory deposit scheme for drinks containers aimed at maximising re-use of such containers and thus protecting the environment[47]; and a Member State cannot ban

---

[44] Case 249/81 *Commission v Ireland* [1982] E.C.R. 4005. In Joined Cases 266 and 267/87 *R v Pharmaceutical Society of Great Britain, ex parte Association of Pharmaeutical Importers* [1989] E.C.R. 1295, para.15 the Court held that measures adopted by a professional body vested with statutory disciplinary powers might constitute "measures" within the scope of Art.28 EC. See also Case C–292//92 *Ruth Hünermund v Landesapothekerkammer Baden-Württemberg* [1993] E.C.R. I–6787, para.15.

[45] Case 222/82 *Apple and Pear Development Council* [1983] E.C.R. 4083; see also Case C–255/03 *Commission v Belgium* judgment of 17/6/04, unreported.

[46] See above para.16–018.

[47] e.g. Case C–309/02 *Radlberger Getränkegesellschaft mbH & Co. and S. Spitz KG* [2004] E.C.R. I–11763. esp. para.81, and the same issue in Case C–463/01 *Commission v Germany* (reusable containers) [2004] E.C.R. I–11705.

transport on wheels of given goods on a part of its territory in order to reduce pollution and shift transport from wheels to trains without leaving traders time to adapt to the new circumstances.[48]

(d) The prohibition in Article 28 EC applies at the marketing stage 16–022 **rather than the production stage.** The Court in the *Kramer* case contrasted the production stage of the economic process with the marketing stage, and indicated that Articles 28 EC *et seq.* applied to the latter but not to the former.[49]

(e) A national restriction offering flexible exemptions may still 16–023 **amount to a measure having equivalent effect.** A defence some-times advanced by national authorities has been that although a particular measure is apparently contrary to Articles 28 *et seq.* it is in fact administered with flexibility, and exceptions may be made. The Court has consistently rejected this argument.[50] As the Court explained in *Kelderman*:

"... a measure caught by the prohibition provided for in Article 30 [now 28] ... does not escape that prohibition simply because the competent authority is empowered to grant exemptions, even if that power is freely applied to imported products. Freedom of movement is a right whose enjoyment may not be dependent upon a discretionary power or on a concession granted by the national administration."[51]

(f) The application of Articles 28–30 EC may not be resisted on the 16–024 **ground that the national rules should have been harmonised.** It is clear that many barriers to intra-Community trade are capable of elimination through the technique of harmonisation of national laws under Article 94 or Article 95 EC. The possibility of harmonisation however, cannot justify derogation from the requirements of Article 28 EC. In *Commission v Italy* the latter Member State argued that the Commission should have sought harmonisation before resorting to Articles 28–30 EC of the Treaty. The Court rejected the argument as follows:

"The fundamental principle of a unified market and its corollary, the free movement of goods, must not under any circumstances be made subject to the condition that there should first

---

[48] Case C–320/03 *Commission v Austria* (motorway ban) [2005] E.C.R. I–9871; on a similar problem see Case C–114/04 *Commission v Germany* (parallel imports of phytosanitary products) judgment of 14/7/05, unreported.
[49] Joined Cases 3/76, 4/76 and 6/76 *Kramer* [1976] E.C.R. 1279, para27.
[50] Case 82/77 *Van Tiggele* [1978] E.C.R. 25; Case 251/78 *Denkavit* [1979] E.C.R. 3369; Case 27/80 *Fietje* [1980] E.C.R. 3839. It is of course otherwise if the restrictions are capable of being justified in accordance with the Treaty, as to which, see below, at para.16–036.
[51] Case 130/80 [1981] E.C.R. 517, para.14. See also Case 124/81 *Commission v United Kingdom* [1983] E.C.R. 203, para.10.

be an approximation of national laws for if that condition had to be fulfilled the principle would be reduced to a mere cipher."[52]

16–025 **(g) The cross-border element and reverse discrimination.** It has been held that the inconsistency of national rules with Articles 28–30 EC is a point which can only be taken in respect of goods imported or to be imported from another Member State.[53] Where Article 28 EC precludes the application of national law to imports, the result may be that domestic products are placed at a disadvantage in comparison with imports. But this is consistent with Community law.[54] It is a consequence of, on the one hand, the choice of the national legislator, and, on the other hand, the fact that the prohibition of quantitative restrictions and measures having equivalent effect applies exclusively to imported products. The position is certainly different where Community rules lay down the same conditions for the marketing of domestic products and imports alike.[55] But in *Pistre*, the Court considered the compatibility with Article 28 EC of national rules restricting use of the description "mountain" to products having links with a specific region of national territory. The reference arose from national criminal proceedings against French nationals prosecuted for marketing French products wrongly bearing the designation in question. The Court rejected the argument that Article 28 EC could have no application since imports were not involved. It noted that nevertheless "the application of the national measure may also have effects on the free movement of goods between Member States, in particular when the measure in question facilitates the marketing of goods of domestic origin to the detriment of imported goods. In such circumstances, the application of the measure, even if restricted to domestic producers, in itself creates and maintains a difference of treatment between those two categories of goods, hindering, at least potentially, intra-Community trade."[56] Since the legislation in issue in the national proceedings discriminated against goods from other Member States, Article 28 EC precluded the application of the rules in question. The ruling in *Pistre* lead to some confusion as to whether Article 28 EC could apply to purely internal situations. However, the ruling in *Guimont* clarified that Article 28 EC does not apply to purely internal situations. The fact that the Court is nonetheless

---

[52] Case 193/80 [1981] E.C.R. 3019, para.17.
[53] See *e.g.*, Joined Cases 314–316/82 *Waterkeyn* [1986] E.C.R. 1855.
[54] Case 355/85 *Driancourt v Cognet* [1986] E.C.R. 3231; Cases 80 and 159/85 *EDAH BV* [1986] E.C.R. 3359.
[55] Case 98/86 *Mathot* [1987] E.C.R. 809.
[56] Joined Cases C–321/94, C–322/94, C–323/94, C–324/94 *Jacques Pistre etc.*, [1997] E.C.R. I–2343, para.45.

willing to accept jurisdiction also in cases which do not have an intra-Community element,[57] seems to be due to the spirit of co-operation with national courts that characterises the relationship between European and domestic judiciary. Thus, since in order to apply their domestic law (usually the Constitutional guarantee of equal treatment) national courts need to assess the extent to which Article 28 EC would apply if it was a cross-border case, the Court is willing to reply to the questions referred so as to allow national courts to settle the (purely domestic) dispute before them.[58]

(h) Article 28 EC applies to Community measures as well as to 16–026 **national measures.** It is established that the prohibition of quantitative restrictions and of all measures having equivalent effect applies not only to national measures but also to measures adopted by the Community institutions.[59]

Measures having equivalent effect to quantitative resrictions on exports

Article 29 EC provides that quantitative restrictions on exports, 16–027 and all measures having equivalent effect, shall be prohibited between Member States. The notion of measures having equivalent effect clearly embraces measures which formally differentiate between domestic trade on the one hand, and the export trade on the other, as the *Bouhelier* case illustrates.[60] In order to ensure quality control, French legislation authorised a public authority to inspect pressed lever watches and watch movements made in France and destined for export to other Member States. If the watches or movements complied with the relevant quality standards, a certificate was issued to that effect. The export of such watches and movements was subject to the grant of a licence, except in the case of consignments in respect of which a standards certificate had been issued. The Court held that Article 29 EC precluded both export licensing and the imposition of quality controls on exports. Since the latter controls were not required in the case of products for the domestic market, their imposition amounted to arbitrary discrimination and constituted an obstacle to intra-Community trade.

The evolution of the case law on measures having equivalent effect to quantitative restrictions on exports has not mirrored that on

---

[57] Case C–448/98 *Guimont* [2000] E.C.R. I–10663, esp. paras 15 and ff. Case C–254/98 *Schutzverband gegen unlauteren Wettbewerb and TK-Heimdienst Sass GmbH* [2000] E.C.R. I–151 also involved a purely internal situation.

[58] For an extensive analysis of these issues, see E. Spaventa "Annotation of *TK-Heimdiest*" (2000) 37 C.M.L.Rev. 1265.

[59] Case 15/83 *Denkavit Nederland v Hoofdproduktschap voor akkerbouwprodukten* [1984] E.C.R. 2171, para.15; Case C–51/93 *Meyhui NV v Schott Zwiesel Glaswerke AG* [1994] E.C.R. I 3879, para.11; Case C–114/96 *René Kieffer and Romain Thill* [1997] E.C.R. I–3629, para.27.

[60] Case 53/86 [1977] E.C.R. 197.

imports. Notwithstanding developments in the *Cassis* doctrine the Court has consistently required a national measure to have discriminatory effects before it could be held to comprise a prohibited restriction on exports. As the Court explained in *Groenveld*:

> "That provision [i.e. Article 29 EC] concerns the national measures which have as their specific object or effect the restriction of patterns of exports and thereby the establishment of a difference in treatment between the domestic trade of a Member State and its export trade in such a way as to provide a particular advantage for national production or for the domestic market of the State in question at the expense of the production or of the trade of other Member States. This is not so in the case of a prohibition like that in question which is applied objectively to the production of goods of a certain kind without drawing a distinction depending on whether such goods are intended for the national market or for export."[61]

The Court has repeated this formulation on numerous occasions.[62] An obligation on producers to deliver poultry offal to their local authority has been held to involve, by implication, a prohibition of exports and to fall accordingly within the scope of application of Article 29 EC.[63] Similarly, an obligation to transport animals for short maximum periods and distances combined with an obligation for all such transport to end at the nearest suitable abattoir in national territory for slaughter was held to amount to a measure having equivalent effect to a quantitative restriction on both imports and exports.[64] And an obligation to bottle the wine in the region of production in order to be able to benefit from the certified denomination of origin also constituted a restriction prohibited by Article 29 EC.[65] In theory, since the scope of Article 29 EC is limited to a prohibition on directly discriminatory restrictions, only the derogations contained in Article 30 EC can be used to justify measures falling within its scope.[66]

---

[61] Case 15/79 [1979] E.C.R. 3409, para.7.

[62] See e.g., Case 155/80 *Oebel* [1981] E.C.R. 1993, para.15; Case 286/81 *Oosthoek's* [1982] E.C.R. 4575, para.13; Case 172/82 *Inter-Huiles* [1983] E.C.R. 555, para.12; Case 237/82 *Jongeneel Kaas v Netherlands* [1984] E.C.R. 483, para.22; Case C–412/97 *ED Srl v Italo Fenocchio* [1999] E.C.R. I–3845, para.10.

[63] Case 118/86 *Nertsvoederfabriek Nederlandse* [1987] E.C.R. 3883.

[64] Case C–350/97 *Wilfried Monsees* [1999] E.C.R. I–2921.

[65] Case C–47/90 *Etablissements Delhaize Frères et Compagnie Le Lion SA v Promalvin SA and AGE Bodegas Unidas SA* [1992] E.C.R. I–3669; the Court changed its mind as to whether such rules were justified in Case C–388/95 *Belgium v Spain* (Rioja) [2000] E.C.R. I–3123, noted E Spaventa (2001) 38 C.M.L.Rev. 211. See also Case C–12/02 *Grilli* [2003] E.C.R. I–11585; see also Case C–469/00 *Ravil* [2003] E.C.R. I–5053, paras 44 and ff.

[66] Although the case law is not entirely consistent in this respect; see e.g. C–209/98 *Entreprenørforeningens Affalds/Miljøsektion (FFAD) v Københavns Kommune* [2000] E.C.R. I–3743, and see discussion about the problems inherent in the fact that Art.30 EC does not expressly mention environmental protection as one of the grounds which allows a Member State to derogate from Art.28 EC, below p.625.

The prohibition in question binds the Community institutions as well as the Member States, and the requirements of Article 29 EC have been held to be satisfied where Community rules made equivalent but not identical provision for administrative supervision both for exports in bulk of compound feeding-stuffs and for the marketing thereof within the Community.[67]

CHARACTERISTICS OF NATIONAL MEASURES HELD TO HAVE EFFECTS EQUIVALENT TO QUANTITATIVE RESTRICTIONS

The general definitions of measures having equivalent effect **16–028** advanced by the Court of Justice in *Dassonville*, *Cassis*, and *Keck*, are of course of enormous importance.[68] But it is also the case that certain factual characteristics of national measures held to comprise measures having equivalent effect do seem to recur, and it may be of some assistance to consider some of the more common examples.

Frontier inspections
So far as health inspections carried out at frontiers are concerned, **16–029** the Court has held that, as a result of the delays inherent in the inspections and the additional transport costs which the trader may incur thereby, the inspections in question are likely to make imports or exports more difficult or more costly and accordingly to amount to measures having equivalent effect, subject to justification.[69] The Court has also held that the principle to be applicable to other types of frontier inspections, in particular national rules which provide for systematic inspections of goods when they cross a frontier.[70]

Import/export licences, declarations, etc.
Apart from the exceptions for which provision is made by **16–030** Community law itself, Articles 28 and 29 EC preclude the application to intra-Community trade of a national provision which

---

[67] Case 15/83 *Denkavit* [1984] E.C.R. 2171.
[68] See above at pp.578–603.
[69] Case 35/76 *Simmenthal v Italian Minister for Finance* [1976] E.C.R. 1871, para.7; Case C–272/95 *Bundesanstalt für Landwirtschaft und Ernährung v Deutsches Milch-Kontor GmbH* [1997] E.C.R. I–1905, para.27.
[70] Case 190/87 *Moormann* [1988] E.C.R. 4689, para.8.

requires, even purely as a formality, import or export licences or any other similar procedure.[71-72]

An obligation imposed by an importing Member State to produce a certificate of fitness issued by an exporting Member State in connexion with the import of a product amounts to a measure having equivalent effect.[73] Confining imports of alcohol to licensed traders who complied with conditions concerning their professional knowledge, financial capacity and possession of storage capacity has been held to amount to a measure having equivalent effect to a quantitative restriction.[74]

However, requiring declarations from importers concerning the origin of goods for the purpose of monitoring the movement of goods does not amount to a measure having equivalent effect provided that the importer is not required to declare more than he or she knows or can reasonably be expected to know, and provided that penalties for failure are not disproportionate.[75]

Preference for domestic or other products

16–031   National measures which express a preference for domestic products or confer some advantage on domestic products will amount to measures having equivalent effect to quantitative restrictions. The Court of Justice has so ruled in the case of a quality designation reserved for alcoholic drinks containing 85 per cent spirits distilled on national territory.[76] Similarly, in *Campus Oil* the Court held that Irish rules requiring importers of petroleum products to purchase a certain proportion of their requirements at prices fixed by the competent minister from a state-owned company operating a refinery in Ireland amounted to a measure having equivalent effect.[77] In *Commission v Greece* it was conceded by the defendant Member State that requiring the Agricultural Bank of Greece not to finance purchases of imported agricultural machinery except upon proof that machinery of that kind was not manufactured in Greece amounted to a measure having equivalent effect. The Court held that the concession was rightly made.[78] In *Du Pont de Nemours Italiana* the

---

[71-72] Note that import licences may in principle be excused in appropriate cases under Art.30 (as to which see below at para.16–036), see Case 124/81 *Commission v United Kingdom* [1983] E.C.R. 203; Case 74/82 *Commission v Ireland* [1984] E.C.R. 317; Case 40/82 *Commission v United Kingdom* [1984] E.C.R. 283

[73] Case 251/78 *Denkavit* [1979] E.C.R. 3369, para.11.

[74] Case C–189/95 *Harry Franzén* [1997] E.C.R. I–5909.

[75] Case 41/76 *Donckerwolcke* [1976] E.C.R. 1921; Case 179/78 *Rivoira* [1979] E.C.R. 1147.

[76] Case 13/78 *Eggers* [1978] E.C.R. 1935; Joined Cases C–321/94, C–322/94, C–323/94, C–324/94 *Jacques Pistre etc.*, [1997] E.C.R. I–2343 (designation "mountain" confined to products linked to region of national territory).

[77] Case 72/83 [1984] E.C.R. 2727. But the Court held that such a measure might in principle be excused under Art.30 EC on grounds of national security.

[78] Case 192/84 [1985] E.C.R. 3967; Case 103/84 *Commission v Italy* [1986] E.C.R. 1759 (subsidies for vehicles of national manufacture); Case C–137/91 *Commission v Greece* [1992] E.C.R. I–4023 (obligation to purchase cash machines comprising at least 35% added value in Greece).

Court held that Article 28 EC precluded national rules which reserved to undertakings established in particular regions of the national territory a proportion of public supply contracts.[79] In *Decker*, the Court considered a national requirement of prior authorisation for reimbursement for spectacles purchased in another Member State, where no such requirement existed for purchase on national territory, and concluded that such a requirement encouraged insured persons to purchase those products on the home market rather than in other Member States, and to curb imports of spectacles assembled in those states.[80] A tender specifying a particular branded product and failing to indicate that equivalents will be considered has been held to amount to a measure having equivalent effect, though the product specified was not a domestic product.[81] It has even been held that State financed publicity campaigns promoting the purchase of national products on the grounds of national origin and disparaging products from other Member States infringe Article 28 EC.[82]

Conditions imposed in respect of imported products only

One of the most easily detected infringements of the Treaty's **16–032** prohibition on measures having equivalent effect to quantitative restrictions is a national rule imposing conditions on imported products which are not imposed on their domestic counterparts. Thus phytosanitary inspections on imports of plant products where no compulsory examination is made of domestic products amounts to a measure having equivalent effect.[83] Again, a national requirement that imported drinks be at least of the alcohol content specified as the minimum in the country of origin, where no minimum alcoholic content was specified for similar domestic products, has been held to be contrary to Article 28 EC.[84] In *Commission v Italy* the Court condemned an Italian measure prohibiting the testing, for the purposes of registration, of buses which were more than seven years old and came from other Member States, where no such prohibition applied to Italian buses.[85]

---

[79] Case C–21/88 [1990] E.C.R. I–889; Case C–351/88 *Laboratori Bruneau Srl* [1991] E.C.R. I–3641.

[80] Case C–120/95 *Nicholas Decker v Caisse de Maladie de Employés Privés* [1998] E.C.R. I–1831. Rules that prescribe technical standards to be satisfied by wheelchairs in order for those to be eligible for reimbursement by the social security system, even when the wheelchairs have a CE trade mark, also breach Art.28 EC, Case C–38/03 *Commission v Belgium*, judgment of 13/01/05, unreported.

[81] Case C–359/93 *Commission v Netherlands* [1995] E.C.R. I–157 (specification of operating system "UNIX", a software system developed by Bell Laboratories of I.T.T. (USA) for connecting several computers of different makes).

[82] Case 249/81 *Commission v Ireland* [1982] E.C.R. 4005; Case 222/82 *Apple and Pear Development Council* [1983] E.C.R. 4083.

[83] Case 4/75 *Rewe* [1975] E.C.R. 843. In this case the measures were justified under Art.30 EC.

[84] Case 59/82 *Schutzverband* [1983] E.C.R. 1217.

[85] Case 50/83 [1984] E.C.R. 1633.

Measures making imports more difficult or more costly

16–033   A ground advanced by the Court for holding frontier checks of imported products to amount to measures having equivalent effect is that such checks make imports more difficult or costly.[86] Examples of national measures which have been held to be contrary to Article 28 EC (subject to appropriate justification in accordance with the Treaty)[87] on this ground are an import deposit scheme for imports for which payment was made in advance[88]; the extension to imported products of national rules which prohibited the sales of silver goods without hall-marking[89]; the extension to imported products of a national rule which required, that margarine be sold in cube shaped packs[90]; the extension to imported products of a requirement that certain information be not provided on the packaging of certain products[91]; the extension to imported products of a national rule which prohibited the sale of goods by retail unless they bore an indication of their country of origin[92]; and the roadworthiness testing of imported vehicles.[93] It is often unclear whether the Court is referring to requirements which make the marketing of imports more difficult or costly than they would otherwise be, or more difficult or costly than imports. In truth, both propositions are usually corrrect, and in the view of the present writer it would be preferable for the Court to accept that measures such as those referred to are indirectly discriminatory.

Impeding access to certain channels of distribution

16–034   The definition of measures having equivalent effect which the Court has adopted has led it to conclude that measures are forbidden which "favour, within the Community, particular trade channels or particular commercial operators in relation to others."[94–95] An example of such a measure is provided by the proceedings in *Procureur du Roi v Dassonville.*[96] The Court reiterated its view that there must be no discrimination between channels of trade in *de Peijper.*[97] Dutch legislation laid down certain safety requirements in the case of imports of medicinal preparations. The

---

[86] Case 4/75 *Rewe* [1975] E.C.R. 843, para.11; Case 42/82 *Commission v France* [1983] E.C.R. 1013, para.50; see also more recently e.g. Case C–448/98 *Guimont* [2000] E.C.R. I–10633, para.26.
[87] As to which see below at para.16–036 *et seq.*
[88] Case 95/81 *Commission v Italy* [1982] E.C.R. 2187
[89] Case 220/81 *Robertson* [1982] E.C.R. 2349.
[90] Case 261/81 *Rau* [1982] E.C.R. 3961.
[91] Case 94/82 *De Kikvorsch* [1983] E.C.R. 947.
[92] Case 207/83 *Commission v United Kingdom* [1985] E.C.R. 1201.
[93] Case 50/85 *Schloh* [1986] E.C.R. 1855.
[94–95] Case 155/73 *Sacchi* [1974] E.C.R. 409, para.8.
[96] See above at para.16–005.
[97] Case 8/74 [1974] E.C.R. 837.

importer was bound to present certain documentation, verified by the manufacturer, to the Dutch public health authorities. Centrafarm purchased quantities of Valium, manufactured by Hoffmann-La Roche in England, from a British wholesaler, packed the tablets in packages bearing the name Centrafarm and marked with the generic name of the product in question, and distributed them to pharmacies in the Netherlands. Centrafarm could not rely on Hoffmann-La Roche's co-operation with regard to the relevant documentation, and was charged under Dutch law. On a reference for a preliminary ruling, the Court ruled that national practices which resulted in imports being channelled in such a way that certain traders could effect these imports, while others could not, constituted measures having equivalent effect.

Price restrictions

The Court has considered on a number of occasions the compat- **16–035** ibility with Article 28 EC of national measures fixing the selling prices of products. Selective price measures taken by national authorities to restrict importation of products from other Member States will clearly be incompatible with Article 28 EC.[98–99] As has been explained, maximum selling prices which make the sale of imported products if not impossible, at any rate more difficult, comprise measures having equivalent effect, as do minimum prices fixed at such a high level that the price advantage enjoyed by imports over domestic goods is cancelled out.

Even if national rules establish different criteria for fixing the selling prices of imports than are established for fixing the selling prices of domestic goods, there will only be a violation of Article 28 EC if imports are actually put at some disadvantage. This follows from the *Roussel* case, in which the Court held that:

> "Legislation . . . which differentiates between the two groups of products, must be regarded as a measure having an effect equivalent to a quantitative restriction where it is capable of making more difficult, in any manner whatever, the sale of imported products."[1]

That separate rules for the price fixing of imports do not of themselves infringe Article 28 EC is confirmed in *Leclerc*, in which the Court condemned separate price fixing rules for imported books

---

[98–99] Case 90/82 *Commission v France* [1983] E.C.R. 2011, para.27.
[1] Case 181/82 [1983] E.C.R. 3849, para.19. If price controls are imposed, it may be necessary for any criteria set to take account of circumstances more likely to affect imports than domestic products.

which were liable to impede trade between Member States.[2] Nevertheless, if price-fixing rules applied exclusively to imported products, this would violate Article 28 EC since it would of itself place imported products at some disadvantage. Following the ruling in *Keck*, price restrictions have been qualified as selling arrangements: therefore the above case law according to which price restrictions are caught by Article 28 EC only insofar as they are discriminatory has been confirmed.[3]

DEROGATIONS FROM ARTICLES 28–29 EC

Article 30 of the EC Treaty
16–036   Article 30 EC of the Treaty provides:

> "The provisions of Articles 28 and 29 EC shall not preclude prohibitions or restrictions on imports, exports or goods in transit justified on grounds of public morality, public policy or public security; the protection of health and life of humans, animals or plants; the protection of national treasures possessing artistic, historic or archaeological value; or the protection of industrial and commercial property. Such prohibitions or restrictions shall not however, constitute a means of arbitrary discrimination or a disguised restriction on trade between Member States."

Grounds of derogation
16–037   Article 30 EC is the only available justification for quantitative restrictions and directly discriminatory measures; it constitutes an exception to the fundamental rule that all obstacles to the free movement of goods between Member States shall be abolished and therefore must be interpreted strictly.[4] It follows that the list of exceptions is exhaustive.[5] Thus the Court has held that Article 30 EC does not justify derogation from Article 28 EC on the grounds of the protection of consumers or the fairness of commercial transactions,[6]

---

[2] Case 229/83 [1985] E.C.R. 2.
[3] Case C–63/94 *Groupement National des Négociants en Pommes de Terre de Belgique v ITM Belgium Sa and Vocarex SA* [1995] E.C.R. I–2467.
[4] Case 46/76 *Bauhuis v Netherlands* [1977] E.C.R. 5; Case 113/80 *Commission v Ireland* [1981] E.C.R. 1625; Case 95/81 *Commission v Italy* [1982] E.C.R. 2187.
[5] Case 95/81 *Commission v Italy* [1982] E.C.R. 2187.
[6] Case 95/81 *Commission v Italy* [1982] E.C.R. 2187; Case 220/81 *Robertson* [1982] E.C.R. 2349; Case 229/83 *Leclerc* [1985] E.C.R. 2. Such considerations may however, in the case of non-discriminatory restrictions, amount to mandatory requirements justifying reasonable restrictions on the free movement of goods in the general interest, see below at para.16–044.

economic policy,[7] or the protection of creativity and cultural diversity,[8] since none of the foregoing are referred to in the Article. While the Court has accepted that the expression "public policy" is capable of embracing a national ban on the export of coins no longer constituting legal tender,[9] it has refused to accept that the expression includes the protection of consumers.[10]

In the absence of harmonised rules at the Community level, recourse to Article 30 EC may entail the application of different standards in different Member States, as a result of different national value-judgments, and different factual circumstances. Thus the Court has stated that:

> "In principle, it is for each Member State to determine in accordance with its own scale of values and in the form selected by it the requirements of public morality in its territory."[11]

Similarly, in the absence of harmonisation at Community level, it is for each Member State to determine the appropriate level of protection which they wish to accord to the protection of human health, whilst taking account of the free movement of goods within the Community.[12] As the Court explained in *Heijn*:

> "In so far as the relevant Community rules do not cover certain pesticides, Member States may regulate the presence of residues of those pesticides in a way which may vary from one country to another according to the climatic conditions, the normal diet of the population and their state of health."[13]

Nevertheless, while a public health risk to consumers is capable of justifying national rules under Article 30 EC, "the risk must be

---

[7] Case 7/61 *Commission v Italy* [1961] E.C.R. 317; Case 95/81 *Commission v Italy* [1982] E.C.R. 2187; Case 238/82 Duphar [1984] E.C.R. 523; Case 72/83 *Campus Oil* [1984] E.C.R. 2727; Case 288/83 *Commission v Ireland* [1985] E.C.R. 1761; Case C–324/93 *R v Home Secretary, ex parte Evans Medical Ltd and Macfarlan Smith Ltd.* [1995] E.C.R. I–563, at para.36. But non-discriminatory measures designed to limit the costs of a state health insurance scheme are compatible with Community law, see Case 238/82 *Duphar* [1984] E.C.R. 523, para.17; see also Case C–120/95 *Nicholas Decker v Caisse de Maladie de Employés Privés* [1998] E.C.R. I–1831, ". . . aims of a purely economic nature cannot justify a barrier to the fundamental principle of the free movement of goods. However, it cannot be excluded that the risk of seriously undermining the financial balance of the social security system may constitute an overriding reason in the general interest capable of justifying a barrier of that kind.", para.39 (though it will be noted that in the latter case the measure was discriminatory.
[8] Case 229/83 *Leclerc* [1985] E.C.R. 2.
[9] Case 7/78 *Thompson* [1978] E.C.R. 22247.
[10] Case 177/83 *Kohl* [1984] E.C.R. 3651.
[11] Case 34/79 *Henn & Darby* [1979] E.C.R. 3795.
[12] Case C–205/89 *Commission v Greece* [1991] E.C.R. I–1361, para.8.
[13] Case 94/83 [1984] E.C.R. 3263; more recently e.g. Case C–366/04 *Schwarz* [2005] E.C.R. I–10139.

measured, not according to the yardstick of general conjecture, but on the basis of relevant scientific research,"[14] and the discretion of the Member States to decide, in the case of a food additive, on the degree of protection of the health and life of humans to be adopted, is one which is retained "in so far as there are uncertainties in the present state of scientific research with regard to the harmfulness" of the additive in question.[15] Thus, Article 28 EC does not have the effect of imposing on Member States a minimum common standard in health protection, and indeed scientific uncertainty regarding the effect of a product is enough for the Member State to be able to invoke the public health derogation (so called precautionary principle).[16]

While Article 30 EC leaves a margin of discretion to the national authorities as to the extent to which they wish to protect the interests listed therein, the discretion is limited by two important principles. Firstly, that any discrimination between imports and domestic products must not be arbitrary. Secondly, that national measures must not restrict trade any more than is necessary to protect the interest in question. Furthermore, the Court has held that Article 30 EC can never be invoked to protect purely economic interests,[17] and that the Member States are under an obligation to respect fundamental rights as general principles of Community law when invoking Article 30 EC (or the mandatory requirement doctrine).[18]

Arbitrary discrimination or a disguised restriction on trade

16–038   Article 30 EC provides that prohibitions or restrictions permitted under that Article shall not however constitute a means of arbitrary discrimination or a disguised restriction on trade between Member States. The purpose of this proviso was described by the Court in *Henn & Darby* as being to:

> ". . . prevent restrictions on trade based on the grounds mentioned in the first sentence of Article 36 [now 30] from being diverted from their proper purpose and used in such a way as either to create discrimination in respect of goods originating in other Member States or indirectly to protect certain national products."[19]

[14] Case C–17/93 *JJJ Van der Veldt* [1994] E.C.R. I–3537, para.17; Case 178/84 *Commission v Germany* [1987] E.C.R. 1227.

[15] Case C–113/91 *Criminal proceedings against Michel Debus* [1992] E.C.R. I–3617, para.13.

[16] Case 174/82 *Sandoz* [1983] E.C.R. 2445; C–192/01 *Commission v Denmark* [2003] E.C.R. I–9693.

[17] e.g. Case C–398/98 *Commission v Greece* (obligation to stock petroleum) [2001] E.C.R. I–7915.

[18] *Mutatis mutanda* Case C–260/89 *ERT* 2925.

[19] Case 34/79 *Henn & Darby* [1979] E.C.R. 3795, para.21; Case 40/82 *Commission v United Kingdom* [1984] E.C.R. 283, para.36.

In determining whether or not discrimination against imported goods is arbitrary, an important yardstick will be a comparison with measures taken *vis-à-vis* domestic goods. As a precaution against transmission of the destructive San José Scale insect, German legislation provided for the phyto-sanitary examination of certain imported fruit and vegetables at point of entry. On a reference for a preliminary ruling, the Court held that such measures must be considered to be justified in principle under Article 30 EC, provided that they did not constitute a means of arbitrary discrimination. This would not be the case where effective measures were taken to prevent the distribution of contaminated domestic products, and where there was reason to believe that there would be a risk of the harmful organism spreading if no inspections were held on importation.[20]

A measure which discriminates against imports and indeed excludes imports may however be justified if it is the only way to achieve the objective of protection for the health and life of humans. Thus in *Evans Medical Ltd and Macfarlan Smith Ltd*, the Court of Justice held that a Member State was entitled to refuse a licence for importation of narcotic drugs from another Member State on the ground that such importation threatened the viability of the sole licensed manufacturer in the former State and jeopardised reliability of the supply of diamorphine for medical purposes, provided that the latter objective could not be achieved as effectively by measures less restrictive of intra-Community trade.[21] If a Member State seeks to preserve an indigenous animal population with distinct characteristics by banning imports of other species which might mate with the indigenous population and endanger its survival, this can be justified under Article 30 EC as a measure to protect the life of animals.[22]

National measures are only justified if they are no more restrictive than is strictly necessary

The Court has emphasised that Article 30 EC is not designed to **16–039** reserve certain matters to the exclusive jurisdiction of Member States, but only permits national laws to derogate from the principle of the free movement of goods to the extent to which such derogation is and continues to be justified for the attainment of the objectives referred to in that Article.[23] The word "justified" is to be construed as meaning "necessary".[24] Application of the Article is

---

[20] Case 4/75 *Rewe-Zentralfinanz v Landwirtschaftskammer* [1975] E.C.R. 843.

[21] Case C–324/93 *R v Home Secretary, ex parte Evans Medical Ltd and Macfarlan Smith Ltd* [1995] E.C.R. I–563, paras 35–39.

[22] Case C–67/97 *Ditlev Bluhme* [1998] E.C.R. I–8033.

[23] Case 5/77 *Tedeschi* [1977] E.C.R. 1556; Case 251/78 *Denkavit* [1979] E.C.R. 3327.

[24] Case 153/78 *Commission v Germany* [1979] E.C.R. 2555, para.8; Case 251/78 *Denkavit* [1979] E.C.R. 3327, para.21.

thus to be conditioned upon compliance with the principle of proportionality.[25] As the Court explained in *Commission v Belgium*:

> "However, [public health] measures are justified only if it is established that they are necessary in order to attain the objective of protection referred to in Article 36 [now 30] and that such protection cannot be achieved by means which place less of a restriction on the free movement of goods within the Community."[26]

Thus, in *de Peijper*,[27] the Court considered the argument that restrictive provisions of Netherlands legislation which favoured imports by dealers securing the co-operation of the manufacturer were justified on the basis that they were necessary for the protection of the health and life of humans. While the Court acknowledged that this interest ranked first among the interests protected by Article 30 EC of the Treaty, it emphasised that national measures did not fall within the exception if the health or life of humans could be as effectively protected by means less restrictive of intra-Community trade. In particular, Article 30 EC did not justify restrictions motivated primarily by a concern to facilitate the task of the authorities, or reduce public expenditure, unless alternative arrangements would impose unreasonable burdens on the administration.

Where a measure having equivalent effect has but a slight impact on trade, this will be relevant in assessing the proportionality of the national measures in question. As the Court explained in *Société Civile Agricole du Centre d'Insémination de la Crespelle*:

> "In order to ascertain that the restrictive effects on intra-Community trade of the rules at issue do not exceed what is necessary to achieve the aim in view, it must be considered whether those effects are direct, indirect or purely speculative and whether those effects do not impede the marketing of imported products more than the marketing of national products."[28]

16–040   Judicial assessment of the proportionality of a measure may well involve a review of possible alternative means of achieving the aim in question,[29] and determining the compatibility with Article 30 EC of

---

[25] As to which, see above at Ch.7.
[26] Case 155/82 [1983] E.C.R. 531. And a consistent case law to this effect, see e.g., Case 97/83 *Melkunie* [1984] E.C.R. 2367, para.12; Case C–189/95 *Harry Franzén*, [1997] E.C.R. I–5909, para.75; Case C–212/03 *Commission v France* (import licences for medicinal products) [2005] E.C.R. I–4213.
[27] Case 104/75 [1976] E.C.R. 613.
[28] Case C–323/93 [1994] E.C.R. I–5077, para.36.
[29] Case C–131/93 *Commission v Germany* [1994] E.C.R. I–3303, para.25.

e.g. a national measure limiting the sulphur dioxide content of beer, can entail a detailed consideration of available scientific evidence as regards the qualities and effects of the additive in question.[30] There can be no doubt that claims to restrict the free movement of goods on public health grounds are not beyond judicial scrutiny, and such matters as the burden of proof,[31] or, in cases on food additives, the tolerated levels of the additive in question in other beverages or food-stuffs, or other conduct of the relevant national authorities which suggests that alternative measures less restrictive of trade would be adequate to achieve the aims in question,[32] may play a large part in the outcome of a case.[33] In adversarial proceedings under Article 226 EC it will be for the Court of Justice to decide whether or not a national measure is proportionate.[34] On a reference for a preliminary ruling the Court of Justice may consider it has enough information to allow it to determine itself whether the requirement of proportionality is satisfied, and do so,[35] or it may leave it to the national court to decide.[36]

As long as the rules relating to health protection in a particular sector have not been harmonised, it is open to the Member States to carry out any necessary inspections at national frontiers.[37] However, the free movement of goods is facilitated by the carrying out of health inspections in the country of production and the health authorities of the importing Member State should co-operate in order to avoid the repetition, in the importing country, of checks which have already been carried out in the country of production.[38] Similar considerations apply to approval by national authorities of products which have been approved on health grounds in other Member States. Whilst a Member State is free to require such products to undergo a fresh procedure of examination and approval,

---

[30] Case C–113/91 *Criminal proceedings against Michel Debus* [1992] E.C.R. I–3617, paras 17–29.

[31] Case C–113/91 *Criminal proceedings against Michel Debus* [1992] E.C.R. I–3617, paras 18, 24; Case C–131/93 *Commission v Germany* [1994] E.C.R. I–3303, para.26; Case C–189/95 *Harry Franzén*, [1997] E.C.R. I–5909, para.76.

[32] Case C–131/93 *Commission v Germany* [1994] E.C.R. I–3303, para.27; also e.g. Case C–41/02 *Commission v Netherlands* [2004] E.C.R. I–11375, where the Court found that the Netherlands had failed to fulfill its obligation under Art.28 EC because it had not carried out an in-depth assessment of given nutrients before banning the imports of products containing them.

[33] Case C–113/91 *Criminal proceedings against Michel Debus* [1992] E.C.R. I–3617, para.25.

[34] See e.g., Case C–131/93 *Commission v Germany* [1994] E.C.R. I–3303, paras 25–27.

[35] Case 315/92 *Verband Sozialer Wettbewerb eV v Clinique Laboratories SNC* [1994] E.C.R. I–317, paras 20–23; though the Advocate General thought that the national court should decide the matter, Opinion of Mr. Gulmann, esp. para.26.

[36] Case C–324/93 *R v Home Secretary, ex parte Evans Medical Ltd and Macfarlan Smith Ltd.* [1995] E.C.R. I–563, where the Court left it to the referring court to determine whether it was necessary to refuse licences for the import of drugs from other Member States to ensure a reliable supply of drugs for essential medical purposes.

[37] Case 73/84 *Denkavit* [1985] E.C.R. 1013.

[38] Case 251/78 *Denkavit* [1979] E.C.R. 3327; Case 73/84 *Denkavit* [1985] E.C.R. 1013; Case C–228/91 *Commission v Italy* [1993] E.C.R. I–2701.

the authorities of that Member State are bound to assist in bringing about a relaxation of the controls applied in intra-Community trade,[39] and are not entitled unnecessarily to require technical or chemical analyses or tests where those analyses or tests have already been carried out in another Member State and their results are available to those authorities, or may at their request be placed at their disposal.[40] The same principles apply to checking for other purposes, for example to confirm the precious metal content of articles.[41]

Disguised restrictions, arbitrary discrimination, and proportionality

16–041   The requirements that measures taken by Member States under Article 30 EC must not constitute a means of arbitrary discrimination, nor a disguised restriction on trade, and must comply with the principle of proportionality, overlap, and should not be considered in isolation. Thus, infringement of the principle of proportionality may lead to a measure being categorised as a disguised restriction on trade.[42] And discrimination between imports and domestic products as regards frequency of testing may lead to the conclusion that the level of scrutiny of imports is disproportionate. Thus in deciding in *Commission v France*[43] whether or not the frequency of French frontier tests of Italian wine complied with the principle of proportionality, the Court of Justice took into account not only the fact that similar checks on Italian wine were carried out by the Italian authorities, but also the fact that the frequency of the French frontier inspections was distinctly higher than the occasional checks carried out on the transportation of French wine within France.

The effect of harmonisation directives and other Community measures on recourse to Article 30 EC

16–042   Recourse to Article 30 EC is no longer justified if Community rules provide for the necessary measures to ensure protection of the interests set out in that Article.[44] This may be the case, e.g. when directives enacted under Article 94 or Article 95 EC or otherwise provide for the full harmonisation of the measures necessary for the protection of animal and human health, and establish the procedures

---

[39] Case 104/75 *de Peijper* [1976] E.C.R. 613; Case 272/80 *Frans-Nederlandse* [1981] E.C.R. 3277.
[40] Case 272/80 *Frans-Nederlandse* [1981] E.C.R. 3277; Case C–373/92 *Commission v Belgium* [1993] E.C.R. I–3107; Case C–228/91 *Commission v Italy* [1993] E.C.R. I–2701.
[41] Case C–293/93 *Houtwipper* [1994] E.C.R. 3159.
[42] Case 272/80 *Frans-Nederlandse* [1981] E.C.R. 3277, paras 13, 14; Joined Cases 2–4/82 *Le Lion* [1983] E.C.R. 2973, para.12
[43] Case 42/82 [1983] E.C.R. 1013, paras 51–57.
[44] Case 72/83 *Campus Oil* [1984] E.C.R. 2727, para.27.

to check that they are observed.[45] Thus, if such a directive places the responsibility for public health inspections of a product upon the Member State of export, the national authorities of the importing Member State will no longer be entitled to subject the product to systematic inspection upon importation; only occasional inspections to check compliance with the Community standards will be permissible.[46] But procedures for checking imports authorised under Community law must not entail unreasonable cost or delay.[47] Where however harmonisation is not complete, Member States may continue to rely upon Article 30 EC.[48]

Burden of proof lies on the national authorities

It is for the national authorities of the Member States to prove **16–043** that their restrictive trading rules may be justified under Article 30 EC. As the Court stated in *Leendert van Bennekom*:

> "it is for the national authorities to demonstrate in each case that their rules are necessary to give effective protection to the interests referred to in Article 36 [now 30] of the Treaty."[49]

Thus, in *Cullet* the French Government defended national rules fixing retail selling prices for fuel on grounds of public order and security represented by the violent reactions which would have to be anticipated on the part of retailers affected by unrestricted competition. The Court rejected this argument summarily:

> "In that regard, it is sufficient to state that the French Government has not shown that it would be unable, using the means at its disposal, to deal with the consequences which an amendment of the rules in question . . . would have upon public order and security."[50]

The burden of proving that Article 30 EC applies accordingly entails:

---

[45] Case 251/78 *Denkavit* [1979] E.C.R. 3369, para.14; Case 227/82 *Leendert* [1983] E.C.R. 3883, para.35; Case 29/87 *Denkavit* [1988] E.C.R. 2965; Case 190/87 *Moormann* BV [1988] E.C.R. 4689; Case C–304/88 *Commission v Belgium* [1990] E.C.R. I–2801; *R v MAFF ex parte Hedley Lomas* [1996] E.C.R. I–2553, para.18; *R v MAFF ex parte Compassion in World Farming Limited* [1998] E.C.R. I–1251, para.47.

[46] Case 35/76 *Simmenthal* [1976] E.C.R. 1871; Cases 2–4/82 *Le Lion* [1983] E.C.R. 2973.

[47] Case 406/85 *Goffette* [1987] E.C.R. 2525.

[48] Case C–323/93 *Société Civile Agricole du Centre d'Insémination de la Crespelle* E.C.R. I–5077, para.35; Case C–39/90 *Denkavit* [1991] E.C.R. I–3069, para.19.

[49] Case 227/82 [1983] E.C.R. 3883, para.40; see also Case 104/75 *de Peijper* [1976] E.C.R. 613; Case 251/78 *Denkavit* [1979] E.C.R. 3369, para.24; Case 174/82 *Sandoz* [1983] E.C.R. 2445, para.22; Joined Cases C–13/91 and C–113/91 *Criminal proceedings against Michel Debus* [1992] E.C.R. I–3617, para.18

[50] Case 231/83 [1985] E.C.R. 306, paras 32, 33.

How restrictive that State activity shows that is justified [handwritten marginal note]

> (i) showing that the national measures in question fall within one of the categories (e.g. public health, public policy or public morality) referred to in Article 30 EC[51];
> (ii) establishing that the measure does not constitute a means of arbitrary discrimination, that is to say, that if it differentiates between domestic products and imports, it does so on objective and justifiable grounds[52];
> (iii) establishing that the measure does not constitute a disguised restriction on trade, that is to say, that any restrictive effect on the free movement of goods is limited to what is necessary to protect the interest in question.[53]

The requirement that national authorities must prove the consistency of national legislation with Article 30 EC may be incapable of application if no national authorities are party to the proceedings in question.[54]

Mandatory requirements in the general interest

16–044   Although the Court has stated repeatedly that the exceptions listed in Article 30 EC are exhaustive,[55] it could be said that in effect it established further grounds upon which Member States may derogate from Article 28 EC in the *Cassis* case, in which it held that obstacles to the free movement of goods in the Community resulting from disparities between national marketing rules must be accepted in so far as they were necessary to satisfy mandatory requirements relating in particular to the effectiveness of fiscal supervision, the protection of public health, the fairness of commercial transactions, and the defence of the consumer.[56] One explanation for this apparent inconsistency is that the *Cassis* list does not so much provide grounds for derogating from Article 28 EC as define the circumstances in which national measures fall within Article 28 EC in the first place.[57] Another explanation is that the indistinctly applicable measures described in the *Cassis* case and in subsequent case law as amounting to measures having equivalent effect are in

---

[51] Above at para.16–037.

[52] Above at para.16–038.

[53] Above at para.16–039. But in direct proceedings if the national authority/Government puts forward convincing reasons why Art.30 EC should apply, it falls upon the Commission to challenge the soundness of such reasons (including scientific opinion); e.g. Case C–24/00 *Commission v France* [2004] E.C.R. I–1277, para.68.

[54] *cf.* Case C–368/95 *Vereinigte Familiapress Zeitungsverlags- und vertriebs GmbH v Heinrich Bauer Verlag* [1997] E.C.R. I–3689, a case involving mandatory requirements where it seems the national court was obliged to resolve the matter on the basis of a study of the market in question.

[55] Above at p.616.

[56] See above at para.16–006.

[57] *cf.* also E. Spaventa "On Discrimination and the Theory of Mandatory Requirements" (2000) 3 C.Y.E.L.S. 457.

truth indirectly discriminatory, and the mandatory requirements amount to grounds which objectively justify the discrimination in question.[58]

In any event it should be noted that mandatory requirements cannot be invoked to justify directly discriminatory measures, and/or quantitative restrictions.[59] Thus in the case of national rules requiring certain imported products but not their domestically produced counterparts to bear an indication of country of origin, the Court held that considerations of consumer protection and the fairness of commercial transactions could have no application.[60] In the case of national rules requiring both domestic goods and imports to bear an indication of country of origin, the Court again refused to consider arguments based on considerations of consumer protection on the grounds that the national rules were in fact discriminatory:

> "The requirements relating to the indication of origin of goods are applicable without distinction to domestic and imported products only in form because, by their very nature, they are intended to enable the consumer to distinguish between those two categories of products, which may thus prompt him to give his preference to national products."[61]

Thus, mandatory requirements are only available for measures that, at least in law, apply to imported and domestic products alike. This said, there have been some exceptions to this principle, and environmental protection (a mandatory requirement of public interest not included in Article 30 EC) has been successfully invoked in some cases which related to discriminatory measures.[62] In order to allow for such justification to be invoked in cases relating to discriminatory measures, the Court has relied also on the fact that a high level of the protection of the environment constitutes one of the objectives of the Treaty. Yet, such cases represent a threat to the consistency of the Court's case law on the respective scope of Treaty derogations and mandatory requirements. For this reason, Advocate General Jacobs has called on the Court to dispose of such distinction and just

---

[58] See above at p.592 for the view that the restrictions such as that involved in *Cassis* are indirectly discriminatory.

[59] Case 113/80 *Commission v Ireland* [1981] E.C.R. 1625, paras 8 and 11; Joined Cases C–321/94, C–322/94, C–323/94, C–324/94 *Jacques Pistre etc.*, [1997] E.C.R. I–2343, at para.52.

[60] Case 113/80 *Commission v Ireland* [1981] E.C.R. 1625.

[61] Case 270/83 *Commission v United Kingdom* [1985] E.C.R. 1201.

[62] Case C–2/90 *Commission v Belgium* [1992] E.C.R. I–4431; Case C–389/96 *Aher-Waggon GmbH v Germany* [1998] E.C.R. I–4473; Case C–203/96 *Chemische Afvalstoffen Dusseldorp v Minister van Volkshuisvesting, Ruimtelijke Ordering en Milieubeheer* [1998] E.C.R. I–4075; Case C–209/98 *Entreprenørforeningens Affalds/Miljøsektion (FFAD) v Københavns Kommune* [2000] E.C.R. I–3743; Case C–379/98 *PreussenElektra Advocate General v Schleswag AG* [2001] E.C.R. I–2099.

consider the mandatory requirements as additional grounds of justification for any type of measure, including discriminatory ones.[63] The Court has not taken the suggestion on board. It could be argued that that is the correct approach and that in any event measures taken to protect the environment could be justified on the grounds of being aimed at protecting the life of humans, animals and plants from a long term threat.[64]

A further difference between the Treaty derogations and the mandatory requirements is that the former cannot pursue economic aims, whilst in relation to the latter economic aims can be taken into consideration, even though they may not be the only reason why the measure was adopted.[65]

16–045   The categories of justification under the *Cassis* formulation are not closed, as appears from the formulation itself, which refers to four categories "in particular". The categories of justification expanded during the period prior to the limitation imposed on the *Cassis* doctrine by *Keck and Mithouard*.[66] While some of the restrictions identified by the pre-*Keck* case law would no longer be regarded as falling within the scope of Article 28 EC unless directly or indirectly discriminatory, the categories of justification upheld in such cases would seem to remain good law. The Court has added to the original *Cassis* list of mandatory requirements *inter alia*, environmental protection,[67] and the encouragement of film-making, upholding on this latter ground national rules providing that video-cassettes of films could not be distributed until one year after the release of the films at the cinema.[68] In *Oebel* the Court stated that legitimate interests of economic and social policy, consistent with the Treaty, might similarly justify impediments to the free movement of goods.[69] And the Court has held that restrictions on imports which result from national rules governing the opening hours of retail premises, in particular as regards Sunday trading, may be justified by reference to national or regional socio-cultural characteristics.[70]

But by far the most invoked requirement of public interest to justify restrictions to intra-Community trade is that of consumer

---

[63] Case C–379/98 *PreussenElektra AG v Schleswag AG* [2001] E.C.R. I–2099, para.226; see also P. Oliver, "Some further reflections on the scope of Art.28–30 (*ex* 30–36) EC" 36 (1999) C.M.L.Rev. 783 and 804; and C. Barnard, "Fitting the remaining pieces into the goods and persons gigsaw" (2001) E.L.Rev. 35, 54.

[64] See further E. Spaventa, "On Discrimination and the Theory of Mandatory Requirements" (2000) 3 C.Y.E.L.S. 457.

[65] This is probably the reason why in Case C–120/95 *N. Decker v Caisse de Maladie des Employés Privés* [1998] E.C.R. I–1831, the Court relied on the mandatory requirement of public health rather than on Art.30 EC.

[66] See above at para.16–009.

[67] Case 240/83 *Brûleurs d'Huiles Usagées* [1985] E.C.R. 532.

[68] Joined Cases 60 and 61/84 *Cinéthèque* [1985] E.C.R. 2605.

[69] Case 155/80 *Oebel* [1981] E.C.R. 1993, para.12.

[70] Case 145/88 *Torfaen BC v B&Q Plc* [1989] E.C.R. 3851, para.14; Case C–332/89 *Andrè Marchandise* [1991] E.C.R. 1027, para.12.

protection. This is natural having regard to the fact that different regulatory environments and mutual recognition might allow into the market products unfamiliar to consumers. Whilst the Court recognises that consumer protection is a valid ground of justification, it scrutinises carefully national measures as to their proportionality. This means that in most cases concerning product requirements, the Court is satisfied that a labelling requirement is enough to ensure that the consumer is not going to be mislead. Furthermore, in deciding whether the measures are necessary to protect the consumer, the Court has had regard to the "reasonably well informed consumer". This majoritarian approach, whereby the Court would accept measures directed at protecting the majority of consumers (the reasonably well informed ones), but not those directed at protecting the more vulnerable consumers (the non reasonably informed) has led to some criticism.[71]

In *Mars*, the defendant launched a campaign to promote some ice cream bars. Those were packaged with a wrapping containing the statement " + 10 per cent". An association fighting unfair competition brought proceedings to restrain Mars from marketing its products in that way arguing, *inter alia*, that the packaging was misleading since the proportion of the wrapping where the "+10 per cent" statement appeared was significantly bigger than 10 per cent of the wrapping thus giving the impression that the product had been increased by a bigger proportion. The Court was seized of the question whether German legislation which would have prevented Mars from wrapping its products in such a way could be justified on consumer protection grounds. After having held that the rules fell within the scope of Article 28 EC, the Court found that they were not justified on consumer protection grounds since: "Reasonably circumspect consumers may be deemed to know that there is not necessarily a link between the size of publicity markings relating to an increase in a product's quantity and the size of that increase".[72] In *Estée Lauder* the Court adopted a more nuanced approach and in relation to the possible misleading effects of the indication "lifting" in relation to a firming cream, it held that whilst the "reasonably circumspect consumer" should not be mislead, the national court could investigate whether German consumers would be mislead. It held: "In particular, it must be determined whether social, cultural or linguistic factors may justify the term 'lifting', used in connection with a firming cream, meaning something different to the German consumer as opposed to consumers in other Member States, or whether the instructions for the use of the product are in themselves

---

[71] e.g. Weatherill "Recent case law concerning the free movement of goods: mapping the frontiers of market deregulation" (1999) 36 C.M.L.Rev. 51.
[72] Case C–470/93 *Verein gegen Unwesen in Handel und Gewerbe Köln e.V. v Mars GmbH* [1995] E.C.R. I–1923, para.24.

sufficient to make it quite clear that its effects are short-lived, thus neutralising any conclusion to the contrary that might be derived from the word 'lifting'."[73]

Other rules might be easier to assess. In *Oosthoek's Uitgeversmaatschaapij B.V.* the Court upheld national measures restricting the giving of gifts as a means of sales promotion, on the grounds of the fairness of commercial transactions and the defence of the consumer, in the following terms:

"It is undeniable that the offering of free gifts as a means of sales promotion may mislead consumers as to the real prices of certain products and distort the conditions on which genuine competition is based. Legislation which restricts or even prohibits such commercial practices for that reason is therefore capable of contributing to consumer protection and fair trading."[74]

16–046   In *GB-INNO-BM,* however, the Court took a different view of the need for state intervention in the interests of consumer protection. A Belgian company had distributed advertising leaflets in Luxembourg as well as on Belgian territory allegedly contrary to Luxembourg rules according to which sales offers involving a temporary price reduction may not state the duration of the offer or refer to previous prices. The Court held that under Community law concerning consumer protection the provision of information to the consumer is considered one of the principal requirements. It followed that Article 28 EC could not be interpreted as meaning that national legislation which denies the consumer access to certain kinds of information might be justified by mandatory requirements concerning consumer protection.[75]

Consumer protection and fair trading raise also issues which extend beyond the market of the importing Member State. In *Prantl*[76] the Court considered trading rules reserving to national wine producers the use of the characteristically shaped *"Bocksbeutel"* bottle. Consumer protection and fair trading were pleaded in support of the national rules. The Court noted however that in the common market consumer protection and fair trading as regards the presentation of wines must be guaranteed "with regard on all sides for the fair and traditional practices observed in the various Member

---

[73] Case C–220/98 *Estée Lauder v Lancaster* [2000] E.C.R. I–117, para.29.
[74] Case 286/81 *Oosthoek's Uitgeversmaatschaapij B.V.* [1982] E.C.R. 4575, para.18. And in Cases C–1/90 and C–176/90 *Aragonesa de Publicidad Exterior SA* [1991] E.C.R. I–4151, the Court upheld on public health grounds restrictions on advertising of certain alcoholic beverages. See also Case 382/87 *Buet* [1989] E.C.R. 1235 (prohibition of door to door canvassing of educational material justified).
[75] Case C–362/88 *GB-INNO-BM* [1990] E.C.R. I–667.
[76] Case 16/83 [1984] E.C.R. 1299.

States."[77] It followed that an exclusive right to use a certain type of bottle granted by national legislation in a Member State could not be used to bar imports of wines originating in another Member State put up in bottles of the same or similar shape in accordance with a fair and traditional practice in that Member State.[78]

Recourse to mandatory requirements is subject to the principle of proportionality, as the Court made clear in the *Rau* case:

> "It is also necessary for such rules to be proportionate to the aim in view. If a Member State has a choice between various measures to attain the same objective it should choose the means which least restrict the free movement of goods."[79]

The Court of Justice, or the competent national court, must determine whether the least restrictive measure has in fact been selected by the national legislature; this in some cases can lead to an extensive review of the rules at issue. For example, the *Familiapress*[80] case concerned a national prohibition on the sale of periodicals containing prize puzzle competitions or games, which the Court of Justice regarded as impairing access of imported periodicals to the market of the Member State in question and as constituting in principle a measure having equivalent effect. Nevertheless, the Court held that "Maintenance of press diversity may constitute an overriding requirement justifying a restriction on the free movement of goods", noting that "Such diversity helps to safeguard freedom of expression as protected by Article 10 of the European Convention on Human Rights and Fundamental Freedoms, which is one of the fundamental rights guaranteed by the Community legal order." The Court went on to examine in detail how the national court should go about assessing the proportionality of the matter in issue. This involved a detailed study by the national court of the economic conditions prevailing on the Austrian press market. The Court stated, *inter alia*,

> "In carrying out that study, it will have to define the market for the product in question and to have regard to the market shares of individual publishers or press groups and the trend thereof.

---

[77] Case 16/83 [1984] E.C.R. 1299, para.27.

[78] The principle may be confined to cases involving similar indirect indications of national provenenance, and the problem in *Prantl* is explained in Case C–3/91 *Exportur SA v LOR SA and Confiserie du Tech SA* [1992] E.C.R. I–5529, para.34, as being "how to reconcile use of an indirect indication of national provenance with concurrent use of an indirect indication of foreign provenance," which was "not comparable to the use of names of Spanish towns by French undertakings, which raises the problem of the protection in one State of the names of another State."

[79] Case 261/81 [1982] E.C.R. 3961, para.12.

[80] Case C–368/95 *Vereinigte Familiapress Zeitungsverlags- und vertriebs GmbH* [1997] E.C.R. I–3689.

Moreover, the national court will also have to assess the extent to which, from the consumer's standpoint, the product concerned can be replaced by papers which do not offer prizes, taking into account all the circumstances which may influence the decision to purchase, such as the presence of advertising on the title page referring to the chance of winning a prize, the likelihood of winning, the value of the prize or the extent to which winning depends on a test calling for a measure of ingenuity, skill or knowledge."[81]

The ruling in *Familiapress* also clarified that whenever the Member States invoke a mandatory requirement to justify a restriction to intra-Community trade they have to respect fundamental rights as guaranteed by the general principles of Community law since the situation falls within the scope of Community law.[82]

THE RELATIONSHIP BETWEEN ARTICLES 28 TO 30 EC AND OTHER PROVISIONS OF THE TREATY

16–047   However, wide the field of application of Articles 28 and 29 EC may be, it does not include obstacles to trade covered by other provisions of the Treaty, such as Articles 23 to 25 EC (customs duties and charges having equivalent effect), Article 90 EC (discriminatory internal taxation), and Articles 87 and 88 EC (state aids).[83] Where national taxes are imposed on an import which lacks a domestic counterpart, the rate of tax must not be so high as to impede the free movement of goods. Such an impediment to free movement would fall to be governed by Articles 28–30 EC, rather than within the framework of Article 90 EC.[84] This extent to which fiscal charges not falling within the scope of Article 25 or Article 90 EC might fall within the scope of Article 28 EC was clarified in *De Danske Billimportører*.[85] Here the claimant argued that a very high registration duty for new cars was an obstacle to trade prohibited by Article 28 EC. Denmark does not produce cars or any product in competition with cars and so there was no issue of discrimination for Article 90 EC purposes. After having found that the charge was of a fiscal nature, the Court held that if such charges are of such an amount as to represent an obstacle to the free movement of goods

---

[81] Case C–368/95 [1997] E.C.R. I–3689, paras 30, 31.
[82] See Ch.8, above.
[83] Case 74/76 *Iannelli & Volpi* [1977] E.C.R. 557; Case 222/82 *Apple and Pear Development Council* [1983] E.C.R. 4083, para.30.
[84] Case C–47/88 *Commission v Denmark* [1990] E.C.R. I–4509.
[85] Case C–383/01 *De Danske Billimportører* [2003] E.C.R. I–6065, and see para.15–016, above.

within the Common Market they might be caught by Article 28 EC. However, in the case at issue, the Court found that the figures communicated by the national court in relation to the number of new vehicles registered in Denmark (and thus imported in that State) did not in any way show that free movement of cars between Denmark and other Member States had been impeded. The Court has also clarified that the non-applicability of Articles 25 and 90 EC by no means triggers the automatic applicability of Article 28 EC.[86] Thus, it is very likely that only in the most extreme of circumstances would a non-discriminatory/non-protectionist tax be qualified as an obstacle to intra-Community trade within the meaning of Article 28 EC (and subject to justifications).

National measures which fail to be scrutinised by the Commission under Articles 87 and 88 EC cannot be categorised as measures having equivalent effect simply by virtue of their effects upon trade, unless the aid in question produces "restrictive effects which exceed what is necessary to enable it to attain the objectives permitted by the Treaty."[87] This may be the case where aid is granted to traders who obtain supplies of imported products through a state agency but is withheld when the products are imported direct, if this distinction is not clearly necessary for the attainment of the objectives of the said aid or for its proper functioning.[88] Furthermore, the Court has held that the possibility that State subsidies to a campaign designed to favour domestic products might fall within Articles 87 and 88 EC does not mean that the campaign itself thereby escapes the prohibitions laid down in Article 28 EC.[89] The fact that a public works contract relates to the provision of services cannot remove a clause in an invitation to tender restricting the material that may be used from the scope of the prohibitions set out in Article 28 EC.[90]

And, a national measure which facilitates an abuse of a dominant position will generally infringe Article 28 EC.[91]

ARTICLE 31 EC—STATE MONOPOLIES OF A COMMERCIAL CHARACTER

Article 31 EC, which reproduces a slightly amended text of former **16–048** Article 37, provides, in part:

---

[86] Joined Cases C–34/01 to C–38/01 *Enirisorse Spa* [2003] E.C.R. I–14243.
[87] Case 74/76 *Iannelli & Volpi* [1977] E.C.R. 557.
[88] Case 74/76 *Iannelli & Volpi* [1977] E.C.R. 557.
[89] Case 249/81 *Commission v Ireland* [1982] E.C.R. 4005, para.18.
[90] Case 45/87 *Commission v Ireland* [1988] E.C.R. 4929.
[91] Case C–179/90 *Merci convenzionali porto di Genova SpA v Siderurgica Gabrielli SpA* [1991] E.C.R. I–5889, para.21.

"1. Member States shall adjust any State monopolies of a commercial character so as to ensure that no discrimination regarding the conditions under which goods are procured and marketed exists between nationals of Member States.

The provisions of this Article shall apply to any body through which a Member State, in law or in fact, either directly or indirectly supervises, determines or appreciably influences imports or exports between Member States. These provisions shall likewise apply to monopolies delegated by the State to others.

Member States shall refrain from introducing any new measure which is contrary to the principles laid down in paragraph 1 or which restricts the scope of the Articles dealing with the abolition of customs duties and quantitative restrictions between Member States."

The provisions of Article 31(2) EC were held to be directly applicable from the date of entry into force of the Treaty in *Costa v ENEL*.[92] Article 37(1) (now 31(1)), which provided prior to its amendment on May 1, 1999 that Member States were to "progressively adjust" state monopolies so as to ensure that no discrimination exists "when the transitional period has ended" was held to have similar effect from the end of the transitional period in *Pubblico Ministero v Flavia Manghera* and *Rewe-Zentrale des Lebensmittel-Grosshandels v Hauptzollamt Landau/Pfalz*.[93] The State monopolies in question are those enjoying exclusive rights in the procurement and distribution of goods, not services,[94] and Article 31 EC applies to monopolies over provision of services only in so far as such a monopoly contravenes the principle of the free movement of goods by discriminating against imported products to the advantage of products of domestic origin.[95] But the existence of national rules requiring the licensing of particular activities is not sufficient to amount to a State monopoly of a commercial character.[96] And Article 31 EC has no application to national legislation which reserves the retail sale of manufactured tobacco products to distributors authorised by the State, provided that the State does not intervene in the procurement choices of retailers.[97]

---

[92] Case 6/64 [1964] E.C.R. 585.
[93] Case 45/75 [1976] E.C.R. 91.
[94] Case 155/73 *Sacchi* [1974] E.C.R. 409; Case 271/81 *Societe d'Insemination Artificielle* [1983] E.C.R. 2057. In the latter case the Court recognised the possibility that a monopoly over the provision of services might have an indirect influence on trade in goods.
[95] Case 271/81 *Amélioration de l' Élevage v Mialocq* [1983] E.C.R. 2057; Joined Cases C–46/90 and C–93/91 *Procureur du Roi v Jean-Marie Lagauche* [1993] E.C.R. I–5267, para.33.
[96] Case 118/86 *Nertsvoederfabriek Nederland BV* [1987] E.C.R. 3883.
[97] Case C–387/93 *Banchero* [1995] E.C.R. I–4663, para.31.

As from the end of the transitional period every national monopoly of a commercial character must have been adjusted so as to eliminate the exclusive right to import from other Member States.[98] Exclusive import rights give rise to discrimination prohibited by Article 31(1) EC against exporters established in other Member States, and such rights directly affect the conditions under which goods are marketed only as regards operators or sellers in other Member States.[99] But for the prohibition of all discrimination between nationals of Member States provided for in Article 31(1) EC to be applicable, it is not necessarily a requirement that the exclusive rights to import a given product relate to all imports; it is sufficient if those rights relate to a proportion such that they enable the monopoly to have an appreciable influence on imports.[1] However, the Court has repeatedly stated that Article 31 EC does not require national monopolies having a commercial character to be abolished but requires them to be adjusted in such a way as to ensure that no discrimination regarding the conditions under which goods are procured and marketed exists between nationals of Member States.[2] The purpose of Article 31 EC of the Treaty is to reconcile the possibility for Member States to maintain certain monopolies of a commercial character as instruments for the pursuit of public interest aims with the requirements of the establishment and functioning of the common market. It aims at the elimination of obstacles to the free movement of goods, save, however, for restrictions on trade which are inherent in the existence of the monopolies in question.[3] Thus Article 31 EC only applies to activities intrinsically connected with the specific business of the monopoly and is irrelevant to national provisions which have no connection with such specific business.[4] While, during the transitional period, Article 31 EC suspended the operation of Article 90 EC, prohibiting discriminatory internal taxation,[5] as of the end of the transitional period, the position of internal taxes has been subject exclusively to Article 90 EC.[6] Furthermore, while Article 31 EC permits the continuation of the obligation to deliver goods to the monopoly, and a corresponding obligation upon the monopoly to purchase such goods, Article 28 EC applies so as to ensure equal treatment of domestic goods and imports.[7] It thus seems that Article 31 EC is cumulatively applicable

---

[98] Case 59/75 *Manghera* [1986] E.C.R. 91.
[99] Case C–157/94 *Commission v Netherlands* [1997] E.C.R. I–5699, para.15.
[1] Case C–347/88 *Commission v Greece* [1990] E.C.R. I–4747, para.44; Case C–157/94 *Commission v Netherlands* [1997] E.C.R. I–5699, para.18.
[2] Case C–189/95 *Criminal proceedings against Harry Franzén* [1997] E.C.R. I–5909, para.38 and cases there cited; see also Case C–438/02 *Hanner* [2005] E.C.R. I–4551.
[3] Case C–189/95 *Criminal proceedings against Harry Franzén* [1997] E.C.R. I–5909, para.39.
[4] Case 86/78 *Grandes Distilleries* [1979] E.C.R. 897.
[5] As to which, see above at Ch.15, para.15–024.
[6] Case 86/78 *Grandes Distilleries* [1979] E.C.R. 897.
[7] Case 119/78 *Grandes Distilleries* [1979] E.C.R. 975.

with the earlier provisions of the chapter on the elimination of quantitative restrictions, and the provisions on customs duties and charges having equivalent effect.

16–049   In the second *Hansen* case,[8] arising from the operation of the German alcohol monopoly, the Court held:

(i) that after the end of the transitional period, Article 31 EC remained applicable wherever the exercise by a state monopoly of its exclusive rights entailed a discrimination or restriction prohibited by that Article;

(ii) that Article 31 EC prohibited a monopoly's right to purchase and re-sell national alcohol from being exercised so as to undercut imported products with publicly subsidised domestic products; and

(iii) that Articles 31 EC and 87/88 EC were capable of cumulative application to one and the same fact situation.

In *Pigs and Bacon Commission v McCarren*[9] the Court held that Article 32(1) EC[10] gave priority to the rules for the organisation of the agricultural markets over the application of Article 31 EC. The better view is that this means merely that Article 31 EC cannot be pleaded by way of derogation from rules imposed by a common organisation: the positive obligations of the Article are surely to be implied into the framework of a common organisation and it is established that common organisations can derogate only in exceptional circumstances from the free movement provisions of the Treaty.[11]

Article 31(3) EC which contains the slightly amended text of that formerly found in Article 37(4) EC, provides:

"If a State monopoly of a commercial character has rules which are designed to make it easier to dispose of agricultural products or obtain for them the best return, steps should be taken in applying the rules contained in this Article to ensure equivalent safeguards for the employment and standard of living of the producers concerned."

In *Charmasson*[12] the Court held that Article 31(3) EC had never allowed any derogation from Article 31 EC, and that the "equivalent safeguards" referred to in Article 31(3) EC must themselves be compatible with the provisions of Article 31(1) and (2) EC.

---

[8] Case 91/78 [1979] E.C.R. 935.
[9] Case 177/78 [1979] E.C.R. 2161.
[10] Art.32(2) provides: "Save as otherwise provided in Arts 33 to 38, the rules laid down for the establishment of the common market shall apply to agricultural products."
[11] Cases 80 and 81/77 *Commissionaires Reunis* [1978] E.C.R. 927; Case 83/78 *Redmond* [1978] E.C.R. 2347.
[12] Case 48/74 [1974] E.C.R. 1383.

ARTICLES 28–30 EC AND INTELLECTUAL PROPERTY RIGHTS

Intellectual property and the common market

The co-existence of separate systems of protection for intellectual **16–050** property rights in the different Member States is capable of conflicting with the objective of creating a single market. For example, if one hypothetically considers for a moment national law in isolation from EC law, and supposes that a company holds a patent right protected under the law of two Member States, A and B, that company might be entitled to rely upon that patent in Member State B to oppose the import into that State of an article manufactured and placed on the market under the patent in Member State A, and *vice versa*, even though it was the company itself, or a licensee, which had itself placed that article on the market in the first place. Similarly, if a company held the rights to a trade mark in each Member State, it might oppose the import into Member State A of an article bearing the trade mark and placed on the market in Member State B, and *vice versa*, even though, once again, it was the company itself, or a licensee, which had placed that article on the market in the first place. In fact, national patent and trade mark rights do not operate in isolation from Community law, and Community law has addressed the above problem from two perspectives. The first is that of the application of Articles 28–30 EC, which have been interpreted by the Court as preventing holders of patents, trade marks, or copyright or other intellectual property rights, from using those rights to prevent the import of goods covered by those rights into one Member State from the territory of another where the holder of the rights in question has consented to their being placed on the market. The second perspective has been the harmonisation of laws. Thus for example there has been harmonisation of national trade mark rules under Directive 89/104 to approximate the laws of the Member States relating to trade marks,[13] while under Regulation 40/94 on the Community Trade Mark,[14] trade mark owners have been able since April 1, 1996 to apply for a single registered trade mark for the whole of the European Community from the Office for Harmonisation in the Internal Market (OHIM), which is located in Alicante, Spain. Since April 1, 2003 it has been possible to apply to the OHIM for a design right for one area comprising all Member States under Regulation 6/2002 on Community designs.[15] Such harmonisation does not however render the case law of the Court of

---

[13] [1989] O.J. L40/1; Consolidated text (Eurlex) (pdf) 1991–12–23; and as amended by EEA Agreement, Art.65(2) and Annex XVII, [1994] O.J. L1/482.
[14] [1994] O.J. L11/36; Consolidated text (Eurlex) (pdf) 2004–12–27.
[15] [2002] O.J. L3/1.

Justice on the free movement of goods provisions redundant, since
EC secondary legislation must be interpreted in the light of the
Treaty rules on the free movement of goods and in particular Article
30 EC.[16] Reference may also be made to other examples of
harmonisation of intellectual property rights (e.g., rental and lending
rights, legal protection of databases, certain aspects of copyright and
related rights, and the protection of designs).[17]

In the field of patent law there has to date been co-ordination at
the level of processing applications for patent protection in the
various Member States, within the framework of the European
Patent Convention. The Convention on the Grant of European
Patents, or European Patent Convention, came into force on
October 7, 1977. The European Patent Office which processes
patent applications, is in Munich, with a branch in the Hague, sub-
offices in Berlin and Vienna, and a bureau in Brussels. An applicant
for a European patent specifies the contracting States in which
protection is sought, and if an application is granted, the patent has
the same effect as a national patent in each of those States.

The Community Patent Convention, which would provide for a
unitary Community patent, superseding national patents after a
transitional period, has not come into force, because it has not been
ratified by a sufficient number of Member States, and it is not
expected that this initiative will be pursued. The Commission in
August 2000 put forward a proposal for a Council Regulation on the
Community patent.[18] Under this proposal, Community Patents
would be issued by the European Patent Office. National and
European Patents would coexist with the Community Patent system,
so that inventors would be free to choose which type of patent
protection best suited their needs. The patent would be valid as
granted by the European Patent Office in one of the three EPO
languages (English, French and German), with translations of the
claims in the other two languages published for information. In
March 2003 the Council agreed a common political approach
whereby translations of the claims of the patent be filed in all
Community languages for the patent to be valid, unless Member
States renounce the requirement for their official languages. Disagreement over the precise legal effect of translations is one reason
why final agreement on the Community patent regulation has yet to

---

[16] Joined Cases C–427/93, C–429/93 and C–436/93 *Bristol-Myers Squibb v Paranova* [1996]
E.C.R. I–3457, para.27.
[17] See e.g., Dir.92/100 on rental right and lending right and on certain rights related to
copyright in the field of intellectual property, [1992] O.J. L346/61; Consolidated text
(Eurlex) (pdf) 2001–06–22; Dir.96/9 on the legal protection of databases, [1996] O.J.
L77/20; Dir.2001/29 on the harmonisation of certain aspects of copyright and related rights
in the information society [2001] O.J. L167/10; Dir.98/71 on the legal protection of designs,
[1998] O.J. L289/28.
[18] COM (2000) 412 final; [2000] O.J. C–337E/278.

be achieved. In the context of continuing efforts to secure agreement on the Community patent the Commission in January 2006 launched a consultation exercise on the patent system in Europe, with a view to organising a hearing in Brussels in early summer 2006 on the basis of the feedback.

The following sections of this chapter deal with the relationship between intellectual property rights and the provisions of the Treaty on the free movement of goods, rather than with harmonising legislation relating to intellectual property, though reference to the latter is made where appropriate.

A distinction between the existence and exercise of intellectual property rights

A question which arose at the outset for the Court in the present **16–051** context was how far it was bound to recognise rights conferred by national laws on holders of intellectual property ("industrial and commercial property" in the language of Article 30 EC of the Treaty), even if the exercise of those rights could lead in certain circumstances to impeding the movement of goods between Member States. The answer to this question, on a superficial reading of the relevant Treaty texts, appeared, and indeed appears, to be that effect must be given to intellectual property rights, even if the result is indeed to prevent imports in certain cases. A general Treaty provision of obvious relevance is Article 295 EC, which provides:

> "This Treaty shall in no way prejudice the rules in Member States governing the system of property ownership."

On the face of it, this might appear to uphold the rights of holders of intellectual property rights to exercise those rights, even if the result were some interference with the free movement of goods. Indeed, Article 30 EC provides, in relevant part:

> "The provisions of Articles 28 and 29 shall not preclude prohibitions or restrictions on imports, exports or goods in transit justified on grounds of . . . the protection of industrial and commercial property. Such prohibitions or restrictions shall not, however, constitute a means of arbitrary discrimination or a disguised restriction on trade between Member States."

While restrictions on imports that are necessary for the protection of industrial and commercial property are exempted from the prohibitions in Articles 28 and 29 EC, it is made clear in the second sentence of the Article that there may be circumstances where, regardless of the rights existing under national law, the prohibition will apply. But where is this line to be drawn as regards intellectual property rights? The judicial answer to this question involves drawing a distinction between the *existence* of intellectual property rights, which remains intact, and the *exercise* of those rights, which must be modified in order to ensure the free movement of goods. This solution is formulated as follows in *Terrapin v Terranova*:

> ". . . whilst the Treaty does not affect the existence of rights recognised by the legislation of a Member State in matters of industrial and commercial property, yet the exercise of those rights may nevertheless, depending on the circumstances, be restricted by the prohibitions in the Treaty. Inasmuch as it provides an exception to one of the fundamental principles of the common market, Article 36 [now 30] in fact admits exceptions to the free movement of goods only to the extent to which such exceptions are justified for the purposes of safeguarding the rights which constitute the specific subject-matter of that property."[19]

The distinction drawn by the Court between the existence of rights and their exercise is evidently inspired by a wish to remain at least within the letter of Article 295 EC. It invites the criticism that a form of property is the bundle of rights recognised by national law under a particular designation, and if Community law prevents any rights in the bundle from being exercised, the property is to that extent diminished. Yet such criticism taken to its logical conclusion would argue that e.g., the Treaty's prohibition of discrimination on grounds of nationality could have no application to the exercise of property rights, so that a municipal authority offering public housing to workers could charge nationals of other Member States a higher rent than nationals, or even exclude non-nationals altogether. What the Court has done, in reality, emerges from the second sentence in the quoted passage. The derogation in Article 30 EC has been confined to rights which, the Court considers, constitute the essential core or "specific subject-matter" of the property in question. The exercise of the "specific subject-matter" of such rights is permitted by Community law, even if it impedes trade or competition, because otherwise it would no longer be possible to say that the property was receiving protection. On the other hand, rights which the Court regards as merely incidental to the property are not allowed to be used to partition the market.

---

[19] Case 119/75 [1976] E.C.R. 1039, para.5; Case C–10/89 *Hag GF* [1990] E.C.R. I–3711, para.12, Case C–61/97 *FDV* [1998] E.C.R. I–5171, para.13; Case C–115/02 *Rioglass SA* [2003] E.C.R. I–12705, para.23.

Free movement of goods—the exhaustion of the rights principle

The exclusive right of an owner of intellectual property to put into **16–052** circulation for the first time goods that are subject to the property is likely to be understood in the law of the Member State concerned (leaving aside Community law considerations) as applying to sale in that State's territory. Sales elsewhere will not count as an exercise of the right—in the jargon of the subject, they are not considered to "exhaust" that right. This means that, as a matter of national law alone, it would be open to the owner of the property to oppose the sale by other traders of imported products acquired in a Member State where they have been marketed by the owner himself, or by a licensee of the owner. It is to be noted that there would be an incentive for such so-called "parallel" importing if, for some reason, the products in question were significantly cheaper in the State of initial distribution than in the one from which it was sought to exclude them.

On the other hand, the Court of Justice has repeatedly stated, as a general principle, that "the proprietor of an industrial or commercial property right protected by the legislation of a Member State may not rely on that legislation in order to oppose the importation of a product which has lawfully been marketed in another Member State by, or with the consent of, the proprietor of the right himself or a person legally or economically dependent on him."[20] Whatever the position in national law, the proprietor's exclusive right is deemed in Community law to be exhausted by putting products into circulation anywhere in the common market. The rationale of the principle is to be found in the limitation of the exception in Article 30 EC by reference to the case law derived concept of the specific subject-matter of the intellectual property in question. Where exhaustion occurs it is because the right to exclude imports originally marketed in another Member State is not seen as part of the specific subject-matter of the property in question. The exercise of the right would, therefore, not be "justified" within the meaning of Article 30 EC as being necessary for the protection of the industrial and commercial property right in question.[21] The principle of exhaustion has been applied by the Court of Justice to most of the important forms of intellectual property, and since the principle is derived from the Treaty itself, it is applicable to Community intellectual property

---

[20] Case 144/81 *Keurkoop v Nancy Kean Gifts* [1982] E.C.R. 2853, para.25; the principle appears in numerous cases, see e.g. Joined Cases C–427/93, C–429/93 and C–436/93 *Bristol-Myers Squibb v Paranova* [1996] E.C.R. I–3457, para.45.
[21] This analysis was applied by the Court for the first time in Case 78/80 *Deutsche Grammophon v Metro* [1971] E.C.R. 487. It is more fully developed in Case 15/74 *Centrafarm v Sterling Drug* [1974] E.C.R. 1147.

rights, and has been incorporated into the Community Regulations establishing such rights.[22]

Free movement of goods and patents

16–053   The leading case on the application of the exhaustion of rights principle to patents is *Centrafarm v Sterling Drug*.[23] Patents for a drug used in the treatment of urinary tract infections were held by Sterling Drug, an American company, in the United Kingdom and the Netherlands. The case originated in the proceedings brought for the infringement of the Dutch patent against Centrafarm, a company famous in the annals of European Court litigation as a parallel importer of pharmaceutical products.[24] Centrafarm's alleged infringement consisted of importing into the Netherlands and offering for sale there quantities of the patented product which had been lawfully marketed by licensees of Sterling Drug in the United Kingdom. This was commercially attractive for Centrafarm, because the price of the drug on the United Kingdom market was only about half the price on the Dutch market. The Court of Justice defined the specific subject-matter of a patent as:

> ". . . the guarantee that the patentee, to reward the creative effort of the inventor, has the exclusive right to use an invention with a view to manufacturing industrial products and putting them into circulation for the first time, either directly or by the grant of licences to third parties as well as the right to oppose infringements."[25]

The essential function of a patent is here acknowledged to be the rewarding of (and hence encouragement of) creative effort. The reward comes from the patentee's ability to earn a monopoly profit through an exclusive right to manufacture the protected product and put it into circulation for the first time. That right may be exploited directly or by appointing licensees. It has, as a corollary, a right to oppose manufacturing or first marketing of the product by third parties.

In the light of that definition the Court went on to consider the circumstances in which the use of a patent to block the importation of protected products from another Member State might be justified.

---

[22] Art.13 of Reg. 40/94 (Community trade mark); Art.21 of Reg. 6/2002 (Community design). It is also to be found in Directives harmonising national rules on intellectual property, see e.g. Dir.89/104 on trade marks, Art.7, and Dir.92/100 on rental right and lending right, Art.9.

[23] Case 15/74 *Centrafarm v Sterling Drug* [1974] E.C.R. 1147.

[24] There were parallel proceedings for the infringement of the Dutch trade mark: Case 16/74 *Centrafarm v Winthrop* [1974] E.C.R. 1183.

[25] [1974] E.C.R. 1147, 1162.

Two cases of possible justification were mentioned: where the product is not patentable in the Member State of origin and has been manufactured there by a third party without the consent of the patentee in the Member State of importation[26]; and where a patent exists in each of the Member States in question but the original proprietors of the patents are legally and economically independent. On the other hand, there could be no justification for opposing importation "where the product has been put onto the market in a legal manner, by the patentee himself or with his consent, in the Member State from which it has been imported, in particular in the case of parallel patents."[27] If a patent could be used in this way, the patentee would be able to cordon off national markets, thereby restricting trade between Member States, "where no such restriction was necessary to guarantee the essence of the exclusive rights flowing from the parallel patents."[28] The objection that national patents were unlikely to be truly parallel, with the result that levels of protection would vary between Member State, was brushed aside. "It should be noted here," the Court said, "that, in spite of divergences which remain in the absence of any unification of national rules concerning industrial property the identity of the protected invention is clearly the essential element of the concept of parallel patents which it is for the courts to assess."[29] The Court concluded:

> ". . . that the exercise, by a patentee, of the right which he enjoys under the legislation of a Member State to prohibit the sale, in that State, of a product protected by the patent which has been marketed in another Member State by the patentee or with his consent is incompatible with the rules of the EEC Treaty concerning the free movement of good within the common market."[30]

The basis of the ruling was not made altogether clear. On the one **16–054** hand, it might be thought that the existence of parallel patents was a crucial factor: a right to oppose the importation of protected products could be regarded as superfluous, because the patentee would already have received the monopoly profit, which was his due, in the Member State where the products were first put on the market. On the other hand, the general terms in which the ruling was expressed, taken with other hints in the judgment,[31] strongly

---

[26] This was the situation in Case 24/67 *Parke, Davis v Centrafarm* [1968] E.C.R. 55. The questions put to the Court were, however, formulated with reference to the competition rules.

[27] [1974] E.C.R. 1147, 1163.

[28] *ibid.*

[29] *ibid.*

[30] *ibid.*

[31] See, in particular, the reference, *ibid.*, to non-patentable goods "manufactured by third parties without the consent of the patentee."

suggested the principle of exhaustion would apply, even where the initial marketing occurred without the benefit of patent protection. If that were so, then the explanation could only lie in the patentee's consent to the marketing. That such was indeed the Court's meaning was shown in the later case of *Merck v Stephar*.[32] The plaintiff in the national proceedings, Merck and Co. Inc., was the holder in the Netherlands of patents relating to a drug used mainly in the treatment of high blood pressure. The proceedings arose because Stephar BV had imported the drug into the Netherlands from Italy where, although it was not patentable, it had been put into circulation by Merck. On Merck's behalf it was argued that the function of rewarding an inventor's creative effort would not be fulfilled if, owing to the impossibility of patenting a product, its sale in the Member State in question did not take place under monopoly conditions. To this the Court replied:

> "That right of first placing a product on the market enables the inventor, by allowing him a monopoly in exploiting his product, to obtain the reward for his creative effort, without, however, guaranteeing that he will obtain such a reward in all circumstances.
>
> It is for the proprietor of the patentee to decide, in the light of all the circumstances, under what conditions he will market his product, including the possibility of marketing it in a Member State where the law does not provide patent protection for the product in question. If he decides to do so he must accept the consequences of his choice as regards the free movement of the product within the Common Market, which is a fundamental principle forming part of the legal and economic circumstances which must be taken into account by the proprietor of the patent in determining the manner in which his exclusive right will be exercised."[33]

This approach seems wrong in principle. The justification for "exhaustion" of patent rights by first sale in a Member State is surely that the patent holder is entitled to exercise the specific subject-matter of his right only once in the Common Market; but in the case of a sale in one Member State of a product not patented there, but entitled to patent protection in other Member States, there has been no exercise of the patent right at all, and the effect of holding that the right cannot be subsequently exercised to prevent parallel imports in the Member States where the product is covered by patent protection is to extinguish the right entirely. The conclusion that it is for the patent holder to make the choice whether or not to

---

[32] Case 187/80 [1981] E.C.R. 2063.
[33] [1981] E.C.R. 2063, 2081–2082.

market patented products in a Member State where the product is not patentable, and must accept the consequences of that decision, rather begs the question as to whether this an appropriate dilemma to impose upon patent holders in the first place.

It used to be debated whether an owner of parallel national patents was entitled to resist the importation into one of the Member States concerned of products manufactured under a compulsory licence issued in respect of his patent in another Member State.[34] The question received a clear affirmative answer in *Pharmon v Hoechst*[35]; a case in which the Court's reasoning appeared to cast some doubt on its approach in *Merck*. Parallel patents in a medicinal product were owned by Hoechst in Germany, the Netherlands and the United Kingdom. A compulsory licence for the manufacture of the product had been obtained in the United Kingdom, and Pharmon had purchased a consignment from the licensee with a view to selling it on the Dutch market. This Hoechst was anxious to prevent. Pharmon rested its case on the exhastion of rights principle, arguing that Hoechst had entered the British market with its eyes open and must be taken to have accepted all the legal consequences flowing from the registration of a parallel patent. The passage quoted above from the judgment in *Merck* seemed to give force to that argument.[36] It was, however, rejected by the Court on the ground that the compulsory character of a licence meant the holder of the patent could not be regarded as having consented to the actions of the licensee. "Such a measure," the Court said, "deprives the patent proprietor of his right to determine freely the conditions under which he markets his products."[37] The provision of the Community Patent Convention excepting from the principle of exhaustion "the case of a product put on the market under a compulsory licence" was thus shown to reflect the law of the Treaty.[38] If *Pharmon*, apart from its intrinsic significance, also implied that the reasoning underlying *Merck* might at least be open to question, a later judgment on the law of copyright was to point strongly in the same direction.

In *Warner Bros. v Christiansen*,[39] the Court of Justice considered **16–055** whether the marketing in the United Kingdom of a video-cassette of the film exhausted the right of the author to control the subsequent hiring out of the video-cassette in Denmark, where Danish law recognised such a right, but where under United Kingdom law the purchase of the video-cassette entitled the purchaser to hire it out without the need for the consent of the author. The Court held that:

---

[34] Under a system of compulsory licensing a patentee may be deprived of his monopoly by an official decision to grant licences to third parties in return for a reasonable royalty.
[35] Case 19/84 [1985] E.C.R. 2281.
[36] [1981] E.C.R. 2063, 2082.
[37] [1985] E.C.R. 2281, para.25.
[38] Community Patent Convention, Art.76(3) (formerly 81(3)).
[39] Case 158/86 [1988] E.C.R. 2605.

"where national legislation confers on authors a specific right to hire out video-cassettes, that right would be rendered worthless if its owner were not in a position to authorise the operations for doing so. It cannot therefore be accepted that the marketing by a film-maker of a video-cassette containing one of his works, in a Member State which does not provide specific protection for the right to hire it out, should have repercussions on the right conferred on that same film-maker by the legislation of another Member State to restrain, in that State, the hiring out of that video-cassette."[40]

If the statement in the second sentence of the above paragraph were applied by analogy to patent rights in the context of circumstances such as those in *Merck*, the result would be that a patent holder could resist the import of products into a Member State where they were patented if they were marketed in a Member State where they could not be patented. The occasion for the Court to reconsider *Merck v Stephar* came in *Merck v Primecrown*,[41] a case which arose in the context of the application of transitional arrangements in the Act of Accession of Spain and Portugal to parallel imports into the United Kingdom from the latter countries. Merck & Co. Inc. argued in reliance *inter alia* on *Pharmon* and *Warner Bros.* that the Court should overrule *Merck v Stephar*. Advocate General Fennelly agreed.[42] But the Court did not. As regards *Pharmon*, the Court distinguished the factual situation in *Merck* (patent holder's consent to marketing) with that in *Pharmon* (marketing under a compulsory licence to which the patent holder had not consented).[43] As regards *Warner Bros.*, the Court briefly stated the facts, prefaced with the words "Unlike the cases now under consideration . . .".[44] In truth, the Court had already given what is perhaps the main reason for its judgment a few paragraphs earlier: the transitional measures provided for in the Act of Accession were adopted in light of the ruling in *Merck* and indicated the intention of the Member States that upon expiry of those transitional arrangements, the free movement of goods provisions of the Treaty, as interpreted in *Merck*, should apply in full to trade between Spain and Portugal. That was an entirely defensible ground for adhering to the result in *Merck* even if the reasoning underlying the original decision could no longer be defended.

---

[40] Case 158/86 [1988] E.C.R. 2605, para.18.
[41] Joined Cases C–267/95 and C–268/95 [1996] E.C.R. I–6285.
[42] This lengthy Opinion is erudite and convincing.
[43] Joined Cases C–267/95 and C–268/95 [1996] E.C.R. I–6285, para.41.
[44] Joined Cases C–267/95 and C–268/95 [1996] E.C.R. I–6285, para.42.

Free movement of goods and trade marks

Exhaustion of rights
Centrafarm v Sterling Drug[45] had a companion case, *Centrafarm v* **16–056**
Winthrop,[46] relating to the infringement of the trade mark, Negram,
under which the imported drug was sold. The conclusion of the
Court of Justice was similar to that in the patent case and was
reached by a similar process of reasoning. The specific subject-
matter of a trade mark was said to be:

> ". . . the guarantee that the owner of the trade mark has the
> exclusive right to use that trade mark, for the purpose of
> putting products protected by the trade mark into circulation
> for the first time, and is therefore intended to protect him
> against competitors wishing to take advantage of the status and
> reputation of the trade mark by selling products illegally
> bearing that trade mark."[47]

The emphasis here is on what makes a trade mark valuable—the
reservation to the owner, through his exclusive right to put trade
marked products into circulation, of the goodwill associated with the
mark. The Court did not on this occasion examine the reason why
such a right should be given, the question of the "essential function"
of a trade mark, but it did so in later cases, in which it described that
essential function as being to guarantee the identity of the trade
marked product to the consumer or ultimate user.[48] The exhaustion
of rights conferred by a trade mark is now dealt with in Article 7 of
the Trade Mark Directive,[49] which states in the relevant part:

> "1. The trade mark shall not entitle the proprietor to prohibit
> its use in relation to goods which have been put on the
> market in a Contracting Party under that trade mark by the
> proprietor or with his consent."

The original text referred to goods put on the market in the
Community, but the text was amended to accommodate the European Economic Area (EEA) Agreement. The EEA comprises the

---

[45] Case 15/74 *Centrafarm v Sterling Drug* [1974] E.C.R. 1147, see above at p.640.
[46] Case 16/74 *Centrafarm v Winthrop* [1974] E.C.R. 1183.
[47] [1974] E.C.R. 1183, 1194.
[48] See Case 102/77 *Hoffmann-La Roche v Centrafarm* [1978] E.C.R. 1139; Case 3/78 *Centrafarm v American Home Products* [1978] E.C.R. 1823; Joined Cases C–427/93, C–429/93 and C–436/93 *Bristol-Myers Squibb v Paranova* [1996] E.C.R. I–3457; Case C–349/95 *Frits Loenderloot v George Ballantine & Son Ltd* [1997] E.C.R. I–6227.
[49] Dir.89/104 [1989] O.J. L40/1; Consolidated text (Eurlex) (pdf) 1991–12–23; as amended by EEA Agrement, Art.65(2) and Annex XVII, [1994] O.J. L1/482.

EC, Iceland, Liechtenstein and Norway. Accordingly, reference to the market in a Contracting Party is a reference to the territory of the EEA.[50] In *Peak Holding AB*[51] the Court was called upon to interpret the reference in Article 7(1) of the Directive to "goods which have been put on the market", and in particular to decide whether goods bearing a trade mark are regarded as having been put on the market in the EEA where the proprietor has imported them with a view to selling them there, or where she/he has offered them for sale to consumers in the EEA, in his own shops or those of an associated company, but without actually selling them. The Court held that where a proprietor merely imports his goods with a view to selling them in the EEA or offers them for sale in the EEA, he does not put them on the market within the meaning of Article 7(1) of the Directive, since such acts do not transfer to third parties the right to dispose of the goods bearing the mark, and do not allow the proprietor to realise the economic value of the trade mark. "Even after such acts," declared the Court, "the proprietor retains his interest in maintaining complete control over the goods bearing his trade mark, in order in particular to ensure their quality."[52]

In *Bristol Myers-Squibb*[53] the Court held that Article 7 comprehensively regulates the question of the exhaustion of trade mark rights for products traded in the Community, and that national rules must be assessed in the light of that Article, but added that "the directive must be interpreted in the light of the Treaty rules on the free movement of goods and in particular Article 36 [now 30]."[54] Citing Article 7(1), the Court stated:

> "That provision is framed in terms corresponding to those used by the Court in judgments which, in interpreting Articles [28 and 30] of the Treaty, have recognised in Community law the principle of the exhaustion of the rights conferred by a trade mark. It reiterates the case law of the Court to the effect that the owner of a trade mark protected by the legislation of a Member State cannot rely on that legislation to prevent the importation or marketing of a product which was put on the market in another Member State by him or with his consent . . ."[55]

It follows from the foregoing that the concept of exhaustion of trade mark rights under Article 7(1) of the Directive and the concept of

[50] EEA Agreement, Art.65(2) and Annex XVII, [1994] O.J. L 1/482.
[51] C–16/03 [2004] E.C.R. I–11313; see Enchelmaier, "The Peak Holding Case: the Notion of Exhaustion of Intellectual Property Rights in the Internal Market Clarified", (2005) *European Current Law*, Part 5 "Focus" p.xi–xv.
[52] *ibid.*, para.42.
[53] Joined Cases C–427/93, C–429/93 and C–436/93 *Bristol-Myers Squibb v Paranova* [1996] E.C.R. I–3457.
[54] *ibid.*, paras 25–27.
[55] *ibid.*, para.31.

exhaustion under Articles 28 and 30 EC are one and the same concept.

The principle of exhaustion of trade mark rights referred to above is of course a concept applicable to the marketing of trade marked goods *within* the EEA. The issue which arose in *Silhouette International*[56] was whether national rules providing for exhaustion of trade-mark rights in respect of products put on the market outside the EEA, were contrary to Article 7(1) of the Directive. The Court concluded that Articles 5 to 7 of the Directive must be considered as embodying a complete harmonisation of the rules relating to the rights conferred by a trade mark, and that accordingly national rules providing for the exhaustion of trade mark rights put on the market *outside* the EEA under that mark by the proprietor or with his consent were contrary to Article 7(1) of the Directive. The Court considered a somewhat different but related issue in *Davidoff*,[57] which arose from proceedings in an English court by proprietors in the United Kingdom of various trade marks, including LEVI'S, against various retailers, including Tesco and Costco, who had sold in the United Kingdom products originally placed on the market in various countries outside the EEA, including the United States. In favour of the United Kingdom retailers it was argued that the proprietor of the trade mark of goods placed on the market *outside* the EEA might nevertheless have consented, expressly or impliedly, to those goods being placed on the market *inside* the EEA, that such consent should be presumed unless the trade mark proprietor proved the contrary, and that a trade mark proprietor wishing her/his exclusive rights to be reserved within the EEA must ensure that the goods bearing the trade mark carry a clear warning of the existence of such reservations, and that the reservations must be stipulated in the contracts for the sale and resale of those goods. These were far-reaching arguments indeed, and were largely rejected by the Court of Justice. The starting point for the Court was that if the concept of consent were a matter for the national laws of the Member States, trade mark protection for proprietors would vary according to the legal system concerned, and this would be contrary to the objective of Directive 89/104 of achieving the same protection under the legal systems of all the Member States. In the Court's view, it fell to it to supply a uniform interpretation of the concept of consent to the placing of goods on the market within the EEA as referred to in Article 7(1) of the Directive. In view of its serious effect in extinguishing the exclusive rights of the proprietors of trade

---

[56] Case C–355/96 *Silhouette International Schmied GmbH & Co. KG v Hatlauer Handelsgesellschaft mbH* [1998] E.C.R. I–4799. See also Case C–173/98 *Sebago Inc. and Ancienne Maison Dubois et Fils SA v GB-Unic SA* [1999] E.C.R. I–4103.

[57] Joined Cases C–414/99 to C–416/99 *Zino Davidoff SA etc.* [2001] E.C.R. I–8691; see Petursson, Dryberg, "What is Consent" (2002) 27 E.L. Rev. 464.

marks, the Court considered that consent must be so expressed that an intention to renounce those rights be unequivocally demonstrated. Such intention would normally be gathered from an express statement of consent, but it was conceivable that consent might, in some cases, be inferred from facts and circumstances prior to, simultaneous with or subsequent to the placing of the goods on the market outside the EEA.[58] The Court did not however consider that implied consent could be inferred from the mere silence of a trade mark proprietor; it was for the trader alleging consent to prove it, and not for the trade mark proprietor to demonstrate its absence. Nor could consent be inferred (a) from the fact that the trade mark proprietor had not communicated his opposition to marketing within the EEA, (b) from the fact that the goods did not carry any warning that it was prohibited to place them on the market within the EEA, (c) from the fact that the trade mark proprietor transferred ownership of the goods bearing the mark without imposing contractual reservations, nor (d) from the fact that, according to the law governing the contract, the property right transferred included, in the absence of such reservations, an unlimited right of resale, or, at the very least, a right to market the goods subsequently within the EEA.[59] The Court concluded that "A rule of national law which proceeded upon the mere silence of the trade mark proprietor would not recognise implied consent but rather deemed consent. This would not meet the need for consent positively expressed required by Community law."[60]

Re-packaging

16–057   One of the boldest aspects of the case law of the Court of Justice in the trade mark field has been the development of its jurisprudence on the extent to which a parallel importer may lawfully re-package a trade marked product and re-affix the mark to the re-packaged product. In *Hoffmann-La Roche v Centrafarm*[61] the Court held that:

> "The proprietor of a trade mark right which is protected in two Member States at the same time is justified pursuant to the first sentence of Article [30 EC] . . . in preventing a product to which the trade mark has lawfully been applied in one of those States from being marketed in the other Member State after it has been repackaged in new packaging to which the trade mark has been affixed by a third party."[62]

---

[58] *ibid.*, paras 45, 46.
[59] *ibid.*, paras 53–57.
[60] *ibid.*, para.58.
[61] Case 102/77 [1978] E.C.R. 1139. See also Case 3/78 *Centrafarm v American Home Products* [1978] E.C.R. 1823.
[62] [1978] E.C.R. 1139, 1164.

It reached that conclusion in the light of the "essential function of the trade mark", which, it said, was "to guarantee the identity of the trade marked product to the consumer or ultimate user, by enabling him without any possibility of confusion to distinguish that product from products which have another origin."[63] The Court took the view that the guarantee of origin meant "that the consumer or ultimate user can be certain that a trade marked product which is sold to him has not been subject at a previous stage of marketing to interference by a third person, without the authorisation of the proprietor of the trade mark, such as to affect the original condition of the product."[64] It followed that the right to prevent any dealing with the marked product which was likely to impair this guarantee formed part of the specific subject-matter of the trade mark right.

The Court concluded that Article 30 EC must be interpreted as meaning that a trade mark owner may rely on his/her rights as owner to prevent an importer from marketing a product put on the market in another Member State by the owner or with her/his consent, where that importer has repackaged the product in new packaging to which the trade mark has been affixed, unless:

— It is established that the use of the trade-mark right by the owner, having regard to the marketing system which she/he has adopted, will contribute to the artificial partitioning of the markets between Member States.
— It is shown that the repackaging cannot adversely affect the original condition of the product.
— The owner of the mark receives prior notice before the repackaged product is put on sale.
— It is stated on the new packaging by whom the product has been repackaged.[65]

In this way the Court sought to reconcile, on the one hand, the legitimate interests of consumers and the trade mark holder, and, on the other hand, the principle of the free movement of goods between Member States, requiring that the seller of the imported goods be given "a certain licence which in normal circumstances is reserved to the proprietor himself."[66]

---

[63] *ibid.*
[64] *ibid.*
[65] See Case 1/81 *Pfizer v Eurim-Pharm* [1981] E.C.R. 2913 (outer wrapping removed from blister strips upon which strips the trade mark Vibramycin Pfizer was printed; each strip packed in a box with a transparent window through which the trade mark was clearly visible; names and addresses of manufacturer and importer on the boxes, with a statement that importer responsible for the packakging; advance warning given to the Pfizer—parallel importer could rely upon Art.28 EC).
[66] [1978] E.C.R. 1139, 1165–1166.

Article 7(2) of the Trade Mark Directive[67] provides that the owner of a trade mark may oppose the further commercialization of products where there is a legitimate reason for doing so, especially where the condition of the products has been changed or impaired since they were put on the market. In *Bristol-Meyers Squibb*[68] the Court, after citing Article 7(2), observed that:

> "Article 7 of the directive, like Article [30] of the Treaty, is intended to reconcile the fundamental interest in protecting trade mark rights with the fundamental interest in the free movement of goods within the common market, so that those two provisions, which pursue the same result, must be interpreted in the same way."[69]

The national proceedings which gave rise to the reference concerned the activities of a parallel importer company called Paranova, which purchased certain products in batches in Member States where prices were relatively low (Greece, the United Kingdom, Spain and Portugal) and imported them into Denmark, where it sold them below the manufacturers' official sale prices while still making a profit. For the purposes of sale in Denmark, Paranova repackaged all the medicines in new external packaging with a uniform appearance and its own style, namely white and coloured stripes corresponding to the colours of the manufacturers' original packaging. That packaging displayed, *inter alia*, the respective trade marks of the manufacturers and the statement that the product had been manufactured respectively by "Bristol Myers-Squibb" etc., together with the indication "imported and repackaged by Paranova." Certain other changes were made to the packaging of the products, including, for example, in the case of one product, replacing the spray in the original packaging with a spray from a source other than Bristol-Myers Squibb.

16–058   Referring to prior case law, the Court stated that Article 7(2) of the directive must therefore be interpreted as meaning that a trade mark owner may legitimately oppose the further marketing of a pharmaceutical product where the importer has repackaged it and re-affixed the trade mark, unless the conditions set out in the *Hoffman-La Roche* judgment have been complied with. The Court went on to explain further the conditions laid down by the latter case.

---

[67] Directive 89/104 [1989] O.J. L40/1. Consolidated text (Eurlex) (pdf) 1991–12–23; and as amended by EEA Agrement, Art.65(2) and Annex XVII, [1994] O.J. L1/482.
[68] Joined Cases C–427/93, C–429/93 and C–436/93 *Bristol-Myers Squibb v Paranova* [1996] E.C.R. I–3457; see also Joined Cases C–71/94, 72/94 and C–73/94 *Eurim-Pharm v Beiersdorf* [1996] E.C.R. I–3603; Case C–232/94 *MPA Pharma v Rhône-Poulenc Pharma* [1996] E.C.R. I–3671; Case C–349/95 *Frits Loenderloot v George Ballantine & Son Ltd* [1997] E.C.R. I–6227.
[69] *ibid.*, para.40.

As to "artificial partitioning of the markets between Member States", the Court said that this did not imply that a parallel importer must prove that the trade mark owner deliberately sought to partition the market between Member States, it simply meant that the owner might always rely on her/his rights as owner to oppose the marketing of repackaged products when such action was justified by the need to safeguard the essential function of the trade mark, in which case the resultant partitioning could not be regarded as artificial.[70] Reliance on trade mark rights by their owner in order to oppose marketing under that trade mark of products repackaged by a third party would contribute to the partitioning of markets between Member States in particular where the owner had placed an identical pharmaceutical product on the market in several Member States in various forms of packaging, and the product could not, in the condition in which it has been marketed by the trade mark owner in one Member State, be imported and put on the market in another Member State by a parallel importer.[71] The trade mark owner could not therefore oppose the repackaging of the product in new external packaging when the size of the packet used by the owner in the Member State where the importer purchased the product could not be marketed in the Member State of importation by reason, in particular, of a rule authorising packaging only of a certain size or a national practice to the same effect.[72] Where, in accordance with the rules and practices in force in the Member State of importation, the trade mark owner used many different sizes of packaging in that State, the finding that one of those sizes was also marketed in the Member State of exportation was not enough to justify the conclusion that repackaging was unnecessary. Partitioning of the markets would exist if the importer were able to sell the product in only part of his/her market.[73] The owner could however oppose the repackaging of the product in new external packaging where this was unnecessary because the importer could achieve packaging which could be marketed in the Member State of importation by, for example, affixing to the original external or inner packaging new labels in the language of the Member State of importation, or by replacing an additional article not capable of gaining approval in the Member State of importation with a similar article that has obtained such approval.[74] The power of the owner of trade mark rights protected in a Member State to oppose the marketing of repackaged products under the trade mark should be limited only in so far as the repackaging undertaken by the importer

---

[70] *ibid..* para.57.
[71] *ibid.,* para.52.
[72] *ibid.,* para.53.
[73] *ibid.,* para.54.
[74] *ibid.,* para.55.

was necessary in order to market the product in the Member State of importation.[75]

The Court also explained that the concept of "adverse effects on the original condition of the product" referred to the condition of the product inside the packaging.[76] The trade mark owner could therefore oppose any repackaging involving a risk of the product inside the package being exposed to tampering or to influences affecting its original condition. To determine whether that applied, account had to be taken of the nature of the product and the method of repackaging.[77] As regards pharmaceutical products, repackaging was to be regarded as having been carried out in circumstances not capable of affecting the original condition of the product where, for example, the trade mark owner had placed the product on the market in double packaging and the repackaging affected only the external layer, leaving the inner packaging intact, or where the repackaging was carried out under the supervision of a public authority in order to ensure that the product remained intact.[78] The mere removal of blister packs, phials, ampoules or inhalers from their original external packaging and their replacement in new external packaging could not affect the original condition of the product inside the packaging.[79] As regards operations consisting in the fixing of self-stick labels to flasks, phials, ampoules or inhalers, the addition to the packaging of new user instructions or information in the language of the Member State of importation, or the insertion of an extra article, such as a spray, from a source other than the trade mark owner, there was nothing to suggest that the original condition of the product inside the packaging was directly affected thereby.[80] The Court however entered the caveat that the original condition of the product inside the packaging might be indirectly affected where, for example, the external or inner packaging of the repackaged product, or a new set of user instructions or information, omitted certain important information or gave inaccurate information concerning the nature, composition, effect use or storage of the product. And the same would be the case if an extra article inserted into the packaging by the importer and designed for the ingestion and dosage of the product did not comply with the method of use and the doses envisaged by the manufacturer.[81]

16–059   The Court also commented on the other requirements to be met by the parallel importer, indicating, *inter alia*, that it was not necessary to require that it be stated on the packaging that the

[75] *ibid.*, para.56.
[76] *ibid.*, para.58.
[77] *ibid.*, para.59.
[78] *ibid.*, para.60.
[79] *ibid.*, para.61.
[80] *ibid.*, para.64.
[81] *ibid.*, para.65.

repackaging was carried out without the authorisation of the trade mark owner, but that a trade mark owner had a legitimate interest in being able to oppose the marketing of a product which had been poorly or untidily repackaged in a way which could damage the trade mark's reputation.[82] Moreover, the trade mark owner must be given advance notice of the repackaged product being put on sale. The owner could also require the importer to supply her/him with a specimen of the repackaged product before it went on sale, to enable him/her to check that the repackaging had not been carried out in such a way as directly or indirectly to affect the original condition of the product, and that the presentation after repackaging was not likely to damage the reputation of the trade mark. Similarly, such a requirement gave the trade mark owner a better chance of protecting himself against counterfeiting.[83] In *Boehringer Ingelheim KG and Others*[84] the referring court asked *inter alia* whether, if the intended repackaging did not in the particular case prejudice the specific subject-matter of the mark, notice was nevertheless necessary. The Court maintained that it was, and added that if the parallel importer did not satisfy the requirement of notice, the trade mark proprietor could oppose the marketing of the repackaged product. Moreover, it was incumbent on the parallel importer itself to give notice to the trade mark proprietor of the intended repackaging. It was not sufficient that the proprietor be notified by other sources, such as the authority which issues a parallel import licence to the importer. As regards the period of notice which should be given to the trade mark proprietor, it was appropriate to allow the latter a reasonable time to react to the intended packaging, regard being had to the parallel importer's interest in proceeding to market the pharmaceutical product as soon as possible after obtaining the necessary licence from the competent authority. While in the event of dispute it was for a national court to assess, in the light of all the relevant circumstances, whether the trade mark owner had a reasonable time to react to the intended repackaging, a period of 15 working days seemed likely to constitute such a reasonable time where the parallel importer had chosen to give notice to the trade mark owner by supplying it simultaneously with a sample of the repackaged pharmaceutical product.[85]

It will be recalled that in *Bristol-Meyers Squibb* the Court held that a trade mark owner could oppose the repackaging of the product in new external packaging where this was unnecessary because the importer could achieve packaging which could be marketed in the Member State of importation by, for example, affixing to the original

---

[82] *ibid.*, paras 72, 75 and 76.
[83] *ibid.*, para.78.
[84] Case C–143/00 [2002] E.C.R. I–3759
[85] *ibid.*, paras 61–67.

external or inner packaging new labels in the language of the Member State or importation. A related question arose in *Mercke, Sharp & Dohme GmbH*,[86] which was whether consumer resistance to overly stickered parallel imports could justify repackaging which would not otherwise be necessary. The Court held that strong consumer resistance could justify repackaging. Resistance to relabelled pharmaceutical products did not always constitute an impediment to market access such as to make replacement packaging necessary, within the meaning of the Court's case law. But there might exist on a market, or on a substantial part of it, such strong resistance from a significant proportion of consumers to relabelled pharmaceutical products that there must be held to be a hindrance to effective market access. In such circumstances, repackaging would not be an attempt to secure a commercial advantage, but simply to achieve effective market access. It would be for the national court to determine whether this was in fact the case.[87]

Whereas the judgments in *Hoffmann-La Roche* and *Bristol-Myers Squibb* concerned cases in which a parallel importer repackaged a trade-marked product and reaffixed the original trade mark thereon, *Centrafarm BV v American Home Products Corporation*,[88] concerned the case of a parallel importer replacing the original trade mark used by the proprietor in the Member State of export by the trade mark which the proprietor used in the Member State of import. In the latter case the Court held that prohibition by the proprietor of such unauthorised use of the mark by a third party would constitute a disguised restriction on trade between Member States within the meaning of the second sentence of Article 30 EC if it were established that the practice of using different trade marks for the same product had been adopted by the proprietor of those trade marks for the purpose of artificially partitioning the markets.[89] In *Pharmacia & Upjohn SA*[90] the Court of Justice considered the meaning of the latter expression, and concluded that the condition of artificial partitioning of the markets between Member States as defined by the Court in *Bristol-Myers Squibb* applied equally in a case where a parallel importer replaced the original trade mark by that used by the proprietor in the Member State of import.[91]

The Court's case law, not least the judgment in *Bristol-Meyers Squibb*, amounts to a code on re-packaging rivalling in detail the terms of any conceivable harmonising legislation on the subject-matter in question.

---

[86] Case C–443/99 [2002] E.C.R. I–3703.
[87] *ibid.*, paras 30–32. See also Case C–143/00 *Boehringer Ingelheim KG* [2002] E.C.R. I–3759, paras 51–53.
[88] Case 3/78 [1978] E.C.R. 1823.
[89] Paras 22, 23 of Judgment.
[90] Case C–379/97 *Pharmacia & Upjohn SA, formerly Upjohn SA, v Paranova A/S* [1999] E.C.R. I–6927.
[91] Para.40 of Judgment.

Common origin

A restriction on the exercise of trade mark rights derived from **16–060** Article 28 EC which represented something of a wrong turning by the Court of Justice was the common origin principle. According to this principle, when trade marks held by different persons in different Member States had a common origin, the sale in a Member State of goods lawfully bearing one of the national marks could not be prevented merely because another of the marks was protected by the law of that State. The source of the common origin principle was the judgment of the Court of Justice in *Van Zuylen v Hag (Hag I)*.[92] The case concerned trade marks for Hag decaffeinated coffee, one held by Hag AG in Germany, and the other held by a successor in title to a Belgian subsidiary of Hag AG in Luxembourg, the Belgian subsidiary having been sequestrated as enemy property at the end of the Second World War. The Court of Justice held that the Luxembourg holder of the Hag mark could not oppose imports bearing the German Hag mark, despite the fact that there were no longer any links whatsoever between the two companies. It was to be fifteen or so years before the Court reversed this decision, in *SA CNL-Sucal NV v Hag GF AG (Hag II)*.[93] The Court observed that trade mark rights constituted an essential element in the system of undistorted competition which the Treaty seeks to establish and maintain. Under that system, an undertaking must be in a position to keep its customers by virtue of the quality of its products and services, something which was possible only if there were distinctive marks which enabled customers to identify those products and services. For the trade mark to be able to fulfil such a role, it had to offer a guarantee that all goods bearing it had been produced under the control of a single undertaking which was accountable for their quality.[94] In the circumstances of the case in point, the Court noted that:

"From the date of expropriation and notwithstanding their common origin, each of the marks independently fulfilled its function, within its own territorial field of application, of guaranteeing that the marked products originated from one single source."[95]

It followed that each of the trade mark proprietors must be able to oppose the marketing, in the Member State in which the trade mark belonged to him/her, of goods originating from the other proprietor,

---

[92] Case 192/73 [1974] E.C.R. 731. The principle was foreshadowed in Case 40/70 *Sirena v Eda* [1971] E.C.R. 69. In that case, however, the reference was made and dealt with by the Court on the basis of the rules of competition.

[93] Case C–10/89 [1990] E.C.R. I–3711.

[94] *ibid.*, para.13 of judgment.

[95] *ibid.*, para.18.

in so far as they were similar products bearing an identical mark or one which is liable to lead to confusion.[96] Consistently with this approach, the Court described the principle of exhaustion of rights as regards trade marks as follows in *IHT Internationale Heiztechnik v Ideal Standard*:

> "That principle, known as the exhaustion of rights, applies where the owner of the trade mark in the importing State and the owner of the trade mark in the exporting State are the same or where, even if they are separate persons, they are economically linked. A number of situations are covered: products put into circulation by the same undertaking, by a licensee, by a parent company, by a subsidiary of the same group, or by an exclusive distributor."[97]

Free movement of goods and copyright and related rights

16–061   The phrase "industrial and commercial property" in Article 30 EC, while it clearly applies to patents and trade marks, is less apt as a description of artistic property.[98] Nevertheless, after some initial hesitation by the Court of Justice[99] it is now beyond doubt that copyright and other rights protecting literary and artistic work are covered.

A right akin to copyright was the subject of the proceedings in *Deutsche Grammophon v Metro*,[1] the earliest case in which the exhaustion of rights principle can be seen at work. Deutsche Grammophon (DG), the plaintiff in the national proceedings, supplied the records it manufactured to retailers in Germany under a retail price maintenance arrangement. It also exported records to France where they were marketed by its subsidiary, Polydor. Metro, the defendant, had succeeded in obtaining records originally sold in France by Polydor, which it then resold in Germany at prices well below the controlled price. DG sought to prevent these sales by invoking against Metro the exclusive right of distribution, akin to copyright, which manufacturers of sound recordings enjoy under German legislation. On a reference from the German court to which the case went on appeal, the Court of Justice held that:

> ". . . it would be in conflict with the provisions prescribing the free movement of products within the common market for a

---

[96] *ibid.*, para.19.

[97] Case C–9/93 [1994] E.C.R. I–2789, para.34.

[98] See the remarks by Advocate General Warner in his Opinion in Case 62/79 *Coditel v Ciné Vog Films* [1980] E.C.R. 881, pp.878–879.

[99] In the *Deutsche Grammophon* case, cited in the following note, the Court left open the question whether a record manufacturer's right analogous to copyright came within the scope of Art.30.

[1] Case 78/70 [1971] E.C.R. 487.

manufacturer of sound recordings to exercise the exclusive right to distribute the selected articles, conferred upon him by the legislation of a Member State, in such a way as to prohibit the sale in that State of products placed on the market by him or with his consent in another Member State solely because such distribution did not occur within the territory of the first Member State."[2]

The conclusion is clear but the steps by which it is reached are less so. The judgment contains the first mention of the limitation of the derogation in Article 30 EC to measures justified for the safeguarding of rights which constitute the specific subject-matter of a form of IP. However, the Court did not go on to define the specific subject-matter of a record manufacturer's exclusive right of distribution; nor did it rule that a right to oppose the sale of records marketed by a manufacturer or with his consent in another Member State could not be included in such subject-matter. It simply reasoned that the purpose of unifying the market could not be attained "if, under the various legal systems of the Member States, nationals of those States were able to partition the market and bring about arbitrary discrimination or disguised restrictions on trade between Member States."[3]

A decade later the principle of exhaustion was applied by the **16–062** Court in *Musik-Vertrieb Membran v GEMA*.[4] The case concerned the importation of records and cassettes into Germany from other Member States, one being the United Kingdom, where they had been manufactured and put on the market with the consent of the copyright owners. The copyright management society, GEMA, claimed that the importation was in breach of the owners' rights in Germany. However, it did not seek to exclude the recordings from the German market but only to recover a sum representing the difference between the royalties payable in Germany and those paid in respect of the initial distribution. It was held that such recovery was contrary to Articles 28 and 30 EC. The ground given by the Court for its ruling was that the exploitation of a copyright in a given market was a matter for the free choice of the owner. "He may," the Court said, "make that choice according to his best interests, which involve not only the level of remuneration provided in the Member State in question but other factors such as, for example, the opportunities for distributing his work and the marketing facilities which are further enhanced by virtue of the free movement of goods within the Community."[5] As a trader within the common market she/he must, in other words, abide by the consequences of his decisions.

---

[2] [1971] E.C.R. 487, 500.
[3] *ibid.*
[4] Joined Cases 55 and 57/80 [1981] E.C.R. 147.
[5] [1981] E.C.R. 147, 165.

GEMA has been distinguished in two subsequent cases. In *Warner Bros. v Christiansen*[6] the plaintiff in the national proceedings was the owner in the United Kingdom of the copyright in the film "Never Say Never Again." The defendant, who managed a video shop in Copenhagen, purchased a copy of the film in London with a view to hiring it out in Denmark and imported it into Denmark for that purpose. Under Danish law the hiring out of a video-cassette was subject to the consent of the author or producer, even after the video-cassette had been marketed, whereas under the law of the United Kingdom, the author had no right to control hiring out after the initial sale of the video-cassette. On a reference to the Court of Justice by a Danish court Warner Brothers claimed that reliance on Danish law to restrict the hiring out of the video-cassette was justified under Article 30 of the Treaty. The defendant Christiansen relied upon GEMA, arguing that if an author chose to market a video-cassette in a country where national rules afforded no right to limit hiring out, he must accept the consequences of this choice and the exhaustion of his right to restrain the hiring out of that video-cassette in any other Member State. The Court rejected this latter view, on the ground that it would render "worthless" the specific right to authorise hiring out if that right were exhausted by sale in a Member State which afforded no specific protection for that right.[7]

In *EMI Electrola v Patricia*[8] the plaintiff in the national proceedings was assignee of the production and distribution rights in Germany of the musical works of Cliff Richard. The defendant sold in Germany sound recordings originating in Denmark which incorporated some of Cliff Richard's works, and resisted the plaintiff's action for an injunction on the ground that the recordings had been lawfully marketed in Denmark after the expiry of the period during which exclusive rights were protected under Danish copyright law. The Court distinguished *GEMA* on the ground that the marketing in Denmark was due, not to an act or the consent of the copyright owner or his licensee, but to the expiry of the protection period under the law of that Member State.

16–063   Copyright and related forms of literary and artistic property[9] are complex forms of property, reflecting the diversity of the works to which they relate. *Deutsche Grammophon* and *GEMA* concerned the aspect of copyright which protects an owner's interest in the reproduction and sale of material objects incorporating creative work—sound recordings, in the cases in point. That kind of interest

---

[6] Case 158/86 [1988] E.C.R. 2605.
[7] *ibid.*, para.18.
[8] Case 34/87 [1989] E.C.R. 79.
[9] The Court has held that the protection of industrial and commercial property within the meaning of Art.30 EC includes literary and artistic property, see Case 262/81 *Coditel v Ciné Vog* [1982] E.C.R. 3381, and in *Warner Bros.*, n.36 above, the Court treated the rights in question as literary and artistic property, *ibid.*, para.13.

is adequately served by the control the copyright owner enjoys over the initial marketing of protected products. But literary and artistic works may be the subject of commercial exploitation by means other than the sale of the recordings made of them.[10] The release into circulation of a sound-recording cannot render lawful other forms of exploitation of the protected work, by such means as rental, and public performance, as the *Warner Bros.* case indicated.[11]

Council Directive 92/100[12] was enacted in order to establish harmonised legal protection in the Community for the rental and lending rights and certain rights related to copyright in the field of intellectual property. Article 1(1) of the Directive requires the Member States to provide a right to authorise or prohibit the rental and lending of originals and copies of copyright works, and other subject-matter. Pursuant to Article 1(4), those rights are not to be exhausted by any sale or other act of distribution. Under Article 2(1) the exclusive right to authorise or prohibit rental and lending is to belong to the author in respect of the original and copies of his/her work, to the performer in respect of fixations of her/his performance, to the phonogram producer in respect of his/her phonograms and to the producer of the first fixation of a film in respect of the original and copies of her/his film. Under Article 9 of the Directive, without prejudice to the specific provisions concerning the lending and rental right, and those of Article 1(4) in particular, the distribution right, which is the exclusive right to make any of the above-mentioned objects available to the public by sale or otherwise, is not to be exhausted except where the first sale in the Community of that object is made by the rightholder or with her/his consent.

In *Metronome Musik Gmbh v Musik Point Hokamp GmbH*[13] the Court of Justice considered whether the introduction of an exclusive rental right pursuant to Directive 92/100/EEC might infringe the principle of exhaustion of distribution rights in the event of the offering for sale, by the rightholder or with his/her consent, of copyright works. Referring to its previous case law,[14] the Court noted that "like the right to present a work by means of public performance . . . the rental right remains one of the prerogatives of the author and producer notwithstanding sale of the physical recording,"[15] and concluded:

> "Thus, the distinction drawn in the Directive between the effects of the specific rental and lending right, referred to in

---

[10] Case C–200/96 *Metronome Musik Gmbh v Musik Point Hokamp GmbH* [1998] E.C.R. I–1953, para.15.

[11] *ibid.*, para.18.

[12] [1992] O.J. L346/61.

[13] Case C–200/96 *Metronome Musik Gmbh v Musik Point Hokamp GmbH* [1998] E.C.R. I–1953.

[14] *viz.*, Joined Cases 55/80 and 57/80 *Musik Vertrieb Membran and K-tel International v GEMA* [1981] E.C.R. 147; Case 58/80 *Dansk Supermarked v Imerco* [1981] E.C.R. 181; Case 158/86 *Warner Brothers and Metronome Video v Christiansen* [1988] E.C.R. 2605.

[15] Case C–200/96, n.13, para.18.

Article 1, and those of the distribution right, governed by Article 9 and defined as an exclusive right to make one of the objects in question available to the public, principally by sale, is justified. The former is not exhausted by the sale or any other act of distribution of the object, whereas the latter may be exhausted, but only and specifically upon the first sale in the Community by the rightholder or with his consent.

The introduction by the Community legislation of an exclusive rental right cannot therefore constitute any breach of the principle of exhaustion of the distribution right, the purpose and scope of which are different."[16]

In *Foreningen af danske Videogramdistributúrer v Laserdisken*,[17] a Danish court asked the Court of Justice whether it was contrary to Article 30 EC or to Directive 92/100 for the holder of an exclusive rental right to prohibit copies of a film from being offered for rental in a Member State even where offering those copies for rental has been authorised within another Member State. In other words, did offering copies of a film for rental in one Member State exhaust the exclusive rental right as regards those copies of the film? The plaintiffs in the national proceedings, the governments submitting observations, and the Commission, argued that it followed from the Court's case law and the Directive that the right to authorise or prohibit the rental of a film is comparable to the right of public performance and, unlike the right of distribution, is not exhausted as soon as it has first been exercised.[18] The Court agreed, holding that just as a rental right remains one of the prerogatives of the author and producer notwithstanding sale of the physical recording, the same reasoning must be followed as regards the effect produced by the offer for rental. The exclusive right to hire out various copies of the work contained in a video film can, by its very nature, be exploited by repeated and potentially unlimited transactions, each of which involves the right to remuneration. "The specific right to authorise or prohibit rental would be rendered meaningless if it were held to be exhausted as soon as the object was first offered for rental."[19] The same result followed from Article 9 of Directive 92/100.[20]

Free movement of goods and other intellectual property forms

16–064   In *Keurcoop v Nancy Kean Gifts BV*[21] the Court of Justice considered the application of Article 30 EC to industrial designs. The case concerned the design of a ladies' handbag which had been

---

[16] Case C–200/96, n.13, paras 19, 20.
[17] Case C–61/97 [1998] E.C.R. I–5171.
[18] *ibid.*, para.11.
[19] *ibid.*, para.18.
[20] *ibid.*, paras 20, 21.
[21] Case 144/81 [1982] E.C.R. 2853.

registered under the Uniform Benelux Law on Designs by Nancy Kean Gifts BV. The registration had been effected without the consent of the American author of the design but this had no bearing on its validity in the Netherlands.[22] The reference to the Court was made in proceedings brought by Nancy Kean Gifts to prevent the sale on the Dutch market of handbags of the same design which had been imported by Keurcoop. It was held by the Court that industrial designs came within the protection afforded by Article 30 EC to "industrial and commercial property" since they had the aim of defining exclusive rights which was characteristic of such property. That protection enabled the owner of the right to a design in a Member State to prevent the sale of identical products imported from another Member State where they had been legally acquired by a third party—the situation described in the reference. However, the Court made it clear that the principle of the exhaustion of rights would apply if the products in question had been put on the market in the Member State of origin by or with the consent of the design owner in the Member State of importation or by a person legally or economically dependent on him.[23]

Analogous principles to those applicable to patents, trade marks, copyright and other artistic and literary property, and industrial designs, no doubt apply to other property rights falling within the term "industrial and commercial property" in Article 30 EC. Rules on the protection of indications of provenance and designations of origin comprise "industrial and commercial property" within the meaning if the latter Article, providing that the protected names have not become generic in the country of origin.[24] And the Court has referred to the specific subject-matter of a trade mark as being applicable by analogy as regards the protection of trade names.[25]

Further reading

Barnard, "Discrimination and Free Movement in EC Law" (1996) 45 I.C.L.Q. 82.

Barnard, "Fitting the remaining pieces into the goods and persons gigsaw" (2001) E.L.Rev. 35.

Killing, D.T. *Intellectual Property Rights in EU Law*, Volume I, Free movement and Competition Law (OUP, Oxford, 2004).

---

[22] One of the questions put by the referring court to the Court of Justice was whether a rule giving an exclusive right to the first person to register a design, irrespective of its authorship, was compatible with Art.30. The Court's response was that, in the absence of standardization or harmonization of laws on industrial designs, it was for national law to lay down the necessary conditions and procedures. See also Case 53/87 *CICRA v Maxicar* [1987] E.C.R. 6039.

[23] [1982] E.C.R. 2853, 2871.

[24] Case C–3/91 *Exportur SA v LOR SA and Confiserie du Tech SA.* [1992] E.C.R. I–5529 paras 37–39.

[25] Case C–255/97 *Pfeiffer Großhandel GmbH v Löwa Warenhandel GmbH* [1999] E.C.R. I–2835, para.22.

Koutrakos, "On Groceries, Alcohol and Olive Oil: More on the Free Movement of Goods after *Keck*" (2001) 26 E.L.Rev. 391.

Maduro, Poiares. "The Saga of Article 30 EC Treaty: To Be Continued" (1998) 5 M.J. 298.

Maduro, Poiares. *We, the Court* (Hart Publishing, Oxford, 1998).

Weatherill, "After *Keck*: some thoughts on how to clarify the clarification" (1996) C.M.L.Rev. 885.

White, "In Search of the Limits to Article 30 of the EEC Treaty" (1989) 26 C.M.L.Rev. 235.

CHAPTER 17

UNION CITIZENSHIP AND THE RIGHTS TO MOVE AND RESIDE IN THE UNION

Guide to this Chapter: The original EEC Treaty granted a right **17–001** to reside in other Member States, together with a right to equal treatment with host-State nationals, only to those nationals of the Member States who migrated in order to pursue an economic activity. Thus non-economically active migrants were not protected by Community law. With time, however, this changed. Firstly, three residence directives were adopted which granted a conditional right of residence to those who had sufficient means to support themselves, including students and pensioners. Secondly, and more importantly, the Maastricht Treaty introduced the notion of Union citizenship; according to Article 18 EC Union citizens have a right to move and reside freely within the territory of any of the Member States subject to the limitations and conditions contained in the EC Treaty and secondary legislation. The European Court of Justice then defined Union citizenship as the "fundamental status" of Union citizens.

As a result of these legislative changes, Union citizens previously excluded from the scope of Community law have gained directly enforceable rights, including a (still) conditional right of residence and a limited right to equal treatment. Furthermore, Council and Parliament recently adopted a new Directive (2004/38) detailing the right of Union citizens, previously contained in several sectorial pieces of secondary legislation. In this chapter we will consider the evolution of the case law on Union citizenship, to then turn to the regime established by the new

Union citizenship Directive. This analysis focuses on the Union citizens' rights of residence and equal treatment. We will then conclude with a brief assessment of the other rights that Union citizens derive from the Treaty.

THE ROAD TO CITIZENSHIP

17–002   Economic migrants, i.e. those who move to another Member State to there exercise an economic activity as an employed or self-employed person, or to receive a service, have always had the right to enter and reside in that Member State. This right derives directly from the Treaty, and is only detailed in secondary legislation.[1] Furthermore, economically active migrants have always enjoyed the right to equal treatment in respect of most benefits.

On the other hand, non-economic migrants, i.e. those who moved for reasons not related to an economic activity, originally did not derive rights from the EEC Treaty. In other words, those who were not economically active, such as pensioners and students, did not have a right to go and reside in other Member States bestowed by the Treaty, and would be thus subject to the national migratory regime. However, in 1990 three residency directives were adopted[2]: those conferred a conditional right of residence to pensioners, students and other non-economic migrants. The right of residence was conditional upon two criteria: first of all, the non-economic migrant needed to have comprehensive medical insurance; secondly, he/she needed to have sufficient resources so as not to become a burden on the social security system of the host Member State.[3] If

---

[1] Then Directive 68/360 on the abolition of restrictions on movement and residence within the Community for workers of Member States and their families [1968(I)] O.J. Spec. Ed.485; Directive 73/148 on the abolition of restrictions on movement and residence within the Community for nationals of Member States with regard to establishment and the provision of services, [1973] O.J. L172/14; both directives have now been repealed by, and subsumed in, Directive 2004/38 on the right of citizens of the Union and their family members to move and reside freely within the territory of the Member States amending Regulation (EEC) 1612/68 and repealing Directives 64/221, 68/360, 72/194, 73/148, 75/34, 75/35, 90/364, 90/365 and 93/96, [2004] O.J. L229/35, hereinafter Directive 2004/38.

[2] Directive 90/364 on a general right to residence [1990] O.J. L180/26 (hereinafter Directive 90/364); Directive 90/365 on retired persons [1990] O.J. L180/28 (hereinafter Directive 90/365); Directive 93/96 on students [1993] O.J. L317/59 (hereinafter Directive 93/96). The Court had already held that students may derive residency rights directly from Art. 12 EC, e.g. Case C–357/89 *Raulin* [1992] E.C.R. I–1027. The students' directive was first adopted in 1990 together with the other directives, but it had to be re-adopted in 1993 following a successful challenge to its legal basis.

[3] Directives 90/365 and 90/364: the claimant must have sufficient resources to avoid becoming a burden on the state's social assistance. Directive 93/96: the student need only assure the national authorities that he/she has sufficient resources to avoid becoming a burden on the state.

those two conditions were fulfilled, the migrant would have a right to reside in any of the Member States bestowed by Community secondary legislation. In 1992, with the Maastricht Treaty, Union citizenship was created and a provision referring to a general right to move and reside everywhere in the Community was introduced. Thus, Article 18 EC (then Article 8a) provides that:

> "Every citizen of the Union shall have the right to move and reside freely within the territory of the Member States, subject to the limitations and conditions laid down in the Treaty and the measures adopted to give it effect."

In the aftermath of the Maastricht Treaty, it was unclear whether Article 18 EC was capable of having direct effect, i.e. whether it could be relied upon in order to establish a right of residence independent from that provided for by another Treaty provision or by secondary legislation. The Court eventually decided that Article 18 EC bestowed on Union citizens a directly effective right, even though subject to some "limitations and conditions".

The introduction of Union citizenship, together with the evolution of the Court's case law, rendered the secondary legislation on free movement of both economic and non-economic citizens rather outdated. Moreover, the fact that a Union citizen should negotiate his/her way through a plurality of different legal instruments to understand her/his rights was considered highly unsatisfactory. For this reason, in April 2004 a new residence directive was adopted: this repeals most of the relevant secondary legislation, so as to provide a single and coherent framework detailing Union citizens' rights of residence in Member States other than that of their nationality; and it codifies some of the recent case law.

In this chapter we are going to look at the evolution of the case law on citizenship, to then consider in detail the new residency directive, and the other rights pertaining to Union citizens (e.g. to vote in local and European elections). The rights which are particular to economic migrants will then be analysed in detail in the chapters on free movement of workers, the right to establishment and the freedom to provide services.

The evolution of the Court's case law on Union citizenship

We have said above that before the adoption of the three **17–003** residency directives only economically active migrants derived rights from Community law.[4] Those who were not engaged in an economic

---

[4] Including workseekers; see para.18–012, Ch.18 below; as we shall see further below the rights of economically active migrants also include the right to have their family with them. As a result also some of the family members of the migrant (i.e. spouse and children) acquire rights in Community law.

activity, however generously construed this notion was, would be subject to ordinary national migration policies. The three residency directives provided for a Community right of residence in any of the Member States for students, retired people, and those who could afford it. However, this right of residence was conditional upon the fulfilment of two criteria: comprehensive medical insurance; and sufficient resources so as not to become a burden on the host welfare system. Those two conditions were included to ensure that the right to reside in any of the Member States would not give rise to so called "welfare tourism", i.e. movement undertaken for the sole purpose of exploiting a more generous welfare system of another Member State.[5] By making the right to reside conditional, the Member States would protect their welfare provision: on the one hand, medical care would not be a problem since the non-active migrant would in any event have medical insurance; on the other hand, the fact that the migrant needed to have "sufficient resources" would disqualify him/her from means-tested benefits. Migration of non-economically active people would therefore come at no expense for the host State's public purse. This framework however came under attack, and very much under strain, after the introduction of Union citizenship. As said above Union citizenship was established in 1992, with the Maastricht Treaty.

Article 17 EC, which established Union citizenship, provides that "every person holding the nationality of a Member State shall be a citizen of the Union". Article 18 EC provides that all Union citizens have the right to move and reside freely within any of the Member States, subject to the limitations and conditions contained in the Treaty and in secondary legislation. Furthermore, Article 12 EC provides that within the scope of the EC Treaty, "and without any prejudice to any special provisions contained therein, any discrimination on grounds of nationality shall be prohibited". The main question for the Court was then whether Article 18 EC granted a right to reside independently from the three residency directives; and whether, as a result of the combined effect of Articles 18 and 12 EC, any Union citizen had the right to be treated equally, especially in relation to welfare provision.

In the case of *Sala*,[6] a Spanish citizen living in Germany was denied a child raising allowance on the grounds that she was not a German national, and she did not have a residence permit. It was not entirely clear whether Mrs Sala, who had been previously employed, could be considered as a worker and thus be entitled to

---

[5] On the impact of EU law on national welfare systems, see generally Dougan and Spaventa (eds), *Social Welfare and EU law* (Hart Publishing, Oxford, 2005); De Búrca, *EU Law and the Welfare State* (OUP, Oxford, 2005).
[6] Case C–85/96 *M. M. Martínez Sala v Freistaat Bayern* [1998] E.C.R. I–2691.

equal treatment in respect of social advantages pursuant to Regulation 1612/68,[7] and family benefits pursuant to Regulation 1408/71.[8] The Court relied partially on the citizenship provisions in order to find that Mrs Sala was protected by the principle of non-discrimination in respect of the allowance, even were she not to be considered a worker. However, the Court preferred not to address the issue of the direct effect of Article 18 EC, rather relying on the fact that Mrs Sala was in any case lawfully resident in Germany under national law (albeit without a residence permit). Since Germany had granted her residency rights, it could not exclude her from the principle of equal treatment. As a result of the ruling in *Sala* then, once a Union citizen is lawfully resident (even independently from Community law) in one of the Member States she/he can rely on the principle of equal treatment to claim welfare benefits.[9] However, following *Sala*, it was unclear exactly which rights were conferred by Union citizenship.[10] In particular it was not clear whether a Union citizen could derive a right to reside directly from Article 18 EC; whether a Union citizen could rely on the non-discrimination obligation when he/she was residing in the host-State by virtue of one of the three residency directives; and, if yes, how far the principle of non-discrimination would stretch. Thus, the key issue was, and is, how far can a Union citizen rely on her/his rights under Article 18 EC in order to demand welfare provision from the host-Member State. Those issues were clarified in subsequent case law.

In *Grzelczyk*,[11] a French citizen who was studying in Belgium **17–004** applied, during the last year of his studies, for the *minimex*, a non-contributory benefit reserved to own nationals and other Member States' citizens covered by Regulation 1612/68.[12] As a student, Mr Grzelczyk derived his right of residence from Directive 93/96, which provides that those enrolled in a recognised educational establishment have a right to reside in the host-State provided they have sufficient resources and comprehensive health insurance. He had supported himself throughout his studies by taking up some jobs, but in his last year he needed economic support because he could not

---

[7] Reg.1612/68 on freedom of movement for workers within the Community [1968(I)] O.J. Eng. Spec. Ed. 475, hereinafter Reg.1612/68.

[8] Reg.1408/71 on the application of social security schemes to employed persons, to self-employed persons and to members of their families, as amended, Consolidated text in Annex A Reg.118/97 [1997] O.J. L28/1; the Regulation will soon be replaced by Reg.883/2004 on the co-ordination of social security systems [2004] O.J. L166/1.

[9] See also Case C–135/99 *Elsen* [2000] E.C.R. I–10409;

[10] *cf.* also Case C–274/96 *Bickel and Franz* [1998] E.C.R. I–7637; Case C–378/97 *Wijsenbeek* [1999] E.C.R. I–6207.

[11] Case C–184/99 *R Grzelczyk v Centre public d'aide social d'Ottignies-Louvain-la-Neuve* [2001] E.C.R. I–6193.

[12] This was consistent with a previous ruling of the Court, Case 197/86 *S. M. Brown v Secretary of State for Scotland* [1988] E.C.R. 3205.

work due to the demands of his course. He therefore applied for the minimex, which would have been available to him had he been a Belgian national. However, since he was a French national he was not entitled to the benefit: the issue was clearly one of discrimination on grounds of nationality and the problem was whether Mr Grzelczyk fell or not within the scope of the Treaty by virtue of the citizenship provisions. Only if he fell within the scope of the Treaty, would he be able to rely on the general prohibition of discrimination on grounds of nationality contained in Article 12 EC. The Court held that since he was a lawfully resident Union citizen he fell within the scope of the Treaty and was therefore protected by the prohibition of non-discrimination on grounds of nationality. It stated:

> "Union citizenship is destined to be the *fundamental status* of nationals of the Member States, enabling those who find themselves in the same situation to enjoy the same treatment in law irrespective of their nationality, subject to such exceptions as are expressly provided for."[13]

The Court then acknowledged that the right to move and reside granted by Article 18 EC was subject to the limitations and conditions contained in the Treaty and in secondary legislation, and especially in the residency directives. Thus, Member States could legitimately require students to fulfil the conditions contained in Directive 93/96, i.e. availability of sufficient resources not to become an unreasonable burden on the welfare system of the host State and comprehensive health insurance. However, this did not mean that the Member State could refuse a welfare benefit to the Union citizen: the only thing that the host State could do was to consider whether, because of a change in circumstances, the Union citizen was no longer fulfilling the conditions provided for in the Directive and thus either withdraw the residence permit or refuse to renew it. But in no event could such action be taken automatically, without taking into consideration the citizen's individual circumstances.

The ruling in *Grzelczyk* confirmed that Union citizens who have moved in another country fall within the scope *rationae personae* of the Treaty, and thus, provided they also fall within the scope *rationae materiae* of the Treaty, they can rely on Article 12 EC to claim equal treatment also in relation to welfare benefits. However, *Grzelczyk* also clarified the scope of the *Sala* ruling: the rights conferred by Article 18 EC can be limited if the citizen becomes an "unreasonable" burden. This was further elaborated in *D'Hoop*,[14] where the issue was whether a Union citizen could rely on Article 18 and 12

---

[13] Case C–184/99 *R. Grzelczyk v Centre public d'aide social d'Ottignies-Louvain-la-Neuve* [2001] E.C.R. I–6193, para.31, emphasis added.
[14] Case C–224/98 *D'Hoop* [2002] E.C.R. I–6191.

EC in order to obtain a tide-over allowance for young people seeking their first employment. One of the conditions to be satisfied in order to be eligible was to have received secondary education in Belgium.[15] Ms D'Hoop was a Belgian national who, having received her secondary education in France, failed to fulfil that condition, even though she had received her university education in Belgium. The Court, consistently with *Grzelczyk*, found that movement together with citizenship is enough to bring oneself within the scope *rationae materiae* and *personae* of the Treaty. Ms D'Hoop fell within the scope of the Treaty because she had moved first to France and then back to Belgium.

The rule was clearly putting those who move, and therefore **17–005** exercise their Treaty rights, at a disadvantage since if Ms D'Hoop had stayed in Belgium for her secondary education, she would have now been eligible for the benefit. The Court held that a difference in treatment between those who have exercised their free movement rights and those who have not, can be accepted only insofar as it is based on objective reasons and it is proportionate to the legitimate aim of the national rules. In the case at issue, the purpose of the restriction was to ensure that there was a *real link* between the applicant and the geographic employment market concerned. However, the rules at issue went beyond what was necessary to ensure this link, since the fact that a person completed her secondary education abroad was not in itself representative of the connection between applicant and geographical labour market.

In the cases examined above, the Court linked Union citizenship rights to lawful residency, to find that once a Union citizen was lawfully resident in the host State, she/he could rely on the principle of non-discrimination to claim welfare benefits (subject to the possibility for the Member States to rely on imperative grounds of public interest to justify discrimination). In *Baumbast*,[16] the Court found that Article 18 EC granted a directly effective (albeit conditional) right to reside in any of the Member States. Here, Mr Baumbast, a German national living in the UK, was denied renewal of his residency permit on the grounds that he did not fulfil the conditions set out in Directive 90/364, which make the right to reside in another Member State conditional upon having sufficient resources and comprehensive health insurance. Although Mr Baumbast had sufficient resources and health insurance in Germany, where he and his family would go to receive health treatment, he did not have insurance for emergency treatment in the UK and thus was not insured for *all* health risks as required by Directive 90/364. The issue was then whether Article 18 EC grants a free standing right to

---

[15] Exception given for children of migrant workers.
[16] Case C–413/99 *Baumbast and R v Secretary of State for the Home Department* [2002] E.C.R. I–7091.

residency even when the situation does not fall within the scope of one of the three residency directives.[17] Further, the Court had to consider what weight should be given to the specification contained in Article 18 EC that the right to move and reside is subject to the limitations contained in the Treaty and by the measures adopted to give it effect. The Court stated that Article 18 EC had conferred "on every citizen the right to move and reside freely within the territory of the Member States".[18] This right is subject to the limitations contained in secondary legislation, i.e. sufficient resources and comprehensive health insurance so as not to become a burden on the host welfare system. However, the Court also found that these limitations and conditions had to be applied consistently with the general principles of Community law and in particular with the principle of proportionality. Not to allow Mr Baumbast to reside in the UK only because he was not covered by emergency treatment insurance would be a disproportionate interference with the substance of the right of residence which he derived directly from the Treaty.

Following these recent developments, the situation for economically inactive people seems to be as follows.[19] First of all, Union citizens who lawfully reside in another Member State are entitled to equal treatment in respect of all benefits. However, excessive reliance on this right might be grounds for the host Member State to terminate the right to residency itself, subject however to the general principles of Community law, and in particular to the principle of proportionality.[20] Secondly, Member States are not prevented from introducing criteria which, whilst distinguishing between Union citizens, are objectively justified and proportionate to the legitimate aim the rules pursue. Thus, the ruling in *D'Hoop* suggests that the Member States might be entitled to make some benefits conditional to a link between the claimant and the territory.[21] Thirdly, Union citizens now derive their right to residency (and movement) directly from Article 18 EC, before having derived it from secondary legislation. That right to residency might be subject to conditions as contained in secondary legislation, and especially the sufficient resources and comprehensive health insurance requirements. Thus, in principle, Union citizenship does not entitle the individual to become an "unreasonable" burden on the welfare system of the

---

[17] Dir.90/364; Dir.90/365; Dir.93/96.
[18] Case C–413/99 *Baumbast and R v Secretary of State for the Home Department* [2002] E.C.R. I–7091, para.81.
[19] These issues have been thoroughly examined in M. Dougan and E. Spaventa "Educating Rudy and the (non-)English patient: A double-bill on residency rights under Article 18 EC" (2003) 28 E.L.Rev. 699, and the conclusions in the text draw from that analysis.
[20] *cf.* Case C–456/02 *Trojani* [2004] E.C.R. I–7574.
[21] See also Case C–138/02 *Collins* [2004] E.C.R. I–2703; Case C–209/03 *Bidar* [2005] E.C.R. I–2119; Case C–258/04 *Ioannidis* [2005] E.C.R. I–8275.

host-State. However, what is to be considered "unreasonable", will very much depend on the case at issue, and in any event the Member States have to comply with the principle of proportionality, and arguably also with fundamental rights as general principles of Community law.

The introduction of Union citizenship has therefore changed the European Union landscape: whilst at the outset only those who actively contributed to the host-society by engaging in an economic activity as either employed or self-employed derived rights from the Treaty, following the introduction of citizenship, economically inactive citizens derive a right to move and to participate in, and benefit from, at least to a certain extent, the host welfare society. In this way, the Union becomes much more than an economic enterprise: without calling into question the strongest bond arising from national citizenship, Union citizenship creates a link between European citizens quite independently from their economic contribution. Thus, even though the Union citizen is not necessarily entitled to claim full solidarity from her/his fellow citizens, she/he can expect some solidarity, in the form of welfare provision, should the need arise. Whilst most of the Member States initially resisted the turn that the case law was taking, they eventually agreed to codify much of it in the new residence directive, which replaces the previous residence directives, together with other secondary legislation. We shall now look in detail at the rights which the new directive confers upon citizens. The reader should in any event remember that most of those rights remain conferred directly by the Treaty.

THE RESIDENCE DIRECTIVE

In May 2001 the Commission proposed a Directive on the "right **17–006** of citizens of the Union and their family members to move and reside freely" within the Union. The basic concept underlying the Commission's proposal was that "Union citizens should, (. . .), be able to move between Member States on similar terms as nationals of a Member State moving around or changing their place of residence or job in their own country. Any additional administrative or legal obligations should be kept to the bare minimum required by the fact that the person in question is a non-national."[22] To this effect, the proposed directive sought to replace the plethora of

---

[22] Proposal for a European Parliament and Council Directive on the right of citizens of their Union and their family members to move and reside freely within the territory of the Member States, COM (2001) 257 final, [2001] O.J. C270 E 23/150, para.13 of the explanatory memorandum.

existing legislation with one single document, as well as to enhance the rights to move and reside of Union citizens and their families.

In this respect, the original proposal was more ambitious than the text which was eventually approved. Thus, the Commission had proposed a six months' time of unconditional temporary residence for all Union citizens and their family members (so that even economically inactive citizens would have a right to reside regardless of resources and health insurance), as well as the right to permanent residency (i.e. the right to stay in the host country unconditionally) after four years for all Union citizens and their families. The Commission also broadened the definition of family member to include unmarried partners when the legislation of the host State treats unmarried couples in a similar way to married ones. This represented a positive step forward in recognising, at least to a limited extent, the right to family life of those who do not want or cannot enter into marriage, and especially of same sex couples. It also removed the oddity in the case law, where the Court defined the right to have a partner reside with the migrant worker as a "social advantage" and therefore covered by the principle of non-discrimination.[23]

The European Parliament went further, and sought to include in the scope of the directive registered partners and unmarried partners in a durable relationship irrespective of their sex, provided that *either* the home *or* the host State recognised their rights in a corresponding manner to married couples.[24] In this way, the Union citizen would have been able to be accompanied by his/her unmarried partner even if the host State did not recognise rights corresponding to those of married couples to partnerships. However, the Council successfully watered down the proposal: thus, as we shall see, Directive 2004/38 grants an unconditional right to reside for three months only, a right to permanent residence after five rather than four years, and adopts a definition of family member narrower than both the one proposed by the European Parliament and that proposed by the Commission.

The personal scope of the Directive

Union Citizens

17–007   The Directive governs the *exercise* of the right to move and reside within the territory of the Member States by the Union citizens and their family members. As said above, the Directive is not constitutive of such rights, since those are bestowed on Union citizens directly by

---

[23] Case 59/85 *Reed* [1986] E.C.R. 1283.
[24] European Parliament Report A5–0009/2003, final.

the Treaty. This means that the Court is not prevented from taking a more generous view as to citizens' rights than those contained in the Directive.

A Union citizen is any person having the nationality of one of the Member States since, as provided by the Treaty, Union citizenship complements rather than replaces national citizenship. It is exclusively for the Member State to decide the conditions upon which nationality is granted, and the other Member States cannot interfere with that decision. Thus, for instance, in *Chen*,[25] a baby was born in Northern Ireland from Chinese parents who had gone to Northern Ireland with the sole intention of gaining Irish nationality for their baby. Apart from having been born there, neither the baby nor her family had any connection to the United Kingdom or to the Republic of Ireland. However, the Republic of Ireland granted Irish nationality to anyone born in the Irish island, including those born in Northern Ireland. Ms Chen therefore acquired Irish citizenship without ever having set foot in the Republic. She then moved to Wales arguing that she (as well as her mother as her primary carer), had a right to reside there because she was a Union citizen. The Court accepted the contention and stated that it was immaterial that Ms Chen had never been in the Republic of Ireland. Since she held the nationality of one of the Member States, she was a Union citizen and as such was protected by the Treaty when residing in a Member State other than that of her nationality. On the other hand, in the case in which a Member State refuses to grant full rights to its nationals, Union citizenship is of no help. Thus, in *Kaur*, Ms Kaur was a British national who had no right to reside in the United Kingdom since she was born in Kenya and gained British nationality as a result of the post-colonial settlement. Ms Kaur attempted to rely on Community law to obtain a right to reside in the United Kingdom. The Court held that it was for the United Kingdom to decide the conditions under which its nationals gained the right to reside in the United Kingdom. Since the UK had made a declaration to the effect that *only* British nationals with full rights to reside were to be considered as Union citizens, the situation fell outside the scope of Community law.[26]

Family members

The Union citizen's willingness to move to another Member State **17–008** would be greatly reduced if she/he had to leave his/her family behind. For this reason, from the very early stage of Community integration, Regulation 1612/68 provided that the worker's spouse

---

[25] Case C–200/02 *Chen* [2004] E.C.R. I–9925; see also Case C–369/90 *Micheletti* [1992] E.C.R. I–4239.
[26] Case C–192/99 *Kaur* [2001] E.C.R. I–1237.

and descendants (i.e. offspring) under the age of 21 or dependent upon the worker, together with the dependent relatives on the ascending line (i.e. the workers' and the workers' spouse parents/ grandparents) had a right to install themselves in the host-Member State with the worker, regardless of their nationality (i.e. even if they were third country nationals).[27] Moreover, Member States had to facilitate the admission of any other family member dependent on the worker, or living with her/him in the country whence he or she came. The worker's spouse and the worker's children had also a right to work and the children had a right to be educated under the same conditions as nationals of the host State. Directive 73/148 provided for almost identical rights for the family members of self-employed (i.e. service providers and those taking advantage of the freedom of establishment).[28] The European Court of Justice interpreted those rights generously; in *Singh*, a British national decided to return to the UK after having spent a period working as a self-employed in Germany.[29] She was married to a third country national, Mr Singh, who was treated for immigration purposes as the spouse of a UK national, rather than as the spouse of a Community (economic) migrant. As the latter regime would have been much more favourable to Mr Singh, he argued that he should be covered by Directive 73/148 and thus have a right to reside granted by Community law. The Court extended the scope of Article 43 EC and Directive 73/148 to embrace also spouses of own citizens returning in their country of origin after having exercised their right to (economic) free movement.

Article 2 of the new residence Directive adds to those which were already listed in the above mentioned secondary legislation, the "partner with whom the Union citizen has contracted a *registered* partnership" if the legislation of the host-State treats registered partnership as *"equivalent"* to marriages and in accordance with the host-State's legislation. Thus, the rights granted to non-married couples are not as extensive as the European Parliament had proposed, since only "registered" partnerships produce rights, and only if the host-State treats those partnerships as equivalent to marriages. It is likely that the assessment of equivalence will give rise to some questions of interpretation, since treatment of registered partnerships, whilst often similar to that of marriages, is seldom identical. In many respects this limitation on the rights of non-married couples is disappointing, especially having regard to emerging case law of the European Court of Human Rights which is more

---

[27] Reg.1612/68 on freedom of movement for workers within the Community [1968] O.J. Spec. Ed. L257/2, 475.

[28] Council Dir.73/148 on the abolition of restrictions on movement and residence within the Community for nationals of Member States with regard to establishment and the provision of services [1973] O.J. L172/14.

[29] Case C–370/90 *Singh* [1992] E.C.R. I–4265.

and more critical of discrimination on grounds of sexual orientation.[30] This said, Article 3 extends the duty of the Member States to facilitate the entry and residence of dependent family members also to the partner with whom the Union citizen has a durable relationship duly attested. Moreover, the directive also provides for the duty of the Member State to facilitate entrance and residence of a Union citizen's family member that, even though not dependent, requires, for serious health grounds, the personal care of the Union citizen. The obligation to "facilitate" admission is also more stringent than was previously the case: the Member State shall take into account the personal circumstances of the applicant and shall justify any denial of entry and residence of non protected family members. Thus, it is clear that in the drafters' view denial of the right to entry and reside should be the exception rather than the rule.

The material scope of the Directive

Right to exit and right to enter

Article 4 provides that Union citizens have a right to leave the **17–009** territory of a Member State on production of a valid identity card or passport; and their family members who are not Union nationals have a right to leave on production of a valid passport. No additional formality can be imposed. Similarly, an identity card or valid passport is all that a Union citizen needs to enter the territory of any of the Member States (Article 5). A third country national family member might be required to have an entry visa according to the provisions of Community or national law.[31] An entry visa shall not be required if the third country national family member has a residence card, i.e. a document attesting the family member's right to establish him/herself in one of the Member States with the Union citizen. An important innovation is contained in Article 5(4) which, codifying the case law,[32] provides that if a Union citizen or his/her family member lack the necessary travel documents or the necessary visa, the Member State has to give them any opportunity to prove identity and/or family ties before turning them back.[33] In practice then,

---

[30] *cf.* the minority opinion of Mr Turco and Mr Capato (M.E.P.s) in the European Parliament Recommendation for the Council's Second Reading, A5–0090/2004, Final.

[31] *cf.* for the Schengen zone Reg.539/2001 listing the third countries whose nationals must be in possession of visas when crossing the external border and those whose nationals are exempt from such requirement [2001] L81/1, as amended by Reg.851/2005 [2005] O.J. L141/3.

[32] Case C–459/99 *MRAX* [2002] E.C.R. I–6591.

[33] Similarly, Member States cannot make recognition of the right of residence for a Union citizen conditional upon the Union citizen producing an identity card or a passport when the Union citizen can prove his/her identity unequivocally by other means, see Case C–215/03 *Oulane* [2005] E.C.R. I–1215.

Union citizens and their family members cannot be turned back at the frontier, but for reasons of public policy/security/health (see below).[34] Once in the territory of the Member State, Union citizens and their family members might be asked to report their presence to the authorities within a reasonable and non-discriminatory period of time, and Member States might impose sanctions for failure to do so.[35] As always in relation to sanctions for behaviour in any way linked to the exercise of a Treaty right, the sanction must be proportionate and non-discriminatory.

Right of temporary residence

17–010   Article 6 of Directive 2004/38 provides for an unconditional right of residence for *all* Union citizens for up to three months. Prior to the Directive, the right to reside even on a temporary basis was conditional upon exercising an economic activity, looking for a job, or satisfying the sufficient resources/health insurance requirement. De facto, however, such a right was easily gained by any Union citizen by relying on Article 49 EC, and argue that she/he was a recipient of services in the host-Member State. This was the case, for instance, for tourists, but also for those who were just passing through a country since they would always receive services of some sort (hotels, restaurants, etc.).

Following the adoption of Directive 2004/38, however, such right is codified and cannot be made subject to any condition other than the requirement to hold a valid identity card or passport; furthermore, the right to temporary residence is granted also to the Union citizen's family. Both Union citizens and their families temporarily resident in a Member State other than that of the Union citizen's nationality enjoy a right to equal treatment with the nationals of the host-Member State. The Commission had originally proposed that the right to equal treatment should be absolute.[36] However, the Council, concerned about the possibility of welfare tourism, modified the Commission's proposal, and Article 24(2) of the Directive now provides that the host-State is not obliged to confer entitlement to social assistance to those who are residing only temporarily in their territory pursuant to Article 6. Furthermore, according to Article 14(1), the right of temporary residence pursuant to Article 6

---

[34] *cf.* Case C–503/03 *Commission v Spain* (Schengen Information System), (Judgment of January 31, 2006, forthcoming).

[35] See e.g. Case 118/75 *Eatson and Belmann* [1976] E.C.R. 1185; Case C–265/88 *Messner* [1989] E.C.R. I–4209.

[36] Proposal for a European Parliament and Council Directive on the right of citizens of their Union and their family members to move and reside freely within the territory of the Member States, COM (2001) 257 final, [2001] O.J. C270/150, Art.21. The original proposal also provided for the right of temporary residence to be for up to 6 rather than 3 months (Art.6).

is retained only as long as the Union citizen and her/his family members do not become an unreasonable burden on the social assistance of the host Member State. This means that even if the host-State confers some social assistance to temporary residents, it is open to such State to terminate temporary residence should the Union migrant rely excessively on social assistance.

Right of residence for more than three months

If the right to residence for up to three months is unconditional, **17–011** Article 7 provides that the right to reside in another Member State for more than three months is conditional upon satisfaction of listed requirements. Those, roughly speaking, reflect the requirements contained in pre-existing legislation, or elaborated by the Court of Justice.

Article 7(1) provides that:

"1. All Union citizens shall have the right of residence on the territory of another Member State for a period longer than three months if they:

(a) are workers or self-employed persons in the host Member State; or

(b) have sufficient resources for themselves and their family members not to become a burden on the social assistance system of the host Member State during their period of residence and have comprehensive sickness insurance cover in the host Member State; or

(c) — are enrolled at a private or public establishment, accredited or financed by the host Member State on the basis of its legislation or administrative practice, for the principle purpose of following a course of study, including vocational training; and
— have comprehensive sickness insurance cover in the host Member State and assure the relevant national authority, by means of a declaration or by such equivalent means as they may choose, that they have sufficient resources for themselves and their family members not to become a burden on the social assistance system of the host Member State during their period of residence; or

(d) are family members accompanying or joining a Union citizen who satisfies the conditions referred to in points (a), (b) or (c)."

The second paragraph of Article 7 provides that the right of residence for family members extends also to those members of the family who are not nationals of a Member State. Article 7(3), provides that in certain circumstances the status of worker/self-employed (with all the advantages deriving from such status) is retained even if the Union citizen is no longer exercising an economic activity. We shall now look more closely at the conditions required for each of the different categories of Union citizens.

Economically active citizens

17–012   As we shall see in more detail in the following chapters, economically active citizens derive extensive rights from the Treaty. In particular, once a Union citizen is engaged in an economic activity either as an employed or a self-employed person, she/he has, upon production of evidence as to their economic activity,[37] a right to reside in the host Member State, provided only that the economic activity is genuine and not on such a small scale so as to be marginal and ancillary. Economically active citizens enjoy a right to be treated equally with own nationals in relation to almost all welfare benefits; furthermore, they retain their status in certain circumstances even once they have ceased their economic activity. Article 7(3) provides that the status as economically active citizen is retained when the Union migrant is (i) unable to work because of illness or an accident; (ii) he/she is in recorded involuntary unemployment after having been employed for more than one year and has registered as a job-seeker with the relevant employment office; (iii) he/she is recorded in involuntary unemployment after having been employed (in a fix-term or indefinite-term capacity) for less than one year and has registered as a work-seeker[38]; in this case the status of worker is retained for at least six months; or (iv) when she/he has embarked on vocational training related to the previous employment; if the worker is involuntarily unemployed the training can be in any area. The possibility to retain the status of economically active is important because it means that the Union citizen can continue to reside in the host Member State without having to satisfy any other condition; and that she/he is entitled to welfare provision. We shall look at those issues in more detail in the chapters dealing with economically active citizens.

Furthermore, and as we shall see more in detail in Chapter 18, Union citizens who move to look for a job in another Member State are also protected by Article 39 EC and by Directive 2004/38. They can stay beyond the initial three months without having to satisfy any additional requirement (i.e. sufficient resources/health insurance) provided that they can demonstrate that they are continuing to seek employment and have a "genuine chance" of being engaged (Article

---

[37] In the case of workers, this takes the form of a confirmation of engagement from the employer; in the case of self-employed proof of activity.
[38] See also, Case C–413/01 *Ninni-Orasche* [2003] E.C.R. I–13187.

14(4)(b). According to Article 24(2) however, Member States are not obliged to confer entitlement to social assistance to work-seekers. As we shall see in Chapter 18, following the ruling in *Collins*,[39] it is not clear how far this exemption applies.[40]

Economically independent citizens

The second category of Union citizens who have a right to reside **17–013** for more than three months in a Member State other than that of their nationality, are those who have "sufficient resources" for themselves and their family members not to become a burden on the social assistance system of the host Member State; and have comprehensive health insurance. Article 7(1)(b) of Directive 2004/38 thus unifies in one category both pensioners and those who are self-sufficient, previously dealt with in two separate directives. The Member State cannot lay down a fixed amount to be considered as "sufficient resources" and have to have due regard to the applicant's individual circumstances; furthermore, in no event can the amount required be higher than the threshold below which nationals of the host Member State receive social assistance; or higher than the minimum social security pension.[41] The Court has clarified that the economic resources referred to in then Directive 90/364, do not need to be the Union citizen's own: thus resources provided by a family member,[42] or by a third party even when there is no legal link between the Union citizen and the person who supplies the resources,[43] have to be taken in the same account as if they were the Union citizen's own resources. As for the comprehensive sickness insurance requirement, it is worth recalling the ruling in *Baumbast* where the Court held that the fact that the Union citizen is only partially insured cannot justify the Member State's refusal to renew his/her residence permit. Thus, both conditions, medical insurance and resources, have to be assessed with due regard to the individual circumstances and the principle of proportionality, and the Member State cannot have a rule which requires automatic expulsion of Union citizens who do not produce the relevant evidence within the prescribed time.[44]

Whilst Article 24 does not exclude economically inactive Union citizens from the scope of the principle of equal treatment, this is

---

[39] Case C–138/02 *Collins* [2004] E.C.R. I–2703, see also M. Dougan "Free Movement: the Workseeker as a Citizen" (2001) 4 C.Y.E.L.S. 94.
[40] See discussion below, para.18–012.
[41] Art.8(4).
[42] Case C–200/02 *Chen* [2004] E.C.R. I–9925.
[43] Case C–408/03 *Commission v Belgium* (citizenship), (Judgment of March 23, 2006, forthcoming).
[44] Case C–408/03 *Commission v Belgium* (citizenship), (Judgment of March 23, 2006, forthcoming).

more limited than in the case of economically active citizens. This is so since, as we have seen above, should a Union citizen who is not economically active rely excessively on the host State's welfare system, he/she could become an "unreasonable burden" and lose her/his right to reside in the host State. However, and as we also saw above, the Court has made clear that before terminating the Union citizen's right to reside in its territory, a Member State must look at the individual circumstances of the citizen; must act proportionally; and must respect fundamental rights including the right to family life.[45] This principle has been codified in Article 14(3) of the Directive which clarifies that "an expulsion measure shall not be the automatic consequence of a Union citizen's or his/her family member's recourse to the social assistance of the host Member State." Should the Member State want to terminate the right to reside of a Union citizen on those grounds, it has to respect the procedural safeguards detailed in relation to the public policy/security/health derogations (i.e. notification, judicial review, etc. see below).

Article 24(2) provides that economically inactive citizens are not entitled to maintenance grants and loans for studies. However, in the case of *Bidar*,[46] the Court held that a French citizen residing in the UK by virtue of Article 18 EC and Directive 90/364 had a right to equal treatment also in relation to a student loan, even though the Member State could legitimately require a certain degree of integration of the Union citizen before awarding such loan. Thus, it is likely that notwithstanding the wording of Article 24(2), the Union citizen might be eligible for students' aid even when he/she is economically inactive, provided that she/he is lawfully residing and sufficiently integrated in the host State.

Students

17–014   Finally, students enrolled in a private or public establishment accredited or financed by the host State, have a right to reside in the host State if they have comprehensive sickness insurance as well as sufficient resources for themselves and their family members. Article 7(1)(c) of Directive 2004/38, like Directive 93/96 before it, provides that students do not need to provide evidence of their financial situation, but merely need to assure the relevant authorities by means of a declaration or by such equivalent means as they may choose. As in the case of economically independent citizens, students are not in principle excluded from the right of equal treatment provided for in Article 24, save as regards maintenance grants and

---

[45] *cf.* Case C–413/99 *Baumbast and R v Secretary of State for the Home Department* [2002] E.C.R. I–7091; Joined Cases C–482/01 and 493/01 *Orfanopoulos and Olivieri* [2004] E.C.R. I–5257.
[46] Case C–209/03 *Bidar* [2005] E.C.R. I–2119.

maintenance loans. However, excessive reliance on the host welfare system might transform them into "unreasonable burdens", and entitle the Member State to terminate (but not automatically) or refuse to renew their residence permit (Article 14(2)).[47] Further-more, Member States might make entitlement to welfare provision conditional upon the Union citizen showing that he/she has a real link with the host State employment market.[48] On the other hand, the ruling in *Bidar* seems to be limited to those Union citizens who reside in another State independently from their status as students, so it is likely that students are excluded from entitlement to maintenance grants and loans without any need for the State to justify such exclusion.[49]

The Union citizens' family

As we have seen above, the Union citizen's spouse, registered **17–015** partner when the host State recognises registered partnerships, children and ascendants (i.e. parents) have a right to install them-selves with the Union citizen, regardless of whether they themselves are Union citizens. However, students do not have a right to bring their parents with them, even though the Member State has a duty to facilitate their entry and residence.

Once they are lawfully resident in the host State, the Union citizen's spouse/partner and children have a right to pursue an economic activity.[50] Whilst the right to reside of family members is dependent upon the right to reside of the Union citizen, Directive 2004/38 has provided that in certain circumstances the family members retain an independent right of residence.

This will be the case first, if the Union citizen dies (Article 12). In this case, her/his family retains the right of residence, provided that, if they are not Union citizens, they have resided in the host State for at least a year before the Union citizen's death.[51]

---

[47] And, according to Art.15 Dir.2004/38, the procedural safeguards provided for in Arts 30 and 31 the Directive apply to termination and refusal to renew residence permits, see below para.17–027.

[48] Case C–184/99 *R Grzelczyk v Centre public d'aide social d'Ottignies-Louvain-la-Neuve* [2001] E.C.R. I–6193 ; Case C–224/98 *D'Hoop* [2002] E.C.R. I–6191.

[49] *cf.* also C. Barnard, "Annotation on *Bidar*" (2005) 42 C.M.L.Rev. 1465; M. Dougan, "Fees, Grants, Loans and Dole Cheques: Who Covers the Costs of Migrant Education Within the EU?" (2005) 42 C.M.L.Rev. 943.

[50] Art.23 Dir.2004/38 (and previously Art.11 Reg. 1612/68). However, they have the right to pursue an economic activity only in the State where they have a right to reside, i.e. a cross border element needs to be present; see Case C–10/05 *Mattern and Cikotik*, (Judgment of March 30, 2006, forthcoming). Family members of economically active citizens benefit of slightly more favourable conditions, for instance maintenance grants and student grants/loans; *cf.* Art.24(2) of Dir.2004/38 as well as Art.12 of Reg.1612/68 which has not been repealed, even though the equal treatment obligation provided therein is subsumed also in the more general provision in Art.24 of the Directive.

[51] The prior regime naturally confined the family's right to stay to families of economically active people; this right is still present in its original formulation, see Art.17(4).

Secondly, family members retain the right to reside in the host State if the Union citizen leaves the host State, provided they are Union citizens. In any event, however, the Union citizen's children and the parent who has custody retain the right to reside in the host-State as long as they are in education (Article 14(3)).

Thirdly, Article 13 provides that the spouse/partner of the Union citizen maintains the right to reside in the host-State upon divorce, annulment of the marriage or termination of the partnership. However, if the spouse/partner is not a Union citizen, maintenance of the right to reside is conditional upon listed requirements. Thus, in order to retain the right to reside, the marriage must have lasted for at least three years, including one in the host State; or the spouse/partner has custody of the children; or she/he has a right to access the children and a court has ruled that such access shall be exercised in the host State; or this is warranted by particularly difficult circumstances such as having been victim of domestic violence.

In any event, though, the family member who retains the right of residence after termination of the relationship with the main right holder (i.e. after the death of the spouse, or after the divorce or annulment of the marriage/partnership) has to satisfy the conditions that are imposed on Union citizens in order to gain residence. Thus, they must be either economically active (employed or self-employed), or possess sufficient resources and comprehensive health insurance so as not to become a burden on the social assistance of the host State.

Finally, and as said above, family members of Union citizens who have moved to another Member State to then come back to their State of origin are protected in the same way as if they were family members of migrant Union citizens.

Administrative formalities

Administrative formalities for Union citizens

17–016   As we have seen above, Union citizens have a right, conferred directly upon them by the Treaty, to reside in any of the Member States provided they satisfy the conditions detailed by Directive 2004/38. This does not mean however that Member States cannot impose administrative formalities upon Union citizens: the Court had already ruled in the past that such formalities are justified by the imperative need for the Member States to know who is present in their territory.[52] Not surprisingly then Article 8 of Directive 2004/38

---

[52] e.g. Case C–265/88 *Messner* [1989] E.C.R. 4209.

authorises Member States to require Union citizens residing in their territory for longer than three months, to register their presence with the relevant authorities. Since, as we saw above, the right of residence of the Union citizen for the first three months is unconditional, the Member States must allow for a minimum period of at least three months from the date of arrival in their territory for the Union citizen to register. Furthermore, the registration certificate has to be issued immediately, stating the date of registration (which is important to evidence length of stay in order to gain permanent residency), as well as the name and address of the applicant.

It should be remembered that the registration certificate is mere evidence of the right to stay in the host State: it is not constitutive of such a right. Accordingly, failure to register can give rise to sanctions: however, those need to be proportionate and non-discriminatory, i.e. not different from sanctions imposed upon nationals for a comparable breach (such as the breach of the obligation to carry identity cards at all times). It is thus very unlikely that the Member States would be able to impose a custodial sentence for a breach of the registration requirement, since this would be disproportionate. In any event, the Member States cannot deport the Union citizen for her/his failure to comply with administrative formalities.[53]

Article 8(3) provides that in order to obtain the certificate, the Union citizen needs only to demonstrate that she/he satisfies the conditions laid down in the directive in order to gain residence. Thus if he/she is the main right-holder, she/he has to provide proof of employment or economic activity; or sufficient resources and health insurance and where applicable student status as detailed above. If the Union citizen is seeking residence by virtue of being a family member of an economically active or financially independent citizen, then she/he has merely to prove identity and the family (or partnership) tie with the main right holder.

Administrative formalities for family members who are not Union citizens

Third country nationals who derive their right of residence in one **17–017** of the Member States by virtue of being a family member of a Union citizen are in a more vulnerable position than Union citizens. Whilst Union citizens (whatever their status) are always protected by the Treaty and are therefore not subjected to ordinary immigration law, third country nationals are subject to migration law unless they can prove that they have a link with a Union citizen entitling them to claim protection under Community law. For this reason, Article 9

---

[53] e.g. Case 48/75 *Royer* [1976] E.C.R. 497.

provides that Member States must provide the third country national family member with a residence card, as evidence of their right to stay in the host Member State; a residence card also allows third country nationals to travel within the Community without having to obtain a visa, where such a visa is usually required.[54] Differently from ordinary migration law, the Member State retains no discretion in issuing a residence card to a third country national who is a protected family member of a migrant Union citizen (exception given for the derogations expressly provided for in the Directive that we shall considered in detail below); and the residence card must be valid for at least five years or for the envisaged period of residence of the Union citizen if that is less that five years. Furthermore, temporary absences do not affect the validity of the residence card. Those are absences not exceeding six months a year, or absences for a longer duration due to compulsory military service, or an absence for a maximum of twelve months for important reasons "such as childbirth, pregnancy, serious illness, study or vocational training, or a posting in another Member State or a third country" (Article 11). The list is clearly not exhaustive and it would be open to the third country national family member to prove that a long absence was due to another, not listed, important reason. As in the case of Union citizens, the third country national only needs to prove identity and entitlement (family tie and dependency where required). However, identity must be proven by means of a passport, rather than just an identity card.

Right of permanent residence

17–018   One of the most significant new features of Directive 2004/38 is the introduction of the right of permanent residence for Union citizens and their family members. Article 16 provides that the right of permanent residence is acquired after five years of continuous legal residence in the host State, and differs in a very important respect from the right of residence for more than three months, since after the Union citizen or his/her family have acquired the right to permanent residence, the Member State cannot impose any additional requirement, i.e. it cannot require the Union citizen and her/his family to be either economically active or financially independent. After five years of continuous residence, then, the Union migrant is deemed to have established a sufficient link with the host society to become almost akin to a national of that State, and has a full right to equal treatment in respect of social assistance. As we shall see more in detail below, the Member States can deport permanent residents only on "serious grounds of public policy and

---

[54] Art.5(2) of Dir.2004/38.

public security" (Article 28(2)); and permanent residents lose their right to residence only if they are absent from the host-State's territory for more than two years (Article 16(4)).

For the purposes of the Directive, continuity of residence is not affected by temporary absences not exceeding six months a year, or for longer absences due to compulsory military service. Furthermore, and as we have seen already in relation to third country national family members, an absence of a maximum of twelve consecutive months does not affect continuity of residence if it is due to "important reasons" such as pregnancy and childbirth, serious illness, study or vocational training or posting to another country (Article 16(3)).

More favourable conditions for formerly economically active people

Consistently with pre-existing Community legislation,[55] Article 17 **17–019** provides a more favourable treatment for those who have reached pensionable age; for those who have had to stop working because of a permanent incapacity; and for "frontier workers".

Those who stop working because they have reached the age that entitles them to an old age pension (or the age of 60 if there is no right to old age pension) or because they have taken early retirement, have a right to permanent residence provided they have worked in the host-State for at least a year, and have resided there for more than three years.

Those who stop working as a result of a permanent incapacity to work acquire the right of permanent residence provided they have resided in the host-State for more than two years. However, if the incapacity is the result of an accident at work or of an occupational disease entitling the person concerned to a benefit payable in full or in part by one of the host-State's institutions, there is no requirement as to length of residence.

Frontier workers, i.e. those who live in a Member State but work in another, do not have to satisfy additional length of residence, if they have worked in the host State where they reside for at least three years before starting to work in another Member State, and provided they retain their residence in the host-State, to which they return as a rule at least once a week.

Continuity of employment is not affected by involuntary unemployment duly recorded; periods not worked for reasons not of the

---

[55] Reg.1251/70 on the right of workers to remain in the territory of a Member State after having been employed in that State, [1970] O.J. L142/24; and Dir.75/34 concerning the right of nationals of a Member State to remain in the territory of another Member State after having pursued therein an activity in a self-employed capacity, [1975] O.J. L14/10; the latter has been repealed by Dir.2004/38. However, and for unclear reasons, Reg.1251/70 has not been repealed. Note also that Art.17 (3) and (4) are not gender neutral; an oversight of drafting no doubt, but a rather unfortunate one.

person's own making; and absences from work or cessation of work due to illness or accident (Article 17(1)).

Finally, the worker or self-employed who is married/partnered with a national of the host-State, or with someone who has lost the nationality of that State through marriage to the worker/self-employed, does not have to satisfy any length of residence since the required connection with the host state is provided by family ties rather than residence (Article 17(2)).

Right of permanent residence of the citizen's family members

17–020   As we have said above, the right of permanent residence accrues also to family members, even if they are third country nationals, once the main right holder has gained such right. Moreover, family members who have remained in the host State after the death of the main right holder, or divorce or annulment of their marriage/ registered partnership, have a right to acquire permanent residence after five years of continuous lawful residence.

And if the main right holder was economically active and died whilst still working, but before he/she acquired the right to permanent residence, her/his family members residing with her/him in the host State acquire the right of permanent residence provided that (a) the main right holder had at the time of death resided in the host State for a continuous period of two years[56]; or (b) the death resulted from an accident at work or an occupational disease; or (c) the surviving spouse has lost the nationality of that Member State following the marriage to the worker or self-employed person. If the above conditions are not satisfied, and provided the conditions in Articles 12 or Article 13 are satisfied, the family members retains the right of residence provided he/she satisfies the conditions of economic activity or economic independence. After five years of continuous residence they will gain the right to permanent residence.

Permanent residence cards

17–021   The right of the Union citizen to permanent residence is evidenced by a document which is to be issued as soon as possible, after the Member State has verified the duration of residence. This document must be of indefinite duration (Article 19).

Member States have also to issue a permanent residence card to third country national family members; this needs to be issued within six months from submission of the application and is renewable automatically every ten years. Article 20(2) makes it a duty for the third country national family member to apply for the permanent

---

[56] This condition was interpreted narrowly in Case C–257/00 *Givane* [2003] E.C.R. I–345.

residence card before the (normal) residence card expires, and provides that failure to comply with such provision might give rise to proportionate and non-discriminatory sanctions. The third country national can also, without affecting the validity of her/his permanent residence card, interrupt her/his residence for a maximum of two consecutive years.

As always the documents attesting residence are merely evidence of the right, which is conferred directly by the Treaty, through the Directive.[57] The host-State can impose on the Union citizen and on the citizens' family members an obligation to carry the residence card with them at all times, but only if it also imposes upon its citizen a duty to carry an identity card at all times. The Member State cannot charge for such documents more than it would charge its own nationals for a similar document.

In order to prove continuity of residence the Union citizen and/or his/her family members can rely on any means of proof in use in the host Member State. This would typically be evidence of employment or gainful activity, rent receipts, etc. Continuity of residence is interrupted in the case of an expulsion decision duly enforced against the person concerned (Article 21).

Rights of residents and permanent residents

The right to reside in the host territory shall cover the entirety of the Member State's territory. Article 22 provides that territorial restriction can be imposed only where the same restrictions apply to own nationals. This provision clearly seeks to codify the ruling in *Rutili*,[58] where the Court held that France could not impose a territorial restriction on Mr Rutili, an Italian trade unionist, if such restriction could have not been imposed on a French citizen for similar reasons. However, some 30 years later, the Court changed its case law and in *Olazabal*[59] upheld the same French legislation which it had found inconsistent with Community law in *Rutili*. In this case, the French authorities imposed a territorial restriction on a convicted ETA sympatiser, Mr Olazabal, who could not reside in any of the districts bordering Spain, and who could not leave the district where he was residing without previously warning the police authorities. Notwithstanding the fact that such a restriction could have not been imposed on a French national, the Court found that it was justified on public policy grounds and therefore compatible with Community law. Following the adoption of the Directive, however, the ruling in *Olazabal* cannot be considered any longer good law, and Member States will not be able to impose territorial restrictions

17–022

---

[57] See Case 157/79 *Pieck* [1980] E.C.R. 2171.
[58] Case 36/75 *Rutili* [1975] E.C.R. 1219.
[59] Case C–100/01 *Olazabal* [2002] E.C.R. I–10981.

on Union citizens and their family members unless they would be able to do so in relation to their own nationals.

As said above, pursuant to Article 24, all Union citizens who are lawfully resident in another Member State have a right to be treated equally with the nationals of the host State.[60] However, Member States may exclude the right to equal treatment in relation to social assistance during the first three months of residence; and for work seekers (we shall look at the regime provided for work-seekers in detail in the next chapter).[61] Furthermore, the right of equal treatment does not embrace, before the acquisition of permanent residence, the grant of maintenance aid for studies (subject to the *Bidar* qualification as seen above) to economically inactive citizens and their families. It should also be recalled that excessive reliance on welfare provision by economically inactive people might mean that they no longer satisfy the requirements of economic independence listed in Article 7; in such a case, according to Article 14, the Member State might terminate/refuse to renew residence.

Third country national family members have a right to work, both as employed and as self-employed, as well as the right to equal treatment as long as they have a right to residence or permanent residence (i.e. with the exclusion of the first three months of residence) (Article 23).

Derogations on the right of entry and residence on the grounds of public policy, public security and public health

17–023   Articles 39(3) and 46 EC provide for the possibility for the Member States to derogate from the Treaty free movement of workers, establishment and free movement of services provisions on the grounds of public policy, public security and public health. Even though there is no similar express derogation for the rights contained in Article 18 EC, the reference in that article to the limitations and conditions contained in the Treaty and in secondary legislation, clearly mean that the derogations apply also to Union citizens' rights.[62] Directive 2004/38, as Directive 64/221 before it, details the modalities according to which the Member States can rely on such derogations, partially codifying the Court's case law. Article 27(1) clarifies that the derogations can never be invoked to serve economic ends.

Public policy and public security

17–024   The possibility of derogating from the Treaty free movement provisions is extremely limited and in forty years of case law the

---

[60] See above p.679.
[61] See para.18–012, Ch.18.
[62] *cf.* Case C–357/98 *Yiadom* [2000] E.C.R. I–9265; Joined Cases C–482/01 and 493/01 *Orfanopoulos and Olivieri* [2004] E.C.R. I–5257, para.47.

Member States have very seldom succeeded in invoking the derogations.[63] Article 27 provides that measures (typically deportation or refusal of residence) taken on grounds of public policy/security shall comply with the principle of proportionality and be based "exclusively on the personal conduct of the individual concerned".

In *Bonsignore* for instance, Carmelo Bonsignore was an Italian worker resident in Germany, who unlawfully acquired a Beretta pistol, with which he accidentally shot his younger brother Angelo. He was fined for unlawful possession of a firearm, and deportation was ordered by the Chief Administrative Office of the City of Cologne. The national court referred a question to the Court of Justice enquiring whether the equivalent provision in Directive 64/221 was to be interpreted as excluding deportation of a national of a Member State for the purpose of deterring other foreign nationals for such offences, or whether expulsion was only permissible when there were clear indications that an (E)EC national, who had been convicted of an offence, would himself commit further offences or in some other way disregard public security or public policy. "As departures from the rules concerning the free movement of persons constitute exceptions which must be strictly construed," declared the Court, "the concept of 'personal conduct' expresses the requirement that a deportation order may only be made for beaches of the peace and public security which might be committed by the individual affected."[64] This principle has now been codified in Article 27(2) of Directive 2004/38 which states that consideration is of general prevention cannot be accepted to justify deportation. Furthermore, previous criminal convictions do not constitute in themselves grounds for an expulsion order, although they might be evidence of the fact that the individual poses a "present threat" to public policy/security. Thus, in *Bouchereau*,[65] the Court held that "the existence of a previous criminal conviction can therefore only be taken into account in so far as the circumstances which gave rise to that conviction are evidence of personal conduct constituting a present threat to the requirements of public policy". Whilst admitting that "in general, a finding that such a threat exists implies the existence in the individual concerned of a propensity to act in the same way in the future," the Court also added that "it is possible that past conduct alone may constitute such a threat to the requirements of public policy."[66]

Directive 2004/38 also codifies the case law in relation to the definition of the conduct which might justify recourse to the public

---

[63] A public policy derogation was successfully invoked in Case 41/74 *Van Duyn* [1975] E.C.R. 1337.

[64] Case 67/74 *Bonsignore* [1975] E.C.R. 297, 307.

[65] Case 30/77 *Bouchereau* [1977] E.C.R. 1999.

[66] Case 30/77 *Bouchereau* [1977] E.C.R. 1999, 2012. For possible circumstances when past conduct may justify deportation, see Wyatt (1978) 15 C.M.L. Rev. 221 224, 225

policy derogation: the conduct of the individual concerned must "represent a genuine, present and sufficiently serious threat affecting one of the fundamental interests of society". In order to pose such a threat the conduct must lead to serious sanctions if performed by own nationals: thus it is very likely that Member States would not be able to invoke the public policy/security derogation if the same conduct would not give rise to criminal liability when performed by own nationals.[67] This said, criminal behaviour in itself is not determinant, since the Member States cannot issue a deportation order as a penalty or legal consequence of a custodial penalty (Article 33), unless the individual poses a genuine and present threat to public policy or public security.[68] Thus, exclusion orders can never be an automatic consequence of a breach of law.[69] Furthermore, if more than two years have elapsed between when the expulsion order was issued as a penalty or result of a custodial penalty and its execution, the Member State must check that the individual concerned is at that time still a current and genuine threat to public policy/security, and whether there has been any material change in the circumstances (such as family circumstances) since the order was first issued.[70]

17–025   In order to ascertain whether the individual represents a genuine, present and sufficient threat to public policy/security, the Member State can exceptionally, and if it considers it essential, request information to the person's State of nationality, or to any other State (Article 27(3)). The Court has also clarified that the safeguards provided by Community law to Union citizens and their family members, apply also in relation to the Schengen Information System.[71] The latter is a system whereby Member States participatory to the Schengen agreement can issue an alert against a non-Community national on grounds of public policy/security, which are more loosely defined than the same concepts in relation to Directive 2004/38.[72] Once the alert has been issued, the other Member States parties to the Schengen agreement have to refuse a visa (save for limited circumstances) to the Schengen area.[73] In *Commission v Spain*,[74] the Commission brought proceedings against Spain because

---

[67] *cf.* Joined Cases 115/81 and 116/81 *Adoui and Cornuaille* [1984] E.C.R. 1665; Case C–268/99 *Jany* [2001] E.C.R. I–8615.

[68] Case 131/79 *Santillo* [1980] E.C.R. 1585.

[69] Art.33; and *cf.* also Case 30/77 *Bouchereau* [1977] E.C.R. 1999.

[70] *cf.* Case 131/79 *Santillo* [1980] E.C.R. 1585; Joined Cases C–482/01 and 493/01 *Orfanopoulos and Olivieri* [2004] E.C.R. I–5257.

[71] Convention Implementing the Schengen Agreement (CISA) [2000] O.J. L239/19, Title IV, Arts 92 and ss.00–00

[72] *cf.* CISA, Art.96, and see Declaration of the Executive Committee established by the CISA of April 18, 1996 defining the concept of alien [2000] O.J. L239/458.

[73] Art.5(1) of the CISA; Art.5(2) provides for the possibility for a Member State to derogate from the obligation to refuse entry/visa on humanitarian grounds, on grounds of national interest, or because of international obligations. However, in this case, the geographic validity of the visa must be limited to the area of the Member State issuing the visa.

[74] Case C–503/03 *Commission v Spain* (Schengen Information System), (Judgment of January 31, 2006, forthcoming).

the latter had refused visas/entry to spouses of Community nationals against whom a Schengen Information System alert had been issued. The Court held that even though inclusion in the Schengen Information System constitutes evidence that there are reasons to refuse the person concerned entry/visa, such evidence must be corroborated by information that enables the Member State to ascertain whether the individual is a *present* and *sufficiently serious* threat affecting one of the fundamental interests of society. In other words, the Schengen Information System cannot be used to circumvent the guarantees and the rights that Union citizens' family members derive from Community law, and entry/visa can be denied only if the narrower definition of public policy/security is met.

Furthermore, before issuing an expulsion order, the Member State has to take into due consideration the personal situation of the Union citizen or his/her family members. In particular, Article 28 of the Directive instructs Member States to take into account the length of stay in the host state, the individual's age, state of health, family and economic situation, social and cultural integration in the host State and the extent of her/his links with the country. Those requirements are clearly an aspect of the proportionality and fundamental rights scrutiny which is always required when a Member State seeks to limit a Union citizen's right.[75] Thus, the more the individual is integrated in the host-society the less likely it is for the Member State to be able to invoke successfully the derogations; that would be especially the case when the individual has established ties (family, friends, work) in the host country. In this respect, a deportation order might also conflict with the right to family life as guaranteed by the general principles of Community law (and by the ECHR).[76] It is not by coincidence then that Article 28(2) provides that those who have a right to permanent residence, and are therefore more integrated in the host-society, cannot be deported from the host-State's territory except on "serious grounds of public policy and security"; and that Article 28(3) provides that those who have resided in the host State for at least 10 years can be deported only for "imperative grounds of public security". Given that the public policy and security derogation are already very narrowly defined, it is only in the most serious of cases that an individual who has lived in the host country for more than five years could be lawfully deported.

The same concern towards the family rights of Union citizens and their family members clearly also inspired the more protective regime set out for minors, who, pursuant to Article 28(3)(b) can only be deported on "imperative grounds of public security" or if the

---

[75] See Ch.8 above.
[76] See Joined Cases C–482/01 and 493/01 *Orfanopoulos and Olivieri* [2004] E.C.R. I–5257; and by analogy Case C–60/00 *Carpenter* [2002] E.C.R. I–6279; Case C–109/01 *Akrich* [2003] E.C.R. I–9607.

expulsion is necessary for the best interests of the child as provided by the UN Convention on the right of the child. In any event though the child's right to family life has to be respected and if her/his family is in the host-State, an expulsion order is very unlikely to succeed.

Public health

17–026   Article 29 provides that Member States can refuse entry as well as refuse to issue the first residence permit on grounds of public health in relation to diseases with epidemic potential (as defined by the World Health Organisation), and other infectious or contagious parasitic diseases if they are subject to protection provisions also in relation to own nationals. In this respect, and only if there are very serious indications that that is necessary, the host State can require the individual (within three months from their arrival) to undergo a medical examination, free of charge; those examinations can never be imposed as a matter of routine. The health derogation can be invoked only during the first three months of stay; after that time the individual cannot be made subject to an expulsion order, since of course, if such a time has elapsed the individual would have either caught the disease in the host-country or have already had the chance to spread it, so that an expulsion would become meaningless. In any event it is very unlikely that a Member State would invoke the health derogation against a given individual (and in fact there is no case law on the issue); rather it is more likely that if such measures were to be necessary they would be adopted in relation to individuals coming from, or having recently visited, a given region (whether within or outside Europe) struck by an epidemic disease.

If a person is validly excluded from the host-State on any ground, he/she shall be allowed to re-enter the territory of the State of origin even if his/her document is no longer valid or if the holder's nationality is disputed (Article 27(4)).

Procedural requirements

17–027   Directive 2004/38, like its precursor 64/221, provides for essential procedural guarantees for those whose right to movement and residence is limited because of a public policy, security or health reasons.

Article 30 provides that the individual concerned must be notified in writing of the decision to exclude/expel him/her, in such a "way that they are able to comprehend its content and the implication for them". This suggests a possible obligation upon the host-State's authorities to write in the individual's language, as well as to write in clear (and not excessively bureaucratic) terms. The written communication needs to state, precisely and in full, the grounds upon which the decision is based unless that would be contrary to the interests of State security. Furthermore, since the individual has a right to appeal granted directly by Community law (*cf.* Article 31), Article 30 provides that the written communication must also provide the details of the competent judicial or (independent) administrative authority to hear the appeal, the time-limit for the appeal, and the time allowed for the person to leave the territory.[77] Such time cannot be less than a month unless there are substantiated cases of urgency. The individual seeking judicial review/appealing (according to the host State's rules) might also ask for an interim order to suspend removal pending the judicial/administrative court's decision on the substance of the matter. In this case, pursuant to Article 31, the host-State's authorities cannot give execution to the order of expulsion until when the competent authority has adjudicated on the interim order, unless the expulsion is based on a previous judicial decision (such as for instance as a result of previous criminal proceedings), or where the person has already had access to judicial review, or when expulsion is based on an imperative requirement of public security in the case of long term and permanent residents. Therefore, even though the appeal might not have automatic suspensory effects,[78] i.e. might not stop repatriation, the Member State has a duty (apart from the narrowly defined exemptions) to wait at least until when the competent court or administrative authority has had the chance to assess the *prima facie* strength of the host State's claim.[79] After that, and if the court/authority has not granted the interim order, the host-State might exclude the individual pending the appeal. However, it has to allow the individual to come back in order to allow her/him the possibility to submit her/his defence in person, unless his/her appearance may cause serious troubles to public policy or security or judicial review concerns a denial of entry to the territory Article 31(4). Denial of entry is narrowly defined, and the Court in *Yiadom* has held that if the person has been allowed temporarily in the host-State's territory pending a decision following investigation of his/her case, as to whether she/he should be allowed leave to enter, and, at least when presence in the territory has been of not inconsiderable length (in the case at issue seven months), the decision refusing leave to enter cannot be considered as a decision concerning entry and therefore full procedural guarantees apply, and the claimant has the right to submit her/his defence in person.[80]

---

[77] *cf.* also Case C–175/94 *Gallagher* [1995] E.C.R. I–4253; the authority can be appointed by the same authority that takes the decision provided it is truly independent from it.

[78] *cf.* also Case 98/79 *Pecastaing* [1980] E.C.R. 691.

[79] And a rule which provides for the possibility to assess only the *prima facie* legality of the measure, but not the substantive grounds for the measure, is incompatible with Community law, Case C–136/03 *Dörr and Ünal* [2005] E.C.R. I–4759.

[80] Case C–357/98 *Yiadom* [2000] E.C.R. I–9265.

As for the appeal proper, Article 31(3) codifies the case law by requiring the competent authority to review not only the legality of the measure (i.e. whether the measure is formally correct) but also, and much more importantly, the substance of the issue and in particular whether deportation is a proportionate reaction to the actual threat that the individual might represent to the requirements of public policy, security or health.[81] Thus, the Directive ensures that exclusion of Union citizens and their family members from the territory of any of the Member States can occur only because of objective (and thus reviewable) considerations, and not as a matter of political (and thus not reviewable) discretion.[82]

Duration and modalities

17-028   As already established by the Court,[83] an exclusion order can never be of permanent duration since that would violate the very requirement that a derogation can be invoked only in relation to individual conduct constituting an "actual" threat to policy/security, and that past conduct alone is not conclusive to that effect. Furthermore, permanent exclusions would run against the principle of proportionality. In the case of health it is only when the individual is actually carrying a disease that an exclusion might be justified (Article 29).

It is not surprising then that Article 32 limits the possibility to exclude a person protected by the directive from the host territory for a given amount of time to cases relating to public policy or public security. After a reasonable amount of time the person so excluded has a right to submit an application for lifting of the exclusion order[84]; what is reasonable will depend on the circumstances of the particular case. In any event though, after three years from enforcement of the final exclusion order the person excluded can put forward arguments to demonstrate that there has been a change in the material circumstances which justified the decision ordering the exclusion. The Member State has then six months to reach a decision on the application for the lifting of the exclusion order. During this time, the person concerned has no right of entry in the territory of the Member State. Article 32 does not specify that the individual has a right to judicial review in those cases; however, it is clear that Article 31 would apply also in these circumstances, since a

---

[81] Joined Cases 115/81 and 116/81 *Adoui and Cornuaille* [1984] E.C.R. 1665, para.15; and also Case C–136/03 *Dörr and Ünal* [2005] E.C.R. I–4759.

[82] National immigration rules in relation to third country nationals not covered by the Directive are usually significantly more restrictive of the procedural rights of individuals, see e.g. the UK policy (*www.ind.homeoffice.gov.uk/ind/en/home/laws—policy/policy—instructions/ table—of—contents.html?*)

[83] *cf.* Case C–348/96 *Calfa* [1999] E.C.R. I–11.

[84] See also Joined Cases C–65/95 and C–111/95 *Shingara and Radiom* [1997] E.C.R. I–3343.

decision of refusal to lift the exclusion order is still a decision taken on grounds of public policy or security according to Article 31(1). Since the decision would be concerning a denial of entry, the person concern would not have, according to Article 31(4) the right to enter to submit his/her defence in person.

Abuse of rights

Article 35 explicitly provides that Member States are entitled to **17–029** refuse, terminate or withdraw any right conferred by the Directive in the case of abuse of rights or fraud, such as marriages of convenience.

The extent to which a Member State will be able to invoke the abuse of rights doctrine seems to be rather limited: the Court has on several occasions refused to consider the exercise of Community rights for a purpose different from the one for which the right was originally granted as an abuse of right.[85] Thus, the fact that a Union citizen moves to another Member State with the sole intention of triggering the Treaty, and therefore benefit from the often more generous Community law regime in relation to the rights of partners and spouses, is immaterial.[86] The same is true in relation to those citizens who seek to return to their Member State of origin after having taken advantage of their free movement right. Upon returning to their State of origin they, and their family members, are protected by Community law even if the only reason why they left in the first place was to be able to rely on the more favourable Community law regime upon returning to their State of origin. The exception of fraudulent use might be relevant only in relation to those family members who were illegally present in the territory of the Community at the time of moving. In *Akrich*,[87] Mrs Akrich was married to a third country national who was illegally present in the United Kingdom. The couple moved to Ireland where Mrs Akrich worked for a while. They then came back to the United Kingdom, and argued that since Mrs Akrich was coming back after she had exercised her right to free movement, Mr Akrich had a Community law right to enter and reside in the United Kingdom. The Court held that that was not the case, as Regulation 1612/68 only applied to movement within the Community and did not govern access by a third country national to the territory of a Member State. Thus, Article 10 of Regulation 1612/68 (and by implication Directive 2004/38) applied only to those spouses who were already lawfully present in the territory of one of the Member States, before moving

---

[85] *cf.* Case C–212/97 *Centros* [1999] E.C.R. I–1459, paras 24 and ff; Case C–109/01 *Akrich* [2003] E.C.R. I–9607.
[86] e.g. Case C–109/01 *Akrich* [2003] E.C.R. I–9607.
[87] Case C–109/01 *Akrich* [2003] E.C.R. I–9607.

to another Member State.[88] As for marriages of convenience, the Court in *Akrich* had clarified that sham marriages constitute an abuse of Community law.[89]

Finally, it should be noted that any right in the Directive is subject to the general principles of Community law. Thus procedural provisions cannot be less favourable than those available to own nationals for similar claims and cannot deprive the rights in the directive of their effectiveness.[90] Sanctions imposed for breach of the directive must be proportionate and are subject to the principle of non-discrimination and must therefore be equivalent to sanctions imposed on nationals for comparable breaches of law (Article 35). Furthermore, since the Directive is a minimum measure it is open to the Member States to provide for a more favourable regime (Article 37).

OTHER RIGHTS PERTAINING TO EU CITIZENS

General right to equal treatment and beyond

17–030   So far, we have focused on the Union citizens' right to reside and on the right to equal treatment in relation to welfare provision. However, the rights granted by the Treaty go further than that, and indeed Articles 17 and 18 EC (read together with Article 12 EC) encompass a more general right to equal treatment, as well as a more general right not to be hindered in one's ability to move.[91] In *Bickel and Franz,* an Austrian and a German national undergoing trial in the bilingual South Tyrol (Italy) claimed a right to have the proceedings conducted in German. Residents in the province had such a right, but non-residents had to face trial in Italian. Given that a residence requirement always amounts to indirect discrimination, the issue for the Court was whether the situation fell within the scope of application of the Treaty so that the principle of non-discrimination would apply. In deciding that it did, the Court

---

[88] This said, Arts 39/43/49/18 EC might still be of help and the Member State has to respect proportionality and fundamental rights when refusing entry to the Union citizen's spouse even when the latter does not have rights under Dir.2004/38, see Spaventa, "Annotation on *Akrich*" (2005) C.M.L.Rev. 225, para.8–011, Ch.8, above.

[89] *cf.* also Council Resolution of December 4, 1997 on measures to be adopted on the combating of marriages of convenience, [1997] O.J. C381/1.

[90] e.g. Joined Cases 115/81 and 116/81 *Adoui and Cornuaille* [1984] E.C.R. 1665, and see Ch.6 above.

[91] *cf.* Case C–224/02 *Pusa* [2004] E.C.R. I–5763; see also Advocate General Geelhoed's Opinion in Case C–406/04 *De Cuyper*, delivered February 2, 2006, case still pending at the time of writing. However, lacking harmonizing legislation (i.e. for non-Schengen countries) Member States retain the right to have border controls to establish identity and entitlement of those entering their territory, Case C–378/97 *Wijsenbeek* [1999] E.C.R. I–6207.

preferred to find in Article 49 EC the trigger for Article 12 EC to apply, rather than to rely directly on the citizenship provisions, which however it mentioned in order to strengthen its reasoning.[92]

In *Garcia Avello*,[93] the right to equal treatment of Union citizens in respect of all matters having an even remote connection with movement rights was more clearly established. The dispute related to Belgian rules on how to determine a child's surname. Mr Garcia Avello was a Spanish national married to a Mrs Weber, a Belgian national. The couple resided in Belgium and had two children, who were born in Belgium and had dual nationality (Belgian and Spanish); following Belgian practice, the children were registered under their father's last name, Garcia Avello. The couple then requested the competent authority to change the name of the children into Garcia Weber, following established Spanish practice whereby the children's last name is the father's last name followed by the mother's last name. In the meanwhile, the couple also registered the children at the Spanish embassy as Garcia Weber. The Belgian authorities rejected the couple's request, merely changing the last name to Garcia, on the grounds that according to Belgian law the children bear their father's last name. Mr Garcia Avello, acting as the legal representative for the children, brought proceedings challenging the Belgian authorities' decision; the Belgian Court referred a question to the European Court of Justice to enquire as to whether Articles 17 and 18 EC prevented the Belgian authorities from rejecting the requested change of name.

The preliminary question for the Court was whether the Treaty had been triggered. The Belgian Government argued that the situation was purely internal since the children were born and had always resided in Belgium. In examining the question, the Court focused on the fact that the children were Spanish nationals residing in Belgium; therefore the cross-border element had been triggered. Having found that the situation fell within the scope of the Treaty, the Court turned to the substantive issue, and in particular to whether the Belgian rules entailed any discrimination prohibited by Article 12 EC, read in conjunction with Article 17 EC. It restated the principle according to which non-discrimination requires that comparable situations should be treated equally, and non-comparable situations should be treated differently. The Belgian rules, however, treated citizens having dual nationality (objectively in a different situation than Belgian citizens), in the same way as it treated Belgian nationals having only that nationality. The Court therefore found that the refusal to allow the Garcia Avello children to register with their father's and mother's last name constituted discrimination caught by Article 12 EC. In bringing the rules on

---

[92] Case C–274/96 *Bickel and Franz* [1998] E.C.R. I–7637, para.15.
[93] Case C–148/02 *Garcia Avello* [2003] E.C.R. I–11613.

names (in principle within the exclusive competence of the Member States) within the scope of the Treaty, the Court relied on the fact that the prohibition to have the same last name as that registered in the Spanish documents might have affected the children's right to move in the future, and especially their right to return to Spain, since all of the Belgian official documents would be drawn using the Belgian surname. The Court found then that the strict practice concerning authorisation to change names was unnecessary to protect risks of confusion as to parentage, as well as being disproportionate.

As a consequence, the ruling in *Garcia Avello* is important for two reasons: first of all the Court seems to suggest that dual nationality is *per se*, and regardless of actual movement, enough to trigger the Treaty. Secondly, the link with the material scope of the Treaty was rather remote, and not entirely convincing: on the one hand, it was based on purely potential factors (i.e. the children's willingness to move in the future), on the other hand, nothing, besides cultural reasons, would have prevented the children to use their Belgian name so as to avoid future confusion. Thus, the ruling in *Garcia Avello* not only further restricts the scope of the "purely internal situation", according to which the Treaty free movement provisions apply only when there is a cross-border element,[94] but also suggests that the effect of the introduction of Union citizenship is to subject an increasing number of national rules to the proportionality assessment,[95] even when those rules only remotely affect their Treaty rights.[96]

Political rights and rights to good administration

17–031   As said above, the Maastricht Treaty established Union citizenship; whilst it was not clear at the time whether Article 18 EC was a mere codification of the status quo, or whether it was going to create more extensive rights of movement and residence than those granted by the three residence directives, the Maastricht Treaty also established new rights.

In particular, Article 19 EC provides that Union citizens residing in a Member State different from that of nationality have the right to vote and to stand in the local elections of the State where she/he

---

[94] See also N. Nic Shuibhne, "Free movement of persons and the wholly internal rule: time to move on?" (2002) 39 C.M.L.Rev. 731.

[95] But not all of them, *cf.* Case C–386/02 *Baldinger* [2004] E.C.R. I–8411, where the Court did not follow Advocate General Ruiz-Jarabo Colomer's Opinion and refused to bring within the scope of Treaty rules concerning compensation for ex-prisoners of war.

[96] See also Advocate General Jacobs' Opinion in Case C–96/94 *Standesamt Stadt Niebüll*, delivered June 30, 2005, judgment of 27/04/06, not yet reported.

resides under the same conditions as nationals of that State. This right is to be exercised subject to detailed arrangements adopted by the Council, which may provide for derogations "where warranted by problems specific to a Member State". Such arrangements have been laid down by Directive 94/80.[97]

The municipal elections concern representative councils and the local government units listed in the Annex to the Directive.[98] Those would be the like of parishes, districts, counties, county boroughs, communities, regions, etc.

Article 5(3), first paragraph, of the Directive provides:

> "Member States may provide that only their own nationals may hold the office of elected head, deputy or member of the governing college of the executive of a basic local government unit if elected to hold office for the duration of his mandate."

This provision is worthy of remark. The right of a citizen of the Union to "stand as a candidate . . . under the same conditions as nationals of that State" would be worthless if he/she were not entitled, if elected, to carry out all the functions and exercise all the prerogatives of an elected member of the nationality of the State in question. It is true that Article 19(1) EC permits derogations, but these must be "warranted by problems specific to a Member State," and the issue addressed by Article 5(3) could not be so described. It appears from the preamble to the Directive that the justification for Article 5(3) is to be found by analogy with Article 55 EC, which provides that the right of establishment for self-employed persons does not apply to activities connected, even occasionally, with the exercise of official authority.[99] This latter provision is the counterpart of Article 39(4) EC, which provides that the right of freedom of movement of workers does not apply to "employment in the public

---

[97] Dir.94/80 laying down detailed arrangements for the exercise of the right to vote and to stand as a candidate in municipal elections by citizens of the Union residing in a Member State of which they are not nationals, [1994] O.J. L368/38, as amended by Dir.96/30 [1996] L122/14 and by the Act of Accession [2003] O.J. L236/33. See also Commission Report on granting a derogation pursuant to Art.19(1) of the Treaty, presented under Art.12(4) of Dir.94/80 on the right to vote and stand as a candidate in municipal elections, COM (2005) 382 final. On the compatibility of the legislation transposing Dir.94/80 with the French Constitution, see Conseil Constitutionnel, Decision 98–400, 20/5/98.

[98] As amended by Dir.96/30.

[99] See Ch.19, para.19–032. The preamble of the Directive states in relevant part: "Whereas, since the duties of the leadership of basic local government units may involve taking part in the exercise of official authority and in the safeguarding of the general interest, Member States should be able to reserve these offices for their nationals; whereas Member States should also be able to take appropriate measures for that purpose; whereas such measures may not restrict more than is necessary for the achievement of that objective the possibility for other Member States' nationals to be elected . . ."

service".[1] It is true that the "public service/authority proviso" comprises one of the "limitations and conditions laid down in this Treaty and by the measures adopted to give it effect" within the meaning of Article 18(1) EC which defines the right of movement and residence referred to in that Article. But it does not follow that a principle based on the official authority/public service proviso may be invoked to limit the right to vote and stand in municipal elections which is laid down in Article 19(1) EC. The official authority/public service proviso is concerned with access to certain remunerated posts in the public service, and seeks to distinguish economic activity from the exercise of powers of governance. But the right to hold elected office in a local government authority intrinsically involves the right to exercise official authority, by way of participation in the exercise of powers conferred by public law (e.g. decisions on licensing, planning permission). Even an allegedly limited and proportionate application of the official authority/public service proviso in the context in question appears to take back by secondary legislation some part of the very right which the Treaty has bestowed. The application of the official authority/public service proviso by way of Article 5(3) of Directive 94/80 appears to be as much an exercise in second thoughts on the part of the Council as regards the implications of bestowing the right to stand for office in the first place, as a laying down of detailed arrangements for the exercise of the right in question.

17–032   Union citizens also have the right to participate in the elections of the European Parliament: as a result, every citizen of the Union residing in a Member State of which she/he is not a national must be given the right to vote and to stand as a candidate in elections to the European Parliament in which she/he resides, under the same conditions as nationals of that State. Directive 93/109 lays down detailed arrangements for the exercise of this right.[2] It is to be noted that the Directive provides that Community voters shall exercise their right to vote either in the Member State of residence or in their home Member State.[3] No person may vote more than once at the same election, and no person may stand as a candidate in more than one Member State at the same election.[4]

Citizenship of the Union also bestows advantages for individuals as regards diplomatic and consular protection in the territory of third countries. Every citizen of the Union shall, in the territory of a third country in which the Member State of which he/she is a national is not represented, be entitled to protection by the diplomatic or consular authorities of any Member State, on the same

---

[1] Ch.18, at para.18–017.
[2] [1993] O.J. L329/34.
[3] *ibid.*, Art.4.
[4] *ibid.*, Art.4; Union citizens have of course the right to vote for the EP in their home-State, see Ch.1.

conditions as the nationals of that State. Member States are obliged to establish the necessary rules among themselves and start the international negotiations required to secure this protection. In accordance with this obligation, the Representatives of the Governments of the Member States meeting within the Council adopted a Decision regarding protection for citizens of the European Union by diplomatic and consular representations.[5] The Decision *inter alia* defines the diplomatic protection to be extended to citizens of the Union, as follows:

"(a) assistance in cases of death;
(b) assistance in cases of serious accident or serious illness;
(c) assistance in cases of arrest or detention;
(d) assistance to victims of violent crime;
(e) the relief and repatriation of distressed citizens of the Union.

In addition, Member States' diplomatic representations or consular agents serving in a non-member State may, in so far as it is within their powers, also come to the assistance of any citizen of the Union who so requests in other circumstances."[6]

Further rights enjoyed by citizens of the Union are the right to petition the European Parliament,[7] the right to apply to the Ombudsman established under Article 195 EC,[8] and the right to write to the Community institutions or the Ombudsman in any of the EC's official languages and to have an answer in the same language.[9]

As mentioned in Chapter 9, the Charter of Fundamental Rights reproduces these rights in its Title V; furthermore the Charter also includes, as Union citizens' rights, the right to good administration, which is not limited to Union citizens, and, has we saw in Chapter 7, is a general principle of Union law; and the right of access to documents which is available to Union residents as well as to Union citizens. The latter is provided for in Article 255 EC, and is detailed in Regulation 1049/2001 on public access to Parliament, Council and Commission documents.[10] Article 255 EC applies also to documents

---

[5] Council Decision 95/553/EC, [1995] O.J. L314/73.
[6] *ibid.*, Art.5.
[7] Art.21 TEC, first paragraph, and Art.194 TEC, which grants the right to petition to all EU residents, and not only to EU citizens. See for instance with reference to a possible violation of the media pluralism in Italy the Report of the European Parliament the on the risks of violation, in the EU and especially in Italy, of freedom of expression and information (Art.11(2) of the Charter of Fundamental Rights) 2003/2237 (INI)) which was drafted following a private citizens' petition. The report albeit clearly scathing about the situation in Italy stopped short of requesting the Council to activate the Art.7 TEU procedure.
[8] Art.21 TEC, second paragraph.
[9] Art.21 TEC, third paragraph.
[10] Reg.1049/2001 regarding public access to European Parliament, Council and Commission documents [2001] O.J. L145/43.

adopted within the field of Common Foreign and Security Policy (the Second Pillar), and Police and Judicial Co-operation in Criminal Matters (the Third Pillar), and so does Regulation 1049/2001. Article 4 of the Regulation provides for exceptions to the principle of open access: those, not surprisingly, concern the Union public interest (such as security, defence, etc.), and the protection of commercial interests, court proceedings, the purpose of investigations, etc. Article 9 provides for treatment of sensitive documents, i.e. those that the institution classifies as secret, top-secret or confidential. Each institution must make the rules concerning sensitive documents public and a refusal of access must be reasoned.

Further reading

Barnard, "EU Citizenship and Social Solidarity" in Dougan and Spaventa (eds) *Social Welfare and EU law* (Hart Publishing, Oxford, 2005).

Dougan and Spaventa, "Educating Rudy and the (non-)English patient: A double-bill on residency rights under Article 18 EC" (2003) 28 E.L.Rev. 699.

Dougan and Spaventa, " 'Wish you weren't here . . .': new models of social solidarity in the European Union" in Dougan and Spaventa (eds) *Social Welfare and EU law* (Hart Publishing, Oxford, 2005).

Everson, "The Legacy of the Market Citizen" in Shaw J. and More G. (eds), *New Legal Dynamics of European Union* (Clarendon, Oxford, 1995).

Ferrara, "Towards an 'Open' Social Citizenship? The New Boundaries of Welfare in the European Union" in De Búrca (ed.) *EU Law and the Welfare State* (OUP, Oxford, 2005).

Fries and Shaw, "Citizenship of the Union: First Steps in the European Court of Justice" (1998) 4 E.P.L. 533.

Hailbronner, "Union citizenship and access to social benefits" (2005) 42 C.M.L.Rev. 1245.

Meehan, *Citizenship and the European Community* (Sage, London, 1993).

O'Leary, *The Evolving Concept of Community Citizenship* (Kluwer, The Hague, 1996).

CHAPTER 18

FREEDOM OF MOVEMENT FOR WORKERS

Guide to this Chapter: The original EEC Treaty provided for a **18–001** right to move and reside across the Community only for economically active (workers and self employed) Union citizens. In this chapter we are going to look at the rights of workers, whilst in the next chapters we will focus on self-employed and corporate actors. Even though the right to free movement was provided with an economic rationale in mind, so that workers could migrate from areas of the Community where there was unemployment to areas where there were jobs available, workers were never treated as mere factors of production. Thus, secondary legislation provided not only for an extensive right to equal treatment, including a right to welfare provision, but also for the right to be joined by one's family, who also derived rights from Community law, for the right to stay in the host-State when involuntarily unemployed, for protection from deportation and so on. The European Court of Justice not surprisingly interpreted the Treaty provisions and the relevant secondary legislation in a generous and purposive way, protecting the worker as a person as well as a "factor of production". In this chapter we will focus on those rights that are peculiar to workers, whilst just recalling the rights that we have already analysed in the previous chapter. In particular we will focus on the personal scope (who is protected) and on the material scope (what constitutes a barrier to movement) of Article 39 EC.

GENERAL

18–002   The Treaties establishing the European Communities each contain provisions designed to facilitate the movement of workers between the Member States. The signatories to the Treaty establishing the European Coal and Steel Community (ECSC) undertook in Article 69 to remove any restrictions based on nationality upon the employment in the coal and steel industries of workers holding the nationality of one of the Member States and having recognised qualifications in coal-mining or steel-making, and a similar provision appears in Article 96 of the Treaty establishing the European Atomic Energy Community (Euratom), declaring the right of nationals of the Member States to take skilled employment in the field of nuclear energy. Acting under this latter Article the Council issued a Directive in 1962[1] defining the scope of skilled employment and requiring that Member States adopt all necessary measures to ensure that any authorisation required for taking up employment in the field specified should be automatically granted.

As Treaties concerned only with limited economic integration, the ECSC and Euratom Treaties naturally only dealt with workers in their respective sectors. The EC Treaty, on the other hand, seeks to promote comprehensive economic integration, and its provisions requiring that "freedom of movement for workers shall be secured within the Community" are applicable to all "workers of the Member States" regardless of occupation.[2] It is with the provision of the EC Treaty, and the implementing legislation made thereunder, that we shall be hereafter concerned.

Since a common market requires the removal of all obstacles to the free movement of the factors of production, as well as of goods and services, the free movement of workers in the Community may be seen simply as a prerequisite to the achievement of an economic objective. Support for this view may be found in the Spaak Report,[3] and in the texts of Articles 39, 40 and 42 EC (ex 48, 49 and 51). Under Article 39 EC, workers of the Member States are to be free

---

[1] [1962] O.J. 1650.
[2] Art.39(1) EC, amending and replacing Art.48(1), by omitting reference to the transitional period, and Art.39(2) (ex 48(2)). But the EC Treaty did not "affect" the provisions of the ECSC Treaty, nor does it "derogate" from those of the Euratom; see Art.305 EC (ex 232).
[3] *Rapport des chefs de délégation aux ministres des affaires étrangéres* (Brussels, April 21, 1956).

to accept offers of employment actually made, and to remain in a Member State for the purposes of carrying on employment. Article 40 EC authorises legislation by the Council to eliminate administrative procedures likely to impede the movement of workers, and to set up machinery for matching offers of employment in one Member State with available candidates in another. The provisions of Article 42 EC, empowering the Council to take legislative action in the field of social security, appear to extend this authorisation only to measures necessary for safeguarding the rights of the migrant worker *stricto sensu.*

Yet such a functional economic approach to the interpretation of **18–003** the free movement provisions is likely to be inadequate for two reasons. First, in the graphic words of Article 6 of the Clayton Anti-Trust Act, because of the notion that "the labour of a human being is not a commodity or article of commerce," or as Advocate General Trabucchi has put it: "The migrant worker is not regarded by Community law—nor is he by the internal legal system—as a mere source of labour but is viewed as a human being."[4] A similar sentiment may be discerned in the fifth recital to the preamble to Regulation 1612/68 of the Council,[5] which speaks of the exercise of workers' rights in "freedom and dignity," and describes freedom of movement for workers as a "fundamental right" and "one of the means by which the worker is guaranteed the possibility of improving his living and working conditions and promoting his social advancement, while helping to satisfy the requirements of the economies of the Member States." As Advocate General Jacobs has observed, "The recital makes it clear that labour is not, in Community law, to be regarded as a commodity and notably gives precedence to the fundamental rights of workers over satisfying the requirements of the economies of the Member States."[6]

But for another reason a purely economic approach is likely to be deficient. The EEC was established after the failure of rather more ambitious attempts to institute a Western European military and political union, and it represented an attempt to achieve a similar political aim by means of economic integration. Thus the first recital to the preamble of the (now) EC Treaty records the determination of the signatories to lay the foundation of an ever closer union among the peoples of Europe, and the eighth records their resolve to strengthen peace and liberty by a pooling of their respective resources. The closing words of Article 2 of the Treaty lays down as

---

[4] Case 7/75 *Mr. and Mrs. F.* [1975] E.C.R. 679, 696.
[5] [1968] J.O. L257/2. The Court has referred to the fifth recital both as a guide to the interpretation of the Regulation, and as an indication of the scope of the application of the Treaty: Case 76/72 *Michel S.* [1973] E.C.R. 457, Case 9/74 *Casagrande* [1974] E.C.R. 773, (interpretation of Reg. 1612/68); Case 152/81 *Forcheri* [1983] E.C.R. 2323 (scope of application of the Treaty).
[6] Case 344/87 *Bettray* [1989] E.C.R. 1621, 1637.

one of the Community's allotted tasks that of promoting economic and social cohesion and solidarity among the Member States. To this extent, there may be said to be a larger objective contained in the provisions relating to the free movement of persons. It is to be noted that the Declaration issued after the Summit Conference of October 1972 included the words: "The Member States re-affirm their resolve to base their Community's development on democracy, freedom of opinion, *free movement of men and ideas* and participation by the people through their elected representatives."[7]

The Court of Justice has sometimes interpreted the provisions of Articles 39–42 EC and the implementing legislation made thereunder, in a rather more liberal manner than would be dictated by a purely functional view of the Treaty based on its economic objectives. In *Maison Singer*[8] a German national on holiday in France had been killed in a road accident. His dependants were paid benefits by a German social security institution, which then brought an action in France against the employer of the driver of the other vehicle, claiming that the French court was bound to recognise the subrogation that German law allowed, by virtue of Article 52 of Regulation 3.[9] In the course of the proceedings before the Court of Justice, it was argued that to apply Article 52 of the Regulation in circumstances such as those before the national court would be incompatible with Article 42 of the EC Treaty, inasmuch as that provision only allowed the Council to adopt such measures as were necessary to provide freedom of movement for workers qua workers, not qua holidaymakers. The Court responded:

> "Since the establishment of as complete as possible a freedom of movement of labour is among the 'foundations' of the Community, it is the ultimate goal of Article 51 [now 42] and, therefore, governs the exercise of the power it confers upon the Council. It would not be in keeping with such a concept to limit the idea of 'worker' to migrant workers strictly speaking or to travel connected with their employment. Nothing in Article 51 requires such a distinction; moreover, such a distinction would make the application of the contemplated rules unfeasible. On the other hand, the system adopted for Regulation No.3, which consists in removing, as much as possible, the territorial limitations for applying the various social security systems, is quite in keeping with the objectives of Article 51 of the Treaty."[10]

---

[7] Emphasis added. Bull. E.C. 10/72, 15.
[8] Case 44/65 [1965] E.C.R. 965.
[9] J.O. [1958], 561.
[10] [1965] E.C.R. 965, 971.

It was in a similar spirit that the Court of Justice considered the **18–004** purpose and effect of Regulation 1612/68[11] in *Commission v Germany*[12] in the following terms:

> "It is apparent from the provisions of the regulation, taken as a whole, that in order to facilitate the movement of members of workers' families the Council took into account, first, the importance for the worker, from a human point of view, of having his entire family with him, and secondly, the importance, from all points of view, of the integration of the worker and his family into the host Member State without any difference in treatment in relation to nationals of that State."[13]

More recently, the introduction of Union citizenship, which clearly transcends the economic requirements of the common market, is in line with the interpretation given by the Court to Article 39 EC, and with the very idea of considering economic migrants as persons rather than mere factors of production.[14] As we said before, the economic free movement provisions take precedence over Article 18 EC, both because they confer more estensive rights and because they are *lex specialis*. This is not to say, however, that the notion of Union citizenship is not relevant to economic migrants: first of all, and as we shall see below, the Court of Justice has partially amended its interpretation of Article 39 EC in the light of the introduction of Union citizenship; secondly, citizenship of the Union gives rights other than residence and equality, and in particular the right to vote for local and European elections in the host country, thus strengthening the link between migrant and host community.

THE AMBIT OF ARTICLE 39 EC

The cross-border element

Article 39 EC aims to secure freedom of *movement* for workers. **18–005** This provision, along with the other provisions of the Treaty relating to freedom of movement for persons are intended to facilitate the pursuit of occupational activities of all kinds throughout the Community and preclude national legislation which might place Community nationals at a disadvantage when they extend their activities beyond a single Member State.[15]

---

[11] [1968] O.J. L257/2.
[12] Case 249/86 *Commission v Germany* [1989] E.C.R. 1263.
[13] [1989] E.C.R. 1263, para.11.
[14] Indeed the free movement provisions, and in particular the regime for workers, have been identified as an embryonic form of European Citizenship; see Meehan, *Citizenship and the European Community* (Sage, London, 1993).
[15] Case C–443/93 *Ioannis Vougioukas* [1995] E.C.R. I–4033, para.39.

In order for Article 39 EC to apply there needs to be a cross-border element. This is present when (i) the worker moves to another Member State to work and reside there; (ii) when the worker resides in a Member State but is employed in another one (frontier worker); (iii) when the worker returns to her/his State of origin after having exercised his/her Article 39 EC rights by working in another Member State. In the latter case, the worker benefits of the protection of Community law against her/his Member State as if she/he were a national of another Member State.[16] Thus, a national who has undertaken a course of study in another Member State and then returned to his/her Member State of origin may rely upon Article 39 EC against that Member State to uphold his/her right to use the postgraduate academic title acquired in that other Member State.[17]

It should be remembered, however, that a cross-border element is always necessary, and Article 39 EC does not extend to situations wholly internal to a Member State,[18] for example the binding over of a person charged within theft on condition that he proceed to Northern Ireland and not return to England or Wales for three years.[19] A worker cannot rely upon Article 39 EC unless he/she has exercised the right to freedom of movement within the Community,[20] or is genuinely seeking to exercise that right. The purely hypothetical possibility that an individual may at some time in the future seek work in another Member State is not sufficient.[21] Thus, whilst a custodial sentence clearly limits the possibility to move, it cannot, for that only reason, be considered as a restriction to one of the free movement provisions since a "purely hypothetical" prospect of exercising a Treaty right is not enough to trigger the necessary cross-border element.[22]

---

[16] Case C–419/92 *Scholz* [1994] E.C.R. I–505, para.9; Case C–443/93 *Ioannis Vougioukas* [1995] E.C.R. I–4033, para.38. A worker working in her State of origin (Germany) who acquired French nationality by marriage (retaining her German nationality) and resided in France is to be regarded as having exercised her right of free movement in order to work in a Member State other than that in which she resides, see Case C–336/96 *Gilly* [1998] E.C.R. I–2793, paras 20, 21.

[17] Case C–19/92 *Kraus* [1993] E.C.R. I–1663; for further discussion of the latter case see below at p.735.

[18] Case 175/78 *Saunders* [1979] E.C.R. 1129; Case 298/84 *Iorio* [1986] E.C.R. 247; Case C–332/90 *Steen* [1992] E.C.R. I–341, and Case C–132/93 *Steen* [1994] E.C.R. I–2715; Joined Cases C–64/96 and C–65/96 *Uecker* [1997] E.C.R. I–3171.

[19] Case 175/78 *Saunders* [1979] E.C.R. 1129. It is to be noted by way of contrast that in the context of the free movement of goods, charges on the intra-State movement of domestic goods are covered by Art.25 EC, Joined Cases C–363/93 *etc., Lancry* [1994] E.C.R. I–3957, esp. paras 27–29, p.541 above.

[20] Joined Cases 35 and 36/82 *Morson* [1982] E.C.R. 3723.

[21] Case 180/83 *Moser* [1984] E.C.R. 2539.

[22] Case C–299/95 *Kremzow* [1997] E.C.R. I–2629.

Vertical, semi-horizontal and horizontal effect

Article 39 EC is directly effective.[23] It can be relied upon by the **18–006** worker, even in a case in which the adverse effects on a worker result from obligations imposed by national law upon the employer,[24] as well as by an employer who wishes to employ, in a Member State in which she/he is established, a worker who is a national of another Member State.[25] As the Court said in *Clean Car Autoservice*, referring to Article 39(1) and (2):

> "While those rights are undoubtedly enjoyed by those directly referred to—namely, workers—there is nothing in the wording of Article 48 [now 39] to indicate that they may not be relied upon by others, in particular employers."[26]

As any directly effective provision, Article 39 EC applies to all rules, acts and practices of public authorities. Furthermore, it also applies to rules of any other nature aimed at regulating gainful employment in a collective manner.[27] Otherwise, the effect of the Treaty would have been greatly reduced since, especially in the continent, a significant proportion of labour relations is regulated by means of collective agreements.

Moreover, the Court has expanded the scope of Article 39 EC to apply (at least partially) also in horizontal situations, i.e. when the claim involves private parties. Thus, in *Angonese* the Court held that the prohibition on discrimination on grounds of nationality contained in Article 39 EC applies also to private employers. The Court drew a parallel with the prohibition of discrimination on grounds of sex (Article 141 EC) which also binds private employers: both provisions, the Court held, are designed to ensure that there is no discrimination in relation to the labour market, and therefore bind private as well as State parties.[28] In *Angonese* the Court was quite careful in delimiting the possibility to rely on Article 39 EC against a private party to claims relating to discrimination on grounds on nationality. To extend the horizontal application of Article 39 EC also to non-discriminatory barriers (see below) would in fact be a step too far in that it would risk unduly limiting the contractual freedom of private parties.[29]

---

[23] Case 48/75 *Royer* [1977] E.C.R. 497, para.23; Case 41/74 *Van Duyn v Home Office* [1974] E.C.R. 1337; Case C–90/96 *David Petrie v Université degli Studi di Verona* [1997] E.C.R. I–6527, para.28.

[24] Case C–27/91 *Union de Recouvrement des Cotisations de Sécurité Sociale et d'Allocations Familiales de la Savoie (URSSAF) v Hostellerie Le Manoir SARL.* [1991] E.C.R. I–5531, para.9.

[25] Case C–350/96 *Clean Car* [1998] E.C.R. I–2521.

[26] *ibid.*, para.19.

[27] Art.7(4) Reg.1612/68; e.g. Case 36/74 *Walrave* [1974] E.C.R. 1405, para.17; Case C–415/93 *Bosman* [1995] E.C.R. I–4921, para.82; and more recently Case C–400/02 *Merida* [2004] E.C.R. I–8471.

[28] Case C–281/98 *Angonese* [2000] E.C.R. I–4139, esp. paras 34–36.

[29] e.g. a clause providing for substantial period of notice for termination of a fixed term contract could be construed as a barrier to movement.

Territorial Application

18–007   The application of Article 39 EC is not conditional upon all conduct pertaining to an economic relationship or activity occurring within the territory of the Member States: it applies in judging all legal relationships which can be localised within the Community, by reason either of the place where they were entered into, or the place where they take effect.[30] In *Boukhalfa* the Court held that the latter principle must be deemed to extend to cases in which there was a sufficiently close link between the employment relationship, on the one hand, and the law of a Member State and thus the relevant rules of Community law, on the other. The Court concluded that Article 39 EC applied where a national of a Member State (a Belgian) permanently resident in a non-Member country (Algeria) was employed by another Member State (Germany) in its embassy in that non-Member country, where that person's contract of employment was entered into and permanently performed in that latter country, and where the plaintiff's situation was subject to the law of the employing State in several respects; the consequence was that the prohibition of discrimination laid down in the Treaty applied as regards all aspects of the employment relationship which were governed by the law of the employing Member State.[31]

THE PERSONAL SCOPE OF APPLICATION OF ARTICLE 39 EC

The concept of "worker"

18–008   Article 39 EC refers to freedom of movement for "workers." Article 1 of Regulation 1612/68 (freedom of movement for workers within the Community) refers to the right to "take up an activity as an employed person." Neither term ("worker" or "employed person") is defined,[32] but the concepts must be interpreted according to their ordinary meaning, and in the light of the objectives of the Treaty.[33] The definition of "worker" in the Community sense rarely causes difficulty because if an economically active migrant is not a

---

[30] Case 36/74 *Walrave* [1974] E.C.R. 1405; Case 237/83 *Prodest* [1984] E.C.R. 3153; Case 9/88 *Lopes da Veiga* [1989] E.C.R. 2989.

[31] Case C–214/94 *Boukhalfa* [1996] E.C.R. I–2253.

[32] Though the concept of "employed person" is defined for the purposes of co-ordination of the national social security systems pursuant to Arts 40 and 308, see Art.1(a) of Reg.118/97 amending and updating Regulation (EEC) 1408/71 on the application of social security schemes to employed persons, to self-employed persons and to members of their families moving within the Community *etc.*, [1997] O.J. L28/1 (Part I of Annex A contains a consolidated text of Reg.1408/71). Most of Reg.1408/71 will be repealed once Reg.883/2004, [2004] O.J. L200/1 enters into force.

[33] Case 53/81 *Levin* [1982] E.C.R. 1035.

worker, he/she is as like as not to be self-employed, in which case either Article 43 EC or Article 49 EC will apply. The Court has held that Articles 39, 43 and 49 EC are based on the same principles both as far as entry and residence and non-discrimination on grounds of nationality are concerned,[34] and so categorisation under Article 39 EC, as opposed to Article 43 or Article 49 EC, will rarely be crucial. Thus, for example, Member States are obliged to issue a residence permit to a national of another Member State if it is not disputed that that person is engaged in economic activity, without its being necessary in that regard to classify the activity as that of an employed or self-employed person.[35] Nevertheless, the distinction may be significant in certain cases, and especially in relation to the transitional period following accession of new Member States when the transitional arrangements allow for a temporary suspension of the free movement of workers provisions whilst guaranteeing full free movement rights to self-employed persons.[36] Furthermore, a person who has worked only in a self-employed capacity in the relevant Member State cannot be regarded as a "worker" within the meaning of Article 39 of the EC Treaty and therefore cannot rely upon that provision.[37]

This said, whilst the distinction between employed and self-employed, and exception given for new Member States, is of limited importance, the distinction between economically active and economically inactive migrants was of paramount importance before the introduction of Union citizenship since, as we said in the previous chapter, Community law conferred at first free movement rights only to economic migrants and their families. But even after the introduction of Union citizenship, the correct identification of the legal basis for the exercise of Community rights is very relevant. As we have seen in the previous chapter, workers (and economically active migrants in general), benefit of more extensive rights than non-economically active Union migrants. In particular, as we saw, economic migrants have an unconditional right of residence (i.e. not dependent upon resources/insurance), as well as a right to access most welfare benefits as if they were nationals of the host-State. Thus, it will be in the interest of the Union citizen to be defined, whenever possible, as a "worker" (or self-employed), rather than just as a Union citizen.

Given the fact that non-economically active migrants were not protected by Community law, it is not surprising that the Court gave a broad and purposive interpretation to who was to be defined as a

---

[34] Case 48/75 *Royer* [1976] E.C.R. 497.
[35] Case C–363/89 *Roux* [1991] E.C.R. I–273.
[36] See below, para.18–031.
[37] Case C–15/90 *Middleburgh* [1991] E.C.R. I–4655.

worker and therefore come within the personal scope of application of Article 39 EC. Thus, the term cannot be defined according to the national laws of the Member States,[38] as otherwise the meaning would vary from State to State, but has a Community meaning.[39] The Court in its case law has held that the essential characteristic of the employment relationship is that for a certain period a person performs services for and under the direction of another person in return for which she/he receives remuneration.[40] Since the concepts of worker and employed person define the field of application of one of the fundamental freedoms guaranteed by the Treaty, they must not be interpreted restrictively.[41] For this reason the Court has held that part-time workers whose activity is genuine and not ancillary are also protected by Article 39 EC. Otherwise a large number of those who seek to improve their living conditions through part-time work would be excluded from the scope of the Treaty.[42] Thus, the Court held in *Levin*:

> "(. . .) Since part-time employment, although it may provide an income lower that what is to be considered to be the minimum required for subsistence, constitutes for a large number of persons an effective means to improve their living conditions, the effectiveness of Community law would be impaired and the achievement of the objectives of the Treaty would be jeopardised if the enjoyment of rights conferred by the principle of freedom of movement of workers were reserved solely to persons engaged in full time employment earning, as a result, a wage at least equivalent to the guaranteed minimum wage in the sector under consideration".[43]

18–009 Part-timers fall within the scope of Article 39 EC even when they work just a few hours a week and their pay falls below the minimum wage so that they have to rely on welfare provision to supplement their earnings. Thus, for instance, in *Kempf*, a German piano teacher giving 12 lessons a week in Belgium was held to be a worker and for this reason was entitled to welfare provision to supplement his salary as well as benefits when he found himself incapable to work for

---

[38] Though to some extent they are defined by reference to coverage of the national social security systems in the context of the co-ordination of the national social security systems for employed and self-employed persons under Reg.1408/71, see n.32.

[39] Case 75/63 *Hoekstra (neé Unger)* [1964] E.C.R. 177; Case 53/81 *Levin* [1982] E.C.R. 1035.

[40] Case 66/85 *Lawrie-Blum* [1986] E.C.R. 2121, paras 16 and 17; Case 85/96 *Martinez Sala* [1998] E.C.R. I–2691, para.32.

[41] Case 53/81 *Levin* [1982] E.C.R. 1035; Joined Cases 389 and 390/87 *Echternach* [1989] E.C.R. 723.

[42] Furthermore since in most industries women form most of the part-time labour force, the exclusion of part-timers from the scope of Art.39 EC would have had sex discrimination implications.

[43] Case 53/81 *Levin* [1982] E.C.R. 1035, para.15.

health reasons.[44] This is the case also for a person engaged in preparatory training in the course of occupational training, who has to be regarded as a worker if the training period is completed under the conditions of genuine and effective activity as an employed person, even if the trainee's productivity is low, and he/she works only a small number of hours per week and consequently receives limited remuneration.[45]

The fact that a worker has worked only for a short period of time in a fixed term contract, does not exclude her/him from the scope of Article 39 EC, provided that the activity was not purely marginal and ancillary. Thus, in *Ninni-Orasche*,[46] the issue for consideration was whether a woman who had worked for just two months and a half could nonetheless be considered a worker, and therefore have a right not to be discriminated against on grounds of nationality in relation to study finance for a university course (Article 7(2) of Regulation 1612/68—see below). The Court of Justice instructed the national court to have sole regard to the nature of the activity, i.e. whether it was genuine and not purely ancillary, in order to determine the status of Ms Ninni-Orasche, and to disregard any other consideration, including the fact that she had taken up the job years after having first entered the host-territory; that soon after taking up the job she obtained a qualification which made her eligible for enrolment in a university; and that she was looking for a job in between finishing her short fixed term employment and enrolling in the university.

The reason why an individual moves to seek work in another Member State is immaterial to her/his classification as a worker. Thus, it is irrelevant that a person has moved for the sole purpose of triggering the Treaty and therefore benefit of rights granted by Community law.[47] However, in *Brown* the Court held that if the primary purpose for which the person has moved is to undertake university education, and the employed activity, whilst being genuine, is purely ancillary to the studies, then the rights to equal treatment in relation to social advantages might be of more limited application, and the worker/student will not be entitled to maintenance grants otherwise available to workers who, after having worked, decide to pursue training relevant to their previous occupation.[48]

It is not clear whether *Brown* is still good law after the ruling in **18–010** *Bidar*.[49] It will be recalled that in that case the Court held that a Union citizen residing in another Member State by virtue of

---

[44] Case 139/85, *Kempf* [1986] E.C.R. 1741.
[45] Case 66/85 *Lawrie-Blum* [1986] E.C.R. 2121, paras 19–21; Case 344/87 *Battray* [1989] E.C.R. 1621, para.15; Case C–3/90 *Bernini* [1992] E.C.R. 1071, paras 15 and 16.
[46] Case C–413/01 *Ninni-Orasche* [2003] E.C.R. I–13187, para.32.
[47] e.g. Case C–109/01 *Akrich* [2003] E.C.R. I–9607.
[48] Case 197/86 *Brown* [1988] E.C.R. 3205; Case C–3/90 *Bernini* [1992] E.C.R. I–1071, paras 20 and 21.
[49] Case C–209/03 *Bidar* [2005] E.C.R. I–2119.

Directive 90/364 on the general right of residence is in principle entitled to equal treatment in relation to all benefits, including maintenance grants, save for the possibility for the Member State to justify denial of the benefit in the case in which the Union citizen had not acquired a sufficient link with the host State.[50] It could be argued then that whether or not a worker who has moved with the main purpose of undertaking higher education is eligible for maintenance grants will very much depend on whether she/he has acquired a sufficient link with the host country. Admittedly, this would be unlikely for those who moved *only* to undertake a university course, since the length of stay prior to enrolment as students would probably not be sufficient to establish the required link. However, if *Brown* has to be reinterpreted in the light of the citizenship provisions, a longer length of stay, even when instrumental, might entitle the Union citizen/worker to equal treatment also in relation to maintenance grants.

Furthermore, even though the concept of worker is generously construed, it still covers only the pursuit of *effective* and *genuine* activities, and not activities on such a small scale as to be regarded as "marginal and ancillary."[51] Work cannot be regarded as an effective and genuine economic activity if it constitutes merely a means of rehabilitation or reintegration for the persons concerned and the purpose of the paid employment, which is adapted to the physical and mental capabilities of each person, is to enable those persons sooner or later to recover their capacity to take ordinary employment or to lead as normal as possible a life.[52] In the case of *Tojani*,[53] a French citizen living in Belgium did about 30 hours work a week for the Salvation Army as part of a personal socio-occupational reintegration scheme; in return for his work he received board, lodging and some pocket money. He then claimed subsistence benefits, which were denied on the grounds that he was not a worker within the meaning of Article 39 EC and was therefore not entitled to social assistance. On a preliminary ruling, the Court of Justice held that in deciding whether work is to be regarded as an "effective and genuine" economic activity the national court:

> "must in particular ascertain whether the services actually performed by Mr Trojani are capable of being regarded as forming part of the normal labour market. For that purpose, account may be taken of the status and practices of the hostel, the content of the social reintegration programme, and the nature and details of performance of the services".[54]

---

[50] See p.680, Ch.17.
[51] Case 197/86 *Brown* [1988] E.C.R. 3205.
[52] Case 344/87 *Battray* [1989] E.C.R. 1621.
[53] Case C–456/02 *Trojani* [2004] E.C.R. I–7574.
[54] Para.24.

This said, the motives which may have prompted a "worker" to seek employment in another Member State are of no account as regards her/his right to enter and reside in the territory of that State, provided that he/she pursues or wishes to pursue an effective and genuine activity.[55]

Retention of Status of Worker

We saw in the previous chapter that an economically active Union **18–011** citizen might retain her/his status as a worker or self employed when she/he is unable to work as a result of illness and accident; she/he is duly recorded in involuntary unemployment having been employed for more than one year and having registered as a work seeker; if the worker has been employed for less than a year the status as a worker is retained for no less than six months; or she/he embarks in vocational training related to the previous employment; in the case of involuntarily unemployment the latter condition does not apply, and the worker can choose any vocational training.[56] The retention of the status of worker is important both in order to establish unconditional residence, and for entitlement to welfare benefits. In relation to vocational training, welfare benefits include maintenance grants during education, and the Directive codifies, seemingly in a slightly more generous way, existing case law.

Thus, in the case of *Lair*,[57] the Court, relying on the fact that secondary legislation provided for rights for workers who are no longer active either because of involuntary unemployment, illness, and retirement, held that migrant workers "are guaranteed certain rights linked to the status of worker even when they are no longer in an employment relationship".[58] It then specified that in the fields of maintenance grant for education there should be either some continuity between the previous occupational activity and the studies undertaken; or the worker has become involuntarily unemployed and is obliged by the conditions of the job market to retrain in another field. As we have seen above, in relation to involuntarily unemployed workers, Article 7(3)(d) of Directive 2004/38 does not link the possibility to retrain in another field to the conditions of the job market.

What constitutes 'involuntarily unemployment' depends on the circumstances; thus, the Court has clarified that a worker might be qualified as involuntarily unemployed even when she/he is unemployed as a result of the expiry of a fixed term contract,[59] i.e. when

---

[55] Case 53/81 *Levin* [1982] E.C.R. 1035; Case C–109/01 *Akrich* [2003] E.C.R. I–9607.
[56] Art.7(3) Dir.2004/38, and see Ch.17, para.17–012.
[57] Case 39/86 *Lair* [1988] E.C.R. 3161.
[58] *ibid.* para.36.
[59] Case C–413/01 *Ninni-Orasche* [2003] E.C.R. I–13187, para.32, and see Art.7(3)(c) of Dir.2004/38.

the unemployment is not caused by dismissal. Whether in such cases the worker is involuntarily unemployed depends on several circumstances and in particular the structure of the labour market in that sector, i.e. whether the fix term contract is usual practice in the sector concerned, whether it is imposed on the worker, etc. Lastly, in order to avoid abuses of Community law directed at exploiting the welfare provision of the host-State, the Court has clarified that the "worker" does not retain her/his status in relation to maintenance grants, when the employment is purely ancillary to the studies about to be undertaken,[60] at least in those cases where the worker has not established a sufficient link with the host country.[61]

Work-seekers

18–012　　Article 39 EC would lose much of its effect if Union citizens were not entitled to move in order to seek work, as it might be difficult to find employment from abroad. For this reason, the Court had no hesitation in holding that Article 39 EC also applies to work-seekers, who have a right to move to another Member State to seek employment and are entitled to stay there for a 'reasonable amount of time' without being deported, and even beyond that time if they can prove that they have genuine chances of being employed.[62] However, the Court originally excluded work-seekers from the right to equal treatment in relation to social and tax advantages, and limited their right to equal treatment to access to the labour market. Thus, even though Union citizens could move to any of the Member States in order to look for a job, they could not claim social assistance from the authorities of the host-State. Rather, the job seeker was (and is) entitled under Regulation 1408/71,[63] to "export", where possible, to the host-State such benefits as she/he would have been entitled to in the home State. This system was clearly inspired by the desire to avoid welfare tourism, i.e. the instrumental use of the free movement provisions for the sole purpose of exploiting the most generous welfare system. However, following the introduction of Union citizenship, the Court has changed its interpretation of Article 39 EC.

In the case of *Collins*,[64] Mr Collins was an Irish citizen who went to the United Kingdom and whilst looking for a job claimed

---

[60] Case 197/86 *Brown* [1988] E.C.R. 3205.

[61] See pp.713–714 above, and Case C–209/03 *Bidar* [2005] E.C.R. I–2119.

[62] Case C–292/89 *Antonissen* [1991] E.C.R. I–745; Case C–344/95 *Commission v Belgium* [1997] E.C.R. I–1035. In *Antonissen*, the Court held that six months was to be considered a 'reasonable time', and in *Commission v Belgium* it held that even three months would be enough.

[63] A new and slightly more relaxed regime is about to enter into force following the adoption of Reg.883/2004, [2004] O.J. L200/1.

[64] Case C–138/02 *Collins* [2004] E.C.R. I–2703.

unemployment benefits. He was denied the benefit on the grounds that he was not habitually resident in the United Kingdom; since he was not a worker but a work-seeker he was not, according to the Court's own previous case law, entitled to equal treatment in relation to welfare benefits. On a preliminary reference, the ECJ decided that the time was ripe for a change in its interpretation of Article 39 EC. Thus, the Court held that that Article had now to be interpreted in the light of the introduction of Union citizenship; since Union citizens are entitled to equal treatment in regard to all matters falling within the material scope of the Treaty,[65] it was no longer possible to exclude from the scope of application of Article 39(2) EC (which provides for the general right to equal treatment) benefits of a financial nature for work-seekers. Thus, work-seekers are now entitled to equal treatment in the host Member State, even in relation to welfare benefits. However, it is open to the Member State to justify indirect discrimination (a residence requirement is always to be so considered), in particular by claiming the necessity to ensure that a genuine link exists between claimant and labour market, therefore limiting, if not eliminating, the possibility of welfare tourism. Thus, a residence requirement is, in principle, an appropriate way of ensuring that the claimant is genuinely seeking work (although, the length of residence required must not go beyond what is necessary).[66]

Part of the case law on work seekers (but not the ruling in *Collins*) has now been codified in Directive 2004/38, which provides for an unconditional right of residence for everyone for up to three months (Article 6) and for the retention of such right for work-seekers who have genuine chances of finding a job (Article 14(4)(b)). However, and contrary to what held in *Collins*, Article 24(2) excludes work seekers from the right to equal treatment in relation to social assistance. It is to be seen whether the Court will be willing to reconsider its ruling in *Collins* in the light of the Directive, or rather whether it will rely on the Treaty to limit the exclusion from the right to equal treatment for welfare benefits to the first three months of temporary residence, which seems in line with the *Collins* ruling, and just ignore that part of the derogation in Article 24(2) which allows the Member States to exclude work-seekers from welfare benefits for longer if they so wish. After all, it could be argued, that if the work-seeker is being allowed to stay in the host-territory because he/she has genuine chances of getting employed, he/she will also have established a genuine link with the employment market, sufficient to entitle them to welfare benefits. Thus, the Court may well require the Member States to justify denial of welfare provision

---

[65] See in particular Case C–184/99 *Grzelcyk* [2001] E.C.R. I–6193 and Case C–224/98 *D'Hoop* [2002] E.C.R. I–6191, and the discussion in para.17–002 of the previous chapter.
[66] The ruling in *Collins* has been confirmed in Case C–258/04 *Ioannidis* [2005] E.C.R. I–8275.

to work seekers who are allowed to remain in the country past the initial period of time.

In any event, a worker seeking employment in a Member State other than his/her own is entitled to receive from the host-State's employment services the same assistance as that afforded to national workers.[67]

REMOVAL OF RESTRICTIONS ON MOVEMENT AND RESIDENCE IN THE MEMBER STATES

18–013   The Treaty provides that freedom of movement for workers shall entail the right to move freely within the Member States for the purpose of accepting offers of employment actually made and empowers the Council to implement this objective by legislation.[68] Acting under this authority the Council issued Directive 68/360[69] on the abolition of restrictions on movement and residence for workers of the Member States and their families, which, as we have seen in the previous chapter, has now been repealed and substituted by Directive 2004/38. The provisions of Article 39 EC are directly effective,[70] as were those of Directive 68/360,[71] and now of Directive 2004/38. The Court explained in *Royer*,[72] "the directives concerned [including 68/360] determined the scope and detailed rules for the exercise of rights conferred directly by the Treaty." As we have seen in the previous chapter, Directive 2004/38 (like Directive 68/360 before it) grants the worker a right to go in any of the Member States in order to seek or take up employment and to reside there. The right to enter, move and reside can be limited only by invoking grounds of public policy, public security, public health. Those are narrowly construed since they constitute derogations from a fundamental Community right.[73]

After five years of lawful residence, the worker (and her/his family) can obtain a right to reside permanently in the host State, and as we have seen in the previous chapter, in certain cases (retirement and incapacity) the right of permanent residence can be acquired before five years.[74] Furthermore, and as we shall see in the

---

[67] Art.5.
[68] Art.39(3)(a) and (b) EC and Art.40 EC.
[69] [1968] J.O. L257/13; O.J. Spec. Ed. 1968 (II), 485.
[70] Case 167/73 *Commission v France* [1974] E.C.R. 359; Case 41/74 *Van Duyn* [1974] E.C.R. 1337.
[71] Case 36/75 *Rutili* [1975] E.C.R. 1219.
[72] Case 48/75 *Royer* [1976] E.C.R. 497.
[73] See Ch.17 above, para.17–023.
[74] Art.17 Directive 2004/38, see Ch.17.

sections below, the worker has the right to equal treatment in relation to all matters falling within the scope of the Treaty, including social advantages, as well as the right not to be "hindered" in his/her possibility to move around the Community to exercise her/his economic activity.

EQUALITY OF TREATMENT

General

Article 39(2) EC provides that freedom of movement for workers **18–014** shall entail the abolition of any discrimination based on nationality between workers of the Member States as regards employment, remuneration and other conditions of work and employment. According to the Court's case law, the prohibition on discrimination on grounds of nationality encompasses both direct and indirect discrimination. Direct discrimination occurs when the national and the non-national are treated differently in law; as we shall see below, such discrimination can only be justified on one of the grounds listed in Article 39(3) and (4) EC. Indirect discrimination occurs when an apparently neutral rule affects non-nationals more heavily than nationals, e.g. a residence requirement is indirectly discriminatory since nationals are more likely to be resident in the national territory than non-nationals. Indirect discrimination can be justified by imperative requirements of public interest.[75] A rule can be justified by an imperative requirement when it pursues an aim compatible with Community law (an interest worthy of protection); and when the restriction it imposes on the enjoyment of the Community right is necessary to achieve that aim, as well as proportionate. Furthermore, and as seen in Chapter 8, when the Member States invoke either a Treaty derogation or an imperative requirement to justify a rule, the situation falls within the scope of Community law and the rule must also respect fundamental rights as general principles of Community law.[76]

Article 39 EC does not exclude the right of Member States to adopt reasonable measures to keep track of the movement of aliens within their territory.[77] On the other hand, while Member States may impose penalties for failure to comply with the requirements of

---

[75] Imperative requirements are akin to the mandatory requirements in the context of the free movement of goods; see Ch.16, para.16–044, above.

[76] See Ch.8, para.8–010, above.

[77] Case 118/75 *Watson and Belmann* [1976] E.C.R. 1185, discussed (1975–76) 1 E.L. Rev. 556. But a requirement that nationals of other Member States make a declaration of residence within three days of arrival is unreasonable and contrary to Community law, Case 265/88 *Messner* [1989] E.C.R. 4209.

Community law relating to migrants, such penalties must be comparable to those attaching to the infringement of provisions of equal importance by nationals, and such punishment must be proportionate to the gravity of the offences involved.[78] However, where Community law permits differentiation between migrants and national workers, for instance in allowing Member States to require the possession of residence permits by aliens,[79] Member States may impose more serious penalties for infractions of such requirements than would be imposed in the case of the commission by nationals of comparable offences, for instance the failure to comply with the requirement that nationals possess identity cards.[80] But while such penalties may be more serious, they may not be disproportionately so.[81]

Whereas Directive 2004/38 ensures entry and residence for Community workers,[82] the right to equal treatment in respect of job opportunity and conditions of employment is detailed by Regulation 1612/68 on freedom of movement for workers within the Community.[83] Part I of the Regulation is now divided into three Titles:

— Eligibility for employment;
— Employment and equality of treatment; and
— Workers' families.

The Title concerning the workers' family has been moved to Directive 2004/38, but for Article 12 which provides for equal treatment in education for the workers' children. It is convenient to adopt the scheme of the Regulation for the purposes of exposition of its terms and discussion of the case law of the Court.

Eligibility for employment

18–015   The Regulation guarantees to workers the right to take up employment in the territory of a Member State with the same priority as the nationals of the State in question.[84] Employees and

---

[78] Case 118/75 *Watson and Belmann* [1976] E.C.R. 1185, para.21.
[79] As to which, see above, Ch.17, para.17–016.
[80] Case 8/77 *Sagulo* [1977] E.C.R. 1495, discussed (1977) 2 E.L. Rev. 445. It may be that Case 118/75 *Watson & Belmann* [1976] E.C.R. 1185, may be explained on the basis that keeping track of aliens constitutes objective differentiation between nationals and non nationals, but it is indirect rather than direct discrimination on grounds of nationality which is normally capable of objective justification.
[81] Case C–24/97 *Commission v Germany* [1998] E.C.R. I–2133.
[82] And such rights were previously ensured by Dir.68/360.
[83] [1968] J.O. L257/2, Spec. Ed.(II), 475. The right to equal treatment is of course granted directly by Art.39 EC and the Court has made clear that Reg.1612/68 is therefore not constitutive of rights granted directly by the Treaty. This means that the fact that a given right is not mentioned in the Regulation is immaterial if that right is seen as to be conferred directly by Art.39 EC.
[84] Art.1(2) Reg.1612/68.

employers are entitled to exchange their applications for, and offers of, employment and to conclude and perform contracts in accordance with "the provisions in force laid down by law, regulation or administrative action, without any discrimination resulting therefrom."[85]

National provisions, whether the result of legal regulation or administrative action, are stated to be inapplicable if they limit explicitly or implicitly the right of workers to take up and pursue employment.[86] An exception is made in the case of linguistic requirements necessitated by the nature of the post to be filled.[87] In the *Groener* case[88] the Court considered the compatibility with Regulation 1612/68 of national rules making appointment to a permanent full time post as a lecturer in public vocational educational institutions conditional upon proof of an adequate knowledge of the Irish language. Knowledge of the Irish language was not required for the performance of the duties which teaching of the kind at issue specifically entailed. The Court held, however, that the post justified the requirement of linguistic knowledge, provided that the requirement in question was imposed as part of a policy for the promotion of the national language which was the first official language, and provided that the request was applied in a proportionate and non-discriminatory manner. A language requirement is considered indirectly discriminatory also when imposed by the employer rather than by legislation. Whilst in this case Article 3 of Regulation 1612/68 is not relevant, the Court has held that the requirement to possess a certificate of bilingualism issued by a local authority, without the applicant being allowed to prove language proficiency by alternative means, infringed the principle of equal treatment (nationals being more likely to reside in the region and therefore acquire the regional language certificate).[89]

Article 3 of the Regulation itemises, as particular instances of the provisions declared inapplicable by the foregoing, those which:

"(a) prescribe a special recruitment procedure for foreign nationals;

(b) limit or restrict the advertising of vacancies in the press or through any other medium or subject it to conditions other than those applicable in respect of employers pursuing their activities in the territory of that Member State;

(c) subject eligibility for employment to conditions of registration with employment offices or impede recruitment of

---

[85] Art.2 Reg.1612/68.
[86] Art.3(1) Reg.1612/68.
[87] Art.3(1), Reg.1612/68, last sub-para.
[88] Case 378/87 [1989] E.C.R. 3967.
[89] Case C–281/98 *Angonese* [2000] E.C.R. I–4139.

individual workers where persons who do not reside in the territory of that State are concerned."

18–016 Article 4 of the Regulation provides that national rules restricting by number or percentage the employment of foreign nationals are to be inapplicable to nationals of the Member States. In *Commission v France*,[90] the Court held that France had infringed Article 39 EC and Article 4 of Regulation 1612/68 by providing for a ratio of maximum one foreigner to three Frenchmen in certain jobs on sea vessels. Faced with the French Government's objection that it had given instructions that such provision should not apply to Community nationals, and that in practice it was not applied to Community nationals, the Court acknowledged that whilst the objective legal situation was clear—namely, that Article 39 of the EC Treaty and Regulation 1612/68 were directly applicable in France—the fact that the non-discriminatory application of the offending rules appeared to be a matter of grace, not of law, brought about an ambiguous situation creating uncertainty for those subject to the law.

Regulation 1612/68 further provides that the engagement or recruitment of a national of one Member State for a post in another Member State shall not depend on medical, vocational or other criteria which are discriminatory by comparison with those applied in the case of national workers.[91] Nevertheless, when an employer actually offers a job to a national of another Member State he/she may expressly condition this offer on the candidate undergoing a vocational test.[92] An eligibility for employment issue which is not addressed by Regulation 1612/68 is that of national requirements to the effect that those carrying on certain activities be in possession of certain qualifications. Such requirements also affect self-employed activities, and the exercise of the right of establishment and the freedom to provide services. The compatibility of such requirements with Articles 39, 43 and 49 EC, and the effect of directives on mutual recognition of qualifications on the exercise of employed and self-employed activities, are considered in some detail in Chapter 19.

The public service proviso

18–017 As we have seen, Member States cannot impose nationality conditions for access to employment. However, there is an exception to this rule, and Member States are entitled to reserve some posts in the public service to their own nationals. Article 39(4) EC provides that the "provisions of this Article shall not apply to employment in the public service." The provision does not apply to all employment

---

[90] Case 167/73 *Commission v France* [1974] E.C.R. 359.
[91] Art.6(1).
[92] Art.6(2).

in the public service, nor does it allow discrimination in the terms and conditions of employment once appointed. This much is clear from the judgment in *Sotgiu*,[93] in which the referring court sought a ruling from the Court of Justice on the question whether or not Article 7 of Regulation 1612/68 was applicable to employees in the German postal service in view of this proviso. The Court replied that since the exception contained in Article 39(4) EC could not be allowed a scope extending beyond the object for which it was included, the provision could be invoked to restrict the admission of foreign nationals to *certain activities* in the public service, but not to justify discrimination once they had been admitted.[94]

The Court further clarified the scope of Article 39(4) in *Commission v Belgium (No.1)* holding that that Article:

> ". . . removes from the ambit of Article 48(1)–(3) [now 39(1) to (3)] a series of posts which involve direct or indirect participation in the exercise of powers conferred by public law and duties designed to safeguard the general interests of the State or of other public authorities. Such posts in fact presume on the part of those occupying them the existence of a special relationship of allegiance to the State and reciprocity of rights and duties which form the foundation of the bond of nationality."[95]

Thus not all posts in the public service fall within the public service proviso. In the Court's view, to extend Article 39(4) EC to posts which, while coming under the State or other organisations governed by public law, still do not involve any association with tasks belonging to the public service properly so called, would be to remove a considerable number of posts from the ambit of the principles set out in the Treaty and to create inequalities between the Member States according to the different ways in which the State and certain sectors of economic life are organised.

Nevertheless, classification of particular posts can cause difficulty. **18–018** In *Commission v Belgium (No.2)*,[96] the Court approved the Commission's concession that the following posts fell within the ambit of Article 39(4) EC: head technical office supervisor, principal supervisor, works supervisor, stock controller, and nightwatchman with the Municipalities of Brussels and Auderghem. The Court also upheld the Commission's view that a number of other jobs with Belgian National Railways, Belgian Local Railways, the City of Brussels, and the Commune of Auderghem, fell outside Article 39(4) EC. These

---

[93] Case 152/73 [1974] E.C.R. 153.
[94] On the point that Art.39(4) cannot justify discrimination if non-nationals are admitted to the public service, see also Case 225/85 *Commission v Italy* [1987] E.C.R. 2625, and Cases 389 and 390/87 *Echternach* [1987] E.C.R. 723.
[95] Case 149/79 [1980] E.C.R. 3881, para.10.
[96] Case 149/79 [1982] E.C.R. 1845.

jobs included railway shunters, drivers, platelayers, signalmen and nightwatchmen, and nurses, electricians, joiners and plumbers employed by the Auderghem.

Participation in the exercise of powers conferred by public law would clearly cover the exercise of police powers not exercisable by the ordinary citizen, and the exercise of other binding powers such as the grant or refusal of planning permissions. A Commission notice has stated that:

> ". . . the derogation in Article 48(4) [now 39(4)] covers specific functions of the State and similar bodies such as the armed forces, the police and other forces for the maintenance of order, the judiciary, the tax authorities and the diplomatic corps . . . The derogation is also seen as covering posts in State Ministries, regional government authorities, local authorities and other similar bodies, central banks and other public bodies, where the duties of the post involve the exercise of State authority, such as the preparation of legal acts, the implementation of such acts, monitoring of their application and supervision of subordinate bodies."[97]

The nature of some of the posts held in *Commission v Belgium* above to fall within the public service proviso seems to suggest that the reference to participation in the exercise of powers conferred by public law includes the exercise of senior managerial powers over state resources. This is confirmed by the judgment of the Court in *Commission v Italy*,[98] in which the Court rejected the proposition that research posts at the national research centre (CNR) could be reserved to Italian nationals, and stated:

> "Simply referring to the general tasks of the CNR and listing the duties of all its researchers is not sufficient to establish that the researchers are responsible for exercising powers conferred by public law or for safeguarding the general interests of the state. Only the duties *of management or of advising the state on scientific and technical questions could be described as employment in the public service within the meaning of Article 48(4)* [now 39(4)]. However, it has not been established that these duties were carried out by researchers."[99] (emphasis added)

The italicised words in the above extract of the Court's judgment certainly suggest that managerial activities and advice to the state are regarded by the Court as falling within the scope of Article 39(4), as interpreted by the Court in *Commission v Belgium*.

[97] [1988] O.J. C72/2.
[98] Case 225/85 [1987] E.C.R. 2625.
[99] *ibid.*, para.9.

Whereas access to the public service posts in question will often be **18–019** direct, it might also be by promotion from other posts which could not be classified along with those "certain activities" to which access may be limited. It would seem to follow that Article 39(4) EC should be read as permitting discrimination against Community nationals already holding posts in the public service, insofar as promotion to "sensitive" posts is concerned. This consideration was argued by the German Government in *Commission v Belgium*[1] to militate against construing Article 39(4) as only applying to certain posts within the public service, rather than to the public service at large. The Court's reply was that applying Article 39(4) EC to all posts in the public service would impose a restriction on the rights of nationals of other Member States which went further than was necessary to achieve the aims of the proviso.[2]

The public service exception can be relied upon even if the employer is a private person/company, provided that the worker would be exercising public law powers (such as the maintenance of law and order on a vessel). However, the Court has clarified that in order for the derogation in Article 39(4) EC to be relied upon, public law powers linked to a given position must be exercised on a regular basis and must not represent a "very minor" part of the worker's activities.[3]

The Court of Justice has held that the following posts do not qualify for application of the public service proviso: a nurse in a public hospital,[4] a trainee teacher,[5] a foreign language assistant at a university,[6] researchers at a national research centre,[7] and numerous posts in the public sectors of teaching, research, inland transport, posts and telecommunications, and water gas and electricity, not being posts involving the direct or indirect participation in the exercise of powers conferred by public law and duties to safeguard the general interests of the State.[8] Article 39(4) cannot be relied upon by private security undertakings which do not as such comprise part of the public service.[9]

---

[1] Case 149/79 [1980] E.C.R. 3881.
[2] Applying the tests laid down by the Court of Justice, the Court of Appeal of Northern Ireland in the *O'Boyle* and *Plunkett* cases [1999] N.I. 126 [2000] Eu.L.R. 637, has found the post of Deputy Chief Fire Officer of Northern Ireland, and the post of Inland Revenue Claims Examiner, to be posts falling within the public service within the meaning of Art.39(4) EC.
[3] Case C–47/02 *Anker* [2003] E.C.R. I–10447; see also Case C–405/01 *Colegio de Oficiales de la Marina Mercante Española* [2003] E.C.R. I–10391.
[4] Case 307/84 *Commission v France* [1986] E.C.R. 1725.
[5] Case 66/85 *Lawrie-Blum* [1986] E.C.R. 2121.
[6] Case 33/88 *Allué and Coonan* [1989] E.C.R. 1591.
[7] Case 225/85 *Commission v Italy* [1987] E.C.R. 2625.
[8] Case C–473/93 *Commission v Luxembourg* [1996] E.C.R. I–3207.
[9] Case C–114/97 *Commission v Spain* [1998] E.C.R. I–6717, para.33.

EQUALITY IN THE EMPLOYMENT CONTEXT AND BEYOND

Direct and indirect discrimination

18–020   Article 39(2) EC provides for the abolition of discrimination based on nationality in terms and conditions of employment and this prohibition is reiterated and expanded in Article 7(1) of the Regulation, as follows:

> "A worker who is a national of a Member State may not, in the territory of another Member State, be treated differently from national workers by reason of his nationality in respect of any conditions of employment and work, in particular as regards remuneration, dismissal, and should he become unemployed, re-instatement or re-employment."

Infringement of the principle of equality will occur where national legislation expressly attaches different terms to the conditions of employment of national workers and workers from other Community countries. In *Marsman*,[10] a Dutch national resident in the Netherlands was employed in Germany. After becoming incapacitated as a result of an accident at work, he was dismissed by his employer. German legislation provided that seriously disabled workers could not be dismissed without the approval of the main public assistance office. While this protection extended to nationals resident outside Germany, it applied only to non-nationals resident within the jurisdiction. Mr Marsman challenged the legality of his dismissal before a German court, which sought a ruling from the Court of Justice as to whether a Community national in the position of Mr Marsman was entitled to the same protection against dismissal as that afforded to German nationals. The Court replied in the affirmative, emphasising that the social law of the Community was based on the principle that the laws of every Member State were obliged to grant nationals of the other Member States employed in its territory all the legal advantages that it provided for its own citizens.

A slightly more complex situation arises when legislation conditions certain advantages on criteria which, although theoretically applicable to nationals and non-nationals alike, will in practice be fulfilled only by nationals. The point is illustrated in *Ugliola*.[11] The respondent in the main suit was an Italian national employed by the appellant in Germany. He performed his military service in Italy between May 1965 and August 1966, and claimed the right to have this period taken into account in calculating his seniority with his

---

[10] Case 44/72 [1972] E.C.R. 1243.
[11] Case 15/69 [1969] E.C.R. 363.

employer. German legislation provided that military service in the German Army was to be taken into account for such purposes, but made no similar provision for services in the forces of other States. The German court seised of the dispute sought a preliminary ruling from the Court of Justice on the question whether Article 7 of Regulation 1612/68 entitled a Community national in the position of Mr Ugliola to have military service in his home country taken into account for the purposes of the German legislation in question. In its observation to the Court, the German Government argued that the Job-protection Law was not discriminatory, since the possibility to have the period spent in the military taken into account (a) did not apply to nationals who served in the forces of other States and (b) applied to non-nationals who served in the German forces. Advocate General Gand regarded such an argument as tempting, but was not convinced, since performance of military service in the Army of a Member State other than the one whose nationality one possessed was a hypothesis which the German Government agreed was quite theoretical. The Court agreed. The provisions of Community law in question prohibited Member States from "indirectly establishing discrimination"[12] in favour of their own nationals in such a way.[13]

The Court was faced with the problem of allegedly indirect discrimination once more in *Sotgiu*.[14] The plaintiff, an Italian whose family lived in Italy, was employed by the German postal service. He received a separation allowance at 7.50 DM per day, on the same basis as workers of German nationality. In accordance with a Government circular the allowance paid to workers residing within Germany at the time of their recruitment was increased to 10 DM per day, while those workers residing abroad at the time of their recruitment—German and foreign alike—continued to receive the allowance at the old rate. Mr Sotgiu invoked Regulation 1612/68 before a German court, which sought a ruling, *inter alia,* on whether Article 7(1) of the Regulation could be interpreted as prohibiting discrimination on the basis of residence as well as on the basis of nationality. In the course of the arguments before the Court it became apparent that although workers residing within Germany at the time of the recruitment indeed received a larger allowance, it was conditional on their willingness to move to their place of work, and in any event was no longer paid after two years. No such conditions were attached to payment of the allowance to workers residing abroad at the time of the recruitment. The Court affirmed that Article 7 prohibited all covert forms of discrimination which, by the application of criteria other than nationality, nevertheless led to

18–021

---

[12] *ibid.*, para.6.
[13] But see Case C–315/94 *de Vos* [1996] E.C.R. I–1417.
[14] Case 152/73 [1974] E.C.R. 153.

the same result.[15] Such an interpretation was consonant with the fifth recital to the Regulation, which required that equality of treatment for workers to be established in fact as well as in law. Application of criteria such as place of origin or residence, reasoned the Court, could, in appropriate circumstances, have a discriminatory effect in practice that would be prohibited by the Treaty and the Regulation. This would not, however, be the case where the payment of a separation allowance was made on conditions which took account of objective differences in the situation of workers, which differences could involve the place of residence of a worker when recruited. Similarly, the fact that in the case of one group of workers allowances were only temporary while in the case of another they were of unlimited duration, could be a valid reason for differentiating between the amounts paid.

In *Biehl*[16] the Court considered a national rule whereby overpaid tax deducted from salaries and wages was not repayable to taxpayers resident during only part of the year in the relevant Member State. The national tax administration argued that a difference in treatment between two distinct categories of taxpayers did not constitute discrimination if it was objectively justified, and that the rule prevented taxpayers from avoiding the effects of progressive taxation by spreading their tax liability between different States. The Court noted that there was a risk that the criterion of permanent residence in the national territory would work in particular against taxpayers who were nationals of other Member States. The Court rejected the justification offered by the national tax authorities since a national rule such as that in issue was liable to infringe the principle of equal treatment in various situations; in particular where no income arose during the year of assessment to the temporarily resident taxpayer in the country which he had left or in which he had taken up residence. In such a situation, the taxpayer would be treated less favourably than a residence taxpayer because he would lose the right to repayment of the over-deduction of tax which a residence taxpayer would always enjoy. It followed in the Court's view that such a measure was contrary to Article 39(2) EC. The *Biehl* case is not entirely satisfactory. Its ruling is based merely on the risk that non-nationals would be treated less favourably than nationals,[17] and the

---

[15] The Court has consistently held that Art.39 EC prohibits not only overt discrimination by reason of nationality, but also all forms of discrimination which, by the application of other distinguishing criteria, lead in fact to the same result, see *e.g.*, Case 111/91 *Commission v Luxembourg* [1993] E.C.R. I–817, para.9; Case C–419/92 *Ingetraut Scholz v Opera Universitaria di Cagliari* [1994] E.C.R. I–505, para.7; Case 278/94 *Commission v Belgium* [1996] E.C.R. I–4307, para.27.

[16] Case C–175/88 *Klaus Biehl v Administration des contributions du grand-duché de Luxembourg* [1990] E.C.R. I–1779.

[17] In Case 33/88 *Allué and Coonan* [1989] E.C.R. 1591 the Court found indirect discrimination where "only" 25 per cent of persons affected were nationals of the host State, see para.32 of Judgment. But a numerical estimate is not a precondition to establishing indirect discrimination, see below, p.725.

consequence of the ruling seems to be that such a national rule cannot be applied by the national court, even in a case in which the rule would produce neutrality as between residents and non residents. Nevertheless, the Court has acknowledged that the coherence of the tax system may sometimes justify measures otherwise contrary to Article 39 EC. Thus in *Bachmann*[18] the Court held that while a national rule making pension contributions tax-deductible but confining this advantage to contributions made in national territory was in principle contrary to Article 39 EC, it could be justified where the counterpart of making such contributions tax-deductible was subjecting the resulting pensions to tax liability.

Unless it is objectively justified and proportionate to its aim, a provision of national law must be regarded as *indirectly* discriminatory if it is intrinsically liable to affect migrant workers more than national workers and if there is a consequent risk that it will place the former at a particular disadvantage.[19] As it is clear from the cases referred to above, the Court has given a broad interpretation of the principle of indirect discrimination and the best formulation of what is to be understood as indirectly discriminatory has been given in the case of *O'Flynn*. In that case an Irish national working in the UK applied for a grant to cover his son's funeral expenses. The British authorities refused to grant the benefit on the grounds that the funeral was taking place outside the UK territory. Mr O'Flynn claimed that such refusal was inconsistent with Article 7(2) of Regulation 1612/68, as the grant was to be considered a social advantage which could not be made conditional upon directly or indirectly discriminatory criteria. The Court agreed. It held that:

> "(. . .) conditions imposed by national law must be regarded as indirectly discriminatory where, although applicable irrespective of nationality, they affect essentially migrant workers (. . .) or the great majority of those affected are migrant workers (. . .), where they are indistinctly applicable but can more easily be satisfied by national workers than by migrant workers (. . .), or where there is a risk that they may operate to the particular detriment of migrant workers (. . .)".[20]

Thus the Court made clear that any rule that even only risks putting foreigners or migrants at a disadvantage has to be considered indirectly discriminatory and needs to be justified by an imperative requirement. Furthermore, the Court also clarified that, differently

---

[18] Case C–204/90 *Hanns-Martin Bachmann v Belgian State* [1992] E.C.R. I–249; in relation to taxation see also Ch.20, para.20–040 below.
[19] Case C–237/94 *John O'Flynn v Adjudication Officer* [1996] E.C.R. I–2617, para.20; Case 57/96 *H. Meints v Minister van Landbouw* [1997] E.C.R. I–6689, para.45.
[20] Case C–237/94 *John O'Flynn v Adjudication Officer* [1996] E.C.R. I–2617, para.18.

from sex discrimination law, it is enough for a rule to "potentially" affect more migrants than nationals, for it to be considered discriminatory. Thus the claimant does not need to prove, with statistical means or otherwise, that the rule imposes a heavier burden on migrants. The mere likelihood of a rule to do so is enough to bring it within the scope of the prohibition on discrimination. Not surprisingly then, the Court held that the rule in *O'Flynn* was indeed indirectly discriminatory since foreigners are more likely to want to have their relatives buried in their country of origin. Nor could the rule be justified by an imperative requirement. The United Kingdom sought to justify the rule having regard to the "prohibitive costs and practical difficulties" of paying a burial taking place outside the United Kingdom. The Court was not persuaded: the cost of transport was not reimbursed, and so higher costs faced in relation to intra-State transport was not an issue; and, as far as the cost of the burial was concerned, the Court simply reminded the United Kingdom that it could adopt other, non-discriminatory, cost containing measures, such as fixing a lump sum or limiting the amount of the reimbursement to a given amount having regard to the normal cost of burial in the United Kingdom.

The Court seems willing to assume, on a common sense basis, that certain distinguishing criteria, especially if they contain a territorial element, such as a period of practical training administered by the authorities of the State in question, will in the vast majority of cases operate to the advantage of nationals rather than non-nationals.[21] The same reasoning imposes upon the Member States the duty to take into account employment in the public service of other Member States, if they take into account experience gained in their own public service.[22]

Equality in social and tax advantages

18-022   In order to ensure equality for Community workers in the employment context, Regulation 1612/68 provides that they shall have "by virtue of the same right and under the same conditions as national workers [. . .] access to training in vocational schools and retraining centres."[23] Freedom from discrimination for Community workers, although limited explicitly to the employment context in the

---

[21] Case C–27/91 *Union de Recouvrement des Cotisations de Sécurité Sociale et d'Allocations Familiales de la Savoie (URSSAF) v Hostellerie Le Manoir SARL* [1991] E.C.R. I–5531, para.11. As indicated above, the Court will sometimes be in a position to make an assessment based on an actual numerical estimate of the relative numbers of nationals and non-nationals involved.

[22] Case C–419/92 *Scholz* [1994] E.C.R. I–505; Case C–15/96 *Schöning* [1998] E.C.R. I–47; Case C–195/98 *Österreichischer Gewerkschaftsbund* [2000] E.C.R. I–10497; Case C–278/03 *Commission v Italy* (State Schools) [2005] E.C.R. I–3747.

[23] Art.7(3).

Treaty, could not be achieved without requiring appropriate adjustments to all fields of national law and practice which might be likely to have an effect on the conditions under which migrants take up and pursue employment. Thus Article 7(2) of the Regulation provides that a national of one Member State employed in another "shall enjoy the same social and tax advantages as national workers." The wording and context of the Article suggest that it might be restricted to social and tax advantages conferred by national law on workers as such, but the Court of Justice has taken a more liberal view, as its judgment in *Cristini* illustrates. French legislation provided that in families of three or more children under the age of 18 years, the father, mother, and each child under 18 years should receive a personal identity card entitling them to a reduction of between 30 and 75 per cent in the scheduled fare charged by French Railways, the SNCF. A French court sought a preliminary ruling from the Court of Justice on the question whether the reduction card issued by the SNCF to large families constituted for the workers of the Member States a "social advantage" within the meaning of Article 7(2) of the Regulation. The SNCF, in its observations to the Court, argued that Article 7(2) referred exclusively to advantages attaching to the nationals of Member States by virtue of their status as workers, and accordingly had no application to a benefit such as the reduction cards issued by the SNCF. The Court rejected this view, reasoning as follows:

> "Although it is true that certain provisions in this article refer to relationships deriving from the contract of employment, there are others, such as those concerning reinstatement and re-employment should a worker become unemployed, which have nothing to do with such relationships and even imply the termination of a previous employment.
>
> It therefore follows that, in view of the equality of treatment which the provision seeks to achieve, the substantive area of application must be delineated so as to include all social and tax advantages, whether or not attached to the contract of employment, such as reductions in fares for large families."[24]

The Court has subsequently held that Article 7(2) applies to any benefit payable by virtue of an individual's status as a worker, or residence on national territory, where the extension of the benefit to nationals of other Member States seems suitable to facilitate free movement of workers.[25] Thus, Article 7(2) has been held to cover seven year interest-free means-tested loans to families in respect of newly born children, even though the loans were of a discretionary

---

[24] Case 32/75 *Cristini v SNCF* [1975] E.C.R. 1985, 1094, 1095.
[25] Case 207/78 *Even* [1979] E.C.R. 2019.

nature[26]; an allowance to handicapped adults covered by Regulation 1408/71 on Social Security[27]; a guaranteed minimum subsistence allowance[28]; the possibility of using one's own language in court proceedings[29]; a special unemployment benefit for young persons falling outside the ambit of Regulation 1408/71[30]; an old age benefit for those lacking entitlement to a pension under the national social security system[31]; a guaranteed minimum income for old persons[32]; and a grant to cover funeral expenses.[33] Finally, in *Reed*, faced with a national rule which provided that nationals could obtain a residence permit for their (unmarried) partners, whilst foreigners could not, the Court held that the right to have one's partner was a social advantage falling within the scope of Article 7(2) and it was thus covered by the principle of non-discrimination.[34] Admittedly, the ruling is rather far fetched; however it shows the Court's willingness to stretch the provisions of Community law to the maximum in order to foster and ensure free movement. This said, the term "social advantage" does not extend to cover benefits awarded because of the "special link of nationality". This would be the case for most benefits awarded as compensation for services rendered to one's country during wartime, or as compensation for military service. This type of benefit is not awarded to the individuals for reason of their being workers; rather, it is awarded because of the special link of nationality that requires individuals to serve in the army. For instance an early retirement on full pension for those in receipt of an invalidity pension granted by an Allied Power in respect of war service[35]; or an advantage comprising partial compensation for those national workers called up for the consequences of the obligation to perform military service[36]; and an allowance for former prisoners of war,[37] are not considered to be social advantages within the meaning of Article 7(2).

Article 7(2) also requires non-discrimination in relation to tax advantages; here the assessment of the existence of indirect discrimination might well be more complicated since taxes (and tax advantages) are inherently territorial. This means that in some cases, a residence requirement in order to benefit of tax advantages, a requirement which would normally be considered indirectly discriminatory, might be compatible with the Treaty since residents and non-

---

[26] Case 65/81 *Reina* [1982] E.C.R. 33.
[27] Case 63/76 *Inzirillo* [1976] E.C.R. 2057.
[28] Case 249/83 *Hoecks* [1985] E.C.R. 973; Case 122/84 *Scrivner* [1985] E.C.R. 1027.
[29] Case 137/84 *Mutsch* [1985] E.C.R. 2681.
[30] Case 94/84 *Deak* [1985] E.C.R. 1873.
[31] Case 157/84 *Frascogna* [1985] E.C.R. 1739.
[32] Case 261/83 *Castelli* [1984] E.C.R. 3199.
[33] Case C–237/94 *John O'Flynn v Adjudication Officer* [1996] E.C.R. I–2617.
[34] The ruling has now been codified in Art.3 of Directive 2004/38.
[35] Case 207/78 *Even* [1979] E.C.R. 2019.
[36] Case C–315/94 *de Vos* [1996] E.C.R. I–417.
[37] Case C–386/02 *Baldinger* [2004] E.C.R. I–8411.

residents are in non-comparable situations in relation to direct taxation. This said, the Court readily scrutinises the tax regime to ensure that there is no discrimination: for instance in *Zurstrassen*, Luxembourg legislation provided that spouses could make a joint tax declaration, which was more convenient from a tax viewpoint, only if both spouses were resident in the national territory. Mr Zurstrassen, was a Belgian national working and residing in Luxembourg. His wife and children continued to reside in Belgium, and as his wife was not earning, she was not liable to tax in Belgium. Mr Zurstrassen was prevented from making a joint tax declaration, and instead was treated as a single person, because of the fact that his wife was resident in Belgium. The Court held that, even though residence might be relevant for tax benefits, in the case at stake the Luxembourg legislation was incompatible with Article 39 EC and 7(2) of the Regulation since Mr Zurstrassen received almost all his income in Luxembourg, and was therefore taxed in Luxembourg. To prevent him from declaring his wife as a dependant on the sole ground that she did not reside in Luxembourg constituted indirect discrimination on grounds of nationality since Luxembourg nationals were more likely to reside in Luxembourg.[38]

Membership of trade unions

Article 8 of the Regulation provides that a worker who is a **18–023** national of a Member State and who is employed in the territory of another Member State shall enjoy equality of treatment as regards membership of trade unions and the exercise of rights attaching thereto, including the right to vote and to be eligible for the administration and management posts of a trade union. He/she may however be excluded from taking part in the management of bodies governed by public law and from holding an office governed by public law. In *ASTI*,[39] a case concerning "occupational guilds" from which non-nationals were excluded, it was denied that the bodies in question comprised trade unions for the purpose of the above-mentioned provision. The Court held that this Article constitutes a particular expression of the principle of non-discrimination in the specific field of workers' participation in trade-union organisation and activities, and could not be limited by reference to the legal form of the body in question. "On the contrary", stated the Court, "the exercise of the trade-union rights referred to in that provision extends beyond the bounds of trade-union organisations in the strict sense and includes, in particular, the participation of workers in bodies which, while not being, in law, trade-union organisations, perform similar functions as regards the defence and representation

---

[38] Case C–87/99 *Zurstrassen* [2000] E.C.R. I–3337.
[39] Case C–213/90 [1991] E.C.R. 3507.

of workers' interests."[40] Once more we are reminded of the inter-relation between the secondary legislation in this field and the fact that it is designed to facilitate the enjoyment of rights conferred directly by the Treaty, and is to be interpreted accordingly.

Housing

18–024   The Regulation recognises the importance of freely available housing to the migrant worker when it provides that he/she shall "enjoy all the rights and benefits accorded to national workers in matters of housing, including ownership of the housing he needs."[41] She/he may also, "with the same right as nationals, put his name down on the housing lists in the region in which he is employed, where such lists exist; he shall enjoy the resultant benefits and priorities."[42] If the worker's family have remained in the country whence he/she came, they must be considered, for the purposes of priority on housing lists, as residing in the area where the worker is employed, where national workers benefit from a similar presumption.[43]

NON-DISCRIMINATORY RESTRICTIONS ON FREEDOM OF MOVEMENT FOR WORKERS

18–025   Article 39(1) EC states that "freedom of movement shall be secured within the Community" and Article 39(2) EC states that such freedom "shall entail the abolition of any discrimination based on nationality" between workers of the Member States. While this formulation makes it clear that freedom of movement *includes* the abolition of discrimination based on nationality, it also leaves room for the possibility that non-discriminatory restrictions which prevent freedom of movement being secured are also prohibited by the Treaty. The Community institutions and the Member States seem to have long proceeded on the basis that a worker of any Member State was in principle entitled to leave the territory of any Member State in order to take up activities as an employed person in the territory of another Member State.[44] This right seems to be derived directly from the right to freedom of movement, rather than the right to equality of treatment. Similarly, the right of installation of those

---

[40] *ibid.*, para.16.
[41] Art.9(1) Reg.1612/68.
[42] Art.9(2) Reg.1612/68.
[43] Art.9(2), Reg.1612/68, second sub-para.
[44] Directive 68/360, Arts 1 and 2 (now Art.4 Dir.2004/38).

members of the family specified in Article 2 of Directive 2004/38[45] does not appear to be a right which is conditional upon the same rights being enjoyed by nationals of the host State in question; it appears to be based on the proposition that without the right of installation in question workers would be prevented from exercising in practice the right to freedom of movement envisaged by the Treaty. An analysis which is consistent with the text of Article 39 EC, and the terms of the secondary legislation referred to above, is that Article 39 EC prohibits all obstacles to freedom of movement, whether discriminatory or not, which impede the entry and residence of a migrant worker in a Member State, and the conditions of access to employment in that State, but that national rules which affect the migrant worker in the pursuit and exercise of activities as an employed person, and in the enjoyment of all the social, health, tax,[46] educational and other advantages normally available for residents, are consistent with the latter Article if they do not discriminate either in law or in fact on grounds of nationality. The case law of the Court of Justice is consistent with the above statement of the law, and for a more complete picture of the place of the non-discriminatory restriction to freedom of movement for workers it is appropriate to turn to that case law.

In *Kraus*[47] the Court of Justice considered a situation in which a German national who had passed the first State examination, went to the United Kingdom, where he took the LLM at Edinburgh University. After returning to Germany, he objected to a German legal requirement that as a precondition to using his Scottish academic title he must obtain authorisation from the competent German authority. The Court noted that a postgraduate academic title was not usually a prerequisite for access to a profession, either as an employee or on a self-employed basis, but that the possession of such a title nevertheless constituted, for the person entitled to make use of it, an advantage for the purpose both of gaining entry to such a profession and of prospering in it.[48] The Court held that Article 39 EC precluded any national measure governing the conditions under which an academic title obtained in another Member State might be used, where that measure, even though it was applicable without discrimination on grounds of nationality, was

---

[45] Previously Art.10 Reg.1612/68.
[46] In relation to cases brought under Art.18 EC, the Court has made clear that "the Treaty offers no guarantee to a citizen of the Union that transferring his activities to a Member State other than that in which he previously resided will be neutral as regards taxation. Given the disparities in the tax legislation of the Member States, such a transfer might be to the citizen's advantage in terms of indirect taxation or not, according to the circumstances", Case C–365/02 *Lindorfs* [2004] E.C.R. I–7183, para.34. See also Case C–403/03 *Schempp* [2005] E.C.R. I–6421; and in relation to Art.39 EC see Case C–387/01 *Weigel* [2004] E.C.R. I–4981, para.55.
[47] Case C–19/92 *Dieter Kraus v Land Baden-Württemberg* [1993] E.C.R. I–1663.
[48] *ibid.*, para.18.

liable to hamper or to render less attractive the exercise by Community nationals, including those of the Member State which enacted the measure, of fundamental freedoms guaranteed by the Treaty. The situation would be different only if such a measure pursued a legitimate objective compatible with the Treaty and was justified by pressing reasons of public interest.[49] It is to be noted that the Court's recourse to a very general test of whether a national measure was "liable to hamper or render less attractive" the exercise of free movement was in circumstances in which a national rule in effect governed the conditions of access (as regards the use of the title) of the worker concerned to the labour market of the Member State in question. It did not follow from *Kraus* that thereafter the above formulation would be applicable in all circumstances and that analysis of the question of discrimination would be rendered superfluous.

In *Bosman*[50] the Court considered the consistency with Article 39 EC of rules laid down by sporting associations under which a professional footballer who is a national of one Member State could not, on the expiry of his contract with a club, be employed by another club (of another Member State) unless the latter club had paid to the former a transfer, training or development fee. The Court held that the rules in question, although they did not discriminate on grounds of nationality, constituted an obstacle to freedom of movement for workers. The Court's reasoning was straightforward. It noted that nationals of Member States have in particular the right, which they derive directly from the Treaty, to leave their country of origin to enter the territory of another Member State and reside there in order to pursue an economic activity.[51] And it added that provisions which preclude or deter a national of a Member State from leaving his/her country of origin in order to exercise his/her freedom of movement constitute an obstacle to that freedom even if they apply without regard to the nationality of the workers concerned.[52] This was the effect of the rules in issue in the national proceedings in the cases in point, even if similar rules also governed transfers between clubs within a single Member State. The Court stated:

> "It is sufficient to note that, although the rules in issue in the main proceedings apply also to transfers between clubs belonging to different national associations within the same Member State and are similar to those governing transfers between clubs

---

[49] *ibid.*, para.32. The Court of Justice in the event held that the national measure in question might be so justified.
[50] Case C–415/93 *Union Royale Belge des Sociétés de Football Association ASBL v Jean-Marc Bosman* [1995] E.C.R. I–4921.
[51] *ibid.*, para.95.
[52] *ibid.*, para.96.

belonging to the same national association, they still directly affect players' *access to the employment market* in other Member States and are thus capable of impeding freedom of movement for workers (emphasis added)."[53]

The Court concluded that the transfer rules constituted an obstacle to freedom of movement for workers prohibited in principle by Article 39 EC. It could only be otherwise if the rules pursued a legitimate aim compatible with the Treaty and were justified by pressing reasons of public interest. In order to be so justified they would have to be appropriate to ensure achievement of the aim in question, and not go beyond what was necessary for that purpose.[54]

In *Terhoeve*[55] the Court considered the position of a migrant **18–026** worker who transferred his residence from one Member State to another. The latter subjected Mr Terhoeve to a heavier social security burden than would have been the case if he, in otherwise identical circumstances, had continued to reside throughout the whole year in the Member State in question. The Court, taking a very similar approach to that in *Bosman*, held that a national of a Member State could be deterred from leaving the Member State in which he resides in order to pursue an activity as an employed person in the territory of another Member State if he were required to pay greater social security contributions than if he continued to reside in the same Member State throughout the year, without thereby being entitled to additional social benefits such as to compensate for that increase.[56] It followed, in the view of the Court, that national legislation of the kind in issue in the main proceedings constituted an obstacle to freedom of movement for workers, prohibited in principle by Article 39 EC, and it was therefore unnecessary to consider whether there was indirect discrimination on grounds of nationality, prohibited by the Treaty or by Article 7(2) of Regulation 1612/68.[57] This case too concerns national rules which specifically affect the exercise of the right to freedom of movement and therefore access to the labour market in another Member State, and is so easily explained.

However, the breadth of the *Bosman* formula, which includes mere discouragement to the willingness to move within the definition of obstacles relevant for free movement purposes, led to a

---

[53] *ibid.*, para.103; the Court thus distinguishes the "selling arrangements" referred to in the context of the free movement of goods in Joined Cases C–267/91 and C–268/91 *Keck and Mithouard* [1993] E.C.R. I–6097, as to which see above, Ch.16, para.16–011.

[54] *ibid.*, para.104. For the proportionality of national measures in the similar contexts of the right of establishment, and freedom to provide services, see Ch.19, para.19–036.

[55] Case C–18/95 *F.C. Terhoeve v Inspecteur van de Belastingdienst Particulieren/Ondernemingen Buitenland* [1999] E.C.R. I–345. For another example of an "exit" restriction see Case C–109/04 *Karl Robert Kranemann v Land Nordrhein-Westfalen* [2005] E.C.R. I–493.

[56] *ibid.*, para.40.

[57] *ibid.*, para.41.

rather imaginative attack on national rules regulating compensation for termination of an employment contract. In *Graf*,[58] Mr Graf quit his employment in Austria to take up a position in Germany. The Austrian legislation provided for compensation for termination of employment when such termination resulted from a decision not attributable to the employee (i.e. when the employee had been dismissed for causes not attributable to her/him). Since Mr Graf had voluntarily quit his occupation, he was not entitled to any compensation. Relying on a literal interpretation of the *Bosman* ruling, Mr Graf argued that the rule constituted an obstacle to his right to move to another Member State to there take up employment, since the prospect of losing the right to be compensated discouraged him from moving. The Court was not impressed by the submission: having found that the rule did not put migrant workers at a disadvantage, it turned to the question as to whether nonetheless the rule could be considered an obstacle to movement. The Court found that that could not be the case, since in order to be considered an obstacle to movement, the rule has to affect "*access of the worker to the labour market*".[59] In the case at issue, that was not so since the compensation for involuntary dismissal was not "dependant upon the worker's choosing whether or not to stay with his current employer but on a future and hypothetical event, namely the subsequent termination of his contract without such termination being at his own initiative or attributable to him".[60] Such an event was "too uncertain and indirect" for such rule to be regarded as an obstacle to free movement falling within the scope of the Treaty. In *Graf* the Court defined more precisely the boundaries of Article 39 EC: not any rule which might potentially discourage movement is an obstacle caught by that Article. Rather, the rule needs to affect access to the employment market in a way which is not too uncertain and indirect.

A few months later, the Court delivered two other important rulings. In *Lehtonen*,[61] the Court held that a rule which imposed a deadline in order to field players for the basketball championship was an obstacle falling within the scope of Article 39 EC. Even though the rule applied regardless of the nationality of the player, the Court found that it restricted the possibility of engaging players from other Member States where they have been engaged after the specified date. The Court accepted that in principle a rule prohibiting late transfers is aimed at ensuring that the strength of the teams does not change substantially just before the end of the championship, and is therefore aimed at pursuing the legitimate aim of ensuring the proper functioning of sport competition. However,

---

[58] Case 190/98 *Graf* [2000] E.C.R. I–493.
[59] Para.23, emphasis added.
[60] Para.24.
[61] Case C–176/96 *Lehtonen* [2000] E.C.R. I–2681.

when the Court turned its attention to assessing the proportionality of the rule, it found that it went beyond what was necessary, since players from a federation outside the Eurozone benefited from a later deadline. Thus, if non-EU players could be engaged at a later date without affecting the proper functioning of the championship, then there was no reason why players from the Eurozone could not also benefit from the extended deadline. In *Deliège*,[62] the Court was once again seized with the question of the compatibility with Community law of rules regulating sporting activity. Even though the case related to the free movement of services, the rationale of the case can be easily transposed to the scope of Article 39 EC. Here, the claimant attacked the selection process to be able to take part in an international judo championship. If the *Bosman* ruling were to be applied mechanically, it could be agued that such rules constituted an obstacle to movement, since the fact that Ms Deliège had not been selected meant that she could not go to another Member State to take part in the championship. The Court, however, wisely avoided such interpretation. It held that even though the rules at issue inevitably limited the possibility to take part to sporting competitions, they "were inherent in the conduct of an international high-level sports event".[63]

The above case law shows the limits of the *Bosman* formula: not **18–027** *all* non-discriminatory rules are to be considered as an obstacle to the free movement of workers, as otherwise all rules regulating any aspect of employment activity would have to be justified according to the imperative requirements doctrine. Rather, the above case law is consistent with the proposition that national measures which apply to the entry and residence of migrants, to their access to the employment market, or apply in any other way specifically to the transfer of the migrant from one Member State to another for the purposes of employment, will be prohibited by Article 39 EC if they restrict or impede freedom of movement for workers, even if they do not discriminate, directly or indirectly, on grounds of nationality. National measures which discriminate, not on grounds of nationality, but by placing at a disadvantage those who have exercised their right of free movement as compared to those who have not, will also be regarded as impeding the exercise of freedom of movement.[64] But once a migrant worker has secured entry and residence in a Member

---

[62] Joined Cases C–51/96 and 191/97 *Deliège* [2000] E.C.R. I–2549.
[63] Para.64.
[64] The Court has held that the provisions of the Treaty relating to the free movement of persons are thus intended to facilitate the pursuit by Community citizens of occupational activities of all kinds throughout the Community, and preclude national legislation which might place Community citizens at a disadvantage when they wish to extend their activities beyond the territory of a single Member State, see Case 143/87 *Christopher Stanton and SA belge d'assurances "L'Étoile 1905" v Inasti (Institut national d'assurances sociales pour travailleurs indépendants)* [1988] E.C.R. 3877, para.13

State, and gained access to the employment market of a Member State, and is pursuing employed activities in that State, it will not be possible to object to national rules concerning, e.g., the terms of conditions and employment, or the tax treatment of residents, solely on the ground that they might be described as excessively burdensome to those subject to them. Once integrated into the economic and social life of the host State, the migrant worker's fundamental right derived from Article 39 EC is the right to equality of treatment, in law and in fact.[65] Yet all that said, the *Kraus* formulation, that any national measures liable to hamper or make less attractive the exercise of a fundamental freedom must be justified, does not in terms prevent a migrant worker objecting to *any* national rule or practice which makes less attractive the exercise of her/his fundamental freedom to move to and reside in other Member States, whether or not it specifically relates to the transfer of the migrant from one Member State to another or affects access to the employment market. A broader reading of the *Kraus* than the "access to the market" reading is certainly possible. Yet that broader reading might seem unduly generous to the migrant. Once a migrant worker has secured entry and residence in a Member State, and gained access to the employment market of a Member State, and is pursuing employed activities in that State, it might be said that it should not be possible to object to national rules concerning, e.g., the terms of conditions and employment, or the tax treatment of residents, solely on the ground that they might be described as excessively burdensome or insufficiently generous to those subject to them. Once integrated into the economic and social life of the host State, it would seem to be entirely reasonable if the migrant worker's fundamental right derived from Article 39 EC were simply to be the right to equality of treatment, in law and in fact.[66]

This proposition is not entirely straightforward, however. The argument against drawing a distinction between national rules which might hinder access to the market, and those which do not, is that such a distinction is difficult to draw in practice, since rules which relate to, say, the terms and conditions of employment, or to the tax treatment of residents, might, if unduly burdensome, be said to deter workers of other Member States from entering the employment market of the host State. And it cannot be said that all the Court's

---

[65] If a restriction on access to the market is imposed on a migrant after his/her integration into the economic and social life of the host State, this does not of course preclude it being regarded as a restriction on access to the market, and it will required to be justified even if non-discriminatory. Thus if a restriction such as that in issue in Case C–19/92 *Dieter Kraus v Land Baden-Württemberg.* [1993] E.C.R. I–1663 is of its nature a restriction on access to the market, it is immaterial whether it is invoked as against a new market entrant, or as against a person already pursuing the relevant economic activity.

[66] See the discussion of Advocate General Fennelly in Case C–190/98 *Volker Graf v Filzmoser Machinenbau Gmbh* [2000] E.C.R. I–493.

case law is consistent with the proposition that non discriminatory rules need only be justified if they hinder access to the employment market. In *Carpenter*,[67] the Court held that a United Kingdom national residing in the United Kingdom and selling advertising space to advertisers in other Member States could rely on Article 49 EC to resist the deportation of his wife, a third country national illegally resident in the United Kingdom, since their separation would be detrimental to their family life, and therefore to the conditions under which the United Kingdom national was exercising a fundamental freedom.[68] While this case is concerned with the provision of services by a self-employed person rather than with the rights of a migrant worker, the proposition that a national measure which is detrimental to the conditions under which an individual exercises a fundamental freedom must be justified would seem capable to be of general application. And as we shall see in the next chapter there are other examples of an expansive interpretation of the free movement provisions, which might well go beyond the "access to the market" criterion.

THE WORKER'S FAMILY

General

We have seen in the previous chapter that Union citizens have a **18–028** right to bring their families in the host-State to which they are migrating. For economically active citizens this right is unconditional, i.e. not dependent upon sufficient resources and health insurance.[69] We have also seen that the spouse,[70] the registered partner when registered partnerships are recognised in the host State, and children under the age of 21 or children who are dependant upon the worker/spouse (regardless as to whether they are children of the couple or of only one of the spouses),[71] as well as dependant relatives in the ascending line, come within the definition

---

[67] Case C–60/00 *Mary Carpenter v Secretary of State for the Home Department* [2002] E.C.R. I–6279.
[68] *ibid.*, para.39. For a critical analysis of *Carpenter*, see (2003) 40 C.M.L.Rev. 537–543, for analysis of related issues, see Spaventa, *From Gebhard to Carpenter: Towards a (non)-Economic European Constitution* (2004) 41 C.M.L.Rev. 743–773.
[69] See Ch.17 para.17–012.
[70] In order to benefit of the rights conferred by Dir.2004/38 the Union citizen's spouse must be lawfully resident in a Member State before moving, see Case C–109/01 *Akrich* [2003] E.C.R. I–9607; if that is not the case, refusal to grant residence rights to a Union citizen's spouse could still be qualified as a barrier to the Union citizen's free movement rights, *cf.* Spaventa, "Annotation on *Akrich*" (2005) C.M.L.Rev. 225. See also Ch.8, p.271, above.
[71] The status of dependency is a result of a factual situation, namely the provision of support by the worker, without there being any need to determine the reasons for recourse to such support, see Case 316/85 *Lebon* [1987] E.C.R. 2811.

of "family member" for Community law purposes.[72] Those have a right to enter and install themselves with the worker (/Union citizen), as well as a right to take up an economic activity and a right not to be discriminated against on grounds of nationality in respect of all matters, including welfare benefits.

Article 3 of Directive 2004/38 further provides that the Member State shall facilitate admission of, and justify any denial of entry for, other members of the family who are dependent on the worker or, even though not dependent, require for serious health grounds the personal care of the worker (Union citizen); or who were living under his/her roof in the country whence she/he came; or the partner with whom the Union citizen has a stable and duly attested relationship.[73]

The third recital of the preamble to Regulation 1612/68 describes freedom of movement as a fundamental right of workers and their families, and indeed, genuine equality for the worker could not be achieved if the members of her/his family could be deprived of social advantages in the host State on account of their nationality. Thus Article 12 of Regulation 1612/68, which has not been repealed by Directive 2004/38,[74] provides that the children of a worker residing in the territory of a Member State shall be admitted to that State's general educational, apprenticeship and vocational training courses under the same conditions as nationals of that State. This provision clearly bestows rights directly upon such children, although the second paragraph of Article 12, to the effect that "Member States shall encourage all efforts to enable such children to attend courses under the best possible conditions," is not directly effective, and provides merely an admonition to Member States as to the spirit in which they should apply the first paragraph of that Article, and a guide to courts in its interpretation.

18–029   The Court of Justice has had cause to interpret Article 12 on several occasions. In *Michel S.*,[75] the plaintiff in the main suit was the mentally handicapped son of a deceased Italian national who had worked as a wage-earner in Belgium. He was refused benefit from a national fund established to assist persons of Belgian nationality whose chances of employment had been seriously diminished by physical or mental handicap. The Court, having declared that Article 7 of the Regulation protected workers, but not their families, went on to consider Article 12, drawing on the wording of the fifth recital of the preamble as an aid to its interpretation. According to the Court, the "integration" contemplated by the preamble presupposed

[72] *ibid.*
[73] See Ch.17, para.17–008.
[74] As we have seen in Ch.17, para.17–022, Art.24(2) of Dir.2004/38 also grants the right to maintenance aids for students to those who are economically active and their families.
[75] Case 76/72 [1973] E.C.R. 457.

that the handicapped child of a foreign worker would be entitled to take advantage of benefits provided by the law of the host country for rehabilitation of the handicapped on the same basis as nationals in a similar position. No conclusion to the contrary could be drawn from the failure of the Council explicitly to mention such benefits in the text of the Article; rather, this omission could be explained by the difficulty of including all possible hypotheses.

The Court's liberal approach to the text of Article 12 in *Michel S.* was followed in *Casagrande*,[76] in which the son of a deceased Italian national who had worked as a wage-earner in the Federal Republic was refused, on grounds of nationality, a means-tested educational grant under a Bavarian Statute. A German court sought a ruling from the Court of Justice on the consistency of such discriminatory provisions with Article 12 of Regulation 1612/68. The Court resorted once again to the fifth recital of the Regulation's preamble. Read with the words of the second paragraph of Article 12, it became apparent that the Article guaranteed not simply access to educational courses, but all benefits intended to facilitate educational attendance. In *Echternach*[77] the Court held that Article 12 of Regulation 1612/68 refers to any form of education, including university courses in economics and advanced vocational studies at a technical college. The Court also accepted that a child of a worker of a Member State, which latter has been in employment in another Member State, retains the status of member of a worker's family within the meaning of the Regulation when that child's family returns to the Member State of origin and the child remains in order to continue his studies, which he or she could not pursue in the Member State of origin. Furthermore, in *Baumbast and R*, the Court held that since the worker's children have a right to remain to complete their education in the host-State even when the worker has returned to her/his country of origin or when the Union citizen has lost his/her right of residence, the (divorced) parent who is the children's guardian/primary carer derives a right to residence from her/his children's right to stay. If the primary carer (in the case of divorce) or the parents were not allowed to stay in the host-country, the children might be deprived of their Community right to be educated in the host-State.[78] The Court's interpretation was clearly purposive and aimed at guaranteeing that the worker's children rights under Community law would not be compromised by a change in their parents' circumstances. As we have seen in the previous chapter, the ruling in *Baumbast* has now been codified in Article 12(3) of Directive 2004/38.

---

[76] Case 9/74 [1974] E.C.R. 773, and see Case 68/74 *Alaimo v Prefect of the Rhone* [1975] E.C.R. 109.

[77] Case 389/87 [1989] E.C.R. 723

[78] Case C–413/99 *Baumbast and R* [2002] E.C.R. I–7091, esp. para.71

In the *Lubor Gaal* case[79] the Court held that Article 12 also covers financial assistance for those students who are already at an advanced stage in their studies, even if they are already 21 years of age or older and are no longer dependants of their parents.

Social and tax advantages

18–030   The Court has retreated from its position in *Michel S.* that Article 7 of the Regulation protects workers but not their families. This will not be the case where the survivors of a worker living in the State where he was last employed claim a social advantage granted to the dependants of survivors of national workers in similar circumstances. In *Cristini*, it will be recalled that the widow of a deceased Italian national applied for a reduced fare card on French national railways. The Court of Justice held that Article 7(2) must be interpreted as meaning "that the social advantages referred to by that provision include fares reduction cards issued by a national railway authority to large families and that this applies, even if the said advantage is only sought after the worker's death, to the benefit of his family remaining in the same Member State."[80] In *Inzirillo*,[81] the Court, dealing with a reference on the scope of Regulation 1408/71 on social security benefits for migrants, observed that the protection of Article 7(2) of Regulation 1612/68 extended to handicapped, dependent adult children of a worker who have installed themselves with the worker in accordance with Article 10 of Regulation 1612/68. And in *Castelli*,[82] and *Frascogna*,[83] the Court has held that Article 7(2) is intended to protect, as well as workers themselves, their dependent relatives in the ascending line who have installed themselves with the worker. It follows from the above cases that any member of a worker's family who is entitled to, and does, install him/herself with the worker, is also entitled to equal treatment with nationals of the host State in the grant of all social and tax advantages.[84] The rationale of this proposition would seem to be the deterrent effect upon free movement for workers which would result from the possibility of discriminating against dependent members of her/his family.[85] In *Bernini*[86] the Court held that study finance

---

[79] Case C–7/94 *Landesamt für Ausbildungföderung Nordrhein-Westfalen v Lubor Gaal* [1995] E.C.R. I–1031.
[80] Case 32/75 *Cristini v SNCF* [1975] E.C.R. 1985, 1095.
[81] Case 63/76 [1976] E.C.R. 2057.
[82] Case 261/83 [1984] E.C.R. 3199.
[83] Case 157/84 [1985] E.C.R. 1739.
[84] In this respect see also Art.24 Dir.2004/38, which extends the equal treatment right to family members of the Union citizen, provided they have the right of residence or of permanent residence.
[85] Case 63/76 *Inzirillo* [1976] E.C.R. 2057, para.17 of the Judgment. And see Case 316/85 *Lebon* [1987] E.C.R. 2811, para.11 of Judgment.
[86] Case C–3/90 *M.J.E. Bernini v Minister van Onderwijs en Wetenshcappen* [1992] E.C.R. 1071, paras 25, 26.

granted by a Member State to the children of workers constitutes a social advantage within the meaning of Article 7(2) of Regulation 1612/68, where the worker continues to support the children,[87] but that the child may himself or herself rely on that Article in order to obtain the financing if under national law it is granted directly to the student. A directly effective Treaty basis of this right to equality in the relatives (as opposed to rights vested in the workers) is to be found in Article 12 EC, which prohibits any discrimination on grounds of nationality within the scope of application of the Treaty. Indeed, the Commission argued as much in *Cristini*. Support for this view is to be found in the *Forcheri*[88] case, which held that discrimination against a national of one Member State lawfully established in another in the provision of vocational training, infringed the Article which is now Article 12 EC. The plaintiffs in the national proceedings were a Commission official and his wife (the latter being the victim of the alleged discrimination). The Court's reasoning appears to be based on Article 12 of the Treaty, the Court being of the opinion that vocational training fell squarely within the "scope of application of the Treaty."

THE TRANSITIONAL ARRANGEMENTS FOR THE NEW MEMBER STATES

As we have seen in Chapter 1, in 2004 the European Union **18–031** increased its population by 75 million people with the accession of 10 new Member States (EU 10).[89] The 2004 enlargement was the largest and most ambitious enlargement in the history of the Union; its magnitude and disparities in the economic conditions between new and old Member States raised concerns about its possible impact on the existing Member States' labour markets,[90] especially at a time when the rate of unemployment in several of the Member

---

[87] Art.7(2) cannot be relied upon to claim study finance for the worker's children, if the worker has ceased his/her occupational activity in the host-State and has moved back to the Member State of origin with her or his children, see Case C–33/99 *Fahmi and Esmoris Cerdeiro-Pinedo Amado* [2001] E.C.R. I–2415.

[88] Case 152/82 [1983] E.C.R. 2323. See also Case 293/83, *Gravier* [1985] E.C.R. 593.

[89] The "new" Member States are commonly referred to as EU 10, whilst the "old" Member States are referred to as EU 15. EU 8 refers to the new Member States minus Malta and Cyprus.

[90] The difference in G.D.P. per capita varied at the moment of accession between 35 per cent (Latvia) to 74 per cent (Slovenia) of the EU15 average, source Eurostat; see the Commission's Communication *More Unity and More Diversity. The Europe Union's Biggest Enlargement* (NA–47-02-389–EN–C) (*www.europa.eu.int/comm/publications/booklets/move/41/index—en.htm*).

States was very high.[91] For this reason, the Treaty of Accession 2003 established transitional arrangements,[92] contained in annexes to the Treaty, which allow for the free movement of workers to be deferred for a maximum period of seven years following accession.[93] The limitation to free movement applies to all the new Member States but Malta and Cyprus (EU 8), whose citizens benefit of full free movement rights.[94]

According to the transitional arrangements, Member States can limit access to their employment market from EU 8 countries (and vice-versa).[95] However, once the worker has gained access to the employment market, equal treatment applies in full, apart from a further derogation from Article 11 of Regulation 1612/68 (now subsumed in Directive 2004/38), in relation to the protected family members' right to work. The transitional arrangements also provide for a stand still obligation, whereby the Member States wishing to derogate from Article 39 EC cannot impose conditions more restrictive than those existing at the date of the signature of the Accession Treaty; and that Member States must give precedence to workers of the Member States to which the arrangements apply over third country nationals in relation to access to their labour market.

Of the EU 15, only the United Kingdom,[96] Ireland and Sweden opened up access to their employment market to EU 8 workers from the moment of accession. All of the other Member States have restricted, in different ways and setting in place bilateral agreements, access to their labour market.

---

[91] e.g. Germany's unemployment rate for 2003 was 9 per cent; Italy's 8.4 per cent; France's 9.5 per cent; Spain's 11.5 per cent. The average unemployment rate for the EU 25 in 2003 was 9 per cent, and 8 per cent for the EU 15. It raised to 9.1 per cent and 8.1 per cent respectively in 2004, and dropped to 8.7 per cent and 7.9 per cent respectively in 2005, source Eurostat.

[92] Annexes V to XV of the Accession Treaty, [2003] O.J. 236/803 and ff.

[93] See generally, Adinolfi "Free movement and access to work of citizens of the new member states: the transitional measures" (2005) 42 C.M.L.Rev. 469; and Dougan, "A spectre in haunting Europe . . . Free movement of persons and the Eastern Enlargement" in Hillion (ed.) *EU Enlargement: A Legal Approach* (Hart, Oxford, 2004). A similar framework is provided in the Treaty of Accession for Bulgaria and Romania.

[94] Although Malta benefits of special arrangements.

[95] Art.39 EC applies but for Arts 1 to 6 of Reg.1612/68 which regulate access to the employment market. Germany and Austria can derogate from Art.49(1) EC in respect of posting workers according to Art.1, Dir.96/71 concerning the posting of workers in the framework of the provision of services [1997] O.J. L18/1; the derogation applies only to listed service sectors (as listed in para.13 of the transitional arrangements).

[96] See the Accession (Immigration and Workers Registration) Regulations 2004; the UK has introduced a system of registration for monitoring purposes; however, it has also provided that in the first year of employment EU 8 nationals do not have a right to have their family members, do not have a right to reside in the first year (for access to benefit purposes), and lose their status as "registered workers" if they are unemployed for more than 30 days even if unemployment is involuntary or due to illness or accident. The extent to which the UK legislation is compatible with EU law is questionable. As said above Member States are only allowed to derogate from provisions relating to access to the labour market; once the worker has gained access they are entitled to full equal treatment.

The transitional arrangements provide that before the end of the **18–032** first phase (2 years from accession) the Commission has to publish a report on the functioning of the Transitional Arrangements; following the Report, the Member States have to notify the Commission whether they want to maintain the transitional arrangement for a further three years; lacking the notification Article 39 EC applies in full. After five years from Accession, a Member State can maintain the restrictions for a maximum of further two years only in case of "serious disturbances of its labour market or threat thereof". The transitional arrangement lasts for a maximum of seven years, after which EU 8 nationals acquire full free movement rights.

The Commission has recently issued its first report,[97] and not surprisingly has called for the Member States to allow for full free movement. It based its request on two main arguments: first of all, migration fluxes have been modest and less than expected; second, the limitation of access to employment might produce social dumping effects, in that it encourages migrants to either pretend to be self-employed, or to work in the black market. For the latter reason, Finland has decided to lift its restrictions, and it is very likely that more Member States will follow.[98] Germany and Austria, however, are likely to keep the restrictions until 2011, mainly out of fear that frontier workers might negatively affect their labour market.

Apart from Germany and Austria, which have negotiated special derogations because of their geographic location,[99] the Member States can derogate only from the free movement of workers provisions. In other words, EU 8 citizens benefit from the freedom to move as EU citizens, as well as for the freedom to move as self-employed. The distinction between workers and self-employed is however not always so clear cut. In *Jany*,[100] a pre-accession case concerning the association agreements with the (then) applicant countries, the issue arose as to whether prostitutes should be considered as employed or self-employed. The claimants were Polish and Czech nationals working as window prostitutes in the Netherlands, where such an activity is lawful. One of the questions for the Court was whether prostitutes are to be considered as employed by their pimp (in which case the claimants would have had no right to be in the Netherlands), or whether they are to be considered as self-employed (in which case they would have a right to reside and carry out their economic activity in the Netherlands). The Court left it to the national court to decide the issue. It however clarified that the

---

[97] Report on the Functioning of the Transitional Arrangements set out in the 2003 Accession Treaty (period May 1, 2004–30 April 2006), COM (2006) 48 final.

[98] *cf.* "Finland opens door to new EU workers" euobserver, March 31, 2006; Spain, Portugal and Greece have indicated a similar intention.

[99] *cf.* para.13 Transitional Agreements that allows for a derogation from Art.49 (1). See above n.95.

[100] Case C–268/99 *Jany* [2001] E.C.R. I–8615.

Netherlands could not operate on the general presumption that the relationship between pimps and prostitutes is equivalent to employment, as otherwise it would put an entire economic activity beyond the freedom of establishment. In order to assess whether the services were provided in a self-employed or employed capacity, the national court has to assess whether the activity is carried out outside any employment relationship concerning the choice of activity, remuneration and working conditions; under that persons' responsibility; and in return for remuneration paid to that person directly and in full.

Further reading

Bernard, "Discrimination and free movement in EC Law" (1996) 45 I.C.L.Q. 82.

Castro Oliveira, "Workers and other persons: step-by-step from movement to citizenship—case law 1995–2001" (2002) 39 C.M.L.Rev. 77.

Daniele, "Non-discriminatory restrictions to the free movement of persons" (1997) 22 E.L.Rev. 191.

O'Keeffe, "Judicial Interpretation of the Public Service Exception to the Free Movement of Workers" in Curtin D. and O'Keeffe D. (eds), *Constitutional Adjudication in European Community Law and National Law* (Butterworths, Dublin, 1992).

Shuibhne, Nic, "Free Movement of Persons and the Wholly Internal Rule: Time to Move on?" (2002) 39 C.M.L.Rev. 731.

Spaventa, "From Gebhard to Carpenter: Towards a (non)-Economic European Constitution" (2004) 41 C.M.L.Rev. 743.

Spaventa, *Free Movement of Persons* (Kluwer International, the Hague, 2006).

White, *Workers, Establishment and Services in the European Union* (OUP, Oxford, 2004).

CHAPTER 19

THE RIGHT OF ESTABLISHMENT AND THE FREEDOM TO PROVIDE SERVICES

Guide to this Chapter: The right of establishment and the **19–001** freedom to provide services are for individuals the self-employed equivalent of the free movement of workers. Self-employed individuals are entitled to carry on economic activities in other Member States on a temporary or permanent basis. The temporary pursuit of a trade or business in another Member State is covered by the Treaty provisions on services; if the economic activities are permanent, the provisions on establishment apply. The right of establishment covers the right to set up and manage businesses, including companies, in other Member States. Companies and firms, as well as individuals, are entitled to freedom of establishment and freedom to provide services. Detailed consideration is given to corporate establishment in Chapter 20. This chapter deals generally with the right of establishment and the freedom to provide services. The case law on establishment and services has seen changes in the Court's approach to the relevant Treaty provisions, and this chapter discusses these changes in detail. Perhaps the most important change has been judicial recognition that non-discriminatory restrictions on establishment and services, as well as discriminatory restrictions, will be prohibited unless justified. Justification may be possible on the basis of express provisions in the EC Treaty, for example on grounds of public policy, or where an activity involves the exercise of official authority. It may also be possible on grounds of imperative requirements in the general interest. National requirements as to professional qualifications may amount to discriminatory or non-discriminatory restrictions on the right of establishment and the freedom to provide services, and such issues are considered from the perspective of the Court's case law on Articles 43 and 49 EC, and in the light of the recent Professional Qualifications Directive (2005/36), and the Directives on Provision of Services (77/249), and Establishment (98/5), by lawyers qualified in a Member State.

ESTABLISHMENT AND SERVICES

Meaning of right of establishment and freedom to provide services

19–002   As well as ensuring the free movement of workers, the Treaty guarantees the right of establishment, and the freedom to provide services between Member States: what Article 39 EC provides for the employee, Articles 43 and 49 EC provide for the employer, the entrepreneur and the professional. The employed and self-employed activities covered by the foregoing provisions may include work done by members of a community based on religion or another form of philosophy, as part of the commercial activities of that community, and as a *quid pro quo* for services provided by it.[1]

The right of establishment is granted to natural and legal persons,[2] and subject to relevant exceptions, it allows all types of self-employed activity to be taken up and pursued on the territory of any other Member State, undertakings to be formed and operated, and agencies, branches and subsidiaries to be set up.[3] It follows that a

---

[1] Case 196/87 *Udo Steymann v Staatssecretaris van Justite* [1987] E.C.R. 6159, paras 14, 16; and see Case C–456/02 *Trojani* [2004] E.C.R. I–7574, Ch.17 at p.714.

[2] As defined in Art.48 EC. For specific treatment of corporate establishment, see Ch.20.

[3] Case C–55/94 *Reinhard Gebhard v Consiglio dell'Ordine degli Avvocati e Procuratori di Milano* [1995] E.C.R. I–4165, para.23.

person may be established, within the meaning of the Treaty, in more than one Member State—in particular, in the case of companies, through the setting up of agencies, branches or subsidiaries, and in the case of the members of professions, by establishing a second professional base.[4] The concept of establishment within the meaning of the Treaty is a very broad one, allowing a Community national to participate, on a stable and continuous basis, in the economic life of a Member State other than his or her State of origin and to profit therefrom, so contributing to economic and social interpenetration within the Community, in the sphere of activities of self-employed persons.[5] The Court has held that an undertaking of one Member State which maintains a permanent presence in another is covered by the provisions on establishment "even if that presence does not take the form of a branch or agency, but consists merely of an office managed by the undertaking's own staff or by a person who is independent but authorised to act on a permanent basis for the undertaking as would be the case with an agency."[6]

The right of establishment is to be contrasted with the freedom to provide services. The former entails settlement in a Member State for economic purposes, and permanent integration into the host State's economy, being generally exercised by a shift of a sole place of business, or by the setting up of agencies, branches or subsidiaries. The latter entails a person or undertaking established in one Member State providing services in another on a temporary basis, as in the case of a doctor established in France visiting a patient in Belgium. The distinction may not always be clear-cut, because the provision of services may involve temporary residence in the host State, as in the case of a German firm of business consultants which advises undertakings in France, or a construction company which erects buildings in a neighbouring country. As long as such residence is temporary the activities in question will fall within the ambit of Articles 49–55 EC, on freedom to provide services[7]; if the activities are carried out on a permanent basis, or, in any event, without a foreseeable limit to their duration, they will not fall within the provisions of the Treaty on the provision of services, but will be regulated by the provisions on the right of establishment.[8] But the fact that the provision of services is temporary does not mean that the provider of services within the meaning of the Treaty may not

---

[4] *ibid.*, para.24.

[5] *ibid.*, para.25.

[6] Case 205/84 *Commission v Germany* [1986] E.C.R. 3755, p.3801, para.21.

[7] Art.50 EC, third para. provides: "Without prejudice to the provisions of the Chapter relating to the right of establishment, the person providing a service may, in order to do so, temporarily pursue his activity in the State where the service is provided, under the same conditions as are imposed by that State on its own nationals."

[8] Case 196/87 *Udo Steymann v Staatssecretaris van Justite* [1987] E.C.R. 6159, para.16.

equip himself with some form of infrastructure in the host Member State, such as an office, chambers or consulting room.[9] The fact that both an established person and a person providing services may carry on business from such an office, consulting room or other place of business means that it may in practice be difficult to distinguish activities subject to the Treaty provisions on establishment from those subject to the Treaty provisions on services. As will be seen in subsequent sections of the present Chapter, the interpretation of the respective provisions of the Treaty on establishment and services by the Court of Justice has reduced, though not eliminated, the significance of such a distinction being drawn. In any event, whether the activities in question are to be regarded as temporary, and so subject to the Treaty provisions on services, rather than on establishment, has to be determined in the light, not only of the duration of the provision of the service, but of its regularity, periodicity or continuity.[10] The Court has admitted that no provision of the Treaty provides a means of determining, in an abstract manner, the duration or frequency beyond which the supply of a service or of a certain type of service in another Member State can no longer be regarded as the provision of services within the meaning of the Treaty.[11] And the Court has held that services may comprise services within the meaning of the Treaty even if supplied over an extended period to persons established in one or more other Member States, for example the giving of advice or information for remuneration.[12] It seems that the provision of services from one Member State to another on a regular basis, accompanied by use of an office or similar facility in the host State, may shade imperceptibly into establishment. But offering the services from an established professional base in the host State is essential if a person is to be regarded as established in that State[13]; the difficulty with insisting on this latter requirement is discussed later.[14]

Scope of the present Chapter

19–003   The right of establishment and the freedom to provide services may be invoked by companies and firms as well as by individuals. The present Chapter will deal generally with the right of establishment and the freedom to provide services. Detailed consideration is given to corporate establishment in Chapter 20. As regards individuals, the rights of movement and residence of Union Citizens who

---

[9] Case C–55/94 *Reinhard Gebhard v Consiglio dell'Ordine degli Avvocati e Procuratori di Milano* [1995] E.C.R. I–4165, para.27.
[10] *ibid.*
[11] Case C–215/01 *Bruno Schnitzer* [2003] E.C.R. I–14847, para.31.
[12] *ibid.*, para.30.
[13] *ibid.*, para.32; Case C–171/02 *Commission v Portugal* [2004] E.C.R. I–5645, para.25; Case C–514/03 *Commission v Spain* Judgment of January 26, 2006, para.22.
[14] Below, at p.781.

are self-employed, and of members of their families, and limitations on those rights, are specified in Directive 2004/38, and are covered in Chapter 17 on Union Citizenship and Rights to Move and Reside in the Union. The Court's general case law on the development of the right of establishment and freedom to provide services, and the limitations on those rights, are covered in the present Chapter, as is the Court's case law on the effect of the right of establishment and the freedom to provide services on national requirements that those pursuing certain activities hold certain professional qualifications. Community rules on mutual recognition of diplomas, and the co-ordination of national qualifications are considered, including the directives on the provision of services by, and establishment of lawyers. It is to be noted that the foregoing rules are applicable to employed as well as to self-employed persons.

THE RIGHT OF ESTABLISHMENT

General scope

Article 43 EC draws a distinction between the right of establish- **19–004** ment of nationals of Member States and the right of establishment of nationals *already established* in the territory of a Member State. The former are entitled to establish themselves in any Member State, that is to say to set up their main establishment, while the latter are entitled to set up agencies and branches. A Member State cannot refuse to accord rights under Article 43 EC to a national of another Member State on the ground that that national also holds the nationality of a third country.[15]

Freedom of establishment includes a number of distinct rights. One is the right of a natural or legal person to leave his/her or its Member State of origin or establishment in order to accomplish a shift in primary establishment, or to set up a secondary establish-ment, in another Member State.[16] Another is the right to have more than one place of business in the Community.[17] A third is the right to carry on business under the conditions laid down for its own nationals by the law of the host Member State.[18] The fourth is a much broader right. It is the right to resist the application of

---

[15] Case C–369/90 *Mario Vicente Micheletti v Delegación del Gobierno en Cantabria* [1992] E.C.R. I–4239; see also Case C–122/96 *Stephen Austin Saldanha and MTS Securities Corporation v Hiross Holding AG* [1997] E.C.R. I–5325; Case C–200/02 *Chen* [2004] E.C.R. I–9925.

[16] Below at p.759. And see Ch.17 on Union Citizenship and the Rights to Move and Reside in the Union.

[17] Below at p.758.

[18] Below at p.767, *et seq.*

national measures which are liable to hinder or make less attractive the exercise of the right of establishment guaranteed by the Treaty.[19] This latter broader right might be said to be confined to situations where national measures comprise a restriction of one sort or another on *access to the relevant market* by nationals of Member States, though it is questionable whether any concept of access to the market operates as a significant limit on the ability of an individual or firm to challenge national rules which hinder or make less attractive the exercise of a fundamental freedom.[20] All the foregoing rights are of course subject to the exceptions and derogations recognised by Community law.[21] It must be noted, however, that Article 43 EC can have no application in a situation which is purely internal to a Member State.[22] The right of establishment guaranteed by Article 43 EC is directly applicable.[23]

Evolution of the Court's case law on the interpretation of Article 43 EC

19–005   The interpretation by the Court of Justice of Article 43 EC has been the subject of a quite significant evolution in two respects. Firstly, as regards the extent to which the provision may be relied upon by a national of a Member State when returning to his or her Member State of origin and as against his or her own national authorities; the Court's early approach, relying upon a literal approach to the text, largely ruled out such reliance, but that approach has not been followed in later case law. The second respect concerns the type of national rule regarded by the Court as comprising a restriction prohibited by Article 43 EC. The Court's case law until the 1990s was to the effect that only discriminatory restrictions could be so regarded, with the exception of measures preventing nationals from leaving their own Member States, and measures which prevented individuals from having a place of business in more than one Member State, or placed such individuals at a disadvantage by virtue of having exercised their right of free movement. But more recently

---

[19] Below at p.770, *et seq.*

[20] As to which, see below at pp.775—776.

[21] As to which see below at pp.795–810 *et seq.* And see Ch.17 on Union Citizenship and the Rights to Move and Reside in the Union.

[22] Case 204/87 *Bekaert* [1988] E.C.R. 2029; Cases C–54/88 *et al. Nino* [1990] E.C.R. I–3537; Case C–152/94 *Openbaar Ministerie v Geert Van Buynder* [1995] E.C.R. I–3981. It appears that a person qualified in a Member State who carries on all his professional activity there may not rely upon Art.43 solely because he resides in another Member State, Case C–112/91 *Hans Werner v Finanzamt Aachen-Innenstadt* [1993] E.C.R. I–429, but the Court has treated a similar situation as being governed by Art.49 EC, see case 39/75 *Coenen* [1975] E.C.R. 1555.

[23] Case 81/87 *R v HM Treasury and Commissioners of Inland Revenue ex parte Daily Mail and General Trust plc* [1988] E.C.R. 3483, para.15; Case C–1/93 *Halliburton Services v Staatssecretaris van Financiën* [1994] E.C.R. I–1137, para.16; Case C–254/97 *Société Baxter v Premier Ministre* [1999] E.C.R. I–4809, para.11.

the Court has adopted a broader approach, which seems to have been inspired by its pre-*Keck* jurisprudence on the free movement of goods, and latterly on the provision of services, which holds that Article 43 EC covers all national measures which are liable to hinder or make less attractive the exercise of the right of establishment. It is appropriate to consider first the text of Article 43, and then to trace the major developments in the Court's interpretation of that text.

Article 43 EC provides that "Within the framework of the provisions set out below, restrictions on the freedom of establish-ment of *nationals of a Member State* in the territory of *another Member State* shall be prohibited." (emphasis added). It is to be noted that the words in italics indicate that the Article covers a national of one Member State exercising self-employed activities in the territory of another, but there is no indication that the scope of the Article extends to the case of a national of a Member State returning to his or her Member State of origin. The wording is however apt to cover restrictions imposed by a Member State of origin on the right of establishment of its own nationals in another Member State. Article 43 goes on to say that "freedom of establish-ment shall include the right to take up and pursue activities as self-employed persons . . .", etc., ". . . under the conditions laid down for its own nationals by the law of the country where such establishment is effected". The use of the word "include" in the latter formulation would seem to be consistent with the proposition that the "restric-tions" on freedom of establishment referred to in the first sentence of the Article, which are to be prohibited, are not confined to discriminatory restrictions. It is also to be noted that the "restric-tions" referred to in the first sentence of the Article refer to the "framework of the provisions set out below", and the provisions in question authorise the issue of EC directives in order "to attain freedom of establishment as regards a particular activity",[24] and in order "to make it easier for persons to take up and pursue activities as self-employed persons" by providing for the "mutual recognition of diplomas, certificates and other evidence of formal qualifications".[25]

In *Reyners v Belgian State* the Court of Justice held that the prohibition of discrimination contained in Article 43 EC was directly applicable, despite the reference in that Article to the prohibition of restrictions on the right of establishment "within the framework" of subsequent Articles of the Treaty providing for the adoption of Community secondary legislation. This judgment was of considerable significance, and it is referred to further below.[26] Other judgments

---

[24] Art.44 EC.
[25] Art.47 EC.
[26] Case 2/74 *Reyners v Belgian State* [1974] E.C.R. 631, see below at p.765.

on the applicability of the prohibition on discrimination followed.[27] But in the first *Auer* case,[28] the Court felt it necessary to address an important issue of principle as to the scope of Article 43 EC. The national proceedings which gave rise to a reference to the Court of Justice involved a Mr Vincent Auer, originally of Austrian nationality, who studied veterinary medicine first in Austria, then in France, and then in Italy, at the University of Parma, where he was awarded in 1956 the degree of doctor of veterinary medicine, and in March 1957 a provisional certificate to practise as a veterinary surgeon. Mr Auer took up residence in France and in 1961 acquired French nationality by naturalization. He then applied, pursuant to a provision of French law allowing veterinary surgeons who have acquired French nationality to be authorised to practise in France despite the absence of a French doctorate. The competent French authority refused to recognise the equivalence of Mr Auer's Italian qualification, but he practised in France nevertheless, and he was prosecuted on several occasions for doing so. One such prosecution led to a reference to the Court of Justice, asking whether the person concerned was in a position to claim in France the right to practise the profession of veterinary surgeon which he had acquired in Italy. The Court noted that the question referred to the situation as it existed at the time when Article 47(1) EC relating to mutual recognition of diplomas, certificates and other qualifications had not yet been applied as regards the practice of the profession of veterinary medicine, though directives on mutual recognition and co-ordination of veterinary qualifications had been adopted subsequently. It remained to be considered whether, and if so to what extent, "nationals of the Member State in which they were established were entitled, at the time in question, to rely on the provisions of Articles 52 to 57 of the Treaty in situations such as that described above."[29] The Court might have proceeded on the basis that a person in the situation of Mr Auer could not rely upon the right of establishment because he had never, as a national of a Member State, exercised his right of free movement. But it did not, it proceeded instead on the basis that the only relevant right under Article 43 EC in such circumstances was the right of non-discrimination, and that right could only be invoked by a national of one Member State in the territory of another. The Court, citing the text of the Treaty, including the reference to "establishment of nationals of one Member State in the territory of another" stated:

---

[27] See for example Case 7/76 *Thieffry* [1977] E.C.R. 765 (refusal of access to the Paris Bar of a Belgian national, on the ground that he did not possess a French law degree, despite the fact that he possessed a Belgian law degree, recognized by the University of Paris as equivalent to a French law degree, held discriminatory).

[28] Case 136/78 *Ministère public v Auer* [1979] E.C.R. 437; see also Case 271/82 *Auer v Ministère public* [1983] E.C.R. 2727.

[29] *ibid.*, para.14.

"In so far as it is intended to ensure, within the transitional period, with direct effect, the benefit of national treatment, Article [43] concerns only—and can concern only—in each Member State the nationals of other Member States, those of the host Member State coming already, by definition, under the rules in question."[30]

The Court went on to explain that in order to ensure complete **19–006** freedom of establishment, the Treaty provided for directives to be adopted on mutual recognition of qualifications, and that such directives could be invoked both by nationals of one Member State in the territory of another, and by the nationals of a Member State in that Member State.[31]

The above judgment supported three related propositions. The first was that the direct effect of Article 43 EC was confined to a guarantee of national treatment; the second was that that guarantee could only by definition be invoked by a national of one Member State in the territory of another; and the third was that any restrictions on freedom of movement caused to nationals of a Member State by national rules on qualifications could be removed by the adoption of directives on mutual recognition of qualifications. Only the last of these propositions was to be confirmed by subsequent case law.

In a judgment given on the same day as *Auer*, in the *Knoors* case,[32] the Court explained the justification for allowing a national of a Member State, who had secured in another Member State a qualification which had been the subject of a directive issued under Article 44 of the Treaty to rely upon the terms of that directive. Referring to the free movement provisions of the Treaty, *viz.*, Articles 39, 43 and 49, the Court stated:

"In fact, these liberties, which are fundamental in the Community system, could not be fully realized if the Member States were in a position to refuse to grant the benefit of the provisions of Community law to those of their nationals who have taken advantage of the facilities existing in the matter of freedom of movement and establishment and who have acquired, by virtue of such facilities, the trade qualifications referred to by the directive in a Member State other than that whose nationality they possess."[33]

This rationale was well suited to the case in point; the plaintiff in the national proceedings was a Netherlands national who had resided in

---

[30] *ibid.*, para.20.
[31] *ibid.*, paras 22–26.
[32] Case 115/78 *Knoors v Secretary of State for Economic Affairs* [1979] E.C.R. 399.
[33] *ibid.*, para.20.

Belgium and there acquired the practical experience as a plumber which, pursuant to the directive, was to be accorded recognition by other Member States. The Court went on:

> "Although it is true that the provisions of the Treaty relating to establishment and the provision of services cannot be applied to situations which are purely internal to a Member State, the position nevertheless remains that the reference in Article [43] to 'nationals of a Member State' who wish to establish themselves 'in the territory of another Member State' cannot be interpreted in such a way as to exclude from the benefit of Community law a given Member State's own nationals when the latter, owing to the fact that they have lawfully resided on the territory of another Member State and have there acquired a trade qualification which is recognised by the provisions of Community law, are, with regard to their State of origin, in a situation which may be assimilated to that of any other person enjoying the rights and liberties guaranteed by the Treaty."[34]

19–007   The effect of the judgment in *Knoors* is that nationals of a Member State may rely upon an "establishment" directive even in their own Member State, where they have acquired a qualification covered by that directive in the territory of another Member State. The justification is that otherwise such nationals would be deprived of the advantages of the exercise of the right of establishment, in those cases where the qualification in question had in fact been secured by the exercise of the right of establishment in the first place.

In *Klopp*[35] the Court held that the right referred to in Article 43 EC to set up agencies and branches was a specific statement of a general principle, applicable equally to the liberal professions, according to which the right of establishment includes the freedom to set up and maintain, subject to observance of the professional rules of conduct, more than one place of work within the Community.[36] It was thus incompatible with freedom of establishment to deny to a national of another Member State the right to enter and to exercise the profession of advocate solely on the ground that he maintained chambers in another Member State, even if the national rules in question applied without discrimination on grounds of nationality. This case provides a good example of a non-discriminatory restriction which falls within the ordinary meaning of the words used in the text of the Treaty. It is thus incompatible with

---

[34] *ibid.*, para.24.
[35] Case 107/83 *Ordre des Avocats au Barreau de Paris v Klopp* [1984] E.C.R. 2971.
[36] The context makes it clear that it is contemplated that the Court is referring to a place of business in more than one Member State.

the right of establishment if national rules place at a disadvantage a person who has a place of business in more than one Member State, as compared to a person whose business activities are located within a single Member State.[37]

In the *Daily Mail* case the Court made it clear that Article 43 EC prohibited restrictions imposed by a Member State on its own nationals, or on a company incorporated under its legislation, seeking to establish themselves in the territory of another Member State. The Court stated:

> "Even though those provisions are directed mainly to ensuring that foreign nationals and companies are treated in the host Member State in the same way as nationals of that State, they also prohibit the Member State of origin from hindering the establishment in another Member State of one of its nationals or of a company incorporated under its legislation which comes within the definition contained in Article [48]."[38]

The foregoing case law indicated that the right of establishment gave to the nationals of a Member State the right to leave that State in order to take up self-employed activities elsewhere, the right to set up a place of business in more than one Member State, and the right to carry on self-employed activities in another Member State under the same conditions as those laid down for nationals of that Member State. That the right to equality of treatment was the "core" guarantee of Article 43 EC, and that that guarantee did not extend to a general prohibition on non-discriminatory measures which might be held to restrict the exercise of the right of establishment in some way, was made clear in *Commission v Belgium*,[39] in which the Commission alleged that non-discriminatory Belgian rules governing the activities of clinical biology laboratories were incompatible with Article 43 EC, on the ground that the rules in question were excessively restrictive, and that the latter Article prohibited not only discriminatory measures, but also "measures which apply to both nationals and foreigners without discrimination where they constitute an unjustified constraint for the latter."[40] The Court rejected this approach to the right of establishment, emphasising that the text of Article 43 EC guaranteed equality of treatment for nationals and non-nationals, and stating:

---

[37] For cases where national rules place at a disadvantage a person who has a place of business in more than one Member State, see Case 143/87 *Stanton* [1988] E.C.R. 3877; Cases 154 and 155/87 *Wolf* [1988] E.C.R. 3897; Case C–53/95 *Inasti v Hans Kemmler* [1996] E.C.R. I–703.

[38] Case 81/87 *R v HM Treasury and Commissioners of Inland Revenue ex parte Daily Mail and General Trust plc* [1988] E.C.R. 3483, para.16.

[39] Case 221/85 [1987] E.C.R. 719.

[40] *ibid.*, para.5.

">. . . provided that such equality of treatment is respected, each Member State is, in the absence of Community rules in this area, free to lay down rules for its own territory governing the activities of laboratories providing clinical biology services."[41]

19-008 It will be recalled that in *Knoors* the proposition that a national in his or her own Member State might rely upon the terms of a directive adopted to secure the implementation of the right of establishment was justified by the fact that such a person might have brought himself or herself within the situation contemplated by the directive by prior exercise of the right of establishment. The Court took the proposition in *Knoors* a small step further in *Bouchoucha*, in that it described the scope of a case of a French national practising in France, while holding a professional diploma issued in another Member State, as "not purely national" and noted that "the applicability of the EEC Treaty provisions on freedom of establishment must be considered."[42]

It fell to the Court in *Surinder Singh*[43] to consider whether a spouse of a national of a Member State who had exercised her right of freedom of movement as an employed person in another Member State and then returned to her own Member State to carry on self-employed activities, was entitled to install himself in the latter Member State. If his wife had been taking up self-employed activities in another Member State, it seemed that he would have derived that right from the applicable secondary legislation. It was argued however by the Member State of origin that the position was different where a national returned to her own Member State; such a situation was, it said, governed by national law. The Court replied as follows:

"However, this case is concerned not with a right under national law but with the rights of movement and establishment granted to a Community national by Articles [39] and [43] of the Treaty. These rights cannot be fully effective if such a person may be deterred from exercising them by obstacles raised in his or her country of origin to the entry and residence of his or her spouse. Accordingly, when a Community national who has availed himself or herself of those rights returns to his or her own country of origin, his or her spouse must enjoy at least the same rights of entry and residence as would be granted

---

[41] *ibid.*, para.9. The Court confirmed this view of the scope of freedom of establishment in Case 198/86 *Erwin Conradi v Direction de la Concurrence et des Prix des Hauts de Seine* [1987] E.C.R. 4469.

[42] Case C-61/89 *Criminal Proceedings against Marc Gaston Bouchoucha* [1990] E.C.R. I-3551, para.11.

[43] Case C-370/90 *R v Immigration and Appeal Tribunal and Surinder Singh ex parte Secretary of State for the Home Department* [1992] E.C.R. I-4265; see Ch.17 at p.674.

to him or her under Community law if his or her spouse chose to enter and reside in another Member State."[44]

This reasoning is worthy of remark. The Court appears disinclined to assert that the Treaty bestows directly on nationals of a Member State the right to enter that Member State—such a right is normally inherent in citizenship and arises under national law. So the Court asserts that an individual may be deterred from exercising his/her right to *leave* his/her own Member State in order to carry on economic activities in another Member State by the prospect of being treated less favourably on his/her return (as regards the right to be accompanied by his/her spouse) than he/she would be treated if he/she sought admission to another Member State instead. This might be plausible in a case in which a national of a Member State took up economic activities in another Member State, married there a national of a third country, and then found himself/herself unable to return to his/her Member State of origin with his/her spouse. In such a case, the person in question would in a sense be disadvantaged as a consequence of having exercised his/her right of free movement. In *Surinder Singh*, however, no such disadvantage seemed to arise. In the later case of *Akrich*,[45] the Court made it clear that the reasoning in *Singh* only applied where the exercise of the right of free movement resulted in the loss of opportunity for an employed person and his or her spouse to live lawfully together. The Court also held that the right under Community secondary legislation of a spouse of a national of one Member State employed in the territory of another Member State to live with that worker in the latter Member State[46] presupposed that the spouse was initially lawfully resident in the first Member State, though the Court added that regard must still be had to the right to family life under Article 8 of the European Convention of Human Rights.[47]

It is noted above that in 1979 the Court in the *Cassis* case **19–009** interpreted the free movement of goods provisions as covering non-discriminatory national measures which made the import of goods more difficult or costly,[48] and in 1991 in the *Säger* case the Court interpreted the provisions of the Treaty on the provision of services as applying to national rules which applied without distinction to nationals and non-nationals but nevertheless restricted the provision of services.[49] In 1993 the Court held in the *Kraus* case[50] that the right

---

[44] *ibid.* para.23.
[45] Case C–109/01 *Secretary of State for the Home Department v Hacene Akrich* [2003] E.C.R. I–9607; see also Ch.17 at p.695.
[46] Art.10 of Reg.1612/68.
[47] *ibid.*, para.58.
[48] Ch.16 at p.579.
[49] Below at p.788.
[50] Case C–19/92 *Dieter Kraus v Land Baden-Württemberg.* [1993] E.C.R. I–1663; see also Ch.18 at p.735.

to freedom of movement for workers applied where a German national who had secured an academic title in the United Kingdom returned to his country of origin, it being the case that the possession of such a title constituted for the person entitled to make use of it, an advantage for the purpose both of gaining entry to such a profession, and of prospering within it. The Court held moreover that Article 39 EC precluded any national measure governing the conditions under which an academic title obtained in another Member State might be used, where that measure, even though it was applicable without discrimination on grounds of nationality, was liable to hamper or to render less attractive the exercise by Community nationals, including those of the Member State which enacted the measure, of fundamental freedoms guaranteed by the Treaty. The situation would be different only if such a measure pursued a legitimate objective compatible with the Treaty and was justified by pressing reasons of public interest.[51] That this latter principle was also applicable in the context of Article 43 EC was made clear in *Gebhard*[52]:

"... national measures liable to hinder or make less attractive the exercise of fundamental freedoms guaranteed by the Treaty must fulfil four conditions: they must be applied in a non-discriminatory manner; they must be justified by imperative requirements in the general interest; they must be suitable for securing the attainment of the objective which they pursue; and they must not go beyond what is necessary in order to attain it." (see Case C–19/92 *Kraus* . . ., para. 32).[53]

In *Asscher* the Court considered whether a national of a Member State pursuing an activity as a self-employed person in another Member State, in which he/she resides, may rely on Article 43 EC as against his/her State of origin, on whose territory he/she pursues another activity as a self-employed person. The Court stated: [54]

"It is settled law that, although the provisions of the Treaty relating to freedom of establishment cannot be applied to

---

[51] *ibid.*, para.32. The Court of Justice in the event held that the national measure in question might be so justified. That a national of a Member State could rely upon the Treaty against his or her Member State of origin was justified in the terms referred to in *Knoors*, above, p.757.

[52] Case C–55/94 *Reinhard Gebhard v Consiglio dell'Ordine degli Avvocati e Procuratori di Milano* [1995] E.C.R. I–4165.

[53] *ibid.*, para.37.

[54] Case C–107/94 *P.H. Asscher v Staatssecretaris van Financiën* [1994] E.C.R. I–1137, para.32, citing Case 115/78 *Knoors v Secretary of State for Economic Affairs* [1979] E.C.R. 399; Case C–61/89 *Criminal Proceedings against Marc Gaston Bouchoucha* [1990] E.C.R. I–3551; Case C–19/92 *Dieter Kraus v Land Baden-Württemberg.* [1993] E.C.R. I–1663; Case C–419/92 *Scholz v Opera Universitaria di Cagliari* [1994] E.C.R. I–505. This formulation may also provide the true explanation of Case C–370/90 *R v Immigration and Appeal Tribunal and Surinder Singh ex parte Secretary of State for the Home Department* [1992] E.C.R. I–4265

situations which are purely internal to a Member State, Article [43] nevertheless cannot be interpreted in such a way as to exclude a given Member State's own nationals from the benefit of Community law where by reason of their conduct they are, with regard to their Member State of origin, in a situation which may be regarded as equivalent to that of any other person enjoying the rights and liberties guaranteed by the Treaty . . ."

It appears from the foregoing survey of the case law that the Court's approach to the interpretation of the Treaty provisions on the right of establishment has been the subject of considerable development, as regards the right of a national of a Member State, and members of the family deriving rights through that person, to invoke the right of establishment against the authorities of that State, and as regards the application of Article 43 EC to non-discriminatory national measures capable of restricting the right of establishment. It will be examined in a subsequent section of this chapter to what extent the formulation of the Court set out in *Gebhard* above is to be taken literally, since it implies that any national regulation of economic activity will have to be justified on grounds compatible with Community law, and in terms of proportionality, lest such regulation burden cross border economic activity.

Abolition of restrictions on the right of establishment

The General Programme and secondary legislation

The Treaty in its original text provided for the abolition of **19-010** restrictions on freedom of establishment in progressive stages *during the transitional period.*[55] Such abolition was, and is to be facilitated by secondary legislation prohibiting discrimination on grounds of nationality,[56] ensuring the mutual recognition of "diplomas and certificates, and other evidence of formal qualifications,"[57] and co-ordinating national requirements governing the pursuit of non-wage-earning activities.[58] Legislation on the abolition of restrictions was to be preceded by a General Programme, which was to be drawn up by the Council before the end of the first stage. The Programme[59] was

---

[55] The words are omitted from the current text because they are now superfluous.
[56] See Art.44(2)(f) EC referring to "effecting the progressive abolition of restrictions on freedom of establishment in every branch of activity under consideration, . . .".
[57] Art.47(1) EC.
[58] Art.47(2) EC.
[59] The General Programme constitutes neither a Regulation, Directive nor Decision within the meaning of Art. 249 of the Treaty. For the view that it bound the Community institutions, but not the Member States, see van Gerven (1966) 3 C.M.L. Rev. 344, 354. There seems to be no reason why it could not bind the Member States, see Case 22/70 *ERTA* [1971] E.C.R. 263

adopted in December 1961,[60] and provided the basis for the Council's subsequent legislative activities in this area.

Abolition of discriminatory restrictions by secondary legislation

19–011   Title III of the General Programme called for the abolition of discriminatory measures which might impair access to the non-wage-earning activities of nationals of the Member States, such as measures which:

— conditioned the access to or exercise of a non-wage earning activity on an authorisation or on the issuance of a document, such as a foreign merchant's card or a foreign professional's card;
— made the access to or exercise of a non-wage earning activity more costly through the imposition of taxes or other charges such as a deposit or surety bond paid to the receiving country;
— barred or limited membership in companies, particularly with regard to the activities of their members.

In addition to measures primarily likely to discriminate against nationals of the Member States with respect of access to non-wage-earning activities, the General Programme condemned specific national practices discriminating against such persons in the exercise of these activities, such as those limiting the opportunity:

— to enter into certain types of transactions, such as contracts for the hire of services or commercial and farm leases;
— to tender bids or to participate as a co-contractor or sub-contractor in public contracts or contracts with public bodies[61];
— to borrow and to have access to various forms of credit;
— to benefit from aids granted by the State.

Subsequently, the Council issued a series of Directives implementing the General Programme, and dealing with the right of establishment in a wide variety of commercial callings, from the wholesale

---

[60] [1974] O.J. Spec. Ed., Second Series, IX, p.7. The Court has referred to the General Programme in its case law, see e.g., Case 7/76 *Thieffry* [1977] E.C.R. 765; Case 136/78 *Auer* [1979] E.C.R. 452; Case 182/83 *Fearon* [1984] E.C.R. 3677; Case 107/83 *Klopp* [1984] E.C.R. 2971.

[61] There has been substantial harmonisation in this field, see in particular Directive 2004/17 of the European Parliament and of the Council, coordinating the procurement procedures of entities operating in the water, energy, transport and postal services sectors, [2004] O.J. L134/1; Directive 2004/18 of the European Parliament and of the Council, on the coordination of procedures for the award of public works contracts, public supply contracts and public service contracts, [2004] O.J. L134/114.

trade to the provision of electricity, gas, water and sanitary services.[62] Many such Directives are applicable to both establishment and the provision of services, emphasising again the close practical relationship between the two. Directive 64/223,[63] concerning the attainment of freedom of establishment and freedom to provide services in respect of activities in the wholesale trade, may be considered for illustrative purposes. Under the Directive Member States are required to abolish the restrictions itemised in Title III of the General Programmes with respect to the commercial activities concerned. Specific legislative provisions in effect in the Member States are singled out for prohibition, such as the obligation under French law to hold a *carte d'identité d'étranger commerçant*,[64] while Member States are obliged to ensure that beneficiaries of the Directive have the right to join professional or trade organisations under the same conditions, and with the same rights and obligations as their own nationals.[65] Where a host State requires evidence of good character in respect of its own nationals taking up the commercial activities concerned, provision is made for accepting appropriate proof from other Member States, and for the taking of a solemn declaration by self-employed persons from such States, where the State in question does not issue the appropriate documentation.[66]

Effect of direct applicability of Article 43 EC on harmonisation programme

Although Article 53 of the EEC Treaty,[67] which prohibited **19–012** Member States from introducing any new restrictions on the right of establishment of nationals of other Member States, was held by the Court to be directly applicable in *Costa v ENEL*,[68] the Council's extensive legislative scheme, based on the General Programme, appears to have been adopted on the basis that the prohibition of discrimination contained in Article 43 EC was ineffective in the absence of implementation. That this was not the case was made clear by the Court of Justice in *Reyners v Belgian State*.[69] The plaintiff in the main suit was a Dutch national resident in Belgium. He had

---

[62] The documents are too numerous to list.
[63] [1963–64(I)] O.J. Spec. Ed. 123.
[64] Art.3.
[65] Art.4.
[66] Art.6.
[67] This Article appeared in the original text of the EEC Treaty, but was repealed as superfluous by the Amsterdam Treaty.
[68] Case 6/64 [1964] E.C.R. 585.
[69] Case 2/74 [1974] E.C.R. 631. For a discriminatory provision remaining on the statute book contrary to Art.43 EC see Case 159/78 *Commission v Italy* [1979] E.C.R. 3247. And see Case 38/87 *Commission v Greece* [1988] E.C.R. 4415. For discriminatory conditions of tender contrary to Art.43 EC, see Case 197/84 *Steinhauser* [1985] E.C.R. 1819.

been born in Belgium, educated there, and taken his *docteur en droit belge*, only to be finally refused admission to the Belgian bar on the ground of his Dutch nationality. On a reference for a preliminary ruling, the Court held that the prohibition on discrimination contained in Article 43 EC was directly applicable as of the end of the transitional period, despite the opening words of the text of that Article, which referred to the abolition of restrictions "within the framework of the provisions set out below." These provisions—the General Programme and the Directives provided for in Article 44 EC—were of significance "only during the transitional period, since the freedom of establishment was fully attained at the end of it." According to the Court, the aim of Article 43 was intended to be facilitated by the Council's Legislative programme, but not made dependent upon it.

The Court's decision had immediate repercussions. The Commission undertook, at a meeting of the Permanent Representatives, to report to the Council its view of the implications of the *Reyners* case for the implementation of the right of establishment. In its promised memorandum,[70] the Commission expressed the view that all the rules and formalities cited in the Directives on the abolition of restrictions were no longer applicable to nationals of the Member States, though, in the interests of legal certainty, the Member States should formally bring their legislation into line with the requirements of Article 43 EC. In view of this, the Commission considered that it was no longer necessary to adopt Directives on the abolition of restrictions, and furthermore, since Directives were by their nature constitutive, that the adoption of such instruments having only declaratory effect would create confusion and protract the work of the Council unnecessarily. The latter view is open to question. Several Directives in the field of free movement of persons have been stated by the Court to give rise to no new rights, but merely to give closer articulation to rights bestowed directly by the Treaty.[71] This would also appear to be the case with Directive 75/117[72] on equal pay, which clarifies but does not add to the material scope of Article 141 EC. It was on this ground that Advocate General Verloren van Themaat urged the Court to hold a Member State in breach of Article 141 EC, rather than the Directive, in proceedings brought by the Commission under Article 226 EC. The Court nonetheless held the Member State in default for failing to implement the Directive.[73] But as the Court commented in *Reyners* itself, Directives already issued under Article 44(2) EC would not lose all interest, since they would "preserve an important scope in the field

---

[70] Commission Communication, SEC (74) Final, Brussels.
[71] Case 43/75 *Royer* [1976] E.C.R. 497.
[72] [1975] O.J. L45/19.
[73] Case 58/81 *Commission v Luxembourg* [1982] E.C.R. 2175.

of measures intended to make easier the effective exercise of the right of freedom of establishment."[74] The Court was no doubt mindful of the value to the individual litigant before a national tribunal of some more precise formulation of his/her rights than the general prohibitions of the Treaty. In any event, the Commission formally withdrew a large number of proposed Directives on abolition of restrictions on freedom of establishment.

The prohibition in Article 43 EC of discrimination on grounds of nationality is not concerned solely with the specific rules on the pursuit of occupational activities but also with the rules relating to the various general facilities which are of assistance in the pursuit of those activities, including access to housing, and to the facilities provided by national authorities to alleviate the financial burden of acquiring housing.[75] For further discussion of the rights of economically active persons and members of their families to equal access to such benefits and facilities in the Member States, see Chapter 18 on Free Movement of Workers.

Direct and indirect discrimination

Article 43 EC prohibits both direct and indirect discrimination on **19–013** grounds of nationality. Direct discrimination takes place when individuals or undertakings are treated differently by reference to their nationality.

Examples of direct discrimination are:

— a requirement that nationals **of other Member States** set up a company incorporated in the host State before obtaining a licence to fish at sea[76];
— a requirement that in order for a ship to qualify for the nationality of a Member State, it must be **owned by nationals of that Member State**.[77]

In such cases the reference to nationality as a ground for differentiation is express, and such discrimination is described as "direct" or "overt".

The Court has held that Article 43 EC prohibits not only direct, or overt discrimination by reason of nationality but also all covert forms of discrimination which, by the application of other criteria of differentiation, lead in fact to the same result.[78] In *Commission v Italy* a national measure providing that only companies in which all

---

[74] [1974] E.C.R. 631, 652.
[75] See e.g. Case 63/86 *Commission v Italy* [1988] E.C.R. 129; Case 305/87 *Commission v Greece* [1989] E.C.R. 1461.
[76] Case C–93/89 *Commission v Ireland* [1991] E.C.R. I–4569.
[77] Case C–221/89 *Factortame* [1991] E.C.R. I–3905.
[78] Case C–3/88 *Commmission v Italy* [1989] E.C.R. 4035.

or a majority of the shares are either directly or indirectly in public or State ownership may conclude agreements for the development of data-processing systems for public authorities was held to be contrary to Article 43 EC.[79] The Court held that although the rules in issue applied without distinction to all companies, they *essentially favoured* domestic companies, and observed that no data-processing companies from other Member States qualified under the criteria in question at the material time.[80] In the *Asscher* case the Court identified as being potentially discriminatory legislation which was "liable to act mainly to the detriment of nationals of other Member States."[81] Criteria which have been identified as potential sources of indirect discrimination include the place of residence of self-employed persons or the principal place of establishment of companies.[82]

However, differentiation between situations on objective grounds consistent with the Treaty does not amount to prohibited discrimination. Although residence requirements may amount in certain cases to indirect discrimination,[83] the Court has held that a national law exempting rural land from compulsory acquisition if the owners have lived on or near the land for a specified period, is consistent with Article 43 EC, where the purpose of the law is to ensure as far as possible that rural land belongs to those who work it, and where the law applies equally to its own nationals and to the nationals of other Member States.[84] Again, in *Commission v France* the Court acknowledged the possibility that a distinction based on the location of the registered office of a company or the place of residence of a natural person might under certain conditions be justified in an area such as tax law.[85] National tax rules are increasingly held to amount to restrictions on freedom of establishment and other fundamental freedoms, and this topic is covered in some detail in Chapter 20.

19–014   The discriminatory effects of national rules or practices contravening Article 43 EC may adversely affect and be challenged by nationals of the offending Member State as well as nationals of other Member States. In *Coname* the Court of Justice considered whether the direct award by a public authority of a management concession for a gas distribution service was compatible with Articles 43 and 49

---

[79] *ibid.*
[80] [1989] E.C.R. 4035, paras 9, 10.
[81] Case C–107/94 *P.H. Asscher v Staatssecretaris van Financiën* [1994] E.C.R. I–1137, para.38.
[82] Case C–1/93 *Halliburton Services v Staatssecretaris van Financiën* [1994] E.C.R. I–1137; Case C–330/91 *R v Inland Revenue Commissioners ex parte Commerzbank* [1993] E.C.R. I–4017; Case C–80/94 *Wielockx v Inspecteur der Directe Belastingen* [1965] E.C.R. I–2493.
[83] Case C–80/94 *Wielockx v Inspecteur der Directe Belastingen* [1995] E.C.R. I–2493; and see Case 152/73 *Sotgiu* and the discussion of indirect discrimination in the context of free movement of workers in Ch.18 at p.727.
[84] Case 182/83 *Fearon* [1984] E.C.R. 3677.
[85] Case 270/83 [1986] E.C.R. 273, para.19.

EC.[86] The direct award of the concession to the Padania company was challenged before an Italian court by Coname, an undertaking which had previously held the concession in question. The Italian court asked whether it was consistent with Articles 43 and 49 EC to award such a concession without an invitation to tender. The Court held that in so far as the contract might also have been of interest to an undertaking located in another Member State, lack of transparency in the award of the contract would amount to a difference in treatment to the detriment of the undertaking located in the other Member State. The Court considered that:

> "Unless it is justified by objective circumstances, such a difference in treatment, which, by excluding all undertakings located in another Member State, operates mainly to the detriment of the latter undertakings, amounts to indirect discrimination on the basis of nationality, prohibited under Articles 43 EC and 49 EC . . .
>
> In those circumstances, it is for the referring court to satisfy itself that the award of the concession . . . complies with transparency requirements which, without necessarily implying an obligation to hold an invitation to tender, are, in particular, such as to ensure that an undertaking located in the territory of a Member State other than that of the Italian Republic can have access to appropriate information regarding that concession before it is awarded, so that, if the undertaking had so wished, it would have been in a position to express its interest in obtaining that concession."

If the national court found that this was not the case, it would have to be concluded that there was a difference in treatment to the detriment of an undertaking located in another Member State. In such an event, the Court of Justice ruled out the possibility that such a difference in treatment could be objectively justified.

Relationship between Article 12 EC and Articles 43 and 49 EC

Article 12 EC prohibits discrimination on grounds of nationality **19–015** within the scope of operation of the Treaty. This general prohibition of discrimination has been implemented as regards freedom of establishment and the provision of services by Articles 43 and 49 of the Treaty.[87] The Court has said that any rules incompatible with the latter articles are also incompatible with Article 12 EC.[88] However,

---

[86] Case C–231/03 *Consorzio Azienda Metana (Coname) v Comune di Cingia de' Botti* Judgment of July 21, 2005.
[87] And as regards freedom of movement for workers, *ibid.*
[88] Case 90/76 *Van Ameyde v UCI* [1977] E.C.R. 1091, p.1126, para.27; Case 305/87 *Commission v Greeece* [1989] E.C.R. 1461, para.12.

non-discriminatory rules which disadvantage a person by virtue of the fact that he has more than one place of business within the Community may be consistent with Article 12 but inconsistent with Article 43.[89] And non-discriminatory rules which amount to restrictions on the provision of services would be incompatible with Article 49 EC, but consistent with Article 12 EC.[90] Furthermore, Article 12 EC "applies independently only to situations governed by Community law in regard to which the Treaty lays down no specific prohibition of discrimination."[91]

Non-discriminatory restrictions on the right of establishment

19–016   It has been noted in the section of this Chapter on the evolution of the Court's case law on Article 43 EC that in the *Gebhard* case[92] the Court adopted the concept of the non-discriminatory restriction on the right of establishment, applicable in circumstances other than those in which an individual or company sought a right of "exit" from a Member State, or asserted the right to a place of business in more than one Member State. A question yet to be resolved is whether the *Gebhard* formulation is to be taken at face value, that is to say, as requiring *all* non discriminatory restrictions likely to hinder or make less attractive the exercise of the right of establishment, to be justified. An alternative possibility is that although all discriminatory restrictions have to be justified, non-discriminatory restrictions only require justification if they restrict access to the market. There are still signs in post *Gebhard* case law that the dominant aim of Article 43 EC is to prohibit discriminatory restrictions on establishment; thus in the *Royal Bank of Scotland* case, the Court states:

> "It is common ground that the essential aim of Article [43] of the Treaty is to implement, in the field of self-employment, the principle of equal treatment laid down in Article [12] of the Treaty."[93]

There has already been some discussion in Chapter 18 on Freedom of Movement for Workers, on the possible scope of the prohibition on non-discriminatory restrictions laid down by Article 39 of the Treaty.[94] That discussion indicated two possible approaches: the first

---

[89] Case 143/87 *Stanton* [1988] E.C.R. 3877; Joined Cases 154 and 155/87 *Wolf* [1988] E.C.R. 3897.

[90] For the scope of Art.49, see below at p.778 *et seq.*

[91] Case 305/87 *Commission v Greece* [1989] E.C.R. 1461, para.13.

[92] Case C–55/94 *Reinhard Gebhard v Consiglio dell'Ordine degli Avvocati e Procuratori di Milano* [1995] E.C.R. I–4165, above at p.762.

[93] Case C–311/97 *Royal Bank of Scotland v Elliniko Dimosio (Greek State)* [1999] E.C.R. I–2651, para.21.

[94] Above at p.734.

being that non-discriminatory national measures need only be justified if they restrict access to the market; the second and broader approach being that all national measures which are detrimental to the conditions under which individuals exercise a fundamental freedom constitute restrictions on the free movement of workers and must be justified. That analysis is in principle equally applicable to Article 43 EC, and the reader is accordingly referred to the relevant passages in their entirety, but it is nevertheless appropriate to consider cases specific to Article 43 EC in which the Court has had recourse to the *Gebhard* formulation.

In *Futura Participations SA* the Court considered Luxembourg rules which allowed the carrying forward of tax losses but limited this possibility to profits and losses arising from Luxembourg activities in the case of non-residents, while imposing no such limitation in respect of residents. The Court applied the test of discrimination to determine the compatibility of the rules in question with Article 43 EC. But there was a second issue in *Futura*, namely, whether it was compatible with Article 43 EC to require non-residents, during the financial year in which the losses the taxpayer sought to carry forward were incurred, to have kept in Luxembourg accounts complying with the relevant national rules. As regards this issue the Court refers to the *Gebhard* test.[95–96] But the Court says of the national requirement in question that it:

> "may constitute a restriction, within the meaning of Article [43] of the Treaty, on the freedom of establishment of a company or firm . . . where that company or firm wishes to establish a branch in a Member State different from that in which it has its seat."[97]

This makes it clear that the Court regards the condition as one **19–017** which specifically restricts the setting up by a company of a secondary establishment in another Member State. The Court goes on to describe the imposition of such a condition as one which "specifically affects companies or firms having their seat in another Member State", which is in principle prohibited by Article 43 EC, since it involves such a company or firm keeping, in addition to its own accounts which comply with the tax accounting rules applicable in the Member State in which it has its seat, separate accounts for its branch's activities complying with the tax accounting rules applicable in the State in which the branch is established. This part of the Court's judgment, however seems to amount to a finding that the measure in question is indirectly *discriminatory*, since it imposes a

---

[95–96] Case C–250/95 *Futura Participations SA v Administrations des Contributions* [1997] E.C.R. I–2471, para.26.
[97] *ibid.*, para.24.

requirement on companies or firms having a seat in another Member State which is in practice more burdensome than that imposed on domestic companies.[98] In these circumstances, recourse to the *Gebhard* formulation as regards the restriction in question seems indistinguishable from asking whether the measure is indirectly discriminatory, and if so, whether it can be objectively justified.

But that is not to say that all the Court's case law dealing with national restrictions which require to be justified in order to be regarded as compatible with Article 43 EC can be rationalized as case law on indirect discrimination. Thus in *Sodemare*[99] the Court considered national rules which limited certain activities to non-profit-making organisations, and whether in particular such a rule amounted to a restriction on the right of establishment of a profit-making private company established in another Member State. In concluding that such a rule was compatible with the Treaty the Court referred to case law which indicated that non-discriminatory restrictions on the free movement of goods could be justified on the basis that Member States retained the power to organise their social security systems and to adopt, in particular, provisions intended to govern the consumption of pharmaceutical preparations in order to promote the financial stability of their health-care insurance schemes.[1] It is true that the Court notes that a restriction such as that in issue does not place profit-making companies from other Member States in a less favourable factual or legal situation than similar domestic companies, but if this were in itself enough to condone the national measure the reference to national competence to organize their social security systems would have been unnecessary.[2] The national rule in *Sodemare* was of course one which restricted the *access* by a foreign company to the domestic market, and it is perhaps on this basis that it was necessary to justify even a non-discriminatory restriction.

Nationality requirements as to companies, shareholders, and directors, defined by reference to the nationality of *any* Member State, rather than the nationality of the host State, may nevertheless constitute restrictions on freedom of establishment. In *Commission v Netherlands,*[3] the Court considered Netherlands rules which conditioned registration of a ship in the Netherlands on the shareholders and directors of a Community company owning the ship being of Community nationality, and required local representatives in the

---

[98] On direct and indirect discrimination, see above at pp.767–768.
[99] Case C–70/95 *Sodemare SA v regione Lombardia* [1997] E.C.R. I–3395.
[1] The Court refers to Case 238/82 *Duphar v Netherlands State* [1984] E.C.R. 523, para.16; see *Sodemare*, para.27.
[2] The same is true of the *Duphar* case; the absence of discrimination referred to in that case was significant since discriminatory national measures could only be justified under Art.30 EC; see Ch.13, at p.616, n.6.
[3] C–299/02 *Commission v Kingdom of the Netherlands* [2004] E.C.R. I–9761.

Netherlands being of Community nationality.[4] The Court noted that if shipowner companies wishing to register their ships in the Netherlands did not satisfy the conditions in issue, their only course of action would be to alter the structure of their share capital or of their boards of directors, and that such changes might entail serious disruption within a company and also require the completion of numerous formalities having financial consequences. The Court considered that the requirements amounted to restrictions which could not be justified. The Court's analysis is consistent with the conclusion that the rules in issue had discriminatory effects; yet the starting point is that even non discriminatory rules which hinder or male less attractive the exercise of a fundamental freedom must be justified.[5]

In *Pfeiffer Großhandel*[6] the Court considered the compatibility **19–018** with Article 43 EC of a restraining order which prevented an Austrian subsidiary of a German parent operating discount stores in Austria from using a trade name used by the German parent in Germany and other Member States. The Court referred to the *Gebhard* test and held that the order in question was "liable to constitute an impediment to the realization by those undertakings of a uniform advertising concept at Community level since it might force them to adjust the presentation of the businesses they operate according to the place of establishment."[7]

It is possible to see in this judgment the basis of a potentially far-reaching principle that any national measure which might constitute an impediment to the realization by a company of a "uniform advertising concept at Community level" is to be treated as prima facie contrary to Article 43 EC and must accordingly be justified by imperative requirements in the public interest. A narrower analysis of the above case is however possible. It is that preventing a national of one Member State or a company with its seat in one Member State from carrying out economic activities in another Member State under a title or trade name which it is entitled to use in the first Member State is to be regarded as in principle a restriction on *access* to the market of that State. This approach would allow at least a broad analogy to be drawn with case law on the movement of goods concerning national rules preventing the marketing of goods under home country designation.[8]

Reference was made in Chapter 16 to the *Keck* case, which held that while non discriminatory rules relating to the composition and

---

[4] EEA nationality was a permissible alternative for shareholders, directors and local representatives.
[5] *ibid.*, para.15.
[6] Case C–255/97 *Pfeiffer Großhandel Gmbh v Löwa Warenahndel Gmbh* [1999] E.C.R. I–2835.
[7] *ibid.*, para.20.
[8] Ch.16, p.581.

packaging of goods, etc. amounted to measures having equivalent
effect to quantitative restrictions, and had to be justified, rules
relating to certain selling arrangements would not have to be
justified provided they applied to all traders operating within the
national territory and provided that they affected in the same
manner, in law and in fact, the marketing of domestic products and
of those from other Member States.[9] Support for the view that
Article 43 EC is to be given an interpretation which, while not
necessarily precisely the same as that of Article 28 EC, post *Keck*, is
at any rate analogous, and will lead to a similar outcome in similar
cases, is to be found in *Semeraro Casa Uno Srl*,[10] in which the Court
considered whether national rules which (save for certain products)
required retail shops to close on Sundays and public holidays, were
contrary to Article 28 EC or Article 39 EC. As regards Article 28 EC
the Court referred to *Keck*, and concluded that such national rules
amounted to non-discriminatory selling arrangements and were
consistent with Article 28 EC. As regards Article 43 EC the Court,
referring to its reasoning concerning Article 28 EC, stated:

> "As far as Article [43] is concerned, suffice it to state that, as
> has been found above, the legislation in question is applicable
> to all traders exercising their activity on national territory; that
> its purpose is not to regulate the conditions concerning the
> establishment of the undertakings concerned; and that any
> restrictive effects which it might have on freedom of establish-
> ment are too uncertain and indirect for the obligation laid
> down to be regarded as being capable of hindering that
> freedom."[11]

19–019   The above formulation is clearly akin to that applicable to "selling
arrangements" pursuant to the *Keck* judgment. But while one would
expect a similar outcome in genuinely similar cases, irrespective of
whether a national measure fell to be assessed under Article 28 EC
or Article 43 EC, or indeed Article 39 EC or Article 49 EC, cases
which are superficially similar may actually raise rather different
issues. Thus reasoning essentially the same as that cited above has
been used to justify the conclusion that national rules on the
licensing of shops are consistent with Article 28 EC[12]; but it would
not automatically follow that such rules would escape scrutiny under
Article 43 EC. Authorisation requirements relating to access to
particular premises from which to pursue an economic activity, such

[9] Joined Cases C–267 and C–268/91 *Keck and Mithouard* [1993] E.C.R. I 6097, paras 15–17; and see Ch.16, pp.588–593.
[10] Joined Cases C–418/93 *etc., Semeraro Casa Uno Srl v Sindaco del Comune di Erbusco etc.* [1996] E.C.R. I–2975.
[11] *ibid.*, para.32.
[12] Joined Cases C–140–142/94 *DIP SpA* [1995 E.C.R. I–3257, para.29.

as office premises, are capable of affecting access to the market by self-employed persons. Refusing a licence to operate a shop on the basis that there were already a sufficient number of such shops to serve local needs would seem to amount to a restriction on freedom of establishment which could not be justified.[13]

The debate about the scope of the *Kraus/Gebhard* formulation has yet to be resolved. In the *CaixaBank France* case[14] the Court considered whether national rules of a Member State prohibiting the remuneration of "sight" current accounts in euros constituted restrictions on the freedom of establishment prohibited by Article 43 EC in so far as they apply to the subsidiary formed in that Member State by a legal person from another Member State. Advocate General Tizzano attempted to "unravel the case law."[15] He found it difficult to accept that national measures could be restrictions contrary to the Treaty for the sole reason that they reduced the economic attractiveness of pursuing an economic activity, if those measures did not directly affect access to that activity and did not discriminate on grounds of nationality. If such measures were restrictions it would enable economic operators, both national and foreign, to oppose all national regulation, and would create a market in which "rules are prohibited as a matter of principle, except for those necessary and proportionate to meeting imperative requirements in the general interest." For that reason he did not consider that that was the right road to take.[16] In his view:

> ". . . *where the principle of non-discrimination is respected*—and hence the conditions for the *taking up and pursuit* of an economic activity are equal *both in law and in fact*—a national measure cannot be described as a restriction on the freedom of movement of persons unless, in the light of its purpose and effects, the measure in question *directly affects market access*."[17]

In the Court's view, the prohibition in issue constituted for companies from Member States other than France "a serious obstacle to the pursuit of their activities via a subsidiary in the latter Member

---

[13] It is common for directives designed to facilitate the right of establishment to prohibit licensing on economic grounds of undertakings wishing carry on certain economic activities, see e.g. Dir.2002/83 concerning life assurance, [2004] O.J. L345/1, Art.6(6); Dir.2005/68/EC on reinsurance, [2005] O.J. L323/1, Art.10. Prior authorisation to acquire property amounts to a restriction on establishment and capital movement in the absence of justification, see e.g. Case C–302/97 *Klaus Konle* [1999] E.C.R. I–3099, paras 22, 49; and Case C–452/01 *Margarethe Ospelt* [2003] E.C.R. I–9743.

[14] Case C–442/02 *CaixaBank France v Ministère de l'Économie, des Finances et de l'Industrie* [2004] E.C.R. I–8961.

[15] Case C–442/02 *CaixaBank France v Ministère de l'Économie, des Finances et de l'Industrie* [2004] E.C.R. I–8961, Opinion of Advocate General, para.58.

[16] *ibid.*, see paras 62, 63.

[17] *ibid.*, para.66.

State, affecting their access to the market."[18] The prohibition deprived out-of-state companies of the possibility of competing more effectively with the banks traditionally established in France, which had an extensive network of branches and therefore greater opportunities for raising capital from the public. It is to be noted that the prohibition in issue discriminated against out-of-state banks seeking to enter the market in France because it reinforced a barrier to market entry in the sector in question (the cost of acquiring an extensive network of branches). It may be that where a national rule reinforces a barrier to market entry, and is accordingly likely to make it difficult for new market entrants to compete with established market entrants, this is enough to attract the application of Article 43, since at the very least some new market entrants will or may be out-of-state operators. But the Court's judgment is not necessarily to be confined to situations where national rule reinforces a barrier to market entry, such as the existence of a branch network, since the Court makes an observation which might be seen as of more general application:

> "Where credit institutions which are subsidiaries of foreign companies seek to enter the market of a Member State, competing by means of the rate of remuneration paid on sight accounts constitutes one of the most effective means to that end. Access to the market by those establishments is thus made more difficult by such a prohibition."[19]

This passage supports the proposition that national rules which deprive a new market entrant of what would be an effective means of competing with established market operators restricts access to the market and hinders the exercise of the right of establishment. National rules which make it more difficult for market operators to compete with each other might well be said to restrict market access even if the rules themselves regulate the conduct of business activities rather than market access as such.

Parallel interpretation of Articles 39, 43 and 49 EC

19–020   Theoretically, problems may arise in differentiating between the employed and the self-employed, and between instances of establishment and provision of services, but it will in many cases be unnecessary to make any hard and fast classification, because the applicable principles will be the same in any event. Thus, in *Procureur du Roi v Royer*,[20] the Court of Justice, considering a

---

[18] Case C–442/02 *CaixaBank France*, [2004] E.C.R. I–8961, para.12 of Judgment.
[19] Case C–442/02 *CaixaBank France*, [2004] E.C.R. I–8961, para.14.
[20] Case 48/75 [1976] E.C.R. 497. And see Case 118/75, *Watson & Belmann* [1976] E.C.R. 1185.

request for a preliminary ruling from a national court which was uncertain whether the subject of the proceedings before it was to be considered as falling within Article 39 EC, Article 43 EC or Article 49 EC, observed:

> ". . . comparison of these different provisions shows that they are based on the same principles both in so far as they concern the entry into and residence in the territory of Member States of persons covered by Community law and the prohibition of all discrimination between them on grounds of nationality."[21]

The distinction between employed and self-employed persons is however important in relation to migrants from the new Member States. As we have seen in the preceding Chapter, the transitional arrangements allow for temporary derogation from the rules guaranteeing non-discriminatory access for workers to the labour market, while freedom of movement for the self-employed is fully guaranteed.[22] The distinction between employed and self-employed persons will thus be significant in this context.

An important corollary of the statement of principle in the *Royer* case quoted above is that Article 43 EC, like Article 39 EC, must be construed as prohibiting discrimination by private parties as well as by public authorities. In *Walrave v Union cycliste internationale*,[23] the Court expressed the opinion that Article 39 of the Treaty extended to agreements and rules other than those emanating from public authorities, citing in support of its view the text of Article 7(4) of Regulation 1612/68, which nullifies discriminatory clauses in individual or collective employment agreements. A similar conclusion was justified in the case of Article 49 EC, since the activities referred to therein were "not to be distinguished by their nature from those in Article [39], but only by the fact that they are performed outside the ties of a contract of employment."[24] It follows that Article 43 EC has a similar ambit.

But while these various Treaty provisions may have similar effects in certain circumstances, this will not be so in all cases (quite apart from the special position of migrants from new Member States). Application in particular of the principle of proportionality may yield different results according to whether or not a particular

---

[21] [1976] E.C.R. 497, 509. For parallel interpretation of Arts. 39 EC and 43 EC see Case C–106/91 *Ramrath v Ministre de la Justice* [1992] E.C.R. I–3351, para.17; and Case C–107/94 *P.H. Asscher v Staatssecretaris van Financiën* [1994] E.C.R. I–1137, para.29.

[22] Currently in relation to workers from the EU 8 (EU 10 minus Cyprus and Malta); similar arrangements are provided in relation to Bulgaria and Romania. See Ch.18, at p.746. The distinction was relevant before accession, see Case C–268/99 *Jany* [2001] E.C.R. I–8615.

[23] Case 36/74 [1974] E.C.R. 1405.

[24] [1974] E.C.R. 1405 at 1419; and see Case C–281/98 *Angonese* [2000] E.C.R. I–4139, Ch.18, at p.709.

individual or undertaking is providing services or established in a Member State. Thus e.g. national rules requiring registration with an appropriate trade or professional body are presumptively not applicable to those providing services but applicable to those established in the Member State in question.[25]

FREEDOM TO PROVIDE SERVICES

General Scope

19–021   Article 49 EC of the Treaty provides that "[w]ithin the framework of the provisions set out below, restrictions on freedom to provide services within the Community shall be prohibited in respect of nationals of Member States who are established in a State of the Community other than that of the person for whom the services are intended." It will be noted that in order to invoke this provision, nationals must be "established" in a Member State. In the case of companies whose registered office is situated inside the Community, but whose central management or principal place of business is not, this requirement is satisfied by their activities having "a real and continuous link with the economy of a Member State, excluding the possibility that this link might depend on nationality, particularly the nationality of the partners or the members of the managing or supervisory bodies, or of persons holding the capital stock."[26] It is to be noted that a company registered in a Member State may be established in that State even if it conducts all its business through an agency branch or subsidiary in another Member State.[27]

"Services" are defined in Article 50 EC, and are considered as such when they are "normally provided for remuneration." One would expect the remuneration to be provided by the receiver of services, but this is not essential. In the *Debauve* and *Coditel* cases, Advocate General Warner expressed the opinion that the purpose of the definition of "services" in Article 50 EC was to exclude those that are normally provided gratuitously. Television broadcasting thus in his view fell within the definition whether it was financed by licence fee, or by advertising. The decision factor was that the broadcasting was remunerated in one way or another.[28] *Bond van*

---

[25] Case C–215/01 *Bruno Schnitzer* [2003] E.C.R. I–14847; Case 292/86 *Gullung* [1988] E.C.R. 111. Thus, Art.4 of Dir. 77/249 on provision of services by lawyers, exempts service providers from registration in the host State, while Art.3 of Dir.98/5 on the establishment of lawyers provides for such registration.

[26] General Programme (Services), [1974] O.J. Spec. Ed., 2nd Series, IX, p.3.

[27] Case 79/85 *Segers v bestuur van de Bedrijfsvereniging voor Bank- en Verzeleringswezen* [1986] E.C.R. 2375; Case C–212/97 *Centros Ltd v Erhvervs- og Selskabsstyrelsen* [1999] E.C.R. I–1458, below at p.842.

[28] Case 52/79 *Procureur du Roi v Marc J.V.C. Debauve* [1980] E.C.R. 833; Case 62/79 SA *Compagnie générale pour la diffusion de la télévision, Coditel v Ciné Vog Films and others* [1980] E.C.R. 881 Opinion at p.876.

Adverteerders v Netherlands State[29] concerned *inter alia* the provision of services by cable television operators in one Member State to broadcasters in another by relaying to network subscribers in the first Member State television programmes transmitted to them by the broadcasters. The Court held that these services were provided for remuneration. The cable network operators were paid, in the form of the fees which they charged their subscribers for the service which they provided to the broadcaster, and it was irrelevant that the broadcasters generally did not themselves pay the cable network operators for relaying their programmes.[30] Similarly, the fact that hospital medical treatment is financed directly by sickness insurance funds on the basis of agreements and pre-set scales of fees does not remove such treatment from the sphere of services within the the the meaning of Article 50 EC.[31]

A non-exhaustive list of services in Article 50 EC specifies activities of an industrial character, activities of a commercial character, activities of craftsmen, and activities of the professions. Where a particular activity falls within the provisions of the Treaty relating to the free movement of goods, capital or persons, however, these latter provisions govern. The Court has held that the broadcasting of television signals,[32] cable transmission,[33] tourism, medical treatment[34] (including the termination of pregnancy[35] and in-patient hospital treatment[36]), education,[37] the importation of lottery advertisements and tickets into a Member State,[38] and unsolicited telephone calls to potential clients,[39] are covered by the provisions on the freedom to provide services. In a different but analogous context the Court has held that prostitution is a provision of services for remuneration.[40]

Without prejudice to the right of establishment, a person providing a service may, in order to do so, "temporarily pursue his activity in the State where the service is provided, under the same conditions as are imposed by that State on its own nationals."[41] The Court of

---

[29] Case 352/85 [1988] E.C.R. 2085.
[30] *ibid.*, para.16.
[31] Case C–157/99 *Smits and Peerbooms* [2001] E.C.R. I–5473, para.56.
[32] Case 155/73 *Sacchi* [1974] E.C.R. 490, para.6.
[33] Case 52/79 *Procureur du Roi v Marc J.V.C. Debauve* [1980] E.C.R. 833, para.8; Case C–23/93 *TV10 SA v Commissariaat voor de Media* [1994] E.C.R. I–1963, para.13.
[34] Case C–157/99 *Smits and Peerbooms* [2001] E.C.R. I–5473.
[35] Case 159/90 *The Society for the protection of Unborn Children Ireland Ltd v Stephen Grogan* [1991] E.C.R. I–4685, para.18.
[36] Case C–157/99 *Smits and Peerbooms* [2001] E.C.R. I–5473.
[37] Joined cases 286/82 and 26/83 *Graziana Luisi and Giuseppe Carbone v Ministero del Tesoro.* [1984] E.C.R. 377
[38] Case C–275/92 *Her Majesty's Customs and Excise v Gerhart Schindler and Jörg Schindler* [1994] E.C.R. I–1039, para.37.
[39] Case C–384/93 *Alpine Investments BV v Minister van Financiën* [1995] E.C.R. I–1141.
[40] Case C–268/99 *Jany* [2001] E.C.R. I–8615, para.49 (interpretation of provision of EC-Poland Association Agreement having the same meaning as Art. 43 EC).
[41] Art. 50 EC, third para.

Justice in *Rush Portuguesa* concluded from these words that an undertaking could accordingly take with it its staff to the territory of another Member State to provide services there:

> "Articles [49 and 50] of the Treaty therefore preclude a Member State from prohibiting a person providing services established in another Member State from moving freely in its territory with all his staff and preclude that Member State from making the movement of staff in question subject to restrictions such as a condition as to engagement *in situ* or an obligation to obtain a work permit."[42]

As observed above,[43] the pursuit of economic activities on a permanent basis in a host State, would amount to establishment, rather than to the provision of services. As the Court explained in *Steymann*:

> "It is clear from the actual wording of [Article 50] that an activity carried out on a permanent basis or, in any event, without a foreseeable limit to its duration does not fall within the Community provisions concerning the provision of services. On the other hand, such activities may fall within the scope of Articles [39 to 42] or Articles [43 to 48] of the Treaty, depending on the case."[44]

19–022 Since the permanent pursuit of economic activities cannot be covered by the Treaty provisions on freedom to provide services, and falls in principle within the Chapter on establishment, it would seem to follow that an individual or company established in one Member State and carrying on all his her or its business in another Member State should be regarded as established in the latter Member State, even in the absence of any place of business in the latter State. Yet the Court's case law indicates that in order to be established in a Member State, the person concerned must have an established professional base in that State.[45] On the other hand, the Court's "anti-circumvention" case law, which holds that if an undertaking is established in one Member State, and directs its activities entirely or principally to the territory of another, without having a place of business in the latter Member State, the latter State may either treat

---

[42] Case C–113/89 *Rush Portuguesa Ldc* [1990] E.C.R. I–1417, para.12; Case C–445/03 *Commission of the European Communities v Grand Duchy of Luxemburg* [2004] E.C.R. I–10191.

[43] At p.751.

[44] Case 196/87 *Udo Steymann v Staatssecretaris van Justite* [1987] E.C.R. 6159, para.16.

[45] Case C–215/01 *Bruno Schnitzer* [2003] E.C.R. I–14847, para.32; Case C–171/02 *Commission v Portugal* [2004] E.C.R. I–5645, para.25; Case C–514/03 *Commission v Spain* Judgment of January 26, 2006, para.22.

the Chapter on establishment as applicable, or treat the person concerned as a domestic undertaking, would seem to imply that otherwise the person concerned could rely on the Chapter on services.[46] In the *Schnitzer* case,[47] which concerned a Portuguese plastering firm engaged to carry out large scale plastering work in Bavaria between November 1994 and November 1997, the Court admitted that no provision of the Treaty provided a means of determining, in an abstract manner, the duration or frequency beyond which the supply of a service or of a certain type of service in another Member State could no longer be regarded as the provision of services within the meaning of the Treaty,[48] and indicated that the Portuguese firm (which did not have an established professional base in Bavaria) should be regarded as providing services. The Court also noted that services may comprise services within the meaning of the Treaty even if supplied over an extended period to persons established in one or more other Member States, for example the giving of advice or information for remuneration,[49] but the Court does not go so far as to suggest that services may be provided indefinitely. One difficulty with the Court's case law is that it seems to suggest that permanent service provision in a Member State without an established professional base comprises neither establishment nor the provision of services. This is hardly satisfactory. It is submitted that an undertaking established in one Member State carrying on economic activity in the territory of another, on a permanent basis, but without a place of business in the latter State, should be regarded as being in principle covered by the chapter on establishment; subject to the Court's case law on circumvention,[50] which would if necessary allow the host Member State to treat the situation as if it were a purely internal one.

A literal interpretation of Articles 49 and 50 EC would guarantee freedom to provide cross-frontier services, in circumstances where provider and recipient remain in their respective Member States, as in the case of financial advice from United Kingdom advisers in the United Kingdom to French clients in France. It would similarly uphold the right of a person established in one Member State to provide services in situ in the territory of another, as in the case of a French doctor practising in France making a house call on a patient in Luxembourg. The text also implies that a potential recipient of services would be entitled to visit another Member State so that those services could be provided there, as in the case of the hypothetical Luxembourg patient referred to above calling at the

---

[46] See below at pp.793–795.
[47] Case C–215/01 *Bruno Schnitzer* [2003] E.C.R. I–14847.
[48] ibid., paras 30, 31.
[49] ibid., para.30.
[50] Below, at p.793.

surgery in France of his or her French doctor. The Court has held that the right freely to provide services may be relied on by an undertaking as against the State in which it is established if the services are provided for persons established in another Member State,[51] and that the right includes the freedom for recipients of services to go to another Member State in order to receive a service there, without being obstructed by restrictions.[52] The Court has furthermore given a rather generous interpretation to the text, in holding that Article 49 of the Treaty "applies not only where a person providing services and the recipient thereof are established in different Member States, but also in cases where the person providing services offers those services in a Member State other than that in which he is established, wherever the recipients of those services may be established."[53] Thus Article 49 EC could be invoked, for example, by a German tourist guide alleging that Greek rules comprised an obstacle to his or her provision of services, in Greece, to German tourists.

National measures affecting both Articles 28 EC and 49 EC

19–023   The cross border provision of services and movement of goods may as a matter of fact be linked, and it may be necessary to determine whether either or both of the provisions of Article 28 EC, on the free movement of goods, or Article 49 EC on the freedom to provide services, apply. Where a national measure affects both the freedom to provide services and the free movement of goods, the Court will, in principle, examine it in relation to just one of those two fundamental freedoms if it is clear that, in the circumstances of the case, one of those freedoms is secondary to the other and may be attached to it for the purposes of legal analysis.[54] Thus, the Court has held that sending advertisements and application forms, and tickets, on behalf of a lottery operator, from one Member State to another, are covered by the freedom to provide services, since they are only steps in the organisation or operation of a lottery and cannot, under the Treaty, be considered independently of the lottery to which they relate, so as to attract the application of Article 28 EC. The Court noted that the importation and distribution of the items referred to were not ends in themselves, and that their sole purpose

---

[51] Case C–70/95 *Sodemare v Regione Lombardia* [1997] E.C.R. I–3395, para.37; Case C–224/97 *Erich Ciola v Land Vorarlberg* [1999] E.C.R. I–2517, para.11.

[52] Joined Cases 286/82 and 26/83 *Graziana Luisi and Giuseppe Carbone v Ministero del Tesoro.* [1984] E.C.R. 377, para.16; Case 186/87 *Cowan v Trésor Public* [1989] E.C.R. 195, para.15.

[53] C–198/89 *Commission v Greece* [1991] E.C.R. I–727, paras 8–10; Case C–398/95 *Syndesmos ton en Elladi Touristikon kai Taxidiotikon Grafeion v Ypourgos Ergasias* [1997] E.C.R. I–3091, para.8.

[54] Case C–36/02 *Omega Spielhallen-und Automatenaufstellungs-GmbH* [2004] E.C.R. I–9609, para.26; Case C–71/02 *Karner* [2004] E.C.R. I–3025, para.46.

was to enable residents of the Member States where the advertisements and forms, etc. were imported and distributed to participate in the lottery.[55] However, a national measure may affect both Article 28 EC and Article 49 EC, without the application of one being subordinate to the other, and it may accordingly be necessary to assess the compatibility of the measure with each. This may be the case, as in *Gourmet International*,[56] where a national rule prohibits advertising of various kinds; the rule in question may amount to a restriction on the free movement of goods, and on the provision of services, and require justification in respect of both Article 28 EC and Article 49 EC.[57]

Abolition of discriminatory restrictions—the General Programme and secondary legislation

Like the original text of Article 44 EC, the original text of Article **19–024** 52 EC provided for the drawing up of a General Programme for the abolition of restrictions on freedom to provide services within the Community. The Programme was adopted in December 1961,[58] and closely resembles the General Programme for the abolition of restrictions on the right of establishment.[59] Thus, e.g. Title III calls for the abolition of restrictions such as those which "condition the provision of services on an authorisation or on the issuance of a document, such as a foreign merchant's card or a foreign professional's card."[60] As indicated earlier, most of the Directives issued to abolish restrictions on the right of establishment apply in addition to freedom to provide services. Thus Directive 64/223, used for illustrative purposes in the context of establishment,[61] also applies, in relation to the wholesale trade, to freedom to provide services. Furthermore, Article 47(2) of the Treaty, which provides for the harmonisation of national rules governing the pursuit of self-employed activities, is applied to the chapter on services by Article 55 EC. Further reference is made to this below.[62]

---

[55] Case C–275/92 [1994] E.C.R. I–1039, paras 21–25.
[56] Case C–405/98 *Gourmet International Products AB (GIP)* [2001] E.C.R. I–1795; see also Ch.16 at p.597.
[57] But see Case C–71/02 *Herbert Karner* [2004] E.C.R. I–3025, para.46, where the Court held that the advertising was secondary to the sale of the goods in question.
[58] [1974] O.J. Spec. Ed., 2nd Series IX, p.3. The programme has been referred to by the Court in a number of cases, see e.g., Case 15/78 *Koestler* [1978] E.C.R. 1971; Case 136/78 *Auer* [1979] E.C.R. 452; Cases 286/82 and 26/83 *Luisi* [1984] E.C.R. 377; Case 63/86 *Commission v Italy* [1988] E.C.R. 29; Case 305/87 *Commission v Greece* [1989] E.C.R. 1461.
[59] See above at p.763.
[60] [1974] O.J. Spec. Ed. 2nd Series IX, at p.4.
[61] See above at p.765.
[62] See below at p.815.

Effect of direct applicability of Article 49 EC on harmonisation programme

19–025   Just as the Court's decision in *Reyners v Belgian State* on the direct applicability of Article 43 EC reduced significantly the importance of Directives requiring the abolition of particular discriminatory restrictions, so its later decision in *Van Binsbergen v Bedrijfsvereniging Metaalnijverheid*, upholding the direct effect of Articles 49 EC, first paragraph and 50 EC, third paragraph, entailed similar consequences for the provisions of Directives concerned with the abolition of restrictions on the supply of services.[63]

It is to be noted that Article 49 EC, like Article 43 EC, is concerned not only with the specific rules on the pursuit of occupational activities but also with the rules relating to the various general facilities which of assistance in the pursuit of those activities, including the right to equal access to housing, and financial facilities to acquire housing.[64]

Prohibition of restrictions in respect of non-residence, nationality or otherwise—evolution of the Court's case law

19–026   It has already been noted that the Court of Justice's interpretation of the Treaty provisions on the free movement of goods, on freedom of movement for workers, and on the right of establishment, have undergone a considerable evolution in the last decade or so, and that the Court has given increased prominence in its judgments to the concept of the non-discriminatory restriction on free movement in the latter contexts.[65] This phenomenon is also true of the case law on freedom to provide services, and the significant stages in that evolution are indicated below. The survey which follows will concentrate principally on identifying restrictions on freedom to provide services which may conflict with the Treaty, referring only *en passant* to justifications for such restrictions; possible justifications for such rules will be considered separately below.[66]

The starting point is the judgment in *Van Binsbergen*.[67] The case involved a Netherlands national who acted as a legal representative in proceedings in the Netherlands where representation by an *advocaat* was not obligatory. As a result of moving house to Belgium (he practised from home[68]) his right to practise before a Netherlands court was called in question by a provision of Netherlands law under

---

[63] Case 33/74 [1974] E.C.R. 1299; and see Case 36/74 *Walrave* [1974] E.C.R. 1405; Case 13/76 *Dona v Mantero* [1976] E.C.R. 133; Cases 110 and 111/78, *Van Wesemael* [1979] E.C.R. 35.
[64] Case 63/86 *Commission v Italy* [1988] E.C.R. 29.
[65] See Ch.16, pp.579 *et seq.*, Ch.18, pp.734 *et seq.*, and this Chapter at p.770 *et seq.*, above.
[66] See the section on the public policy proviso, at pp.798 *et seq.* and that on mandatory requirements in the general interest, at pp.801 *et seq.*
[67] Case 33/74 *Van Binsbergen v Bedrijfsvereniging Metaalnijverheid* [1974] E.C.R. 1307.
[68] Advocate General Mayras at [1974] E.C.R. at p.1314.

which only persons established in the Netherlands could act as legal representatives before that court. The Court identified the national measures covered by the prohibition in these Articles as follows:

> "The restrictions to be abolished pursuant to Articles [49 and 50] include all requirements imposed on the person providing the service by reason in particular of his nationality or of the fact that he does not habitually reside in the state where the service is provided, which do not apply to persons established within the national territory or which may prevent or otherwise obstruct the activities of the person providing the service.
>
> In particular, a requirement that the person providing the service must be habitually resident within the territory of the state where the service is to be provided may, according to the circumstances, have the result of depriving Article 49 of all useful effect, in view of the fact that the precise object of that article is to abolish restrictions on freedom to provide services imposed on persons who are not established in the state where the service is to be provided."

The Court's judgment thus identifies discrimination on grounds of nationality and by reference to residence outside national territory as being characteristics of national measures prohibited by the Treaty. It appears from the text and context that the reference to the incompatibility with the Treaty of the residence requirement in issue was not based on the premise that such a requirement amounted to indirect discrimination *on grounds of nationality*. As regards the text, this follows from the terms of the Court's ruling on the direct effect of Articles 49 and 50 EC, to the effect that those Articles "have direct effect . . . at least in so far as they seek to abolish any discrimination against a person providing a service by reason of his nationality *or of the fact that he resides in a Member State other than that in which the service is to be* provided."[69] As regards the context, it will be noted that the plaintiff in the national proceedings was a Netherlands national, and so no question of discrimination against him on grounds of nationality in the Netherlands arose. The statement by the Court that a residence requirement would deprive Article 49 of all useful effect has been endorsed in a consistent subsequent case law. In *Commission v Germany* the Court described the requirement of a permanent establishment as "the very negation" of freedom to provide services. "It has", said the Court, "the

---

[69] For further rulings on direct effect, see e.g., Case 36/74 *Walrave v Union Cycliste Internationale* [1974] E.C.R. 1405; Joined Cases 110 and 111/78. *Ministère public and "Chambre syndicale des agents artistiques et impresarii de Belgique" ASBL v Willy van Wesemael* [1979] E.C.R. 35; Case 279/80. *Criminal proceedings against Alfred John Webb* [1981] E.C.R. 3305.

result of depriving Article [49] of the Treaty of all effectiveness, a provision whose very purpose is to abolish restrictions on the freedom to provide services of persons who are not established in the State in which the service is to be provided."[70]

19–027   In *van Wesemael*[71] the Court had to consider *inter alia* the extent to which national rules of one Member State could impose a licensing requirement on an employment agency established in another Member State placing employees in the first Member State. The Court repeated the proposition that Articles 49 and 50 EC "abolish all discrimination against the person providing the service by reason of his nationality or the fact that he is established in a Member State other than that in which the service is to be provided."[72] As regards the application of the licensing requirement, the Court held that it would be incompatible with the Treaty for a Member State to impose a licensing requirement on an employment agency established in another Member State, which was supervised and licensed in its home State, unless the requirement was objectively justified by the need to ensure observance of professional rules of conduct or the protection of the entertainers placed by the agency.[73] In the event, the Court held that such a requirement was not justified when the service was provided by an employment agency which was licensed in its home State under conditions comparable to those applicable in the host State and subject to the supervision of its home State authorities as regards all its activities in the Member State.[74] It follows from the reasoning in the latter case that it might be discriminatory to apply to a service provider established in another Member State all the requirements of host State law, and in the later case of *Webb*[75] (involving a "manpower" agency licensed in one Member State providing services in another) the Court, confirming that the Treaty provisions on provision of services prohibited all discrimination against the person providing the service by reason of his or her nationality or the fact that he or she is established in a Member State other than that in which the service is provided, added that the reference in Article 50 EC, para.3 to equality of treatment with nationals did not mean "that all national legislation applicable to nationals of that State and usually applied to the permanent activities of undertaking established therein may be similarly applied in its entirety to the temporary

---

[70] Case 205/84 *Commission v Germany* [1988] E.C.R. 3755, para.52, citing Case 39/75 *Coenen* [1975] E.C.R. 1547, and Case 76/81 *Transporoute* [1982] E.C.R. 417. See also Case C–101/94 *Commission v Italy* [1996] E.C.R. I–2691, para.31; and Case C–222/95 *Société Civile Immobilière Paroldi v Banque H. Albert de Bary et Die* [1997] E.C.R. I–3899, para.31.

[71] Joined Cases 110 and 111/78. *Ministère public and "Chambre syndicale des agents artistiques et impresarii de Belgique" ASBL v Willy van Wesemael* [1979] E.C.R. 35.

[72] *ibid.*, para.27 of Judgment.

[73] *ibid.*, para.29.

[74] *ibid.*, para.30

[75] Case 279/80 *Criminal proceedings against Alfred John Webb* [1981] E.C.R. 3305.

activities of undertakings which are established in another Member State."[76]

In *Commission v Germany*[77] the Court considered the compatibility with Article 49 EC of German rules requiring *inter alia* that insurance companies established in other Member States, and authorised and supervised in those Member States, obtain a separate German authorisation for their activities in Germany. The Court repeated its customary formulation to the effect that Article 49 EC covered discrimination on grounds of nationality or by reference to establishment in another Member State.[78] It reiterated the proposition that national rules could not necessarily be applied in their entirety to a service provider established in another Member State, but added that specific requirements could nevertheless be imposed on such a provider if the provisions in question were justified in the public interest, to the extent that the relevant public interest was not safeguarded by the provisions to which the provider was subject in the Member State of establishment. The Court says that "*In addition* such requirements must be objectively justified by the need to ensure that professional rules of conduct are complied with and that the interests which such rules are designed to safeguard are protected" (emphasis added).[79] The above formulation is significant, since it indicates that even national supervisory requirements which do not duplicate those applied in the Member State of establishment may only be applied to the out of State provider if they are objectively necessary. This is borne out by the Court's observation that the requirement of authorisation may not be justifiable on grounds relating to the protection of policy-holders and insured persons in all fields of insurance, and its suggestion that in the field of commercial insurance the policy-holders might simply not need the protection of mandatory rules of national law.[80] Whether the proposition can be said to emerge from the prior case law or not, the proposition emerges from this case that to impose national supervisory requirements on service providers who are established in other Member States where they are authorised to provide the service in question will be regarded as discriminatory on grounds of nationality or by reference to establishment in another Member State if *the need for the supervisory requirements of the host State* cannot be objectively justified. This conclusion is borne out by the judgment in *Commission v Greece*, in which the Court holds that it is discriminatory on grounds of nationality, or on the ground that the persons providing the service is established in another Member State, for one Member

---

[76] *ibid.*, para.16.
[77] Case 205/84 *Commission v Germany* [1988] E.C.R. 3755.
[78] *ibid.*, para.25.
[79] *ibid.*, para.27.
[80] *ibid.*, para.49.

State to insist that tourist guides established in another Member State possess the qualifications of the first Member State.[81]

It follows in particular from the last two cited cases that the Court had developed a broad concept of discrimination by reference to nationality, or by reference to establishment in another Member State, which was infringed if the host State, without objective justification, imposed the same qualification on a service provider established in another Member State as it imposed on services providers established in the host State. Thus an out-of-State service provider qualified in his or her home State must be allowed access to the host State market in the relevant services unless there are sound objective grounds to refuse him or her access. This is indistinguishable from the approach in the *Cassis* case in all but name; but it is a legal development which took place within the analytical framework of discrimination.[82] In fact, a conceptual sea-change was about to take place.

19–028   Very shortly after *Commission v Greece*, referred to above, the Court decided *Säger v Dennemeyer & Co. Ltd.*[83] The national proceedings arose from a legal action by a patent agent in Munich against a company incorporated in England and Wales. The plaintiff was a specialist in patent renewal services who claimed that the provision of such services by the defendant was contrary to German rules reserving such activities exclusively to persons possessing the relevant professional qualification. The provision of patent renewal services was not subject to regulation in the United Kingdom. The German court seised of the dispute asked the Court of Justice whether rules such as those in issue were compatible with Article 49 EC. It is to be noted that the approach adopted by the Court of Justice in *Commission v Germany* and *Commission v Greece*, above, would have pointed towards the German rules in issue being treated as *discrimination* on grounds of nationality or on grounds that the service provider was established in another Member State, unless they could by justified by reference to the need to protect the interests asserted to be at stake. Instead, the Court adopted an analysis rather closer to that adopted in the *Cassis* case,[84] as follows:

> "It should first be pointed out that Article [49] of the Treaty requires not only the elimination of all discrimination against a person providing services on the ground of his nationality but also the abolition of any restriction, even if it applies without distinction to national providers of services and to those of

---

[81] Case C–198/89 [1991] E.C.R. I–727, paras 16, 18. And see Case C–154/89 *Commission v France* [1991] E.C.R. I–4221.
[82] Ch.16, at para.16–010.
[83] Case C–76/90 *Manfred Säger v Dennemeyer & Co. Ltd* [1991] E.C.R. I–4221.
[84] Ch.16, at para.16–006.

other Member States, when it is liable to prohibit or otherwise impede the activities of a provider of services established in another Member State where he lawfully provides similar services."[85]

The Court adopted the same approach to justification as it had adopted in *Commission v Greece*, above.[86] If Article 49 EC is read as laying down a general prohibition on non-discriminatory restrictions, then national rules prohibiting certain services outright will be subject to judicial scrutiny to determine whether such a general ban can be upheld. Even in a case where most Member States banned a particular service, it seems that the final decision as to the sustainability of such a ban would lie in the hands of the judges, rather than national legislative authorities. In *Schindler*[87] the Court considered national rules which prohibited (with certain exceptions) lotteries in the United Kingdom, and prohibited the import of lottery tickets. If the pre-*Säger* case law had been applied, the first question to be addressed would be whether the measure discriminated on grounds of nationality or on the ground that the service provider was established in another Member State. Since the Court regarded such national rules as non-discriminatory, that would have been the end of the matter.[88] But the Court applied the *Säger* formulation, which meant that it was necessary to address the issue of objective justification, and proportionality. The Court noted that the regulation of lotteries raised wide issues, including moral, religious and cultural issues, and the risk of crime and fraud.[89] Instead of applying an objective test, the Court adopted a subjective test, allowing Member States "to assess not only whether it is necessary to restrict the activities of lotteries but also whether they should be prohibited, providing that those restrictions are not discriminatory."[90] The Court referred to the "peculiar nature of lotteries, which has been stressed by many Member States."[91] It is tempting to draw the conclusion that the Court, having developed the concept of the non-discriminatory restriction on the provision of services, found that its strict application could lead to a result which was rather obviously inappropriate, and that it found it necessary to adjust its reasoning accordingly.

---

[85] *ibid.*, para.12.
[86] Case C–198/89 [1991] E.C.R. I–727.
[87] Case C–275/92 *Her Majesty's Customs and Excise v Gerhart Schindler and Jörg Schindler.* [1994] E.C.R. I–1039; and subsequent cases on similar subject matter, e.g. Case C–60/01 *Anomar* [2001] E.C.R. I–8621.
[88] Para.48.
[89] *ibid.*, para.60.
[90] *ibid.*, para.61.
[91] *ibid.*, para.59; 11 governments intervened in the proceedings.

19–029   In *Säger*, it will be recalled that the Court held that Article 49 EC prohibits not only discrimination on grounds of nationality against providers of services established in other Member States, but also any restriction liable to prohibit or otherwise impede the activities of a service provider established in another Member State where he lawfully provides similar services. The Court has added that Article 49 precludes the application of any national rules which have the effect of making the provision of services between Member States more difficult than the provision of services purely within one Member State.[92] In *Smits and Peerbooms* the Court held that restrictions in the latter category include rules of a Member State to the effect that reimbursement of the cost of hospital treatment from a sickness insurance fund be subject to prior authorisation where the hospital treatment is received in another Member State, where such authorisation is unnecessary where the hospital treatment is received in the first Member State.[93] In *Coster* the Court made a similar finding as regards a municipal tax on satellite dishes in Belgium. The tax did not apply to the reception of programmes transmitted by cable. Since broadcasters established in Belgium enjoyed unlimited access to cable distribution for their programmes in that Member State, while broadcasters established in certain other Member States did not, the Court regarded the tax as impeding more the activities of operators established in other Member States than those of operators established in Belgium.[94]

In *Gourmet International*,[95] the Court considered a ban on advertising of alcoholic beverages on TV and radio and in periodicals and other publications other than publications distributed solely at point of sale. The Court held that this ban was a restriction under Article 49 because it restricted the right of advertisers to offer advertising space to potential advertisers in other Member States.[96] This is an extension of the principle recognised in *Säger v Dennemeyer & Co. Ltd* which dealt with restrictions on the cross frontier provision of *services lawfully provided in the Member State of origin*.[97] For the principle in *Gourmet* to apply, it is necessary only that a service would be provided in a Member State, were it not for a restriction on the provision of that service, and that there are potential customers in other Member States. It is true that the Court observed in *Gourmet* that a measure such as that in issue "even if it is non-discriminatory, has a particular effect on the cross-border supply of

---

[92] See e.g. Case C–158/96 *Kohll* [1998] E.C.R. I–1931, para.33.
[93] Case C–157/99 *Smits and Peerbooms* [2001] E.C.R. I–5473, para.61.
[94] Case C–17/00 *Coster* [2001] E.C.R. I–9445, paras 30–35.
[95] Case C- 405/98 *Gourmet International Products AB (GIP)* [2001] E.C.R. I–1795.
[96] *ibid.,* paras 37, 38. The Court held the restriction could be justified on grounds of public health, subject to the principle of proportionality, which was a matter for the national court, see paras 40, 41.
[97] Case C–76/90 *Manfred Säger v Dennemeyer & Co. Ltd* [1991] E.C.R. I–4221, para.12.

advertising space, given the international nature of the advertising market in the category of products to which the prohibition relates", but it is difficult to read this as placing much in the way of a limit on the general proposition that where a national rule can be shown to prevent a potential in-state service provider from supplying a potential out of state customer, Article 49 applies. This ruling erodes the distinction between those restrictions on the supply of services which are purely internal to a Member State, and those which affect the freedom to provide services to customers across national borders.

Prohibition of non discriminatory restrictions on freedom to provide services

The formulation in *Säger*, covering as it does both discriminatory **19–030** and non-discriminatory restrictions, has been applied on numerous occasions by the Court, and there are few signs that the Court acknowledges that a class of cases exists to which it does not apply.

Yet it is nevertheless possible that the test is only applicable to national rules which restrict access to the market, or rather, that a category of cases exist in which national rules will not be regarded as restricting access to the market and will be compatible with Article 49 provided they do not discriminate on grounds of nationality or by reference to establishment in another Member State. In *Alpine Investments*[98] the Court of Justice considered whether rules of a Member State prohibiting providers of services established in its territory from making unsolicited telephone calls to potential clients established in other Member States in order to offer their services constituted a restriction on freedom to provide services covered by Article 49 EC. Reference was made in Chapter 16 to the *Keck* case, which held that while non discriminatory rules relating to the composition and packaging of goods, etc. amounted to measures having equivalent effect to quantitative restrictions, and had to be justified, rules relating to certain selling arrangements would not have to be justified provided they applied to all traders operating within the national territory and provided that they affected in the same manner, in law and in fact, the marketing of domestic products and of those from other Member States.[99] The Netherlands and the United Kingdom argued by analogy with *Keck*, that non-discriminatory rules such as those in issue, since they were selling arrangements, should not be regarded as falling within Article 49 EC at all. The Court rejected this argument, saying *inter alia*, that a

---

[98] Case C–384/93 *Alpine Investments BV v Minister van Financiën* [1995] E.C.R. I–1141.
[99] Joined Cases C–267 and C–268/91 *Keck and Mithouard* [1993] E.C.R. I 6097, paras 15–17; and see Ch.16, at p.588.

prohibition such as that in issue "directly affects *access to the market in services* in the other Member States and is thus capable of hindering intra-Community trade in services" (emphasis added).[1] The Court has subsequently held that a prohibition on advertising in one Member State of services available in the territory of another amounts to a restriction on the freedom to provide services.[2] The Court also continues to rely on the principle that Article 49 EC precludes the application of any national rules which have the effect of making the provision of services between Member States more difficult than the provision of services purely within one Member State.[3] Equally, cases in which the latter formulation is invoked more often than not concern national measures which are discriminatory, and/or amount to restrictions on access to the market.[4] In *Deliège*, the Court rejected the proposition that certain selection rules applicable to sporting activities comprised restrictions on freedom to provide services, observing, in particular, that "the selection rules at issue . . . do not determine the conditions governing *access to the labour market* by professional sportsmen and do not contain nationality clauses limiting the number of nationals of other Member States who may participate in a competition."[5] However, in *Carpenter* the Court considered a decision to deport the wife (a national of a third country) of a United Kingdom national resident in the United Kingdom who provides services to customers in other Member States, and says that "it is clear that the separation of Mr and Mrs Carpenter would be detrimental to their family life and, therefore, to the conditions under which Mr Carpenter exercises a fundamental freedom . . .".[6] This approach seems inconsistent with the proposition that non discriminatory restrictions on freedom to provide services only require justification if they restrict access to the market. Restrictions on access to the market are generally contrasted with those alleged restrictions which arise solely from the unattractiveness of the regulatory conditions under which a particular activity is exercised. Yet, as noted above,[7] one difficulty with seeking to draw

---

[1] Case C–384/93 *Alpine Investments BV v Minister van Financiën* [1995] E.C.R. I–1141, para.38.
[2] Case C–294/00 *Gräbner* [2002] E.C.R. I–6515, para.68.
[3] Case C–158/96 *Raymond Kohll v Union des Caisses de Maladie* [1998] E.C.R. I–1931, para.33; Case C–157/99 *Smits and Peerbooms* [2001] E.C.R. I–5473; para.61.
[4] Case C–272/94 *Guiot* [1996] E.C.R. I–1905; Case C–3/95 *Broede* [1996] E.C.R. I–6511; Case C–398/95 *Syndesmos ton en Elladi Touristikon kai Taxidiotikon Grafeion v Ypourgos Ergasias* [1997] E.C.R. I–3091; Case C–157/99 *Smits and Peerbooms* [2001] E.C.R. I–5473, para.69.
[5] Case C–51/96 *Deliège* [2000] E.C.R. I–2549, para.61.
[6] Case C–60/00 *Carpenter* [2002] CR I–6279, para.39; see 40 C.M.L.Rev. 2003, pp.537–543; For an excellent analysis of related issues, see Spaventa, "From Gebhard to Carpenter: Towards a (non)-Economic European Constitution" 41 C.M.L.Rev. 2004, 743–773.
[7] Ch.18, p.740.

this distinction is that unattractive conditions for the carrying on of a particular activity might be held to deter operators from taking up the activity, and thereby to restrict access to the market. Certainly regulatory conditions which make it more difficult for market operators to compete with other market operators can be regarded as affecting access to the market, since they may have a particularly adverse effect on new market entrants, including importers.[8]

All that said, problems which have arisen in the context of the free movement of goods because of the indiscriminate development of the concept of the non-discriminatory trade restriction, are also capable of arising in the context of the provision of services, and principles analogous to those contained in the *Keck* judgment ought in principle to be applicable. It has been noted that the Court has held that restrictions on Sunday trading are not caught by Article 28 (because of the application of the "selling arrangements" proviso in *Keck*),[9] or Article 43 (because of the conclusion that any effects on the right of establishment were too "uncertain and indirect"),[10] and it would seem to follow that analogous principles also apply to ensure that such national measures are not covered by Article 49 EC. At the end of the day, it might be that the only national rules which might "impede" the activities of a service provider within the meaning of the *Säger* formulation, but which do not require justification, are those whose effects on the freedom to provide services are too "uncertain and indirect" to be regarded as affecting the freedom to provide services.

Establishment and services—National measures to prevent circumvention, and derogation on express or implied grounds

National measures to prevent circumvention of national rules in the context of the right of establishment and freedom to provide services

The Court of Justice has indicated in a number of cases that **19–031** provisions of Community law should not be interpreted in such a way as to facilitate the wrongful avoidance of national rules.[11] It will

---

[8] *cf.* Case C–442/02 *Caixa Bank France v Ministère de l'Économie, des Finances et de l'Industrie* [2004] E.C.R. I–8961, above at p.775.
[9] Joined Cases C–418/93 *Semeraro Casa Uno Srl v Sindaco del Comune di Erbusco etc.,* [1996] E.C.R. I–2975, see this Chapter, p.774.
[10] *ibid.*
[11] Case 115/78 *Knoors* [1979] E.C.R. 399, para.25; Case 61/89 *Bouchoucha* [1990] E.C.R. I–3557, para.14.

be noted that in the *Centros* case,[12] Danish nationals resident and carrying on business in Denmark incorporated a company to carry on that business and incorporated that company in England rather than Denmark in order to avoid the relatively high minimum capital requirement attendant upon incorporation in Denmark. The Danish authorities argued that those nationals could not rely upon the Treaty provisions on the right of establishment, since the sole purpose of the company formation in England was to circumvent the application of the Danish rules governing formation of private limited companies and therefore constituted abuse of the freedom of establishment.[13] The Court referred to its case law on wrongful circumvention of national rules,[14] and explained it as follows. That case law allowed national courts to take account, case by case, and on the basis of objective evidence, of abuse or fraudulent conduct on the part of the persons concerned in order, where appropriate, to deny them the benefit of provisions of Community law on which they relied. But it was nevertheless necessary to assess such conduct in the light of the objectives pursued by the provisions of Community law in question.[15] The Court noted that in the case in point, "the provisions of national law, application of which the parties concerned have sought to avoid, are rules governing the formation of companies and not rules concerning the carrying on of certain trades, professions or businesses."[16] The Court went on to note that the provisions of the Treaty on freedom of establishment were intended specifically to enable companies of one Member State to pursue activities in other Member States through an agency branch or subsidiary, and held that that being so, the fact that a national of a Member State who wished to set up a company chose to form it in the Member State whose rules of company law seemed to him or her the least restrictive, and to set up branches in other Member States could not, in itself constitute an abuse of the right of establishment.[17]

From the outset the case law on freedom to provide services indicated that the Treaty did not prohibit Member States from taking appropriate steps to prevent the wrongful circumvention of national rules. The Court in *Van Binsbergen* stated:

> "Likewise, a member state cannot be denied the right to take measures to prevent the exercise by a person providing services whose activity is entirely or principally directed towards its territory of the freedom guaranteed by Article 49 for the

---

[12] Case C–212/97 *Centros Ltd v Erhvervs- og Selskabsstyrelsen* [1999] E.C.R. I–1458, see below at p.841.
[13] Case C–212/97 *Centros Ltd v Erhvervs- og Selskabsstyrelsen* [1999] E.C.R. I–1458, para.23.
[14] *ibid.*, para.24.
[15] *ibid.*, para.25.
[16] *ibid.*, para.26.
[17] *ibid.*, paras 26, 27; and see below, Ch.20, at p.841.

purpose of avoiding the professional rules of conduct which would be applicable to him if he were established within that State; such a situation may be subject to judicial control under the provisions of the chapter relating to the right of establishment and not of that on the provision of services."[18]

It is to be noted that the Court clearly presupposed that control under the provisions of the Chapter relating to the right of establishment would involve a greater ability to impose requirements on economic operators than would be possible under the Chapter on the provision of services. While such a difference exists today in principle it seems that the extent of that difference has diminished,[19] and this perhaps explains why the Court's formulation of national anti-circumvention competence has evolved over the years. Thus in *Veronica*[20] the Court of Justice repeated the above formulation, but omitted the reference to the situation being subject to judicial control under the provisions of the Chapter relating to the right of establishment, and in *TV10 SA* the Court repeated the latter formulation, but added that it would therefore be compatible with the provisions of the Treaty on freedom to provide services to treat such organisations *as domestic organisations*. It is argued above that the better view is to regard an undertaking established in one Member State carrying on economic activity in the territory of another, on a permanent basis, but without a place of business in the latter State, as being covered in principle by the Chapter on establishment, though this should not displace the Court's case law on circumvention should supervision under the Chapter on establishment be inadequate, and require supervision as if the situation were a purely internal one.[21]

Articles 45 and 55 EC—exception in the case of activities connected with the exercise of official authority

Article 45 EC provides that the provisions of the Chapter on **19–032** establishment shall not apply, "so far as any given Member State is concerned, to activities which in that State are connected, even occasionally, with the exercise of official authority." Pursuant to

---

[18] Case 33/74 *Van Binsbergen v Bedrijfsvereniging Metaalnijverheid* [1974] E.C.R. 1307, at para.13. This formulation was repeated *verbatim* by the Court in Case 205/84 *Commission v Germany* [1986] E.C.R. 3755, para.22.

[19] For example, national rules on registration with professional bodies are presumptively applicable as regards those who are exercising the right of establishment, but not as regards those providing services. Thus, Art.4 of Dir. 77/249 on provision of services by lawyers, exempts service providers from registration in the host State, while Art.3 of Dir.98/5 on the establishment of lawyers provides for such registration.

[20] Case C–148/91 *Vereniging Veronica Omroep Organisatie v Commissariaat voor de Media.* [1991] E.C.R. I–487, para.12

[21] Above at p.781.

Article 55 EC this latter provision also applies to the Chapter on freedom to provide services. This exception constitutes a derogation from a fundamental Treaty rule, and must be interpreted strictly, so as not to exceed the purpose for which it was inserted.[22]

In *Reyners v Belgian State*,[23] it was argued that the profession of *avocat* was exempted from the chapter on establishment because it involved the exercise of official authority. The Court held that Article 45 EC applied only to those activities which, taken on their own, involved a direct and specific connection with the exercise of official authority,[24] and added that:

> "Professional activities involving contracts, even regular and organic, with the courts, including even compulsory co-operation in their functioning, do not constitute, as such, connexion with the exercise of official authority. The most typical activities of the profession of *avocat*, in particular, such as consultation and legal assistance and also representation and the defence of parties in court, even when the intervention or assistance of the *avocat* is compulsory or is a legal monopoly, cannot be considered as connected with the exercise of official authority. The exercise of these activities leaves the discretion of judicial authority and the free exercise of judicial power intact."[25]

This latter observation certainly implies that the exercise of a judicial function by an advocate would amount to the exercise of official authority, which is in any event self-evident. Advocate General Mayras described official authority as "that which arises from the sovereignty and majesty of the State; for him who exercises it, it implies the power of enjoying the [sic] prerogatives outside the general law, privileges of official power and powers of coercion over citizens."[26] This is consistent with the approach of the Court of Justice in *Commission v Belgium*, on the ambit of Article 39(4) EC.[27] In the latter case the Court held that Article 39(4) EC covers posts which involve direct or indirect participation in the exercise of powers conferred by public law and duties designed to safeguard the general interests of the State.[28] Article 39(4) EC and Article 45 have essentially the same aim, and should be interpreted in an analogous way. As an exception to a fundamental principle, Article 45 EC is

---

[22] Case 2/74 *Reyners v Belgian State* [1974] E.C.R. 631; Case 152/73 *Sotgiu v Deutsche Bundespost* [1974] E.C.R. 153; see Ch.18, at p.723.
[23] Case 2/74 [1974] E.C.R. 631.
[24] *ibid.*, para.45.
[25] *ibid.*, paras 51–53.
[26] [1974] E.C.R. 631, 664.
[27] Case 149/79 [1980] E.C.R. 3881.
[28] *ibid.*, para.10. See in general Ch.18, at p.722 *et seq.*

given a strict construction.[29] Thus the Court has held that the activity of traffic accident expert does not involve the exercise of official authority where the reports of these experts are not binding on the courts, leaving the discretion of the judiciary and the exercise of judicial power intact.[30] Similarly, the Court has held that the "auxiliary and preparatory functions" of an "approved commissioner" *vis-à-vis* an "Insurance Inspectorate," which latter body was a body exercising official authority by taking the final relevant decision, could not be regarded as having a direct and specific connection with the exercise of official authority.[31] Security undertakings and security staff lacking legal powers of constraint cannot be described as exercising official authority because they make a contribution to the maintenance of public security, which any individual may be called upon to do.[32]

Article 45 EC refers to "activities" connected with the exercise of **19–033** official authority, rather than "to professions." The Court of Justice in *Reyners* made it clear that while certain "activities" forming part of a particular profession might fall within Article 45 EC, the profession as a whole might nevertheless be subject to the right of establishment. This would be the case wherever the activities could be "severed" from the profession concerned, as they could be so severed, it would seems, in the case of an advocate called upon to perform occasional judicial functions. The Court took the view that the exception allowed by Article 45 EC could only be extended to a whole profession where the activities in question "were linked with that profession in such a way that freedom of establishment would result in imposing on the Member State concerned the obligation to allow the exercise, even occasionally, by non-nationals of functions appertaining to official authority."[33] It is certainly the case that the text of Article 45 EC seems to rule out requiring a Member State to tolerate even the occasional exercise of official authority. It is interesting to consider by way of contrast the Court's interpretation of Article 39(4) EC in *Colegio de Oficiales de la Marina Mercante Española*; the Court held that the posts of master and chief mate in the Spanish merchant navy are posts in which the exercise of rights under powers conferred by public law is, in practice, only occasional, and it would be disproportionate to exclude those posts from the scope of Article 39 EC if the rights in question were exercised only exceptionally *by nationals of other Member States*.[34] On the face of it, it would seem that employment will not be excluded from the scope

---

[29] Case 2/74 *Reyners* [1974] E.C.R. 631, para.43.
[30] Case C–306/89 *Commission v Greece* [1991] E.C.R. I–5863, para.7.
[31] Case C–42/92 *Adrianus Thijssen v Controledienst voor de verzekeringen*. [1993] E.C.R. I–4047, para.22.
[32] Case C–114/92 *Commission v Spain* [1990] E.C.R. I–6717, para.37.
[33] Case 2/74 *Reyners* [1974] E.C.R. 631, para.46.
[34] Case C–405/01 [2003] E.C.R. I–10391, paras 44, 45.

of Article 39 EC solely because it entails the occasional exercise of powers under public law by foreign nationals, while in the case of Article 45 EC even the occasional exercise of official authority will wholly exclude the *activity* in question, while leaving open the possibility that that activity might be severed from the relevant profession or overall self-employed activities carried on by the individual in question. While Article 39(4) EC is to be interpreted and applied in an analogous way to Article 45 EC, the outcome in comparable cases will not always be identical

In view of the Court's decision in *Sotgiu v Deutsche Bundespost*, it would seem that Article 45 EC should be interpreted as applying only to *access* to activities connected with the exercise of official authority; not as authorising discriminatory conditions of work once a person had been allowed to take up such activities.[35]

The second paragraph of Article 45 EC provides that the Council may rule "that the provisions of this Chapter shall not apply to certain activities." It seems that these words must be construed subject to the text of the previous paragraph, i.e. as involving activities connected with exercise of official authority. The authority bestowed thereby upon the Council would thus seem to be rather limited. In applying Article 45 EC to a particular profession, it is necessary to establish the ambit of the "activities" which "taken on their own, constitute a direct and specific connection with the exercise of official authority."[36] While the "exercise of official authority" is a concept of Community law, the question of "direct and specific connection" with such exercise is one of fact which, unresolved, can lead to uncertainty on the part of those subject to the law. It seems that the Council's function under this provision is limited to establishing that certain activities do indeed have a "direct and specific connection" with the exercise of official authority. The Council has not exercised the power conferred by this provision.

Articles 46 and 55 EC—the public policy proviso

19–034   Article 46 EC provides that the provisions of the Chapter on establishment and measures taken in pursuance thereof shall not prejudice the applicability of provisions providing for special treatment for foreign nationals on grounds of public policy, public security or public health. And Article 55 EC makes the same provision as regards the Chapter on provision of services. The scheme of Articles 39 to 55 EC, and the parallel interpretation given to these provisions in relation to discrimination, entry and

---

[35] Ch.14, at p.723.
[36] Case 2/74 *Reyners* [1974] E.C.R. 631, para.45.

residence,[37] and the fact that the public policy provisos of Article 39(3) EC and Article 46 EC are implemented by one and the same Directive—Directive 2004/38—suggests that Article 46 EC is to be interpreted in an analogous manner to that of Article 39(3) EC.[38] Thus, for instance, it would seem to follow that Article 46 EC must be interpreted as permitting derogation from the chapter on establishment only in respect of entry and residence—not in respect of the terms and conditions under which occupational activities are carried on.[39] For a detailed analysis of the terms of Directive 2004/38, and an examination of the Court's jurisprudence on the public policy proviso in Article 39(3) EC, the reader is referred to the chapter on Union Citizens and their rights of movement and residence.[40]

In the context of the right of establishment, the Court has said that while the need to combat fraud may justify a difference in treatment on grounds of nationality in certain circumstances, the mere risk of tax avoidance cannot justify discriminatory treatment.[41] Article 46 EC permits derogation from the right of establishment in the case of foreign nationals, but since this provision, by virtue of Article 55, also applies as an exception to the Treaty's prohibition on restrictions to provide services, and since the latter prohibition covers national measures which discriminate not only on grounds of nationality, but also by reference to the place of establishment of the provider,[42] or the place of residence of the recipient,[43] discrimination on these latter grounds also falls within the scope of this provision, and direct discrimination on any of these above grounds may be justified only by this provision or another express term of the Treaty.[44]

The Court held in the *Omega* case that the concept of public policy includes respect for human dignity as a general principle of law, and may justify prohibiting the commercial exploitation of games (and thereby placing restrictions on the freedom to provide services) which involve the simulated killing of human beings.[45]

---

[37] Above at p.776.

[38] As indicated in Ch.17, Dir.2004/38/EC lays down (a) the conditions governing the exercise of the right of free movement and residence within the territory of the Member States by Union citizens and their family members, (b) the right of permanent residence in the territory of the Member States for Union Citizens and their family members, and (c) the limits placed on the rights set out in (a) and (b) on grounds of public policy, public security or public health; see Art.1.

[39] Case 152/73 *Sotgiu* [1974] E.C.R. 153; Case 15/69 *Ugliola* [1969] E.C.R. 363; above at p.723.

[40] Ch.17, pp.688 *et seq.*

[41] Case 79/85 *Segers v bestuur van de Bedrijfsvereniging voor Bank- en Verzeleringswezen* [1986] E.C.R. 2375, para.17.

[42] Case C–484/93 *Svensson et Gustavsson v Ministre du Logement et de l'Urbanisme* [1995] E.C.R. I–3955, para.15.

[43] Case C–224/97 *Ciola v Land Voralrberg* [1999] E.C.R. I–2517, para.16.

[44] Case C–484/93 *Svensson et Gustavsson v Ministre du Logement et de l'Urbanisme* [1995] E.C.R. I–3955, para.15; Case C–224/97 *Ciola v Land Voralrberg* [1999] E.C.R. I–2517, para.16; and see below at p.807.

[45] Case C–36/02 *Omega Spielhallen-und Automatenaufstellungs-GmbH* [2004] E.C.R. I–9609.

19–035   In the *Kohll* case, the Court noted that the Treaty allowed
Member States to limit freedom to provide services on grounds of
public health, but added that that did not permit them to exclude the
public health sector, as a sector of economic activity and from the
point of view of the freedom to provide services, from the application of the fundamental principle of freedom of movement.[46] It
did however permit Member States to restrict the freedom to
provide medical and hospital services in so far as the maintenance of
a treatment facility or medical service on national territory is
essential for the public health and even the survival of the population.[47] Public health considerations justify a Member State in prohibiting television advertising for alcoholic beverages marketed in
that State, in the case of indirect television advertising resulting from
the appearance on screen of hoardings visible during the retransmission of bi-national sporting events taking place in other Member
States.[48]

It is established that economic aims do not constitute grounds of
public policy within the meaning of Article 46 of the Treaty.[49] Nor
do the aims of reinforcing the financial soundness of companies in
order to protect public and private creditors.[50] Nor have the aims of
avoiding diminution in tax revenue and erosion of the tax base been
regarded as falling within Article 46 EC in the cases in which the
argument to the contrary has been put.[51]

In order to justify a national measure on the basis of Article 46
EC, it is necessary to demonstrate that it is indispensable for
achieving one of the aims referred to.[52] In upholding the right of a
Member State, on grounds of public policy and respect for human
dignity, to prohibit the commercial exploitation of games involving
the simulated killing of human beings, the Court emphasised the
requirement of proportionality and noted that by prohibiting only
the variant of the laser game the object of which was to fire on actual
human targets and thus "play at killing" people, the national

---

[46] Case C–158/96 *Raymond Kohll v Union des Caisses de Maladie* [1998] E.C.R. I–1931,
para.46.
[47] *ibid.*, para.51; the Court refers by analogy to Case 72/83 *Campus Oil v Minister for Industry
and Energy* [1984] E.C.R. 2727, paras 33–36, which deals with public security within the
meaning of Art.30 of the Treaty. See also Case C–157/99 *Smits and Peerbooms* [2001]
E.C.R. I–5473, paras 72–74; and case C–372/04 *Watts* Judgment of 16/05/06, para.75.
[48] Case C–429/02 *Bacardi France SAS* [2004] E.C.R. I–6613.
[49] Case C–288/89 *Stichting Collectieve Antennevoorziening Gouda v Commissariaat voor de
Media* [1991] E.C.R. I–4007, para.11; Case C–484/93 *Svensson et Gustavsson v Ministre du
Logement et de l'Urbanisme* [1995] E.C.R. I–3955, para.15.
[50] Case C–212/97 *Centros Ltd v Erhvervs- og Selskabsstyrelsen* [1999] E.C.R. I–1458, paras
32–34.
[51] See e.g. Case C–330/91 *ICI v Colmer (Her Majesty's Inspector of Taxes)*, para.28; Case
C–168/01 *Bosal Holdings BV v Staatssecretaris van Financiën* [2003] E.C.R. I–9409, para.42.
[52] Case C–3/88 *Commission v Italy* [1989] E.C.R. 4035, para.15; Case C–101/94 *Commission v
Italy* [1996] E.C.R. I–2691, para.26.

measure did not go beyond what was necessary to attain the objective pursued by the competent national authorities.[53]

Imperative requirements in the general interest

General

It has been noted in the last section that restrictions on the right **19–036** of establishment and the freedom to provide services may be justified on grounds of public policy, public security or public health. But these are not the only grounds upon which measures which hinder the exercise of fundamental freedoms may be justified. The Court has interpreted the relevant Treaty provisions in such a way that restrictions which arise from certain imperative requirements, which are imposed in the general interest, are not regarded as comprising prohibited obstacles to the right of establishment or the freedom to provide services. At first sight the admissibility of implied imperative requirements in addition to express derogations on grounds of public policy, etc. seems to contradict the proposition that exceptions to general principles must be construed narrowly. But a plausible theory underlying the concept of imperative require-ments which justify derogation from fundamental freedoms (the concept is also applicable in the field of free movement of goods[54]), is that the relevant Treaty provisions prohibit some national mea-sures *per se*, subject to application of the express exceptions in the Treaty, while other national measures are only prohibited if their restrictive effects cannot be justified on grounds compatible with Community law, and consistently with the principle of propor-tionality. Thus, for example, direct discrimination on grounds of nationality is prohibited *per se*, and can be justified only in accord-ance with express derogations in the Treaty, such as Articles 39(3) EC, 39(4) EC, 45 EC, and 46 EC (these latter two articles in conjunction as appropriate with Article 55 EC).[55] For example, the Court has held that national rules which restrict the ability to form undertakings (tax advice centres) carrying on certain activities reserved exclusively to them (tax advice), to certain legal entities already established in the Member State in question, are inconsistent with Articles 43 and 49 EC, are discriminatory, and can be justified only under Article 46 and 55 EC.[56]

---

[53] Case C–36/02 *Omega Spielhallen-und Automatenaufstellungs-GmbH* [2004] E.C.R. I–9609, para.39.

[54] See Ch.16, at p.624.

[55] Case C–388/01 *Commission v Italy* [2003] E.C.R. I–721, para.19; Case C–311/97 *Royal Bank of Scotland v Elliniko Dimosio (Greek State)* [1999] E.C.R. I–2651, para.32; Case C–451/03 *Servizi Ausiliari Dottori Commercialisti Srl* Judgment of March 20, 2006, para.36.

[56] Case C–451/03 *Servizi Ausiliari Dottori Commercialisti Srl* Judgment of March 20, 2006, para.36.

But alleged indirect discrimination can be justified on objective grounds consistent with Community law (a concept akin to imperative requirements), and non discriminatory restrictions on fundamental freedoms alleged to hinder or make less attractive the exercise of fundamental freedoms can similarly be justified on the basis of imperative requirements. It is accordingly appropriate to consider below, *inter alia*, the evolution of the Court's case law in this regard; the categories of general interest, or public interest, which may justify restrictions; the application of the principle of proportionality; and the line of demarcation between the restrictions which may be so justified, and the discriminatory restrictions which the Court has stated on numerous occasions to be capable of justification exclusively by an express provision of the Treaty, and in particular by Articles 46 and 55 of the Treaty.

The Court's case-law on imperative requirements in the general interest in the context of the right of establishment

19–037   In the context of the right of establishment, it has only been with the development of the concept of the non-discriminatory restriction on this right, that recourse to imperative requirements has become of some significance. That is not to say that the question of justification of restrictions did not arise before the advent of the non discriminatory restriction, but that it arose in the context of alleged indirect discrimination on grounds of nationality, which would not be prohibited by the provisions of the Treaty if objectively justified.[57] The concept of objective justification, and the concept of imperative requirements, are clearly closely related. The question of justification of indirect discrimination on grounds of nationality arising from national tax rules by reference to the "cohesion of the tax system", discussed in the next Chapter, is relevant in this respect.[58] Where national rules have been held to comprise a restriction on the right of establishment, not by discrimination on grounds of nationality, nor by totally prohibiting cross-frontier activity, but by placing at a disadvantage those with a place of business in more than one Member State, or hindering the right of establishment, the Court accepts that justification on grounds of imperative requirements is in principle possible.[59] Where national rules have the effect of prohibiting cross border activity, it is less clear that imperative requirements can justify such a restriction. Reference has already been made to

---

[57] See Ch.14, on indirect discrimination and jusification in the context of the free movement of workers, at pp.719 *et seq.*, and this Chapter, p.768 above.

[58] Ch.20, at pp.898 *et seq.*

[59] Case 143/87 *Stanton v Inasti* [1988] E.C.R. 3877, para.15; Case C–53/95 *Inasti v Kemmler* [1996] E.C.R. I–703, para.13; C–255/97 *Pfeiffer Großhandel Gmbh v Löwa Warenahndel Gmbh* [1999] E.C.R. I–2835, para.21.

the *Klopp* case,[60] in which the Court considered a national rule requiring an advocate to practise from a single set of chambers. The Court noted that Article 43 EC entitles a person established in one Member State to establish an agency or branch in another, and held that for an advocate this meant being entitled to practise from chambers in more than one Member State. It is true that the Court refers to a host State having the right to require that lawyers enrolled at a bar in its territory practise in such a way as to maintain sufficient contact with their clients and the judicial authorities and abide by the rules of their profession, but the Court adds that "such requirements must not prevent the nationals of other Member States from exercising properly the right of establishment guaranteed them by the Treaty."[61] A restriction such as that in issue in *Klopp* should probably be regarded as being capable of justification only on the basis of an express derogating provision in the Treaty.

With the development of the concept of the non-discriminatory restriction on the right of establishment has come the "rolled up" formulation, in which the definition of the restriction and the possibilities for its justification are presented in a simple, apparently straightforward formulation, as the following statement of the Court in the *Gebhard* case indicates:

> ". . . national measures liable to hinder or make less attractive the exercise of fundamental freedoms guaranteed by the Treaty must fulfil four conditions: they must be applied in a non-discriminatory manner; they must be justified by imperative requirements in the general interest; they must be suitable for securing the attainment of the objective which they pursue; and they must not go beyond what is necessary in order to attain it . . ."[62]

Application of the above criteria for justification can involve some fairly intensive proportionality review, as is illustrated by the Court's analysis in the *Centros* case.[63] In this case it was argued for the Danish authorities that they were justified in refusing to register a branch of an English company in Denmark, where the English company carried on no business in England, and did not meet the minimum capital requirements laid down for Danish companies. The share capital of the English company was £100, and the sole reason the Danish nationals set up a company in the United Kingdom rather than Denmark, was to secure the advantages of limited

---

[60] Case 107/83 *Ordre des avocats au Barreau de Paris v Onno Klopp.* [1983] E.C.R. 2971; see above, p.758.

[61] *ibid.*, paras 20, 21.

[62] Case C–55/94 *Gebhard v Consiglio dell'Ordine degli Avvocati e Procuratori di Milano* [1995] E.C.R. I–4165, para.37.

[63] Case C–212/97 *Centros Ltd v Erhvervs- og Selskabsstyrelsen* [1999] E.C.R. I–1458.

liability without having to meet the cost of the £20,000 minimum capital requirement then prevailing in Denmark. The Danish authorities emphasised that had the company done any business at all in England, they would registered the branch in Denmark, and argued that refusing to register the branch was the least restrictive means available of reinforcing the financial soundness of companies so as to protect the interests of public and private creditors (i.e., tax authorities), and in particular the latter, who, unlike private creditors, were not in a position to secure their debts by obtaining personal guarantees from the directors of debtor companies.[64]

19–038   The Court did not deny that interests such as those referred to might in principle justify measures such as those in issue, but rejected the arguments made on proportionality grounds. In the first place, the Court held that the refusal to register the company was not such as to attain the objective of protecting creditors, since, if the company concerned had conducted business in the United Kingdom, its branch would have been registered in Denmark, even though Danish creditors might have been equally exposed to risk. The Court next emphasised that the English company held itself out as such, and not as a company governed by Danish law, and that it followed that its creditors were on notice that it was covered by laws different from those governing Danish companies. The Court clearly attached significance to this, and added that creditors could refer to certain rules of Community law which protected them. These latter rules were disclosure rules designed to enable third parties to be able to check on the financial position of companies, and in particular branches of foreign companies.[65] The Court concluded that it was possible to adopt measures which were less restrictive, or which interfered less with fundamental freedoms, by, for example, making it possible in law for public creditors to obtain the necessary guarantees.[66] The Court's assessment amounts to this: it is disproportionate to require out of state private companies to comply with a minimum capital requirement in order to protect the interests of private creditors and national tax authorities, and private and public creditors can adequately protect their interests by being aware of the legal status and financial position of such companies and being placed in a position where they can secure guarantees from those managing such companies. The present writer fully agrees with the Court's conclusion, but would emphasise that in coming to it the Court is engaging in fairly intensive proportionality review.

---

[64] *ibid.*, para.32. See also Ch.20, p.841.
[65] The Court refers to the Fourth Council Directive 78/660 on the annual accounts of certain types of companies [1978] O.J. L222/1, and to Eleventh Council Directive 89/666 concerning disclosure requirements in respect of branches opened in a Member State by certain types of company governed by the law of another State [1989] O.J. L395/36.
[66] *ibid.*, para.37.

Industrial and commercial property has been held to justify a restriction on the right of establishment,[67] and the effectiveness of fiscal supervision constitutes an "overriding requirement of general interest" capable of justifying a restriction on the exercise of fundamental freedoms guaranteed by the Treaty.[68] As regards the categories of mandatory requirement which may be invoked to justify national rules which might restrict the exercise of the right of establishment, reference by analogy may be made in particular to the case law on the free movement of goods,[69] and on freedom to provide services. Protection of public health may justify restrictions resulting from special treatment for foreign nationals pursuant to Article 46(1) EC, and is therefore in principle also capable of justifying national measures which apply indiscriminately, such as a measure reserving to persons holding certain qualifications the right to carry out certain medical procedures.[70]

The Court's case law on overriding reasons in the general interest in the context of freedom to provide services

In the *van Binsbergen* case the Court of Justice stated that **19–039** restrictions on freedom to provide services would not be prohibited by the Treaty where they had the purpose of applying:

> "professional rules justified by the general good—in particular rules relating to organisation, qualifications, professional ethics, supervision and liability—which are binding upon any person established in the state in which the service is provided, where the person providing the service would escape from the ambit of those rules being established in another Member State."[71]

It is to be noted that the Court did not make any reference to Article 46 EC, and seemed to countenance that, in principle, and in an appropriate case, a Member State might insist on establishment within national territory to ensure application of national rules such as those referred to. In *Ramrath* the Court held that a requirement that auditors maintain an establishment in national territory was justified in order to secure the application of national rules in the public interest designed to uphold the integrity and independence of

---

[67] Case C–255/97 *Pfeiffer Großhandel Gmbh v Löwa Warenahndel Gmbh* [1999] E.C.R. I–2835, para.21.
[68] Case C–254/97 *Société Baxter v Premier Ministre* [1999] E.C.R. I–4809, para.18; this category of mandatory requirement was recognized as a justification for restricting the free movement of goods in the *Cassis* case, see Ch.16, at p.624.
[69] Chapter 16, pp.624 *et seq.*
[70] Case C–108/96 *Dennis MacQuen* [2001] E.C.R. I–837.
[71] Case 33/74 *Van Binsbergen v Bedrijfsvereniging Metaalnijverheid* [1974] E.C.R. 1307, para.12.

those practising the profession in question.[72] This latter case is the only one in which the Court has upheld such a requirement, and may be wrongly decided. In *van Binsbergen* the national rules identified as comprising restrictions on the freedom to provide services comprised those discriminating on grounds of nationality and those which discriminated by reference to the place of establishment of the service provider[73]—a formulation to be repeated in the Court's subsequent case law.[74] Yet in *van Binsbergen* and *Ramrath* the reference to national rules applicable to all persons pursuing the activities in the State in question suggests that the Court had in mind rules which, while they might differentiate between individuals by reference to their place of establishment, would nevertheless not discriminate on grounds of nationality, at any rate not directly.[75]

In *Seco* the Court considered an obligation imposed by national law on employers to pay social security contributions on behalf of their employees, which was also applicable to employers who were established in other Member States and temporarily providing services in the host State, and who were already liable to make similar contributions under the legislation of the Member States where they were established. The Court held that this amounted to indirect discrimination on grounds of nationality, which could not be justified on account of the general interest in providing workers with social security, since no benefits were payable to the employees in such circumstances. It will be noted that in this case the examination of justification in the general interest is in fact an assessment of whether or not the indirect discrimination can be objectively justified.[76] More recent case law treats the application of national measures of social protection in such cases of posted workers as restrictions on the provision of services without the need to establish that the measures are indirectly discriminatory, and considers justification by reference to overriding requirements in the general interest. Thus the Court in *Arblade* reiterated its approach in *Seco* as regards social contributions payable in respect of posted workers, which could not be levied in respect of protection essentially similar to that afforded by the rules of the Member State of establishment of their employer, but held that provisions of a Member State's legislation or collective labour agreements which guarantee minimum wages may in principle be applied to employers providing

---

[72] Case C–106/91 *Ramrath v Ministre de la Justice, and L'Institut des réviseurs d'entreprises* [1992] E.C.R. I–3351.

[73] See above at p.785.

[74] Above at p.786.

[75] Case 33/74 *Van Binsbergen v Bedrijfsvereniging Metaalnijverheid* [1974] E.C.R. 1307, para.12; Case C–106/91 *Ramrath v Ministre de la Justice, and L'Institut des réviseurs d'entreprises* [1992] E.C.R. I–3351, para.29.

[76] Joined Cases 62 and 63/81 *Société anonyme de droit français Seco et Société anonyme de droit français Desquenne & Giral v Etablissement d'assurance v la vieillesse et l'invalidité* [1982] E.C.R. 223, paras 8–10.

services within the territory of that State, regardless of the country in which the employer is established.[77] In *Mazzoleni*, another case involving the payment of the minimum wage specified by the host-State to posted workers, the Court distinguished between construction workers posted to another Member State for varying periods in order to carry out a specific project in another Member State, and workers employed by an undertaking established in a frontier region, some of whose employees might be required, on a part-time basis and for brief periods, to carry out a part of their work in the adjacent territory of a Member State other than that in which the undertaking is established. In the former case the minimum wage must be paid; in the latter case it might be neither necessary nor proportionate to the objective pursued to insist on the payment of the minimum wage, and competent authorities in the host State should undertake a careful evaluation of all the circumstances.[78]

In *Bond van Adverteerders* the Court stated that national rules **19–040** which "are not applicable to services without distinction as regards their origin and which are therefore discriminatory are compatible with Community law only if they can be brought within the scope of an express derogation", such as Article 46 EC.[79] In *Gouda* the Court repeated and expanded upon this earlier statement. While national rules which discriminated against services by reference to their origin could only be justified if brought within an express provision of the Treaty, such as Article 46 EC,[80] the position was different for national rules which restricted the freedom to provide services by virtue of their effects on service providers established in the territory of another Member State who already had to satisfy the requirements of that State's legislation.[81] As regards restrictions in this latter category:

"such restrictions come within the scope of Article [49] if the application of the national legislation to foreign persons providing services is not justified by overriding reasons relating to the public interest or if the requirements embodied in that legislation are already satisfied by the rules imposed on those persons in the Member State in which they are established."[82]

---

[77] Joined Cases C–369 and 376/96 *Arblade* [1999] E.C.R. I–8453, esp. at paras 46, 53, 54.

[78] Case C–165/98 *Mazzoleni* [2001] E.C.R. I–2189; see also Case C–164/99 *Portugaia Construções Lda* [2002] E.C.R. I–787; Joined Cases C–49/98 etc. *Finalarte et al.* [2001] E.C.R. I–7831.

[79] Case 352/85 *Bond van Adverteerders v The Netherlands State* [1988] E.C.R. 2085, para.32.

[80] Case C–288/89 *Stichting Collectieve Antennevoorziening Gouda v Commissariaat voor de Media* [1991] E.C.R. I–4007, para.11.

[81] *ibid.*, para.12.

[82] *ibid.*, para.13.

The Court goes on to list overriding reasons relating to the public interest which the Court had recognised to date.[83] It appears from that list that the Court regards the second category to which it has referred, which covers restrictions which need not be justified by reference to Article 46 (in conjunction with Article 55 EC), as covering both national rules which discriminate indirectly on grounds of nationality (where the overriding reasons in the general interest in effect amount to objective justification),[84] and national rules which discriminate indirectly by reference to the fact that the service provider is established in another Member State.

The Court of Justice has also held that national rules which are not applicable to services without distinction as regards the place of residence *of the recipient* are discriminatory and can be justified only by an express derogation such as Article 46.[85]

19–041   The case law is not really consistent. It would appear from the judgments of the Court in *Bond van Adverteerders* and *Gouda* that the proposition maintained in *van Binsbergen* and *Ramrath* that a service provider might be excluded from providing services in one Member State on the ground that he is established in another Member State and not the host State can be upheld only if the considerations of public interest can be regarded as falling within the scope of Article 46 of the Treaty, and not if such considerations are "mere" overriding reasons in the general interest. On the other hand, prohibiting the provision of services on the sole ground that the service provider is not established in the same Member State as the service recipient is as much the very mischief at which Article 49 is in terms aimed as the direct discrimination on grounds of nationality prohibited by the Treaty which the Court has emphasised can only be justified by reference to express derogating provisions in the Treaty.[86] The Court's "re-alignment" of its case law in *Bond van*

---

[83] The Court listed professional rules intended to protect recipients of the service (Joined Cases 110/78 and 111/78 *Van Wesemael* [1979] E.C.R. 35, para.28); protection of intellectual property (Case 62/79 *Coditel* [1980] E.C.R. 881); the protection of workers (Case 279/80 *Webb* [1981] E.C.R. 3305, para.19); Joined Cases 62/81 and 63/81 *Seco v EVI* [1982] E.C.R. 223, para.14; Case C–113/89 *Rush Portuguesa* [1990] E.C.R. I–1417, para.18); consumer protection (Case 220/83 *Commission v France* [1986] E.C.R. 3663, para.20; Case 252/83 *Commission v Denmark* [1986] E.C.R. 3713, para.20; Case 205/84 *Commission v Germany* [1986] E.C.R. 3755, para.30; Case 206/84 *Commission v Ireland* [1986] E.C.R. 3817, para.20; Case C–180/89 *Commission v Italy* [1991] E.C.R. I–709, para.20; and Case C–198/89 *Commission v Greece,* [1991] E.C.R. I–727, para.21), the conservation of the national historic and artistic heritage (*Commission v Italy*, cited above, para.20); turning to account the archaeological, historical and artistic heritage of a country and the widest possible dissemination of knowledge of the artistic and cultural heritage of a country (*Commission v France*, cited above, para.17, and *Commission v Greece*, cited above, para.21).

[84] Note that the Court refers to the *Seco* case, which, as shown above, concerns in reality the question of objective justification for indirect discrimination.

[85] Case C–224/97 *Ciola v Land Vorarlberg* [1999] E.C.R. I–2517, para.16.

[86] Case C–388/01 *Commission v Italy* [2003] E.C.R. I–721, para.19; Case C–311/97 *Royal Bank of Scotland v Elliniko Dimosio (Greek State)* [1999] E.C.R. I–2651, para.32; and see above at p.801.

Adverteerders and *Gouda* seems in principle to be correct. However, it has continued to consider possible justification of national measures which discriminate against out of State providers by reference to mandatory requirements.[87] Thus in *Commission v Italy*,[88] the Court considered Italian rules requiring *inter alia* undertakings engaged in the provision of temporary labour established in other Member States to maintain their registered office or a branch office on Italian territory. Relying on *Gouda*, the Commission argued that these requirements could only be justified under Articles 46 and 55 EC, and that no such justification could be made out. The Court noted that it followed from the Court's case law (citing, *inter alia, Gouda*!) that "the protection of workers is among the overriding reasons of public interest capable of justifying a restriction on the freedom to provide services", though it held, predictably, on proportionality grounds, that this could not justify the Italian requirements in issue.[89] The Court is, it seems, more attached to flexibility than to legal principle or consistency. In *Danner*, Advocate General Jacobs noted the existence of two inconsistent lines of case law on the question whether national rules which discriminate as regards the origin of a service can be justified by reference to imperative requirements or solely by reference to Articles 45 and 46 EC. He considered the state of uncertainty to be unsatisfactory, advocated a solution whereby all restrictions on the provision of services should be capable of justification on grounds of imperative requirements, and expressed the view that the Court should clarify the position.[90] The Court in *Danner* did not do so.

The Court in *Gouda*, after listing the categories of public interest referred to above, ended with a reference to the need for national measures being appropriate and proportionate in order to be justified:

"Lastly, as the Court has consistently held, the application of national provisions to providers of services established in other Member States must be such as to guarantee the achievement of the intended aim and must not go beyond what is necessary

---

[87] Case C–158/96 *Raymond Kohll v Union des Caisses de Maladie* [1998] E.C.R. I–1931, paras 34 and 41. Case C–410/96 *André Ambry* [1998] E.C.R. I–7875, paras 28 to 31. In Case C–484/93 *Svensson et Gustavsson v Ministre du Logement et de l'Urbanisme* [1995] E.C.R. I–3955, the Court repeated the proposition that a national rule which discriminates by reference to place of establishment can only be justified by reference to Art. 46 EC, but then goes on to examine whether the measure may nevertheless be justified by the ned to maintain cohesion of the tax system; paras 15, 16.

[88] Case C–279/00 [2002] E.C.R. I–1425.

[89] *ibid.*, paras 19–25.

[90] Case C–136/00 [2002] E.C.R. I–8147, paras 34–40. Advocate General Jacobs adds that "the same solution may be appropriate for the free movement of goods. That solution would meet the need to give equal weight, when assessing restrictions on the free movement of goods, to interests no less vital than those set out in Art.30 EC, notably the protection of the environment," see para.40; and see Ch.16, at p.616.

in order to achieve that objective. In other words, it must not be possible to obtain the same result by less restrictive rules . . ."[91]

While the above test for the proportionality of national measures is almost invariably an objective one, it seems that in exceptional cases the importance and sensitivity of the issues of public interest involved allow Member States a wide discretion to judge whether it is necessary to restrict and/or prohibit certain activities.[92]

The Court's analysis of "overriding reasons in the general interest" has continued to follow the pattern established prior to the development of the concept of the non-discriminatory restriction in the *Säger* case.[93] The Court has upheld national rules which prohibit lotteries on grounds of consumer protection and the maintenance of order in society,[94] and national rules which confine the judicial recovery of debts to members of the legal profession on the grounds of consumer protection and safeguarding the proper administration of justice.[95] The Court has also acknowledged that the risk of seriously undermining the financial balance of the social security system may constitute an overriding reason in the general interest capable of justifying a Member State requiring authorisation for dental treatment in another Member State, at the expense of a social security fund covered by national rules in the first Member State, where no such authorisation was required for treatment in the first Member State; once again, such a restriction, since it directly discriminates against out of state providers, should in principle be justifiable solely by reference to Article 46 EC (*in casu* public health).[96]

MUTUAL RECOGNITION OF DIPLOMAS, TRAINING, AND EXPERIENCE, AND THE CO-ORDINATION OF NATIONAL QUALIFICATIONS

Direct applicability of Articles 43 and 49 EC (and Article 39 EC)

Principles applicable where no relevant harmonisation directives have been adopted

19–042   Article 47(1) EC provides that the Council shall issue directives for the mutual recognition of diplomas, certificates, and other

---

[91] Case C–288/89 *Stichting Collectieve Antennevoorziening Gouda v Commissariaat voor de Media* [1991] E.C.R. I–4007, para.15.

[92] Case C–275/92 *Her Majesty's Customs and Excise v Gerhart Schindler and Jörg Schindler.* [1994] E.C.R. I–1039, para.61. Lotteries alone appear to fall into this category.

[93] Case C–76/90 *Manfred Säger v Dennemeyer & Co. Ltd* [1991] E.C.R. I–4221.

[94] Case C–275/92 *Her Majesty's Customs and Excise v Gerhart Schindler and Jörg Schindler.* [1994] E.C.R. I–1039, para.61.

[95] Case C–3/95 *Broede v Sandker* [1996] E.C.R. I–6511.

[96] Case C–158/96 *Raymond Kohll v Union des Caisses de Maladie* [1998] E.C.R. I–1931, para.41

evidence of formal qualifications. Article 47(3) EC provides that in the case of the medical and allied and pharmaceutical professions, the progressive abolition of restrictions shall be dependent upon coordination of the conditions for their exercise in the various Member States. But even in the absence of directives under Article 47 EC, recognition of foreign diplomas may be required by the prohibitions on discrimination contained in Articles 43 and 49 EC, and indeed Article 39 EC, on the free movement of workers. *Thieffry v Paris Bar Council*,[97] concerning the application of Article 43 EC, is illustrative. A Belgian national held a Belgian law degree recognised by the University of Paris as equivalent to a French law degree. He acquired the qualifying certificate for the profession of advocate, but the Paris Bar Council refused to allow him to undergo practical training on the ground that he did not possess a French law degree. The Court of Justice held that such a refusal could amount to indirect discrimination prohibited by Article 43 of the Treaty. As the General Programme for the abolition of restrictions on freedom of establishment made clear in Title III(B), the Council proposed to eliminate not only overt discrimination, but also any form of disguised discrimination, including "Any requirements imposed . . . in respect of the taking up or pursuit of an activity as a self-employed person where, although applicable irrespective of nationality, their effect is exclusively or principally to hinder the taking up or pursuit of such activity by foreign nationals."[98] It would be for the competent national authorities, taking account of the requirements of Community law, to judge whether a recognition granted by a university authority could, in addition to its academic effect, constitute valid evidence of a professional qualification.

The Court emphasised in *Vlassopoulou* that a Member State, dealing with a request for authorisation to practise a profession access to which is under national legislation subject to the holding of a diploma or professional qualification, is obliged to take into account qualifications acquired in another Member State, by carrying out a comparison between the skills evidenced by those diplomas and the knowledge and qualifications required by national rules.[99] In the context of that review a Member State might take into consideration objective differences relating to the legal context of the profession concerned in the Member State or origin and its field of

---

[97] Case 71/76 [1977] E.C.R. 765. See Case 11/77 *Patrick* [1977] E.C.R. 119; and Case 65/77 *Razanatsimba* [1977] E.C.R. 2229 (Lomé Convention, Art. 62).
[98] [1974] O.J. English Spec. Ed., Second Series, IX, p.8.
[99] Case C–340/89 *Vlassopoulou v Ministerium für Justiz, Bundes- und Europaangelegenheiten Baden-Württemberg* [1990] E.C.R. I–2327; citing Case 222/86 *UNECTEF v Heylens* [1987] E.C.R. 4097.

activity.[1] If such a comparison indicates the possession of a qualification equivalent to that required by the national law of the host State,
the Member State is bound to accept the person concerned as being
qualified. If the comparison shows only partial equivalence, the host
State has the right to require that the person concerned should
demonstrate that he or she has acquired the additional knowledge
and qualifications needed.[2] Comparison of the national qualifications
must be carried out according to a procedure complying with the
requirements of Community law relating to the effective protection
of fundamental rights conferred by the Treaty on nationals of
Member States.[3] It follows that it must be possible for any decision
to be made the subject of judicial proceedings in which its legality
under Community law can be reviewed and it must be possible for
the person concerned to ascertain the reasons for the decision.[4] In
Bobadilla,[5] a case involving Article 39 EC, the Court added where no
general procedure for official recognition has been laid down at
national level by the host Member State, or where that procedure
does not comply with the requirements of Community law, it is for a
public body seeking to fill the post itself to investigate whether the
diploma obtained by the candidate in another Member State,
together, where appropriate, with practical experience, is to be
regarded as equivalent to the qualification required. In the case in
point, the public body in question (the Prado) had made a grant to
the candidate to enable him to pursue his studies in another
Member State and had already employed him on a temporary basis
in the post to be filled. The Court of Justice held that in such a case,
the public body was ideally placed to assess the candidate's actual
knowledge and abilities compared to the knowledge and abilities of
holders of the national diploma.[6]

*Principles applicable in the absence of harmonisation directives also
applicable after harmonisation to situations not covered by relevant
directives*

19–043   In *Hocsman*[7] the Court rejected the argument that the above
principles were only applicable in the absence of harmonisation of
relevant qualifications, and thus had no application to the free
movement of doctors, whose qualifications were exhaustively regulated by Directive 93/16.[8] Where requirements such as those set out

---

[1] Case C–340/89 *Vlassopoulou* [1990] E.C.R. I–2327, para.18.
[2] *ibid.*, para.19.
[3] *ibid.*, para.22.
[4] *ibid.*, para.22.
[5] See Case C–234/97 *Teresa Fernández de Bobadilla v Museo Nacional del Prado, Comité de
Empresa del Museo Nacional del Prado and Ministerio Fiscal* [1999] E.C.R. I–4773.
[6] *ibid.*, paras 34, 35.
[7] Case C–238/98 *Hocsman* [2000] E.C.R. I–6623.
[8] [1993] O.J. L165/24.

in Directive 93/16 were satisfied, mutual recognition of the diplomas in question rendered superfluous their recognition under the general principles developed by the Court. However, those principles remained relevant in situations not covered by such directives. In the case in point, Dr Hocsman, of Argentine origin, acquired Spanish nationality in 1986, and French citizenship in 1998. He had been refused authorisation to practise medicine in France on the ground that he did not hold qualifications obtained in a Member State. He held an Argentine medical diploma recognised in Spain as equivalent to the Spanish University degree in medicine and surgery, so allowing him to practise medicine in Spain and train there as a specialist. The Court held that the authorities of the Member State to which Dr Hocsman had applied were bound to carry out the comparative assessment referred to in Vlassopoulou and *Bobadilla*. In particular, it would be necessary to verify whether recognition in Spain of Dr Hocsman's diploma from Argentina as equivalent to the Spanish degree in medicine and surgery was given on the basis of criteria comparable to those whose purpose, in the context of Directive 93/16, was to ensure that Member States may rely on the quality of the diplomas in medicine awarded by the other Member States.[9]

A national requirement that a person possess a particular qualification in order to carry on a particular occupational activity is in itself a restriction on a fundamental freedom which must be justified

Failure to recognise that a foreign national has qualifications **19–044** equivalent to national qualifications may thus hinder or make less attractive the exercise of a fundamental freedom. But it is also the case that national rules requiring that certain activities be reserved to those with certain qualifications can itself hinder or make less attractive the exercise of the right of establishment or freedom to provide services, and require justification. The Court has subjected claims of justification to fairly searching scrutiny as regards proportionality, though unsurprisingly accords rather more deference to claims based on the protection of public health than to claims based on other grounds.

Thus in *MacQuen*,[10] national rules reserving to opthalmologists the right to carry out certain eyesight operations was held to be a restriction on the right of establishment, though one which could in principle be justified on grounds of protection of public health. The Court noted however that the national rule in issue was not expressly provided for in legislation, but resulted from national judicial interpretation "based on an assessment of the risks to public health

---

[9] *ibid.*, esp. paras 33–39; see also Case C–319/92 *Haim* [1994] E.C.R. I–425.
[10] Case C–108/96 *MacQuen* [2001] E.C.R. I–837

which might result if opticians were authorised to carry out certain eyesight operations."[11] The Court observed that an assessment of this kind was liable to change with the passage of time, particularly as a result of scientific and technical progress, and concluded that it was for the national court to assess, in the light of the Treaty requirements relating to freedom of establishment and the demands of legal certainty and the protection of public health, whether the interpretation of domestic law adopted by the competent national authorities in that regard remained valid.[12]

The occupational activity considered by the Court in *Gräbner*[13] was that of "Heilpraktiker" (or lay health practitioner) under German law, which was a professional or commercial activity involving the diagnosis, treatment or alleviation of illness, pain or physical injury. Austrian law recognised no such category, reserving all these latter activities to doctors. It was undisputed that the Austrian rules constituted a restriction on the exercise of the right of establishment and freedom to provide services; the main issue was whether the Austrian prohibition was a necessary and proportionate means of protecting human health. The Court repeated its observation in *MacQuen*, that assessments such as that made by the Austrian legislature are liable to change over time, but concluded without more that the Austrian rule did not go beyond what was necessary to protect public health.[14]

19-045   In *Commission v Greece*, the Court considered a national rule of one Member State requiring that tourist guides travelling with a group of tourists from another Member State to show them around places of interest and historic sites, have a licence requiring specific training evidenced by a diploma. The Court held that this was a restriction on the freedom to provide services which could not be justified by a Member State's general interest in the proper appreciation of its artistic and archaeological heritage, since the requirements imposed were disproportionate, in view of the fact that the tourist guides in question provided their services to a closed group with whom they travelled from the Member State of establishment to the Member State to be visited.[15]

In *Säger v Dennemeyer*, the Court considered the application to service providers established in other Member States of a national rule requiring providers of patent renewal services (monitoring patents by a computerised system and advising them when renewal payments are due) to hold a special professional qualification, such as patent agent. The Court held that the rule in question was a

---

[11] *ibid.*, para.35.
[12] *ibid.*, 36, 37.
[13] Case C–294/00 *Gräbner* [2002] E.C.R. I–6515.
[14] *ibid.*, para.50.
[15] Case C–198/89 [1991] E.C.R. I–727, paras 16, 18. And see Case C–154/89 *Commission v France* [1991] E.C.R. I–4221.

restriction on the freedom to provide services, which could not be justified on grounds of protecting clients, since the services provided comprised advising clients on when renewal fees had to be paid in order to prevent a patent from lapsing, requesting them to state whether they wish to renew the patent, and paying the fees on their behalf if they so desired. Those tasks were essentially of a straightforward nature and did not call for specific professional aptitudes, as was indicated by the high level of computerization which appeared to have been attained by the defendant in the main proceedings. The Court added that the risk for the holder of a patent of the failure by a company entrusted with monitoring German patents to fulfil its obligations was very limited, since two months after the date for renewal, the German patent office sends a reminder to the holder of a patent pointing out that, failing payment of the fee, increased by a surcharge of 10 per cent, the patent will expire four months after the sending of the reminder.

Where national requirements reserving a particular occupational activity to those holding a particular qualification can be justified, nationals of other Member States can be required to hold that qualification or its equivalent. That may in turn raise the question whether a particular individual, qualified or experienced in one Member State, may rightly claim to be appropriately qualified or experience in another Member State. The Treaty rules on establishment and services may be directly invoked in such cases, as discussed above. Increasingly, Community legislation lays down specific rules on the mutual recognition of qualifications for particular professions, or general rules for assessing the compatibility of qualifications or experience gained in one Member State with the lawful requirements for pursuit of occupational activities in another. The most important Community legislation in this field is discussed below.

Mutual recognition of diplomas and the co-ordination of national qualifications by Community rules

Introduction

Paragraphs (1) and (2) of Article 47 EC provide, respectively, for **19–046** the "mutual recognition of diplomas, certificates, and other evidence of formal qualifications," and for "the coordination of the provisions laid down by law, regulation or administrative action in Member States concerning the taking up and pursuit of activities as self-employed persons." Article 47(3) EC provides that in the case of the medical and allied and pharmaceutical professions, the progressive abolition of restrictions shall be dependent upon coordination of the conditions for their exercise in the various Member States. By far the single most important legislation adopted under Article 47(1) and

(2) EC is Directive 2005/36 of the European Parliament and of the Council on the recognition of professional qualifications.[16] This Directive supersedes more than a dozen prior directives, and lays down the framework for application of a number of others. It will be referred to in the subsequent discussion as "the PQ Directive". This Directive does not prescribe a single approach or blueprint for dealing with mutual recognition, but combines a number of approaches, which vary according to the types of qualification, training or experience involved, and according to whether individuals are seeking mutual recognition in the context of exercise of the right of establishment, or the freedom to provide services. The aim of the following treatment is to provide understanding of the scheme of the PQ Directive, and of its central principles, rather than to offer a comprehensive handbook on its detailed provisions. The PQ Directive establishes rules according to which a Member State which makes access to a pursuit of a regulated profession[17] in its territory contingent upon possession of specific professional qualifications (referred to in the Directive as the host Member State), shall recognise professional qualifications obtained in another Member State (referred to as the home Member State), and which allow the holder of these qualifications to pursue the same profession there, for access to and pursuit of that profession.[18] The Directive applies to all nationals of a Member State wishing to pursue a regulated profession in a Member State, including those belonging to the liberal professions, *other than that in which they obtained their professional qualifications*, on either a self-employed or employed basis.[19] The recognition of professional qualifications by the host Member State allows the person concerned to gain access in that Member State to the same profession as that for which he is qualified in the home Member State and to pursue it in the host Member State under the same conditions as its nationals.[20]

Freedom of establishment—recognition on the basis of coordination of minimum training conditions—Chapter III of Title III of the PQ Directive

19–047   It has been noted above that Article 47(3) EC requires that for certain professions, the abolition of restrictions shall be dependent upon coordination of the conditions for their exercise. Chapter III of

---

[16] [2005] O.J. L255/22.
[17] Art.3(a) of the PQ Dir. defines "regulated profession" as "a professional activity or group of professional activities, access to which, the pursuit of which, or one of the modes of pursuit of which is subject, directly or indirectly, by virtue of legislative, regulatory or administrative provisions to the possession of specific professional qualifications; in particular, the use of a professional title limited by legislative, regulatory or administrative provisions to holders of a given professional qualification shall constitute a mode of pursuit." Other professional activities are *treated* as regulated professions, see Art.3(2) of the PQ Dir.
[18] PQ Dir., Art.1.
[19] PQ Dir., Art.2(1).
[20] PQ Dir., Art.4(1).

Title III of the PQ Directive deals with those professional activities for which mutual recognition has proceeded on the basis of the coordination of minimum training conditions. The activities covered are those of doctor (with basic training and specialised), nurse (general care), midwife, dental practitioner (and specialised dental practitioner), veterinary surgeon, pharmacist, and architect. Under the principle of automatic recognition laid down in the PQ Directive,[21] detailed rules are laid down which identify the qualifications awarded in Member States which other Member States are bound to recognise. Each Member State is obliged to make access to and pursuit of the professional activities of all those referred to above (except architects) subject to possession of evidence of the formal qualifications referred to, attesting that the person concerned has acquired, over the duration of his or her training, and where appropriate, the knowledge and skills which are spelled out in the Directive.[22] Without underestimating their significance, it must be said that the requirements laid down in the PQ Directive are of necessity spelled out in fairly general terms. Thus, by way of example, the specification for "basic medical training" in the PQ Directive is as follows[23]:

"1. Admission to basic medical training shall be contingent upon possession of a diploma or certificate providing access, for the studies in question, to universities.
2. Basic medical training shall comprise a total of at least six years of study or 5500 hours of theoretical and practical training provided by, or under the supervision of, a university.

For persons who began their studies before January 1, 1972, the course of training referred to in the first subparagraph may comprise six months of full-time practical training at university level under the supervision of the competent authorities.
3. Basic medical training shall provide an assurance that the person in question has acquired the following knowledge and skills:

(a) adequate knowledge of the sciences on which medicine is based and a good understanding of the scientific methods including the principles of measuring biological functions, the evaluation of scientifically established facts and the analysis of data;
(b) sufficient understanding of the structure, functions and behaviour of healthy and sick persons, as well as

---

[21] PQ Dir., Art.21.
[22] PQ Dir., Art.21(6).
[23] PQ Dir., Art.24.

relations between the state of health and physical and social surroundings of the human being;

(c) adequate knowledge of clinical disciplines and practices, providing him with a coherent picture of mental and physical diseases, of medicine from the points of view of prophylaxis, diagnosis and therapy and of human reproduction;

(d) suitable clinical experience in hospitals under appropriate supervision."

Apart from the periods of training specified, requirements of this generality are close to non-justiciable, and it seems that coordination of minimum training conditions based on such requirements is based on an implicit assumption that the quality and intensity of medical training in the various Member States is and will remain essentially comparable.

Freedom of establishment—recognition of professional experience—Chapter II of Title III of the PQ Directive

19–048   Chapter II of Title III of the PQ Directive deals with situations where access to or pursuit of one the activities listed in Annex IV of the Directive is in a Member State contingent upon possession of general commercial or professional knowledge and aptitudes. In such a case, the Member State shall recognise previous pursuit of the activity in another Member State as sufficient proof of such knowledge and aptitudes.[24] Chapter II deals with activities covered by a dozen or so earlier directives which provide for recognition of commercial or professional activity in other Member States. Chapter II groups the activities into three lists in Annex IV, the purpose of the groupings being to distinguish, as appropriate, the requisite period of experience, or combination of experience and training, required in each case, for self-employed activities in one Member State to qualify for recognition in another. Thus, to take an example from the numerous categories covered by List I, a self-employed person falling within a specified category in the field of manufacture of textiles (or footwear, or wearing apparel, or mattresses and bedding, etc. and so forth), would qualify for recognition if he or she had previously pursued the relevant activity: (a) for six consecutive years on a self-employed basis or as a manager of an undertaking; or (b) for three consecutive years on a self-employed basis or as a manager of an undertaking, where the beneficiary proves that he or she has received at least three years previous training for the activity in question, which has been appropriately evidenced; or (c) for four

---

[24] PQ Dir., Art.16.

consecutive years on a self-employed basis or as a manager of an undertaking, where the beneficiary can prove that he or she has received, for the activity in question, two years' previous training, which has been appropriately evidenced; or (d) for three consecutive years on a self-employed basis, if the beneficiary can prove that he or she has pursued the activity in question on an employed basis for at least five years; or (e) for five consecutive years in an executive position, of which at least three years involved technical duties and responsibilities for at least one department of the company, if the beneficiary can prove that he or she has received, for the activity in question, at least three years appropriately evidenced previous training. In cases (a) to (d), the activity must not have finished more than 10 years before the date on which the person concerned applies to the competent authority of a Member State for recognition of his previous experience and training.[25] There is similar provision, with slight variation in the details of periods of self-employed experience, appropriately evidenced previous training, employed experience, etc., for the dozens and dozens of activities included in list II and list III of Annex IV.[26]

Freedom of establishment—the general system—Chapter I of Title III of the PQ Directive

(a) Introduction. Chapter I of Title III applies to all professions **19–049** which are not covered by Chapters II and III and to certain cases in which a person, for specific and exceptional reasons, does not satisfy the conditions laid down in those Chapters.[27] The component parts of the mechanism of the general system should be seen as a whole; taking any one part out of context can be misleading. Particular note must be taken of (a) the different levels of qualification; (b) the conditions for recognition; and (c) compensation measures.

(b) The different levels of qualification. The different levels of **19–050** qualification "are established only for the purpose of the operation of the general system, have no effect upon the national education and training structures nor upon the competence of Member States . . ."[28] There are five levels of qualification identified in the PQ Directive, ranging from an attestation of competence (level (a)), to three or four year university or equivalent degrees, combined with the professional training which might be required in addition to those courses (levels (d) and (e)).[29]

---

[25] PQ Dir., Art.17.
[26] PQ Dir., Arts 18, 19.
[27] PQ Dir., Art.10.
[28] PQ Dir., preamble, recital (13).
[29] PQ Dir., Art.11.

19–051 **(c) The conditions for recognition.**   As regards the conditions for recognition, the general principle is that if access to or pursuit of a regulated profession in a host Member State is contingent upon possession of specific professional qualifications, the competent authority of that Member State shall permit access to and pursuit of that profession, under the same conditions as apply to its nationals, to applicants possessing the attestation of competence or evidence of formal qualifications required by another Member State in order to gain access to and pursue that profession in its territory.[30] For this general principle to apply, attestations of competence or evidence of formal qualifications shall satisfy two conditions. The first is that they have been issued by a designated competent authority. The second is that they shall attest a level of professional qualification "at least equivalent to the *level immediately prior* to that which is required in the host Member State . . .".[31] The reference to an immediately prior level is at first sight curious, since it seems to require Member States to recognise "inferior" qualifications. But two points must be made. The first is that differences in the duration of courses leading to particular qualifications in different Member States do not automatically allow conclusions to be drawn as regards the rigorousness of a course, or the quality of the qualification awarded at the end of it. In some Member States the typical pattern of a undergraduate course at university is three or four years; in other Member States the typical pattern is four or five years. Thus, for example, a typical three year law degree in the United Kingdom, accompanied by appropriate professional training (level (d)) would rank as equivalent to a five year law degree accompanied by appropriate professional training in a Member State in which that represented the normal pattern. The second point is a reiteration of that made earlier; the various components of the general system should be seen as a whole rather than in isolation. In this regard, the general principle of recognition should be considered in conjunction with the provisions on compensation measures.

19–052 **(d) Compensation measures—adaptation period or aptitude test.**   In principle, compensation measures are an exception to a general principle of recognition, and must be construed and applied strictly, in accordance with the principle of proportionality. In practice, and in view of the diversity of national systems of qualification and training, compensation measures operate in conjunction with the general principle of recognition, to make what would

---

[30] PQ Dir., Art.13(1), first sub-para.

[31] PQ Dir., Art.13(1)(b). There are further and slightly different rules in Art.13(2) dealing with the situation where a person has pursued the relevant profession on a full-time basis for two years during the previous ten years in another Member State which does not regulate that profession.

otherwise be an unworkable principle in many, if not most cases, workable in practice.

The general principle of recognition referred to above does not preclude the host State from requiring, in certain circumstances, the person concerned to complete an adaptation period of up to three years or to take an aptitude test. It is appropriate to offer a brief explanation of these requirements. By "adaptation period" is meant the pursuit of the regulated profession in the host Member State under the responsibility of a qualified member of that profession, such period of supervised practice possibly being accompanied by further training. The period of supervised practice shall be the subject of an assessment. The detailed rules governing the adaptation period and its assessment as well as the status of the migrant under supervision shall be laid down by the competent authority in the host Member State.[32] The "aptitude test" referred to is a test limited to the professional knowledge of the person concerned, set by the competent authorities of the host Member State with the aim of assessing the ability of the person concerned to pursue a regulated profession in that Member State. In order to permit this test to be carried out, the competent authorities shall draw up a list of subjects which, on the basis of a comparison between the education and training required in the Member State and that received by the person concerned, are not covered by the evidence of formal qualifications possessed by the latter.[33]

The Member State is entitled to require the person concerned to complete an adaptation period, or to take an aptitude test, in three situations. The first is where the duration of the training of which he or she provides evidence is at least one year shorter than that required by the host Member State. The second is where the training received by the person concerned covers substantially different matters than those covered by the evidence of formal qualifications required in the host Member State. The third is where the regulated profession in the host Member State comprises one or more regulated professional activities which do not exist in the corresponding profession in the home Member State of the person concerned, and that difference consists in specific training which is required in the host Member State and which covers substantially different matters from those covered by the attestation of competence or evidence of formal qualifications of the person concerned.[34] The reference in the second and third cases just mentioned to "substantially different matters" means matters of which knowledge is essential for pursuing the profession and with regard to which the training received by the migrant shows important differences in

---

[32] PQ Dir., Art.3(1)(g).
[33] PQ Dir., Art.3(1)(h).
[34] PQ Dir., Art.14(a)(b)(c).

terms of duration or content from the training required by the host Member State.[35] Furthermore, recourse by a Member State to the possibility of requiring the person concerned to complete an adaptation period or to take an aptitude test is to be applied with due regard to the principle of proportionality. In particular, if the host Member State intends to impose such a requirement, it must first ascertain whether the knowledge acquired by the person concerned in the course of his or her professional experience in a Member State or in a third country, is of a nature to cover, in full or in part, the "substantial difference" already referred to.[36]

19–053 **(e) Extent of migrant's choice between adaptation period and aptitude test.** If the host Member State makes use of the option to require an adaptation period or aptitude test, it must in principle offer the person concerned a choice between the two.[37] However, where a Member State considers, with respect to a given profession, that it is necessary to derogate from the requirement that it offer the person concerned a choice, it shall inform the other Member States and the Commission in advance and provide sufficient justification for the derogation.[38] If, after receiving all necessary information, the Commission considers that such derogation is inappropriate or that it is not in accordance with Community law, it shall, within three months, ask the Member State in question to refrain from taking the envisaged measure. In the absence of a response from the Commission within the abovementioned deadline, the derogation may be applied.

Quite apart from the possibility of a Member State seeking to over-ride the choice of the migrant on the above basis, Member States are entitled to stipulate either an adaptation period or an aptitude test, for professions "whose pursuit requires precise knowledge of national law and in respect of which the provision of advice and/or assistance concerning national law is an essential and constant aspect of the professional activity".[39]

Common Provisions on establishment—Chapter IV of Title III of the PQ Directive

19–054 **(a) Documentation and formalities and procedure for mutual recognition of professional qualifications.** Where the competent authorities of the host Member State decide on an application for authorisation to pursue the regulated profession in question by

---

[35] PQ Dir., Art.14(4).
[36] PQ Dir., Art.14(5).
[37] PQ Dir., Art.14(2), first sub-para.
[38] PQ Dir., Art.14(2), second sub-para.
[39] PQ Dir., Art.14(3), first sub-para.

virtue of Title III, they may demand various documents and certificates specified in Annex VII, including proof of nationality, copies of evidence of formal qualifications giving access to the profession in question, etc.[40] In the event of "justified doubts", the host Member State may require from the competent authorities of a Member State confirmation of the authenticity of the attestations and evidence of formal qualifications awarded in that other Member State, as well as, where applicable, confirmation of the fact that the beneficiary fulfils, for the professions referred to in Chapter III of Title III, the minimum training conditions set out in the relevant provisions of the PQ Directive.[41] Where a host Member State requires its nationals to swear a solemn oath or make a sworn statement in order to gain access to a regulated profession, and where the wording of that oath or statement cannot be used by nationals of the other Member States, the host Member State shall ensure that the persons concerned can use an appropriate equivalent wording.

The competent authority of the host Member State shall acknowledge receipt of the application within one month of receipt and inform the applicant of any missing document.[42] The procedure for examining an application for authorisation to practise a regulated profession must be completed as quickly as possible and lead to a duly substantiated decision by the competent authority in the host Member State in any case within three months after the date on which the applicant's complete file was submitted. This deadline may be extended by one month in cases falling with Chapters 1 and II of Title III.[43] The decision, or failure to reach a decision within the deadline, shall be subject to appeal under national law.[44]

(b) Use of professional titles. If, in a Member State, the use of a **19–055** professional title relating to one of the activities of the profession in question is regulated, nationals of the other Member States who are authorised to practise a regulated profession on the basis of Title III shall use the professional title of the host Member State, which corresponds to that profession in that Member State, and make use of any associated initials.[45]

---

[40] PQ Dir., Art.50.

[41] There is also provision fpr verification in the case of "justified doubt" as regards evidence of formal qualifications issued by a competent authority in a Member State where the evidence includes training received in whole or in part in an establishment legally established in the territory of another Member State, see Art.50(3).

[42] PQ Dir., Art.51(1).

[43] PQ Dir., Art.52(2).

[44] PQ Dir., Art.52(3).

[45] PQ Dir., Art.52(1). For the position where a profession is regulated by an association or organisation within the meaning of Art.3(2) of the PQ Dir., see Art.52(2).

Freedom to provide services—pursuit of activities under home title—
Title II of the PQ Directive

19–056 (a) Principle of the Free Provision of Services.   For services, Title II of the PQ Directive declares the principle that Member States shall not restrict, for any reason relating to professional qualifications, the free provision of services in another Member State: (a) if the service provider is legally established in a Member State for the purpose of pursuing the same profession there (the Member State of establishment), and (b) where the service provider moves. As regards the movement of the service provider, the Directive draws a distinction between regulated professions and others. If the profession is not regulated in the Member State of establishment, the person concerned must have pursued that profession in that State for at least two years during the 10 years preceding the provision of services; but this condition does not apply when either the profession or the education and training leading to the profession is regulated.[46] The provisions of Title II apply only where the service provider moves to the territory of the host Member State to pursue the profession in question, on a temporary and occasional basis, and the temporary and occasional nature of the provision of services shall be assessed case by case, in particular in relation to its duration, its frequency, its regularity and its continuity.[47] The latter formulation is clearly derived from the *Gebhard* case.[48] The preamble to the Directive notes that in view of "the different systems established for the cross border provision of services on a temporary and occasional basis on the one hand, and for establishment on the other, the criteria for distinguishing between these two concepts in the event of the movement of the service provider to the territory of the host State should be clarified."[49] Simple repetition of the wording in the *Gebhard* case does not however amount to such clarification. Moreover, it is to be noted that for a service provider to equip himself or herself with an office or consulting room is not incompatible with the temporary and occasional nature of service provision.[50] Where a service provider moves, he or she is subject to those rules applicable in the host State to professionals who pursue the same profession in that Member State, which are of a professional, statutory or administrative nature and which are directly linked to professional qualifications, such as the definition of the profession, the use of titles, and serious professional malpractice which is directly and

---

[46] PQ Dir., Art.5(1)(b).
[47] PQ Dir., Art.5(2).
[48] Case C–55/94 *Reinhard Gebhard v Consiglio dell'Ordine degli Avvocati e Procuratori di Milano* [1995] E.C.R. I–4165; see above, at p.752.
[49] Recital (5) of preamble of PQ Dir.
[50] Above, at pp.751–752.

specifically linked to consumer protection and safety, as well as disciplinary provisions.[51]

(b) Exemptions. The host Member State shall exempt service **19–057** providers established in another Member State from the requirements which it places on professionals established in its territory relating to authorisation by, registration with or membership of a professional organisation of body. However, in order to facilitate the application of disciplinary provisions in force on their territory, Member States may provide either for automatic temporary registration with or for pro forma membership of such a professional organisation or body, provided that such registration or membership does not delay or complicate in any way the provision of services and does not entail any additional costs for the service provider.[52] The host Member State shall also exempt service providers established in another Member State from the requirement it places on professionals established in its territory relating to registration with a public social security body for the purpose of settling accounts with an insurer relating to activities pursued for the benefit of insured persons.[53] This provision is particularly relevant for the provision of medical and social services. The service provider shall, however, inform in advance, or in an urgent case, afterwards, the body referred to in point (b) of the services which he or she has provided.[54]

(c) Declaration to be made in advance if the service provider **19–058** **moves.** Member States may require that, where the service provider first moves from one Member State to another in order to provide services, he/she shall inform the competent authority in the host Member State in a written declaration to be made in advance including the details of any insurance cover or other means of personal or collective protection with regard to professional liability. Such declaration shall be renewed once a year if the service provider intends to provide temporary or occasional services in that Member State during that year. The service provider may supply the declaration by any means.[55] Moreover, for the first provision of services, or if there is a material change in the situation substantiated by the documents, Member States may require that the declaration be accompanied by the following documents: (a) proof of the nationality of the service provider; (b) an attestation certifying that the holder is legally established in a Member State for the purpose

---

[51] PQ Dir., Art.5(3).
[52] PQ Dir., Art.6, first sub-para.(a).
[53] PQ Dir., Art.6, first sub-para.(b).
[54] PQ Dir., Art.6, second sub-para.
[55] PQ Dir., Art.7(1).

of pursuing the activities concerned and that he or she is not prohibited from practising, even temporarily, at the moment of delivering the attestation; (c) evidence of professional qualifications; (d) for cases where it is a precondition of movement by the service provider that he or she has pursued the activity in question for at least two years during the previous 10 years, any means of proof of that fact; (e) for professions in the security sector, where the Member State so requires for its own nationals, evidence of no criminal convictions.[56]

19–059 **(d) Services provided under home-country professional title.** The services under discussion shall be provided under the professional title of the Member State of establishment, in so far as such a title exists in that Member State for the professional activity in question. That title shall be indicated in the official language or one of the official languages of the Member State of establishment in such a way as to avoid any confusion with the professional title of the host Member State. Where no such professional title exists in the Member State of establishment, the service provider shall indicate his or her formal qualification in the official language or one of the official languages of that Member State. By way of exception, the service shall be provided under the professional title of the *host Member State* for cases referred to Chapter III of Title III.[57]

19–060 **(e) Regulated professions having public health or safety implications.** For the first provision of services, in the case of regulated professions having public health or safety implications, which do not benefit from automatic recognition under Chapter III of Title III, the competent authority of the host Member State may check the professional qualifications of the service provider prior to the first provision of services. Such a prior check shall be possible only where the purpose of the check is to avoid serious damage to the health or safety of the service recipient due to a lack of professional qualification of the service provider and where this does not go beyond what is necessary for that purpose.[58] Within a maximum of one month of receipt of the declaration and accompanying documents, the competent authority shall endeavour to inform the service provider either of its decision not to check his or her qualifications or of the outcome of such check. Where there is a difficulty which would result in delay, the competent authority shall notify the service provider within the first month of the reason for the delay and the timescale for a decision, which must be finalised within the second month of receipt of completed documentation.[59]

---

[56] PQ Dir., Art.7(2).
[57] PQ Dir., Art.7(3).
[58] PQ Dir., Art.7(4), first sub-para.
[59] PQ Dir., Art.7(4), second sub-para.

Where there is a substantial difference between the professional qualifications of the service provider and the training required in the host Member State, to the extent that that difference is such as to be harmful to public health or safety, the host Member State shall give the service provider the opportunity to show, in particular by means of an aptitude test, that he or she has acquired the knowledge or competence lacking. In any case, it must be possible to provide the service within one month of a decision being taken in accordance with the timescale referred to above.[60] In the absence of a reaction of the competent authority within the deadlines referred to above, the service may be provided.[61]

It is to be noted that where qualifications have been verified under the requirements referred to above, the service shall be provided under the professional title of the host Member State.[62]

(f) Administrative co-operation. The competent authorities of the **19–061** host Member State may ask the competent authorities of the Member State of establishment, for each provision of services, to provide any information relevant to the legality of the service provider's establishment and his or her good conduct, as well as the absence of any disciplinary or criminal sanctions of a professional nature. The competent authorities of the Member State of establishment shall provide this information in accordance with the duties of mutual and close collaboration applicable to the authorities of home and host Member State.[63] The competent authorities shall ensure the exchange of all information necessary for complaints by a recipient of a service against a service provider to be correctly pursued. Recipients shall be informed of the outcome of the complaint.[64]

(g) Information to be given to recipients of the service. In cases **19–062** where the service is provided under the professional title of the Member State of establishment or under the formal qualification of the service provider, in addition to the other requirements relating to information contained in Community law, the competent authorities of the host Member State may require the service provider to furnish the recipient of the service with certain information, including registration details, if applicable, of the service provider; the name and address of any competent authorising body in the Member State of establishment; and details of any insurance cover or other means of personal or collective protection with regard to professional liability.

---

[60] PQ Dir., Art.7(4), third sub-para.
[61] PQ Dir., Art.7(4), fourth sub-para.
[62] PQ Dir., Art.7(4), fifth sub-para.
[63] PQ Dir., Art.8(1), referring to Art.56.
[64] PQ Dir., Art.8(2).

Right of Establishment under home title?

19–063   The rights of individuals under the PQ Directive, as regards establishment on the one hand, and service provision on the other, are in some cases similar, and in others markedly dissimilar. As regards a doctor or nurse qualified within the meaning of Chapter III of Title III, the main difference as regards service provision and establishment would be that in the former case the person concerned would be exempt from authorisation by or registration with or membership of a professional organisation or body, and from registration with any relevant public social security body, but would be subject to obligations as regards relevant declaratory, documentary and information requirements; in the latter case (establishment) the same conditions as apply to nationals would apply to the person concerned. In either case the activities would be carried out under the professional title of the host Member State. In the case of a person engaged in a regulated profession having public health or safety implications, the person concerned would be subject to the exemptions and requirements just referred to in the case of service provision, but his or her qualifications would be subject to verification, including an aptitude test if there were a substantial difference between his or her professional qualifications and the training required in the host Member State. If such a person were to exercise the right of establishment, the substantial difference referred to would enable the host Member State to require the migrant to undertake an aptitude test or adaptation period, with the migrant having the right to choose, unless grounds existed to derogate from the requirement of choice. In the case of service provision or establishment, the activities would be carried out under the professional title of the host Member State.

There are a number of cases however, where the PQ Directive implies that a person carrying on a professional activity in one Member State who wishes to extend those activities to a second Member State, will be able to do so under home title by way of provision of services, but will have to undertake an aptitude test or adaptation period in order to exercise the right of establishment, and thereby to carry on their activities under the professional title of the host Member State. This would be the case for a person whose training in his or her home Member State is shorter, or substantially different, from that of the intended host Member State. A point which the Directive does not directly address is whether an individual who is entitled under Title II of the PQ Directive to carry on professional activities under home title by way of provision of services, can operate *permanently* in the host Member State, and become established there, under the professional title of the home Member State, complying only with relevant non discriminatory rules regarding registration with professional bodies, etc. and relying not on the Directive, but directly on Article 43 EC. It would seem that the answer is in principle in the affirmative. The PQ Directive does not guarantee such a right, but nor does it, nor could it, exclude it. It has already been noted that to insist on a qualification for a particular activity is in principle a restriction on the right of establishment, which has to be justified by imperative requirements in the general interest.[65] It is difficult to see how a Member State could justify restricting the permanent exercise of professional activities under home title of a person entitled to provide the services in question under home title on a temporary and occasional basis. Transition from service provision to establishment might be gradual and difficult to determine with certainty, particularly if professional activities are carried on from an office or consulting room, which, as noted above, is in itself compatible with both service provision and establishment. It may be difficult in many cases to determine whether a person established in one Member State and engaged in professional activities under home title in another Member State, is doing so on a temporary or occasional basis, or has become established in the second Member State as well as the first. This should not necessarily cause difficulty; the main consequence of becoming established is likely to be a duty to register with relevant professional bodies. Whether established or providing services, the person concerned will be subject to at least certain rules of professional conduct of both the home Member State and host Member State.

Other Specific Arrangements for a given regulated profession

Other specific arrangements directly related to the recognition of **19–064** professional qualifications may apply instead of the arrangements in the PQ Directive.[66] In particular, the Directive does not affect the operation of Council Directive 77/249 to facilitate the effective exercise by lawyers of freedom to provide services (hereafter the Lawyers' Services Directive),[67] or of Directive 98/5 of the European Parliament and of the Council to facilitate practice of the profession of lawyer on a permanent basis in a Member State other than that in which the qualification was obtained (hereafter the Lawyers' Establishment Directive).[68] As indicated below, these Directives provide in each case for practise under home title, and in the case of the latter Directive, it is provided that practice under home title may amount to an adaptation period for the purposes of acquiring the qualification of the host Member State. However, the recognition of professional qualifications for lawyers for the purpose of immediate

---

[65] Above, at para.19–044.
[66] PQ Dir., Art.2(3), recital (42) of preamble.
[67] [1977] O.J. L78/17.
[68] [1998] O.J. L77/36.

establishment under the professional title of the host Member State is covered by the PQ Directive.

Lawyers—freedom to provide services

19–065   Under the Lawyers' Services Directive, Member States must recognise designated legal practitioners as "lawyers" for the purpose of pursuing "the activities of lawyers pursued by way of provision of services."[69] Since the substantive content of legal training differs in the Member States, and the Directive contains no provisions for the mutual recognition of diplomas, a designated legal practitioner must adopt the professional title used in the Member State from which he or she comes, expressed in the language of that State, and with an indication of the professional organisation by which he or she is authorised to practise.[70] Member States may reserve to prescribed categories of lawyers the preparation of formal documents for obtaining title to administer estates of deceased persons, and the drafting of formal documents creating or transferring interests in land.[71]

Activities relating to the representation of a client in legal proceedings or before public authorities shall be pursued in each host Member State under the conditions laid down for lawyers established in that State, with the exception of any conditions requiring residence, or registration with a professional organisation, in that State.[72] A lawyer pursuing these activities shall observe the rules of professional conduct of the host Member State, without prejudice to his or her obligations in the Member State from which he or she comes.[73] For the pursuit of these activities a Member State may require the lawyers to which the Directive applies (a) to be introduced, in accordance with local rules or customs, to the presiding judge and, where appropriate, to the President of the relevant Bar in the host Member State; and (b) to work in conjunction with a lawyer who practises before the judicial authority in question and who would, where necessary, be answerable to that authority, or with an "avoué" or "procuratore"[74] practising before it.[75] The Court has held that the purpose of the requirement that a lawyer providing services "work in conjunction with" a local lawyer is intended to provide him or her with the support necessary to enable him or her to act within a judicial system different from that to which he or she is accustomed and to assure the judicial authority

---

[69] Art. 1(2), 2.
[70] Final recital to preamble, and Art.3.
[71] Art. 1(1), second sub-para.
[72] Art. 4(1).
[73] Art. 4(2).
[74] No longer relevant; this profession was abolished in 1997.
[75] Art.5.

concerned that the lawyer providing services actually has that support and is thus in a position fully to comply with the procedural and ethical rules that apply.[76] But national implementing measures must not lay down disproportionate requirements in this regard, such as a requirement that a local lawyer be present throughout the oral proceedings, or a requirement that the local lawyer be the authorised representative or defending counsel.[77] The German Government sought to justify such requirements on the not implausible ground that a foreign lawyer practising under home title might not be familiar with German law. The Court's response was that any problem of possibly inadequate knowledge of German law "forms part of the responsibility of the lawyer providing services *vis-à-vis* his client, who is free to entrust his interests to a lawyer of his choice."[78] The Court held in *AMOK Verlags GmbH* that national rules which preclude a successful litigant from recovering the costs of the local lawyer in addition to that of the foreign lawyer are incompatible with Article 49 EC, since such a rule "is liable to make the transfrontier provision by a lawyer of his services less attractive. Such a solution may have a deterrent effect capable of affecting the competitiveness of lawyers in other Member States . . .".[79]

A lawyer pursuing activities other than those relating to the representation of a client in legal proceedings shall remain subject to the conditions and rules of professional conduct of the Member State from which he or she comes without prejudice to respect for the rules, whatever their source, which govern the profession in the host Member State, especially those concerning the incompatibility of the exercise of the activities of a lawyer with the exercise of other activities in that State, professional secrecy, relations with other lawyers, the prohibition on the same lawyer acting for parties with mutually conflict interests, and publicity.[80] The latter rules are applicable only if they are capable of being observed by a lawyer who is not established in the host Member State and to the extent to which their observance is objectively justified to ensure, in that State, the proper exercise of a lawyer's activities, the standing of the profession and respect for the rules concerning incompatibility.[81]

Lawyers—freedom of establishment
Perhaps the most interesting directive adopted under Article 47(1) **19–066** and (2) EC, in terms of the techniques which it uses to remove obstacles to freedom of movement of those engaged in a profession,

---

[76] Case 427/85 *Commission v Germany* [1988] E.C.R. 1123.
[77] *ibid.*, and see Case C–294/89 *Commission v France* [1991] E.C.R. I–3591.
[78] Case C–427/85 *Commission v Germany* [1988] E.C.R. 1123, para.27.
[79] Case C–289/02 *AMOK Verlags GmbH v A & R Gastronomie GmbH* [2003] E.C.R. I–15059, para.36.
[80] Art.4(4).
[81] Art.4(4).

and to secure "integration into the profession of lawyer in the host Member State", is the Lawyers' Establishment Directive. The Directive provides two options for lawyers; the first is permanent practice under home title; the second is acquisition of the professional title of the host Member State after a period of practice under home title, which serves as an adaptation period for the purposes of securing qualification in the latter State. The Directive applies both the self-employed and employed activities of lawyers.[82]

The Directive lists lawyers qualified under the laws of the Member States, and provides that any such lawyer shall be entitled to pursue on a permanent basis, in any other Member State under his home-country professional title, the activities specified in the directive.[83] These activities are described as the "same professional activities as a lawyer practising under the relevant professional title used in the host Member State and may, *inter alia*, give advice on the law of his home Member State, on Community law, on international law and on the law of the host Member State."[84] There are two exceptions or qualifications to the foregoing. The first applies where a Member State authorises in its territory a prescribed category of lawyers to prepare deeds for obtaining title to administer estates of deceased persons and for creating or transferring interests in land which, in other Member States are reserved for professions other than that of lawyer. In such a case the Member State may exclude from such activities lawyers practising under a home-country professional title conferred in one of the latter Member States.[85] The second qualification to the right to practise under home-country title applies to the pursuit of activities relating to the representation or defence of a client in legal proceedings where the law of the host Member State reserves such activities to lawyers practising under the professional title of that State. In such circumstances the host Member State may require lawyers practising under their home-country professional title to work in conjunction with a lawyer who practises before the judicial authority in question and who would, where necessary, be answerable to that authority or with an "avoué" practising before it. It will be noted that the latter safeguards are the same as those applicable under the Lawyers' Services Directive.

A lawyer who wishes to practise on a permanent basis in a Member State other than that in which he or she obtained his or her professional qualification shall register with the competent authority in that State.[86] The latter authority shall register the lawyer upon presentation of a certificate attesting to his or her registration with

---

[82] Art.1(1).
[83] Arts 1(2), 2.
[84] Art.5(1).
[85] Art.5(2).
[86] Arts 1, 3(1).

the competent authority in the home Member State. It may require that, when presented by the competent authority of the home Member State, the certificate be not more than three months old. It shall inform the competent authority in the home Member State of the registration.[87] Irrespective of the rules of professional conduct to which he or she is subject in his or her home Member State, a lawyer practising under his home-country professional title shall be subject to the same rules of professional conduct as lawyers practising under the relevant professional title of the host Member State in respect of all the activities he or she pursues in its territory.[88] The host Member State may require such a lawyer either to take out professional indemnity insurance or to become a member of a professional guarantee fund in accordance with the rules which that State lays down for professional activities pursued in its territory, unless he or she already has equivalent cover in accordance with the rules of the home Member State.[89] In the event of failure by a lawyer practising under his or her home-country professional title to fulfil the obligations in force in the host Member State, the rules of pro-cedure, penalties and remedies provided for in the host Member State shall apply.[90]

Integration into the profession of lawyer in the host Member State **19–067** is achieved *inter alia* as follows. A lawyer practising under his or her home-country professional title who has "effectively and regularly pursued for at least three years an activity in the host Member State in the law of that State including Community law shall, with a view to gaining admission to the profession of lawyer in the host Member State, be exempted from the conditions set out" in Article 14(1) of the PQ Directive.[91] The conditions referred to are those relating to the requirement of an adaptation period or aptitude test, as explained above, in the context of discussion of the PQ Directive. It is for the lawyer concerned to furnish the competent authority in the host Member State with proof of effective regular pursuit for a period of at least three years of an activity in the law of the host Member State.[92]

It is at first sight curious that a lawyer qualified in, say, Germany, and working with a law firm in Berlin, could transfer to that firm's London office, spend three years there working on mergers and acquisitions, or, for that matter, UK and EU competition law, and emerge as a solicitor, fully qualified to draw up a will or defend a

---

[87] Art.3(2).
[88] Art.6(1).
[89] Art.6(3).
[90] Art.7(1).
[91] Art.10, first sub-para. The text of Art.10 refers to Art.4(1) (b) of Dir. 89/48. Art.62(1) of the PQ Dir. repeals Dir. 89/48 with effect from October 20, 2007, and provides that references to Dirs repealed by Art.62 shall be understood as references to the PQ. Dir.
[92] Art. 10, second sub-para.

client in criminal proceedings before a magistrates' court. It certainly must be doubted whether three years of specialised legal practice of the kinds referred to could provide overall knowledge and under-standing of the laws and legal system of England and Wales. Related but slightly different misgivings were expressed by Luxembourg in a vigorously argued challenge to the validity of Directive 98/5. The Court of Justice considered these arguments in *Luxembourg v Parliament and Council*.[93] It is to be noted that Spain, the Nether-lands and the United Kingdom intervened in support of the Parlia-ment and Council, as, predictably, did the Commission. Luxembourg's main concern was that the Directive allowed migrant lawyers to set up permanent practice under home title despite lack of knowledge of host State law, which failed to protect the interests of consumers and the proper administration of justice. Yet the Court held that consumer protection and the administration of justice were adequately protected by various provisions of the Directive. The Court emphasised that a lawyer practising under his or her home-country professional title is required to do so under that title, so that consumers are informed that the professional to whom they entrust the defence of their interests has not obtained his or her qualifica-tion in the host Member State and that his or her initial training did not necessarily cover the host Member State's national law.[94] The Court also referred to the possibility of the host State requiring (a) that certain activities be reserved to host State lawyers, and/or (b) that the migrant "work in conjunction" with an appropriately qualified host State lawyer when representing a client in legal proceedings.[95] The Court added, *inter alia*, that the Directive makes a lawyer practising under home title subject not only to the rules of professional conduct applicable in his home State, but also to the same rules of professional conduct as lawyers practising under host State title,[96] and that the host Member State was entitled to require appropriate professional indemnity cover.[97] The final point made by the Court related to rules of professional conduct. Those rules applicable to lawyers generally entail, observed the Court:

> "like Article 3.1.3 of the Code of Professional Conduct adopted by the Council of the Bars and Law Societies of the European Union (CCBE), an obligation, breach of which may incur disciplinary sanctions, not to handle matters which the profes-sionals concerned know or ought to know they are not compe-tent to handle."

---

[93] Case C–168/98 *Grand Duchy of Luxembourg v European Parliament & Council* [2000] E.C.R. I–9131.
[94] *ibid.*, para.34.
[95] *ibid.*, para.35.
[96] *ibid.*, para.36.
[97] *ibid.*, para.37.

The Court concluded that the arguments of Luxembourg as regards consumer protection and the administration of justice should be rejected.

The Lawyers' Establishment Directive is certainly a significant initiative in promoting freedom of movement both for self-employed and salaried lawyers, and a possible model for transition from service provision to establishment for other professional activities. The difficulties which it appears to pose, both as regards practise under home title, and as regards acquisition of host State title after three years' practise under home title, probably loom rather larger in theory than in practice. The hypothetical example of the German lawyer practising in mergers and acquisitions, and then emerging to draft a will or defend a client in criminal proceedings, is more rhetorical flourish than balanced assessment. Those engaging in specialised legal practice, whatever their original qualifications and training, become speedily unfit for unprepared forays into other specialist fields, including those of the high street solicitors' practice. Furthermore, the discipline imposed by professional bodies, the need to secure insurance, and the imperatives of the market place, are, as the Court of Justice implies, not to be underestimated. In many if not most cases, a lawyer qualified in one Member State wishing to join a legal practice in another Member State, in which the laws differ substantially from that of the first, will find it essential to prepare for and to take an aptitude test in host State law; the legal practice or law firm he or she wishes to join will simply insist on that for obvious reasons. In other cases, to return to our hypothetical German lawyer with a taste for mergers and acquisitions, the "adaptation period" of practice under home title under the Lawyers' Establishment Directive, can provide for convenient and appropriate transition to the acquisition of a second legal qualification; not least for those whose practice is in fields of law containing a substantial element of EU law.

Further reading

Barnard, C., *The Substantive Law of the EU, The Four Freedoms* (OUP, Oxford, 2004), Chs 12–14.

Giesen, R., "Posting: Social Protection of Workers v Fundamental Freedoms?" (2003) 40 C.M.L.Rev. 143.

Hörnle, J., "Country of Origin Regulation in cross-border media: one step beyond the freedom to provide Services?" (2005) 54 I.C.L.Q. 89.

Spaventa, E., "From *Gebhard* to *Carpenter*: Towards a (non-)economic European constitution" (2004) 41 C.M.L.Rev., 743–773.

Spaventa, E., "*Caixa-Bank France*" (2005) 42 C.M.L.Rev. 1151.

CHAPTER 20

CORPORATE ESTABLISHMENT, CROSS-BORDER ACQUISITIONS, COMPANY LAW HARMONISATION, AND THE IMPACT OF NATIONAL TAX RULES ON THE INTERNAL MARKET

Guide to this Chapter: This chapter considers elements of four **20–001** distinct but related topics. The first is the application of the Treaty provisions on establishment to legal persons—companies and firms—and the significance of the case law of the Court of Justice on the interpretation of the relevant Treaty provisions. The right of establishment includes the right of undertakings to incorporate in a Member State of choice, and to engage in mergers and acquisitions across national frontiers. This leads into the second topic, which is cross-border acquisitions. Holding or acquiring shares in a company across national frontiers can involve exercise both of the right of establishment and the right of capital movement where the shareholding gives the investor definite influence over the company's decisions and allows the investor to determine its activities; where the cross-frontier investment does not give to the investor such influence it is known as "portfolio" investment and falls solely under the Treaty provisions on capital movement. It is the former aspect which is addressed in particular in this chapter and there is discussion of the compatibility with Community law of "special" or "golden" shares which grant national authorities powers of intervention in the decision making of corporate bodies—often formerly state owned and recently privatised companies providing services in fields such as energy or transport. The third topic addressed is company law harmonisation. The relevance of company law harmonisation to corporate establishment is that the Treaty basis for such harmonisation is the chapter on establishment—the rationale of company law harmonisation is not to harmonise company law for its own sake but to remove obstacles to the cross-frontier activities of individuals and companies. Thus mergers and acquisitions, as well as falling within the scope of directly applicable Treaty provisions on establishment (and on capital movement), may also be the subject matter of company law harmonisation. The final topic addressed is the extent to which national tax rules amount to obstacles to the exercise of fundamental freedoms which are either prohibited or eligible for harmonisation. The link here with corporate establishment is that while national tax rules may in principle and in practice hinder or make less attractive the exercise of any of the fundamental freedoms by individuals as well as companies, there is no doubt that disparities between national tax regimes pose particular problems for companies exercising the right of establishment via subsidiaries in other Member States. A chapter dealing with corporate establishment issues thus provides a logical place to consider the relationship between national tax rules and fundamental freedoms, and to give at least brief consideration to the possibility and desirability of harmonisation of those national tax rules of particular significance to cross-frontier corporate activity.

CORPORATE ESTABLISHMENT

Secondary establishment by companies and firms—agencies, branches and subsidiaries

The freedom of establishment is enjoyed by companies and firms, **20–002** as well as by natural persons. Article 48 EC, first paragraph, provides:

> "Companies or firms formed in accordance with the law of a Member State and having their registered office, central administration or principal place of business within the Community shall, for the purposes of this Chapter, be treated in the same way as natural persons who are nationals of Member States."

Article 48 EC states furthermore that:

> " 'Companies or firms' means companies or firms constituted under civil or commercial law, including co-operative societies, and other legal persons governed by public or private law, save for those which are non-profit making."

A company formed in accordance with the law of a Member State is entitled to exercise the right of establishment if it has its registered office, its central administration, or its principal place of business within the Community.

The Court has said that the "immediate consequence" of Article 48 EC is that "those companies are entitled to carry on their business in another Member State through an agency, branch of subsidiary", and that the location of their registered office, central administration or principal place of business "serves as the connecting factor with the legal system of a particular State in the same way as does nationality in the case of a natural person".[1]

The Court has also held that Articles 43 EC and 48 EC confer a **20–003** "right of exit" on corporate bodies:

> "Even though those provisions are directed mainly at ensuring that foreign nationals and companies are treated in the host Member State in the same way as nationals of that State, they

---

[1] Case C–212/97 *Centros Ltd v Erhvervs- og Selskabsstyrelsen* [1999] E.C.R. I–1459, para.20, citing Case 79/85 *Segers v Bedrijfsvereniging voor Bank-en Verzekeringswegen, Groothandel en Vrije Beroepen* [1986] E.C.R. 2375, para.13; Case 270/83 *Commission v France* [1986] E.C.R. 273, para.18; Case C–330/91 *R v Inland Revenue Commissioners ex parte Commerzbank AG* [1993] E.C.R. I–4017, para.13; Case C–264/96 *ICI v Colmer (Her Majesty's Inspector of Taxes)* E.C.R. I–4695, para.20.

also prohibit the Member State of origin from hindering the establishment in another Member State of one of its nationals or of a company incorporated under its legislation which comes within the definition contained in Article [48]"[2]

As the Court has observed:

"In the case of a company, the right of establishment is generally exercised by the setting up of agencies, branches or subsidiaries, as is expressly provided for in the second sentence of the first paragraph of Article [43]."[3]

An undertaking of one Member State which maintains a permanent presence in another "comes within the scope of the provisions of the Treaty on the right of establishment, even if that presence does not take the form of a branch or agency, but consists merely of an office managed by the undertaking's own staff or by a person who is independent but authorised to act on a permanent basis for the undertaking, as would be the case with an agency."[4]

The Court has held that to allow a Member State in which a company carried on its business to treat that company in a different manner solely because its registered office was in another Member State would deprive Article 48 EC of all meaning.[5] Furthermore, discriminatory tax treatment as between companies of the host Member State and branches of companies registered in other Member States is contrary to Article 43 EC, and such discrimination cannot be justified on the ground that companies registered in other Member States are at liberty to establish themselves by setting up a subsidiary in order to have the benefit of the tax treatment in question.[6] As the Court has emphasised:

"The second sentence of the first paragraph of Article [43] expressly leaves traders free to choose the appropriate legal form in which to pursue their activities in another Member State and that freedom of choice must not be limited by discriminatory tax provisions."[7]

---

[2] *ibid.*, para.16.

[3] *ibid.*, para.17.

[4] Case 205/84 *Commission v Germany* [1986] CCR 3755, para.21.

[5] Case 79/85 *Segers v Bedrijfsvereniging voor Bank- en Verzekeringswegen, Groothandel en Verije Beroepen* [1986] E.C.R. 2375, para.14, citing Case 270/83 *Commission v France* [1986] E.C.R. 273, para.18.

[6] Case 270/83 *Commission v France* [1986] E.C.R. 273; and see Case C–307/97 *Compagnie de Saint-gobain, Zweighniederlassung Deutschland v Finanzamt Aachen-Innenstadt* [1999] E.C.R. I–6161.

[7] Case 270/83 *Commission v France* [1986] E.C.R. 273, para.22.

The *Sodemare* case indicates that even non-discriminatory restrictions on the legal form in which a company incorporated in another Member State may carry on business in the host State will require justification if they are to be compatible with Article 43 EC.[8]

Right of primary establishment of companies

Article 43 EC draws a distinction between setting up a primary **20–004** establishment in another Member State, and setting up a secondary establishment, in the form of a branch or a subsidiary. In the former case the only qualifying characteristic is the nationality of a Member State, while in the latter there must be an existing establishment in one of the Member States.[9] The General Programme construed this qualification as requiring, in the case of companies having only the seat prescribed by their statutes in the Community, a "real and continuous link with the economy of a Member State."[10] In *Segers*[11] the Court of Justice regarded a company registered in one Member State and undertaking *all* its business through a subsidiary in another Member State as entitled to exercise its right of establishment in the second Member State. Thus registration of a company in a Member State of itself amounts to establishment in that State, even if the company does no business in that Member State, and all its shareholders are nationals of the Member State in which it transacts all its business through an agency branch or subsidiary (for such was the position in *Segers*). In *Centros*[12] the Court considered a situation in which Danish nationals resident in Denmark and carrying on business in Denmark set up a limited liability company in England whose only business activities would be carried out by a branch in Denmark. The share capital of the English company was £100, and the sole reason the Danish nationals set up a company in the United Kingdom rather than Denmark, was to secure the advantages of limited liability without having to meet the cost of the £20,000 minimum capital requirement then prevailing in Denmark. When the Danish nationals sought to register the Danish branch of the company, the Danish authorities refused to do so, since that branch would be the principal establishment of the English company, which would do no business in the United Kingdom, and since the sole purpose of setting up the English company was the avoidance of

---

[8] Case C–70/95 *Sodemare SA, etc. v regione Lombardia* [1997] E.C.R. I–3395.
[9] The second sentence of Art.43 EC refers to the setting up of agencies, branches or subsidiaries by nationals of any Member State *established* in any Member State (emphasis added).
[10] Title I, [1974] O.J. Spec. Ed., Second Series, IX, p.7.
[11] Case 79/85 *Segers v bestuur van de Bedrijfsvereniging voor Bank- en Verzeleringswezen* [1986] E.C.R. 2375.
[12] Case C–212/97 *Centros Ltd v Erhvervs- og Selskabsstyrelsen* [1999] E.C.R. I–1458. See also *Kamer van Koophandel en Fabrieken voor Amsterdam v Inspire Art Ltd*. [2003] E.C.R. I–10155.

Danish minimum capital requirements. The Danish authorities regarded the situation as in reality being internal to Denmark, but made it clear that they would have registered the branch if the company had been also carrying on business in the United Kingdom. The Court of Justice referred to *Segers*, confirming that a company formed in one Member State, for the sole purpose of establishing itself in another, where its main or even sole business activities were to be carried on, could rely on the right of establishment, and added that the fact that the company was set up by nationals of the latter Member State resident in that State for the sole purpose of avoiding the minimum capital requirements of that State was immaterial.[13] The Court's judgment is most worthy of remark for its strong endorsement of the rights of individuals to choose the least restrictive corporate form of those available in the Member States as the vehicle of their entrepreneurial ambitions. The Court stated:

> "The provisions of the Treaty on freedom of establishment are intended specifically to enable companies formed in accordance with the law of a Member State and having their registered office, central administration or principal place of business within the Community to pursue activities in other Member States through an agency, branch or subsidiary.
>
> That being so, the fact that a national of a Member State who wishes to set up a company chooses to form it in the Member State whose rules of company law seem to him the least restrictive and to set up branches in other Member States cannot, in itself, constitute an abuse of the right of establishment. The right to form a company in accordance with the law of a Member State and to set up branches in other Member States is inherent in the exercise, in a single market, of the freedom of establishment guaranteed by the Treaty."[14]

The Court held that the refusal in such circumstances of the national authorities in which the branch was to be formed to register that branch amounted to an infringement of the right of establishment, which could not be justified by mandatory requirements in the public interest, or on the ground of improper circumvention of national rules.[15] The Danish authorities argued that refusing to register the branch was the least restrictive means available of reinforcing the financial soundness of companies so as to protect the interests of public and private creditors, and in particular public creditors, who, unlike private creditors, were not in a position to secure their debts by obtaining personal guarantees from the directors of debtor

---

[13] *ibid.*, paras 17, 18.
[14] *ibid.*, paras 26, 27.
[15] As to the argument alleging improper circumvention of national rules, see Ch.19, at p.793.

companies.[16] The Court did not deny that interests such as those referred to might in principle justify measures such as those in issue, but rejected the argument on the ground that it was possible to adopt measures which were less restrictive, or which interfered less with fundamental freedoms, by, for example, making it possible in law for public creditors to obtain the necessary guarantees.[17] This is a radical judgment. It might be said to imply the Court's lack of faith in the efficacy of capital requirements. And it might have contributed to a tendency to eliminate capital requirements for private companies.[18]

It seemed initially that enjoyment in practice of the right of establishment endorsed by the Court in this case might be subject to limitation *vis-à-vis* those Member States which do not recognise that a company may be validly incorporated in a Member State other than that of its company headquarters or central administration. While the *Centros* case nominally involved a "branch" of the company in question, that "branch" comprised its sole place of business and its central administration.

A change of primary establishment involving a transfer of com- **20–005** pany headquarters or central management may be hindered by national legal provisions to the effect: (a) that a company transferring its central administration out of the jurisdiction loses it corporate personality; or (b) that a company wishing to establish its central administration within the jurisdiction must be newly constituted there. These requirements amount to a refusal to recognise the legal personality of a company incorporated in a Member State other than where its actual central administration is located. This principle is sometimes described as the "real seat" doctrine.[19] It had always been arguable that to deny recognition to a company satisfying the requirements of the first paragraph of Article 48 EC amounts to a denial of that company's right of establishment.[20] However, in *Ex parte Daily Mail* and *General Trust Plc* the Court held that the differences in national legislation concerning the required connecting factor between a company and the Member State under which it is incorporated, and the question whether—and if so how—the registered office or real head office of a company incorporated under national law may be transferred from one Member State to

---

[16] *ibid.*, para.32.

[17] *ibid.*, para.37.

[18] See Becht, Mayer and Wagner, "Corporate Mobility Comes to Europe: The Evidence", a paper presented in November 2005 which suggests that *Centros* has generated regulatory responses in *inter alia* France, which in 2000 introduced legislation which has led to the abolition of minimum capital requirements for the SARL.

[19] See R. R. Drury, "Migrating Companies" (1999) 24 E.L.Rev. 354; for a discussion of "incorporation theory jurisdictions" and "real seat jurisdictions" see Wymeersch, "The Transfer of the Company's Seat in European Company Law", (2003) C.M.L.Rev. 661, 666–673.

[20] Everling, *The Right of Establishment in the Common Market* (CCH, Chicago, 1964), p.71.

another, were problems which were not resolved by the Treaty rules concerning the right of establishment, but were to be dealt with by future legislation or conventions.[21] It seemed to follow that Articles 43 and 48 of the Treaty could not be interpreted as conferring on companies incorporated under the law of a Member State a right to transfer their central management and control and their central administration to another Member State while retaining their status as companies incorporated under the legislation of the first Member State.[22] Did the *Daily Mail* ruling mean that the corporate establishment rights upheld by the Court in *Centros* could be resisted if asserted against a host State subscribing to the "real seat" doctrine?

The Court gave a negative response to this question in *Überseering*.[23] In this case the Court considered a situation in which a company incorporated under Netherlands law, Überseering BV, acquired land in Düsseldorf, engaged NCC to undertake work on the site, then subsequently sued NCC in Düsseldorf for breach of contract in relation to that work. Prior to initiation of the legal proceedings in question, German nationals residing in Düsseldorf had acquired all the shares in Überseering BV. The central administration of the company thus became established in Germany. Under German law a company could only be recognised if it was incorporated under the law applicable in the place where its actual central administration was located. The Bundesgerichtschof considered whether, in view of the *Centros* case, the Treaty provisions on freedom of establishment precluded application of the German "real seat" doctrine when the consequence would be to refuse to recognise the legal capacity of a company validly incorporated in another Member State and to deny its capacity to bring legal proceedings in Germany. On a reference for a preliminary ruling the Court of Justice regarded the *Daily Mail* case as concerning only the compatibility with Article 43 EC of restrictions imposed by the law of the State of incorporation of a company, and did not resolve the question raised in *Überseering* as to whether a Member State was entitled to refuse to recognise the legal personality of a company validly incorporated under the law of another Member State. The Court held that the companies and firms referred to in Article 48 EC which were formed in accordance with the law of a Member State and had their registered office, central administration or principal

---

[21] *R v HM Treasury and Commissioners of Inland Revenue ex parte Daily Mail and General Trust Plc* [1988] E.C.R. 5483, para.23.
[22] *ibid.*, para.24. Tridimas argued with foresight that the *Daily Mail* limitation on the scope of Art.43 EC only applied to restrictions imposed by the Member State of origin on the right of establishment and did not authorise a Member State of destination to refuse to recognise a transfer of primary establishment by a company authorised so to do by rules of the Member State of origin; "Case Law on Corporate Entities" (1993) 13 Y.E.L. 335.
[23] Case C–208/00 *Überseering BV v Nordic Construction Company Baumanagement GmbH (NCC)* [2002] E.C.R. I–9919.

place of business within the Community, were "entitled to carry on their business in another Member State,"[24] and added that "[a] necessary precondition for the exercise of the freedom of establishment is the recognition of those companies by any Member State in which they wish to establish themselves."[25] The German rules in issue left a company in the position of Überseering BV with no choice but to reincorporate in Germany if it wished to enforce before a German court its rights under a contract entered into with a company incorporated under German law. It followed in the Court's view that the refusal by the German courts to recognise the legal capacity and capacity to be a party to legal proceedings of a company validly incorporated in another Member State constituted a restriction on freedom of establishment.[26] While the Court accepted that it was "not inconceivable" that overriding requirements relating to the general interest, such as the protection of the interests of creditors, minority shareholders, employees and even the taxation authorities might, in certain circumstances and subject to certain conditions, justify restrictions on freedom of establishment, such objectives could not justify a denial of legal capacity and capacity to bring legal proceedings, which was tantamount to "an outright negation of the freedom of establishment conferred on companies by Articles 43 and 48 EC."[27]

A question increasingly asked after *Überseering* is whether application by a Member State of the "real seat" doctrine to deny to companies incorporated under its law the right to move their primary establishment to another Member State without dissolution under the law of the first Member State and reincorporation under the law of the second, amounts to a restriction on the right of establishment.[28] As noted above, *Überseering* distinguishes the *Daily Mail* case and does not call into question the reasoning or ruling in the latter case. Ebke nevertheless argues that it is "inconceivable" that the Court would treat an "emigration" or "exit" case (such as that under discussion) more restrictively than an "immigration" or "entry" case such as *Überseering*—in other words the Court of Justice is bound to modify its ruling in the *Daily Mail* case, or its interpretation of that ruling.[29] Wymeersch considers that "emigration should, from the angle of free movement, be dealt with along the same lines as immigration."[30] There must at the very least be a

---

[24] *ibid.*, paras 56, 57.

[25] *ibid.*, para.59.

[26] *ibid.*, paras 78–82.

[27] *ibid.*, para.93.

[28] See e.g. Wymeersch, "The Transfer of the Company's Seat in European Company Law", (2003) C.M.L.Rev. 661, 690.

[29] Ebke, "The European Conflict-of-Corporate-Laws Revolution: *Überseering, Inspire Art,* and Beyond" [2005] E.B.L.R. 13, 23.

[30] Wymeersch, "The Transfer of the Company's Seat in European Company Law" (2003) C.M.L.Rev. 661, 677.

real possibility that this will indeed be the approach of the Court of Justice in future cases. It should be added that national systems of company law which apply the real seat principle may place restrictions not only on the right of establishment of companies incorporated under their laws, but also on the rights of individuals and companies seeking to acquire control of companies incorporated under their laws. It is explained later that an individual or company acquiring a controlling stake in the shares of a company registered in another Member State is exercising the right of establishment.[31] Denial of Überseering BV's right to sue was assessed by the Court of Justice in terms of a restriction on the right of establishment of the latter company, but that denial operated no less as a restriction on the right of establishment of the German nationals residing in Düsseldorf, who had acquired all the shares in that company, thereby precipitating a shift in its central administration from the Netherlands to Germany, and resulting in the loss of the company's right to sue in a German court. As the proceedings in *Überseering* illustrate, one consequence of investors residing in one Member State buying most or all of the shares in a company from shareholders residing in another Member State, may be a shift in the real seat of that company from the second Member State to the first. If such a purchase of shares results in a transfer to another Member State of the real seat of a company incorporated under the law of a Member State applying the real seat doctrine, the effect may be that acquisition of the company results in its non-existence. If the principles reflected in *Überseering* apply to "immigration" or "entry" situations but not to "emigration" or "exit" situations, it would mean that German shareholders precipitating a shift of the real seat of a Netherlands company by acquiring all its shares would be protected by the right of establishment, whereby Netherlands shareholders precipitating shift of the real seat of a German company by acquiring all its shares would not be.

The judgments of the Court of Justice in *Centros* and *Überseering* were bold initiatives of the Court. It is not inconceivable that *Centros* might have been decided differently. The reference in Article 43 EC to the right to set up secondary establishments in other Member States being reserved to nationals of Member States *established* in a Member State could have been interpreted as requiring more of a limited company than that it be *registered* in a Member State, while undertaking its entire business elsewhere. Nor is it inconceivable that *Überseering* might have been decided differently, as the *Daily Mail* judgment suggested that it would be. But in each case such an alternative reading of the Treaty would have been unfortunate, because these judgments go a long way towards giving reality to

---

[31] Below at p.853, and see Case C–208/00 *Überseering BV v Nordic Construction Company Baumanagement GmbH (NCC)* [2002] E.C.R. I–9919, para.77

corporate establishment in the internal market, and to promoting regulatory competition. A provisional assessment of the evidence by Becht, Mayer and Wagner indicates that there is a highly significant post *Centros* and *Überseering* effect in the use of private limited companies incorporated in England and Wales for the conduct of business in other Member States, accompanied by regulatory responses to liberalise or consider liberalising company law in France, Spain, Germany and the Netherlands.[32]

Parent company may implement uniform advertising concept at Community level through subsidiaries in other Member States

In *Pfeiffer Großhandel*[33] the Court considered the compatibility **20–006** with Article 43 EC of a restraining order pursuant to national law which prevented an Austrian subsidiary of a German parent operating 139 discount stores in Austria from using a trade name owned by the parent company which the subsidiary had begun to use to market its goods. The parent company was active in the discount store sector in Germany, Italy, Spain, the Czech Republic and Hungary under the trade name in question and the parent company's aim was for all its stores throughout Europe to adopt the same style of presentation, making it possible to use the same advertising material across Europe and to go on to develop a "corporate identity". The Court stated:

> "A restraining order of the type sought by the plaintiff in the main proceedings operates to the detriment of undertakings whose seat is in another Member State where they lawfully use a trade name which they would like to use beyond the boundaries of that State. Such an order is liable to constitute an impediment to the realization by those undertakings of a uniform advertising concept at Community level since it may force them to adjust the presentation of the businesses they operate according to the place of establishment."[34]

It is possible to see in this judgment the basis of a potentially far-reaching principle that any national measure which might constitute an impediment to the realization by a company of a "uniform advertising concept at Community level" is to be treated as prima facie contrary to Article 43 EC and must accordingly be justified by imperative requirements in the public interest (the restriction in issue in *Pfeiffer* was in fact held to be justified on intellectual property grounds).[35]

---

[32] See Becht, Mayer and Wagner, "Corporate Mobility Comes to Europe: The Evidence", a paper presented in November 2005 in Oxford.
[33] Case C–255/97 *Pfeiffer Großhandel Gmbh v Löwa Warenahndel Gmbh* [1999] E.C.R. I–2835.
[34] *ibid.*, at para.20.
[35] For a narrower analysis, see Ch.19, p.773.

National rules reinforcing barriers to market entry hinder market access of subsidiaries and must be justified

20–007   In the *CaixaBank France* case[36] the Court was asked to indicate whether national rules of a Member State prohibiting the remuneration of 'sight' current accounts in euros constitute restrictions on the freedom of establishment prohibited by Article 43 EC in so far as they apply to the subsidiary formed in that Member State by a legal person from another Member State. The Court's analysis was as follows:

> " That prohibition hinders credit institutions which are subsidiaries of foreign companies in raising capital from the public, by depriving them of the possibility of competing more effectively, by paying remuneration on sight accounts, with the credit institutions traditionally established in the Member State of establishment, which have an extensive network of branches and therefore greater opportunities than those subsidiaries for raising capital from the public.
>
> Where credit institutions which are subsidiaries of foreign companies seek to enter the market of a Member State, competing by means of the rate of remuneration paid on sight accounts constitutes one of the most effective methods to that end. Access to the market by those establishments is thus made more difficult by such a prohibition."[37]

There seem to be two distinct strands to this reasoning. One (in the first paragraph cited) is that the national rule in question reinforces a barrier to market entry. The barrier to market entry is the existence of an extensive network of branches, and the rule prohibiting the payment of interest reinforces that barrier by prohibiting a potential means of competing with established market operators. The second strand (see the second paragraph cited) is simply that prohibiting a potential means of competing with established market operators is a restriction on access to the market which must be justified.

Harmonisation at Community level to achieve freedom of establishment

Article 44(1) and 44(2)(f) EC
20–008   Article 44(1) EC provides that in order to attain freedom of establishment as regards a particular activity, the Council, acting in accordance with the procedure referred to in Article 251 EC and

---

[36] Case C–442/02 *CaixaBank France v Ministère de l'Économie, des Finances et de l'Industrie* [2004] E.C.R. I–8961.
[37] *ibid.*, paras 13–14.

after consulting the Economic and Social Committee, shall act by means of directives. Under Article 44(2) EC the responsibilities of the Council and Commission are more specifically defined.

Article 44(2)(f) EC (which refers to every branch of activity) provides lawmaking competence for *inter alia* the abolition of restrictions on the transfer of personnel from the main establishment to managerial or supervisory posts in its branches or subsidiaries. In the event of such personnel holding the nationality of a Member State, they will, of course, be entitled to assert an independent right of entry and residence under the provisions of the Treaty guaranteeing freedom of movement for workers.[38] The implication is that certain senior personnel may be transferred under Article 44(2)(f) EC who would not otherwise be entitled to a right of residence under the Treaty. The principal reason for such lack of entitlement is likely to be that they are nationals of third countries. An undertaking providing services in another Member State may bring its workforce with it, irrespective of whether the employees concerned enjoy an independent right of free movement.[39] It would seem to follow that in principle a national of a third country may be posted from the main establishment to a *senior* post in a branch or subsidiary in another Member State, and that workers employed by an undertaking established in a Member State may, *irrespective of status*, be posted on a temporary basis to another Member State under Article 49 EC. This distinction between the scope of Article 43 and 49 EC as regards the status of employees who may be entitled to residence as a result of a posting would seem to reflect the permanent nature of establishment as against the temporary and sporadic nature of the provision of services, and the intent of the draftsman of the Treaty to place a clear limit on the duty of Member States to grant a right of residence to nationals of third countries. It might be questioned however whether it is necessary to adopt rules under Article 44(2)(f) EC in order to abolish the restrictions on the transfer of the staff referred to, since the objective in question would seem achievable by means of the direct effect of Article 43 EC.

Company law harmonisation to facilitate freedom of establishment

The prospect of firms incorporated under the law of one Member **20–009** State being free to establish themselves in another led those who drafted the Treaty to insert Article 44(2)(g) EC, which requires the

---

[38] See Ch.18.
[39] Case C–113/89 *Rush Portuguesa Ldc* [1990] E.C.R. I–1417; C–369/96 *Criminal proceedings against Jean-Claude Arblade and Arblade & Fils SARL* [1999] E.C.R. I–8453; Case C–49/98 *alarte Sociedade de Construção Civil Ldã* [2001] E.C.R. I–7831; Case C–445/03; *Commission of the European Communities v Grand Duchy of Luxemburg* [2004] E.C.R. I–10191. And see Dir.96/71 on the posting of workers in the framework of the provision of services [1996] O.J. L18/1.

co-ordination of the provisions of national company law which safeguard the position of investors and "others". The rationale of such harmonisation is that in its absence the existence of different national rules could discourage the exercise of the right of establishment, and deter third parties from dealing with companies having their seats in other Member States. This provision provides the legal basis for company law harmonisation, which is considered later in this Chapter.

Mergers and acquisitions as aspects of freedom of corporate establishment

20–010   The Court has held that "a national of a Member State who has a holding in the capital of a company established in another Member State which gives him definite influence over the company's decisions and allows him to determine its activities is exercising his right of establishment".[40] It follows that an individual or company seeking to acquire such a holding would also fall within the scope of the right of establishment, and this is consistent with the adoption of a directive on takeovers under Article 44(1) EC, which is considered later in this chapter. It might also follow that certain activities of the board of a target company which have the aim of frustrating a takeover bid might amount to restrictions on the freedom of establishment of the bidding company, and this too is considered later in this Chapter.

The Court of Justice has confirmed that mergers fall within the scope of Articles 43 and 48 EC. In *SEVIC Systems AG*[41] the Court of Justice considered a reference from a national court in which a German company had challenged the refusal of the competent German authority to register in the national commercial register the merger between the German company in question and a company established in Luxembourg. The ground for refusal was that the German law on company transformations provided only for mergers between companies established in Germany. The merger contract concluded in 2002 beween the German and Luxembourg company provided for the dissolution without liquidation of the latter company and the transfer of the whole of its assets to the former, without any change in the name of the transferee. The Court of Justice rejected contentions of the German Government and the Netherlands Government that Article 43 EC had no application to a merger situation such as that in issue in the national proceedings, in the following terms:

[40] Case C–251/98 *C. Baars v Inspecteur der Belastingen Particulieren/Ondernemingen Gorinchem* [2000] E.C.R. I–2787, paras 21, 22.
[41] Case C–411/03 Judgment of December 13, 2005.

> "Cross-border merger operations, like other company transfor-
> mation operations, respond to the needs for co-operation and
> consolidation between companies established in different Mem-
> ber States. They constitute particular methods of exercise of the
> freedom of establishment, important for the proper functioning
> of the internal market, and are therefore amongst those
> economic activities in respect of which Member States are
> required to comply with the freedom of establishment laid
> down by Article 43 EC."[42]

The Court considered that since under national rules recourse to
such a means of transformation was not possible where one of the
companies was established in a Member State other than the Federal
Republic of Germany, German law established a difference in
treatment between companies according to the internal or cross-
border nature of the merger, which was likely to deter the exercise of
the freedom of establishment laid down by the Treaty.[43]

*The Court also rejected the argument that such a blanket restriction
was justified on proportionality grounds.[44]*

CROSS-BORDER ACQUISITIONS

Free Movement of Capital
  In considering cross-border investment issues as they affect **20–011**
acquisition it is necessary to consider the Treaty provisions on
capital movement as well as those on the right of establishment.
Within the framework of the Chapter on capital and payments, all
restrictions on the movement of capital and on payments between
Member States and between Member States and third countries are
prohibited.[45] These provisions are without prejudice to the right of
Member States to apply relevant provisions of their tax law which
distinguish between taxpayers who are not in the same situation with
regard to their place of residence or with regard to the place where
their capital is invested.[46] This possibility is considered later in this
Chapter.[47] Member States may also take all requisite measures to
prevent infringements of national law and regulations, in particular

---

[42] *ibid.*, paras 18–19.
[43] *ibid.*, paras 22–23.
[44] *ibid.*, paras 24–30.
[45] Art.56 EC.
[46] Art.58(1)(a) EC.
[47] p.904.

in the field of taxation and the prudential supervision of financial institutions, or to lay down procedures for the declaration of capital movements for purposes of administrative or statistical information, or to take measures which are justified on grounds of public policy or public security.[48] The provisions of the Chapter on capital and payments are stated to be without prejudice to the applicability of restrictions on the right of establishment which are compatible with the Treaty.[49] The rights of Member States to apply the foregoing national measures shall not however constitute a means of arbitrary discrimination or a disguised restriction on the free movement of capital and payments.[50]

Meaning of "capital movement"—"direct investment" and "portfolio investment"

20–012   Although the Treaty does not define the terms "movement of capital" and "payments", the case law of the Court of Justice has indicated that Directive 88/361,[51] together with the nomenclature annexed to it, may be used for the purposes of defining what constitutes a capital movement.[52] Capital movements comprising "direct investment" may be contrasted with "portfolio investment". Direct investment is defined as follows by the Court of Justice in *Commission v Belgium*[53]:

> "Points I and III in the nomenclature set out in Annex I to Directive 88/361, and the explanatory notes appearing in that annex, indicate that direct investment in the form of participation in an undertaking by means of a shareholding or the acquisition of securities on the capital market constitute capital movements within the meaning of Article [56] of the Treaty. The explanatory notes state that direct investment is characterised, in particular, by the possibility of participating effectively in the management of a company or in its control."

Referring to the same Directive, the Commission describes "portfolio investment" as follows in its 1997 Communication on Certain Legal Aspects concerning intra-EU Investment:[54]

---

[48] Art.58(1)(b) EC.
[49] Art.58(2) EC.
[50] Art.58(3) EC.
[51] [1988] O.J. L178/5
[52] Case C–222/97 *Trummer and Mayer* [1999] E.C.R. I–1661, paras 20, 21.
[53] Case C–503/99 [2002] E.C.R. I–4809, para.38.
[54] [1997] O.J. C220/15. See also The Commission's 2005 Communication on Intra-EU investment in the financial services sector [2005] O.J. C293/2.

"In the Directive, the heading 'Acquisition . . . of domestic securities . . .' includes, among others, the transaction 'acquisition by non-residents' of shares and bonds in domestic companies on pure financial investment grounds, that is, without the aim of exerting any influence in the management of the company. Thus, this transaction is considered as a form of capital movement. It is also usually known in the financial literature as 'portfolio investment'."

Cross-border acquisitions involve free movement of capital and right of establishment

In the present context, *viz.*, cross-border acquisitions, it is direct **20–013** investment which will be considered, without losing sight of parallel application of the right of establishment. In its 1997 Communication referred to above, the Commission noted that[55]:

"At the same time, the acquisition of controlling stakes in a domestic company by an EU investor, in addition to being a form of capital movement, is also covered under the scope of the right of establishment . . . Thus, nationals of other EU Member States should be free to acquire controlling stakes, exercise voting rights and manage domestic companies under the same conditions laid down in a given Member State for its own nationals (i.e. the application of the 'national treatment' principle to other EU investors)."

National rules on surveillance and control of cross-border investments and free movement of capital

National rules requiring the prior declaration of capital move- **20–014** ments amount in principle to restrictions on capital movement but may be justified for the purposes of administrative or statistical information, or to take measures which are justified on grounds of public policy or public security.[56]

National rules requiring prior declarations must not be subject to disproportionate penalties, nor require those concerned to provide more information than they can reasonably be expected to have.[57] In the case of direct foreign investments which constitute a genuine and sufficiently serious threat to public policy or public security, a system

---

[55] *ibid.*, para.4.
[56] Art.58(1)(b) of the EC Treaty; Joined Cases C–358/93 and C–416/93 *Bordessa* [1995] E.C.R. I–361.
[57] Case 52/77 *Cayrol* [1977] E.C.R. 2261; Case 179/78 *Rivoira* [1979] E.C.R. 651.

of prior declaration may prove to be inadequate to counter such a threat, and call for a system of prior authorisation.[58] National rules which make a direct investment subject to prior authorisation require justification, even if consent is deemed to be given if no objection is made after the lapse of a time-limit.[59] In the case of direct foreign investments, the difficulty in identifying and blocking capital once it has entered a Member State may make it necessary to prevent, at the outset, transactions which would adversely affect public policy or public security.[60]

Systems of prior authorisation must comply with the principle of legal certainty. A system of prior authorisation which does not make it clear which investments require authorisation will not comply with the principle of legal certainty.[61] Nor will a system of prior authorisation which indicates which transactions require authorisation but which gives "no indication whatever as to the specific objective circumstances in which prior authorisation will be granted or refused. Such lack of precision does not enable individuals to be apprised of the extent of their rights and obligations deriving from Article [56] of the Treaty."[62] The Court has observed that "Such a wide discretionary power constitutes a serious interference with the free movement of capital, and may have the effect of excluding it altogether."[63]

Restrictions on capital movement arising from "special" shares or "golden" shares

The trend to privatisation

20–015   In recent years a definite trend has been discernible in the Member States—the tendency to move wholly or partly into the private sector undertakings previously owned and controlled by the State and carrying on economic activities of public importance, e.g. energy supply, air-lines, telecommunications, etc. With the reduction in equity participation by the State in the undertakings carrying on such activities came a reduction in the control exercised by the State both in the strategic direction and the day to day management of these undertakings. A second and linked trend has been to set up in place of public undertakings new undertakings in which public authorities and private investors provide investment and participate

---

[58] Case C–54/99 *Association Église de Scientologie de Paris and the Prime Minister* [2000] E.C.R. I–1335.
[59] *ibid.*
[60] *ibid.*
[61] *ibid.*
[62] Case C–483/99 *Commission v France* [2002] E.C.R. I–4781, para.50.
[63] *ibid.*, para.51.

to greater or lesser extent according to circumstances in corporate governance. Because of national perceptions of the importance of the services provided by such undertakings safeguards of various kinds have been adopted when privatizations have taken place or when joint public and private ventures have been established.

"Special" or "golden" shares

(a) The Commission's 1997 Communication. The safeguards **20–016** referred to above have sometimes taken the form of "special" or "golden" shares, being rights of the government to appoint directors and/or veto certain decisions of the company relating to the mortgage or transfer of important assets of the company in question, and/ or to restrict acquisition of a controlling interest in the company.

In the 1997 Communication mentioned above, the Commission referred to certain types of national arrangements which amounted in its view to unlawful restrictions on the free movement of capital/ right of establishment. The arrangements included:

— a "prohibition on investors from another EU country acquiring more than a limited amount of voting shares in domestic companies . . ."
— "measures applied without distinction to all investors, . . . in particular general authorisation procedures whereby, for example, any investor (EU and national alike) wanting to acquire a stake in a domestic company above a certain threshold . . . [must be authorised]
— the rights given to national authorities, in derogation of company law, to veto certain major decisions to be taken by the company, as well as the imposition of a requirement for the nomination of some directors as a means of exercising the right of veto, etc."

The first category of measure referred to above is discriminatory on grounds of nationality. Measures of this kind clearly infringe Article 43 EC. The second category covers restrictions on access to the market, which are incompatible with Article 43 EC in the absence of justification—a requirement of a general authorisation for the acquisition of property or shares is in principle contrary to Article 56 EC.[64] The third category referred to is less obviously, or was less obviously at the time—a restriction requiring justification as regards either the movement of capital or the right of establishment. The basis for this proposition in the Commission's document is that such

---

[64] See e.g. Case C–302/97 *Klaus Konle* [1999] E.C.R. I–3099.

a power hindered or made less attractive the exercise of fundamental freedoms within the meaning of the *Gebhard* formulation.[65] But the proposition that the power of a national authority to intervene in the decision making of a company is itself a restriction on capital movement/freedom of establishment was not clearly established at the time of the issue of the Commission's Communication. Subsequent infraction proceedings launched by the Commission were to confirm that the analysis of the Commission contained in its 1997 Communication was correct.

20–017 (b) A test case Strategy? The Commission launched what was in effect a test case strategy to combat the "special share" phenomenon which it saw as a threat to cross-border acquisitions. Its first action was against Italy and challenged Italian rules providing for the reserve of special powers to the State and public bodies in privatised companies in the defence, transport, telecommunications, energy and other public service sectors. The special powers included a power to grant express approvals, a power to appoint a minimum of one or several directors and an auditor, and the right to veto certain decisions. The Commission relied on its Communication of 1997 before the Court of Justice, citing relevant parts of it as established law, which the Commission considered it to be. The Italian rules challenged by the Commission proved to be something of a "soft target", since Italy conceded the case, and the Court held the contested measures to be incompatible with the provisions on capital movement and establishment.[66] Since important issues in the case had been conceded, the Court's judgment was not as convincing a vindication of the legal position of the Commission on "special shares" as it might have been. The Advocate General in subsequent "special share" cases, Mr D. Ruiz-Jarabo Colomer, described the ruling as "disturbing" since it seemed to accept that the parties were free to decide how an action for failure to fulfil obligations under the Treaty was to be disposed of. He suggested that the Court of Justice attribute no significance to this precedent.[67]

The most vigorously contested of the "special share" cases were those brought against France, Belgium and the United Kingdom.[68] In all three cases the Commission was successful in upholding its view of the ways in which "special shares" amounted to restrictions on capital movement, though in the proceedings against Belgium the Court accepted that the restrictions in issue were justified.

---

[65] Case C–55/94 *Gebhard v Consiglio dell'Ordine degli Avvocati e Procuratori di Milano* [1995] E.C.R. I–4165, para.37.

[66] Case C–58/99 *Commission v Italian Republic* [2000] E.C.R. I–3811.

[67] See Case C–483/99 *Commission v France* [2002] E.C.R. I–4781, paras 76–77 of Opinion; Case C–503/99 *Commission v Belgium* [2002] E.C.R. I–4809, paras 76–77 of Opinion.

[68] See Case C–483/99 *Commission v France* [2002] E.C.R. I–4781; Case C–503/99 *Commission v Belgium* [2002] E.C.R. I–4809; and Case C–98/01 *Commission v United Kingdom* [2003] E.C.R. I–4641.

(c) France's "golden share" in Elf-Aquitaine. In the proceedings 20–018
against France the Commission challenged French rights attached by
legislation to the French State's "golden share" in the national
company Elf-Aquitaine. These rights in the first place required prior
approval of the relevant French minister whenever certain percentage thresholds were reached for holdings in the capital of the
company. In the second place they allowed the French state to
oppose decisions to transfer or use as security or collateral the
majority of the capital of four subsidiaries of Elf. The Court held
that these rights were incompatible with the free movement of
capital:

> "Even though the rules in issue may not give rise to unequal
> treatment, they are liable to impede the acquisition of shares in
> the undertakings concerned and to dissuade investors in other
> Member States from investing in the capital of those undertak-
> ings . . . They are therefore liable, as a result, to render the free
> movement of capital illusory."[69]

Although the reference in the passage cited is to investors in general
the Court refers in a previous paragraph to direct investment in
particular, and to the fact that it is characterised by the possibility of
participating effectively in the management of a company or in its
control.[70] What is particularly significant is that it seems that the
rights of a State under a "golden share" will amount to a restriction
on capital movement on the sole ground that the State has reserved
a right to interfere with the managerial decision making of the
company. The reasoning is that since investors seeking a controlling
stake in the company are seeking control, placing restrictions on that
control will deter them and amount to a restriction on capital
movement which must be justified. And the Court rejected France's
arguments that the special rights in issue were justified. The Court
accepted that the objective pursued by the legislation at issue,
namely the safeguarding of supplies of petroleum products in the
event of a crisis, amounted to a legitimate public interest. But the
rights conferred wide discretionary powers, lacked precision, and
were disproportionate.

(d) Belgium's "golden shares" in SNTC and Distrigaz. In the 20–019
proceedings against Belgium, the Court considered that the rules
vesting in the Kingdom of Belgium "golden shares" in SNTC and
Distrigaz, entitling that Member State to oppose, first, any transfer,
use as security or change in the intended destination of lines and
conduits or of certain other strategic assets and, second, certain

---

[69] See Case C–483/99 *Commission v France* [2002] E.C.R. I–4781, paras 41–42.
[70] See Case C–483/99 *Commission v France* [2002] E.C.R. I–4781, para.37.

management decisions regarded as contrary to the guidelines for the country's energy policy, constituted a restriction on the movement of capital between Member States. Noting that the Belgian Government did not deny, in principle, that the restrictions to which the legislation in issue gave rise fell within the scope of the free movement of capital, the Court turned its attention to justification; and on justification the Court found for Belgium. The aim of the rules was compatible with Community law—to ensure a minimum level of energy supplied in the event of a genuine and serious threat to those supplies. The regime was not one of prior authorisation, but of *ex post facto* opposition by the government subject to a strict timetable. The regime was limited to certain decisions concerning the strategic assets of the companies in question and to such specific management decisions relating to those assets as might be called in question in any given case. Finally, the minister could only intervene where there was a threat to the objectives of national energy policy, any such intervention had to be supported by a formal statement of reasons, and could be made the subject of effective judicial review.

On any view the rulings in the above proceedings against France and Belgium are significant. The Court adopts a wide view of restrictions on capital movement. Interfering with the managerial prerogatives of the company is seen as a restriction on capital movement, since direct investment involves the right to participate in the management of the company. And justification is given the usual narrow construction. In particular, it seems that a precondition of relying on justification in any analogous future case would be (a) the publication in advance of sufficiently precise criteria for the exercise of special powers and (b) an *ex post facto* system of challenge by a reasoned decision of the state subject to judicial review.

20–020 **(e) The United Kingdom's Special Share in BAA.** The proceedings against the United Kingdom differed in one respect from those against Italy, France and Belgium, which is at least worthy of remark. In the latter cases the actions challenged provisions of national legislation. In the former case the action against the United Kingdom challenged provisions in the Articles of Association of the British Airports Authority. Under the Airports Act 1986 the British Airports Authority (BAA), which used to own and operate seven international airports in the United Kingdom, was privatised. Under that Act, the Secretary of State had power to approve with or without modifications the Articles of Association of the company nominated to take over the British Airports Authority's functions. BAA was formed for that purpose in 1987. A £1 Special Share was created and was held by the Secretary of State for Transport. This Special Share allowed the Secretary of State to veto (a) the winding up of BAA and (b) the sale of a "designated airport" (Heathrow, Gatwick, etc.). The articles also prohibited any shareholder holding more than 15 per cent of the equity of BAA. The Court of Justice held that the foregoing veto power and the equity limitation amounted to restrictions on capital movement. Two arguments advanced by the United Kingdom were rejected by the Court. The first was that the rights exercisable by the Secretary of State under the Special Share were not discriminatory and did not amount to restrictions on access to the market.[71] The Court dismissed this argument in the same terms as those used in its judgment in respect of the French golden share in Elf-Aquitaine, adding that the restrictions in question were "liable to deter investors from other Member States from making such investments and, consequently, affect access to the market . . .".[72] The second argument of the United Kingdom rejected by the Court of Justice was that the alleged restrictions did not fall within the scope of the Commission's 1997 Communication, since they were all provisions contained in the Articles of Association of BAA, and were not "in derogation of company law" as were restrictions in the third category referred to by the Commission in its Communication. The Court responded as follows:

> "The United Kingdom Government's argument that what is concerned here is solely the application of private company-law mechanisms cannot be accepted. The restrictions at issue do not arise as the result of the normal operation of company law. BAA's Articles of Association were to be approved by the Secretary of State pursuant to the Airports Act 1986 and that was what actually occurred. In those circumstances, the Member State acted in this instance in its capacity as a public authority . . . Consequently, the rules at issue constitute a restriction on the movement of capital for the purposes of Article 56 EC."

It is worth considering the extent to which it is significant whether or not restrictions such as those under discussion in the BAA case— restrictions according special rights to a particular class of shares, and/or prohibiting any shareholder from holding a controlling proportion of the equity shares in the company—should be classified on the one hand as ordinary mechanisms of private law, or, on the other hand, as acts of the state "in derogation of company law".

---

[71] The argument was based by analogy on Joined Cases C–267 and C–268/91 *Bernard Keck and Daniel Mithouard* [1993] E.C.R. I 6097, and Case C–384/93 *Alpine Investments BV v Minister van Financiën* [1995] E.C.R. I–1141.

[72] Case C–98/01 *Commission v United Kingdom* [2003] E.C.R. I–4641, para.47; and see above at p.857.

20–021 **(f) Can action taken by shareholders or directors under the corporate constitution amount to restrictions on capital movement or freedom of establishment in the absence of state intervention?** An argument can be made for the position taken by the Commission in its 1997 Communication, to the effect that it is only powers of veto over corporate decision making which are "in derogation of company law" which amount to restrictions on capital movement or the right of establishment; despite the unfortunate imprecision of the latter expression. The argument is essentially as follows. In the first place, standard formulations in the Court's case law define restrictions on fundamental freedoms as "national measures" which hinder or make less attractive the exercise of those freedoms; the exercise of rights under private law will not normally amount to restrictions on fundamental freedoms. In the second place, the right of establishment, the freedom to provide services, and the free movement of capital, are freedoms of market operators to carry on economic activities. The fact that the Treaty prohibits restrictions on these freedoms indicates that a distinction is to be drawn between the activities of operators *in the market*, who are the beneficiaries of fundamental freedoms, and activities *external* to the market, which are prohibited by the Treaty, unless they can be justified. In this scheme of things, it could be said to be necessary to distinguish between rights of national authorities to veto corporate decisions, and nominate directors in accordance with company law, and rights of national authorities to do so "in derogation of" company law. For example, a national authority owning all the shares in a company may be entitled to veto corporate decisions or nominate directors, and that national authority may resolve to maintain its shareholding rather than to place a controlling stake on the market. This state of affairs cannot be said in itself to amount to a restriction on the fundamental freedoms of potential investors in the company. Where, by way of contrast, a national authority holds special shares which, irrespective of their value, grant to it the power to veto corporate decisions or nominate directors, with a view to ensuring that the company concerned acts in accordance with the public interest, the position is different, even if the special shares are derived from, and exercisable via mechanisms of private law. In the latter case the Court's case law makes it clear that the existence of the special shares and the powers of the national authority derived therefrom may amount to a restriction on the exercise of fundamental freedoms. The essential difference between the two situations is that in the former the State's powers are intrinsic to its activities as a market participant, while in the latter case its powers are a means of regulating the market, rather than participating in it. This is the distinction which it seems the Commission was seeking to draw in its reference in its 1997 Communication to powers to veto corporate decisions and to nominate directors *in derogation of company law* and this is the distinction which the Court of Justice seems to endorse in the passage in its BAA judgment, cited above, in which it refers to the Secretary of State acting in his capacity as a public authority when he endorsed the Articles of Association of BAA which created the rights under the Special Share and limited any single shareholding in BAA to 15 per cent. This line of argument seems essentially correct, and it prevents a Member State from relying on the fact that its regulatory powers are derived from, and exercisable via mechanisms of private law, such as the corporate constitution, in order to deny that such powers may amount to restrictions on a fundamental freedom. It is not, however, a line of argument which excludes the possibility that the actions of private operators under private law, may amount to restrictions on fundamental freedoms.

The Court's case law holds that the collective regulation of economic activities by private operators under private law may amount to a restriction on fundamental freedoms, including non discriminatory restrictions on access to the market.[73] In such circumstances private operators act as regulators, and are accordingly subject to the Treaty's prohibition of restrictions on fundamental freedoms. It cannot, however, necessarily be assumed that the activities of private regulatory bodies comprise the sole activities of private operators which might be regarded as external to the market and be capable of amounting to a restriction on fundamental freedoms. Certainly, non discriminatory activities by or on behalf of market operators to improve their market position *vis-à-vis* their competitors or their suppliers or customers, would not seem in principle and in general capable of amounting to restrictions on the fundamental freedoms of others. But discriminatory conduct on the part of market operators, or action which restricts access to the market of other market operators, would seem capable of amounting to a restriction on a fundamental freedom. If this line of argument is correct, it is possible that certain action taken by shareholders, or by the directors of a company, to prevent a bidder acquiring a controlling stake in a public company, might amount to a restriction on a fundamental freedom.[74]

In the first place it seems clear that provisions of the corporate constitution which discriminate on grounds of nationality (e.g. by prohibiting non nationals from acquiring shares) are incompatible with the right of establishment, or, in cases where acquisition of control is not in issue, with the general prohibition on discrimination

---

[73] Case 36/74 *Walrave v Union cycliste internationale* [1974] E.C.R. 1405; Case C–415/93 *Union Royale Belge des Sociétes de Football Association ASBL v Jean-Marc Bosman* [1995] E.C.R. I–4921.

[74] Art.43 EC seems capable of direct application to private parties; the provisions of the Treaty on free movement of capital bind Member States, but probably do not bind private parties.

on grounds of nationality laid down in Article 12 EC.[75] It is also clear that an equity limitation such as that involved in the BAA special share case, discussed above, has restrictive *effects* which may hinder the right of establishment. The question which arises is whether those restrictive effects nevertheless fall outside the scope of the Treaty if such a provision is adopted without the prompting or endorsement of the authorities of a Member State.[76] It is to be noted that such a limitation does not enable potential bidders, share-holders, or the company itself, to maintain or improve their position on the market; it entrenches the position of the board of the company, and denies access to the market in corporate control by preventing such a market from operating. It would seem to amount to a serious restriction on the right of establishment, and it is not easy to see how it might be justified by imperative requirements in the general interest.[77] A similar argument might well apply to provisions of a corporate constitution, or to measures permitted by or adopted under a corporate constitution, or to agreements appli-cable in connection with the exercise of the right of shareholders, which are intended to and do restrict access to the market in corporate control. Into this category might fall certain conduct of the kind referred to in Article 9(2) of Directive 2004/25 on take-over bids, taken to frustrate a bid, without the consent of the general meeting, where a Member State has opted out of the latter provision.[78] It might be objected that such a conclusion would be inconsistent with the regime established by the latter Directive, which authorises certain measures by the board which might frus-trate a bid, where a Member State has exercised its right to opt out of Article 9(2) of the Directive. That is a point meriting further comment in the section of this Chapter which follows, on company law harmonisation.[79]

It should be added that conduct of the board of the kind referred to would also seem to have restrictive effects on the free movement of capital. Whatever limitations may exist in this context on the horizontal effect of the Treaty provisions on capital movement, or indeed freedom of establishment, it is established that Member

---

[75] Art.39 EC directly binds employers as regards its prohibition of discrimination on grounds of nationality, see Case C–281/98 *Angonese* [2000] E.C.R. I–4139, esp. paras 34–36, discussed in Ch.18 at p.709. It is difficult to avoid the conclusion that the prohibition of discrimination in Art.43 EC applies directly to the terms of a corporate constitution, whether its securities are traded on a regulated market or not.

[76] It is not argued that such arrangements are likely to be encountered in practice; the point is addressed as a matter of principle.

[77] Where rules of private law regulate economic activity mandatory requirements in the general interest may in principle be pleaded by way of justification, see Case C–415/93 *Union Royale Belge des Sociététes de Football Association ASBL v Jean-Marc Bosman* [1995] E.C.R. I–4921, paras 86, 104.

[78] See below at pp.883–884.

[79] See below at pp.883–884.

States are obliged to take all appropriate measures to ensure that private individuals do not interfere with the effective exercise of fundamental freedoms.[80] This obligation would seem to require each Member State to ensure that its national system of company law contains rules to ensure that company boards do not engage in conduct which might prevent shareholders from accepting an advantageous bid. It might be that national rules implementing Directive 2004/25 on takeover bids achieve in full the requirements of the Treaty provisions on capital movement as well as those on freedom of establishment in this respect. The latter Directive is discussed in the following section of this Chapter.[81]

COMPANY LAW HARMONISATION

Company law harmonisation designed to promote freedom of establishment

The Treaty makes provision in Article 44(2)(g) EC for the **20–022** adoption of legislation designed to co-ordinate the:

> "safeguards which, for the protection of the interests of members and others, are required by Member States of companies or firms within the meaning of the second paragraph of Article 48 with a view to making such safeguards equivalent throughout the Community."

The aim of this legislation is made clear in Article 44(1) EC; it is to "attain freedom of establishment". Edwards has argued that "While company law harmonisation is not an end in itself, so that Article [44(2)(g)] EC undoubtedly requires a link between the legislation adopted thereunder and the facilitation of companies' right of establishment,[82] that goal calls for a generous construction in accordance with the general approach developed by the Court of Justice over the last three decades to the interpretation of Treaty provisions."[83] Nevertheless, a slightly stricter approach to Treaty base may be necessary today. The Court of Justice has emphasised

---

[80] Case C–26595 *Commission v France* [1997] E.C.R. I–6959; Case C–112/00 *Schmidberger* [2003] E.C.R. I–5659. These cases involve private action interfering with the free movement of goods, but para.62 of the latter case refers to "restrictions on the exercise of a fundamental freedom . . .".

[81] See below at p.880.

[82] See, e.g. Case C–122/96 *Saldanha and MTS Securities Corporation v Hiross Holding* [1997] E.C.R. I–5325, where the Court of Justice stated that Art.54(3)(g) "empowers the Council and the Commission, for the purpose of giving effect to the freedom of establishment, to coordinate to the necessary extent the safeguards . . ." (para.23).

[83] Edwards, *EC Company Law*, (OUP, Oxford, 1999), p.7.

that legislation adopted to improve the functioning of the internal market must genuinely have as its object the improvement of the conditions for the establishment and functioning of the internal market. This means, in the present context, that such legislation must remove barriers to cross-frontier business activity and/or or eliminate appreciable distortions of competition.[84] And today such legislation should also aim to reduce the transaction costs involved in cross-border business activity, and thus to contribute to the overall competitiveness of the European market, in order to promote the "high degree of competitiveness" which it is the task of the Community to promote.[85]

The provisions of Article 44(1) and 44(2)(g) EC are not the only legal basis for Community legislation regulating the structure of corporate bodies at European level. Recourse has also been had to Article 308 EC, in particular as regards the European Economic Interest Grouping (EEIG), and the European Company Statute. In both cases the Council adopted regulations. The legal argument for use of Article 308 EC rather than Article 44 EC is that the latter Article provides a basis for directives requiring Member States to adopt common national rules whereas in the case of the EEIG and the European Company what was needed were directly applicable European regimes establishing European corporate entities operating in parallel with existing national company law regimes. This approach also has the convenient political result of requiring unanimous agreement in Council. Use of Article 308 EC would not seem however to dispense with the need to link European rules on corporate structure with the exercise of fundamental freedoms, since Article 308 EC applies "in the course of operation of the common market", while the "objectives of the Community" applicable in such a context are internal market/common market objectives.

Edwards has argued that company law harmonisation measures "which prima facie have little immediate impact on cross-border establishment will in any event normally be found on closer scrutiny indirectly to smooth the path of cross-border establishment."[86] This observation was probably not intended to damn with faint praise, but it might be questioned whether it should be regarded as appropriate today for the Community institutions to adopt measures of company law harmonisation unless direct gains to the internal market are likely to result. As Edwards indicates, however, company law harmonisation measures can at least be rationalised in terms of making some contribution to freedom of establishment.

---

[84] Case C–376/98 *Germany v Council and Parliament* [2000] E.C.R. I–8419.
[85] Art.2 EC.
[86] Edwards, *EC Company Law*, (OUP, Oxford, 1999), p.7.

Obstacles to establishment addressed by company law harmonisation measures

The obstacles to establishment of companies addressed by harmo- **20–023** nisation measures can be broadly grouped into three categories.

- Differences between national rules which deter cross-frontier activity to the extent that economic operators in one Member State are unfamiliar with rules in another (psychological obstacles)
- Differences between national rules which necessitate compliance with further requirements by virtue of establishment in another Member State
- National rules which (whether or not they vary from State to State) inhibit establishment in another Member State.

Psychological obstacles to dealing with foreign companies, unfamiliarity with regimes applicable to foreign companies, and promoting legal certainty

The First Council Directive 68/151[87] concerned publicity require- **20–024** ments relating to companies, the circumstances in which company transactions would be valid, and the rules relating to the nullity of companies. The preamble of the directive is not particularly informative as regards the cross-frontier advantages likely to result from the directive, though these might have seemed obvious. The preamble refers to the coordination referred to in Article 44(2)(g) EC and states that that coordination and that provided for in the General Programme for the abolition of restrictions on freedom of establishment "is a matter of urgency, especially in regards to companies limited by shares or otherwise having limited liability, since the activities of such companies often extend beyond the frontiers of national territories."

The Court of Justice considered the rationale of the disclosure requirements to be as follows:

> "the objective of the directive, . . . is to guarantee legal certainty in dealings between companies and third parties in view of the intensification of trade between Member States following the creation of the common market . . ."[88]

---

[87] [1968(I)] O.J. English Spec. Ed.; Series I Chapter, p.41; as last amended by Directive 2003/58 [2003] O.J. L221/13.
[88] Case 32/74 *Haaga* [1974] E.C.R. 1205, para.6.

The Court makes the same legal certainty point about the nullity provisions in the *Marleasing* case.[89] It is indeed possible that third parties might be deterred from doing business with or investing in foreign companies by uncertainty as to the requirements applicable to such companies. This might have an adverse effect on the right of establishment of companies, or on the right of establishment of investors seeking a controlling stake in foreign companies. Third parties might be concerned as to whether they might be afforded a lesser degree of legal protection in dealings with foreign companies than in dealings with companies incorporated in their own Member States, and information about foreign companies might not dispel such concerns if published in an unfamiliar format, or if compiled on the basis of different rules. Such considerations, as well providing a case, in terms of promoting freedom of establishment, for the First Directive, also provide a justification for other measures of company law harmonisation, such as the Fourth Council Directive 78/660 on the annual accounts of certain types of companies.[90] The preamble of this Directive refers to it being necessary to "establish in the Community minimum equivalent legal requirements as regards the extent of the financial information that should be made available to the public by companies that are in competition with another another." The Fourth Directive was supplemented by the Seventh Council Directive 83/349 on Consolidated Accounts.[91] Under Article 51 of the Fourth Directive, companies must have their annual accounts audited by one or more persons authorised by national law to audit accounts. The Eighth Council Directive 84/253 on the approval of persons responsible for carrying out the statutory audits of accounting documents, provided for the harmonisation of the qualifications of such persons.[92]

It is to be noted that disparities between disclosure requirements could also comprise obstacles falling with the second category referred to above if not harmonised—disparities between national company law rules which might result in further, and perhaps varying, requirements being imposed on a company extending its activities beyond its State of origin. Edwards points out, as regards the Eleventh Council Directive on disclosure by branches, that "certain Member States had imposed their own disclosure require-ments on branches, which differed between Member States, leading to further discrepancies within the Community."[93]

The Council Regulation establishing the EEIG[94] aims to promote cross-border co-operation between individuals and companies, and

[89] Case C–106/89 [1990] E.C.R. I–4135. para.12.
[90] [1978] O.J. L222/11.
[91] [1983] O.J. L193/1.
[92] [1984] O.J. L126/20.
[93] Edwards, *EC Company Law*, (OUP, Oxford, 1999), p.212.
[94] Council Reg.2137/85 [1985] O.J. L199/1.

its preamble refers to "legal, fiscal or *psychological* difficulties" (emphasis added) in the way of such co-operation, which would be addressed by the Regulation. The preamble of the Council Regulation on the statute for a European Company (SE)[95] similarly argues that restructuring and co-operation operations involving companies from different Member States "give rise to legal and psychological difficulties . . .". These references to psychological difficulties seem to be references to the unfamiliarity and uncertainty which might arise when dealing with foreign companies and legal regimes, which are discussed above.

Differences between national rules which unless harmonised might necessitate compliance with further and varying requirements by virtue of establishment in another Member State

Reference has already been made to the Eleventh Directive on disclosure by branches. The preamble to this Directive refers to the First, Fourth, Seventh and Eighth Directives, and notes that whereas these Directives apply to companies as such, they do not apply to their branches. The preamble points out that this lack of coordination as regards branches, in particular concerning disclosure, leads to disparities in the protection of shareholders and third parties, and between companies which operate in other Member States by opening branches and those which operate there by creating subsidiaries. The preamble adds that differences in the laws of the Member States might interfere with the exercise of the right of establishment. As indicated above, the case for this Directive in terms of promoting the right of establishment is two fold. In the first place it assists companies wishing to set up branches in other Member States by countering the unfamiliarity of third parties with disclosure requirements in the country in which the branch is established. In the second place it assists such companies by laying down uniform disclosure requirements to be fulfilled by their branches in the Member States in which they are established. The compulsory disclosure is limited to documents specified including the accounting documents of the company as drawn up, audited and disclosed pursuant to the law of the Member State by which the company is governed in accordance with Third, Fourth and Seventh Directives.[96] The Member State in which the branch has been opened may stipulate that the documents relating to the activities of the company and its accounting documents must be published in another official language of the Community (no doubt the Member State would specify its own language) and that the translation of such documents

20–024.1

---

[95] Council Reg.2157/2001 [2001] O.J. L294/1.
[96] Eleventh Directive, Art.3.

must be certified.[97] In the *Centros* case, discussed above, the Court of Justice found support in the Fourth and Eleventh Directives for its rejection of the arguments of the Danish authorities that refusing to register the Danish branch of an English company had been justified by the need to protect the interests of public and private creditors of the company:

> "Since the company concerned in the main proceedings holds itself out as a company governed by the law of England and Wales and not as a company governed by Danish law, its creditors are on notice that it is covered by laws different from those which govern the formation of private limited companies in Denmark and they can refer to certain rules of Community law which protect them, such as the Fourth Council Directive 78/660/EEC . . . on the annual accounts of certain types of companies . . ., and the Eleventh Council Directive 89/666/EEC . . . concerning disclosure requirements in respect of branches opened in a Member State by certain types of company governed by the law of another State . . ."[98]

Another company law directive whose Treaty basis can at any rate in part be justified by the need to remove obstacles to corporate establishment resulting from disparities between national laws is the Second Council Directive 77/91, which deals with the formation of public limited liability companies and the maintenance and alteration of their capital.[99] Article 6 of the Directive provides that the laws of the Member States shall require that, in order that a company may be incorporated or obtain authorisation to commence business, a minimum capital shall be subscribed the amount of which shall not be less than 25,000 European units of account. Edwards notes that the original Member States had minimum capital requirements ranging from 20,000 to 160,000 units of account, and that the United Kingdom and Ireland had no such requirement. As she points out, such wide divergences in the requirement were capable of affecting freedom of establishment, and distorting competition, for example by discouraging companies from setting up cross-border subsidiaries in Member States with higher limits. It should be added that such disparities might also encourage Member States to refuse to allow branches of companies incorporated in Member States with lower capital requirements to carry on business in their territory, or to subject such activity of branches to similar capital requirements as were applicable to the formation of companies. Considerations such

---

[97] Eleventh Directive, Art.4.
[98] Case C–212/97 *Centros Ltd v Erhvervs- og Selskabsstyrelsen* [1999] E.C.R. I–1458, para.36.
[99] [1977] O.J. L26/1.

as these gave rise to the proceedings in the *Centros* case.[1] In the latter case the Court held that a Member State could not justify placing restrictions on the activities of a "branch" of a private company incorporated in another Member State on grounds of protection of public and private creditors. One of the Court's reasons for rejecting this justification was that arrangements might be made for public creditors to obtain guarantees from the proprietors of the company. Such considerations would not be applicable to public companies. The amount of paid up capital provided for under the Second Directive is however a minimum requirement, and has never been increased in the three decades since the Directive was adopted, though there is provision for review every five years.[2] As Edwards comments, "The figure is unquestionably on the small side if the purpose is to ensure that the company's capital is a genuine guarantee for third parties and to reserve the public company for undertakings of a certain scale."[3]

The recent Directive 2005/56 of the European Parliament and Council on cross-border mergers of limited liability companies[4] seeks to overcome "the many legislative and administrative difficulties" which mergers between companies registered in different Member States encounter in the Community. The obstacles facing companies were described by the Commission in the explanatory memorandum accompanying its proposal in the following terms:

> "At present, as Community law now stands, such mergers are possible only if the companies wishing to merge are established in certain Member States. In other Member States, the differences between the national laws applicable to each of the companies which intend to merge are such that the companies have to resort to complex and costly legal arrangements. These arrangements often complicate the operation and are not always implemented with all the requisite transparency and legal certainty. They result, moreover, as a rule in the acquired companies being wound up—a very expensive operation."[5]

In order to facilitate cross-border merger operations, the Directive provides that each company taking part in a cross-border merger, and each third party concerned, remains subject to the provisions and formalities of the national law which would be applicable in the case of a national merger.[6] Employee participation in the newly

---

[1] Case C–212/97 *Centros Ltd v Erhvervs- og Selskabsstyrelsen* [1999] E.C.R. I–1458.
[2] Second Directive, Art.6(3).
[3] Edwards, *EC Company Law*, (OUP, Oxford, 1999), pp.60, 61.
[4] [2005] O.J. L310/1.
[5] COM (2003) 0703 final, p.2.
[6] Directive 2005/56 of the European Parliament and Council on cross-border mergers of limited liability companies, [2005] O.J. L310/1, esp. Art.4(1)(b).

created company will be subject to negotiations based on the model of the European Company Statute, which is discussed below. The proposal was designed in particular to benefit "small and medium-sized enterprises, which stand to benefit because of their smaller size and lower capitalisation compared with large enterprises and for which, for the same reasons, the European Company Statute does not provide a satisfactory solution."[7]

National rules or practices which (whether or not they vary from state to state) inhibit cross-border establishment

20–025 Some national rules, whether contained in legislation, or in the articles of association of companies, may inhibit the right of establishment. Such restrictions do not result from disparities between national rules in one or more Member States, but from the fact that the rules in question, or practices authorised by such rules, are intrinsically capable of inhibiting cross-frontier establishment. Restrictions falling within this category were the target of one of provisions of the proposed directive on takeover bids. Article 9(2) of the Commission's proposal of 2002 provided as follows:

> "During the [relevant period][8] . . . the board of the offeree company must obtain the prior authorisation of the general meeting of shareholders given for this purpose before taking any action other than seeking alternative bids which may result in the frustration of the bid and in particular before issuing any shares which may result in a lasting impediment to the offeror in obtaining control over the offeree company."[9]

The Commission's explanatory memorandum says of this part of the proposal:

> "Where control of the offeree company is at stake, it is important to ensure that its fate is decided by its shareholders. The authorisation of the general meeting must therefore be given explicitly with a view to responding to a specific bid . . . The Directive does not define the measures which can frustrate a bid. In general, such measures may be all operations which are not carried out in the normal course of the company's business or not in conformity with normal market practices."[10]

Such action as that referred to is clearly capable of inhibiting cross-frontier merger. The Commission's proposal was finally adopted in modified form as Directive 2004/25, and is discussed below.[11]

---

[7] COM(2003) 0703 final, p.2.
[8] From the time the board of the offeree company receives information concerning the bid and until the result of the bid is made public or the bid lapses; see Art.9(2) of the proposal.
[9] COM (2002) 534 final.
[10] *ibid.*, at p.8.
[11] Below, at p.880.

Whether company law harmonisation has made an effective contribution to the internal market is an open question

Assessing the effectiveness of the contribution of harmonisation to **20–026** the internal market is difficult in this area as it is in others. Even if legislation in principle can be said to address obstacles to establishment, it is difficult to establish that the net effect of harmonisation will be or has been increased cross-frontier activity, or less costly cross-frontier activity. The press release accompanying the adoption of Directive 2005/56 of the European Parliament and Council on cross-border mergers of limited liability companies,[12] stated that the Directive "is expected to reduce costs, while guaranteeing the requisite legal certainty and enabling as many companies as possible to benefit. It is one of the key actions for growth and employment under the Lisbon agenda." Yet the Commission acknowledged in an earlier published memo that there had been no economic analysis quantifying the likely benefits of the Directive, adding that "EU companies have been calling for many years for such a measure to be adopted, so clearly they believe it will benefit them even if it would be very difficult to quantify these benefits."[13] In fact it seems a fair assessment of the directive in question that it will reduce the future costs of cross-border mergers, at any rate for companies registered in Member States whose legislation previously excluded the possibility of such cross-border mergers.[14]

On the other hand, economic operators have always had to negotiate differences between national laws, and negotiating such differences does not always impose substantial costs, particularly where the law of the host Member State is relatively business friendly. The adverse impact of psychological obstacles or uncertainty factors is difficult to measure. So is the beneficial impact of adopting measures designed to counteract such considerations. Furthermore, if harmonisation takes place at the level of the more highly regulated Member States, the net cost of economic activity in Europe, including the cost of cross-frontier activity, might be more after harmonisation, than before. Until recently, the extent to which measures of company law harmonisation might promote freedom of establishment was approached more as a matter of principle, than of detailed empirical analysis. The results of some company law harmonisation initiatives at least have left doubts as to their practical contribution to the internal market. Perhaps an over cited statistic is that applicable to the Fourth Directive on annual accounts which left no fewer than 41 options to the Member States in addition to 35 options to the business enterprises themselves.[15] The significance of

---

[12] [2005] O.J. L310/1; see press release IP/05/1487, Brussels, November 29, 2005.

[13] MEMO/03/233 Brussels, November 18, 2003.

[14] According to MEMO/03/233, the countries referred to are the Netherlands, Sweden, Ireland, Greece, Germany, Finland, Denmark and Austria.

[15] Edwards, *EC Company Law* (OUP, Oxford, 1999), p.117, citing Buxbaum, and Hopt, citing Niehus.

multiple options in a measure of harmonisation is that it places in doubt the extent to which the harmonisation in question is worthy of the name, and might be said to imply that the objective of achieving solutions at European level has overshadowed the aim of promoting cross-border business activity.[16] One reason why the effectiveness or not of measures of company law harmonisation to promote freedom of establishment has proved difficult to assess is that until recently it has not been thought appropriate to put in place mechanisms to attempt to evaluate the contribution by the legislation in question to the internal market. It is clear however that at least some initiatives designed to promote cross-frontier establishment of firms and corporate bodies have proved less successful than hoped.

Claims to promote cross-frontier activity have not always been made good—the EEIG

Characteristics of the EEIG

20–027   Council Regulation 2137/85 on the European Economic Interest Grouping (EEIG)[17] was adopted on the basis of Article 308 EC. According to its preamble it aims to provide the means for natural persons, companies, firms and other legal bodies to co-operate effectively across frontiers. The preamble notes that co-operation of this nature can encounter legal, fiscal or psychological difficulties, and that the creation of an appropriate Community legal instrument in the form of an EEIG would contribute to such co-operation.

The EEIG is based on a written contract, which contains its name, its official address, the names of its members, and the duration of the contract. The EEIG must comprise at least two persons, natural or legal, from at least two Member States. Activities of the EEIG must be ancillary to the main businesses of its members, it must not make profits for itself and it cannot practise a profession. The organs of the EEIG are its members acting collectively and its manager or managers. The grouping shall be registered in the country in which it has its official address and in each country in which it has an establishment. The official address must be in the EC and either be where the EEIG has its central administration or where one of its members has its central administration or principal place of business. Registration involves filing of information about the grouping e.g. the contract, the managers and their powers. The law applying to the internal organisation of the EEIG is the law of the state in which the official address is situated. But the EEIG is subject to the law of the

---

[16] Though Edwards argues that "the achievement of the Fourth Directive in imposing certain common minimum standards should not be underestimated", *ibid.*, p.117.
[17] [1985] O.J. L199/1.

relevant host state as regards its day to day activities and relations with third parties in that country, e.g. employment of staff and insolvency.

Profits or losses resulting from the activities of the EEIG shall be taxable only in the hands of its members.[18] Profits resulting from a grouping's activities shall be deemed to be the profits of its members and shall be apportioned among them in the proportions laid down in the contract for the formation of the grouping or in the absence of any such provision in each equal shares.[19]

Drawbacks of the EEIG

The Regulation claims that creation of the EEIG will remove **20–028** obstacles to cross-frontier business co-operation. Yet it is not clear that it does so. The preamble refers to the fact that cross-frontier business co-operation of the kind envisaged can encounter legal and psychological difficulties. Clearly such difficulties include the need for participants from different Member States to deal with the legal systems of other Member States. Yet the first thing the members have to do is to choose which national law will govern the internal organisation of the EEIG, and hence their legal relationship, just as would be the case if parties from different Member States were seeking more *ad hoc* joint venture arrangements. But the EEIG is not in other respects a particularly attractive framework for business co-operation. In particular, an EEIG cannot make profits for itself, which significantly reduces its attractiveness as a vehicle for cross-frontier business co-operation. It is difficult to avoid the impression that Member States only agreed to the EEIG on terms which excluded any possibility that it might compete in any significant way with national alternatives.

The Commission has sought to find niche uses for EEIGs, such as encouraging their use for consortia bidding for European projects. Yet the Economic and Social Committee[20] and the Court of Auditors have been critical of the EEIG even in such specialist contexts. The Court of Auditors observed:

> "The Commission promotes the possibility of using a European Economic Interest Grouping (EEIG) as a mechanism for

---

[18] Art.40.

[19] Art.21.

[20] See the Opinion of the Economic and Social Committee on the "Communication from the Commission to the Council, the European Parliament, the Economic and Social Committee and the Committee of the Regions on Public-Private Partnerships in Trans-European Transport Network projects" [1998] O.J. C129/14, "The European Economic Interest Grouping (EEIG) statute is a good instrument in the early phases of a project, but it is not well adapted to the requirements of the construction and operation phases."

participating in RTD programmes . . . Out of the 17 audited JOULE projects, six were coordinated by three different EEIGs. Although the consortium partners were satisfied that the administrative tasks were delegated to a separate entity,which in two cases was located close to the Commission, in none of the cases had the use of an EEIG resulted in easier or faster contract negotiations. On the contrary,there were several additional problems . . ."[21]

Positive aspect of the EEIG as an additional option contributing to regulatory competition

20–029 An important positive feature of the EEIG was that it represented a new approach to European law-making in this field. It offered an additional *option* which did not limit in any way existing options which might be available under national law. This was in terms of technique a contrast to measures of company law harmonisation under Article 44(2)(g) which have replaced the diversity of national rules with a uniform, or at any rate more uniform solution. Such additional European options as that offered by the EEIG Regulation contribute to regulatory competition, even if in the event they do not compete very effectively. It is also possible to evaluate whether such initiatives promote cross-frontier activity by monitoring the take up by businesses of the opportunities they offer.

The need for empiricism—evaluation and feedback on European legislation

20–030 Today, more empiricism is regarded as necessary in the legislative process than has been the case in the past, both in general and in the company law harmonisation area in particular. In the Commission's *White Paper on European Governance*,[22] the Commission declares itself committed to an efficient and empirical approach to regulation:

"The European Union will rightly continue to be judged by the impact of its regulation on the ground. It must pay constant attention to improving the quality, effectiveness and simplicity of regulatory acts . . .

---

[21] Special Report No.17/1998 on support for renewable energy sources in the shared-cost actions of the JOULE-THERMIE Programme and the pilot actions the Altener Programme together with the Commission's replies (Submitted pursuant to Art.188c(4)(2) of the EC Treaty) [1998] O.J. C356/03.

[22] Brussels, COM (2001) 428 final, July 25, 2001.

— First, proposals must be prepared on the basis of an effective analysis of whether it is appropriate to intervene at EU level and whether regulatory intervention is needed. If so, the analysis must also assess the potential economic, social and environmental impact, as well as the costs and benefits of that particular approach. A key element in such an assessment is ensuring that the objectives of any proposal are clearly identified.

— Sixth, a stronger culture of evaluation and feedback is needed in order to learn from the successes and mistakes of the past. This will help to ensure that proposals do not over-regulate and that decisions are taken and implemented at the appropriate level.[23]

New values and company law harmonisation

The constitutional framework for harmonisation has not stood **20–031** still. New legal values have taken their place in the Community legal system. After ratification of the Maastricht amendments it was for the first time a declared aim of the European project to strengthen the competitiveness of Community industry. With the Amsterdam amendments in 1997 came an addition to the tasks of the Community—to achieve a high level of competitiveness. These textual changes have been reflected in the ostensible political direction of the European Union. In the year 2000 the Lisbon summit committed the European Union to the aim of being the most competitive knowledge based economy in the world by 2010.[24] These legal and political signals may have some significance. There are signs of a shift in emphasis, from a model of the internal market in which the price of freedom of movement might be harmonisation bringing with it uncompetitive levels of regulation, towards a model of the internal market in which freedom of movement, regulatory competition and overall competitiveness play a larger and more significant role.

Reports of the High Level Group of Company Law Experts

Some evidence of a shift of the kind referred to above came with **20–032** the decision of the European Commission to appoint a High Level Group of Company Law Experts (hereafter the HLG) which was to prove a positive factor as regards the future direction of proposals

---

[23] *ibid.*, at p.22
[24] Presidency Conclusions of the Lisbon European Council of March 23 and 24, 2000, Press release nr: 100/1/00, 24/3/2000, published on the website of the Council of the European Union (*http://ue.eu.int*).

for company law harmonisation. Internal Market Commissioner
Frits Bolkestein referred to the setting up of the HLG as facilitating
the goal set by the Lisbon Summit of restructuring the European
economy to make it the most competitive in the world by 2010.[25] The
First Report of the HLG was on the proposed Take-over Directive
and was presented in January 2002. The market orientated approach
of the HLG is revealed in the opening words of the Report's
Summary:

> "An important goal of the European Union is to create an
> integrated capital market in the Union by 2005. The regulation
> of takeover bids is a key element of such an integrated market.
>   In the light of available economic evidence the Group holds
> the view that the availability of a mechanism for takeover bids
> is basically beneficial. Takeovers are a means to create wealth
> by exploiting synergies and to discipline the management of
> listed companies with dispersed ownership, which in the long
> term is in the best interests of all stakeholders, and society at
> large. These views also form the basis for the Directive."[26]

The Final Report of the HLG was on "A Modern Regulatory
Framework for Company Law in Europe" and was presented in
November 2002.[27] In order to include in its work the broadest
possible spectrum of opinions, the Group published a Consultative
Document in April 2002, in which it asked those interested in and
concerned with company law in Europe to comment on issues
relating to modernising the regulatory framework for company law
in Europe. The HLG's commitment to competitiveness and empiricism is demonstrated in the following extract from Chapter 2 of its
Second Report:

> "Company law should first of all facilitate the running of
> efficient and competitive business enterprises. This is not to
> ignore that protection of shareholders and creditors is an
> integral part of any company law. But going forward the Group
> believes that an important focus of the EU policy in the field of
> company law should be to develop and implement company law
> mechanisms that enhance the efficiency and competitiveness of
> business across Europe. Part of the focus should be to eliminate
> obstacles for cross-border activities of business in Europe. The
> European single market is more and more becoming a reality

---

[25] See Annex I of the First Report on Takeover Bids, containing the terms of reference laid
down by the Commission for the HLG; see following footnote for reference.
[26] Report of the High Level Group of Company Law Experts on issues related to takeover
bids, Brussels, January 10, 2002, p.2. *http://europa.eu.int/comm/internal—market/company/
docs/takeoverbids/2002–01-hlg-report—en.pdf.*
[27] *http://europa.eu.int/comm/internal—market/company/docs/modern/report—en.pdf.*

and business will have to become competitive in this wider arena. In order to do so, it will have to be able to efficiently restructure and move across-borders, adapt its capital structures to changing needs and attract investors from many Member States and other countries."

The Commission's response—modernising company law and enhancing corporate governance in the European Union

In May 2003 the Commission gave a strong endorsement to the HLG's approach in a Communication to the Council and European Parliament entitled "Modernising Company Law and Enhancing Corporate Governance in the European Union—A Plan to Move Forward".[28] The Commission opens its Communication with a reference to the need for competitiveness: **20–033**

> "Good company law, good corporate governance practices throughout the EU will enhance the real economy:
> An effective approach will foster the global efficiency and competitiveness of businesses in the EU . . ."[29]

And in defining guiding political criteria for its company law Action Plan the Commission gives pride of place to subsidiarity:

> "In developing this Action Plan, the Commission has paid particular attention to the need for any regulatory response at European level to respect a number of guiding criteria:
>
> — It should fully respect the subsidiarity and proportionality principles of the Treaty and the diversity of many different approaches to the same questions in the Member States, while at the same time pursuing clear ambitions (strengthening the single market and enhancing the rights of shareholders and third parties) . . ."[30]

The Action Plan recognises the importance of expert and public consultation as an integral part of the development of company law and corporate governance at Community level, and in April 2005 the Commission established a group of non-governmental experts on corporate governance and company law, "to serve as a body for reflection, debate and advice to the Commission . . . in particular in connection with the measures foreseen in the Action Plan."[31] At the

---

[28] COM (2003) 284 final.
[29] A Modern Regulatory Framework for Company Law in Europe, *http://europa.eu.int/comm/internal—market/company/docs/modern/report—en.pdf, p.3.*
[30] *ibid.*, p.4.
[31] Commission Decision 2005/380/EC [2005] O.J. L126/40, see in particular, preamble, recital (3).

fourth meeting of the Advisory Group in January 2006 the general
view was that "the new Action Plan should bring about initiatives
that are more flexible, leave more choice to the Member States and
companies and remove barriers that hinder entrepreneurship . . . the
EU should, instead of regulating, lay down principles that Member
States would follow or promote, . . . let the market regulate more
and intervene only if this mechanism fails."[32]

Is the promise of more empirical, more decentralised and more
pro-competitive European legislation being realised? It is possible to
attempt a tentative answer by considering two recent initiatives
which in conception were claimed to make significant contributions
to promoting cross-border business activity—the European Company Statute, and the Takeover Directive.

20–034 **(a) The European Company Statute.** Council Regulation
2157/2001 provides the basis for the Statute for a European Company (SE).[33] The Statute is supplemented by Council Directive
2001/86 on the involvement of employees.[34] The Regulation and
Directive were adopted by unanimity under Article 308 EC and
securing agreement on these instruments took many years; the
project for a European Company was first subject to a Commission
proposal in 1970[35] and was referred to in the Internal Market White
Paper of 1985. The European Company Statute (ECS) is a measure
designed to contribute to the internal market, and provides an
option for companies wishing to merge, create a joint subsidiary, or
convert a subsidiary into an SE. The SE is a corporate form only
available to existing companies incorporated in different Member
States. The ECS does not identify in a very specific way, in its
preamble, the obstacles which it seeks to remove, though it implies
that it will help to counter "legal and psychological difficulties . . .".
It was originally intended that the ECS would comprise a self-
contained European regime, but that aim proved impossible to
achieve. While an SE must comply with mandatory rules laid down
in the ECS, it has been noted that the latter refers on 84 occasions to
the laws of the Member States.[36] Once an SE is established, it will be
able to transfer its head office to another Member State without
winding up.

The HLG refers to the SE in the following terms in their Final
Report:

---

[32] Minutes of the Meeting of January 27, 2006 of the Advisory Group on Corporate
Governnance and Company Law, MARKT/F2/LZ/MFS: D(2005) *http://europa.eu.int/
comm/internal—market/company/ docs/advisory-committee/minutes4—en.pdf.*
[33] [2001] O.J. L294/1.
[34] [2001] O.J. L294/22.
[35] Edwards, "The European Company-Essential Tool or Eviscerated Dream" (2003) 40
C.M.L.Rev. 443, 444.
[36] Siems, "The Impact of the European Company (SE) on Legal Culture" (2005) 30 E.L.Rev.
431, 432, citing Brandt and Scheifele (2002) *Deutsches Steuerrecht—D.St.R.* 547.

"The SE represents a major breakthrough, especially because it makes it possible for European companies to merge across-borders and to transfer their seat from one Member State to another. Moreover, it may be important for a company to do business as a European company and not as an Italian, German or French company. This latter objective of the SE, however, is only partly achieved, as the Statute often refers to the law of the Member State of incorporation and, as a result, different types of SEs will come to exist depending on where they have been incorporated."[37]

The SE has a number of mandatory European elements, though many features of the SE remain determined by national company law. The subscribed capital of an SE shall not be less than €120,000.[38] The laws of a Member State requiring a greater subscribed capital for companies carrying on certain types of activity shall apply to SEs with registered offices in that Member State.[39] Subject to the foregoing, the capital of the SE, its maintenance and changes thereto, together with its shares, bonds, and other similar securities shall be governed by the provisions which would apply to a public limited liability company with a registered office in the Member State in which the SE is registered.[40] Article 7 of the ECS provides that the registered office of an SE shall be located within the Community, in the same Member State as its head office, thus applying the "real seat" doctrine to the SE.[41] The ECS gives SEs the choice of opting for a one-tier or two-tier board system.[42]

The ECS and the Directive on the involvement of employees at **20–035** board level provides for the protection of the rights of employees. Davies has summarised the position as follows:

"In general, one can say that no SE will be formed without either some special employee involvement provisions in place or an explicit decision on the part of the representatives of the employees that they do not want to have special involvement provisions for the SE."[43]

Board level participation is required, as the default position in an SE, i.e., in default of agreement by the representatives of employees,

---

[37] A Modern Regulatory Framework for Company Law in Europe, *http://europa.eu.int/comm/internal—market/company/docs/modern/report—en.pdf*, p.3., p.113.
[38] Council Reg.2157/2001 Art.4(1).
[39] *ibid.*, Art.4(2).
[40] *ibid.*, Art.5.
[41] For the view that this requirement is incompatible with the judgment in Case C–208/00 *Überseering BV v Nordic Construction Company Baumanagement GmbH (NCC)* [2002] E.C.R. I–9919, see Wymeersch, "The Transfer of the Company's Seat in European Company Law", C.M.L.Rev. 2003 661, 692.
[42] *ibid.*, Art.38.
[43] Davies, "Workers on the Board of the European Company?" 32 Indus. L.J. 75, 79.

only where such requirements are part of the mandatory national law governing a substantial part of the workforce who will be employed by the SE after it is formed.[44] These provisions have led to suggestions that companies registered in Member States whose laws provide for high levels of employee participation will not prove attractive partners to companies registered in Member States which do not provide for employee participation at board level.[45] Unlike the board level rules, the information and consultation provisions are effectively mandatory for all SEs.[46]

It remains to be seen whether the features of the SE make it a sufficiently attractive option to secure significant numbers of registrations in future. Edwards considers "that the balance sheet is not obviously favourable, and time alone will tell whether the European Company will prove to have been worth the long wait."[47] The fact that the ECS is a parallel optional regime is an important feature; it makes the regime self-evaluating. The pattern of registrations, and non-registrations, will reveal the perceptions of economic operators as to when the ECS is more cost-effective or otherwise attractive than compliance with national corporate forms. The ECS is in truth an example of regulatory competition. But not regulatory competition between the Member States; the Community has entered the market in competition between legal orders and is in competition with the systems of company law of the Member States.

While it is possible to be enthusiastic about a *method* of company law harmonisation which provides new European options without limiting the number of existing national options, it is appropriate to recall why it took so long to secure agreement on the ECS. While regulatory competition promotes competitiveness, relatively heavily regulated Member States tend to see relatively less heavily regulated regimes as a form of "unfair" competition, and as providing possibilities for circumvention of elements of national law which are considered to be essential e.g. the protection of employees. It was putting in place mechanisms to limit the possibility of such circumvention that prolonged discussion of the ECS for so long.

20–036 **(b) Directive 2004/25/EC on Takeover Bids**[48]. Reference has been made to Commission proposals for a Directive on takeover bids. The Council and the European Parliament failed to adopt the Directive

---

[44] Davies, p.76.
[45] Davies, p.76; Siems, "The Impact of the European Company (SE) on Legal Culture" (2005) 30 E.L.Rev. 431, 441.
[46] Davies, p.81.
[47] Edwards, "The European Company-Essential Tool or Eviscerated Dream" (2003) 40 C.M.L.Rev. 443, 464.
[48] Dir.2004/25 of the European Parliament and of the Council of April 21, 2004 on takeover bids, [2004] O.J. L108/38; I am grateful to Jonathan Rickford, Director of the Company Law Centre of the British Institute of International and Comparative Law, for his comments on an earlier draft of this part and related parts of this Chapter. For the views expressed I am solely responsible.

in the form advocated by the Commission. In the form proposed by the Commission the Directive would have had distinctive pro market and pro competitive features; these features survive but are made subject to opt-out arrangements which reduce their effectiveness.

In the first place, the Directive provides that during the period a bid is pending, the board of an offeree company shall obtain the prior authorisation of the general meeting of shareholders given for this purpose before taking any action, other than seeking alternative bids, which may result in the frustration of a bid and in particular before issuing any shares which may result in a lasting impediment to the offeror's acquiring control of the offeree company (Article 9(2)). Mention has already been made of this provision in draft.[49] It is a significant provision of the Directive, and merits further remark. Various steps might be taken by a board (subject to company law and practice in the relevant Member State) to frustrate a bid.[50] One step is to seek an alternative bid from a more acceptable bidder, sometimes known as the "white knight" defence, and as noted above this is permitted by Article 9(2). The "poison pill" is a rights plan that entitles existing shareholders to securities or cash if a hostile bidder takes control, while being redeemable at the option of the board, should a friendly acquirer take control[51]; the "sale of crown jewels" is selling valuable assets of the company; "lock-up" options involve granting preferential options over shares or assets to white knights or other persons; "green mail" involves paying the hostile bidder to withdraw its bid; the "Pac Man defence" involves launching a bid for the bidder itself; while "golden parachutes" involve contractually binding the target company to make large severance payments to incumbent managers in the event of a change of control.[52] The effect of Article 9(2) is that, apart from seeking alternative bids, the board is precluded from adopting any of the foregoing "defensive" measures without the prior consent of the general meeting, if they may result in the frustration of the bid.

The Directive further provides that any restrictions on the transfer of securities provided for in the articles of association of the offeree company, or provided for in contractual arrangements between the offeree company and holders of its securities, or in contractual arrangements between holders of the offeree company's securities entered into after the adoption of the Directive, shall not apply *vis-*

---

[49] Above, at p.870.

[50] See Kirchner and Painter, "Takeover Defenses under Delaware Law, the Proposed Thirteenth EU Directive and the New German Takeover Law: Comparison and Recommendations for Reform" (2002) 50 Am. J. Comp. L. 451.

[51] *Kirchner and Painter, op. cit.*, at p.452.

[52] The definitions and descriptions are from Kirchner and Painter, op. cit., at p.452; but the terms are widely used in commercial and academic literature and in judicial decisions, see for example *Criterion Properties Plc v Stratford UK Properties LLC* [2004] U.K.H.L. 28; [2004] 1 W.L.R. 1846 (HL) ("poison pill" agreement).

à-vis the offeror during the time allowed for acceptance of the bid
(Article 11(2)). Furthermore, multiple voting rights shall carry only
one vote each, and restrictions on voting rights provided for in the
articles of association of the offeree company, or provided for in
contractual agreements between the offeree company and the
holders of its securities, or in contractual agreements between
holders of the offeree company's securities entered into after the
adoption of the Directive, shall not apply, at any general meeting
which decides on defensive measures in accordance with Article 9
(Article 11(3)).

20-037 These provisions of the Directive, if not subject to opt-out
arrangements, would have improved competitiveness in the internal
market by preventing self-serving defensive measures by company
boards. But pressure from the European Parliament and certain
Member States led to these provisions of the Take-over Directive
being considerably weakened.[53] Article 12(1) of the Directive allows
Member States to opt out of the rules on defensive measures/voting
rights in Articles 9 and/or 11 of the Directive for companies
registered in their territories. Companies registered in those Member
States which have opted out must nevertheless be allowed to opt
into the regime of Articles 9 and/or 11 if they wish (Article 12(2)).
And Member States may authorise companies otherwise subject to
Articles 9 and/or 11 not to apply these Articles if they are the subject
of a takeover by a company which does not apply that regime
(Article 12(3)). So in countries which apply Articles 9 and/or 11,
target company boards cannot frustrate bids by home companies, but
may be entitled to frustrate bids by companies subject to the law of a
Member State which has opted out of Articles 9 and/or 11, unless
the bidding company in question has opted into the latter regime. In
a Member State which has opted out of Article 9 and/or 11, the
board of a target company which has opted into either or both of
these Articles, may frustrate a bid by another company registered in
that same Member State which has not opted in, but may not
frustrate a bid by a company registered in that same Member State
which has opted in, or by a company registered in any other Member
State which is subject to the relevant articles, either because the
relevant Member State has not opted out, or because although the
relevant Member State has opted out, the bidder has opted in. As
noted above, this reciprocity regime may lead to a bid from a
company in the same Member State being subject to Articles 9 and/
or 11, while a bid from a company registered in another Member
State is not; this might seem to amount to indirect discrimination on
grounds of nationality contrary to Article 43 EC. Yet any such

---

[53] Rickford, "Takeovers in Europe, etc.", Ch.4 in Grant, (ed.), *European Takeovers—the Art
of Acquisition* (Euromoney, 2005); Baums and Cahn, (eds.), *Das neue Europäische
Übernahmerecht—Umsetzungsfragen und Perspektiven* (Walter De Gruyter, 2006).

difference in treatment is not in truth by reference to Member State of registration of the company, but by reference to differences in the legal regimes which may be applicable in different Member States, and indeed within the same Member State; differences moreover which reflect not only Member State choices but also the choices of individual companies.

The Commission's proposal was for a European wide take-over regime that would have made for a more competitive Europe. It was modified into a regime which allows Member States to adopt protectionist opt outs, and target companies to invoke reciprocity against bidders, both of which seem difficult to reconcile with the aims of the Chapter on establishment. The main argument in favour of the regime is that it was the best package available and that it allows and perhaps encourages the existence of a market in corporate control applicable to and between a constellation of companies across the European Union, creating in the process more freedom of establishment (and incidentally more freedom of capital movement) than would otherwise have been the case.

Rickford argues strongly against the "international trade policy" logic which underlies reciprocity, saying, "There is a fear of 'one way traffic' in corporate control with 'national assets' being 'stolen'. This general policy argument is likely to be completely irrelevant to the merits of the bid, and not a matter which should be of concern to the target board."[54]

A possible legal argument against the opt out and reciprocity provisions of the Directive is that they authorise at least *some* defensive conduct by the board of an offeree company which would seem to amount to an infringement of the right of establishment of a bidding company.[55] The rationale of the takeover Directive, referring in its preamble first and foremost to Article 44(1) EC, which has as its aim freedom of establishment, is clearly to achieve freedom of establishment, and the assumption underlying Article 9(2) of the Directive, which prohibits conduct likely to frustrate a bid without the prior authority of the general meeting, seems to be that such defensive conduct, unless taken with the prior authorisation of the general meeting, constitutes an obstacle to the freedom of establishment.

Yet the fact that Article 9(2) is drafted so as to cover all defensive conduct of the board likely to hinder exercise of the right of establishment does not necessarily mean that *all* conduct incompatible with the latter Article would also be incompatible with the right of establishment of a bidder. Article 9(2) is a prophylactic rule which protects the interests of bidder and shareholders by requiring the consent of the general meeting in all cases to action of the kind

---

[54] *loc. cit.*
[55] See above at pp.862, 863.

referred to. So if the general meeting of a company gives authority to the board, in advance of any bid being made, to adopt certain defensive measures to protect shareholders from inadequate offers, and on the basis that such defensive measures are likely to increase the ability of the target company to negotiate a higher premium, it will be inconsistent with Article 9(2) for the board to take such defensive measures. Yet it is not at all clear that action taken by the board in such circumstances should be considered to amount to an infringement of Article 43 EC. It is suggested above[56] that non-discriminatory activities by or on behalf of market operators to improve their market position *vis-à-vis* their competitors or their suppliers or customers, are not in principle and in general to be regarded as restrictions on the fundamental freedoms of others, though discriminatory conduct on the part of market operators, or activities which restrict the access to the market of other market operators, would seem capable of amounting to such restrictions. If this analysis is correct, conduct of the kind described above; *viz.*, defensive measures authorised in advance of a bid but with a view to protecting shareholders from inadequate bids, cannot be regarded as a restriction on the right of establishment.[57] On the other hand, Article 43 EC would seem to impose some limits on the consequences of opting out of Article 9(2), as would Article 3(c) of the Directive, and the latter provision might be read as aiming in part to ensure that opting out of Article 9(2) remains compatible with Article 43 EC. Opting out of Article 9(2) does not suspend or create an exception to application of the general principle laid down in Article 3(c) of the Directive, to the effect that "the board of an offeree company must act in the interests of the company as a whole and *must not deny the holders of securities the opportunity to decide on the merits of the bid*" (emphasis added). Opting out of Article 9(2) thus does not authorise defensive action by a board which frustrates a bid by pre-empting decisions of shareholders and thereby denying them the opportunity to decide on the merits of the bid. To read Article 9(2) otherwise would be incompatible with Article 3(c) and with Article 43 EC. It follows that, in the view of the present writer, opting out of Article 9(2) will still leave certain conduct caught by the latter Article prohibited by the Directive, because it would place the board in default of Article 3(c) and of Article 43 EC. An example of such conduct would be action taken by the board, without the authorisation of the general meeting, to break up the

---

[56] Above, at p.861.
[57] *Kirchner and Painter, loc cit.*, at p.458, cite Bergström, *et al.*, *Regulation of Corporate Acqusitions*, (1995) Colum. Bus. L.Rev. 495, 510, "A conclusion that defensive measures should be prohibited is too simplistic. The matter is complicated because defensive measures also increase a target company's ability to negotiate a higher premium," and add that "The higher premiums paid for US companies than for their European counterparts support this observation."

offeree company, in order to frustrate the hostile bid, and prevent shareholders of the target company acting on the favourable assessment the board considered they were likely to make of the bid.[58]

Some conclusions about company law harmonisation

It has always been possible to rationalise measures of company 20–038 law harmonisation in terms of promotion of cross-border business activity. It is more difficult to testify to the practical effectiveness of such measures in this regard. The Commission's approach to company law harmonisation has however changed. The Commission has sought to utilise company law harmonisation as a means of promoting cross-border business activity to a greater extent than in the past, which accords with the logic of the Treaty basis for harmonisation being located in the chapter of establishment. The Commission has also embraced an approach to the internal market which lays greater emphasis on the global competitiveness of the internal market than has been the case in the past. All this is consistent with the greater emphasis placed on competitiveness in the EC Treaty post-Maastricht. But the change in the Commission's approach is also explicable on broader political grounds, reflected in the conclusions of the Lisbon Presidency 2000, and its aim to make the EU the most competitive knowledge based economy in the world.

Not all Member States have responded favourably to Commission proposals designed to strengthen the internal market by liberalising it. Negotiation of the ECS was heavily influenced by the desire of some Member States to prevent circumvention of their national rules on employee participation at board level. Although the ECS is a far cry from the EEIG, the preoccupation of some Member States with preventing European joint venture or corporate models from effectively competing with their own national models has in each case reduced the attractiveness of the European model which has emerged from the negotiating process. One saving grace of the EEIG and the SE is that they have been free-standing European initiatives which have not limited the options open to businesses under the various national laws of the Member States. The European legal order has entered into competition with the national legal orders, rather than harmonising national options out of existence. Where the Commission has rightly sought to harmonise national options out of existence, because those national options maintain the fragmentation of the internal market in corporate control, it has failed. The Commission's proposal for a Directive on Takeovers was probably the best proposal for company law harmonisation the

---

[58] The example is taken from Kirchner and Painter, loc cit., at p.468, though they are commenting on the scope of the German takeover code which came into force on January 1, 2002, rather than on the issues discussed in the text.

Commission has ever made; its dilution by opt out arrangements has been a set back for the internal market.

THE IMPACT OF NATIONAL TAX RULES ON THE INTERNAL MARKET

Harmonisation in the field of taxation—facilitating the operation of the internal market

20–039 There is competence to harmonise indirect taxation under Article 93 EC and direct taxation under Article 94 EC. Article 93 EC provides for such harmonisation as "is necessary to ensure the establishment and functioning of the internal market". Article 94 EC provides for the issue of directives for the approximation of such laws, etc. "as directly affect the establishment or functioning of the common market". The rationale for European tax harmonisation is thus to improve the functioning of the internal/common market. Both Article 93 EC and Article 94 EC require unanimity in the Council. Article 95 (which provides for qualified majority voting in the Council) excludes harmonisation of "fiscal provisions" (Article 95(2)).[59] It follows that all tax harmonisation requires unanimity. The internal/common market justification of harmonisation of direct taxation is generally to remove obstacles to the free movement of persons, including corporate persons, freedom to provide services, and freedom of capital movement, and/or to remove appreciable distortions of competition.

Some harmonisation of direct taxation has taken place in the name of promoting cross-frontier activities. Two directives adopted in 1990 were designed to promote freedom of establishment. One was Council Directive 90/434 of July 23, 1990 on the common system of taxation applicable to mergers, divisions, partial divisions, transfers of assets and exchanges of shares concerning companies of different Member States and to the transfer of the registered office, of an SE or European Co-operative Society (SCE), between Member States.[60] The preamble of the Directive notes that mergers,

---

[59] For the meaning of "fiscal provisions," see Case C–338/01 *Commission v Council* [2004] E.C.R. I–4829; Case C–533/03 *Commission v Council*, Judgment of January 26, 2006.

[60] [1990] O.J. L225/1. See Case C–28/95 Leur-Bloem [1997] E.C.R. I–4161; Case C–43/00 *Andersen og Jensen ApS v Skatteministeriet* [2002] E.C.R. I–379. The Directive, and its title, was amended by Directive 2005/19/EC [2005] O.J. L58/19. The amendments *inter alia* added to those entities covered by the Directive, the European Company (SE), and the European Co-operative Society (SCE). The amendments also introduce rules governing the transfer of the registered office of the SE. The applicable tax regime is found under a new Title IVb, Arts 10b–10d. The SE transferring its registered office will enjoy tax deferral on capital gains where its assets remain connected with a permanent establishment situated in the Member State from which it is moving. The shareholders of the SE should not be liable to tax on this occasion.

divisions, transfers of assets and exchanges of shares concerning companies of different Member States may be necessary in order to create conditions analogous to those of an internal market, and that such operations ought not to be hampered by restrictions, disadvantages or distortions arising in particular form the tax provisions of the Member States. The directive aims to establish common rules which are as far as possible *tax neutral* as regards the transactions concerned.

The second directive adopted in 1990 was Council Directive 90/435 of July 23, 1990 on the common system of taxation applicable in the case of parent companies and subsidiaries of different Member States.[61] This Directive aims to prevent profits made by a subsidiary being taxed both in the State of the subsidiary, as income of the subsidiary, and in the State of the parent company, as dividends. The aims of the measure are described in the preamble, which refers to the need for the grouping together of companies of different Member States in order to create conditions analogous to those of an internal market. The preamble notes that such grouping together may result in the formation of groups of parent companies and subsidiaries, but adds that national tax provisions which govern the relations between parent companies and subsidiaries of different Member States vary and "are generally less advantageous than those applicable to parent companies and subsidiaries of the same Member State". The preamble concludes that "it is necessary to eliminate this disadvantage by the introduction of a common system". Under the common system for which the directive provides, where a parent company by virtue of its association with its subsidiary[62] receives distributed profits, the State of the parent company must either refrain from taxing such profits, or tax such profits while authorising the parent company to deduct from the amount of tax due that fraction of the corporation tax paid by the subsidiary and any lower tier subsidiary which relates to those profits.[63] The Court of Justice has explained the rationale of the Directive in the following terms:

> "The need for the Directive results from the double taxation to which groups comprising companies established in a number of States may be subject.

---

[61] [1990] O.J. L225/6. The Directive was amended by Dir.2003/123, [2004] O.J. L7/41. The amendments include updating the list of companies that the Directive covers, and the new list includes the SE and the CSE.

[62] Under the original text of Art.3 of the Directive a company may be subsidiary if another holds 25 per cent of its capital. This minimum will be 20 per cent from January 1, 2005 to December 31, 2006; 15 per cent from January 1, 2007 to December 31, 2008; and 10 per cent from January 1, 2009. The amendments also provide that Member States must impute against the tax payable by the parent company any tax on profits paid by successive subsidiaries downstream of the direct subsidiary. This ensures that the objective of eliminating double taxation is better achieved.

[63] Art.4(1) of the Directive.

> If there is no specific exemption granted by States either unilaterally or under bilateral agreements, profits made by a subsidiary are liable to be taxed both in the State of the subsidiary, as operating income of the subsidiary, and in the State of the parent company, as dividends."[64]

There is no doubt that the requirement that harmonisation measures under Article 94 EC be adopted by unanimity has inhibited the adoption of European legislation in the field of direct taxation. Lack of harmonisation has not however inhibited the development of the case law of the Court of Justice on the interpretation of Treaty Articles on fundamental freedoms as they apply to national tax provisions.

National tax measures as restrictions on fundamental freedoms

Residence a legitimate distinguishing factor for the purposes of tax law but suggestive of indirect discrimination from the perspective of the internal market

20–040   National tax rules are capable of constituting restrictions on the free movement of persons, services and capital. Analogous principles apply to all the relevant Treaty provisions as regards the concept of a restriction on a fundamental freedom, and as regards the possibility of justifying derogation. The discussion which follows refers to case law involving all the above freedoms, but with some emphasis on impediments posed by the national tax rules to the cross-frontier activities of corporate bodies.

In *Commission v France* the Court *inter alia* endorsed three propositions of considerable importance as regards the relationship between the right of establishment and the application of national tax legislation. The first proposition was that as regards the exercise of the right of establishment by companies, it was the location of their registered office, or central administration, or principal place of business, which served as the connecting factor with the legal system of a particular State, like nationality in the case of natural persons, and for a company seeking to establish itself in another Member State to be treated differently solely by reason of the fact that its registered office, *etc.* was situated in another Member State would

---

[64] Case C–294/99 *Athinaïki Zythopoiia AE v Elleniko Dimosio* [2001] E.C.R. I–2797, paras 5, 6. See also on the interpretation of the Directive, Joined Cases C–283/94, C–291/94 and C–292/94 *Denkavit International BV* [1996] E.C.R. I–5063; Case C–375/98 *Epson Europe* [2001] E.C.R. I–4243; Case C–168/01 *Bosal Holding BV* [2003] E.C.R. I–9409; Case C–58/01 *Océ Van der Grinten NV* [2003] E.C.R. I–9809.

deprive the right of establishment of all meaning.[65] The second proposition was that nevertheless the possibility could not "altogether be excluded" that a distinction based "on the location of the registered office of a company or the place of residence of a natural person may, under certain conditions, be justified in an area such as tax law."[66] The third proposition was that where national tax rules treat two forms of establishment in the same way for the purposes of taxing their profits (in the case in point, companies with a registered office in France on the one hand, and branches in France of companies with a registered office in another Member State on the other), that amounts to an admission that there is no objective difference between their positions as regards the detailed rules and conditions relating to that taxation which could justify different treatment.[67]

Even those with but the briefest familiarity with the intricacies of tax law will be aware that it frequently lays down different rules for residents and non-residents, whether they be individuals or companies. Yet it has been noted above that national rules which distinguish between individuals on the basis of their residence may amount to indirect discrimination on grounds of nationality, contrary to the provisions of the Treaty on the free movement of workers or right of establishment.[68] And it will be noted that the criteria referred to in the second and third propositions derived from the judgment of the Court in *Commission v France*, which allot to a company a status akin to that of the nationality, are also criteria

---

[65] Case 270/83 [1986] E.C.R. 273, para.18. It seems from the context and from later case law that what the Court means is that it is the registered office, central administration or principal place of business which determines the seat of the company, in accordance with relevant national rules, which comprises the relevant connecting factor, and that discrimination solely by reference to the fact that a company's seat is in another Member State is contrary to Art.43 EC, see Case C–311/97 *Royal Bank of Scotland plc v Elliniko Dimosio (Greek State)* [1999] E.C.R. I–2651, para.23.

[66] *ibid.*, para.19. The better view is that this amounts to justification of indirect discrimination on grounds of nationality, rather than justification of direct discrimination, since the connecting factors referred to in Art.48 EC, *viz.*, registered office, *etc.*, not only comprise a link analogous to that of nationality, but may also be indicative of residence for tax purposes. Even if it is the case that direct discrimination on grounds of nationality cannot normally be justified, differentiation on grounds of residence may be so justified, perhaps particularly in the tax context, and it is to this latter possibility that the Court is referring in para.19. Furthermore, the Court has accepted that it is consistent with Art.39 EC for Member States to define nationality as one of the criteria for allocating their powers of taxation as between themselves, with a view to eliminating double taxation, see Case C–336/96 *Mr and Mrs Robert Gilly v Directeur des Services Fiscaux du Bas-Rhin* [1998] E.C.R. I–2793, para.30.

[67] Case 270/83 [1986] E.C.R. 273, para.20.

[68] See Ch.18 at p.719, and Ch.19 at p.768. For the proposition that differentiating between individuals on grounds of residence will amount to indirect discrimination on grounds of nationality unless justified, in the contest of freedom of movement for workers, see Case 152/73 *Sotgiu v Deutsche bundespost* [1974] E.C.R. 153; it is a case cited by the Court in support of the same proposition as regards companies in the context of Art.43 EC, see Case C–330/91 *R v Inland Revenue Commissioners ex parte Commerzbank AG* [1993] E.C.R. I–4017, para.14.

used to determine the residence of a company. The result is that the application to individuals and companies of the residence criteria which are such a commonplace of the national tax regimes seem almost intrinsically to raise a question as to compatibility with Article 43 EC or other fundamental freedoms. The case law certainly holds that the fact that a residence criterion is applied in the tax context is no guarantee of immunity from successful challenge under the Treaty.

Thus in *Commerzbank*[69] the Court of Justice considered a national tax rule which restricted repayment supplement (a payment analogous to an interest payment) on overpaid tax to companies resident for tax purposes in the Member State in question. In the case in which the question arose a non-resident company had received a repayment of overpaid tax by virtue of non-residence, pursuant to a double tax convention, but been denied repayment supplement pursuant to the contested rule. The Court considered the rule was discriminatory, as follows:

> "Although it applies independently of a company's seat, the use of the criterion of fiscal residence within national territory for the purpose of granting repayment supplement on overpaid tax is liable to work more particularly to the disadvantage of companies having their seat in other Member States. Indeed, it is most often those companies which are resident for tax purposes outside the territory of the Member State in question."[70]

The Member State in question argued that non-resident companies in the position of the claimant in the national proceedings, far from being discriminated against, enjoyed privileged treatment. They were exempt from tax normally payable by resident companies. In such circumstances there was no discrimination with respect to repayment supplement: resident companies and non-resident companies were treated differently because, for the purposes of corporation tax, they were in different situations.[71] The Court, however, did not accept that argument. The rule the benefit of which the non-resident company was denied was a rule allowing repayment supplement when tax was overpaid; the fact that the exemption from tax which gave rise to the refund was available only to non-resident companies could not justify a rule of a general nature withholding the benefit.[72]

---

[69] Case C–330/91 *R v Inland Revenue Commissioners ex parte Commerzbank AG* [1993] E.C.R. I–4017.
[70] *ibid.*, para.15.
[71] *ibid.*, para.16.
[72] *ibid.*, paras 18, 19.

It is appropriate to organise discussion of the impact of national tax rules on the internal market under various heads, distinguishing between types of restriction, and examining the scope for justification of such restrictions. As regards restrictions on fundamental freedoms, we shall consider discrimination against non residents generally; discrimination against out of state parent companies as regards their dealings with their subsidiaries; and restrictions which inhibit persons established in a Member State from extending their activities to another Member State.

Discrimination against non-residents

The second of the three propositions referred to above as having **20–041** been endorsed by the Court of Justice in *Commission v France*, to the effect that the possibility could not "altogether be excluded" that a distinction based "on the location of the registered office of a company or the place of residence of a natural person may, under certain conditions, be justified in an area such as tax law"[73] seemed to understate the significance of individual or corporate residence as a connecting factor with a State for tax purposes, and in later cases the Court allowed that "in relation to direct taxes, the situations of residents and of non-residents in a given State are not generally comparable, since there are objective differences between them from the point of view of the source of the income and the possibility of taking account of their ability to pay tax or their personal and family circumstances."[74] While the Court has acknowledged that "direct taxation does not as such fall within the purview of the Community", it has emphasised that "the powers retained by the Member States must nevertheless be exercised consistently with Community law",[75] and this in turn means examining in detail the distinctions drawn between resident and non-resident tax-payers to establish whether they are indeed compatible with Community law.

While the situation of residents and of non-residents are not generally comparable, if they are in fact comparable, and yet the non-resident is treated less favourably than the resident, this will amount to discrimination, and be contrary to Article 43 EC.[76] Thus in *Schumacker* the Court held that it will not be discriminatory to deny to a non-resident certain tax benefits paid to a resident, where

---

[73] Case 270/83 [1986] E.C.R. 273, para.19.
[74] Case C–279/93 *Finanzamt Köln-Alstadt v Schumacker* [1995] E.C.R. I–225, para.31; Case C–80/94 *Wielockx v Inspecteur der Directe Belastingen* [1995] E.C.R. I–2493, para.18; Case C–107/94 *P.H. Asscher v Staatssecretaris van Financiën* [1994] E.C.R. I–1137, para.41.
[75] See e.g. Case C–279/93 *Finanzamt Köln-Alstadt v Schumacker* [1995] E.C.R. I–225, para.21, citing Case C–246/89 *Commission v United Kingdom* [1991] E.C.R. I–4585, para.12.
[76] See e.g. Case C–279/93 *Finanzamt Köln-Alstadt v Schumacker* [1995] E.C.R. I–225 (the case concerns Art.39 EC); Case C–80/94 *Wielockx v Inspecteur der Directe Belastingen* [1995] E.C.R. I–2493 (Art.43 EC).

the major part of the income of the resident is concentrated in the State of residence, and the latter State has available all the information needed to assess the taxpayer's overall ability to pay, while this is not so in the case of the non-resident.[77] But the Court added that the position will be different where the non-resident receives no significant income in the State of his or her residence and obtains the major part of his or her taxable income from an activity performed in the State of employment, with the result that the State of his or her residence is not in a position to grant him or her the benefits resulting from the taking into account of his or her personal and family circumstances.[78] The Court concluded that there was no objective difference between the situations of such a non-resident and a resident engaged in comparable employment, such as to justify different treatment as regards the taking into account for taxation purposes of the taxpayer's personal and family circumstances.[79]

In *Asscher*,[80] the question arose before the referring court whether it was compatible with Article 43 EC for the Netherlands to tax a person resident in Belgium and carrying on business in its territory at a higher rate than a resident, in order to offset the fact that certain non-residents escape the progressive nature of the Netherlands tax system because their tax obligations are confined to income received in the Netherlands. The Court of Justice noted that it was open to Belgium, the state of residence, pursuant to the relevant double taxation convention between Belgium and the Netherlands, to take account of income earned in the Netherlands in order to apply progressive rates of tax when taxing income arising in Belgium. The Court of Justice concluded that the fact that the taxpayer was a non-resident did not enable him to avoid, in the circumstances under consideration, the application of progressive rates of tax, and that resident and non-resident taxpayers in the Netherlands were thus in a comparable situation as regards the application of progressive rates of tax. It is to be noted that the Court treats as comparable to a Netherlands resident taxpayer who will have *Netherlands progressive tax rates* calculated by reference to the resident's entire income and applied to his Netherlands income, a Belgian resident taxpayer who works in the Netherlands and who will not have *Netherlands* progressive rates applied to take account of his income outside the Netherlands but will have *Belgian progressive tax rates* calculated by reference to his Netherlands income and imposed on his Belgian income. This seems an analogous approach to that recognised as applicable where, pursuant to Article 39 EC an employer in one

---

[77] Case C–279/93 *Finanzamt Köln-Alstadt v Schumacker* [1995] E.C.R. I–225, paras 33–35.
[78] *ibid.*, para.36. *Schumacker* is distinguished in Case C–391/97 *Frans Gschwind v Finanzamt Aachen-Außenstadt* [1999] E.C.R. I–5451.
[79] *ibid.*, para.37.
[80] Case C–107/94 *P.H. Asscher v Staatssecretaris van Financiën* [1994] E.C.R. I–1137.

Member State is obliged to take account of military service, or public employment, in another Member State.[81]

Discrimination against out of state parent companies as regards their dealings with their subsidiaries

It is not uncommon for national tax rules to subject relations **20–042** between resident subsidiaries and non resident parent companies to less favourable treatment than relations between resident subsidiaries and resident parent companies—a phenomenon referred to in the preamble to Directive 90/435, and noted above.

In *Halliburton Services*[82] the Court considered the compatibility with Article 43 EC of an exemption from property transfer tax applicable in the case of an internal reorganisation of public limited companies and private limited companies, subject to the proviso that the companies party to the transfer were incorporated under the law of the Member State in question. The effect of the application of the Netherlands law in the national proceedings was that a transfer of property in the Netherlands from a German subsidiary of a United States company to a Netherlands subsidiary of the same United States company involved the liability of the latter subsidiary to the tax which would not have been payable if the transferor had also been a Netherlands company.

The Netherlands Government argued that no discrimination was involved because the person liable to pay the tax was not the Germany company but the Netherlands company, which meant that the situation was purely internal to the Netherlands, and Community law was not involved. The Court rejected this argument, noting that "payment of a tax on the sale of immovable property constitutes a burden which renders the conditions of sale of the property more onerous and thus has repercussions on the position of the transferor".[83] The Court concluded that although "the difference in treatment has only an indirect effect on the position of companies constituted under the law of other Member States, it constitutes discrimination on grounds of nationality" prohibited by Article 43 EC.[84] The Netherlands Government argued that the restriction of the exemption to companies constituted under national law was necessary because the competent tax administration was unable to check whether the legal forms of entities constituted in other Member States were equivalent to those of public and private limited companies within the meaning of the relevant national

---

[81] See Case 44/72 *Marsman v Rosskamp* [1972] E.C.R. 1243; Case C–419/92 *Scholz v Opera Universitaria di Cagliari* [1994] E.C.R. I–505.

[82] Case C–1/93 *Halliburton Services BV v Staatssecretaris van Financiën* [1994] E.C.R. I–1137.

[83] *ibid.*, para.19.

[84] *ibid.*, para.20.

legislation. The Court rejected this argument because information relating to the characteristics of the forms in which companies can be constituted in other Member States could be obtained pursuant Community legislation on mutual assistance by the competent authorities of the Member States in the field of direct taxation.[85]

20–043   An example of national tax rules treating relations between resident subsidiaries and non-resident parent companies less favourably than relations between resident subsidiaries and resident parent companies was to be found in the provisions on advance corporation tax (ACT) in the United Kingdom prior to April 6, 1999. ACT was payable by a company resident in the United Kingdom when it made certain distributions, such as a payment of dividends to its shareholders. ACT was not a sum withheld on a dividend, which was paid in full, but was rather corporation tax borne by the company distributing dividends, paid in advance and set off against the mainstream corporation tax (MCT) payable in respect of each accounting period. Two companies resident in the United Kingdom, one of which held at least 51 per cent of the other, could make a group income election. The result of such election was that the subsidiary did not pay ACT on the dividends which it paid to its parent company, unless it gave notice that it did not wish the election to apply to a particular distribution of dividends.[86] In *Metallgesellschaft Ltd and others* and *Hoechst AG, Hoechst UK Ltd*,[87] companies resident in the United Kingdom paid dividends to their respective German resident parent companies, and paid the ACT due on those dividends. The parent companies maintained that, because it was impossible for them and their subsidiaries to make a group income election which would have enabled the subsidiaries to avoid payment of ACT, those subsidiaries suffered a cash flow disadvantage which subsidiaries of parent companies resident in the United Kingdom did not incur. By making a group income election, the latter were able to retain, until the date when the MCT to which they were liable fell due, the sums which would otherwise have had to pay as ACT on the distribution of dividends to their parent companies. In their view, that disadvantage amounted to indirect discrimination on grounds of nationality contrary to Article 43 EC.

The Court of Justice upheld the claims of the taxpayer companies, as regards the discriminatory nature of the national rules, in the following terms[88]:

---

[85] *ibid.*, para.22.
[86] For a fuller description of the relevant tax provisions, see Case C–397/98 *Metallgesellschaft Ltd* and Case C–410/89 *Hoechst AG, Hoechst UK Ltd* [2001] E.C.R. I–1727, paras 3-25.
[87] Case C–397/98, etc., *loc. cit.*
[88] Case C–397/98 *Metallgesellschaft Ltd* and Case C–410/89 *Hoechst AG, Hoechst UK Ltd* [2001] E.C.R. I–1727, paras 42–44.

". . . Acceptance of the proposition that the Member State in which a company seeks to establish itself may freely apply to it a different treatment solely by reason of the fact that its registered office is situated in another Member State would thus deprive Article [43] of all meaning . . .

With regard to the right to make a group income election, the legislation in question creates a difference in treatment between subsidiaries resident in the United Kingdom depending on whether or not their parent company has its seat in the United Kingdom. Resident subsidiaries of companies having their seat in the United Kingdom may, subject to certain conditions, avail themselves of the group income election regime and thus be relieved of the obligation to pay ACT when distributing dividends to their parent companies. By contrast, that advantage is denied to the resident subsidiaries of companies not having their seat in the United Kingdom and which are therefore obliged to pay ACT whenever they distribute dividends to their parent companies.

It is not disputed that this gives the subsidiary of a parent company resident in the United Kingdom a cashflow advantage inasmuch as it retains the sums which it would otherwise have had to pay by way of ACT until such time as MCT becomes payable, that is to say, for a period of between eight and a half months, at the least, and 17 and a half months, at the most, depending on the date of distribution."

A further example of national tax rules treating relations between resident subsidiaries and non resident parent companies less favourably than relations between resident subsidiaries and resident parent companies were those at issue before the referring court in *Lankhorst-Hohorst.*[89] German rules on corporation tax ("thin capitalisation rules") provided that repayments in respect of loan capital which a company limited by shares subject to unlimited taxation had obtained from a shareholder not entitled to corporation tax credit, which had a substantial holding in its share capital, should be regarded as a covert distribution of profits. The reference to a shareholder "not entitled to corporation tax credit" did apply to *some* German companies but applied to *all* non-resident companies. The essential facts of the case before the referring court were that a Netherlands company LT BV owned all the shares in the Netherlands company LH BV, which in turn owned all the shares in the German company Lankhorst-Hohorst GmbH (LH). LT BV gave a loan to LH repayable with interest over 10 years in annual instalments. The loan, which was intended as a substitute for capital, was

---

[89] Case C–324/00 *Lankhorst—Hohorst GmbH v Finanzamt Steinfurt* [2002] E.C.R. I–11779.

accompanied by a "letter of support" under which LT BV waived repayment if third party creditors made claims against LH. The competent German tax authority took the view that interest paid to LT BV under the loan agreement was equivalent to a covert distribution of profits. Before the Court of Justice the German tax authority argued that the distinction drawn by the German rules between persons who are entitled to tax credit and those who are not did not amount to disguised discrimination on the basis of nationality, since those rules also excluded several categories of German taxpayers from entitlement to tax credit. The Court of Justice rejected this argument, on ground that in "... the large majority of cases, resident parent companies receive a tax credit, whereas, as general rule, non-resident parent companies do not."[90] The Court concluded:[91]

> "Such a difference in treatment between resident subsidiary companies according to the seat of their parent company constitutes an obstacle to the freedom of establishment which is, in principle, prohibited by Article 43 EC. The tax measure in question in the main proceedings makes it less attractive for companies established in other Member States to exercise freedom of establishment and they may, in consequence, refrain from acquiring, creating or maintaining a subsidiary in the State which adopts that measure."

Restrictions which inhibit individuals and companies established in a Member State from extending their activities to another Member State

20–044   It is established that Article 43 EC prohibits "exit" restrictions, i.e., restrictions which deter natural or legal persons from extending their activities to other Member States.[92] National tax rules which have this tendency amount to restrictions on Article 43 EC.

In *Hughes de Lasteyre du Saillant*[93] the Court of Justice considered national tax rules which provided that taxpayers intending to transfer their residence for tax purposes outside France were to be subject to immediate taxation on increases in value that had not yet been realised, and which would not be taxed if those taxpayers retained their residence in France. The Court noted that even if the rules in question did not prevent a French taxpayer from exercising his or her right of establishment, they were nevertheless of such a kind as

---

[90] *ibid.*, para.28.
[91] *ibid.*, para.32.
[92] See e.g. Case 81/87 *R v HM Treasury and Commissioners of Inland Revenue ex parte Daily Mail and General Trust plc* [1988] E.C.R. 3483, para.16.
[93] Case C–9/02 [2004] E.C.R. I–409.

to restrict the exercise of that right, having at the very least a dissuasive effect on taxpayers wishing to establish themselves in another Member State.[94] The Court held that the national rules in question amounted to an inappropriate and disproportionate means of achieving their alleged aim—to prevent temporary transfers of tax residence outside France exclusively for tax reasons.[95]

In *Bosal*[96] the issue before the national court was the compatibility with Article 43 EC of Netherlands tax rules which when determining the tax on profits of a parent company established in the Netherlands, made the deductibility of costs in connection with the company's holding in the capital of a subsidiary established in another Member State subject to the condition that such costs were indirectly instrumental in making profits which were taxable in the Netherlands. The Court of Justice held that these rules constituted a hindrance to the establishment of subsidiaries in other Member States. A parent company might be dissuaded from carrying on its activities through the intermediary of a subsidiary established in another Member State since, normally, such subsidiaries do not generate profits that are taxable in the Netherlands.

In *ICI v Colmer (Her Majesty's Inspector of Taxes)*[97] the Court **20–045** considered whether Article 43 EC precluded United Kingdom legislation which, in the case of companies resident in that State belonging to a consortium which controls a holding company, makes a particular form of tax relief ("consortium relief") subject to the requirement that the holding company's business consist *wholly or mainly* in the holding of shares in subsidiaries that have their seat in the Member State concerned. The effect of the tax rules in question was that the setting up of a consortium company in another Member State could deprive a resident consortium company of relief on losses of another resident consortium company. The logic of placing a limit on the number of non-resident subsidiaries was from the United Kingdom's point of view *inter alia* to prevent charges being shifted to resident companies and profits being shifted to non resident companies.[98] The Court considered that the requirement that the above mentioned subsidiaries be wholly or mainly United Kingdom resident subsidiaries could inhibit exercise of the right of establishment by the holding company in a Member State other than the United Kingdom.

In the *Marks & Spencer* case,[99] the Court of Justice considered United Kingdom tax rules on group relief. These rules allowed

---

[94] *ibid.*, para.45.
[95] *ibid.*, paras 50–58.
[96] Case C–168/01 *Bosal Holdings BV v Staatssecretaris van Financiën* [2003] E.C.R. I–9409.
[97] Case C–330/91 [1998] E.C.R. I–4695.
[98] *ibid.*, para.25.
[99] Case C–446/03 *Marks & Spencer plc v David Halsey (HM Inspector of Taxes)*, Judgment of December 13, 2005.

transfers of losses from a resident subsidiary to a resident parent company, but did not allow such transfers from a non resident subsidiary. Through the intermediary of a holding company established in the Netherlands, Marks and Spencer plc (M&S), resident in the United Kingdom, had subsidiaries in Germany, Belgium and France. From the middle of the 1990s, those subsidiaries began to record losses. During 2001, M&S divested itself of its European activities. M&S submitted group relief claims to the competent tax authority in respect of losses incurred by certain of its EU subsidiaries for the years 1998 to 2001. These claims were rejected on the ground that the group relief scheme did not apply to subsidiaries which were neither resident nor economically active in the United Kingdom. The Court of Justice noted that group relief such as that at issue constituted a tax advantage for the companies concerned, and added that:

> "The exclusion of such an advantage in respect of the losses incurred by a subsidiary established in another Member State which does not conduct any trading activities in the parent company's Member State is of such a kind as to hinder the exercise of that parent company of its freedom of establishment by deterring it from setting up subsidiaries in other Member States.
>
> It thus constitutes a restriction on freedom of establishment within the meaning of Articles 43 and 48 EC, in that it applies different treatment for tax purposes to losses incurred by a resident subsidiary and losses incurred by a non-resident subsidiary."[1]

Possible justification for national tax rules which restrict the exercise of fundamental freedoms

20–046 **(a) The principle of "cohesion of the tax system" may justify restrictions on fundamental freedoms.** In the *Bachmann* case[2] the Court introduced a potentially significant ground of justification for national tax rules restricting the exercise of fundamental freedoms— "the need to preserve the cohesion of the tax system." In the case in question a German national employed in Belgium, who made payments in respect of sickness invalidity and life insurance in Germany under arrangements made prior to his arrival in Belgium, challenged Belgian tax rules whereby contributions to sickness and

---

[1] *ibid.*, paras 33, 34.
[2] Case C–204/90 *Bachmann v Belgian State* [1992] E.C.R. I–249; see also Case C–300/90 *Commission v Belgium* [1992] E.C.R. I–305.

invalidity and life insurance contracts were only tax deductible if paid to insurers based in Belgium. The Court noted that workers who have carried on an occupation in one Member State and who are subsequently employed in another Member State will normally have concluded their pension and life assurance contracts or invalidity and sickness insurance contracts with insurers established in the first State. It followed that there was "a risk that the provisions in question may operate to the particular detriment of those workers who are, as a general rule, nationals of other Member States." The Court however found that the restriction on freedom of movement involved could be justified, since there existed under Belgian law a connection between the deductibility of contributions and the liability to tax of sums payable by insurers under pension and life assurance contracts; under the tax system in question the loss of revenue resulting from the deduction of contributions was offset by the taxation of pensions, annuities or capital sums payable by the insurers. The Court stated:

> "The cohesion of such a tax system, the formulation of which is a matter for each Member State, therefore presupposes that, in the event of a State being obliged to allow the deduction of life assurance contributions paid in another Member State, it should be able to tax sums payable by insurers"[3]

Since it was not possible to guarantee that sums payable in other Member States could be subject to such tax to compensate for the tax deductibility of the contributions, the rules in question comprised the least restrictive rules possible, compatible with maintaining the cohesion of the tax system in question.

The *Bachmann* case seemed to recognise that loss of revenue to the national exchequer amounted to a legitimate justification for placing restrictions on the exercise of a fundamental freedom. As the Court observed, ". . . in such a tax system the loss of revenue resulting from the deduction of life assurance contributions from total taxable income . . . is offset by the taxation of pensions . . . payable by the insurers."[4] Subsequent case law on the scope of the "cohesion of the tax system" justification indicated that its scope was very limited indeed—perhaps limited to its own facts. In the first place, the Court of Justice has held that for an argument based on such a justification to succeed, a direct link had to be established between the tax advantage concerned and the offsetting of that advantage by a particular deduction, and that such a direct link required that the advantage and the deduction relate to the same tax and the same taxpayer.[5]

[3] Case C–204/90, para.23.
[4] Case C–204/90, para.22.
[5] Case C–35/98 *Staatssecretaris van Financiën v B.G.M. Verkooijen* [2000] E.C.R. I–4071, paras 57, 58. The case involves the Treaty provisions on capital movement.

20–047 This narrow formulation led the Court in *Verkooijen* to hold that the "cohesion" argument could not be invoked to justify a Member State limiting exemption from income tax payable on dividends to natural persons who are shareholders to cases where the dividends are paid by a company whose seat is in that Member State—in such circumstances the relevant advantage was granted to individual taxpayers in respect of income tax while the intended offsetting advantage was corporation tax payable by resident (but not non resident) companies.[6] Nor was the "cohesion" argument available in the *ICI* case, referred to above, since there was no direct link between the consortium relief granted for losses incurred by a resident subsidiary and the taxation of profits made by non resident subsidiaries.[7]

In *Manninen* the Court of Justice placed a further principled limitation on the "cohesion" argument. In this case there were in issue Finnish rules allowing to an individual a tax credit on dividends from resident but not from non resident companies. A Finnish taxpayer claimed a tax credit in respect of dividends from a Swedish company which had already paid corporation tax on the profits from which the dividends were paid. Intervening Member States sought to distinguish *Verkooijen* on the ground that in *Manninen* the tax credit was granted to shareholders only on condition that the company had actually paid the tax on its profit in respect of which the tax credit was granted. The aim of the tax credit in *Manninen* (as had been the case in *Verkooijen*) was to avoid double taxation of company profits in the hands of the company and individual shareholders. The Court held that even if a direct link did exist in the instant case, the legislation in question did not appear *necessary* to preserve the cohesion of the tax system in question. The aim of the Finnish tax rules in question was to avoid double taxation. This aim would be achieved whether the profits from which the dividends were derived had paid tax in Finland or in Sweden. The Court noted that in *Bachmann* the aim of the national rules had also been to avoid double taxation.[8] The Court's approach in this case is highly significant. A Member State cannot rely upon the principle of "cohesion" to ensure that relief from its tax is matched by tax collected by *its authorities*. It is obliged to treat tax collected by another Member State as equivalent to tax it collects itself.

In *Marks and Spencer*, referred to above, the Court of Justice held that allowing group relief in respect of resident subsidiaries while refusing such relief in respect of non resident subsidiaries amounted

---

[6] *ibid.*, para.58.
[7] Case C–330/91 *ICI v Colmer (Her Majesty's Inspector of Taxes)* [1998] E.C.R. I–4695, para.29
[8] Case C–19/02 *Petri Manninen* [2004] E.C.R. I–7477, paras 45–48. The case involves the Treaty provisions on capital movement.

to a restriction on freedom of establishment. Advocate General Maduro suggested that the criteria for application of the principle of cohesion of the tax system should be relaxed. "Cohesion must first and foremost be adjudged," he argued, "in light of the aim and logic of the tax regime at issue." The aim of the UK system of group relief was to ensure fiscal neutrality by permitting the circulation of losses within a group. It followed in the view of the Advocate General that it would be necessary to take account of the treatment applicable to losses of subsidiaries in the State in which they were resident, and that justification based on cohesion of the system of relief could be accepted only if the foreign losses could be accorded equivalent treatment in the State in which the losses arose. The Court of Justice came to a conclusion similar to that of the Advocate General, but did not base that analysis on the principle of fiscal cohesion. The Court accepted that the UK rules identified as restrictive pursued legitimate objectives and constituted overriding reasons in the public interest, and that they were apt to achieve the attainment of those objectives. The Court however considered that the rules were disproportionately restrictive where two conditions were satisfied. The first condition was that the non-resident subsidiary had exhausted the possibilities available in its State of residence of having the losses taken into account for the accounting period concerned by the claim for relief and also for previous accounting periods, if necessary by transferring those losses to a third party or by offsetting the losses against the profits made by the subsidiary in a previous period. The second condition was that there was no possibility for the foreign subsidiary's losses to be taken into account in its State of residence for future periods either by the subsidiary itself or by a third party, in particular where the subsidiary had been sold to that third party.

The fact that the Court of Justice in *Marks and Spencer* did not base its analysis on the principle of cohesion of the tax system may be significant. If it had followed the lead of the Advocate General the result would have been to expand the possibilities for Member States to plead justification for national tax rules inhibiting the exercise of fundamental freedoms. The Court might not have wanted to do this. The reasoning offered by the Court instead is somewhat open ended. It relies on three justifications, taken together.

> "First, in tax matters profits and losses are two sides of the same coin and must be treated symmetrically in the same tax system in order to protect a balanced allocation of the power to impose taxes between the different Member States concerned. Second, if the losses were taken into consideration in the parent company's Member State they might well be taken into account twice. Third, and last, if the losses were not taken into

account in the Member State in which the subsidiary is established there would be a risk of tax avoidance."[9]

The Court's reliance on all three considerations in conjunction preserves room for manoeuvre for itself in future cases rather than laying down clear guidance for taxpayers or national tax administrations.

20–048 **(b) Avoiding tax fraud and the risk of tax avoidance.** The Court has held that while the need to combat fraud may justify a difference in treatment on grounds of nationality in certain circumstances, the mere risk of tax avoidance cannot justify discriminatory treatment.[10] The prevention of tax avoidance and the need for effective fiscal supervision may be relied upon to justify restrictions on the exercise of fundamental freedoms guaranteed by the Treaty,[11] but a general presumption of tax avoidance or fraud is not sufficient to justify a fiscal measure which compromises the objectives of the Treaty.[12] The Court has refused to accept arguments of justification based on avoiding the risk of tax avoidance where the national legislation did not have "the specific purpose of preventing wholly artificial arrangements"[13]

20–049 **(c) Avoiding the diminution of tax revenue cannot justify restrictions on fundamental freedoms.** In the *ICI* case, referred to above, one of the United Kingdom's arguments by way of justification for the rule that the majority of relevant subsidiaries must be resident companies was that revenue lost through the granting of tax relief on losses incurred by resident subsidiaries could not be offset by taxing the profits of non resident companies. The Court rejected that argument, pointing out:

"that diminution of tax revenue occurring in this way is not one of the grounds listed in Article [46] of the Treaty and cannot be regarded as a matter of overriding general interest which may be relied upon in order to justify unequal treatment that is, in principle, incompatible with Article [43] of the Treaty."[14]

---

[9] *Marks and Spencer*, cited above, para.43. The risk of tax avoidance is the risk that within a group of companies losses will be transferred to companies established in the Member States which apply the highest rates of taxation and in which the tax value of the losses is therefore the highest (para.49).

[10] Case 79/85 *Segers v bestuur van de Bedrijfsvereniging voor Bank- en Verzeleringswezen* [1986] E.C.R. 2375, para.17.

[11] C–254/97 *Baxter* [1999] E.C.R. I4809, para.18,

[12] C–334/02 *Commission v France* [2004] E.C.R. I–2229, para.27.

[13] Case C–330/91 *ICI v Colmer (Her Majesty's Inspector of Taxes)* [1998] E.C.R. I–4695, para.26.

[14] Case C–330/91 *ICI v Colmer (Her Majesty's Inspector of Taxes)* [1998] E.C.R. I–4695, para.28. The point is reiterated in a consistent case law, see for example, Case C–397/98 *Metallgesellschaft Ltd* and Case C–410/89 *Hoechst AG, Hoechst UK Ltd* [2001] E.C.R. I–1727, para.59.

In the *Bosal* case, referred to above,[15] the Court rejected an argument of the Netherlands and the Commission that the limitation on deductibility in issue in that case was justified by the aim of avoiding an erosion of the tax base going beyond mere diminution of tax revenue, concluding that such a justification did not differ in substance from that concerning the risk of diminution of tax revenue.[16] The Court of Justice has never offered a satisfactory explanation of why diminution of revenue/erosion of the tax base should not qualify as a matter of overriding general interest which might justify restrictions on fundamental freedoms. In *X, Y v Riksskatteverket*[17] the Court stated that the aim of avoiding a reduction in tax revenue was "purely economic" and could not, according to settled case law, constitute an overriding reason in the general interest. This analysis is unconvincing. It is true that economic aims, in the sense of protectionist aims,[18] have been rightly ruled out as justifying restrictions on fundamental freedoms, but it does not follow that national measures aiming to avoid reduction in tax revenue should also be ruled out.[19]

(d) The principle of territoriality may justify differentiation between 20–050
residents and non residents. In *Futura Participations SA*[20] a non-resident taxpayer complained that Luxembourg rules allowing the carrying forward of tax losses limited this possibility to profits and losses arising from Luxembourg activities as regards non-residents, but imposed no such limitation in respect of residents. The Court held that "such a system, which is in conformity with the fiscal principle of territoriality, cannot be regarded as entailing any discrimination, overt or covert, prohibited by the Treaty." The Court means by its reference to the principle of territoriality that a State is entitled to tax residents on worldwide income but only to tax non residents on income arising in its territory. In *Marks and Spencer*, the Court of Justice referred to the principle of territoriality in these terms, but rejected the proposition that the fact that the United

---

[15] Case C–168/01 *Bosal Holdings BV v Staatssecretaris van Financiën* [2003] E.C.R. I–9409.

[16] *ibid.*, para.42.

[17] Case C–436/00 [2002] E.C.R. I–829. The case involves the Treaty provisions on capital movement.

[18] In this (protectionist) sense, see e.g. Case 352/85 *Bond van Adverteerders v The Netherlands State* [1988] E.C.R. I–2085, para.34; Case C–224/97 *Ciola* [1999] E.C.R. I–2517, para.16; Case C–164/99 *Portugaia Construções Lda* [2002] E.C.R. I–787, para.26.

[19] In *X,Y* at para.50 the Court supports its reference to "economic aims" by reference to para.48 of its judgment in Case C–35/98 *Staatssecretaris van Financiën v B.G.M. Verkooijen* [2000] E.C.R. I–4071. In fact the reference in the latter case to "aims of a purely economic nature" is a reference to an argument of the United Kingdom that a provision such as that in issue might be justified by the intention to promote the economy of the Netherlands by encouraging investment in the Netherlands. This is an argument which can correctly be described as supporting an economic, in the sense of protectionist, objective.

[20] Case C–250/95 *Futura Participations SA v Administrations des Contributions* [1997] E.C.R. I–2471.

Kingdom does not tax the profits of the non-resident subsidiaries of a parent company might justify restricting group relief to losses incurred by resident companies.[21]

20–051 (e) Article 58(1)(a) EC as a justification for restrictions on capital movement. Article 58(1)(a) EC provides that the provisions of Article 56 EC, which prohibits all restrictions on capital movement as between Member States and between Member States and third countries shall be prohibited, shall be without prejudice to the right of Member States "(a) to apply the relevant provisions of their tax law which distinguish between taxpayers who are not in the same situation with regard to their place of residence or with regard to the place where their capital is invested." In *Manninen*, the Court rejected the argument of the Finnish, French and United Kingdom governments that Article 58(1)(a) EC showed that Member States are entitled to reserve the benefit of a tax credit for in respect of dividends for dividends paid by companies established in their territory. The Court noted (a) that Article 58(1)(a) must be interpreted strictly, and (b) that Article 58(1)(a) is qualified by Article 58(3), which provides that national provisions referred to in Article 58(1) "shall not constitute a means of arbitrary discrimination or a disguised restriction on the free movement of capital and payments as defined in Article 56." It followed in the Court's view that a "distinction must therefore be made between unequal treatment which is permitted under Article 58(1)(a) EC and arbitrary discrimination which is prohibited by Article 58(3)." This meant in turn that any difference in treatment must concern situations which are not objectively comparable or are justified by overriding reasons in the general interest, such as the cohesion of the tax system.[22] In truth, the Court's interpretation of Article 58(1)(a) EC treats it as simply declaratory of principles developed in cases such as *Schumacker* and *Bachmann*.[23]

Assessment of the Court's case law on national tax provisions and the internal market

20–052 The Court's identification of national tax rules as restrictions on fundamental freedoms, particularly as restrictions on freedom of establishment and capital movement, is consistent with the approach it has adopted to the interpretation and application of the relevant

---

[21] Case C–446/03 *Marks & Spencer plc v David Halsey (HM Inspector of Taxes)*, n.99, paras 39, 40. The Court rejected an argument based on fiscal territoriality in Case C–168/01 *Bosal Holdings BV v Staatssecretaris van Financiën* [2003] E.C.R. I–9409, paras 37 *et seq.*, and in Case C–19/02 *Petri Manninen* [2004] E.C.R. I–7477, paras 31 *et seq.*

[22] Case C–19/02 *Petri Manninen* [2004] E.C.R. I–7477, paras 27–29.

[23] This is made clear in Case C–35/98 *Staatssecretaris van Financiën v B.G.M. Verkooijen* [2000] E.C.R. I–4071, paras 43 and 44, cited by the Court in *Manninen* at para.29.

Treaty provisions in other areas of national regulatory competence. This is a realistic approach. Application of national tax rules—in particular differentiation between individuals and companies on the basis of residence—can certainly hinder cross-border activities. The Court's approach to *justifications* for such restrictions is more questionable. Having accepted the principle of cohesion of the tax system as a basis for justifying restrictions on freedom of movement, the Court of Justice has defined the principle so narrowly as to deprive it of useful effect. It is unfortunate that the proposal of Advocate General Maduro in *Marks and Spencer* to revisit and develop that principle did not meet with the Court's explicit approval. At least the result in the latter case is a reminder that it is not impossible to justify restrictions on fundamental freedoms which result from the application of national tax laws. But it is certainly arguable that the Court's case law lacks sufficient recognition of the legitimacy of national policies which aim to avoid diminution of tax revenue through erosion of the tax base. The power of the State to levy tax underpins all other activities of the State. The Court's case law recognises the effectiveness of fiscal supervision as a mandatory requirement in the general interest,[24] yet denies that maintenance of the tax base amounts to such a requirement. It cannot be a satisfactory basis for this approach that the latter interest is "purely economic". *Protectionist* interests are incompatible with fundamental freedoms. Economic interests as such are not. An express ground for derogation from Article 30 is protection of industrial and commercial property, and such protection also amounts to a mandatory requirement in the general interest as regards other fundamental freedoms[25]—yet national measures in this field essentially have the aim of protecting *economic interests*. Furthermore, the Court has held that while economic aims cannot justify restrictions on freedom of movement, it is not impossible that the risk of seriously undermining the financial balance of the social security system may constitute an overriding reason in the general interest.[26] Again, the Court has referred to, without ruling out, the possibility that the concern of a Member State to encourage long-term saving might justify restrictions on the right of establishment.[27] To exclude absolutely from the category of mandatory requirements in the general interest national measures which have the aim of avoiding diminution of tax revenue

---

[24] See e.g. Case C–39/04 *Laboratoires Fournier SA v Direction des verification nationales et internationals* [2005] E.C.R. I–2057, para.24.

[25] See e.g. Case C–255/97 *Pfeiffer Großhandel Gmbh v Löwa Warenahndel Gmbh* [1999] E.C.R. I–2835, para.21, protection of industrial and commercial property justifies restrictions on right of establishment.

[26] Case C–322/01 *Deutscher Apothekerverband eV v 0800 DocMorris NV and Jacques Waterval* [2003] E.C.R. I–14887, para.122, and cases cited there.

[27] Case C–442/02 *CaixaBank France v Ministère de l'Économie, des Finances et de l'Industrie* [2004] E.C.R. I–8961, para.23.

or of avoiding the erosion of the tax base is difficult to justify on legal grounds. One result of such exclusion is that Member States are increasingly forced to treat tax collected in another Member State as equivalent to tax collected by them in their own Member States, for purposes such as giving tax credits to shareholders in respect of corporation tax paid by non resident companies in other Member States. Such a result might be said to have effects more akin to those of positive measures of harmonisation adopted under Article 94 EC, rather than to those of the "negative harmonisation" which results from the application of directly effective Treaty provisions; indeed the obligation of a Member State under the Treaty provisions on free movement of capital to give tax credits to individual shareholders in respect of corporation tax paid by companies resident in other Member States is analogous to the obligations imposed on Member States pursuant to Directive 90/435.[28] Another result of such exclusion is that Member States may be required to give reliefs in respect of activities not themselves subject to or yielding tax.[29] It might be that one effect of the Court's case law is to encourage Member States along the road to harmonisation,[30] but such a consideration should not influence the Court's reasoning in particular cases.

While the Court's minimalist approach to justification of restrictions on fundamental freedoms resulting from national provisions may be open to criticism, this criticism should be kept in perspective. Even if the Court did adopt a more positive approach to possible justifications for restrictions resulting from the application of national tax rules, it is likely that the outcome in the great majority of cases would be the same. In many cases Member States have had difficulty in formulating convincing grounds for differential treatment of non residents, either in general, or in the case in point, and the "blanket" approach of some such rules would rule out justification on proportionality grounds.[31] And in terms of overall outcome,

---

[28] See above at p.887.

[29] Case C–446/03 *Marks & Spencer plc v David Halsey (HM Inspector of Taxes)* n.99, above falls into this category. Another case which might be criticised on this ground is Case C–168/01 *Bosal Holdings BV v Staatssecretaris van Financiën* [2003] E.C.R. I–9409.

[30] See Wathelet, "Free Movement and National Taxation" (2001) 20 Y.E.L. 1, "It may be that, if there is a continuing increase in the number of cases brought, either before the Court of Justice or before the national courts, that will force the Member States to accelerate moves towards a harmonisation of national laws"; at p.33. Mr Wathelet was a judge at the Court of Justice until 2003 and was reporting judge in a number of cases on national tax provisions and fundamental freedoms.

[31] For example, Case C–279/93 *Finanzamt Köln-Alstadt v Schumacker* [1995] E.C.R. I–225; Case C–330/91 *R v Inland Revenue Commissioners ex parte Commerzbank AG* [1993] E.C.R. I–4017; Case C–1/93 *Halliburton Services BV v Staatssecretaris van Financiën* [1994] E.C.R. I–1137; Case C–397/98 *Metallgesellschaft Ltd* and Case C–410/89 *Hoechst AG, Hoechst UK Ltd* [2001] E.C.R. I–1727; Case C–324/00 *Lankhorst-Hohorst GmbH v Finanzamt Steinfurt* [2002] E.C.R. I–11779; Case C–9/02 *Hughes de Lasteyre du Saillant* [2004] E.C.R. I–409.

the Court's case law in this field, as in others, is having a positive and beneficial impact in removing obstacles to the cross-frontier activity of individuals and companies. For those who see a functioning and effective internal market as the most significant contribution of the EU to the well being of its peoples, this is no small countervailing consideration.

The European Commission considers judicial developments and ad hoc responses by Member States as being less satisfactory than harmonisation

The European Commission sees harmonisation rather than *ad hoc* **20–053** responses to the Court's case law as being more likely to contribute to an effective internal market. The Commission's Communication of November 24, 2003 on an Internal Market without Company Tax obstacles states[32]:

> "If individual Member States delay corrective action until these contraventions are confirmed in ECJ decisions they are then faced with having to make hurried and uncoordinated changes to their tax systems. This approach is inefficient, fails to address the fundamental problems, and often leaves open tax planning opportunities. Furthermore, inasmuch as investment decisions are driven by such 'tax engineering' considerations, rather than by expectations about the pure economic return, this is also particularly detrimental to an optimal allocation of capital and thus the above-mentioned 'Lisbon-objectives'."

The reference to the Lisbon objectives is to the Lisbon summit which in the year 2000 committed the European Union to the aim of being the most competitive knowledge based economy in the world by 2010.[33]

Commission initiative for a common consolidated corporate tax base

The Commission's policy for advancing the Lisbon agenda in face **20–054** of obstacles to cross-border business activity posed by the different systems of company taxation is to seek to secure a common consolidated corporate tax base ('CCCTB') for EU businesses. In its

---

[32] Brussels, COM (2003) 726 final, November 24, 2003, Communication from the Commission to the Council, the European Parliament and the European Economic and Social Committee—An Internal Market without company tax obstacles: achievements, ongoing initiatives and remaining challenges, at p.6.

[33] Presidency Conclusions of the Lisbon European Council of March 23 and 24, 2000, Press release No.: 100/1/00, March 24, 2000, published on the website of the Council of the European Union (*http://ue.eu.int*).

Communication of October 2005 on The Contribution of Taxation and Customs Policies to the Lisbon Strategy, the Commission summarises the problems as it sees them and the possible solution in the form of a CCCTB:[34]

"The present co-existence of 25 different and sometimes even mutually incompatible corporation tax systems in the EU *de facto* imposes supplementary compliance costs and offers few opportunities for cross-border loss compensation, even though such loss compensation frequently exists for purely domestic situations. This should not happen in a truly single market. While in their commercial activities (research, production, inventories, sales, etc.) companies increasingly tend to treat the EU as one single market, they are obliged, for tax purposes alone, to segment it into national markets. Corporate tax rules treat cross-border activities in the EU differently and frequently less favourably than similar purely domestic activities. This encourages firms to invest domestically and deters participation in foreign companies and the establishment of subsidiaries abroad. At the same time, inconsistencies between national systems open possibilities for tax avoidance.

The Commission policy of working towards a Common Consolidated Corporate Tax Base ("CCCTB") dates back to 2001[35] and was confirmed in 2003.[36] A CCCTB would enable companies operating in the internal market to follow the same rules for calculating their tax bases in different Member States of the EU. The Commission does not intend to propose a harmonised corporate income tax rate. However, a Common Consolidated Corporate Tax Base would permit cross-border offsetting of losses and would solve the current tax problems linked to cross-border activities and restructuring of groups of companies. A method for sharing the consolidated tax base between Member States so that each State could apply its own tax rate to its share of the consolidated base would have to be agreed. This method should lead to a simpler and more transparent corporate tax system in the EU. This is a challenging exercise, but the Commission intends to carry out the necessary preparatory work towards a Common Consolidated Tax Base during the next three years in order to present a Community legislative measure by 2008."

---

[34] COM (2005) 532 final, at p.5.
[35] Commission, COM (2001) 582 and SEC (2001) 1681.
[36] Commission, COM (2003) 726.

The Commission and the European Parliament continue to argue that the CCCTB should initially be proposed as optional for companies and would not entail the replacement of national tax bases.[37] Not all companies operate in more than one Member State and there is no need for such companies to change their tax base.[38] The Commission accepts that the simultaneous operation of two corporate tax bases—the CCCTB and the national tax base—might raise issues for national tax administrations, but considers that an optional CCCTB would be more likely to gain the support of all Member States and of business than a compulsory CCCTB.[39] For enterprises, using only one tax base rather than up to 25 would be much simpler, while designing the CCCTB as optional also creates an incentive for its design to be as competitive as possible.[40] The introduction of a common tax base in the EU would mean allowing EU firms to reduce their compliance costs by being able to compute their aggregate profits in the internal market according to a single set of tax rules. Implementing such a strategy would however mean that a formula would have to be developed to distribute the common tax base across the Member States.[41] If it is possible to secure agreement on a CCCTB, it could provide a valuable optional alternative regime for companies seeking to avoid obstacles to cross-border activity resulting from disparities between national tax regimes. As an optional alternative regime it would compete with purely national options rather than foreclosing options and limiting competition between Member States in the provision of business friendly tax systems. A CCCTB Working Group was established in 2004 and a work programme established and implemented involving initially four sub-groups dealing with (a) Assets and Depreciation (b) Provisions, Reserves and Liabilities; (c) Taxable Income; and (d) International Aspects. Their work is expected to be broadly completed by the end of 2006.[42]

---

[37] COM (2006) 157 Final, Implementing the Community Lisbon Programme: Progress to date and next steps towards a CCCTB, point 3.4.

[38] *ibid*.

[39] *ibid*.

[40] *ibid*.

[41] Although EU Member States currently do not use formulary methods to distribute a common consolidated tax base across national boundaries, Canada and the United States have extensive experience using formulary methods to distribute income across sub-national boundaries; see Tax Papers, Formulary Apportionment and Group Taxation in the European Union: insights from the United States and Canada By Joann Martens Weiner Working paper No.8 March 2005 *http://europa.eu.int/comm/taxation—customs/ resources/documents/taxation/gen—info/economic—analysis/tax—papers/2004—2073—EN —web—final@20version.pdf*. Although published by the Commission D-G on Taxation and the Customs Union working papers in this series represent the views solely of their authors.

[42] COM(2006) 157 Final, point 3.1.

While Commission policy is to advance the CCCTB initiative, and the CCCTB Working Group has been active,[43] even within the Commission the view has not been unanimous that the CCCTB comprises a viable exercise. A pessimistic view on the CCCTB, and a less than enthusiastic view on broader issues of tax harmonisation, has been expressed by Mr McCreevy, Commissioner for the internal market and services:

"The Commission has started preparatory work on harmonising the corporate tax base across Europe with a view to aiding simplification for pan-European companies and investors. It is not an area where I have direct responsibility in the Commission although as a Member of the Competitiveness Group of Commissioners I have a keen interest in the role that a sensible taxation environment can play in enhancing Europe's economic prospects. So lets consider the proposal for a harmonised tax base in this light . . . First, it is inevitable that any exercise involving tax base harmonisation will have winners and losers. Those winners and losers will be determined by the basis on which the cake is divided or in other words how the allocation of a company's pan-European profits across the Member States is broken down for the purposes of levying the tax. The major challenge is to determine what criteria are used for determining the size of each slice of the cake . . . To establish a common tax base we will need first to get agreement on what constitutes taxable profits. At the moment there are wide divergences between Member States—in terms of what interest expense is tax deductible and what isn't, what capital spending is allowable and what isn't, over what period assets can be depreciated and what depreciation is allowable and what isn't, how and when income is recognised in different circumstances for tax purposes, to what extent and in what circumstances tax losses can be carried forward and for how long . . .

I am not going to anticipate what progress will be made on advancing the consolidated tax base idea . . .

My colleague Lazlo Kovacs has been making excellent progress with a whole series of proposals for simplifying and easing the burden of administration of tax and customs obligations for companies operating across Member States. I believe that this will make a meaningful contribution over time towards reducing the regulatory and cost burdens for businesses trading across-borders.

---

[43] The CCCTB Working Group held its first meeting on November 23, 2004, four meetings in 2005, a meeting in March 2006, with a seventh meeting scheduled for June 2006. At the outset two Member States indicated that a distinction was to be drawn between technical participation and the political aspects of the common tax base project. The two Member States in question remained politically opposed to a common tax base.

But let me reiterate that I am emphatically opposed to tax harmonisation—be it by the front door or the back."[44]

Nevertheless, the Commission has reiterated the aim of presenting a comprehensive Community legislative CCCTB measure at the end of 2008.[45] It is as yet unclear whether a CCCTB will prove feasible, and if feasible whether it will prove an attractive option for companies.

The broader perspective

The need for unanimity makes far-reaching tax harmonisation **20–055** under Article 94 EC unlikely; though recourse to enhanced co-operation under Article 43 TEU would be a possibility. In the short term at least, *ad hoc* responses by individual Member States to rulings of the Court of Justice are likely to overshadow collective initiatives. This might be no bad thing. The negative harmonisation of Court judgments removes obstacles to cross-border business activity, and promotes overall economic welfare. For the time being that is a worthy European priority.

Further reading

Ebke, "The European Conflict-of-Corporate-Laws Revolution: *Überseering, Inspire Art,*and Beyond" [2005] E.B.L.R. 13.

Edwards, *EC Company Law* (OUP, Oxford, 1999).

Edwards, "The European Company-Essential Tool or Eviscerated Dream" (2003) 40 C.M.L.Rev. 443.

Johnston, Andrew, "The European Takeover Directive: ruined by protectionism or respecting diversity?" (2004) 25(9) Comp. Law. 270–276.

Kirchner and Painter, "Takeover Defenses under Delaware Law, the Proposed Thirteenth EU Directive and the New German Takeover Law: Comparison and Recommendations for Reform" (2002) 50 Am. J. Comp. L. 451–476.

Knudsen, Jette Steen, "Is the Single European Market an illusion? Obstacles to reform of EU takeover regulation." (2005) 11(4) E.L.J. 507–524.

du Plessis, Jean J., and Sandrock, Otto, "The German corporate governance model in the wake of company law harmonisation in the European Union" (2005) 26(3) Comp. Law. 88–95.

Rickford (ed.), *The European Company* (Intersentia, 2003).

Roth, W.H., "From *Centros* to *Überseering:* Free Movement of Companies, Private International Law, and Community Law" (2003) 52 I.C.L.Q. 177.

---

[44] "Tax Harmonisation—No thanks", speech for European Business Initiative on Taxation, Brussels, November 10, 2005, SPEECH/05/679.
[45] COM (2006) 157 Final, point 3.5.

Szyszczak, Erika, "Golden Shares and Market Governance, Legal Issues in European Integration" (2002) 29(3) 255.

Siems, "The impact of the European Company (SE) on legal culture" (2005) 30 E.L.Rev. 431–442.

Wathelet, "Free Movement and National Taxation" (2001) 20 Y.E.L. 1.

Wymeersch, "The Transfer of the Company's Seat in European Company Law" (2003) C.M.L.Rev. 661.

CHAPTER 21

COMPLETING THE INTERNAL MARKET[1]

Guide to this Chapter: This Chapter is about the powers that **21–001** are available under the EC Treaty, and the steps that have been taken by the Union's Institutions and Member States, to complete the task of establishing a single market within which the free movement of goods, persons, services and capital can be fully realised. The Chapter begins by recalling the legislative programme that was initiated by a Commission White Paper in the mid-1980s, with the aim of putting in place the legal framework of the internal market by the beginning of 1993. While remarkable progress was made, it will be seen that, even today, the goal of a unified market remains elusive; it is now being pursued within the wider socio-economic strategy laid down in March 2000 by the European Council of Lisbon. Measures designed to remove impediments to the establishment and functioning of the internal market are enacted, using legal machinery that was initially created by amendments to the EC Treaty by the SEA. That machinery is closely analysed, in particular Article 14 EC, which defines the internal market project, and Article 95 EC, which is the main legal basis for adopting internal market measures. The criteria that govern the choice between Article 95 EC, and other legal bases that may be available for the adoption of legislation affecting the internal market, are then considered. There follows

---

[1] The present chapter was, in its original version, largely a reworking of a report by Alan Dashwood on research carried out within the Centre for Studies and Research of The Hague Academy of International Law at its 1991 session: see *The Legal Implications of 1993 for Member and Non-Member Countries of the EEC* (Martinus Nijhoff, 1992), pp.91 *et seq.* The authors express their thanks to the Curatorium of the Academy for their kind permission to draw on that report.

an examination of common labelling rules to illustrate the relationship between harmonisation and the free movement of goods.
The real virtue of common labelling rules is that they make it
easier to produce multi-lingual labels—the hallmark of a product
which is as near as it is possible to get to a product which is
genuinely "European", in that it can be packaged and labelled in
a way which makes it marketable across the EU. The relationship
between the mutual recognition principle resulting from the *Cassis*
judgment, and legislation at Community level is also examined.
While the former in general requires national rules simply to be
disapplied, the role of Community rules is normally to set common standards where Member States can justify refusing to
recognise product standards adopted in other Member States
and maintaining their own rules. Community rules may also be
appropriate, however, to deal with national rules that are simply
prohibited by Community law. The Chapter ends with a discussion of the Commission's proposal for a general directive on
services in the internal market. The original idea was that the
directive would establish the principle that service providers
should be supervised exclusively by the authorities of their
Member State of establishment (known as "the country of origin
principle")—an innovation that would have swept away many of
the restrictions that are inhibiting the development of the market
for services. Unfortunately, as we shall see, the Commission has
been forced by political pressures to abandon that idea, seriously
weakening its proposal in a way that bodes ill for the continuing
liberalisation of the market.

Unfinished business

The single market programme of the Delors Commission

21–002   As previous chapters will have made clear, when the 12-year
transitional period for the establishment of the common market
ended on December 31, 1969, "the elimination of all obstacles to
intra-Community trade in order to merge the national markets into a
single market bringing about conditions as close as possible to those
of a genuine internal market"[2] was still far from having been
achieved. The rapid development of the case law of the Court of
Justice on the scope and the direct effect of the prohibitions
contained in such provisions of the EC Treaty as Articles 28, 29, 43
and 49 EC allowed a great variety of discriminatory or otherwise

---

[2] Case 15/81 *Schul v Inspecteur de Invoerrechten en Accijnzen* [1982] E.C.R. 1409, 1431–1432;
[1982] 3 C.M.L.R. 11.

unjustifiable interferences with freedom of movement to be challenged successfully, but the completion of the internal market could not be achieved by judicial action alone. A major legislative effort was needed, and this was finally set in train by the Commission which took office in January 1985 under the Presidency of Mr Jacques Delors.

Responding to an invitation issued at the Brussels meeting of the European Council in March 1985, the Commission prepared a White Paper[3] on completing the internal market, which it presented at the Milan meeting in June of that year. The White Paper set out a detailed legislative programme for the unification of the market, focusing on the removal of the remaining physical, technical and fiscal barriers to freedom of movement for goods, persons, services and capital. Annexed to the programme was a timetable for the adoption of the specific measures the Commission considered necessary to achieve the desired unification. The deadline fixed for the final establishment of the internal market was December 31, 1992, which gave a period of some eight years (corresponding, at the time, to two Commission terms of office), for the enactment of the necessary measures. The European Council welcomed the Commission's White Paper and instructed the Council to initiate a precise programme of action based upon it.

New legal machinery for the attainment of the political objectives stated in the White Paper and endorsed by the European Council was included in the SEA which represented the outcome of inter-governmental negotiations undertaken in the light of the conclusions reached at the Milan meeting. The SEA was signed on February 17, 1986, and entered into force, after ratification by the Member States, on July 1, 1987. The provisions relating to the internal market which the SEA added to the EC Treaty were broadly of two kinds: general principles defining the project to be implemented by the end of 1992, which are to be found, notably, in Article 14 EC; and new or modified legal bases for the enactment of internal market legislation, notably Article 95 EC which applies where measures are needed for the approximation of provisions laid down by law, regulation or administrative action in Member States.[4]

Progress in the implementation of the legislative programme contained in the White Paper of 1985 was the subject of annual reports submitted by the Commission to the Council and the European Parliament. The seventh, and last, such report,[5] which the Commission presented in September 1992, noted that, of the 282

---

[3] COM (85) 310.

[4] For a full analysis of the background to the SEA and of its provisions, see J. De Ruyt, *L'Acte unique européen* (Editions de l'Université de Bruxelles, 1987). On the internal market aspects of the SEA, see A. Mattera, *Le marché unique européen* (2nd ed., Jupiter, 1990).

[5] COM (92) 383 final.

measures proposed in the White Paper, 32 remained to be adopted by the Council; nine of these were of low priority, not being linked to the removal of frontier controls, so that there were only 23 measures which, in the Commission's view, the Council needed to tackle as a matter of urgency, if necessary by holding special meetings.[6] As for the rate of transposition of directives by the Member States, this was estimated by the Commission as 75 per cent (89 per cent in the case of directives that were in force in June 1991).[7] The Commission's overall assessment was that "in view of the decisions already in force, the economic framework for the single market is now in place, with people, goods, capital and services able to move around freely either on the basis of harmonised or common rules or on the basis of mutual recognition".[8] In similar vein, the 27th General Report spoke of the White Paper programme's "having been all but completed".[9]

The internal market and the Lisbon Strategy

21-003 There is nothing in the wording of Article 95 EC, or of the other legal bases for internal market measures, to suggest it was intended that their force should be spent once the deadline of December 31, 1992 was reached: indeed, the reference in Article 95(1) EC to "the establishment *and functioning* of the internal market"[10] indicates the opposite. Since 1992, legislation has continued to be enacted on the basis of Article 95, though at a lower level of intensity. Reacting to the recommendations of a study group, which was set up under one of its former Members, Mr Sutherland, and which reported in October 1992,[11] the Commission has sought ways of ensuring that the internal market operates so as to produce the expected benefits. An attempt has been made to organise legislative activity in a series of framework programmes, setting strategic targets and identifying the specific measures needed to achieve them.

The process of completing the internal market has now been subsumed within the wider socio-economic strategy that was laid down for the European Union by the special meeting of the European Council held in Lisbon on March 23 and 24, 2000. At that meeting, the European Council set, as a goal for the European Union over the next decade, "to become the most competitive and dynamic knowledge-based economy in the world, capable of sustainable economic growth with more and better jobs and greater social cohesion".[12] The environmental aim of "sustainable development"

---

[6] At points 17-19.
[7] *ibid.*, point 11.
[8] *ibid.*, point 1.
[9] 27th Gen. Rep. EC, p.36, point 70.
[10] Emphasis added.
[11] 26th Gen. Rep. EC, p.37, point 70.
[12] Lisbon Conclusions, point 5.

has since been added to that already ambitious agenda. Progress in implementing the "Lisbon strategy" is reviewed annually at the Spring meeting of the European Council. At the mid-term review in March 2005, it had to be acknowledged that the results to date had been "mixed".[13] The European Council meeting in Brussels on March 22 and 23, 2005 sought to relaunch the strategy, by identifying two priorities on which urgent action was needed: stronger and more sustainable growth, and more and better jobs.[14] At the time of writing, it was unclear whether the political will would be found at Member State level to carry out the structural reforms, especially of labour markets, that were widely perceived to be necessary in order to increase the competitiveness of European businesses. The agreement by the French Government to scrap an employment law reform, following violent demonstrations by students and trade unionists in the Spring of 2006, was symptomatic of a discouraging political conjuncture.

As to the internal market, the Lisbon Presidency Conclusions described it, rather optimistically, as "largely complete . . .".[15] Nevertheless, it was said, "[r]apid work is required in order to complete the internal market in certain sectors and to improve under-performance in others in order to ensure the interests of business and consumers".[16] This should take place within "[a]n effective framework for ongoing review and improvement.[17] The currently applicable framework was established by a Commission Communication of May 7, 2003, defining an "Internal Market Strategy" for the period 2003 to 2006.[18] The progress made, and the difficulties encountered in various sectors of the internal market, are recorded in a "scoreboard", which is published periodically by the Commission.[19]

The Internal Market Strategy highlights the importance of the integration of services markets. The main instrument designed by the Commission to eliminate the many obstacles to the development of service activities in the internal market, is its proposal for a general directive on services, which was submitted to the Council early in 2004.[20] At the time of writing, it seemed that the Services Directive, as we shall call it,[21] would be capable of being adopted

---

[13] Gen. Rep. EU 2005, pp.47–49.
[14] *ibid.*
[15] Lisbon Conclusions, point 3.
[16] *ibid.*, point 16.
[17] *ibid.*
[18] COM (2003) 238 final.
[19] See, e.g. Annex 1 to Second Implementation Report of the Internal Market Strategy 2003–2006, COM (2005) 11 final.
[20] COM (2004) 2 final/3.
[21] The proposal is also known as "the Bolkenstein Directive", after the Commissioner responsible for the internal market at the time when it was drafted, who was a strong supporter of its liberalising tendency.

only in a severely weakened form; the proposal is further considered in the final section of the present chapter. The political opposition it has encountered gives an indication that the business of establishing a truly open and competitive market within the EU for the full range of goods and services is likely to remain unfinished for some time to come.

Article 14: the internal market project
21–004   Article 14 EC, as amended by the TA, provides as follows:

> "1. The Community shall adopt measures with the aim of progressively establishing the internal market over a period expiring on December 31, 1992, in accordance with the provisions of this Article and of Articles 15, 26, 47(2), 49, 80, 93 and 95 and without prejudice to the other provisions of this Treaty.
> 2. The internal market shall comprise an area without internal frontiers in which the free movement of goods, persons, services and capital is ensured in accordance with the provisions of this Treaty.
> 3. The Council, acting by a qualified majority on a proposal from the Commission, shall determine the guidelines and conditions necessary to ensure balanced progress in all the sectors concerned".[22]

Paragraph (1) of the Article created an obligation for "the Community" to achieve a specified object (the establishment of the internal market) within a specified time-limit (December 31, 1992) and by specified means (the adoption of "measures" in accordance with certain Articles of the EC Treaty, but without prejudice to its other provisions). Paragraph (2) defines the notion "internal market". Although, for convenience in presentation, we examine the two paragraphs separately, it is important to stress that the Article must be read as a whole, the second paragraph merely clarifying the object to be achieved within the deadline, and by the means, laid down in the first paragraph. The provisions of paragraph (3) were previously contained in the second paragraph of Article 7b, which was repealed by the TA.

The obligation in the first paragraph
21–005 The obligation imposed on "the Community" was for its institutions to use their respective powers under the Treaty to adopt the measures necessary for the completion of the internal market before

---

[22] Art.14 was originally numbered Art.8. This was changed to Art.7a by the TEU. Para. (3) was added to the Article by the TA.

1993. Article 14 EC does not directly address the Member States but they are bound, pursuant to Article 10 EC, to co-operate fully in the internal market project.[23] The nature and scope of the obligation falling on the Market States will be examined below.

The provisions referred to in Article 14(1) EC are, besides that Article itself: Article 15 EC requiring allowance to be made, in the drafting of internal market proposals, for the effort demanded of "certain economies showing differences in development"; Article 26 EC on the fixing of Common Customs Tariff duties; Article 47(2) EC on the co-ordination of provisions concerning the taking up and pursuit of self-employed activities; Article 49 EC on the abolition of restrictions on the freedom to provide services; Article 80 EC on sea and air transport; Article 93 EC on harmonisation of indirect taxation; and Article 95 EC, as to which, see below.

However, it is expressly stipulated that the list of provisions in Article 14(1) EC is without prejudice to the other provisions of the Treaty. This is important for two reasons.

Firstly, by no means all of the legal bases central to the internal market project are mentioned in the list. For example, veterinary and plant health measures, necessary for the removal of obstacles to trade in live animals and plants, and in the whole range of animal and plant products, fall within the purview of Article 37 EC, the general basis of legislation for the purposes of the common agricultural policy.[24] Similarly, the liberalisation of transport services by rail, road or inland waterway has been pursued on the basis of Article 71 EC.

Secondly, Article 14 EC does not derogate from Article 30 EC, or from other similar provisions of the Treaty allowing freedom of movement to be restricted for certain narrowly-defined, non-economic reasons.[25] Nor does it modify the rule, which was confirmed by the *Cassis de Dijon* line of authority, that the Treaty does not prohibit the non-discriminatory application of national provisions that are necessary to serve important purposes of public interest, even where, owing to disparities between the legal solutions adopted by different Member States, such application may result in impediments to free movement.[26] Thus a major part of the task for the Community institutions consisted of removing the justification

---

[23] On the principle of loyal co-operation in Art.5 EC, see de Cockborne *et al.*, *Commentaire Mégret* (2nd ed., éditions de l'Université de Bruxelles, 1992), Vol.1, Ch.II.

[24] See the discussion of Art.37 as a basis for internal market legislation, below.

[25] *cf.* proviso to Art.39(3) EC, and para.(4) of the same Article (workers); Art.46(1) EC (establishment and services). Such exceptions to fundamental Community principles are very narrowly construed. As to goods, see Case 46/76 [1977] E.C.R. 5; Case 251/78 *Denkavit Futtermittel* [1979] E.C.R. 3369; [1980] 3 C.M.L.R. 513. As to persons, see Case 30/77 *Bouchereau* [1977] E.C.R. 1999; [1977] 2 C.M.L.R. 800.

[26] The abundant case law on the limits of the directly effective prohibitions imposed by the relevant Treaty Articles has been analysed in previous chapters in this book.

hitherto available to Member States under the Treaty for maintaining restrictive national provisions, through the enactment of harmonised rules or of measures for the mutual recognition of standards and qualifications that would adequately protect the interests in question.

The definition in the second paragraph

21–006   The definition of the internal market in the second paragraph of Article 14 EC comprises two elements—absence of internal frontiers and the free movement of goods, persons, services and capital. Those elements may be contrasted in terms of their relative precision and scope.

The first element, a space without internal frontiers, sets the Community institutions the measurable objective of securing the abolition of all frontier controls on goods or persons moving between the Member States. As long as any such controls remain in place, it will be clear that the objective has not been achieved. The second element, consisting of the realisation of the four freedoms, is more elusive: there is simply no way of identifying the exact moment at which the requisite degree of liberalisation will have been attained.

On the other hand, for all its psychological importance, the complete removal of physical frontiers will not, in itself, ensure freedom of movement. For instance, divergent national rules on such things as maximum levels of food additives or the labelling of foodstuffs, could be enforced, even in the absence of frontier controls, by inspection at the retail stage of distribution. Similarly, immigration controls are not the only way of restricting the entry and residence of non-nationals (although perhaps a uniquely effective one in the case of the insular Member States). Controls can be exercised, for example, through hotels or lodging houses, through employers or by spot checks in public places.

21–007   Indeed, for certain kinds of restriction on freedom of movement, the abolition of physical frontiers would have little or no impact. An example, of the greatest importance for the internal market in goods and, to some extent, in services, is the protection of intellectual property rights, still largely organised at the level of individual Member States[27]: such protection is achieved not by checks on imports but by infringement proceedings brought by interested parties in national courts. Another, very obvious, example affecting the free movement of persons is that of differences between Member States as to professional qualifications or the conditions of access to business activities, where impediments can only be removed by harmonisation or mutual recognition.[28]

---

[27] See Chap.16.
[28] See Chap.19, above.

A question that arises is whether the unqualified reference in the second paragraph of Article 14 to the free movement of *persons* can be taken at face value, or whether it must be interpreted in the sense of Title III, Chapters 1 to 3 of Part Three of the Treaty, as relating only to Community nationals who travel to another Member States to carry on employed or self-employed activities, or as providers or recipients of services, i.e. as market actors. It is submitted that the wider interpretation is the correct one. Not only does it correspond to the letter of Article 14 EC (as well as to that of Article 3(c) EC) but it is also necessary to ensure the *effet utile* of the removal of internal frontiers since, if controls are retained for any categories of travellers, they are liable to be applied to all.[29]

The four freedoms are to be ensured "in accordance with the provisions of this Treaty". This confirms the point made in relation to the first paragraph that Article 14 EC does not derogate from the provisions under which certain justified restrictions are tolerated by the Treaty, despite their incompatibility with a single market. The strategy of the Article is to implement a legislative programme removing any such justification, thereby enabling the basic Treaty provisions on freedom of movement to apply with full effect.[30]

A final question is how the notion of the internal market, as defined by Article 14 EC, relates to that of the common market with which it has co-existed in the EC Treaty since the SEA. It would be confusing if, as is sometimes said, the two notions were simply interchangeable. "Common market" is nowhere defined in the Treaty but its primary meaning can be gathered from Article 2 EC, where it is juxtaposed with economic and monetary union and the implementation of the common policies and activities referred to in Article 3 and 4 EC, as one of the principal means by which the Community is to carry out its task. Here "common market" seems to be used as a term of art, covering not only the four economic freedoms highlighted by Article 14 EC but a range of flanking policies, as well as the social dimension of the market. Legislative practice over the years suggests that a similarly broad meaning has been given to the term in Article 94 EC and Article 308 EC. The internal market should, therefore, be regarded as the more specific notion, introduced to provide a sharper focus for the project that was set in motion by the 1985 White Paper.

The legal effects of Article 14

Effects for the Community institutions
Did Article 14 EC impose on the Community institutions involved in **21–008**
the legislative process a *legally* binding obligation? Or was the commitment expressed in the Article to the task of establishing the

---

[29] On the rights of free movement of Union citizens, see Ch.17.
[30] On the same lines, see de Cockborne *et al.*, *op.cit.* n.22, above pp.20 *et seq.*

internal market before the deadline of December 31, 1991 purely political?

The Declaration on Article 14 EC annexed to the Final Act of the SEA might seem to indicate the latter, since it states:

> "The Conference wishes by means of the provisions in Article 8a to express its firm political will to take before January 1, 1993 the decisions necessary to complete the internal market defined in those provisions, and more particularly the decisions necessary to implement the Commission's programme described in the White Paper on the Internal Market.
>
> Setting the date of December 31, 1992 does not create an automatic legal effect".

However, it is thought the Declaration does not express any view as to the nature of the obligation resulting from the Article *for the Community institutions.* The reference in the final sentence to the date of December 31, 1992 as not creating "an automatic legal effect" suggests that the issue the Conference intended to address was that of the possible direct effect of the Article, if the necessary legislation had not been enacted by that date. This is an altogether different issue, to which we return when we examine the effects for the Member States. It is, therefore, submitted that the mandatory language of Article 14(1) EC ("The Community *shall* adopt".) must be given its plain meaning.

21–009   It does not necessarily follow that the admitted failure to ensure, before December 31, 1992, the complete realisation of the internal market as envisaged by Article 14 EC, exposed the Commission (or the Council, in matters in respect of which proposals were lying unadopted on its table) to an adverse finding pursuant to Article 232 EC. Whether an infringement of the Treaty, through the inaction of the institution concerned, could be established, would depend on the test that was formulated by the Court of Justice in Case 13/83, where proceedings under Article 175 EC were brought against the Council by the European Parliament in respect of the failure to introduce a common transport policy before the end of the transitional period.[31] According to that test, the measures which are the subject of the allegation of a failure to act must be defined with sufficient precision for them to be identified individually, and adopted in compliance with the Court's judgment, pursuant to Article 233 EC. This cannot be the case where discretionary power is given to the institution concerned, allowing it to make policy choices the content of which is not specified by the Treaty.

In applying the test laid down in the *Transport* case to Article 14 EC, it is useful to recall what was said in the previous section about

---

[31] Case 13/83 *European Parliament v Council* [1985] E.C.R. 1513. See, more particularly, 1592–1593 and 1596–1597; [1986] 1 C.M.L.R. 138

the two elements of the definition of the internal market in paragraph (2) of the Article.

Ensuring the free movement of goods, persons, services and capital, with all that implies in terms of the harmonisation or mutual recognition of standards, qualifications and control procedures, is too general an objective, and its attainment too fraught with policy choices, to be the subject of proceedings under Article 232 EC: it would not be possible, if the Court found there had been a failure to act, to specify the legislative steps that would have to be taken to comply with the judgment.

Turning to the other element of the definition, the absence of internal frontiers, a further distinction needs to be drawn—between controls on goods and controls on persons. On the one hand, the Commission was able to spell out with reasonable precision the measures necessary to allow the removal of internal physical frontiers in respect of goods[32] (which is not the same as saying that the adoption of such measures proved to be politically a straightforward matter). The measures in question related essentially to the administration of systems of indirect taxation, commercial policy matters affecting Member States individually, human, animal and plant health, the requirements of transport policy and the collection of statistics. In the event, the Commission could declare in its 27th General Report that "border checks on goods are now a thing of the past".[33] On the other hand, the abolition of checks on persons at the common borders of Member States could be achieved only after a range of matters, such as the effective control of external borders and visa requirements for third country nationals, had been regulated. Decisions on these matters clearly involved discretionary choices. In the event, it proved politically possible to make the necessary choices within the context of the "Schengen" agreements, which were concluded outside the constitutional order of the EU by the Member States other than Ireland and the United Kingdom (see below).

In summary, there is a fundamental difference between the legal position in respect of persons and that in respect of goods: namely that, for persons, the Community has no equivalent to the CCT, nor any principle corresponding to that of the free circulation of third country products once these have cleared customs. We conclude that, whereas proceedings under Article 232 EC might have been brought successfully against the Commission or the Council, if the legislative steps necessary for the removal of border controls on goods had not been taken by the date specified in Article 14 EC, the

---

[32] White Paper, points 24–26.
[33] At p.37, para.70. On the final legislative steps in the process, see 26th Gen. Rep. EC, p.38, para.70.

failure to secure the abolition of border controls on persons would not have passed the test of justiciability in the *Transport* case.[34]

Effects for the Member States

21–010 Here the main question is whether, or to what extent, Article 14 EC may be directly effective. Does the Article leave the Member States free to apply their national rules in areas where internal market legislation is not yet in place or where it has not yet been fully implemented, despite the tendency of such rules to restrict the free movement of goods, persons, services or capital? Or would individuals affected by such rules have the right, pursuant to Article 14 EC, to resist their continued application, and would national courts be required to recognise and give effect to that right?

The conditions under which provisions of the EC Treaty and of acts of the institutions produce direct effects for the subjects of the Community legal order, as established in the case law of the Court of Justice, were discussed in Chapter 5. To summarise: the provision in question must be clear and unconditional; and it must also be complete, in the sense of being immediately usable by the Court of Justice or by national courts in determining the rights and obligations of individuals, without any need for further definition of those rights and obligations by the legislator.

Article 14 EC would not seem to fulfil those conditions since, as we have seen, the creation of an area without internal frontiers in which the four freedoms are ensured *in accordance with the provisions of the Treaty* requires the enactment of Community measures making recourse to restrictive national provisions, in the cases allowed by the Treaty, no longer justifiable. Given the need for such legislation, until this is fully in place certain impediments to freedom of movement, resulting from the application of national provisions, will continue.

21–011 That analysis appears to be consistent with the Declaration to Article 14 EC, cited above, in which it was stated that the setting of the end of 1992 deadline "does not create an automatic legal effect". While the case law of the Court of Justice casts doubt on the interpretative value of statements entered in the minutes of the

---

[34] The opposite view was taken by the European Parliament. After calling upon the Commission to put forward proposals for the abolition of border controls on persons, and having received what it regarded as an unsatisfactory reply, the Parliament brought proceedings under Art.232 EC against the Commission in November 1993: see Case C–445/93 [1994] O.J. C1/12. In July 1995, the Commission submitted to the Council proposals for three measures, founded on provisions of the EC Treaty, with a view to securing the free movement of persons, including third country nationals, across internal Community frontiers: see Editorial Comments in (1996) 33 C.M.L.Rev. 1. These made no headway within the Council. The proceedings in Case C–445/93 were terminated in July 1996.

Council,[35] a published declaration of a negotiating conference is in a quite different category. The Declaration in question made manifest the intention of the Conference of the Representatives of the Government of the Member States, at the time of signing the SEA, to avoid the result that, independently of the state of implementation of the White Paper, complete freedom of movement might be legally a *fait accompli* after December 31, 1992.[36] It has sometimes been claimed that the maintenance of controls at the internal frontiers of the Community has been absolutely prohibited since December 31, 1992. The Commission seemed, at one time to believe that Article 14 EC, taken together with Article 10 EC, imposed such a prohibition.[37] If that were correct, any Member State which had not dismantled internal frontier controls by the end of 1992 would have been in breach of the Treaty and liable to be condemned in enforcement proceedings under Article 226 EC or Article 227 EC, and it would also run the risk of having to pay compensation to undertakings or individuals suffering loss as a result of the failure to abolish controls.[38]

However, as the foregoing analysis will have made clear, the matter is more complicated. Border controls on movement between Member States become illegal if, but only if, they are no longer necessary to safeguard interests recognised as legitimate by the Treaty. That will obviously be the case where harmonised rules, standards or qualifications are *fully* in place. It is further submitted that, even where the legislative framework remains incomplete, the combined effect of Article 14 EC and the obligation of loyal co-operation in Article 10 EC will prevent Member States from having recourse to frontier controls, if the interests in question could be protected by some other means. The principle of proportionality,

---

[35] Case 38/69 *Commission v Italy* [1970] E.C.R. 47; [1970] C.M.L.R. 77; Case 237/84 *Commission v Belgium* [1986] E.C.R. 1247. More recently in Case C–292/89 *Antonissen* [1991] E.C.R. 745, 778; [1991] 2 C.M.L.R. 373, the Court said: ". . . a declaration cannot be used for the purpose of interpreting a provision of secondary legislation where, as in this case, no reference is made to the content of the declaration in the wording of the provision in question".

[36] On the effect of the Declaration, see the article by Judge F. Schockweiler, (1991) R.M.C. 882. As to the effect in international law of such interpretative declarations, see Art.31(3) of the Vienna Convention of 1969 on the law of Treaties. In Case C–378/97 *Criminal proceedings against Florus Arieël Wijsenbeek* (see below), Advocate General Cosmas expressed the opinion that the rule of international law could not be transposed into Community law: once amending provisions become part of the EC Treaty, they acquire a legal force independent of their authors' wishes. See his Opinion, paras 51–54. We respectfully disagree. It must be possible for the supreme constitutional authority of the European Union as determined by Art.48 TEU, to decide the scope and legal effect of amending provisions, and to make its intentions clear in a published text.

[37] See the Commission's Communication of May 18, 1992 (SEC (92) 877 final). See also the remarks by Vice-President Bangemann reported in *Agence Europe*, February 26, 1992, pp.9 and 10. However, the Commission appeared to change its mind: see Case C–378/97, considered below.

[38] On the doctrine of state liability, see Ch.5, above.

too, would seem to require, in the conditions of the internal market, that frontier controls be retained only where they are truly indispensable.[39] So, while there was no automatic obligation to abolish all controls at the Community's internal frontiers before January 1, 1993, as from that date the burden of proof has been upon Member States to justify the retention of such controls.

The continuing justification for Member States' requiring persons crossing one of the Community's internal borders to produce a passport or other proof of nationality, was at issue in the *Wijsenbeek* case.[40] The proceedings arose out of the prosecution of a Dutch national for refusing to show his passport or to prove his nationality by other means, on re-entry into the Netherlands. His claim that, since January 1, 1993, there had been a directly effective prohibition against internal border controls, was rejected by the Court. Article 14 EC, the Court said, "cannot be interpreted as meaning that, in the absence of measures adopted by the Council before December 31, 1992 requiring the Member States to abolish controls of persons at the internal frontiers of the Community, that obligation automatically arises from expiry of that period".[41] Such an obligation presupposed harmonisation of national laws on the crossing of external borders, immigration, the granting of visas and asylum, and the exchange of information on those matters. Mr Wijsenbeek also invoked his right of free movement as a citizen of the Union, pursuant to Article 18(1) EC; but here, again, the Court held that it remained justifiable for the authorities to insist upon proof of nationality.

21–012   The Court referred in its judgment both to the Declaration on Article 14 EC, and to another Declaration adopted on the occasion of the signing of the Final Act of the SEA and relating to Articles 13 to 19 of that Treaty, which states: "Nothing in these provisions shall affect the right of Member States to take such measures as they consider necessary for the purpose of controlling immigration from third countries, and to combat terrorism, crime, the traffic in drugs and illicit trading in works of art and antiques". However, there is no discussion in the judgment as to the legal effect of the two Declarations.

It is important to be clear that, in *Wijsenbeek*, the Court was not saying that Articles 14 and 18 EC are incapable, in principle, of conferring rights on individuals. Without specifically addressing the issue of the direct effect of those Articles, the Court observed that, even if they did confer on nationals of the Member States an

---

[39] See the discussion of the proportionality principle in Ch.7.
[40] Case C–378/97 [1999] E.C.R. I–6207. See also, in the field of social security, Case C–297/92 *Baglieri* [1993] E.C.R. I–5211, paras 16–17.
[41] At para.40 of the *Wijsenbeek* judgment. See also the Opinion of Advocate General Cosmas, para.77.

"unconditional right" of internal free movement, it was still open to the authorities to carry out identity checks "in order to be able to establish whether the person concerned is a national of a Member State, thus having the right to move freely within the territory of the Member States, or a national of a non-member country, not having that right".[42]

The *Wijsenbeek* judgment confirms the foregoing analysis of Article 14 EC. The passing of the deadline set by the Article did not have the "automatic legal effect" of prohibiting the imposition of internal border controls. These may be retained, however, only as long as they can be justified in accordance with the provisions of the Treaty.

Schengen and the abolition of internal border controls

Although interesting in principle, the issue of the direct effect of **21–013** Article 14 EC has lost much of its practical significance since the entry into force of the TA. Of the then 15 Member States, 13 have achieved the abolition of checks at their common borders on the basis of a body of law that was originally developed outside the Treaty framework, under the so-called Schengen Agreement of 1985 and the Schengen Implementing Convention of 1990. Moreover, the 10 new Member States are legally committed to join in "Schengen co-operation", subject to the provisions of the Treaty of Accession. However, the United Kingdom and Ireland have been given the right, at the level of primary Union law, to continue to apply their national systems of border control, including in the face of any possible direct effect of Article 14 EC.

The rather disparate body of legal elements constituting the "Schengen *acquis*" was incorporated into the law of the EU pursuant to a Protocol, which was annexed to the EC Treaty and the TEU by the TA.[43] Under the arrangements there laid down, the Council was given the task of assigning to each of the provisions and decisions contained in the Schengen acquis a legal basis either in Title IV of Part Three of the EC Treaty[44] or in Title VI of the TEU, as appropriate.[45] Proposals and initiatives to build upon the *acquis* are adopted under the relevant Treaty provisions.[46]

The United Kingdom and Ireland are not bound by the Schengen *acquis*,[47] and they have a choice as to whether they wish to take part

---

[42] At para.43. For the direct effect of Art. 18 EC, see Ch.17.
[43] Protocol on integrating the Schengen acquis into the framework of the European Union. The components of the acquis are identified in an Annex to the Protocol.
[44] This is the EC Treaty Title on "Visas, asylum, immigration and other policies related to free movement of persons", comprising elements that fell within the Third Pillar of the Union as originally established by the Maastricht version of the TEU.
[45] See Council Dec. 1999/436/EC, [1999] O.J. L176/17.
[46] Schengen Protocol, Art.5(1), first subpara.
[47] *ibid.*, Arts 1 and 4.

in measures building upon it.⁴⁸ As explained in Chapter 4, above, the
mechanisms of the Schengen Protocol provide an instance of
"primary flexibility". The Member States other than the United
Kingdom and Ireland are authorised by Article 1 of the Protocol to
establish enhanced co-operation among themselves, within the scope
of the Schengen *acquis* as defined by the Annex. Article 4 provides
that the United Kingdom and Ireland may at any time request to
take part in some or all of the provisions of the *acquis*; however,
contrary to the principle of openness applicable to enhanced co-
operation of a "secondary" kind,⁴⁹ their admission requires a
unanimous decision of the Council, presumably in order to respect
the original international character of the obligations in question. A
different type of enhanced co-operation mechanism is provided by
Article 5, with respect to measures building on the Schengen *acquis*.
This places the onus on the two non-Schengen Member States to
notify the President of the Council, if they wish to take part in a
given measure. Where neither of them notifies, the Schengen
Member States are automatically authorised to proceed without
them, by way of enhanced co-operation as provided for by Article 11
EC or Article 40 TEU (depending on the legal basis of the measure
in question). Where one or other notifies, then that Member State
will be included, along with the Schengen Member States, in the
authorisation to proceed with enhanced co-operation. If both Ireland and the United Kingdom notify, this de-activates the special
enhanced co-operation mechanism, allowing the measure in question to be adopted as a Union act, applicable in the normal way to
all the Member States.⁵⁰

Pursuant to another Protocol, which was also annexed to the TEU
and the EC Treaty by the TA,⁵¹ the United Kingdom and Ireland
have been authorised, notwithstanding Article 14 EC or any other
provision of the Treaties or measures adopted under them, to go on
applying border controls, for the purpose of verifying the right of
entry of Union citizens (or the citizens of non-Union EEA countries,
who have similar rights) or of controlling the entry of other
persons.⁵² Those two Member States are, therefore, protected
against the legal consequences of the interaction between Article 14

---

⁴⁸ *ibid.*, Art.5 (1).
⁴⁹ See Art.43b TEU.
⁵⁰ At the time of writing, the issue as to whether the mechanism of Art.5(1) of the Schengen
  Protocol allows the United Kingdom and Ireland to participate in measures developing
  some aspect of the (original) Schengen *acquis* which they have not opted into under Art.4,
  was the subject of proceedings before the Court of Justice: see Case 77/05, *United Kingdom
  v Council* and Case C–137/05, *United Kingdom v Council*.
⁵¹ Protocol on the application of certain aspects of Art.14 of the Treaty establishing the
  European Community to the United Kingdom and to Ireland. Art.2 of the Protocol
  provides for the continuance of the Common Travel Area between the two countries (which
  explains why Ireland wished to be covered by the special arrangements).
⁵² See Art.1 of the Protocol.

EC and future Community measures, which may render such controls unlawful. As long as the special arrangements of the Protocol apply, other Member States will be entitled, notwithstanding Article 14 EC, to exercise similar controls on persons (of whatever nationality) arriving from the United Kingdom and Ireland.[53]

Article 95: approximation by qualified majority

It has been said that the central idea which dominated the inter-governmental negotiations leading to the signature of the SEA was that wider recourse to the qualified majority was essential for the attainment of the objective of completing the internal market before January 1, 1993.[54] The most significant of the amendments to the EEC Treaty giving effect to that idea was the introduction of Article 95 EC as a general legal basis for the adoption of "measures for the approximation of the provisions laid down by law, regulation or administrative action in Member States which have as their object the establishment and functioning of the internal market". After being left intact by the TEU, Article 95 EC was amended by the TA in several respects, including through the substitution of co-decision for co-operation as the procedure for enacting the measures provided for.   **21–014**

Article 95 EC operates by way of derogation from Article 94 EC which enables the Council, acting *unanimously*, to issue directives for the approximation of national provisions directly affecting the establishment or functioning of the common market.[55] Article 94 EC has thus been reduced to a residual role. It is available, for example, in the cases expressly excluded by paragraph (2) of Article 95 EC from the scope of that Article (see below), as well as in respect of matters not linked with the establishment or functioning of the internal market but covered by the broader notion of the common market.

In its turn, Article 95 EC is a residual provision, since it applies "save where otherwise provided in this Treaty". This means that the specific legal bases provided by the Treaty in areas such as the common agricultural policy, the right of establishment, freedom to provide services and the common transport policy,[56] should be used, in preference to Article 95 EC, for the adoption, in those areas, of

---

[53] See Art.3 of the Protocol.
[54] See J.-L. Dewost in Capotorti *et al.* (eds), *Du droit international au droit communautaire, Liber amicorum Pierre Pescatore* (Nomos, 1998), pp.167 *et seq.*
[55] On the approximation of laws pursuant to Art.100, see Mégret *et al., Le droit de la CEE* (éditions de l'Université de Bruxelles, 1973), Vol.5, pp.152 *et seq.*; A Dashwood in Wallace, Wallace and Webb (eds), *Policy-making in the European Community* (2nd ed., John Wiley & Sons, 1983), Ch.6.
[56] See, respectively, Art.37 EC, Art.44 EC, Art.47 EC and Arts 71 and 80(2) EC.

legislation having as its object the establishment and functioning of the internal market. Some problems of choosing between Article 95 EC and other available legal bases are discussed in the next section of this chapter.

21–015 The reference to "measures" in Article 95(1) EC leaves the institutions the choice as to the particular form of act appropriate in a given case, in contrast to Article 94 EC which only allows the adoption of directives. In practice, however, the Council has shown a clear preference for using directives for the enactment of approximation measures under Article 95 EC, even in cases where an act in the form of a regulation has been proposed by the Commission.

The prospect of having approximation measures adopted by majority decision prompted concerns among the different Member States, which could only be assuaged by subjecting the power created by Article 95(1) EC to a number of qualifications. Thus it is expressly provided by paragraph (2) of the Article that paragraph (1) does not apply to fiscal provisions[57] or to provisions relating to the free movement of persons[58] or to the rights and interests of employed persons.[59] By paragraph (3) the Commission is required, in the proposals it makes concerning health, safety, environmental protection and consumer protection, to take as a base a high level of protection: account must be taken, in particular, of any new development based on scientific facts. The European Parliament and the Council have been placed under a similar obligation, when carrying out their respective roles in the legislative process. In paragraph (10) it is recalled that harmonisation measures may include safeguard clauses authorising Member States "to take, for one or more of the non-economic reasons referred to in Article 30 EC, provisional measures subject to a Community control procedure".

It is, however, paragraphs (4) to (9) of Article 95 EC that require special attention, because of the exception created to the fundamental principles of the uniform application of Community law and the unity of the market.[60] Those six paragraphs were inserted into Article 95 by the TA, replacing the original paragraph (4), which dated from the SEA. They provide as follows:

---

[57] The legal basis for the harmonising of indirect taxation is Art.93 EC, which requires the Council to act unanimously on a proposal from the Commission and after consulting the European Parliament and the Economic and Social Committee. There is no specific legal basis provided for the harmonisation of direct taxation, so it is necessary to fall back on the general power of approximation in Art.94 EC.

[58] As we have seen, the legal bases for legislating on the free movement of persons are now to be found in Title IV of Part Three. The procedure prescribed by Art.87 EC during a transitional period of five years, is a variant of the consultation procedure, with the Council acting by unanimity. At the end of the transitional period, the Council has power to substitute co-decision for consultation. See Ch.3, above.

[59] See the extensive powers provided for by Art.137(2) EC which are exercisable by co-decision.

[60] See Opinion of Advocate General Tesauro in Case C–41/93 *France v Commission* [1994] E.C.R. I–1829, at I–1833, para.4.

"4. If, after the adoption by the Council or by the Commission of a harmonisation measure, a Member State deems it necessary to maintain national provisions on grounds of major needs referred to in Article 30, or relating to the protection of the environment or the working environment, it shall notify the Commission of these provisions as well as the grounds for maintaining them.

5. Moreover, without prejudice to paragraph 4, if, after the adoption by the Council or by the Commission of a harmonisation measure, a Member State deems it necessary to introduce national provisions based on new scientific evidence relating to the protection of the environment or the working environment on grounds of a problem specific to that Member State arising after the harmonising measure, it shall notify the Commission of the envisaged provisions as well as the grounds for introducing them.

6. The Commission shall, within six months of the notifications as referred to in paragraphs 4 and 5, approve or reject the national provisions involved after having verified whether or not they are a means of arbitrary discrimination or a disguised restriction on trade between Member States and whether or not they shall constitute an obstacle to the functioning of the internal market. In the absence of a decision by the Commission within this period the national provisions referred to in paragraphs 4 and 5 shall be deemed to have been approved.

   When justified by the complexity of the matter and in the absence of danger for human health, the Commission may notify the Member State concerned that the period referred to in this paragraph may be extended for a further period of up to six months.

7. When, pursuant to paragraph 6, a Member State is authorised to maintain or introduce national provisions derogating from a harmonisation measure, the Commission shall immediatly examine whether to propose an adaptation to that measure.

8. When a Member State raises a specific problem on public health in a field which has been the subject of prior harmonisation measures, it shall bring it to the attention of the Commission which shall immediately examine whether to propose appropriate measures to the Council.

9. By way of derogation from the procedure laid down in Articles 226 and 227, the Commission and any Member State may bring the matter directly before the Court of Justice if it considers that another Member State is making improper use of the powers provided for in this Article".

21–016 Essentially, this allows an escape route for a Member State which considers that harmonised rules, adopted under Article 95 EC, do not constitute a sufficient guarantee of attaining certain important public interest objectives. In effect, the fulfilment of the prescribed substantive and procedural condition prevents the operation, in respect of the Member State concerned, of the general rules of Community law that, once the standards protecting the interests in question have been fully harmonised, recourse to national provisions previously allowed under the Treaty despite potential interference with freedom of movement, can no longer be justified.[61]

According to paragraph (4), after a "harmonisation measure" has been adopted by the Council or the Commission, a Member State which "deems it necessary to *maintain* national provisions on grounds of major needs referred to in Article 30 EC, or relating to the protection of the environment or the working environment".[62] should notify those provisions to the Commission, specifying the grounds on which it relies. The paragraph, as amended by the TA, thus caters for the situation where a Member State wishes to continue applying provisions already in force at the time of the enactment of the Community measure in question.

A first comment on the paragraph relates to the term "harmonisation measure", which is also found in paragraph (5). The reference is manifestly to measures of the kind provided for by paragraph (1) of the Article, there described as "measures for the *approximation* of the provisions laid down by law, etc". (emphasis added). That "harmonisation" and "approximation" should be treated, within the same Article, as interchangeable terms, is strong evidence that no difference of substance is indicated by the draftsman's choice of one term or the other, elsewhere in the Treaty.[63]

21–017 Secondly, the harmonisation measure from which derogation is sought may be one which has been adopted by either the Council or the Commission. Of course, only the Council is empowered (with the European Parliament) to act directly on the basis of Article 95 EC. The mention of the Commission, added by the TA, is presumably to make clear that derogation obtained in respect of primary legislation will also cover any implementing measures adopted under powers which have been created pursuant to Article 202, third indent EC.[64]

Thirdly, the justification for maintaining national provisions has to be found among the "major needs" (*exigences importantes*) mentioned in Article 30 EC to which are added the protection of the

[61] See Case 251/78 *Denkavit Futtermittel*, n.19, above. On the background to the inclusion of original para.(4) in Art.100a, see De Ruyt, *op.cit.* n.5, above, pp.170 *et seq.*
[62] Emphasis added.
[63] See, e.g. Art.93, which refers to "harmonisation", and Art.94, which refers, like Art.95, to "approximation".
[64] See, e.g. Case C–359/92 *Germany v Council* [1994] E.C.R. I–3681; [1995] 1 C.M.L.R. 413. See also Case C–66/04, *UK v Parliament and Council,* judgment of December 6, 2005, not yet reported, para.50.

environment and the working environment. Consistently with the requirement of strict interpretation,[65] the catalogue of possible justifications must be taken to be exhaustive, unlike the open-ended list of "mandatory requirements" which, according to the *Cassis de Dijon* line of authority, may justify the application of disparate national provisions until harmonisation rules are in place.[66] The onus is on the Member State invoking the safeguard to prove that its national provisions, which give a higher standard of protection of the interests expressly indicated by Article 95(4) EC, than the relevant Community measure, are necessary and proportionate.[67]

A fourth comment concerns the former limitation of the safeguard clause to cases where a harmonisation measure had been adopted by the Council acting by a qualified majority, so that it was not available where a compromise solution commanding unanimity had been arrived at. Some writers drew the conclusion that the clauses could only be relied on by Member States which had voted against the measure in question.[68] In a previous edition of this work, we pointed out that the benefit of paragraph (4), as then drafted, was not expressly confined to those forming part of the outvoted minority; and such a restriction would have detracted from the *effet utile* of a provision designed to facilitate the formation of qualified majorities, since a Member State, wanting to have the right to apply its national rules but otherwise willing for a given measure to be passed, would have been forced to join with those irreconcilably opposed to the measure, in voting it down.[69] The controversy has been laid to rest by the TA, which deleted the reference to a qualified majority decision from paragraph (4). It is now clear that the escape clause can be resorted to, regardless of whether a given harmonisation measure was adopted unanimously or by a qualified majority; and, in the latter event, whether the Member State concerned voted for or against the measure. Paragraph (5) of Article 95 EC disposes of another old controversy from the period prior to the TA: whether national provisions introduced subsequently to a Community harmonisation measure may be saved by the escape clause. The paragraph recognises this possibility, but subject to conditions more restrictive than those applicable to pre-existing national provisions.[70] The provisions it is sought to introduce must be "based on new scientific evidence relating to the protection of the environment or the working environment" (so that the justifications in Article 30 EC are

---

[65] See Ch.16.
[66] *ibid.*
[67] See the Opinion of Advocate General Tesauro in Case C–41/93 *France v Commission* [1994] E.C.R. at I–1834, para.7.
[68] *cf.* De Ruyt, *op.cit.* n.5, above, pp.171 and 174.
[69] Third edition, at p.365.
[70] The Case C–512/99 *Germany v Commission* [2003] E.C.R. I–845; Case C–3/00, *Commission v Denmark* [2003] E.C.R. I–2643.

not available); and their introduction must be considered necessary "on grounds of a problem specific to that Member State arising after the adoption of the harmonisation measure".

21–018   The procedure under which the Commission is required to deal with notifications pursuant to paragraphs (4) and (5) is laid down by paragraph (6). The Commission has six months in which to approve or reject the national provisions involved "after having verified whether or not they are a means of arbitrary discrimination or a disguised restriction on trade between Member States and whether or not they shall constitute an obstacle to the functioning of the internal market". The last-mentioned element, added by the TA, gives scope for a denial of authorisation, even where a genuine need for the provisions, on one of the specified public interest grounds, has been made out to the satisfaction of the Commission, if the well functioning of the internal market is put at risk.

Commission decisions pursuant to Article 95(6) EC are constitutive, and not merely declaratory, in their effects. Unless and until approval is obtained, either by a decision or through the expiry of the six-month time-limit, the continued application (or the introduction) of the national provisions in question is unlawful: their notification to the Commission does not give provisional exemption, and the Community harmonisation measure, if it satisfies the criteria of direct effect, may be relied on by individuals in the courts of the Member State concerned.[71]

The point may be illustrated by the *Kortas* case from Sweden, which arose out of the prosecution of a shopkeeper, for selling imported confectionery products containing the colorant E124 (or cochineal red). Use of the latter in foodstuffs was authorised by Directive 94/36,[72] but banned under the relevant Swedish legislation. The case fell to be decided on the basis of the pre-Amsterdam version of Article 95 EC, which fixed no time-limit for the Commission to decide on notifications: the Swedish authorities had notified their national provisions to the Commission, with a request for a derogation, in November 1995, but had still received no reply in July 1998. Even in those circumstances, however, the Court refused to countenance the unilateral disapplication of the Directive. If the Commission was in breach of its obligation to act with all due diligence in discharging its responsibilities, then the proper remedy would have been an action under Article 232 EC; such action, the Court noted, could be accompanied, where appropriate, by an application for interim relief. However, the failure of the Commission to act with due diligence could not affect the full application of the Directive concerned.[73] The strict attitude of the Court is

---

[71] Case C–319/97 *Criminal proceedings against Antoine Kortus* [1999] E.C.R. I–3143..
[72] European Parliament and Council Dir.94/36 on colours for use in foodstuffs, [1994] O.J. 237/13.
[73] Case C–319/97, para.36.

explained by the logic of the internal market, where the emphasis is on the removal of impediments to free movement and of elements liable to distort the play of competition, through harmonisation measures. Article 95(6) EC effectively empowers the Commission to grant individual Member States *ad hoc* derogations from common standards which have been judged by the Community legislator adequately to protect the interests referred to in Article 30 EC (and, in matters of health, safety, the environment and consumer protection, to do so at the "high level" prescribed by Article 95(3)) EC. In *Kortas*, Advocate General Saggio drew a contrast between a safeguard clause of that kind, which cuts across the objective of harmonised legislation and must, therefore, be kept severely within bounds; and Article 176 EC, where the more stringent measures the Member States are authorised to maintain or introduce, would be serving the same purpose (of protecting the environment) as the corresponding Community measures, so that a lighter control regime is justified.[74]

The Commission must satisfy itself that all the conditions which **21–019** allow a Member State to invoke the safeguard clause are fulfilled. In particular, it must establish whether the national provisions in question are justified on the grounds specified, respectively, by paragraphs (4) and (5) of Article 95 EC, and also that they do not constitute a means of arbitrary discrimination or a disguised restriction on trade between Member States, or an obstacle to the functioning of the internal market.[75]

If authorisation is given, the reasons of fact and law explaining why all of the prescribed conditions are to be regarded as fulfilled in the case in point, must be set out by the Commission in its decision. The very first Commission Decision granting a derogation under Article 95 EC was annulled by the Court of Justice for not being adequately reasoned.[76] It concerned German provisions prohibiting the substance pentachlorophenol (PCP), which were significantly more restrictive than the rules applicable under the relevant Community Directive.[77] According to Advocate General Tesauro, the Commission failed to mention any factors justifying the application in Germany of national rules assuring a higher degree of protection than that provided by the Community.[78] On the issue of the proportionality of the German rules, the Advocate General said: ". . . I think it would have been appropriate for the decision to have

---

[74] At para.26 of his Opinion. Under Art.176 EC the Member State concerned must notify to the Commission any measures it wishes to maintain or introduce, but there is no special vetting procedure.
[75] Case C–41/93 *France v Commission* [1994] E.C.R. I–1829, para.27 of Judgment.
[76] *ibid.*
[77] Council Dir. 91/173 amending for the ninth time Council Dir. 76/769 concerning PCP [1991] O.J. L85/34.
[78] Case C–41/93 [1994] E.C.R. at I–1838, para.14.

specified to what extent the additional protection of health and the environment guaranteed by the German rules justifies the possibility of greater barriers to intra-Community trade; or, again, for it to have examined the consequences of the need to use other products instead of PCP".[79] As to the verification the Commission was required to undertake, in order to establish that the German rules did not result in arbitrary discrimination or a disguised restriction on trade between Member States, the decision was criticised by the Advocate General for confining itself to repeating slavishly the relevant wording of Article 95 EC, "without the statements made being in any way supported by any consideration which might justify the Commission's conclusions".[80] The judgment of the Court, though expressed less concretely and trenchantly, was in the same sense.[81]

The case on the PCP Decision was specifically concerned with the inadequacy of the statement of reasons furnished by the Commission, which was in contravention of Article 253 EC. However, the analysis undertaken by Advocate General Tesauro provides valuable insight into the delicately nuanced judgment the Commission is called upon to make, when acting under the safeguard clause of Article 95 EC. The interests of the Member State wishing to maintain or introduce provisions giving a higher level of protection, are not to be considered paramount. They have to be carefully weighed against the possibly adverse consequences for the well functioning of the internal market.[82]

21–020   Paragraphs (7) and (8) of Article 95 EC are designed to activate the legislative process of the Community, where appropriate, in the light of concerns brought forward by a particular Member State. Under paragraph (7), the Commission, if it authorises a Member State to maintain or introduce provisions derogating from a harmonisation measure, must immediately examine whether it should propose that the measure be amended. Under paragraph (8), a Member State seised of a public health problem in a field which has been the subject of prior harmonisation measures, must bring this

---

[79] *ibid.*, 1839.
[80] *ibid.*
[81] Case C–41/93 [1994] E.C.R. at I–1829, 1850, paras 35–37.
[82] The Danish Government made a unilateral Declaration to the Final Act of the SEA, in these terms:

> "The Danish Government notes that in cases where a Member State is of the opinion that measures adopted under Art.100a do not satisfy higher requirements concerning the working environment, the protection of the environment or the needs referred to in Art.36, the provisions of Art.100a(4) *guarantee* that the Member State in question can apply national provisions. Such national provisions are to be taken to fulfil the above-mentioned aim and may not entail hidden protectionism" (emphasis added).

If the Danish Government's interpretation of the provisions now contained in paras. (4)–(6) of Art.95 EC were correct, the vetting of notifications by the Commission would have been a pure formality. We contested that interpretation in the third edition of this work, and the case law has now confirmed that it is untenable.

immediately to the attention of the Commission, which must examine whether it should make a proposal to the Council.

Should a Member State be suspected of making improper use of the safeguard clause in Article 95 EC, an enforcement action can be brought against it by the Commission or another Member State, using the accelerated procedure provided for by paragraph (9).[83] In such circumstances, the Court of Justice might also be persuaded to issue an interim order prohibiting the application of the provision pending the outcome of the proceedings.

At the time of the signature of the SEA, it was feared by some critics of the new Treaty that the then paragraph (4) of Article 100a would undermine the case law of the Court of Justice on Article 30 EC.[84] There would, indeed, be a danger, if the safeguard clause in Article 95 EC were very frequently resorted to, that the effectiveness of the Article as an instrument for achieving the single market objectives of Article 14 EC might be compromised. However, in practice this has not happened. Why should the dire predictions of eminent commentators have proved so wrong? Three reasons may be hazarded. First, the common political will to complete the internal market within the time-limit set by Article 14(1) EC must have helped to overcome inhibitions. Secondly, Member States which may have hoped to use the safeguard clause to protect the high health status of their livestock industries have been prevented from doing so by the evolution of the case law on Article 37 EC which has shown that Article to be the appropriate legal basis for internal market legislation in the veterinary field.[85] Thirdly, the obligation imposed by Article 95(3) EC to propose high common standards of consumer and environmental protection may have helped to deter Member States from having recourse to the safeguard clause, as it was clearly intended to do.

A final question is how the mechanism relates to the practice known as "minimal harmonisation". The latter occurs when Community legislation lays down certain minimum standards which must be observed in all the Member States, while authorising any Member State that so wishes to apply stricter standards in respect of the same matters.[86] The answer to the question is that paragraphs (4) and following only come into play once the rules relating to the matters in question have been fully harmonised: minimal harmonisation represents a step in a process which remains incomplete, leaving it open for Member States to invoke, as the case may be, Article 30 or

---

[83] *cf.* the accelerated procedure under Art.88(2).
[84] Notably P. Pescatore in J.-V. Lous (ed.), *L'acte unique européen* (Journée d'études, Bruxelles, March 1, 1986), pp.39 *et seq.*; *contra*, H.-L. Glaesner, (1986) R.M.C. p.321.
[85] See the cases cited in n.96, below
[86] An example of a minimal harmonisation measure adopted on the basis of Art.100a is Council Dir.90/31 on package holidays [1990] O.J. L158/59. See also Council Dir.91/477 of June 18, 1991 on the acquisition and detention of weapons, [1991] O.J. L256/51.

one of the "mandatory requirements" recognised under the *Cassis de Dijon* doctrine. Step-by-step harmonisation is, in principle, a legitimate strategy for the Community legislator to adopt,[87] bearing in mind, however, the time-limit that was fixed by Article 14(1) EC for the completion of the internal market.

Prior to its amendment by the TA, the EC Treaty included an Article 100b creating a mechanism under which steps could have been taken, in the last year of the programme for the completion of the internal market (1992), to compel the mutual recognition by the Member States of national laws, regulations and administrative provisions falling within the scope of Article 95 (Article 100a, as it then was), but which had not been harmonised. The mechanism remained unused and Article 100b EC was one of the provisions repealed by the TA.

Legal bases for internal market legislation

Choice of legal bases

21–021   The issue addressed in this section is that of the selection of the correct legal basis for a given piece of internal market legislation. In practice, disputed choices are generally between Article 95 EC and some other provision of the EC Treaty. Preferences are liable to be influenced by the perception of political advantage (or disadvantage) in the procedure for the adoption of harmonisation measures by the Council acting by a qualified majority by way of co-decision with the European Parliament, on the one hand, or in the escape route the Article may offer from the consequences of such measures, on the other. Disputes may arise between different Community institutions, especially where the Council has amended by unanimity the legal basis proposed by the Commission, or between the Council and one or more of the Member States, when a proposal has been adopted in the face of minority opposition.

General principles governing the choice of the legal basis of Community acts have been laid down by the Court of Justice. According to those principles, the choice must be made in the light of objective factors capable of being the subject of judicial review,[88] in particular the aim and content of the act.[89] Where examination of the relevant factors shows that the act is concerned with two or more distinct matters which are dealt with in separate provisions of the EC Treaty, a dual or multiple legal basis may be required.[90] However,

---

[87] See Case 215/87 *Heinz Schumacher v HZA Frankfurt-am-Main* [1989] E.C.R. 638; [1990] 2 C.M.L.R. 465; Case C–42/90 *Bellon* [1990] E.C.R. 4863.
[88] Case 45/86 *Commission v Council* [1987] E.C.R. 1493; [1988] 2 C.M.L.R. 131.
[89] Case C–300/89 *Commission v Council (Titanium Dioxide Waste)* [1990] E.C.R. 2867.
[90] Case 165/87 *Commission v Council* [1988] E.C.R. 5545; [1990] 1 C.M.L.R. 457.

legal bases must not be combined if the procedures which they prescribe are incompatible.[91]

The leading authority on the choice of Article 95 EC as a legal basis is *Tobacco Advertising*.[92] The Court of Justice held that the Article was an inappropriate choice for a directive imposing a comprehensive ban on the advertising and sponsorship of tobacco products. In the words of the Court, "the measures referred to in Article [95 (1)] are intended to improve the conditions for the establishment and functioning of the internal market".[93] For the Article to be construed as vesting in the Community legislator "a general power to regulate the internal market" would not only be contrary to its express provisions but would also be incompatible with the principle of conferred powers enshrined in Article 5.[94] Owing to its general scope, the Directive could not be seen either as genuinely contributing to the elimination of obstacles to the free movement of goods or to eliminating appreciable distortions of competition.[95]

The choice between Article 95 EC and Article 37 EC
The leading cases concern legislation pre-dating the SEA, when the **21–022** disputed demarcation was between Article 37 EC and Article 94 EC. However, the lessons to be drawn from those cases are equally applicable to the demarcation between Article 37 EC and Article 95 EC.

Article 37 EC does not prescribe the co-decision procedure but only consultation of the European Parliament. The Council acts by a qualified majority, so the choice of legal basis does not affect the voting rule but does limit the degree of the Parliament's involvement. There is also the possibility of invoking the safeguard clause of Article 95 EC, which has no equivalent in Article 37 EC. Delegations wishing to maintain national rules guaranteeing, as they claim, a higher health status for their countries than harmonised rules which it is proposed to adopt on veterinary or plant health matters, may accordingly press for the proposal to be based on Article 95 EC.

The cases establish that Article 37 EC is the correct legal basis for legislation satisfying two conditions: it must relate to the production or marketing of the agricultural products listed in Annex II to the EC Treaty; and it must contribute to the attainment of one or more of the objectives of the common agricultural policy set out in Article

---

[91] Case C–300/89 *Commission v Council (Titanium Dioxide Waste)* [1990] E.C.R. 2867. See the discussion of this case with respect to the choice between Art.95 and Art.175.
[92] Case C–376/98 *Germany v European Parliament and Council.*[2001] E.C.R. I–8419; and see Case C–210/03 *Swedish Match* [2004] E.C.R. I–11893.
[93] *ibid.*, para.83.
[94] *ibid.*
[95] *cf.* Case C–491/01, *ex parte BAT* [2002] E.C.R. I–11453.

33 EC of the Treaty.[96] It has further been held that, where the bulk of the products to which legislation applies are Annex II products, the fact that the legislation may also apply, in an accessory way, to certain non-Annex II products does not take it outside the scope of the common agricultural policy[97]; nor does the fact that the legislation pursues, at the same time, certain general aims, such as the protection of health.[98]

Applying those principles, the Court has found that Article 37 EC was the correct legal basis for a ban on the administration of growth hormones to livestock,[99] a directive laying down conditions for the treatment of battery hens,[1] a directive relating to the importation of animal glands and organs for use by the pharmaceutical industry,[2] a directive on undesirable substances in animal feeding stuffs,[3] and a regulation establishing a system for the identification and registration of bovine animals and the labelling of beef.[4]

On the other hand, where internal market measures apply equally to certain agricultural and non-agricultural products, a dual legal basis, Article 37 EC together with Article 95 EC, seems both desirable and possible, since there is no difference of Council voting rule liable to distort the operation of the co-decision procedure (see the discussion of the *Titanium Dioxide Waste* case below).

The choice between Article 95 EC and Article 175 EC

21–023 A Title on the Environment, comprising Articles 174 to 176 EC was added to Part Three of the EC Treaty by Article 25 of the SEA. Article 174 EC defines the objectives and the general principles of action by the Community relating to the environment. The legislative procedure originally laid down by Article 175 EC was for the Council to act by unanimity after consulting the European Parliament and the Economic and Social Committee. The TEU substituted the co-operation procedure for simple consultation, except in respect of a few matters considered especially sensitive politically; and the TA replaced co-operation with co-decision. So under the EC

---

[96] See, in particular, Case 68/86, *United Kingdom v Council* [1988] E.C.R. 855; [1988] 2 C.M.L.R. 543; Case 131/86 *United Kingdom v Council* [1988] E.C.R. 905; [1988] 2 C.M.L.R. 364; Case 13/87
Commission v Council [1989] E.C.R. 3743; Case 11/88 *Commission v Council* [1989] E.C.R. 3799.
[97] Case 11/88, *loc. cit.*
[98] See cases cited *ibid.*
[99] Council Dir.87/519 of October 19, 1987, [1987] O.J. L304/38.
[1] Council Dir.86/113 of March 25, 1986, [1986] O.J. L95/45.
[2] Council Dir.87/64 of December 30, 1986, [1987] O.J. L34/52.
[3] Council Dir.87/519 of October 19, 1987, [1987] O.J. L304/38. See also Joined Cases C–164 and 165/97, judgment of February 25, 1999, [1999] E.C.R. I–1139, where the choice of legal basis was between Art.37 and Art.175.
[4] Council Reg.820/97 of April 21, 1997, [1997] O.J. L117/1. See Case C–269/97, *Commission v Council* [2000] E.C.R. I–2257.

Treaty, as amended, the choice between Article 95 EC and Article 175 EC will no longer make any difference, in most cases, as to the procedure to be used for adopting measures. The difference that remains—and it is significant—relates to the ability of Member States to maintain or introduce higher protective standards than those provided for by the Community. As we have seen, the conditions of the safeguard clause under Article 95 EC are much stricter than those imposed by Article 176 EC.

Articles 174 to 176 EC were clearly intended to provide a coherent framework for organising a Community environmental policy. Like regional policy or social policy, this is a Community policy applying in an area where the Member States enjoy concurrent competence ("Community policy on the environment still contribute . . .", as Article 174(1) EC puts it). It is to be contrasted with the common policies in the fields of agriculture and transport, where Community competence is potentially exclusive, and actually so, once it has been exercised.

However, it is equally clear that Article 95 EC was intended to serve as the legal basis of measures for the approximation of national provisions on the protection of the environment, where such measures have as their object the establishment or functioning of the internal market. This follows from the reference in Article 95(3) EC to Commission proposals "concerning . . . environmental protection". There is a fine dividing line between such harmonisation measures and the specific Community action in relation to the environment which is the province of Article 175 EC.

An uncontroversial example of the use of Article 95 EC would be **21–024** the harmonisation of legislation laying down technical specifications, with a view to the protection of the environment, for certain manufactured products which are traded within the internal market. By removing disparities between national provisions, while guaranteeing a high level of environmental protection throughout the Community, the harmonising measure would obviously contribute towards ensuring the free movement of the products in question. Article 95 EC was thus correctly chosen as the legal basis for Community measures in relation to the control of emissions from motor vehicles.

A more difficult case is that of Community measures designed to protect the environment against the harmful consequences of industrial processes, such as legislation on the disposal of industrial waste. Such measures cannot be regarded as removing impediments to the free movement of goods within the internal market. However, since pollution control is expensive for the undertakings concerned, disparities between the levels of protection prescribed by the legislation of different Member States may result in distortions of competition, which the harmonisation of national provisions would help to remedy. The Court of Justice has said that action by the Community for the approximation of national rules relating to conditions of production in a given industrial sector, with a view to eliminating distortions of competition in that sector, is capable of contributing to the attainment of the internal market and, accordingly, falls within the purview of Article 95 EC.[5] On the other hand, if that logic is pressed too far, it would completely exclude Article 175 EC as a basis for legislation on such matters as the control of industrial pollution, which lie at the very heart of any policy on the protection of the environment. This seems inconsistent with the letter and spirit of the Treaty Title on the Environment.

The choice between Article 95 EC and Article 175 EC (in their previous versions) was the subject of the litigation in Case C—300/89 concerning the Council Directive of June 21, 1989, on the harmonisation of national programmes for the reduction, with a view to its elimination, of pollution caused by the titanium dioxide waste industry.[6] The Directive was annulled by the Court on the ground that Article 95 EC, as proposed by the Commission, and not Article 175 EC, substituted by the Council, was the correct legal basis. Analysis of the aim and content of the Directive led the Court to conclude that it was a measure with the dual object of protecting the environment and removing distortions of competition, which seemed to point to the requirement of a dual legal basis. However, that solution had to be rejected since, in the Court's view, the unanimity rule then applicable to all legislation adopted under the Title on the Environment was incompatible with the co-operation procedure prescribed by Article 95 EC. A choice had, therefore, to be made, and the Court opted for Article 95 EC, apparently because it considered both the objects of the Directive could effectively be pursued on that legal basis, although the judgment does not explain why they could not be pursued, as effectively and appropriately, on the basis of Article 175 EC.

The judgment in *Titanium Dioxide Waste* is explained by the drafting of the Directive in question. This emphasised the dual object of the measure; while the normal expedient of providing a dual legal basis could not be adopted, because, as the Court saw it, the respective decision making procedures of Articles 95 EC and 175 EC, in their original versions, were mutually incompatible. In subsequent cases, relating to measures the aim and content of which showed that their essential object was the protection of the environment, Article 175 EC has been confirmed as the correct legal basis.[7] The mere fact, the Court of Justice has said, that the establishment

---

[5] Case C–300/89, *Commission v Council (Titanium Dioxide Waste)* [1990] E.C.R. 2867, para.23.
[6] [1989] O.J. L201/6.
[7] Case C–155/91 *Commission v Council* [1993] E.C.R. I–939; Case C–187/93, *European Parliament v Council* [1994] E.C.R. I–2857; [1995] 2 C.M.L.R. 309.

or functioning of the market is affected, is not sufficient for Article 95 EC to apply. Recourse to that Article is not justified where the measure to be adopted has only the *incidental* effect of harmonising market conditions within the Community.[8]

Other cases

The exclusions in paragraph (2) of Article 95 EC may sometimes **21–025** give rise to difficult borderline cases.

For instance, it was a question whether the Regulation on the elimination of controls and formalities applicable to the cabin and hold baggage of persons taking an intra-Community flight and the baggage of persons making an intra-Community sea crossing should have been based on Article 95 EC, as a measure facilitating the movement of goods, or on Article 94 EC, as a measure facilitating the movement of persons.[9] The choice of Article 95 EC seems correct, since the provisions of the Regulation apply specifically to controls on baggage. The fact that baggage is accompanied by its owner when frontiers are crossed does not prevent it from being regarded as "goods" within the meaning of the Treaty. Similar reasoning justified the choice of Article 95 EC as the legal basis for the Directive on the acquisition and detention of weapons.[10] A different position was taken by the Council in the case of the Regulation on co-operation between tax authorities, the aim of which was to ensure the effective collection of revenue, while avoiding interference with the free movement of goods.[11] Since the administrative arrangements in question were ancillary to the objective of levying taxation, the right legal basis for the measure was thought to be Article 93 EC.

A limitation on the scope of Article 95 EC that must not be forgotten is that it only applies to measures for the approximation of national provisions. The hallmark of approximation measures is that they are designed to remove obstacles to the establishment or functioning of the internal market, which result from actual or potential disparities between such provisions.[11A] For instance, national rules on the protection of intellectual property rights may be the subject of harmonisation measures adopted pursuant to Article 95 EC; but for the creation of entirely new property forms, protected by Community law independently of the law of the Member States, recourse must be had to Article 308 EC.

---

[8] See *ibid.* and Case C–70/88 *European Parliament v Council* [1991] E.C.R. I–2041; [1991] E.C.R. I–4529; [1992] 1 C.M.L.R. 91.

[9] See Council Reg. 3925/91 of December 19, 1991, [1991] O.J. L374/4. This has been supplemented by Commission Reg.1823/92 of July 3, 1992 laying down detailed rules.

[10] Council Dir.91/477 of June 18, [1991] O.J. L256/51.

[11] Council Reg.218/92 of January 27, 1992, [1992] O.J. L24/1.

[11A] The Community legislator has discretion as to the particular method of approximation that may be appropriate in the circumstances: Case C–66/04 *loc. cit.* n.64, para.45; Case C–217/04, judgment of May 2, 2006, not yet reported.

A case study in harmonisation: common rules on labelling

21–026   A brief examination of common labelling rules may help to illustrate the relationship between harmonisation and the removal of obstacles to the free movement of goods. The Court's case law establishes that national labelling requirements may restrict free movement. Where such requirements cannot be justified, they are prohibited.[12] The Court has held that a labelling requirement to indicate the ingredients, in descending order of their proportion, of compound feeding stuffs on the label of such products, can be justified by the public interest in the protection of the health of humans and animals, within the meaning of Article 30 EC, and also by the requirements of consumer protection and fair trading, constituting a potential barrier to trade.[13] Thus the preamble of Directive 67/548 on the classification, packaging and labelling of dangerous substances states that "the differences between the national provisions of the . . . Member States on the classification, packaging and labelling of dangerous substances and preparations hinder trade in these substances", making it "necessary to remove such hindrances"; and this "entails approximating the laws, regulations and administrative provisions on classification, packaging and labelling". Articles 6 and 7 lay down the content and size of labels to be affixed to the products in question. The Directive has been amended on numerous occasions and remains in force as amended.[14] Other examples of common labelling rules are provided by Council Directive 76/768 on cosmetic products,[15] and Directive 2000/13 of the European Parliament and of the Council on the labelling, presentation and advertising of foodstuffs.[16]

Harmonising national labelling rules does not in itself make it possible for a commercial operator to print a single label for a product which will comply with the labelling requirements of all Member States. The inhabitants of 25 Member States speak almost as many languages; and some Member States have more than one official language—Belgium, for instance, has three (French, Flemish and German). In Luxembourg the official languages are French and German, while "Lëtzebuergesch" is the national language, and is the everyday spoken language of the people of Luxembourg. Labelling rules invariably require the use of a language which will readily be understood by consumers—usually an official language of the State concerned. This in itself amounts to a restriction on the free movement of goods, yet Member States are for obvious reasons entitled to insist on such a requirement on grounds of consumer

---

[12] Case 27/80 *Fietje* [1980] E.C.R. 3839; Case 94/82 *De Kikvorsch* [1983] E.C.R. 947.
[13] C–39/90 *Denkavit Futtermittel GmbH* [1991] E.C.R. I–3069.
[14] O.J. English Spec. Ed. Series 1, Ch.1967, p. 234, as amended.
[15] [1976] O.J. L262/169, as amended, and consolidated text of April 21, 2002.
[16] [2000] O.J. L109/29. This Directive consolidates the much amended Directive 79/112.

protection.[17] The Court of Justice has held that, where a labelling directive fully harmonises the language requirements applicable for a given product, the Member States cannot impose additional language requirements.[18] Where there is only partial Community harmonisation or none at all, the Member States in principle retain the power to impose additional language requirements,[19] though such language requirements must be proportionate to the aim pursued.[20] Proportionality in this context requires that a measure requiring the use of a language which consumers can readily understand must not exclude the possible use of other means of informing them, such as designs, symbols or pictograms.[21] Proportionality also requires that a language requirement be restricted to the information made mandatory by the Member State concerned.[22] Furthermore, such requirements can be justified only in so far as they are indistinctly applicable, and must not fall solely upon imported products, so that products from other language areas of the Member State concerned are not at an advantage compared with products coming from other Member States.[23]

The existence of linguistic diversity in the EU, and the fact that Member States can insist on labelling in the local language or languages, means that a product labelled in a single language, whether pursuant to common labelling rules or not, is unlikely to be eligible to be placed on the market in more than one Member State. There are one or two exceptions, where more than one country shares a single official or national language for labelling purposes, e.g. Austria and Germany. But even where countries share a single official language, a product appropriately labelled for one of those countries might not be appropriately labelled for the other; e.g. the information and warnings on a packet of cigarettes written in French for the French market would be intelligible to French speakers in Belgium and Luxembourg, but the label would not comply with the labelling requirements in either of the latter countries because Belgium would require also Dutch and German, while Luxembourg would require also German.[24] Similarly, packets of cigarettes labelled for Belgium and Luxembourg would not comply with the rules applicable in France, despite the fact that the information and warnings would appear in French, since the size of the information and warnings in French would be inadequate.[25]

---

[17] Case C–33/97 *Colim NV* [1999] E.C.R. I–3175, para.36.
[18] Case C–33/97, *loc. cit.*, para.34.
[19] Case C–33/97, *loc. cit.*, para.35.
[20] Case C–33/97, *loc. cit.*, para.40.
[21] Case C–33/97, *loc. cit.*, para.41.
[22] Case C–33/97, *loc. cit.*, para.42.
[23] Case C–33/97, *loc. cit.*, para.43.
[24] Dir.2001/37 of the European Parliament and Council on the manufacture presentation and sale of tobacco products, Art.5(6)(e).
[25] Dir.2001/37, Art.5(6)(e).

21–027   It might seem to follow that common labelling rules serve little useful purpose: since languages vary from country to country, commercial operators are compelled to label products in a way which is country specific. And if commercial operators label products in a way which is country specific it would not seem to matter whether the rules in different Member States have been harmonised or not. It is of course the case that it is easier to check on the current state of national rules if they have been harmonised. But the point is not of great practical significance if a commercial operator is affixing different labels to a product for different countries. Common labelling rules are invariably adopted by the Directive, and require implementation by national rules. Member States are usually given some discretion in matters of detail,[26] and commercial operators will be well advised to and will in practice consult the national rules implementing the relevant labelling directive.

In fact, the real virtue of common labelling rules is that they make it easier to produce multi-lingual labels. The multi-lingual label is the hallmark of a product which is as near as it is possible to get to being genuinely "European"—one that is packaged and labelled in a way that makes it marketable across the EU. Let us take a hypothetical example of a packet of spaghetti produced in a Member State and labelled, in accordance with the national rules implementing Directive 2000/13 on the labelling, presentation and advertising of of foodstuffs, in Italian, Dutch, English, French and German. Labelling a product in this way, which allows it to be sold in seven Member States (including Belgium and Luxembourg) is more commercially advantageous than labelling products separately for the various countries. In the latter case a supplier seeking to supply outlets in various Member States has in effect to keep stocks of spaghetti packaged for the UK, stocks packaged for France, and so on. If stocks of spaghetti with English labels are exhausted, more spaghetti will have to be packaged in English, even if the supplier has surplus stocks of "spaghetti for Germany" and "spaghetti for France". In other words, multi-lingual packaging in a common format for a number of European countries allows for economies of scale and flexibility of supply. It might be said that the same objective could be achieved without common rules; and so it could, though the exercise might be more commercially risky. Labelling rules, particularly those affecting foodstuffs, seem prone to frequent change; this is reflected in the numerous amendments to the European rules. The possibility of a change in the labelling rules of any one Member State on the market of which a product was to be placed might deter a commercial operator from producing large quantities of the product in multi-lingual packaging, or could lead to

---

[26] See e.g. Dir.2000/13, Art.16, as to languages; Dir.2001/37, Art.5(8), as to requirement of a reference, outside the warnings box, to the issuing authority.

changes in the packaging to omit for the time being one or more countries thought likely to change their labelling rules. Keeping track of prospective changes in labelling rules across the EU is certainly easier where the rules are harmonised than when they are not, and in this context this probably amounts to an advantage. The presence of foodstuffs and cosmetics on sale in the shops of Member States bearing multi-lingual labelling is an indication that common labelling rules are of some commercial value in the internal market.

Reference was made above to a multi-lingually labelled product being as close as it is possible to get to a genuinely European product, which is in principle a product which can be packaged and labelled in a way which allows it to be placed on the market in all Member States. Because of the extent of linguistic diversity in Europe, and the size limitations on placing multilingual labelling on the packaging of products, the most that can be achieved in practice in many cases is a product which can be placed on the market in *a number* of Member States. In the *Schwarzkopf* case,[27] the Court of Justice was called upon to interpret Directive 76/768 on cosmetic products, which required certain obligatory warnings to appear on cosmetic products in the national or official language or languages of the Member State of marketing. The Court noted that the Directive itself was subject to the requirements of Article 28 EC, and offered two conclusions which are of general significance. The first conclusion was that "the obligation to put the obligatory warnings on cosmetic products in full must not make it excessively difficult for cosmetic products having the same get-up to be marketed in several Member States."[28] This proposition is significant since it acknowledges that the rationale of common labelling rules is the possibility of multilingual labelling, and implies that a directive laying down common labelling rules which does *not* facilitate multilingual labelling would be invalid for inconsistency with Article 28 EC. The second conclusion drawn by the Court is the practical one that "the marketing of cosmetic products cannot be considered to be made excessively difficult if secondary law is interpreted as preventing a producer or distributor wishing to market his products in nine languages, including eight official languages of the Community, from invoking practical impossibility so as to avoid the obligation to place the compulsory warnings in full on the container and packaging".[29] The Court noted that national linguistic requirements such as those authorised by the Directive in issue constituted an obstacle to intra-Community trade in that the products had to be given quite different labelling according to the language or languages prescribed in the Member State in which the products are marketed, which entailed

---

[27] Case C–169/99 *Hans Schwarzkopf GmbH & Co. KG* [2001] E.C.R. I–5901.
[28] Case C–169/99, *loc. cit.*, para.41.
[29] Case C–169/99, *loc. cit.*, para.41.

supplementary packaging costs. But the Court regarded these obstacles as justified by the public interest objective of protecting public health; the prescribed information would be of no practical use unless given in a language which could be understood by those for whom it was intended.

21–028   It might be thought that the gains for the internal market of common labelling rules are likely to be modest, if the most that can be required of such rules is that they must not make it "excessively difficult for . . . products having the same get-up to be marketed in several Member States". "Several"means more than two, and it seems that in the *Schwarzkopf* case it was, according to Advocate General Mischo "possible to print the warning, in three languages, on the tube and corresponding packaging".[30] But at least in the latter case the interpretation given to the labelling rules pays some regard to the requirements of Article 28 EC and the internal market aims of the Treaty provision upon which they were based. The original Treaty basis was Article 100 EC, and any substantive amendments going beyond adaptation to technical progress are adopted under Article 95 EC.

In the *Tobacco Advertising* case[31] the Court held that the measures referred to in Article 95(1) "are intended to improve the conditions for the establishment and functioning of the internal market"[32] and a measure adopted on the basis of this provision "must genuinely have as its object the improvement of the conditions for the establishment and functioning of the internal market."[33] In the same case, the Court holds that once the conditions for recourse to Article 95 and other internal market provisions are fulfilled, the Community legislature cannot be prevented from relying on that legal basis on the ground that "public health protection is a decisive factor in the choices to be made."[34] In the *Schwarzkopf* case the Court struck a balance between the requirements of Article 28 EC and the aims of the common rules in question, on the one hand, and public health on the other, and the outcome was an interpretation of common labelling rules which allowed those rules to make a contribution to the internal market while upholding the public health aims underlying the labelling requirements.

In the case of common rules for the labelling of tobacco products, internal market aims appear to have been lost sight of both by the Community lawmaker and by the Court of Justice itself. The preamble of Council Directive 89/622 on the labelling of tobacco products[35] referred to differences between national rules on labelling

---

[30] Para.96 of the Advocate General's Opinion.
[31] Case C–376/98 *Federal Republic of Germany v European Parliament and Council of the European Union* [2000] E.C.R. I–8419.
[32] *ibid.*, para.83.
[33] *ibid.*, para.84.
[34] *ibid.*, para.88.
[35] [1989] O.J. L359/1.

of tobacco products and to the fact that those differences were likely to constitute barriers to trade. Provision was made for all unit packets of tobacco products to carry, "on the most visible surface, the following general warning in the official language or languages of the country of final marketing: 'Tobacco seriously damages health'."[36] With regard to cigarette packets, the "other large surface of the packet shall carry, in the official language or languages of the country of final marketing" various specific warning selected from the Annex and alternating as specified.[37] On cigarette packets the warnings referred to must cover "at least 4 per cent of each large surface of the unit packet".[38] In the United Kingdom the Directive was implemented by the Tobacco Products Labelling (Safety) Regulations 1991,[39] which provided that the warnings were to cover "at least six per cent" of the relevant surface area for *domestic products*.[40] In the *Gallaher* case[41] various tobacco companies challenged the latter provisions on the ground that all Member States were bound to implement the Directive by providing that warnings cover "at least four per cent" of the relevant surface area, rather than "at least six per cent". The effect of the rules adopted by the United Kingdom was that domestically produced cigarettes were required to carry larger health warnings than imported cigarettes. The issue was referred to the Court of Justice before which the Commission and the United Kingdom advanced the argument that the reference in the Directive to "at least four per cent" gave Member States a discretion to require that the warnings cover a larger surface area if they so wished, in the case of domestic products. The Advocate General pointed out that a similar issue had arisen before the Court in the *Ratti* case,[42] in which the Court of Justice had interpreted Directive 73/173 on the classification, packaging and labelling of dangerous preparations. In that case the Court had held that Member States were not entitled to maintain, parallel with the rules laid down by the Directive for imports, *different rules* for the *domestic market*. The rules laid down by the Directive included a provision that the label must be "at least" a certain dimension. The Advocate General (Mr Lenz) argued: "That which is valid in this regard for Directive 73/173 must *a fortiori* also be valid for the present Directive, as it must be borne in mind that the Community legislature would have been aware of the Ratti judgment when it

---

[36] Art.4(1).
[37] Art.4(2).
[38] Art.4(4). This percentage was increased to 6 per cent for countries with two official languages and to 8 per cent for countries with three official languages. *ibid.*
[39] S.I. 1991/1530.
[40] Regs. 5(2)(d) and 6(3)(b).
[41] Case C–11/92 *The Queen v Secretary of State for Health, ex parte Gallaher Ltd, Imperial Tobacco Ltd and Rothmans International Tobacco (UK) Ltd.* [1993] E.C.R. I–3545.
[42] Case 148/78 *Pubblico Ministero v Ratti* [1979] E.C.R. 1629.

adopted Directive 89/622."[43] Mr Lenz concluded that "at least four per cent" meant that all Member States must adopt the rule that warnings must cover at least four per cent of the unit packet and that there was no discretion in Member States to prescribe a larger warning for domestic products. He reasoned as follows:

> "42. This conclusion is consistent with the objective pursued by the Directive both with regard to the easing of restrictions on the movement of goods and the approximation of conditions of competition.
>
> As the applicants in the United Kingdom proceedings correctly argued, a manufacturer wishing to export his produce from Member State A, which imposes a more stringent spatial requirement than that laid down by the Directive, to Member State B, which has the same official language as Member State A, would have to change his packaging if Member State B treats a spatial requirement of 4 per cent as adequate. Although the product labelled in accordance with the provisions of Member State A would also be marketable in Member State B (if one subscribes to the views expressed by the Commission and the United kingdom), those imports would be placed at a commercial disadvantage vis-à-vis domestic goods produced in Member State B if the manufacturer were not to adapt to the less stringent requirements existing in the latter State. The liberalization of trade and the approximation of conditions of competition, as objectives of the Directive, would here be placed in equal jeopardy.
>
> 43. . . . This conclusion is all the more justified when one considers that the Directive (if understood as laying down a minimum limit) does not specify any maximum limit for the percentage which may be imposed by Member States. Consequently, that figure could—theoretically—lie any-where between 5 per cent and 100 per cent. I cannot imagine that those who drafted the Directive intended to bring about such a position in law."

21–029 The Court of Justice, however, appeared to conclude that such a position could indeed have been intended. The Court took the view that the expression "at least" was to be interpreted as giving to Member States a discretion to decide that the indications and warnings are to cover a greater surface area than four per cent. The Court noted that in the *Ratti* case the Court had not had to rule

---

[43] Case C–11/92 *The Queen v Secretary of State for Health, ex parte Gallaher Ltd, Imperial Tobacco Ltd and Rothmans International Tobacco (UK) Ltd.* [1993] E.C.R. I–3545, para.26 of Opinion.

specifically on the labelling provision but on "other provisions of that directive and on the nature of its provisions in general."[44] The Court accepted that this interpretation of the provisions of the Directive "may imply less favourable treatment for national products in comparison with imported products and leaves in existence some inequalities in conditions of competition", but regarded these consequences as being "attributable to the degree of harmonisation sought by the provisions in question, which lay down minimum requirements."[45] The difficulty with the Court's conclusion is that it deprives the Directive of virtually all useful effect as regards removing obstacles to trade or eliminating distortions of competition, as the Advocate General so clearly demonstrates. It was noted above that the chief benefit of common labelling rules at the European level is that they make possible multilingual labelling. Certainly a "four per cent rule" applicable in the way suggested by the Advocate General would make multilingual labelling possible; a packet of cigarettes could be labelled for the UK, France and Belgium with health warnings covering only 16 per cent of the large surface areas. Yet as the Advocate General points out, the Court's interpretation would allow a Member State to require such a large size label for sale of domestic production on its own market that it would be impossible in practice to label for other Member States as well.

The provisions on labelling of tobacco products were amended by Article 5(2) of Directive 2001/37 of the manufacture, presentation and sale of tobacco products.[46]

Each unit packet of tobacco products must carry a general warning, on the most visible surface of the unit packet, and an additional warning, on the other most visible surface. The general warning "shall cover not less than 30 per cent of the external area of the corresponding surface of the unit packet . . . on which it is printed. That proportion shall be increased to 32 per cent for Member States with two official languages and 35 per cent for Member States with three official languages". The additional warning "shall cover not less than 40 per cent of the external area of the corresponding surface of the unit packet of tobacco on which it is printed. That proportion shall be increased to 45 per cent for Member States with two official languages and 50 per cent for Member States with three official languages."[47] Member States are furthermore entitled to stipulate that the warnings referred to are to be accompanied by a reference, outside the box for warnings, to the issuing authority.[48]

---

[44] *ibid.*, para.21.
[45] *ibid.*, para.22.
[46] [2001] O.J. L194/26.
[47] Art.5(5) of Dir.2001/37.
[48] Art.5(8) of Dir.2001/37.

A challenge to the validity of the Directive by various tobacco companies in the English High Court led to a reference to the Court of Justice.[49] The applicants argued that Article 5 of the Directive was invalid because, contrary to the requirements of the *Schwarzkopf* case, that provision made it at the very least excessively difficult for tobacco products complying with the labelling rules in question to be marketed in several Member States, to the point that parallel imports would in practice be excluded, and tobacco products would continue to be labelled exclusively for the Member State in which they are to be marketed.[50] The Court simply does not address these points. It refers to its judgment in the *Gallaher* case for the proposition that "some provisions contained in the Community harmonisation measures already adopted merely laid down minimum requirements leaving the Member States a degree of discretion to adapt them".[51] It also refers to the fact that certain recitals in the preamble "refer to the fact that different Member States have different laws with regard to the presentation of warnings".[52] The Court goes on to note that the Directive guarantees the free movement of products which comply with its requirements,[53] and concludes that "the Directive genuinely has as its object the improvement of the conditions for the functioning of the internal market".[54] This reasoning is at a level of generality which does not engage with the argument referred to above to the effect that the size requirements for the warning labels make it impossible or excessively difficult for a commercial operator to label for "several Member States". Furthermore, the Court says nothing to indicate that the reasoning adopted in the *Gallaher* case and referred to above does not apply to the Directive under consideration. The references in Article 5(2) to warnings covering "not less than" 30 per cent, etc. would seem capable of being construed as minimum standards still allowing to Member States a discretion to require larger labels for domestic products. Yet quite apart from this, the labelling requirements in Article 5, far from facilitating cross frontier trade in tobacco products, ensures that such trade is close to impossible. The internal market aims claimed by the Directive appear to have been wholly subordinated to public health aims.

---

[49] *The Queen on the Application of (British American Tobacco (Investments) Limited, Imperial Tobacco Limited v The Secretary of State for Health, HM Attorney General* [2001] W.L. 1676838.

[50] Report for the Hearing, paras 73–75.

[51] Case C–491/01 *The Queen v Secretary of State for Health ex parte British American Tobacco (Investments) Ltd and Imperial Tobacco Ltd* [2002] E.C.R. I–11453, para.66.

[52] *ibid.*, para.72.

[53] *ibid.*, para.74.

[54] *ibid.*, para.75.

Mutual recognition, and why negative harmonisation is not always enough

National rules incompatible with Article 28 EC should be disapplied—harmonisation is normally reserved for obstacles to trade justified under Article 30 EC or on the basis of mandatory requirements

It was suggested in Chapter 16 that the judgment of the Court of 21–030 Justice in the *Cassis* case was one of the great formative events in the establishment of the internal market. The judgment provided the basis for a principle of "mutual recognition" which is relevant today not only to the free movement of goods, but also to the free movement of persons and of services. This principle promotes both free trade and national and local diversity, while minimising the need for harmonisation of national rules. The impact which the *Cassis* judgment would have on harmonisation was noted at once by the Commission and commented on in its Communication of October 3, 1980, as follows:

> "The Commission's work of harmonisation will henceforth have to be directed mainly at national laws having an impact on the functioning of the common market where barriers to trade to be removed arise from national provisions which are *admissible* under the criteria set by the Court." (emphasis added)

The national provisions referred to by the Commission, as being "admissible" under the criteria set by the Court, are those that are genuinely necessary for the purposes of the derogations in Article 30, or of mandatory requirements in the general interest. Where disparities between national rules create barriers to trade which can be justified, these barriers can be eliminated by adopting common rules which eliminate the disparities from which the barriers arise. An example would be disparities between national rules on permitted levels of certain additives in foodstuffs. Member States maintaining such rules might well be able to justify them, but differences between the national rules in question might lead to products of certain Member States being excluded from the markets of certain others. If all Member States adopt the same rule as regards the additives in question, foodstuffs placed on the market in one Member State can be marketed in any other.

The significant and abiding achievement of the *Cassis* judgment is that it meant Member States could no longer *automatically* rely upon national standards relating to the composition, packaging etc. of products, as justifying the exclusion from their markets of non-compliant products which had been allowed onto the market in other Member States. As the 1980 Communication noted:

"The Commission will therefore have to tackle a whole body of commercial rules which lay down that products manufactured and marketed in one Member State must fulfil technical or qualitative conditions in order to be admitted to the market of another and specifically in all cases where the trade barriers occasioned by such rules are inadmissible according to the very strict criteria set out by the Court. The Commission is referring in particular to rules covering the composition, designation, presentation and packaging of products as well as rules requiring compliance with certain technical standards."

The "tackling" of national rules that impede the free movement of goods without justification—since the rules in question amount to infringements of the EC Treaty—would involve the Commission's requesting Member States to amend or repeal offending provisions and if necessary initiating infraction proceedings pursuant to Article 226 EC. Harmonisation would not, on the face of it, be an appropriate mechanism for dealing with rules which ought simply to be *disapplied*; harmonisation was designed to substitute common rules at the European level for rules adopted at the national level, which addressed genuine issues of public interest but which by their diversity caused obstacles to trade.

It does not however follow that legislation at Community level has no role to play in dealing with national rules that are simply prohibited by Community law. In the first place, a Community measure may require a Member State to notify other Member States and the Commission of proposed national rules, relating in particular to the characteristics, packaging and labelling of products, which might affect the free movement of goods. The aim of such notification is to allow sufficient time for the Commission and the Member States to raise objections to a proposed measure, where necessary, in order to secure the removal or reduction of possible impediments it may cause to the free movement of goods, if adopted.[55] Secondly, even in cases where national rules are prohibited by Article 28 EC, Community measures may provide a useful way of laying down specific rules declaratory of the scope of the requirements of the Article, putting Member States under an obligation to adopt mechanisms and procedures to make it possible in practice for interested parties to place products on the market in all Member States.

Transparency, and the enforcement in practice of Article 28 EC

21–031 The case law of the Court of Justice on Articles 28 and 30 EC and the principle of mutual recognition represent an approach to the free movement of goods which respects diversity and maximises

---

[55] See Dir.98/34 of the European Parliament and of the Council laying down a procedure for the provision of information in the field of technical standards and regulations, [1998] O.J. L204/3.

consumer choice. A major difficulty which arises in practice is that the rights of importers and the obligations of national authorities are to be found in the *European Court Reports* and in the debates of jurists in the law journals rather than in any clear legal texts which are in terms addressed to those concerned. The truth is that rights created or confirmed by EC Directives and implemented by national rules are in practice more accessible and enforceable than directly applicable rights arising solely from the provisions of the EC Treaty. Implementation of Directives requires Member States to adopt binding national rules which are clear and precise, are made known to those subject to the law, and establish a specific legal framework both as regards substantive and procedural rules and enforcement mechanisms.[56] The position is somewhat different as regards directly applicable Treaty provisions. The principal legislative obligations of Member States as regards directly applicable Treaty provisions are (a) to recognise and ensure the full force and effect of such provisions and (b) to disapply national rules which are inconsistent with such provisions.[57] But the duty to implement the Treaty by adopting national measures is not confined to a duty to disapply inconsistent national rules; it may amount to a further duty to adopt positive rules and procedures to ensure that individuals can exercise the rights contemplated by the Treaty.[58] In practice Member States are much more systematic in implementing Directives by the adoption of national rules than they are in adopting national legal frameworks for the enjoyment of specific Treaty rights, and Commission enforcement under Article 226 EC does not appear to prioritise actions against Member States for shortcomings of the latter type. Against this background it is appropriate to consider the Commission's Interpretative Communication of 2003 (IC2003) on the practical application of mutual recognition.[59]

IC2003 states that a large number of economic operators and national administrations are unfamiliar with the principle of mutual recognition in the area of the free movement of goods. This uncertainty encourages economic operators to adapt their products to the rules (composition, packaging labelling, etc.) of the importing Member State, and competent authorities to err on the side of caution and refuse access to the market to non conforming imports. The Commission indicates that in order to comply with Articles 28 and 30 EC the examination by an importing Member State of the

---

[56] See Ch.5, p.164.
[57] Ch.5, p.144.
[58] Ch.5, p.144. Case C–375/92 *Commission Kingdom of Spain* [1994] E.C.R. I–923. See also to similar effect in the context of a regulation, Case 72/85 *Commission v Netherlands* [1986] E.C.R. 1219.
[59] Commission interpretative communication on facilitating the access of products to the markets of other Member States: the practical application of mutual recognition, [2003] O.J. C 265/2.

fitness of marketing of a product manufactured in another Member State can be divided into three stages.

— Collecting the necessary data.
— Verifying equivalence.
— Results of the assessment and communicating them to the applicant.

The first port of call as regards collection of data is the relevant economic operator such as the importer who should be able to provide relevant technical information including a sample to the competent authority within a reasonable time (the Commission suggests 20 working days). Necessary data includes information on the conformity of the product with the rules of the Member State of origin. The competent authority has the right to take samples of a product in order to examine its conformity with its rules. The number of samples must be proportionate to the potential risk the product may pose. But the competent authority of the importing Member State cannot duplicate controls which have already been carried out in the same State or in another Member State. Evidence of controls and/or the technical or scientific reports may be obtained from the scientific operator in question or, as appropriate, from the competent authorities in the Member State of origin. The importing Member State will only have the right to require additional testing in certain circumstances, e.g. the tests which have been carried out have not been carried out by a body providing equivalent guarantees to those required for national bodies.

21–032 It is the second stage referred to by the Commission in IC2003 which poses most difficulties in practice—verification of the equivalence of levels of protection. The Commission points out that when the authorities of the importing Member State learn that a product complies with the rules of one or more Member States of origin, it may be aware, by virtue of administrative co-operation between Member States, of the minimum level of protection provided by the legislation of the State or States in question. If this level is equivalent to that of the importing Member State, a more detailed examination of the product will not be necessary. When an importing Member State has no technical rules for the marketing of products on its territory, in principle the marketing of a product will not be restricted there. This will generally be the case for simple or well known products, which do not pose any risk to health or safety, under normal conditions of use. If however the importing Member State lays down technical rules for the marketing of products on its territory, the competent authority should examine relevant documentation relating to the product and, if necessary, the product itself, in the light of these rules. This examination makes it possible to determine the technical rules to which the product does not conform, and it is these latter rules which will be the basis for examining the proportionality of the application of these rules in the case in question. IC2003 briefly summarises the effect of the Court's case law on the free movement of goods as regards mandatory requirements and the proportionality. The Communication notes that examination of the possible application of a technical rule to an imported product may mean that domestic products "are treated differently, perhaps even more severely" than the imported product, but the competent authority "cannot regard such different treatment as a decisive factor."[60]

The third stage referred to by the Commission involves the results of the assessment and communicating them to the applicant. When an importing Member State has examined the product in question, the results of this assessment, whether positive or negative, must be communicated as soon as possible to the economic operator concerned. The Commission emphasises the procedural rights of economic operators, which include being informed in writing of those elements of the national technical rules which prevent the marketing of the product in question, having the opportunity to submit any comments within a reasonable period before any decision is taken to restrict the marketing of the product, and, once the individual measure restricting the marketing of the product has been taken, being notified of the decision and of available methods of appeal.

Perhaps the most interesting feature of IC2003 is the Commission's proposed "mutual recognition clause", which appears under the heading "Some advice to Member States", and the suggestion that Member States are under a legal duty to incorporate an appropriately worded clause into national law. As regards the latter legal duty, the Commission states:

> "In fact, the principles of legal certainty and the protection of individuals require, in areas covered by Community law, that the Member States' legal rules should be worded unequivocally so as to give the persons concerned a clear and precise understanding of their rights and obligations and enable national courts to ensure that those rights and obligations are observed. The Commission considers that the mutual recognition clause is a valid means to implement these principles."[61]

The above statement of the Commission seems correct, for the **21–033** reasons given above,[62] though the Commission does not refer to the case law of the Court on the point. The Commission had in fact referred to mutual recognition clauses in its 1999 Communication to

---

[60] [2003] O.J. C265/9, para.4.2
[61] [2003] O.J. C265/10, para.6.1
[62] p.955.

the Council and the European Parliament.[63] The reference there was
to the judgment of the Court of Justice in *Commission v France*.[64]
The Commission had objected to a draft Decree notified to it[65] on
the ground that it reserved certain trade descriptions to preparations
with foie gras as a base which met various conditions as to their
quality and composition laid down by the Decree and in so far as it
made no provision for a mutual recognition clause for products
lawfully marketed in the other Member States. The Court of Justice
upheld the contentions of the Commission. But the mutual recognition clauses referred to in IC2003 seem to go rather further than that
referred to by the Court of Justice and by the Commission in its
1999 Communication.

The Commission suggests that a mutual recognition clause can
take one of two forms. The first is "a simple clause, when other parts
of national laws already include the administrative guarantees outlined in this communication".[66] The second is "a clause which makes
provision for a more detailed procedure, in compliance with the
principles outlined in this communication."[67] There is an example of
a detailed mutual recognition clause, which is drafted as follows:

> "The requirements of this law do not not apply to products
> lawfully manufactured and/or marketed in another Member
> State of the European Union . . .
>
> If the competent authorities have proof that a specific
> product lawfully manufactured and/or marketed in another
> Member State . . . does not provide a level of protection
> equivalent to that sought by this law, they may refuse market
> access to the product or have it withdrawn from the market,
> after they:
>
> — have informed the manufacturer or the distributor in
>   writing which elements of the national technical rules
>   prevent the marketing of the product in question, and
> — have proved, on the basis of all the relevant scientific
>   elements available to the the competent authorities, that
>   there are overriding grounds of general interest for
>   imposing these elements of the technical rule must be
>   imposed on the product concerned and that less restric-
>   tive measures could not have been used, and

---

[63] Communication on Mutual recognition in the context of the follow-up to the Action Plan
for the Single Market, COM (99) 0299 final, p.11.
[64] Case C–184/96 [1998] E.C.R. I—6197
[65] Pursuant to Council Directive 83/189 laying down a procedure for the provision of
information in the field of technical standards and regulations, [1983] O.J. L109/8, the
predecessor of Directive 98/34, n.1 above.
[66] [2003] O.J. C265/111, para.6.1
[67] *ibid*.

      — have invited the economic operator to express any comments he may have within a period of (at least four weeks or 20 working days), before issuing an individual measure against him restricting the marketing of this product, and

      — have taken due account of his comments in the grounds of the final decision. The competent authority shall notify the economic operator concerned of individual measures restricting the marketing of the product, stating the means of appeal available to him."[68]

IC2003 and the mutual recognition clause which it contains are worthy of remark. The Commission's communication recognises the pratical difficulties which economic operators and competent national authorities are likely to encounter in negotiating the direct applicability of Articles 28 and 30 EC. It goes on to summarise the substantive and procedural requirements of these Articles as indicated by the case law of the Court of Justice. This summary is in turn in part further summarised in the "mutual recognition" clause, which the Commission commends as a suitable way for Member States to ensure that their national legal rules are compliant with the Articles in question. Such a clause, if adopted by legislation in Member States, would amount to the sort of specific legal framework referred to above[69] which one would expect to find as the result of implementation of a Directive. The Communication and the Mutual Recognition clause are thus a kind of "soft law" or "quasi" Directive. It must be added that there seems no reason at all why the Commission should not make a proposal for a Directive under Article 95 EC in terms similar to those incorporated in the mutual recognition clause.

The Services Directive
The proposal for a directive on services in the internal market is a **21–034** central plank of the Internal Market Strategy, 2003–2006, to which reference was made in the opening section of this chapter. The proposal was formally transmitted by the Commission to the European Parliament and the Council on February 6, 2004.[70] Almost at once, its radical features, in particular the adoption of the "country of origin" principle (of which more below), provoked a storm of controversy; and, although it was firmly based on principles derived from the existing EC Treaty, the proposal became one of the themes of the bitterly fought referendum campaigns on the ratification of

---

[68] [2003] O.J. C 265/11.
[69] At p.955.
[70] COM (2004) 2 final.

the Constitutional Treaty in France and the Netherlands, and is believed to have been a factor in the rejection of the Treaty by the electorates of those countries. At the time of writing, the Commission had recently presented an amended proposal.[71] This incorporates many, though not all, of the amendments put forward by the European Parliament in its legislative resolution at first reading, adopted on February 16, 2006.

The 2004 version of the Services Directive drew a sharp distinction between freedom of establishment for service providers, which was the subject of Chapter II, and "free movement of services" (in other words, the supply of services *between* Member States, where either the provider or the recipient moves to another Member State), which was the subject of Chapter III. In broad terms, the proposal took as its starting point the case law of the Court of Justice on establishment and services, which was discussed in Chapter 19, above; however, the main thrust of the provisions in the respective chapters was very different.

As regards the establishment of service providers, the proposal accepted the continuing right of Member States to impose authorisation requirements, subject to a set of principles laid down by Article 9, which is clearly modelled on the *Gebhard* test.[72] Establishment was to be facilitated, however, in a practical way, by measures of administrative simplification: for instance, the establishment of "single points of contact", at which service providers could complete the formalities relevant to their activities,[73] and be able to do so by electronic means.[74] There was also a provision banning certain legal requirements regarded as especially restrictive (e.g. that service providers should not be established in more than one Member State or should not belong to professional bodies in more than Member State)[75]; and a provision requiring Member States to evaluate a further list of requirements,[76] in order to assess their compatibilty with principles once again based upon the *Gebhard* test.[77] Although adding nothing of substance to the existing case law, the specific identification of prohibited and reviewable requirements can be seen as contributing usefully to the aim, discussed in the previous section, of enhancing legal transparency.

21–035   As regards the free movement of services, the centrepiece of the original proposal was the country of origin principle enshrined in Article 16. This is the principle according to which service providers

---

[71] COM (2006) 160 final.
[72] Case C–55/94, *Reinhard Gebhard v Consiglio dell'Ordine degli Avvocatie Procuratori di Milano* [1995] E.C.R. I–4165. See Ch.19, pp.762 *et seq.*
[73] Art.5.
[74] Art.8.
[75] Art.14.
[76] Art.15(1) and (2).
[77] Art.15(3).

are subject only to the national provisions of their Member State of origin (i.e. the Member State where they are established[78]). The Member State of origin was to be responsible for supervising both the provider and the service provided, including where this took place in another Member State.[79] Member States would be explicitly prohibited from, among other things, imposing on the provider an obligation to have an establishment in their territory or an obligation to obtain an authorisation from their competent bodies or to registerwith a professional body in their territory.[80] Not surprisingly, given the radical nature of the country of origin principle, it was thought necessary to lay down a long list of general derogations, some relating to whole economic sectors (e.g. postal services and electricity, gas and water distribution services), others to matters covered by existing provisions of Community law, such as on the recognition of professional qualifications.[81] In addition, there would be temporary derogations (applicable during a transitional period to, for instance, gamblig activities, including lotteries and betting trans-actions)[82] and the possibility of case-by-case derogation (e.g. in relation to the exercise of a health profession).[83]

Other features of the proposal were various concrete measures designed to protect the rights of recipients of services[84]; and pro-visions clarifying the allocation of tasks between the Member State of origin and the Member State of destination in cases where workers, including third country nationals, are "posted" to the territory of another Member State in order to provide a service there.[85]

The 2006 version of the proposal leaves the chapter relating to establishment largely unchanged in substance. However, the pro-visions on administrative simplification have been moved into a separate chapter, evidently intended to apply to service activities in general, and not only to establishment. That alteration to the structure of the draft is explained by the main change in the new version of the Services Directive: the Commission has followed the legislative resolution of the European Parliament in eliminating the country of origin principle as the basis of the free movement of services. Article 16(1) EC now imposes a general obligation on the Member States to respect "the right of service providers to provide services in a Member State other than that in which they are established". It is stated that Member States "shall *not* make access to or exercise of a service activity in their territory subject to

---

[78] Art.4(4).
[79] Art.16(2).
[80] Art.16(3).
[81] Art.17.
[82] Art.19.
[83] Art.19.
[84] Arts 20–23. And see Ch.19.
[85] Arts 24, 25.

compliance with any requirements which do *not* respect" a set of principles reflecting a muscular version of the *Gebhard* test: justification is restricted to reasons of public policy, public security, public health and the protection of the environment. The double negative construction of that sentence makes crystal clear that Member States have the right to impose requirements compliant with the prescribed principles (hence the relevance of administrative simplification). The provisions relating to recipients of services mostly survive, but those on the posting of workers have been deleted.

The least that can be said is that the Commission's new proposal is a severely watered-down version of the original one. The most innovative, and potentially liberalising, mechanism of the first draft—a country of original principle that would operate without Member States' being able to justify restrictions—has been lost; but the *quid pro quo* for that innovation—the list of derogations in Article 17—has been retained, and in some respects strengthened. For instance, the utilities mentioned in the original list are now treated as mere illustrations, under the heading "Services of General Economic Interest", and the treatment of waste has been added. There is a real risk that, if eventually enacted in something like its present form, the Directive could represent a retreat from the Community *acquis* in the field of services, with serious consequences for legal certainty.[86]

That is a sombre note, indeed, on which to end a chapter on the completion of the internal market. It remains to be seen whether it is realistic to insist, as the European Council of March 2006 did, that "the internal market for services must be made fully operational, *while preserving the European social model*".[87]

Further reading

Barnard, C., *The Substantive Law of the EU—The Four Freedoms* (Oxford, 2004), Ch. 18.

Barnard, C. and Scott, J. (eds.), *The Law of the Single European Market* (Hart, Oxford, 2002).

Bieber, R., "Legislative Procedure for the Establishment of the Single Market" (1988) 25 C.M.L.Rev. 711.

C.E.L.S. Occasional Paper No.5, 2000, *The ECJ's Tobacco Advertising Judgment*.

Dougan, M., "Minimum Harmonisation and the Internal Market" (2000) 37 C.M.L.Rev. 853.

Pescatore, "Some Critical Remarks on the 'Single European Act' " (1987) 24 C.M.L.Rev. 9.

---

[86] See the critical Editorial in the April 2006 issue of C.M.L.Rev. This relates to the Parliament's legislative resolution but the comments are, in the main, equally pertinent to the amended proposal.

[87] Presidency Conclusions, para.57. Emphasis added.

PART VI

COMPETITION POLICY

INTRODUCTION TO THE RULES ON COMPETITION

Guide to this Chapter: This Chapter identifies the myriad func- **22–001** tions of competition law in its specific EC context, distinguishing between its early focus upon buttressing the single market and its more modern place in the post-Lisbon competitiveness agenda. Analysis of the personal scope of the competition rules emphasises the flexibility of the central concept of an "undertaking", especially when applied to state organisation of health care and other activities. The material, territorial and temporal dimensions of the competition rules are also discussed with attention paid to the extra-territorial application of EC law and the increasing importance of bilateral and multilateral competition agreements involving non-EU States. The Chapter concludes with a brief appraisal of the constitutional significance of EC competition law.

Competition in its European Context

The list of "activities of the Community" in Article 3(g) EC **22–002** includes the institution of "a system ensuring that competition in the internal market is not distorted." Article 4 EC provides for economic policy to be "conducted in accordance with the principle of an open market economy with free competition." These seemingly mild references belie the importance attached to competition law and policy in securing the broad objectives laid down for the Community in Article 2.

Competition, at least in a commercial context, describes a struggle for superiority in the market place. It is an essential aspect of the market mechanism because the availability of choice between goods and services establishes a link between the success of an undertaking and its ability to satisfy consumers' wishes. However, this idea is not the perfect competition model of neo-classical economics, in which efficiency is maximised by equilibrium between consumer demand and producer supply. Instead, EC law has adapted this theoretical paradigm to develop competition law in the light of evolving policies and priorities. Following a sustained period where the focus was upon the relationship between competition law and the single market, the modern agenda[1] is to ensure competitiveness in the "new economy".

The early focus upon the market

22–003   In the introduction to its *First Report on Competition Policy* the Commission wrote:

> "Competition is the best stimulant of economic activity since it guarantees the widest possible freedom of action to all. An active competition policy pursued in accordance with the provisions of the Treaties establishing the Communities makes it easier for the supply and demand structure continually to adjust to technological development. Through the interplay of decentralized decision making machinery, competition enables enterprises continuously to improve their efficiency, which is the sine qua non for a steady improvement in living standards and employment prospects within the countries of the Community. From this point of view, competition policy is an essential means for satisfying to a great extent the individual and collective needs of our society."[2]

This early statement clearly portrayed competition policy as ensuring that the common market envisaged by the Treaty functioned as a genuine *market*. The importance of this focus was equally reflected in the emphasis placed by the European Court upon the notion of *workable* competition. This expresses the "degree of competition necessary to ensure the observance of the basic requirements and attainment of the objectives of the Treaty, in particular the creation of a single market achieving conditions similar to those of a domestic market."[3] The idea of workable competition, not being anchored in any particular economic doctrine, permitted pragmatic responses to diverse and complex issues. Among the disparate areas which competition policies might address are the following: consumer welfare, the redistribution of wealth, the protection of small and medium-sized enterprises,[4] regional, social or industrial considerations and the integration of the single market. These concerns are not necessarily mutually compatible or easily reconciled in any given

---

[1] See *A proactive Competition Policy for a Competitive Europe,* COM (2004) 293 final.
[2] (1971) Comp. Rep. 11.
[3] Case 26/76 *Metro v Commission* [1977] E.C.R. 1875, 1904.
[4] Specifically mentioned in the EC Treaty as part of Art.157 in Title XVI Industry.

situation. Questions as to how they are to be balanced or, indeed, whether they are legitimate elements in competition policy at all, remain controversial for lawyers and economists alike.[5]

Many factors affecting competition and competition policy, such as industrial or social policy, are not peculiar to the European context. The exception, of course, is the influence wrought by the drive to create a single internal market.[6] Here competition policy reinforces the provisions of the Treaty aiming at the removal of barriers between the economies of the Member States. Dismantling those (mainly) public obstacles to trade will hardly be effective if they are simply replaced by private ones. It would be futile to attempt to create a single market without internal frontiers in goods, persons, services and capital, as required by Article 14 EC, if the isolation of national markets could effectively be maintained by restrictive practices on the part of undertakings, or by State aid policies giving competitive advantages to national industries. As will be seen in the discussion of Articles 81 and 82 in succeeding chapters, market partitioning is a particularly serious infringement of the rules on competition.

It must be emphasised that although more modern preoccupations with competitiveness have emerged in the conduct of competition policy (see below), the connection with the internal market remains a significant element in case law developments. Indeed, the extent of convergence between concepts underpinning the single market and competition rules is an active area of research and commentary.[7] In particular, the relevance of "rule of reason" arguments or non-economic justifications to Article 81 and the scope of the competition and free movement rules in relation to services such as health care provision have fuelled debates about the cross-fertilisation and consistency in application of core ideas.

Post-"Lisbon" policy: competitiveness, consumer welfare and efficiency

As the internal market has come closer to realisation, so its **22–004** position as the pre-eminent driver of competition policy has diminished. The so-called Lisbon strategy,[8] adopted in 2000, committed

---

[5] See, *inter alia*, the discussion of so-called Harvard and Chicago School economic theories by Burton, "Competition over competition analysis: a guide to some contemporary economics disputes" in Lonbay (ed.), *Frontiers of Competition Law* (Wiley Chancery Law, 1994), Ch. 1. Also Bork, *The Antitrust Paradox: A Policy at War with Itself* (Basic Books, 1978, reprinted with new Introduction and Epilogue 1993); D. Hildebrand, "The European School in EC Competition Law" (2002) 25 World Comp. 3.
[6] See Ehlermann, "The contribution of EC competition policy to the Single Market" (1992) 29 C.M.L.Rev. 257.
[7] See, e.g. K. Mortelmans, "Towards convergence in the application of the rules on free movement and competition?" (2001) 38 C.M.L.Rev. 613; J. Baquero Cruz, *Between Competition and Free Movement* (Hart, Oxford, 2002); R. O'Loughlin, "EC Competition Rules and Free Movement Rules: an Examination of the Parallels and their Furtherance by the ECJ *Wouters* Decision" [2003] E.C.L.R. 62.
[8] An agenda first adopted in March 2000, then re-launched in March 2005.

Member States to make the EU "the world's most competitive and dynamic knowledge-based economy" by 2010. In 2004 the Commission set out its ideas for a "pro-active competition policy",[9] characterised by:

> "— improvement of the regulatory framework for competition which facilitates vibrant business activity, wide dissemination of knowledge, a better deal for consumers, and efficient restructuring throughout the internal market; and
> — enforcement practice which actively removes barriers to entry and impediments to effective competition that most seriously harm competition in the internal market and imperil the competitiveness of European enterprises."

The goal of such a policy "is to support the competitive process in the internal market and to induce firms to engage in competitive and dynamically efficiency-enhancing behaviours".[10] As an OECD report has observed,[11] the Commission's contentions just about cover all bases. What is clear, however, is the instrumentalism of competition law and policy. As the Commission explicitly acknowledged, ". . . competition is not an end in itself. It is a vital market process which rewards firms offering lower prices, better quality, new products, and greater choice."[12]

EC competition policy is thus in a state of transition, visible in various aspects of the application of its fundamental rules . The "workable" competition of the older case law is being reshaped by the Commission in terms of economic principle.[13] The reforms of 2004 made to Article 81 EC cartels and merger control emphasise that market effects should underpin legal regimes. Similarly, the Commission's review of Article 82 EC[14] is likely to embrace a more functional and effects-based analysis of abuses of dominant position. Proponents of this approach claim[15] at least two complementary goals are served. First, it ensures that anti-competitive behaviour does not outwit legal provisions. This also ensures consistency in the treatment of commercial practices. Secondly, an economic approach guarantees that legal rules do not unduly thwart pro-competitive strategies, the emphasis from a regulatory perspective being placed

---

[9] See n.1, above.
[10] *ibid.*, para.2.2.
[11] *Competition Law and Policy in the European Union* (OECD, 2005). This report was the basis for a peer review examination of the European Commission in the OECD Competition Committee, October 2005. Available from *www.oecd.org*.
[12] *op. cit.*, n.1 above, para.2.1.
[13] OECD report, n.11 above, p.12.
[14] Staff discussion paper December 2005 reviewing the application of Art.82 EC to exclusionary abuses.
[15] e.g. Report by EAGCP, *An economic approach to Art.82* (July 2005), Coordinator Patrick Rey.

upon controlling the more important competitive harms whilst preserving and encouraging efficiency.

The other major overhaul of EC competition law concerns enforcement. The OECD report of 2005[16] succinctly summarised the position:

"Modernisation of the enforcment process, by eliminating notification and prior approval of exemptions while sharing enforcement responsibility with national agencies, is designed, among other things, to redirect resources so that DG Comp can concentrate on complex, Community-wide issues and investigations. Modernisation shares competence with national institutions in a different way than the Community usually does. It does not follow the paradigm of a directive from Brussels to be implemented through national laws. There are no EU-level directives requiring national governments to adopt a particular substantive competition law, and modernisation does not require substantive harmonisation. Rather, it builds on the fact that national competition law systems have co-evolved along with the Community system, so that over the years most national governments (and all of the pre-accession Members) have adopted substantive rules that are generally consistent with those of the EU without being required to do so."

Decentralisation of enforcement, of course, carries its own risks regarding the effectiveness of ensuring compliance with EC requirements. If, as seems clear, the Commission is concentrating its own resources on large cartels, a large dose of self-help by victims of other anti-competitive behaviour appears necessary alongside the enhanced monitoring roles assigned to national agencies. Consequently, the Commission has issued a Green Paper[17] inviting comments on various options for promoting damages actions for breaches of EC competition rules. Linking this to the changed priorities for competition policy, the Green Paper notes that private as well as public enforcement of antitrust law is an important tool to create and sustain a competitive economy.[18]

EC Sources of Competition Law

The preamble to the Treaty and the general provisions of Articles **22–005** 2 and 3 have played a significant part in the development of the case law on competition.[19] The primary Treaty provisions in which the

---

[16] *op.cit.*, n.11 above, p.61.
[17] *Damages actions for breach of the EC antitrust rules* COM (2005) 672 final.
[18] *ibid.*, para.1.1.
[19] See, e.g. Case 32/65 *Italy v Council and Commission* [1966] E.C.R. 389, 405; Case 6/72 *Europemballage and Continental Can v Commission* [1973] E.C.R. 215, 243–244.

substantive law on the topic is to be found are Articles 81 to 89. Together, these form the framework for competition law applicable to private undertakings, public enterprises and States. In addition, EC secondary legislation provides the detailed substance for merger control and enforcement action. The whole scheme of competition law is increasingly supplemented by "soft law" devices, such as Guidelines, Notices and Communications, which provide important signals to business and legal communities as to the Commission's thinking and operation of key ideas such as market definition, fines and leniency policies and a framework for public service compensation.

The principal Treaty provisions

22–006   So far as the behaviour of undertakings is concerned, the Treaty adopts a distinction which is familiar in competition law (or, to use the American term, "antitrust law"[20]) between two types of problem that may arise. The first concerns restrictive agreements or practices involving a degree of collusion between undertakings that are economically independent of each other. Such combinations in restraint of trade are often referred to as "cartels". Examples can be found in agreements between A and B to keep out of each other's markets or to fix prices. Article 81 of the Treaty is designed to deal with such situations. It is considered in Chapter 23, below. The second type of problem arises where a single undertaking or a group of undertakings has reached a position of such strength on a given market that the normal constraints of the competitive process no longer apply to it. This is known in Community law as a "dominant position". Dominant undertakings represent a danger to other operators on the same market and to their customers or suppliers. They may, for example, drive the remaining participants in the same market out of business or charge unreasonably high prices for their products. Such abuses of dominance are discussed in Chapter 24 below. One way of averting the problems of market power is to attack the fact of dominance itself, by seeking to prevent the growth of undertakings beyond a certain point, and by taking power to break up any that may succeed in doing so. An alternative approach is to attempt to regulate the behaviour of dominant undertakings. Here regulatory power is used as a constraining influence, to compensate for the absence of effective competition. Initially the latter approach was adopted by the EC Treaty in its focus upon the "abuse" of dominance. Subsequently, the European Court held that, in certain circumstances, a further accretion of market power to a dominant undertaking may, in itself, constitute an abuse. This latter,

---

[20] In the nineteenth century anti-competitive arrangements were often carried out in the USA through trusts, hence this term.

structural, issue will now normally fall within the Merger Regulation,[21] at least where there is the requisite Community dimension in turnover and geographical terms.

Provision for the application of the substantive rules in Articles 81 and 82 is made by Articles 83 to 85 of the Treaty. Article 83 empowers the Council, acting by a qualified majority on a proposal from the Commission and after consulting the European Parliament, to adopt implementing regulations or directives. This power was used for the enactment of, *inter alia*, Regulation 17/62, which established the basic machinery for the execution of EC competition policy, giving primary responsibility to the Commission in a system originally contemplating *ex ante* notification.[22] This enforcement regime was dismantled and replaced by a new, decentralised regime in the form of Council Regulation 1/2003,[23] which became effective from May 1, 2004 and utilises national courts and national competition authorities as well as the European Commission. These arrangements, discussed further in Chapter 25 below, rely on *ex post facto* control of anti-competitive conduct.

Problems arising from the relationships between governments, on the one hand, and public undertakings or undertakings which have been entrusted with the performance of certain tasks in the public interest, on the other, are the subject of Article 86. This relationship, although clearly liable to affect the conditions of competition, has a wider significance for the operation of the common market. In particular, Article 86(2) provides an opportunity for entrusted undertakings to escape the application of "normal" Treaty rules.[24] A particular issue which has arisen in recent years has been the provision of state support to undertakings charged with the operation of services of general economic interest. The significance of Article 86 and its interaction with other Treaty rules are discussed in Chapter 26, below.

Under Articles 87 to 89 the Community institutions, and in particular the Commission, have supervisory powers over the granting of aids to industry in the various Member States. The general principle is that aid must not be granted if it distorts or threatens to distort competition by favouring certain undertakings or forms of production, in so far as trade between Member States may be affected. However, exceptions are permitted in relation to a number

---

[21] Council Reg.139/2004 [2004] O.J. L24/1. Detailed examination of this provision is outside the scope of this book, although comparisons are made where relevant with mergers case law for the purposes of explaining the more general rules of competition law.

[22] [1962] J.O. 204; [1959–1962] O.J. 87.

[23] [2003] O.J. L1/1.

[24] See J. Baquero Cruz, "Beyond competition: services of general interest and European Community Law" in G. de Búrca (ed.), *EU Law and the Welfare State, In Search of Solidarity* (OUP, Oxford, 2005); also T. Prosser, *The Limits of Competition Law, Markets and Public Services* (OUP, Oxford, 2005), esp. Chs 6–8.

of economic, regional, social and cultural concerns, enabling the Commission to take account of the various pressures to which the Member States are subject. These provisions are discussed in Chapter 27, below.

Other sources of EC competition law

22–007   Besides the EC Treaty itself, the principal sources of EC competition law are regulations pursuant to Article 83, the case law of the Court of Justice and the Court of First Instance, and the administrative practice of the Commission.

Regulations on competition have been adopted by both the Council and the Commission, the latter acting under delegated powers. Regulation 1/2003, the general implementing measure, has already been mentioned. The Court of Justice has played a vital part in the development of the rules on competition, as of other areas of Community law. Competition matters normally come to the European courts by way of proceedings under Article 230 EC for the review of decisions of the Commission applying the rules, or through references under Article 234 from national courts before which the rules have been invoked. In addition, the Court of Justice has unlimited jurisdiction to hear appeals against the imposition by the Commission of fines or periodic penalty payments for infringements of the rules.[25] Proceedings under Article 230 relating to the implementation of the competition rules of the EC must be brought before the Court of First Instance.[26] Appeal lies to the Court of Justice from the Court of First Instance only on points of law.[27]

As a result of this realignment of responsibilities, the Court of Justice no longer has quite the same opportunities to influence the development of competition law.[28] After the early heady days in which the Commission's desire to secure an effective regulatory regime gained judicial endorsement, the Court of Justice was instrumental in ensuring that the Commission is itself subject to rule of law considerations, requiring it to provide more detailed economic evidence in support of its conclusions and establishing procedural rights for undertakings.[29] The Court of First Instance has in turn taken a robust approach to factual issues in competition cases. As the OECD 2005 Report noted, "since the CFI was created the courts have not given the Commission much leeway about evidentiary matters. The potential for judicial review and annulment

---

[25] See Reg.1/2003, Art.31.
[26] Art.3(1)(c) of Council Dec.88/591, Establishing an EC Court of First Instance [1988] O.J. L319/1.
[27] Art.51 of the Statute of Court of Justice as amended by Art. 7 Council Dec.88/591.
[28] See generally Gerber, *Law and Competition in Twentieth Century Europe: Protecting Prometheus* (Clarendon Press, Oxford, 1998).
[29] Arnull, *The European Union and its Court of Justice* (OUP, Oxford, 1999), p.397.

shores up deficiencies of the Commission decision process under principles of European human rights law about impartiality and independence."[30]

The Commission is the authority charged with the administration **22–008** of the competition system at Community level. For this purpose it has been empowered to take decisions, *inter alia*, to order termination of infringements,[31] to make findings of inapplicability[32] and to impose fines[33] or periodic penalty payments.[34] In addition to its decisions in individual cases, the Commission's policy and practice can also be discerned from its Annual Reports on Competition Policy. Moreover, in recent years the Commission has increasingly made greater use of 'soft law' mechanisms such as Notices. These have covered a variety of topics, including market definition, *de minimis* rules, and the Commission's own relationship with national courts in the disposal of individual cases. Notices are technically not binding but will be influential in the areas they cover, offering guidance and some element of certainty for the business community.

Finally, it may be noted, the directly effective provisions of Articles 81 and 82 invite recourse to national courts for the application of EC competition law. This is particularly true since the modernisation reforms of 2004 removed the Commission's previously exclusive power over Article 81(3) individual exemptions. National courts may accordingly now apply all of the provisions of Articles 81 to 82.[35] As part of the same reform package, national competition authorities are now also an integral part of the enforcement mechanism for EC competition law. Acting on their own initiative or on a complaint, such authorities may take decisions requiring infringements to be brought to an end, ordering interim measures, accepting commitments or imposing fines, periodic penalty payments or any other penalty provided for in their national law.[36]

The scope of the EC competition rules

Personal scope

The rules in Articles 81 and 82 apply to "undertakings". No **22–009** definition of this concept for the purposes of competition law is provided by the EC Treaty. However, the Court has taken an

---

[30] n.11, above, p.64.
[31] Reg.1/2003, Art.7.
[32] Reg.1/2003, Art.10.
[33] Reg.1/2003, Art.23.
[34] Reg.1/2003, Art.24.
[35] Reg.1/2003, Art.6.
[36] Reg.1/2003, Art.5.

expansive and functional view of the notion, holding that it "encompasses every entity engaged in an economic activity, regardless of the legal status of the entity and the way in which it is financed."[37] The requirement of participation in economic activities must be understood in a wide sense. It covers not only the production and distribution of goods but also the provision of services.[38] A body that exists for a non-economic purpose but engages in certain operations of a commercial nature will be, to that extent, an undertaking[39]: for example a public service broadcasting establishment when it licenses the manufacture of toys based on a popular children's series.[40] Nor is there any need for the body in question to be motivated by the pursuit of profits. Thus societies that manage the rights of authors and performing artists on a non-profit making basis qualify as undertakings because they provide a commercial service.[41]

The entities accepted as undertakings by the Court of Justice and the Commission exhibit a wide range of legal forms. They include companies, partnerships,[42] co-operatives[43] and foreign trade associations.[44] Individuals may be undertakings, not just self-employed professionals[45] but also inventors who grant licences for the use of their patents[46] or opera stars who contract to perform for a television company.[47] However, individuals who are "workers" within the meaning of Article 39 EC will not be undertakings. Thus in *Becu*[48] "recognised dockers" were found to perform their work for and under the direction of undertakings, thus satisfying the definition of "worker".[49] Since they were, for the duration of that relationship, incorporated into the undertakings concerned and formed an economic unit with each of them, the dockers did not in themselves constitute undertakings within the meaning of Community competition law.[50] Nor could the recognised dockers viewed collectively in a port area be regarded as an undertaking.[51]

---

[37] Case C–41/90 *Höfner v Macrotron* [1991] E.C.R. I–1979, para.21.
[38] Case 155/73 *Sacchi* [1974] E.C.R. 409; [1974] 2 C.M.L.R. 177.
[39] *ibid.*
[40] *Re BBC* [1976] 1 C.M.L.R. D89.
[41] Case 127/73 *BRT v SABAM* [1974] E.C.R. 51 and 313; [1974] 2 C.M.L.R. 238; Case 7/82 GVL v Commission [1983] E.C.R. 483; [1983] 3 C.M.L.R. 645.
[42] e.g. *Re William Prym-Werke* [1973] J.O. L296/24; [1973] C.M.L.R. D250.
[43] e.g. Re Rennet [1980] O.J. L51/19; [1980] 2 C.M.L.R. 402. The decision was upheld by the Court in Case 61/80 *Co-operatieve Stremsel-en-Kleurselfabriek v Commission* [1981] E.C.R. 851; [1982] 1 C.M.L.R. 240.
[44] Even if under their domestic law they have no identity separate from the state: *Re Aluminium Imports from Eastern Europe* [1985] O.J. L92/1; [1987] 3 C.M.L.R. 813.
[45] Case C–309/99 *Wouters and others* [2002] E.C.R. I–1577, [2002] 4 C.M.L.R. 913.
[46] See e.g. Re AOIP/Beyrard [1976] O.J. L6/8; [1976] 1 C.M.L.R. D14.
[47] *Re Unitel* [1978] O.J. L157/39; [1978] 3 C.M.L.R. 306.
[48] Case C–22/98 *Becu* [1999] E.C.R. I–5665, [2001] 4 C.M.L.R. 968.
[49] See Case C–170/90 *Merci Convenzionali v Porto di Genova* [1991] E.C.R. I–5889.
[50] Case C–22/98 *Becu*, n.48 above, para.26.
[51] *ibid.*, para.27.

The broad approach taken by the Court in *Höfner v Macrotron*[52] has not proved sufficient on its own to resolve complex situations which may arise in relation to the application of the competition rules to activities carried on by a State or State entity. As Advocate General Poiares Maduro has observed,[53] in this area "the Court is entering dangerous territory, since it must find a balance between the need to protect undistorted competition on the common market and respect for the powers of the Member States." One explanatory formulation often adopted by the Court is the notion of market participation or at least the exercise of functions in a market context, expressed in a number of cases in the proposition that "any activity consisting in offering goods and services on a given market is an economic activity."[54] A line is accordingly drawn between market, economic engagement and the exercise of public authority for regulatory functions.

Thus, in *SAT v Eurocontrol*,[55] the body involved was an inter- **22–010** national organisation charged with supervising air traffic control services within the air space of the States party to the Convention under which it was established, and to collect the charges levied for those services. In the Court's view, Eurocontrol was carrying out, on behalf of the Contracting States, tasks in the public interest aimed at contributing to the maintenance and improvement of air navigation safety. Collection of route charges, the subject of the dispute in the case, could not be separated from the organisation's other activities as they were merely the consideration, payable by users, for the obligatory and exclusive use of air navigation control facilities and services. Thus, taken as a whole, Eurocontrol's activities were connected with the exercise of powers relating to the control and supervision of air space which are typically those of a public authority. They were not of an economic nature justifying the application of the Treaty rules of competition.[56] Similarly, charges levied by a body made responsible by the State for anti-pollution surveillance at a particular port were held to be integral to its general surveillance activities and outside the scope of Article 82.[57]

There is perhaps a whiff of circularity in some of these arguments. The capacity to undermine the goals of competition policy can itself become the "economic" character that leads to application of the Treaty provisions. This purposive approach has its champions. As Advocate General Jacobs has argued[58]:

---

[52] n.37, above.
[53] Case C–205/03P *FENIN* (Opinion, November 10, 2005, para.26).
[54] Joined Cases C–180/98 to C–184/98 *Pavlov* [2000] E.C.R. I–6451, [2001] 4 C.M.L.R. 30, para.75; Case C–475/99 *Ambulanz Glöckner* [2001] E.C.R. I–8089, [2002] 4 C.M.L.R. 726, para.19; Case C–309/99 *Wouters* [2002] E.C.R. I–1577, [2002] 4 C.M.L.R. 913, para.47.
[55] Case C–364/92 *SAT Fluggesellschaft v Eurocontrol* [1994] E.C.R. I–43; [1994] 5 C.M.L.R. 208.
[56] *ibid.*, para.30.
[57] Case C–343/95 *Calì & Figli v SEPG* [1997] E.C.R. I–1547, [1997] 5 C.M.L.R. 484.
[58] Opinion in Joined Cases C–264/01, C–306/01, C–354/01 and C–355/01 *AOK Bundesverband* [2004] E.C.R. I–2493.

> "In assessing whether an activity is economic in character, the basic test appears to me to be whether it could, at least in principle, be carried on by a private undertaking in order to make profits. If there were no possibility of a private undertaking carrying on a given activity, there would be no purpose in applying the competition rules to it."

In short, this is an effectiveness argument based on the need to avoid any distortions of competition in the market caused by the conduct of any entity, whether public or private.[59] However, as discussed below, the Court has been careful not to rely on such undisguised elasticity. Yet it has equally eschewed the trap of over-prescription in relation to 'non-economic' characteristics. Indeed, as the Commission has observed,[60] it is very difficult to envisage compiling a list of activities that would not *a priori* be economic, let alone one that could ever be up to date given the political choices made by Member States in areas such as health care or pensions.

These latter areas have generated many of the most recent refinements in the case law determining the point at which competition rules apply. The focus of the Court's tests, explicitly or implicitly, is the extent to which the schemes and systems in question exhibit dimensions of solidarity. This notion is likely to be demonstrated on a number of levels,[61] particularly by reference to the characterisation of a system in terms of its membership, funding and benefits. Thus, in *Poucet and Pistre*,[62] the Court held that the concept of undertaking did not encompass organisations charged with the management of certain compulsory social security schemes. Indicators were provided by the fact that the sickness and maternity benefits involved were the same for all beneficiaries, regardless of contributions. The retirement pensions also operated on the basis that entitlements were not proportional to contributions paid into the scheme. Finally, schemes with a surplus contributed to the financing of those with structural financial difficulties. Consequently, taking all considerations together, the Court concluded that "those schemes pursue a social objective and embody the principle of solidarity."

22–011   In contrast, a non-profit-making organisation which managed a pension scheme intended to supplement a basic compulsory scheme, established by law as an optional scheme and operating according to the principles of capitalisation, was held to be an undertaking.[63]

---

[59] Noted expressly by Advocate General Jacobs in Case C–222/04 *Ministero dell'Economia e delle Finanze v Cassa di Risparmio di Firenze SpA* (Opinion October 27, 2005)

[60] *Non-Paper on Services of Economic Interest and State Aid*, para.37 (November 12, 2002).

[61] See V. Hatzopoulos, "Health Law and Policy: The Impact of the EU" in G de Búrca (ed.) *EU Law and the Welfare State—In Search of Solidarity* (Oxford, OUP 2005).

[62] Case C–160/91 *Poucet and Pistre* [1993] E.C.R. I–637.

[63] Case C–244/94 *Fédération Française des Sociétés d'Assurance v Ministère de l'Agriculture et de la Pêche* [1995] E.C.R. I–4013.

Benefits depended solely on the amount of the contributions paid by the beneficiaries and on the financial results of the investments made by the managing organisation, thus implying that the organisation carried on an economic activity in competition with life assurance companies. A similar result was reached in *Albany International*,[64] even though affiliation in that case was compulsory for workers in the relevant industrial sector.

Solidarity is a matter of degree, and it is the measurement of its predominance that will seemingly decide whether an entity's activities are deprived of their economic nature to render competition law inapplicable. For example, in *AOK*[65] the dispute at issue concerned the way in which German sickness funds were authorised to set maximum amounts to be paid for medicinal products. Pharmaceutical companies who objected to these limits argued that the sickness funds were in fact competing strongly with each other in relation to the amount of contributions, the benefits offered and the management and organisation of their services. Having noted that the sickness funds were obliged by national law to offer essentially identical obligatory benefits which did not depend on the amount of contributions, the Court then observed:

> "The latitude available to the sickness funds when setting the contribution rate and their freedom to engage in some competition with one another in order to attract members does not call this analysis into question. As is apparent from the observations submitted to the Court, the legislature introduced an element of competition with regard to contributions in order to encourage the sickness funds to operate in accordance with principles of sound management, that is to say in the most effective and least costly manner possible, in the interests of the proper functioning of the German social security system. Pursuit of that objective does not in any way change the nature of the sickness funds' activity."[66]

The Court thus concluded that the sickness funds did not constitute undertakings within the meaning of Articles 81 to 82 EC. However, it also acknowledged that the funds might engage in operations that would step outside their social functions. But this was not the case in relation to the setting of maximum amounts, which was held by the Court to be inseparable from the exclusively social objective of the sickness funds.

The extent of severability of functions is thus highly relevant to any assessment of the economic character of an entity. The State

---

[64] Case C–67/96 *Albany International BV v Stichting Bedrijfspensioenfonds Textielindustrie* [1999] E.C.R. I–5751, [2000] 4 C.M.L.R. 446.
[65] n.58 above.
[66] *ibid.*, para.56.

cannot shelter behind the pretext of solidarity in order to avoid economic operators being subject to competition law.[67] But whether activities can be neatly demarcated is not an easy task, as shown by the *FENIN* case involving alleged abuses of Article 82 EC by public bodies responsible for the management of the Spanish national health system ("the SNS"). FENIN, an association of undertakings which marketed medical goods and equipment used in Spanish hospitals, complained that the 26 bodies (including three ministries) running the SNS only paid sums invoiced after considerable delays of around 300 days on average. The Commission's rejection of the complaint was upheld by the Court of First Instance,[68] which held that purchasing activities linked to a non-economic, solidarity-based entity were to be classified in the same way. On subsequent appeal to the Court of Justice, FENIN claimed that the Court of First Instance had erred in law by taking too narrow a view of economic activity and too wide a view of solidarity.

22–012   Advocate General Poiares Maduro took the Court of First Instance to task over its analysis of FENIN's complaint. In particular, it had adopted a single, global, classification of the SNS instead of distinguishing between its activities. On the one hand, SNS managed the health insurance system in Spain. On the other, it was also responsible for providing health care services to its members. According to the Advocate General, the Court of First Instance had simply taken the solidarity case law relevant to the first activity and subsumed the second within it without identifying the different factors which might apply. Drawing upon case law from the free movement of services,[69] but at the same time recognising that the inferences did not have to be identical, the Advocate General concluded that there was insufficient information from which to determine if health care provision was in fact economic. He accordingly recommended that the case be referred back to the Court of First Instance for it to make the necessary findings in order to determine whether public and private health sectors existed in Spain or whether the solidarity present in the provision of health care free to all was predominant.

As will be seen in Chapter 26 below, determining that an entity is not an undertaking by virtue of its lack of economic character is a different task from relieving an undertaking with special responsibilities from the full rigour of the competition rules by reference to the derogation for services of general economic interest set out in Article 86(2) EC. Thus, in *Albany International*, the Court acknowledged that the pursuit of a social objective, the presence of

---

[67] Advocate General Poiares Maduro in Case C–205/03P *FENIN*, n.53 above.
[68] Case T–319/99 [2003] E.C.R. II–357
[69] Particularly Case C–385/99 *Müller-Fauré* [2003] E.C.R. I–4509, [2004] 2 C.M.L.R. 33 and Case C–157/99 *Smits and Peerbooms* [2001] E.C.R. I–5473

solidarity features in the scheme and various restrictions on investments made by the sectoral fund might make its service less competitive than comparable services rendered by insurance companies. Although these considerations did not prevent the fund being an undertaking, they could be taken into account when applying Article 86(2).[70]

A final aspect of the meaning of 'undertaking' concerns the application of the rules on competition to groups of companies. Here the Court of Justice does not hesitate to go behind the facade of separate corporate personality. This pragmatic approach is illustrated by the *Hydrotherm* case[71] which concerned the block exemption granted by Regulation 67/67[72] to certain categories of exclusive dealing agreements. The exemption was expressly limited to agreements "to which only two undertakings are party."[73] That condition was held to be fulfilled where the parties to a contract were, on the distribution side, a German company, and on the manufacturing side, the Italian developer of a product and two legally independent firms controlled by him. The Court explained that "In competition law, the term 'undertaking' must be understood as designating an economic unit for the purpose of the subject-matter of the agreement in question even if in law that economic unit consists of several persons, natural or legal."[74] In practice, the main impact of the "enterprise entity" doctrine has been on two issues: the assertion of jurisdiction against a parent company established in a third country which has subsidiaries within the common market; and the application of Article 81 to agreements and practices between parent companies and subsidiaries. These issues are examined further below.

Material scope

The EC rules on competition apply generally, to all sectors of the **22–013** economy, except where express derogations are provided in other Articles of the Treaty.[75] The expiry of the ECSC Treaty on July 23, 2002 means that the coal and steel industries are now within the EC regime of competition law. However, the Commission has signalled[76] that no proceedings will be instigated in relation to agreements authorised under the ECSC Treaty unless "substantial factual or legal developments" render them obviously not entitled to exemption.

---

[70] *Albany International*, n.64 above, para.86.
[71] Case 170/83 *Hydrotherm* [1984] E.C.R. 2999.
[72] [1967] J.O. 849. [1967] O.J. 10.
[73] *ibid.*, Art.1(1).
[74] [1984] E.C.R. 2999, 3016.
[75] Joined Cases 209–213/84 *Ministère Public v Asjes* [1986] E.C.R. 1425.
[76] [2002] O.J. C152/5.

The approach taken by the EC Treaty to agriculture reflects the potential tension between the objectives of the common agricultural policy established by Title II and the notion of undistorted competition envisaged by Article 3(g). The extent to which the competition rules apply was made a matter for the discretion of the Council in what is now Article 36. In exercising that discretion the Council differentiated between the rules applicable to undertakings and the rules on State aids. The former were extended to agricultural products by Regulation 26,[77] subject to an exemption from the prohibition in Article 81(1) for the benefit of agreements that form an integral part of a national market organisation or that are necessary for the attainment of the objectives of the EC's common agricultural policy set out in Article 33 EC. The exception has been narrowly interpreted and is of limited practical significance.[78] There is no derogation from the impact of Article 82. In the case of State aids, effect has been given to the relevant provisions of the EC Treaty by the basic regulations of the various common organisations of national markets.

Special mention should also be made of the transport sector. Whilst the Treaty provisions on competition apply,[79] separate arrangements have been made for their implementation.[80] The Commission is contemplating significant reform of the block exemption relating to the shipping sector.[81]

Territorial scope

22–014 The prohibition in Article 81 applies to arrangements between undertakings "which may affect trade between Member States and which have as their object or effect the prevention, restriction or distortion of competition within the common market", and that in Article 82 to any abuse of a dominant position "within the common market or in a substantial part of it . . . in so far as it may affect trade between Member States." This wording makes it clear that the target of the prohibitions is behaviour having an actual or intended impact on the conditions of competition in the territory over which

---

[77] [1962] J.O. 993; [1959–62] O.J. 129.

[78] The first limb of the exception ceased to be available once a common organisation of the market had been established in respect of the product in question: Case 83/78 *Pigs Marketing Board v Redmond* [1978] E.C.R. 2347, 2369–2370; [1979] 1 C.M.L.R. 177. To satisfy the second limb of the exception, an agreement must be shown to be necessary for the attainment of all five of the objectives in Art.33 EC: Case 71/74 *FRUBO v Commission* [1975] E.C.R. 563, 582–583.

[79] Joined Cases 209–213/84 *Ministère Public v Asjes*, n.75 above.

[80] See Reg.1017/68 (road, rail and inland waterways), Reg.4056/86 (maritime transport) and Reg.3975/87 (air transport). The procedural elements of each are amended by Reg.1/2003, Arts 36–43.

[81] See Commission proposal to repeal Reg.4056/86 COM (2005) 651 Final, December 14, 2005.

the common market extends, i.e. the territory of the Community as defined by Article 299 EC.

It follows that undertakings carrying on business in the Community are free under the EC rules on competition to participate in agreements or practices that may interfere with the functioning of the market mechanism in third countries, so long as the consequences are unlikely to spill back into the common market.[82] Thus, in its *VVVF* Decision[83] the Commission allowed a Dutch association of paint and varnish manufacturers to continue a system of minimum prices and uniform conditions of sale in respect of exports by its members outside the common market, after securing the abolition of the system in respect of intra-Community trade.

The converse case is where undertakings not physically present on Community territory behave in ways that are liable to affect competition on the common market. How far does the Community claim extraterritorial jurisdiction in competition matters? In addressing this question it is useful to bear in mind the distinction drawn by international lawyers between "prescriptive jurisdiction" (the power to make rules and to take decisions under them) and "enforcement jurisdiction" (the power to give effect to such rules or decisions through executive action).[84] The assertion of either form of jurisdiction, but especially the latter, against an undertaking located on another state's territory raises legal and political issues of some delicacy. Three possible bases for the application of the EC rules in such cases fall to be considered.

First, it is generally accepted in international law that a state is **22–015** entitled to jurisdiction where activity which was commenced abroad is brought to consummation on its territory. This is known as the "objective territorial principle." It would, for example, allow the Commission to apply Article 81 to a contract made in a third country but substantially performed, at least on one side, within the Community.

Secondly, and more controversially, the Court of Justice has developed a doctrine of enterprise entity as a basis of jurisdiction against a parent company which has subsidiaries inside the Community, though situated itself on the outside. Under the doctrine, where material aspects of the subsidiary's commercial policy are controlled by the parent company, behaviour of the former in contravention of the rules on competition may be imputed to the latter. The leading case remains *Dyestuffs*,[85] which concerned a

---

[82] However, the application of bilateral and multilateral agreements containing rules analogous to EC law may of course reduce the scope of such freedom.

[83] [1969] J.O. L168/22; [1970] C.M.L.R. D1.

[84] See M. Shaw, *International Law* (5th ed., CUP, Cambridge, 2003), Ch.12.

[85] There was, in fact, a group of cases brought by different addressees of the decision in question, to which this collective designation is given. See, in particular, Case 48/69 *ICI v Commission* [1972] E.C.R. 619; [1972] C.M.L.R. 557.

decision by the Commission that a group of major manufacturers of aniline dyes had been guilty on three separate occasions of concerted price fixing. The addressees of the decision included ICI (at that time the United Kingdom was not a Member State) and certain Swiss companies. Objections by these companies to the jurisdiction of the Commission were dismissed by the Court on the ground that all of them had subsidiaries within the common market for whose decisions on pricing they could be held responsible.

This approach to parent-subsidiary relationships has received regular judicial affirmation. In the context of fines, for example, the Court of First Instance has observed:

> "It is well-established that the fact that a subsidiary has separate legal personality is not sufficient to exclude the imputation of its conduct to the parent company, especially where the subsidiary does not determine its conduct independently but in all material respects carries out the instructions given to it by the parent company."

Whilst there may still be some room for doubt in individual cases about the point at which autonomy exists in the subsidiary, the main indicators will be the size of the parent's shareholding, its control of the subsidiary's board of directors and other organs and the parent's general ability to influence decisions.[86] In the *PVC Cartel II* case,[87] the Court of First Instance ruled that since the subsidiary was wholly owned by the parent it was superfluous to inquire whether the latter was able to exercise a decisive influence on the former's commercial behaviour.

22–016   The enterprise entity doctrine has been used by the Court and the Commission to found not only prescriptive but also enforcement jurisdiction. Thus competition proceedings may be validly initiated against the foreign parent of a Community subsidiary by sending it a statement of objections through the post,[88] and the final decision finding the company guilty of an infringement of the rules may be similarly served.[89] Fines may be imposed on the parent company for the infringement, and it may be ordered to take remedial action. In *Commercial Solvents*,[90] for example, an American multinational corporation was found to have abused its dominant position under Article 82 by refusing, through its Italian subsidiary, to supply a

---

[86] *cf.* the notions of "control" set out in the Merger Reg.139/2004, Art.3(2), referring to the "possibility of exercising decisive influence on an undertaking".

[87] Joined Cases T–305–307, 313–316, 318, 325, 328–329 and 335/94 *Re the PVC Cartel II: Limburgse Vinyl Maatschappij NV v Commission* [1999] E.C.R. II–931, [1999] 5 C.M.L.R. 303, para.984.

[88] See, *e.g.*, Case 52/69 *Geigy v Commission* [1972] E.C.R. 787.

[89] Case 6/72 *Europemballage and Continental Can v Commission*, n.19 above.

[90] Joined Cases 6 and 7/73 *Commercial Solvents Corporation v Commission* [1974] E.C.R. 223.

customer with a product in which it held the world monopoly. The Court did not question the power of the Commission, besides fining Commercial Solvents, to require it to make an immediate delivery of a specified quantity of the product in question to the customer and to submit proposals for longer term supply arrangements. Of course, if fines are not paid, they can only be enforced by levying execution on property of the parent or subsidiary which is on the territory of a Member State.[91]

A third, and still more controversial, basis for the extraterritorial application of competition law is the so-called "effects doctrine." Broadly, the doctrine holds that a state is entitled to assert jurisdiction in respect of non-nationals abroad, where these produce effects felt within the state's own territory. In EC law, the question is whether the Court of Justice has followed the approach of American courts in constructing a principle of jurisdiction based on direct, substantial and foreseeable effects.[92] The leading case is *Wood Pulp*,[93] where the Commission imposed fines on various American and Scandinavian producers of wood pulp for concertation on the fixing of prices at which they supplied the paper industry in the common market. The activities regarded by the Commission as constituting the concertation took place in the producers' home countries, and several of those involved had no establishment and no subsidiaries within the Community.

When the applicants challenged the Commission's decision before the Court, Advocate General Darmon proposed the adoption of a qualified effects doctrine of the type used in American competition law. However, the Court did not grasp this particular nettle, instead expressing its view in terms of an 'implementation' test as follows:

> "If the applicability of prohibitions laid down under competition law were made to depend on the place where the agreement, decision or concerted practice was formed, the result would obviously be to give undertakings an easy means of evading those prohibitions. The decisive factor is therefore the place where it is implemented.
>
> The producers in this case implemented their pricing agreement within the common market. It is immaterial in that respect whether or not they had recourse to subsidiaries, agents, sub-agents or branches within the Community in order to make their contacts with purchasers within the Community.

---

[91] See Art.256 EC.

[92] The classic US statement can be found in *US v Aluminium Co. of America* 148 F.2d 416 (1945) where it was said that "any state may impose liabilities, even upon persons not within its allegiance, for conduct outside its borders that has consequences within its borders which the state reprehends." This was modified in later cases such as *Timberlane Lumber Co. v Bank of America* 549 F.2d 597 (1976).

[93] Joined Cases 89, 104, 114, 116, 117 and 125 to 129/85 *Åhlström v Commission* [1988] E.C.R. 5193.

Accordingly the Community's jurisdiction to apply its competition rules to such conduct is covered by the territoriality principle as universally recognised in public international law."[94]

The scope of this concept of implementation, and its relationship to any effects doctrine, is still not entirely free from doubt.[95] In particular, it may be asked whether it applies to situations where the distortion to intra-Community trade is caused by the parties diverting their goods away from the Community as distinct from, say, fixing the prices at which those goods will eventually be sold on Community territory. It might be hard to see how refraining from trade would amount to an 'implemented' agreement although it might equally well be said that this would also produce insufficiently direct consequences to be caught by an effects doctrine. Thus there may be little difference in real outcomes, despite the different language used by the Court.

In the later *Gencor* case,[96] decided in relation to the Merger Regulation, the Court of First Instance took the view that the *Wood Pulp* implementation criterion was satisfied by mere sale within the Community, irrespective of the sources of supply and the production plant. Moreover, the Court of First Instance also noted that application of the Merger Regulation was "justified under public international law when it is foreseeable that a proposed concentration will have an immediate and substantial effect in the Community."[97]

22–017   Ultimately, the delicate issues raised in cases with extra-territorial dimensions are perhaps best solved by international co-operation over the allocation of jurisdiction, rather than unilateral assertions of extensive jurisdiction. Certainly, it is one thing to claim jurisdiction over particular activities, but quite another to exercise it. That decision may be influenced by considerations relating to the impact it would have on the relationship with authorities of another jurisdiction. Vigorous pursuit of an effects doctrine, for example, might provoke harmful retaliatory action by the home state of a parent company. Self-restraint may therefore be a preferable course in the light of these factors of comity. The Commission has recognised the presence of such influences, although it has on occasions been highly reluctant to concede them.[98]

Comity considerations can be given a more formal status by the adoption of agreements between the EC and individual states. Prime

---

[94] *ibid.*, paras 16–18 of Judgment.
[95] See Lange and Sandage, "The *Woodpulp* decision and its implications..." (1989) 26 C.M.L.Rev. 137. *cf.* Mann, "The public international law of restrictive trade practices in the ECJ" (1989) 38 I.C.L.Q. 375.
[96] Case T–102/96 *Gencor v Commission* [1999] E.C.R. II–753, [1999] 4 C.M.L.R. 971.
[97] *ibid.*, para.90
[98] *Aluminium Imports from Eastern Europe* [1985] O.J. L92/1; [1987] 3 C.M.L.R. 813.

examples can be seen in the two agreements drawn up between the EC and the USA, originally adopted in 1991[99] and subsequently elaborated in 1998.[1] The 1991 Agreement provides for the competition authorities of the parties to notify each other where enforcement activities affect important interests of the other. It also seeks to avoid conflicts over enforcement by adoption of a so-called 'negative comity'clause.[2] This states that "each party shall consider important interests of the other party in decisions as to whether or not to initiate an investigation or proceeding, the scope of an investigation or proceeding, the nature of the remedies or penalties sought, and in other ways, as appropriate". Use of this provision was made in the controversy surrounding the *Boeing/McDonnell Douglas* merger.[3] The concentration in question reduced the number for manufacturers of large commercial aircraft from three to two, leaving Airbus Industrie (the European producer) up against a single dominant American competitor. The merger was cleared by the American authorities, but authorisation was only given by the European Commission after last-minute assurances as to Boeing's future conduct.

According to the 1998 EU-USA Positive Comity Agreement,[4] the competition authorities of one party may request the competition authorities of the other to investigate and, if warranted, to remedy anti-competitive activities in accordance with the requested party's competition laws. Such a request may be made regardless of whether the activities also violate the requesting party's competition laws, and regardless of whether the competition authorities of the requesting party have commenced or contemplate taking enforcement activities under their own competition laws. Article IV sets out the conditions on which the competition authorities of the requesting party will normally defer or suspend their own enforcement activities in favour of those of the requested party. *Inter alia*, these require that the adverse effects on the interests of the requesting party can be and are likely to be fully and adequately investigated and, as appropriate, eliminated or adequately remedied. The competition authorities of the requested party must devote adequate resources to the investigation, carry it out promptly and use their best efforts to pursue all reasonably available sources of information, including such sources of information as may be suggested by the competition authorities of the requesting party.

---

[99] [1991] 4 C.M.L.R. 823 but struck down by the Court of Justice in Case C–327/91 *France v Commission* [1994] E.C.R. I–3641. It was then re-adopted with proper ratification by the Council as Decision 95/145, [1995] O.J. L95/45, corrected by [1995] O.J. L131/38, and taking effect from its original date.

[1] *Agreement between the European Communities and the Government of the United States of America on the application of positive comity principles in the enforcement of their competition laws* O.J. 1998 L173/28; [1999] 4 C.M.L.R. 502. It does not apply to mergers.

[2] 1991 Agreement, Article VI.

[3] [1997] O.J. L336/16.

[4] n.1, above, Art.III.

As well as bilateral agreements of this type,[5] multilateral arrangements also provide for the application of competition rules akin to EC provisions in other territories. The European Economic Area ("EEA") Agreement was concluded[6] between the EC and the EFTA states, with the exception of Switzerland. It applies the fundamental freedoms and some of the horizontal policies of the EC, such as competition and social policies, to the EEA. As a number of former members of EFTA have since become full members of the EC, the importance of the EEA agreement has declined. Only Iceland, Norway and Liechtenstein remain as contracting states outside membership of the EC. Articles 53 and 54 EEA replicate for practical purposes Articles 81 and 82 EC, whilst Article 57, 59 and 61–64 EEA essentially incorporate the EC Merger Regulation and the rules on public undertakings and State aids. It is also provided that in the application of the rules the principles of the European Commission's notices must be taken into account.

Temporal scope

22–018   The rules on competition came into force under the EEC Treaty with effect from January 1, 1958. Each time the Community has been enlarged, a new range of agreements and practices has been brought within the purview of the competition rules from the date of accession. It must, however, be remembered that undertakings established on the territory of a new Member State may have been subject to the rules even prior to accession, for example as parties to an agreement to be performed in the EC or because they had subsidiaries there.[7]

The prohibitions in Article 81(1) and Article 82 began to have direct effect for the general class of agreements and practices from the date when Regulation 17 (now superseded) with its implementing machinery came into force, *viz. March 13, 1962.*[8]

Wider Perspectives on EC Competition Law

Developments towards international regulation or co-operation

22–019   The trends in EU competition law should not be considered in isolation, despite the rather inchoate state of globalised competition regulation and policy co-operation. Competition policy was not

---

[5] See also the Competition Laws Co-operation Agreement 1999 between the EC, ECSC and Canada [1999] O.J. L175, [1999] 5 C.M.L.R. 713. The OECD report, n.11 above, remarks that bilateral relationships have been "particularly continuous" with Australia, China, Korea, Mexico and Brazil.

[6] [1994] O.J. L1/3.

[7] See the discussion of the enterprise entity doctrine, above.

[8] Case 13/61 *Bosch v de Geus* [1962] E.C.R. 45; [1962] C.M.L.R. 1.

included in the original remit of the World Trade Organisation (WTO),[9] but a Working Group on the interaction between trade and competition policy was established at the Singapore Ministerial Conference in December 1996, producing a report in December 1998.[10] The 2001 Doha Minsterial Declaration listed the interaction between trade and competition policy as part of its work pro-gramme.[11] However, following deadlock at the 2003 Cancún Minis-terial Conference, the WTO General Council dropped this item from the work programme in August 2004 for the remainder of the Doha Round. Even though WTO discussion has been about neither the creation of some supranational antitrust agency nor the harmo-nisation of national competition laws,[12] competition developments remain stalled within the WTO framework.

A much more visible, distinctive but entirely different form of co-operation can be seen in the development of the International Competition Network (ICN),[13] launched in October 2001. According to its own mission statement,[14] the ICN:

> "is unique in many ways. It is the only international body devoted exclusively to competition issues. Members are not States or governments, but competition authorities, bodies entrusted with the enforcement of competition laws. Member-ship is voluntary and currently 90 such agencies are ICN members. There is no permanent secretariat, and no headquar-ters, which leads to the ICN often being described as a 'virtual forum'. The ICN co-operates closely with and seeks input from existing international organisations (such as the OECD, WTO and UNCTAD) and is assisted by experts from outside compe-tition authorities, for example from the legal and economic professions, consumer organisations, academia etc. . . ."

The ICN's goals are to achieve better competition enforcement and better competition advocacy, i.e. the promotion of competition

---

[9] For documentation on developments in relation to trade and competition policy see the WTO's website on *www.wto.org*.

[10] Including matters such as the impact of anti-competitive practices of enterprises and associations on international trade; the impact of state monopolies and exclusive rights; the relationship between the trade-related aspects of intellectual property rights and competi-tion policy; the relationship between investment and competition policy and the impact of trade policy on competition.

[11] The areas to be addressed being identified as: core principles including transparency, non-discrimination and procedural fairness, and provisions on "hardcore" cartels (i.e. cartels that are formally set up); ways of handling voluntary co-operation on competition policy among WTO member governments; support for progressive reinforcement of competition institutions in developing countries through capacity building.

[12] See F. Souty, "Is there a need for additional WTO competition rules promoting non-discriminatory competition laws and competition institutions in WTO Members?" in E-U Petersmann (ed.), *Reforming the World Trading System* (OUP, Oxford, 2005).

[13] See *www.internationalcompetitionnetwork.org*.

[14] "A Statement of Mission and Achievements Up Until May 2005", on website above, n.112.

culture among governments, the private sector and public awareness. There is no aspiration to harmonisation of competition law and policies throughout the world. Instead, the emphasis is on exchanging experience and best practice in procedures, systems and techniques. The European Commission, alongside the competition authorities of the Member States, is a member of the ICN.

The constitutional significance of EC competition law

22–020   As the instrument to give effect to competition policies, competition law is hardly neutral.[15] Its attempts to de-regulate may substitute re-regulation of particular markets or sectors. In this sense it is different from the negative integration which flows from the implementation of the fundamental freedoms. By curtailing or accepting the freedom of action of particular parties, competition law makes judgments about the content of notions of consumer welfare and other objectives, and the best means of promoting them. Market regulation by law in this way raises in turn much wider issues about the scope for and extent of any "economic constitution" in the EC.[16]

Moreover, as already seen in parts of this Chapter, competition law meets State sovereignty head-on in a number of situations. Most obviously, EC law may restrict the freedom of States to act as market regulators, facilitators (e.g. through providing State aid) or participants. More subtly, the notion of 'undertaking' is ultimately not about form but instead requires analysis of why it should be the case that the activity in question falls within the scope of EC competition law competence. The asymmetries between competition law and free movement reflect a somewhat inconsistent stance towards the choices to be made—variously represented as state/market, economic/non-economic, public/private or EC/national divisions. As will be seen in later Chapters, a different kind of choice must be exercised when it comes to assessing conduct or measures which prima facie fall within the compass of the competition regime. The extent to which competition concerns can be trumped by other, often non-economic, values surfaces not just in the explicit context of Article 86(2) but also in relation to Article 81(1) and (3) and, as will be pursued in Chapter 26, Article 16 EC. In this sense, analysis of the competition rules is every bit as revealing about the state of EU evolution as other developments covered in this book such as fundamental rights and citizenship.

---

[15] See generally G. Amato, *Antitrust and the Bounds of Power* (Hart, Oxford, 1997).
[16] This idea is not pursued in detail in this book. However, for a flavour of the arguments, see Micklitz and Weatherill, *European Economic Law* (Ashgate, Dartmouth, 1997); also Joerges, "Law, Economics and Politics in the Constitutionalisation of Europe" (2002–03) 5 C.Y.E.L.S. 123.

Further reading

Boni, S. and Manzini, P., "National Social Legislation and EC Antitrust Law" (2001) 24 World Comp. 239.

Ehlermann, C. D., "The modernisation of EC antitrust policy: a legal and cultural revolution" (2000) 37 C.M.L.Rev. 537.

Louri, V., " 'Undertaking' as a Jurisdictional Element for the Application of EC Competition Rules" (2002) 29 *Legal Issues of European Integration* 143.

Monti, G., "Article 82 EC and New Economy Markets" in Graham C. and Smith, F., (eds), *Competition, Regulation and the New Economy* (Hart, Oxford, 2004), Chap.2.

Odudu, O., "The meaning of undertaking within 81 EC" (2004–05) 7 C.Y.E.L.S. 211.

CHAPTER 23

ARTICLE 81: CARTELS AND RESTRICTIVE PRACTICES

Guide to this Chapter: This Chapter deals with collusive **23–001** behaviour between undertakings, covering agreements between undertakings, decisions of associations of undertakings and concerted practices. The overlap between these concepts is illustrated by reference to the tests of concurrence of wills and the necessary evidentiary proof. The other constituent elements of the prohibition contained in Article 81(1) are analysed in the case law, secondary legislation, Commission Guidelines and other forms of practice Notices. In particular, the notion of a "restriction on competition" is assessed in the context of whether any "rule of reason" arguments about the balancing of pro- and anti-competitive concerns or non-competition values are recognised in an Article 81(1) analysis. The case law and legislative developments reveal an increasing emphasis upon market impact and economic analysis in the application of all stages of an Article 81 assessment. Horizontal and vertical agreements attract differential treatment as a result, with the latter being given a lighter regulatory touch except for "hardcore" restrictions. The exemption criteria set out in Article 81(3) are examined in outline, together with the umbrella block exemption in favour of vertical restraints. The Chapter concludes with a discussion of the Court's limited use of Article 81 in conjunction with Article 10 of the Treaty where Member States reinforce anti-competitive agreements or delegate their legislative powers to private economic operators.

Introduction

Article 81 EC addresses the problem of interference with competi- **23–002** tion resulting from collusion between market participants over their business decisions. The strategy of the Article is to prohibit such interference subject to the possibility of justification for arrangements, which, on balance, are judged to be economically beneficial.

The Article provides:

"1. The following shall be prohibited as incompatible with the common market: all agreements between undertakings, decisions by associations of undertakings and concerted practices which may affect trade between Member States and which have as their object or effect the prevention, restriction or distortion of competition within the common market, and in particular those which:

   (a) directly or indirectly fix purchase or selling prices or any other trading conditions;
   (b) limit or control production, markets, technical development, or investment;
   (c) share markets or sources of supply;
   (d) apply dissimilar conditions to equivalent transactions with other trading parties, thereby placing them at a competitive disadvantage;
   (e) make the conclusion of contracts subject to acceptance by the other parties of supplementary obligations which, by their nature or according to commercial usage, have no connection with the subject of such contracts.

2. Any agreements or decisions prohibited pursuant to this Article shall be automatically void.

3. The provisions of paragraph 1 may, however, be declared inapplicable in the case of:

   — any agreement or category of agreements between undertakings;
   — any decision or category of decisions by associations of undertakings;
   — any concerted practice or category of concerted practices;

which contributes to improving the production or distribution of goods or to promoting technical or economic progress, while allowing consumers a fair share of the resulting benefit, and which does not:

   (a) impose on the undertakings concerned restrictions which are not indispensable to the attainment of these objectives;
   (b) afford such undertakings the possibility of eliminating competition in respect of a substantial part of the products in question".

The scope of paragraph (1) is potentially wide indeed. Its list of examples of prohibited arrangements is non-exhaustive and there is no attempt to distinguish between so-called horizontal and vertical arrangements (i.e. between economic operators at the same or different stages of the economic chain respectively). However, as we shall see, a more lenient view has generally been taken of vertical restrictions between, for example, producer and distributor, and this stance has been embodied in legislative changes. Paragraph (1) is also silent on the meaning of its primary elements, allowing controversy to develop as to the degree of distortion of competition required and the scope for weighing the pros and cons of particular arrangements or the relevance of non-competition criteria. Or, to put it in the language familiar from other areas of EC law, whether a "rule of reason" can apply to paragraph (1).

Paragraph (2) of Article 81 identifies a particular consequence for breach of the prohibition, although additional remedies may be available in national law.[1] Paragraph (3) sets out the criteria that must be met by arrangements prima facie within paragraph (1), in order to benefit from a declaration of the inapplicability of the paragraph. This power to exempt was previously reserved exclusively by Regulation 17[2] to the Commission, but was opened up as part of modernisation proposals[3] designed to promote the decentralised enforcement of EC competition law. The position since 2004[4] is that national courts and competition authorities may apply the exception.

Indeed, the reforms of 2004, together with other shifts in emphasis discussed in Chapter 22 above, have had a significant impact on the problems and priorities that form the modern view of Article 81. What was once perhaps a sweeping prohibition subject to narrow and tightly controlled exceptions has become a more sophisticated instrument which permits pragmatic assessments of collusive arrangements to be made in the light of their effects in the relevant market. These assessments are more firmly anchored in economics and market analysis, with a stronger focus on whether anti-competitive effects really do flow from particular conduct or arrangements. The precise effects of the post-2004 enforcement system are still emerging, although the relationship between paragraphs (1) and (3) may be expected to take on a rather different aspect than hitherto, as discussed further at various points in this Chapter.

---

[1] Enforcement of both Arts 81 and 82 is discussed further in Ch.25, below.

[2] Reg.17/62 [1962] J.O. 204; [1959–1962] O.J. 87.

[3] *White Paper on Modernisation of the Rules Implementing Arts 85 and 86 of the EC Treaty*, April 28, 1999.

[4] Reg.1/2003 *On the Implementation of the Rules on Competition Laid Down in Articles 81 and 82 of the Treaty* [2003] O.J. L1/1, which came into force on May 1, 2004.

Collusive market behaviour between undertakings: concurrence of wills

23–003   The target of the prohibition in Article 81(1) is co-operative or collusive market behaviour between undertakings. As was seen in Chapter 22, the notion of "undertakings" as independent economic entities limits the scope of Article 81 in relation to parent-subsidiary relationships,[5] some acts of public authorities[6] and the delivery of solidarity-based schemes.[7] Similarly, agreements within a pure agency relationship may fall outside the provision where the agent acts in the name and for the account of his principal, taking none of the risks of a transaction upon himself.[8] Such an agent, the Court of Justice has said, when working for his principal can be regarded "as an auxiliary organ forming an integral part of the latter's undertaking bound to carry out the principal's instructions and thus, like a commercial employee, forms an economic unit with this undertaking".[9] An agreement by the agent not to trade in goods competing with the products of his principal would not in these circumstances fall within Article 81(1).[10]

A question which has arisen more recently has been the extent to which ostensibly unilateral conduct might be caught by the Article. At first sight, the obvious source available to combat anti-competitive acts by single undertakings is Article 82. However, this is limited to firms occupying dominant positions, implying that unilateral conduct by non-dominant individual firms was not seen as a threat to competition by the drafters of the Treaty. But this does not mean that acts in furtherance of a contract escape prohibition under Article 81(1) merely because they are performed by a single party. In the *AEG* case[11] the Court of Justice was called upon to assess the compatibility with that Article of a system of selective distribution. Under such a system the resale of goods is limited to a network of "approved" dealers. One of the arguments put forward by AEG was that refusal to admit prospective dealers to its network was a unilateral act and therefore not within the scope of the prohibition. The argument was rejected by the Court on the ground that refusals

---

[5] There will be no agreement between undertakings for the purposes of Art.81 where the subsidiary enjoys no real freedom to determine its course of action on the market: Case 22/71 *Béguelin Import Co. v SA GL Import Export* [1971] E.C.R. 949; [1972] C.M.L.R. 81; Case C–73/95P *Viho Europe BV v Commission* [1996] E.C.R. I–5457; [1997] 4 C.M.L.R. 419.

[6] The key question being whether such a body is acting as a public authority at the time: see Case30/87 *Bodson v Pompes Funèbres* [1988] E.C.R. 2479; [1989] 4 C.M.L.R. 984.

[7] Case C–160/91 *Poucet and Pistre* [1993] E.C.R. I–637. The issue was discussed more fully in Ch.22, above.

[8] Joined Cases 40–48, 50, 54–56, 111, 113 and 114/73 *Suiker Unie v Commission (Sugar)* [1975] E.C.R. 1663; [1976] 1 C.M.L.R. 295.

[9] *ibid.*, [1975] E.C.R. 1663, at 2007.

[10] *ibid.* In the instant case the relationship between a German sugar producer and its trade representatives was found not to be such as to escape the prohibition.

[11] Case 107/82 *AEG v Commission* [1983] E.C.R. 3151; [1984] 3 C.M.L.R. 325.

of approval were acts performed in the context of AEG's contractual relations with approved dealers.[12]

However, in recent years the European Courts have resisted attempts by the Commission to stretch the boundaries of tacit acceptance or acquiescence. Thus, in *Bayer AG v Commission*,[13] the Court of First Instance overturned the Commission's finding of an agreement in the system operated by Bayer's subsidiaries in Spain and France in relation to supplies of the heart drug Adalat. In order to prevent the high prices which could be charged in the United Kingdom from being threatened by quantities of parallel imports through wholesalers located in Spain and France, Bayer's subsidiaries restricted supplies of Adalat to the latter to the amounts needed to satisfy domestic demand. There was evidence that the wholesalers had tried different tactics to obtain extra supplies, but that these were detected and countered by Bayer. The Commission had taken the view that the monitoring and supply restrictions constituted an agreement between Bayer's subsidiaries and the wholesalers to restrict exports. According to the Commission, an agreement for the purposes of Article 81(1) required an interest of two parties in concluding an agreement, without there being any need for that interest to be held in common. In this case Bayer's interest was in preventing, or at least reducing, parallel imports. The wholesalers' interest was to avoid a reduction in supplies of Adalat.

In forcefully rejecting the Commission's approach, the Court of **23–004** First Instance underlined the need for a "concurrence of wills" to exist in order to support the finding of an agreement within Article 81(1). Whilst this would be satisfied where an "apparently" unilateral measure adopted by a manufacturer was shown to receive at least tacit acquiescence by the wholesalers, there was no evidence in the case to show that the latter had aligned themselves to Bayer's policy designed to reduce parallel imports. The Court of Justice subsequently endorsed the Court of First Instance's ruling, observing:

> ". . . the mere fact that a measure adopted by a manufacturer, which has the object or effect of restricting competition, falls within the context of continuous business relations between the manufacturer and its wholesalers is not sufficient for a finding that . . . an agreement exists."[14]

The Court proceeded to distinguish the earlier *AEG* and *Ford* decisions on the basis that the *existence* of an agreement had not

---

[12] See also Joined Cases 25–26/84 *Ford v Commission* [1985] E.C.R. 2725; [1985] 3 C.M.L.R. 528.

[13] Case T–41/96 *Bayer* [2000] E.C.R. II–3383; [2001] 4 C.M.L.R. 126.

[14] Cases C–2 and 3/01P, *Bundesverband der Arzneimittel-Importeure EV and Commission v Bayer AG* [2004] E.C.R. I–23, [2004] 4 C.M.L.R. 653.

been at issue in those cases. Instead, they had been decided on whether the measures adopted by the manufacturers concerned fell within the scope of the agreement.

Proof of acquiescence is required to defeat "apparent" unilateral conduct. This is not altogether surprising given the financial consequences for firms on the wrong end of Article 81(1) proceedings. A fine of €30.96 million was overturned in *Volkswagen v Commission*[15] in relation to the "strict price discipline" alleged to have been the subject of agreement between the car manufacturer and its German dealers. The Commission sought to persuade the CFI that, in a selective distribution system such as this, the dealers agreed when signing up in the first place to any subsequent calls by the manufacturer in relation to dealers' activity. However, the Court of First Instance made it clear that "a concurrence of wills must cover particular conduct, which must, therefore, be known to the parties when they accept it."[16] Moreover, the part of the dealership terms which required distributors to "defend and promote in every way the interests of Volkswagen . . ." could only be interpreted as referring to lawful means and could not be construed as a reservation clause which would connote dealer acquiescence in any later calls by the manufacturer of any description.

Forms of co-operation

23-005   Article 81(1) refers to three forms of co-operation on which the prohibition may bite: agreements between undertakings, decisions of associations of undertakings and concerted practices. Something will be said about each of these forms, as there are some important differences when it comes to their conceptualisation. However, there is substantial practical overlap between them and it is important to remember that the real borderline is between unlawful collusion evidenced by any of these forms and independently determined behaviour that will not be caught by Article 81(1) at all.

Agreements between undertakings

23-006   There is no need for an arrangement to be legally binding for it to be treated as an agreement for the purposes of Article 81(1). In the *Quinine* cases,[17] for instance, the Court had to consider the application of the rules to arrangements between European producers of quinine and quinidine contained in an "export agreement" and a "gentlemen's agreement": the former, which was signed and made public, purported to apply only to trade with third countries but its

---

[15] Case T–208/01 *Volkswagen v Commission* [2003] E.C.R. II–5141, [2004] 4 C.M.L.R. 727.
[16] *ibid.*, para.56.
[17] See Joined Cases 41, 44–45/69 *ACF Chemiefarma v Commission* [1970] E.C.R. 661.

provisions were extended by the latter, which remained unsigned and secret, to trade within the (then) EEC. In view of its clandestine character, let alone its name, the gentlemen's agreement cannot have been intended to be legally enforceable. The parties had, however, made clear that it faithfully expressed their joint intention as to their conduct and that they considered themselves no less bound by it than by the export agreement. The Court accepted it as an agreement. The decisive test, that there has been an expression by the participating undertakings of their joint intention to conduct themselves on the market in a specific way, has been consistently relied upon by the Court in subsequent cases.[18] As expressed by the Court of First Instance, the requirement is for "a concurrence of wills between at least two parties, the form in which it is manifested being unimportant so long as it constitutes the faithful expression of the parties' intention."[19]

Decisions of associations of undertakings

A typical example would be a resolution of a trade association **23–007** laying down standard terms on which its members are required to do business. The express reference to "decisions of associations of undertakings" makes it possible, in an appropriate case, for the Commission to impose a fine on the trade association itself.[20] The Court of Justice is inclined to brush aside technical arguments about the precise legal character of acts of trade associations. Its attitude is summed up by the remark in the *FRUBO* judgment[21] that Article 81(1) "applies to associations in so far as their own activities or those of the undertakings belonging to them are calculated to produce the results to which it refers".[22] For example, the constitution of an association has sometimes been treated as a decision[23] and sometimes as an agreement.[24] A Regulation issued by the Netherlands Bar in relation to the terms on which partnerships could be established between members of the Bar and other professions was deemed to be a decision adopted by an association of undertakings.[25]

---

[18] e.g. Case C–49/92P *Commission v Anic Partecipazioni SpA* [1999] E.C.R. I–4125, para.130.

[19] Case T–41/96 *Bayer v Commission* n.13 above.

[20] See, e.g. *Re AROW/BNIC* [1982] O.J. L379/1; [1983] 2 C.M.L.R. 240.

[21] Case 71/74 *FRUBO v Commission* [1975] E.C.R. 563; [1975] 2 C.M.L.R. 123.

[22] [1975] E.C.R. 563, 583. See also Case T–193/02 *Piau v Commission* (CFI judgment January 26, 2005), paras 68–79.

[23] *Re ASPA* [1970] J.O. L148/9; [1970] C.M.L.R. D25.

[24] *Re Nuovo CEGAM* [1984] O.J. L99/29; [1984] 2 C.M.L.R. 484.

[25] Case C–309/99 *Wouters* [2002] E.C.R. I–1577, [2002] 4 C.M.L.R. 913, para.71. Ultimately, there was no infringement of Art.81 as the prohibition on multi-disciplinary partnerships did not amount to a "restriction"; see p.1013 below.

There is no more need for "decisions" than for "agreements" to be legally binding. In *Re Fire Insurance*[26] the Commission applied Article 85 (as it was then) to a "recommendation" by an association of insurers in Germany that premiums for various classes of policy be raised by a stipulated percentage. Although described in its title as "non-binding" the recommendation was found to constitute a decision within the meaning of the first paragraph. "It is sufficient for this purpose", the Commission said, " that the recommendation was brought to the notice of members as a statement of the association's policy provided for, and issued in accordance with, its rules".[27] In other cases a pattern of past compliance with recommendations has been emphasised.[28] The conclusive factor, it is submitted, is the ability of the association, in fact if not in law, to influence its members' conduct. But where an association plays no distinguishable role in the implementation of an anti-competitive arrangement, or where its acts are not severable from those of its members, it may escape liability or the imposition of fines.[29]

Concerted practices

23–008   The concept of a concerted practice represents the outer limits of the prohibition on collusion imposed by Article 81(1). It has at times provoked controversy and uncertainty in the case law, both as regards the elusiveness of its boundaries and in respect of the evidence necessary to establish it. However, a rigid categorisation of particular circumstances as either agreements or concerted practices is not demanded. Indeed, where a number of firms are engaged to varying degrees in complex infringements, it is possible to treat those patterns of conduct as manifestations of a single infringement, made up partly of agreements and partly of concerted practices without having to specify exact borderlines between them.[30] According to the Court, agreements and concerted practices "are intended to catch forms of collusion having the same nature and are only distinguishable from each other by their intensity and the forms in which they manifest themselves".[31]

The Court's first attempts at defining a concerted practice treated it as "a form of coordination between undertakings which, without having been taken to a stage where an agreement properly so called

[26] [1985] O.J. L35/20. The Decision was upheld by the Court of Justice in Case 45/85 *Verband der Sachversicherer* [1987] E.C.R. 405; [1988] 4 C.M.L.R. 264.
[27] [1985] O.J. at L35/20, 24.
[28] See, in particular, Joined Cases 209–215 and 218/78 *Van Landewyck v Commission (FEDETAB)* [1980] E.C.R. 3125; [1981] 3 C.M.L.R. 134; Joined Cases 96–102, 104, 105, 108 and 110/82 *IAZ v Commission* [1983] E.C.R. 3369; [1984] 3 C.M.L.R. 276.
[29] Joined Cases 89, 104, 114, 116, 117 and 125–128/85 *A. Ahlström Oy v Commission ("Wood Pulp")* [1988] E.C.R. 5193; [1988] 4 C.M.L.R. 901, para.27.
[30] Case C–49/92P *Commission v Anic Partecipazioni SpA*, n.18, above
[31] *ibid.*, para.131.

has been concluded, knowingly substitutes practical co-operation between them for the risks of competition".[32] These criteria of coordination and co-operation are to be understood in the light of the concept inherent in the provisions of the Treaty relating to competition, according to which each economic operator must determine independently the policy which he intends to adopt on the market.[33] According to the Court:

> "although that requirement of independence does not deprive economic operators of the right to adapt themselves intel-ligently to the existing and anticipated conduct of their com-petitors, it does however strictly preclude any direct or indirect contact between such operators, the object or effect whereof is either to influence the conduct on the market of an actual or potential competitor or to disclose to such a competitor the course of conduct which they themselves have decided to adopt or contemplate adopting on the market, where the object or effect of such contact is to create conditions of competition which do not correspond to the normal conditions of the market in question, regard being had to the nature of the products or services offered, the size and number of the undertakings and the volume of the said market".[34]

This approach makes the question of "contact", whether direct or indirect, central to the idea of a concerted practice. An example of how such contact may be established can be seen from the various infringements known collectively as the *Polypropylene* cases.[35] Fol-lowing its investigations into the relevant market, the Commission had concluded that between 1977 and 1983 producers had regularly set target prices by way of a series of price initiatives and brought about a system of annual volume control to share out the available market between them according to agreed percentage or tonnage targets. The Commission cited the following evidence to support its allegations of agreements and concerted practices: contact through regular meetings in secret to discuss and determine commercial policies; the setting of target or minimum prices for sales in each Member State; the exchange of detailed information on deliveries, a

---

[32] Case 48/69 *ICI v Commission* [1972] E.C.R. 619, 655; [1972] C.M.L.R. 557; reiterated in Joined Cases 40–48, 50, 54–56, 111, 113 and 114/73 *Suiker Unie v Commission ("Re Sugar")*, n.8, above; Joined Cases 89, 104, 114, 116, 117 and 125–128/85 *A. Ahlström Oy v Commission ("Wood Pulp")*, [1993] E.C.R. I–1307; [1993] 4 C.M.L.R. 407 para.63; Case C–49/92P *Commission v Anic Partecipazioni SpA*, n.18, above.

[33] *Re Sugar*, n.8, above, para.173; Case 172/80 *Züchner* [1981] E.C.R. 2021; [1982] 1 C.M.L.R. 313, para.13; Case C–7/95P *John Deere v Commission* [1998] E.C.R. I–3111; [1998] 5 C.M.L.R. 311, para.86.

[34] Case C–49/92P *Commission v Anic Partecipazioni SpA*, n.18, above, para.117, citing the cases listed in n.33, above.

[35] For the Commission's original Decision, see [1986] O.J. L230/1; [1988] 4 C.M.L.R. 347.

system of "account management" designed to implement price rises to individual customers; simultaneous price increases implementing the said targets; and a limitation on monthly sales by reference to some previous period. The ensuing protracted litigation focused, *inter alia*, upon whether the Commission had been entitled to characterise the infringements as agreements *and* concerted practices, the requisite levels of intention and market effect for each and the extent to which each party could be responsible for the acts of others.

The Court of First Instance[36] held that if a company participated in meetings of the type in question then it and the other undertakings could not fail to take into account, directly or indirectly, the information obtained during the course of those meetings. However, this was an erroneous approach according to the Court of Justice. In its view, "a concerted practice implies, besides undertakings' concerting together, conduct on the market pursuant to those collusive practices, and a relationship of cause and effect between the two".[37] This observation points to a conceptual difference between agreements and concerted practices by requiring subsequent conduct in relation to the latter. However, the Court of Justice has minimised the practical extent of that distinction by its location of the burden of proof:

> ". . . subject to proof to the contrary, which it is for the economic operators concerned to adduce, there must be a presumption that the undertakings participating in concerting arrangements and remaining active on the market take account of the information exchanged with their competitors when determining their conduct on that market, particularly when they concert together on a regular basis over a long period."[38]

In short, it appears that it is the collusion, rather than the presumed subsequent conduct, which is the driving determinant. As the Commission has observed,[39] a concerted practice is caught by Article 81(1) even in the absence of anti-competitive effects on the market.

Proof and responsibility

23–009   Proving that a concerted practice exists may be a delicate task. It will be especially difficult in those cases that tread the key borderline between co-ordinated market behaviour prohibited by Article 81(1)

---

[36] e.g. Case T–6/89 *Enichem Anic v Commission* [1991] E.C.R. II–1623. By the time of the appeal to the Court of Justice as Case C–49/92P, n.18, above, the company was known as Anic.

[37] Case C–49/92P, n.18, above, para.118. The Court of Justice went on to find that, despite faulty reasoning on this point, the operative part of the judgment of the Court of First Instance was well-founded on other legal grounds.

[38] *ibid.*, para.121.

[39] *Decision re Interbrew and Alken-Maes* [2003] O.J. L200/1, para.222.

and parallel behaviour resulting from decisions independently arrived at by traders. Since it will often be the existence of parallel conduct that gives rise to the suspicion of concertation, it may become a matter of fine judgment as to whether what is going on is simply the right of a party to "adapt intelligently" to the decisions of competitors or whether collusion has indeed been present.

Direct evidence of relevant contact between the parties may be available in the form of letters, faxes, emails, or records of telephone conversations or meetings. Where direct evidence of concertation is lacking or inconclusive, the Commission has to rely on circumstantial evidence, i.e. on the inferences that can be drawn from the behaviour of the alleged parties, in the light of an analysis of conditions on the market in question.[40] In such cases the Commission, and ultimately the Court, must be satisfied that there can be no reasonable explanation of the parties' behaviour other than the existence of a concerted practice between them.

The point is well illustrated by the *Zinc Products* case.[41] The concerted practice in issue was allegedly designed to protect the German market for rolled zinc products, where prices were higher than elsewhere in the Community, against parallel imports. A French producer, CRAM, and a German producer, Rheinzink, had delivered quantities of zinc products to a Belgian dealer, Schiltz, under contracts which stipulated that the products be exported to Egypt. Schiltz, however, relabelled them and sent them back to Germany, where they were sold below the normal price. It was common ground that employees of Rheinzink found out about the reimports towards the end of October 1976 and that CRAM and Rheinzink discontinued their deliveries to Schiltz on, respectively, 21st and 29th of that month. In its Decision[42] the Commission had taken the view that the cessation of deliveries by CRAM and Rheinzink could only be explained as the result of an exchange of information for the purpose of preventing imports into Germany. "Faced with such an argument", the Court said, "it is sufficient for the applicants to prove circumstances which cast the facts established by the Commission in a different light and which thus allow another explanation of the facts to be substituted for the one adopted by the contested decision".[43] In the event, CRAM was able to point to two such circumstances: the fact that, when it ceased deliveries on October 21, it had completed a particular order from Schiltz; and the fact that there had been difficulties over obtaining payment for products supplied to Schiltz in September (and there were similar

---

[40] Case 48/69 *ICI v Commission*, n.32, above, at 655.
[41] Joined Cases 29 and 35/83 *CRAM and Rheinzink v Commission* [1984] E.C.R. 1679; [1985] 1 C.M.L.R. 688.
[42] *Re Rolled Zinc Products and Zinc Alloys* [1982] O.J. L362/40 [1983] 2 C.M.L.R. 285.
[43] [1984] E.C.R. 1679, 1704.

difficulties in respect of the October delivery). The Court concluded that the Commission had failed to provide "sufficiently precise and coherent proof" of a concerted practice.[44]

23–010   Oligopolistic markets present particular difficulties for the application of the prohibition in Article 81(1). Such markets[45] are typically characterised by small numbers of participants with roughly equal shares and, crucially, a mutual dependence that invites parallel conduct. There is likely to be transparency in market information and little incentive to compete on price. Changes in market strength are likely to arise from either investment in advertising or acquisition of competitors. In the absence of collusive agreements between the parties, any application of Article 81(1) will require proof that they have gone beyond independently acting in parallel to a point where concertation has been reached.

The *Wood Pulp* saga[46] indicates the problems in policing this particular line. At the heart of this epic[47] was an alleged concertation on prices between woodpulp producers mainly located in Finland, Sweden, Canada and the United States. In the Commission's view, concertation could be found in the virtually simultaneous and identical quarterly price announcements made by the producers. These announcements, though made to customers, circulated quickly through the trade press and agents who acted for more than one producer. Having ruled out the Commission's documentary evidence,[48] the Court of Justice considered the nature of the market in the light of the evidence provided by experts it had appointed.

According to the Court, the Commission had failed to establish a "firm, precise and consistent body of evidence".[49] In particular, it had not excluded other plausible explanations for the parallel conduct of the producers. Pulp buyers tended to spread their sources and habitually disclosed to producers the prices of competitors. Market transparency was further enhanced by rapid communication and a dynamic trade press. The net result was that the Court relied on the experts' evidence that the features of the market were at least as likely an explanation of price movements as any alleged concertation. Contrary to the inferences drawn by the Commission, the system of price announcements was a rational response to the fact that the pulp market constituted a long-term market and to the need

---

[44] *ibid.*
[45] See Whish and Sufrin, "Oligopolistic markets and EC competition law" (1992) 12 Y.E.L. 59.
[46] Joined Cases C–89, 104, 114, 116, 117 and 125–128/85 *A. Ahlström Oy v Commission*, n.32, above.
[47] The Commission's original contested Decision was issued in 1984 but the Court's judgment on the merits was only given in 1993, having made a separate ruling on jurisdictional matters in 1988: see n.29, above.
[48] Inadmissible on several grounds, including the Commission's failure to identify all the parties adequately.
[49] Para.127 of Judgment.

felt by both buyers and sellers to limit commercial risks. The coincidence of timing in announcements could be attributed to market transparency and the parallelism of the prices could be satisfactorily explained by the oligopolistic tendencies of the market.[50] Article 1(1) of the Commission's decision in relation to collusion was therefore annulled by the Court.

The Court's approach in *Wood Pulp* reflects the position suggested **23–011** by Advocate General Cosmas that parallelism of conduct is an evidential issue, not an element of the concept of concerted practice.[51] As expressed subsequently by the Court of First Instance, where the Commission relies upon bare parallelism it is sufficient for the parties to prove circumstances which cast the facts established by the Commission in a different light, allowing another explanation of the facts to be substituted for the one adopted by the Commission.[52] The burden is different in cases where other documented evidence of concertation is available. In those circumstances, the onus is on the parties not merely to submit an alternative explanation for the facts found by the Commission but to challenge the existence of those facts established on the basis of the documents produced by the Commission.[53] Once the Commission establishes that undertakings have participated in regular meetings exchanging information with other producers, a presumption is created that the undertakings participating in those sessions and remaining active on the market take account of the information exchanged with their competitors when determining their conduct, especially when the concertation has taken place on a regular basis over a long period.[54] It is therefore for the economic operators to adduce evidence to rebut that presumption.

Almost inevitably, cases which arouse suspicions of concerted practices are likely to involve multiple parties and thus give rise to questions as to the extent of collective responsibility. Not every party will always have attended every meeting or received every circular or fax. In one of the appeals arising from the *Polypropylene* cases, the Court of Justice noted the contradiction in the Court of First Instance's judgment, whereby the latter had accepted the Commission's claim that Anic had been a participant to a single extended

---

[50] But *cf.* the outcome in Case C–7/95P *John Deere v Commission*, n.33, above. Here the information exchanged was between only the main suppliers on the relevant market instead of to purchasers. The information went beyond price announcements and amounted to business secrets enabling traders to know the market positions and strategies of their competitors. Unlike the situation in *Wood Pulp*, such exchanges lessened each undertaking's uncertainty as to the future attitude of its competitors.

[51] Para.188 of Opinion.

[52] Joined Cases T–305–307, 313–316, 318, 325, 328–329 and 335/94 *Re PVC Cartel II: Limburgse Vinyl Maatschapij NV v Commission* [1999] E.C.R. II–931, [1999] 5 C.M.L.R. 303, para.725.

[53] *ibid.*, para.728.

[54] Case C–49/92P *Commission v Anic Partecipazioni SpA*, n.18, above, para.121. To the same effect, see Case C–199/92P *Hüls v Commission* [1999] E.C.R. I–4287; [1999] 5 C.M.L.R. 1016, para.162. The parties in these cases failed to provide the necessary rebuttal.

infringement made up of several agreements and practices with the same economic objective in common, but at the same time had condemned the Commission's failure to prove the extent of Anic's participation in particular meetings or conduct. The Court of Justice set out the relevant test as follows:

> "the Commission must, in particular, show that the undertaking intended to contribute by its own conduct to the common objectives pursued by all the participants and that it was aware of the actual conduct planned or put into effect by other undertakings in pursuit of the same objectives or that it could reasonably have foreseen it and that it was prepared to take the risk".[55]

In the Court's view, the findings of fact made by the Court of First Instance supported the fixing of responsibility upon Anic for conduct followed by other undertakings in the period after it had stopped participating in meetings mid-1982. Anic was perfectly aware of all the elements of the single infringement by virtue of its participation in regular meetings over a period of years and must have assumed that they would continue after mid-1982.[56]

Ultimately, the policy underpinning the concepts of agreement and concertation serves to establish the importance of uncertainty in a functioning competitive market. Of course, it is perhaps ironic[57] that firms may well spend huge amounts of money and effort in second-guessing their rivals' intentions—and, if they do it successfully, they will achieve competitive advantage as a reward for the risk undertaken. Yet, to gain the same information about policies by exchange is to fall into the legal mire of concertation.[58]

Restricting competition

23–012   Article 81(1) refers to agreements, etc.[59] "which have as their object or effect the prevention, restriction or distortion of competition within the common market". This phrase has proved to be the very nub of the provision, its deceptive simplicity conflating a bundle

---

[55] Case C–49/92P *Commission v Anic Partecipazioni SpA*, n.18, above, para.87. See also the views of the Court of First Instance in Case T–334/94 *Sarrió v Commission* [1998] E.C.R. II–1439; [1998] 5 C.M.L.R. 195 arising from a cartonboard cartel, paras 164–171.

[56] *ibid.*, para.206. However, it is clear that the Court of Justice sees marginal participation as relevant to a reduction in any fine. See further, Ch.24 on enforcement of competition law, below.

[57] See R. Lane, *EC Competition Law* (Longman, Pearson Education, Harlow, 2000), pp.59–60.

[58] Information exchange is often unproblematic (e.g. statistics in industrial sectors). However, unusual or unjustifiably detailed information may attract suspicion: see Commission Dec.2001/418/EC *Amino Acids* [2001] O.J. L152.

[59] References hereinafter to "agreements" should be understood as applying also to decisions and concerted practices unless the context indicates otherwise.

of fundamental issues relating not just to the scope of the prohibition but also the methodology of investigation. These questions include whether the same test should be applied to all types of agreements, the nature and extent of economic market analysis required, the thresholds of scale and foreseeability to determine anti-competitive effects and the relevance of any offsetting benefits. Interpretative approaches to these problems have evolved over time in response to changes in the economic and political context in which Article 81 must operate. On the one hand, the advancing process of market integration and economic re-appraisal of certain types of activity have led to some of the strictest applications of the prohibition being relaxed—for example, in relation to vertical restraints. On the other, workload pressures facing the Commission and recurring calls for decentralisation have led to re-allocation of institutional enforcement responsibilities which could in turn influence the holistic conceptual development of Article 81.

The phrase "object or effect" must be read disjunctively.[60] The precise purpose of the agreement must first be ascertained by examining its terms in the particular context in which they will have to be performed. Where it can be seen that the purpose, if achieved, will entail the prevention, restriction or distortion of competition to an appreciable degree,[61] there will be no need to go on and show that such has in fact been the outcome. Where, however, the implications an agreement may have for competition are less clear-cut, it will be necessary to undertake an analysis of economic conditions on the relevant market to assess the extent of any adverse impact.[62] This, however, is not a matter of measuring actual effects on trade between Member States but a question of whether the agreement is capable of such effects.[63] Nothing turns on the distinction between "prevention", "restriction" and "distortion" of competition. The *Consten and Grundig* judgment,[64] for instance, describes the agreement in question as being "such as to *distort* competition in the common market", while a few lines later it refers to "the above-mentioned *restrictions*"[65] (emphasis added). The three terms express, with varying emphasis, the basic idea of a change in the state of competition.

The starting point for an inquiry into the implications of an agreement for competition is the situation as it would have been if

---

[60] Case 56/65 *Société Technique Minière v Maschinenbau Ulm* [1966] E.C.R. 235, [1966] 1 C.M.L.R. 357; confirmed in Case C–219/95P *Ferrière Nord SpA v Commission* [1997] E.C.R. I–4411, [1997] 5 C.M.L.R. 575. In the latter case the Court held that the Italian version of the Treaty, referring to object *and* effect, could not prevail over the unambiguous and express use of the disjunctive in all the other language versions.

[61] On the *de minimis* rule, see p.1015, below.

[62] Case 56/65 *Société Technique Minière*, n.60 above, at 249.

[63] Case 19/77 *Miller Schallplatten v Commission* [1978] E.C.R. 131; [1978] 2 C.M.L.R. 334.

[64] Joined Cases 56 and 58/64 *Consten and Grundig v Commission* [1966] E.C.R. 299; [1966] C.M.L.R. 418.

[65] [1966] E.C.R. 299, 343.

the agreement did not exist.[66] Without some competition capable of being restricted by the agreement, there can be no infringement of Article 81. Lack of competition in a market may, for example, be the result of government intervention.[67] In the *Sugar* judgment[68] the Court of Justice held that measures taken to regulate the market in Italy had fundamentally restricted the scope for competition between sugar producers. The Commission's finding of an infringement of Article 81 was, therefore, quashed, although it was manifest that concertation had taken place between the Italian producers and exporters from other Member States. Where, however, despite intervention by the public authorities, some room remains for competitive pressures to influence the decisions of market participants, further restriction of competition through an agreement between undertakings is liable to fall foul of Article 81(1). Indeed, the Commission contends that in such circumstances the anti-competitive effects of private arrangements are all the more significant.[69] The need for there to be some competition capable of restriction may be a further explanation why Article 81 is consistently held not to apply as between parent and subsidiary companies within a single economic entity.[70]

In assessing restrictions, the Commission has come to use the language of "hardcore" restraints to describe their most objectionable forms.[71] Such restrictions are generally considered by the Commission to constitute restrictions by *object*.[72] For horizontal agreements, these will include price-fixing, limitation of output and the sharing of markets or customers. As evidenced by block exemptions,[73] hardcore restraints in vertical relationships are likeliest to be found in resale price maintenance or excessive territorial restraints. If an agreement is not restrictive by object then it must be examined according to whether there are restrictive *effects* on competition. This means that the agreement "must affect actual or potential competition to such an extent that on the relevant market negative

---

[66] Case 56/65 *Société Technique Minière*, n.60 above, at 250. See also Case C–7/95P *John Deere v Commission*, n.33, above, para.76.

[67] The extent to which Art.81, in combination with Art.10 of the Treaty, may give rise to state responsibility is discussed further at the end of this Chapter.

[68] n.8, above.

[69] See, e.g. *Re Stichting Sigarettenindustrie Agreements* [1982] O.J. L232/1; [1982] 3 C.M.L.R. 702. The point is mentioned in Joined Cases 209–215 and 218/78 *Van Landewyck v Commission*, n.28, above, at 3261.

[70] Case 22/71 *Béguelin Import Co. v SA GL Import Export*, n.5 above; see also W. Wils, "The undertaking as subject of EC Competition Law and the Imputation of Infringements to Natural or Legal Persons" (2000) 25 E.L.Rev. 99.

[71] See *Guidelines on the Application of Article 81(3) of the Treaty* [2004] O.J. C101/08 for the Commission's position on the scope and application of Art.81(1) as well as the exemption provisions that provide the somewhat misleading title to this Notice.

[72] *ibid.*, para.23.

[73] Reg.2790/1999 on the application of Art.81(3) to categories of vertical agreements and concerted practices [1999] O.J. L336/21.

effects on prices, output, innovation or the variety or quality of goods and services can be expected with a reasonable degree of probability."[74]

The economic context

As summarised by the Court of First Instance, in assessing the **23–013** effect of an agreement under Article 81(1),

> ". . . the examination of conditions of competition is based not only on existing competition between undertakings already present on the relevant market but also on potential competition, in order to ascertain whether, in the light of the structure of the market and the economic and legal context within which it functions, there are real concrete possibilities for the undertakings concerned to compete among themselves or for a new competitor to penetrate the relevant market and compete with the undertakings already established".[75]

This market-based analysis has not always been the basis for applying Article 81(1). Certainly, back in the 1960s, a much more abstract view of the potential for competition to be restricted was visible in judical reasoning.[76] However, it is clear now that an "effects" approach requires the agreement or practice to be situated within the market in which it operates. Particular guidance on the so-called "network" effect of agreements can be seen from the Court's judgment in *Delimitis*,[77] a case concerning "tie" arrangements between brewers and cafe owners whereby the latter were committed to purchases from the former. A single agreement of this type might not be especially significant, but the overall impact of many similar tied contracts in a market could effectively foreclose competition. The Court of Justice ruled that such a beer supply agreement infringed Article 81(1) if two cumulative conditions were met:

> "The first is that, having regard to the economic and legal context of the agreement at isue, it is difficult for competitors who could enter the market or increase their market share to gain access to the national market for the distribution of beer in premises for the sales and consumption of drinks . . . The second condition is that the agreement in question must make a

---

[74] *Guidelines on the Application of Art.81(3) of the Treaty*, n.71, above, para.24.
[75] Joined Cases T–374–375, 384 and 388/94 *European Night Services v Commission* [1998] E.C.R. II–3141; [1998] 5 C.M.L.R. 718, paras 136–137.
[76] Joined Cases 56 and 58/64 *Consten and Grundig*, n.64, above.
[77] Case C–234/89 *Delimitis v Henninger Bräu* [1991] E.C.R. I–935; [1992] 5 C.M.L.R. 210.

significant contribution to the sealing-off effect brought about by the totality of those agreements in their economic and legal context. The extent of the contribution made by the individual agreement depends on the position of the contracting parties in the relevant market and on the duration of the agreement."[78]

This judicial blessing for an economic approach to Article 81 has led the Commission to expand in detail upon its methodology. Thus, in a 2004 Notice, it noted that when analysing restrictive effects, besides having to define the relevant market,

"It is normally also necessary to examine and assess, *inter alia*, the nature of the products, the market position of the parties, the market position of competitors, the market position of buyers, the existence of potential competitors and the level of entry barriers. In some cases, however, it may be possible to show anti-competitive effects directly by analysing the conduct of the parties to the agreement on the market. It may for example be possible to ascertain that an agreement has led to price increases . . ."[79]

A rule of reason in Article 81(1)?

23–014   The fact that the possibility of a "rule of reason" in Article 81(1) has remained a long-standing question[80] for both scholars and practitioners reflects the confluence of a number of rather different considerations and circumstances. As a term, "rule of reason" has a different pedigree according to which side of the Atlantic has legal jurisdiction. In the EC context, it is tempting to equate the concept with its more familiar historic attachment to the single market and the fundamental freedoms. A further complication is added by the fact that the specific character of Article 81 involves not only the separation of the prohibition in paragraph (1) from the exceptions in paragraph (3), but also a fundamental change in how the Article is enforced following the 2004 reforms. These factors are elaborated further below, although it should be stressed that ultimately the interpretation of Article 81 must be a teleological one based on its position within the competition rules and the wider Treaty context, rather than any notion transplanted from elsewhere.

As applied to competition law, the use of "rule of reason" can be traced to US antitrust law,[81] where this idea arose to mitigate the

---

[78] *ibid*, para.27.
[79] *Guidelines on the Application of Art.81(3) of the Treaty*, n.71 above, para.27.
[80] See, *e.g.*, R. Wesseling, "The Rule of Reason and Competition Law: Various Rules, Various Reasons" in A. Schrauwen (ed.) *Rule of Reason, Rethinking Another Classic of European Legal Doctrine* (Europa Law Publishing, Groningen, 2005), Ch.4.
[81] See Peeters, "The rule of reason revisited: prohibition on restraints of competition in the Sherman Act and EEC Treaty" (1989) A.J. Comp.Law 521; Forrester and Norall, "The laïcization of Community law: self-help and the rule of reason: how competition law is and could be applied" (1984) 21 C.M.L.Rev. 11.

rigour of the prohibition in section 1 of the Sherman Act against contracts in restraint of trade.[82] The rule of reason applies to agreements other than those, such as horizontal price-fixing agreements, which are treated by the American courts as illegal *per se*. Essentially, a court is required under the rule to consider the overall impact of the agreement in question on competition within the relevant market. This involves, in particular, identifying any pro-competitive effects the agreement may have and weighing them against its anti-competitive effects. However, the importance in American antitrust law of the rule of reason is explained by the absence of any "gateway" through which a restrictive agreement which is felt, nevertheless, to be economically beneficial may escape prohibition. Where application of the rule leads to a favourable assessment of an agreement under the Sherman Act, that will be because the agreement is judged, on balance, not to be restrictive of competition.

In EC law, on the other hand, an agreement that restricts competition within the meaning of Article 81(1) may still qualify for exemption under Article 81(3). At first sight, therefore, it might be assumed that pro-competitive aspects of an agreement will only be taken into account in assessing the economic benefits that may justify a grant of exemption, especially now that national courts and competition authorities are competent to take decisions on the latter. Certainly, in cases[83] pre-dating the 2004 reforms, the Court of First Instance expressly rejected the existence of a rule of reason in this "weighing up" sense. In particular, it observed that much of the effectiveness of Article 81(3) as a precision framework would be lost if pro- and anti-competitive factors were to be balanced under paragraph (1). However, the Court of First Instance conceded that other case law[84] signalled a broader treatment of Article 81(1) to the extent that account needed to be taken of the actual context in which any agreement functioned.

Any scope for "rule of reason" arguments therefore seems to **23–015** depend on the "context" that is capable of appropriation by analysis within Article 81(1). At its narrowest, discussed above, it is confined to the economic arena yet rules out balancing pro-competitive features. This leaves at least two further possibilities. The first engages a legal context expressed in terms of necessary or inherent elements of an agreement which must survive in order to make it work. It would perhaps seem curious to use the term "rule of reason" here, although the case law discussed below clearly supports

---

[82] The rule is summarised by Whish and Sufrin (1987) 7 Y.E.L. 1, 4–12. See also Black, "Per se rules and rules of reason: what are they?" [1997] 3 E.C.L.R. 145.

[83] Case T–112/99 *Métropole Télévision (M6) v Commission* [2001] E.C.R. II–2459, [2001] 5 C.M.L.R. 1236 and Case T–65/98 *Van den Bergh Foods v Commission* [2003] E.C.R. II–4653, [2004] 4 C.M.L.R. 1.

[84] e.g. *Delimitis*, n.77, above; also the 'ancillary restraints' cases, discussed further below.

this margin of appreciation within Article 81(1). A second possibility, and much more redolent of the balancing characteristics of EC free movement "rule of reason" applications,[85] is that Article 81(1) permits or requires the balancing of competition and non-competition concerns as part of the "actual context" of the agreement.

To illustrate the first group, the Court has held in a number of cases that contractual provisions giving a measure of protection against competition do not fall within Article 81(1) if they are genuinely necessary to enable a partner to be found in a business transaction. The earliest reference to this "indispensable inducement" rationale was in *Société Technique Minière v Maschinenbau Ulm*[86] which concerned an exclusive distribution agreement. Under the agreement the supplier promised not to appoint another distributor in the concession territory or to sell the goods there himself, but no protection was provided against parallel imports. The Court said that "it may be doubted whether there is an interference with competition if the said agreement seems really necessary for the penetration of a new area by an undertaking".[87] The case is distinguishable from *Consten and Grundig*,[88] where the absolute territorial protection sought by the parties could not be regarded as "really necessary" to secure access for Grundig products to the French market. A further example is *Remia*,[89] where the Court accepted that the seller of a business could be put under an obligation not to compete with the buyer, while emphasising that "such clauses must be necessary to the transfer of the undertaking concerned and their duration and scope must be strictly limited to that purpose".[90] The Court refused to interfere with the Commission's finding that four years' protection for the buyer of a sauce-manufacturing business would have been enough to cover the introduction of a new trademark and to win customer loyalty, instead of the 10-year period which had been agreed.

In a rather different vein, the Court held in *Pronuptia*[91] that various provisions in an agreement forming part of a distribution franchise system did not restrict competition within the meaning of Article 81(1) because they were necessary to the successful functioning of the system. This approach goes beyond the analysis of the cases just referred to: the issue is not whether, apart from the

---

[85] See generally, A. Schrauwen (ed.), *op.cit.* n.80, above.
[86] Case 56/65, n.60, above.
[87] [1966] E.C.R. 235, 250. The lack of further authority on "indispensable inducement" in respect of exclusive distribution agreements is due, presumably, to the enactment of a block exemption regulation soon afterwards.
[88] n.64, above.
[89] Case 42/84 *Remia v Commission* [1985] E.C.R. 2545; [1987] 1 C.M.L.R. 1.
[90] See para.20 of Judgment.
[91] Case 161/84 *Pronuptia de Paris v Schillgalis* [1986] E.C.R. 353; [1986] 1 C.M.L.R. 414.

provisions in question, a bargain could have been struck but whether the essential aims of the transaction (considered to be one that competition law ought not to disfavour) could have been realised. As applied by the Court the analysis comprised four logical steps: (i) definition of the salient features of the transaction; (ii) finding that the transaction is not in itself restrictive of competition; (iii) identification of the conditions that have to be met to enable such a transaction to be satisfactorily performed; (iv) identification of the contractual terms indispensable to the fulfilment of those conditions. In other words, the Court's approach acknowledged an ancillary restraints element in the assessment of restrictions.

Distribution franchising, the Court explained, is a marketing **23–016** system under which an established distributor whose success is associated with a certain trademark and certain commercial methods (the franchisor) puts his mark and methods at the disposal of independent traders (the franchisees) in return for the payment of a royalty. This has the advantage to the franchisor of enabling him to exploit his know-how without having to commit his own capital; and to the franchisees of giving them access to methods they could otherwise only have acquired through prolonged effort and research, while also allowing them to profit from the reputation of the mark. The success of such a system depends on two things: the franchisor must be able to communicate his know-how to the franchisees and help them in putting his methods into practice without running the risk that his competitors might benefit, even directly; and he must be able to take appropriate measures to preserve the identity and reputation of the network symbolised by the mark. Under the agreement in question the franchisee had undertaken not to open a shop selling competing goods and not to dispose of the franchise premises except with the prior consent of the franchisor. These terms imposed quite severe restraints on the running of the franchisee's business but they were found to be indispensable to the fulfilment of the first condition and so outwith Article 81(1). Among the terms excluded from Article 81(1) by the second condition was the franchisee's obligation to obtain stock only from the franchisor or from suppliers chosen by him. This helped to protect the reputation of the network by ensuring that the public would find goods of uniform quality in all Pronuptia shops. Given the character of the franchise products (wedding dresses and formal wear) it would, in the Court's view, have been impossible to achieve that result by formulating a set of objective quality specifications.

The *Pronuptia* case, representing at the time a new form of business model for evaluation against competition rules, followed earlier judgments by the Court that had similarly focused upon the merit and purpose of another business method, selective distribution. Although now largely overtaken by block exemption legislation,[92] a series of cases established that selective distribution agreements based on objective quality criteria which are applied in a non-discriminatory way are compatible with Article 81(1).[93] Under such a system, for example, a manufacturer may limit the outlets for a product which is expensive and technically complex to dealers able and willing to promote it effectively and to provide presales advice, and an after-sales maintenance and repair service, for customers.[94] Selectivity is likely, on the one hand, to result in higher prices. On the other, opportunities are created for competition between manufacturers in respect of the customer services associated with their brands. The rationale of the Court's approach to selective distribution can be seen from the *AEG* case,[95] where it said:

> ". . . there are legitimate requirements, such as the maintenance of a specialist trade capable of providing specific services as regards high-quality and hightechnology products, which may justify a reduction of price competition in favour of competition relating to factors other than price. Systems of selective distribution, in so far as they aim at the attainment of a legitimate goal capable of improving competition in relation to factors other than price, therefore constitute an element of competition which is in conformity with Article 85(1)".[96]

In essence, the Court's approach to franchising and selective distribution exhibits a willingness to weigh the pros and cons of different *forms* of competition against each other (in the sense of quality versus price). This could be seen as a rather sophisticated application of a "rule of reason", buttressed by an application of the ancillary restraints idea to ensure that the merit of the business technique is rendered operational. Thus the Court still refused to uphold *quantitative* conditions, such as limits on numbers of outlets, resale price maintenance[97] or export bans,[98] without specific exemption even though, arguably,[99] the purpose of their inclusion in an

---

[92] Reg.2790/1999, n.73, above.
[93] See, in particular, Case 26/76 *Metro* [1977] E.C.R. 1875, [1978] 2 C.M.L.R. 1; Joined Cases 253/78 and 1–3/79 *Guerlain, Rochas, Lanvin and Nina Ricci (Perfumes)* [1980] E.C.R. 2327; [1981] 2 C.M.L.R. 99; Case 86/82 *Hasselblad v Commission* [1984] E.C.R. 883; [1984] C.M.L.R. 559; Case 75/84 *Metro v Commission (no 2)* [1986] E.C.R. 3021; [1987] 1 C.M.L.R. 118; Case C–376/92 *Metro v Cartier* [1994] E.C.R. I–15; [1994] 5 C.M.L.R. 331; Case T–19/92 *Groupement D'Achat Edouard Leclerc v Commission* [1996] E.C.R. II–1961; [1997] 4 C.M.L.R. 995.
[94] The *Perfumes* cases, n.93, above, illustrate selective distribution of another kind of product thought to require special handling, *viz.* luxury items.
[95] Case 107/82 *AEG v Commission*, n.11, above.
[96] *ibid.*, at 3194.
[97] *ibid.*
[98] See, *Perfumes* cases, n.93, above.
[99] See Chard, "The Economics of the Application of Article 85 to Selective Distribution Systems" (1982) 7 E.L.Rev. 83.

agreement may be to ensure a sufficient turnover for the dealer to support the desired range of customer services.

Perhaps the most modern evidence of the "rule of reason" in its **23–017** EC competition context is provided by the cases in which the "context" surrounding an agreement extends beyond economic analysis or ancillary requirements. Instead, the Court treats Article 81(1) as inapplicable because of some other public interest consideration that trumps the restrictive element of the agreement. The most potentially far-reaching example is provided by *Wouters*,[1] a case concerning Regulations issued by the Netherlands Bar which prohibited multi-disciplinary partnerships between members of the Bar and other professions, including accountants. The Court of Justice first decided that members of the Bar were undertakings carrying on an economic activity and that the Bar itself was an association of undertakings when it adopted Regulations of the type in question. The Court then observed the adverse effect on competition that resulted from the prohibition against partnerships with accountants,[2] particularly in terms of preventing a wider range of services, maybe even new ones, from emerging in a one-stop shop structure for business clients. However, the Court proceeded to override this limitation of production and development[3] as follows:

> ". . . not every agreement between undertakings or every decision of an association of undertakings which restricts the freedom of action of the parties or of one of them necessarily falls within the prohibition laid down in [Article 81 EC]. For the purposes of application of that provision to a particular case, account must first of all be taken of the *overall context in which the decision of the association of undertakings was taken or produces its effects*. More particularly, account must be taken of its objectives, which are here connected with the need to make rules relating to organisation, qualifications, professional ethics, supervision and liability, in order to ensure that the ultimate consumers of legal services and the sound administration of justice are provided with the necessary guarantees in relation to integrity and experience . . . *It has then to be considered whether the consequential effects restrictive of competition are inherent in the pursuit of those objectives*."[4] [emphasis added]

In conclusion, the Court held that the Regulation in issue could therefore "reasonably be considered to be necessary in order to

---

[1] n. 25, above.

[2] Described by the Dean of the Bar as a marriage between a mouse and an elephant in the light of the gigantic size of accountants' firms compared with Bar practices.

[3] A specific example of anti-competitive practice listed in Art.81(1).

[4] *Wouters* judgment, n.25 above, para.97.

ensure the proper practice of the legal profession, as it is organised in the Member State concerned."[5]

This controversial judgment may usefully be contrasted with the Opinion of Advocate General Léger in the same case. Having decided that all the alleged "rule of reason" cases about Article 81(1)[6] confined themselves to pro-competitive concerns rather than public interest factors, he took the view the wider justifications being invoked in *Wouters* were not incapable of falling within Article 81(3) exemptions or, more likely, the provisions of Article 86(2) available to entrusted undertakings.[7] He therefore recommended that the Regulation be referred back to the national court for it to assess the need to safeguard lawyers' independence and professional secrecy against the tests of Article 86(2).[8]

The novelty of the *Wouters* judgment is twofold. Firstly, it clearly finds a negative effect on competition but discounts it because of wider public interest concerns. This balancing is not a purely competition-led inquiry. Secondly, this resemblance to a "rule of reason" borrowed from the single market is not wholly followed through, as the usual proportionality requirements are not strictly applied. The *Wouters* case was subsequently adopted by the Commission as part of its alternative reasoning in relation to anti-doping rules applicable to professional sport. However, the Court of First Instance[9] distinguished *Wouters* as a case based on market conduct whereas, in its view, the doping rules were "purely" sporting legislation and outwith Articles 81 and 82 altogether.

The controversy about which test to use to mark the outer limits of application of the Treaty's competition rules thus persists. As seen in Chapter 22, above, the notion of "undertaking" has increasingly performed this role in relation to systems of health care or pension arrangements. *Wouters* appears to offer the opportunity, albeit half-grasped, to develop a convergence with free movement case law by concentrating on how to measure a "restriction", whilst the Court of First Instance's *Meca-Medina* approach clings to a more artificial classification of activities which fall within (or outside) the competition arena.

---

[5] *ibid.*, para.107.

[6] Including the ones discussed above, such as *Pronuptia* and the selective distribution cases.

[7] The individual lawyers, rather than the Bar, being the "entrusted" undertakings for this purpose. At this time, the national court could not have applied Art.81(3), which might explain the Advocate General's stronger reliance upon use of Art.86(2).

[8] Discussed below, Ch.26.

[9] Case T–313/02 *Meca-Medina and Majcen v Commission* (Judgment of the CFI, September 30 2004), criticised by S. Weatherill, "Anti-Doping Rules and EC Law" [2005] E.C.L.R. 416.

Appreciable effects on competition and on trade between Member States

For Article 81(1) to apply, the agreement must restrict competi- **23–018** tion to an appreciable extent. This *de minimis* rule is a further illustration that the prohibition contained in the Article must be adapted to practical contexts. Given the instrumentalism of competition law, discussed in Chapter 22 above, there would be little point in regulating potential infringements of Article 81 which had no real impact on the single market or the free play of competition. At the same time, there will be no breach of Article 81 without an appreciable effect on trade between Member States. This notion serves a jurisdictional role, since if it is not satisfied then any regulation of the agreement will flow from national competition rules rather than the EC regime. These two applications of appreciability are discussed in turn below.

The de minimis rule applied to restrictions on competition

This was first laid down by the Court of Justice in *Völk v* **23–019** *Vervaecke*,[10] where the manufacturer in question held only around 0.2 per cent of the market. Following the Court's lead, the Commission adopted, and periodically revised, guidance Notices for business on when agreements will be deemed to lack the appreciable effect necessary for the purposes of a restriction under Article 81(1). The 2001 Notice[11] is built upon market share criteria, the relevant figures being 10 per cent for agreements between competitors and 15 per cent for those between non-competitors.[12] Where there is doubt as to which category applies, the 10 per cent figure is to be used. For agreements with network effects the figures across the board are reduced to five per cent.[13] But in any event, the *de minimis* thresholds do not apply to agreements containing any of the hardcore restrictions identified in paragraph 11 of the Notice, such as price-fixing or market partitioning.

Some care must be exercised when seeking to apply the Notice. As a piece of "soft" law, it is not legally binding and, in particular, is subject to the jurisprudence of the Court.[14] Market shares above the thresholds of the Notice will not inevitably mean an appreciable

---

[10] Case 5/69 *Völk v Vervaecke* [1969] E.C.R. 295; [1969] C.M.L.R. 273.
[11] *Notice on Agreements of Minor Importance* [2001] O.J. C368/13, [2002] 4 C.M.L.R. 699.
[12] *ibid.*, para.7.
[13] *ibid.*, para.8. However, the same provision notes that a cumulative foreclosure effect is unlikely to exist if less than 30 per cent of the relevant market is subject to parallel network agreements having similar effects.
[14] *ibid.* para.6.

effect is established.[15] The Notice does, however, drive the Commission's thinking and conduct. Thus in cases covered by it, the Commission will not institute proceedings either upon application or upon its own initiative. Where undertakings assume in good faith that an agreement falls within the Notice, the Commission will not impose fines.[16]

Appreciable effect on trade between Member States

23–020   The purpose of the condition in Article 81(1) relating to the effect of an agreement on trade between Member States is, in the words of the Court of Justice, "to define, in the context of the law governing competition, the boundary between the areas respectively covered by Community law and the law of the Member States".[17] The line of demarcation is the same under both Articles 81 and 82.[18] The test in the case law, first formulated in *Société Technique Minière*, is that "it must be possible to foresee with a sufficient degree of probability on the basis of a set of objective factors of law or of fact that the agreement in question may have an influence, direct or indirect, actual or potential, on the pattern of trade between Member States".[19] The crucial element is the diversion of trade flows from the pattern they would naturally follow in a unified market. Where trade has been so diverted, it is immaterial that the agreement may have led to an increase in the volume of goods or services reaching the market in other Member States. Thus in *Consten and Grundig*,[20] trade was held to be affected in the necessary sense, regardless of any increase in imports of Grundig products into France, because not only were all such imports to be channelled through Consten but their re-exportation to the Member States was prohibited.

As part of the switch to decentralised enforcement of Article 81, the Commission issued an expansive Notice in 2004 on the meaning of the effect on trade requirement.[21] Building on the case law elaboration of the test, the Notice stresses that the concept of "trade" is not limited to traditional exchanges of goods and services across borders. Instead, it is a wider concept, covering all cross-

---

[15] *ibid.*, para.2. See also Case T–7/93 *Langnese-Iglo v Commission* [1995] E.C.R. II–611; [1995] 5 C.M.L.R. 602. In Joined Cases T–374, 375, 384 and 388/94 *European Night Services v Commission*, n.75, above, the Commission disputed the claims of the parties that their market shares fell below the then threshold figure of 5%. The Court of First Instance ruled that the Commission had failed to provide adequate reasoning, but that in any event a slight excess over the 5 per cent Notice threshold would not in itself indicate an appreciable effect.

[16] 2001 *Notice*, n.11 above, para.4.

[17] Case 22/78 *Hugin v Commission* [1979] E.C.R. 1869, 1899; [1979] 3 C.M.L.R. 345.

[18] [1979] E.C.R. 1869, 1899.

[19] Case 56/65 *Société Technique Minière*, n.60, above, at 249.

[20] Joined Cases 56 and 58/64, n.64, above.

[21] *Guidelines on the effect on trade concept contained in Articles 81 and 82 of the Treaty* [2004] O.J. C101/7.

border activity including establishment.[22] Trade will also be affected where the competitive structure of the market is put at risk by the elimination or threatened elimination of a competitor.[23] The impact on trade is to be measured against the *Technique Minière*[24] test of "direct or indirect, actual or potential" effects. However, the Notice makes it clear that this does not mean that the analysis can be based on remote or hypothetical effects.[25]

The Notice focuses on the concept of appreciability, setting out some general principles before providing examples of their application to particular types of agreement.[26] Whilst acknowledging that the assessment of appreciability depends on the circumstances of each individual case, the Notice sets out a negative rebuttable presumption expressed somewhat inelegantly as the Non-Appreciable Affectation of Trade (NAAT) rule.[27] This applies to all agreements within the meaning of Article 81(1) irrespective of the nature of the restrictions contained in the agreement, including hardcore restraints.[28] Thus, an agreement will not be capable of appreciably affecting trade where the following cumulative conditions are met:

(a) the aggregate market share of the parties on any relevant market within the Community affected by the agreement does not exceed 5 per cent, and

(b) in the case of horizontal agreements, the aggregate annual Community turnover of the undertakings concerned in the products covered by the agreement does not exceed €40 million; in the case of vertical agreements the aggregate annual Community turnover of the supplier in the products covered by the agreement does not exceed €40 million.[29]

Where the agreement is one which by its very nature is capable of affecting trade, for example by governing imports and exports or covering several Member States, the Commission will apply a positive presumption that trade is affected once the above thresholds are met.[30]

---

[22] *ibid.*, para.19.

[23] *ibid,* para.20. This is most likely in the context of abuses of dominance, discussed in Ch.24 below. See Joined Cases 6–7/73 *Commercial Solvents Corporation v Commission* [1974] E.C.R. 223; [1974] 1 C.M.L.R. 309.

[24] n.60, above.

[25] Notice, n.120 above, para.43.

[26] In particular, distinguishing between agreements and abuses that cover several Member States and those which are confined to a single Member State or part thereof. The detail is omitted here; see paras.58–109 of the Notice.

[27] *ibid.*, para.50.

[28] *ibid.*

[29] *ibid.*, para.52, with further refinements to the tests in paras.53–57.

[30] *ibid.*, para.53.

The Notice assumes particular importance for national courts and competition authorities now charged with the enforcement of Articles 81 and 82. According to Article 3 of Regulation 1/2003, such bodies, when applying national competition rules, must also apply Articles 81 and 82 where the agreement or abuse affects trade between Member States.

Exemptions under Article 81(3)

23–021　　Agreements that appreciably affect competition may nevertheless bring significant economic advantages. Accordingly, the prohibition of Article 81(1) is tempered by the possibility of exemption under Article 81(3). According to the latter, the provisions of Article 81(1) may be declared inapplicable to "any agreement or category of agreements". The power to grant individual exemptions was originally reserved by Regulation 17/62 to the Commission, but this was removed by the reforms implemented in 2004. There is no longer any requirement for exemptions to be obtained in advance, so national courts and competition authorities may now simply apply paragraph (3) where the validity of an agreement is at stake. However, the 2004 changes do not alter the position regarding so-called "Block" exemptions, which are regulations of the Commission adopted under powers delegated by the Council in accordance with Article 83 EC and applicable to categories of agreement. Such categories include: vertical agreements,[31] specialisation[32], research and development [33] and technology transfer.[34] The detailed contents of these block exemptions are not examined in this work, although their principles are discussed further below after consideration of the specific elements of Article 81(3).

In principle, any agreement, no matter how restrictive of competition, is capable of being justified under Article 81(3).[35] From interpretative and policy perspectives, the function of paragraph (3) must be seen against the "rule of reason" discussed earlier in this Chapter in the context of paragraph (1).[36] As seen from cases such as *Wouters*,[37] the Court appears to accept that non-competition criteria can be deployed as part of the "overall context" of an agreement when measuring the limits of application of the prohibition in paragraph (1). The question therefore arises whether a similar degree of contextual breadth attaches to consideration of the exemption criteria set out in paragraph (3). In its guidance Communication,[38] the Commission firmly rejects this by stating that

---

[31] Reg.2790/1999 [1999] O.J. L336/21, [2000] 4 C.M.L.R. 398.
[32] Reg.2659/2000 [2000] O.J. L304/3, [2001] 4 C.M.L.R. 800.
[33] Reg.2659/2000 [2000] O.J. L304/7, [2001] 4 C.M.L.R. 808.
[34] Reg.772/2004 [2004] O.J. L123/18.
[35] Case T–17/93 *Matra Hachette v Commission* [1994] E.C.R. II–595.
[36] See text accompanying n.80, above.
[37] See n.25, above.
[38] *Guidelines on the application of Art.81(3) of the Treaty* [2004] O.J. C101/97.

paragraph (3) deals with the assessment of the positive *economic* effects of restrictive agreements.[39]

Article 81(3) sets out two positive criteria and two negative ones. An exemption must satisfy all the criteria, so that if it fails on one there is no need to go on and examine the others.[40] The burden of proof lies on the parties seeking the protection of the exemption.[41] The benefits required do not necessarily have to occur within the territory of the Member State or States in which the undertakings party to the agreement are established.[42] The four criteria for exemption under Article 81(3) are discussed in turn below.

Efficiency gains

The first of the positive criteria identifies in broad terms a number **23–022** of economic benefits that provide the rationale for refraining from applying Article 81(1). The agreement must contribute "to improving the production or distribution of goods or to promoting technical or economic progress". Only one from this list of efficiency gains needs to be satisfied. Although the reference is explicitly to goods, the Commission treats the provision as applicable by analogy to services.[43]

It is not sufficient merely that the parties themselves may secure advantages in their production and distribution activities.[44] As set out in the Commission's Guidelines, all efficiency claims must be substantiated so that the following can be verified[45]: (a) the *nature* of the claimed efficiencies; (b) the *link* between the agreement and the efficiencies; (c) the *likelihood* and *magnitude* of each claimed efficiency; and (d) *how* and *when* each claimed efficiency would be achieved. In essence, efficiencies flow from an integration of economic activities whereby undertakings combine their assets to achieve what they could not achieve as efficiently independently or whereby they entrust another undertaking with tasks that can be performed more efficiently by the latter.[46] Benefits from efficiencies may broadly be divided into cost and qualitative categories, both of which are given extensive elaboration in the Commission's Guidelines.[47]

---

[39] *ibid.*, para.32. In para.11 the Commission alludes to the balancing of pro-competitive and anti-competitive effects being conducted "exclusively" within the framework of Art.81(3).
[40] Case C–137/95P *Vereniging van Samenwerkende Prijsregelende Organisaties in de Bouwnijverheid (SPO) v Commission* [1996] E.C.R. I–1611.
[41] Joined Cases 43, 63/82 *VBVB and VBBB v Commission* [1984] E.C.R. 19, [1985] 1 C.M.L.R. 27. Now legislatively enshrined in Art.2 of Reg.1/2003.
[42] Case C–360/92P *Publishers Association v Commission* [1995] E.C.R. I–25; [1995] 5 C.M.L.R. 33.
[43] *Guidelines* n.38, above, para.48.
[44] Joined Cases 56 and 58/64 *Consten and Grundig v Commission*, n.64, above.
[45] *Guidelines*, n.38, above, para.51.
[46] *ibid.*, para.60.
[47] *ibid*, paras 64–68 (cost) and 69–72 (qualitative).

"Economic progress" seems at first sight to be the widest of the four criteria identified in the first positive condition of Article 81(3). Indeed, there is evidence from the pre-2004 case law that it, rather than Article 81(1), incorporates any "rule of reason"that might be legitimately invoked. In particular, some older decisions paid particular attention to crisis cartels, formed to enable an industry to adapt in an orderly way to adverse economic conditions such as a decline in the overall market for its products. In *Re Synthetic Fibres*[48] an agreement providing for joint measures to cut capacity, in an industry where the trend in demand had not kept pace with increased output resulting from rapid technical advances, was considered eligible for exemption. The advantages identified by the Commission included the shedding of the financial burden of keeping under-utilised capacity open, the achievement of optimum plant size and specialisation in the development of products adapted to user's requirements. "The eventual result", the Commission said, " should be to raise the profitability and restore the competitiveness of each party".[49]

Social factors, too, have occasionally fallen within the heading of "economic progress".[50] Among the elements mentioned in support of the *Synthetic Fibres* exemption was the possibility of cushioning the social effects of restructuring by making suitable arrangements for the retraining and redeployment of redundant workers. Environmental concerns might also seem arguable as economic benefits, especially since environmental protection is to be integrated into all Community policies,[51] but the Commission's older practice appeared to place them within the second positive criterion, benefit to consumers. As it noted in *Philips/Osram*,[52] "The use of cleaner facilities will result in less air pollution, and consequently in direct and indirect benefits for consumers from reduced negative externalities. This positive effect will be substantially reinforced when R&D in the field produces lead-free materials".

The key question as yet not fully resolved is whether the Commission's narrow, economic approach in its 2004 Guidelines to the criteria of Article 81(3) will withstand any future judicial scrutiny. The Court's judgment in *Wouters*,[53] using wider public interest tests to discount the restrictive elements of Article 81(1), gave an implicit green light to the Commission's view of the narrower balancing

[48] [1984] O.J. L207/17; [1985] 1 C.M.L.R. 787.
[49] *ibid.*, at para.36.
[50] The creation of employment is mentioned by the Court in Case 26/76 *Metro*, n.93, above, para.43. Also Case 42/84 *Remia*, n.89, above.
[51] Art.6 EC, inserted by the Treaty of Amsterdam.
[52] Dec.94/986, para.27. See also Dec.91/38 *KSB/Goulds/Lowara/ITT* [1991] O.J. L19/25; Dec.2000/475 *CECED* [2000] O.J. L187/47, [2000] 5 C.M.L.R. 635.
[53] n.25, above and discussed at 23–017.

exercise to be undertaken for the purposes of Article 81(3).[54] Until such time as a national court chooses to refer the matter under Article 234 EC, it may be safer to assume that any "rule of reason" is best argued within the parameters of the prohibition of Article 81(1).

Benefit to consumers

The second positive benefit is that consumers must receive a fair **23–023** share of the benefit resulting from the restriction of competition. At first sight, the use of the term "consumer" suggests that only the consuming public, or end consumer, is meant. Such a construction, however, would have the effect of severely limiting the scope of possible exemptions, because in many cases the parties to the agreement cannot by themselves do anything to ensure that the condition is met. It is not therefore surprising that the Commission has taken the view that consumers are the customers of the parties to the agreement and subsequent purchasers.[55]

According to the Commission's Guidelines[56]:

> "The concept of *"fair share"* implies that the pass-on of benefits must at least compensate consumers for any actual or likely negative impact caused to them by the restriction of competition found under Article 81(1). In line with the overall objective of Article 81 to prevent anti-competitive agreements, the net effect of the agreement must at least be neutral from the point of view of those consumers directly or likely affected by the agreement."

Thus, pursuing this idea of compensation, if an agreement is likely to lead to higher prices then consumers must be compensated through increased quality or other benefits.[57] A benefit now is worth more than one in the future, so that in calculating the compensatory effects a discount will be applied to future benefits.[58] The detailed Guidelines express the commitment of the Commission to economic analysis, fleshing out an analytical framework for the assessment of pass-on gains. Thus, in establishing the extent to which cost efficiencies are likely to be passed on to consumers, all of the following

---

[54] *cf.* Advocate General Léger in *Wouters*, who had noted that "Professional rules which . . . produce economic effects which are positive, taken as a whole, should therefore be eligible for exemption under [Art.81(1)]".

[55] *Guidelines*, n.38, above, para.84. In any event, the term "consumer" in English may have a narrower connotation than the term used in other language texts: the French text uses the term *utilisateur*.

[56] *ibid.*, para.85

[57] *ibid.*, para.86.

[58] *ibid.*, para.88.

factors must normally be considered: (a) the characteristics and structure of the market; (b) the nature and magnitude of the efficiency gains; (c) the elasticity of demand; and (d) the magnitude of the restriction of competition.[59]

Where the purported benefits of an agreement are qualitative, the application of Article 81(3) is much more of a value judgment since the obtaining of a new or improved product is less susceptible to precise measurement.[60] Careful scrutiny will be required in situations where such qualitative benefits are needed to offset price increases.

No restrictions that are not indispensable

23–024 Turning to the negative criteria of Article 81(3), the first is that exemption cannot be given to restrictions of competition which are not indispensable to the attainment of the efficiency gains. In other words, the adverse effects on competition must be proportionate to the benefits made out for the agreement.[61] During the days of its exclusive powers in relation to exemption, the Commission adopted a robust approach to this particular requirement in order to extract modifications to agreements before granting authorisation. The new, decentralised, *ex post facto* system of enforcement gives less opportunity for this particular strategy.

The Commission's 2004 Guidelines indicate that the indispensability condition amounts to a two-fold test. First, the restrictive agreement as such must be reasonably necessary in order to achieve the efficiencies.[62] In other words, taking a market assessment and a realistic view of the parties' position, were there no other economically practicable and less restrictive means of achieving the benefits? The second stage is to ask whether individual restrictions within the agreement are reasonably necessary to achieve the efficiencies. The more restrictive the restraint, the more difficult it will be for the parties to establish its indispensability. Hardcore restrictions, such as those prohibited by block exemptions, are unlikely to gain protection.[63] However, for example, where the success of the product is uncertain, a restriction may be more likely to be seen as indispensable in order to secure gains. Any refusal of an exemption by the Commission without countering the evidence put forward by the parties in respect of indispensability will, of course, provide grounds for review of the decision.[64]

---

[59] *ibid.*, para.96.
[60] *ibid.*, para.103.
[61] Case T–17/93 *Matra Hachette*, n.35, above, para.135.
[62] *Guidelines*, n.38, above, para.73.
[63] *ibid.*, paras 79–80.
[64] See, e.g. Case C–360/92P *Publishers Association v Commission*, n.42, above. In the Court's view the Commission (and indeed the Court of First Instance) had failed to address properly the parties' claim that a collective system of fixed prices for books was indispensable.

No possibility of eliminating competition

The final criterion is that the agreement must not afford the **23–025** parties the possibility of eliminating competition in respect of a substantial part of the products in question. Its presence in the assessment process underlines a key point of competition policy. As the Commission's Guidelines observe:

"Ultimately the protection of rivalry and the competitive process is given priority over potentially pro-competitive efficiency gains which could result from restrictive agreements .... When competition is eliminated the competitive process is brought to an end and short-term efficiency gains are outweighed by longer term losses stemming *inter alia* from expenditures incurred by the incumbent to maintain its position (rent seeking), misallocation of resources, reduced innovation and higher prices."[65]

Elimination of competition has its own meaning within Article 81(3),[66] and will depend on the degree of competition existing prior to the agreement and the reduction brought about by the agreement.[67] A "realistic" market analysis is required, establishing the various sources of competition, the level of competitive constraint that they impose on the parties to the agreement and the impact of the agreement on this competitive restraint. Both actual and potential competition should be considered.[68]

If the pre-2004 application of this criterion is continued, then an agreement which clearly satisfies the other criteria in Article 81(3) is unlikely to fail under this one.

Block exemptions

An agreement that would otherwise be liable to prohibition under **23–026** Article 81(1) will automatically escape this fate if it fulfils the terms of a block exemption regulation. The use of block exemptions proliferated under the pre-2004 notification regime because parties to qualifying agreements were saved the uncertainty and delay of seeking individual exemption. The price to be paid for those

---

[65] *Guidelines*, n.38, above, para.105.

[66] See Case T–395/94 *Atlantic Container Line* [2002] E.C.R. II–875, [2002] 4 C.M.L.R.28 at para.330: "... the prohibition on eliminating competition is a narrower concept than that of the existence or acquisition of a dominant position, so that an agreement could be regarded as not eliminating competition within the meaning of Article [81](3)(b) of the Treaty, and therefore qualify for exemption, even if it established a dominant position for the benefit of its members."

[67] *Guidelines*, n.38, above, para.107. Hypothetical examples of the analysis required are given in para.116.

[68] *ibid.*, para.108.

advantages was that the regulations often imposed a degree of *dirigisme*, since the parties to a prospective agreement were inevitably under pressure to conduct their affairs so as to meet the terms and conditions tolerated or outlawed by a block exemption. However, even prior to the 2004 enforcement reforms, the style of block exemptions changed to promote a more flexible and market-based analysis.

The "new" approach is typified by the Regulation on vertical restraints.[69] The treatment of vertical agreements between market participants at different levels of economic activity has always been more lenient in EC law than that of horizontal agreements between competitors. In a typical arrangement between producer and distributor, the producer can concentrate on the efficiencies of production whilst the marketing of the product or service is undertaken by a specialist. The classic economic problems created by such systems (e.g., exclusive or selective distribution models) reflect their different effects on inter-brand and intra-brand competition. Depending on the amount of territorial protection provided, intra-brand competition can almost be wiped out as the privileged distributor will be the outlet for most customers. On the other hand, inter-brand competition may be stimulated by the efforts made by the distributor to promote the product. Vertical restraints may well encourage non-price competition and encourage improved quality in services. There may, however, be a question as to whether the efficiency savings of distribution agreements are passed on to customers. With these issues in mind, the Commission adopted a block exemption in 1999 declaring that Article 81(1) does not apply "to agreements or concerted practices entered into between two or more undertakings each of which operates, for the purposes of the agreement, at a different level of the production or distribution chain, and relating to the conditions under which the parties may purchase, sell or resell certain goods or services."[70]

In essence,[71] Regulation 2790 creates a presumption of legality for vertical agreements generally,[72] subject to two fundamental limitations. First, the "safe harbour" protection is lost if a particular market share is exceeded. This is set at 30 per cent and will usually refer to the market share of the supplier. However, in cases of

---

[69] Reg.2790/1999 on the application of Art.81(3) to categories of vertical agreements and concerted practices [1999] O.J. L336/21. It expires on May 31, 2010.

[70] *ibid.*, Art. 2(1).

[71] For a more detailed view, see A. Jones and B. Sufrin, *EC Competition Law Text, Cases and Materials* (2nd ed., OUP, Oxford, 2004), Ch.9.

[72] Thus addressing objections to the Commission's previous practice of drawing up Regulations for specific types of agreement. Notably, the umbrella protection of Reg.2790 covers selective distribution, a form of dealing not previously exempted by legislation.

exclusive supply obligations the relevant share relates to the buyer's market power.[73] Secondly, there is no protection for hardcore restraints. According to Article 4, the exemption does not apply to vertical agreements which "directly or indirectly, in isolation or in combination with other factors under the control of the parties, have as their object" a list of particular restraints. In line with the Commission's policy view of the risks attached to vertical agreements outlined above, the main targets are those restrictions which most significantly affect intra-brand competition. Thus provisions which impose resale price maintenance or which seek to restrict the territory into which, or the customers to whom, the buyer may sell will be treated as hardcore restraints.[74] So too will particular restrictions in selective distribution agreements.[75]

The nuanced approach taken by the block exemption can be demonstrated by a more detailed examination of the way in which the territorial and customer hardcore restrictions operate. As the Commission's Guidelines[76] explain, the hardcore restraint set out in Art. 4(b) seeks to prevent market partitioning by territory or by customer and covers not just direct limitations but also indirect measures aimed at inducing the distributor not to sell to certain customers. However, the Regulation identifies four exceptions, the first of which allows:

> "the restriction of active sales into the exclusive territory or to an exclusive customer group reserved to the supplier or allocated by the supplier to another buyer, where such a restriction does not limit sales by the customers of the buyer".

In other words, the key idea behind this exception is that some degree of parallel trade in the goods or services in question must be possible. As the Commission makes clear in its Guidelines,[77] the essential distinction is between "active" and "passive" sales. Examples of the first, prohibited, group are direct mail shots to individual customers in another exclusive distributor's territory or establishing a warehouse or distribution outlet in such a territory. On the other hand, passive, permitted, sales mean responding to unsolicited requests from individual customers or general advertising which reaches customers in other exclusive territories but which is a reasonable way of reaching customers outside those territories. Every distributor must be free to use the Internet to advertise or to

---

[73] Reg.2790, Art.3.
[74] *ibid.*, Art.4 (a) and (b), although the latter also identifies exceptions.
[75] *ibid.*, Art.4(c) and (d).
[76] Commission *Notice on Guidelines on Vertical Restraints* [2000] O.J. C291/1.
[77] *ibid.*, para.50.

sell products.[78] In the Commission's view, the fact that such advertising will have effects outside the distributor's territory is a result of the technology and should not be classed as "active". Sending a direct email to a customer in another territory would, however, be an infringement. Suppliers may nevertheless insist on quality controls for the use of the Internet in the same way that they might demand quality standards for a distributor's shop or general promotion.

As a final observation on block exemptions more generally, it must be stressed that the validity and enforceability of block exemptions is not called into question by the shift to the new institutional arrangements post-2004. National competition authorities, by virtue of Article 29(2) of Regulation 1/2003 may withdraw the benefit of a block exemption in respect of its territory (or part thereof) if that territory has all the characteristics of a distinct geographic market. National courts have no such power. Nor, obviously, can they modify the scope of a block exemption so as to extend them to agreements not within the exemption.[79]

National legislation and Article 81

23–027   Although the discussion of Article 81 has focused on the collusive behaviour of undertakings, there is also a well-established strand of case law dealing with situations in which restrictive practices and distortions of competition are linked in some way to specific legislation or the general legal framework of a Member State.[80] The Court of Justice has consistently maintained that although Article 81 is concerned solely with the conduct of undertakings, that provision, in conjunction with Article 10 of the Treaty, requires the Member States not to introduce or maintain in force measures, even of a legislative or regulatory nature, which may render ineffective the competition rules applicable to undertakings.[81] In the context of their economic policy, the activities of the Member States must observe the principle of an open market economy with free competition.[82] However, it is clear from the case law that a Member State will not be made liable for every anti-competitive consequence of

---

[78] *ibid.*, para.51.
[79] See *Guidelines on Application of Article 81(3)*, n.38, above, para.37.
[80] For the liability of Member States under Art.86 and discussion of situations involving public undertakings and undertakings entrusted with services of general economic interest, see Ch.26, below.
[81] Case 267/86 *Van Eycke* [1988] E.C.R. 4769; [1990] 4 C.M.L.R. 330, para.16; Case C–185/91 *Reiff* [1993] E.C.R. I–5801, para.14; Case C–153/93 *Delta Schiffahrts- und Speditionsgesellschaft* [1994] E.C.R. I–2517, para.15; Case C–35/96 *Commission v Italy (Re CNSD)* [1998] E.C.R. I–3851, [1998] 5 C.M.L.R. 889; Case C–35/99 *Arduino* [2002] E.C.R. I–1529, para.34; Case C–198/01 *Consorzio Industrie Fiammiferi (CIF) v Autorità Garante della Concorrenza e del Mercato* [2003] E.C.R. I–8055, para.45.
[82] Case C–198/01 *CIF*, above n.81, para.47. See P. Nebbia, case note (2004) 41 C.M.L.Rev. 839.

legislation, however tenuous or remote. Instead, the Court has indicated that liability can only attach to the Member State if either (a) it requires or favours the adoption of agreements, decisions or concerted practices contrary to Article 81, or reinforces their effects, or (b) deprives its own rules of the character of legislation by delegating to private economic operators responsibility for taking decisions affecting the economic sphere. Each of these two tests is discussed further below.

Requiring or favouring anti-competitive agreements, or reinforcing their effects

Although the Court repeatedly refers to this formula,[83] examples **23–028** of direct influence are unusual. However, an enforcement action brought by the Commission against Italy in relation to its rules governing customs agents provides a case in point.[84] According to Italian Act No.1612/1960 the National Council of Customs Agents (CNSD) was made responsible for setting the tariff for services provided by customs agents. This tariff was compulsory and anyone contravening it was liable to disciplinary action, including suspension or removal from the register of customs agents. The Commission took action against Italy on the basis that the tariff-fixing was a decision of an association of undertakings, for which the Member State was responsible. The Court agreed. Having found that in adopting the tariff, the CNSD infringed Article 81,[85] it went on to condemn Italy's direct participation, observing:

> "By adopting the national legislation in question, the Italian republic clearly not only required the conclusion of an agreement contrary to [Article 81] and declined to influence its terms, but also assists in ensuring compliance with that agreement".[86]

A more likely, if more problematic, application of the Court's formulation concerns the reinforcing of anti-competitive agreements since this could embrace looser forms of influence than those where the State directly requires anti-competitive conduct. However, it appears that the Court only entertains its application in relation to

---

[83] e.g. Case 229/83 *Leclerc v Sarl "Au Blé Vert"* [1985] E.C.R. 1; [1985] 2 C.M.L.R. 286, para.15; Joined Cases 209–213/84 *Ministère Public v Asjes* [1986] E.C.R. 1425; [1986] 3 C.M.L.R. 173, para.72; Case 311/85 *VZW Vereniging van Vlaamse Reisbureaus v VZW Sociale Dienst* [1987] E.C.R. 3801; [1989] 4 C.M.L.R. para.10; Case 254/87 *Syndicat des Libraires de Normandie v L'Aigle Distribution* [1988] E.C.R. 4457.

[84] Case C–35/96 *Commission v Italy (Re CNSD)*, n.81, above.

[85] The Court had no difficulty treating the activity of customs agent as economic and finding that the CNSD was an association of undertakings regardless of its national public law categorisation.

[86] [1998] E.C.R. I–3851, para.55.

legislation that adopts or reinforces previous private arrangements. In *Van Eycke*,[87] for example, holders of certain Belgian savings accounts could get tax exemptions provided that the bank kept interest rates to below maximum levels specified in a Royal Decree. This Decree was alleged to reinforce a previous arrangement between banks and financial institutions restricting interest rates. However, the Court of Justice left it to the national court to decide whether this was indeed the case.[88]

In later cases it proved difficult to persuade the Court of the reinforcing effects of national legislation. Thus, in *Meng*[89] the relevant German rules forbade insurance agents from sharing their commission with customers. Faced with the argument that this legislation restricted the competitiveness of agents, the Court declined to accept that it fell within the reach of Article 81 in combination with Article 10. In its view, the measure was no more than regulation by the State of the insurance market. This reluctance on the part of the Court coincided with its drawing of lines in the sand in relation to other areas of market regulation under EC law.[90]

Legislation deprived of its State character by delegation

23–029   Member States cannot absolve themselves from responsibility by simply delegating or transferring decision making powers to private bodies. The question is whether the legislation is deprived of its state character, a conclusion that the Court again appears reluctant to draw. In *Reiff*,[91] for example, it was called upon to consider German legislation under which the rates for the carriage of goods by road were set by tariff boards made up of industry representatives appointed by the relevant Minister. The Court noted that the industry representatives were not bound by instructions from the undertakings from which they were drawn and as such were not representatives of those undertakings. Moreover, the Minister was able to take part in meetings of the tariff boards and held powers to substitute his own tariffs in substitution for those of the boards. These features, the Court concluded, meant that the system was not a delegation of the State's powers.[92]

---

[87] Case 267/86 n.81, above.
[88] The evidence of direct reinforcement was much clearer in Case 311/85 *Van Vlaamse*, n.83, above.
[89] Case C–2/91 *Meng* [1993] E.C.R. I–5751; see also Case C–245/91 *Ohra* [1993] E.C.R. 5851.
[90] Notably Cases C–267–268/91 *Keck and Mithouard* [1993] E.C.R. I–6097; [1995] 1 C.M.L.R. 101. See Reich, "The 'November Revolution' of the European Court of Justice: *Keck, Meng* and *Audi* revisited" (1994) 31 C.M.L.Rev. 459.
[91] Case C–185/91, n.81, above.
[92] See also Joined Cases C–140, 141, 142/94 *DIP v Commune di Bassano del Grappa* [1995] ECRI–3257.

The objection to States delegating their powers to private bodies is found in the scope thereby conferred for those bodies to take anti-competitive decisions in their own favour. Consequently, it seems there will be no breach by the State if the transfer includes requirements to take public interest considerations into account. In the Italian customs agents case,[93] for example, the Court noted that Italian Act 1612/90 neither obliged nor even encouraged the members of the CNSD to take into account not only the interests of the undertakings which appointed them but also the general interest and the interests of undertakings in other sectors or users of the services in question.[94] Instead, the legislation "wholly relinquished"[95] to private economic operators the powers of the public authorities as regards the setting of tariffs. The Italian Republic had accordingly failed to fulfil its obligations under Articles 10 and 81 of the Treaty.

The most recent line of case law on delegation has concerned the fixing of scales of lawyers' fees and has raised again the interaction of competition and free movement provisions of the Treaty. Where, as in the *Arduino* case,[96] a Member State required a professional body to produce a draft tariff for minimum and maximum fees for lawyers' services, the Court rejected the view that this constituted delegation such as to trigger Articles 10 and 81. As a draft, the tariff could be reviewed by the appropriate Minister and no approval could be given without opinions from two public bodies. The Court found that the legislation setting out the process "does not contain either procedural arrangements or substantive requirements capable of ensuring, with reasonable probability, that, when producing the draft tariff the CNF [members of the Bar] conducts itself like an arm of the State working in the public interest."[97]

This ruling proved contentious, and subsequent references were **23–030** made by Italian courts on other aspects of the same legislation. In particular, they asked whether the *Arduino* ruling governed derogation from the fixed scales[98] or their application to out-of-court services.[99] Advocate General Poiares Maduro's Opinion in both cases sought to reconcile the refusal of the Court to apply the competition rules in *Arduino* with the criticisms voiced by other Advocates General.[1] Firstly, he identified that the danger in this area is that a legislative provision might have the sole purpose of protecting certain private interests from the elements of

---

[93] Case C–35/96, n.81, above.
[94] *ibid.*, para.44.
[95] *ibid.*, para.57.
[96] C–35/99 n.81, above.
[97] *ibid.*, para.39.
[98] Case C–94/04 *Cipolla v Fazari* (Judgment pending).
[99] Case C–202/04 *Macrino, Capodarte v Meloni* (Judgment pending).
[1] Especially Advocate General Jacobs in Joined Cases C–180/98 to C–184/98 *Pavlov* [2000] E.C.R. I–6451 and Advocate General Léger in Case C–35/99 *Arduino*, n.81 above.

competition, to the detriment of the public interest.[2] Secondly, Advocate General Poiares Maduro pointed to the need to ensure effective supervision by the State, including examination of the decision making process leading to adoption of the rule in question.[3] Whilst not wishing to disturb the particular ruling of the Court in *Arduino*, the Advocate General seized on the capacity within the Italian rules for courts to disregard the fixed fee scales, including for out-of-court services. Applying the *Pfeiffer*[4] ruling in relation to the interpretative duties of national courts, he therefore recommended that Article 81 in conjunction with Article 10 EC did not preclude national measures of the types in question so long as they had been subjected to effective supervision by the State and where interpretative powers of the national courts were exercised in accordance with Community law to limit the anti-competitive effects of those measures.[5]

It should be noted that professional services constitute an area of particular current difficulty for the purposes of application of Community competition rules. The Court's treatment of *Wouters* displayed a retreat to a "rule of reason" for justification, whilst its *Arduino* judgment also demonstrated a reluctance to apply the combined effects of Articles 81 and 10 without an obvious failure of State supervision in the legislative process.[6] The Commission has signalled its consideration of action under Article 86(3)[7] in this area.[8]

Further reading

Capobianco, A., "Information Exchange under EC Competition Law" (2004) 41 C.M.L.Rev. 1247.

Monti, G., "Article 81 EC and Public Policy" (2002) 39 C.M.L.Rev. 1057.

Odudu, O., "Interpreting Article 81(1): Object as Subjective Intention" (2001) 26 E.L.Rev. 60.

---

[2] Opinion in *Cipolla* and *Macrino*, (February 1, 2006), nn.98–99 above, para.33.
[3] *ibid.*, para.37.
[4] Joined Cases C–397/01 to C–403/01 *Pfeiffer* [2004] E.C.R. I–8835; see Ross,"Effectiveness in the European legal order(s):Beyond Supremacy to Constitutional Proportionality?" (2006) 31 E.L.Rev. 474.
[5] The Advocate General also concluded that the measures infringed the free movement of services.
[6] See also Case C–250/03 *Mauri* (ECJ Order February 17, 2005), where the Court applied *Arduino* and held that the State had exercised sufficient supervision over the professional examining process relating to advocates to conclude that it had not delegated its powers to private economic operators.
[7] The legislative powers conferred by this provision are considered more closely in Ch.26 below.
[8] See *"Professional Services—Scope for More Reform"* COM (2005) 405 final, which was a follow-up to the Commission's earlier *Report on Competition in Professional Services*, COM (2004) 83.

Odudu, O., "Interpreting Article 81(1): Demonstrating Restrictive Effect" (2001) 26 E.L.Rev. 261.

Rousseva, E., "Modernizing by Eradicating: How the Commission's New Approach to Article 81 EC Dispenses with the Need to Apply Article 82 EC to Vertical Restraints" (2005) 42 C.M.L.Rev. 587.

van de Gronden, J., "Rule of Reason and Convergence in Internal Market and Competition Law" in A Schrauwen (ed.), *Rule of Reason—Rethinking Another Classic of European Legal Doctrine* (Europa Law Publishing, Groningen, 2005), Ch.5.

Whish, R., "Regulation 2790/99: the Commission's New Style Block Exemption for Vertical Agreements" (2000) 37 C.M.L.Rev. 887.

ABUSE OF DOMINANCE: ARTICLE 82

Guide to this Chapter: Article 82 EC prohibits abuses by **24–001** dominant firms, individually or collectively. This Chapter broadly adopts the three-stage analysis that has tended to prevail in the Commission's decisions and the case law of the European Courts. First, the relevant market is defined, using tests from the case law and the Commission's 1997 Notice. Secondly, dominance is discussed, exploring the range of possible criteria and the particular significance of market shares. Thirdly, the concept of abuse as non-justifiable behaviour prejudicial to competition as an institution is examined in the light of a number of commercial practices. These include pricing policies, rebates, bonuses, tying arrangements and refusals to supply. The Chapter also identifies elements of the agenda to reform Article 82 in the wake of changes in other areas of EC competition law (e.g. cartels, mergers and enforcement). The Commission's Discussion Paper published in 2005 is likely to lead to policy and methodology more closely reflecting the economics-based and effects-oriented developments in those other fields. Where appropriate, implications of likely reform for the existing body of law under Article 82 are incorporated throughout the Chapter, together with a brief summary of key ongoing themes at its end.

Introduction: the purpose of Article 82

The Court of Justice has said that Articles 81 and 82 EC "seek to **24–002** achieve the same aim on different levels, *viz*, the maintenance of effective competition within the common market".[1] The "level" at which Article 82 operates is that of seeking to neutralise the adverse consequences of an absence of effective competition. In short, it is about restraining market power. Explaining the balance between the two leading Treaty competition provisions, the Court has observed:

> "[Article 81] of the Treaty applies to agreements, decisions and concerted practices which may appreciably affect trade between Member States, regardless of the position on the market of the undertakings concerned. [Article 82] of the Treaty, on the other hand, deals with the conduct of one or more economic operators consisting in the abuse of a position of economic strength which enables the operator concerned to hinder the maintenance of effective competition on the relevant market by allowing it to behave to an appreciable extent independently of its competitors, its customers and, ultimately, consumers."[2]

The rationale of Article 82 has been expressed more recently in the following terms by Advocate General Kokott:

> ". . . Article 82, like the other competition rules of the Treaty, is not designed only or primarily to protect the immediate interests of individual competitors or consumers, but to protect the *structure of the market* and thus *competition as such (as an institution)*, which has already been weakened by the presence of the dominant undertaking on the market. In this way, consumers are also indirectly protected. Because where competition as such is damaged, disadvantages for consumers are also to be feared."[3] (emphasis original, citations omitted).

This formulation is strikingly closer to the effects-led proposals being discussed as part of a review of Article 82 announced by the Commission in 2005.[4]

Article 82 provides:

---

[1] Case 6/72 *Europemballage and Continental Can v Commission* [1973] E.C.R. 215, 244; [1973] C.M.L.R. 199.
[2] Joined Cases C–395/96P and C–396/96P *Compagnie Maritime Belge Transports, Compagnie Maritime Belge SA and Dafra Lines A/S v Commission* [2000] E.C.R. I–1365, para.34, [2000] C.M.L.R.1076.
[3] Case C–95/04P *British Airways v Commission (other party Virgin Atlantic Airways)* (Opinion February 23, 2006, para.68; Judgment pending).
[4] Commissioned by the Chief Economist of DG Competition, the Economic Advisory Group for Competition Policy produced a report ("the EAGCP Report"—"An Economic Approach to Art.82") in July 2005. The thinking therein underpinned a speech by the Competition Commissioner, Neelie Kroes, to the Fordham Corporate Law Institute in New York on September 23, 2005. The Commission published a staffing paper in December 2005, "*DG Competition Discussion Paper on the Application of Art.82 of the Treaty to exclusionary abuses*", open for public consultation.

"Any abuse by one or more undertakings of a dominant position within the common market or in a substantial part of it shall be prohibited as incompatible with the common market in so far as it may affect trade between Member States. Such abuse may, in particular, consist in:

(a) directly or indirectly imposing unfair purchase or selling prices or other unfair trading conditions;

(b) limiting production, markets or technical development to the prejudice of consumers;

(c) applying dissimilar conditions to equivalent transactions with other trading parties, thereby placing them at a competitive disadvantage;

(d) making the conclusion of contracts subject to acceptance by the other parties of supplementary obligations which, by their nature or according to commercial usage, have no connection with the subject of such contracts".

The provision accordingly only prohibits abuse, not dominance itself. The abuses listed are purely illustrative, and not exhaustive.[5] Article 82 is directly effective and can be applied by national courts and competition authorities.[6]

Dominant undertakings may conduct their business efficiently, keeping down prices and maintaining or improving the quality of their product; indeed, the existence of a dominant position may have positive economic advantages, for example enabling the undertaking in question to pursue an adventurous research and development policy. On the other hand, insulation from competitive pressure is liable to encourage bad habits: for example an undertaking may choose to limit its output and charge higher prices. The function of Article 82 is to ensure that the market conduct of dominant undertakings remains consistent with the objectives of the EC Treaty. As the Court explained in the original *Michelin* case:

"A finding that an undertaking has a dominant position is not in itself a recrimination but simply means that, irrespective of the reasons for which it has such a dominant position, the undertaking concerned has a special responsibility not to allow its conduct to impair genuine undistorted competition on the common market".[7]

Moreover, whilst the fact that an undertaking is in a dominant position cannot deprive it of its entitlement to protect its own

---

[5] *Continental Can*, n.1, above, para.26; Joined Cases 6–7/73 *Istituto Chemioterapico Italiano SpA and Commercial Solvents Corpn v Commission* [1974] E.C.R. 223, [1974] 1 C.M.L.R. 309.

[6] Reg.1/2003, Arts 1(3), 5, 6.

[7] Case 322/81 *NV Nederlandsche Banden-Industrie Michelin v Commission* [1983] E.C.R. 3461, 3511; [1985] 1 C.M.L.R. 282. (Now known as *Michelin I*).

commercial interests when they are attacked, and whilst such an undertaking must be allowed the right to take such reasonable steps as it deems appropriate to protect those interests, such behaviour will not be allowed if its purpose is to strengthen that dominant position and thereby abuse it.[8] Dominant undertakings are thus subject to legal obligations which are not incumbent on those with less economic power.

Investigation under Article 82 classically follows three stages: first, defining the relevant market as the precondition[9] for the second stage, establishing dominance, followed by the final (and determinative) issue of whether there has been an abuse. This will also be the pattern followed for analysis in this Chapter. Other key elements of Article 82, such as the meaning of "undertaking" and the notion of affecting inter-State trade, have been dealt with earlier in Chapters 22 and 23 respectively.

However, two caveats apply. First, the separation of market, dominance and abuse is not to be undertaken mechanistically since there are linkages between the elements. Indeed, the question of whether conduct constituting the abuse can also be used as an index of dominance has been a long-running criticism of some enforcement decisions in practice. Secondly, the reforms being mooted for Article 82 would, if applied, focus more on foreclosure in the market and the protection of effective competition rather than over-formalised conceptual distinctions. There is already some divergence between older, but unretracted, judicial authority and modern Commission thinking. A "new" approach to Article 82 could force those differences into the open more starkly.

Establishing the relevant market

24–003   The EC Treaty defines neither markets nor dominance,[10] but the meaning and scope of these concepts have been clarified by the approach of the Commission and the case law of the Court of Justice. Although the latter is, of course, the sole arbiter of the meaning of EC law concepts, the Commission adopted a Market Definition Notice[11] in 1997 which has become an established reference point for day-to-day practice. Indeed, it has been relied upon by the Court of First Instance.[12] The point of a market assessment,

---

[8] Case 27/76 *The United Brands Company v Commission* [1978] E.C.R. 207, para.189; [1978] 1 C.M.L.R. 429.

[9] Case T–62/98 *Volkswagen v Commission* [2000] E.C.R. II–2707, para.230; [2000] 5 C.M.L.R. 948.

[10] *cf.* Art.66(7) ECSC which spoke of undertakings holding or acquiring "a dominant position shielding them against effective competition in a substantial part of the common market".

[11] [1997] O.J. C372/5; [1998] 1 C.M.L.R. 177.

[12] Joined Cases T–346/02 and T–347/02, *Cableuropa SA v Commission* [2003] E.C.R. II–4251, albeit in the context of a concentration.

and dominance within it, is to establish the extent to which a firm is subject to competitive pressure and restraint. This is done by differentiating between those performances of other undertakings which must be taken into account in evaluating the position of the undertaking subject to the investigation, and those which can safely be left out of account for this purpose. The two main questions to be answered are how wide a range of products, and what geographical distribution of offers, should be covered by the evaluation. The timing of the offers is also likely to be significant. These three criteria of relevance—product, geographic and temporal—are examined separately below.

The relevant product or service market

The definition of the product market is not always an easy matter **24–004** because, on the one hand, things which are physically dissimilar may be in competition with regard to a particular application (e.g., oil and gas domestic heating systems) while on the other hand, things which are physically similar may not be in competition (e.g., tyres for heavy vehicles and tyres for vans or motor cars).[13] It will usually be an advantage for the undertaking in question to have the product market defined as widely as possible, since the greater the variety of products involved, the more difficult it will be to make out the existence of a dominant position.

In the case law, the fundamental test for product differentiation is that of the interchangeability of product X and product Y as to their end uses. In the words of the European Court:

"... the possibilities of competition must be judged in the context of the market comprising the totality of the products which, with respect to their characteristics, are particularly suitable for satisfying constant needs and are only to a limited extent interchangeable with other products".[14]

The Court has stressed, however, that examination should not be limited to the objective characteristics of the products in question: "the competitive conditions and the structure of supply and demand on the market must also be taken into consideration".[15] In essence the test involves "cross-elasticity of demand". By this is meant the degree to which sales of X increase in response to an increase in the

---

[13] See Case 322/81 *Michelin I*, n.7, above and the discussion, below, of the issue of the relevant product market in that case.

[14] Case 31/80 *L'Oréal v PVBA De Nieuwe AMCK* [1980] E.C.R. 3775, 3793; [1981] 2 C.M.L.R. 235.

[15] Case 322/81 *Michelin I*, n.7, above, at 3505.

price of Y; high elasticity, i.e. a substantial increase in the quantity of
X sold when the price of Y rises only slightly, provides a clear
indication of competition between the two products. There is also
the narrower test in the case law of "peculiar characteristics and
uses", which makes the common sense point that highly specialised
products are likely to be found on a separate market.[16]

The Commission's Market Definition Notice of 1997[17] starts from
the premise that there are three main sources of competitive
restraints: demand substitution, supply substitutability and potential
competition. It specifically takes up the cross-elasticity approach,
treating demand substitution as the "most immediate and effective
disciplinary force on the suppliers of a given product, in particular in
relation to their pricing decisions."[18] In an attempt to provide firms
with transparency and certainty of guidance, the Commission's test[19]
is whether the parties' customers would switch to readily available
substitutes or to suppliers located elsewhere in response to a
hypothetical Small but Significant (in the range 5 to 10 per cent)
Non-transitory Increase in the Price of products (the so-called
SSNIP test). This test does not as such contradict the Court's case
law and should be seen more as a refinement of it to enable a more
robust economic measurement. Nor is it always applied by the
Commission.[20]

24–005   The SSNIP test to measure substitutability carries its own difficulties. Foremost among these is the so-called "cellophane fallacy".[21]
This problem arises because the SSNIP approach normally assumes
that the benchmark price for the analysis of substitutes comes from
prevailing prices. In Article 82 cases, the prevailing price may
already be high because the existence of dominance has allowed it to
be significantly increased. The danger, therefore, is that the market
may be assessed too widely as it might include products or geographic areas which only provide competitive restraints because the
prevailing price is already above competitive levels. The Commission
recognises this issue[22] and claims that in most cases a market

---

[16] e.g. the different groups of vitamins in Case 85/76 *Hoffman-La Roche v Commission* [1979]
E.C.R. 461, [1979] 3 C.M.L.R. 211.
[17] n.11, above.
[18] *ibid.*, para.13.
[19] *ibid.*, para.17.
[20] It was not used, for example, by the Commission in *Michelin II* [2001] O.J. L143/1, [2002] 5
C.M.L.R. 388. Michelin did not challenge the definition of market on appeal: Case
T–203/01*Manufacture française des pneumatiques Michelin v Commission* [2003] E.C.R.
II–4071, [2004] 4 C.M.L.R. 923
[21] Taking its name from a United States case involving a producer of cellophane: *United States
v E.I.du Pont de Namours & Co.* 351 U.S. 377, 76 S.Ct 994 (1956).
[22] See Market Definition Notice, n.11, above, para.19; also see *DG Competition Discussion
Paper on the Application of Art.82 of the Treaty to exclusionary abuses*, n.4 above, para.13–17.

decision will have to be based on the consideration of a number of criteria and different items of evidence.[23] Paragraphs 38 to 43 of the Market Definition Notice develop a number of factors which might be relevant to determining whether two products are demand substitutes: evidence of substitution in the recent past; quantitative econometric tests; views of customers and competitors; consumer preferences and marketing studies; barriers and costs associated with switching demand to potential substitutes; and different categories of customers and price discrimination.

The Court's position may be illustrated by its attitude to inter-changeability in the *United Brands*[24] case on the supply of bananas to certain of the Member States. The proceedings arose out of the condemnation of the supplier concerned, the United Brands Company (UBC), by the Commission on four counts of abusive conduct. According to the Commission, the product market consisted of "bananas of all varieties, where branded or unbranded". On the other hand, UBC argued that bananas formed part of the general market for fresh fruit: in other words, customers make their choice freely between bananas and other varieties of fruit on the basis of availability and relative prices. If this were so, even a very large supplier of bananas like UBC would not be at liberty to set prices within a wide range, since allowance would have to be made for the risk of potential customers altering their preferences (assuming of course that the same company did not control the supply of other fruits). The Court said that:

> "For the banana to be regarded as forming a market which is sufficiently differentiated from other fruit markets it must be possible for it to be singled out by such special features distinguishing it from other fruits that it is only to a limited extent interchangeable with them and it is only exposed to their competition in a way that is hardly perceptible".[25]

In the Court's view, the test was satisfied. It noted, in particular, the year-round excess of banana supplies over demand, which enabled marketing to be adapted to the seasonal fluctuations of other fruits. There was no evidence of "significant long term cross-elasticity", nor of "seasonal substitutability in general between the banana and all the seasonal fruits", the latter occurring only in Germany in respect of peaches and table grapes. Bananas, also, had characteristics enabling them to play an important part in the diet of a large section of the population comprising the very old, the very young and the sick. The constant needs of such consumers, and the limited and

---

[23] Market Definition Notice, n.11, above, para.25.
[24] n.8, above.
[25] [1978] E.C.R. 207, 272.

sporadic nature of the competition, justified recognition of the separate entity of the banana market.

Interchangeability may also be considered on the supply side of the market. This will certainly be the case where, according to the Market Definition Notice, its effects are equivalent to those of demand substitution in terms of effectiveness and immediacy.[26] It will be relevant, for example,[27] in situations where companies market a wide range of qualities or grades of one product; even if for a given final customer or group of consumers, the different qualities are not substitutable, the different qualities will be grouped into one product market, provided that most of the suppliers are able to offer and sell the various qualities immediately and without incurring significant additional costs or risks. The Commission cites paper[28] as a practical example, so that standard writing paper and high quality artwork paper might not be interchangeable in terms of demand yet would still fall within the same product group on the basis that paper plants are prepared to switch swiftly, with negligible costs and no particular difficulties of distribution, between the different qualities.

24–006   Supply-side considerations were responsible for the Court's quashing of the Commission's Decision in *Continental Can*.[29] The Commission had found that the acquisition of a Dutch packaging firm, TDV, by the Continental Can subsidiary, Europemballage Corporation, amounted to an abuse of the dominant position which the American firm enjoyed, through its German subsidiary, SLW, on the market in Germany for meat tins, fish tins and metal closures for glass jars; the abuse consisting of an unacceptable strengthening of SLW's position on the markets concerned since, in the Commission's view, TDV had been a potential competitor of SLW. The main ground for the annulment of the Decision was that the Commission had not shown convincingly why manufacturers, for example of tins for vegetables, condensed milk, olive oil or fruit juice could not, by making some adaptation to their product, enter the field as serious competitors to SLW, if the latter raised its prices unduly. The Commission was also criticised for not dealing adequately with the possibility that SLW's major customers might begin to manufacture the relevant types of container themselves. The essence of these objections was that potential competition from new products or new producers ("elasticity of supply") had not been ruled out.

On occasions it may be necessary to combine demand and supply substitution tests in order to define the relevant market. This was the case in *Michelin I*,[30] concerning a Decision of the Commission that

---

[26] Market Definition Notice, n.11. above, para.20.
[27] *ibid.*, para.21.
[28] *ibid.*, para.22.
[29] n.1, above.
[30] n.7, above

NBIM, the Dutch subsidiary of the Michelin tyre group, was guilty of infringing the predecessor of Article 82 because of certain terms included in the contracts under which it supplied dealers. The Court of Justice approved the Commission's definition of the market as that in new "replacement" tyres for heavy vehicles. This market was distinguishable from: (a) the market in "original equipment" tyres; (b) the market in tyres for cars and light vans; and (c) the market in retreads. As to (a), it was common ground that the structure of demand for replacements was entirely different from that for original equipment tyres, although they were identical products: while the former were supplied to dealers for retail sale, the latter were supplied to manufacturers to be fitted to new vehicles. As to (b), besides the lack of interchangeability at user level between car and van tyres and heavy vehicle tyres, there was again a difference of demand structures. For car and van drivers the purchase of tyres was an occasional event; whereas buyers of heavy vehicle tyres were normally haulage undertakings for which tyres represented an important business cost and which expected specialised advice and services from dealers. Nor was there elasticity of supply between tyres for light and heavy vehicles: the time and expenditure needed to switch production from one to the other made this impracticable as a way of responding to fluctuations in demand.[31] As to (c), the Court acknowledged that retreads were to some extent interchangeable, and hence in competition, with new tyres, but not sufficiently to undermine a dominant position on the market for the latter. Some consumers had reservations, whether rightly or wrongly, about the safety and reliability of retreads. In addition, a significant proportion of retreads used by transport undertakings were made to order from their own tyre carcasses. These would not compete with new tyres, since their production involved the provision of a service directly by retreading firms to the tyre owners. A further consideration was the dependence of the market for retreads, with respect to price and supply, on the market for new tyres. Every retread must have started life as a new tyre; and there was a limit to the number of times retreading could be done. So a dominant supplier of new tyres would have a privileged position *vis-à-vis* retreading undertakings.

Prior economic choices by a consumer may narrow the range of offers from which future demands have to be met, a phenomenon sometimes referred to as "lock-in". It operates where the opportunity cost of reversing a choice is felt to outweigh the advantages in the longer term of doing so. For instance, oil, gas and other

---

[31] The Court noted that in 1977, when there was a shortfall in the supply of heavy vehicle tyres, NBIM chose to grant an extra bonus rather than use surplus car tyre capacity to meet demand; [1983] E.C.R. 3461, 3506. *cf. Continental Can*, n.1, above, where the Decision of the Commission adverted to the barriers to market entry confronting possible competitors, notably the size of the necessary investments, but the Court did not think the burden of proof had been discharged.

domestic fuels may form a single market from the point of view of a person contemplating the installation of a new central heating system, but not after one or other system has been installed.

24–007   Similar reasoning may apply to so-called "aftermarkets" where a product or service follows on from another. An obvious example is where spare parts for a consumer durable are available only from the manufacturer. In such situations the spare parts from another product may be wholly useless for the durable in question. Moreover, supply-side substitution may be impossible because of the existence of intellectual property rights. In *Hugin*,[32] the Court found that most of the spare parts for Hugin cash registers were not interchangeable with parts made to fit any other type of machine, so that the operator of an independent maintenance, repair or reconditioning business, was entirely dependent on Hugin for supplies. The relevant market was, accordingly, that for Hugin spare parts required by such businesses. This was a crucial issue in the case, since the share held by Hugin of the market for cash registers as such was very modest.[33] A similarly restricted view of the relevant market was taken in *Hilti*,[34] where nails and cartridges were seen as distinct markets from the nail guns in which they were to be used as fastenings in the construction industry. This finding was based not on classes of user, as in *Hugin*, but primarily on the existence of independent suppliers of nails and cartridges for use in Hilti nail guns, together with the fact that nails and nail guns are not necessarily purchased together.

Market definition may also prove problematic in relation to raw materials which yield derivative or end products competing on wider markets. The Court first had to grapple with this question in *Commercial Solvents*.[35] The case arose from a complaint to the Commission by the Italian pharmaceutical firm, Zoja, that CSC, through its Italian subsidiary, Istituto, had refused to supply it with aminobutanol, the base product for the manufacture of the drug ethambutol, which was used in the treatment of tuberculosis. CSC contended, *inter alia*, that the relevant market could not be that for aminobutanol, on which its dominance was relatively easy to prove, since the derivative, ethambutol, formed part of a wider market for anti-tubercular drugs. With this the Court disagreed:

> "... it is in fact possible to distinguish the market in raw material necessary for the manufacture of a product from the

---

[32] Case 22/78 *Hugin Kassaregister AB v Commission* [1979] E.C.R. 1869; [1979] 3 C.M.L.R. 345. For criticism, see Baden Fuller "Article 86 EEC: Economic Analysis of the Existence of a Dominant Position" (1979) 4 E.L.Rev. 423, 426–427.

[33] Hugin had a market share of 12 per cent in the common market as a whole and 13 per cent in the UK Its largest competitor, the American company, National Cash Register had shares of 36 per cent and 40 per cent respectively.

[34] Case C–53/92P *Hilti A.-G. v Commission* [1994] E.C.R. I–667; [1994] 4 C.M.L.R. 614, upholding the findings of the Court of First Instance in Case T–30/89 [1991] E.C.R. II–1439; [1992] 4 C.M.L.R. 16.

[35] n.5, above.

market on which the product is sold. An abuse of a dominant position on the market in raw materials may thus have effects restricting competition in the market on which the derivatives of the raw material are sold and these effects must be taken into account when considering the effects of an infringement, even if the market for the derivative does not constitute a self-contained market".[36]

Thus, according to the Court, the raw material may constitute a relevant market in its own right; but it may still be valid, in determining whether a dominant position on that market has been abused, to take into account any anti-competitive effects which may have been felt on the market for the derivative. This problem of the relevance of potentially separate markets is especially acute in the context of vertically integrated organisations, whose behaviour in one market may produce or be directed towards effects in others.[37]

Although much of the case law concerns dominance held by producers or suppliers, it should be remembered that *buyer* power may also lead to abuses under Article 82. A leading example is provided by a case involving British Airways (BA). Following a complaint by Virgin Atlantic, the Commission investigated the allegedly abusive terms on which BA bought services from travel agents. The market here was therefore not BA's own services in operating air routes for passengers but, in the Commission's view, the services which airlines purchased from travel agents for the purposes of marketing and distributing their airline tickets. As the Court of First Instance concluded, upholding the Commission's findings:

"That specific nature of the services provided to airlines by travel agents, without any serious possibility of the airlines substituting themselves for the agents in order to carry out the same services themselves, is corroborated by the fact that, at the time of the events of which complaint is made, 85 per cent of air tickets sold in the territory of the United Kingdom were sold through the intermediary of travel agents.

The Court therefore considers that the services of air travel agencies represent an economic activity for which, at the time of the contested decision, airlines could not substitute another form of distribution of their tickets, and that they therefore constitute a market for services distinct from the air transport market."[38]

---

[36] *ibid.*, at 249–250.

[37] See also Case C–62/86 *AKZO v Commission* [1991] E.C.R. I–3359; [1993] 5 C.M.L.R. 215, discussed further, below, in relation to abusive predatory pricing.

[38] Case T–219/99 *British Airways plc v Commission* [2003] E.C.R. II–5917, paras 99–100; [2004] 4 C.M.L.R. 19; BA's further appeal, n.3, above, related only to the abuses, not market definition or dominance—see para.24–026 below.

The emergence of new products, services and forms of competition test the utility and robustness of market definition criteria. As an example, the "new economy" based on technological change can be seen as driven by competition over innovation rather than price—in which case the SSNIP test, discussed above, may be less than a precision tool. Such challenges to date over market definition have tended to occur in the arena of mergers and concentrations rather than Article 82, but this will inevitably change.[39]

Finally, it may be noted that *potential* competition does not usually feature in assessment of the relevant product market. As the Commission observes in its Market Definition Notice, although potential competition is a source of competitive restraint it will normally only come into consideration "once the position of the companies involved in the relevant market has already been ascertained, and when such position gives rise to concerns from a competition point of view."[40]

The geographic market

24–008   It is necessary in defining a relevant market for the purpose of Article 82 to identify the specific territory within which the interplay of supply and demand is to be considered. Once the relevant geographic market has been established, a further question arises as to whether it constitutes a sufficiently "substantial part of the common market" as specifically mentioned in the Treaty text.

The approach to the opening question is well settled. In the *British Airways* case[41] the Court of First Instance stated:

"consistent case law shows that it may be defined as the territory in which all traders operate in the same or sufficiently homogeneous conditions of competition in so far as concerns specifically the relevant products or services, without it being necessary for those conditions to be perfectly homogeneous."[42]

In its Market Definition Notice[43] the Commission lists the type of evidence relevant to determine a geographic market as follows: past evidence of diversion of orders to other areas, basic demand characteristics (such as preferences for national brands, language,

---

[39] See J. Lücking, "B2B E-Marketplaces: A New Challenge to Existing Competition Law Rules?" in C. Graham and F. Smith (eds), *Competition, Regulation and the New Economy* (Hart, Oxford, 2004), Ch.4.

[40] n.11, above, para.24.

[41] Case T–219/99, n.38, above.

[42] *ibid.*, para.108, citing Case T–83/91 *Tetra Pak v Commission* [1994] E.C.R. II–755, [1997] 4 C.M.L.R. 726, confirmed on appeal in Case C–333/94P *Tetra Pak v Commission (Tetra Pak II)* [1996] E.C.R. I–5951, [1997] 4 C.M.L.R. 662.

[43] n.11, above, paras 44–52.

culture and life style), views of customers and competitors, current geographic pattern of purchases, trade flows/patterns of shipments (where statistics are sufficiently detailed for the relevant products) and barriers and costs connected with switching orders to companies in other areas. The impact of transportation costs is particularly relevant for the last-mentioned consideration, especially in relation to bulky, low-value products.

It might have been expected that the significance of distinct national geographic markets would diminish as integration continued in the context of an evolving single Community-wide market.[44] Nevertheless, numerous examples can still be found of geographic markets which present sufficiently distinctive national conditions. In *Tiercé Ladbroke*[45] the Court of First Instance found that the conditions existing on the market in sound and pictures for horse races taking place in France had to be considered in relation to betting outlets. This was because the latter constituted the demand-side for sound and pictures for retransmission to final consumers (the punters), with the result that the conditions in which the downstream market in sound and pictures operated were determined by the conditions under which the main betting market was conducted.[46] The conditions in which the main betting market operated were characterised by close geographical links between punters and betting outlets, insofar as the mobility of punters is necessarily limited and marginal. The effect of that proximity was that competition between betting outlets developed within geographical areas which, considered as a whole, could not in any event extend beyond national boundaries, even though pictures of the races were available in France, Germany and Belgium. Since the geographic betting market was national, ie Belgium in this case, this also had to be the case for the ancillary market in sound and pictures.[47]

Having identified the appropriate geographic area, it must then be considered whether it amounts to a "substantial part" of the common market. The test to be applied is not the geographic extent of the territory in question but the economic importance of the market situated there. This was made clear in the *Sugar* judgment, where the Court said:

> "For the purpose of determining whether a specific territory is large enough to amount to 'a substantial part of the common market' . . . the pattern and volume of the production and

[44] Indeed, the whole of the EC was taken to be the geographical market in *Tetra Pak I*, n.42, above.
[45] Case T–504/93 *Tiercé Ladbroke v Commission* [1997] E.C.R. II–923, [1997] 5 C.M.L.R. 309.
[46] *ibid.*, para.103 of Judgment.
[47] *ibid.*, paras 106–107.

consumption of the said product as well as the habits and economic opportunities of vendors and purchasers must be considered".[48]

On this basis the Belgo-Luxembourg market and the southern part of Germany were considered a substantial part of the common market.

A market amounting to a substantial part of the common market may cover a number of Member States or a single Member State[49] or parts of one or more Member States. In a number of cases single ports or other economic hubs have been held to satisfy the "substantial" criterion. Thus, in *Merci Convenzionali Porto di Genova*[50] the Court held that regard must be had to the volume of traffic in the port in question and its importance in relation to maritime import and export operations as a whole in the Member State concerned.

The temporal market

24–009   Market power will only give a dominant position if it is capable of enduring for a considerable time. The prospect of substitutes becoming available in the short run limits freedom of action because of the risk of future defections by customers.[51] The market on which an undertaking operates may fluctuate from time to time with respect both to the range of products and the geographical area covered. For example, if the view had been taken in *United Brands* that the demand for bananas was seriously affected by the availability of various seasonal fruits, it might have concluded that bananas formed part of a series of different markets at different times of the year; and it would have followed that the position of UBC must be examined in relation to each of these markets. Another example is provided by *Commercial Solvents*, where it had been argued by CSC that the manufacture of ethambutol was possible by processes other than that involving aminobutanol. However, the Court held that the processes in questions were still of an experimental nature and incapable at the material time of being used for production on an industrial scale. They, therefore, did not constitute a realistic alternative for the customer, Zoja.[52]

---

[48] Joined Cases 40–48, 50, 54–56, 11, 113 and 114/73 *Suiker Unie v Commission* [1975] E.C.R. 1663, 1977; [1976] 1 C.M.L.R. 295.

[49] Case 322/81 *Michelin I*, n.7, above; Case C–323/93 *Centre d'Insémination de la Crespelle* [1994] E.C.R. I–5077; Case C–7/97 *Bronner* [1998] E.C.R. I–7791, [1999] 4 C.M.L.R. 112.

[50] Case C–179/90 [1991] E.C.R. I–5889, para.15; [1994] 4 C.M.L.R. 422. See also Case C–163/96 *Raso* [1998] E.C.R. I–533; [1998] 4 C.M.L.R 737 where the port of La Spezia was also held to a substantial part of the common market, being the leading Mediterranean port for container traffic. In Case C–163/99 *Commission v Portugal* [2001] E.C.R. I–2613 the three mainland airports of Portugal (Lisbon, Oporto and Faro) were taken together as a substantial part of the common market as regards the provision of intra-Community services.

[51] Gyeselen and Kyriazis, "Art.86: Monopoly Power Measurement Issue Revisited" (1986) E.L.Rev. 134, stress that market power only gives cause for concern if it is a long-run phenomenon.

[52] n.5, above, at 248.

Dominance

This central element of Article 82 refers to the economic power of **24–010** the undertaking concerned, which frees it from the constraints normally imposed by competing on the merits. This liberation is qualified, since the Court speaks of the "power to behave *to an appreciable extent* independently".[53] So understood, a dominant position is compatible with the survival of some competition.[54] It will be sufficient if the undertaking in question is able "at least to have an appreciable influence on the conditions under which that competition will develop, and in any case to act largely in disregard of it so long as such conduct does not operate to its detriment".[55] More recently, the Commission has explained dominance as conferring substantial market power to "influence market prices, output, innovation, the variety or quality of goods and services, or other parameters of competition on the market for a significant period of time.[56] Dominant positions often relate to the supply of goods or services, but they may also exist on the demand side.[57] Dominance may arise in relation to one undertaking or collectively[58] in relation to two or more undertakings.

The existence of dominance may derive from several factors which, taken separately, are not necessarily decisive. The most frequently used indicators are discussed below.

Market shares

The most important factor is the size of the undertaking's share of **24–011** the relevant market. According to the Court, extremely large market shares are in themselves, save in exceptional circumstances, evidence of the existence of a dominant position.[59] Not surprisingly, monopolies will constitute dominance even where that position is the result of statute or other legal means.[60] A market share of over 50 per cent will also in itself give rise to dominance.[61] Where the share of the market held by the undertaking is smaller, other factors take

---

[53] Used by the Court of Justice in *Michelin I*, n.7, above, and reiterated routinely since.

[54] Case 85/76 *Hoffman-La Roche*, n.16, above. Also, Case T–395/94 *Atlantic Container Line AB v Commission* [2002] E.C.R. II–875.

[55] Case 85/76 *Hoffman-La Roche*, n.16, above, at 520.

[56] *Discussion Paper on the Application of Article 82 of the Treaty to exclusionary abuses*, n.4, above, para.24.

[57] See Case 298/83 *C.I.C.C.E. v Commission* [1985] E.C.R. 1105, [1986] 1 C.M.L.R. 486; also Case T–219/99 *British Airways*, n.38, above.

[58] Collective dominance is discussed further, para.24–014 below. See Joined Cases C–395/96P and C–396/96P, n.2, above.

[59] Case 85/76 *Hoffmann-La Roche*, n.16, above; Case C–62/86 *AKZO*, n.37, above.

[60] Case 26/75 *General Motors Continental v Commission* [1975] E.C.R. 1367; [1976] 1 C.M.L.R. 95; Case 13/77 *INNO v ATAB* [1977] E.C.R. 2115; [1978] 1 C.M.L.R. 283; Case 41/83 *Italy v Commission (British Telecom)* [1985] E.C.R. 873; [1985] 2 C.M.L.R. 368; Case C–163/96 *Raso*, n.50, above

[61] Case C–62/86 *AKZO*, n.37, above, para.60.

on increased significance. Thus, in *United Brands*, the European Court cited as a consideration affording evidence of "preponderant strength" the fact that UBC's percentage of the market was several times greater than that of its nearest competitor (16 per cent), with the remaining market participants well behind.[62] Similarly, market shares below 40 per cent can be considered dominant, depending on the strength and numbers of competitors.[63]

In its 2005 Discussion Paper on possible reform,[64] the Commission points to the importance of market shares being qualified by an analysis of the degree of product differentiation in the market. Thus, to take its hypothetical example, it may be that a rival with a 10 per cent market share presents a greater competitive restraint on an undertaking with a 50 per cent market share than another competitor which might supply 20 per cent of the market. This might be the case where the allegedly dominant firm and the lower rival each sell premium branded products whereas the holder of the 20 per cent share sells a bargain brand.[65]

A tendency has also emerged towards the use of "super-dominance"[66] to describe market shares in some cases. The significance of this development seems to be that there may be either more types of conduct that become abusive at that threshold or that an abuse is more easily inferred.[67]

Barriers to market entry or expansion by rivals

24–012   Even a very large market share can be rapidly eroded when the market is penetrated by lively new competitors. A careful analysis of a dominant position should, therefore, refer to any advantages enjoyed by the undertaking in question, or to any difficulties in the way of potential market entrants, making it unlikely that the structure of the market will change radically in the shorter run. Barriers should also be considered in relation to the scope for

---

[62] [1978] E.C.R. 207, 282–283. See also Case 85/76 *Hoffmann-La Roche v Commission*, n.16, above, where the smallness of its competitors' market shares helped to establish the dominance of Roche on the markets for Vitamins A, C and E.

[63] The relevant market share in the *British Airways* case, n.38, above, was 39.7 per cent with BA having more than seven times the share of Virgin, its nearest competitor. In Case C–250/92 *Gottrup-Klim v Dansk Landbrugs* [1994] E.C.R. I–5641 the Court treated shares of 36 per cent and 32 per cent as insufficient on their own to constitute conclusive evidence of dominance.

[64] n.4, above.

[65] *ibid.*, para.33.

[66] See Joined Cases C–395/96P and C–396/96P, n.2, above, where Advocate General Fennelly expressly uses this term at para.137 of his Opinion. The Court's Judgment, para.119, pointedly refers to the fact that there was dominance amounting to 90 per cent with only one competitor. See also *1998 Football World Cup* [2000] O.J. L5/55, [2000] 4 C.M.L.R. 963.

[67] Discussed further, below, in relation to the concept of abuse and its application.

expansion by existing rivals. In its 2005 Discussion Paper, the Commission observed:

"If the barriers to expansion faced by rivals and to entry faced by potential rivals are low, the fact that one undertaking has a high market share may not be indicative of dominance. Any attempt by an undertaking to increase prices above the competitive level would attract expansion or new entry by rivals thereby undermining the price increase.

In assessing whether expansion or entry has been, would have been or is likely to be timely, the Commission will look at whether any such expansion or entry has been or would be or will be sufficiently immediate and persistent to prevent the exercise of substantial market power. The appropriate time period depends on the characteristics and dynamics of the market. The period of time needed for undertakings already on the market to adjust their capacity can be used as a yardstick to determine this period. Expansion or entry which is not of sufficient scope and magnitude is not likely to constitute an effective constraint on the undertaking concerned. Small-scale entry, for instance, into some market 'niche', may not be considered sufficient."[68]

Barriers to entry and expansion may accordingly require examination of the history of the industry in question.

The presence of barriers can be found across a wide spectrum of situations. Thus, it may be that an undertaking controls essential patents or know-how; or because, like United Brands, it is vertically integrated, with privileged access to supplies, means of transport and distribution outlets[69]; or because, like Michelin, it has a well-developed network of commercial representatives providing continuous contact with customers[70]; or because of its technical superiority,[71] its range of products[72] or a strong brand image resulting from advertising.[73] Established consumer preferences may also act as barriers, as in *British Midland/Aer Lingus*[74] where the Commission noted that Irish nationals preferred to use the national flagship airline.

---

[68] n.4, above, paras.34–35.

[69] n.8, above, at 278–280.

[70] n.7, above, at 3511. See also the reference to "a highly developed sales network" in *Hoffmann-La Roche*, n.16, above, at 524.

[71] Case C–53/92 P *Hilti*, n.34, above.

[72] *Michelin I*, n.7, above.

[73] *United Brands*, n.8, above.

[74] Dec. 92/213 [1992] O.J. L96/34; [1993] 4 C.M.L.R. 596. Aer Lingus' market share was also high, being 75 per cent of the London Heathrow—Dublin route.

From the point of view of a potential competitor the chief difficulty in overcoming such advantages would be that of cost. Very large resources may be needed, for example, to finance independent research or countervailing advertising. These are often sunk costs which cannot be recovered in the case of exit and therefore may entry more risky. The crucial consideration will be the range within which the undertaking is free to fix its prices without making it commercially attractive for others to risk the investment required in order to mount a challenge. Also in the present context it is important to bear in mind the time factor. The possibility that, at the end of a very long period of development, another undertaking may succeed in establishing itself as a serious competitor would not normally be sufficient to impair an existing dominant position.[75]

Conduct and performance of the undertaking

24–013   Market shares and barriers to entry and expansion are indicative of the structure of the market and the state of competition in it. A rather less clear issue in relation to the criteria for measuring dominance concerns the relevance of an undertaking's conduct or performance. Certainly, there is a real risk of circularity if the fact that particular behaviour, alleged to be abusive, could occur at all becomes the rationalisation for the existence of dominance.

Nevertheless, there is evidence that conduct or performance can affect decisions in relation to market power under Article 82. For example, the Court of First Instance in *Hilti*[76] endorsed the Commission's view that it was highly improbable that a non-dominant undertaking would have acted in the way that Hilti did in terms of its intellectual property rights. The Commission also claimed in *Michelin II*[77] that the firm's behaviour was strong evidence of dominance. The Court has also rejected arguments that tried to plead the absence of dominance on the basis of poor profitability.[78] Indeed, in its view, the ability to weather losses, at least temporarily, might suggest the exact opposite, i.e. that the undertaking has the economic strength to absorb them.

The concept of joint or collective dominance

24–014   The concept of an undertaking was examined in Chapter 22. It will be remembered that legally distinct companies may be regarded as forming a single undertaking, if in practice they are subject to

---

[75] See the very full analysis of those features of UBC's banana operation which the European Court regarded as contributing to its retention of a large market share: [1978] E.C.R. 207, 278–281.

[76] n.34, above.

[77] n.20, above.

[78] e.g. both *Michelin I*, n.7 above, and *United Brands*, n.8, above; also Case C–497/99P *Irish Sugar v Commission* [2001] E.C.R. I–5333.

common control. The importance of this principle in the context of Article 82 is that, in determining whether the conduct of one member of a group constitutes an abuse of a dominant position on a relevant market within the common market, it may be possible to take into account the economic strength of other members of the group, some or all of them established in third countries. For example, in *Commercial Solvents*[79] it was CSC's control over world supplies of aminobutanol that gave Istituto a dominant position on the common market; CSC was legally answerable for Istituto's refusal to supply Zoja.

The more controversial use of the phrase "one or more undertakings" in Article 82 involves its attachment to so-called joint or collective dominance by non-connected firms. After early resistance by the European Court to the idea,[80] it is now clear that collective dominance is embraced by Article 82. The first real judicial endorsement came from the Court of First Instance in *Italian Flat Glass*,[81] where it stated:

> "There is nothing, in principle, to prevent two or more independent economic entities from being, on a specific market, united by such economic links that, by virtue of that fact, together they hold a dominant position *vis-à-vis* the other operators on the same market. This could be the case, for example, where two or more independent undertakings jointly have, through agreements or licences, a technological lead affording them the power to behave to an appreciable extent independently of their competitors, their customers and ultimately of their consumers".[82]

On the facts, the Commission had failed to adduce sufficient evidence to make out its claim. Nevertheless, the principle of collective dominance has been subsequently developed by the Court of Justice in the context both of Article 82 and the Merger Regulation.[83]

The leading statement by the Court is found in the *Compagnie Maritime Belge* cases[84]:

---

[79] Cases 6–7/73, n.5, above.
[80] See Case 85/76 *Hoffmann-La Roche*, n.16, above; also Case 247/86 *Alsatel* [1988] E.C.R. 5987; [1990] 4 C.M.L.R. 434, where the Court did not take up the Commission's arguments.
[81] Joined Cases T–68, 77 and 78/89 *SIV v Commission* [1992] E.C.R. II–1403; [1992] 5 C.M.L.R. 302.
[82] *ibid.*, para.358.
[83] Reg.139/2004 on the control of concentrations between undertakings [2004] O.J. L24/1; supplemented by implementing Reg.802/2004 [2004] O.J. C77/1 together with Notices on the interpretation of provisions.
[84] n.2, above.

". . . the expression 'one or more undertakings' in Article [82] of the Treaty implies that a dominant position may be held by two or more economic entities legally independent of each other, provided that from an economic point of view they present themselves or act together on a particular market as a collective entity."[85]

To establish such a collective entity it is necessary to examine the economic links or factors which give rise to a connection between the undertakings concerned. The existence of an agreement or concerted practice within Article 81(1) is not of itself sufficient to establish such a link. However:

"The existence of a collective dominant position may . . . flow from the nature and terms of an agreement, from the way in which it is implemented and, consequently, from the links or factors which give rise to a connection between undertakings which result from it. Nevertheless, the existence of an agreement or of other links in law is not indispensable to a finding of a collective dominant position; such a finding may be based on other connecting factors and would depend on an economic assessment and, in particular, on an assessment of the structure of the market in question."[86]

These cases confirm that a joint dominant position consists in a number of undertakings being able together, in particular because of factors giving rise to a connection between them, to adopt a common policy on the market.[87] In *Almelo*, for example, the issue left to be determined by the national court was whether the requisite links between the regional electricity suppliers in question were "sufficiently strong". One such factor was that the contracts between the regional distributors and local purchasers had common exclusive purchasing conditions. The links allegedly present in the *Flat Glass* case included structural ties relating to production in the form of systematic exchange of products between the three producers. In *Irish Sugar*[88] the Court of First Instance did not disturb the Commission's findings that Irish Sugar occupied a joint dominant position on the Irish granulated sugar market with Sugar Distribution Holdings

---

[85] *ibid.*, para.36.
[86] *ibid.*, para.46.
[87] Case C–393/92 *Almelo* [1994] E.C.R. I–1477, para.42; Case C–96/94 *Centro Servizi Spediporto v Spedizioni Marittima del Golfo* [1995] E.C.R. I–2883, paras 32–33; [1996] 4 C.M.L.R. 613; Joined Cases C–140–142/94 *DIP* [1995] E.C.R. I–3257, para.26; [1996] 4 C.M.L.R. 157; Case C–70/95 *Sodemare v Regione Lombardia* [1997] E.C.R. I–3395, paras 45–46; [1998] 4 C.M.L.R. 667.
[88] Case T–228/97 *Irish Sugar plc v Commission* [1999] E.C.R. II–2969; upheld by the ECJ in Case C–497/99P, n.78, above.

(SDH), the latter being the parent company of the principal distributor (SDL) in that market. The factors relied upon by the Commission were Irish Sugar's 51 per cent shareholding in SDH, its representation on the boards of SDH and SDL, the policy-making structure of the companies and the communication process established to facilitate it, and the direct economic ties constituted by SDL's commitment to obtain its supplies exclusively from Irish Sugar and the latter's financing of all consumer promotions and rebates offered by SDL to its customers.

The precise application of collective dominance for the purposes **24–015** of Article 82 is complicated by the fact that the case law, at least prior to the revised Merger Regulation of 2004, was intertwined with that developed in relation to concentrations. The essential difference between the provisions in this context is that whereas Article 82 is concerned only with abuses of market power, the rationale of the Regulation is based on the curbing of prospective concentrations which would undermine an effective market structure. This might explain any apparent divergence in the language used in the case law from the two areas. In *France and others v Commission*,[89] the first case to uphold the application of joint dominance to the Merger Regulation,[90] the Court of Justice referred to the need to establish an impediment to effective competition arising in particular from "correlative factors" existing between the undertakings involved in the concentration.

In the *Airtours*[91] case, also brought in relation to the Merger Regulation prior to its 2004 amendment, the CFI fleshed out the conditions for collective dominance as follows:

"As the applicant has argued and as the Commission has accepted in its pleadings, three conditions are necessary for a finding of collective dominance as defined:

— first, each member of the dominant oligopoly must have the ability to know how the other members are behaving in order to monitor whether or not they are adopting the common policy. As the Commission specifically acknowledges, it is not enough for each member of the dominant oligopoly to be aware that interdependent market conduct is profitable for all of them but each member must also have a means of knowing whether the other operators are adopting the same strategy and whether they are maintaining it. There must, therefore, be sufficient market transparency for all members of the dominant oligopoly to be

---

[89] Joined Cases C–68/94 and C–30/95 [1998] E.C.R. I–1375, para.221; [1998] 4 C.M.L.R. 829.
[90] This being the previous version: Reg.4064/89 [1989] O.J. L395/1.
[91] Case T–342/99 *Airtours plc v Commission* [2002] E.C.R. II–2585.

aware, sufficiently precisely and quickly, of the way in which the other members' market conduct is evolving;

— second, the situation of tacit coordination must be sustainable over time, that is to say, there must be an incentive not to depart from the common policy on the market. As the Commission observes, it is only if all the members of the dominant oligopoly maintain the parallel conduct that all can benefit. The notion of retaliation in respect of conduct deviating from the common policy is thus inherent in this condition. In this instance, the parties concur that, for a situation of collective dominance to be viable, there must be adequate deterrents to ensure that there is a long-term incentive in not departing from the common policy, which means that each member of the dominant oligopoly must be aware that highly competitive action on its part designed to increase its market share would provoke identical action by the others, so that it would derive no benefit from its initiative . . .

— third, to prove the existence of a collective dominant position to the requisite legal standard, the Commission must also establish that the foreseeable reaction of current and future competitors, as well as of consumers, would not jeopardise the results expected from the common policy."[92]

The introduction of the revised Merger Regulation in 2004 with a more detailed set of appraisal criteria for evaluating concentrations suggests that future case law might not encourage such an easy interchangeability between it and Article 82 in relation to the conceptualisation and requisite proof of collective dominance.[93]

The concept of an abuse

24–016   The wording of Article 82 indicates that the existence of a dominant position does not in itself attract the prohibition contained in the Article.[94] But whilst not unlawful, it is clear that dominance creates special obligations for the undertakings concerned,[95] so that they must not abuse their power. There is no definition of abuse in

---

[92] *ibid.*, para.62.

[93] It may be noted that the Commission adopts the *Airtours* criteria for its discussion of Art.82 collective dominance in its 2005 Discussion Paper, n.4, above, paras.48–50.

[94] *cf.* Art.86 (Ch.26, below), where the Court at one point developed an "inevitable abuse" doctrine in relation to certain situations involving the creation and exercise of exclusive rights; see principally Case C–41/90 *Höfner v Macrotron* [1991] E.C.R. I–1979; [1993] 4 C.M.L.R. 306; also Case C–55/96 *Job Centre Coop* [1997] E.C.R. I–7119, paras 34–35; [1998] 4 C.M.L.R. 708.

[95] See the passage quoted from the *Michelin I* Judgment, text accompanying n.7, above.

the EC Treaty, and the instances listed in Article 82 itself (such as unfair pricing or limiting production) are only non-exhaustive examples. However, the Court of Justice gave what has become a benchmark test of abuse in *Hoffmann-La Roche*:

"The concept of abuse is an objective concept relating to the behaviour of an undertaking in a dominant position which is such as to influence the structure of a market where, as a result of the very presence of the undertaking in question, the degree of competition is weakened and which, through recourse to methods different from those which condition normal competition in products or services on the basis of the transactions of commercial operators, has the effect of hindering the maintenance of the degree of competition still existing in the market or the growth of that competition".[96]

Recurring conceptual issues
A number of general observations may be made from this starting **24-017** point and its later applications.

Firstly, there is a potential tension in the notion of abuse in so far as it is not expressly directed at the protection of one particular set of interests.[97] So-called exploitative abuses, such as excessive pricing, tend to harm consumers. On the other hand, anti-competitive conduct, such as predatory pricing, tying contracts or refusals to supply,[98] may more directly affect other actual or potential firms in the market (whilst having repercussions for consumers). Both types of abuse are caught by Article 82. In addition, it was made clear at an early stage in the case law that the provision was not confined to behavioural abuses but could also cover the strengthening of dominance by structural means such as the acquisition of competitors.[99]

Secondly, abuse is an objective concept, generally requiring neither an intention to harm nor any morally reprehensible dimension. However, intent may be of real significance in relation to specific

---

[96] Case 85/76, n.16, above at 541.
[97] Although in Case C–7/97 *Bronner*, n.49, above, Advocate General Jacobs observed that the "primary" purpose of Art. 82 was to protect consumers, rather than safeguarding the position of particular competitors. See also Advocate General Kokott's observations in C–95/04P *British Airways v Commission*, quoted at text accompanying n.3, above.
[98] These examples are also often referred to as "exclusionary" abuses; this group exclusively forms the target of the Commission's 2005 Discussion Paper for reform, n.4, above.
[99] Case 6/72 *Continental Can*, n.1, above. However, this application of Art.82 has been effectively superseded by the creation of merger control at EC level, at least where concentrations having a community dimension within the meaning of Reg.139/2004 are concerned; n.83, above.

abuses, such as predatory pricing.[1] There is no formal exception incorporated in to the text of Article 82 that corresponds to Article 81(3), but conduct may escape condemnation as abuse if it can be objectively justified. For example, there is considerable room for debate whether particular conduct is a firm's rational response to meet the challenge of competition or if it is abusive. This problem is particularly highlighted in developments concerning discriminatory pricing,[2] discussed below. Other potential justifications may arguably stem from efficiencies, at least for some types of abuse that are non-exploitative.

24–018   A third thread of difficulty relates to the question of causation. Must the undertaking have used its power as the means of achieving the result which is regarded as abusive? Ever since *Continental Can* it has been clear that the Court does not require a strict causal relationship of this type. As a result, an allegation of abuse cannot be negated by evidence that the same conduct is pursued by non-dominant firms or is a normal practice in the market concerned. Moreover, the abuse does not necessarily have to be committed in the same market as the one in which the firm is dominant. It may affect downstream or neighbouring markets, as in the *CBEM* case,[3] where action by an undertaking dominant on the television broadcasting market had abusive effects in the telemarketing services market. Conversely, conduct on a different market which strengthens the undertaking's position in the dominated market will also be caught.[4] In some situations the reach of Article 82 may go even further, so long as there are some "associative" links between the markets in which the dominance and abuse are found.

The extent of this more controversial notion was tested in the *Tetra Pak* litigation. The Court of First Instance[5] had upheld a Commission decision fining Tetra Pak for abusing its dominant position in the markets for aseptic liquid repackaging machinery and aseptic cartons. The abusive conduct included predatory pricing and tying contracts undertaken on the non-aseptic machinery and carton markets in which Tetra Pak had not been established as dominant. According to the Court of First Instance, application of Article 82 was justified by the situation on the different markets and the close associative links between them, noting that Tetra Pak occupied a "leading position" in the non-aseptic market whilst holding a quasi-

---

[1] Discussed further below; see para.24–021 below.
[2] e.g. Case T–228/97 *Irish Sugar*, [1999] E.C.R. II–2969.
[3] Case 311/84 *Centre Belge d'Etudes de Marché Télémarketing v CLT* [1985] E.C.R. 3261; [1986] 2 C.M.L.R. 558.
[4] Case C–310/93P *BPB Industries and British Gypsum v Commission* [1995] E.C.R. I–865; [1997] 4 C.M.L.R. 238. See also Case T–219/99 *British Airways*, n.38, above; although the case was brought in relation to a loyalty reward system operated in the market of airline travel agency services, the 'real' fruits of that conduct would be for the benefit of BA (especially *vis-à-vis* Virgin) in the different market of passenger air travel.
[5] n.42, above.

monopolistic 90 per cent share of the aseptic sector, and that its customers in one sector were also potential customers in the other. On appeal, the Court of Justice observed:

> "It is true that application of Article [82] presupposes a link between the dominant position and the alleged abusive conduct, which is not normally present where conduct on a market distinct from the dominated market produces effects on that distinct market. In the case of distinct, but associated, markets, as in the present case, application of Article [82] to conduct found on the associated, non-dominated, market and having effects on that associated market can only be justified by special circumstances".[6]

However, it then adopted the "associative" approach of the Court of First Instance to find that such special circumstances existed, concluding that Tetra Pak was placed in a situation "comparable to that of holding a dominant position on the markets in question as a whole".[7]

Fourthly, the notion of abuse is coming under increasing scrutiny in the context of the economics and effects-led arguments which have dominated reforms elsewhere in EC competition law. In the extract from *Hoffman-La Roche* quoted at the start of this section, the Court of Justice referred to abuses being judged against "normal" competition, an arguably question-begging view that perhaps chimes with rather loose notions of "workable" or "unfair" competition that might emanate from lawyers rather than economists. As the discussions about reforming Article 82 develop, it is increasingly clear that one of the areas of economic debate concerns the extent to which a real anti-competitive effect must be felt on the market before an abuse should be considered established. The case law at present is not entirely unequivocal. In one of the fullest discussions of the point, the CFI in *Michelin II*[8] observed:

> "Unlike Article 81(1) EC, Article 82 EC contains no reference to the anti-competitive aim or anti-competitive effect of the practice referred to. However, in the light of the context of Article 82 EC, conduct will be regarded as abusive only if it restricts competition."[9]

This might be seen as offering comfort to those seeking to prevent Article 82 applying to only foreseeable or potential harm. However, the Court of First Instance then recapitulated on this by stating:

---

[6] [1996] E.C.R. I–5951, para.27.
[7] *ibid.*, para.31.
[8] n.20, above.
[9] *ibid.*, para.237.

> "it is sufficient to show that the abusive conduct of the undertaking in a dominant position tends to restrict competition *or, in other words*, that the conduct is *capable of* having that effect."[10] [emphasis added]

The Court of First Instance's subsequent conclusion did little to kill off the doubts about the role of intent and effect in the measurement of abuse:

> "It follows that, for the purposes of applying Article 82 EC, establishing the anti-competitive object and the anti-competitive effect are one and the same thing . . . If it is shown that the object pursued by the conduct of an undertaking in a dominant position is to limit competition, that conduct will also be liable to have such an effect."[11]

Apart from indicating that object and effect have a close correlation, this formulation unfortunately does not explain whether it is a general rule for all abuses, whether object or intent are necessary conditions, or whether there are such things as *per se* abuses. The latter issue has also become a pressing policy concern in the light of the trend towards recognition of super-dominance.

A number of the issues raised by these recurrent themes are applied below in the course of a more detailed view of conduct frequently treated as abusive in the case law.

Examples of abuses

24–019   The following, non-exhaustive, examples represent the most frequent or important manifestations of abuses in the case law. The subdivisions therefore reflect a variety of different commercial practices rather than a typology of conceptual categories such as exploitative versus exclusionary or anti-competitive abuses.

Pricing policies

24–020   **(a) Excessively high prices.**   This is probably the first example of an abuse of a dominant position which would occur to most people, because of the direct impact felt by consumers. However, competition authorities are not usually over-anxious to intervene on high prices alone. In particular, it is not easy to formulate theoretically adequate and practically useful criteria for determining where the line between fair and unfair prices should be drawn in a given case.

---

[10] *ibid.*, para.239.
[11] *ibid.*, para.241.

Nevertheless, the Court of Justice in its *United Brands* judgment spoke of a price being excessive "because it has no reasonable relation to the economic value of the product supplied".[12] It went on to approve as one test of excess over economic value, a comparison between the selling price of a product and its cost of production, which would disclose the size of the profit margin. As the Court said, the question was "whether the difference between the costs actually incurred and the price actually charged is excessive" and if so, "whether a price has been imposed which is either unfair in itself or when compared to competing products".

Such a test may attract criticism. High profits may be the result of a firm's efficiency which deserves to be rewarded (although it is reasonable to require some element of cost saving to be handed on to consumers); while low profits may be the result of inefficiency, in which case prices may still be excessive. The task of assessing how efficiently a dominant undertaking employs its resources is likely to be a formidable one.[13] There is also the question of the proportion of indirect costs. and general expenditure which should be allocated to the cost of putting a particular product on the market. The structure of the undertaking, the number of subsidiaries and their relationship with each other and with their parent company, may cause further complications. However, it is clear that the Court was aware of these problems and intended the test to be applied sensitively, with due regard to its limitations. In the case of the banana market, the Court was of the opinion that a satisfactory estimate could have been arrived at.

From *United Brands* it seems that any attempt to establish an abuse in the form of unfairly high prices should normally proceed by way of an analysis of the cost structure of the undertaking concerned. However, other methods of proving unfairness will continue to be acceptable, if the Court is satisfied of their appropriateness in the specific circumstances of the case. For example, in *Bodson*[14] the Court noted that since in more than 30,000 communes in France the provision of the relevant funeral services was unregulated or operated by the communes themselves, there would be comparisons available to provide a basis for assessing whether the prices charged by the holders of exclusive concessions for those services were

---

[12] [1978] E.C.R. 207, 301, echoing its judgment in *General Motors*, n.60, above.
[13] See Commission Decs COMP/A.36.568 *Scandlines v Port of Helsingborg* and COMP/A.36.570 *Sundbusserne v Port of Helsingborg* (both July 23, 2004), where the Commission rejected complaints lodged by ferry operators alleging abuses involving excessive port fees. The Commission cited insufficient evidence and the lack of useful benchmarks for establishing excessive levels.
[14] Case 30/87 *Bodson v SA Pompes funèbres des regions liberées* [1988] E.C.R. 2479; [1989] 4 C.M.L.R. 984.

indeed excessive.[15] Legislation may also on occasion lend assistance
to the evaluative task.[16]

24–021 **(b) Predatory prices.** A dominant seller may adopt a tactic of
pricing its goods very low, or even below cost, in order to drive out
of business competitors with more limited resources who cannot for
long sustain the losses occasioned by matching the terms it is
offering. Consumers, of course, benefit from price reductions in the
short run but risk finding themselves even more at the mercy of the
dominant undertaking after it has captured a larger share of the
market.

The application of Article 82 to predatory price cutting was first
clearly established In the *AKZO* case.[17] AKZO was the EC's major
supplier of a chemical substance, benzoyle peroxide, which is used in
the manufacture of plastics and in the blanching of flour.[18] The
Commission found that, in order to deter ECS, a small competitor in
the market in flour additives, from expanding its business into the
market in organic peroxides for plastics, AKZO had first threatened
and later implemented a campaign of price cuts aimed at important
customers of ECS in the former market. If successful, the campaign
would not only have eliminated ECS as a competitor in the supply of
organic peroxides; it would also have discouraged other potential
challenges to AKZO's established position. AKZO's appeal against
the decision was dismissed.[19]

Having indicated that not all forms of price competition were
legitimate, the Court proceeded to set out a twofold test for
determining whether an undertaking has practised predatory pricing,
stating:

> "Prices below average variable costs (that is to say, those which
> vary depending on the quantities produced) by means of which
> a dominant undertaking seeks to eliminate a competitor must
> be regarded as abusive. A dominant undertaking has no interest
> in applying such prices except that of eliminating competitors
> so as to enable it subsequently to raise its prices by taking
> advantage of its monopolistic position, since each sale gener-
> ates a loss, namely the total amount of the fixed costs (that is to

---

[15] See also Case 395/87 *Ministère Public v Tournier* [1989] E.C.R. 2521; [1991] 4 C.M.L.R. 248
and Cases 110 and 241–242/88 *Lucazeau v SACEM* [1989] E.C.R. 2811, paras 38 and 25
respectively of the Court's Judgments; [1991] 4 C.M.L.R. 248.

[16] Case 66/86 *Ahmed Saeed* [1989] E.C.R. 803; [1990] 4 C.M.L.R. 102, in which a Directive on
air fares was used as a reference point, albeit with criteria not unlike the judicial approach
in *United Brands*.

[17] Case C–62/86, n.37, above.

[18] AKZO estimated its share of the relevant market as 50 per cent or more. It was equivalent
to those of all the remaining producers together.

[19] After considerable delay, the Commission's Decision being in 1985 and the Court's
Judgment in 1991. The fine was reduced for several reasons, and allegations of discrimination were held to be unfounded.

say, those which remain constant regardless of the quantities produced) and, at least, part of the variable costs relating to the unit produced. Moreover, prices below average total costs, that is to say, fixed costs plus variable costs, but above average variable costs, must be regarded as abusive if they are determined as part of a plan for eliminating a competitor".[20]

This approach was affirmed by the Court in *Tetra Pak*,[21] together with the additional observation that it was not necessary for the purposes of establishing predatory pricing to prove that the company had a realistic chance of subsequently recouping its losses. According to the Court, it must be possible to penalise predatory pricing whenever there is a risk that competitors will be eliminated. The aim pursued, which is to maintain undistorted competition, rules out waiting until such a strategy leads to the actual elimination of competitors.[22]

These principles have been criticised, especially the need for a **24–022** plan to eliminate competition before predatory pricing can be established under the second limb of the *AKZO* test. The requisite element of intention can only be inferred from the surrounding evidence, such as the duration, continuity and scale of the losses made.[23] Commentators[24] have argued that the emphasis on intention is arbitrary, and fails to take account of a firm's rational economic behaviour. Instead, contrary to the Court's position in *Tetra Pak*, it is argued that any assessment should first entail a structural analysis with a view to establishing whether market conditions favour the undertaking being able to recoup its losses, since it is only the latter prospect which would rationally induce the undertaking to engage in predatory activity.[25] As the Commission has recognised,[26] predatory pricing is a risky strategy because the self-inflicted losses may not be regained if the predator makes a mistake about the market conditions.

In opening the discussion for Article 82 reform in relation to exclusionary abuses such as predatory pricing, the Commission proposes adopting cost benchmarks based on either the alleged dominant firm or, if not available, an "apparently efficient competitor".[27] It also sets out in detail[28] the kind of evidence that it believes

---

[20] At paras 71–72 of Judgment.
[21] Case C–333/94P, n.42, above.
[22] *ibid.*, para.44.
[23] Not all companies will be so obliging as AKZO, which had committed its plans to paper.
[24] e.g. Mastromanolis, "Predatory pricing strategies in the European Union: a case for legal reform" [1998] E.C.L.R. 211; J. Temple Lang and R. O'Donoghue, "Defining Legitimate Competition: How to Clarify Pricing Abuses under Art.82 EC" (2002) 26 Fordham Int.L.J. 83.
[25] See COMP/38.233 *Wanadoo Interactive*, July 16, 2003, for an example of the Commission engaging in the attempt to assess recoupment. On appeal as Case T–340/03, [2003] O.J. C289/34.
[26] 2005 *Discussion Paper*, n.4, above, para.97.
[27] *ibid.*, para.103.
[28] *ibid.*, paras.106–129.

relevant to establishing a plausible case of predation, depending on which cost benchmark is applicable. The Commission also suggests that a dominant firm should have the defence of showing that its conduct will not have the alleged exclusionary effect or that recoupment will never be possible and that consumers are not and will not be harmed.[29] Predatory pricing should normally be reserved to situations where the dominant firm is using it to protect or strengthen its market power. The only exception envisaged by the Commission is where dominance is derived from a legal monopoly, in which case the legitimate target for the use of Article 82 is to prevent the monopolist drawing upon the protected position to establish or defend itself in unrelated markets through cross-subsidisation.[30]

24–023   **(c) Discriminatory prices.** A dominant undertaking may fall foul of Article 82 by charging different prices in respect of equivalent transactions without objective justification. If the customers concerned are "trading parties", i.e. the purchase is made for the purposes of an economic activity in which they are engaged, the objectionable feature of such a pricing policy is found in the competitive disadvantage suffered by those called upon to pay the higher prices, and the case falls precisely within Article 82(c). However, even in transactions with ultimate consumers, discriminatory pricing may be abusive, if incompatible with any aims of the Treaty.

An abuse may take the form of discriminating between customers within the same market or of following different pricing policies on different markets, although in the latter case objective justification may be more readily available. It should be noted that the customers concerned need not be in competition with each other: the one paying the higher price suffers a "competitive disadvantage" simply because he is, to that extent, less well equipped to meet competition, whatever quarter it may come from.

The *United Brands* case highlighted the particular problem of how far it is permissible for dominant undertakings to adapt their pricing policies to take account of the diversity of marketing conditions in the various Member States.[31] For instance, there may be significant disparities in rates of taxation, freight charges or the wages paid to workers for assembling or finishing the product, which may influence costs; or in other factors relevant to a marketing strategy, such as consumer preferences or the intensity of competition. In addition,

---

[29] *ibid.*, para.123.
[30] See Dec.2001/354 *Deutsche Post* [2001] O.J. L125/27.
[31] Case 27/76 n.8, above, at 294 *et seq.* The Commission found that UBC's differential pricing policy amounted to a separate head of abuse, and this part of the Decision was upheld by the Court of Justice.

price differences may result from government action over which a supplier has no control, for example, the imposition of a price freeze on certain products. Some convergence of these conditions may be expected as progress to the single market and economic and monetary union develops, but markets within the Community are bound to retain a degree of territorial specificity (although not necessarily along national lines) due, for example, to climate, geography and cultural differences.

UBC had put forward, as objective justification for its policy of **24–024** charging different prices for its bananas depending on the Member State where the ripened fruit was to be sold, the continuing division of the market for bananas along national lines. Each of the national markets had its own internal characteristics, and accordingly different price levels; and the prices to the ripener/distributors in a given week were intended to reflect as accurately as possible the prices which ripened bananas were expected to fetch on the individual markets during the following week. The defect which the European Court found in this argument was that UBC did not operate directly on the retail markets. It was not, therefore, entitled to take account of market pressures which only made themselves felt at the retail stage. However, not all commentators find this convincing,[32] resisting in particular the suggestion that a producer can be immune from the risks of demand conditions at the retail level.

Attempts have been made by dominant firms to justify discriminatory pricing on the basis of the need to meet competition. Thus, in *Irish Sugar*,[33] the dominant party granted discounts to customers situated near the boundary with Northern Ireland in order to counter the effects of cheap imports into the Republic of Ireland from across that border. Irish Sugar accused the Commission of failing properly to take account of the fact that price competition in the United Kingdom had widened the gap in prices between Northern Ireland and the Republic, that part of the border trade was illegal and that, at that time, Irish Sugar was incurring considerable losses. Irish Sugar also asserted that it had the right to defend its market position by meeting competition through selective, but non-predatory, pricing tactics.

The Court of First Instance gave short shrift to these arguments. Firstly, the influence of the pricing differential in the United Kingdom was "of the very essence"[34] of a common market, so that obstacles to its enjoyment raised by a dominant firm were abusive. This was all the more so since the lower prices outside Ireland were not themselves below cost. Secondly, Irish Sugar could not use its

---

[32] See W. Bishop, "Price discrimination under Art. 86: political economy in the European Court" (1981) 44 M.L.R. 282.
[33] Case T–228/97, n.2, above.
[34] *ibid.*, para.185.

financial situation in the way it claimed without making a "dead letter"[35] of the Treaty rule. Thirdly, on the question of defensive pricing, the Court of First Instance noted that Irish Sugar was defeated by its own arguments. By claiming that it did not have the financial resources to offer discounts and rebates throughout the Irish territory, the undertaking was in effect admitting that it was subsidising the discounts for border customers from the high prices being charged in the rest of the country. This practice was preventing the development of free competition on the market and distorting its structures, in relation to both purchasers and consumers.[36] If "meeting competition" was available as an argument to a dominant firm in Irish Sugar's position at all then, at the very least, it would have to satisfy criteria of economic efficiency and be consistent with the interests of consumers.[37] The position adopted by the Court of First Instance[38] is a further example of how difficult it is to mount a defence to discriminatory pricing where the core values of market integration are threatened by that policy, in particular the inhibition of parallel imports.

However, commentators[39] have taken issue with the general aversion to price discrimination adopted by the European Courts. According to the EAGCP Report,[40] even when a firm has enough market power to be dominant, the ability to engage in price discrimination might actually *reduce* its market power. A ban on price discrimination, so the argument runs, removes the bilateral bargaining between dominant firm and customers which might otherwise arise—especially in relation to customers in downstream markets who might be competing against each other.[41] The absence of price discrimination actually assists the dominant firm to resist requests for lower prices and, thus, to exploit its market power. The same Report acknowledges that there are also anti-competitive effects of price discrimination. However, this is normally when discrimination is combined with other strategies such as selective predatory pricing or rebates (see below). In such situations, according to the Report, it is the particular harm that should form the focus of Article 82 rather than a formal condemnation of price discrimination.

---

[35] *ibid.*, para.186.

[36] *ibid.*, para.188.

[37] *ibid.*, para.189.

[38] The Court of Justice dismissed Irish Sugar's appeal without discussing the discrimination point: see Case C–497/99P, n.78, above.

[39] See W. Bishop, *op.cit.*, n.32, above; D. Ridyard, "Exclusionary pricing and price discrimination abuses under Art.82: An Economic Analysis" [2002] E.C.L.R. 286; T. Eilmansberger, "How to Distinguish Good from Bad Competition Under Art.82 EC: In Search of Clearer and More Coherent Standards for Anti-Competitive Abuses" (2005) 42 C.M.L.Rev. 129, 139; J. Temple Lang and R. O'Donoghue, *op. cit.*, n.24, above.

[40] n.4, above.

[41] *ibid.*, p.33.

(d) Margin squeezing. This typically occurs in situations where a 24–025 firm is dominant in one market but can use a pricing strategy to squeeze out competitors in downstream markets. The product price is set "at such a level that those who purchase it do not have a sufficient profit margin on the processing to remain competitive on the market for the processed product".[42] Vertically integrated firms are thus particularly able to squeeze out non-integrated rivals. As the Commission's 2005 Discussion Paper points out,[43] this behaviour is often to be construed as a constructive refusal to supply or termination of a supply relationship. An example is *British Sugar/Napier Brown*,[44] where British Sugar was dominant in the industrial sugar market but also operated in the downstream, retail, market. The margin between its two prices was below its own repackaging and selling costs. Napier, a retail competitor, depended on supplies from British Sugar and could not viably operate against British Sugar's low pricing tactics.

A more recent example shows the squeeze at the upstream point. In *Deutsche Telekom*,[45] the dominant firm (DT) in the wholesale broadband market charged such high prices that competitors could not then supply retail access at prices below those charged by the dominant firm itself. Part of the importance of the Commission's decision is in its methodology,[46] whereby it asserted that DT would not be able to offer its own retail services without incurring a loss if it needed to pay its own wholesale prices. According to the Commission, a margin squeeze, and therefore an abuse, occurred when the spread between DT's retail and wholesale prices was either negative or at least insufficient to cover DT's own downstream costs. DT's wholesale prices were actually higher than its retail levels.

Rebates, single branding and discounts

Rebates, discounts and other "incentives" come in a multitude of 24–026 forms.[47] They will often be part of a wider range of strategies and so their market impact may not always be uniform or easily demarcated. Single branding obligations require the buyer to concentrate its purchases to a large degree with one supplier. Such obligations also embrace "English clauses", whereby the buyer has to report any better offer to the supplier and can only take it up if the latter does not match it.[48] Rebates may be unconditional or conditional. The

---

[42] Case T–5/97 *Industrie des Poudres Sphériques v Commission* [2000] E.C.R. II–3755.
[43] n.4, above, paras.219–225.
[44] [1988] O.J. L284/41, [1990] 4 C.M.L.R. 196.
[45] [2003] O.J. L263/9, now under appeal as Case T–271/03.
[46] See also *Notice on the Application of Competition Rules to Access Agreements in the Telecommunications Sector* [1998] O.J. C265/2.
[47] See the Commission's 2005 *Discussion Paper*, n.4, above, paras.134–141.
[48] See Case 85/76 *Hoffmann-La Roche*, n.16, above. Moreover, if the buyer has to disclose the identity of the better offer, this will reinforce the knowledge of the dominant party about the market.

former, whilst granted to some customers and not others, are applied without reference to customer behaviour—for example, to customers in border regions who might otherwise be tempted to seek foreign suppliers. Conditional rebates reward certain (purchasing) behaviour by customers—such as on the basis of previous amounts purchased or percentages of requirements taken from that supplier. As Advocate General Kokott observed in the *British Airways* case[49]:

> "loyalty rebates and loyalty bonuses can in practice bind business partners so closely to the dominant undertaking (the 'fidelity-building effect'), that its competitors find it inordinately difficult to sell their products ('exclusionary' or 'foreclosure' effect), with the result that competition itself can be damaged and, ultimately, the consumer can suffer.

In the sense that they are likely to target particular customers, or apply differently to selected traders, discounts and rebates also often imply discrimination.[50]

Nevertheless, there may be benefits to be derived. Simple "quantity" discounts are not likely to be seen as anti-competitive where these correlate to cost savings for the supplier. The use of rebates in vertical relationships may induce efficient behaviour by retailers insofar as increased retail margins on additional volumes encourage retailers to promote the product. By allowing high and low demand elasticity consumers to be treated differently, rebates will impact upon margins. The result is that there is at least an open question as to whether the net effect on consumer welfare is positive or negative.[51] However, general economic intuition is that pure quantity rebates are more likely to be motivated by efficiency considerations than fidelity rebates.[52]

Rebates and bonuses can also operate in relation to buyer power. Thus, in *Virgin/British Airways*,[53] the Commission fined BA for its systems of financial incentives in relation to travel agencies providing airline ticket and promotional services. All the schemes were geared to meeting targets for sales growth and shared one key characteristic: the commission increased in relation to *all* tickets sold by an agent in the reference period, not just the ones sold after the target was reached. This meant that whenever a travel agent was close to reaching the trigger sales threshold for an increase in commission rates, selling relatively few extra BA tickets could have a significant impact on commission income. Any competitor (such as Virgin)

---

[49] Case C-95/04P, n.3, above.
[50] Although discrimination is not a precondition for a rebate or bonus to constitute an abuse: see *Michelin I*, n.7, above, para.120.
[51] See EAGCP Report, n.4, above, p.36.
[52] *ibid.*
[53] Dec. 2000/74 [2000] O.J. L30/1.

would therefore have to pay a much higher rate of commission to an agent to divert some of its sales to the competitor's tickets in order to overcome that effect. The Court of First Instance, upholding the Commission's findings, accepted that this "very noticeable effect at the margin"[54] would also mean that an agent could suffer significant financial losses for even a small drop in turnover in BA tickets.

On appeal to the Court of Justice, BA sought to challenge the findings of abuse. In particular, it claimed that the performance rewards were objectively justified and that the Court of First Instance had failed to require the concrete effects of the schemes to be established. These arguments were all dismissed in turn by Advocate General Kokott. In her view, the Court of First Instance had rightly resisted judging behaviours by labels and had correctly applied the tests of objective justification. She noted:

> "Independently, however, of the use of the terms 'quantity rebate' and 'fidelity rebate', the question of the economic justification for such rebates or bonuses is always to be determined by reference to all the circumstances of the individual case. The determining factor is whether the foreclosure effect of the rebates or bonuses, which is detrimental to competition, can be compensated for, or more than compensated for, by *efficiency advantages* which also demonstrably enure to consumers. It is thus ultimately a question of balancing the advantages and disadvantages for competition and consumers against one another. If the foreclosure effect of a dominant undertaking's bonus or rebate scheme bears no discernible relation to advantages for competition or consumers, or if it goes beyond what is necessary to achieve those advantages, that bonus or rebate scheme is to be regarded as abusive."[55] (original emphasis)

Turning to the question of the anti-competitive effect of the abuses, the Advocate General observed that "a line of conduct of a dominant undertaking is abusive as soon as it runs counter to the purpose of protecting competition in the internal market from distortions". What needed to be established was:

> "the mere *likelihood* of the conduct in question hindering the maintenance or development of competition still existing in the market by means other than competition on the merits . . ."[56] (original emphasis)

---

[54] Case T–219/99, n.38, above, para.272.
[55] Case C–95/04P, n.3, above, para.59.
[56] *ibid.*, para.71.

This rather general test then had to be applied in the specific case situation of making it difficult or impossible for BA's competitors to have access to the market and its business partners to choose between various sources of supply and various business partners.[57] In the Advocate General's view, the Court of First Instance had properly observed the requirements of proof of likelihood in the particular market.

Tying and bundling

24–027   The illustrative abuses listed in Article 82(d) specifically include "tying" arrangements, where a person is required to accept, as a condition of entering into a contract, "supplementary obligations which, by their nature or according to commercial usage, have no connection with the subject of such contracts". In simple terms this can mean that to order X good (the tying good) the customer must also take quantities of Y (the tied good) as well. X and Y may be complementary, independent or substitutes. Similarly, services may be tied so that the purchase of a heating system may include an obligation to sign up for a five-year service contract. Tying thus makes the sale of one item conditional upon the purchase of another. Bundling, however, describes the situation where two or more products are sold together. It may be "pure" (the component goods can only be bought together) or "mixed" (where the components are also available separately but the bundle comes at a discount on the price of the separate components).

The main objection to tying, the so-called leverage argument, is that it enables a dominant position on one market to be used in order to gain a competitive advantage on another. It may also be directly oppressive to consumers in the first market. Thus, in *Hilti*[58] it was held to be an abuse for Hilti to supply cartridge strips to certain end-users or distributors on terms that the requisite complement of nails was purchased as well. Hilti claimed as an objective justification that its policy was based on safety grounds, alleging that other manufacturers' nails were dangerous when used in the Hilti system. This argument was forcefully rejected by the Court of First Instance, noting that it was not for Hilti to take unilateral action in that way; safety issues could be referred to the relevant public authorities. Even in relation to products where tied sales are part of commercial usage, the possibility of such practice being an abuse cannot be ruled out.[59]

Bundling is a common phenomenon and is by no means confined to dominant firms. It can often be used as a means to increase the

---

[57] *ibid.*, para.73.
[58] Case C–53/92P, n.34, above.
[59] Case C–333/94P *Tetra Pak*, n.42, above, para.37.

appeal of the product with which the second component is bundled.[60] However, when adopted by dominant firms bundling may produce abusive leveraging effects. This was the Commission's claim in relation to Microsoft's bundling of its Windows Media Player (WMP) with its PC operating systems.[61] Customers therefore had no choice to obtain Windows without WMP. Nor was there any ready means to un-install WMP. In the Commission's view, even though customers obtained WMP "for free", alternative suppliers of media players were put at a disadvantage by Microsoft's bundling. Citing recent Court of First Instance judgments[62] in relation to the requisite burden of proof in relation to anti-competitive effects, the Commission claimed that the bundling was liable to foreclose competition in the market for media players. The Commission considered, essentially, that the presence of WMP in all Microsoft's PC operating systems gave content providers and applications manufacturers an incentive to design their products on the basis of WMP. In other words, the detriment to competition would result from these indirect network effects. The Commission also rejected Microsoft's arguments that it had in fact created a single integrated product (rather than a bundle). Microsoft further claimed that consumers benefited from having a set of default options in a personal computer "out of the box" ready to run. However, in the Commission's view, the benefit of pre-installation needed to be distinguished from Microsoft making that selection itself.

Microsoft appealed against the Commission's Decision. Its request for the application of interim measures was dismissed.[63] However, the President of the Court of First Instance accepted that a number of Microsoft's arguments could not be regarded as prima facie unfounded. In particular, there was a "complex question" whether, and if so on what conditions, the Commission could rely on the probability that the market would "tip" in Microsoft's favour as a result of indirect network effects as the basis for imposing sanctions in respect of tying or bundling.

The Commission's Decision in *Microsoft* has been criticised for treating bundling in the same way as tying.[64] The EAGCP Report[65] stressed the need to consider tying and bundling in their individual circumstances:

---

[60] See T. Eilmansberger, *op.cit.*, n.39, above, at p.154. He uses the example of a sports section to boost sales of a newspaper.

[61] COMP/C–3/37.792 *Microsoft* (March 24, 2004). The interoperability aspect of the Decision is dealt with below in the section on refusals to supply. See also J. Appeldoorn, "He who spareth his rod, hateth his son? Microsoft, superdominance and Art.82 EC" [2005] E.C.L.R. 653.

[62] In particular, Case T–65/98 *Van den Bergh Foods* [2003] E.C.R. II–4653, *Michelin II*, n.20, above and *British Airways*, n.38, above.

[63] Case T–201/04R *Microsoft v Commission* [2005] 4 C.M.L.R. 406.

[64] see T. Eilmansberger, *op.cit.*, n.39, above (but not disputing the ultimate finding of abuse). See also D. Ridyard, "Tying and Bundling—Cause for Complaint?" [2005] E.C.L.R. 316.

[65] n.4, above.

"depending on the nature of competition, the cost structure on the tied market, the magnitude of costs savings associated with bundling, and the existence of strategic reasons, bundling can have exclusionary or pro-competitive effects and should thus be analyzed in the light of the effects of the practice. The potential for efficiency gains is more limited when the linkage is achieved through pricing schemes and bundling than when it is achieved through technological integration."[66]

The Commission's 2005 Discussion Paper[67] concentrates on developing tests for the measurement of foreclosure effects.[68]

Refusals to supply

24–028   Freedom of contract implies that any economic operator should be able to determine whom to supply, or not, as the case may be.[69] Dominant firms enjoy that presumption too, but it is also the case that discontinuations, refusals or threats of refusals to supply may constitute abuse when dominant firms' special responsibilities are considered in particular circumstances. The notion of refusal to supply has become something of an umbrella term and can embrace "constructive" refusals which at first sight take different forms, such as delaying tactics or pricing practices.[70]

The line of case law with the longest pedigree concerns termination of existing supply. However, more recent developments have seen abuses against first-time customers, especially where the refusal amounts to a form of leveraging which prevents access to a supply (or, in economic terms, an input) which is necessary for a downstream market. The case law is complex because the developments in this area are drawn from two rather different factual contexts which have become cross-referenced in the case law. On the one hand, there are refusals to license intellectual property rights (IPRs), particularly the *Magill*,[71] *IMS Health*[72] and *Microsoft*[73] cases. On the other, in cases such as *Bronner*[74] which do not entail intellectual property rights, there are denials of access to inputs allegedly indispensable to downstream activities which have been argued, explicitly or by analogy, in support of a so-called essential facilities

---

[66] *ibid.*, p.41.
[67] n.4, above.
[68] *ibid.*, paras.188–203.
[69] See also the Opinion of Advocate General Jacobs in Case C–7/97 *Bronner*, n.49, above, paras.58–62.
[70] e.g. margin squeezes, discussed above.
[71] Joined Cases C–241–242/91P *RTE and ITP v Commission* [1995] E.C.R. I–743, [1995] 4 C.M.L.R. 718.
[72] Case C–418/01 *IMS Health v Commission* [2004] E.C.R. I–5039, [2004] 4 C.M.L.R. 1543.
[73] Case T–201/04 (Judgment pending)
[74] n.49, above.

doctrine. The policy undercurrents in these two modern strands of case law are not the same. In relation to IPRs the issue is whether competition concerns can trump legally-conferred monopoly rights. The problem posed by any imposition of a duty to share essential facilities lies in the interference with freedom of contract and (arguably) the potential protection of competitors rather than competition. The challenge for competition enforcement agencies and the European Courts is thus whether the competitive harm in all these cases should be treated identically or whether the policy values involved demand differential treatment.

With the necessary caveat that the Court has never been inhibited from drawing upon all strands of case law to analyse any particular context, the discussion below first examines terminations of existing supply before looking at essential facilities and the intellectual property cases.

(a) **Termination of existing supply.** The case law suggests a **24–029** distinction between termination of an existing relationship and a refusal to start dealing with a new customer. The earliest case on refusal to deal was *Commercial Solvents*.[75] The refusal from the end of 1970 to supply Zoja with aminobutanol required for the manufacture of the derivative, ethambutol, was the result of a policy decision by the CS group to manufacture and sell the derivative on its own account. The Court said:

> ". . . an undertaking being in a dominant position as regards the production of raw material and therefore able to supply to manufacturers of derivatives, cannot, just because it decides to start manufacturing these derivatives (in competition with its former customers) act in such a way as to eliminate their competition which in the case in question, would amount to eliminating one of the principal manufacturers of ethambutol in the common market".[76]

Three main points emerge from this passage. In the first place, Zoja was an established customer of CSC. Admittedly, at the beginning of 1970 Zoja had cancelled its orders under the current supply contract, but the Court regarded this as irrelevant because CSC had anyway decided to cut off the supplies once deliveries under the contract had been completed. Secondly, the effect of withholding supplies of the raw material was likely to be serious, namely the elimination of a major producer from the market for the derivative. Thirdly, the reason for driving Zoja out of the market was to smooth CSC's own entry. The Court made it clear that the conduct in question could not be justified as a legitimate competitive tactic.

---

[75] Cases 6–7/73, n.5, above.
[76] *ibid.*, at 250–251.

The *United Brands* judgment contains an even more forthright condemnation of refusal to supply:

> ". . . it is advisable to assert positively from the outset that an undertaking in a dominant position for the purpose of marketing a product—which cashes in on the reputation of a brand name known to and valued by the consumers— cannot stop supplying a long standing customer who abides by regular commercial practice, if the orders placed by that customer are in no way out of the ordinary".[77]

The victim was the Danish ripener/distributor, Olesen, which UBC had refused to supply with "Chiquitas" after it had taken part in a sales campaign mounted by the rival supplier, Castle and Cooke. That collaboration was not regarded by the Court as justifying the refusal. Even a dominant undertaking may act in defence of its commercial interests, but such action must be reasonable and proportional to the threat, which that taken against Olesen had not been.

The apparent importance of distinguishing carefully between different categories of customer was highlighted by the *BP*[78] judgment, in which the Court annulled the Decision of the Commission that BP had abused the dominant position which it enjoyed in relation to its Dutch customers during the oil supply crisis of 1973–74 by reducing deliveries of motor spirit to a particular customer, ABG, more drastically than to others. The Court found that BP had given notice of the termination of its supply contract with ABG in November 1972, and that at the time when the crisis broke, ABG's relationship with BP, so far as concerned supplies of motor spirit, was that of a casual customer. BP could not, therefore, be blamed for treating ABG less favourably than its regular customers, since the latter would have received a substantially smaller quantity than they were entitled to expect, if a standard rate reduction had been applied.[79] However, not all prioritising of customers will be objectively justified. In *BPB Industries*,[80] the Court of First Instance found that BG was abusing its dominance in the plasterboard market by favouring customers who were not importers of plaster-board from other sources. It accordingly dismissed BG's argument that this was

---

[77] n.8, above, at 292.

[78] Case 77/77 [1978] E.C.R. 1513, [1978] 3 C.M.L.R. 174.

[79] As Advocate General Warner pointed out, a legal and moral right to security of supplies is the counterpart, for a contractual customer, of his loss of freedom to seek the best available bargain at a given moment, and the loyalty of regular, though non-contractual, customers also merits special consideration.

[80] Case T–65/89 *BPB Industries and British Gypsum v Commission* [1993] E.C.R. II–389; [1993] 5 C.M.L.R. 32; this aspect of the case was not dealt with on appeal in Case C–310/93P, [1995] E.C.R. I–865.

justified prioritisation for the benefit of regular customers in times of shortage. Whilst selection criteria can be adopted in such circumstances, they must be objectively justified and observe the rules governing fair competition between economic operators.

This older case law in relation to treatment of existing customers may seem rather removed from a close economic analysis of effects. They contain at the very least a nod in the direction of more nebulous notions of fair dealing. By contrast, it is perhaps noteworthy that the Commission's explanation of the relevance of existing customer relationships in its 2005 Discussion Paper is that they create a (rebuttable) presumption that their continuation is pro-competitive.[81]

(b) Essential facilities. As with some other developments in EC **24–030** competition law, such as the rule of reason,[82] the concept of essential facilities has a counterpart originating in the United States.[83] Put shortly, the idea requires that dominance over key facilities, such as transport or other infrastructure, requires access to be opened up to other users in particular circumstances. The American case law, as discussed by Advocate General Jacobs in *Bronner*, contains five conditions. Firstly, an essential facility is under the control of a monopolist. Secondly, a competitor is unable practically or reasonably to duplicate the essential facility. Thirdly, the use of the facility is denied to a competitor, even on reasonable terms. Fourthly, it is feasible for the facility to be provided and, fifthly, there is no legitimate business reason for refusing access to the facility.

The term essential facilities has been expressly adopted in Community law by the Commission, although the Court's position is less clear. In *Sea Containers v Stena Sealink*[84] the Commission decided that Sealink's refusal, as operator of the port of Holyhead, to allow access on reasonable and non-discriminatory terms to a potential competitor on the market for ferry services was an abuse of a dominant position. A facility will be essential if the handicap to a new entrant resulting from denial of access is one that can reasonably be expected to make competitors' activities in the market in question either impossible or permanently, seriously and unavoidably uneconomic.[85] This test is to be applied objectively, so that the special vulnerability of a particular competitor is irrelevant.

---

[81] n.4, above, para.217.
[82] See Ch.23, above
[83] Although its existence even in the USA is now viewed with scepticism: see *Verizon Communications Inc. v Law Offices of Curtis V. Trinko*, LLP 540 US 682 (2004).
[84] Dec. 94/19 [1994] O.J. L15/8.
[85] Temple Lang, "Defining legitimate competition: companies duties' to supply competitors, and access to essential facilities" (1994) 18 *Fordham International Law Journal* 245, quoted by Advocate General Jacobs in *Bronner*, n.49, above.

In *Bronner* the claimant, a small newspaper, sought access to the national home-delivery network for newspapers established by Mediaprint, which held 40 per cent of the Austrian newspaper market. Advocate General Jacobs emphasised the policy context which might discourage extensive resort to any essential facilities notion. In particular, he pointed to the right to choose one's trading partners and freely to dispose of one's property as generally recognised principles in the laws of the Member States, in some cases with constitutional status. Furthermore, from a competition perspective, the long-term interests of consumers might be better served by allowing the undertaking to keep its facilities. Otherwise, automatic rights for new entrants would act as a disincentive to those parties to develop competing facilities. Short-term gains by opening access might well thus be offset by longer-term disadvantages. In relation to the specific circumstances of the case, Advocate General Jacobs noted that although the applicant might be unable to duplicate that network it still had a variety of other distribution options open to it. The case thus fell "well short" of the type of situation in which it might be appropriate to impose an obligation on a dominant undertaking to allow access to a facility which it has developed for its own use.

24–031   The Court of Justice, notably, reformulated the question in *Bronner* in terms of a refusal to supply and did not expressly articulate an essential facilities doctrine. However, it took a narrow view of the requirements necessary to make out a breach of Article 82, observing that not only would the refusal of access have to be likely to eliminate all competition in the daily newspaper market on the part of the person requesting the service and that such refusal be incapable of being objectively justified, but that the service must also be indispensable to carrying on that person's business. The last requirement was not satisfied in the particular case since Bronner could choose other methods of distributing its newspapers besides home delivery. The Court also emphasised that in order to demonstrate that it had no realistic alternatives, the applicant could not just assert that it would not be economically viable to set up its own distribution network for the small circulation of its newspapers. This view acknowledges criticisms prior to the judgment expressing fears about the rising tide of essential facilities doctrine.[86]

The indispensability requirement in *Bronner* thus displays twin features.[87] In addition to the generic question of whether home delivery as such was indispensable to the distribution of newspapers, it was also necessary to assess the specific question of whether

---

[86] e.g. D. Ridyard, "Essential facilities and the obligation to supply competitors under UK and EC competition law" [1996] E.C.L.R. 438.

[87] See Doherty, "Just what are essential facilities?" (2001) 38 C.M.L.Rev. 397.

Mediaprint's facility could be duplicated. In a judgment[88] delivered after the Opinion in *Bronner*, the Court of First Instance had also ruled that a facility could only be essential if there were no substitutes. This more rigorous standard casts doubt on the Commission's previous approach in cases such as *London European v Sabena*,[89] where the refusal to allow access to a computer reservation system was condemned without a particularly rigorous assessment of Sabena's market position.

The message from *Bronner*, if not all its ramifications, is clear: imposing a duty to share facilities will be an exceptional, not a routine, event.

(c) Intellectual property: licensing and interoperability issues. In 24–032 its *Bronner* judgment, the Court of Justice carefully avoided commenting on whether its previous case law on refusal to license IPRs was of general application. The key previous decision was *Magill*,[90] a saga concerning access to rights protected by copyright. The three television companies involved had previously reproduced advance weekly listings of their programmes in separate magazines. Magill, which wanted to launch a single publication containing all the listings, was refused access to this information by the various copyright-holding companies. The Commission treated this refusal as an abuse, a view upheld by the Court of First Instance on the basis that preventing the emergence of a new product for which there was potential consumer demand went further than was necessary for protection of the essential function of copyright. The Court of Justice endorsed this conclusion, adding a direct reference to *Commercial Solvents*[91] and treating the programme scheduling as the indispensable raw material for the compilation of a new final magazine product.

Critics of the *Magill* judgment claimed that it took insufficient account of the rights and interests of holders of intellectual property rights, to the point of undermining the Court's own often-stated position that a refusal to license such rights was not itself an abuse.[92] However, subsequent cases have allayed these early fears. First, the Court of First Instance in *Tiercé Ladbroke*[93] expressly rejected the application of the *Magill* judgment on the footing that the copyright holders who were refusing to license their television rights for transmission in Belgium were not themselves already exploiting

---

[88] Cases T–374, 375, 384 and 388/94 *European Night Services v Commission* [1998] E.C.R. II–3141, [1998] 5 C.M.L.R. 718, (although in relation to Art.81, not Art.82).
[89] Dec.88/589; [1988] O.J. L317/47.
[90] n.71, above.
[91] Cases 6–7/73, n.5, above.
[92] Case 238/87 *Volvo v Erik Veng* (UK) [1988] E.C.R. 6211; [1989] 4 C.M.L.R. 122; Case 53/87 *Maxicar v Renault* [1988] E.C.R. 6039.
[93] Case T–504/93, n.45, above.

them on the Belgian market. In his *Bronner* Opinion, Advocate General Jacobs described the *Magill* judgment as having special circumstances: the existing weekly guides were inadequate, the provision of copyright protection for television listings was hard to justify in any event, and, since the shelf-life of listings was short, any refusal to supply the information was bound to act as a permanent barrier to a new product.

The limits to *Magill* were confirmed by the Court's judgment in *IMS Health*,[94] a case which, like *Magill*, concerned copyright protection—and again in an arguably rather weak version. IMS was dominant in the production of data on deliveries by wholesalers of pharmaceuticals in Germany. It had developed, with its customers (pharmaceutical companies), a so-called brick structure—1860 blocks based on postcodes which contained data on pharmacies and drug prescription levels to track regional sales. Newcomers introduced modified versions of the 1860 brick structure, which were then challenged by IMS as breach of its copyright. Having first affirmed that indispensability would only be satisified by showing that alternatives would not be viable for production on a scale comparable to that of IMS, the Court turned to the particular context of IPR licensing. Basing its argument on *Magill* and *Bronner*, the Court observed:

> "It is clear from that case law that, in order for the refusal by an undertaking which owns a copyright to give access to a product or service indispensable for carrying on a particular business to be treated as abusive, it is sufficient that three cumulative conditions be satisified, namely, that the refusal is preventing the emergence of a new product for which there is a potential consumer demand, that it is unjustified and such as to exclude any competition on a secondary market."[95]

The clarification, or shift, here is the statement that these three elements are cumulative.

24–033   Moreover, the first condition, the emergence of a new product, suggests a distinguishing requirement additional to cases about IPRs but absent from other putative essential facilities claims. The new product, and its demand, were clearly available in *Magill* in the form of the all-in-one TV listings journal. However, in *IMS Health*, the Court of Justice left to the national court the task of deciding whether an undertaking requesting an IPR licence was merely "limiting itself essentially to duplicating the goods or services already offered on the secondary market" or whether there would indeed be

---

[94] n.72, above. See E. Derclaye, "The *IMS Health* Decision and the Reconciliation of Copyright and Competition Law" (2004) 29 E.L.Rev. 687.
[95] *IMS Health*, n.72, above, para.38.

a new product. It seems clear from *IMS Health* that the "new product" requirement was expressly inserted as the means of balancing the interests of IPR holders against detriments to consumers.

As regards the exclusion of competition on a secondary market, several points may be noted. Firstly, this condition confirms the requirement that there must be an upstream and (secondary) downstream market before there can be a possible abuse in relation to a refusal to grant access. However, this can still be satisfied where there is no separate marketing of one of them (as was the case in *Bronner*, for example). Indeed, the Court in *IMS Health* specifically stated that "it is sufficient that a potential market or even hypothetical market can be identified."[96] What is required is that they are interconnected, insofar as the upstream product is indispensable for the downstream one. The breadth of this leaves some doubts about the parameters of *IMS Health*. After all, the brick structure (which in effect became an industry standard) was only developed to provide the data reports for sale. In this sense the case is very different from both *Magill* and *Bronner* where the secondary markets were not central to the dominant firms.

The remaining condition identified, but not explored, by the Court was objective justification. Arguments made by dominant firms will tend to rely on the substantial investments (and risks) involved in securing their IPRs or in establishing their hold on what turns out to be an essential facility. At the very least, such arguments might support a sufficient period of protection from competition in order to obtain an adequate return on investment.[97] This view also chimes with that expressed by Advocate General Jacobs in *Bronner* about the need to preserve incentives for innovation.[98]

Issues of justification are at the heart of the appeal arising from the Commission's investigation of Microsoft. The point at issue of importance at this juncture[99] concerns the ways in which Microsoft had restricted the interoperability between its Windows operating system and other work group server operating systems. In its Decision, the Commission had emphasised that Microsoft had changed its practices in relation to the disclosure of interoperability information, i.e. the complete and accurate specifications for all the Protocols implemented in Windows work group server operating systems. In the early 1990s competitors (such as Novell) had established a distinct technological lead in relation to group networks that contained non-Microsoft work group servers. Thus, according to the Commission, for that period Microsoft had an

24-034

---

[96] *ibid.*, para.44.
[97] See *European Night Services*, n.88, above.
[98] See also his Opinion in Case C–53/03 *Syfait v GlaxoSmithKline* [2005] E.C.R. I–4609; the Court, however, declined to accept jurisdiction under Art.234.
[99] The bundling aspects relating to the WMP were discussed above, para.24–027.

incentive to have its client PC operating system interoperate with non-Microsoft group server systems. But once its own group server operating system had gained acceptance, holding back information relating to interoperability with the Windows environment began to make sense. Microsoft accordingly reduced the release of information pertaining to core tasks expected from group systems, especially in relation to the provision of group and user administration services.

Although Microsoft failed to obtain interim relief before the Court of First Instance,[1] the President acknowledged there were live issues of substance to be considered in the main proceedings. In particular, he noted[2] that the information sought (secret, valuable and allegedly IPR-protected) was fundamentally different from that at issue in *Magill* and *IMS Health*. In those cases the information at issue was widely known in the sector: the television programme listings were sent free of charge to newspapers every week and the map of Germany was in reality an industry standard for the presentation of sales figures.

On the question of justification, the President observed that it would be for the Court of First Instance to determine if the Commission had committed a manifest error in the evaluation of the interests involved, "in particular in connection with the protection of the intellectual property rights relied on and the requirements of free competition enshrined in the EC Treaty."[3] The Commission had rejected any objective justification on the grounds that the possible negative impact of an order to supply on Microsoft's incentives to innovate was outweighed by its positive impact on the level of innovation of the whole industry (including Microsoft).

By way of conclusion to this section, the question might be posed as to whether the Microsoft saga is best discussed in terms of *IMS Health* and *Bronner* at all. Part of the nub of the Commission's objections stemmed from Microsoft *changing* its policy to one of not providing information. In other words, was this exclusionary conduct closer to the termination of existing supply as demonstrated in *Commercial Solvents*? It may be recalled that the Court itself used the latter case as the foundational analogy for its analysis in *Magill*.

Reforming Article 82

24–035   Numerous references have been made in this Chapter regarding the reform of Article 82 to keep pace with the changes in emphasis and methodology seen in other aspects of EC competition law. The Commission's 2005 Discussion Paper[4] in effect sets out what a

---

[1] Case C–201/04R, n.63, above.
[2] *ibid*., para.207.
[3] *ibid*., para.224.
[4] n.4, above (consultation closed March 31, 2006).

Guidelines-type Notice might look like in relation to the application of Article 82 to exclusionary abuses. Several aspects of the discussion in this Chapter perhaps bear out the views of critics who see reform as long overdue.[5] For example, the claims that abuses have hitherto been too much determined by legal pigeonholes rather than anti-competitive effects might justifiably point to demarcation lines that have emerged in case law between types of transaction rather than impact on the market. Similarly, the apparent new category of super-dominance[6] fuels criticism that the proliferation of legal conceptual layers obscures the proper issues: competition on the merits and restraints on market power. Indeed, some critics have posed the question whether a "dominance" test is required at all.[7]

The Competition Commissioner, launching the review, claimed that the eventual outcome was not meant to be a radical shift in enforcement policy.[8] However, the questions already being discussed range from the detail of the relevance and measurement of intention, actual market effects or justificatory efficiencies to wider engagement with the functions (and limits) of competition law. As seen from examples in relation to refusals to grant access to facilities or IPRs, competition law treats innovation rather differently from the assumptions of IP law.

What seems highly likely is that the analysis to be carried out by enforcers of Article 82 will in future be less able to rely on a blanket ban on particular practices and will require more careful proof of the abusive elements. Of course, however, opening up the possibilities for justification does not necessarily mean that they will succeed. The Court of First Instance's role in reviewing Commission action will be critical. "Competition on the merits" is already in the judicial lexicon but its measurement awaits explanation and definition in the reform process.

Further reading

Arowolo, O., "Application of the Concept of Barriers to Entry under Article 82 of the EC Treaty: is there a Case for Review?" [2005] E.C.L.R. 247.

Eilmansberger, T., "How to Distinguish Good from Bad Competition Under Article 82 EC: In Search of Clearer and More Coherent Standards for Anti-Competitive Abuses" (2005) 42 C.M.L.Rev. 129.

---

[5] See B. Sher, "The Last of the Steam-Powered Trains: Modernizing Article 82" [2004] E.C.L.R. 243.

[6] n.66, above. The Commission stressed the "extraordinary" market strength of Microsoft: Decision, n.61, above, point 586.

[7] D. Ridyard, "The Agenda for Art.82 Reform—Eight Key Economic and Policy Issues" (2005 Autumn) *Lawyers' Europe*, 10; also A. Majumdar, "Whither Dominance" [2006] E.C.L.R. 161.

[8] Neelie Kroes, speech September 23, 2005, text on Commission's website.

Gérardin, D., "Limiting the Scope of Article 82 EC: What can the EU Learn from the US Supreme Court's Judgment in *Trinko* in the Wake of *Microsoft, IMS* and *Deutsche Telekom*" (2004) 41 C.M.L.Rev. 1519.

Maher, I., "The Interface of EC Competition Law and Intellectual Property Rights: The Essential and the Creative" (2004–05) 7 C.Y.E.L.S. 189.

Oliver, P., "The Concept of 'Abuse' of a Dominant Position under Article 82 EC: Recent Developments in Relation to Pricing" (2005) 2 E.C.L.J. 315.

Sinclair, D., "Abuse of Dominance at a Crossroads: Potential Effect, Object and Appreciability under Article 82 EC" [2004] E.C.L.R. 491.

Wind, E., "Remedies and Sanctions in Article 82 of the EC Treaty" [2005] E.C.L.R. 659.

CHAPTER 25

ENFORCEMENT OF ARTICLES 81 AND 82

Guide to this Chapter: This Chapter examines enforcement of **25–001**
Article 81 to 82 in the light of Regulation 1/2003, guidance
Notes, fundamental rights protection and the general norms of
effectiveness developed by the case law of the European Courts.
Analysis concentrates on four principal areas: the distribution of
responsibilities between Commission, national courts and national
competition authorities under the umbrella of the European Competition Network; the main stages and limitations of an investigation, including information-gathering, inspections and rights of the
defence; public enforcement demonstrated by the fining policies
of the Commission, including its Guidelines on fines and its
Leniency Notice; and, finally, the increasing emphasis being put
upon private enforcement by competitors and other injured
parties in the pursuit of civil remedies in national courts. The
post-2004 enforcement regime, centred upon Regulation 1/2003,
offers a much more decentralized model than previously. The
Chapter concludes by briefly considering the Commission's 2005
Green Paper that seeks to promote damages actions for breach
of the EC antitrust rules.

Introduction

The enforcement system for EC competition law underwent a **25–002**
major overhaul with the introduction of Regulation 1/2003[1] in May
2004. This ended the Commission's exclusive powers of granting

---

[1] Council Reg.1/2003 *On the Implementation of the Rules on Competition Laid Down in Articles
81 and 82 of the Treaty* [2003] O.J. L1/1. More detailed rules for the conduct of proceedings
by the Commission are set out in Commission Reg.773/2004 [2004] O.J. L123/18.

exemptions under Article 81(3) and marked a significant shift in both the institutional distribution of enforcement powers and in the ethos and assumptions underpinning the effective application of Articles 81 and 82. In short, the new system is characterised by decentralization and privatization. National courts and national competition authorities (NCAs) are now lynchpins in the enforcement system alongside the Commission. At the same time, the new arrangements assume and encourage a change in competition culture by anticipating a much greater willingness among competitors and consumers to resort to litigation in national courts to obtain remedies such as damages for breaches of EC competition rules. These changes can be seen as representing a closer alignment than previously between competition law enforcement and the "usual" rules of effective protection of EC law rights through national processes and remedies. Nevertheless, the Commission still retains considerable powers and, crucially, is enabled (in theory, at least) to focus its resources in pursuit of the most pernicious and significant cartels.[2]

This Chapter does not purport to describe in detail every aspect of the procedures for investigation and hearing of complaints or the voluminous case law that has been generated by appeals alleging infringements by the Commission of the rights of the defence or errors in the gathering of evidence and calculations of fines. Instead, it first sets out the key structural elements in the distribution of enforcement powers between institutions, with a view to signposting some of the potential tensions or difficulties in their interrelationship. Secondly, the core stages in an investigation or complaint are identified, together with the protections available to undertakings, particularly in the light of fundamental principles derived from general EC law and in the context of the provisions of the ECHR. The Chapter moves on to address the two principal outcomes envisaged by the new enforcement processes—either a fine imposed by the Commission or an NCA as public authorities, or a private remedy (most likely, but not exclusively, for compensation in damages) pursued through national courts.

The institutional structures for enforcement

25–003   Regulation 1/2003 builds an enforcement regime around three key centres of authority: the Commission, the NCAs and national courts. To this end it spells out the powers of each authority and also the relationship between EC law and national law in competition cases.

---

[2] The ability to prioritise its work was one of the explicit rationales adopted by the Commission in 1999 when putting forward the precursor of change, its *White Paper on Modernisation* [1999] O.J. C132/1. The reasoning is also included in Recital (3) of Reg.1/2003, n.1, above.

In relation to both dimensions there are significant departures in detail from the previous regime under Regulation 17/62.[3] The most striking features are that the notion of advance notification under Article 81 has disappeared, along with the Commission's exclusive power of exemption under Article 81(3). The exception contained in the latter provision may now be applied by any of the enforcement agencies. A European Competition Network (ECN) is established between the Commission and the various NCAs of the Member States, with a number of provisions promoting the exchange of information between members.

The Commission's powers
The Commission is able to act on a complaint or its own initiative **25–004** and may determine that an infringement of Article 81 or Article 82 has occurred. It may by decision require the undertaking(s) concerned to bring such infringement to an end and for this purpose may impose any "behavioural or structural remedies which are proportionate to the infringement committed and necessary to bring the infringement effectively to an end."[4] The Commission is also able to accept offers of commitments made by undertakings after a preliminary assessment by the Commission that it intends to adopt a decision requiring an infringement to be brought to an end. In such a case the Commission can by decision make those commitments binding on the undertaking.[5] Regulation 1/2003 also empowers the Commission to adopt, on its own initiative, a decision such that Article 81 or Article 82 is not applicable to an agreement, decision or conduct.[6] However, this latter provision has not hitherto been exercised and any fears that it might tend towards old-style "negative clearance" appear unfounded. As under the pre-2004 system, the Commission retains the power to impose fines. These may not exceed 10 per cent of total turnover of the undertaking in the case of intentional or negligent infringements of Articles 81 to 82 or failure to comply with commitments.[7] In relation to the supply of incorrect or misleading information and similar defaults, the maximum for an intentional or negligent failure is 1 per cent of total turnover in the preceding business year.[8] The Commission also retains its ability to adopt block exemptions although, as was seen in Chapter 23 above, these have become less common in practice.

---

[3] [1962] O.J. Spec. Ed. 87; repealed and replaced by Reg.1/2003 with effect from May 1, 2004.
[4] Reg.1/2003 Art.7.
[5] Art.9.
[6] Art.10.
[7] Art.23(2).
[8] Art.23(1).

The National Competition Authorities

25–005 Article 5 of Regulation 1/2003 confers on NCAs the power to apply Articles 81 and 82 of the Treaty in individual cases. Acting on their own initiative or on a complaint they may take the following decisions:

— requiring that an infringement be brought to an end;
— ordering interim measures;
— accepting commitments;
— imposing fines, periodic penalty payments or any other penalty provided for in their national law

According to Article 11 of the Regulation, the Commission and the NCAs shall apply the Community competition rules "in close co-operation". This is done by forming together a network of public authorities,[9] which has come to be designated the ECN. The mechanisms for operating this network have been fleshed out in a Commission notice (the "Network" Notice),[10] which describes the ECN as the "basis for the creation and maintenance of a common competition culture in Europe."[11] The Notice also claims that the ECN "should ensure both an efficient division of work and an effective and consistent application of EC competition rules".[12] As discussed further below, the exchange of information between NCAs, and exchanges with the Commission, have proved controversial.

The principal procedural obligation of NCAs is that when acting under Article 81 or Article 82 they must inform the Commission in writing before or without delay after commencing the first formal investigative measure. This information may also be made available to the competition authorities of the other Member States.[13] Similarly, not later than 30 days before adopting a decision about infringement, accepting commitments or withdrawing the benefit of a block exemption, an NCA must inform the Commission.[14] Again, this may be made available to the NCAs of other Member States. There is a general power of NCAs to consult the Commission on any case involving the application of Community law. Where, however, the Commission itself initiates proceedings for the adoption of a decision, this shall relieve the competition authorities of the Member States of their competence to apply Articles 81 and 82.[15] If a

---

[9] Recital (15).
[10] *Commission Notice on Co-operation within the Network of Competition Authorities* [2004] O.J. C101/43.
[11] *ibid.*, para.1.
[12] *ibid.*, para.3.
[13] Reg.1/2003, Art.11(3).
[14] *ibid.*, Art.11(4).
[15] *ibid.*, Art.11(6).

competition authority is already acting on a case, the Commission shall only initiate proceedings after consulting with that NCA.[16]

National courts

According to Article 6 of Regulation 1/2003, national courts shall **25–006** have the power to apply Articles 81 and 82 of the Treaty. In one sense this is not wholly new, insofar as it is over 30 years since the Court of Justice ruled that the prohibitions of those provisions were directly applicable by national courts.[17] The key difference under the new system is that, in addition to application of the prohibitory aspects, the exception of Article 81(3) now also falls within the jurisdiction of national courts for the first time.

As part of the 2004 modernisation "package", the Commission also issued a Notice in relation to co-operation with national courts.[18] For obvious and understandable reasons relating to the function and independence of the judiciary, national courts cannot be members of the ECN[19] with the Commission and NCAs. Nor can the Cooperation Notice bind national courts. However, it does set out useful guidance which in part draws upon established case law[20] of the European Court but also explains the Commission's view of the new arrangements under Regulation 1/2003.

As will be discussed further below, the value of the national court in competition law enforcement is in providing a decentralised opportunity for injured competitors and consumers (and, in some cases, even parties to the unlawful activity) to obtain remedies for infringements of Articles 81 and 82. This private aspect of enforcement, in parallel with the fining powers of the public authorities, sets up a system of dual enforcement that matches more closely the wider development of EC law as a result of the general principles established by the Court of Justice.[21] The latter, specifically the principles of equivalence and effectiveness, are underlined in the Cooperation Notice.[22]

---

[16] *ibid.*
[17] Case 127/73 *BRT and SABAM* [1974] E.C.R. 51, para.16.
[18] *Commission Notice on the Co-operation Between the Commission and the Courts of the EU Member States in the Application of Articles 81 and 82 EC Treaty* [2004] O.J. C101/54. This replaced the previous such Co-operation Notice [1993] O.J. C39/6.
[19] Although it is possible for a national court to be designated as a national competition authority: Art.35(1) of Reg.1/2003. In such a case, the court (*qua* NCA) would be covered by the Network Notice, n.10, above.
[20] Especially Case 14/68 *Walt Wilhelm* [1969] E.C.R. 1; Case C–2/88 *Zwartveld* [1990] E.C.R. I–4405; Case C–234/89 *Delimitis* [1991] E.C.R. I–935; Case C–344/98 *Masterfoods* [2000] E.C.R. I–11369.
[21] See Ch.5, above.
[22] Co-operation Notice, n.18, above, para.10.

Relationship of national competition laws and Article 81 and Article 82 EC

25–007   This question is explicitly addressed in Article 3 of Regulation 1/2003, although it should be remembered that other more general principles of supremacy will also be relevant. The specific obligation created by Article 3(1) is that where NCAs or national courts apply national law to an agreement or an abuse for the purposes of Articles 81–82 of the Treaty which affects trade[23] between Member States, they *shall also* apply Articles 81 to 82. This outcome was not the one originally canvassed by the Commission when putting forward its draft proposals.[24] Member States are required by Regulation 1/2003 to forward to the Commission any written judgment of its national courts deciding on the application of Article 81 or Article 82.[25]

The extent to which national competition law can impose stricter requirements depends upon whether it is Article 81 or Article 82 that is in question. Where an agreement would not be prohibited by Article 81(1), or where the conditions for exception under Article 81(3) or a block exemption regulation are fulfilled, it cannot be prohibited by national law. However, Member States are not precluded from adopting and applying stricter laws in relation to unilateral conduct engaged in by undertakings.[26] It is also possible for NCAs and national courts to apply provisions of national law "that predominantly pursue an objective different from that pursued by Articles 81 and 82."[27] In this regard, Recital (9) of Regulation 1/2003 specifically alludes to national legislation on unfair trading practices. It would also seem that sectoral regulators can apply stricter national rules without reference to Articles 81 and 82 under this provision, subject of course to the general requirements of EC law.

As part of the need to secure uniform application of Community competition law, Article 16 of Regulation 1/2003 requires that national courts must avoid giving decisions which would conflict with a decision contemplated by the Commission in proceedings it has initiated. To that effect, the national court may assess whether it is necessary to stay its proceedings. As a further device to enhancing consistency and co-operation, NCAs, on their own initiative, may submit written observations to the national courts of their Member

---

[23] The meaning of this requirement, applicable to both Arts.81 and 82, was discussed in Ch.23, above.
[24] The original proposal sought to make Arts.81–82 *exclusively* applicable to situations where inter-State trade was affected.
[25] Reg.1/2003, Art.15(2). The non-confidential reports of these judgments are filed on the Commission's website at *http://europa.eu.int/comm/competition/antitrust/national—courts/index—en.html*.
[26] *ibid.*, Art.3(2).
[27] *ibid.*, Art.3(3).

State on issues relating to the application of Article 81 and Article 82.[28] With the permission of the court in question, NCAs may also make oral observations. The Commission enjoys similar powers, except that its observations are confined to situations "where the coherent application of Article 81 or Article 82 so requires". This, the Commission states, means that it will limit its observations "to an economic and legal analysis of the facts underlying the case pending before the national court."[29]

National courts dealing with proceedings for the application of Article 81 or Article 82 may also ask the Commission for information or its opinion on questions concerning Community competition rules.[30] This power is, of course, without prejudice to any national court's ability to seek a preliminary ruling from the Court of Justice using the Article 234 procedure.[31]

The ECN in operation

As stated above, the ECN[32] consists of the Commission and the **25–008** NCAs. Although the need for a network is recognised in Regulation 1/2003 and its operation is detailed in the Network Notice, the ECN is in many ways a remarkably informal arrangement.[33] In particular, there is no specific tool or authority to determine case allocation between the different potential arms of enforcement. Instead, the Network Notice refers to "principles of allocation"[34] which might result in an investigation either being undertaken by one NCA, or by several NCAs acting in parallel or by the Commission. The byword for choice among these parallel competences is efficiency, and the touchstone for exercising it is the notion of which institution is "well placed" to do so. This latter criterion adopts a more jurisdiction-led nexus to establish case allocation.[35]

According to paragraph 8 of the Network Notice, an authority can be considered well placed if the following three cumulative conditions are met:[36]

---

[28] *ibid.*, Art.15(3).
[29] Co-operation Notice, n.18, above, para.32.
[30] Reg.1/2003, Art.15(1). In 2004 nine such requests were made to the Commission, six of them by Spanish courts on a similar type of distribution agreement. See Comp.Rep. 2004, SEC (2005) 805 final, point 112.
[31] See Chap.14, above.
[32] Note that the ECN is not to be confused with the ICN, discussed briefly in Ch.22, above.
[33] See *http://europa.eu.int/comm/competition/antitrust/ecn/ecn—home.html* for the "one-stop access" website launched in Spring 2006. This page is nested within the Commission's Competition site. From its inception on May 1, 2004 to the end of the first quarter of 2006, the ECN had been informed of 550 investigations applying Art.81 or Art.82 (or both). Of these 427 had been initiated by NCAs and 123 by the Commission.
[34] n.10, above, para.5.
[35] See further, S. Brammer, "Concurrent Jurisdiction under Reg.1/2003 and the Issue of Case Allocation" (2005) 42 C.M.L.Rev. 1383.
[36] The Notice goes on to give illustrations of how these tests might apply: see paras.10–14.

— the agreement or practice has substantial direct or foresee-able effects on competition within its territory, is imple-mented within or originates from its territory;

— the authority is able to effectively bring to an end the entire infringement, ie it can adopt a cease-and-desist order the effect of which will be sufficient to bring an end to the infringement and it can, where appropriate, sanction the infringement adequately;

— it can gather, possibly with the assistance of other author-ities, the evidence required to prove the infringement.

The Notice provides that the Commission will be "particularly well placed" to deal with a case where "it is closely linked to other Community provisions which may be exclusively or more effectively applied by the Commission, if the Community interest requires the adoption of a Commission decision to develop Community competi-tion policy when a new competition arises or to ensure effective enforcement."[37]

Paragraph 7 of the Network Notice indicates a preference for a single well placed authority as often as possible, and this might frequently prove to be settled uncontroversially. However, there seems to be no final arbiter in the case of a number of NCAs being concerned and none willing to withdraw. Since each ECN member retains "full discretion" in deciding whether to pursue a case, there could be parallel proceedings in up to three Member States.[38] It has been suggested[39] that there may be competition between NCAs in the light of differences in legal culture and traditions, expertise, experience, staffing and reputation. NCAs looking to build up and enhance experience and reputation may encourage parallel inves-tigations at the expense of efficient case allocation.

The Commission and the NCAs have the power to provide one another with and use in evidence any matter of fact or of law, including confidential information.[40] There are restrictions as to use, so that the information exchanged can only be used for the purpose of applying Article 81 or Article 82 and in respect of the subject-matter for which it was collected by the transmitting authority. Further limitations apply if the exchanged information is to be used to impose sanctions on natural persons. Here the law of both the transmitting and receiving ECN authority must foresee penalties of "a similar kind" for infringements of the Treaty rules. Failing that, the information must have been collected in such a way as to respect

---

[37] *ibid.*, para.15.
[38] Where more than three Member States are affected the expectation must be that the Commission takes action since Art.14 of the Network Notice identifies it as "best placed" in this scenario.
[39] Brammer, *op.cit.*, n.35, above, at 1404.
[40] Reg.1/2003, Art.12(1).

the same level of protection of the rights of the defence of natural persons as provided for under the rules of the receiving authority.[41]

However, concern has been expressed that the exchange arrangements may prove detrimental to undertakings and other parties, especially in relation to confidentiality.[42]

The conduct of proceedings by the Commission

The carrying out of an investigation is undertaken against the **25–009** legislative framework provided by Regulation 1/2003 and Regulation 773/2004,[43] together with the detailed guidance set out in the Commission's Notices.[44] Of course, the general principles of EC law developed by the Court of Justice and Court of First Instance also apply. These have been particularly influential and, at times, have adopted controversial positions when seen against interpretations of the ECHR by the Court of Human Rights. The discussion below broadly divides into two stages of an investigation: first, the gathering information and evidence, where the Commission has a range of weapons available to combat reluctant undertakings; and secondly, the rights of the defence once the Commission has moved to a formal statement of objections.

Information and evidence

Undertakings are unlikely to be shouting their anti-competitive **25–010** practices from the roof-tops. The Commission is therefore enabled to seek information and establish evidence in a variety of ways. Its powers under Articles 18 to 21 of Regulation 1/2003 broadly correspond to, but go further than, its former position under Regulation 17/62. Given the intrusiveness of some of these powers, the European Courts are frequently called upon to determine the boundary between the effective enforcement of the competition rules and the legitimate interests of the undertakings.

(a) requests for information and power to take statements. By **25–011** virtue of Article 18, the Commission may, by simple request or by decision, require undertakings and associations to provide all "necessary" information. This is now a choice for the Commission and not, as was previously the case, a two-stage procedure. A failure to respond to a simple request will not lead to penalty, although supplying false or misleading information will.[45] If, however, the

---

[41] *ibid.*, Art.12(3).
[42] e.g. D. Reichelt, "To what Extent does the Co-operation within the European Competition Network Protect the Rights of Undertakings?" (2005) 42 C.M.L.Rev. 745.
[43] n.1, above.
[44] See especially, the *Notice on the Handling of Complaints by the Commission under Articles 81 and 82* [2004] OJ C101/5.
[45] Reg.1/2003, Art.18(2).

request is by decision then penalties may be imposed for non-compliance.[46] The Commission must forward copies of any request to the NCA of the Member State in whose territory the seat of the undertaking is located and the NCA of the Member State whose territory is affected.[47] At the request of the Commission, governments of the Member States and NCAs shall provide the Commission with all necessary information to carry out its duties under the Regulation.[48]

Case law from the similar provisions of the previous regime of Regulation 17/62 has been influential in shaping the current position under Regulation 1/2003. For example, the information to be supplied must not be disproportionate to the requirements of the investigation.[49] More fundamentally, in *Orkem*[50] the undertaking claimed that it had been forced into giving answers of a self-incriminating nature pursuant to an order under Regulation 17. The Court of Justice, whilst apparently denying the existence of any rule against self-incrimination as such in EC law, nevertheless held that the Commission could not compel an undertaking "to provide it with answers which might involve an admission on its part of the existence of an infringement . . . which it is incumbent upon the Commission to prove".[51] The Court of First Instance in a later ruling indicated that the acknowledgement of any absolute right to silence would constitute an unjustified hindrance to the Commission's performance of its duty to ensure that the rules on competition within the common market are observed.[52] This case law seems to be captured by Recital 23 of Regulation 1/2003, which provides:

> "When complying with a decision of the Commission, undertakings cannot be forced to admit that they have committed an infringement, but they are in any event obliged to answer factual questions and to provide documents, even if this information may be used to establish against them or against another undertaking the existence of an infringement."

However, the Court's position in *Orkem* has persistently caused rumblings from undertakings claiming incompatibility with Article 6 ECHR and the right to silence as part of a fair trial. Nevertheless, the Court, whilst acknowledging developments in the jurisprudence

---

[46] *ibid.*, Art.18(3).
[47] *ibid.*, Art.18(5).
[48] *ibid.*, Art.18(6).
[49] Case T–39/90 *Samenwerkende Electriciteits-produktiebedrijven (SEP) v Commission* [1991] E.C.R. II–1497, [1992] 5 C.M.L.R. 33.
[50] Case 374/87 *Orkem v Commission* [1989] E.C.R. 3283; [1991] 4 C.M.L.R. 502.
[51] [1989] E.C.R. 3283, para.35. See also Case 27/88 *Solvay v Commission* [1989] E.C.R. 3255 (summary publication).
[52] Case T–112/98 *Mannesmannröhren-Werke AG v Commission* [2001] E.C.R. II–729, para.66.

of the European Court Human Rights, has not seen the need to reverse its own case law.[53] This stance has been recently defended by Advocate General Geelhoed,[54] arguing that subsequent ECtHR rulings offer no cogent reasons to change the *Orkem* position:

"First, it must be borne in mind that that case law concerned natural persons in the context of 'classical' criminal procedures. Competition law concerns undertakings. The Commission is only allowed to impose fines on undertakings and associations of undertakings for violations of Articles 81 EC and 82 EC. It is not possible simply to transpose the findings of the [European Court of Human Rights] without more to legal persons or undertakings . . .

Second, there is no dispute that the [European Court of Human Rights] extended certain rights and freedoms to companies and other corporate entities. The same is true under Community law and under the Charter of Fundamental Rights of the European Union. That being said, the [European Court of Human Rights] also makes a distinction between the level of protection conferred on natural persons on the one hand and legal persons on the other. That may be inferred from other fundamental rights in the Convention, such as Article 8 . . .

Third, what is decisive, however, so far as Article 6 of the Convention is concerned, is that a request for documents is not contrary to the right to remain silent. The [European Court of Human Rights] did not recognise an absolute right to remain silent. It held in *Saunders* that "[t]he right not to incriminate oneself is primarily concerned, however, with respecting the will of an accused person to remain silent. As commonly understood in the legal systems of the Contracting Parties the Convention and elsewhere, it does not extend to the use in criminal proceedings of material which may be obtained from the accused through the use of compulsory powers but which has an existence independent of the will of the suspect such as, *inter alia*, *documents* acquired pursuant to a warrant, breath, blood and urine samples and bodily tissues for the purpose of DNA testing." That finding has been recently confirmed in *J.B. v Switzerland.*

Thus, the right not to make self-incriminating statements does not extend to information which exists independently of the will of the suspect such as, *inter alia*, documents. The production of those documents may be requested and they may

---

[53] Joined Cases C–238/99P, C–244/99P, C–245/99P, C–247/99P, C–250/99P to C–252/99P and C–254/99P, *PVC Cartel II* [2002] E.C.R. I–8375.
[54] Case C–301/04P *Commission v SGL Carbon*, Opinion January 19, 2006, Judgment pending. This case is an appeal from Case T–239/01, n.27, below.

be used as evidence. In that regard, I would refer in particular to documented information relating to and used in the internal processing and decision making of an undertaking, such as, for example, marketing or pricing strategies. Such information, available for internal use, may be requested. Possibly, it may reveal the likelihood of a cartel or concerted practice, but that as such is not self-incriminating. It is still possible to rebut that likelihood. To go further would be to take away the objective element of the Courts' case law, which would disturb the balance of enforcement."

The Advocate General's robust endorsement of the existing case law insists that the balance between effective enforcement of competition law and the rights of the defence is currently correctly drawn.

A new power introduced by Article 19 of Regulation 1/2003 and elaborated upon in Article 3 of Regulation 773/2004 allows the Commission to take statements from persons who give their consent to interview for the purpose of collecting information relating to the subject-matter of an investigation. The interview may be conducted by any means, including telephone or electronic, it may be recorded in any form and a copy made available to the person interviewed for approval.[55] It would seem that this kind of consensual interview will most likely apply to competitors or customers giving information about cartels or abuses.

25–012 **(b) Inspections.**   The power to inspect premises has always been the most invasive of the Commission's weapons, giving rise to the notorious, but temporally-misleading, epithet of the "dawn raid". Article 20 of Regulation 1/2003 authorises Commission officials to conduct all necessary inspections of undertakings and associations of undertakings. In particular,[56] they may enter any premises, land and means of transport of the undertaking, examine books and other records irrespective of the medium in which they are stored, take copies, seal any premises or records and to ask any representative or member of staff of the undertaking for explanations. Undertakings are required to submit to inspection ordered by decision of the Commission.[57] Where an undertaking opposes an inspection, the Member State concerned must provide the Commission officials with necessary assistance, including the assistance of the police or equivalent authority.[58]

If such assistance requires authorisation from a judicial authority according to national rules, that authorisation shall be applied for. According to Article 20(8), that national judicial authority

---

[55] Reg.773/2004, Art.3(2) and (3).
[56] Reg.1/2003, Art.20(2).
[57] *ibid.*, Art.20(3).
[58] *ibid.*, Art.20(6).

"shall control that the Commission decision is authentic and that the coercive measures envisaged are neither arbitrary nor excessive having regard to the subject-matter of the inspection. In its control of the proportionality of the coercive measures, the national judicial authority may ask the Commission, directly or through the Member State competition authority, for detailed explanations in particular on the grounds the Commission has for suspecting infringement of Articles 81 and 82 of the Treaty, as well as on the seriousness of the suspected infringement and on the nature of the involvement of the undertaking concerned. However, the national authority may not call into question the necessity for the inspection nor demand that it be provided with the information in the Commission's file. The lawfulness of the Commission decision shall be subject to review only by the Court of Justice."

Authorisation from the national judicial authority must be sought if the Commission wishes to inspect *other* premises, land or means of transport on the basis of a reasonable suspicion that books or other records may be kept there which may be relevant to prove a serious violation of Article 81 or Article 82. This extends to the homes of directors, managers and other members of staff, but with additional conditions.[59]

Not surprisingly, inspections conducted by the Commission have provoked defences based on fundamental rights protection, in particular by reference to the impact of the ECHR. At an early stage in the case law, the Court of Justice held[60] that the unannounced nature of a dawn raid of business premises under Regulation 17/62 did not infringe Article 8(1) of the ECHR relating to the protection of private and family life, home and correspondence. This was developed further in *Hoechst*,[61] where the Court explicitly stated that the protective scope of Article 8(1) ECHR was concerned with the development of man's personal freedom and could not be extended to business premises.[62] However, *Hoechst* was decided at a time when there was no direct interpretation on this issue by the European Court of Human Rights at Strasbourg. Its subsequent ruling in *Niemitz*[63] determined that Article 8(1) included certain professional or business activities or premises since self-employed persons could engage in business activities at home and private activities at their place of work.

---

[59] *ibid.*, Art.21. This provision did not exist under the old regime of Reg.17/62.
[60] Case 136/79 *National Panasonic v Commission* [1980] E.C.R. 2033, [1980] C.M.L.R. 169.
[61] Joined Cases 46/87 and 227/88 *Hoechst v Commission* [1989] E.C.R. 2859, [1991] 4 C.M.L.R. 410.
[62] *ibid.*, para.18.
[63] *Niemitz v Germany*, Series A, No.251-B, (1993) 16 E.H.R.R. 97, para.31.

Nevertheless, despite *Niemitz* and other European Court of Human Rights rulings,[64] the European Courts have maintained the *Hoechst* approach. The Court of First Instance, for example, stated in *PVC Cartel II*[65] that those developments did not directly affect the solutions adopted in *Hoechst*. The issue was raised again in *Roquette Frères*,[66] a request for a preliminary ruling made by a French court in relation to the authorisation of assistance by national authorities for an inspection. Advocate General Mischo carefully analysed the *Niemitz* reasoning and understood it to accept that the professional sphere does not necessarily, or, in every respect, deserve protection as extensive as that enjoyed by the private sphere.[67] In his view, inspections properly made pursuant to the competition rules of the Treaty and its own protections were therefore subject to safeguards equivalent to those inferred by the European Court of Human Rights from Article 8 ECHR. The Court of Justice dealt with the matter by recalling its own *Hoechst* ruling, which had established that:

> "the need for protection against arbitrary or disproportionate intervention by public authorities in the sphere of the private activities of any person, whether natural or legal, constitutes a general principle of Community law . . .
>
> For the purposes of determining the scope of that principle in relation to the protection of business premises, regard must be had to the case law of the European Court of Human Rights subsequent to the judgment in *Hoechst*. According to that case law, first, the protection of the home provided for in Article 8 of the ECHR may in certain circumstances be extended to cover such premises (see, in particular, the judgment of April 16, 2002 in *Colas Est and Others v. France*) and, second, the right of interference established by Article 8(2) of the ECHR might well be more far-reaching where professional or business activities or premises were involved than would otherwise be the case (*Niemietz v. Germany*)."[68]

These attempts at reconciliation of the ECHR and EC competition law positions are likely to be tested further once the new powers to carry out inspections at homes are exercised. Article 21 of Regulation 1/2003 provides for additional procedural hurdles beyond "normal" inspections, in particular the requirement of authorisation

---

[64] *Funke v France*, Series A, No.256–A, (1993) 16 E.H.R.R. 297.
[65] Joined Cases T–305–307, 313–316, 318, 325, 328–329 and 335/94 *Limburgse Vinyl Maatschappij v Commission* [1999] E.C.R. II–931; [1999] 5 C.M.L.R. 303.
[66] Case C–94/00 *Roquettes Frères SA v Directeur général de la concurrence, de la consommation et de larépression des fraudes* [2002] E.C.R. I–9011, [2003] 5 C.M.L.R. 53.
[67] *ibid.*, Opinion, para.38.
[68] *ibid.*, Judgment, paras 27 and 29.

from the national judicial authority for the execution of the Commission's decision. The national court's control role includes consideration of the seriousness of the suspected infringement, the importance of the evidence sought, the involvement of the undertaking concerned and the reasonable likelihood that business records relating to the subject-matter of the inspection are kept in the premises for which authorisation is requested.[69]

(c) **Professional privilege.** A final concern in gathering information 25–013 is that the Commission may be denied access to documents protected by professional privilege, the principle of the confidentiality of communications between lawyer and client. This principle was recognised by the Court of Justice in the *AM&S* case.[70] Protection of confidentiality was held to be subject, in effect, to three conditions. First, the communication must be "made for the purposes and in the interests of the client's rights of defence." That extended, in particular, to "all written communications exchanged after the initiation of the administrative procedure under Regulation 17 [as it was] which may lead to a decision on the application of [Articles 81 and 82] or to a decision imposing a pecuniary sanction on the undertaking,"[71] as well as to "earlier written communications which have a relationship to the subject-matter of that procedure."[72] Secondly, the communication must "emanate from independent lawyers, that is to say, lawyers who are not bound to the client by a relationship of employment."[73] Thirdly, the lawyers in question must be entitled to practise their profession in one of the Member States. Communications with two classes of lawyers are accordingly outside the privilege, viz. in-house lawyers, even in those Member States where they are subject to professional ethics and discipline, and lawyers from non-EU countries in the absence of any reciprocal arrangements with the EU.

The *AM&S* rule has been heavily criticised, particularly in the context of the advent of the 2004 changes to the enforcement system.[74] In *Akzo Nobel Chemicals v Commission*,[75] the President of the Court of First Instance acknowledged that a genuine issue existed, noting that:

> "The evidence therefore tends to show that increasingly in the legal orders of the Member States and possibly, as a consequence, in the Community legal order, there is no presumption

---

[69] Reg.1/2003, Art.21(3).
[70] Case 155/79 *AM & S v Commission* [1982] E.C.R. 1575, [1982] 2 C.M.L.R. 264.
[71] [1982] E.C.R. 1575, 1611.
[72] *ibid.*
[73] *ibid.*
[74] See representations made on the White Paper on Modernisation, n.1, above.
[75] Joined Cases T–125/03R and T–253/03R, *Akzo Nobel Chemicals Ltd, Akcros Chemicals Ltd v Commission* [2003] E.C.R. II–4771.

that the link of employment between a lawyer and an undertaking will always, and as a matter of principle, affect the independence necessary for the effective exercise of the role of collaborating in the administration of justice by the courts if, in addition, the lawyer is bound by strict rules of professional conduct, which where necessary require that he observe the particular duties commensurate with his status."[76]

The President accordingly made an order which maintained the confidentiality of material, including emails, between in-house lawyers and their undertaking, until the substantive hearing of the appeal.

The right to a hearing

25-014   Before it adopts a decision applying Article 81 or Article 82 the Commission is required, pursuant to Article 27 of Regulation 1/2003, to give the undertakings concerned the opportunity of being heard on the matters to which the Commission has taken objection. The exercise of the right to heard is set out in more detail in Regulation 773/2004 on the conduct of proceedings.[77] These provisions implement in the sphere of competition the general principle of law that a person whose interests are liable to be adversely affected by an individual decision of a public authority has a right to make his views known to the authority before the decision is taken. The key stages, and the issues about protection which they raise, are briefly discussed below.

25-015 **(a) The statement of objections and the Hearing Officer.**   In order for a person effectively to exercise his right to a hearing, he must be informed of the facts and considerations on the basis of which the responsible authority is minded to act.[78] Article 10(1) of Regulation 773/2004 places the Commission under a duty to inform the parties in writing of the objections raised against them. The issuing of a "statement of objections" marks the formal initiation of proceedings that may culminate in a finding that Article 81 or Article 82 has been infringed. Article 27 of Regulation 1/2003 provides that the Commission can only base its decisions on objections on which the parties concerned have been able to comment.[79]

---

[76] *ibid.*, para.126.
[77] n.1, above.
[78] Case 17/74 *Transocean Marine Paint v Commission*, [1974] E.C.R. 1063, [1974] 2 C.M.L.R.459.
[79] The undertakings may waive their right to a hearing: Joined Cases T–213/95 and 18/96 *SCK and FNK v Commission* [1997] E.C.R. II–1739; [1998] 4 C.M.L.R. 259. However, this must be unambiguously done if the Commission is to be able to omit to communicate documents: Case T–30/91 *Solvay v Commission* [1995] E.C.R. II–1775, para.57; [1996] 5 C.M.L.R. 57.

The statement of objections thus provides the boundaries of the case. The Court of Justice has repeatedly affirmed that it must set forth clearly all the essential facts upon which the Commission relies against the respondent undertakings.[80] A fairly succinct summary may be judged adequate for this purpose,[81] although the Commission must identify in the objections each of the infringements which it alleges to have occurred.[82] The final decision need not be an exact replica of the statement of objections, since the Commission must take into account factors which emerge during the administrative proceedings: some objections may be abandoned altogether, and different arguments may be put forward in support of those which are maintained.[83] Where, however, the Commission wishes to introduce fresh objections, a supplementary statement should be sent to the respondents.[84]

Once the statement of objections has been issued, the parties have a right of access to the Commission's file. The Commission must give the addressees of the statement of objections the opportunity to develop their arguments at an oral hearing, if they so request.[85] Hearings are conducted by a Hearing Officer "in full independence".[86] The principal task of the Hearing Officer is to ensure that the effective exercise of the right to be heard is respected in competition proceedings before the Commission. There are currently two Hearing Officers, who report to the Competition Commissioner but are not part of the Competition Directorate. The Hearing Officer may allow the parties to whom the statement of objections has been addressed, the complainants, other persons invited to the hearing, the Commission services and NCAs to ask questions during the hearing.[87]

(b) Access to the file.   One of the most frequently contested aspects **25–016** of the rights of defence in competition cases down the years has concerned access to the Commission's file. The evolution of

---

[80] See, e.g. Case 45/69 *Boehringer v Commission* [1970] E.C.R. 769; Case 85/76 *Hoffmann-La Roche v Commission* [1979] E.C.R. 461; [1979] 3 C.M.L.R. 211; Joined Cases 43 and 63/82 *VBVB and VBBB v Commission* [1984] E.C.R. 19; [1985] 1 C.M.L.R. 27.

[81] Case 48/69 *ICI v Commission* [1972] E.C.R. 619, 650–651; [1972] C.M.L.R. 557; Joined Cases 100–103/80 *Musique Diffusion Française v Commission* [1983] E.C.R. 1825; [1983] 3 C.M.L.R. 221.

[82] Joined Cases C–89/85 etc *Ahlström Oy v Commission ("Wood Pulp")* [1993] ECR I–1307. [1993] 4 C.M.L.R. 407.

[83] Joined Cases 209–215 and 218/78 *Van Landewyck v Commission* [1980] E.C.R. 3125; [1981] 3 C.M.L.R. 134, paras 68–70. See also Joined Cases T–305–307, 313–316, 318, 325, 328–329 and 335/94 *Re the PVC Cartel II: Limburgse Vinyl Maatschappij v Commission* [1999] E.C.R. II–931; [1999] 5 C.M.L.R. 303.

[84] Case 54/69 *Francolor v Commission* [1972] E.C.R. 851; [1972] C.M.L.R. 557.

[85] Reg.773/2004, Art.12.

[86] *ibid.*, Art.14. For the terms of reference for Hearing Officers, see Commission Dec.2001/462, [2001] O.J. L162/21.

[87] Reg.773/2004, Art.14(8).

principle in this area again displays the tensions between efficient and effective enforcement on the one hand, and fundamental rights and due process on the other. Establishing clear rules is not made any easier by the confidential and commercially-sensitive nature of many documents in competition cases. According to Article 27(2) of Regulation 1/2003:

> "The rights of defence of the parties concerned shall be fully respected in the proceedings. They shall be entitled to have access to the Commission's file, subject to the legitimate interest of undertakings in the protection of their business secrets. The right of access to the file shall not extend to confidential information and internal documents of the Commission or the competition authorities of the Member States . . ."

These requirements are developed in Articles 15 to 16 of Regulation 773/2004 and largely reflect the significant contributions of the case law in formulating the content of the rights of the defence.

Thus, for example, the Court of First Instance had held in *Hercules*[88] that the Commission was not able to depart from the standards it had voluntarily set for itself in its *Twelfth Report on Competition Policy*. As a result, the Commission was obliged to make available to the undertakings involved in proceedings under Article 81(1) all documents, whether in their favour or otherwise, which it had obtained during the course of the investigation, save where the business secrets of other undertakings, the internal documents of the Commission or other confidential information were involved.[89]

The Court of Justice has always refrained from holding the right of access to the file to be absolute. Instead, it has concentrated on the need for effective defence. It has summarised its case law as follows[90]:

> "A corollary of the principle of respect for the rights of the defence, the right of access to the file means that the Commission must give the undertaking concerned the opportunity to examine all the documents in the investigation file which may be relevant for its defence . . . Those documents include both incriminating evidence and exculpatory evidence, save where the business secrets of other undertakings, the internal documents of the Commission or other confidential information are involved . . .

[88] Case T–7/89 *Hercules Chemicals v Commission* [1991] E.C.R. II–1711; [1992] 4 C.M.L.R. 84, para.53, relying on Case 81/72 *Commission v Council* [1973] E.C.R. 575; [1973] C.M.L.R. 639.
[89] [1991] E.C.R. II–1711, at para.54.
[90] Joined Cases C–204/00 P, C–205/00 P, C–211/00 P, C–213/00 P, C–217/00 P and C–219/00 P *Aalborg Portland A/S v Commission* [2004] E.C.R. I–123.

It may be that the undertaking draws the Commission's attention to documents capable of providing a different economic explanation for the overall economic assessment carried out by the Commission, in particular those describing the relevant market and the importance and the conduct of the undertakings acting on that market.

The European Court of Human Rights has none the less held that, just like observance of the other procedural safeguards enshrined in Article 6(1) of the ECHR, compliance with the adversarial principle relates only to judicial proceedings before a tribunal and that there is no general, abstract principle that the parties must in all instances have the opportunity to attend the interviews carried out or to receive copies of all the documents taken into account in the case of other persons.

The failure to communicate a document constitutes a breach of the rights of the defence only if the undertaking concerned shows, first, that the Commission relied on that document to support its objection concerning the existence of an infringement and, second, that the objection could be proved only by reference to that document."[91] (citations omitted)

(c) Final decision. The Commission has a number of powers at its **25–017** disposal once it has concluded that there has been an infringement of Article 81 or Article 82. Article 7 of Regulation 1/2003 provides that the Commission may by decision order an infringement to be brought to an end. Termination may involve positive action on the part of the addressee or addressees, and the decision may specify the steps to be taken. Thus in *Commercial Solvents*,[92] a case involving an abuse of a dominant position, the Commission imposed on CSC and Instituto an obligation to deliver an initial quantity of aminobutanol to Zoja within 30 days and to submit within two months a plan for making supplies available in the longer term. A periodic penalty payment may be attached to the order to ensure that it is complied with.

The *Microsoft* saga[93] illustrates the extent to which positive action may be required. It will be recalled[94] that the Commission found two abuses under Article 82, one relating to Microsoft's refusal to disclose information which would allow interoperability and one concerning the bundling of WMP with its Windows PC operating

---

[91] *ibid.*, paras 68–71.
[92] Joined Cases 6 and 7/73 *Commercial Solvents Corporation v Commission* [1974] E.C.R. 223, [1974] 1 C.M.L.R. 309. The abuse consisted of a refusal to supply; see further, Ch.24.
[93] COMP/C–3/37.792 *Microsoft* (March 24, 2004); on appeal as Case T–201/04; for the consideration of interim measures, see Case T–201/04R *Microsoft v Commission* [2005] 4 C.M.L.R. 406
[94] Ch.24, above.

system. The Commission imposed positive obligations on Microsoft to disclose accurate interface documentation and to offer to PC manufacturers a version of its operating system withou WMP. The Commission added:

> "As a result of the Commission's remedy, the configuration of such bundles will reflect what consumers want, and not what Microsoft imposes. Microsoft retains the right to offer a version of its Windows client PC operating system product with WMP. However, Microsoft must refrain from using any commercial, technological or contractual terms that would have the effect of rendering the unbundled version of Windows less attractive or performing. In particular, it must not give PC manufacturers a discount conditional on their buying Windows together with WMP.
>
> The Commission believes the remedies will bring the anti-trust violations to an end, that they are proportionate, and that they establish clear principles for the future conduct of the company.
>
> To ensure effective and timely compliance with this decision, the Commission will appoint a Monitoring Trustee, which will, *inter alia*, oversee that Microsoft's interface disclosures are complete and accurate, and that the two versions of Windows are equivalent in terms of performance."

Those obligations were suspended pending the Court of First Instance's consideration of Microsoft's request for interim measures. After these were rejected, the Commission market-tested the inter-operability "solutions" before issuing a further decision on November 10, 2005 pursuant to Article 24(1) of Regulation 1/2003. This warned that if Microsoft did not comply by December 15, 2005 with its obligation to: (i) supply complete and accurate interoperability information; and (ii) make that information available on reasonable terms, it would face a daily fine of up to €2 million. On December 22, 2005, the Commission sent Microsoft a Statement of Objections. However, the revised interoperability documentation which was then released to the Trustee was described as unusable by experts' reports. The case had still not been satisfactorily resolved by the end of March 2006.[95]

The extensive, pro-active, use of remedies in relation to Article 82 may be compared to the more circumspect approach historically taken by the Commission under Article 81. In *Automec II*,[96] for

---

[95] Microsoft had requested an oral hearing for March 30–31, 2006. The Commission was contemplating ordering the imposition of a fine to run from December 2005 until eventual compliance.

[96] Case T–24/90, *Automec v Commission* [1992] E.C.R. II–2223; [1992] 5 C.M.L.R. 431.

example, the Commission claimed that it had no power in the circumstances of the case to require the positive action sought from the applicant in order to remedy an infringement of Article 81(1). In particular, it claimed it lacked the competence to order BMW to resume deliveries to its distributor and that this could only be done on the basis of national law. The Commission expressly distinguished between cases under Article 82, where specific acts of abuse could be remedied, and Article 81, where the infringing element must be the agreement. Therefore, it argued, its only power available under Article 3 of Regulation 17/62 with regard to the latter was to compel the parties to bring the agreement to an end. But in the case in question Automec wanted to be included in the agreement (i.e. the selective distribution network), not to see it terminated. This step, the Commission also argued, would be too great an incursion into freedom of contract. The Court of First Instance endorsed the Commission's position, stressing that "the Commission undoubtedly has power to find the existence of the infringement and order the parties concerned to end it, but it is not for the Commission to impose upon the parties its own choice among the different potential courses of action which all conform to the Treaty."[97]

However, caution should be exercised in drawing too many inferences from this case. In particular, it should be remembered that Article 7 of Regulation 1/2003 now refers to "any behavioural or structural remedies" necessary to bring the infringement to an end and that these can apply to either Article 81 or 82.

Public enforcement: fines and other penalties

Regulation 1/2003 identifies a number of remedies available for penalising infringements of Articles 81 and 82. This section will concentrate on the powers of the Commission to impose fines on undertakings and the restraints on their exercise arising either from the Commission's own guidelines or review by the European Courts. It should also be noted that Article 5 of Regulation 1/2003 also authorises NCAs to impose fines, penalty payments "or any other penalty provided for in their national law." The latter may result in stricter regimes in some cases. For example, the Enterprise Act 2002 in the United Kingdom establishes a cartel offence[98] for which individuals may be punished by imprisonment for up to five years. The same Act also provides for disqualification from office as a director on certain conditions.[99] The Commission's fining powers, on

25–018

---

[97] *ibid.*, para.52.
[98] Enterprise Act 2002, s.188.
[99] *ibid.*, s.204.

the other hand, are restricted to the undertaking committing the infringement.[1]

It may, of course, be asked why there is such a heavy reliance on fining as a sanction. There is a considerable literature[2] on the pros and cons of fining as a deterrent in relation to anti-competitive conduct. Without discussing these in detail, recurring questions address issues such as whether it is undertakings or individuals who should be the subject of penalties, whether fines are passed on in terms of prices or if they are budgeted for anyway in advance; and whether undertakings positively measure the risks of detection against benefits to be obtained in the short-run and conduct themselves accordingly. Regardless of the criminological, economic or sociological answers to these questions, it is clear that fines represent a major element of the Commission's enforcement policy.

Calculating fines: the Guidelines Notice

25–019   Fines under Article 23(2) of Regulation 1/2003 relate to intentional or negligent infringements of Article 81 or Article 82, contravention of interim measures or failing to comply with binding commitments.[3] The ceiling for each infringing undertaking is 10 per cent of turnover in the preceding business year. With regard to the amounts and calculation of fines, Article 23(3) of Regulation 1/2003 stipulates only that "regard shall be had both to the gravity and to the duration of the infringement". In 1998 the Commission adopted a Guidelines Notice[4] to establish a "new method" of determining fines with enhanced transparency and certainty. Although this is not legislation in the sense of Article 249 EC, case law makes it clear that it will be deemed to generate legitimate expectations in the wider world.[5] In the *Pre-Insulated Pipes* cartel case,[6] its leading judgment on fining policy, the Grand Chamber of the Court of Justice expressed the position as follows:

> "In adopting such rules of conduct and announcing by publishing them that they will henceforth apply to the cases to which they relate, the institution in question imposes a limit on the

---

[1] This may in itself be problematic. "Undertaking" is construed widely (see Ch.22 above) for the purposes of establishing a breach of the EC competition rules; but enforcement must be against a legal personality.

[2] See, *inter alia*, M Ermann and R Lundmann (eds), *Corporate and Governmental Deviance* (Oxford, OUP, 1978); W Wils, 'EC competition fines; to deter or not to deter' (1995) 15 Y.E.L. 17.

[3] *i.e.* decisions under Art.9 of Reg.1/2003, discussed above.

[4] *Guidelines on the Method of Setting fines* [1998] O.J. C9/3.

[5] For a wider discussion, see H. Hofmann, "Negotiated and Non-Negotiated Administrative Rule-Making: The Example of EC Competition Policy" (2006) 43 C.M.L.Rev. 153.

[6] Joined Cases C–189/02P, C–202/02P to C–208/02P and C–213/02P *Dansk Rørindustri*, [2005] E.C.R. I–5425.

exercise of its discretion and cannot depart from those rules under pain of being found, where appropriate, to be in breach of the general principles of law, such as equal treatment or the protection of legitimate expectations. It cannot therefore be excluded that, on certain conditions and depending on their conduct, such rules of conduct, which are of general application, may produce legal effects."[7]

Thus, whilst the Commission has a discretion when determining the amount of each fine and is not required to apply a precise mathematical formula,[8] it may not depart from the rules which it has imposed on itself. As the Court of First Instance has also observed:

"Since the Guidelines are an instrument intended to define, while complying with higher-ranking law, the criteria which the Commission proposes to apply in the exercise of its discretion when determining fines, the Commission must in fact take account of the Guidelines when determining fines, in particular the elements which are mandatory under the Guidelines."[9]

At the heart of the Guidelines is the idea that gravity and duration of the infringement are used to determine a basic amount for the fine, which can then be increased or reduced in the light of the aggravating or attenuating circumstances of the particular case. The guidelines divide both gravity and duration into three categories. Thus, in relation to gravity, infringements may be "minor", "serious" or "very serious", examples respectively being vertical restraints with limited market impact, vertical or horizontal restrictions with more extensive effects and horizontal cartels engaging in price-fixing or market-sharing. The basic element of the fine for these three types of gravity is likely to comprise up to €1 million for minor infringements, up to €20 million for serious ones, and above that for the very serious category. The three categories which make up duration are "short", "medium" and "long", representing periods of, respectively, up to one year, five years or longer. Nothing is to be added to the gravity sum for short infringements, but medium-term breaches may increase it by up to 50 per cent and long violations may add on 10 per cent of the gravity amount per year of the duration.

The Court of First Instance has also stressed[10] the significance of the requirement in the Guidelines to take account of the effective

---

[7] *ibid.*, para.211.
[8] Case T–150/89 *Martinelli v Commission* [1995] E.C.R. II–1165, para.59.
[9] Case T–15/02 *BASF v Commission* forthcoming, Judgment March 15, 2006, para.119, citing Joined Cases T–67/00, T–68/00, T–71/00 and T–78/00 *JFE Engineering v Commission* [2004] E.C.R. II–2501.
[10] *BASF*, n.9, above, para.120.

economic capacity of offenders to cause significant damage to other operators, particularly consumers, and to set the fine at a level which ensures that is has a sufficiently deterrent effect. However, the objective of deterrence is not a separate factor in the calculation of the level of fine. Instead, it operates as a reference point for the Commission that underpins the entire process of the calculation.[11] This means that it is not open to an undertaking to claim lack of reasoning by the Commission in failing specifically to verify the likelihood of repeat infringements.[12] The fact that the Guidelines do not include multipliers for deterrence does not preclude the Commission from applying them.[13] Similarly, the Guidelines cannot give rise to a legitimate expectation as to the level of the starting amount, of amounts added to it other than for reasons of the duration of the infringement and, thus, of the final figure for fines to be imposed in respect of very serious infringements.[14] The deterrence consideration is accordingly hugely influential in the final sum imposed and will lead to different amounts according to circumstances. Thus, in *BASF*, the particular undertaking had considerable financial resources when compared to other members of the cartel. In the Court of First Instance's view, this allowed it to raise the funds for the fine more readily and therefore justified the imposition of a fine proportionately higher than that imposed in respect of the same infringement committed by an undertaking without those resources.[15] More generally, the Court of Justice has repeatedly held that the proper application of the Community competition rules requires that the Commission may at any time adjust the level of fines to meet policy needs.[16]

25–020   Having determined the basic amount according to gravity and duration, the Commission also takes into account aggravating and attenuating circumstances in coming to the final amount to be imposed. Examples of the former listed in the Guidelines are: repeated infringements of the same type, attempts to obstruct the Commission's investigations, acting as leader or instigator of the infringement, retaliatory measures to enforce practices and the need to increase the penalty to exceed the gains improperly made if the latter are objectively possible to estimate. However, exercising its rights of defence must not be construed as obstruction of the Commission's investigation by the undertaking.[17]

In *BASF*, the Court of First Instance emphasised that "instigator" and "leader" are two different concepts: whereas instigation is

---

[11] *ibid.*, paras.226, 238.
[12] In *BASF* the Commission had doubled the "gravity" element for deterrence purposes.
[13] *BASF*, n.9, above, para.253.
[14] *ibid.*, para.252.
[15] *ibid.*, para.235.
[16] Joined Cases 100/80 to 103/80 *Musique Diffusion française v Commission* [1983] E.C.R. 1825.
[17] *Pre-Insulated Pipes*, n.6, above, para.353.

concerned with the establishment or enlargement of a cartel, leadership is concerned with its operation.[18] To be classified as an instigator:

"an undertaking must have persuaded or encouraged other undertakings to establish the cartel or to join it. By contrast, it is not sufficient merely to have been a founding member of the cartel. Thus, for example, in a cartel created by two undertakings only, it would not be justified automatically to classify those undertakings as instigators. That classification should be reserved to the undertaking which has taken the initiative, if such be the case, for example by suggesting to the other an opportunity for collusion or by attempting to persuade it to do so."[19]

Leadership may be joint, and for that purpose does not have to be equal in degree with other members of the cartel. This will obviously be a matter of detailed investigation, and individual acts are not as such determinative. For example, in the part of the *BASF* decision relating to restrictions applied to Vitamin C production by BASF, Roche, Takeda and others, the Court of First Instance rejected the Commission's finding that BASF had been the leader. A number of proposals about production quotas had been put forward; the fact that the proposal finally adopted was that of BASF as a compromise between the positions or Roche and Takeda did not make BASF a leader.[20] Roche, on the other hand, was the only undertaking which could conceivably be classified as a leader—it had organised a significant number of meetings, had met separately with cartel members in order to represent them in other further meetings, collected the sales figures of cartel members and reported to them overall results by undertaking.[21]

Attenuating circumstances in the Guidelines include: a purely passive or "follow-my-leader" role in the infringement, non-implementation in practice of agreements, prompt termination of the violation as soon as the Commission intervenes, reasonable doubt on the part of the undertaking as to whether its conduct constitutes an infringement, negligent or unintentional breaches and effective co-operation beyond the scope of the Leniency Notice.[22] In *BASF*, the Court of First Instance rejected the applicant's attempt to make an attenuating circumstance out of the measures it had taken after the infringements had come to an end. The company had

---

[18] *BASF*, n.9, above, para.316.
[19] *ibid.*, para.321.
[20] *ibid.*, para.392.
[21] *ibid.*, para.404.
[22] Discussed further, para.25–021 below.

dismissed senior executives, adopted internal competition compliance programmes and instituted staff awareness training. These
steps, it argued, reduced the risk of future infringement and
accordingly should reduce the need for a deterrence component in
the fine. The Court of First Instance ruled that the preventive
measures placed 'no duty whatsoever'[23] on the Commission to
reduce the fine, even though it had taken compliance programmes
into account in other previous cases.[24]

As the Court of First Instance has made clear,[25] the objective of
the Guidelines is transparency and impartiality, not the foreseeability of the level of the fines. Moreover, the European Courts
recognise the considerable discretion held by the Commission. The
Court of First Instance's review is confined to the legality of the
Commission's decision. It is therefore only possible for the Court to
exercise its unlimited jurisdiction under Article 229 EC and Article
31 of Regulation 1/2003 if it makes a finding of illegality affecting
that decision and accordingly moves to annul or adjust the fine if
necessary. The Court of Justice, in turn, will not interfere with the
Court of First Instance's assessment:

> "it is not for the Court, when ruling on questions of law in the
> context of an appeal, to substitute, on grounds of fairness, its
> own assessment for that of the Court of First Instance exercis-
> ing its unlimited jurisdiction to rule on the amount of fines
> imposed on undertakings for infringements of Community law.
> The Court cannot therefore, at the appeal stage, examine
> whether the amount of the fine fixed by the Court of First
> Instance, in the exercise of its unlimited jurisdiction, is propor-
> tionate in relation to the gravity and duration of the infringe-
> ment as established by the Court of First Instance on
> completion of its appraisal of the facts"[26]

Proportionality is, of course, a principle of EC law which can be
invoked in order to contest the legality of the Commission's original
fining decision. However, an undertaking will only be able to pursue
such a claim based on its particular circumstances and not by trying
to establish generalities from levels of multipliers applied by the
Commission in other cases.[27]

---

[23] *BASF*, n.9, above, para.266.
[24] e.g. Case T–7/89 *Hercules Chemicals v Commission* [1991] E.C.R. II–1711; Case T–13/89 *ICI v Commission* [1992] E.C.R. II–1021; Case T–28/99 *Sigma Tecnologie v Commission* [2002] E.C.R. II–1845 and Case T–23/99 *LR AF 1998 v Commission* [2002] E.C.R. II–1705.
[25] e.g. *BASF*, n.9, above, para.250.
[26] Case C–338/00 *Volkswagen v Commission* [2003] E.C.R. I–9189, para.151.
[27] e.g. A multiplier of 2.5 (i.e. 150 per cent) was treated as excessive by the CFI in Joined Cases T–236/01, T–239/01, T–244/01 to T–246/01, T–251/01 and T–252/01 *Tokai Carbon v Commission* [2004] E.C.R. II–1181 on the basis of a comparison with multipliers applied against other members of the same cartel; but it had not interfered with the same multiplier figure in T–31/99 *ABB Asea Brown Boveri v Commission* [2002] E.C.R. II–1881.

Uncovering cartels: leniency incentives

Obviously, there can be no effective enforcement of the competi- **25–021** tion rules so long as cartels remain secret. The Commission's desire to detect as well as deter has led to its adoption of Leniency Notices,[28] which seek to reward (by immunity or reduced fines) participants in cartels who "blow the whistle" about their existence. Not surprisingly, such an attractive carrot comes with conditions, explained more fully below. The position is complicated by the fact that NCAs, or at least many of them,[29] also run their own leniency programmes. As these can differ from each other, and from the scheme contained in the Commission's Notice, there is a practical issue about whether multiple applications are necessary or desirable in the absence of a "one-stop shop" for leniency.[30] Certainly, the Network Notice indicates than an application to one ECN authority is not to be considered as an application for leniency to any other authority and underlines that it is for the applicant to take the steps which it considers appropriate to protect its position.[31] The discussion below is confined to the Commission's arrangements.

The 2002 Leniency Notice concerns "secret cartels between two or more competitors aimed at fixing prices, production or sales quotas, sharing markets including bid-rigging or restricting imports or exports."[32] The requirements for obtaining leniency differ according to whether the undertaking is seeking immunity or a reduction in fines. In the case of immunity applications, the undertaking must be either the first to submit evidence which in the Commission's view may enable it to adopt a decision to carry out a cartel investigation[33] or the first to submit evidence which in the Commission's view may enable it to find a cartel infringement of Article 81(1).[34] The first of these avenues corresponds to the situation where the evidence allows the Commission to carry out a surprise inspection and depends on the Commission not already having sufficient evidence itself. The second category is used in practice[35] to deal with requests for immunity made after an inspection has already occurred. This route is subject to an extra requirement, namely that no conditional

---

[28] The current version came into force from February 14, 2002: *Notice on immunity from fines and reduction of fines in cartel cases* [2002] O.J. C45/3; this replaced the original Notice [1996] O.J. C207/4. In the first three and a half years of operation of the 2002 Notice, double the number of leniency applications had been made when compared to the entire six years for which the 1996 Notice applied.

[29] Seventeen at the time of writing.

[30] See M. Reynolds and D. Anderson, "Immunity and Leniency in EU Cartel Cases: Current Issues" [2006] E.C.L.R. 82.

[31] Network Notice, n.10, above, para.38.

[32] n.28, above, para.1.

[33] *ibid.*, para.8(a).

[34] *ibid.*, para.8(b).

[35] See B. van Barlingen and M. Barennes, "The European Commission's 2002 Leniency Notice in Practice" (Autumn 2005) *Competition Newsletter* 6 (accessible via Commission website).

immunity has already been given to an undertaking on the basis of the first path. Immunity either way is subject to the following cumulative conditions: (a) that the undertaking co-operates fully, on a continuous basis and expeditiously throughout the Commission's administrative procedure; (b) that the undertaking ends its involvement in the suspected infringement no later than the time at which it submits evidence; and (c) that the undertaking did not take steps to coerce other undertakings to participate in the infringement.[36]

Firms that do not meet the conditions for immunity may nevertheless still benefit from a reduction in the fine that would otherwise be imposed. The basic requirement here is that an undertaking "must supply the Commission with evidence of the suspected infringement which represents significant added value with respect to the evidence already in the Commission's possession and must terminate its involvement in the suspected infringement no later than the time at which it submits the evidence." [37] In any final decision adopted at the end of the administrative procedure, the Commission will determine whether the evidence indeed represented significant added value and set out the level of reduction to be applied. The benefit, in the form of a reduction relative to the fine which would otherwise be imposed, is 30 to 50 per cent for the first undertaking, 20 to 30 per cent for the second undertaking and up to 20 per cent for subsequent undertakings.[38]

25–022   According to the Notice, the concept of "added value" refers to the extent to which the evidence strengthens, by its very nature and/ or its level of detail, the Commission's ability to prove the facts in question.[39] The question of whether it is "significant" will of course have to be measured in the context of specific case circumstances. However, the fact that undertakings are able to apply for both immunity and a reduction in fines under the Leniency Notice suggests that a reduction may be available for information which, whilst not enough to gain immunity, satisfies the significance test for a reduction. Particular possibilities include the corroboration of other evidence, identifying a larger geographical application or wider range of activities of the cartel then hitherto believed, or allowing the Commission to prove that the cartel has been in operation for longer than it could previously demonstrate. However, as it is the Commission that will decide what is "significant" and, moreover, only do so at the end point of the administrative process, an application for leniency carries its own risks. Some firms may take the view that a possibility of securing, say, 10 per cent off an as yet unquantified fine is not a gamble worth taking.

---

[36] 2002 Notice, n.28, above, para.11.
[37] *ibid.*, para.21.
[38] *ibid.*, para.23.
[39] *ibid.*, para.22.

There are other problems associated with the operation of leniency applications. A particular criticism has been made in relation to the possibility that corporate statements given to the Commission in the course of a leniency application can become more widely available through discovery procedures in later civil proceedings (especially in third countries, such as the United States). The Commission has addressed this by proposing an amendment to the 2002 Notice[40] which would establish a special procedure for such statements. Under this proposal, undertakings will be able to provide statements in oral form, recorded and kept by the Commission. Access to the file, including corporate statements, will be given only for the purposes of Article 81 proceedings and no mechanical copies of corporate statements will be allowed.

The Commission certainly claims success for its Leniency Notice in terms of uncovering secret cartels. The danger, perhaps, is that requests for immunity and/or reductions clog up the very system that is intended to assist the targeting of the most objectionable anti-competitive practices. In any event, the 2002 Leniency Notice does not affect the civil liability of an undertaking for breach of Article 81. It is to the private enforcement of infringements of the competition rules that we now turn.

Private enforcement: remedies before national courts

The point has already been made that the modernisation reforms 25–023 adopted in 2004 were premised on a view that more use could and should be made of private remedies at local level. This argument was not confined to the perceived benefits to be achieved from freeing up the Commission's time to devote to hardcore cartels. After all, a competitor, customer or consumer injured by an undertaking in breach of Article 81 or Article 82 does not derive any great or direct benefit from seeing the perpetrator fined by the Commission or NCA. In the case law immediately preceding the 1999 White Paper on Modernisation,[41] the Commission had pointed to the value of private action with increasing frequency and had successfully invoked the availability of alternative redress to justify refusals to take complaints forward.[42]

Nevertheless, the incorporation of this privatization tendency into the operating framework since 2004[43] still represents a significant

---

[40] Draft amendment open for consultation until March 2006.

[41] n.2, above.

[42] *e.g.* Case C–91/95 *Tremblay v Commission* [1996] E.C.R. I–5574; [1997] 4 C.M.L.R. 211, where the CFI referred to the Commission being able to reject a complaint "provided that the rights of the complainant ... can be adequately safeguarded, in particular, by the national courts".

[43] See the *Commission Notice on the Handling of Complaints by the Commission under Articles 81 and 82 of the EC Treaty* [2004] O.J. C101/65.

leap of faith. As Advocate General Geelhoed observed in relation to a number of cases referred by Italian courts on whether damages were available to consumers injured by concerted practices adopted by insurance companies:

"... private enforcement in Europe is still in its infancy, or at least it is clearly not practised on the scale familiar from other jurisdictions, especially that of the United States, where some 90 per cent of antitrust proceedings are initiated by private parties. In the European Union the emphasis has traditionally lain on public enforcement, both by the European Commission and by national authorities."[44]

The Advocate General summarised the arguments in favour of private enforcement thus:

"Besides the sanction of invalidity ensuing from Article 81(2) EC, an advantage mentioned in this context is that national courts may award damages. A court should also give a ruling in any dispute brought before it, and it should protect the rights of individuals. As public enforcers, on the other hand, act in the general interest, they often have certain priorities, and not every complaint is therefore considered as to its substance. Furthermore, civil actions may have a deterrent effect on (potential) offenders against the prohibition of cartels and so contribute to the enforcement of that prohibition and to the development of a culture of competition among market operators."[45]

However, the Advocate General added a word of caution:

"The growth in private enforcement may, however, vary from one Member State to another, depending on procedural culture, the restrictions imposed on jurisdiction, rules on the burden of proof, the possibility of class actions, etc. The effectiveness of that enforcement is, of course, partly determined by the accessibility of the national courts."[46]

There are thus a number of improbables involved in assessing whether the actual take-up of opportunities for local redress will match the Commission's strenuous advocacy. In purely doctrinal terms, it is important to clarify the exact basis of such claims. More specifically, the question to be examined is whether a *Francovich-*

---

[44] Joined Cases C–295/04 to C–298/04 *Manfredi* (Opinion, January 26, 2006), para.29.
[45] *ibid.*, para.30.
[46] *ibid.*, para.31.

type[47] autonomous remedy exists at the private level for damages against undertakings in breach of Article 81 or Article 82, or whether the enforcement mechanism amounts to a set of disparate (albeit perhaps converging) national remedies and claims regulated or supervised within the "usual" twin themes of equivalence and effectiveness.

The case in favour of a Community right to damages against individuals who infringe Treaty rules had been forcefully presented by Advocate General van Gerven in *H. Banks & Co Ltd v British Coal Corporation*,[48] a case following shortly on the heels of *Francovich*. The Advocate General pointed to the remedy as both the logical consequence of horizontal direct effect and an important step in the more effective enforcement of decentralised competition law. However, the Court of Justice avoided the need to discuss these questions by finding that the rules of the ECSC at issue in that case were not directly effective in the first place. This particular discussion was only kick-started again by the Court's judgment in *Courage v Crehan*,[49] a decade after it had decided *Francovich*.

The "Courage" doctrine: a communautaire horizontal remedy for private parties?

The case arose from a reference made under Article 234 EC by **25-024** the English Court of Appeal in the context of a tied-pub contract. Two key aspects of the case formed the context for the request: first, it was one of the parties to the contract who was seeking to claim damages on the basis that it infringed Article 81; secondly, as presented by the referring court, English law treated contracts in breach of Article 81 as illegal and that, consequently, parties to an illegal contract could not recover damages as a matter of English law. The answers given by the Court of Justice spawned a critical literature[50] which principally engaged with whether the Court had created a right to damages for breach of Article 81 as a matter of Community law or whether it had, more narrowly, applied its general effectiveness principles to the particular context of Article 81. If the latter, then damages might be seen as the usual expectation as a national remedy but not mandated by EC law as such.

The key passages of principle are, indeed, strikingly reminiscent of the Court's reasoning earlier when unveiling state liability in

---

[47] Joined Cases C–6 and 9/90 *Francovich v Italy* [1991] E.C.R. I–5357; [1993] 2 C.M.L.R. 66; discussed above, Ch.6.

[48] Case C–128/92 [1994] E.C.R. I–1209; [1994] 5 C.M.L.R. 30.

[49] Case C–453/99 *Courage v Crehan Ltd* [2001] E.C.R. I–6314.

[50] See in particular, A. Komninos, "New Prospects for the Private Enforcement of EC Antitrust Rules before National Courts" (2002) 39 C.M.L.Rev. 447; O. Odudu and J. Edelman, "Compensatory Damages for Breach of Art.81" (2002) 27 E.L.Rev. 327; N. Reich, "The 'Courage' Doctrine: Encouraging or Discouraging Compensation for Antitrust Injuries?" (2005) 42 C.M.L.Rev. 53.

damages to individuals in *Francovich*. Having referred to its *SABAM* ruling[51] in relation to national courts and the EC competition rules, the Court continued:

> "It follows . . . that *any individual* can rely on a breach of [Article 81(1)] of the Treaty before a national court even where he is a party to a contract that is liable to restrict or distort competition within the meaning of that provision . . .
>
> The full effectiveness of [Article 81] of the Treaty and, in particular, the practical effect of the prohibition laid down in [Article 81(1)] would be put at risk if it were not open to any individual to claim damages for loss caused to him by a contract or by conduct liable to restrict or distort competition.
>
> Indeed, *the existence of such a right* strengthens the working of the Community competition rules and discourages agreements or practices, which are frequently covert, which are liable to restrict or distort competition. From that point of view, *actions for damages before the national courts can make a significant contribution to the maintenance of effective competition* in the Community.
>
> There should not therefore be any absolute bar to such an action being brought by a party to a contract which would be held to violate the competition rules."[52] (emphasis added)

Clearly, this passage can be read very widely if so desired. The italicised parts were couched in more general terms than required by the circumstances of the case. Moreover, as was also the case in the *Francovich* ruling, the structure of the *Courage* judgment is to set out general observations and then move to the particular context.

It is at this second stage that the *Courage* judgment could be read as a marginal retreat from a full-blown endorsement of any autonomous *communautaire* entitlement to damages. The final sentence in the above extract is much more redolent of the *Factortame*[53] dispute, where a particular remedy in English law was also unavailable[54] at the time of the request for an interpretation under Article 234. Indeed, in the later passages of *Courage*, the Court restricts the discussion to the effectiveness of the national (lack of) remedy in protecting an individual's enjoyment of his rights under the EC competition rules. The Court specifically acknowledged that there could be circumstances where the right to damages could be limited in relation to a party responsible for the restriction on competition.

---

[51] n.17, above.
[52] *Courage*, n.49, above, paras.24–28, citations omitted.
[53] Case C–213/89 *R v Secretary of State for Transport, ex p. Factortame* [1990] E.C.R. I–2433; [1990] 3 C.M.L.R. 375.
[54] i.e. interim relief against the Crown.

Nevertheless, it now seems clear that the broader sense of the *Courage* judgment has gained currency. The Cooperation Notice, for example, puts *Courage* and *Francovich* together as examples where individuals should, under certain conditions, be able to ask a national court for damages.[55] More forcefully, the Commission's Green Paper of 2005[56] declares that "individuals who have suffered a loss arising from an infringement of Articles 81 or 82 have the right to claim damages." Advocate General Geelhoed, in his *Manfredi* Opinion,[57] used *Courage* to give an affirmative answer to the national court's specific question as to the right of a third party to claim damages where there is a causal relationship between the agreement or practice and the harm.

Nullity of prohibited agreements

In the case of Article 81 the civil consequences of infringement **25–025** are spelt out by the second paragraph, which provides: "Any agreements or decisions prohibited pursuant to this Article shall be automatically void". The automatic nullity in Article 81(2) "applies to those parts of the agreement affected by the prohibition, or to the agreement as a whole if it appears that those parts are not severable from the agreement itself".[58] Whether any offending clauses can be severed, leaving the main part of the agreement intact, falls to be determined under the law of the Member State concerned.[59] In a case involving the combined application of Article 10 and Article 81,[60] the Court of Justice ruled that the national competition authority had a duty to disapply the offending national legislation and could apply penalties in relation to infringing conduct.

The Commission's Green Paper

The Green Paper[61] advocates damages claims as a way of boosting **25–026** both the remedies for consumers and injured firms whilst improving the efficiency and effectiveness of competition law more generally. However, the Commission acknowledges that many obstacles still exist to the pursuit of claims at national level. The many questions

---

[55] *Co-operation between the Commission and the Courts, op. cit.*, n.18, above, para.10.
[56] *Green Paper, Damages Actions for Breach of the EC Antitrust Rules*, COM (2005) 672 final.
[57] n.44, above, paras 56–58.
[58] Case 56/65 *Société Technique Minière v Maschinenbau Ulm* [1966] E.C.R. 235; [1966] C.M.L.R. 357.
[59] Case C–230/96 *Cabour SA and Nord Distribution Automobile SA v Automobiles Peugeot SA and Automobiles Citröen SA* [1998] E.C.R. I–2055; [1988] 5 C.M.L.R. 679. See also Joined Cases T–185 and 190/96 *Riviera Auto Service Etablissements Dalmasso v Commission* [1999] E.C.R. II–93; [1999] 5 C.M.L.R. 31.
[60] Case C–198/01 *Consorzio Industrie Fiammiferi (CIF) v Autorità Garante della Concorrenza e del Mercato* [2003] E.C.R. I–8055.
[61] *op.cit.*, n.56, above.

on which the Green Paper sought consultation included: access to evidence, quantum of damages, the availability of a passing-on defence (whereby an undertaking subjected to an anti-competitive practice may have passed on the overcharge to its own customers), the desirability of group actions on behalf of consumers, and questions of jurisdiction and applicable law.

The future of enforcement of competition law thus depends upon a balance between the public and private approaches. Advocate General Geelhoed has noted[62] that a possible civil claim for damages, in addition to or separate from a fine, may increase the deterrent effect and enhance enforcement. But, unlike the US federal antitrust legislation, there is no EC provision for "treble damages" for deterrence purposes. In the absence of a harmonised system of remedies for antitrust infringements, the normal principles of equivalence and effectiveness will come under greater scrutiny in a competition context.

Further reading

Armengol O., and Pascual, A., "Some Reflections on Article 9 Commitment Decisions in the Light of the Coca-Cola Case" [2006] E.C.L.R. 124.

Brammer, S., "Concurrent Jurisdiction under Regulation 1/2003 and the Issue of Case Allocation" (2005) 42 C.M.L.Rev. 1383.

Gerber D., and Cassinis, P., "The 'Modernisation' of EC Competition Law: Achieving Consistency in Enforcement" [2006] E.C.L.R. 10 (Part I) and 51 (Part II).

Monti, G., "Anticompetitive Agreements: the Innocent Party's Right to Damages" (2002) 27 E.L.Rev.282.

Reich, N., "The 'Courage' Doctrine: Encouraging or Discouraging Compensation for Antitrust Injuries?" (2005) 42 C.M.L.Rev. 53.

Reynolds M., and Anderson, D., "Immunity and Leniency in EU Cartel Cases: Current Issues" [2006] E.C.L.R. 82.

Venit, J., "Brave New World: The Modernization and Decentralization of Enforcement under Articles 81 and 82 of the EC Treaty" (2003) 40 C.M.L.Rev. 537.

---

[62] *Manfredi*, n.44, above, para.65.

CHAPTER 26

MEMBER STATES, PUBLIC AND ENTRUSTED UNDERTAKINGS: ARTICLE 86

Guide to this Chapter: Article 86 EC is a complex provision **26–001** which governs the extent to which the usual competition rules apply to Member States and to undertakings given special rights or privileges by States. After a brief discussion of the general policy issues affecting the relationship between States, markets and public services, the Chapter then analyses the three separate paragraphs of Article 86. It discusses the conditions upon which States will be legally responsible under Article 86(1) for infringements by undertakings of other rules of the Treaty, such as Article 82, paying particular attention to the notion of "inevitable abuse" that the Court has been willing to apply in some situations. Article 86(2), which allows undertakings entrusted with services of general economic interest to escape the full rigour of the Treaty rules, is shown to have evolved from a strict derogation to a mechanism for balancing of competition and public interest concerns. The Commission's special supervisory and legislative powers under Article 86(3) are also briefly examined. The Chapter concludes with a discussion of Article 16 EC, which stresses the value attached by the European Union to services of general economic interest and which has the capacity to become an important constitutional principle.

Introduction to Article 86 EC

The influence of the State in the economies of the European **26–002** Union may appear in a variety of forms, whether as regulator,[1]

---

[1] State measures of this type may, for example, fall within Art.28 EC; Ch.16, above.

participant or provider of resources.[2] This Chapter concentrates upon the Community rules which apply in relation to undertakings which are State controlled or which enjoy a privileged legal status, normally in return for carrying out certain tasks deemed to be of public importance. Activities which have often been undertaken in this way to varying degrees in the Member States include the energy utilities, railway and other transport services, postal and telecoms services, broadcasting and many other public services.[3] The organisation of Member State participation may be at national, regional or local level.

The extent to which the competition rules of the Treaty are applied to public or privileged undertakings has fundamental implications for the relationship between State and market. A number of approaches can be envisaged for the treatment of legal monopolies.[4] At one end of the spectrum, for example, the State might be said to have absolute sovereignty to grant exclusive rights. At the other, a paradigm of absolute competition could hold such exclusivity to be an infringement *per se* of the competition rules by creating a dominance in which abuses could be pursued. The case law of the Court indicates a middle ground, sometimes favouring a limited form of sovereignty and intervening only when abuses necessarily flow from the grant of exclusivity, but on other occasions adopting a limited competition model in which the existence of a monopoly requires justification against higher interests recognised in Community law. Certainly, the Court recognises that the full force of the competition rules cannot always be applied. In the specific context of undertakings falling within the scope of Article 86(2) (see below), the Court has observed that Member States:

> "cannot be precluded, when defining the services of general economic interest which they entrust to certain undertakings, from taking account of objectives pertaining to their national policy or from endeavouring to attain them by means of obligations and constraints which they impose on such undertakings".[5]

Taking the Treaty at face value, the approach taken by Community law to public and privileged undertakings would seem that, while

---

[2] e.g. in the form of state aid; see Ch.27, below.
[3] This is not a Treaty term and is only used here as a general shorthand. The notion of "services of general economic interest" is central to Art.86(2), discussed fully below. However, a number of Member States attach particular meaning to public services in national law, e.g. France (*ordre public*) and Italy (*servizio pubblico*). See T. Prosser, *The Limits of Competition Law, Markets and Public Services* (Oxford, OUP, 2005), Ch.5.
[4] Edward and Hoskins, "Art.90: Deregulation and EC law, reflections arising from the XVI FIDE conference" (1995) 32 C.M.L.Rev. 157.
[5] Case C–157/94 *Commission v Netherlands* [1997] E.C.R. I–5699, para.40.

there can be no objection in principle to their special relationship with the State,[6] whatever legal form this may take, their behaviour as market participants is governed by the same rules as those applicable to purely private undertakings, except where the Treaty itself specifically permits some derogation. The first limb of this proposition depends in part upon Article 295 EC, preserving intact the systems of property ownership in the Member States, which are therefore free to determine the extent and internal organisation of their public sectors; and in part upon the clear inference to be drawn from Article 86(1) EC that the conferment of special or exclusive rights upon an undertaking does not, in itself, constitute an infringement of any Treaty rule.[7] Support for the second limb of the general proposition can be found in the unqualified reference to "undertakings" in Articles 81 and 82, and in the limited exemption contained in Article 86(2) for the benefit of entrusted undertakings and fiscal monopolies which would have been formulated differently if the rules of the Treaty did not normally apply to public undertakings.

However, this general proposition does not wholly encapsulate the case law developments, particularly since the 1990s as the tensions between market concerns, national policy goals and other, non-economic, values in the Treaty have repeatedly come before the Court. Faced with these sensitive and highly politically charged choices, the Court has adopted a variety of approaches. One method has been to jettison jurisdiction by arguing that the activity, or the way it is organised, falls outside the scope of the Treaty's competition rules. It has already been seen[8] that the key concept of "undertaking" can be used for this gatekeeping role in relation to some solidarity-based healthcare and welfare systems. However, this line-drawing can produce uncomfortable contortions as to whether something is "economic" or not, and the extent to which some activities or functions can be severed from others.[9] A different approach is to apply the Treaty but to utilise the scope provided by Article 86(2) to mitigate the impact of the competition rules on a case-by-case basis. As will be seen below, the methodology adopted by the Court for the application of this provision has changed considerably over recent years. Whether Article 86(2) is accurately described now as an exception or a balancing exercise will be

---

[6] Although Art.4(1) EC assumes "an open market economy with free competition".

[7] So held by the Court in Case 155/73 *Sacchi* [1974] E.C.R. 409; [1974] 2 C.M.L.R. 177, and affirmed on numerous occasions since. See, for example, Case C–266/96 *Corsica Ferries France* [1998] E.C.R. I–3949; [1998] 5 C.M.L.R. 402.

[8] See Ch.22, above, particularly the arguments applied in Case C–160/91 *Poucet and Pistre* [1993] E.C.R. I–637; Case C–67/96 *Albany International BV v Stichting Bedrijfspensioenfonds Textielindustrie* [1999] E.C.R. I–5751, [2000] 4 C.M.L.R. 446; Joined Cases C–180/98 to C–184/98 *Pavlov* [2000] E.C.R. I–6451, [2001] 4 C.M.L.R. 30; Joined Cases C–264/01, C–306/01, C–354/01 and C–355/01 *AOK Bundesverband* [2004] E.C.R. I–2493.

[9] See Advocate General Poiares Maduro's Opinion in Case C–205/03P *FENIN* (November 10 2005, Judgment pending).

considered in more detail below. In addition, Article 16 EC, introduced by the Treaty of Amsterdam, reinforces the particular position occupied by services of general economic interest in the values of the European Union, although the legal effects of this provision await more precise elaboration.

The present Chapter is primarily concerned with Article 86 EC. Another provision of the Treaty, Article 31, relates to a particular category of public undertakings, namely state monopolies of a commercial character.[10] However, since Article 31 constitutes a specialised regime for the removal of obstacles to the free movement of goods which may be associated with the arrangements under which such monopolies operate, it was dealt with in Chapter 16, above. It should be remembered, however, that Article 86(2), discussed fully in this Chapter, is applicable to Article 31 monopolies.[11]

26–003   Article 86 EC provides as follows:

"1. In the case of public undertakings and undertakings to which Member States grant exclusive or special rights, Member States shall neither enact nor maintain in force any measure contrary to the rules contained in this Treaty, in particular to those rules provided for in Article 12 and Articles 81 to 89.

2. Undertakings entrusted with the operation of services of general economic interest or having the character of a revenue producing monopoly shall be subject to the rules contained in this Treaty, in particular to the rules on competition, insofar as the application of such rules does not obstruct the performance, in law or in fact, of the particular tasks assigned to them. The development of trade must not be affected to such an extent as would be contrary to the interests of the Community.

3. The Commission shall ensure the application of the provisions of this Article and shall, where necessary, address appropriate directives or decisions to Member States".

The scheme of the Article contemplates State responsibility in the situations embraced by paragraph (1), relief from the obligations of the Treaty for the undertakings satisfying the criteria of paragraph

---

[10] Arts 86 and 31 belong to a wider group of "provisions relating to infringements of the normal functioning of the competition system by actions on the part of the States": see Case 94/74 *IGAV v ENCC* [1975] E.C.R. 699; [1976] 2 C.M.L.R. 37. The Court also mentioned in this connection what are now Arts 87–89 (state aid) and Arts 96 and 97 (distortions in competition resulting from differences between Member States).

[11] Case C–438/02 *Hanner* [2005] E.C.R. I–4551, para.47, citing Case C–157/94 *Commission v Netherlands*, n.5, above. Revenue-producing monopolies are, in any event, expressly identified in the terms of Art.86(2).

(2) and a mechanism for supervision and enforcement using the legislative machinery provided by paragraph (3). As summarised by the Court of Justice, the provision:

". . . concerns only undertakings for whose actions States must take special responsibility by reason of the influence which they may exert over such actions. It emphasises that such undertakings are subject to all the rules laid down in the Treaty, subject to the provisions contained in paragraph (2); it requires the Member States to respect those rules in their relations with those undertakings and in that regard imposes on the Commission a duty of surveillance which may, where necessary, be performed by the adoption of directives and decisions addressed to Member States".[12]

The use of Article 86 has changed drastically over time. Starting from a prolonged period in which the provision was hardly invoked at all, the influence of the single market imperative gave rise to a vigorous application of State responsibility and a flurry of legislative liberalisation activity. The position has now been reached where the rigour of paragraph (1) is seemingly tempered by a more generous use of paragraph (2). Examination of how readily the latter is applied (and the full rigour of market rules thus restrained), illuminates the extent of the European Union's evolution in its ordering of social and economic concerns.

Article 86(1): the responsibility of Member States
Article 86(1) constitutes a particular application of the general **26–004** principle contained in the second paragraph of Article 10 EC that Member States are required to abstain from measures which are liable to jeopardise the attainment of the objectives of the Treaty.[13] The inclusion of a specific provision concerning the relationship between the State and public and privileged undertakings served both to highlight the particular seriousness of the problems which may arise, and to clarify the extensive nature of the responsibility imposed upon Member States in this situation.

The categories of undertaking in Article 86(1)
The effect of Article 86(1) is that undertakings for whose actions **26–005** States must take special responsibility by reason of the influence which they may exert over such actions are subject to all the rules

---

[12] Joined Cases 188–190/80 *France, Italy and the United Kingdom v Commission* [1982] E.C.R. 2545; [1982] 3 C.M.L.R. 144.
[13] Case 13/77 *INNO v ATAB* [1977] E.C.R. 2115, 2144–2145; [1978] 1 C.M.L.R. 283.

laid down in the Treaty, and in particular to the competition provisions.[14] That responsibility arises in relation to public undertakings and undertakings to whom States grant special or exclusive rights. It will be recalled from the detailed discussion in Chapter 22 that the Court has formulated the notion of "undertaking" in a number of ways.

As was seen, the Court has found the "undertaking" requirement not to be satisfied in solidarity-based health and insurance schemes[15] and in relation to contexts where the body was acting *qua* State rather than undertaking.[16] Not surprisingly, the close interest and involvement of the State in many types of public services means that the application of Article 86 will often require an analysis of "undertaking". In one such case, the Court observed:

> "the concept of an undertaking, in the context of competition law, covers any entity engaged in an economic activity, regardless of the legal status of the entity or the way in which it is financed. Any activity consisting in offering goods and services on a given market is an economic activity."[17] (citations omitted)

The functional approach taken by the Court thus asks not so much *who* is the undertaking but *what* is the activity.[18] In *Ambulanz Glöckner*, the provision of both emergency transport services and non-emergency patient transfer services had been assigned to non-profit making medical aid organisations. The Court of Justice noted that "such activities have not always been, and are not necessarily, carried on by such organisations or by public authorities" and accordingly treated the organisations as undertakings. Moreover, the fact that being subject to public service obligations may render the provision of some services less competitive than comparable services undertaken by other operators without such obligations does not prevent those activities from being regarded as economic.[19]

26–006 **(a) Public Undertakings.**   Public undertakings are specifically mentioned in Article 86(1), but not defined therein. Clearly, there would be no consistency in application if it were necessary to rely upon the widely varying classifications of undertakings as "public" or "private" in national legal systems. The Commission adopted a definition for the purposes of the Transparency Directive[20] in 1980, and this was

---

[14] Advocate General Stix-Hackl in Joined Cases C–34/01 to C–38/01 *Enirisorse* [2003] E.C.R. I–14243, Opinion para.38.
[15] See cases listed in n.8, above; also Case C–218/00 *Cisal* [2002] E.C.R. I–691, [2002] 4 C.M.L.R. 24.
[16] Case C–364/92 *Eurocontrol* [1994] E.C.R. I–43, [1994] 5 C.M.L.R. 208.
[17] Case C–475/99 *Ambulanz Glöckner* [2001] E.C.R. I–8089, [2002] 4 C.M.L.R. 726, para.19.
[18] See O. Odudu, "The Meaning of Undertaking Within 81 EC" (2004–05) 7 C.Y.E.L.S. 210.
[19] *Ambulanz Glöckner*, n.17, above, para.21.
[20] Dir. 80/723 [1980] O.J. L195/35.

upheld by the Court of Justice when the legality of that measure was challenged.[21] According to Article 2 of the Directive, a public undertaking is:

> "any undertaking over which the public authorities may exercise directly or indirectly a dominant influence by virtue of their ownership of it, their financial participation therein, or the rules which govern it".

The same provision also establishes certain presumptions, so that a "dominant influence" will be taken to exist where the public authorities: hold the major part of the undertaking's subscribed capital; or control the majority of the votes attaching to shares issued by the undertaking; or can appoint more than half of the members of the undertaking's administrative, managerial or supervisory body. The Court held that this definition of a public undertaking did not amount to an abuse by the Commission of its powers under Article 86(3), since the financial criteria which the Directive adopted reflected the substantial forms of influence exerted by public authorities over the commercial decisions of public undertakings and were thus compatible with the Court's view of Article 86(1).[22]

A rather different form of words, but deriving its teleological support from the same notions of influence and opportunity, was used by Advocate General Ruiz-Jarabo Colomer in cases arising from so-called "golden shares" cases involving privatised companies in strategically important parts of the economy:

> "it may be inferred from a purposive interpretation that the distinction between public and private undertakings, for the purposes of the Treaty, cannot be based merely on the identity of its various shareholders, but depends on the opportunity available to the State to impose specific economic policies other than the pursuit of the greatest financial gain which characterises private business."[23]

Public undertakings are always within the scope of application of Article 86(1) EC, whether or not they have also been granted special or exclusive rights.[24]

(b) Undertakings granted special or exclusive rights. The second **26–007** category of undertakings referred to in Article 86(1) are those to which Member States grant special or exclusive rights. Such rights

---

[21] Joined Cases 188–190/80 *France, Italy and the United Kingdom v Commission*, n.12, above.
[22] The Court has also applied this definition in Case 118/85 *Commission v Italy* [1987] E.C.R. 2599.
[23] Joined Cases C–463/00 *Commission v Spain* and C–98/01 *Commission v United Kingdom* [2003] E.C.R. I–4581, Opinion para.56.
[24] Advocate General Stix-Hackl, Opinion in *Enirisorse*, n.14, above.

may be granted to public or private undertakings. The rationale behind the category is the fact that the State has deliberately intervened to relieve the undertaking concerned either wholly or partially from the discipline of competition, and must bear responsibility for the consequences. A right conferred by national legislation upon those carrying on an economic activity which is open to anyone, who thus form an indefinite class, is unlikely to be regarded as "exclusive".[25] Similarly, undertakings which are licensed to engage in an activity on the basis of their fulfilment of certain objective conditions (e.g. the financial safeguards imposed in the public interest upon insurance businesses) would be excluded from the category. The mere assignment of a public service through an authorisation procedure does not as such constitute a special or exclusive right in so far as it does not affect the ability of competing operators to offer the same services.[26] The mode of granting the right (whether by an act under public law, for example a statute, regulation or administrative order, or by a private contract) is immaterial, again because formal differences between the legal systems of the various Member States cannot be allowed to interfere with the operation of Article 86(1).

Even though Article 295 EC, which preserves national systems of property ownership, presupposes the existence of undertakings which have special or exclusive rights, it does not follow that all such rights are necessarily compatible with the Treaty.[27] In particular, Article 295 does not have the effect of exempting the Member States' systems of property ownership from the fundamental rules of the Treaty.[28]

There is nothing in the wording of Article 86(1) to explain the notion of "special or exclusive" rights. Early legislation adopted by the Commission failed to define such rights to the satisfaction of the Court.[29] However, in an amended version of the directive on competition in the markets for telecommunications services[30] the following definitions were used:

> " 'exclusive rights' means the rights that are granted by a Member State to one undertaking through any legislative, regulatory or administrative instrument, reserving it the right to provide a telecommunication service or undertake an activity within a given geographical area.

---

[25] See Case 13/77 *INNO v ATAB*, n.13, above at 2146.
[26] Advocate General Jacobs in *Ambulanz Glöckner*, n.17, above; Opinion paras.92–95.
[27] Case C–202/88 *France v Commission* [1991] E.C.R. I–1223; [1992] 5 C.M.L.R. 552, para.22.
[28] Joined Cases C–463/00 *Commission v Spain* and C–98/01 *Commission v United Kingdom*, n.23, above, para.67 of Judgment.
[29] See proceedings arising from the Telecommunications Terminal Equipment Dir.88/301 [1988] O.J. L131/73: Case C–202/88 *France v Commission* n.27, above. Also Joined Cases C–271, 281 and 289/90 *Spain v Commission* [1992] E.C.R. I–5833 in relation to Dir.90/388 on the markets for telecommunications services.
[30] Dir.94/96; [1994] O.J. L268/15.

'special rights' means the rights that are granted by a Member State to a limited number of undertakings through any legislative, regulatory or administrative instrument which, within a given geographical area,

— limits to two or more the number of such undertakings authorised to provide a service or undertake an activity, otherwise than according to objective, proportional and non-discriminatory criteria, or

— designates, otherwise than according to such criteria, several competing undertakings as being authorised to provide a service or undertake an activity, or

— confers on any undertaking or undertakings, otherwise than according to such criteria, legal or regulatory advantages which substantially affect the ability of any other undertaking to provide the same telecommunications service or to undertake the same activity in the same geographical area under substantially equivalent conditions."

Examples of exclusive rights have included exclusive concessions to funeral enterprises in French communes,[31] statutory monopolies in the field of broadcasting,[32] the exclusive right of insemination centres authorised to serve defined areas[33] and rights given to three undertakings to recover building waste produced within the municipality of Copenhagen and to process it.[34]

In relation to special rights, it now seems clear that not all the criteria set out in the legislative example above need to be satisfied for general classification. The reference to "objective, proportional and non-discriminatory criteria" was not cited by the Court in its *Ambulanz Glöckner* judgment.[35] Instead, it observed that:

"the reservation of patient transport services to the medical aid organisations entrusted with the public ambulance service is sufficient for that measure to be characterised as a special or exclusive right within the meaning of [Article 86(1)] of the Treaty, for protection is conferred by a legislative measure on a limited number of undertakings which may substantially affect

---

[31] Case 30/87 *Bodson v Pompes Funèbres des Régions Libérées SA* [1988] E.C.R. 2479; [1989] 4 C.M.L.R. 984.
[32] Case 155/73 *Sacchi*, n.7 above.
[33] Case C–323/93 *Société Civile Agricole du Centre d'Insémination de la Crespelle v Coopérative d'Elevage et d'Insémination Artificielle du Département de la Mayenne* [1994] E.C.R. I–5077.
[34] Case C–209/98 *FFAD v Københavns Kommune* [2000] E.C.R. I–3743, [2001] 2 C.M.L.R. 936. Whether three undertakings may each have the same exclusive rights seems questionable, but in any event the "special" threshold would be met.
[35] n.17, above. Advocate General Jacobs had expressly limited the phrase to the liberalisation process in the telecommunications sector; Opinion, paras.88–89.

the ability of other undertakings to exercise the economic activity in question in the same geographical area under substantially equivalent conditions."

The mere allocation of funds does not make the recipient a holder of special or exclusive rights, since this ignores the influence on the market that such rights entail.[36]

The scope of the obligation imposed on Member States under Article 86(1)

26–008   The phrase "shall neither enact nor maintain in force any measure" is wide enough to cover any forms of positive action taken by a Member State, or the failure to remedy such action previously taken. The notion of "measure" is also open, and has been described by the Court as "any law, regulation or administrative provision."[37] Article 86(1) cannot be applied in isolation, but must always be used in tandem with another EC provision.

The first decision under Article 86(3) (see below) to challenge specific legislation of the type prohibited by Article 86(1) was issued by the Commission in 1985.[38] This related to a measure requiring all public property in Greece to be insured with a Greek State-owned insurance company, and also obliging State banks to recommend customers seeking a loan to take out associated insurance with a State-owned company. In the Commission's view, the preferential treatment accorded to domestic State-owned companies had the effect of excluding from large sections of the Greek insurance market not only Greek private insurers but also insurance companies from other Member States with subsidiaries or branches in the country. The legislation thus amounted to a restriction on freedom of establishment, enacted by Greece in contravention of Article 86(1).[39]

A literal view of Article 86(1) clearly embraces a standstill obligation upon Member States and the need to take positive action to undo prohibited measures. Additionally, the paragraph impliedly makes Member States accountable for the behaviour of public and privileged undertakings. In other words, responsibility under Article 86(1) does not presuppose positive action by the Member State

---

[36] Advocate General Stix-Hackl, Opinion in *Enirisorse*, n.14, above.
[37] Case C–203/96 *Chemische Afvalstoffen Dusseldorp BV v Minister van Volkhuisvesting, Ruimtelijke Ordening en Milieubeheer* [1998] E.C.R. I–4075, at para.61; [1998] 3 C.M.L.R. 873; repeated in Case C–462/99 *Connect Austria Gesellschaft für Telekommunikation GmbH v Telekom-Control-Kommission* [2003] E.C.R. I–5197. It is of course well established that "state measures" for the purposes of Art.28 EC embrace single acts or administrative practices; see Case 249/81 *Commission v Ireland* [1982] E.C.R. 4005, [1983] 2 C.M.L.R. 104.
[38] Dec.85/726 [1985] O.J. L152/25.
[39] Greece did not comply with the Decision, giving rise to enforcement proceedings: Case 226/87 *Commission v Greece* [1988] E.C.R. 3611.

itself: it suffices merely that a public undertaking or an undertaking granted special or exclusive rights has been guilty of conduct which, on the part of the State, would have involved a Treaty violation. In such a situation the Member State is under an obligation to take any remedial steps which may be necessary; and if its existing legal powers are inadequate, it may be required by the Commission to equip itself with additional powers.

Interpreting the notion of maintaining a measure in force in this **26–009** way is consistent with the obligation to take general and particular measures imposed on Member States by Article 10 and with the policy of Article 86(1). If State responsibility under this paragraph is derived, respectively, from the ability to influence public undertakings and from the assumption of the risk inherent in the deliberate distortion of competition by a grant of special or exclusive rights, it ought to make no difference whether the role of the State has been active, in imposing or encouraging certain behaviour, or passive, in failing to correct it.[40] As the Court has put it, the purpose of Article 86(1) is to prevent Member States from adopting or maintaining in force measures which deprive the Community's competition rules of their effectiveness.[41]

The responsibility of a Member State under Article 86(1) is independent of any violation of Community law by the undertaking in question: it is not based upon a theory of imputation, like the joint liability of a parent company for infringements of the competition rules by a subsidiary which it controls.[42] The undertaking's own conduct may be unimpeachable, for example where it has been compelled by the State to enter a cartel, so that the element of agreement required by Article 81 is missing. However, there must be a causal link between a Member State's legislative or administrative intervention on the one hand and anti-competitive behaviour of undertakings on the other.[43] The Court has held that in the context of Article 86(1) alleged abuses must be the "direct consequence" of the national legal framework.[44]

One of the most difficult questions pertaining to the scope of the obligation in Article 86(1) is whether the mere grant of exclusive or special rights can itself constitute a "measure" susceptible to challenge. In *Höfner v Macrotron*[45] the Court was asked whether a national law conferring exclusive rights over the placement of business executives constituted an abuse under Article 82. It was acknowledged that in practice some competition in the market for

---

[40] *cf.* the position in relation to State measures and Art.81; discussed in Ch.23 above.
[41] Case C–260/89 *ERT* [1991] E.C.R. I–2925, at para.35; [1994] 4 C.M.L.R. 540.
[42] See the discussion of "undertaking" in Ch.22, above.
[43] Advocate General Jacobs in Case C–67/96 *Albany International BV*, n.8 above, para.388 of Opinion.
[44] Case C–323/93, n.33, above
[45] Case C–41/90 *Höfner and Elser v Macrotron* [1991] E.C.R. I–1979; [1993] 4 C.M.L.R. 306.

business placements was tolerated despite the legal monopoly. The Court observed in relation to Articles 82 and 86(1) that:

> "A Member State is in breach of the prohibition contained in those two provisions only if the undertaking in question, merely by exercising the exclusive rights granted to it, cannot avoid abusing its dominant position".[46]

Albeit with some nuances in wording along the way,[47] this approach remains the one used by the Court. Thus, in an Italian case[48] in which national legislation reserved exclusively to a particular undertaking the right to pursue certain tax advice and assistance activities, the Court observed:

> "the mere creation of a dominant position through the grant of special or exclusive rights within the meaning of Article 86(1) EC is not in itself incompatible with Article 82 EC. A Member State will be in breach of the prohibitions laid down by those two provisions only if the undertaking in question, merely by exercising the special or exclusive rights . . . is led to abuse its dominant position or where such rights are liable to create a situation in which that undertaking is led to commit such abuses."[49]

The idea that granting special or exclusive rights may, in some circumstances "inevitably" bring about an abuse has been applied in a number of situations.

26–010   Thus, in *Höfner* itself, the decisive feature was that the undertaking which had been granted an exclusive right was "manifestly not in a position to satisfy demand" prevailing on the market for activities of that kind.[50] The fact that infringers of the monopoly had been able to set up in business and obtain clients made it rather easier to identify such failure, although this might not be so blatant in other cases. In *Ambulanz Glöckner*, Advocate General Jacobs attempted to set out some guidance for the national court when assessing this kind of "manifest failure". First, he suggested that a Member State should only be liable under Article 86(1) where there is a failure in

---

[46] *ibid.*, para.29.
[47] The broadest standard being in the *Dusseldorp* judgment, n.37, above, where the Court said that a State would infringe Art.86(1) if it "enabled" a privileged undertaking to abuse its dominant position.
[48] Case C–451/03 *Servizi Ausiliari Dottori Commercialisti v Calafiori* (forthcoming, Judgment March 30, 2006); however, the Court ruled there was insufficient evidence supplied by the national court to determine whether either dominance or abuse were established.
[49] *ibid.*, para.23, citing *Ambulanz Glöckner*, n.17, above. Similar formulations can be seen in *Corsica Ferries France*, n.7, above, and *Albany International*, n.8, above.
[50] *Höfner*, n.45, above, para.31. To similar effect, see Case C–55/96 *Job Centre Coop* [1997] E.C.R. I–7119; [1998] 5 C.M.L.R. 167, paras 34–35.

the system which it has set up, i.e. where abuse is the consequence of its regulatory or decisional intervention. There would accordingly be no breach of that provision if the reason for failing to satisfy demand was the medical aid organisation's inefficient management. Secondly, the Advocate General argued, the Member States must enjoy a certain discretion in deciding whether a monopolist will or will not be able to satisfy demand. Thus any review by the courts must be limited to national provisions which are *manifestly* inappropriate. Thirdly, as rapid and high quality ambulance services are literally a question of life and death, the Advocate General suggested that the national court should analyse primarily whether authorisations for independent operators might contribute to shorter arrival times and to generally higher quality services The decisive factor should, in his view, be the ability of the public ambulance service to provide rapid and high quality services even at peak hours. If the capacities of the public ambulance service are insufficient at those times (such as regular delays of non-emergency transport in towns), systematic refusals to authorise independent operators would be unacceptable.

However, the Court in *Ambulanz Glöckner* made no comment about this suggested "systemic" requirement.[51] Instead, it held that the German law, providing for prior consultation with the medical aid organisations in respect of any application from an independent operator for authorisation to provide non-emergency patient transport, gave an advantage to those organisations (which already held an exclusive right on the urgent transport market). This had the effect of limiting markets to the prejudice of consumers within the meaning of Article 82(b) of the Treaty by reserving to the medical aid organisations an ancillary transport activity which could be carried on by independent operators.

Advocate General Jacobs had also tried to restrict the application of the *Höfner* approach in *Dusseldorp*, arguing that although the exclusive rights over waste management granted by the Netherlands Government to a particular undertaking (AVR) might facilitate the charging of unfair prices by the latter for its services, there was no inevitability about that outcome. But because the Court seized upon the restriction of outlets as the abuse, rather than unfair pricing, the prima facie breach by the Netherlands would in fact have satisfied even the narrower versions of the test. As a result of the exclusive responsibility entrusted to AVR, businesses in effect had to deliver their waste to AVR even though the quality of processing available in another Member State was comparable to that provided by AVR. The Court ultimately left it to the national court to ascertain whether the national rules did indeed have the effect of favouring the national undertaking and increasing its dominant position. The

---

[51] Similar claims for a "systemic" test had been made by Advocate General Fennelly in Case C–163/96 *Raso and others* [1998] E.C.R. I–533; [1998] 5 C.M.L.R. 737, Opinion, para.66.

Court also indicated that it was for the national court to decide whether the derogation of Article 86(2), discussed further below, might apply.

26–011   The scope of the notion of "inevitable abuse" thus remains problematic, at least as regards the shades of difference between State measures which enable, induce or unavoidably lead to anti-competitive results. For example, the grant of exclusive rights to French insemination centres was not seen as necessarily leading them to charge excessive prices for their services.[52] However, on the other hand, it is clear that an extension of a monopoly by granting special or exclusive rights in an adjacent or ancillary market will be prohibited where there is no objective justification.[53] In such cases, a conflict of interest is certain to arise between the existing monopolist and the competitive situation in the allied market. Thus, in *ERT*,[54] the monopolist was a broadcasting undertaking which not only held the exclusive right to broadcast its own programmes but also to retransmit foreign broadcasts. In the Court's view this created a situation in which the undertaking would be liable to infringe Article 82 by virtue of a discriminatory policy favouring its own pro-grammes. Quite clearly, if a Member State actually directly imposes abusive behaviour on an undertaking there will be a breach of Article 86(1) by that State.[55]

As the Court put it in *Connect Austria*, "if inequality of oppor-tunity between economic operators, and therefore distorted competi-tion, results from a State measure, such a measure constitutes an infringement of Article 86(1) EC in conjunction with Article 82 EC."[56] Under the national legislation at issue in that particular case, additional frequencies in the band reserved for the DCS 1800 standard could be allocated to the dominant privileged undertaking already holding a GSM 900 licence without a separate fee being required, whereas a new entrant had to pay a fee for the DCS 1800 licence. However, the Court was careful to point out that there would not be an abuse if the fees imposed on the dominant undertaking for its GSM licence, taking account of the fact that it

---

[52] Case C–323/93, n.33, above. Similarly, in the *FFD* case, n.34, above, there was no infringement where prices for waste processing were freely determined by the holders of the rights.

[53] Case C–18/88 *RTT v GB-Inno-BM* [1991] E.C.R. I–5941; also *Ambulanz Glöckner*, n.17, above.

[54] Case C–260/89, n.41, above; see also Case C–179/90 *Merci Convenzionali Porto di Genova* [1991] ECR I–5889; [1994] 4 C.M.L.R. 422; Case C–163/96 *Raso*, n.51, above.

[55] e.g. the discriminatory tariffs applied as a result of a State administrative act by an airport authority holding exclusive rights in *Re Discount on Landing Fees at Zaventem*: Dec.95/364 [1995] O.J. L216/8; also the situation where an exclusive right holder is paid for services which it has not itself supplied: Case C–340/99 *TNT Traco v Poste Italiane* [2001] E.C.R. I–4109.

[56] Case C–462/99, n.37, above, para.84.

did not pay for the DCS licence, were equivalent to that imposed on the new entrant.

The discussion above indicates that the weight of the case law, including even the *Höfner* thread where abuses "inevitably" follow from privilege, restricts State responsibility under Article 86(1) to abuses caused by the State's privileging of the relevant undertakings. However, this reasoning does not seem to explain *Corbeau*,[57] one of the cases at the "high-tide" of early 1990s case law in the wake of *Höfner*. The *Corbeau* case arose from a prosecution for violation of the monopoly rights of the Belgian postal service, the *Régie des Postes*. Corbeau had set up a private courier service which could undercut the monopoly on certain services. His defence to the criminal prosecution was to challenge the legality of the exclusivity conferred upon the *Régie des Postes*. At no point in the judgment, or the report, was there any discussion of what constituted the abuse. Instead, the focus of the Court's reasoning was upon the justifications that might exist for the monopoly under Article 86(2),[58] thus apparently reversing the burden of proof and implying that monopolies need justification to remain in existence. This is not the same as pointing to market failure as the evidence of abuse.

It may not be particularly fruitful to exaggerate the significance of *Corbeau* in relation to the Article 86(1) discussion. A number of special factors may have applied, not least the fact that this was a "Euro-defence" to a criminal charge rather than a claim from an abused complainant or injured competitor. The Court also treated the first two paragraphs of Article 86 as interdependent, which might suggest that glossing over the foundations for responsibility under paragraph (1) was less important to it at the time than taking the opportunity for lengthier treatment of justifications under paragraph (2). If rationalisation of *Corbeau* is needed, then it is arguable that the "basic" monopoly and special courier services are different markets and that the abuse strengthens dominance to cover an ancillary activity.[59] Similarly, Corbeau's activities might be proof of a *Höfner*-type market failure. But, it must be stressed, these perspectives were not discussed by the Court. However,[60] one lasting contribution of the Court's reasoning might be that part of a Member State's responsibilities under Article 86(1) is to keep changing market conditions under review—and take appropriate actions.

---

[57] Case C–320/91 *Corbeau* [1993] E.C.R. I–2533, [1995] 4 C.M.L.R. 621.
[58] Art.86(2) is discussed in detail in the next section, below.
[59] This could be the Court's own explanation when distinguishing *Corbeau* in *Ambulanz Glöckner*, n.17, above, although the remarks are in the context of Art.86(2) and purportedly to identify "core" activity.
[60] L. Hancher, casenote on *Corbeau* (1994) 31 C.M.L.Rev. 105.

Article 86(2): entrusted undertakings and fiscal monopolies

26–012   Article 86(2) is drafted in terms which first emphasise that "undertakings entrusted with the operation of services of general economic interest or having the character of a revenue-producing monopoly" are normally subject to the rules of the Treaty and then go on to exclude the application of the rules where the performance of the particular tasks assigned to the undertakings is liable to be obstructed. This is subject to a proviso which states that "the development of trade must not be affected to such extent as would be contrary to the interests of the Community". The case law of the Commission and Court initially showed a marked disinclination to accept the application of what was seen to be a derogation from the Treaty. However, the greater use of the competition rules to curb monopolies and public undertakings in the 1990s saw a corresponding development of arguments justifying the activities of such bodies by reference to Article 86(2). The position today is that obtaining the benefit of the provision is no longer the impossible task it once was, at least for undertakings charged with providing universal services of public interest. Indeed, from an analytical perspective, it may be time to re-assess the status and effect of Article 86(2) and to see it less as an exception to the Treaty to be narrowly construed but more as a particular regime to balance the delivery of effective public services in a modern Union with market economies.[61]

The categories of undertaking in Article 86(2)

26–013   There is nothing in the text of the Article that would restrict the categories of undertaking in the second paragraph to those covered by the first. However, undertakings called upon to perform services of the type envisaged by Article 86(2) are often either State controlled or given a *quid pro quo* in the form of special or exclusive rights. The more important of the two categories in Article 86(2) is that of entrusted undertakings. Because of the possible derogation which may be involved, the European Court said in an early case that the category must be strictly defined.[62]

It is immaterial whether the undertaking concerned is public or private, provided that the service has been *entrusted* to it "by an act of the public authority".[63] This does not imply that the act need be in

---

[61] In broad terms, the "exception" approach is that taken by J. L. Buendía Sierra, *Exclusive Rights and State Monopolies under EC Law* (Oxford, OUP, 1999); the "balancing" view is taken by J. Baquero Cruz, "Beyond Competition: Services of General Interest and European Community Law" in G. de Búrca (ed.), *EU Law and the Welfare State* (Oxford, OUP, 2005), p.169.
[62] Case 127/73 *BRT v SABAM* [1974] E.C.R. 313; [1974] 2 C.M.L.R. 238.
[63] [1974] E.C.R., 313, 318.

any particular form[64]; the essential point is that the State must have taken legal steps to secure the provision of the service by the undertaking in question. Thus an undertaking created as a result of private initiative and managing the intellectual property rights of its members on an ordinary contractual basis, could not be an entrusted undertaking, even if it happened to serve public purposes.[65] The same is true where legislation only *authorises* an undertaking to act, even though some supervision of those activities may be exercised by a public agency. Thus, in *GVL v Commission*,[66] the Court held that the relevant German legislation did not confer the management of copyright and related rights on specific undertakings but defined in a general manner the rules applying to the activities of companies which intended to undertake the collective exploitation of such rights. Similarly, the fact that Member States had given express approval to the Eurocheque clearing system did not "entrust" the banks concerned.[67]

The phrase "operation of services" seems to have been chosen advisedly to indicate the organisation of some kind of regular performance, for example a public utility.[68] It is generally agreed that the definition of "services" in Article 50 EC, as a residual concept relating to types of performance not governed by the provisions on the free movement of goods, persons or capital, does not apply in the context of Article 86(2). The Commission, in a document forming the background to the eventual adoption of Article 16 EC,[69] expressly distinguished between services of general economic interest and those (such as compulsory education, diplomacy or the register of births, deaths and marriages) which are non-economic or prerogatives of the State and for which any Community action can be at most complementary. As Advocate General Jacobs has pointed out,[70] the reason for the assignment of particular tasks to undertakings is often that the tasks need to be undertaken in the public interest but might not be undertaken, usually for economic reasons, if the service were to be left to the private sector.

The requirement that services must be "of general economic **26–014** interest" may seem slightly odd at first sight, since in reality it is the service, rather than the interest, which will need to be economic.[71]

---

[64] See also Case C–159/94 *Commission v France* [1997] E.C.R. I–5815, para.66. In a slightly narrower context, the Commission's *Community Framework for State Aid in the Form of Public Service Compensation* (May 2004) refers to the need to assign a specific public service obligation "by way of an official act that . . . may take the form of a legislative or regulatory act or a contract." (para.9).

[65] SABAM was such an undertaking.

[66] Case 7/82 [1983] E.C.R. 483; [1983] 3 C.M.L.R. 645.

[67] *Uniform Eurocheques* [1985] O.J. L35/43, [1985] 3 C.M.L.R. 434.

[68] The relevant phrase in the other official versions of the Treaty has been chosen with equal care to denote the conduct of a service rather than the provision of services.

[69] *Services of General Interest in Europe* [1996] O.J. C281/03.

[70] Case C–203/96 *Dusseldorp*, n.37, above.

[71] This also harks back to the discussion of "undertaking", see Ch.22, above.

SGEIs, as they are rather clumsily known, embrace a wide range of activities beyond the very obvious examples such as water companies,[72] energy[73] and telecoms[74] utilities and postal services.[75] Waste management functions may also properly qualify, particularly where the service is designed to deal with an environmental problem.[76] In *Ahmed Saeed*[77] the Court noted that Article 86(2) may be applied to airline carriers who may be obliged, by the public authorities, to operate on routes which are not commercially viable but which it is necessary to operate for reasons of the general interest. This was also the view of the Court of First Instance in *Air Inter*[78] in the context of an airline running unprofitable routes to open up French cities and regions as part of regional development. In *Campus Oil*[79] the Court of Justice apparently did not dispute the Greek Government's contention that a State-owned oil refinery could be an undertaking operating a service of general economic interest.[80]

The Commission, in its *White Paper on Services of General Interest*,[81] studiously avoided a strict definition of an SGEI but observed that there was "broad agreement" that the term refers to services of an economic nature which the Member States or the Community subject to specific public service obligations by virtue of a general interest criterion. Member States have a broad margin of discretion regarding the nature of services that could be classified as SGEIs. The Commission accordingly sees its task as being to ensure that such choices are not made with manifest error.[82]

---

[72] *The Community v ANSEAU-NAVEWA* [1982] 2 C.M.L.R. 193; challenged on other issues in Joined Cases 96–102, 104–105, 108 and 110/82 *IAZ International Belgium v Commission* [1983] E.C.R. 3369; [1984] 3 C.M.L.R. 276.

[73] e.g. Case C–393/92 *Almelo* [1994] E.C.R. I–1477; Case C–19/93P *Rendo NV v Commission* [1995] E.C.R. I–3319.

[74] *Telespeed Services v United Kingdom Post Office* [1982] O.J. L360/36; [1983] 1 C.M.L.R. 457. The Commission's Decision was unsuccessfully challenged in Case 41/83 *Italy v Commission (British Telecom)* [1985] E.C.R. 873, [1985] 2 C.M.L.R.368; see also Case C–18/88 *RTT*, n.53, above.

[75] Case C–320/91 *Corbeau*, n.57, above.

[76] Case C–209/98 *FFAD*, n.34, above, para.75.

[77] Case 66/86 *Ahmed Saeed Flugreisen v Zentrale zur Bekampfung unlauteren Wettbewerbs* [1989] E.C.R. 803; [1990] 4 C.M.L.R. 102.

[78] Case T–260/94 *Air Inter v Commission* [1997] E.C.R. II–997; [1997] 5 C.M.L.R. 851, although the other conditions of the derogation were not actually made out.

[79] Case 72/83 *Campus Oil Ltd v Minister for Industry and Energy* [1984] E.C.R. 2727; [1984] 3 C.M.L.R. 544.

[80] *ibid.*, paras 18–19 of Judgment.

[81] COM (2004) 374; the same terminology had been adopted in the Green Paper COM (2003) 270.

[82] *Community Framework for State Aid in the Form of Public Service Compensation* (May 2004), para.8. See also Case T–106/95 *FFSA v Commission* [1997] E.C.R. II–229, para.99; Opinion of Advocate General Leger in Case C–438/02 *Hanner*, n.11, above, para.139.

The general interest element can still be satisfied where the benefit of the service may be enjoyed by specific recipients.[83] On the other hand, a bank will not perform such a service when transferring customers' funds from one Member State to another.[84] Nor, it seems,[85] would the management company in the *GVL* case have fulfilled the criterion, since the collecting society was only engaged in the furtherance of the interests of private artistes. In *Merci Convenzionali Porto di Genova*[86] the Court held that on the evidence submitted, dock work consisting of the loading, unloading, transhipment and storage of goods was not necessarily of general economic interest. However, in *Corsica Ferries France*[87] the Court accepted that the provision of mooring services had special characteristics sufficient to bring them within the scope of Article 86(2). In particular, the grantees of the exclusive rights in question were obliged to provide at any time and to any user a universal mooring service, for reasons of safety in port waters.

Undertakings "having the character of a revenue-producing monopoly", the second category in Article 86(2), are distinguished by the overriding purpose of raising revenue for the national exchequer through the exploitation of their exclusive right. They are normally combined with commercial monopolies, so that they must also satisfy the requirements of Article 31 EC.[88] In an important series of energy cases[89] decided in 1997 the Court ruled that the derogation of Article 86(2) could be applied to the grant of exclusive rights to Article 31 monopolies.

In the discussion that follows references to entrusted undertakings should be understood to include fiscal monopolies, unless the context indicates otherwise.

Application of the conditions in Article 86(2)

The view that this paragraph is best categorised as an exception **26–015** stems from the fact that it is capable of restricting the application of any Community provision, including Article 86(1). It makes no

---

[83] In Case 90/76 *Van Ameyde v UCI* [1977] E.C.R. 1091; [1977] 2 C.M.L.R. 478 the Commission argued that the national insurers' bureau responsible for the settlement of claims in relation to damage caused by foreign vehicles in Italy did not qualify as an entrusted undertaking "since its activities do not benefit the whole of the national economy", but this view seems too restrictive. The Court seems to have taken for granted that the bureau would so qualify: *ibid.*, at 1126.

[84] Nor was the bank "entrusted".

[85] *per* Advocate General Reischl.

[86] Case C–179/90, n.54, above. The Court reiterated this view in Case C–242/95 *GT-Link A/S v De Danske Statsbaner* [1997] E.C.R. I–4449; [1997] 5 C.M.L.R. 601.

[87] Case C–266/96, n.7, above.

[88] See Ch.16, above.

[89] Case C–157/94 *Commission v Netherlands*, n.5, above; Case C–158/94 *Commission v Italy* [1997] E.C.R. I–5789; Case C–159/94 *Commission v France* [1997] E.C.R. I–5815; Case C–160/94 *Commission v Spain* [1997] E.C.R. I–5851; [1998] 2 C.M.L.R. 373.

difference whether the rule in question is one designed primarily to influence the conduct of undertakings, for example Article 81 or Article 82, or that of States, for example Article 28 or Article 87.[90] To benefit from Article 86(2), an undertaking must show that application of the Treaty rules would obstruct the performance of the tasks assigned to it. This standard has been expressed in a variety of ways in the case law, although the strictest formulations tied to the impact upon the undertaking's economic viability have been relaxed in more recent years, at least in the context of undertakings entrusted with the provision of universal services for the public benefit.

Thus, early examples of restrictive interpretation include the Commission's declaration that Article 86(2) could only apply in the event that the undertaking concerned had no other technically and economically feasible means of performing its particular task.[91] In similar vein, Advocate General Rozès argued in the *Tobacco Margins* case[92] that the undertaking must have no choice but to infringe Treaty rules before the conditions for the exception would be satisfied. The Court's original position[93] was that rules of the Treaty continued to apply so long as it was not shown that their prohibitions were "incompatible" with the performance of the undertaking's tasks.

However, these approaches must now be read in the light of the Court's subsequent analysis of the scope of the exception in numerous cases involving the tension between the recognition of legitimate public service obligations imposed by States and the Community's drive towards liberalisation of sectors in pursuit of the single market. The flurry of cases expanding the scope of Article 86(1) (see above) brought in turn a reappraisal of the conditions needed to satisfy paragraph (2). Cases such as *Corbeau*[94] indicated that in principle there could be a "core" monopoly activity worthy of relief from the full force of the competition rules, even though in that particular case the core provision of basic postal services was not actually threatened by the peripheral competition posed by Corbeau's specialised premium-rate services. Significantly, the Court recognised that the obligation to perform the relevant services in conditions of economic equilibrium presupposed that it would be

---

[90] The application of Art.86(2) to the state aid rules was expressly recognised in Case C–174/97P *FFSA v Commission* [1998] E.C.R. I–1303, extending Case C–387/92 *Banco Exterior de España* [1994] E.C.R. I–877; [1994] 3 C.M.L.R. 473. State aid is discussed in Ch.27, below.

[91] *The Community v ANSEAU-NAVEWA*, n.72, above.

[92] Case 78/82 *Commission v Italy* [1983] E.C.R. 1955. The Court found no breach of Art.31 and accordingly did not discuss the exception.

[93] Case 155/73 *Sacchi*, n.7, above, and repeated in Case 311/84 *CBEM Télé-Marketing v Compagnie Luxembourgeoise de Télédiffusion and Information Publicité Benelux* [1985] E.C.R. 3261; [1986] 2C.M.L.R. 558.

[94] n.57, above.

possible to offset less profitable sectors against the profitable ones to some degree.

The limits to cross-subsidy were explored by the Court in **26–016** *Ambulanz Glöckner*.[95] Comparing the two cases, the Court observed:

"It is true that, in paragraph 19 of *Corbeau*, the Court held that the exclusion of competition is not justified in certain cases involving specific services, severable from the service of general interest in question, if those services do not compromise the economic equilibrium of the service of general economic interest performed by the holder of the exclusive rights.

However, that is not the case with the two services now under consideration, for two reasons in particular. First, unlike the situation in *Corbeau*, the two types of service in question, traditionally assumed by the medical aid organisations, are so closely linked that it is difficult to sever the non-emergency transport services from the task of general economic interest constituted by the provision of the public ambulance service, with which they also have characteristics in common.

Second, the extension of the medical aid organisations' exclusive rights to the non-emergency transport sector does indeed enable them to discharge their general-interest task of providing emergency transport in conditions of economic equilibrium. The possibility which would be open to private operators to concentrate, in the non-emergency sector, on more profitable journeys could affect the degree of economic viability of the service provided by the medical aid organisations and, consequently, jeopardise the quality and reliability of that service.

However, as the Advocate General explains in point 188 of his Opinion, it is only if it were established that the medical aid organisations entrusted with the operation of the public ambulance service were manifestly unable to satisfy demand for emergency ambulance services and for patient transport at all times that the justification for extending their exclusive rights, based on the task of general interest, could not be accepted."[96]

This benign view had also been visible a few months earlier in a ruling of the Court's Sixth Chamber in relation to Italian postal services.[97] The Court found that it could be necessary not just to permit the universal service provider to engage in cross-subsidy but also to require suppliers of postal services not subject to those universal service obligations to contribute to the financing of the

---

[95] n.17, above.
[96] *ibid.*, paras.59–62.
[97] Case C–340/99, n.55, above.

universal service and "in that way" to enable the entrusted undertaking to perform its task.[98] Such amounts, however, must not exceed the losses incurred by the universal service undertaking.

To sum up, the focus of the Court's approach in its case law since *Corbeau* has been directed towards ensuring that the disturbances to the market and competitive conditions resulting from granting the protection of Article 86(2) are restricted to those necessary for performance of the legitimate service by the undertaking. Explicit confirmation that the derogation is not solely concerned with the economic viability of the undertaking was given by the Court in the 1997 energy cases[99] and applied subsequently in a non-utility context. Thus, dealing with the pension fund arrangements in *Albany International*,[1] the Court summarised its position regarding the conditions for Article 86(2) as follows:

> ". . . it is not necessary . . . that the financial balance or economic viability of the undertaking entrusted with the operation of a service of general economic interest should be threatened. It is sufficient that, in the absence of the rights at issue, it would not be possible for the undertaking to perform the particular tasks entrusted to it, defined by reference to the obligations and constraints to which it is subject . . . or that maintenance of those rights is necessary to enable the holder of them to perform tasks of general economic interest which have been assigned to it under economically acceptable conditions".[2]

Although this approach is very much the standard, there are instances of different formulations. In the *Dusseldorp* case,[3] for example, the Court was not persuaded that the exclusive rights over waste management granted by the Netherlands to AVR were justified. Undertakings were required to deliver waste to AVR unless processing in another Member State would be of higher quality. In the Court's view, Article 86(2) could only be invoked if the Netherlands Government could show to the satisfaction of the national court that the entrusted objectives "could not be achieved equally well by other means". However, it seems unlikely that this rather stricter requirement would have been made out as the only argument advanced by the Netherlands was that exclusivity would reduce AVR's costs and make it economically viable.

Despite the greater scope for application of Article 86(2) as a result of the recent case law, the burden of proof remains on the

---

[98] *ibid.*, para.55.
[99] n.69, above.
[1] n.17, above.
[2] *ibid.*, para.107 of Judgment.
[3] Case C–203/96, n.37, above.

undertaking (or State) to show that compliance with the Treaty would "obstruct" the performance of the entrusted tasks. Thus, in *Air Inter*,[4] the applicant merely asserted that cross-subsidy between its profitable and unprofitable routes was justified without putting a figure on the probable loss of revenue if other air carriers were allowed to compete with it on its exclusive routes. Nor had it shown that any such loss of income would be so great as to force it to abandon certain routes within its network. In the "golden share" cases, the Court rejected Spain's reliance on Article 86(2) for failing to set out in detail the reasons why the entrusted undertaking's tasks would be jeopardised in the event of removing the contested measures.[5] On the other hand, in the 1997 energy cases[6] the Court made it clear that the burden of proof did not extend so far as to require the State to prove positively that no other conceivable measure, which by definition would be hypothetical, could enable the entrusted tasks to be performed under the same conditions.

The proviso to Article 86(2)

The proviso in the second sentence of Article 86(2) states that the **26–017** development of trade must not be affected to such an extent as would be contrary to the interests of the Community. It thus identifies the point at which it still becomes necessary to apply the relevant provisions of Community law, even at the cost of preventing an entrusted undertaking or a fiscal monopoly from performing its allotted task. However, the proviso has received remarkably little discrete interpretation, mainly because for many years attempts to rely on Article 86(2) were consistently rejected on other grounds. Advocate General Cosmas in the 1997 energy cases suggested that the draftsmen of the Treaty inserted the proviso to exclude use of the derogation of Article 86(2) in relation to measures which, in addition to *potentially* restricting trade in the Community, have *in practice* done so, the restrictive effects being so great that intra-Community trade in the sector in question is practically non-existent.[7] The Court in the same cases ruled that the Commission had failed to explain why the Community interest was adversely affected by the exclusive import and export rights which formed the subject-matter of the infringement proceedings. Evidence presented to the Court indicated that there had been increasing inter-State trade in electricity and natural gas despite the existence of the exclusive rights. Accordingly, the Commission was obliged to define the Community interest against which the development of trade was

---

[4] Case T–260/94, n.78, above

[5] Case C–463/00, n.23, above.

[6] n.89, above.

[7] *ibid.*, para.126 of Opinion.

said to be affected. However, it had not done so; in particular, it had not shown why, in the absence of a common policy in the area concerned, development of direct trade between producers and consumers, in parallel with the development of trade between major networks, would have been possible having regard in particular to the existing capacity and arrangements for transmission and distribution.

Advocate General Léger has more recently[8] endorsed the arguments put forward by Advocate General Cosmas, explicitly calling for proof that the measure in issue has in fact had a substantial effect on intra-Community trade.

Direct effect of Article 86(2)

26–018   It has long been clear that a national court may decide whether an undertaking qualifies as "entrusted" within the meaning of Article 86(2).[9] Any lingering doubts as to the powers of national courts in relation to whether undertakings are "obstructed" in the performance of their tasks were removed by the Court's judgment in *ERT*.[10] National courts are accordingly competent to apply the first sentence of Article 86(2) either in favour of or against an undertaking. This does not, of course, diminish the complexity of the task involved in deciding the point at which relief from the full force of the competition rules is no longer necessary to secure the undertaking's entrusted aims. Nor are national courts assisted by different expressions in the European case law of the extent to which Article 86(2) requires a proportionality assessment.[11]

Strictly speaking, the applicability of the proviso contained in the second sentence of the exception still awaits definitive resolution by the Court. The point was sidestepped in *Rendo*,[12] where part of the challenge to the ruling by the Court of First Instance was on the basis that it had erroneously distinguished between the two sentences of the derogation. The Court of Justice merely observed[13] that the second sentence had not arisen before the Court of First Instance and so there was no reason to treat the latter's judgment as having impliedly given exclusive competence over the proviso to the Commission. Advocate General Tesauro had argued that the derogation was "commonly" applied in its entirety[14] and that the

---

[8] Opinion in Case C–438/02 *Hanner*, n.11, above.
[9] Case 127/73 *BRT v SABAM*, n.62, above
[10] Case C–260/89, n.41, above.
[11] Advocate General Léger in *Hanner*, n.11 above, states that proportionality *and* necessity tests are applicable; obstacles to free competition are allowed only "in so far as they are necessary in order to enable the undertaking entrusted with such a task of general interest to perform it. The proportionality test therefore means verifying whether the undertaking's specific task could be performed with less restrictive measures." (para.142).
[12] Case C–19/93P, n.73, above.
[13] *ibid.*, para.19 of Judgment.
[14] *ibid.*, para.38 of Opinion.

Court had never drawn a distinction between the first and second sentences. On this view, a national court can only consider if particular conduct is necessary for the performance of an undertaking's task by taking an holistic approach to Article 86(2). It has also been claimed[15] that the very scheme of Article 86 invites the direct effect of paragraph (2), citing in evidence the Court's own statements elsewhere that Article 86 "confers powers on the Commission only in relation to State measures"[16] leaving the regulation of acts by undertakings on their own initiative for decisions under Articles 81 and 82.

It is thus increasingly difficult to resist the conclusion that a national court is empowered in respect of every aspect of Article 86(2). The case is perhaps even more persuasive now that the provision seems to have been increasingly subjected to holistic interpretation rather than reduced to its component concepts and elements. Moreover, if the constitutional significance of Article 86(2) is on the ascendancy it would seem even less justifiable to treat it as having an economic analysis built in to the proviso that only the Commission could determine.

Article 86(3): the supervisory and legislative competence of the Commission

By Article 86(3) the Commission is both placed under an obliga- **26–019** tion to ensure the application of the Article and equipped with a special power to issue directives or decisions for this purpose. Directives or decisions under Article 86(3) can only be addressed to Member States. However, where appropriate the Commission may have recourse to other powers, for example under Regulation 1/2003, against the undertaking concerned. There is, of course, nothing in Article 86 to prevent the Commission, if it so chooses, from issuing non-binding recommendations. The existence of a special enactment competence vested in the Commission sits uncomfortably against the other law-making processes of the Union, and it is hardly surprising that Member States, in particular, have sought to tame it. As the discussion below indicates, the case law has drawn sharp distinctions between decisions and directives issued under Article 86(3). The result is that the Commission's power is probably more accurately described as one of surveillance rather than legislative.

Article 86(3) became an immediate subject of controversy when it was eventually brought into play. In the first of the challenges[17] to

---

[15] Advocate General Darmon in *Almelo*, n.73, above, at paras 132–134 of Opinion.
[16] Case C–202/88 *France v Commission*, n.27, above, at para.55 of Judgment; also Joined Cases C–271, 281 and 289/90 *Spain v Commission* [1992] E.C.R. I–5833 at para.24 of Judgment.
[17] Joined Cases 188–190/80, n.12, above.

directives adopted under the provision, the Court was called upon to examine the validity of the so-called Transparency Directive.[18] This legislation sought to ensure the transparency of financial relations between Member States and public undertakings, and required Member States to keep available for five years relevant information and to supply it on request to the Commission. The preamble to the Directive stressed the Commission's duty to ensure that Member States did not grant undertakings, public or private, aids incompatible with the common market, and the need for equal treatment of public and private enterprises. The complexity of financial relations between Member States and public undertakings hindered the achievement of that equality, and provided the rationale for the measure. The Court upheld the Commission's power to adopt the Directive in the face of arguments that it could only have been adopted by the Council using its legislative powers in relation to State aids. According to the Court, the Commission's power depended on the needs inherent in its duty of surveillance provided for in Article 86.

A challenge was also mounted, this time by France and supported by Italy, Belgium, Germany and Greece,[19] against the next principal Directive issued under what was then Article 90(3), relating to telecommunications terminal equipment.[20] This measure provided, *inter alia*, that Member States which had granted special or exclusive rights for the importation, marketing, connection, bringing into service of telecommunications terminal equipment and/or the maintenance of such equipment were to ensure that those rights were withdrawn. One argument advanced to challenge the Commission's competence was that the provision constituted a normative act which could only properly belong under the rules concerning competition or the single market (thereby requiring Council action). Following its earlier reasoning in the *Transparency Directive* case, the Court ruled that the duty imposed upon the Commission under what was then Article 90 was more specific than the other general competences conferred on the Council.

26–020   A further argument raised in the *Telecommunications Directive* case was the relationship between the Commission's specific powers and general enforcement actions under what is now Article 226. According to the Court, the specific legislative powers of Article 86 allow the Commission to define in a general way the obligations which the Treaty imposes upon Member States. The directive in question satisfied these normative criteria. However, if a Member State does not comply, the default can then only be pursued by

---

[18] n.20, above.
[19] Case C–202/88, n.27, above.
[20] Dir.88/301; [1988] O.J. L131/73.

recourse to normal infringement proceedings.[21] The need for comparability between the Commission's specific power under Article 86(3) and its general enforcement capacity under Article 226 may also explain the Court's later ruling[22] that the Commission was not responsible to individuals for the exercise of its surveillance powers. In particular, individuals could not force the Commission to take a position under Article 86(3).

Directives and decisions are to be distinguished when considering the Commission's powers under Article 86(3). The choice depends on whether the Commission's objective is to specify in general terms the obligations arising under the Treaty, or to assess a specific situation in one or more Member States in the light of Community law and determine the consequences arising for the Member State or States concerned.[23] An example of the latter involved Netherlands express delivery services,[24] although the Court ultimately annulled the particular decision on the basis that the Commission had given neither the Netherlands Government nor the PTT a fair hearing.

Strengthened by early judicial support, the Commission proceeded to seek liberalisation of particular sectors by measures adopted under Article 86(3).[25] However, there is no power to harmonise under Article 86(3) and so legislation has more recently been enacted by the Council and Parliament using other Treaty bases. Thus the Directive on developing the internal market for postal services[26] was eventually enacted on the basis of the Treaty rules applicable to establishment, services and the single market. Other legislation is now in place for energy markets.[27] Nevertheless, the Commission has not abandoned Article 86(3) and has recently been drafting a decision and a directive to take account of judicial developments in relation to State aid and compensation for SGEIs in the delivery of their obligations.[28]

---

[21] As happened in the context of the Transparency Directive when Italy refused to supply requested information. See Case 118/85 *Re AAMS: Commission v Italy* [1987] E.C.R. 2599; [1988] 3 C.M.L.R. 255.

[22] Case C–141/02P *Commission v T-Mobile Austria, formerly max.mobil* (forthcoming, Judgment February 22, 2005), overturning the CFI's decision in Case T–54/99 *max.mobil v Commission* [2002] E.C.R. II–313. See casenote by F. Castillo de la Torre (2005) 42 C.M.L.Rev. 1751.

[23] Case C–163/99 *Portugal v Commission* [2001] E.C.R. I–2655.

[24] Joined Cases C–48 and 66/90 *Netherlands, Koninklijke PTT Nederland NV and PTT Post BV v Commission* [1992] E.C.R. I–565; [1993] 5 C.M.L.R. 316.

[25] For example, Dir.90/388 on telecommunications services; [1990] O.J. L192/10; Dir.95/51 on the use of cable television networks [1995] O.J. L256/49; Dir.96/2 on mobile and personal communications; [1996] O.J. L20/59.

[26] Dir.97/67 [1998] O.J. L15/14; further opened up by Dir. 2002/39 [2002] O.J. L176/21.

[27] *e.g.* Dir.2003/54 [2003] O.J. L176/1 in relation to electricity; Dir.2003/55 in relation to gas.

[28] Decision on the application of Art.86 to state aid in the form of public service compensation granted to certain undertakings entrusted with the operation of services of general economic interest; draft Directive amending the Transparency Directive (both texts available from Commission's website). The compensation issue and its associated case law are discussed in Ch.27, below.

Article 16 EC and services of general economic interest

26–021   The case law of the 1990s and the different views among Member States as to the role of public service obligations led to discussion of possible reforms.[29] For the Commission,[30] services of general interest form a key element in the European model of society:

> "European societies are committed to the general interest services they have created which meet basic needs. These services play an important role as social cement over and above practical considerations. They also have a symbolic value, reflecting a sense of community that people can identify with. They form part of the cultural identity of everyday life in all European countries".[31]

Rather modestly, the Commission sought to amend Article 3 EC to add "a contribution to the promotion of services of general economic interest" to the list of Community activities. The Reflection Group Report on the 1996 InterGovernmental Conference referred to the "majority" view in favour of reinforcement of the concept of public service utilities (*services publics d'intérêt général*) as a principle supplementing market criteria. In its final form, the Treaty of Amsterdam inserted a new provision into the EC Treaty as Article 16:

> "Without prejudice to Articles 73, 86 and 87, and given the place occupied by services of general economic interest in the shared values of the Union as well as their role in promoting social and territorial cohesion, the Community and the Member States, each within their respective powers and within the scope of application of this Treaty, shall take care that such services operate on the basis of principles and conditions which enable them to fulfil their missions".

The scope of this Article, which might be seen as a triumph for ambiguous drafting,[32] has yet to receive definitive determination by the Court. However, Advocate General Alber has noted that:

> "The newly promulgated Article 16 and Article 36 of the Charter of Fundamental Rights of the European Union underline the importance of [Article 86(2)] as an expression of a fundamental value judgment of Community law."[33]

---

[29] France, for example, initially wanted the Treaty competition rules to be disapplied in their entirety from public services provision.

[30] *Services of General Interest in Europe*, n.69, above.

[31] *ibid.*, para.6.

[32] See Ross, "Art.16 EC and services of general interest: from derogation to obligation?" (2000) 25 E.L.Rev. 22. Also T. Prosser, *op.cit.*, n.3, above, pp.138–141.

[33] Opinion in Case C–340/99 *TNT Traco*, n.55, above; see also Advocate General Jacobs, who noted that Art.16 emphasises the "special importance" of SGEIs in his Opinion in *Ambulanz Glöckner*, n.17, above.

It therefore remains to be seen whether Article 16 satisifies the wish of some Member States to provide further security for public services against the full impact of the competition rules of the Treaty. Certainly, the reference to being without prejudice to Article 86 must mean that Article 16 cannot be used to make it more difficult for providers of universal services to escape the rigours of Community competition law. As discussed above, the case law under Article 86(2) already exhibits an increasingly benign view of entrusted undertakings.

Perhaps the greatest interest in the legal development of Article 16 is to be found in its latent acknowledgment of a Community notion of general interest services, and the extent to which this may prove different from national concepts. Indeed, the fact that it is not exclusively tied to Article 86(2) and the competition rules indicates that it is capable of being relevant to all aspects of Community activity. Whilst it does not confer a specific legislative power on the Community for further action, Article 16's position in the part of the Treaty headed "Principles" might suggest an importance going beyond mere rhetoric. Certainly, it is interesting to note that the equivalent of Article 16 in the Constitutional Treaty, Article III–122, goes further in this regard. Having largely repeated the current provision to the extent that the Union and the Member States shall take care that SGEIs operate on the basis of principles and conditions, in particular economic and financial conditions, which enable them to fulfil their missions, the Constitutional Treaty adds the following:

> "European laws shall establish these principles and set these conditions without prejudice to the competence of Member States, in compliance with the Constitution, to provide, to commission and to fund such services."

This express legal basis for action is a modified version of the original suggestion, which had not included the contents of the "without prejudice" rider.

Even in its current form, the express references in Article 16 to shared Union values and to the particular objectives of social and territorial cohesion upgrade regard for general interest services into a positive horizontal policy-shaping consideration for both Member States and the Community institutions. The Commission has already placed Article 16 at the forefront of its policy documents in relation to SGEIs.[34] Put another way, the provision captures the tension at the heart of the Union's current process of development: the balancing or prioritising of market-based considerations and those

---

[34] See, e.g. its White Paper on SGEIs, *op.cit.*, n.81, above, emphasising the "shared responsibility" of the Union and its Member States.

more concerned with cohesion and social solidarity.[35] Article 16's strength accordingly comes from its capacity as a constitutional principle that repositions or reconciles those forces, especially alongside (or as the justification for) other substantive developments in relation to SGEIs, fundamental rights and citizenship.

Further reading

Baquero Cruz, J., "Beyond Competition: Services of General Interest and European Community Law" in G. de Búrca (ed.), *EU Law and the Welfare State* (Oxford, OUP, 2005), p.169.

Moral Soriano, L., "How Proportionate should Anti-Competitive State Intervention Be?" (2003) 28 E.L.Rev. 112.

Napolitano, G., "Towards a European Legal Order for Services of General Economic Interest" (2005) 11 E.P.L. 565.

Prosser, T., "Competition Law and Public Services: From Single Market to Citizenship Rights?" (2005) 11 E.P.L. 543.

Ross, M., "The Europeanization of Public Services Supervision: Harnessing Competition and Citizenship?" (2004) 23 Y.E.L. 303.

Szyszczak, E., "State Intervention in the Market" in Tridimas, T., and Nebbia, P., (eds), *EU for the 21st Century: Rethinking the New Legal Order*, Vol.2 (Hart, Oxford, 2004).

---

[35] See Freedland and Sciarra (eds), *Public Services and Citizenship in European Law* (Clarendon Press, Oxford, 1998).

CHAPTER 27

STATE AID

Guide to this Chapter: This Chapter examines the rules and **27–001** enforcement of Articles 87 to 89 EC in relation to State aid. These provisions apply to advantages, such as subsidies, preferential loans and other support, conferred upon selected undertakings by the State or through State resources and which distort competition. The essential features of the system are that Member States should notify new aid to the Commission for approval against criteria set out in the Treaty. Only the Commission can declare aid incompatible with the Treaty, although national courts have been given an increasing role in upholding the procedural safeguards of the Treaty rules and ensuring that individuals are protected against failures by Member States to comply. The Chapter begins by discussing the concept of aid for the purposes of Article 87, focusing on the controversial aspects of the case law relating to its requisite constituent elements. It then moves to an overview of the justifications for aid under the mandatory and discretionary exceptions of Article 87(2) and (3) respectively. The particular controversies surrounding State support to services of general economic interest are explored against recent case and legislative developments, including the relationship of the aid rules with Article 86(2). The procedural requirements for supervising aid are summarised by reference to EC secondary legislation. State aid is now being given the modernisation treatment already applied to the general competition rules of Articles 81 to 82, and so the Chapter concludes by considering the enforcement of the aid rules, with particular attention being paid to obstacles to the recovery of unlawful aid and the extent to which private remedies are available against States or beneficiaries of aid.

Introduction: State aid and the modernisation agenda

27–002   By curtailing the freedom of Member States to pursue unilateral industrial strategies, State aid control has been described as "clearly the most original of the EU's competition policies".[1] The unfettered grant of State aid would be liable to cause serious difficulties in a system which has as a primary objective the creation and maintenance of a single internal market. As the Court of Justice has observed:

> "The aim of [Article 87] of the Treaty is to prevent trade between Member States from being affected by advantages granted by public authorities".[2]

The evolution and future shape of State aid regulation must be seen in the context of the developments already discussed in relation to the general competition rules.[3] In particular, the competitiveness agenda set out in the so-called Lisbon strategy is now driving the reform of State aid policy. In 2005 the Commission announced a State Aid Action Plan[4] which, according to a speech by Neelie Kroes[5]:

> "has a key role to play in managing the economic reform agenda . . . Effective State aid control maintains a level playing field for free and fair competition in the single market, the key to competitiveness. We control state subsidies, because in general they distort the market, which results in lower competitiveness for our businesses, less innovation, and higher prices for consumers. But efficient and equitable State aid can also stimulate competition and support the economic reform process in new ways, acting as a driver for the virtuous circle of economic growth, better standards of living, and more and better jobs."

Calling for an economics-focused approach, she added that State aid should only be used:

---

[1] M. Cini and L. McGowan, *Competition Policy in the European Union* (Macmillan Press, Basingstoke, 1998), p.135.
[2] Case C–39/94 *SFEI v La Poste* [1996] E.C.R. I–3547, para.58.
[3] See Ch.22, above.
[4] COM (2005) 107 final, *State Aid Action Plan—Less and Better Targeted State Aid: A Roadmap For State Aid Reform 2005–2009*.
[5] Competition Commissioner, speech July 14, 2005, London, available on Commission's website.

"when it is an appropriate instrument for meeting a well defined objective of common interest; when it creates the right incentives and is proportionate to the problem; and when it distorts competition to the least possible extent."

The Action Plan recognises that State aid is not to be universally condemned, pointing out that:

"State aid policy safeguards competition in the Single Market and it is closely linked to many objectives of common interest, like services of general economic interest, regional and social cohesion, employment, research and development, environmental protection and the protection and promotion of cultural diversity. It must contribute by itself and by reinforcing other policies to making Europe a more effective place to invest and work, building up knowledge and innovation for growth and creating more and better jobs."[6]

The steps advocated for State aid reform are strongly resonant of developments in relation to Articles 81 to 82: more economic analysis of distortions and market failures; more networking between EU and national agencies; more guidance documentation from the Commission; and greater participation in enforcement from private parties and national courts.

Certainly, it may be said that the operation and effectiveness of State aid supervision is a good litmus test of the EU's maturity as a legal order.[7] After years as a legal backwater of interest to only the most idiosyncratic practitioners and academics, State aid has become a mainstream political and legal issue. It took, for example, until 1999 for there to be a procedural and enforcement Regulation[8] in State aid matters to supply a counterpart to the 1962 Regulation in competition law more generally.[9] However, the regime of State aid control remains both distinctive and fraught with controversy. As will be seen from this Chapter, some familiar questions arise—is market distortion measured by conceptual possibility or actual impact, does financial support to services of general economic interest require justification, what is the most effective balance of public and private enforcement?

The original inclusion of State aid in the EEC Treaty might have been as an element towards a common industrial policy to be formulated at Community level. However, the only option that was politically feasible was to allow the Member States to continue

---

[6] n.4, above, para.15.
[7] M. Ross, "State Aids: Maturing into a Constitutional Problem" (1995) 15 Y.E.L. 79.
[8] Reg.659/1999 [1999] O.J. L83.
[9] Reg.17/62, replaced by Reg.1/2003, see Ch.25, above.

granting aids but to establish a system of supervision by the Community institutions. Hence the system of notification and authorisation which was put in place by what are now Articles 87 to 89 of the Treaty. It is to the detailed analysis of these arrangements that we now turn.

The structure of Article 87 EC

27–003   Article 87 EC sets out the principles on the basis of which the compatibility of State aids with the common market is to be judged.[10] Paragraph (1) of the Article lays down the general principle that State aid fulfilling certain broadly defined criteria is incompatible with the common market. The paragraph does not expressly declare incompatible aids to be prohibited (*cf.* the drafting of Articles 81 and 82 EC) but the European Court has accepted that it contains an implied prohibition, though neither absolute nor unconditional.[11]

The general principle in Article 87(1) is qualified by mandatory exceptions listed in paragraph (2) and discretionary exceptions listed in paragraph (3). If an aid is found to be within one of the categories in paragraph (2), it must, as a matter of law, be regarded as compatible with the common market. On the other hand, the compatibility of aids falling within the categories in paragraph (3) is a discretionary matter, requiring an assessment of the positive and negative effects of the aid form the point of view of the Community as a whole. Under the machinery of Article 88 (see below) that discretion is exercised by the Commission, subject to reserve powers of the Council and the usual review criteria of the European Court. The latter's case law has also significantly enhanced the responsibilities of national courts in relation to the protection of individuals against failure by Member States to observe their duties under Article 88(3). Enabling legislation agreed by the Council in 1998[12] permits the Commission to adopt Regulations setting out block exemptions for certain types of aid. Aid falling within a block exemption does not need to be notified.[13] Aspects of State aid procedure and enforcement have been set out in detail by Regulation.[14]

---

[10] For further comment, see C. Quigley and A. Collins, *EC State Aid Law and Policy* (Hart, Oxford, 2003); A. Biondi, P. Eeckhout and J. Flynn (eds), *The Law of State Aid in the European Union* (OUP, Oxford, 2004).

[11] See the references to "an aid which is prohibited" in Case 6/69 *Commission v France* [1969] E.C.R. 523; [1970] C.M.L.R. 43 and "the prohibition in [Art.87](1)" in Case 78/76 *Firma Steinike und Weinlig v Germany* [1977] E.C.R. 595; [1977] 2 C.M.L.R. 688.

[12] Council Reg.994/98; [1998] O.J. L142/1. Examples include Reg.69/2001 on De Minimis Aid [2001] O.J. L10/30; Reg.70/2001 on Aid for Small and Medium-Sized Enterprises (SMEs) [2001] O.J. L10/33; Reg.2204/2002 on Employment Aid [2002] O.J. L337/3.

[13] Although Member States must keep records and must submit annual reports to the Commission on aid granted under these Regulations.

[14] Respectively, Reg.659/1999, n.8, above; Reg.794/2004 [2004] O.J. L140.

Article 87(1) provides:

"Save as otherwise provided in this Treaty, any aid granted by a Member State or through State resources in any form whatsoever which distorts or threatens to distort competition by favouring certain undertakings or the production of certain goods shall, in so far as it affects trade between Member States, be incompatible with the common market."

A general definition of State aid for the purposes of the EC Treaty was offered by the European Court in Case 61/79 *Amministrazione delle finanze dello stato v Denkavit*,[15] where it said that paragraph (1) of the Article:

"refers to the decisions of Member States by which the latter, in pursuit of their own economic and social objectives give, by unilateral and autonomous decisions, undertakings or other persons resources or procure for them advantages intended to encourage the attainment of the economic or social objectives sought".[16]

State aid is thus to be understood in terms of its function as an instrument of national economic and social policy involving the provision of some kind of tangible benefit for specific undertakings.[17]

It is immaterial what form the benefit may take or what particular goal of policy it may be designed to serve. The European Court has repeatedly held that the prohibition in paragraph (1) does not distinguish between measures of State intervention by reference to their causes or aims but defines them in relation to their effects.[18] A still useful list of forms of aid was given by the Commission in reply to a Written Question in 1963,[19] comprising: direct subsidies; exemption from duties and taxes; exemption from parafiscal charges; preferential interest rates; guarantees of loans on especially favourable terms; making land or buildings available either gratuitously or on especially favourable terms; provision of goods or services on preferential terms; indemnities against operating losses; or any other measure of equivalent effect. Further examples may be added, such as deferred collection of fiscal or social contributions, direct and

---

[15] [1980] E.C.R. 1205; [1981] 3 C.M.L.R. 694.
[16] [1980] E.C.R. at 1228; repeated by the CFI in Case T–351/02 *Deutsche Bahn v Commission* (forthcoming, Judgment April 5, 2006).
[17] "Undertakings" may include individuals if the usual tests of economic activity are satisfied; see Ch.22, above; in the state aid context, see Case C–172/03 *Heiser* [2005] E.C.R. I–1627, involving dental practitioners.
[18] Case 173/73 *Italy v Commission* [1974] E.C.R. 709; [1974] 2 C.M.L.R. 593; Case C–241/94 *France v Commission* [1996] E.C.R. 4551; [1997] 1 C.M.L.R. 983.
[19] [1963] J.O. 2235.

indirect State participation in share capital and logistical or commercial assistance granted in return for unusually low consideration. The catalogue should not, of course, be regarded as exhaustive, although it covers the forms of aid most frequently granted by the Member States. Since 2001, the Commission's website[20] has maintained a State Aid Scoreboard. During 2005,[21] excluding information reports relating to block exemptions, there were 764 cases registered with the Commission: 663 of these were notified by Member States, 84 were non-notified cases initiated by the Commission and 17 cases examined "existing"[22] aid. Of that total, 34 per cent of cases concerned aid in the agricultural sector, 52 per cent from manufacturing and service sectors, 9 per cent related to transport and energy and 4 per cent covered fisheries.

Defining State aid: the conditions of Article 87(1)

27–004   The concept of "aid" provides the trigger for the application of Articles 87 to 89 and, therefore, the Community regime of supervision. According to the Court of Justice, Article 87(1) lays down the following conditions:

> "First, there must be an intervention by the State or through State resources. Second, the intervention must be liable to affect trade between Member States. Third, it must confer an advantage on the recipient. Fourth, it must distort or threaten to distort competition."[23]

Although not always consistently identified and ordered in this way by either courts or commentators, these are cumulative requirements[24] and are discussed in turn below.

Intervention by the State or through State resources

27–005   To fall within the scope of Article 87(1) the aid must be granted "by a Member State or through State resources". Although the Court refers to this as one condition, it has also made it clear that it comprises two separate but cumulative elements.[25] Not only must the aid be granted directly or indirectly through state resources but it

---

[20] See: *http://europa.eu.int/comm/competition/state—aid/scoreboard/*.
[21] Statistics taken from Scoreboard Spring 2006 update, COM (2006) 130 final.
[22] Discussed further below.
[23] Case C–280/00 *Altmark Trans* [2003] E.C.R. I–7747, para.75.
[24] Case C–142/87 *Belgium v Commission (Tubemeuse)* [1990] E.C.R. I–959, para.25; Joined Cases C–278/92 to C–280/92 *Spain v Commission* [1994] E.C.R. I–4103, para.20; Case C–482/99 *France v Commission ("Stardust Marine")* [2002] E.C.R. I–4397, para.68; Case C–280/00 *Altmark Trans*, n.23, above, para.74.
[25] Case C–482/99, n.24 above, para.24.

must be imputable to the State.[26] In other words, the phrase used in Article 87(1) is not as wide as might otherwise appear. The reference to "or through State resources" serves to bring within the definition of aid, in addition to benefits granted directly by the State, those granted by a public or private body designated or established by the State. Thus, as Advocate General Ruiz-Jarabo Colomer has observed:

> "Any attempt to list the conditions which have to be fulfilled in order for resources to be regarded as 'State' resources must refer, firstly, to the requirement that such resources should be linked to the State, or to a body which forms part of the structure of the State or exercises any of the powers characteristically vested in it.
>
> Secondly, those resources must be attributable to the State or to the relevant public body in such a way that it is able to exercise a sufficient degree of control over them."[27]

Clearly, the conditions will be satisfied by grants by regional or local authorities as well as by central government. Moreover, State resources do not always have to be under the control of the Treasury. As the Court observed in *Preussen Elektra*[28]:

> "Article [87(1)] of the Treaty covers all the financial means by which the public sector may actually support undertakings, irrespective of whether or not those means are permanent assets of the public sector. Consequently, even though the sums involved in the measure . . . are not permanently held by the Treasury, the fact that they constantly remain under public control, and therefore available to the competent national authorities, is sufficient for them to be categorised as State aid."

However, the question of whether an alleged aid has come from State resources has proved controversial. Thus, in *Sloman Neptun*,[29] German legislation created a shipping register which allowed ships flying under the German flag but employing non-EC crew to escape the full rigours of German labour law. Advocate General Darmon argued that the effect of reducing those shipowners' costs was equivalent to a state-authorised fund for their benefit. However, the Court rejected this view on the basis that there was no burden on

---

[26] Case C–345/02 *Pearle v Hoofdbedrijfschap Ambachten* [2004] E.C.R. I–7139, para.35.
[27] Opinion in *Pearle*, n.26, above, para.67.
[28] Case C–379/98 *Preussen Elektra* [2001] E.C.R. I–2099.
[29] Joined Cases C–72–73/91 *Firma Sloman Neptun Schiffahrts A.-G. v Seebetriebsrat Bodo Ziesmer, Sloman Neptun Schiffahrts AG* [1993] E.C.R. I–887; [1995] 2 C.M.L.R. 97. A similar approach was taken in Case C–189/91 *Kirsammer-Hack v Sidal* [1993] E.C.R. I–6185.

State resources. It confirmed this approach in *Epifanio Viscido v Ente Poste Italiane*,[30] where the provision in question gave relief to Poste Italiane from the normal rule of Italian law that employment contracts were of indefinite duration. The flexibility of fixed-term contracts, whilst arguably conferring benefits or saved costs for the undertaking, did not involve any direct or indirect transfer of State resources to it.

Nevertheless, the value of the State resources test in its *Sloman Neptun* form continues to be criticised. In *Enirisorse v Sotacarbo*,[31] Italian law provided that, in derogation from the general law,[32] members of a company controlled by the State could withdraw from that company on condition they relinquished all claims over that company's assets. The Italian Government submitted that the rules did not place any "additional burden" on the State budget. Any advantage to the company was financed from the private share-holders. Moreover, in its view, as the company had been set up with State funds, relieving it from the obligation of redemption was not the source of a fresh burden. Advocate General Poiares Maduro accepted that application of the *Sloman Neptun* approach would not treat the scenario as a transfer of State resources. However, he expressed strong dissatisfaction with the substance of that test, whilst accepting the legitimacy of a need to place Article 87(1) within limits. Explaining the Court's position, he noted:

> "In its case law, the Court seems to wish to draw a distinction between distortions resulting from the adoption of measures to regulate economic activities and those caused by a transfer of public resources to certain undertakings. Only the latter are such as to affect the competitive environment. The former must be accepted in as much as their only purpose is to establish the parameters within which business is carried on and goods and services produced.
>
> The reason for the distinction is clear to see. The Court is seeking to guard against the scope of the Community rules being broadened to cover distortions of competition that are simply the result of differences in legislative policy between Member States. That caution stems from a concern not to encroach on powers reserved to the Member States. There is a danger that over-extension of the State aid rules might result in all economic policy decisions of Member States being brought under the scrutiny of the Community authorities, without any

---

[30] Joined Cases C–52–54/97 *Epifanio Viscido v Ente Poste Italiane* [1998] E.C.R. I–2629; [1998] 3 C.M.L.R. 184. See also *Preussen Elektra*, n.28, above.

[31] Case C–237/04, forthcoming, Opinion January 12, 2006, Judgment March 23, 2006.

[32] Whether in fact derogation was possible in the general law was not entirely clear, a point stressed by the Advocate General.

distinction being made between direct interventions in the market and general measures to regulate economic activities. It would also result, besides, in a substantial increase in the workload of the Community's supervisory authorities, the Commission and the Court."[33]

According to the Advocate General, however, a more workable and effects-based test would be one based on selective advantage.[34] The Court, however, adhered to the language of *Sloman Neptun* and observed that the national law merely prevented the company's budget from being burdened with a charge which, in a normal situation, would not have existed.[35]

For Article 87(1) to apply there must be imputability to the State. **27–006** The way in which this is an additional requirement beyond the state resources element can be illustrated by the *Stardust Marine* case.[36] Here the financial measures which had been attacked as aid by the Commission were implemented by public undertakings. The Commission had automatically deemed that status to be sufficient basis for imputability to the State. Whilst accepting that the State was in a position to exercise dominant influence over those undertakings using the tests of control set out in the Transparency Directive,[37] the Court insisted that it was necessary to go further and examine whether the public authorities had been involved, in one way or another, in the adoption of the aid measures. Without imposing a level of strictness which would demand proof of the State inciting a body to take particular measures, the Court listed factors which might indicate a sufficient degree of involvement. These included: the legal status of the public undertaking (whether subject to public law or company law, for example), the intensity of the supervision exercised by the public authorities over the management of the undertaking or deductions about State involvement to be drawn from the compass of the measures, their content or the conditions they contain. The Court accordingly annulled the Commission's decision.

The imputability test will clearly be satisfied if the State has chosen to act through the agency of some public or private body. Community law does not permit the rules on State aid to be circumvented merely through the creation of autonomous institutions charged with allocating aid.[38] However, where the State has

---

[33] Opinion, paras.44–45; see also Case C–345/02 *Pearle*, n.26, above, para.36, also applying *Sloman Neptun*.
[34] The advantage condition is discussed separately, below.
[35] Judgment, para.48.
[36] Case C–482/99, n.24, above.
[37] Dir. 80/723 [1980] O.J. L195/35; discussed further in Ch.26, above.
[38] Case T–358/94 *Air France v Commission* [1996] E.C.R. II–2109, para.62; [1997] 1 C.M.L.R. 492.

enacted its obligations under an EC directive and an advantage results, this will not be treated as an aid imputed to the State. Thus, in *Deutsche Bahn*,[39] Germany had relieved commercial airlines from excise duty on fuel in accordance with EC directives. The operators of high-speed trains, who competed with budget airlines on some routes, were thus not exempt and claimed unfair competition based on State aid. However, the Court of First Instance rejected the argument by observing that the German rules were only implementing Community provisions in accordance with their Treaty obligations and thus not imputable to the State.

Liable to affect trade between Member States

27–007   The prohibition in Article 87(1) requires that the aid distorts or threatens to distort competition in so far as it affects trade between Member States. These tests, whilst integral to satisfying the need to reason decisions under Article 253 EC, have not been given much detailed analysis in the case law. Indeed, in *Philip Morris Holland v Commission*[40] the Court came close to enunciating a *per se* rule as to the effect on inter-state trade which would result from aids designed to enable a cigarette manufacturer to close one of of its two factories in the Netherlands and to expand production at the other. The Court said that:

> "When financial aid strengthens the position of an undertaking as compared with other undertakings competing in intra-Community trade the latter must be regarded as affected by that aid".[41]

The reasons for adopting this somewhat less than rigorous stance may well be explained historically by the need to ensure that the State aid regime, toothless enough in the past, was not made even more difficult to apply. Moreover, the lack of intensity in market analysis suggests that the inter-State trade element of Article 87(1) is a measurement of jurisdiction rather than economic impact. This may therefore become increasingly out of step with changes of policy in the modernisation of State aid law.

Nevertheless, it is still the Court's formal position that there is no threshold or percentage below which it may be considered that trade between Member States is not affected.[42] Indeed, in *Heiser*, the Court's formulation was as broad as ever—since it was "not inconceivable" that medical practitioners specialising in dentistry might be

---

[39] Case T–351/02, n.16, above.
[40] Case 730/79 [1980] E.C.R. 2671; [1981] 2 C.M.L.R. 321.
[41] *ibid.*, para.11.
[42] Case C–172/03 *Heiser*, n.17, above, para.32.

in competition with colleagues established in another Member State, the inter-State trade condition was satisfied.[43] Moreover, application of the condition does not depend on the local or regional character of the services supplied or on the scale of the field of activity concerned.[44] Whether aid is "capable" of having an impact on trade between Member States remains the judicial test.[45]

The Court's approach thus does not sit entirely easily with the practice of the Commission, which has applied a *de minimis* policy since 1992.[46] This currently[47] means that aid of an amount less than €100,000 granted to an undertaking over a period of three years does not require notification for approval since it is deemed to have only negligible effects on competition and trade between Member States. The Commission has proposed[48] amending the Regulation to increase the *de minimis* "ceiling" to €150,000, to extend its coverage to some agricultural products and, depending on consultation outcomes, possibly transport. It may be noted, however, that in *Heiser*, the Court did not consider it to have been established that the amount of aid involved, said by the parties to be €30,000 at most over the period 1997–2004, was definitely protected by the *de minimis* Notice applicable at the time.[49]

Conferring an advantage on the recipient

The third condition within the notion of aid is the requirement **27–008** that it must "favour" certain undertakings or the production of certain goods. This formulation suggests at least two ideas, advantage and selectivity, but the interplay between them has created difficulties in the case law. As Advocate General Cosmas has pointed out,[50] there is an elliptical quality to the Treaty expression, since it impliedly requires some comparison to be made between the treatment accorded to the alleged beneficiary and the position of other undertakings. Put another way, "the prohibition of State aid appears as the result of the general principle of equality and the rule derived from it that a like rule should apply to like situations".[51]

The notion of advantage has been expressed in a variety of ways, but all are driven by a quest to establish whether the transaction,

---

[43] *ibid.*, para.35.
[44] *ibid.*, para.33; also Case C–280/00 *Altmark Trans*, n.23, above.
[45] e.g. Joined Cases T–195/01 and T–207/01 *Government of Gibraltar v Commission* [2002] E.C.R. II–2309.
[46] *cf.* Case 142/87 *Belgium v Commission (Re Tubemeuse)* n.24, above, para.43, where the Court expressly rejected the contention put forward by the Belgian Government that the 5 per cent threshold then used by the Commission in general competition matters should also apply to state aids.
[47] Commission Reg.69/2001, n.12, above
[48] March 2006.
[49] the 1996 version, the ceiling being €100,000.
[50] Case C–353/95P *Tiercé Ladbroke v Commission* [1997] E.C.R. I–7007.
[51] *ibid.*, at 7021.

activity or conduct amounts to a normal commercial transaction or rational market behaviour. Of course, these are to some degree question-begging labels that require further unpacking and application. Different contexts will demand nuanced tests, but two particular themes in the case law are sufficiently prevalent to merit closer discussion below. Firstly, there is a well-established principle that applies a hypothetical market investor (or creditor) test as the benchmark. However, there may be circumstances where this kind of comparison is impossible. Secondly, a discernible thread has arisen in recent years which is capable of denying the presence of an advantage where the alleged benefit can be described as "inherent" in the scheme or system being investigated or challenged. This line of argument, if not carefully applied, runs the risk of conflating advantage and justification.

27–009 **(a) Market investor/creditor tests.** This approach had its origins in the cases of the 1980s which established that equity participation by the State in corporate financing could in principle amount to aid within the meaning of Article 87(1). Thus, in *Re Boch*[52] the Court observed:

> "In the case of an undertaking whose capital is almost entirely held by the public authorities, the test is, in particular, whether in similar circumstances a private shareholder, having regard to the foreseeability of obtaining a return and leaving aside all social, regional policy and sectoral considerations, would have subscribed the capital in question".

In the wake of this judicial support, the market investor principle was refined and elaborated beyond the context of capital investment. The key question has essentially become whether the recipient undertaking receives an economic advantage which it would not have obtained under normal market conditions.[53] Expressions of the principle can be found, for example, in relation to loans and interest rates thereon,[54] guarantees[55] and the renegotiation of credit terms.[56] Put shortly, the Court will only find that an aid exists if the State has been acting other than as an "ordinary economic agent".[57] This

---

[52] Case 40/85 *Re Boch: Belgium v Commission* [1986] E.C.R. 2321; [1998] 2 C.M.L.R. 301. See also Joined Cases 296 and 318/82 *The Netherlands and Leeuwarder Papierwaren fabriek BV v Commission* [1985] E.C.R. 809; [1985] 3 C.M.L.R. 380; Joined Cases C–278–280/92 *Spain v Commission*, n.24, above.

[53] Case C–39/94 *SFEI v La Poste*, n.2, above, para.60.

[54] Case T–214/95 *Vlaams Gewest v Commission* [1998] E.C.R. II–717; Case T–16/96 *Cityflyer Express v Commission* [1998] E.C.R. II–757; [1998] 2 C.M.L.R. 537.

[55] Joined Cases C–329/93 and C–62–63/95 *Germany v Commission, Hanseatische Industrie Beteiligungen GmbH v Commission, Bremer Vulkan Verbund A.-G. v Commission* [1996] ECRI–5151.

[56] Case C–256/97 *DMT* [1999] E.C.R. I–3913.

[57] Case C–56/93 *Belgium v Commission* [1996] E.C.R. I–723.

accordingly means that failure by the Commission to make proper assessments of costs, valuations and other economic criteria will undermine any allegation of aid.[58] The reference point for comparison must be taken at the contemporaneous period of the financial support measures.[59]

It was suggested by the applicant in *Italy v Commission*[60] that a private holding company might provide money to ailing subsidiaries for reasons other than profitability, such as the desire to maintain the group's image or to redirect its activities. The Court replied that capital provided by a public investor who is not interested in profitability, even in the long term, must be regarded as an aid for the purposes of the EC rules. In another judgment on the same day,[61] the Court went further and held that the concept of the private investor, whilst not limited to one placing capital for a short- or medium-term profit, must at least relate to a private holding company or private group of undertakings carrying out a global structural policy or one limited to a particular sector which is guided by the prospects of profit in the longer term. On this test, therefore, the Commission was entitled to find that the capital contributions in question which had been made to car companies were beyond the contemplation of private investors and should be seen as solely designed to absorb the debts of the recipient undertaking in order to ensure that it survived.

However, the "normal market conditions" comparison will break down if the operation in question is a universal service network which would never have been created by a private undertaking. This was the situation in *Chronopost*,[62] where La Poste held a monopoly in ordinary mail delivery in France. It had provided various logistical and commercial assistance to its subsidiary Chronopost, providing the latter with access to its postal infrastructure for the collection and transport of Chronopost's express courier deliveries and access to La Poste's customers and enjoyment of its goodwill. The Commission had originally rejected the existence of aid, but this decision had been annulled by the Court of First Instance[63] on application by Chronopost's express courier delivery competitors. On appeal to the Court of Justice, the Court of First Instance's approach was held to have been flawed in law. In particular, an undertaking such as La Poste was in a situation "very different" from that of a private undertaking acting under normal market conditions. Moreover, the provision of logistical and commercial assistance was inseparably

---

[58] See Case T–98/00 *Linde AG v Commission* [2002] E.C.R. II–3961.
[59] Case C–482/99 *France v Commission*, n.24, above.
[60] Case C–303/88 *Italy v Commission* [1991] E.C.R. I–1433; [1993] 2 C.M.L.R. 1.
[61] Case C–305/89 *Italy v Commission* [1991] E.C.R. I–1603.
[62] Joined Cases C–83/01P, C–93/01P and C–94/01P, *Chronopost v Ufex* [2003] E.C.R. I–6993.
[63] Case T–613/97 *Ufex v Commission* [2000] E.C.R. II–4055. Ufex was the successor to SFEI–see Case C–39/94, n.2, above.

linked to the La Poste network, since it consisted precisely in making available that network which had no equivalent on the market. Thus, according to the Court:

> "in the absence of any possibility of comparing the situation of La Poste with that of a private group of undertakings not operating in a reserved sector, normal market conditions, which are necessarily hypothetical, must be assessed by reference to the objective and verifiable elements which are available."

The Court accordingly referred the case back to the Court of First Instance for an assessment of how far payments by Chronopost covered La Poste's costs.

27–010   Judging whether aid exists because the State fails to demand money owed to it, or is prepared to delay its recovery, presents a further issue as to what is to be construed as "normal". Hence, and rather later than the invention of the market investor comparison, the case law has also spawned a "hypothetical private creditor" approach. This may not always be easy to apply, as can be seen from *Spain v Commission*.[64] Tubacex, a company in provisional insolvency, restructured its wage bills with Fogasa, a State-controlled organisation charged with paying employees in the event of their employer's insolvency. Tubacex also made arrangements with the Social Security Fund, whereby debts on social security payments were to be repaid over extended instalments at nine per cent interest, the legal rate for default interest at the time. The Commission treated the interest rate as an aid, deeming it preferential when compared to the rates charged by banks on private loans. However, the Spanish Government claimed that neither Fogasa nor the Social Security Fund were acting as loan providers but were instead renegotiating the terms of existing debts. This view was accepted by the Court in annulling the Commission's decision.[65] In contrast, Advocate General La Pergola had analysed the arrangements as containing an aid element, not because of the rate of interest but because of the fact that the debt rescheduling had occurred at all at a time when Tubacex was deeply in crisis. According to the Advocate General, the "normal" response of creditors to such a grave economic situation would be to prevent the opening of fresh credit.

As Advocate General Poiares Maduro has since indicated, the hypothetical private creditor is a diligent and efficient market operator, capable of discerning and using the most appropriate means of achieving a certain result, i.e. the recovery of its debts.[66] In

---

[64] Case C–342/96 *Spain v Commission* [1999] E.C.R. I–2459.
[65] See also Case C–256/97 *DMT*, n.56, above. Case T–36/99 *Lenzing v Commission* [2004] E.C.R.
[66] Case C–276/02 *Spain v Commission* [2004] E.C.R. I–8091, Opinion, para.36.

his view, choosing to waive a debt temporarily while the debtor continues its activities must satisfy three conditions to avoid constituting an aid: it must be possible in principle to make the undertaking economically viable and to improve its financial position; everything possible must be done to prevent further credit being run up and new debts accumulated; and the State must be able to rely on the recovery of the debts owed to it within a reasonable period.[67] In the same case, the Advocate General identified key differences between the investor and creditor models of comparsion for aid measurement:

"The investor is in a position to choose the investment which seems to him to be the most profitable. In theory, the capital which he is prepared to invest in an undertaking is available, under the same conditions, to all operators on the market. This is not the creditor's situation. A creditor is already in a privileged relationship with a debtor undertaking to which he may be prepared to grant further advantages in the form of a waiver or debt rescheduling. The capital which is at stake in these circumstances is not 'on the market'. It is not available, under the same conditions, to other economic operators. Such capital is allocated in consideration only of the interests of the two parties. The effect of this difference between the two situations is, in my opinion, a difference in the manner of assessing the comparison between the conduct of public authorities and that of a private operator. In an investment situation, the comparison is carried out 'in normal market conditions'. If the capital is allocated under favourable conditions for the investor, even to an undertaking in difficulty, so that the investor may expect a more or less long-term financial profit, there is no advantage and competition is not distorted. The situation is different in a creditor-debtor relationship. They can only be in 'similar market conditions'. It is a question of assessing the situation of debtor undertakings with regard to the situation of undertakings with the same difficulties rather than with regard to the situation of their competitors on the market. Then one should consider not only whether there is an economic advantage, as there is no doubt on that score, but also whether that advantage is a 'selective' advantage, in that it would have the effect of granting an undertaking preferential treatment, without any justification in accordance with the logic of economic efficiency. In that case, the decisive test is not whether there is an economic advantage, but whether that advantage amounts to treatment which is more favourable than

---

[67] *ibid.*, para.40.

that which would be granted, under similar conditions, by a private creditor to a debtor undertaking."[68]

Having made some arrangement with a debtor over waiver, the creditor must exercise due diligence in monitoring and enforcing against further failures to try to recover at least a marginal amount of the money owed.[69]

27–011 **(b) Selectivity.** Article 87(1) EC requires it to be determined whether, under a particular statutory scheme, a State measure is such as to favour "certain undertakings or the production of certain goods" in comparison with others which, in the light of the objective pursued by the system in question, are in a comparable legal and factual situation.[70] A distinction is, therefore, drawn between general measures of economic policy, such as the easing of credit controls or a specific tax regime for the self-employed, which may very well improve the position of undertakings in the country concerned *vis-à-vis* their competitors elsewhere in the Community, and measures giving a competitive advantage to particular undertakings or industrial sectors. The fact that the number of undertakings able to claim entitlement under the measure at issue is very large, or that they belong to different sectors of activity, is not sufficient to call into question its selective nature and thus rule out its classification as a State aid.[71] In Cases 6 and 11/69 *Commission v France*[72] the European Court held that a preferential discount rate for exports must be regarded as an aid falling within the Treaty supervisory regime, despite the fact that it applied to all national products without distinction. The explanation seems to be[73] that some undertakings would be producing solely for the domestic market so that not all undertakings would in fact be claiming the preferential entitlement.

This distinction between aids and general measures is sometimes slippery. Where the scope of rules is defined by regional location,

---

[68] *ibid.*, para.24.
[69] In C–276/02 *Spain v Commission*, n.66, above, the Court annulled the Commission's decision because it had paid insufficient attention to evidence that the Spanish authorities had taken some steps for enforcement of tax and social security obligations. The CFI has subjected the Commission's application of the creditor tests to considerable scrutiny; see also Case T–152/99 *HAMSA v Commission* [2002] E.C.R. II–3049; Joined Cases T–228/99 and T–233/99 *Westdeutsche Landesbank Girozentrale v Commission* [2003] E.C.R. II–435.
[70] Case C–308/01 *GIL Insurance* [2004] E.C.R. I–4777, citing Case C–143/99 *Adria-Wien Pipeline and Wietersdorfer & Peggauer Zementwerke* [2001] E.C.R. I–836; Case C–409/00 *Spain v Commission* [2003] E.C.R. I–1487; see also Case C–172/03 *Heiser*, n.17, above, para.40.
[71] Case C–172/03 *Heiser*, n.17, above, para.42 (in relation to VAT exemptions for medical practitioners).
[72] [1969] E.C.R. 523; [1970] C.M.L.R. 43.
[73] Following the Opinion of Advocate General Roemer, at 552. For a later example of aid covering a whole sector see Case C–95/97 *Belgium v Commission* [1999] E.C.R. I–3671.

industrial sector or size of undertaking selectivity is clearly present, but problems may arise where criteria for the provision of resources appear to be universal. The key indication in such cases is whether the application of the measure rests upon discretion. According to the Court in the *DMT* case:

> "where the body granting financial assistance enjoys a degree of latitude which enables it to choose the beneficiaries or the conditions under which the financial assistance is provided, that assistance cannot be considered to be general in nature".[74]

The Court then left to the national court the question of whether the practices of the national social security office, which had included allowing payments from the undertaking to be postponed for eight years, were indeed part of a discretionary system.

Examples of the interaction of selectivity criteria can be seen in cases involving the special insolvency procedure of Italian law. By Act No.95/79 large companies in difficulties could continue trading subject to Ministerial supervision. Certain thresholds had to be satisfied for the law to apply, including a minimum number of employees and a minimum level of debt owed to particular types of creditor, including the State. One of the consequences of applying the law was that the undertaking had exemption from fines and penalties which would otherwise arise from failure to meet social security contributions. In a case arising under the ECSC Treaty[75] selectivity was held to exist in both the conditions dictating whether an undertaking qualified to take advantage of the law at all and in the discretionary nature of the dispensation to continue trading which was vested in the relevant Minister.[76] This approach was confirmed in the *Piaggio*[77] case, where the Court added that:

> "even if the decisions of the Minister . . . to place the undertaking in difficulties under special administration and to allow it to continue trading are taken with regard, as far as possible, to the interests of the creditors and, in particular, to the prospects for increasing the value of the undertaking's assets, they are also influenced . . . by the concern to maintain the undertaking's economic activity in the light of national industrial policy considerations".[78]

---

[74] *DMT* case, n.56 above, para.27.

[75] Case C–200/97 *Ecotrade v AFS* [1998] E.C.R. I–7907; [1999] 2 C.M.L.R. 833.

[76] See also the observations of Advocate General La Pergola in Case C–342/96 *Spain v Commission* [1999] E.C.R. I–2459.

[77] Case C–295/97 *Piaggio* [1999] E.C.R. I–3735. Although the wording of the ECSC Treaty was different, the notion of selectivity was treated as being the same as that for an aid under the EC Treaty.

[78] *ibid.* para.38.

One effect of using the operation of discretionary rules as a measure of selectivity is to invite a closer scrutiny of national decision making processes than is the case in relation to other, more self-evident, criteria such as those based upon membership of a particular industrial sector.

The Court accepts that there is no selectivity where, although an advantage accrues to its recipient, a measure is justified by the nature or general scheme of the system of which it is part, provided the system in question has a legitimate purpose. As Advocate General Poiares Maduro has explained:

> "It is only where the special treatment cannot be justified on the basis of a general system or where it does not result from a consistent application of the system to which it belongs that the measure can be said to be *selective*. In those circumstances, it is reasonable to assume that the measure has no other justification than to afford preferential treatment to a certain class of economic agents. It is therefore not the measure's legally exceptional character alone that makes it State aid. In this matter, it is necessary to look to the substance and not to the form. A measure is selective if it serves to place certain undertakings in a more favourable economic position than undertakings in a comparable situation, without the resulting costs to the wider community being clearly justified by a system of fairly shared charges."[79]

However, the Court has been reluctant to allow the "inherent" claim to succeed too readily. In *Adria-Wien*,[80] for example, the Court rejected the advice of Advocate General Mischo, who had taken the view that an Austrian tax rebate granted only to undertakings whose activity consisted primarily in the manufacture of goods was not an aid. In particular, the Court noted that undertakings supplying services could incur similar energy taxes yet not be able to claim the rebate. Ecological arguments were similarly undermined, since energy consumption by service providers was just as damaging to the environment; thus relief for one sector could not be justified. The Court has been equally robust in other contexts.[81]

---

[79] Case C–237/04, n.31, above; Opinion, para.52.
[80] Case C–143/99, n.70, above.
[81] See Case C–409/00 *Spain v Commission*, n.70, above, Case C–159/01 *Netherlands v Commission* [2004] E.C.R. I–4461; the Court, however, accepted the argument in Case C–308/01 *GIL Insurance*, n.70, above. For an example of its unsuccessful application before the CFI, see Joined Cases T–346/99, T–347/99, T–348/99 *Disputación de álava* [2002] E.C.R. II–4259, paras.58–64.

Distortion of competition

This is the fourth and final condition cited by the Court of Justice **27–012** as necessary to establish an aid within the meaning of Article 87(1). It is in practice linked closely with the question of effect on inter-state trade, discussed above. The Court has been relatively lax in relation to both requirements. Consequently, the amount of aid can be very little, yet still be held to distort competition.[82] For example, in *Vlaams Gewest*[83] the Court of First Instance swiftly dismissed a claim by the beneficiary airline that the measly amount of aid it had received, described as a few Belgian francs per passenger, could scarcely have enabled it to avoid increasing its fares or ward off insolvency. Nor can a beneficiary use the fact that other undertakings are receiving aids (even illegal ones) from their States to argue that its own aid is only neutralising other distortions.[84] Aid intended to relieve undertakings of all or part of the expenses which they would normally have had to bear in their day-to-day management or usual activities, in principle distorts competition.[85]

In a more economically-focused programme of State aid modernisation there is perhaps scope for a more robust application of the distortion requirement. At present, the fairly light inquiry is whether the recipient would be worse off competitively without the aid. However, there are instances where failure to identify the proper market has been fatal to a decision taken by the Commission.[86]

Justifications for aid: mandatory exceptions under Article 87(2)

Article 87(2) provides that the following categories of aid shall be **27–013** compatible with the common market.

"(a) aid having a social character, granted to individual consumers, provided that such aid is granted without discrimination related to the origin of the products concerned"

The scope of this exception is limited, especially by the require- **27–014** ment that the aid must be for final consumers. Intervention by the State to buy wheat and then resell it at a discount to enable cheaper bread to be available for consumers might conceivably qualify.[87] The Commission cites the possible application of the exception where an

---

[82] Joined Cases C–278–280/92 *Spain v Commission*, n.24, above, para.42.

[83] Case T–214/95 *Vlaams Gewest v Commission*, n.54, above.

[84] *ibid.*

[85] Case T–228/99, n.69, above.

[86] Case T–155/98 *SIDE v Commission* [2002] E.C.R. II–1179; see also the rigorous approach to distorting competition taken by the CFI in Case T–93/02, *Confédération nationale du Crédit Mutuel* [2005] E.C.R. II–143.

[87] Case 52/76 *Benedetti v Munari* [1977] E.C.R. 163. However, as pointed out by Advocate General Reischl at 190, the problem in this case was that the benefit appeared to go to the flour mills, not just the final consumers.

air route concerns an underprivileged region, such as an island. Aid to transport facilities for the island's population could fall within paragraph (a).[88] A travel voucher subsidy scheme was held to fall outside the scope of the provision as it had not been made available to ultimate consumers on a non-discriminatory basis.[89]

"(b)aid to make good the damage caused by natural disasters or exceptional occurrences"

27–015   Aid to make good the damage caused by natural disasters is an obvious candidate for automatic exemption from the general principle in Article 87(1). Italian measures which the Commission has treated as falling under this heading were the assistance given in Liguria to repairs and reconstruction required as a result of the floods in 1977, and the provision in Friuli-Venezia Giulia of low interest loans and subsidies for the reconstruction of industrial plant destroyed by the earthquake in 1976.[90] The aid must be to make good the damage, rather than just promote the industrial development of the area. However, the latter could still qualify for exemption under the discretionary provisions of Article 87(3)(a) or (c).

The notion of "exceptional circumstances" is very vague, but is taken to extend the scope of Article 87(2)(b) to "man-made" damage such as that caused by war, terrorism,[91] marine pollution or catastrophic transport accidents. On the other hand, its applicability in the case of difficulties of an exclusively economic nature is more doubtful. The exceptional aid measures adopted by the Member States in the face of the serious recession which began to affect the Community from the second half of 1974 onwards were dealt with by the Commission under the predecessor to Article 87(3)(b). There must be a sufficient causal link between the disaster or exceptional circumstance and the economic disadvantage sustained.[92]

---

[88] Application of Arts 92 and 93 EC and Art.61 EEA to state aids in the aviation sector; [1994] O.J. C350/5, para.24.

[89] Joined Cases T–116/01 and T–118/01 *P & O Ferries (Vizcaya) SA v Commission* [2003] E.C.R. II–2957, para.167.

[90] [1978] Comp.Rep. point 164.

[91] Including compensation to airlines for the losses sustained as the result of the closure of US airspace and increased insurance premiums in the wake of the terrorist attacks on New York in September 2001.

[92] See Case C–278/00 *Greece v Commission* [2000] E.C.R. I–8787, where there was insufficient connection between the Chernobyl nuclear disaster and a legal provision enabling Greece to settle a whole range of debts owed by agricultural co-operatives.

"(c) aid granted to the economy of certain areas of the Federal Republic of Germany affected by the division of Germany, in so far as such aid is required in order to compensate for the economic disadvantage caused by that division"

Since the unification of Germany in 1990[93] the State aid rules have **27–016** applied with full effect throughout the State. The Commission has consistently taken the view that the exemption must now be applied restrictively[94] and that the provisions of the discretionary exemptions of Article 87(3) are adequate to deal with remaining problems.[95] However, this point was contested in the *Saxony* and *Volkswagen* cases.[96] It was submitted by the company and Government that as sub-paragraph (c) had been left intact by the Maastricht and Amsterdam Treaties, its modern purpose must extend to use in compensating disadvantages experienced by the East in its exposure to a market economy. The Court of First Instance rejected this argument, noting that the difficulties of economic transition were caused not by the division of Germany as such but, in particular, by the nature of the politico-economic regime which then applied. The Commission, accordingly, had not erred in law in taking the view that new aid by investment in the car industry was to be assessed against the criteria of Article 87(3) rather than Article 87(2)(c).

The Court of Justice has maintained this position, emphasising that paragraph (c) only covers the economic disadvantages caused by the 1948 division stemming from the establishment of a physical frontier, such as the breaking of communication links or the loss of markets as a result of the breaking off of commercial relations between the two parts of German territory. The economic disadvantages suffered by the new Länder as a whole following division have not been directly caused by the geographical division of Germany within the meaning of Article 87(2)(c) EC. Differences in development between the original and the new Länder are explained by causes other than the geographical rift caused by the division of Germany and in particular by the different politico-economic systems set up in each part of Germany.[97]

---

[93] Monetary union came into effect on July 1 and political union on October 3.

[94] e.g. in relation to investment aids for Volkswagen, Commission Dec. 94/1068, [1994] O.J. L385/1.

[95] *Aid to Buna;* [1996] O.J. L239/1; the Commission did not regard the difficulties facing companies of the former GDR in meeting the challenges of EU competitors as disadvantages caused by the division of Germany.

[96] Joined Cases T–132 and 143/96 *Freistaat Sachsen and Volkswagen v Commission* [1999] E.C.R. II–3663.

[97] Case C–156/98 *Germany v Commission* [2000] E.C.R. I–6857; repeated in Case C–334/99 *Germany v Commission* [2003] E.C.R. I–1139; Case C–277/00 *Germany v Commission* [2004] E.C.R. I–3925.

Discretionary exceptions under Article 87(3)

27–017   The discretion given to the Commission under Article 87(3) is a wide one. Advocate General Capotorti described it in *Philip Morris Holland* as "implying an assessment of an economic, technical and policy nature".[98] The Court said that the exercise of the discretion "involves economic and social assessments which must be made in a Community context".[99]

When applying the discretionary exceptions, the Commission seeks to ensure that aid measures are approved only if they both promote recognised Community objectives and do not frustrate the maintenance of the internal market. The Commission only has power to authorise aids which are necessary for the furtherance of one of the objectives listed in paragraph (3). In 1980 it adopted the principle of compensatory justification whereby, to gain approval, any aid proposal:

> "must contain a compensatory justification which takes the form of a contribution by the beneficiary of aid over and above the effects of normal play of market forces to the achievement of Community objectives".[1]

The Court upheld this principle in *Philip Morris Holland*, ruling that an aid purporting to be an incentive for investment that would have been made in any event was ineligible, on that ground alone, for exemption.

In more recent times the Commission has established detailed Guidelines covering a range of aid areas (e.g. employment, R&D, rescue and restructuring of companies). These documents, which are not explored in detail here, typically set out methods for the calculation of aid, the eligibility of recipients and the overall "intensity" of permitted levels of aid. Not surprisingly, the legal status of such Guidelines has become contentious. In a case concerning the regional aid Guidelines, the Court observed more generally:

> "It should be noted at the outset that, in the exercise of the powers conferred on it by Articles 87 EC and 88 EC, the Commission may adopt guidelines designed to indicate how it intends, under those articles, to exercise its discretion in regard to new aid or in regard to existing systems of aid.
>
> When they are based on Article 88(1) EC, those guidelines constitute one element of the regular and periodic co-operation under which the Commission, in conjunction with the Member States, must keep under constant review existing systems of aid

---

[98] [1980] E.C.R. 2671, 2701
[99] *ibid.*, at 2691.
[1] [1980] Comp.Rep. point 213.

and propose to them any appropriate measures required by the progressive development or by the functioning of the common market. In so far as these proposals for appropriate measures are accepted by a Member State, they are binding on that Member State."[2]

A similar statement is to be found in the procedural Regulation governing State aid.[3]

The categories of aid that the Commission may determine to be compatible with the common market in accordance with Article 87(3) are as follows.

"(a) aid to promote the economic development of areas where the standard of living is abnormally low or where there is serious under-employment"

The economic problem of the region in question must be more **27–018** serious to fall for consideration under this exception than to attract the general exception relating to sectoral and regional aids in paragraph (c) (see below). The use of the words "abnormally" and "serious" restricts the scope for invoking paragraph (a) by requiring assessment of socio-economic problems to be made in a Community, not a national, context.[4] Using the Commission's Guidelines,[5] the conditions are fulfilled if the region has a per capita gross domestic product of less than 75 per cent of the Community average. Exemption is normally only granted for multisectoral aid under this heading, not aid to a single undertaking. The Court has made it clear that the assessment to be made under paragraph (a) is not confined to whether the measures will contribute effectively to the economic development of the regions concerned, but must also evaluate the impact of the aid on trade between Member States, and in particular to assess the sectorial repercussions they may have at Community level.[6]

"(b) aid to promote the execution of an important project of common European interest or to remedy a serious disturbance in the economy of a Member State"

The exception applies to two completely different types of aid. **27–019**
Originally seen as covering infrastructure or technological

---

[2] Case C–242/00 *Germany v Commission* [2002] E.C.R. I–5603.
[3] Reg.659/1999, n.8 above, Art.19.
[4] Case 248/84 *Germany v Commission* [1987] E.C.R. 4013, para.19; [1989] 1 C.M.L.R. 591.
[5] *Guidelines on National Regional Aid* [1998] O.J. C74/9, amended by [2000] O.J. C258. New Guidelines operate for 2007–2013: [2006] O.J. C54/8; the 75 per cent GDP figure is retained.
[6] Case C–114/00 *Spain v Commission* [2002] E.C.R. I–7657, para.81.

advancement,[7] it is now clear that there will be no common European interest in a scheme "unless it forms part of a transnational European programme supported jointly by a number of governments of the Member States, or arises from concerted action by a number of Member States to combat a common threat such as environmental pollution".[8] The Court has indicated that research and development projects do not *per se* qualify.[9]

As for the second category under Article 87(3)(b), serious disturbances, the Commission used it as a safety valve in the economic troubles besetting Member States which followed the energy crisis of 1974.[10] Disturbances must relate to the whole of a national economy, not just one region or sector.[11] In the latter case the appropriate tool is Article 87(3)(c).

"(c) aid to facilitate the development of certain economic activities or of certain economic areas, where such aid does not adversely affect trading conditions to an extent contrary to the common interest"

27–020   This is the most important of the exceptions to the general principle in Article 87(1). It enables the Commission to authorise aids to particular industrial sectors, aids which promote certain "horizontal" policies, and aids to particular regions of a Member State. Sectors to attract attention have been those in difficulties (such as textiles, shipbuilding, motor vehicles, coal and steel), those for which the Community has established policies (agriculture, fisheries and transport) and sectors which merit particular promotion (such as energy). "Horizontal" policies address common themes and problems which may arise in any industry. The areas for which frameworks and guidelines have been developed include the following: small and medium-sized enterprises (SMEs)[12] ; research and development (R&D)[13]; environmental protection[14]; employment[15]; training[16] and rescue and restructuring.[17] Aid schemes which might otherwise be deemed incompatible with the common market may be justified against these horizontal considerations.

---

[7] e.g. a common standard for the development of high-definition colour television: see [1989] Comp.Rep. point 151.

[8] Joined Cases 62/87 and 72/87 *Executif Regional Wallon and Glaverbel v Commission* [1988] E.C.R. 1573; [1989] 2 C.M.L.R. 771.

[9] *ibid.*

[10] See [1975] Comp.Rep. point 133.

[11] Case C–301/96 *Germany v Commission* [2003] E.C.R. I–9919 where the German Government merely referred to a serious disturbance in the economy of Saxony and made no allegation about serious disturbances for the German economy.

[12] See Reg.70/2001, [2001] O.J. L10/33 and Reg.364/2004 [2004] O.J. L63/22.

[13] See [1996] O.J. C45/5, amended by [1998] O.J. C48. This framework expired on December 31, 2005 but is being applied by the Commission until a new one is agreed during 2006.

[14] See [2001] O.J. C37; these Guidelines expire at the end of 2007.

[15] See Reg.2204/2002, [2002] O.J. L337.

[16] See Reg.68/2001, [2001] O.J. L10/20, amended by Reg.363/2004 [2004] O.J. L63/20.

[17] See [2004] O.J. C244.

The legal limits of the Commission's discretion under paragraph (c) are defined by the notion of facilitating the development of the activities or areas concerned and by the proviso that aid must not have an adverse effect on trading conditions "to an extent contrary to the common interest". A crucial distinction between Article 87(3)(a) and (c) when applied to regional aid is that the latter allows for aid to develop areas which are disadvantaged in relation to the national, as distinct from Community, average.[18]

"Development" presupposes some improvement in economic performance or prospects. Thus aids of a purely conservatory nature, designed to prevent undertakings in a given industry or area from going out of business, thereby creating unemployment, do not fall within the exception.[19] Recipients of aid must be at least potentially competitive. It seems to follow that financial assistance to an undertaking should normally be temporary and given on a declining scale (also referred to as "degressive" or "one time, last time" aid). The purpose of the aid must be the development of the sector or region in question and not of particular undertakings within it. In the *Belgian Textile Aid* case the Advocate General was of the opinion that the Commission ought not to have authorised grants to certain weak undertakings, given the relative strength of the market sector as a whole.[20]

The proviso about common interest in paragraph (c) imposes a **27–021** limit, albeit a flexible one, on the extent to which the disruption of the market mechanism may be tolerated for the sake of the socio-economic benefit sectoral or regional aids may bring. Its operation can be illustrated by Case 47/69 *France v Commission*.[21] The aid in question took the form of contributions towards research and the restructuring of French textile undertakings, and seemed prima facie to be exactly the type of sectoral aid to which paragraph (c) was intended to apply. However, the Commission objected to the fact that the aid was financed out of a parafiscal charge imposed both on textile products manufactured in France and on imports. The European Court agreed with the Commission that the method of financing an aid system was one of the factors to be taken into account in assessing its compatibility with the common market. It was capable of adding to the disturbance of trading conditions, thus rendering the system as a whole contrary to the common interest. That was the case here, because of the protective effect of applying the charge to imports. The amount of aid available increased automatically in proportion to any increase in revenue, so that the

---

[18] Case 248/84 *Commission v Germany* [1987] E.C.R. 4013; [1989] 1 C.M.L.R. 591.
[19] See the remarks of Advocate General Slynn in Case 84/82 *Germany v Commission (Belgian Textile Aid)* [1984] E.C.R. 1451; [1985] 1 C.M.L.R. 153.
[20] *ibid.* at 1504.
[21] [1970] E.C.R. 487.

more undertakings from other Member States succeeded in making sales in France, the more they would have to contribute for the benefit of their French competitors, who might not have made similar efforts.

In that case, the Court seems to have assessed the extent to which trading conditions were liable to be adversely affected independently of the benefits expected to flow from the aid. Its approach was that, however worthwhile the objective being pursued, disruption of the market beyond a certain point must be judged contrary to the common interest. In applying the proviso, account must be taken of any factors that may moderate the anti-competitive impact of an aid. In its *Intermills* judgment the Court said that "the settlement of an undertaking's existing debts in order to ensure its survival does not necessarily affect trading conditions to an extent contrary to the common interest, as provided in [Article 87(3)], where such an operation is, for example, accompanied by a restructuring plan".[22] Failure to show that the possibly mitigating effects of restructuring had been adequately considered was one of the reasons for the annulment of the decisions of the Commission in the *Intermills* and *Leeuwarder*[23] cases.

"(d) aid to promote culture and heritage conservation where such aid does not affect trading conditions and competition in the Community to an extent that is contrary to the common interest"

27–022   This exception was inserted into the EC Treaty by the Treaty on European Union with effect from November 1, 1993, although aids to support culture had previously been capable of consideration under paragraph (c).[24] It has been used by the Commission on a number of occasions, especially in relation to films and books. However, its decisions approving aid to support the export of books in the French language to non-French-speaking countries were overturned by the Court of First Instance for errors in market assessment.[25] The proviso attached to paragraph (d) is the same as for paragraph (c), with the express addition of competition as a consideration pertinent to the common interest, presumably to take account of the particular impact that aids in the fields of broadcasting, media and other conduits of cultural expression might have. Where, for example, broadcasting undertakings are given support in return for carrying out specific public service obligations, other considerations may also apply (in particular Article 86(2), dealt with in Chapter 26, above).

---

[22] Case 323/82 *Intermills v Commission* [1984] E.C.R. 3809, 3832.
[23] Joined Cases 296 and 318/82, n.52, above
[24] e.g. Dec.89/441, [1989] O.J. L208/3 in relation to Greek aid to the film industry for the production of Greek films.
[25] Case T–49/93 *SIDE v Commission* [1995] E.C.R. II–2501; Case T–155/98 *SIDE v Commission* [2002] E.C.R. II–1179.

Authorisation of aid by the Council

The Council's powers to authorise State aids are limited, being **27–023**
confined to Article 87(3)(e) and Article 88(2) third sub-paragraph.
The former represents the last in the list of express discretionary
exceptions, namely: "(e) such other categories of aid as may be
specified by decision of the Council acting by a qualified majority on
a proposal from the Commission". A series of directives on aids to
shipbuilding in the Member States was adopted under this provision,
although shipbuilding is now regulated by a "standard" framework.[26]

Authorisation by the Council under Article 88(2) third sub-
paragraph is expressly reserved for exceptional circumstances, and
has been described as one of the safety valves of the Treaty.[27] The
third and fourth sub-paragraphs provide:

> "On application by a Member State, the Council may, acting
> unanimously, decide that aid which that State is granting or
> intends to grant shall be considered to be compatible with the
> common market, in derogation from the provisions of Article
> 87 or from the regulations provided for in Article 89, if such a
> decision is justified by exceptional circumstances. If, as regards
> the aid in question, the Commission has already initiated the
> procedure provided for in the first sub-paragraph of this
> paragraph, the fact that the State concerned has made its
> application to the Council shall have the effect of suspending
> that procedure until the Council has made its attitude known.
>
> If, however, the Council has not made its attitude known
> within three months of the said application being made, the
> Commission shall give its decision on the case".

The case law interpreting this provision is limited, but most examples are to be found in the agricultural sector.[28] The Court has made
it clear that where a decision finding an aid incompatible with the
common market has been adopted by the Commission, the Council
cannot paralyse the effectiveness of that decision by itself declaring
the aid compatible with the common market on the basis of the third
subparagraph of Article 88(2) EC.[29] The Court added, in the same
case:

> "the Council cannot, on the basis of that provision, validly
> declare compatible with the common market an aid which
> allocates to the beneficiaries of an unlawful aid, which a

---

[26] See Framework on Shipbuilding [2003] O.J. C317, replacing Council Reg.1540/98.
[27] Advocate General Cosmas in Case C–122/94 *Commission v Council* [1996] E.C.R. 881, at
para.62.
[28] For figures on the increasing use of the provision, see the Opinion, *ibid.*
[29] Case C–110/02 *Commission v Council* [2004] E.C.R. I–6333.

Commission decision has previously declared incompatible with the common market, an amount designed to compensate for the repayments which they are required to make pursuant to that decision."[30]

By their very nature, "exceptional circumstances" are hardly susceptible to definition. Advocate General Cosmas has suggested[31] that the idea means "something extraordinary and unforeseen, or at least something not permanent or continuous and of course something other than normal". In other words, taking a regime subject to common organisation as an example, the Council's intervention must be needed for the adoption of measures to deal with a short-term dysfunction that might more particularly affect one Member State against others. The Court of Justice will not interfere with the Council's finding of exceptional circumstances unless there has been a manifest error of assessment. Thus, in a case arising from the common organisation in wine,[32] the Court accepted the Council's view that the aids in question were necessary to avoid the risk in Italy of serious economic and social repercussions, in particular for small producers and co-operative wine cellars, and, in France, the risk of engendering a critical situation.

Article 87 and services of general economic interest (SGEIs)

27–024   Special mention should be made of the treatment in EC law of financial support granted by States to SGEIs. It will be recalled[33] that such undertakings are expressly mentioned in Article 86(2) EC. In particular, that provision relaxes the full rigour of the competition rules where their application would constitute an obstacle to fulfilment of the tasks assigned. From 2000, the Court was confronted by the question of whether financial support to the providers of public services to offset the charges or losses incurred in meeting their obligations constituted aid. Two particular conceptual issues fell to be determined: firstly, whether such support was aid (hence notifiable under Article 87 and requiring justification) or compensation (taking it outside Article 87 altogether); secondly, what role, if any, was left to Article 86(2) in relation to such cases.

Aid or compensation

27–025   The problem posed by the SGEI cases was not entirely novel. The notion of an aid as a "gratuitous advantage"[34] had previously posed

---

[30] *ibid.*, para.47.
[31] Case C–122/94 *Commission v Council*, n.27, above.
[32] *ibid.*
[33] Ch.26, above.
[34] See Case 78/76 *Firma Steinike und Weinlig v Germany*, n.11, above.

the question of what would happen where that advantage was effectively wiped out by the cost of meeting the criteria of eligibility.[35] However, the issue starkly resurfaced in *Ferring*,[36] a case concerning a special French sales tax applicable to pharmaceutical laboratories selling directly to pharmacies. Prima facie, this looked like a selective advantage insofar as it did not attach to wholesale distributors and thus was arguably a tax exemption in favour of the latter. However, the wholesale distributors had particular obligations imposed on them: in particular, they had to hold a permanent range of products to meet demands over a specific geographical area and to deliver requested supplies within a very short time over all that area. The Court's judgment entertained the possibility that the sales tax imposed on the pharmaceutical distributors might be compensation for the services provided by the wholesalers if there was the necessary equivalence between the exemption and the additional costs of meeting the public service elements.

The *Ferring* judgment immediately received robust attention from Advocates General. In particular, Advocate General Léger in *Altmark Trans*[37] argued that the compensation approach undermined Article 86(2) by conflating the questions of aid and justification at the Article 87(1) stage of analysis and disturbing the Commission's surveillance role. In his view, Article 86(2) was the "central Treaty provision for reconciling Community objectives".[38] A rather less strident approach was adopted by Advocate General Jacobs in *GEMO*,[39] arguing that some cases might be assessed under the aid rules and others could be properly treated as compensation, according to how clearly the entrusted obligation had been identified and linked to the State support. Advocate General Stix-Hackl[40] described *Ferring* as a departure both from the Court's previous case law and the Commission's practice.

Notwithstanding these criticisms, the Court affirmed its position in *Altmark* but took the opportunity to clarify the conditions necessary for compensation to escape classification as State aid:

"First, the recipient undertaking must actually have public service obligations to discharge, and the obligations must be clearly defined . . .

Second, the parameters on the basis of which the compensation is calculated must be established in advance in an objective and transparent manner, to avoid it conferring an economic

---

[35] see J. Winter, "Re(de)fining the Notion of State Aid in Art.87(1) of the EC Treaty" (2004) 41 C.M.L.Rev. 475.
[36] Case C-53/00 *Ferring v ACOSS* [2001] E.C.R. I-9067.
[37] Case C-280/00, n.23, above.
[38] *ibid.*, Opinion, para.80.
[39] Case C-126/01 *GEMO* [2003] E.C.R. I-13769.
[40] Case C-34/01 *Enirisorse v Amministrazione delle Finanze* [2003] E.C.R. I-3609.

advantage which may favour the recipient undertaking over
competing undertakings . . .

Third, the compensation cannot exceed what is necessary to
cover all or part of the costs incurred in the discharge of public
service obligations, taking into account the relevant receipts
and a reasonable profit for discharging those obligations.
Compliance with such a condition is essential to ensure that the
recipient undertaking is not given any advantage which distorts
or threatens to distort competition by strengthening that undertaking's competitive position.

Fourth, where the undertaking which is to discharge public
service obligations, in a specific case, is not chosen pursuant to
a public procurement procedure which would allow for the
selection of the tenderer capable of providing those services at
the least cost to the community, the level of compensation
needed must be determined on the basis of an analysis of the
costs which a typical undertaking, well run and adequately
provided with means of transport so as to be able to meet the
necessary public service requirements, would have incurred in
discharging those obligations, taking into account the relevant
receipts and a reasonable profit for discharging the
obligations."[41]

These are cumulative critera, so that failure to comply with any one
of them will render the financial contribution an aid for the purposes
of Article 87(1).

These conditions owe much to the tenor, if not the actual detail,
of the comments made by Advocate General Jacobs. They provide a
checklist for scrutiny that goes some way towards allaying fears that
the Court might be prepared to jettison the entire supervisory
regime of EC law in relation to SGEIs. Post-*Altmark*, the Court of
First Instance has annulled Commission decisions for failing to apply
the criteria adequately.[42] As will be discussed further below, national
courts are empowered to determine whether a measure or package
of measures amounts to aid and so will therefore need to apply the
Altmark tests. An interesting scenario arose in relation to Italian
laws which reserved various tax assistance activities (e.g. advice and
filing of returns) exclusively to CAF. One of the questions referred
to the European Court[43] was whether remuneration paid to CAF

[41] *Altmark*, n.23, above, paras.89–93.
[42] e.g. In Case T–157/01, *Danske Busvognmænd v Commission* [2004] E.C.R. II–917; Case
T–274/01 *Valmont Nederland BV v Commission* [2004] E.C.R.; also Case T–93/02,
Confédération nationale du Crédit Mutuel, n.86, above (although not exclusively decided
upon compensation aspects).
[43] Case C–451/03 *Servizi Ausiliari Dottori Commercialist v Calafiori*, forthcoming, Judgment
March 30, 2006. The case provides interesting issues on the co-existence and interrelationship of the aid and free movement rules since the establishment and services rules were
also invoked.

from State funds amounted to aid. The Court observed that the function of CAF could "conceivably" be a public service and that the €14 paid for each declaration might be objectively and transparently set in advance. However, it referred the third and fourth *Altmark* conditions back to the national court for appraisal in the particular context of the case.

It is the fourth condition that is perhaps the most far-reaching, since it digs further into the procedural context in which "compensation" payments are made by a State. A certain degree of coercion is thus applied: either comply with the steps of *Altmark* or take the risk of having to justify an aid in a different forum.[44]

Article 86(2)after Altmark

The Court was conspicuously silent in *Altmark* as to where its 27–026 pronouncements left Article 86(2). At first glance, since the tests were set up in relation to demarcating aid from compensation for the purposes of Article 87(1), a measure in relation to an entrusted undertaking that does not satisfy the criteria for compensation can still seek to take the benefit of Article 86(2). However, in *Heiser*,[45] the Court noted that:

> "the derogation provided for by [Article 86(2)] of the Treaty does not prevent a measure from being classified as State aid ... Nor could it, once such a classification has been made, allow the Member State concerned not to notify the measure pursuant to [Article 88(3)] of the Treaty."[46]

Moreover, it might be wondered how far the practicalities of a failure to meet the *Altmark* conditions would allow Article 86(2) to be applied in an undertaking's favour. To clarify this, the Commission has adopted detailed measures, discussed below.

Legislation post-Altmark in relation to SGEIs

The real impact of *Altmark* was to trigger a legislative response 27–027 from the Commission which sought to provide affirmation of the protection for compensation to providers of SGEIs. In 2005 it adopted a package of measures, consisting of an amendment to the Transparency Directive, a Decision on the conditions of compensation and a Framework for the measurement of compatibility with the

---

[44] See M. Ross, "The Europeanization of Public Services Supervision: Harnessing Competition and Citizenship?" (2004) 23 Y.E.L. 303.

[45] Case C–172/03, n.17, above.

[46] *ibid.*, para.51, citing Joined Cases C–261/01 and C–262/01 *Van Calster* [2003] E.C.R. I–12249.

aid rules for measures which go further than compensation. The Decision[47] specifies the conditions for qualification as compensation and applies to amounts of less than €30 million per year provided its beneficiaries have an annual turnover of less than €100 million. Compensation provided to hospital and social housing for SGEIs is covered irrespective of amounts. Where the Decision applies, there is no need to notify the compensation since it does not constitute aid within the meaning of the Treaty.

The Commission's Framework,[48] on the other hand, governs public service compensation that does not take the benefit of Decision 2005/842 and which must therefore be notified as aid. The point of the Framework, without prejudice to Articles 81 and 82 EC and the public procurement rules, is to spell out the conditions under which such aid may be justified under Article 86(2). In particular, it requires the entrusting of SGEI responsibilities to specify the following: the precise nature and the duration of the public service obligations; the undertakings and territory concerned; the nature of any exclusive or special rights assigned to the undertaking; the parameters for calculating, controlling and reviewing the compensation; and the arrangements for avoiding and repaying any over-compensation.[49] Taking the fourth condition of the *Altmark* judgment as its departure point, the Framework fleshes out the notions of costs, compensation and reasonable profit. The Framework is to apply for six years.

Enforcement of the State aid rules: the legislative machinery

27–028   We have seen that State aid meeting the criteria in Article 87(1) is not automatically to be regarded as incompatible with the common market, since it may fall within one of the excepted categories in paragraphs (2) and (3) of the Article, or be exempted using the special powers of the Council. Moreover, the application, in particular, of Article 87(3) entails a complex appreciation of economic and social factors in the light of the overall Community interest. The approach adopted by the Treaty is to make the Community institutions responsible in the first instance for giving concrete effect to the principles of Article 87, and machinery for this purpose has been provided in Articles 88 and 89.

The corollary of the provision of special machinery at Community level is that national courts may not rule on the compatibility of an

---

[47] Dec.2005/842 [2005] O.J. L312/67 *On the Application of Art.86(2) to State Aid in the Form of Public Service Compensation Granted to Certain Undertakings Entrusted with the Operation of Services of General Economic Interest.* This was adopted on the basis of Art.86(3); see Ch.26, above.

[48] *Community Framework for State Aid in the Form of Public Service Compensation* [2005] O.J. C297/4.

[49] *ibid.*, para.12.

aid with the common market.[50] In this sense, Article 87 is not directly effective. However, it does not follow that national courts may not sometimes have to interpret Article 87, for example to decide whether a measure introduced by a Member State without obtaining clearance under Article 88(3) constitutes "aid". Such scrutiny forms part of the general obligation upon national courts to provide effective protection of individuals' rights conferred by these procedural requirements.[51] National courts are also empowered to determine whether an aid falls within the scope of a relevant block exemption.

Procedural legislation in the State aids field akin to that prevalent in general competition law matters took years to materialise. However, in 1999 the Council finally used its powers under Article 89 to adopt Regulation 659/1999, which came into force on April 16, 1999.[52] This ("Procedural") Regulation was aimed at codifying case law practices and making the procedural rules more transparent and accessible. A further Council ("Implementing") Regulation[53] was adopted in 2004 as part of the general modernisation package for EC competition law and deals with matters such as the forms for notification, the determination of time-limits and the calculation of interest rates when pursuing recovery of aid.

The 1999 Regulation distinguishes four different situations for procedural purposes: notified aid, unlawful aid, misuse of aid and existing aid schemes, each governed by a different chapter. These are discussed further below.

Notified aid

Article 88(3) of the Treaty provides: **27–029**

> "The Commission shall be informed, in sufficient time to enable it to submit its comments, of any plans to grant or alter aid. If it considers that any such plan is not compatible with the common market having regard to Article 87, it shall without delay initiate the procedure provided for in paragraph 2. The Member State concerned shall not put its proposed measures into effect until this procedure has resulted in a final decision".

The paragraph establishes a system of prior control which is designed to prevent any aid incompatible with the common market from being introduced. Member States are required to notify the

---

[50] Case 78/76 *Firma Steinike und Weinlig v Germany*, n.11, above.
[51] Case C–39/94 *SFEI v La Poste*, n.2, above.
[52] [1999] O.J. L83/1. See Sinnaeve and Slot, "The new regulation on State aid procedures" (1999) 36 C.M.L.Rev 1153.
[53] Reg.794/2004, n.14, above.

Commission of plans to grant or alter aid sufficiently in advance of the date set for their implementation to enable it to examine the plans and form a view as to whether the procedure under Article 88(2) should be initiated against them. According to Article 2 of Regulation 659, the notification requirement relates to "any plans to grant new aid", aid being defined in Article 1 as any measure fulfilling all the criteria laid down in Article 87(1) of the Treaty. This means that notification is not required for all measures which might constitute aid, but only for those which embrace each of the elements of Article 87(1). There is thus the capacity for "existential" uncertainty[54] because of the potential gap between a Member State's view as to whether a measure, for example, affects inter-state trade or represents a sufficiently significant distortion of competition, compared to the Commission's *ex post facto* assessment of the situation. Aid falling within group exemptions need not be notified, nor in principle is notification required for individual applications of an approved aid scheme.[55] However, the principle of effectiveness requires that a Member State is required not only to notify the planned aid in the narrow sense but also the method of financing the aid inasmuch as that method is an integral part of the planned measure.[56]

The last sentence of Article 88(3) imposes a "standstill" obligation upon the Member State proposing to introduce an aid.[57] This applies during the period of preliminary review by the Commission and, if the procedure under Article 88(2) is initiated, continues until a final decision is reached. *A fortiori*, a Member State is prohibited from putting an aid into effect without notifying it at all. The Court has explained this preliminary stage as follows:

> "The preliminary stage provided for in [Article 88(3)] of the Treaty is intended merely to allow the Commission a sufficient period of time for reflection and investigation so that it can form a *prima facie* opinion on the draft aid plans notified to it, thus enabling it either to conclude, without the need for detailed examination, that the aid is compatible with the common market or, by contrast, to make a finding that the content of those plans raises doubts as to that compatibility.
>
> In that respect, the Commission is required to examine all the facts and points of law brought to its notice by persons, undertakings and associations whose interests may be affected

---

[54] *ibid.*, p.1165.
[55] Under Reg.659, such an individual application constitutes "existing aid".
[56] Joined Cases C–261/01 and C–262/01 *Van Calster*, n.145, above. On the notion of "integral" see Case C–175/02 *Pape* [2005] E.C.R. I–127 and Case C–174/02 *Streekgewest Westelijk Noord-Brabant* [2005] E.C.R. I–85.
[57] Case 84/82 *Germany v Commission*, n.19, above. This is now also stated in Art.3 of Reg.659.

by the granting of the aid. It is therefore in the light of both the information notified by the State concerned and that provided by any complainants that the institution must make its assessment in the context of the preliminary examination provided for in [Article 88(3)] of the Treaty."[58]

Where aid is notified, Article 4 of Regulation 659 provides for three outcomes to be determined in the form of a decision by the Commission after conducting a preliminary examination. Firstly, it may record that the notified measure does not constitute aid at all. Secondly, it may decide not to raise objections, specifying which exception of the Treaty has been applied. It does not appear that the Commission could attach conditions to such a finding, as these would imply incompatibility with the common market requiring a formal investigation.[59] Thirdly, if doubts are raised as to the compatibility of the aid with the common market the Commission shall take a decision to initiate the formal investigation procedure of Article 88(2). One of these decisions must be taken within two months commencing the day following a complete notification.[60] Following the expiry of that period without a decision by the Commission the aid shall be deemed to have been authorised and the Member State may implement the measures after giving the Commission prior notice.[61]

Where an aid proposal is altered after having been notified to the **27–030** Commission, the latter must be informed of the amendment, although this may be done in the course of consultations arising from the original notification.[62] Failure to bring amendments to the attention of the Commission will cause the standstill under Article 88(3) to remain in force against a scheme which has otherwise been found compatible with the common market. However, the Court recognises that not every technical modification to an existing aid must be notified. Thus in the *Namur* case,[63] Belgian legislation endowed OND with particular advantages such as State guarantees and State bonds, to carry out its function of assisting exports through reduction of credit risks. OND's actual market conduct was restricted as a result of agreement between it and COBAC, a private creditinsurance undertaking, as to the type of risk each would undertake to cover. That agreement was then terminated by instructions given to OND by its supervising ministers, thereby for practical

---

[58] Case C–204/97 *Portugal v Commission* [2001] E.C.R. I–3175. See also Case C–400/99 *Italy v Commission* [2005] E.C.R. I–3657.
[59] *cf.* Reg.659, Art.7(3) and closure of the formal investigation procedure.
[60] Reg.659, Art.4(5). Case law had established a two month period as early as 1973 in Case 120/73 *Lorenz* [1973] E.C.R. 1471.
[61] Reg.659, Art.4(6).
[62] Joined Cases 91 and 127/83 *Heineken Brouwerijen* [1984] E.C.R. 2435; [1985] 1 C.M.L.R. 389.
[63] Case C–44/93 *Namur-Les Assurances du Crédit SA v Office National du Ducroire and Belgium* [1994] E.C.R. I–3829.

purposes enlarging OND's areas of activity although the legislation itself remained intact. The Commission unsuccessfully contended that this practical change constituted aid.

Detailed rules for the operation of the formal investigation procedure are set out in Article 6 of Regulation 659. A decision to open this procedure must summarise the relevant issues of fact and law, include a preliminary assessment of the Commission as to the aid character of the proposed measure and set out the doubts as to its compatibility with the common market. Member States and interested parties must be invited to submit comments within a prescribed period, normally not exceeding one month. Comments received are to be communicated to the Member State concerned, although a third party may request its identity to be withheld on grounds of potential damage.

Closure of the formal investigation procedure must follow the paths indicated by Article 7 of Regulation 659. Thus, as with the ending of the preliminary stage, the Commission may decide that no aid is involved. However, unlike the position under Article 4, closure of the formal investigation in this way may follow modification of the measure by the Member State concerned. This provision emphasises that negotiations between State and Commission should be confined to the formal, and not the preliminary, stage of investigation.[64] A second possibility is a positive decision confirming the aid and specifying which Treaty exception is being relied upon. The Commission has the power[65] to attach conditions to a positive decision. Finally, the Commission may adopt a negative decision ruling that the notified aid is not compatible with the common market.

Decisions taken under Article 7 are, as far as possible, to be taken by the Commission within a period of 18 months from the opening of the formal investigation procedure.[66] After the expiry of this period, the Member State may request the Commission to take a decision within two months. The overall length of the investigation period has been criticised,[67] not least because the necessity might be questioned of any aid project which takes almost two years to be approved.[68] However, it may be noted that compatibility is the commonest outcome of State aid cases. In 2005, for example, the Commission took 646 final decisions. Of these, 89 per cent did not even need a formal investigation to allow the Member States to

---

[64] Confirming Case 84/82 *Germany v Commission*, n.19, above.

[65] Art.7(4) of the Regulation.

[66] *ibid.*, Art.7(6). According to the CFI, a period of 22 months cannot be considered unreasonable merely because it exceeds 18 months, which is an objective to be observed and not a mandatory time-limit: Case T–190/00 *Regione Siciliana v Commission* [2003] E.C.R. II–5015, para.139.

[67] See Sinnaeve and Slot, *op. cit*, n.52, above.

[68] At least two months for the preliminary stage, 18 months under Art.7(6) and the additional two months afterwards.

proceed with awarding aid. A further 8 per cent of the total represented decisions that were either positive, conditional or "no-aid" decisions. Only 3 per cent of all decisions in 2005 were findings of incompatibility.[69]

Unlawful aid

According to Article 1(f) of Regulation 659, unlawful aid is new **27–031** aid put into effect in contravention of Article 88(3) of the Treaty. Thus it covers not only aid which has not been notified at all, but also aid which is notified but implemented prior to authorisation and aid implemented in breach of the terms of authorisation. Where the Commission has in its possession information from whatever source regarding alleged unlawful aid it shall examine that information without delay.[70] Although the time-limits for the preliminary assessment of a properly notified aid do not apply, the Commission must still act within a reasonable time.[71]

Regulation 659 authorises three types of injunction for the Commission to use in the context of possible unlawful aid. Firstly,[72] it can issue an injunction requiring a Member State to submit information, failure to comply giving the Commission the right to take a decision on the basis of the information it already has. Secondly,[73] the Commission may, after giving the Member State concerned the opportunity to submit its comments, adopt a decision requiring the Member State to suspend any unlawful aid until the Commission has taken a decision on the compatibility of the aid with the common market. Thirdly,[74] the Commission has the power to issue a decision requiring the Member State provisionally to recover any unlawful aid until the Commission has taken a decision on the compatibility of the aid. Such an injunction can only be used, however, where according to established practice there are no doubts as to the aid character of the measure, there is an urgency to act and there is a serious risk of substantial and irreparable damage to a competitor. Non-compliance with either a suspensory or pro-visional recovery injunction will entitle the Commission to refer the matter to the European Court direct and apply for a declaration that the failure constitutes an infringement of the Treaty.

Where the Commission adopts a negative decision in cases of unlawful aid, it is obliged to issue a recovery decision requiring the Member State concerned to take all necessary measures to recover

---

[69] All figures taken from State Aid Scoreboard, Spring 2006 Update, n.21, above.
[70] Art.10(1) of Reg.659.
[71] Case T–95/96 *Gestevisión Telecinco v Commission* [1998] E.C.R. II–3407; [1998] 3 C.M.L.R. 1112.
[72] Art.10(3) of Reg.659.
[73] Art.11(1).
[74] Art.11(2).

the aid from the beneficiary.[75] Whilst the power of the Commission to order recovery is well-established in earlier case law,[76] the obligation to do so is a new feature established in Regulation 659. Article 14(2) provides that recovery shall not be required if this would be contrary to a general principle of Community law. However, this restriction is likely to apply only in exceptional situations. It is clear from the Court's previous case law that beneficiaries will not normally be able to invoke the protection of legitimate expectations as a reason for resisting recovery. The reason for this is that a diligent business person should normally be able to determine whether the procedural requirements of Article 88 of the Treaty have been observed.[77] Unjustified delays by the Commission in reaching decisions might give rise to legitimate expectations that the aid was not objectionable,[78] although the timetables introduced by the Regulation will usually pre-empt recourse to this route.

27–032   Any use by the Commission of its powers to order recovery is subject to a limitation period of ten years.[79] This runs from the day on which the unlawful aid is awarded to the beneficiary either as individual aid or as aid under an aid scheme. Any interruption, such as the result of the Commission making a request for information, starts the time period running afresh. There is no obligation to notify the beneficiary of such an interruption.[80] In any event the distortive effects of an aid which has operated undetected and without complaint for ten years must be open to doubt.

Once the Commission has made an order against a Member State seeking recovery, it is for the State to execute it using national laws and procedures. By Article 14(3) of Regulation 659 "recovery shall be effected without delay and in accordance with the procedures under the national law of the Member State concerned, provided that they allow the immediate and effective execution of the Commission's decision". This provision, described as a "real innovation",[81] allows the Commission to act against delaying procedures in Member States so that measures by national judges merely ordering suspensive effects of an aid could be seen as contrary to Regulation 659.

Prior to enactment of the Regulation, the Court had taken a strict view as to the nature of the obligation to repay in a line of cases

---

[75] Art.14(1).
[76] Case 70/72 *Commission v Germany* [1973] E.C.R. 813; [1973] C.M.L.R. 741.
[77] Case 301/87 *France v Commission (Boussac)* [1990] E.C.R. I–307, para.14; see also Case T–109/01 *Fleuren Compost* [2004] E.C.R. II–127, paras.135–137.
[78] Case 223/85 *Rijn-Schelde-Verolme (RSV) Maschinefabrieken en Scheepswerven NV v Commission* [1987] E.C.R. 4617; [1989] 2 C.M.L.R. 259, where the Commission delayed proceedings by 26 months.
[79] Art.15(1) of Reg.659. This rule was inserted into the Regulation by the Council and did not form part of the Commission's original proposal.
[80] Case C–276/03P *Scott v Commission* [2005] E.C.R. I–8437.
[81] Sinnaeve and Slot, *op. cit*, n.52, above

following *Commission v Belgium*[82] where it emphasised the need to consider whether it was *impossible* for the Member State to comply with the Commission's decision. The mere fact that beneficiaries of the aid might suffer financial hardship from its revocation is not sufficient to thwart recovery.[83] Nor is conflict with national rules of company law in cases where undoing aid in the form of equity participation may run counter to standard principles about priorities between creditors and shareholders.[84] Apart from satisfying orthodox doctrines concerning the supremacy of Community law and the need to achieve effectiveness of enforcement, this position also makes clear that repayment is not a matter of countering improper benefits but is an absolute consequence of infringement of the obligations under the aids supervisory regime. Thus in *Re Tubemeuse*,[85] the beneficiary was in liquidation, so that it was no longer able to take advantage of the unlawfully paid aid. Any repayment would in effect come from the company's other creditors, who would be disadvantaged *pro tanto* by the State's claim. The Court, citing previous authority,[86] ruled that:

> "recovery of unlawful aid is the logical consequence of finding that it is unlawful. Consequently, the recovery of State aid unlawfully granted for the purpose of re-establishing the pre-viously existing situation cannot in principle be regarded as disproportionate to the objectives of the Treaty in regard to State aids".

One situation where it would seem impossible to recover aid is illustrated by the *Boussac* case.[87] The aid had consisted of capital injections, loans and reductions in employers' social security contri-butions. However, the Commission ruled out of account the sums paid out by Boussac to meet the cost of transferring certain production sites and employees to independent companies which had subsequently ceased production. These amounts were treated as lost and impossible to recover. The Court accepted this view and, moreover, cited the pursuit by the Commission of only partial repayment as an answer to the French Government's claim that the recovery of aid was disproportionate to the effect on competition. It is submitted that the statement of principle made in *Re Tubemeuse*, above, is better preserved if the *Boussac* observation is seen as a statement that the test of impossibility was satisfied, rather than one applying proportionality criteria. Impossibility is not for the State

---

[82] Case 52/84 *Commission v Belgium* [1986] E.C.R. 89; [1987] 1 C.M.L.R. 710.
[83] Case 63/87 *Commission v Greece* [1988] E.C.R. 2875; [1989] 3 C.M.L.R. 677.
[84] See Case C–142/87 *Re Tubemeuse: Belgium v Commission*, n.24, above.
[85] *ibid.*
[86] Case 310/85 *Deufil v Commission* [1987] E.C.R. 901; [1988] 1 C.M.L.R. 553.
[87] n.77, above.

merely to assert; it must be demonstrated after an active search for a solution in the context of a dialogue between the Commission and the State concerned.[88]

It is not enough where the Government in question merely informs the Commission of the legal, political or practical difficulties involved in recovery and without proposing to the Commission any alternative arrangements.[89]

Misuse of aid

27–033   The notion of misuse appears in the Treaty itself in Article 88(2):

"If, after giving notice to the parties concerned to submit their comments, the Commission finds that aid granted by a State or through State resources is not compatible with the common market having regard to Article 87, *or that such aid is being misused*, it shall decide that the State concerned shall abolish or alter such aid within a period of time to be determined by the Commission". (emphasis added).

Misuse is further defined in Article 1(g) of Reg.659 as aid used by the beneficiary in contravention of a decision taken under the Regulation not to raise objections at the preliminary stage or a decision closing a formal investigation on the basis of either a positive or conditional approval. The key difference between misuse and unlawful aid is that in the former case it the beneficiary who has brought about the infringement whereas the Member State is responsible for unlawful aid. Procedurally, the reference in Article 88(2) means that misuse cannot be addressed without opening a formal investigation. Subject to this important limitation, Regulation 659 adopts the same principles *mutatis mutandis* for enforcement against misuse as for unlawful aid. The only exception is that a provisional recovery injunction under Article 11(2) is not available to the Commission.

Existing aids

27–034   Article 88(1) of the Treaty provides:

---

[88] Case C–349/93 *Commission v Italy* [1995] E.C.R. I–343. See also Case C–6/97 *Commission v Italy* [1999] E.C.R. I–2981 where the fact that Italy had taken no steps to recover the tax credit in question meant that implementation of the recovery decision could not be shown to be impossible.

[89] Case C–415/03 *Commission v Greece* [2005] E.C.R. I–3875. Unsurprisingly, the Court did not view the transfer of assets of the beneficiary (Olympic Airways) to a new company (Olympic Airlines) to make recovery from the former impossible as acceptable!

"The Commission shall, in co-operation with Member States, keep under constant review all systems of aid existing in those States. It shall propose to the latter any appropriate measures required by the progressive development or by the functioning of the common market".

The notion of existing aid comprises the following categories: (i) all aid which existed prior to the entry into force of the Treaty in the respective Member States or before acceding to the Community or Union; (ii) aid schemes or individual aids authorised by the Commission or Council; (iii) aid authorised by default[90]; (iv) aid deemed to be existing by operation of the 10 year limitation period for recovery; (v) aid which is deemed to be an existing aid because it can be established that at the time when it was put into effect it did not constitute an aid, and subsequently became an aid due to the evolution of the common market and without having been altered by the Member State.[91]

It would clearly make no sense for the maintenance of the single market if aids were only subject to controls at the time of their proposal. Article 88(1) thus provides for ongoing supervision and review of existing measures. Under Article 17(1) of Regulation 659 the Commission shall obtain all necessary information for this purpose and, if it forms a preliminary view that existing aid is not, or is no longer, compatible with the common market, it shall inform the Member State of that view and give it one month to submit comments. If it remains of its adverse opinion, the Commission shall then address recommendations to the Member State.[92] Ultimately, if the Member State does not accept those recommendations, the Commission must initiate the formal investigation procedure. However, because of the existing status of the aid, it is not open to the Commission to use the enforcement mechanisms appropriate for unlawful aid. Instead, once a negative decision is finally adopted at the end of a formal investigation, the existing aid scheme is at that point rendered unlawful for the future if it remains in force.

Rights of interested parties

In the absence of secondary legislation in the early days of State 27–035 aid law, the rights of interested third parties developed in the case law as *ad hoc* responses to challenges to Commission decisions.

---

[90] e.g. using Art.4(6) of Reg.659 where the Commission fails to comply with the two-month time-limit to make a decision.

[91] Sinnaeve and Slot, *op. cit.*, above n.52, suggest that this might apply to an activity or product for which the State provides support and for which there is at the time no Community market or trade.

[92] Art.18 of Reg.659.

However, the advent of Regulation 659 codified much of those principles. The Court, sitting as the Grand Chamber, has recently summarised the development of its principles as follows:

"In the case of a Commission decision on State aid, it must be borne in mind that, in the context of the procedure for reviewing State aid provided for in Article 88 EC, the preliminary stage of the procedure for reviewing aid under Article 88(3) EC, which is intended merely to allow the Commission to form a prima facie opinion on the partial or complete conformity of the aid in question, must be distinguished from the examination under Article 88(2) EC. It is only in connection with the latter examination, which is designed to enable the Commission to be fully informed of all the facts of the case, that the EC Treaty imposes an obligation on the Commission to give the parties concerned notice to submit their comments.

Where, without initiating the formal review procedure under Article 88(2) EC, the Commission finds, on the basis of Article 88(3) EC, that aid is compatible with the common market, the persons intended to benefit from those procedural guarantees may secure compliance therewith only if they are able to challenge that decision before the Community judicature. For those reasons, the Court declares to be admissible an action for the annulment of such a decision brought by a person who is concerned within the meaning of Article 88(2) EC where he seeks, by instituting proceedings, to safeguard the procedural rights available to him under the latter provision.

The parties concerned, within the meaning of Article 88(2) EC, who are thus entitled under the fourth paragraph of Article 230 EC to institute proceedings for annulment are those persons, undertakings or associations whose interests might be affected by the grant of the aid, in particular competing undertakings and trade associations.

On the other hand, if the applicant calls in question the merits of the decision appraising the aid as such, the mere fact that it may be regarded as concerned within the meaning of Article 88(2) EC cannot suffice to render the action admissible. It must then demonstrate that it has a particular status within the meaning of the *Plaumann v Commission* case law. That applies in particular where the applicant's market position is substantially affected by the aid to which the decision at issue relates."[93]

---

[93] Case C–78/03P *Commission v Aktionsgemeinschaft Recht und Eigentum*.

Since, in the case in hand, the relevant party was not seeking to contest a failure to intiate an Article 88(2) procedure but was instead in reality seeking to have a contested decision annulled on substantive grounds, the Court went on to apply the "usual" *Plaumann* tests of locus standi.[94] The Court accordingly proceeded to set aside the Court of First Instance's judgment.[95] Even though members of the trade association concerned were economic operators who could be viewed as direct competitors of the beneficiaries of the aid, it did not follow that they were individually concerned for the purposes of *Plaumann* since all farmers in the European Union could be regarded as competitors of the beneficiaries of the land acquisition scheme.

This judgment followed an Opinion from Advocate General Jacobs, who had described the case law up until that point as "plainly unsatisfactory, being complex, apparently illogical, and inconsistent."[96] He had canvassed a return to the terms of Article 230(4) of the Treaty and the tests of direct and individual concern, irrespective of the grounds on which the action was brought, but without the strictness of *Plaumann*. The Court, instead, underscored the earlier case law[97] distinctions whilst maintaining the view that Article 88(2) decisions require applicants to demonstrate a particular status whereby their market positions are substantially affected.[98]

The role of national courts

Although national courts are unable to rule on the compatibility **27–036** of aid with the common market, their role in the supervisory regime is highly significant because of the responsibilities placed upon them in relation to safeguarding the rights of individuals against non-observance by Member States of the procedural rules. As the previous discussion in this Chapter has shown, the European Court's case law requires four cumulative conditions to be established before an aid is present for the purposes of Article 87(1). Thus, to secure the necessary protection for individuals against a Member State's failure to notify, national courts must be able to evaluate the application of each of those criteria.

That the standstill clause of Article 88(3) could create directly effective rights was established as early as 1973 in the *Lorenz* case.[99]

---

[94] Case 25/62 *Plaumann v Commission* [1963] E.C.R. 95; see Ch.13, above.
[95] Case T–114/00 *Aktionsgemeinschaft Recht und Eigentum v Commission* [2002] E.C.R. II–5121.
[96] Case C–78/03P, n.93 above, para.138.
[97] Case C–198/91 *Cook v Commission* [1993] E.C.R. I–2487; Case C–225/91 *Matra v Commission* [1993] E.C.R. I–3203; Case C–367/95P *Commission v Sytraval and Brink's Finance* [1998] E.C.R. I–1719.
[98] See Case 169/84 *Cofaz v Commission* [1986] E.C.R. 391.
[99] Case 120/73 *Lorenz* [1973] E.C.R. 1471.

This was elaborated upon by the Court in its so-called *French Salmon* ruling,[1] stressing the fundamental difference between the central executive role performed by the Commission and the task of national courts. Whilst the Commission was required to examine the compatibility of the planned aid with the common market, even in cases where the Member State infringed the prohibition of implementing aid measures, national courts merely safeguarded, pending a final decision by the Commission, the rights of individuals against any disregard by the State authorities of the prohibition contained in the last sentence of Article 88(3). A decision in that regard by a national court did not amount to an adjudication on the compatibility of the aid with the common market. Nevertheless, the national court had to ensure that individuals were in a position to enforce rights of action in respect of any disregard of Article 88(3), from which all the proper consequences would follow, in accordance with their national law, both regarding the validity of acts involving the implementation of aid measures and the recovery of financial support granted in breach of that provision or of any provisional measures.

It is clear that a finding by a national court that an aid has been granted in breach of Article 88(3) "must in principle lead to its repayment in accordance with the procedural rules of domestic law".[2] Nevertheless, as Advocate General Jacobs pointed out,[3] there might exceptionally be situations in which a repayment order might be inappropriate. These might arise where there was considerable delay in any simultaneous Commission investigation or where the aid character of the measures at stake was not self-evident. Even if the Commission subsequently declares the aid compatible with the common market, this does not regularise a previous violation by the State of its notification obligations so that a national court's power to order repayment of aid already paid out is unaffected. Recovery of the aid alone may not be sufficient to give effective protection for individuals. Since the rights of individuals flow from the Member State's breach of the duty to notify under Article 88(3), claims for liability in damages may apply if the principles of *Francovich*[4] and *Brasserie du Pêcheur and Factortame*[5] are satisfied.[6]

27–037   It seems clear that where the obligation to notify includes the method of financing the aid, protection under Article 88(3) will

---

[1] Case C–354/90 *Fédération Nationale du Commerce Extérieur des Produits Alimentaires v France* [1991] E.C.R. I–5505

[2] Case C–39/94 *SFEI v La Poste* , n.2, above.

[3] *ibid.*

[4] Joined Cases C–6, 9/90 *Francovich and another v Italy* [1991] E.C.R. I–5357; [1993] 2 C.M.L.R. 66.

[5] Joined Cases C–46 and 48/93 *Brasserie du Pêcheur v Germany, R. v Secretary of State for Transport, ex p. Factortame* [1996] E.C.R. I–1029; [1996] 1 C.M.L.R. 889.

[6] See Hernandez, "The principle of non-contractual State liability for breaches of EC law and its application to State aids" [1996] 6 E.C.L.R. 355.

extend in principle to reimbursement of charges or contributions levied specifically for that purpose.[7] Moreover, the Court's approach in the *Pape* and *Streekgewest Brabant* cases[8] confirms that national procedural rules may be challengeable if they represent obstacles to the effectiveness of the State aid rules. The Court in the latter case observed:

"An individual may have an interest in relying before the national court on the direct effect of the prohibition on implementation referred to in the last sentence of [Article 88(3)] of the Treaty not only in order to erase the negative effects of the distortion of competition created by the grant of unlawful aid, but also in order to obtain a refund of a tax levied in breach of that provision. In the latter case, the question whether an individual has been affected by the distortion of competition arising from the aid measure is irrelevant to the assessment of his interest in bringing proceedings. The only fact to be taken into consideration is that the individual is subject to a tax which is an integral part of a measure implemented in breach of the prohibition referred to in that provision."

Locus standi rules will thus have to address when an individual is sufficiently affected.

As noted in Chapter 26, national courts may also incur responsibilities in the context of the application of the derogation set out in Article 86(2). Undertakings entrusted with services of general economic interest may invoke this provision to justify State aids in their favour.[9] However, the limits of Article 86(2) in relation to SGEIs have been noted earlier.

Finally, national courts cannot be used by disgruntled competitors where the real nature of the claim is one which should have been protected by recourse to Article 230. In a case where the beneficiary of an aid had not used its undoubted position as an individually concerned undertaking to challenge an adverse decision addressed to the granting Member State,[10] the Court refused to allow the validity of the Commission's decision to be challenged via Article 234 in national proceedings arising from the recovery procedure.

---

[7] Joined Cases C–261/01 and C–262/01 *Van Calster*, n.46, above, para.54.
[8] n.56, above.
[9] Case C–174/97P *FFSA v Commission* [1998] E.C.R. I–1303, extending Case C–387/92 *Banco Exterior de España* [1994] E.C.R. I–877; [1994] 3 C.M.L.R. 473. See Hancher and Buendia Sierra, "Cross-subsidization and EC law" (1998) 35 C.M.L.Rev. 901, esp. 938–942.
[10] Case C–188/92 *TWD Textilwerke Deggendorf GmbH v Germany* [1994] E.C.R. I–833; [1995] 2 C.M.L.R. 145.

Decentralisation, national courts and more effective enforcement

27-038   As noted at the outset of this Chapter, the State Action Plan of 2005 seeks to proceed with modernisation of State aid law. This includes the encouragement of greater reliance upon national level enforcement. A study which reported in March 2006[11] identified the continuing difficulties and obstacles in this area, despite a significant increase in cases since the previous report made in 1999.[12] It remains the position that by far the commonest scenario before national courts, amounting to half the total number of cases, concerns private parties who seek to avoid a burden on themselves that has not been imposed on the aid beneficiary (most usually a tax exemption). Direct actions against competitors are still limited, and most of these result in injunctive relief to suspend aid. The authors of the report could find no examples of monetary damages being awarded on the basis of an illegal aid granted to a competitor. Most actions were brought against Member States, not against beneficiaries. The Report particularly stresses the diversity of procedures and substantive rules at the level of national law as an explanation of the continued infancy of local enforcement of State aid law. Its recommendations include: a new Notice based on the 1995 Cooperation Notice[13] but wider in scope; the adoption of a Remedies Directive to include a minimum standard of protection for competitors; discussion with Member States of the desirability of creating uniform conditions for the award of damages to competitors for infringement of Article 88(3); and the adoption of best practice guidelines in relation to recovery of State aid.

On the basis of the evidence supplied by the 2006 Report, the inference is that the problem for decentralised enforcement by private action is now not so much a lack of awareness of State aid rules any more, but, instead, the obstacles in the national legal arena to effective enjoyment of the protection afforded by Article 88(3). Originally, the supervisory regime established for State aid did not replicate the system for competition law enforcement generally. It focused instead upon dialogue between Member States and the Commission and use of a two-stage procedure of preliminary and formal investigation. The role of national courts, however, is now being prioritised despite their inability to rule on questions of compatibility of aid. In time, therefore, the balance between public and private enforcement may reflect more closely the model seen elsewhere.

---

[11] *Study on the Enforcement of State Aid Law at National Level* (Coordinated by T. Jestaedt, J. Derenne and T. Ottervanger), available on the Commission's website.

[12] The 1999 study was considered in the 4th edition of this work, p.706. The 2006 Report identified 357 cases before national courts over the study period, compared with 116 in the 1999 report.

[13] *Commission Notice on Cooperation Between National Courts and the Commission in the State Aid Field* [1995] O.J. C312/8; notably, the 2006 Report could find no instance of a request being made by a national court under this Notice.

Further reading

Bovis, C., "Financing Services of General Interest in the EU: How do Public Procurement and State Aids Interact to Demarcate between Market Forces and Protection?" (2005) 11 E.L.J. 79.

Nicolaides, P., "Compensation for Public Service Obligations: the Floodgates of State Aid?" [2003] E.C.L.R. 561.

Ross, M., "Decentralization, Effectiveness and Modernization: Contradictions in Terms?" in Biondi, A., Eeckhout P., and Flynn J., (eds), *The Law of State Aid in the European Union* (OUP, Oxford, 2004), 85.

Winter, J., "Re(de)fining the Notion of State Aid in Article 87(1) of the EC Treaty" (2004) 41 C.M.L.Rev. 475.

INDEX